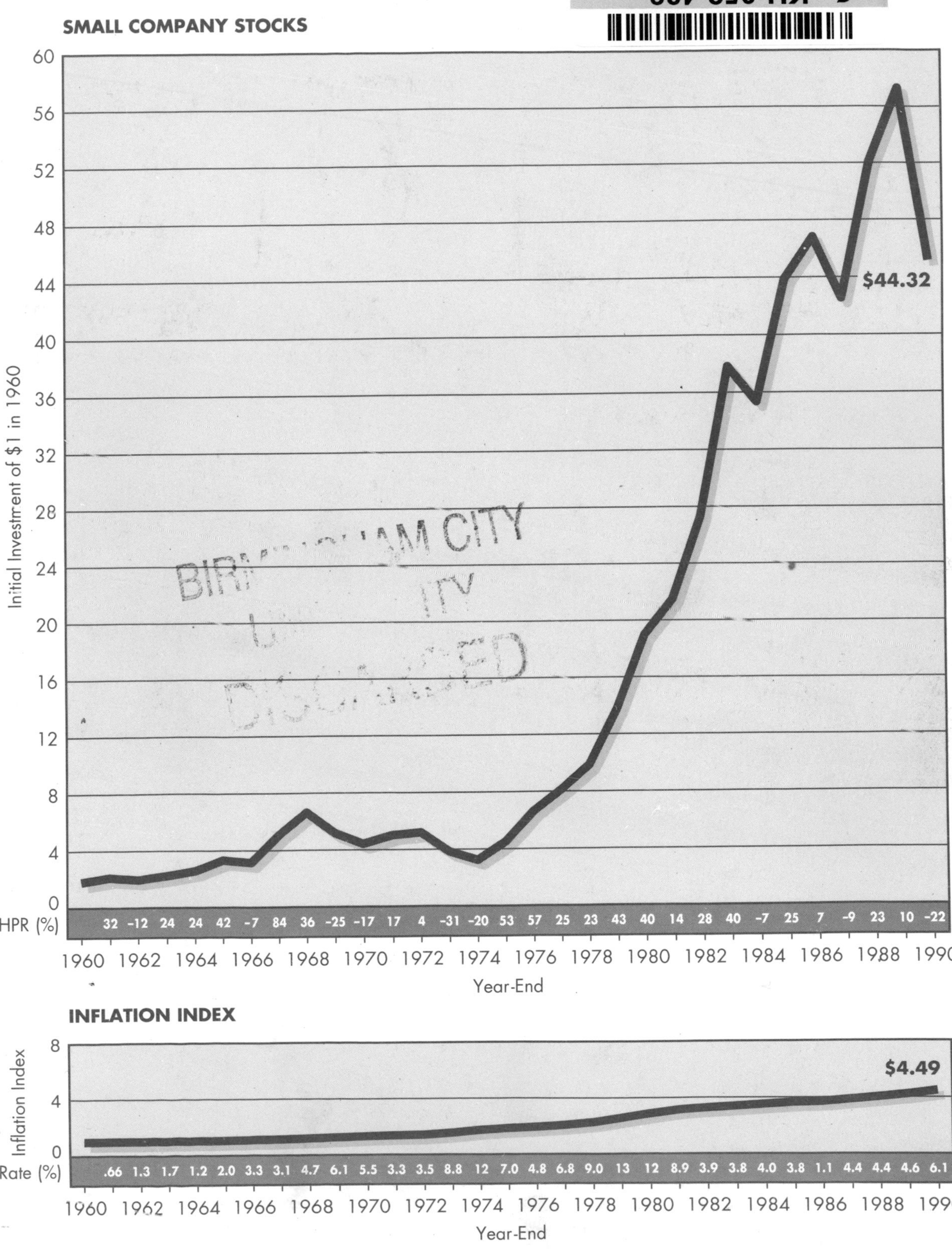
SMALL COMPANY STOCKS
60
56
52
48
44
40
36
32
28
24
20
16
12
8
4
0
Initial Investment of $1 in 1960
$44.32
HPR (%)
32 -12 24 24 42 -7 84 36 -25 -17 17 4 -31 -20 53 57 25 23 43 40 14 28 40 -7 25 7 -9 23 10 -22
1960 1962 1964 1966 1968 1970 1972 1974 1976 1978 1980 1982 1984 1986 1988 1990
Year-End
INFLATION INDEX
8
4
0
Inflation Index
$4.49
Rate (%)
.66 1.3 1.7 1.2 2.0 3.3 3.1 4.7 6.1 5.5 3.3 3.5 8.8 12 7.0 4.8 6.8 9.0 13 12 8.9 3.9 3.8 4.0 3.8 1.1 4.4 4.4 4.6 6.1
1960 1962 1964 1966 1968 1970 1972 1974 1976 1978 1980 1982 1984 1986 1988 1990
Year-End

Fundamentals of Investments

JOHN M. CHENEY

University of Central Florida

EDWARD A. MOSES

Rollins College

Crummer Graduate School of Business

Fundamentals of Investments

WEST PUBLISHING COMPANY

St. Paul
New York
Los Angeles
San Francisco

PRODUCTION CREDITS
Copyediting • Patricia Lewis
Text Design • Katherine Townes
Illustrations • Miyake Illustration and Design
Composition and film • G&S Typesetters, Inc.
Cover Image • David McGlynn, FPG International

Production, Prepress, Printing and Binding by West Publishing Company.

PHOTO CREDITS
2, 3, 5, 27 Ed Pritchard, Tony Stone Worldwide; **60, 61, 63, 89, 119, 161, 195** Doug Armand, Tony Stone Worldwide; **220, 221, 223, 265** Peter Gridley, FPG International; **310, 311, 313, 347** Telegraph Colour Library, FPG International; **400, 401, 403, 431, 455** George Hall, Woodfin Camp & Associates; **iv, v, 488, 489, 491, 529, 565, 613** Mark Segal, Tony Stone Worldwide; **644, 645, 647, 685, 729** Ken Biggs, Tony Stone Worldwide; **770, 771, 773** Jeremy Walker, Tony Stone Worldwide.

610 Opperman Drive
P.O. Box 64526
St. Paul, MN 55164-0526

Printed in the United States of America
99 98 97 96 95 94 93
8 7 6 5 4 3 2 1

LIBRARY OF CONGRESS CATALOGING-IN-PUBLICATION DATA
Cheney, John M.
Fundamentals of investments / John M. Cheney, Edward A. Moses,
p. cm.
Includes bibliographical references.
ISBN 0-314-93360-3 (hard)
1. Investments. 2. Portfolio management. 3. Stocks. 4. Bonds. I. Moses, Edward A. II. Title.
HG4521.C45354 1992
332.6—dc20 91-35170
CIP

To my wife Anne and
my daughter Cheryl—JMC

To my wife Susan and
my children, Lynne
and Daniel—EAM

Brief Contents

Contents

Appendixes

Interest Boxes

Research Boxes

Preface

Students usually begin their first course in investments with great expectations and are excited and interested in the subject matter. It is the responsibility of the professor and the selected textbook not to disappoint the student. Our overriding objective in writing *Fundamentals of Investments* was to provide the student and professor with a comprehensive book that is readable, presents complex concepts in an understandable manner, incorporates the latest advances in theory and practice, and is organized in such a way that the student's expectations of gaining insightful and usable investment information are met.

The dramatic changes the securities markets have undergone in recent years have added significantly to the complexities of personal and institutional investment management. As a result of what is known as financial engineering, new investment products have proliferated. In addition, specialized mutual funds, innovative insurance products, and the emergence of international financial markets have made new alternatives available to the individual investor. Increasing volatility in the securities markets and the continuing changes in the tax code are examples of additional factors investors must consider in developing and implementing investment strategies.

Accompanying these changes has been the ongoing development and empirical testing of investment theories and techniques. These include hypothesis related to the efficiency of financial markets, portfolio and capital market theory, arbitrage pricing theory, option pricing models, program trading, and portfolio insurance to name just a few. The necessity to cover these developments, along with the need to provide investors with an understanding of investment basics, creates quite a challenge for the student of investments, the professor, and, we might add, the authors of investment books.

The purpose of this book is to provide information and procedures that will enable individual investors to make informed investment decisions. The strategies of practicing investment professionals as well as results from theoretical and empirical research are used to introduce students to the practical aspects of investing. The techniques and procedures for active investment strategies presented in this book recognize that there is strong evidence that financial markets are efficient. An underlying proposition throughout the book is that investors should appreciate the pitfalls and complications that occur in pursuing an active investment strategy in an efficient market.

Fundamentals of Investments is intended for use in a first course in investments. While the topics are covered in a comprehensive fashion, the book presents material requiring quantitative analysis in an easily understandable manner. The intended prerequisite for an investments course using this book is the introductory managerial finance course.

DISTINGUISHING PEDAGOGICAL FEATURES

The book has been designed to make the study of investments a meaningful and interesting learning experience for the student. To achieve this goal, we have included a number of pedagogical features, including a somewhat distinctive and flexible organization, the most up-to-date information available, knowledge-level objectives for each chapter, Interest and Research Boxes, numerous examples, tables, and figures, a rich set of end-of-chapter materials, a Glossary of Key Terms, and some very helpful appendixes.

• Organization

Careful consideration was given to the sequencing of chapters in the book, while at the same time allowing the professor flexibility in the design of the course. An examination of the Contents reveals the logic of the organization. This text begins with a discussion of investment fundamentals, including a case example that outlines the challenges facing the individual investor, and an introduction to risk and return. The next two parts examine the investment environment and introduce valuation concepts and analysis. The next three parts present the fundamental analysis of bonds, preferred and common stocks, and alternative investments. The seventh part explores portfolio and capital market theory in detail as well as the analysis of portfolio performance and market efficiency. The book concludes with a separate section on personal investment management that reexamines the personal investment case study presented in Chapter 1.

Several aspects of the organization deserve special mention. The early presentation of risk and return in Chapter 2 includes an overview of portfolio and capital market theory. This overview is sufficient to enable students to understand the use of these concepts in the ensuing chapters. Professors who desire a more detailed treatment of these topics may wish to assign Chapters 19 and 20 early on in the course.

In Part II, The Investment Environment, we have included separate chapters on mutual funds and investing internationally. We feel these topics are important to the individual investor and deserve their location and emphasis in the book. These topics are also further examined throughout the book in appropriate chapters.

A separate chapter on investment strategies is also presented in Part II. This chapter describes the different investment approaches an investor can employ and provides an anchor point for assessing how the different investment alternatives can fit into an individualized investment strategy.

Finally, because the book is written with the investment decision-making process of the individual investor in mind, personal investment management is treated as a separate part at the end of the book.

• Timeliness

Advances in investment theory, practice, and products are occurring at an almost dizzying pace. Although theory precedes practice by a considerable interval of time (sometimes forever) in many disciplines, this is not the case in the area of investments. With the so-called rocket scientists with strong academic credentials in heavy demand on Wall Street, the distinction between theory and practice is not so clear. We have made every effort to include the most up-to-date information possible in the book. The currency of the material is reflected in the examples, tables, and figures throughout the book as well as in the Interest Boxes, Research Boxes, and references at the end of the chapters.

• Knowledge-Level Objectives

Each chapter begins with a list of knowledge-level objectives. This pedagogical feature is designed to give the student an immediate awareness of the important concepts presented in the chapter as well as an overview of the contents of the chapter.

• Interest Boxes

The Interest Boxes discuss contemporary, real-world situations or events relevant to the surrounding text. These boxes, which are sometimes humorous as well as informative, can be assigned at the option of the professor.

• Research Boxes

The Research Boxes present the results of interesting research on a particular topic discussed in the surrounding text. We have carefully selected and summarized this material to provide students with additional information on topics of special interest. These boxes can be assigned at the option of the professor.

• Examples, Tables, and Figures

We have used numerous examples, tables, and figures throughout the book. These illustrations have been selected to enhance the student's understanding of a particular topic. Whenever possible, we have used real-world data to make the illustrations as realistic as possible.

• End-of-Chapter Features

A number of important pedagogical features are included in the end-of-chapter material. These features should help students test their understanding of the chapter material and assist them in applying the investment concepts presented in the chapter.

- *Summary.* Each chapter contains a summary that briefly discusses the key concepts presented in the chapter. Reading the chapter summary and the knowledge-level objectives prior to reading the chapter will provide the student with a complete overview of the chapter's contents.
- *Key terms.* The key terms, which are set in boldface type when they are introduced in a chapter, are also listed in alphabetical order at the end of the chapter. The Glossary of Key Terms at the end of the book contains definitions of these terms.
- *Concept applications.* Consistent with the applications orientation of the book, this feature lists the important investment concepts presented in the chapter and explains how the individual investor can apply each concept.
- *Questions and problems.* Each chapter contains a number of questions and problems that can be assigned by the professor. These questions and problems are designed to test the students' understanding of the concepts and applications presented in the chapter. In many instances, the problems employ data and situations from publicly traded companies.
- *Key to the Investment Analysis Software.* This feature summarizes the access procedures for performing the calculations in a chapter using the *Investment Analysis Software (IAS)* that accompanies this book. Each of the calculations for which a template is available in IAS is indicated by a computer symbol (as shown to the left) in the text preceding the equation for the calculation. This section also includes a page reference to Appendix A-1, The Investment Analysis Software, which provides a detailed description of the access procedures for a particular calculation. IAS can be helpful in solving many of the end-of-chapter problems.

- *End-of-chapter references.* We have provided the interested student and professor with a broad selection of references at the end of each chapter. These references range from academic journals to the more popular investment-related periodicals. They include "classic" academic articles as well as recent articles from publications such as *Barron's,* the *Wall Street Journal, Fortune,* the *Journal of Portfolio Management,* and *Financial Analysts Journal,* to name just a few.

• End-of-Chapter Appendixes

At the end of several chapters we have included material in an appendix. While this practice is not widespread throughout the book, we felt that professors might wish to exclude certain topics from the assigned readings. Thus, placing this material in an appendix adds to the flexibility of the book.

• End-of-Book Appendixes

Five appendixes that should be quite useful to the student appear at the end of the book. Appendix A-1 contains a complete description of the Investment Analysis Software that accompanies the book. The appendix provides a step-by-step guide for the use of the software. Appendix A-2 contains a brief review of analytical techniques used in the book. This summary of analytical techniques provides a quick refresher for statistical and other analytical calculations. Appendix A-3 presents the mathematical terms, symbols, and key formulas used in the book. It provides a quick reference for the student who has forgotten the meaning of a previously defined term or symbol or the equation for a particular calculation. Appendixes A-4 and A-5 contain the compound value and present value financial tables as well as tables for the standard normal cumulative probability distribution and a table for the student *t* distribution for hypothesis testing.

EDUCATIONAL AIDS AND SUPPLEMENTS

Fundamentals of Investments and its ancillary materials are designed to maximize the learning experience of the student and assist the professor in using the book.

• Study Guide

The *Study Guide to Accompany Fundamentals of Investments,* written by Phillip T. Kolbe of Memphis State University, and the authors of the book, is designed to enrich the student's learning experience. The study guide contains a chapter outline and a discussion of the key points in the outline. In addition, multiple-choice and true-false tests, with answers, enable the student to assess his or her knowledge. Further, the study guide contains problems with solutions as well as a matching exercise involving the key terms.

• The Investment Analysis Software

The Investment Analysis Software that accompanies the book was written specifically for *Fundamentals of Investments* by Carol J. Billingham of Central Michigan University. It is designed for IBM personal computers and compatibles. The software, using Lotus 1-2-3 templates, may be run from either a floppy disk drive or a hard disk drive.

All equations in the book preceded with a computer symbol are included in the software. In addition, the Investment Analysis Software contains Personal Financial Planning and Analysis programs that can be used for preparing personal financial statements, maintaining records for analyzing personal portfolios, and performing a rent-versus-buy analysis for a personal residence.

• Instructor's Manual

The Instructor's Manual, written by the authors, is designed to help professors prepare and teach a course in investments using *Fundamentals of Investments.* The manual contains suggested syllabi for courses taught in both the quarter and semester systems. Outlines for possible class projects on economic, industry, and security analysis are also included. Each chapter in the Instructor's Manual includes a detailed outline for the corresponding chapter in the book, teaching suggestions with appropriate class discussion questions, suggested answers to end-of-chapter questions, and solutions to end-of-chapter problems. The manual also contains a test bank consisting of true-false and multiple-choice questions and problems.

• Transparency Masters

A separate pack of transparency masters of key tables and figures in the book is available on a complimentary basis to adopters of the book.

ACKNOWLEDGMENTS

The authors gratefully acknowledge the significant efforts of the many contributors to this book. Without their expertise, suggestions, and support, this book would not have been possible.

Working from first draft to final manuscript requires the help of reviewers who not only have expertise in the area of investments but also have the classroom experience to improve the clarity of the presentation. We are deeply indebted for the excellent reviews of a portion or all of the manuscript provided by the following individuals:

Carol J. Billingham, Central Michigan University; Paul J. Bolster, Northeastern University; Carroll Broome, DePaul University; Richard A. DeFusco, University of Nebraska, Lincoln; Richard J. Dowen, Northern Illinois University; Hassan B. Ehsani, Suffolk University; Thomas H. Eyssell, University of Missouri, St. Louis; James F. Feller, Middle Tennessee State University; George L. Granger, East Tennessee State University; Robert T. Kleiman, Oakland University; Phillip T. Kolbe, Memphis State University; Steven T. Mann, University of South Carolina; Joel Morse, University of Baltimore; Philip Pfaff, Canisius College; Grady Perdue, University of Houston, Clcar Lake; Richard PonArul, California State University, Chico; Gary E. Powell, American University; Thomas V. Schwarz, Southern Illinois University at Carbondale; Howard E. Van Auken, Iowa State University; Herbert J. Weinraub, University of Toledo; Richard E. Williams, Wright State University; Tony R. Wingler, University of North Carolina, Greensboro.

A book such as *Fundamentals of Investments* covers a wide range of topics. In order to ensure that we covered the topics accurately and completely, we used the expertise of a number of our colleagues. We would like to thank Stan Atkinson, Wallace Reiff, and Sharon Graham of the University of Central Florida; Jeff Madura of Florida Atlantic University; and Richard White and Charles Jones of the University of North Florida.

We are deeply appreciative of the expertise and loving care for details demonstrated by Florence Rendulic in typing the entire manuscript. Sue Crabill's help in typing the appendixes for the book and the Instructor's Manual is deeply appreciated. We are also grateful for the research assistance of Howard Fraser.

We are deeply indebted to the professionals at West Publishing Company, Richard Fenton, Nancy Hill-Whilton, and Mark Jacobsen, for their expertise, hard work, creativity, and encouragement in our effort to bring this book to life. Pat Lewis did an exceptional job in editing the original manuscript.

Our wives, Anne and Susan, and our children Cheryl, Lynne, and Daniel, deserve our special thanks for their support and understanding during the preparation of this book. The writing of a book is truly a family effort.

JOHN M. CHENEY
EDWARD A. MOSES

Fundamentals of Investments

PART I

Investment Fundamentals

CHAPTER 1

An Overview of Investments

CHAPTER 2

Investment Risk and Return

INTRODUCTION

The word *investments* brings forth visions of profit, risk, speculation, and wealth. For the uninformed, investing may result in disaster. For the knowledgeable, the investment process can be financially rewarding and exciting. This chapter introduces the basic concepts of investing and the myriad decisions facing the individual investor. It presents a brief overview of the many investment alternatives available to individual investors, with references to the chapters in which these alternatives are discussed. The choice among investment alternatives is strongly influenced by the investor's investment objective(s) and time horizon. In attempting to achieve the objective(s), the investor must consider the expected return and risk of the portfolio and must also develop an appropriate investment strategy. The investment environment has undergone a rapid transformation since the 1950s, and this chapter examines some of the changes that have occurred. The chapter concludes with a brief discussion of the organization and some features of the book.

The following hypothetical case illustrates many of the issues that are addressed in this book. While the case is somewhat abbreviated, it presents many of the complex problems facing investors in today's environment.

THE DECISION TO INVEST: A CASE STUDY

Bill and Martha Stanton, both 49 years old, are concerned about their financial security after retirement. They were married 25 years ago, shortly after graduating from college. They have three children: Roger, aged 20; Sarah, 17; and Tim, 15. Roger is currently a senior finance major at a state university. Sarah and Tim plan to go to college. Bill and Martha currently have savings of $62,000. They are concerned that after they pay for all three college educations, they will have very little left in savings for their retirement years.

The Stantons' principal asset is their "dream" home that they bought three years ago. The house has an estimated fair market value of $130,000 and is mortgaged for 22 more years, with a balance owing of $83,000. The Stantons enjoy their home, however, and have no plans to sell it.

Bill and Martha also own 50 percent of a small retail carpet company that employs 14 people. They started the business 20 years ago with Bill's brother. The business has been reasonably successful, and Bill and Martha's current share of the earnings is about $68,000 per year. It appears that the company will continue its modest growth. Bill and Martha save approximately $6,000 per year after living expenses and taxes.

Bill and Martha have never considered selling their share of the business. They hope that one of the children will eventually come into the business with them so that they can spend less time at work. They realize that their income from the business would probably decline if one of the children joined the business, but they have always wanted to travel. Thus, if one of the children entered the business, Bill and Martha would realize two dreams: they

CHAPTER 1

An Overview of Investments

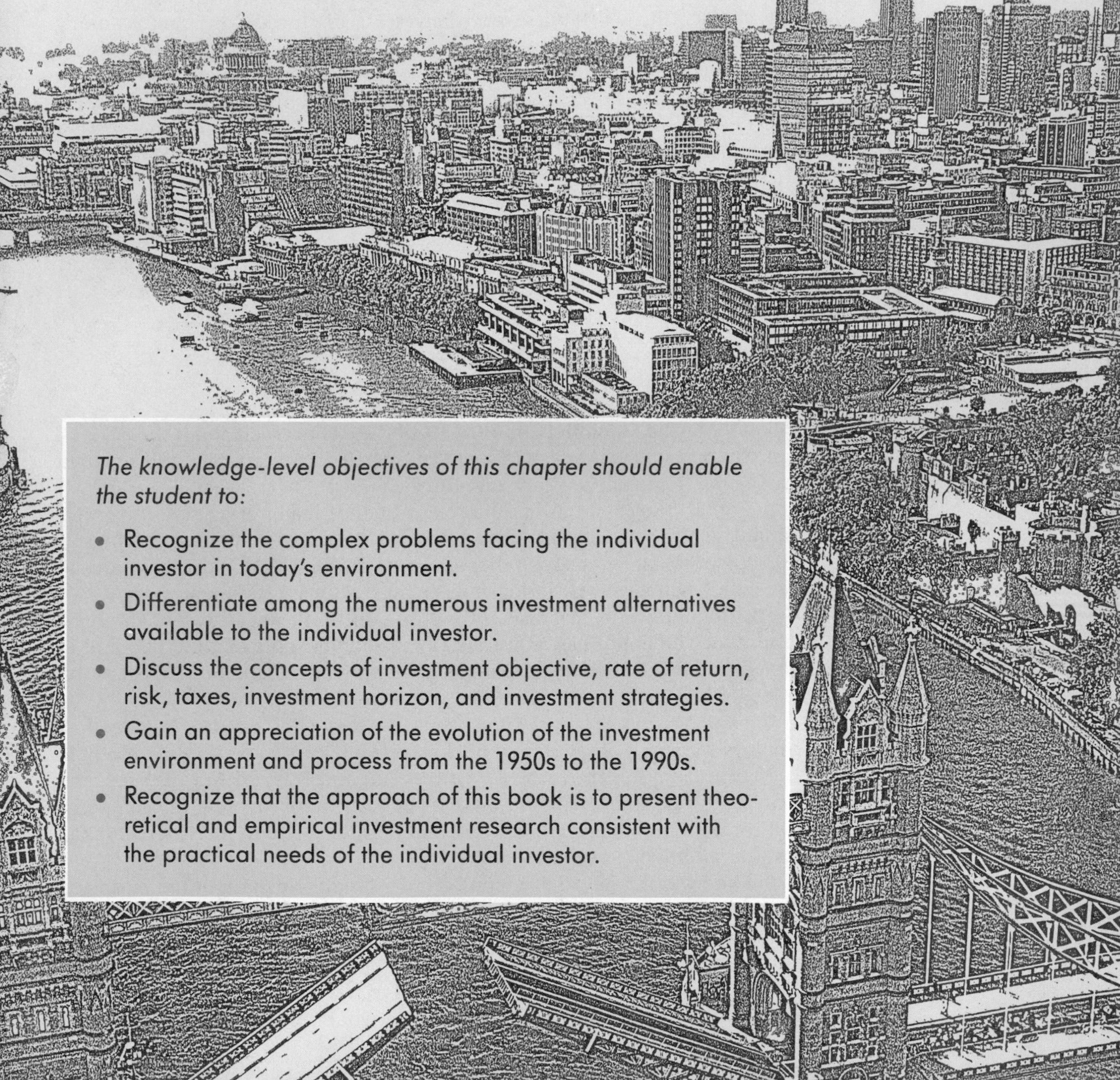

The knowledge-level objectives of this chapter should enable the student to:

- Recognize the complex problems facing the individual investor in today's environment.
- Differentiate among the numerous investment alternatives available to the individual investor.
- Discuss the concepts of investment objective, rate of return, risk, taxes, investment horizon, and investment strategies.
- Gain an appreciation of the evolution of the investment environment and process from the 1950s to the 1990s.
- Recognize that the approach of this book is to present theoretical and empirical investment research consistent with the practical needs of the individual investor.

could travel, and they could leave their share of the business to one of their children.

Bill and Martha know that they need to plan for their retirement. As small business owners, they never established a company retirement plan, and they realize that their retirement income, other than their Social Security benefits, is their responsibility. They also are considering whether they should change the amount of their insurance coverage. Currently, Bill has $200,000 of decreasing term life insurance on himself, and Martha has $100,000 of decreasing term. The company provides the Stantons with long-term disability and medical insurance.

In an effort to begin a financial plan, Bill and Martha have created an initial list of questions:

1. If they decide to retire from the business when they are both 60, how much income will they need to maintain their desired life-style? How much should they be saving and investing per year toward retirement? How much of their savings should be left in a liquid asset?
2. Should the savings program be administered through the family-owned company, or should Bill and Martha set up their own tax-sheltered retirement plan?
3. What should they do about their life insurance?
4. Where should they invest their savings? Should they explore mutual funds, bonds, common stocks, real estate, and other investment alternatives, or should they seek out a professional for financial advice?
5. Where can they find information about investment alternatives?
6. Once they have identified the investment alternatives, how can the investments be analyzed and combined into a portfolio?
7. What impact will selection, timing, and diversification (including international investments) have on their investment decisions?
8. How much risk are they willing to assume? How are expected risk and return calculated? How are expected risk and return related?
9. How can they evaluate the performance of their investments?

Many of these questions require complex answers. More importantly, the answers are interrelated. Each of the questions points to two issues: (1) How can Bill and Martha best provide for their retirement? and (2) How can Bill and Martha create the maximum amount of wealth, consistent with their risk preference, before retirement? Part of the wealth will come from their annual savings, which could be increased by increasing salary income or reducing living expenses. Additional wealth could also be generated by increasing the earnings from invested funds, which may require increased risk. Finally, since the government taxes most sources of income, reducing taxes will always add wealth.

Most individuals want or need to generate enough wealth to permit them to satisfy their personal life-styles and objectives. Frequently, these desires require expenditures in a given period that exceed income for the same period. For example, the Stantons' annual income probably is not large enough to pay all their living expenses and support two children in college in one year. They also realize that their retirement income may not be large enough to support their planned retirement life-style. Because of this mismatch between income and expenses, individuals frequently plan ahead for activities that will require significant expenditures. They hope that with proper planning they will have the necessary wealth by the time the money is needed. When per-period income is less than current expenses, the needed funds are obtained from the individuals' assets or from borrowing.

Investments play two roles in this situation. First, the investment medium or vehicle must ensure that money will be available when it is needed. Second, the invested money should grow because a dollar's real value today is greater than a dollar's value tomorrow in a world of inflation.

OVERVIEW OF INVESTMENT ALTERNATIVES

A wide range of investment alternatives is available to individual investors. In addition to the traditional common stock, preferred stock, and bond alternatives, other **financial assets**—such as convertibles, warrants, rights, commodity futures, financial futures, and options on individual common stocks, commodity futures, and financial futures—are examined in this book. **Real asset** alternatives—such as real estate, precious metals, and collectibles—are also considered.

Table 1.1 provides an overview of the investment alternatives discussed in this book. These alternatives fall into eight major categories: (1) equity securities; (2) short-term debt securities; (3) intermediate- and long-term debt securities; (4) hybrid securities; (5) derivative securities; (6) real assets; (7) international investments; and (8) other investment alternatives.

The table also briefly describes the categories and types of investment alternatives and indicates the market or method of trading associated with each of them. The organized exchanges mentioned in the table include the New York Stock Exchange, the American Stock Exchange, and the regional exchanges. The other major market is the over-the-counter (OTC) market where numerous stocks, bonds, and other types of securities are traded. Some investment alternatives are not traded in the traditional securities markets. Real estate and collectibles, for example, are usually bought through individual brokers and dealers.

The last column in Table 1.1 indicates the chapter(s) that provide the major coverage of the investment alternatives. However, a number of alternatives, such as common stocks, are discussed throughout the book. The subject index should be consulted to determine where specific details about each alternative are presented.

TABLE 1.1 • Overview of Investment Alternatives

	Brief description	Market or method of trading	Coverage in text
Equity Securities			
A. Common stock	Represents ownership interest in issuing corporation.		
1. Class A	Nonvoting common stock entitled to receive dividends.	Organized exchanges and OTC market	Chapters 12–14, 21
2. Class B	Voting common stock not entitled to receive dividends.	Organized exchanges and OTC market	Chapters 12–14, 21
B. Preferred stock	Usually nonvoting but has priority over common stock in dividend and liquidation rights.	Organized exchanges and OTC market	Chapters 12–14
Short-Term Debt Securities	Obligations that mature in one year or less.		
A. Negotiable certificates of deposit	Issued by federally insured commercial banks with a minimum face value of $100,000.	Money market	Chapter 3
B. Commercial paper	Promissory negotiable notes issued by larger, well-known corporations.	Money market	Chapter 3
C. Banker's acceptances	Used by importers to secure trade credit from exporters. The accepting bank guarantees payment by borrower.	Money market	Chapter 3
D. Treasury bills	Obligations issued by U.S. Treasury, sold at a discount from face value.	Money market	Chapters 10 & 17
Intermediate- and Long-Term Debt Securities	Obligations that mature in more than one year.		
A. U.S. government securities			
1. Treasury notes	Issued by U.S. Treasury with maturities between 1 and 10 years; sold at face value with a specified interest payment.	OTC market	Chapters 10 & 17
2. Treasury bonds	U.S. Treasury securities with maturities over 10 years.	OTC market	Chapters 10 & 17
3. Savings bonds	Nonnegotiable savings instruments issued by U.S. Treasury.	OTC market	Chapter 10

TABLE 1.1 • Overview of Investment Alternatives (continued)

	Brief description	Market or method of trading	Coverage in text
Intermediate- and Long-Term Debt Securities (continued)			
B. U.S. agency securities			
1. Government National Mortgage Association	Mortgage-backed, pass-through debt security.	OTC market	Chapter 10
2. Federal Home Loan Mortgage Corporation	Mortgage-backed, pass-through debt security.	OTC market	Chapter 10
3. Federal National Mortgage Association	Mortgage-backed, pass-through debt security.	OTC market	Chapter 10
C. Municipal securities	Debt obligations issued by state or local governments and agencies		
1. Revenue bonds	Issued to obtain financing for specific projects such as sewer facilities and hospitals. Revenues from these projects are earmarked to meet interest and principal payments.	OTC market	Chapter 10
2. General obligation bonds	The general revenues (tax receipts) of the issuer provide funds to meet interest and principal payments.	OTC market	Chapter 10
D. Corporate bonds	Debt obligations issued by corporations. Many types of corporate bonds exist; they differ in the way the principal and interest payments are made and in the collateral used to back the bonds.	Organized exchanges and OTC market	Chapters 10–11
Hybrid Securities	Securities that have characteristics of both equity and debt.		
A. Convertible preferred stock	The convertible feature allows the investor to convert the preferred stock to a specified number of shares of common stock.	Organized exchanges and OTC market	Chapter 16
B. Convertible bonds	The convertible feature allows the investor to convert the bond to a specified number of shares of common stock.	Organized exchanges and OTC market	Chapter 16

Derivative Securities	Securities that derive their value from the value of an underlying asset.		
A. Options	Provide the right to buy or sell shares of common stock of a specific corporation within a limited period of time at a designated price.	Chicago Board of Trade; American Stock Exchange; other exchanges and markets	Chapter 15
B. Commodity futures	Provide the contract holder the right to sell a specified amount of an agricultural or natural resources commodity at a designated price within a specified period of time.	Chicago Board of Trade; Kansas City Board of Trade; other markets	Chapter 17
C. Financial futures	Provide the contract holder the right to sell a specified amount of a common stock index, bonds, or foreign currencies at a designated price within a specified period of time.	International Monetary Market; Chicago Board of Trade; other exchanges	Chapter 17
D. Options on futures	Provide the right to buy or sell a specified commodity or financial future within a limited period of time at a designated price.	Chicago Board of Trade; Chicago Mercantile Exchange; other exchanges	Chapters 15 & 17
E. Rights	Issued by a corporation to existing common stockholders in connection with the sale of additional shares of stock.	Organized exchanges and OTC market	Chapter 16
F. Warrants	Issued by a corporation; provide holder the right or option to purchase additional bonds or shares of common stock from the issuing corporation at a specified price within a designated period of time.	Organized exchanges and OTC market	Chapter 16
Real Assets	Nonfinancial assets.		
A. Precious metals	Includes gold, silver, platinum, and other metals in the form of coins, bullion, or depository certificates.	Individual dealers	Chapter 18
B. Real estate	Includes single- and multifamily residences, undeveloped land, commercial property, and farmland.	Individual brokers	Chapter 18
C. Collectibles	Includes diamonds, prints, fine art, numismatic coins, stamps, and other categories.	Individual dealers	Chapter 18

TABLE 1.1 • Overview of Investment Alternatives (continued)

	Brief description	Market or method of trading	Coverage in text
International Investments	Investments by individuals in debt or equity securities issued by organizations outside the country of residence of the investor.		
A. Multinational corporations	Stocks and bonds issued by large corporations with significant business interests in more than one country.	Organized exchanges and OTC market	Chapter 6
B. Foreign stocks traded on a local exchange	Stocks of large firms that have established trading for their securities on domestic as well as foreign exchanges.	Organized exchanges and OTC market	Chapter 6
C. American Depository Receipts (ADRs)	Securities issued by large banks that represent ownership of foreign securities. ADRs can represent shares of stock of foreign companies as well as the debt of foreign governments.	Organized exchanges and OTC market	Chapter 6
Other Investment Alternatives			
A. Pension funds	Public or private investment funds that provide retirement and other benefits to eligible employees.	Not marketable	Chapter 22
B. Mutual funds	Investment companies that sell shares of common stock that represent an ownership interest in a portfolio of domestic and/or foreign securities.	OTC market and direct transactions with individual funds	Chapters 5 & 21
C. Closed-end companies	Investment companies with a fixed number of shares of common stock outstanding. These companies can take the form of a closed-end fund, unit trust, dual fund, and primes and scores.	Organized exchanges and OTC market	Chapter 5

• INTEREST BOX

Number of Investors in Common Stocks Increases

In mid-1990, the New York Stock Exchange conducted a survey of 5,000 U.S. households in order to estimate the number of U.S. residents owning shares of common stock. The results indicated that more than one in five U.S. residents, or a total of 51 million, own common stocks directly or invest in mutual funds containing common stocks.

The strong equity markets during the first half of the 1980s encouraged common stock ownership. According to the survey results, 13.5 percent of the U.S. population owned stock in 1980. By mid-1990, this percentage had risen to 21.1 percent. Since 1985, the number of investors owning stock through mutual funds has increased by 130 percent. The typical investor in common stocks has the following profile:

- *Male.* Age 45; household income of $46,000 per year; college graduate; and owns an average of 3.4 stocks in a portfolio worth $13,500.
- *Female.* Age 44; household income of $39,000 per year; some college; and owns an average of 3 stocks in a portfolio worth $7,200.

SOURCE: Adapted from Beth Batton, "Stocks More Popular Than Ever, NYSE Says," *USA Today,* May 22, 1991, p. 38.

FACTORS TO CONSIDER IN CHOOSING AMONG INVESTMENT ALTERNATIVES

The major factors that should be considered in making investment decisions include (1) the basic investment objective, (2) the expected rate of return, (3) the expected risk, (4) taxes, (5) the investment horizon, and (6) investment strategies.

• Investment Objective

The **investment objective** is to increase systematically the individual's wealth, defined as assets minus liabilities. Investing requires that an individual invest money in assets that will generate the desired wealth when it is needed for retirement, children's education, or other financial goals. Consequently, most investments are undertaken to provide an increase in wealth.

The higher the level of desired wealth, the higher the return that must be received. An investor seeking higher returns must be willing to face higher levels of risk, however. While wealth maximization may remain an investor's investment objective over a lifetime, age or family circumstances will necessarily force the investor to change his or her investment approach. Consider further the example of Bill and Martha Stanton. Twenty-five years ago, when they were first married and had no children, their investment objective should logically have been wealth maximization, just as it is today. In their earlier years, however, they would have been willing to face high levels of risk to achieve this objective. Today, with children to educate and concerns about retirement, they cannot afford to expose themselves to the high levels of risk they were willing to accept in their earlier years. They still desire to maximize their wealth, but only at a level of risk consistent with their current circumstances. Thus, the Stantons are more risk-averse today than they were early in their careers. Yet, even as their acceptable level of risk decreases, they still desire to maximize their return (wealth).

Most investors do not necessarily have a single investment objective at any point in time. In the case of the Stantons, they have at least two simultaneous investment objectives: college education for their children and retirement. These two objectives will help dictate the composition of their investment portfolio. As to the first objective, the Stantons must be certain that the funds will be available when Sarah and Tim need them for college. The Stantons may consider bonds that have maturities matching these needs for a portion of their investment portfolio. On the other hand, their retirement planning allows the Stantons to consider additional types of investments, such as common stocks with growth potential.

A third investment objective the Stantons should consider is the establishment of an emergency fund equal to some proportion of their annual living expenses. This investment objective would dictate that a portion of their investment portfolio be invested in very safe, highly liquid assets. An example of an asset meeting this criterion is a money market mutual fund.

• Rate of Return

When selecting investment alternatives, the easiest task is to identify the amount or **rate of return** that you want—you always want the most you can get. With most investments, however, the forecast return may not be absolutely accurate. Since it is a forecast, there is usually some variability about the precise amount of the return. This variability requires an analysis of risk.

Rates of return can vary greatly between investment alternatives and over time. Figure 1.1 provides a vivid illustration of this point. Part (a) provides the average annual rates of return on 13 alternatives calculated for the 10-year period from June 1979 to June 1989. The rate of inflation, as indicated by the Consumer Price Index (CPI), is also provided. Notice that, with the exception of coins, the financial assets (stocks, bonds, and Treasury bills) produced much higher returns than did real assets over this 10-year period of relatively low inflation.

Figure 1.1b indicates the returns for the one-year period ending June 1, 1990. Notice that real assets, such as old masters and Chinese ceramics, provided much higher returns than did financial assets over this one-year period.

The large differences in returns among investment alternatives and the changing ranking of returns over time indicate the importance of a careful analysis of alternatives. The returns shown in Figure 1.1 do not necessarily reflect what will occur in the future.

Risk

Risk can be defined as the variability of possible returns around the expected return of an investment. For some investments, this variability can be quite small. For example, the short-term debt securities described in Table 1.1 have very little variability around their expected return because of their relatively short term to maturity (very low interest rate risk), and the issuer has a very

FIGURE 1.1 • Rates of Return on Investment Alternatives

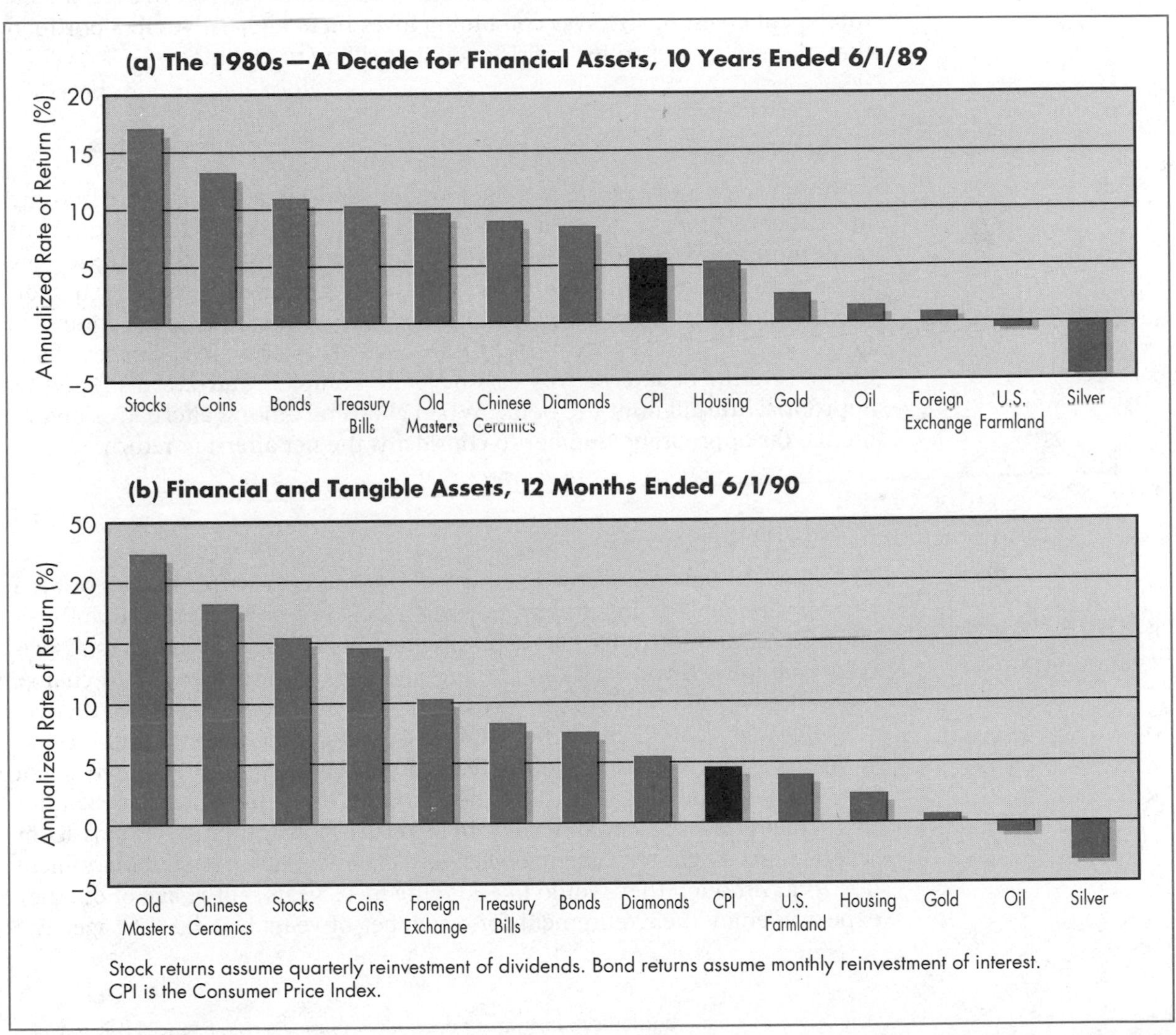

Stock returns assume quarterly reinvestment of dividends. Bond returns assume monthly reinvestment of interest. CPI is the Consumer Price Index.

SOURCES: *The Price Report* (Baltimore: T. Rowe Price, Fall 1989 and 1990). Reprinted by permission of T. Rowe Price Associates, Inc.

low probability of defaulting. On the other hand, commodity futures are an example of a high-risk investment alternative because of the high variability in the prices of the underlying agricultural or natural resources commodities.

Each investor has his or her own attitude about risk and how much he or she can tolerate. Since investment alternatives have different types of risks associated with them, the investor must determine which combination of alternatives matches his or her particular risk tolerances.[1]

Most investors know that there is no free lunch; that is, the return you can expect is a function of the risk you take. Those investors who can tolerate higher levels of risk should be rewarded with higher levels of return. Most empirical studies of historical risk-return relationships support this statement. Intelligent investing involves combining investment alternatives in a portfolio that offers a fair return for the risk you are willing to assume.

• Taxes

Although risk and return are the primary considerations when choosing investments, other factors must be weighed as well. Since the government taxes most sources of income received by individuals, the **tax consequences** must be considered. In the United States, tax rates are progressive, based upon levels of income. The tax laws also provide many deductions in the computation of taxable income. Because of these features, the tax consequences of different investment alternatives can be quite complex and are discussed as appropriate throughout the book. When choosing among alternative investments, the appropriate number to consider is the net after-tax return.

• Investment Horizon

The length of time money will be invested, or the **investment horizon,** is a critical variable. The investment horizon affects not only the return and risk characteristics of the alternatives but frequently the tax consequences associated with the return. For example, the investor's income level could change dramatically over the life of the investment, and the tax code could be revised. These changes would affect the net after-tax return the investor will receive.

An investor's investment objective(s) is closely related to the investment horizon. Returning to the case of the Stantons, their investment horizon for their children's educational needs will be relatively short term, perhaps six or seven years. Their retirement objective dictates a much longer investment horizon. Although they would like to retire in 11 years, at the age of 60, they expect to enjoy their retirement for a number of years beyond that age. The

---

[1]The factors that may contribute to investment uncertainty (business risk, financial risk, liquidity risk, default risk, interest rate risk, management risk, and purchasing power risk) are discussed in Chapter 2.

• INTEREST BOX

Taxes and Investment Decisions

Those "painless" tax-shelter write-offs of yesterday have turned into today's litigation headaches. The Internal Revenue Service is challenging every shelter in sight.

Though the promises sounded like genuine plums—a four-dollar tax deduction for every dollar invested in a shelter—many proved to be only sugarplums dancing in the heads of those who invested.

The IRS, with congressional support and one of the largest task forces ever assembled by the agency, has uncovered a galaxy of tax shelters and has decided to disallow every shelter deduction it can find. The question facing many shelter investors now is whether to litigate.

Before taking on the IRS in a possibly expensive fight, a taxpayer should assess the chances for victory. Clues can be found in recent court actions, such as the decision in the case of Edward M. Becker.

Becker, an airline pilot, was prospecting for a tax-sheltered investment when he learned about a South American gold mine called "Gold for Tax Dollars." The promotional material told of a $100,000 deduction for a $25,000 investment. An investor who was in the then-highest tax bracket of 70 percent could save $70,000 in income taxes for a cash outlay of $25,000.

After several months, Becker wanted to see where he had sunk his $11,000 investment. So he flew to Guyana and then on to Paramaribo, Surinam; he took a ferry across a river and caught a bus for St. Laurent, French Guiana. In two such trips to the site—there were some mining operations there—he never found so much as a gold nugget. "I didn't know if I was going to get out alive," he later said in court.

If a person didn't get killed looking for his gold mine investment, Becker discovered, he might be ambushed by the IRS through a disallowance of his tax deduction. When he deducted his losses, he became one of 3,025 investors in "Gold for Tax Dollars" challenged by the IRS. He was also one of those brave enough to plead his case in court.

The courts decided Becker and his fellow litigants invested primarily to save taxes, not to make a profit, so they lost. There is no deduction unless there is a profit motive. In a decision in the U.S. Court of Appeals for the Seventh Circuit, Judge William J. Campbell said: "It is unfortunate that in their haste to obtain deductions, taxpayers have put their common sense behind them and have become easy targets for tax-shelter charlatans. . . . The freedom to arrange one's affairs to minimize taxes does not include the right to engage in financial fantasies."

SOURCE: A.J. Cook, "The Roof Is Off Tax Shelters," *Nation's Business*, August 1988, pp. 42 and 44. Used by permission. Copyright 1988, U.S. Chamber of Commerce.

length of the investment horizon is an important determinant of the types of assets selected for an investor's portfolio.

• Investment Strategies

In addition to selecting appropriate investment alternatives, an investor needs to consider strategies dealing with selection, timing, and diversification. These ideas are briefly introduced in this section and are discussed in greater detail throughout the book.

SELECTION As Table 1.1 illustrates, investors have numerous investment options. Even within categories there are abundant choices. For example, within the common stock category, an investor can select from thousands of different common stocks. Thus, once the decision is made to invest in common stocks, the investor must still identify individual stocks that provide the best investment opportunities. **Investment selection** decisions, therefore, involve two aspects: (1) identifying appropriate investment alternatives or categories and (2) selecting individual securities or assets in each category.

Selection strategies may use different approaches. For example, in the selection of common stocks, technical and/or fundamental analysis can be employed. These strategies and the impact of an efficient market upon them are discussed in more detail in Chapter 7.

TIMING **Investment timing,** another critical variable in the selection of any investment alternative, refers to purchasing an asset just before it is likely to increase in value and selling the asset just before it is likely to decrease in value. This decision assumes, of course, that the prices of assets follow some pattern and that the investor can accurately forecast the change in prices. Forecasting the change in prices can be quite difficult. Nevertheless, you do not have to be a mathematician to employ a timing strategy. For example, consider the purchase of a home. Real estate prices tend to reflect the level of inflation. If inflation is quite high, real estate prices tend to go up. Therefore, deciding to purchase a home when economists forecast increases in inflation may be a good timing strategy.

Some investors, particularly those investing in mutual funds, avoid the investment timing issue altogether through a strategy called **dollar-cost averaging.** Instead of trying to time the highs and lows, the individual invests the same amount of money at regular intervals over a long period of time. The logic underlying this strategy is that in periods of high prices the equal-dollar investment buys fewer shares, and during periods of low prices, more shares are bought with the same investment dollars. Thus, the average cost per share to the investor is less than the higher prices over the period but greater than the lower prices.

The potential rewards and risks from timing decisions involving financial assets are illustrated in Figure 1.2. The figure shows average annual rates of return, calculated over the period 1926–1983, for market timing versus a buy-and-hold strategy. Market timing in this example consists of transferring funds between common stocks and Treasury bills. "Perfect" market timing occurs when all funds are invested in common stocks prior to a "bull" (increasing) market and all funds are invested in Treasury bills prior to a "bear" (decreasing) market. The figure shows that if an investor correctly forecast each bull and bear market over the period 1926–1983 and used this information to move funds between common stocks and Treasury bills, the average annual rate of return would have been 18.2 percent. On the other hand, if the investor correctly forecast only 50 percent of the bull and bear markets, the average annual rate of return would have been 8.1 percent. This

FIGURE 1.2
Market Timing Using Financial Assets

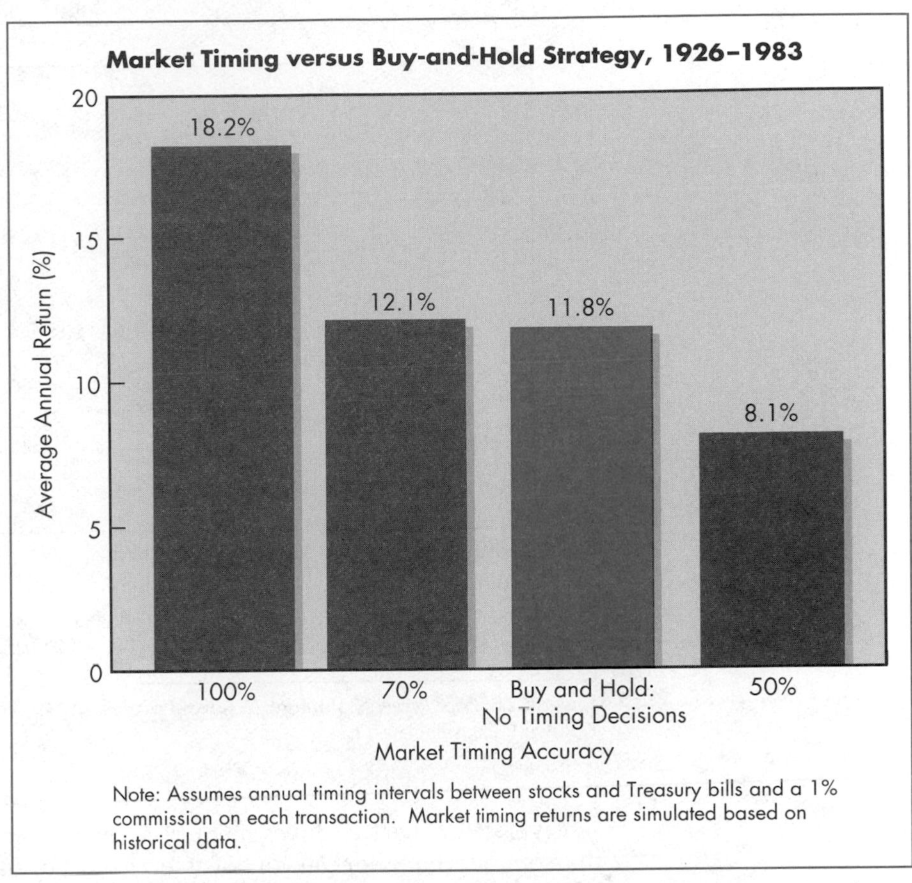

SOURCE: *The Price Report* (Baltimore: T. Rowe Price, Fall 1987). Reprinted by permission of T. Rowe Price Associates, Inc.

rate is significantly below the rate of 11.8 percent that resulted from a simple buy-and-hold strategy using only common stocks.

Figure 1.3 further demonstrates the risk associated with investment timing. The figure indicates that $1 invested in the stock market in 1979 would have grown to $4.52 by 1988. Over this same period, $1 invested in Treasury bills would have grown to only $2.39. If the investor had made the mistake of switching out of stocks into Treasury bills during the five best months of stock market performance over the entire 10-year period, $1 invested in 1979 would have grown to only $2.68. As this graph illustrates, incorrect timing decisions may have significant financial consequences.

Figures 1.2 and 1.3 demonstrate the potential rewards and risks associated with market timing. To be successful at market timing relative to a buy-and-hold strategy, an investor must correctly forecast market movements over 50 percent of the time. Less accurate forecasts result in greatly diminished returns.

FIGURE 1.3
The Risk of Timing the Stock Market: Return on Stocks and Treasury Bills, 1979–1988

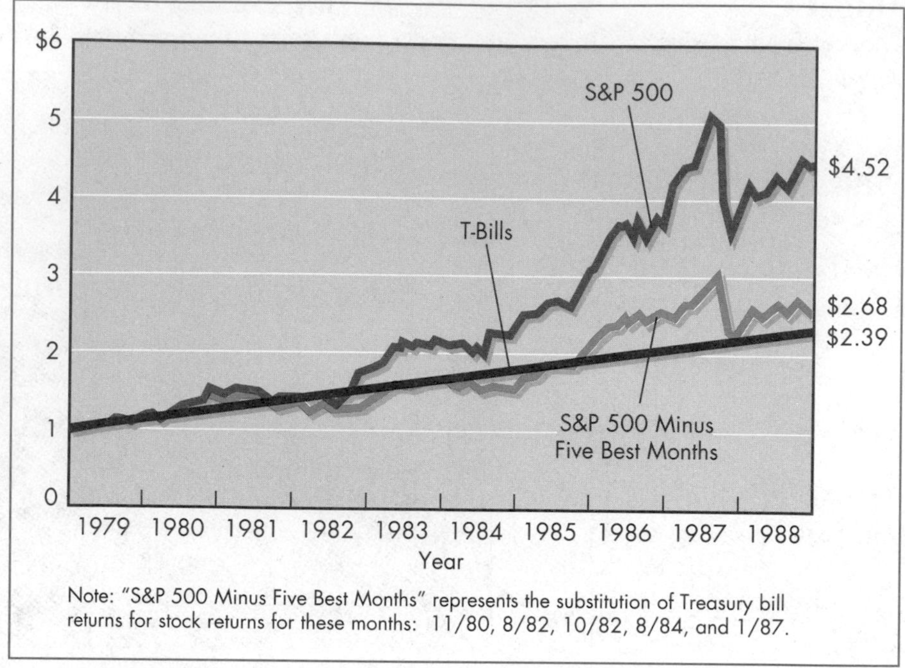

SOURCE: *The Price Report* (Baltimore: T. Rowe Price, Fall 1989). Reprinted by permission of T. Rowe Price Associates, Inc.

DIVERSIFICATION Investment risk can be reduced by including more than one alternative or category of assets in the portfolio and by including more than one asset from each category. This naïve form of **diversification** may significantly reduce risk without a corresponding reduction in the expected rate of return on the portfolio. The importance of diversification and its impact on risk are discussed in Chapters 2 and 19.

An individual investor can achieve a diversified portfolio in several ways. One possibility is to undertake an investment strategy in which the investor personally constructs the portfolio. In applicable chapters throughout the book, we discuss diversification considerations for each investment alternative. Another option is to use professionally managed portfolios, such as mutual funds, to achieve diversification. The rapid growth in the assets of mutual funds during the 1980s suggests that many individual investors are using this approach to achieve diversification. Quite often an investor's portfolio will include more than one professionally managed portfolio in order to achieve proper diversification.

In summary, the decision to invest is usually related to some planned or unplanned expenditure in the future. Most investors prefer to place the invested money in an asset that will yield the highest return. However, other factors, such as risk, after-tax return relative to the risk, investment horizon, selection, timing, and diversification must also be considered. Frequently, these factors are all interrelated.

THE EVOLUTION OF THE INVESTMENT ENVIRONMENT AND PROCESS

• The 1950s and 1960s

During the 1950s and early 1960s, the typical young adult got married, had children, purchased whole life insurance, bought a home, and perhaps purchased a few stocks or bonds for retirement when there was extra discretionary income. Most people planned to pay for their home within 10 to 20 years and to retire and live on their income from their few stocks and bonds as well as their Social Security benefits.

During the late 1960s, individuals' lifetime consumption increased dramatically. More money was needed for the children's education as the cost of a college education increased. Companies expanded their pension plans to include more employees and provide higher benefits. Now pensions supplement most retirees' Social Security income. Most individuals still saved some money to invest in a few good growth stocks or bonds.

• The 1970s

The investment environment began to change significantly in the 1970s. The rate of inflation grew dramatically. The financial community, in particular, felt the impact of rapidly increasing wages and prices, as well as the restructuring of the relationships between wages and prices. In response to these changing patterns of return, risk, and prices, individuals began to realize that certain assets, such as real estate, might be a good investment in an inflationary environment. Other investments, however, were not as likely to provide a return sufficient to offset inflation. The financial community responded by creating a multitude of new investment products. Investments in money market alternatives, such as certificates of deposit, grew at a rapid rate during this period and sometimes yielded rates of return of 15 percent or more. Individual investors realized that the savings and loan associations could not compete and shifted much of their money to the higher-yielding money market instruments. Insurance companies also saw a drain on their capital as individuals borrowed against their whole life insurance policies at very low rates of interest and invested the proceeds in money market alternatives. Real estate partnerships began to be formed. The traditional stock and bond investment alternatives did not appear to promise the same rate of return as the new, exciting products.

Interest rates on borrowed money also changed. In response, the mortgage market invented **adjustable rate mortgages,** which had interest rates below those of fixed rate mortgages, but carried the risk of higher interest rates and thus higher monthly payments. The world struggled to invent new ways to deal with an inflationary environment not fully understood. Many individual investors tended to move out of the traditional stock and bond markets and into other markets such as precious metals, real estate, and money market securities. This shift left institutional investors, like insurance companies and pension funds, dominant in the traditional financial markets.

• The 1980s

Although the rate of inflation decreased significantly by the mid-1980s, interest rates continued to fluctuate. Rates on money market securities declined significantly to reflect the lower rates of inflation. Real estate prices did not rise as rapidly as before and actually declined in some parts of the country. The world, however, was more complex than it had been before the inflationary period of the 1970s. The stock and bond markets were still dominated by large institutional investors. Once again, the financial community responded by creating new products with different patterns of return and risk. Mutual funds grew rapidly during this period, both in dollar size and number of funds. Insurance companies introduced new products such as universal life insurance with both insurance and investment features. Thanks to the Tax Reform Act of 1986, investors had new tax consequences to consider. Technological developments also added to the complexities. Microcomputers came into widespread use, speeding the flow of information and enabling it to be analyzed faster and more thoroughly. Investment decisions could now be made almost instantaneously with the arrival of new information.

The stock market experienced a bull market during the 1980s that ranked as the strongest market since the decade of the 1950s. Figure 1.4 indicates the movement in stock prices over the period 1949–1987. In addition to showing the trend, Figure 1.4 provides percentage changes for the bull and bear markets that occurred over this period. For example, the bull market beginning in August 1982 and ending in August 1987 resulted in a 228.8 percent increase in common stock prices.

Beginning on August 25, 1987, however, the stock market experienced the second worst bear market since World War II. The market declined 33.2 percent in approximately 2 months. Declines of this magnitude typically take 6 to 21 months. Even more amazing than the 33.2 percent decline was the behavior of the market on October 19, 1987, or "Black Monday."

On Black Monday, the Dow Jones Industrial Average declined 508 points (22 percent), and the Standard & Poor's 500 Stock Composite Index declined 57.6 points (20.5 percent) on record trading volume. This decline was significantly greater than the 12.8 percent decline that occurred on "Black Tuesday," October 29, 1929.

FIGURE 1.4 • Bull and Bear Stock Markets, 1949–1987

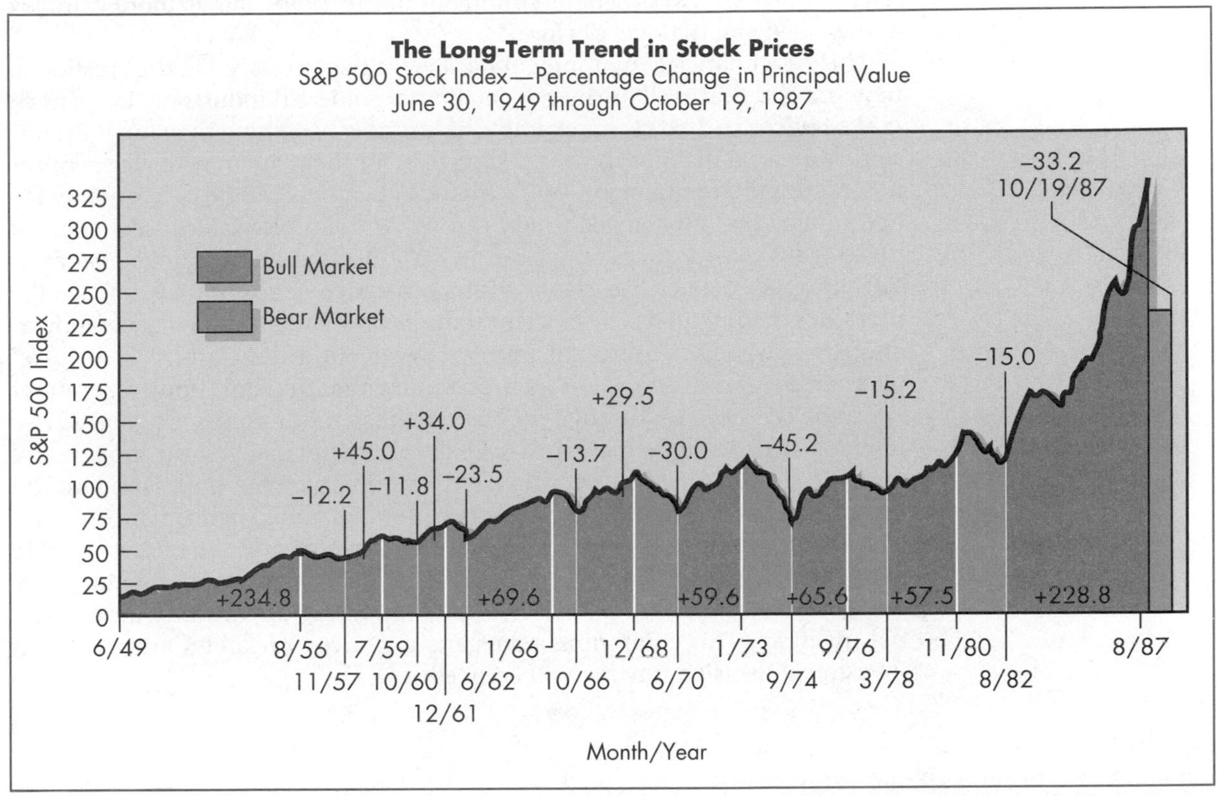

SOURCE: *The Price Report* (Baltimore: T. Rowe Price, Winter 1987). Reprinted by permission of T. Rowe Price Associates, Inc.

The volatility of the stock market during the late 1980s caused many investors to sell common stocks and to reassess their investment strategies. In addition to the domestic stock markets, foreign markets experienced increased volatility. Other investment alternatives, such as long-term bonds and precious metals, also demonstrated volatile prices. It took almost two years for the Standard & Poor's 500 Stock Composite Index to return to the level it had reached on August 25, 1987.

• The 1990s

Even with these environmental changes, the individual investor still has the same basic objective: to save money from current income so that more money can be spent in later years. This investor still wants the highest level of return possible for the risk that he or she assumes. The difference is that the investment-choice set has grown substantially. In addition to a number of new, domestic investment choices, the investor is becoming more aware of the potential portfolio advantages of diversifying internationally. These changes have created an investment environment in the 1990s that is more complex and challenging than ever before.

This new financial environment has been a major catalyst in the creation of new industries as well as the reformation of some old industries. The **financial services industry,** for example, is just now beginning to mature. Professional financial planners help investors plan for their children's college education and/or their retirement. While financial planners can help, frequently tax accountants are also needed to sort through the complex tax consequences of these plans. Many investors also rely on a professional portfolio manager. This manager may be associated with a brokerage house or may manage the investor's mutual fund. The efficient transfer of wealth from one generation to another may now require not only a lawyer but a tax planner, a financial planner, and an insurance broker. The individual investor, however, cannot leave the decisions to the advisers. Rather, the investor must seek good advice about alternative investments, analyze the alternatives, invest the money, and periodically review the performance of the investments (i.e., compare the actual performance of the investments with the planned performance).

In order to undertake these activities, the investor must be knowledgeable about the fundamentals of investments. The investment environment of the 1990s offers a challenging but potentially rewarding opportunity for individual investors. This environment suggests a strategy of careful and informed investment decision making will be needed.

ORGANIZATION AND FEATURES OF THE BOOK

Although this book may not make you wealthy, studying it carefully should enable you to make wiser and more informed investment decisions. Drawing upon results from investment research, each chapter presents material consistent with the practical needs of the individual investor. Where appropriate, the chapter sets out the underlying theoretical framework and then applies that framework to investment decisions faced by individuals.

The text is organized into eight sections. Part 1 (Chapters 1 and 2) provides an overview of investing and introduces measures of investment risk and return. Part 2 (Chapters 3 through 7) examines the environment in which investors operate. In addition to chapters describing the operations and regulations of securities markets and sources of investment information, Part 2 includes chapters on investing in mutual funds and investing internationally. These two chapters appear early in the book because we believe that these two topics are highly significant for investors in the 1990s. The final chapter in this part describes various investment strategies for individual investors.

Part 3 (Chapters 8 and 9) examines various approaches to economic, market, and industry analysis as well as financial statement analysis. In Part 4 (Chapters 10 and 11), bond fundamentals, valuation, and bond investment strategies are discussed. Part 5 (Chapters 12 through 14) examines the important analytical tools and valuation concepts used in the fundamental analysis of preferred and common stocks. Part 6 (Chapters 15 through 18) provides information on other investment opportunities, including options, warrants, rights, convertible securities, commodity and financial futures, and real assets such as precious metals, real estate, and collectibles. A detailed examination of portfolio and capital market theory is provided in Chapters 19 and 20 of Part 7. In addition, Chapter 21 examines techniques for the analysis of portfolio performance and discusses the degree to which security markets are efficient. While this chapter summarizes the evidence for market efficiency, the efficiency of the various markets in which assets are traded is examined in appropriate chapters throughout the book. Finally, Part 8 (Chapter 22) is devoted entirely to individual investment decision making. The Stanton case introduced in this chapter is used to illustrate personal financial planning.

Because this book stresses investment decision making for the individual investor, we have provided a Concept Applications box in the Summary section of appropriate chapters. This feature identifies how the important concepts introduced in the chapter can be applied in the investment decision-making process.

Because the microcomputer has become so important in the investment decision process, a complete investment analysis software package has been developed to accompany this book. A computer symbol like the one in the left margin appears next to equations where applications from the investment software package are available. At the end of appropriate chapters, the access procedures for problem solving using the investment analysis software are also provided. These keys, along with a full explanation of the software in Appendix A-1, should prove helpful in solving many of the end-of-chapter problems.

SUMMARY

Bill and Martha Stanton's desire to provide for their children's education and their retirement years is not based on "get-rich-quick" schemes. Their investment objectives are similar to those of most individuals in the 1990s. While the Stantons' past strategy of investing in their business has been successful, they recognize that their future financial goals will have to be realized in a very complex environment with numerous investment alternatives. The reality of the situation is that they will probably need to obtain financial advice from a variety of sources, including a financial planner, a tax accountant, a lawyer, and an insurance broker.

It is important that the investor set an appropriate investment objective(s) and the accompanying investment horizon. In addition, in developing investment strategies to achieve the objective(s), the investor must understand the tax consequences and expected risk and return associated with the various investment alternatives. Perhaps most importantly, the investor should recognize that achieving an investment objective involves the creation of a portfolio of assets and not a collection of individual assets. How these assets interact with each other is of paramount importance in determining the expected risk with each other is of paramount importance in determining the expected risk of the investor's portfolio. An individual asset considered in isolation may be very risky. Combining this asset into a portfolio of other assets may actually reduce the risk of the overall portfolio. These topics are carefully developed throughout the remainder of the book from the perspective of an individual investor.

• KEY TERMS

Adjustable rate mortgages
Diversification
Dollar-cost averaging
Financial assets
Financial services industry
Investment horizon
Investment objective
Investment selection
Investment strategies
Investment timing
Rate of return
Real assets
Risk
Tax consequences

• QUESTIONS

1. Briefly define selection, timing, and diversification. In your opinion, is one of these three decisions more important to an individual investor than the others?
2. Explain why many individuals are willing to save rather than consume some of their current income.
3. What are some of the advantages of including real assets as investment alternatives for individuals?
4. Explain why taxes are an important consideration in the investment decision-making process. Why is it important to consider investment approaches that allow you to defer taxes? What is the risk of adopting this approach?
5. Using Figure 1.1, discuss the significance of the difference in the returns of the investment alternatives over the 10-year period, June 1980 to June 1989, and the 1-year period ending June 1, 1990.
6. Define the investment horizon, and indicate why it is an important factor to consider in choosing among investment alternatives.
7. Using Figures 1.2 and 1.3, indicate the potential risks and rewards associated with market timing using common stocks and Treasury bills. In your opinion, is market timing a viable strategy for individual investors?
8. Explain how an individual investor can diversify a portfolio. What are the advantages of diversification?
9. Compare and contrast the investment environment of the 1970s with that of the 1990s. What are the implications of this changing environment for individual investors?
10. Based on your current situation, describe an appropriate investment objective(s). What is the investment horizon associated with your investment objective(s)?

CHAPTER 2

Investment Risk and Return

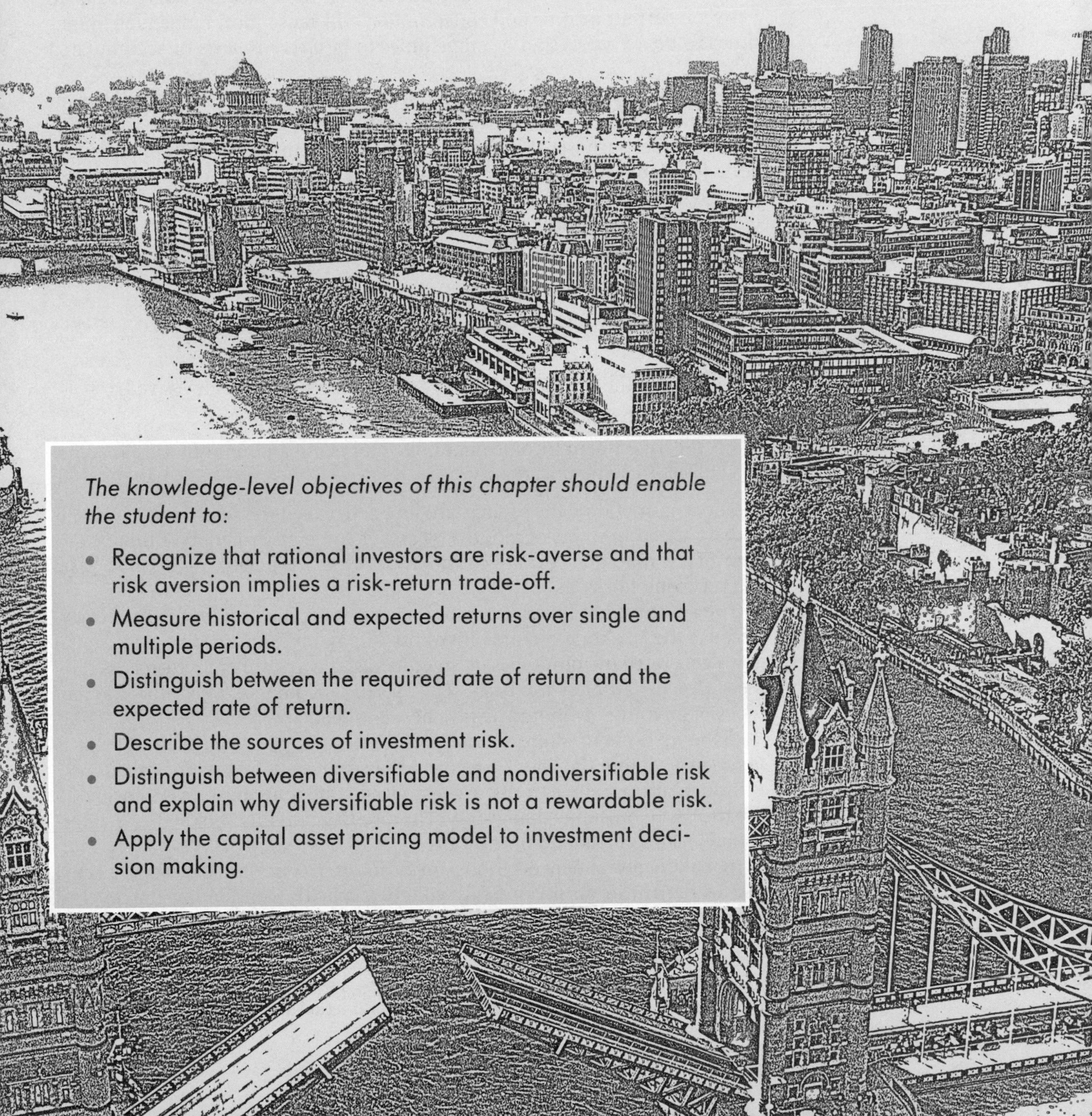

The knowledge-level objectives of this chapter should enable the student to:

- Recognize that rational investors are risk-averse and that risk aversion implies a risk-return trade-off.
- Measure historical and expected returns over single and multiple periods.
- Distinguish between the required rate of return and the expected rate of return.
- Describe the sources of investment risk.
- Distinguish between diversifiable and nondiversifiable risk and explain why diversifiable risk is not a rewardable risk.
- Apply the capital asset pricing model to investment decision making.

INTRODUCTION

Most individuals need to earn enough money to satisfy their consumption desires and long-run objectives.[1] Frequently, their desired life-style requires expenditures that exceed their income for a given time period. During other income periods, expenditures may be less than their income. This imbalance between current income and consumption will cause most individuals sometimes to be *net savers* and at other times to be *net consumers* of accumulated wealth.

While one could bury savings in the yard, the financial system allows an individual to earn additional income on money set aside for future consumption or other purposes. This trade-off in which current consumption is forgone for higher levels of future consumption is the essence of the investment process. If asked, "How much future consumption do you want?" most individuals would respond, "As much as I can have." Unfortunately, the amount of future consumption is affected by several factors, including the following:

- How long will the savings be invested?
- How much will be saved or consumed in future income periods?
- What will be the future rate of inflation?
- What are the tax consequences associated with the money saved?
- How much will the invested income earn after taxes?
- Is the investment income guaranteed, or is the amount of future income subject to some uncertainty?

The length of time the savings are invested, called the *investment horizon*, is usually stated in terms of months, years, or some other period of time. Horizons of less than one year are considered very short; periods of 20 or 30 years are very long horizons.

The amount that invested money will earn is called the *investment return*. Because the tax code requires investors to pay taxes on income and capital gains generated by most types of investments, the investment return is usually measured on an after-tax basis. The specific income-tax effect for different types of investments should always be identified.

If the investment after-tax rate of return is not guaranteed, then there is *uncertainty* about the rate of return. Uncertainty is frequently called *risk*. Although uncertainty and risk are technically different, most investors tend to use the two words interchangeably. The discussion in this book will not differentiate between risk and uncertainty.

In making investment decisions, investors often concentrate on the expected rate of return on an investment without explicitly considering the level of expected risk. The historical performance of investment alternatives is often

[1] This chapter uses a number of basic statistical concepts, such as expected value, variance, and standard deviation. Appendix A-2, Review of Analytical Techniques, provides an explanation of these concepts.

TABLE 2.1 • Compound Annual Rates of Return over Varying Holding Periods

	Twenty years		Ten years		Five years		One year	
	Return	*Rank*	*Return*	*Rank*	*Return*	*Rank*	*Return*	*Rank*
Coins	16.6%	1	12.9%	2	14.5%	4	30.2%	3
Chinese ceramics	13.3	2	8.7	6	12.2	5	40.3	2
Gold	11.5	3	2.8	9	−1.6	10	−20.5	12
Old-master paintings	10.9	4	9.6	5	18.4	2	50.7	1
Diamonds	10.4	5	8.3	7	10.7	6	15.5	5
Stocks[a]	10.3	6	17.0	1	20.1	1	24.5	4
Treasury bills	8.6	7	10.0	4	7.2	7	7.8	7
Bonds[b]	8.6	7	10.9	3	17.6	3	11.2	6
Oil	8.3	8	1.2	10	−10.7	12	3.2	10
Housing	7.6	9	5.5	8	5.1	9	6.6	8
Farmland	6.0	10	−0.5	12	−5.3	11	5.9	9
Silver	5.5	11	−4.6	13	−11.2	13	−23.2	13
Foreign exchange	4.0	12	0.9	11	7.1	8	−13.3	11

SOURCE: *Medical Economics*, September 18, 1989, p. 34. Reprinted by permission.
[a]Assumes quarterly reinvestment of dividends.
[b]Assumes monthly reinvestment.

evaluated the same way. In Table 2.1, the historical performances of 13 asset categories are ranked over both short- and long-run periods based totally on their compound annual rates of return. But is it reasonable to assume that the risk of collectibles, such as old-master paintings, was at the same level over the various periods as the risk of Treasury bills? The tendency to emphasize investment return and neglect investment risk can, perhaps, be traced to the fact that measures of return are intuitively easier to understand than measures of risk.

The major factors in the decision to consume now or to invest and consume later can be summarized by considering the after-tax return relative to the risk over the investment horizon. Rational investors are considered to be risk-averse and believe that the expected return from an investment should increase as risk increases and that the return should increase as the investment horizon lengthens since long horizons involve more uncertainty.

The degree of risk aversion varies among individual investors. For example, a highly risk-averse investor would require a large increase in required return for a small increase in risk. Although they are not considered to be rational, investors may also be "risk-neutral" (increased risk does not change the required return) or "risk-takers" (increased risk reduces the required return).

This chapter begins by examining an investment's expected rate of return or holding period return. Return is measured over a single period as well as over several periods. The investor's required rate of return and the expected rate of return for an investment are distinguished. In establishing the required rate of return, consideration must be given to the risk of an asset. Sources of investment risk, various measures of investment risk, and the integration of investment risk and the required rate of return are discussed. The chapter concludes with an application demonstrating risk and return concepts.

INVESTMENT RETURN

While the rate of return may be intuitively easy to understand, the time horizon can make the computation complex. Therefore, it is necessary to examine how the rate of return is measured over different periods of time.

• Single-Period Measure of Return

The *investment return* is defined as the after-tax increase in the value of the initial investment. The increase in value can come from two sources: a direct cash payment to the investor or an increase in the market value of the investment relative to the original purchase price. For example, suppose you own shares of common stock that you bought one year ago for \$20,000. Under the Tax Reform Act of 1986, no distinction is made, for tax purposes, between cash dividends and capital gains. If during the year you received \$500 in cash dividends on an after-tax basis and the stock could be sold today for a net after-tax receipt of \$25,000, then your total after-tax return would be \$5,500, calculated as follows:

$$\$500 + (\$25{,}000 - \$20{,}000) = \$5{,}500 \tag{2.1}$$

Because the dollar amount of the return is related to the dollar amount of the initial investment, investors prefer to express return as a percentage. This is calculated by comparing the return to the amount initially invested. The *rate of return* over the holding period, or **holding period return** (**HPR**), is computed as

$$\text{HPR} = \frac{(\text{ending price} - \text{beginning price}) + \text{cash receipts}}{\text{beginning price}} \tag{2.2}$$

Applying Equation 2.2 to the common stock example gives the HPR over the one-year period:

$$\text{HPR} = \frac{(\$25{,}000 - \$20{,}000) + \$500}{\$20{,}000} = 27.5\% \tag{2.3}$$

The after-tax HPR of 27.5 percent has two components: a 25 percent increase in price or capital appreciation (\$5,000 ÷ \$20,000), and a 2.5 percent dividend return (\$500 ÷ \$20,000).

Holding period returns are often calculated for periods other than one year; for this reason, the length of the holding period must always be indicated for a specific HPR. Many HPRs over periods shorter or longer than one year are "annualized." In general, if the length of the holding period is not specified, it is assumed to be one year.

• Measures of Return over Several Periods

Suppose that you have the following data on the performance of your Individual Retirement Account (IRA) tax-deferred portfolio:

	Market value	Income distribution
January 1, 1990	$ 8,000	—
December 31, 1990	8,100	$ 500
December 31, 1991	11,000	1,000

Using Equation 2.2, the HPR for 1990 is 7.50 percent {[($8,100 − $8,000) + $500]/$8,000}, and the HPR for 1991 is 48.15 percent {[($11,000 − $8,100) + $1,000]/$8,100}. How can a two-year HPR be calculated? The correct calculation would consider the timing of the income distribution as well as the appreciation in the market value of the portfolio.

Two assumptions can be made about the income distribution of $500 paid on December 31, 1990. Under one assumption, the $500 distribution would be treated as income that was *not* reinvested, giving a two-year HPR of

$$HPR_{p,2t} = \frac{\$11{,}000 - \$8{,}000 + \$500 + \$1{,}000}{\$8{,}000} \tag{2.4}$$

$$= 56.25\%$$

Under the second, more accurate, assumption, the $500 is assumed to be reinvested when it was received on December 31, 1990. It is reinvested for one year at the HPR of 48.15 percent for 1991:

$$HPR_{p,2t} = \frac{\$11{,}000 - \$8{,}000 + \$500(1 + .4815) + \$1{,}000}{\$8{,}000} \tag{2.5}$$

$$= 59.26\%$$

• Annualized Holding Period Returns

The preceding examples assumed a two-year holding period and calculated a two-year HPR. Typically, however, HPRs are reported as an annual equivalent. How should the annualized HPR be calculated for the IRA portfolio example? One possibility is to take the simple arithmetic average of the annual HPRs computed by

$$\overline{\text{HPR}} = \sum_{t=1}^{n} (\text{HPR}_t)/n \qquad (2.6)$$

The simple arithmetic average, $\overline{\text{HPR}}$, of the IRA portfolio would be 27.825 percent and would be calculated as

$$(.0750 + .4815)/2 = 27.825\%$$

The simple average, however, ignores the compounding effect that results if the $500 received on December 31, 1990, is reinvested. In addition, the result of an arithmetic average return can be distorted if there are large differences in the rates of return across time periods. A rather extreme example will illustrate the problem. Suppose rental property increases 300 percent in the first year but loses 75 percent of its value in the second year. The arithmetic average is computed as

$$\overline{\text{HPR}} = [3.00 + (-.75)]/2 = 112.5\% \qquad (2.7)$$

If you initially invested $50,000 in the property, at the end of the first year the investment would be worth $200,000 [50,000 + (50,000)(3)], but by the end of the second year, your property would be worth only the original $50,000 [200,000 + (200,000)(−.75)]. Although the arithmetic average rate of return is 112.5 percent, this investment really generated zero return over the two-year holding period.

Although this example may be extreme, large differences in the periodic rates of return over longer investment horizons will cause the arithmetic rate of return to be misleading.

The **geometric mean** rate of return does not suffer from this flaw. The geometric mean rate of return, $\overline{\text{HPR}}_g$, is defined as the rate of return that would make the initial investment equal to the ending investment value. In our rental property example, the geometric mean rate of return would be 0 percent since a 0 rate of return makes the initial investment equal to the ending investment value.

The $\overline{\text{HPR}}_g$ is calculated by taking the nth root of the product of one plus the individual rates of return. The formula for the geometric mean rate of return is

$$\overline{\text{HPR}}_g = \prod_{t=1}^{n} (1 + \text{HPR}_t)^{1/n} - 1.0 \qquad (2.8)$$

where Π represents the product (the result of multiplying). The individual rates of return, represented by HPR_t, are expressed as 1 plus the individual rate of return. For example, a 10 percent HPR would be 1.10, and a loss of 20 percent would be represented by .80 [1 + (−.20)]. The n-term exponent represents the number of time intervals over the investment horizon.

The 0 percent $\overline{\text{HPR}}_g$ from the rental property example is calculated as follows:

$$\begin{aligned}\overline{\text{HPR}}_g &= \{(1 + 3)[1 + (-.75)]\}^{1/2} - 1.0 \\ &= [(4)(.25)]^{1/2} - 1.0 \\ &= (1)^{1/2} - 1 \\ &= \sqrt{1} - 1 \\ &= 1 - 1 \\ &= 0\%\end{aligned} \tag{2.9}$$

Returning to the IRA portfolio example and using Equation 2.8, the geometric mean of the annual HPRs can be calculated as

$$\begin{aligned}\overline{\text{HPR}}_g &= \prod_{t=1}^{n} (1 + \text{HPR}_t)^{1/n} - 1.0 \\ &= [(1.075)(1.4815)]^{1/2} - 1.0 = 26.2\%\end{aligned} \tag{2.10}$$

Thus, assuming annual compounding and reinvestment of income, the two-year HPR would be

$$\text{HPR}_{p,2t} = (1.2620)^2 - 1 = 59.26\% \tag{2.11}$$

The geometric mean HPR is, therefore, consistent with the assumption of reinvesting income when it is received. This point is illustrated by comparing the results from Equations 2.5 and 2.11. Also note that for the IRA example the arithmetic mean (27.825%) is larger than the geometric mean (26.2%). Due to the inherent bias in the arithmetic mean, the geometric mean will always be equal to or less than the arithmetic mean. The arithmetic mean and geometric mean will only be equal when the HPRs are constant over the investment horizon. If the compound rate of return during the time intervals composing the investment horizon is considered, the geometric mean rate of return is similar to the rate of interest used in compound interest calculations.

In summary, all income distributions over the holding period should be considered. In most cases, income distributions are assumed to be reinvested at the HPRs for the following periods. These assumptions can be correctly incorporated into the calculation of annualized HPRs by calculating the annual HPRs using Equation 2.2, and then calculating the geometric mean HPR using Equation 2.8.

• Required Rate of Return

When setting the **required rate of return** on an investment, an investor must consider the real rate of return, expected inflation, and risk. Because consumption is forgone today, the investor is entitled to a rate of return that compensates for this deferred consumption. Since the investor expects to receive an increase in the *real* goods purchased later, and assuming, for the moment, zero expected inflation and risk, the required rate could equal the **real rate of return,** in which case it would represent the pure time value of money. The capital markets determine this rate based upon the supply of money to be invested relative to the demand for borrowed money.

For example, if an investor plans to lend $500 today in exchange for consumption at some later date (assuming no inflation and risk), then the lender may expect to receive $515 at the expected time of consumption. The $15 return on the investment of $500, or 3 percent, represents the pure time value of money, the real return paid to compensate the investor for deferred consumption.

Now, if the investor expects that the prices of the goods to be consumed will have increased by the time the investment provides a return, then the investor will also require that the return be adjusted for those price increases. In other words, the investor will require compensation for the rate of inflation in addition to the real return. For example, if the investor expects inflation to be 5 percent over the period of the loan, then he or she would expect to receive a total of $540, which includes $15 for the real return and $25 (.05 × $500) to compensate for the 5 percent rate of inflation.

Investment returns are usually not guaranteed. If an investor is uncertain about future returns, he or she will expect to be compensated for that uncertainty and will require an additional return from the borrower. The investor in our example above may want to add a 2 percent additional return for risk. Then the required rate of return would be 10 percent. The total required return of 10 percent pays the investor 3 percent for the time value of money, 5 percent for expected inflation, and 2 percent for risk. The return for expected inflation and risk, or 7 percent, is called the **risk premium.** Estimation of the required return will be demonstrated later in the chapter.

• Expected Rate of Return

If an investment is to be made, the **expected rate of return,** or the expected holding period return, should be equal to or greater than the required rate of return for that investment. The expected rate of return is based upon the expected cash receipts (e.g., dividends or interest) over the holding period and the expected ending, or selling, price. The expected rate of return is an **ex-ante,** or unknown, future return. Unless the rate of return is guaranteed, most investors recognize that several rates of return are possible. Investors summarize these possible rates of return into a single number called the expected rate of return. The remainder of this section examines three techniques for calculating the expected return.

If the investor can describe the possible variables that will influence each of the possible rates of return and assign probabilities to these outcomes, the expected rate of return should equal the weighted average of the various possibilities. Listing the possible investment results and assigning probabilities to each of these outcomes is the same as creating a probability distribution in statistics. Probability distributions are used to describe possible outcomes and to assign individual probabilities, from zero (no chance of occurring) to one (full certainty that the outcome will happen), to each possible outcome.

For example, an investor who believes that an investment will provide different rates of return under different economic conditions might construct a probability distribution for those returns. If the economy is strong, as evidenced by strong real economic growth, the investment might yield a 20 percent rate of return. The investor may think that if the economy exhibits moderate real growth, the investment will yield a 10 percent rate of return. Finally, the investor may forecast that if the economy weakens, the investment will provide a return of negative 10 percent. The investor estimates the probabilities for each of these economic scenarios as a 30 percent chance of a strong economy, a 40 percent chance of a moderate economy, and a 30 percent chance of a weakened economy. This information can be summarized as follows:

State of the economy	Probability, P_j	Rate of return, HPR_j
Strong growth	.30	20%
Moderate growth	.40	10
Weak growth	.30	−10
	1.00	

Thus, the investor has forecast three possible outcomes, each based upon a possible state of the economy. Each economic state will result in a different expected rate of return. Subjective probabilities, P_j, were assigned to each outcome. The overall expected rate of return, $E(\text{HPR})$, can be calculated as a weighted average of the three forecasts:

$$E(\text{HPR}) = \sum_{j=1}^{n} P_j \text{HPR}_j \tag{2.12}$$

The $E(\text{HPR})$ can be estimated as

$$\begin{aligned} E(\text{HPR}) &= (.3)(.20) + (.4)(.1) + (.3)(-.1) \\ &= .06 + .04 - .03 \\ &= 7.0\% \end{aligned}$$

In this example, the investor assigned probabilities to each of the three possible economic conditions and estimated the expected rate of return under each condition. This task is usually quite difficult. The investor is attempting to develop accurate forecasts of uncertain economic events and the rates of return that will result under each economic environment.

Often, forecast probabilities are calculated by applying statistical sampling techniques to historical data. In this second approach, actual historical, or

ex-post, rates of return are collected. Then the percentage of observations that represent each of the economic conditions is computed. For example, assume that 100 historical observations were collected and categorized as strong, moderate, or weak economic conditions. If 30 observations were categorized as strong economic conditions, 40 as moderate, and the rest as weak, then on the basis of these historical observations, the forecaster could estimate the probabilities of a strong, moderate, or weak economy as 30 percent, 40 percent, and 30 percent, respectively.

The corresponding rates of return could then be estimated from the ex-post rates of return in each category (e.g., the average rate of return for all observations occurring during the period categorized as strong economic conditions might be 30 percent). While this technique of using historical relationships to forecast future possibilities has its limitations, it does at least provide an initial forecast that the investor can use as a guide in creating a forecast. Another advantage is that the technique is relatively straightforward and easy to use.

A third technique for estimating the expected rate of return is to collect a sample of ex-post rates of return that represent the distribution of the rates of return over the forecast horizon. Then, assuming that the observations have equal probabilities of occurring, compute the statistical average. For example, consider an investor who has a one-quarter investment horizon and has collected quarterly rates of return for the past five years. By assuming that each observed rate of return has an equal chance of occurring next quarter, the investor can calculate the expected return by using a simple arithmetic average. Table 2.2 provides the data that would be needed for this calculation.

Assuming that each of the ex-post rates of return in Table 2.2 has an equal probability of occurring during the forecast period, the probability of each return is 5 percent. The expected rate of return, $E(\text{HPR})$, can then be calcu-

TABLE 2.2 • Quarterly Ex-Post Holding Period Returns

Quarter	Quarterly ex-post HPRs	Quarter	Quarterly ex-post HPRs
1	15.87%	12	−2.03%
2	5.38	13	10.05
3	4.84	14	5.61
4	6.07	15	10.57
5	−4.44	16	3.03
6	6.20	17	−1.08
7	0.19	18	16.38
8	2.73	19	14.15
9	−1.93	20	15.95
10	11.46	Total	130.65%
11	11.65		

lated using Equation 2.12. Alternatively, since each outcome has an equal probability of occurring, the $E(\text{HPR})$ can be calculated using a simple arithmetic average. Using Equation 2.6 and the information in Table 2.2, this calculation would result in the following expected quarterly rate of return:

$$\begin{aligned} E(\overline{\text{HPR}}) &= 130.65\%/20 \\ &= 6.53\% \end{aligned}$$

The three estimation techniques discussed here are relatively simple forecasting tools. More sophisticated forecasting techniques could also be used to derive the estimated probability distribution. Regardless of the forecasting technique used, the goal is the same. The investor is attempting to describe the possible events that could influence the expected rate of return. The process helps the investor accomplish two objectives: to compute the expected rate of return from the distribution of possible outcomes and simultaneously to describe the uncertainty or risk associated with the investment. For example, Figure 2.1 depicts the distribution associated with the data in Table 2.2. The wide dispersion of historical returns shown in the figure indicates that great uncertainty is associated with the expected return estimated from these holding period returns.

FIGURE 2.1 • Frequency Distribution

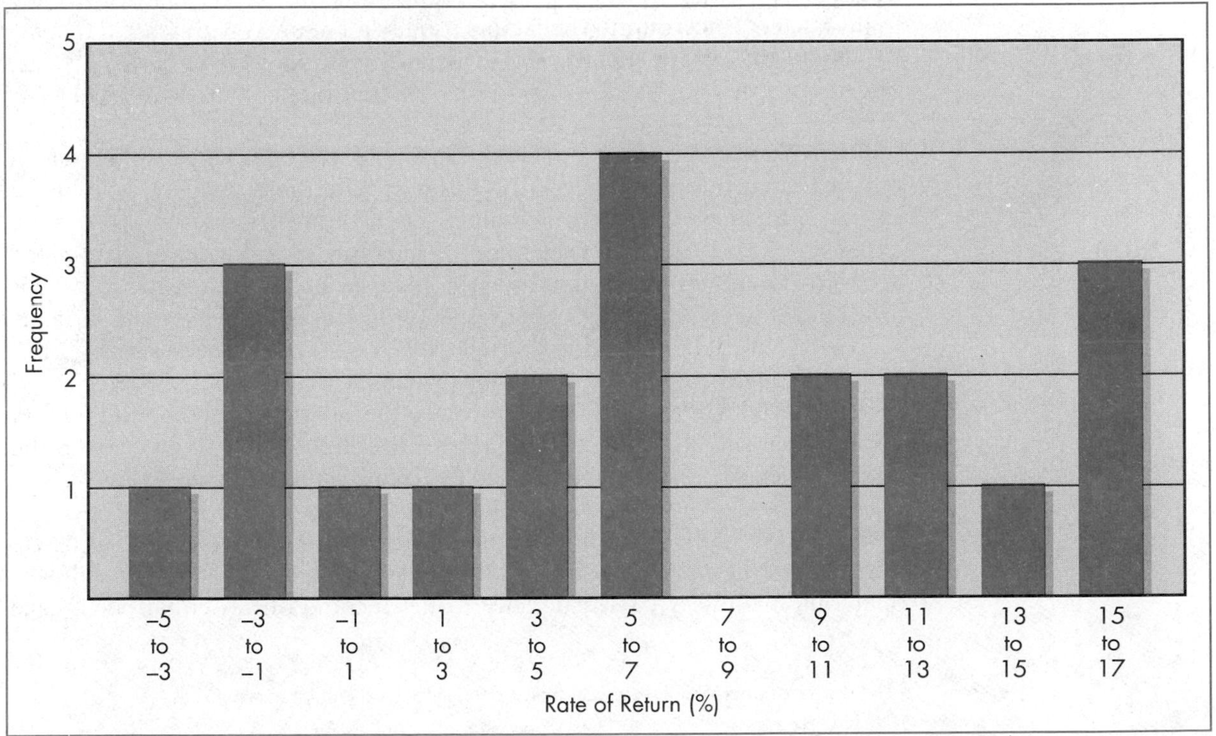

INVESTMENT RISK

• Sources of Investment Risk

Rational investors would agree that an investment's required return should increase as the risk of the investment increases. Most investors would also agree on how the expected rate of return should be calculated. But when the discussion turns to risk, the debate begins.

As discussed earlier, the real return will provide a rate of return that compensates the investor for deferred consumption. To this rate of return should be added an additional rate of return that provides for expected inflation and other types of risk. But how much additional return should be added to this rate to compensate the investor for risk? This relationship can be illustrated as

$$E(R_j) = \text{RR} + \text{RP}_j \quad \textbf{(2.13)}$$

where

$E(R_j)$ = required rate of return for asset j
RR = real rate of return
RP_j = risk premium for asset j

Although a single risk premium must compensate the investor for all the uncertainty associated with the investment, numerous factors may contribute to investment uncertainty. The factors usually mentioned with respect to marketable securities are business risk, financial risk, liquidity risk, default risk, interest rate risk, management risk, and purchasing power risk.

BUSINESS RISK **Business risk** refers to the uncertainty about the rate of return caused by the nature of the business. The most frequently discussed causes of business risk are uncertainty about the firm's sales and operating expenses. Clearly, the firm's sales are not guaranteed and will fluctuate as the economy fluctuates or the nature of the industry changes. A firm's income is also related to its operating expenses. If all operating expenses are variable, then sales volatility will be passed directly to operating income. Most firms, however, have some fixed operating expenses (for example, depreciation, rent, salaries). These fixed expenses cause the operating income to be more volatile than sales. Business risk is related to sales volatility as well as to the operating leverage of the firm caused by fixed operating expenses.[2]

FINANCIAL RISK The firm's capital structure or sources of financing determine **financial risk.** If the firm is all equity financed, then any variability in operating income is passed directly to net income on an equal percentage

[2]The degree of operating leverage at a particular sales level can be measured as

$$\frac{(\text{sales} - \text{variable operating costs})}{(\text{sales} - \text{variable operating costs} - \text{fixed operating costs})}$$

basis. If the firm is partially financed by debt that requires fixed interest payments or by preferred stock that requires fixed preferred dividend payments, then these fixed charges introduce financial leverage. This leverage causes net income to vary more than operating income. The introduction of financial leverage causes the firm's lenders and its stockholders to view their income streams as having additional uncertainty. As a result of financial leverage, both investment groups would increase the risk premiums that they require for investing in the firm.[3]

LIQUIDITY RISK **Liquidity risk** is associated with the uncertainty created by the inability to sell the investment quickly for cash. An investor assumes that the investment can be sold at the expected price when future consumption is planned. As the investor considers the sale of the investment, he or she faces two uncertainties: (1) What price will be received? (2) How long will it take to sell the asset? An example of an illiquid asset is a house in a market with an abundance of homes relative to the number of potential buyers. This investment may not sell for several months or even years. Of course, if the price is reduced sufficiently, the real estate will sell, but the investor must make a selling price concession in order for the transaction to occur.

In contrast, a U.S. Treasury bill can be sold almost immediately with very little concession on selling price. Such an investment can be converted to cash almost at will and for a price very close to the price the investor expected.

The liquidity risk for common stocks is more complex. Because they are traded on organized and active markets, common stocks can be sold quickly. Some common stocks, however, have greater liquidity risk than others due to a *thin* market. A thin market occurs when there are relatively few shares outstanding and investor trading interest is limited. The thin market results in a large price *spread* (the difference between the *bid* price buyers are willing to pay and the *ask* price sellers are willing to accept). A large spread increases the cost of trading to the investor and thus represents liquidity risk. Investors considering the purchase of illiquid investments—ones that have no ready market or require price concessions—will demand a rate of return that compensates for the liquidity risk.

DEFAULT RISK **Default risk** is related to the probability that some or all of the initial investment will not be returned. The degree of default risk is closely related to the financial condition of the company issuing the security

---

[3] The degree of financial leverage at a particular level of operating income can be estimated as

$$\frac{\text{operating income}}{(\text{operating income} - \text{interest expense} - \text{before-tax equivalent of preferred dividends})}$$

The before-tax equivalent of preferred dividends can be estimated by dividing the preferred dividends by one minus the marginal tax rate. As the formulas for estimating the degree of operating leverage and the degree of financial leverage indicate, the higher the fixed operating costs and fixed financing costs, the larger will be the impact of a change in sales on operating income and net income.

and the security's rank in claims on assets in the event of default or bankruptcy. For example, if a bankruptcy occurs, creditors, including bondholders, have a claim on assets prior to the claim of common stockholders.

INTEREST RATE RISK Because money has time value, fluctuations in interest rates will cause the value of an investment to fluctuate also. Although **interest rate risk** is most commonly associated with bond price movements (as discussed in Chapter 11, rising interest rates cause bond prices to decline and declining interest rates cause bond prices to rise), movements in interest rates affect almost all investment alternatives. For example, as illustrated in Chapter 14, a change in interest rates will impact the discount rate used to estimate the present value of future cash dividends from common stocks. This change in the discount rate will materially impact the analyst's estimate of the value of a share of common stock.

MANAGEMENT RISK Decisions made by a firm's management and board of directors materially affect the risk faced by investors. Areas affected by these decisions range from product innovation and production methods (business risk) and financing (financial risk) to acquisitions. For example, acquisition or acquisition-defense decisions made by the management of such firms as Ames Department Stores, Harcourt Brace Jovanovich, Inc., and R.J. Reynolds materially affected the risk of the holders of their companies' securities.

PURCHASING POWER RISK **Purchasing power risk** is, perhaps, more difficult to recognize than the other types of risk. It is easy to observe the decline in the price of a stock or bond, but it is often more difficult to recognize that the purchasing power of the return you have earned on an investment has declined (risen) as a result of inflation (deflation). It is important to remember that an investor expects to be compensated for forgoing consumption today. If an individual is invested in dollar-denominated assets such as bonds, Treasury bills, or savings accounts during a period of inflation, the *real*, or inflation adjusted, rate of return will be less than the nominal, or stated, rate of return. Thus, inflation erodes the purchasing power of the dollar and increases investor risk.

While most investors would agree that business, financial, liquidity, default, interest rate, management, purchasing power, and other risks are basic risks associated with investment decisions, most would not agree on how to convert these sources of risk into a single risk-premium measure.

• Measures of Investment Risk

The measurement of risk has always been a subject for debate in the investment industry. This disagreement stems primarily from the various ways investors perceive risk. Many investors, such as banks, may view their major risk as the uncertainty of whether the money they lend will be returned. To these investors, the risk of bankruptcy or default is the major source of risk. A stockholder of a firm considers not only bankruptcy risk but also the risk that the firm will yield a rate of return below some targeted rate. While both of these measurements are intuitively appealing, combining the sources of investment risk into a single statistical measure is quite difficult.

This section introduces two traditional measures of investment risk: the **range** (maximum return − minimum return) and the **standard deviation.** As the discussion expands from individual securities to portfolios of securities, other risk measures are introduced in a later section of this chapter.

While the range communicates the difference between the best possible return and the worst possible return, it does not provide any information about the distribution of rates of return between the extremes. The standard deviation provides more information about the risk of the asset; its advantage is that the uncertainties of returns can be summarized into a single, easily calculated number. The major disadvantage is that the standard deviation considers possible returns above the expected value to be as risky as returns below the expected value.

The standard deviation of a distribution is the square root of the **variance** of the returns around the mean, $\overline{\text{HPR}}$. This measure considers both the rate of return, HPR_j, and the probability, P_j, associated with the return. The variance of a distribution of holding period returns is computed by

$$\sigma_j^2 = \sum_{j=1}^{n} (P_j)(\text{HPR}_j - \overline{\text{HPR}}_j)^2 \quad (2.14)$$

Using the data presented earlier in Table 2.2 for estimating the expected rate of return, Table 2.3 summarizes the calculations required in computing a standard deviation for a distribution with equal probabilities of outcomes. Table 2.4 summarizes the necessary calculations if the HPR probabilities are unequal.

• Coefficient of Variation

An advantage of the standard deviation as a measure of risk is that it can be related to the expected return. The investment community would agree that expected return should increase as risk increases. If risk is measured by the standard deviation, then risk per unit of expected return can be measured by the **coefficient of variation (CV)**. The coefficient of variation is defined by

$$\text{CV}_j = \frac{\sigma_j}{\overline{\text{HPR}}_j} \quad (2.15)$$

The example from Table 2.3 yields a coefficient of variation of

$$\text{CV}_j = \frac{6.35\%}{6.53\%} = .97 \quad (2.16)$$

TABLE 2.3 • Computation of Standard Deviation: Equal Probabilities of Outcome

Quarter	HPR	$HPR_j - \overline{HPR}_j$	$(HPR_j - \overline{HPR}_j)^2$
1	15.87%	9.34%	87.2356*
2	5.38	−1.15	1.3225
3	4.84	−1.69	2.8561
4	6.07	−0.46	0.2116
5	−4.44	−10.97	120.3409
6	6.20	−0.33	0.1089
7	0.19	−6.34	40.1956
8	2.73	−3.80	14.4400
9	−1.93	−8.46	71.5716
10	11.46	4.93	24.3049
11	11.65	5.12	26.2144
12	−2.03	−8.56	73.2736
13	10.05	3.52	12.3904
14	5.61	−0.92	0.8464
15	10.57	4.04	16.3216
16	3.03	−3.50	12.2500
17	−1.08	−7.61	57.9121
18	16.38	9.85	97.0225
19	14.15	7.62	58.0644
20	15.95	9.42	88.7364
Total	130.65%		805.6195

$$\sigma_j^2 = 805.6195/20 = 40.2810$$

$$\overline{HPR}_j = 130.65\%/20 \qquad \sigma_j = \sqrt{40.2810}$$

$$= 6.53\% \qquad \sigma_j = 6.35\%$$

*Note that the unit of measurement for these numbers is the percentage squared rather than percents.

TABLE 2.4 • Computation of Standard Deviation: Unequal Probabilities of Outcome

State of economy	Probability (P_j)	HPR_j	$(P_j)(HPR_j)$	$(HPR_j - \overline{HPR}_j)^2$	$P_j(HPR_j - \overline{HPR}_j)^2$
Strong growth					
Moderate growth	.4	10	4.0	9.0	3.60
Weak growth	.3	−10	−3.0	289.0	86.70
	1.0		$\overline{HPR}_j = 7.0\%$		$\sigma_j^2 = 141.00$
					$\sigma_j = \sqrt{141.00}$
					$\sigma_j = 11.87\%$

*Note that the unit of measurement for these numbers is the percentage squared rather than percents.

If investors believe that the rate of return should increase as the risk increases, then CV_j provides a quick summary of the relative trade-off between expected return and risk. Consider two investments. Investment A has an expected return of 10 percent and a standard deviation of 2 percent. Investment B has an expected return of 11 percent and a standard deviation of 3 percent. The coefficients of variation for the two investments are as follows:

	Investment A	Investment B
Expected return	10%	11%
Standard deviation	2%	3%
Coefficient of variation	2%/10% = .2	3%/11% = .2727

The coefficients of variation indicate that investment A might be preferred by investors since the risk per unit of return is less than that for investment B. The use of the coefficient of variation to rank investments assumes that the investor should expect higher returns for facing higher total risk as measured by the asset's standard deviation (a constant risk-return tradeoff). As we shall see in the next section, this is not necessarily true, and using this measure for ranking purposes may result in suboptimal investment decisions.

BETA: ANOTHER MEASURE OF INVESTMENT RISK[4]

The standard deviation is a measure of the *total* risk of the asset. That is, it measures the dispersion of returns around the mean return. Earlier it was suggested that rational investors should expect higher returns at higher levels of investment risk. Does this mean that the higher the standard deviation of an asset's returns, the higher the required return? The **capital asset pricing model (CAPM)**, which is discussed in detail in Chapter 20, suggests that the answer to this question is not as straightforward as it would seem on the surface.

The CAPM suggests that total risk, as measured by the standard deviation, contains two parts—diversifiable and nondiversifiable risk—and that total risk is equal to the sum of its parts, or

$$\text{total risk} = \text{diversifiable risk} + \text{nondiversifiable risk}$$

The ability of an investor to diversify away a portion of the risk allows for a distinction to be drawn between **diversifiable** and **nondiversifiable risk.**

[4]The material in the remaining portion of this chapter introduces portfolio and capital market theory, or what has become known as modern portfolio theory. The concepts presented here are referred to in a number of the remaining chapters in the book. Chapters 19 and 20 discuss portfolio and capital market theory in detail.

Diversifiable risk, also known as **unsystematic risk,** is risk that has as its source company or industry factors. For example, the unexpected movement of a discount grocery chain, such as Food Lion, into a market dominated by a traditional grocery chain, such as Winn-Dixie, may have a significant effect on Winn-Dixie's earnings and the price of its common stock. In this example, the factor that has affected the common stock of Winn-Dixie is not common to all marketable securities but rather is company- or industry-specific.

This source of risk can be diversified away by combining the asset with a portfolio of other assets. This reduction in total risk resulting from combining securities into a portfolio is called the **portfolio effect.** Consider the hypothetical example of the Black Ink Company (BIC), which does quite well when the economy is in a strong growth mode, and the Red Ink Company (RIC), which performs well when the economy is faltering. As individual assets, each may be considered quite risky due to fluctuations in the economy. But by combining RIC and BIC into a portfolio, the investor may smooth out these fluctuations and reduce the risk.

The return patterns for BIC and RIC and a portfolio consisting of BIC and RIC are shown in Figure 2.2. As shown in the figure, by combining BIC and RIC into a portfolio, the volatility (risk) of the portfolio's returns is reduced relative to the volatility in returns of the individual assets. This reduction in volatility occurs because the returns of BIC and RIC do not move together. When the return on BIC rises, the return on RIC declines. This relationship

FIGURE 2.2
Return Patterns for BIC, RIC, and a Portfolio Comprised of BIC and RIC.

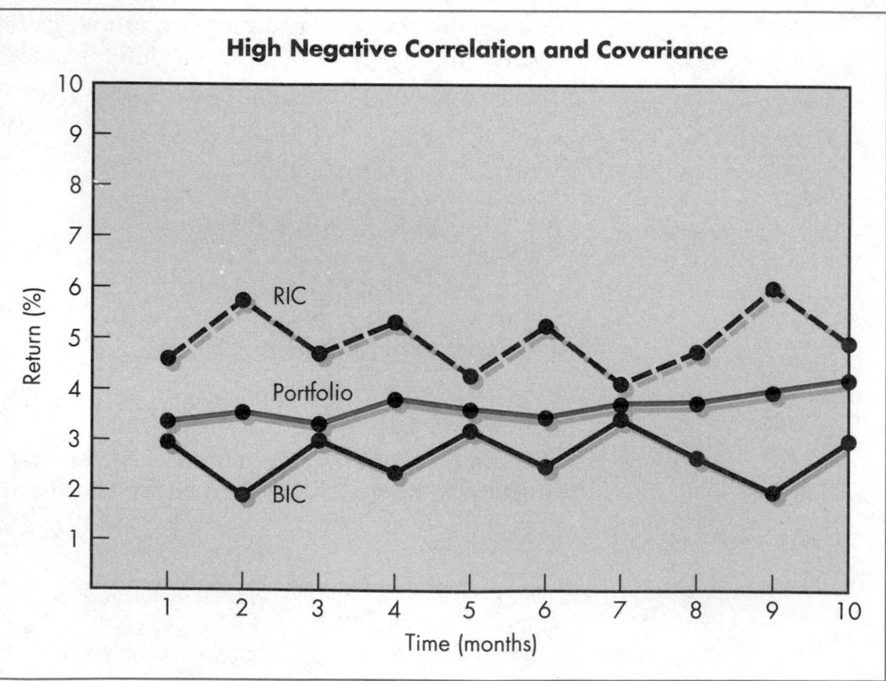

can be described by the **correlation coefficient** between the returns of BIC and RIC.[5] In this example, BIC and RIC have a very high, negative correlation. Normally, the correlation between two financial assets is not as extreme as in this example.

Because it is necessary to consider the correlations of the returns of assets in a portfolio, the standard deviation of a portfolio normally *cannot* be estimated as an average of the standard deviations of the individual assets in the portfolio. Returning to the BIC and RIC example, the rates of return of the two assets are not perfectly positively correlated and this risk-reducing aspect must be taken into consideration in calculating the total risk of the portfolio. Thus, the name portfolio effect.

A number of studies have been conducted to determine how many common stocks must be included in a portfolio in order to eliminate diversifiable risk. The results show that between 10 to 15 stocks will remove a large portion of the unsystematic or diversifiable risk and that adding stocks beyond this number only marginally reduces the unsystematic risk of the portfolio. Thus, since this risk can be diversified away, investors should not expect any additional return for facing this portion of total risk.

Nondiversifiable risk, also referred to as **systematic risk,** has as its source factors that affect all marketable assets and thus cannot be diversified away. For example, a change in expectations about the rate of inflation is pervasive; it will have an influence on all marketable assets and cannot be avoided by diversification. This risk cannot be diversified away, and investors should expect to receive additional returns associated with systematic risk.

How can systematic risk be measured? Since the sources of systematic risk are market-pervasive, it is logical to measure systematic risk as the **covariance** between the return of an individual asset or portfolio and the returns of the "market" portfolio. The **market portfolio** would include a composite of all risky assets, which is very difficult to measure. Thus, a proxy for the market portfolio, such as the Dow Jones Industrial Average or the Standard & Poor's Composite 500 Index, is used as a substitute for the market portfolio. This measure of systematic risk is represented by **beta** ($\boldsymbol{\beta_j}$) and can be calculated by

$$\beta_j = \frac{\text{Cov}_{jM}}{\sigma_M^2} \tag{2.17}$$

where j indicates the individual asset and Cov_{jM} is the covariance of the individual asset returns with the returns of the market portfolio (M).

The beta of the market portfolio is by definition equal to 1 (the covariance of an asset with itself is its variance; thus, $\text{Cov}_{MM} = \sigma_M^2$), and beta values for

[5] Recall from statistics, the correlation coefficient can take on a range of values between +1.0 and −1.0. Perfectly positive correlation, +1.0, indicates that the two sets of numbers move together perfectly and perfectly negative correlation, −1.0, indicates the numbers move inversely to each other. A review of the correlation coefficient and covariance can be found in Appendix A-2, Review of Analytical Techniques.

assets generally range between +.5 and 2.0. Securities with betas above 1.0 are classified as "aggressive" since they are expected to have more volatile returns than the market. Assets with betas less than 1.0 are classified as "defensive" since their volatility is expected to be less than that of the market. For example, if an asset has a beta of 1.2 and the market's return is expected to increase by 10 percent, then the asset's expected return will increase by 12 percent. Of course, this works in the opposite direction as well. If the market's return is expected to decrease by 10 percent, the asset's expected return is expected to decrease by 12 percent. Many large brokerage firms (e.g., Merrill Lynch) and subscription services (e.g., Value Line) provide estimates of betas.

Beta estimates are based on the assumption that the historical relationship between an asset's return and the return of the market will continue into the future. Many studies have examined the stationarity of beta. In general, they have concluded that betas for individual assets are not very stationary over time, but that as the number of assets in a portfolio increases, the stationarity of the portfolio's beta improves significantly.

RELATING BETA AND THE REQUIRED RETURN

The measure of systematic risk permits an investor to evaluate an asset's required return relative to the systematic risk of the asset. In general, the CAPM indicates that an asset's required return should be related to the risk-free rate of return[6] plus a risk premium based on the beta of the asset. The required return for an asset is given by

$$E(R_j) = R_f + \beta_j[E(R_M) - R_f] \quad \textbf{(2.18)}$$

where

$E(R_j)$ = the required rate of return of asset j
R_f = the nominal risk-free rate of return (the real risk-free rate of return plus a risk premium for inflation)
β_j = asset j's beta
$E(R_M)$ = the expected rate of return on the market portfolio

Equation 2.18 is the equation for the **security market line** (**SML**), which is illustrated in Figure 2.3. Figure 2.3 shows the relationship between the measure of systematic risk, β_j, and the required return of an asset. Note that

[6]In order for an asset to be considered riskless, its expected rate of return must be known with certainty. In other words, there is no deviation around the expected return. The yield on U.S. Treasury bills is often used as a proxy for the risk-free rate. Because of their short maturity and backing by the U.S. government, Treasury bills have relatively stable returns, and the risk of default is nil.

FIGURE 2.3
The Security Market Line

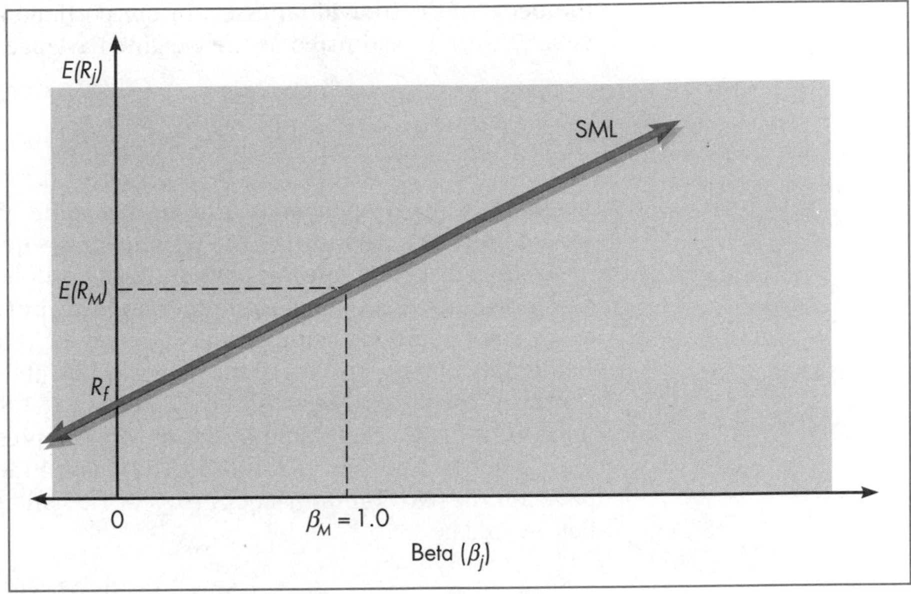

the line in the figure is upward sloping, confirming that investors are risk-averse; the higher the risk (β_j), the higher the required return.

From Equation 2.18 for the SML, the required return of an asset is a function of the return on the risk-free asset, the risk premium in the market $[E(R_M) - R_f]$, and the asset's β_j. Only the last measure, β_j, is asset-specific; thus, an asset's required return will be higher or lower than other assets' expected returns, based upon its relative level of covariance with the market.

An example may help illustrate the relationships between an asset's systematic risk, β_j, and the required return on the asset, $E(R_j)$. Assume that the risk-free rate is 6 percent, the expected return on the market over the next year is 14 percent, the beta of the common stock of Compaq Computer, β_{CC}, is 1.55, and the beta of Cincinnati Bell, β_{CB}, is .75. Using Equation 2.18, the required return for the common stock of these two companies would be

$$\begin{aligned} E(R_{\text{CC}}) &= .06 + 1.55(.14 - .06) \\ &= 18.4\% \\ E(R_{\text{CB}}) &= .06 + .75(.14 - .06) \\ &= 12.0\% \end{aligned}$$

For Compaq Computer and Cincinnati Bell, the expected holding period return over the next year must be greater than 18.4 percent and 12.0 percent, respectively, to justify an investment in these assets.

The relationship expressed by the SML holds for individual assets as well as for a portfolio of assets. The beta of a portfolio can be estimated in the same way as the beta of an individual asset by using Equation 2.17. Alternatively, if the betas of the individual assets in the portfolio are known, the portfolio's beta, β_p, can be estimated as the weighted average of the individual betas:

$$\beta_p = \sum_{j=1}^{n} X_j \beta_j \tag{2.19}$$

where X_j is the proportion of the market value of the total portfolio represented by asset j. The sum of the weights must equal 1 (i.e., $\Sigma_{j=1}^{n} X_j = 1$).

Assume that an investor is considering a portfolio of 100 shares each of the common stock of Compaq Computer and Cincinnati Bell.[7] The current price of a share of Compaq Computer is $38, and the price of a share of Cincinnati Bell is $23. The proportion of the market value of the portfolio represented by Compaq Computer, X_{CC}, will be 62 percent ($3,800/$6,100), and the proportion of the market value of the portfolio represented by Cincinnati Bell, X_{CB}, will be 38 percent ($2,300/$6,100). Given the previous estimates of the betas for the two common stocks ($\beta_{CC} = 1.55$ and $\beta_{CB} = .75$), the portfolio's beta would be

$$\begin{aligned} \beta_p &= (.62)(1.55) + (.38)(.75) \\ &= 1.25 \end{aligned}$$

Using Equation 2.18 and the earlier estimates of a risk-free rate of 6 percent and an expected return on the market of 14 percent, the required return of the portfolio, $E(R_p)$, would be

$$\begin{aligned} E(R_p) &= .06 + 1.25(.14 - .06) \\ &= 16.0\% \end{aligned}$$

In order to justify investing in a portfolio of these two securities, the expected holding period of the portfolio, $E(\text{HRP}_p)$, must be equal to or greater than 16 percent. Once the expected holding period returns of the individual securities are estimated, it is a rather easy task to calculate $E(\text{HPR}_p)$:

$$E(\text{HPR}_p) = \sum_{j=1}^{n} X_j E(\text{HPR}_j) \tag{2.20}$$

where X_j is as defined earlier and $E(\text{HPR}_j)$ indicates the individual asset's expected holding period return.

Suppose we have estimated the expected holding period return for Compaq Computer, $E(\text{HPR}_{CC})$, to be 19 percent and the expected holding period return for Cincinnati Bell, $E(\text{HPR}_{CB})$, to be 13 percent, then $E(\text{HPR}_p)$ would be

$$\begin{aligned} E(\text{HPR}_p) &= (.62)(.19) + (.38)(.13) \\ &= 16.7\% \end{aligned}$$

[7] In order to make the example rather simple, only two assets are being considered. In reality, an investor would consider 10 to 15 assets for a portfolio in order to diversify away the unsystematic risk.

Since the $E(\text{HPR}_p)$ of 16.7 percent is greater than the 16.0 percent required return, the investment in the portfolio is justified.

APPLICATION: THE YOUNG INVESTORS

Mike and Sue O'Brian have been married for three years. They have been saving toward the purchase of their first home. Currently, they have $12,500 invested in a certificate of deposit (CD), which will mature in a few days. If they reinvest the $12,500 in a new one-year CD, the bank will guarantee a 7 percent rate of return.

The mortgage company estimates that they can afford payments on a $70,000 house, assuming that they make a 20 percent down payment and finance the house for 25 years. In addition to the $14,000 down payment, closing costs for the loan are estimated at approximately $3,500, for a total cash requirement of $17,500.

Based on their budget for next year, Sue thinks they can apply their combined year-end bonus of $3,500 to the purchase of the home. If their current savings of $12,500 are reinvested in a one-year CD, they will earn $875, which will bring their total savings to $16,875. They would still lack $625 and would have to postpone the purchase of the home for several months.

Mike discussed the situation with his parents. His father suggested that perhaps they could earn the necessary money by investing their current savings in higher-yielding securities. Although Mike's parents are not wealthy, they agreed to give Mike and Sue the money to cover the taxes and transaction costs from their investment. Thus, Mike and Sue could concentrate on the investment's gross return.

Mike called his friend John, a stockbroker. John suggested two possible investments. One was a mutual fund that had yielded a rate of return of 12 percent (dividends and capital appreciation) during the most recent period of strong economic growth. The alternative investment was a common stock that John thought would be an excellent performer over the next year. The stock could earn as much as 15 percent if the strong economy continued. John cautioned Mike that neither investment might provide the indicated return if the economy weakened, since both alternatives involved risk. John sent Mike and Sue some basic information on the two investment alternatives.

Sue recalled from her college investments course that they needed to compare the expected returns and risk of the three alternative investments. Upon receiving the information from John, she identified the possible returns for each of the investments. She had difficulty estimating the probabilities for each of the possible economic states, so she gave each of the economic scenarios an equal weight. With the aid of her old investments book, Sue calculated the beta coefficients, expected returns, standard deviations, coefficients of variation, and the expected return per unit of systematic risk for each of the three investments. She also estimated the dollar return for each alternative under each economic scenario. Table 2.5 shows the results of Sue's calculations.

TABLE 2.5 • Choices for the Young Investors

Current savings	$12,500
Year-end bonuses	3,500
	$16,000
Down payment on house	$14,000
Closing costs	3,500
	$17,500
Additional funds needed	$ 1,500

		Percentage Returned			Cash Return on $12,500		
	Probability	*Mutual fund*	*Common stock*	*Certificate of deposit*	*Mutual fund*	*Common stock*	*Certificate of deposit*
State of economy							
Weak growth	33%	8.00%	6.00%	7.00%	$1,000	$ 750	$875
Moderate growth	33%	10.00%	12.00%	7.00%	1,250	1,500	875
Strong growth	33%	12.00%	15.00%	7.00%	1,500	1,875	875
Beta		1.0	1.2	0.00			
Expected return		10.00%	11.00%	7.00%			
Standard deviation		1.63%	3.74%	0.00%			
Coefficient of variation		0.16	0.34	0.00			
Expected return/ systematic risk (beta)		10.00%	9.17%				

Mike was impressed by Sue's knowledge of investments but still did not know which alternative to select. Sue explained that although the common stock had an expected return of 11 percent, which was greater than the expected return of the mutual fund, the stock was more risky. The standard deviation of the stock's return was 3.74 percent, compared to the 1.63 percent standard deviation of the mutual fund's return. On a relative basis, the mutual fund provided a much better risk-return trade-off since the coefficient of variation for the mutual fund was only 0.16, compared to the common stock's 0.34 coefficient of variation. The mutual fund also provided a higher return per unit of systematic risk (10.0 percent) than the common stock (9.17 percent). Sue concluded that the common stock would be a good investment for a diversified portfolio, but as a single investment, it was too risky for her. She preferred the mutual fund, based on the return per unit of risk—both total risk (coefficient of variation) and systematic risk.

Mike kept looking at the projected cash value of the returns. He could not help noticing that the mutual fund investment would provide them the $1,500 only if the economy was strong. The common stock would provide them the necessary money even if the economy slowed to moderate. The return on the common stock was below the return on the CD, however, if the economy weakened, as some economists were predicting. Mike decided that he preferred the common stock. He thought the CD should be eliminated from consideration because it would not provide the needed return and because the mutual fund provided a higher expected return than the CD, regardless of the economic state.

Sue recalled her finance professor's discussion of portfolio diversification. She suggested that perhaps they could compromise and invest in both the mutual fund and common stock. She calculated the possible portfolio returns, based upon several dollar allocation schemes between the alternatives. Table 2.6 shows the possible portfolio returns, the expected portfolio returns, the risk measures, and the portfolio cash value returns.

A comparison of the risk and return measures in Tables 2.5 and 2.6 reveals some interesting relationships. First, the standard deviations of the three portfolios in Table 2.6 are essentially a weighted average of the standard deviations of the individual assets. This occurs because the correlation coefficient between the mutual fund and the common stock is 0.97. This almost perfectly

TABLE 2.6 • Portfolio Return and Risk

		Portfolios of mutual fund (MF) and common stock (CS)		
	Probability	$X_{MF} = .75$ $X_{CS} = .25$	$X_{MF} = .5$ $X_{CS} = .5$	$X_{MF} = .25$ $X_{CS} = .75$
State of economy				
Weak growth	33%	7.50%	7.00%	6.50%
Moderate growth	33%	10.50%	11.00%	11.50%
Strong growth	33%	12.75%	13.50%	14.25%
Beta of portfolio		1.05	1.10	1.15
Expected return		10.25%	10.50%	10.75%
Standard deviation		2.14%	2.68%	3.21%
Coefficient of variation		0.21	0.26	0.30
Expected return/systematic risk		9.76%	9.55%	9.35%
Portfolio dollar returns for one year, based on an initial investment of $12,500				
	Probability	$X_{MF} = .75$ $X_{CS} = .25$	$X_{MF} = .5$ $X_{CS} = .5$	$X_{MF} = .25$ $X_{CS} = .75$
State of economy				
Weak growth	33%	$ 938	$ 875	$ 813
Moderate growth	33%	1,313	1,375	1,438
Strong growth	33%	1,594	1,688	1,781

positive correlation eliminates most of the potential benefits of diversification or the portfolio effect. Second, the expected returns on the portfolios are a simple weighted average of the mutual fund and common stock expected returns. Finally, the expected return per unit of systematic risk for the mutual fund is higher than for the three portfolios in Table 2.6.

Mike still preferred to investigate the portfolio cash returns. As he examined each of the portfolios, Mike discovered that the worst-case returns for the portfolios were always less than the mutual fund worst case of $1,000. Even his initial guess of a 50–50 compromise portfolio seemed risky if the economy slowed to weak growth, since the cash return would be only $875. After all of Sue's hard work, Mike agreed that perhaps the best investment was the mutual fund. Clearly, the mutual fund exhibited the best expected return per unit of systematic risk. Mike promised to call the stockbroker the next morning. Mike and Sue were aware that if the economy worsened, the mutual fund was expected to generate only $1,000 of the $1,500 they needed to buy the home next year. Both promised to monitor the mutual fund's performance during the year, so that they could plan the purchase of their new home.

SUMMARY

The investment process helps individuals match the timing of their income with the timing of their consumption decisions. Net savers—investors—expect net borrowers not only to repay the money borrowed but also to pay a rate of return that compensates investors for the time value of money, inflation, and risk. The risk premium must compensate investors for business, financial, liquidity, default, interest rate, management, purchasing power, and other sources of risk. These risks are interrelated and are often measured by the standard deviation of the expected return, which indicates the total risk of the security.

Total risk, however, may not be the appropriate risk measure. The capital asset pricing model indicates that total risk is composed of diversifiable and nondiversifiable risk. Diversifiable or unsystematic risk can be eliminated by proper diversification of a portfolio. Thus, the market will only reward investors for facing nondiversifiable or systematic risk. This latter risk can be measured by the beta of the individual asset or portfolio. Using the security market line, the investor can relate an asset or portfolio's beta to the required return of the asset. A comparison of the required return and the estimated expected return indicates whether or not an investment is justified.

The young investors' case illustrates a number of basic investment principles presented in the chapter. Mike and Sue O'Brian are attempting to determine an appropriate risk-return trade-off. Mike appears to be willing to assume higher levels of risk, while Sue is more risk-averse. The estimates of risk and rates of return provide useful information for the O'Brians' analysis. Since they have a one-year investment horizon and require a minimum

• CONCEPT APPLICATIONS

Investment Concept	Concept Application
Holding period return	A holding period return (HPR) can be calculated using ex-post (historical) information or ex-ante (future) information. Typically, HPRs are reported as an annual equivalent, and all income distributions are assumed to be reinvested. The geometric mean HPR calculation is the preferred approach for investors to use in calculating annualized HPR.
Required rate of return	The required rate of return is a function of the real rate of return and risk; it is the minimum rate of return an investor will accept. The required rate of return for an asset or portfolio of assets can be estimated using the equation for the security market line suggested by the capital asset pricing model.
Expected rate of return	The expected rate of return, or holding period return, is based upon the expected cash receipts over the holding period and the expected ending, or selling, price. Depending upon the assumptions made about cash receipts and ending price, a number of expected rates of return are possible. These possible rates of return estimated by the investor are summarized in an expected rate of return. The expected rate of return must be greater or equal to the required rate of return in order for the investor to find the investment acceptable.
Beta	The beta coefficient is a measure of nondiversifiable or systematic risk. An asset or portfolio with a beta greater than 1.0 is considered to be aggressive (more risky than the market), and an asset or portfolio with a beta less than 1.0 is considered to be defensive (less risky than the market). An investor can use the beta measure to assess the risk level of an asset or portfolio.
Compensation for investment risk	Rational investors are considered to be risk-averse. As such, they require higher returns for facing higher levels of risk. Investors are not compensated for total risk. Rather, they are compensated in the market for facing nondiversifiable or systematic risk. Diversifiable or unsystematic risk can be eliminated by properly diversifying a portfolio. The level of systematic risk can be represented by the asset or portfolio's beta coefficient. The investor's required compensation for rewardable systematic risk can be estimated by multiplying the beta coefficient times the risk premium in the market or $\beta_j[E(R_M) - R_f]$.

investment return of $1,500, the dollar returns from each alternative for each possible state of the economy are also useful. Based on their available information, the mutual fund appears to be their best investment. Because of an uncertain economic environment, however, the O'Brians recognize the need to monitor the fund's performance closely during the next year.

• KEY TERMS

Beta
Business risk
Capital asset pricing model (CAPM)
Coefficient of variation (CV)
Correlation coefficient
Covariance
Default risk
Diversifiable risk
Expected rate of return
Ex-ante returns
Ex-post returns
Financial risk
Geometric mean
Holding period return (HPR)
Interest rate risk
Liquidity risk
Management risk
Market portfolio
Nondiversifiable risk
Portfolio effect
Purchasing power risk
Range
Real rate of return
Required rate of return
Risk premium
Security market line (SML)
Standard deviation
Systematic risk
Unsystematic risk
Variance

• QUESTIONS

1. Explain how financial markets can be used to facilitate decisions concerning consumption versus savings.

2. Compare and contrast the arithmetic and geometric means. Which "average" is more appropriate for analyzing rates of return over a number of holding periods?

3. In subjective terms, how do individuals usually define the concept of "risk"? Do empirical measures of risk match the subjective definition of risk?

4. Explain why the length of the investment horizon is related to the risk of the investment.

5. Compare and contrast the required rate of return with the expected rate of return. How are these two return measures used in making investment decisions?

6. Briefly discuss the real rate of return, expected inflation, and risk components of the required rate of return.

7. Explain how ex-post holding period returns can be used to forecast expected or ex-ante holding period returns. Do you think that this approach is a viable alternative to an investment analysis directed at providing an estimate of the expected return of an investment alternative? Why or why not?

8. Explain why probabilities for each investment outcome are useful in estimating the expected rate of return for an investment. What techniques can be used to estimate probabilities?

9. Discuss business, financial, default, liquidity, interest rate, management, and purchasing power risks as sources of investment risk. Compare the impact of these sources of risk on common stocks and corporate bonds.

10. Does the standard deviation of ex-post holding period returns reflect default risk for a common stock? Explain how default risk might be incorporated into an estimate of the expected return for a common stock.
11. Discuss the advantages and disadvantages of the standard deviation as a measure of risk for individual securities and portfolios of securities.
12. Explain how the coefficient of variation measures the total risk per unit of expected return, and discuss the advantages and disadvantages of this measure.
13. Explain the difference between diversifiable and nondiversifiable risk. Why is an investor compensated for facing nondiversifiable risk but not for facing diversifiable risk?
14. Explain how the beta coefficient can be used to estimate the required return for an individual asset or portfolio.
15. The example of the young investors illustrated how the concepts of risk and return can be applied to individual investment alternatives and to portfolios constructed from the alternatives. Explain why the analysis indicated that an investment in a single asset (mutual fund) appeared to be more attractive than the other portfolio alternatives.

• KEY TO THE INVESTMENT ANALYSIS SOFTWARE

Calculation	Appendix A-1 Page Reference	Access Procedure
Holding period return	A-8	BEGIN, HPR, ONE or MANY
Arithmetic mean holding period return	A-8	BEGIN, HPR, MANY
Geometric mean holding period return	A-7	BEGIN, HPR, MANY or BEGIN, STATISTICAL, GEOM
Expected rate of return	A-7	BEGIN, STATISTICAL, DISCRETE
Variance and standard deviation	A-7	BEGIN, STATISTICAL, DESCRIP
Coefficient of variation	A-7	BEGIN, STATISTICAL, DESCRIP
Covariance and correlation	A-7	BEGIN, STATISTICAL, CORR

Calculation	Appendix A-1 Page Reference	Access Procedure
Security beta	A-12	BEGIN, CAPITAL, CAPM
Portfolio beta	A-7	BEGIN, STATISTICAL, DISCRETE
Security market line (SML) and required rate of return	A-12	BEGIN, CAPITAL, CAPM

• PROBLEMS

1. An investor purchased 100 shares of common stock at $20 per share one year ago. The company declared and paid a dividend of $2 per share during the year. The investor sold the stock for $21 per share after the one-year holding period.

a. Calculate the dollar return from this investment.

b. Calculate the HPR for this investment.

c. Partition the HPR into its dividend and capital appreciation components.

2. Consider the following ex-post HPRs:

Year	*Investment A*	*Investment B*
1	10%	14%
2	15	−10
3	8	30

a. Calculate the arithmetic mean HPR for each investment.

b. Calculate the geometric mean HPR for each investment.

c. Explain why the arithmetic and geometric means are different.

d. Assume that investments A and B have equal risk. Which investment provides the "best" return performance? (*Hint:* Assume that $10,000 was invested in each alternative and then calculate the dollar value of the investment at the end of year 3, using the geometric means.)

3. Consider the following subjective probability distribution for a potential investment:

State of the economy	*Probability*	*Estimated rate of return*
Strong growth	.1	25%
Moderate growth	.4	15
Weak growth	.4	10
Recession	.1	−12

a. Calculate the expected rate of return.

b. Calculate the variance.

c. Calculate the standard deviation.

d. Calculate the coefficient of variation.

e. Interpret your answers to parts (a)–(d).

4. Consider the following ex-post quarterly HPRs provided by a common stock:

Quarter	*Quarterly HPR*
1	−4.3%
2	−1.0
3	1.5
4	3.0
5	6.0
6	2.0
7	0.0
8	−2.5

a. Assuming that each of the ex-post quarterly returns has an equal probability of occurring, calculate the *expected* HPR for quarter 9 using Equation 2.12.

b. Using the assumption in part (a), calculate the variance and standard deviation.

c. Assume that the HPRs for quarters 1, 2, and 8 occurred during a recessionary environment and that the HPR for quarters 4 and 5 occurred during a period of rapid economic growth. The remaining HPRs occurred during quarters of moderate economic growth. Calculate the probability that quarter 9 will be (1) a period of rapid economic growth, (2) a recessionary period, and (3) a period of moderate economic growth.

d. Use the probabilities calculated in part (c) to calculate the expected return, variance, and standard deviation of the common stock's quarterly HPRs.

e. What are the weaknesses of the forecasting techniques used in parts (a) and (d)?

5. The risk-free rate is 8 percent, and the expected return on the market is 16 percent. The betas for the common stock of five companies are as follows:

Common stock	*Beta*
1	1.60
2	.80
3	.70
4	1.20
5	1.40

a. Draw the security market line (SML).

b. Locate each common stock on the SML.

c. Based on your answer to part (b), estimate the required return for each stock. Verify your answer by using Equation 2.18.

6. Assume the betas of two common stocks are $\beta_1 = .9$ and $\beta_2 = 1.3$. If the risk-free rate of return is 8 percent and the expected return on the market portfolio is 12 percent:
   a. Calculate the required returns for each common stock using the capital asset pricing model.
   b. Do the required returns calculated in part (a) include a return to compensate the investor for unsystematic risk? Explain.
   c. If the expected return of stock 1 is 12 percent and the expected return of stock 2 is 14 percent, should the investor buy either stock? Why or why not?
7. Assume that in the example of the young investors, the risk-free rate is 6 percent and the expected return on the market is 10 percent.
   a. Verify the betas for the three portfolios in Table 2.6.
   b. Verify the expected return for the three portfolios in Table 2.6.
   c. Estimate the required return for the three portfolios in Table 2.6.
   d. Compare the expected returns verified in part (b) with the required returns estimated in part (c). Do the portfolios provide an acceptable level of expected return commensurate with their systematic or nondiversifiable risk?

• REFERENCES*

Fouse, William L. "Risk and Liquidity Revisited." *Financial Analysts Journal* (January-February 1977): 40–45.

Fuller, Russell J., and Wenchi G. Wong. "Traditional versus Theoretical Risk Measure." *Financial Analysts Journal* (March-April 1988): 52–57, 67.

Gray, William S. "The Anatomy of a Stock Market Forecast." *Journal of Portfolio Management* (Fall 1989): 36–44.

Lev, Baruch. "On the Association between Operating Leverage and Risk." *Journal of Financial and Quantitative Analysis* 9 (June 1974): 627–41.

Reichenstein, William. "On Standard Deviation and Risk." *Journal of Portfolio Management* (Winter 1987): 39–40.

Winger, Bernard J., and Nancy K. Mohan. "Investment Risk and Time Diversification." *Journal of Financial Planning* (July 1988): 45–48.

* An extensive list of references for topics covered in this chapter is provided at the end of Chapters 19 and 20.

PART II

The Investment Environment

CHAPTER 3
Security Markets: Operations and Regulations

CHAPTER 4
Investment Information

CHAPTER 5
Investing in Mutual Funds

CHAPTER 6
Investing Internationally

CHAPTER 7
Investment Strategies

CHAPTER 3

Security Markets: Operations and Regulations

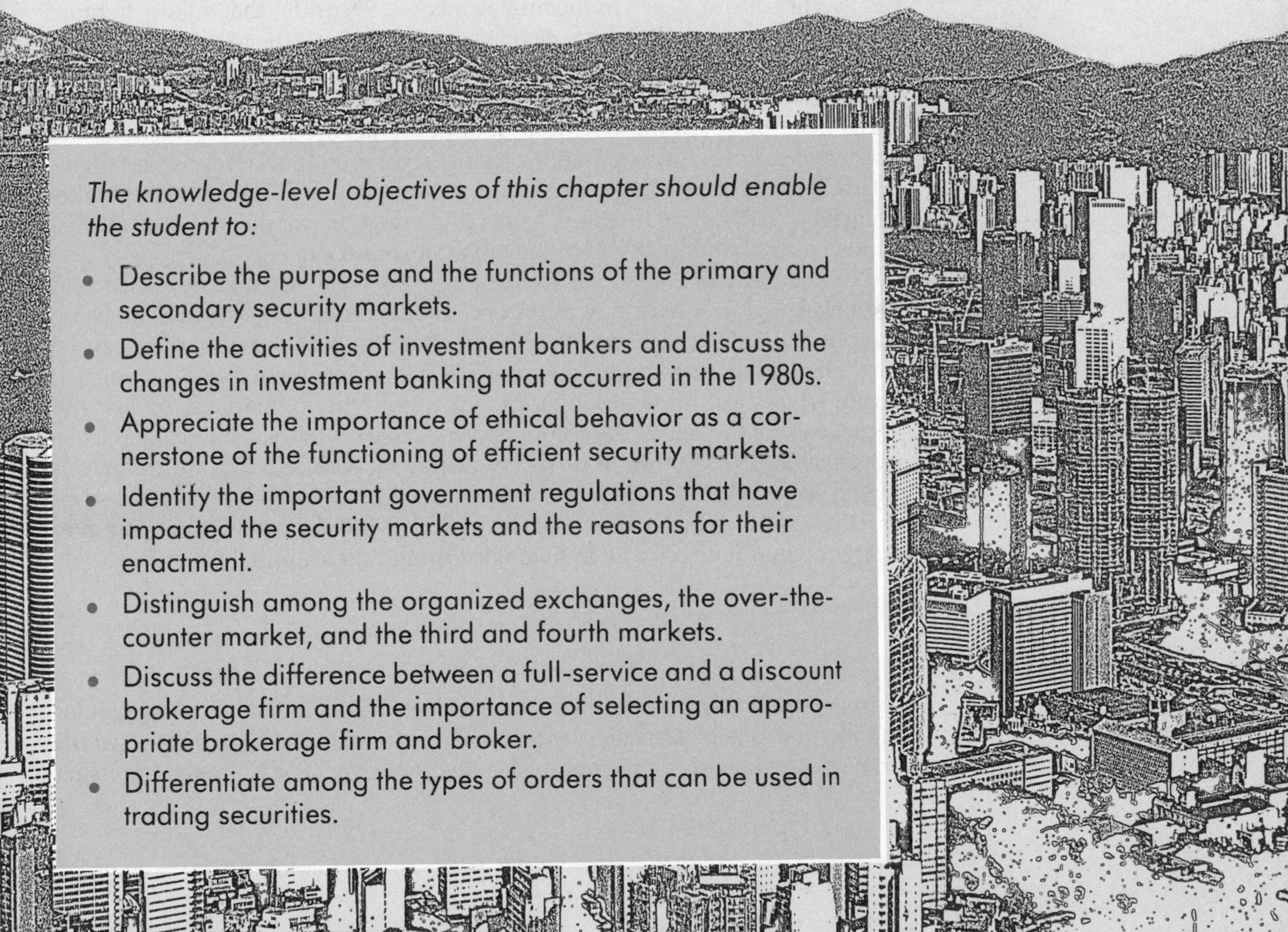

The knowledge-level objectives of this chapter should enable the student to:

- Describe the purpose and the functions of the primary and secondary security markets.
- Define the activities of investment bankers and discuss the changes in investment banking that occurred in the 1980s.
- Appreciate the importance of ethical behavior as a cornerstone of the functioning of efficient security markets.
- Identify the important government regulations that have impacted the security markets and the reasons for their enactment.
- Distinguish among the organized exchanges, the over-the-counter market, and the third and fourth markets.
- Discuss the difference between a full-service and a discount brokerage firm and the importance of selecting an appropriate brokerage firm and broker.
- Differentiate among the types of orders that can be used in trading securities.

INTRODUCTION

The growth of the U.S. economy has been due in large part to the strength and efficiency of its security markets. This chapter will discuss the functions, structures, operations, and regulations of the major U.S. security markets. The importance of an efficient, broadly based security market for a country's economy is demonstrated by the fact that one of the top priorities of the emerging Eastern European countries is the establishment of security markets. In converting from a centrally planned economy to a market-based system, the Eastern European countries are establishing an environment in which businesses can operate. This includes creating a new framework of commercial law, setting up autonomous and decentralized systems of wholesale and retail distribution, establishing a banking system, and providing sources of debt and equity capital for businesses through efficiently operated security markets.

Security markets can be classifed in several ways. One way is by the maturity of the securities traded in the market. The *money market* is made up of securities that mature in one year or less. As Table 1.1 indicated, short-term debt securities are traded in the money market. Securities that mature in more than a year are traded in the *capital market.* While both the money and capital markets provide liquidity for the investor, money market securities have little or no risk of default and do not contain significant price risk because of their short maturities. For these reasons, money market securities represent attractive opportunities for corporations to invest their temporary excess cash balances. Because of the large, minimum denominations of most money market securities, individual investors generally invest in money market mutual funds rather than directly in money market securities.

Another way of classifying security markets is by whether new securities are being sold (the **primary markets**) or already-issued securities are being bought and sold (the **secondary markets**). Both of these markets can be further divided into stock, corporate bond, government bond, municipal bond, futures, commodities, options, and other types of markets. To give you some sense of the size of the secondary stock market in the United States, consider that in 1965 common stocks owned by individuals were worth an estimated $600 billion. In 1990, it was estimated that individuals owned stock worth over $2 trillion, which did not include $170 billion worth of common shares owned indirectly by individuals through their mutual funds.[1]

PRIMARY MARKETS

As mentioned above, the term *primary market* is used to denote the market for the original sale of securities by an issuer to the public. The use of the words *original sale* may be somewhat misleading, however. For example, the issuer

[1] Richard L. Stern, "When Wall Street Sneezes, Middle America Laughs," *Forbes*, March 19, 1990, pp. 36, 68.

may initially have sold common stock to the public several years ago (an **initial public offering,** or **IPO,** by a not-yet-public company) and has now decided to issue additional shares of common stock (a secondary offering). These additional shares will be sold in the primary market, and once the sale is completed, the new shares will be indistinguishable from the shares sold in the initial public offering. The issuer receives cash that may then be invested in productive assets, or the net proceeds from the sale may be used for other purposes. For example, the proceeds from the sale of common stock may be used to retire outstanding debt. The public receives the newly issued securities for the cash invested.

The volume of new issues in the primary market, particularly of common stocks, is directly related to market conditions. When the market is high or rising, the number of new issues being offered to the public rises, and when the market is low or falling, the number declines. For example, during the first 140 days of 1991, a period of rising prices in the stock market, $18.2 billion in new common stock was issued. This represents a significant increase over the same period in 1990.

• Role of the Investment Banker

Investment bankers are responsible for the placement of billions of dollars worth of new securities each year. The term **investment banker** is something of a misnomer, however, because investment bankers are not bankers in the traditional sense of taking deposits and making loans. Although commercial banks may have investment banking divisions, the vast majority of investment banking "deals" are executed by brokerage firms such as Merrill Lynch Capital Markets; Shearson Lehman Brothers, Inc.; Goldman, Sachs & Co.; First Boston Corporation; Paine Webber, Inc.; and others. The Glass-Steagall Act bars commercial banks from many investment banking activities. Congress is currently considering the repeal of Glass-Steagall, which would allow commercial banks to expand their investment banking activities. Given the increasing number of commercial bank failures or potential failures, it is questionable whether Congress will repeal the act.

Brokerage firms are ideally suited to the traditional investment banking function since they already have a large base of security holders as clients as well as a nationwide infrastructure enabling them to sell securities at any time. This allows the investment banker to offer its services at a relatively low cost to a firm desiring to raise money through a new security offering. Investment bankers offer three basic services: (1) advice and counsel, (2) underwriting, and (3) distribution.

ADVICE AND COUNSEL In addition to corporations, governmental units and not-for-profit organizations go to the marketplace to raise money. Since they issue securities so infrequently, they do not have the "in-house" expertise to undertake the considerable paperwork associated with a new issue. In addition, the issuer of securities needs investment bankers to evaluate market conditions in order to determine whether an offering can be made; at what price the security can be sold; whether the security should be debt or equity; and any special characteristics that must be considered, such as convertibility, callability, coupon rate, and maturity.

Some new issues, particularly bonds, are not sold to the general public. Rather, they are sold directly to financial institutions such as pension funds and life insurance companies. These direct sales are called **private placements.** In a private placement, the issuing firm does not have to meet the public notice and disclosure requirements involved in a public offering, which can be a cost savings to the issuer. The assumption is that the financial institution is a sophisticated investor and can acquire the necessary financial information. In addition to cost savings, a private placement has the advantage of allowing the issuer and the financial institution to structure the issue in such a way that it meets the specific needs of all parties involved in the transaction.

UNDERWRITING Once the investment banker has determined the type of security, price, issue date, and any special features, the issue is ready to market to the public. If the investment banking firm **underwrites** the issue, it agrees to purchase the securities in the hope of reselling them at a higher price to the public. The investment banker has assumed the *price risk.* This difference is known as the **spread,** and its size varies with the type of issue (e.g., bonds have a smaller spread than common stocks) and the perceived difficulty of marketing the issue. The size of the spread also varies with the dollar value of the new issue. Because of the large fixed costs associated with bringing a new issue to market, larger issues have lower spreads than smaller issues.

If the investment banking firm acts only as an agent, it assumes no obligation to purchase any of the securities. This is known as a **best-efforts offering.** Under a best-efforts offering, the investment banker does not underwrite the issue but merely uses its best efforts to sell the issue to the public. All unsold securities are returned to the issuer. Best-efforts offerings are usually made for small, unknown firms, where the risk of underwriting is too great, or for well-known firms that are confident the public will purchase their securities.

DISTRIBUTION The investment banking firm that obtains a commitment from the issuer to sell the new security is called the *originator.* As managing underwriter, the originator will form an *underwriting group* to spread the price risk if market conditions suddenly change and to reduce the amount of cash that any one investment banking firm must raise to purchase the issue. Finally, a *selling group* is created comprising both members of the underwriting group and other retail brokerage houses. Each of the brokerage houses will then be allocated a portion of the new issue to sell.

The originating investment banker must file a **registration statement** with the Securities and Exchange Commission (SEC) that provides information on the firm, the type and amount of the security being offered, and the proposed use of the proceeds from the sale.[2] While the registration statement is being evaluated by the SEC, the investment banking firm may issue a *preliminary prospectus,* also known as a **red herring** because of the red ink on its cover. The red herring states that the information in the prospectus is being reviewed by the SEC and that the prospectus is not a solicitation to sell. The difference between the preliminary prospectus and the **prospectus** is that the preliminary prospectus does not state the price or the date of the offering. The offering price is determined immediately prior to the sale; since market conditions can change dramatically, it is not feasible to establish a price until the day of the offering.

Once the registration statement has been approved, the final prospectus is printed—with the price, offering date, underwriting discount, and any new financial information—and delivered to potential investors. The SEC requires that all investors receive a copy of the prospectus before they purchase new securities. The SEC does not approve or disapprove the investment value of the issue. Its approval merely means that sufficient information has been provided for an intelligent investor to make a rational decision on the investment merits of the issue. The front page of a final prospectus is shown in Figure 3.1.

The pricing of initial public offerings involves the security valuation procedures described in later chapters of this book. However, other elements are involved in pricing new issues as opposed to issues already traded in the market. The underwriter is concerned about price risk, and the issuer is interested in netting the maximum proceeds from the new issue. The issuer does not want to leave too much "on the table," while the underwriter does not want to face resistance from investors in marketing the new issue. An additional pricing problem is related to the fact that the new issue is untested, in the sense that market participants have not independently set a price for the security through the market process. While the financial fundamentals of publicly traded securities of comparable companies will be used in setting the price, the fact remains that there is uncertainty about the market's acceptance of the price.[3]

---

[2] In late 1983, the SEC adopted *Rule 415,* which allows larger firms contemplating a future issue of stocks or bonds to bypass investment bankers' involvement in the registration process. Under Rule 415, issuers can register securities with the SEC up to two years before the securities are issued. This "shelf registration" allows the issuer the opportunity to issue the securities at an advantageous time (both in terms of the market price of the securities being offered and the timing of the cash needs of the issuer) and reduces the cost of the underwriting since the issuer, not the investment banker, handles the registration process.

[3] A number of interesting articles have been written on the pricing of initial public offerings. For example, see Michael L. McBain and David S. Krause, "Going Public: The Impact on Insiders' Holdings on the Prices of Initial Public Offerings," *Journal of Business Venturing* (November 1989): 419–28; Seha M. Tinic, "Anatomy of Initial Public Offerings of Common Stock," *Journal of Finance* (September 1988): 789–822; and James M. Johnson and Robert E. Miller, "Investment Banker Prestige and the Underpricing of Initial Public Offerings," *Financial Management* (Summer 1988): 19–29.

FIGURE 3.1
An Example of a Final Prospectus

PROSPECTUS

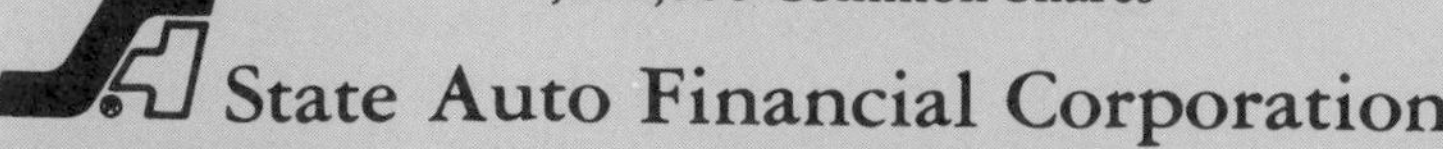

All the Common Shares offered hereby are being sold by State Auto Financial Corporation (the "Company"). Prior to this offering, there has been no public market for the Common Shares. See "Underwriting" for information relating to the factors considered in determining the initial public offering price.

All the Common Shares of the Company are currently owned by State Automobile Mutual Insurance Company, an Ohio mutual insurance company ("Mutual"), which, after the completion of this offering, will own approximately 70% of the Common Shares (67% if the Underwriters' over-allotment option is exercised in full). The Company's operations are interrelated with the operations of Mutual.

Up to a maximum of 168,000 Common Shares offered hereby are being reserved for sale at the initial public offering price to the Company's and Mutual's employees, directors and independent insurance agents. See "Underwriting."

Prospective investors should carefully consider the factors set forth in "Certain Considerations."

THESE SECURITIES HAVE NOT BEEN APPROVED OR DISAPPROVED BY THE SECURITIES AND EXCHANGE COMMISSION OR ANY STATE SECURITIES COMMISSION NOR HAS THE SECURITIES AND EXCHANGE COMMISSION OR ANY STATE SECURITIES COMMISSION PASSED UPON THE ACCURACY OR ADEQUACY OF THIS PROSPECTUS. ANY REPRESENTATION TO THE CONTRARY IS A CRIMINAL OFFENSE.

	Price to Public	Underwriting Discounts and Commissions(1)	Proceeds to Company(2)
Per Share	$13.50	$.95	$12.55
Total(3)	$22,680,000	$1,596,000	$21,084,000

(1) For information regarding indemnification of the Underwriters, see "Underwriting."
(2) Before deducting expenses of the offering estimated at $750,000 payable by the Company.
(3) The Company has granted the Underwriters a 30-day option to purchase up to 252,000 additional Common Shares at the Price to Public, less the Underwriting Discounts and Commissions, solely to cover over-allotments, if any. If the Underwriters exercise such option in full, the total Price to Public, Underwriting Discounts and Commissions and Proceeds to Company will be $26,082,000, $1,835,400 and $24,246,600, respectively. See "Underwriting."

The Common Shares are being offered by the several Underwriters when, as and if delivered to and accepted by them and subject to their right to withdraw, cancel or reject orders in whole or in part. Delivery of certificates for the Common Shares is expected to be made at the offices of Smith Barney, Harris Upham & Co. Incorporated, 110 Wall Street, New York, New York 10005, on or about July 8, 1991.

Smith Barney, Harris Upham & Co.
Incorporated

A.G. Edwards & Sons, Inc.

The Ohio Company

June 28, 1991

SOURCE: Reprinted by permission of Smith Barney, Harris Upham & Co.

The pricing problem extends to the investor in initial public offerings, particularly common stock. If the price set by the underwriter is perceived by the market to be too low, the issue will be oversubscribed, and the availability to the small individual investor may be quite limited. Often in these instances the first price in the secondary market may be substantially above the offering price. If, on the other hand, the market believes the original price is too high, the new issue will be made abundantly available to all investors by the members of the selling group. Unless the underwriter has indicated to the SEC its intent to stabilize the price by buying back the newly issued securities at or near the offering price, the investor in a new issue may find that the price set by the market is below that of the initial offering price.[4]

The prices of initial public offerings in the first days of trading are difficult to predict. For example, Duracell International, Inc., had a new common stock issue in May 1991. In its first day of trading, the price of Duracell's common stock appreciated by 38 percent. In the same month, AnnTaylor Stores Corporation also had a new common stock issue, and its price rose only 3.37 percent in its first day of trading. Merrill Lynch Capital Markets was the lead underwriter or investment banker for both issues.

• Investment Bankers and Banking in the 1980s: A Decade of Innovations and Ethical Problems

Historically, the investment banking business was built on close personal relationships between a limited number of key investment bankers and corporate executives. The industry had a reputation of hiring only a limited number of individuals with the "right" family and educational background.

In the 1980s, the activities of investment bankers expanded beyond their traditional role of helping corporations raise external funds. Although investment bankers continued to provide these services, the restructuring of corporations in the United States and the tremendous changes in the financial markets required changes on the part of investment bankers. They had to become increasingly proactive in order to maintain a competitive edge. In addition to being advisers in mergers and acquisitions and hostile takeover bids, they became partners, lenders, and often principals in their clients' deals. For example, investment bankers provide **bridge loans** to clients. A bridge loan spans the time between when cash is needed and when permanent financing can be acquired. In Robert Campeau's $6.7 billion acquisition of Federated Department Stores, investment bankers First Boston, Inc., Dillon Read, and Paine Webber provided bridge financing of $2.1 billion.[5] The permanent financing quite often took the form of high-yield or **junk bonds.** Junk bonds are defined as publicly traded debt obligations rated as noninvestment grade by at least one of the major independent rating agencies.

Investment bankers also created a generation of innovative products in which they acted as originators. An example of these new products is **asset-backed securities** in which existing assets, such as automobile loans, credit

---

[4] Jay R. Ritter, "The Costs of Going Public," *Journal of Financial Economics* (December 1987): 269–81, presented evidence that the two quantifiable costs of going public—direct expenses and underpricing—averaged 21.22 percent of the realized market value of the securities issued by underwriting and 31.87 percent for best-efforts offers. The study covered the period 1977–1982.

[5] Tom Bancroft, "Psst!! Wanna Buy a Bridge?" *Financial World*, April 3, 1990, pp. 26–27.

card receivables, and home mortgages, are packaged into new securities. *Collateralized mortgage obligations* (*CMOs*) and *stripped mortgage-backed securities* (*SMBSs*) are examples of asset-backed securities. CMOs are collateral-backed bonds that are issued by business entities that purchase mortgages or mortgage securities as collateral for the CMOs. These derivative securities are popular with investors because they offer various payment schedules and maturities, both fixed and variable rate interest payments, and, perhaps most importantly, protection from the risk associated with the unpredictable nature of mortgage repayment schedules. Since the first CMO was issued by the Federal Home Loan Mortgage Corporation in June 1983, total issuance has exceeded $100 billion.

In the case of SMBSs, mortgage securities are usually used as collateral to provide the interest and principal cash flows that are separated and directed to the "stripped" securities. The principal cash flow from the underlying collateral is directed to a *Principal Only* (*PO*) security; the interest cash flow is directed to the *Interest Only* (*IO*) security. As of mid-1989, the Federal National Mortgage Association had more than $10 billion in SMBSs outstanding.

As a result of these activities, the investment banking industry came to be viewed as the dominant force in the securities business. For example, in 1986 the Securities Industry Association estimated that investment bankers represented 2 percent of the New York Stock Exchange member firms dealing with the public but accounted for 50 percent of the total pretax profit of the entire U.S. securities business. In addition, the 10 largest investment banking firms earned one-third of the total revenue of all securities firms.

The growth in employment in the investment banking industry was also phenomenal. The total number of employees for the 10 largest firms was less than five thousand in the late 1970s. From 1980 to 1987, employment more than doubled in the 10 largest firms. This rate of employment growth was much faster than for other sectors of the securities industry. Employment growth was profitable for investment banking firms. In 1985, revenues per employee were estimated to be $.5 million, with pretax profits per employee in excess of $65,000.

One of the investment banking/brokerage firms that helped to revolutionize the industry was Drexel Burnham Lambert, Inc. This firm pioneered the use of junk bonds to finance leveraged buyouts and takeovers. The profitability of merger and takeover activities can be much greater than that of traditional underwriting activities because the firm can collect a fee for advising its client, earn commissions on the publicly or privately placed junk bonds, and earn brokerage commissions by providing a secondary market for the junk bonds. If the takeover is successful, corporate assets may be liquidated to help pay off some of the debt and provide profits for the acquiring group. The investment banking firm may be involved in providing financing for the purchaser of the assets and earn additional fees and commissions. In 1986, Drexel had pretax profits of $1.1 billion, due largely to its leveraged buyout and takeover activities. For reasons explained below, Drexel filed for bankruptcy protection in 1990.

Investment banking firms have been accused of charging excessive fees for their role in mergers and takeovers. An interesting case involved the takeover attempt by The Limited, Inc., of Carter Hawley Stores, Inc. The management of Carter Hawley retained Morgan Stanley & Co. to help fight the takeover. Morgan Stanley's fee is estimated to have been in excess of $50 million plus expenses that exceeded an "eight-figure range." The fee (ignoring expenses) exceeded the total net profit of Carter Hawley for all of 1985 and represented more than 3 percent of the firm's total capitalization.[6] Morgan Stanley estimated that it spent 10,000 hours working on the project, suggesting a fee in excess of $5,000 per hour. Not only were the fees criticized as excessive but they were also questioned in terms of the benefit to the stockholders. In essence, stockholder wealth was used to fight a takeover that might have been in their own best interests.

In addition to criticisms about fees, a number of well-known investment banking firms and investment bankers have been convicted of participating in illegal insider-trading activities involving mergers and takeover attempts. The most highly publicized cases involved Ivan F. Boesky, Michael R. Milken, and Drexel Burnham Lambert, Inc. Boesky was convicted of violating security laws in 1986 and 1987 by trading on insider information provided by Dennis Levine of Drexel. Boesky agreed to pay $100 million in civil penalties and was sentenced to three years in prison. He cooperated with the investigation, and his testimony resulted in Drexel pleading guilty to six felony charges and agreeing to pay a fine of $650 million. In February 1990, Drexel's holding company filed for Chapter 11 bankruptcy protection. Milken also pleaded guilty to security law violations, was fined $600 million, and was sentenced to a jail term.

• Investment Banking in the 1990s

The investment banking industry in the 1980s was very creative and successful in developing new services and entering new businesses. The controversy concerning the economic benefit of takeovers and leveraged buyouts, combined with the involvement of some firms and investment bankers in illegal activities, damaged the reputation of the industry. The excesses of the 1980s will have a direct impact on investment banking in the 1990s. The difficulty some junk bond issuers have had in meeting interest and principal payments will make it harder to use this vehicle to finance leveraged buyouts and corporate takeovers in the future. In addition, commercial banks may become more actively involved in investment banking activities, increasing competition and reducing fees. Further, the excesses of the 1980s may lead to increased government regulation of the security industry.

---

[6] Benjamin J. Stein, "A Saga of Shareholder Neglect: Whose Interest Was This Management Protecting?" *Barron's,* May 4, 1987, pp. 8–9, 70–75.

In the 1990s, U.S. investment bankers will also face the issues of *distintermediation* and *global competition*. Disintermediation occurs when consenting institutional investors and borrowers work out a transaction among themselves, eliminating the need for the services of an investment banker. The impetus for direct dealing is being provided by the large amount of dollars being managed by institutions, rapid technological developments such as CapitaLink, an electronic bond auction system backed by Morgan Guaranty, and the need for specialized products to meet the specific demands of issuers and buyers of securities.

The arrival of a global marketplace will also create increased competition for investment bankers. As Europe becomes a unified financial marketplace and the Japanese markets open, competition will be worldwide. For example, Nomura Securities, the largest financial institution in the world, with a market capitalization of Y1.3 trillion and more than Y52 trillion in customer assets, hired Max C. Chapman, former president of Kidder Peabody, as co-chairman. The purpose of this appointment was to make Nomura a key player in international investment banking.[7]

SECONDARY MARKETS[8]

After securities have been purchased in the primary markets, they can be traded in the *secondary markets.* The secondary markets comprise the organized securities exchanges and the over-the-counter (OTC) markets. The majority of all capital market transactions occur in the secondary markets. The proceeds from sales of securities in the secondary markets do not go to the original issuer but to the owners (sellers) of the securities.

The function of the secondary markets is to provide liquidity for securities purchased in the primary markets. Once investors have purchased securities in the primary markets, they need a place to sell those securities. Without the liquidity of the secondary market, firms would have difficulty raising funds for productive purposes in the primary markets.

• New York Stock Exchange

The **New York Stock Exchange** (**NYSE**) is the largest of the organized securities exchanges in the United States. It was established in 1817 and was originally called the New York Stock and Exchange Board. Its current name was adopted in 1863. Securities of over 1,700 companies are currently traded on the NYSE, with approximately 2,200 common and preferred stocks and 2,300 bonds listed. Listing requirements for the NYSE are given in Table 3.1.

[7] "Investors Chronicle," *Business*, February 1990, pp. 104–6.

[8] Foreign stock exchanges, options exchanges, and futures exchanges are discussed in later chapters of the book, which focus on these topics.

TABLE 3.1 • Listing Requirements for the NYSE

Initial Listing Requirements

1. Earning power
   a. Minimum of $2.5 million earnings before taxes for most recent year
   b. Minimum of $2.0 million earnings for each of the preceding two years, or an aggregate for the last three fiscal years of $6.5 million with a minimum in the most recent year of $4.5 million (all three years must be profitable)
2. Minimum net tangible assets: $18 million
3. Minimum market value of publicly held shares: $18 million (as of 12/31/88)
4. Minimum shares publicly held: 1,100,000 shares
5. Either a minimum 2,000 holders of 100 shares or more, or 2,200 total stockholders together with average monthly trading volume (for the most recent six months) of 100,000 shares

Continued Listing Requirements

1. At least 1,200 round-lot stockholders
2. At least 600,000 shares in public hands
3. Aggregate market value of publicly held shares of $5 million or more

Alternate Listing Standards for Foreign Companies

1. Pretax income: $100 million cumulative in the latest three years with a minimum of $25 million in any one of the three years
2. Minimum net tangible assets of $100 million worldwide
3. Minimum aggregate market value of publicly held shares of $100 million worldwide
4. Minimum number of publicly held shares: 2.5 million shares
5. Minimum 5,000 holders of 100 shares or more

SOURCE: *The NYSE Fact Book 1989* (New York Stock Exchange, Inc.), pp. 22–25.

The "Big Board," as the NYSE is called, accounts for approximately 80 percent of all shares traded on the organized exchanges. The volume of trading on the NYSE has grown rapidly in the past 24 years. In 1967, the average daily volume was 10 million shares. By 1977, the average volume had doubled to 21 million, and by 1990, the average daily volume had risen to approximately 158 million shares. On October 20, 1987, the volume on the NYSE was over 608 million shares.[9]

The NYSE is a corporation with 1,444 members, including 1,366 members who own a "seat." Most of the seats are owned by brokerage firms. The cost of a seat fluctuates with the volume of trading activity on the exchange. Seats have sold for as little as $14,000, in 1876 and 1878, and for as much as

[9] *The NYSE Fact Book 1989* (New York Stock Exchange, Inc.), p. 70.

$1,150,000, in 1987. In April 1991, a seat on the NYSE sold for $350,000. Members are classified into four categories, as follows:

1. *Commission brokers* **Commission brokers** are employees of a member brokerage firm who execute buy and sell orders for the firm's clients. Major brokerage firms have more than one commission broker.
2. *Floor brokers* Independent **floor brokers** own their own seats on the exchange. They are also known as "broker's brokers." When trading activity is high, they accept and execute orders for the commission brokers and receive a fee in return.
3. *Floor traders* **Floor traders** are members of the NYSE who buy and sell solely for their own accounts. They can react quickly to changes in exchange activity and information on securities since they are located on the floor of the exchange. Small price changes in securities can generate profits for them since they pay no commissions.
4. *Specialists* Probably the most important and controversial members of the exchange, **specialists** are responsible for maintaining a "fair and orderly market" in the securities to which they are assigned. There are approximately 50 specialist firms, and each listed stock is assigned to one or more specialists. Specialists perform two functions. First, as *brokers,* they must handle "limit" and other special orders entered in their book for commission brokers. Second, they act as *dealers,* buying and selling the stocks they are assigned in order to maintain an orderly market.

• American Stock Exchange

The **American Stock Exchange (AMEX)** is the other major national exchange. It is often referred to as "the Curb" because it was originally located outside on the corner of Wall and Hanover Streets in New York. Listing requirements for the AMEX are less stringent than those for the NYSE (see Table 3.2). The approximately nine hundred companies listed on the AMEX tend to be smaller and less seasoned than the firms listed on the NYSE. As the firms grow in size and strength, they often move their listings to the NYSE because of the increased prestige. The average daily volume on the AMEX has increased from approximately 1 million shares in 1960 to more than 12 million shares in 1991. The AMEX, like the NYSE, uses the specialist system to maintain a fair and orderly market.

Four types of memberships are available on the AMEX—regular, options principal, associate, and allied. Regular and options principal members, commonly called "seats," provide direct access to the trading floor. The record high price for a seat was $420,000 in 1987, and the all-time low price of $650 was set in 1942.

The AMEX differs from the NYSE in several respects. The first is the smaller size of the firms listed on the AMEX due to the less stringent listing require-

• INTEREST BOX

Electronic Trading Systems

Until recently, the NYSE had little competition. Now, however, a number of NYSE member firms, such as Morgan Stanley, Salomon Brothers, and Bear, Stearns, and institutional investors, such as pension funds and mutual funds, are doing some of their computerized trading off-exchange in order to save commission costs. Some of this off-exchange trading is taking place on foreign exchanges, particularly London, while other transactions are occurring directly between institutional buyers and sellers through the use of electronic trading systems (the fourth market). Three off-exchange electronic trading systems are currently in place:

- *Instinet Crossing Network.* Owned by Reuters Holding, Instinet allows institutions to enter large orders without revealing their identity. At 5:45 P.M. each trading day, the buy and sell orders are electronically matched, based on the NYSE closing price for that day. These trades are reported on the national market system's consolidated tape the next day.
- *Portfolio System for Institutional Investors* (*Posit*). This electronic trading system is owned by the Jefferies Group. For Posit, the matching of institutional buy and sell orders, or crossing, occurs daily at a randomly selected time between 1:00 P.M. and 2:00 P.M. The market price of the stocks at the randomly selected time becomes the crossing price. The trades for Posit are reported on the national market system's consolidated tape when they occur.
- *Single Price Auction Network* (*Spaworks*). Spaworks, the newest electronic trading system, was conceived by former Kidder, Peabody vice president, R. Steven Wunsch, and designed by Cray Research. Unlike Instinet and Posit, Spaworks does not use NYSE quoted prices to set transaction prices. Rather, buy and sell orders (number of shares and price range) are collected without identifying the potential buyer or seller and made available to traders on their computer screens. In a sense, the computer screen is much like the specialist's book, but it is open to all participants. At 5:15 P.M. on Mondays and Wednesdays and at 9:00 A.M. on Fridays, the orders are matched at the price at the intersection of the demand (buy) and supply (sell) curves. For example, if the curves intersect at $50\frac{1}{2}$ for a stock, all orders to buy at $50\frac{5}{8}$ or higher will be executed at $50\frac{1}{2}$, and all orders to sell at $50\frac{3}{8}$ or lower will be executed at $50\frac{1}{2}$. Orders to buy or sell at $50\frac{1}{2}$ will be executed in the order of their arrival at Spaworks. Buy orders below $50\frac{1}{2}$ and sell orders above $50\frac{1}{2}$ will not be executed.

These electronic trading systems may represent the first step in developing a continuous electronic market without an exchange floor and specialists. These developments help explain why the prices of seats on the NYSE have declined, and the NYSE recently extended its trading hours using an electronic trading system.

SOURCE: Adapted from Richard L. Stern, "A Dwindling Monopoly," *Forbes*, May 13, 1991, pp. 64–66.

ments. Second, the AMEX demonstrated innovativeness and aggressiveness by trading warrants before they were allowed to be traded on the NYSE. It was also the first to trade American Depository Receipts (ADRs), securities issued by banks that represent holdings of shares in foreign companies. Further, the AMEX has been very aggressive in introducing option trading for individual

TABLE 3.2 • Listing Requirements for the AMEX

Minimum Initial Listing Requirements

1. Pretax income: $750,000 latest fiscal year or two of the last three fiscal years
2. Minimum stockholders' equity: $4,000,000
3. Minimum shares publicly held: 500,000
4. Minimum market value of publicly held shares/price per share: $3,000,000/$3.00
5. Number of stockholders: 800 holders of round lots if public float is less than 1 million shares, 400 if float is at least 1 million shares

The exchange may also consider listing a company's securities if the company has a minimum of 500,000 shares publicly held and a minimum of 400 shareholders, and the daily volume of trading in the issue has been approximately 2,000 shares or more for the six months preceding the date of application.

Minimum Requirements for Continued Listing

1. Shares publicly held: 200,000
2. Market value of publicly held shares: $1,000,000
3. Number of round-lot holders: 300

Delisting guidelines make a company eligible for removal if (1) it has stockholders' equity of less than $2,000,000 and sustained net losses in two of its three most recent fiscal years; or (2) it has stockholders' equity of less than $4,000,000 and sustained losses in three of its four most recent fiscal years; or (3) it has sustained net losses in its five most recent fiscal years.

SOURCE: *The American Stock Exchange Fact Book of 1989* (American Stock Exchange), p. 11.

stock options, broad-based index options, industry-based index options, and interest rate options. A large number of corporate, U.S. Treasury, and federal government agency bonds are listed on the AMEX.

• Regional Exchanges

There are several **regional exchanges,** including the Pacific Stock Exchange (San Francisco–Los Angeles), the Philadelphia Exchange (Philadelphia-Pittsburgh), the Midwest Stock Exchange (Chicago), the Boston Stock Exchange (Boston), and the Cincinnati Stock Exchange (Cincinnati). The regional exchanges operate in basically the same manner as the national exchanges, although their listing requirements are more lenient.[10]

[10]The Spokane Stock Exchange, the smallest regional stock exchange, closed in May 1991. The exchange had been in operation for 94 years, and most of the 45 companies traded on the exchange are engaged in regional metals mining. The closing of the exchange was blamed on investors' lack of interest in small gold and silver mining companies. Also, the exchange could

The regional exchanges provide two basic functions. First, they list the securities of firms that are too small to meet the listing requirements of the national exchanges. Second, they list dually the securities of firms on the national exchanges. Dual listing allows small brokerage firms, which cannot afford a seat on the national exchanges but can afford membership in a regional exchange, to buy and sell stock in the dually listed firms. The majority of the regional exchanges' equity volume is in the dually listed securities.

• Over-the-Counter Market

The **over-the-counter market** (**OTC**) refers to all security transactions not taking place on the organized exchanges. The OTC has no central location as the major and regional exchanges do; instead, it is a network of brokers-dealers who deal (negotiate) for their own accounts with each other over the telephone or through computer terminals. For this reason, the OTC market is a "negotiated market" in contrast to the auction markets of the organized exchanges. In an auction market, a third party, in this case a specialist, facilitates the transaction.

Securities traded in the OTC market tend to be those of small regional businesses, banks, finance companies, and mutual funds. In addition, most corporate, municipal, and United States government bonds are traded OTC.

All brokers and dealers in the OTC market must belong to the National Association of Security Dealers (NASD). The NASD has developed the **National Association of Security Dealers Automated Quotation (NASDAQ) system,** a computerized network for obtaining bid and ask quotes on NASDAQ securities. To be included in the NASDAQ system, a security must have at least two market makers who are willing to trade a minimum number of shares and must meet certain requirements regarding capital and assets. Slightly more than one-half of the NASDAQ securities meet the SEC-approved criteria for inclusion in the NASDAQ National Market System list; these requirements involve the number and market value of publicly held shares, trading volume, price, and number of market makers. Smaller and less actively traded companies are included in the NASDAQ National and Supplemental lists. Quotes on stock prices for these smaller companies are usually not carried in local newspapers but can be found in *Barron's* and Monday's *Wall Street Journal.* The NASDAQ carries over 4,400 companies and over 5,100 issues. It is estimated that about 1,600 companies on the NASDAQ system could qualify for listing on the AMEX, 600 of which could also qualify for listing on the NYSE.[11]

---

not afford to convert from a chalkboard quotation system to an electronic computer tie-in with national quotation services as required by federal rules.

[11] Claudia Freeman and Edward Rosenbaum, "A Survey of Management's Attitudes toward Stock Exchange Delisting and the NASDAQ National Market System," *Akron Business & Economic Review* (Summer 1987): 19–30.

• **INTEREST BOX**

Extended Trading Hours on the Exchanges

On June 13, 1991, the NYSE extended its trading hours beyond the traditional 4:00 P.M. close by adding two sessions, one beginning at 4:15 P.M. and ending at 5:00 P.M. (Session 1) and a second session beginning at 4:00 P.M. and ending at 5:15 P.M. (Session 2). Session 1 is for individual and institutional investors, and a computer (not a specialist) is used to match the buy and sell orders. The individual investor, as usual, places an order through a broker. There are two rules for executing orders in Session 1. First, the buyer or seller must be willing to trade precisely at the 4:00 P.M. closing price of the stock. Second, in order for the buy or sell order to be executed, there must be a corresponding order on the other side. For example, if there are orders to buy a total of 3,000 shares of IBM at the 4:00 P.M. closing price and orders to sell only 1,000 shares, then only the first 1,000 shares will be traded, and the offers to buy the other 2,000 shares will expire.

Session 2 is for larger investors and must involve at least 15 different NYSE-listed stocks with a market value of $1 million or more. The NYSE will report only the total trading volume for Session 2 after the 5:15 P.M. close, and the large investors have three days before the details of their trades, including prices, are made public. This allows the large traders, particularly those with positions in thinly traded stocks, to complete their transactions before the information becomes public.

The NYSE instituted the extended trading hours, particularly Session 2, to try to regain the business lost to the London stock exchange, the electronic trading networks, and the later trading hours available on the Pacific Stock Exchange. The NYSE is hoping to recapture the 10 to 15 million shares in daily trading it has lost to these rivals. The extended hours, however, do not create 24-hour trading consistent with the globalization of financial markets. Other exchanges are planning more dramatic changes to meet the needs of a global market. The National Association of Securities Dealers has applied to the SEC for approval to begin trading at 3:30 A.M., consistent with the opening of the London stock exchange. The American Stock Exchange is working with the Chicago Board Options Exchange, the Cincinnati Stock Exchange, and Reuters to trade stocks and options on a 24-hour global electronic trading system.

• Third and Fourth Markets

The **third market** refers to OTC transactions in securities listed on the organized exchanges. It is composed primarily of large institutional investors that dislike having to pay set commissions when trading large blocks of stocks on the NYSE. To reduce the commission costs, they trade blocks of securities in the OTC market where they can negotiate the transaction costs. The third market flourished during the 1960s and early 1970s, but it has gradually declined with the onset of negotiated commissions in 1975.

Crossing, also known as the **fourth market,** refers to security transactions directly between a buyer and seller. The broker-dealer is eliminated from the transaction, which is usually between large institutions trading big blocks of stocks, although the term would also apply to the small investor selling a hundred shares of stock to a friend. The fourth market for institutional investors has gained popularity in recent years due to its lower brokerage costs and to the growth of *index funds,* semipassive funds that are not based on brokerage research. In addition, the development of institutional electronic trading systems such as Reuters' Instinet Crossing Network, the Jefferies Group's Portfolio System for Institutional Investors (Posit), and the Single Price Auction Network (Spaworks) has increased activity in the fourth market.[12]

TRADING MECHANICS

• Overview

The first step in investing in securities is usually the selection of a brokerage firm. The investor must decide between a **full-service** brokerage firm and a **discount** brokerage firm. A full-service brokerage firm, such as Merrill Lynch, not only executes orders but also maintains a research staff that provides economic reports and information on industries and firms to its customers. Many full-service brokerage firms not only trade in stocks and bonds but also offer a variety of other services such as mutual funds, limited partnerships, life insurance, and estate planning.

By not providing the research and advice, discount brokers are able to charge commissions that are between 20 and 70 percent less than those charged by full-service brokers. The largest discount brokers, Charles Schwab, Fidelity Brokerage Services, and Quick & Reilly, account for approximately 70 percent of the discount business. There are also "bare-bones" discounters, such as Bidwell and York Securities, that offer even less services and lower fees than the larger discounters. Brokerage fees charged by banks generally fall between those of the full-service brokers and the discount brokers. It should be noted that brokerage commissions can be negotiated, particularly for larger customers.

Two other types of brokerage firms deserve mention. *Regional brokerage firms* are often the only source of research information on small regional companies. Some of these regional companies may have excellent growth and financial characteristics but are simply too small for the major brokerage firms to spend time analyzing them. Second, the number of *"penny stock" brokerage firms* has increased in recent years. Penny stocks are securities trading for less than $5 per share and often less than $1 per share. Commission rates at some penny stock firms are as high as 50 percent of the value of the transaction. In addition to the high risk of the penny stock companies themselves and high commission rates, a penny stock broker may use a technique called "crossing," or simultaneous transactions, in which the broker arranges for one cli-

---

[12]The operation of these electronic trading systems is described in the Interest Box: Electronic Trading Systems.

ent to sell a stock and another client to buy the stock at an additional markup. Thus, it may be difficult to make a profit when trading at one of these firms.

After selecting a brokerage firm, the next step is selecting a broker (also called an account executive or financial consultant). The potential investor can ask other investors for recommendations, the same way a person who is new to an area would select a doctor, a dentist, or an attorney. Investors should select brokers who understand their investment objectives and risk orientation and are willing to operate within these constraints. For example, a retired couple seeking income from their retirement funds may not relate well to a broker who feels that active management of a stock portfolio is the best or only investment approach. The investor should also remember that the broker makes his or her living through buying and selling securities for customers. This creates a potential conflict of interest and can cause complications between the broker and the investor.

Opening an account at a brokerage firm is very simple. The investor must fill out an application that asks for personal information (name, address, telephone number, and Social Security number); financial information (salary, assets, liabilities, other investments); and investment objectives (income, appreciation, preservation of principal, tax savings).

Two basic types of accounts are available to the customer: cash and margin. The most common account is the *cash account,* in which the customer pays the full price of any securities purchased. A *margin account* allows the customer to pay 50 percent (currently) of the price of the securities purchased and to borrow the rest from the brokerage firm. Brokerage firms try to determine that investors have sufficient knowledge of the security markets and the risks involved before allowing customers to open margin accounts. The risk and return characteristics of margin trading are discussed in connection with trading investment strategies in Chapter 7. The account can be opened as a *single* or *joint* account. Joint accounts are generally shared by a husband and wife or a parent and a minor child under the age of 18. The latter is called a *custodial* account and requires the permission of a parent or guardian before any trade can be undertaken. Investors should read agreements carefully before signing any contract with a brokerage firm.

• Types of Orders

Stock orders are normally placed in **round lots**—100 shares. A transaction of less than 100 shares is referred to as an **odd-lot transaction.** The commission cost per share for odd lots is higher than for round lots. Generally, an odd-lot transaction will cost the investor an eighth of a point, or 12.5 cents, per share more than a round-lot transaction. The odd-lot transaction cost does not apply for very high-priced stocks. Historically, there were odd-lot dealers who handled odd-lot orders. Today, specialists perform this function on the exchanges.

MARKET ORDER The most common order is a **market order.** When a customer places a market order, it is transacted at the best price available when the order reaches the floor of the exchange. The advantage of a market order is that it will be executed immediately. The disadvantage is that the investor does not know at exactly what price the transaction will occur. Market orders are normally *day orders* that expire at the end of the day. If there is a chance that the order cannot be executed, the investor may leave the expiration date of the order open by placing a *good-till-canceled order* (*GTC*).

LIMIT ORDER A **limit order** requires that the order be transacted at the limit price or at a better price. For example, assume that you want to buy a stock that is currently selling for $20 a share, but you want to pay only $18 a share. You call your broker and place a limit buy order at $18. The order is sent to the firm's commission broker on the floor of the exchange. The order is then taken to the "post" where the stock is being traded. If the order cannot be transacted, the commission broker will leave the order with the specialist, who puts it in the book. If the price of the stock drops to $18 or lower, the specialist will transact the order. If you want to sell a stock, the limit order is placed above the current price of the stock. Assume that you own 100 shares of IBM, which is currently trading at $105 a share. You think that the stock will rise at least $10 a share over the next few weeks. In an attempt to maximize your profit, you place a limit sell order at $115. If the stock sells for $115 or higher, your order will be executed.

It is possible that a limit order will not be executed when the price is reached. When the specialist enters the limit order in the book, the order enters a queue. In the preceding example, there may already have been an order to sell 400 shares of IBM at $115 a share in the book. If only 400 shares transact at $115 a share, your order will not be executed, but it will now move to the top of the list, and the next buy order at $115 a share will cause the order to be executed.

The major disadvantage in using limit orders is that you may "miss" the market. If IBM stock rose to $114⅞ a share and then dropped to $90 a share, your order would not be executed, and for one-eighth of a point you would suffer a significant decline in net worth. Likewise, placing a limit buy order below the market price when a stock is rising may mean that you miss the price move that you would have gotten if you had placed a market order.

STOP ORDER A **stop order,** also called a *stop-loss* order, is a special order that is placed in the specialist's book. Assume that you bought a stock at $20 per share, and the stock price has risen to $30. Your profit will be $10 a share if you sell the stock. To protect yourself against a drop in the price, you enter a stop-loss order at $27. If the price drops to $27 a share, the stop order will become a market order and will be executed at the highest bid available on the specialist's book. Although you will suffer a slight decline from the $30 price, you will also have protected a portion of the price appreciation in the stock (approximately $7 gain). Of course, there is no guarantee that you will receive $27 per share. If the stock declines rapidly, the market order may be transacted at less than $27. To protect against this possibility, an investor can place a *stop-limit* order. Under this type of order, once the stock price reaches $27, the stop order becomes a limit order at $27 or better. The major disadvantage of a stop order is that if the stock was merely fluctuating within a price range but was still in an uptrend, you will have sold the stock because of a temporary decline in the stock's price.

Limit buy and stop-loss orders are normally reduced in price on the date the stock goes ex-dividend. This is logical since the value of the stock is reduced by the amount of the per-share cash dividend on the ex-dividend date. The amount of price reduction is rounded to the nearest eighth of a point. For example, a limit buy at $18 GTC for Baxter Corporation is placed with the specialist. The next week the stock goes ex-dividend by $.50 per share. The limit buy order would be changed to $17½. If the dividend had been $.34, the order price would have declined three-eighths of a point ($.375). Orders may be marked "DNR" (do not reduce) if desired.

MISCELLANEOUS ORDERS A number of miscellaneous orders are available for large investors. A *fill or kill* (*FOK*) order means to fill the order immediately in one trade or cancel the order completely. An *all or none* (*AON*) order means fill the order in one day or cancel the order completely. The *immediate or cancel* (*IOC*) order means that the broker must immediately fill as much of the order as possible in one trade and then cancel the remainder of the order. A *not held* (*NH*) order grants some discretion to the registered representative (and hence the commission broker) to do as he or she sees fit. The specialist will not receive the order. When the commission broker arrives at the post where the stock is traded, he can immediately try to execute the order, or he can wait if he thinks the price will become more favorable.

REGULATION OF SECURITY MARKETS

There was very little regulation of the security markets in the United States prior to 1933. The 1920s were a time of fraudulent trading practices, speculative excesses with borrowed funds, dissemination of fraudulent securities information, and trading on insider information. These undesirable practices contributed to the market crash of 1929 and the subsequent enactment of legislation governing the securities industry.

The increases in stock market volatility as evidenced by the stock market "crashes" in October 1987 and 1989 and the recent disclosure of unethical and illegal activities in the security markets have created an impetus for additional regulation of the security markets. Many believe that fraudulent activities, such as insider trading, have undermined the fiduciary relationship that lies at the heart of the securities industry. In most instances, regulations are already in place to curb securities fraud, but detecting trading abuses in order to enforce the regulations is difficult. Brokerage houses, stock exchanges, and the OTC are working to develop electronic surveillance and reporting procedures to uncover insider trading and other forms of trading abuses.

• Securities Act of 1933

The Securities Act of 1933 is also known as the "truth in securities act." The act requires all new securities issues and certain secondary offerings to be registered with the federal government. Offerings exempt from the law include government and municipal issues; intrastate offerings (and secondary sales out of state after nine months); Regulation A offerings (issues of less than $1.5 million); issues covered by the Interstate Commerce Commission, such as those of railroads, airlines, and trucking companies; and private placements to a small number of investors.

The primary purpose of the act is to provide full disclosure about securities so that rational investors can make intelligent investment decisions. The law requires the filing of a registration statement that includes information about the firm, a list of its officers and directors, audited financial statements, and the proposed use of the funds to be raised by the offering. After filing the statement, the firm must wait 20 days before it can issue the new securities. While the federal government is evaluating the registration statement, the firm may publish a "tombstone" advertisement (see Figure 3.2) and send a preliminary prospectus (red herring) to potential investors. The final prospectus must be provided to all purchasers of the new security.

The act also provides for civil and criminal penalties for fraud or misrepresentation. If an investor suffers a monetary loss due to fraudulent information or misrepresentation in a security offering, he or she may sue to recover the lost funds.[13]

• Securities Exchange Act of 1934

A number of factors make the Securities Exchange Act of 1934 important to investors. It extends disclosure requirements to securities traded in the secondary markets (NYSE, AMEX, OTC, and regional exchanges). A firm is required to file an annual registration statement (called a 10–K report), as well as other periodic reports, with the SEC. The act was amended in 1964 to require large OTC firms to file annual registration statements.

The act also established the Securities and Exchange Commission (SEC). The SEC is charged with the regulation of security markets and establishes

---

[13] Studies have examined the behavior of investment banks and the pricing of unseasoned new equity offerings, both before and after the Securities Act of 1933. For example, see Seha M. Tinic, "Anatomy of Initial Public Offerings of Common Stock," *Journal of Finance* (September 1988): 789–822; and Carol J. Simon, "The Effect of the 1933 Securities Act on Investor Information and the Performance of New Issues," *American Economic Review* (June 1989): 295–318.

FIGURE 3.2
A Tombstone Advertisement

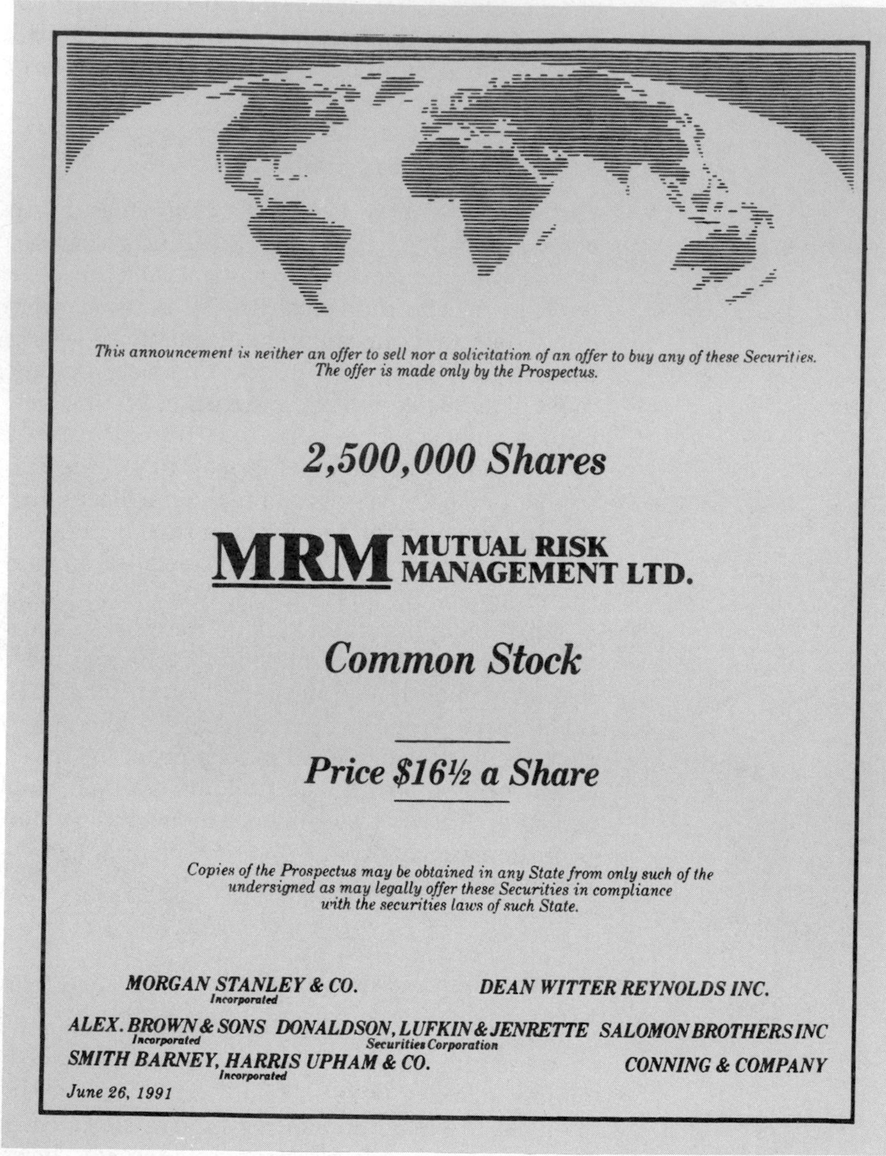

SOURCE: *The Wall Street Journal,* June 26, 1991, p. C17. Reprinted by permission.

trading policies for the exchanges. It may penalize exchanges that do not conform to its guidelines. All organized exchanges are required to register with the SEC.

The SEC also establishes regulations for proxy solicitations and insider information. *Insiders* are the officers and directors of a firm and individuals who own more than 10 percent of the firm's outstanding shares. All insiders are required to file reports on their trading activities with the SEC. The SEC also prohibits manipulation of stock prices through the use of pools (individuals banding together to profit from the manipulation of stock prices), wash sales (the buying and selling of the same security to affect the price or give the impression of activity in the stock), and other practices that could destabilize stock prices.

• Maloney Act of 1936

The Maloney Act provides for the establishment of self-regulatory associations in the OTC market. The only organization to register with the SEC is the National Association of Securities Dealers (NASD). The NASD requires all potential brokers to pass a proficiency test (Series 7 Exam) before they can trade securities. The NASD may also penalize members, with fines or suspension, for misconduct.

• Insider Trading and Securities Fraud Enforcement Act of 1988

The Insider Trading and Securities Fraud Enforcement Act imposes certain new responsibilities on broker-dealers and investment advisers to prevent insider trading. It also imposes substantial penalties on all controlling parties for failure to detect insider trading. At the same time, the act preserves the right of investment analysts to continue to receive legitimate information from corporate issuers of securities.

• Other Regulations

The Investment Company Act of 1940 requires investment companies to register with the SEC and provide information to potential investors. This act is discussed in more detail in Chapter 5. The Investment Advisors Act of 1940 requires individuals and firms that sell advice about investments to register with the SEC. The Securities Investor Protection Act of 1970 established the **Securities Investor Protection Corporation (SIPC)**, which provides insurance to protect investors in the event that brokerage firms fail. Customer accounts are insured for up to $500,000. Only $100,000 of the amount applies to cash balances.

SUMMARY

This chapter discussed the structure and operation of security markets. Primary markets trade new issues of securities. Investment bankers play a critical role in the primary market through (1) advice and counsel, (2) underwriting, and (3) distribution of securities. In the 1980s, the activities of investment bankers

• CONCEPT APPLICATIONS

Investment Concept	Concept Application
Operations and regulations of security markets	The investor must be aware of how the security markets operate and the protection and rights provided by the various regulatory acts.
The importance of selecting a broker	The selection of an appropriate broker and brokerage house and an understanding of trading mechanics are important first steps in the investment process. For a significant number of individual investors, investment information and suggestions will be initiated by a broker. It is important that the broker understands the investor's investment objectives and risk orientation and operates within these constraints. It is also important that the investor does not lose sight of long-term investment objectives as a result of changes in the market. The five-year period preceding the stock market "crash" of 1987 illustrates how investors, quite often encouraged by brokers, abandoned their investment objectives and desired risk levels. During this period, the stock market experienced an appreciation in value in excess of 200 percent. Individual investors, wanting to take advantage of this "bull" market, were encouraged to switch from the more traditional investments in stocks and bonds to the more risky investments in stock options, futures, and options on futures. When the stock market experienced a significant reversal in October 1987, investors suffered extensive losses because of their increased risk exposure.

expanded significantly beyond their traditional role of helping corporations raise external funds. Along with the expanded activities and increased profitability, there were instances of abuses and ethical misconduct.

The secondary market trades securities that are already issued. Trading of securities in the secondary market takes place on the organized security exchanges and the OTC. The NYSE and AMEX are the primary organized exchanges. The OTC market, dealing with security transactions away from the organized exchanges, is an informal network of brokers and dealers who trade through the NASDAQ system.

It is necessary that investors understand the importance of selecting a brokerage house and a broker as well as the mechanics of trading. Investors may use cash or borrow through margin accounts. Investors must also know the difference between market orders, limit orders, and stop orders.

The fraudulent trading practices in the security markets during the 1920s led to the legislation regulating the security markets in effect today. The primary laws are the Securities Act of 1933, which required full disclosure of information, and the Securities Exchange Act of 1934, which created the SEC, required disclosure of information on issued securities, and prohibited fraudulent practices. Other laws include the Maloney Act of 1936, from which the

NASD was created, the Investment Company Act of 1940, the Investment Advisors Act of 1940, the Securities Investor Protection Act of 1970, and the Insider Trading and Securities Fraud Enforcement Act of 1988. Brokerage houses, stock exchanges, and the OTC are continuing to develop electronic surveillance and reporting procedures to uncover illegal trading practices.

• KEY TERMS

American Stock Exchange (AMEX)
Asset-backed securities
Best-efforts offering
Bridge loans
Commission brokers
Crossing
Discount brokers
Floor brokers
Floor traders
Fourth market
Full-service broker
Initial public offering (IPO)
Investment banker
Junk bonds
Limit order
Market order
NASDAQ
New York Stock Exchange (NYSE)
Odd lot transaction
Over-the-counter market (OTC)
Primary markets
Private placement
Prospectus
Red herring
Regional exchanges
Registration statement
Round lot
Secondary markets
Securities Investor Protection Corporation (SIPC)
Specialists
Spread
Stop order
Third market
Underwriting

• QUESTIONS

1. How does the primary market differ from the secondary market?
2. What role do investment bankers play in the primary market? What is a best-efforts offering?
3. What are the basic differences between the listing requirements of the NYSE and the AMEX?
4. What is the OTC market? Differentiate the NASDAQ, the third market, and the fourth market.
5. Under what conditions would you want to go to a full-service broker instead of a discount broker?
6. Explain the role of the specialist.
7. Discuss the advantages and disadvantages of using a market order and a limit order.
8. How do limit orders and stop orders differ?

9. Why are certain securities exempt from registration under the Securities Act of 1933?
10. What are the major features of the Securities Exchange Act of 1934?
11. A customer of a failed brokerage firm had $300,000 worth of common stock and $200,000 in a cash account, for a total of $500,000. How much of the account value will be covered by the SIPC?
12. Explain the differences between a commission broker and a floor broker.
13. How did the traditional activities of investment banking firms differ from their activities in the 1980s?
14. Discuss the importance of ethical conduct in the security markets, both from the perspective of an individual investor and in terms of its impact on the securities industry.
15. Congress has enacted a number of statutes regulating security markets in the United States. What are the purposes of these acts and what are the implications of government intervention in the security markets?

• REFERENCES

Freeman, Claudia, and Edward Rosenbaum. "A Survey of Management's Attitudes toward Stock Exchange Delisting and the NASDAQ National Market System." *Akron Business & Economic Review* (Summer 1987): 19–30.

Johnson, James M., and Robert E. Miller. "Investment Banker Prestige and the Underpricing of Initial Public Offerings." *Financial Management* (Summer 1988): 19–29.

Lewis, Michael. *Liar's Poker.* New York: W.W. Norton & Co., 1989.

McBain, Michael L., and David S. Krause. "Going Public: The Impact on Insiders' Holdings on the Prices of Initial Public Offerings." *Journal of Business Venturing* (November 1989): 419–28.

Ritter, Jay R. "The Cost of Going Public." *Journal of Financial Economics* (December 1987): 269–81.

Simon, Carol J. "The Effect of the 1933 Securities Act on Investor Information and the Performance of New Issues." *American Economic Review* (June 1989): 295–318.

Tinic, Seha M. "Anatomy of Initial Public Offerings of Common Stock." *Journal of Finance* (September 1988): 789–822.

CHAPTER 4

Investment Information

The knowledge-level objectives of this chapter should enable the student to:

- Discuss the importance of investment information in making investment decisions.
- Become aware of the amount of information available to assist investors in making investment decisions.
- Recognize that the type of information an investor needs is related to the investor's investment strategy.
- Analyze the value of information and relate the value to the cost of obtaining and using the information.
- Recognize the importance of computers and data bases, and their limitations, in making investment decisions.
- Describe the various indicators of stock market performance and understand their importance, construction, and weaknesses.

INTRODUCTION

Informed investment decisions are made through the careful evaluation of available information. Investors cannot make good investment decisions if they lack sufficient information and the knowledge of how to evaluate the potential risk and return associated with the investment. The quantity of investment information available to investors has been growing at an almost exponential rate. It is important for the investor to determine what type of information is needed and the appropriate sources for obtaining the information. The investment strategy undertaken by the investor will help determine the type of information required. In a *passive investment strategy*, the investment horizon is long term, and the investor makes very little effort to revise the portfolio through security selection or market timing. With this strategy, the investor's information needs might be limited to information about mutual funds.

At the other extreme, investors engaged in *active investment strategies* in which they manage their own portfolios will need investment information on the economy, industries, and individual companies. This chapter provides the investor with these sources of investment information (investment strategies are discussed in detail in Chapter 7).

New technology has become a dominant force in the dissemination of investment information. In addition to the "hard-copy" traditional sources of information, such as government publications, investors' subscription services, and investment advisory services and newsletters, individual investors can use personal computers to access a wide array of investment services and data bases.

This chapter will discuss and illustrate a variety of investment information sources that are available to investors. The presentation follows a "top-down" approach in that it starts with information related to the macro analysis of the economy and industries and then examines company, or micro, sources of information. Although many of these sources can be obtained free or at a nominal charge, some are fairly expensive, such as the *Value Line Investment Survey*. However, the more costly information may be available free at a public or university library.

The investor should remember that there is a trade-off between the time and cost of obtaining investment information and the potential increased return and/or risk reduction to be derived from the effort. For example, computer-aided investing can be very expensive, with the computer, software products, and a modem for receiving and sending data over the telephone costing $2,000 to $3,000. These costs do not include the expenses of accessing the financial data bases and the software programs for analyzing the data. One rule of thumb used by experts is that computer-aided investing should be considered if the cost of the computer and software is less than 8 percent of the portfolio's value. Additionally, the quality of investment advice can be good or bad. High cost does not guarantee high-quality information.

This chapter also includes a discussion of market indexes. A variety of measures are used to gauge market movement, and the more widely used indexes are discussed. Market indexes are used for (1) evaluating portfolio performance, (2) establishing the relationships between economic variables and overall market movements, (3) forecasting future market movements, and (4) measuring stock or portfolio systematic risk. Therefore, market indexes can be an important source of information.

ANALYSIS OF ECONOMIC CONDITIONS

The federal government is the primary source of raw economic data. The two major government publications are the *Federal Reserve Bulletin* and the *Survey of Current Business.* The *Federal Reserve Bulletin* is a monthly publication of the Board of Governors of the Federal Reserve System. It provides statistical data on monetary aggregates, interest rates, gross national product (GNP), credit, labor, and output. Often, data can be grasped more readily from graphs than from a series of numbers. The *Federal Reserve Monthly Chart Book* depicts monetary and economic data from the *Federal Reserve Bulletin* graphically. The *Historical Chart Book,* also published by the Federal Reserve, contains long-run business and financial charts.

The 12 federal reserve district banks also publish information on economic conditions. For example, the St. Louis Federal Reserve Bank publishes weekly and monthly economic reports that are free and contain some of the best economic analyses available. The *Survey of Current Business* is a monthly publication of the U.S. Department of Commerce. It provides excellent information on all sectors of industrial production in the economy as well as statistics on prices, wages, interest rates, and national income.

Until recently, the Department of Commerce published the findings of the National Bureau of Economic Research (NBER) in a monthly publication called the *Business Conditions Digest.* The NBER's time series of economic indicators are now published in the *Survey of Current Business.* These economic time series can be used to indicate future trends in the economy (**leading indicators**), current trends in the economy (**coincident indicators**), and past trends in the economy (**lagging indicators**). Examples of leading indicators include stock prices as measured by the S&P 500 Common Stock Index, worker productivity, consumer spending, and new business formations. Coincident indicators include unemployment and industrial production. Lagging indicators include such measures as the prime rate and the level of inventories. (A full discussion of these economic indicators is provided in Chapter 8).

Other government publications include the *Economic Report of the President,* an annual report that discusses past economic events and forthcoming economic problems; *The Statistical Abstract of the United States,* an annual publication of the Bureau of Census containing summary statistics from public and private sources on industrial, economic, political, and social trends; and *Economic Indicators,* a monthly publication of the President's Council of Economic Advisers. Information about other government publications can be obtained from the Superintendent of Documents, U.S. Government Printing Office, Washington, D.C. 20402.

INDUSTRY ANALYSIS

Once investors have achieved an understanding of current economic conditions and formulated an opinion of future economic activity, they can focus on specific industries. Information for industry analysis is available from a number of sources. Federal government publications, such as the *Quarterly Financial Report for Manufacturing Corporations,* published by the Federal Trade Commission, present aggregate financial information for all manufacturing companies. The information is broken down by industry and asset size. Business and financial publications, such as *Business Week, Forbes, Fortune, Barron's, Investor's Daily,* and *The Wall Street Journal,* also contain a great deal of information about particular industries, in addition to forecasts and analyses of general economic conditions.

Most industries have trade associations that publish statistical information about conditions in their industry. Examples of such organizations include the American Iron and Steel Institute, the American Petroleum Institute, the National Paper Trade Association, and the Rubber Manufacturers Association.

Trade Journals are also excellent sources of industry information. Examples of trade journals include *Chemical Week, Iron Age, American Banker, Oil and Gas Journal, Public Utilities Fortnightly, Rubber Age,* and *Steel.*

Standard & Poor's *Industry Survey* provides considerable information on various industries. The survey is divided into current and basic analysis sections. The current analysis section discusses the latest developments and prospects for the industry; it also includes statistical data. The basic analysis section looks at the trends and prospects of the industry from a historical perspective.

The *Value Line Investment Survey* reports on 93 industries. The reports include an evaluation of prospects for the industry as well as composite statistics. Figure 4.1 shows a Value Line report on the publishing industry. Value Line also prepares recommendations on individual stocks, which will be discussed later in the chapter.

Excellent sources of current industry analysis (as well as general economic conditions and company information) are the reports published by the full-service brokerage firms. These research reports are generally available to customers of the brokerage firms on request. Finally, *The Wall Street Transcript* usually discusses two industries each week. The paper conducts in-depth interviews with chief executives and security analysts in the highlighted industries. The paper costs approximately $1,300 per year, however, putting it beyond the reach of the average investor.

FIGURE 4.1 • An Industry Report on the Publishing Industry from *Value Line Investment Survey*

INDUSTRY TIMELINESS: 46 (of 97)

A major task confronting investors now is to determine whether the recent surge in stock prices is an accurate forecast of an impending end to the recession or the result of exuberance over America's success in the Persian Gulf war and the Federal Reserve's easing of monetary policy.

Proponents of the efficient market theory argue that the stock market, which supposedly discounts all available information, is a proven leading indicator of future economic health. This argument, however, hasn't proven infallible in view of the false signals that it has given off in the past. Also, the economy has to contend with various new and daunting structural problems, including the banking crisis and related consumer and business overleveraging.

The issue of an economic recovery is especially important for investors interested in publishing stocks. Most of the companies in our Publishing Industry group are extremely vulnerable in a weak economic climate as they, for the most part, are highly dependent on advertising-related revenues. Indeed, ad budgets are one of the first targets of companies maneuvering to cut costs.

This group, with few exceptions, has performed admirably since our December 7, 1990 review. Most have topped the gains achieved by both the Dow and broader S&P 500 stocks, with many (including *Time Warner, Reader's Digest, Bowne, and R.R. Donnelly*) appreciating more than 20%. Oddly enough, one of the two issues that did not participate in the rally was *Harcourt Brace Jovanovich*, which is currently in the process of being taken over.

Textbook and Magazine Publishers

This year promises to be a far better year (for textbook publishers) than last. This optimism is based on the fact that adoption opportunities will be greater, with Georgia, Mississippi, North Carolina, New Mexico, Oklahoma, and Idaho, as well as many school districts in the open territories, making decisions on reading materials—which is the largest segment of the textbook market—versus only Florida in 1990. Six states are also slated to make purchases of social studies programs, another large segment of the market. And at this stage in the selling season, it appears that *Houghton Mifflin* will emerge as one of this year's winners. Prospects, however, don't seem too promising for the magazine publishers. *Meredith, Time Warner, and McGraw-Hill* continue to feel the impact of the depressed ad market. Indeed, even *Reader's Digest*, which in the past has proven quite resilient, is starting to experience some softening.

Printers

Check printers, *Harland* and *Deluxe*, are seeing pricing pressures from their financially-strapped banking customers. Commercial printers, too, which are dependent to a large extent on advertising-related revenue, will probably continue to find the going rough, at least until the economy rebounds. However, if the positive rumblings on Wall Street thus far this year do, in fact, prove precursory, then prosperity may not be far away. The industry-specific recession, which started well before and is deeper than the one afflicting the overall economy, has narrowed the field, leaving stronger contenders. These contenders will probably emerge leaner and more efficient competitors. And if this year's stock price ascent remains on course, the financial printers could witness a windfall in work associated with initial stock offerings and takeover-related activity, which have been in holding patterns since the October 1987 stock market crash.

Investment Advice

Given the rather indiscriminate upward movement in the stock market since the January 16th outbreak of war, investors should exercise extreme caution prior to making any new commitments: Many bad stocks moved in tandem with the good ones. Indeed, business prospects for this rather diverse group are mixed, making even more important, at this juncture, the need to scrutinize individual reports. None of the issues here is top-ranked for the year ahead and only two investment quality equities (*Deluxe* and *Banta*) are pegged to outleg the market during this period. Moreover, if the recent surge in stock prices proves to be a false signal of an impending economic recovery, then some of our publishing shares stand to lose much of their recent gains.

George I.H. Rho

Composite Statistics: Publishing Industry

1986	1987	1988	1989	1990	1991		93-95E
15528	18773	22253	25710	*31000*	*33700*	Sales ($mill)	*43900*
18.6%	19.8%	19.5%	18.1%	*14.5%*	*18.0%*	Operating Margin	*19.5%*
697.4	910.0	1078.2	1447.3	*2085*	*2050*	Depreciation ($mill)	*2300*
1243.7	1419.4	1676.6	957.2	*1150*	*1625*	Net Profit ($mill)	*3150*
43.4%	44.5%	39.2%	45.2%	*42.0%*	*38.0%*	Income Tax Rate	*41.0%*
8.0%	7.6%	7.5%	3.7%	*3.7%*	*4.8%*	Net Profit Margin	*7.2%*
2530.9	2545.6	3218.0	2658.8	*3425*	*3975*	Working Cap'l ($mill)	*5000*
2038.9	3928.0	4618.4	13380	*14250*	*14000*	Long-Term Debt ($mill)	*11700*
6848.3	5993.5	7455.2	13361	*13100*	*13550*	Net Worth ($mill)	*17600*
14.6%	15.8%	15.9%	6.1%	*4.0%*	*6.0%*	% Earned Total Cap'l	*11.0%*
18.2%	23.7%	22.5%	7.2%	*8.0%*	*10.0%*	% Earned Net Worth	*18.0%*
10.9%	NMF	14.8%	2.4%	*2.5%*	*5.5%*	% Retained to Comm Eq	*11.5%*
40%	NMF	40%	83%	*72%*	*55%*	% All Div'ds to Net Prof	*37.0%*
20.9	19.7	16.8	33.5	*Bold figures are*		Avg Ann'l P/E Ratio	*15.0*
1.42	1.32	1.45	2.38	*Value Line*		Relative P/E Ratio	*1.3*
1.9%	9.5%	2.4%	2.5%	*estimates*		Avg Ann'l yield	*2.3%*

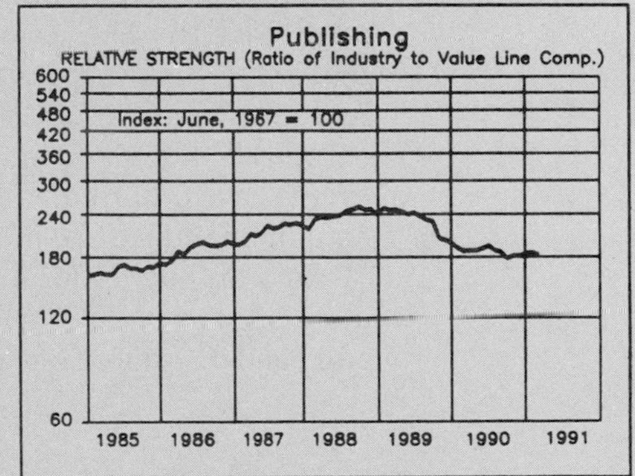

SOURCE: *Value Line Investment Survey,* "Ratings and Reports," 46, *Value Line,* March 8, 1991, p. 1788.

COMPANY INFORMATION

After the investor determines the likely industries for investment, the next step is to analyze specific firms within each industry. In addition to analysts' reports on individual firms provided by full-service brokerage firms, investors should be aware of current events that may impact the firm. This type of information can be obtained by a careful reading of publications such as the *Wall Street Journal,* and *Barron's.* Most full-service brokerage firms also have online services, such as the Dow Jones News/Retrieval Service, that allow the broker to access current information about individual firms.

An important source of information about a firm is the firm itself. All publicly traded firms must publish and distribute an **annual report** to their stockholders. Nonstockholders can obtain a copy of the annual report by writing to the firm. Annual reports may also be found in libraries and at brokerage firms.

The annual report contains audited financial information including the balance sheet, income statement, and statement of changes in financial position for the most recent and earlier periods. Notes to the financial statements provide additional information that can be useful in evaluating the financial condition of the firm. The annual report also discusses the operations of the firm over the preceding year and the future prospects for the company. The quality and amount of specific financial information in annual reports vary. During the year, publicly traded firms publish and distribute quarterly financial reports to their stockholders. These reports give sales and earnings figures for the previous quarter and for the same period in the previous year. These reports are unaudited and do not contain as much detail as the financial statements in the annual report. Many of the figures in the quarterly reports may be adjusted at the end of the year.

In addition to the annual and quarterly reports sent to stockholders, publicly traded firms are required to file a series of reports with the Securities and Exchange Commission (SEC) and other regulatory agencies. As discussed in Chapter 3, a firm issuing new securities is required to file a registration statement with the SEC prior to selling the new issue. In addition, the firm is required to issue a prospectus, which is made available to the public. Firms registered with the SEC must also file a copy of their annual registration statement, called a 10–K form, an 8–K form in any month in which significant events have occurred within the firm, an unaudited quarterly report (10–Q), and an unaudited six-month report (9–K); insiders must file a report within 10 days on any trades they have made in the firm's securities. These reports quite often contain details that are not published in the firm's annual report and can be a source of valuable information for the investor.

INVESTMENT ADVISORY SERVICES

A variety of **investment advisory services** and newsletters provide details and advice on specific industries and firms. The annual cost of these services ranges from approximately one hundred dollars to several thousand dollars.

Investors may want to check with their local libraries since the cost of these services may not be justified, given the size of most portfolios.

A number of investment advisory services are available that use objective procedures and provide detailed information on a range of stocks; however, only the three major services will be discussed here. **Investment newsletters** will be briefly discussed at the end of this section.

• Standard & Poor's Corporation

The Standard & Poor's Corporation publishes a number of reports that can be useful for investors:

1. *Corporate Records* Six volumes of reports are published, with updates in a seventh volume, "Daily News." Each report contains detailed financial information on publicly traded firms under the following headings: Capitalization, Corporate Background, Bond Description, Stock Data, Earnings and Finances, and Annual Report with income statements for three years and balance sheets for two years.
2. *Stock Reports* This publication contains information on recent developments in the firm as well as a 10-year summary of income, balance sheet, and share data. The reports also include a price chart and a summary of business activities. Reports are prepared on the more active NYSE, AMEX, and OTC stocks. An example of a stock report is presented in Figure 4.2.
3. *Stock Guide* This is a pocket-sized monthly publication containing basic financial information on over five thousand common and preferred stocks and mutual funds. The guide gives information on price, earnings, dividends, debt, industry classification, institutional holdings, and quality rankings for each security. Two partial pages from the *Stock Guide* are shown in Figure 4.3. Notice that the lower portion of Figure 4.3 provides additional information about the 15 companies identified in the top portion of the figure.
4. *Bond Guide* Also a monthly publication, the *Bond Guide* contains financial information on over four thousand corporate bonds, municipal bonds, and foreign bonds. Figure 4.4 shows a page from the *Bond Guide*.
5. *Outlook* This publication presents a weekly commentary on the stock market, recommendations on particular industries and firms, and a market forecast.

• Moody's Investor Service

Moody's Investor Service publishes a number of manuals and reports:

1. *Manuals* Moody's publishes an annual set of volumes entitled *Moody's Manuals: Municipal and Government; Industrial; Bank and Finance; Public Utility; Transportation; OTC-Industrial; International.* The manuals contain information on thousands of firms. For each firm,

FIGURE 4.2
A Sample Report from *Standard & Poor's Stock Reports*

Knight-Ridder 1308

NYSE Symbol KRI Options on Phila (Jan-Apr-Jul-Oct) In S&P 500

Price	Range	P–E Ratio	Dividend	Yield	S&P Ranking	Beta
Feb. 6'91	1991					
$50\frac{5}{8}$	$51\frac{5}{8}$–$44\frac{1}{8}$	17	1.40	2.8%	A+	1.17

Summary

Knight-Ridder is one of the largest newspaper publishers in the U.S., and has important interests in the electronic distribution of information. As part of a major restructuring, KRI has sold certain assets, including its eight TV stations, in order to emphasize publishing and information services. KRI's and Gannett's Detroit newspapers began to implement a joint operating agreement in November, 1989.

Current Outlook

Earnings for 1991 are projected at $2.75 a share, down 6.5% from the $2.94 reported for 1990.

The dividend was recently raised 6.1%, to $0.35 quarterly from $0.33.

Revenues for 1991 are expected to decline some 1% from those of 1990 as weakness in advertising should more than offset the positive impact of widespread circulation price increases during the year. Operating costs are expected to rise slightly, despite operating efficiencies and soft newsprint pricing. Thus, operating income would drop. The decline in net income will be limited, however, by reduced interest expense. There should also be fewer average shares outstanding.

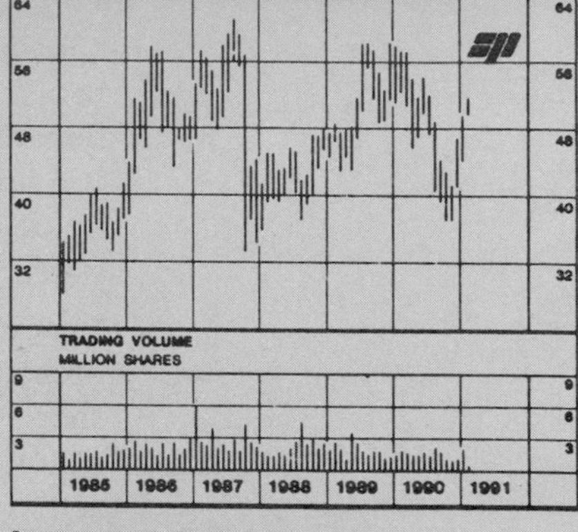

Operating Revenues (Million $)

Quarter:	1990	1989	1988	1987
Mar.	555	541	490	489
Jun.	592	579	516	527
Sep.	571	541	503	500
Dec.	588	608	575	557
	2,305	2,268	2,083	2,073

Revenues for 1990 (preliminary) rose 1.6% from those of 1989. Operating income fell 6.6%. There was a 24% drop in interest expense. However, in the absence of a $0.57 per share gain from the sale of the Pasadena Star-News, net income fell 40%. Share earnings were $2.94, against $3.43, which excludes $1.28 income from discontinued operations.

Common Share Earnings ($)

Quarter:	1990	1989	1988	1987
Mar.	0.50	0.39	0.57	0.49
Jun.	0.88	1.35	0.73	0.73
Sep.	0.73	0.65	0.53	0.57
Dec.	0.85	1.05	0.76	0.86
	2.94	3.43	2.59	2.65

Important Developments

Dec. '90— Dialog Information Services was granted exclusive distribution rights outside Japan to an English-language corporate database from Teikoku Databank Ltd. The database on some 50,000 Japanese firms will mark the first time such information will be available in English. Earlier, Dialog Business Connection announced that its service was being expanded to include information on 1.3 million companies outside the U.S. and that information was being added on thousands on privately-held U.S. companies.

Oct. '90— KRI said that about 2.6 million shares of its common stock had been repurchased during the first nine months of 1990, and that roughly 3 million shares remained to be purchased under outstanding authorization.

Next earnings report expected in late April.

Per Share Data ($)

Yr. End Dec. 31	1990	1989	[1]1988	1987	[1]1986	[2]1985	[1]1984	[1]1983	[1]1982	[1]1981
Tangible Bk. Val.	NA	3.33	1.18	3.50	1.58	6.48	9.01	7.49	7.03	5.63
Cash Flow	NA	5.49	4.27	4.04	3.65	3.19	2.93	2.47	2.13	2.02
Earnings[3]	2.94	3.43	2.59	2.65	2.41	2.19	2.15	1.80	1.57	1.55
Dividends	1.340	1.245	1.145	1.030	0.910	0.790	0.670	0.580	0.460	0.430
Payout Ratio	46%	36%	41%	39%	38%	34%	31%	31%	29%	28%
Prices—High	58	$58\frac{3}{8}$	$47\frac{3}{4}$	$61\frac{1}{4}$	$57\frac{7}{8}$	$41\frac{3}{8}$	31	$30\frac{3}{8}$	$25\frac{7}{8}$	$20\frac{7}{8}$
Low	37	$42\frac{7}{8}$	$35\frac{3}{4}$	$33\frac{1}{4}$	$37\frac{1}{2}$	28	$21\frac{1}{4}$	$22\frac{1}{8}$	$13\frac{5}{8}$	$13\frac{1}{2}$
P/E Ratio—	20–13	17–13	18–14	23–13	24–16	19–13	14–10	17–12	16–9	14–9

Data as orig. reptd. Adj. for stk. div(s). of 100% Nov. 1983. 1. Reflects merger or acquisition. 2. Reflects merger or acquisition and accounting change. 3. Bef. results of disc. opers. of +1.28 in 1989, +0.17 in 1988. NA-Not Available.

Standard NYSE Stock Reports
Vol. 58/No. 32/Sec. 10

February 14, 1991

Standard & Poor's Corp.
25 Broadway, NY, NY 10004

SOURCE: *Standard & Poor's Stock Reports,* February 14, 1991, p. 1308. Reprinted by permission.

FIGURE 4.2

A Sample Report from *Standard & Poor's Stock Reports* (continued)

Income Data (Million $)

Year Ended Dec. 31	Revs.	Oper. Inc.	% Oper. Inc. of Revs.	Cap. Exp.	Depr.	Int. Exp.	[6]Net Bef. Taxes	Eff. Tax Rate	[6]Net Inc.	% Net Inc. of Revs.	Cash Flow
1989	2,268	430	19.0	124	108	84.6	300	38.3%	180	7.9	288
[1]1988	2,083	366	17.6	102	95	62.5	240	36.7%	147	7.0	242
1987	2,073	391	18.9	114	82	49.6	285	43.9%	155	7.5	237
[2]1986	1,911	353	18.5	100	72	33.9	271	46.8%	[4]140	7.3	212
[3]1985	1,730	307	17.8	106	69	22.6	242	43.9%	133	7.7	194
[2]1984	1,665	313	18.8	106	58	10.9	265	45.8%	141	8.5	192
[2]1983	1,473	265	18.0	78	52	6.7	222	45.3%	119	8.1	164
[2]1982	1,328	217	16.4	88	43	12.7	183	42.7%	103	7.8	140
[2]1981	1,237	221	17.9	76	37	13.0	192	46.5%	100	8.1	131
[2]1980	1,099	200	18.2	60	33	[4]7.2	174	45.6%	93	8.5	121

Balance Sheet Data (Million $)

Dec. 31	Cash	Curr. Assets	Curr. Liab.	Curr. Ratio	Total Assets	Ret. On Assets	Long Term Debt	Common Equity	Total Inv. Capital	% LT Debt of Cap.	% Ret. on Equity
1989	60.6	416	346	1.2	2,135	8.1%	661	917	1,737	38.0	21.0
1988	32.2	687	603	1.1	2,357	7.0%	727	822	1,692	43.0	17.6
1987	72.6	409	349	1.2	1,985	7.9%	508	901	1,546	32.9	18.1
1986	99.0	421	336	1.3	1,947	8.3%	621	816	1,565	39.7	18.4
1985	80.1	380	285	1.3	1,394	10.4%	271	697	1,068	25.4	17.8
1984	97.4	378	236	1.6	1,348	11.1%	78	922	1,080	7.2	16.2
1983	43.6	276	206	1.3	1,180	10.8%	77	808	951	8.1	15.3
1982	30.3	236	184	1.3	1,051	10.0%	36	764	851	4.2	14.2
1981	59.5	274	194	1.4	985	10.8%	61	679	778	7.8	15.6
1980	58.1	247	169	1.5	862	11.6%	54	597	680	7.9	16.4

Data as orig. reptd. 1. Excl. disc. opers. and reflects merger or acquisition. 2. Reflects merger or acquisition. 3. Reflects merger or acquisition and accounting change. 4. Reflects accounting change. 5. Incl. equity in earns. of nonconsol. subs. 6. Bef. results of disc. opers. in 1989, 1988.

Business Summary

Knight-Ridder (formerly Knight-Ridder Newspapers) derives some 89% of revenues from newspaper publishing. The company is also engaged in cable TV operations, electronic distribution of commodity and financial news and market quotes, newsprint production, book publishing, and selected computerized information retrieval services. As part of a restructuring announced in October, 1988, KRI has completed the sale of its eight TV stations in order to emphasize newspaper publishing, electronic information and cable television.

KRI owns 29 daily newspapers in 15 states, with average daily and Sunday circulations of 3.90 million and 4.86 million, respectively. The larger papers include the Miami Herald, Philadelphia Inquirer and Philadelphia Daily News, the Detroit Free Press, the San Jose Mercury and San Jose News. KRI also publishes six non-daily suburban newspapers and partially owns three other dailies.

Dialog Information Services, acquired in August 1988, maintains the world's largest computer-based databank, with nearly 370 databases. Other operations include Vu/Text, MoneyCenter, Tradecenter, Commodity News Services, the Journal of Commerce, a partial interest in a newsprint mill, and cable television joint ventures serving over 291,000 basic subscribers. KRI also owns Commodity Research Bureau, a charting and newsletter advisory firm serving the futures industry; and 49.5% of the voting and 65% of the non-voting common stock of Seattle Times Co.

Dividend Data

Dividends have been paid since 1941. A dividend reinvestment plan is available. A "poison pill" stock purchase right was adopted in 1986.

Amt of Divd. $	Date Decl.	Ex-divd. Date	Stock of Record	Payment Date
0.33	Mar. 22	Mar. 30	Apr. 5	Apr. 13'90
0.33	Jun. 28	Jul. 9	Jul. 13	Jul. 23'90
0.33	Sep. 24	Oct. 1	Oct. 5	Oct. 13'90
0.35	Dec. 20	Dec. 31	Jan. 7	Jan. 15'91

Next dividend meeting: late Mar. '91.

Capitalization

Long Term Debt: $769,920,000.

Common Stock: 49,337,881 shs. ($0.02 1/12 par). About 24% controlled by directors; institutions hold about 59%.

Shareholders of record: 11,200.

Office—One Herald Plaza, Miami, Fla. 33101. **Tel**—(305) 376-3800. **Chrmn & CEO**—J. K. Batten. **Pres**—P. A. Ridder. **VP-Secy**—D. C. Harris. **VP-Fin & Treas**—L. A. Levine. **VP & Investor Contact**—F. N. Hawkins, Jr. **Dirs**—J. K. Batten, R. G. Capen, J. R. Challinor, A. H. Chapman, Jr., C. M. Clifford, P. C. Goldmark, Jr., B. B. Hauptfuhrer, J. Hill, Jr., W. S. Lee, P. McColough, B. Morris, T. L. Phillips, B. H. Ridder, Jr., E. Ridder, P. A. Ridder, R. F. Singleton, B. T. Toomey, J. L. Weinberg. **Transfer Agent & Registrar**—Manufacturers Hanover Trust Co., NYC. **Incorporated** in Ohio in 1941; reincorporated in Florida in 1976. **Empl**—21,000.

 William H. Donald

FIGURE 4.3 • Sample Pages from *Standard & Poor's Stock Guide*

120 KLO-LAN

Standard & Poor's Corporation

¶S&P 500 •Options Index	Ticker Symbol	Name of Issue (Call Price of Pfd. Stocks)	Market	Com. Rank. & Pfd. Rating	Par Val.	Inst. Hold Cos	Inst. Hold Shs. (000)	Principal Business	Price Range 1971-88 High	1971-88 Low	1989 High	1989 Low	1990 High	1990 Low	Jan. Sales in 100s	January, 1991 Last Sale Or Bid High	Low	Last	%Div Yield	P-E Ratio
1	KLOFY	Kloof Gold Mining ADR[51]	OTC	NR	[51]R.25	18	4717	South Africa gold mining	16⅛	13/16	12½	7½	13⅞	7¾	10206	9¾	7¼	7 3/16B	3.5	6
¶2•[1]	KM	K mart	NY,B,C,M,P,Ph	A−	1	634	153431	Operates discount dept strs	48⅜	10⅛	44⅞	32½	37¼	23⅜	113087	31	25⅝	31	5.5	9
3	KMSI	KMS Indus	OTC	B	8¢	7	40	Scientific R&D for U.S. govt	152	1	8¼	3⅛	4⅞	1⅝	1609	1 15/16	1⅜	1¾B	6.9	5
4	KNE	KN Energy	NY,M	NR	5	67	4638	Nat'l gas,mineral resources	56	10	25⅝	17⅝	26½	21¼	2266	23⅝	20⅞	22	5.1	11
5	KNAP	Knape & Vogt Mfg	OTC	B+	2	26	851	Mfr specialty hardware	20½	2⅛	18⅞	12½	15¼	11	834	13⅞	12¼	13½B	†4.9	6
¶6•[2]	KRI	Knight-Ridder Inc	NY,B,M,P	A+	21/12¢	243	29054	Newspapers:business info svs	61¼	3⅜	58⅜	42⅞	58	37	20327	49⅝	44⅛	49½	2.8	17
7	KNO	Knogo Corp	NY,B,M,Ph	B−	1¢	22	1369	Electronic detector systems	29⅝	3/16	17½	12¼	13½	6¼	4712	8¼	6⅜	8⅛	3.7	68
8	KNOW	KnowledgeWare Inc	OTC	NR	No	53	4663	Dvlp IBM compatible software	....	....	17⅛	12½	27½	10	60470	29	19¼	28¾B	...	31
9	KOA	Koala Technologies	AS	C	No	2	137	Mfrs video image digitizers	3⅜	¼	½	1/16	⅜	1/16	550	⅛	⅛	⅛	...	d
10	KE	Koger Equity	AS,M	NR	1¢	41	3606	Real estate investment trust	20⅛	18¼	20¾	16⅞	19¼	6⅝	4558	9⅜	7½	9	14.4	6
11	KOG	Koger Properties	NY,M	NR	10¢	69	4394	Dev & construct office bldgs	34	4	28⅛	22¼	23⅞	3¾	16699	7⅞	4¼	6¼	16.0	d
12	KOL	Kollmorgen Corp	NY,M,Ph	B−	2½	47	4485	Motor/ctrls,elec optic instr	36¾	1 3/16	25⅞	11⅜	13½	5¾	5744	9½	7½	8⅞	3.6	18
13	KMAG	Komag Inc	OTC	NR	1¢	54	4449	Mfr thin film computer disks	15¼	6	11½	6⅜	16⅛	8½	35787	15¾	10¾	15⅛B	...	23
14•	KF	Korea Fund	NY,B,M	NR	1¢	48	3060	Closed-end investment co	29¾	4	43⅛	25¼	34⅜	11⅜	13998	13⅜	11⅜	12¼	...	..
¶15•[3]	KR	Kroger Co	NY,B,C,M,Ph	B	1	194	27308	Supermkt chain,drug stores	59	3⅝	19¾	8⅜	17	10⅝	43855	17⅜	12⅝	17¼	...	31

Common and Convertible Preferred Stocks

KLO-LAN 121

Splits ◆ Index	Cash Divs. Ea. Yr. Since	Dividends Latest Payment Period $	Date	Ex. Div.	Total $ So Far 1991	Ind. Rate	Paid 1990	Financial Position Mil-$ Cash& Equiv.	Curr. Assets	Curr. Liab.	Balance Sheet Date
1	1970	[52]0.121	2-22-91	12-21	[52]0.121	0.26	0.328	67.8	129	141	j6-30-90
2◆	1913	Q0.43	3-11-91	2-8	0.43	1.72	1.70	443	9504	6070	10-31-90
3◆	1989	Q0.03	12-14-90	11-8	...	0.12	0.12	3.45	9.57	3.13	9-30-90
4◆	1937	Q0.28	12-31-90	12-10	...	1.12	1.06	11.7	103	116	9-30-90
5◆	1934	Q0.14	3-1-91	2-11	0.14	0.66	†0.62½	0.99	43.0	10.9	9-30-90
6	1941	Q0.35	1-15-91	12-31	0.35	1.40	1.32	17.9	380	353	9-30-90
7	1987	Q0.075	12-5-90	10-31	...	0.30	0.30	Equity per shr $14.53			8-31-90
8	....	None Since Public			...	Nil	....	32.8	55.2	20.1	9-30-90
9	....	None Paid			...	Nil	....	0.01	2.97	2.63	9-30-90
10	1988	Q0.32½	4-23-91	3-22	0.32½	1.30	1.67½	Equity per shr $18.32			9-30-90
11	1975	[54]Q0.25	4-23-91	3-22	[54]0.50	1.00	2.80	Equity per shr $0.01			9-30-90
12	1943	Q0.08	12-4-90	11-14	...	0.32	0.32	28.6	157	68.2	9-30-90
13	....	None Since Public			...	Nil	....	46.2	82.9	23.2	9-30-90
14◆	1985	[56]0.75	1-22-91	12-26	[56]0.75	⊙Nil	©1.94	Net Asset Val $10.03			1-25-91
15◆	....	†[58]40.00	12-2-88	12-5	...	Nil	....	105	1958	2148	10-06-90

Index	Capitalization Lg Trm Debt Mil-$	Shs. 000 Pfd.	Com.	Earnings $ Per Shr. Years End	1986	1987	1988	1989	1990	Last 12 Mos.	Interim Earnings Period	$ per Shr. 1989	1990	Index
1	120	...	±121100	Je	0.94	1.51	1.68	1.33	1.35	1.35	No interim reporting			1
2	3059	...	199632	Ja	□2.98	3.40	4.00	1.61	E3.65	1.67	9 Mo Oct	1.71	1.77	2
3	0.37	...	2493	Dc	*0.24	*0.04	0.32	0.40	....	0.36	9 Mo Sep	0.30	0.26	3
4	141	214	9541	Dc	0.72	△0.90	△d0.89	1.40	....	1.95	12 Mo Sep	△d1.95	△1.95	4
5	8.75	...	±4253	Je	1.13	1.00	±△1.03	1.19	▲2.26	2.40	6 Mo Dec	0.50	0.64	5
6	770	...	49338	Dc	2.41	2.65	2.76	4.71	P2.94	2.94				6
7	p44.6	...	5253	Fb	1.25	0.16	0.65	0.09	....	0.12	9 Mo Nov	0.25	0.28	7
8	....	...	11186	Je	d0.54	d0.45	0.24	0.74	0.83	0.94	6 Mo Dec	0.34	0.45	8
9	1.59	...	18474	Je	*0.04	*△0.03	d0.50	d0.10	d0.04	d0.03	3 Mo Sep	Nil	0.01	9
10	85.5	...	14301	Dc	...	...	§[53]0.59	1.68	P1.48	1.48				10
11	624	...	26926	Mr	0.51	p△d0.17	□0.15	0.04	....	d0.27	6 Mo Sep	0.30	d0.01	11
12	55.3	...	10317	Dc	d1.96	0.03	1.34	d2.99	E0.50	0.05	9 Mo Sep	d1.47	1.57	12
13	21.9	...	14503	Dc	d0.11	*0.50	*0.58	d0.46	....	0.65	9 Mo Sep	d0.55	*0.56	13
14	....	...	20967	Je	§7.46	§11.13	§13.97	§16.84	§14.45	....				14
15	4495	...	85744	Dc	■0.55	△2.20	■0.24	□d0.23	E0.55	0.25	40 Wk Oct	□d0.30	0.18	15

SOURCE: *Standard & Poor's Stock Guide,* February 1991. Reprinted by permission.

FIGURE 4.4 • A Sample Page from *Standard & Poor's Bond Guide*

Corporate Bonds — KIN-LAC 109

Title-Industry Code & Co. Finances (In Italics) / Individual Issue Statistics: Exchange	Ind / Interest Dates	Fixed Charge Coverage 1987 / S&P Debt Rating	Date of Last Rating Change	1988 / Prior Rating	1989 / Eligible	Year End / Bond Form	Million $ Cash & Equiv. / Redemption Provisions: Regular Price	Curr. Assets / Regular (Begins) Thru	Curr. Liab. / Sinking Fund Price	Balance Sheet Date / Sinking Fund (Begins) Thru	L. Term Debt (Mil $) / Refund/Other Restriction Price	Refund/Other Restriction (Begins) Thru	Capitalization (Mil $) / Outst'g (Mil $)	Total Debt % Capital / Underwriting Firm	Underwriting Year	Price Range 1991 High	Price Range 1991 Low	Mo. End Price Sale(s) or Bid	Curr. Yield	Yield to Mat.
Kings County El Lt & Pr	***75***	***Assmd by Consol Edison NY, see***																		
• PM Mtg 6s '97	aO	NR	6/80	A	X	C	NC	....	....	....	....	....	1.45	F4	1898	86⅝	82	86¾	6.92	8.65
K mart	***58g***	***4.27***		***4.29***	***3.76***	***Ja***	***443.0***	***9504***	***6070***	***10-31-90***	***3059***		***9746***	***47.7***						
• Deb 8⅛s '97	Jj	A			X	R	100	(7-1-93)	....	....	....	....	200	M6	'86	97½	95	96⅜	8.43	8.92
Deb 12½s 2005	Ms	A	5/86	A+	X	R	NC	....	....	....	....	....	100	G2	'85	115¼	112⅞	114¼	10.94	10.53
• Deb 8⅜s 2017	Jj15	A			X	R	106.70	1-14-92	100	(1-15-98)	®104.19	1-14-97	300	M6	'87	88⅝	85½	s87⅛	9.61	9.74
Deb 10½s 2017	jD	A			X	R	108.93	11-30-91	100	(12-1-98)	®105.25	11-30-97	200	M6	'87	108¾	107¾	108⅜	9.69	9.62
• Nts 12⅛s '95	Ms	A	5/86	A+	X	R	NC	....	....	....	....	....	150	D9	'85	No Sale		113	10.73	8.30
KN Energy[1]	***73b***	***1.79***		***1.70***	***2.30***	***Dc***	***11.70***	***103.0***	***116.0***	***9-30-90***	***141.0***		***355.0***	***44.2***						
SF Deb 9⅞s '95	Jj	A−	1/89	BBB	X	R	101.48	1-1-92	100	....	....	....	11.1	M3	'75	101⅛	101⅛	101⅛	9.77	9.52
SF Deb 9s '96	Jj	A−	1/89	BBB	X	R	101.79	1-1-92	100	....	....	....	12.2	M3	'76	101⅜	100¼	101⅛	8.90	8.71
SF Deb 10⅜s 2008	mS	A−	1/89	BBB	X	R	109.32	8-31-91	100	(9-1-99)	®107.17	8-31-93	35.0	M3	'88	108¾	107¼	108⅝	9.90	9.72
SF Deb 9.95s 2020	Ao	A−			X	R	103.58	(4-1-00)	100	(4-1-01)	....	....	20.0	M3	'90	101⅜	99⅞	101⅜	9.82	9.80
Knight-Ridder Inc[2]	***53c***	***6.56***		***4.69***	***3.87***	***Dc***	***17.90***	***380.0***	***353.0***	***9-30-90***	***770.0***		***1658***	***47.6***						
Deb[3] 9⅞s 2009	Ao15	AA−			X	R	NC	....	....	....	....	....	200	G2	'89	104¼	102⅞	104⅛	9.48	9.39
Nts 7¼s '92	Jj15	AA−			X	R	100	....	....	....	....	....	160	G2	'87	99⅞	99¾	99⅞	7.26	7.38
Nts 7⅞s '93	Ao15	AA−			X	R	100	(4-15-91)	....	....	....	....	100	G2	'86	99⅝	99	99⅝	7.90	8.05
Nts 8s '96	Ao15	AA−			X	R	100	(4-15-93)	....	....	....	....	100	G2	'86	97¼	96⅛	97	8.25	8.72
Knoll Int'l	***48b***	***Acq by Westinghouse Elec,see***																		
Sr Sub Deb 11⅜s 2001	Ao15	A+	9/90	B−	X	R	107.31	(4-15-91)	100	(4-15-94)	....	....	[4]47.8	D9	'86	101½	101½	101½	11.21	11.12
[5]***Koch(R.N.),Inc***	***59***	***0.83***		***d0.01***	***1.09***	***Dc***	***0.26***	***40.00***	***34.90***	***9-30-90***	***37.10***		***70.20***	***81.2***						
Sr Nts 12¾s '95	mS15	NR				R	105.67	9-14-91	100	(9-15-92)	....	....	[6]30.0	D9	'85	39½	39½	39½	....	....
Koger Co[7]	***38***	[8]***0.66***		***1.06***	***0.76***	***Mr***	***3.18***			***9-30-90***	***286.0***		***295.0***	***96.9***						
• RE[9]Apprec[10]Nts[11] 8s 2000	[12]Jd	BB−	1/91	BBB		R	107.50	(6-1-95)	....	....	....	....	[6]19.5	B10	'82	No Sale		133⅝	5.99	3.70
◆Sr Nts[12] 8.40s '97	Jj15	BB−	1/91	BBB		R	NC	....	....	....	....	....	75.0	D3	'87	No Sale		98⅝	8.52	8.70
[13]***Kraft Inc***[14]	***27***	***7.77***		[15]***4.25***	***2.04***	***Dc***	***1999***	***8816***	***8241***	***9-29-90***	***9833***		***26515***	***47.2***						
• SF Deb 6⅞s '96	Ao	A	11/88	AA	X	R	100.30	3-31-91	100	....	....	....	26.1	G2	'71	92	91	90⅞	7.57	9.13
• SF Deb 8⅜s 2004	Ao15	A	11/88	AA	X	R	102.745	4-14-91	100	....	....	....	72.2	G2	'74	95⅜	95⅜	89¼	9.38	9.84
• SF Deb 7.60s 2007	Jj15	A	11/88	AA	X	R	103.344	1-14-92	100	....	....	....	90.0	G2	'77	No Sale		80⅝	9.43	10.06
SF Deb 8½s 2017	Fa15	A	11/88	AA	X	R	106	2-14-92	100	(2-15-98)	®103.75	2-14-97	200	G2	'87	74⅝	73½	74½	11.41	11.63
Kroger Co.	***58c***	***3.81***		***2.17***	***0.96***	***Dc***	***105.0***	***1958***	***2148***	***10-6-90***	***4495***		***1715***	***271.0***						
Sr Nts[16] 11⅛s '98	Ms15	B			Y	R	105	(3-15-94)	....	....	[17]Z111	3-14-91	250	G2	'90	101⅜	94½	101⅜	10.97	10.84
Sub Deb[16] 13⅛s 2001	Jj15	B−			Y	R	109.375	(1-15-92)	100	(1-15-00)	[17]Z110.625	1-14-92	625	G2	'89	102	98¾	102	12.87	12.76
Sr Sub Deb[16] 12⅞s '99	Jj15	B−			Y	R	108.575	(1-15-92)	....	....	[17]Z110.008	1-14-92	625	G2	'89	101	97¾	101	12.75	12.67
Laclede Gas Co.	***73b***	***△4.41***		***△3.67***	***△2.78***	***Sp***	***9.87***	***99.40***	***71.20***	***9-30-90***	***130.0***		***323.0***	***42.7***						
1st 5¾s '91	Ao15	AA	5/70	A	X	CR	100	....	100	....	....	....	6.00	D10	'66	99½	99¼	99½	5.78	8.09
1st 7s '93	Mn	AA	5/70	A	X	R	100.71	4-30-91	100.34	4-30-91	....	....	6.70	D10	'68	98⅝	98	98⅝	7.10	7.67
1st 9½s '95	Jd	AA			X	R	102	5-31-91	100	....	....	....	7.68	F2	'75	101¾	101¾	101¾	9.34	9.00
1st 7½s '97	Ms15	AA			X	R	102.11	3-14-91	100.44	3-14-91	....	....	12.8	S12	'72	95¼	94⅜	95¼	7.87	8.51
1st[18] 9⅝s '98	[19]Mn15	AA			X	R	100	(5-15-93)	Z100	....	....	....	25.0	M6	'88	103¼	101¾	103⅛	9.33	9.03
1st 8⅞s '99	Ms15	AA			X	R	103.38	3-14-91	100.77	3-14-91	....	....	11.8	F2	'74	101	99⅜	100¾	8.81	8.74
1st 9¾s '99	jJ15	AA			X	R	104.11	7-14-91	100	....	....	....	11.2	P1	'79	103¾	103¾	103¾	9.40	9.10
1st 8½s 2004	mN15	AA			X	R	NC	....	Z100	....	....	....	25.0	S1	'89	95⅞	93½	94⅝	8.98	9.19
1st 9s 2011	Mn	AA			X	R	106.72	4-30-91	Z100	....	®106.27	4-30-91	30.0	M6	'86	97½	96⅛	97⅜	9.24	9.29

Uniform Footnote Explanations-See Page 1. Other: [1] Was Kansas-Nebraska Natural Gas. [2] Was Knight-Ridder Newspapers. [3] (HRO)To 4-15-99 at 100, for an Event, etc. [4] Defeased, funds deposited w/trustee. [5] Subsid & data of Lori Corp. [6] Incl disc. [7] Subsid of Koger Properties. [8] Year Dec '87 & prior. [9] Add'l int accrues ea Dec 31,on property val. [10] Prin amt $1500:(HRO) On 6-1-94 at 100. [11] Int fixed to 6-1-94,adj aft,as defined. [12] Asmd by Koger Properties. [13] See Gen'l Foods, Mallory(P.R.)&Nat'l Dairy Prod. [14] Now Kraft Gen'l Foods. [15] 4 Wk Dec'88. [16] (HRO)At 101 for a Redemption Event. [17] Upon a Redemption Event. [18] (HRO)On 5-15-98 at 100. [19] Due 5-15-13.

SOURCE: *Standard & Poor's Bond Guide,* February 1991. Reprinted by permission.

there is a brief history, a business summary, financial statements for two years, and a description of the firm's financial structure. All manuals are updated twice a week in separate binders. The information in *Moody's Manuals* is similar to but more complete than that published in *Standard & Poor's Corporate Records.*

2. *Handbook of Widely Held Common Stocks* This handbook is issued four times each year and gives a one-page write-up on more than one thousand common stocks. The *Handbook* includes a stock price chart, background on the company, financial statistics, recent developments, and prospects for each stock. A page from the *Handbook* is shown in Figure 4.5.
3. *Bond Survey* This weekly publication provides information on bond market trends, prospective issues, and investment recommendations. It also provides ratings on new preferred stocks, bank ratings, and commercial paper and a list of Prospective Offering—Shelf Registrations under SEC Rule 415.
4. *Bond Record* The *Bond Record* covers over 48,200 issues and situations, with detailed information on approximately 9,100 corporate, municipal, and foreign bonds. The *Record* also rates preferred stocks, commercial paper, and shelf registrations, as well as industrial development revenue bonds and pollution and environmental control revenue bonds.

• Value Line

The *Value Line Investment Survey* is one of the most popular advisory services used by individual investors. It is published each week and reports on over 1,700 stocks in 93 industries. Each stock is covered once a quarter, and the "Ratings and Reports" section provides a weekly stock update to keep the reports current. The "Summary and Index" section provides a weekly update of the ratings on each stock.

Each week Value Line evaluates specific industries and the major firms within the industries. As shown in Figure 4.6, each report provides a wide variety of information including a brief discussion of business prospects, financial and operating statistics, a graph of stock prices in relation to cash flow, and prospects for the common stock. Value Line also projects the firm's financial and operating ratios and estimates its price performance over the next three to five years. A unique feature of the *Investment Survey* is its scoring system (see the top, left portion of Figure 4.6). Each stock is ranked from 1 to 5 for timeliness (relative price performance over the next 12 months) and for safety. A score of 5 represents the lowest expected performance or safety, and a score of 1 represents the highest performance or safety. An estimate of the stock's beta is also provided. Value Line also publishes *Value Line Options* and *Value Line Convertibles* and reports on OTC situations.

FIGURE 4.5

A Sample Page from *Moody's Handbook*

KNIGHT-RIDDER INC.

LISTED	SYM.	LTPS♦	STPS♦	IND. DIV.	REC. PRICE	RANGE (52-WKS.)	YLD.	DIV. ACH.
NYSE	KRI	88.9	90.0	$1.32	37	58 - 37	3.6%	21 yrs.

INVESTMENT GRADE. THE COMPANY SHOULD GROW THROUGH ACQUISITIONS AND PRICE INCREASES.

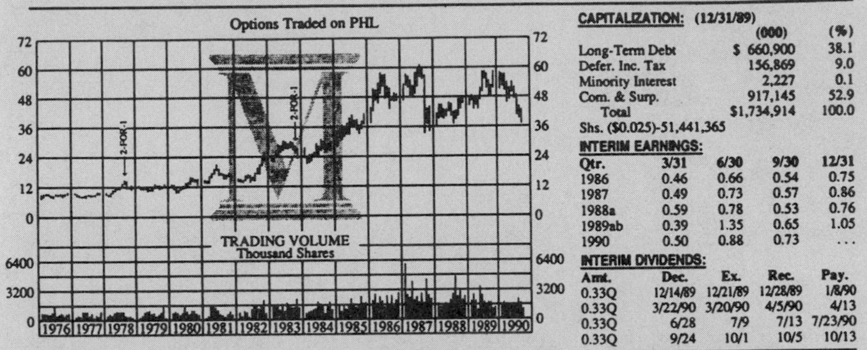

CAPITALIZATION: (12/31/89)

	(000)	(%)
Long-Term Debt	$ 660,900	38.1
Defer. Inc. Tax	156,869	9.0
Minority Interest	2,227	0.1
Com. & Surp.	917,145	52.9
Total	$1,734,914	100.0

Shs. ($0.025)-51,441,365

INTERIM EARNINGS:

Qtr.	3/31	6/30	9/30	12/31
1986	0.46	0.66	0.54	0.75
1987	0.49	0.73	0.57	0.86
1988a	0.59	0.78	0.53	0.76
1989ab	0.39	1.35	0.65	1.05
1990	0.50	0.88	0.73	...

INTERIM DIVIDENDS:

Amt.	Dec.	Ex.	Rec.	Pay.
0.33Q	12/14/89	12/21/89	12/28/89	1/8/90
0.33Q	3/22/90	3/20/90	4/5/90	4/13
0.33Q	6/28	7/9	7/13	7/23/90
0.33Q	9/24	10/1	10/5	10/13

BACKGROUND:

Knight-Ridder Inc. (formerly Knight-Ridder Newspapers, Inc.) is a nationwide information and communications company engaged in newspaper publishing, business news and information services, electronic retrieval services, news graphics and photo services, cable television an newsprint manufacturing. Knight-Ridder's various information services reach more than 100 million people in 129 countries. In 1989, Newspapers accounted for 88% of sales and Business Information contributed 12%.

RECENT DEVELOPMENTS:

For the quarter ended 9/30/90, income from continuing operations increased 7% to $36.6 million compared with $34.0 million a year ago. Revenues rose 6% to $570.5 million from $541.0 million. Earnings benefitted from softer newsprint prices, an improved performance in Detroit operations, and continued growth in the Business Information Services division. Knight-Ridder has repurchased 2,597,500 shares in the nine month period. Growth from the Information Services Division continued and results from Dialog and MoneyCenter were favorable

PROSPECTS:

Earnings per share in the near-term may be flat or down slightly if the weakness in general markets continues. The Company is well positioned to absorb a soft advertising environment in which moderate newsprint price increases are expected in 1991. Results will benefit from lower interest costs. KRI will continue to see softness of advertising linage in many of its publications, but the strengthening of retail advertising sales in some of its markets is encouraging. Good performances from Dialog and other business information services operations should continue as the number of Dialog customers continues to rise. Revenue growth from MoneyCenter's international operations should continue to contribute to results.

STATISTICS:

YEAR	GROSS REVS. ($mill.)	OPER. PROFIT MARGIN %	RET. ON EQUITY %	NET INCOME ($mill.)	WORK CAP. ($mill.)	SENIOR CAPITAL ($mill.)	SHARES (000)	EARN. PER SH.$	DIV. PER SH.$	DIV. PAY. %	PRICE RANGE	P/E RATIO	AVG. YIELD %
80	1,098.5	15.2	15.6	92.9	77.9	53.7	63,732	1.44	0.37	25	16⅛ - 9½	8.9	2.8
81	1,237.1	14.9	14.8	100.4	80.6	60.9	64,416	1.55	0.42	27	20⅞ - 13⅜	11.1	2.4
82	1,327.7	13.1	13.5	102.9	51.8	36.0	65,234	1.57	0.46	29	25¾ - 13⅝	12.5	2.3
83	1,473.4	14.5	14.8	119.4	69.7	77.0	64,155	1.80	0.54	30	30½ - 22⅛	14.6	2.1
84	1,664.7	15.3	15.3	140.8	142.2	77.7	65,043	2.15	0.64	30	31 - 21¼	12.2	2.4
85	1,729.6	13.8	19.0	132.7	95.4	271.5	56,285	2.19	0.76	35	41⅜ - 28	15.8	2.2
86	1,910.7	14.7	17.2	140.0	85.1	621.5	57,131	2.41	0.88	37	57⅞ - 37½	19.8	1.8
87	2,072.6	14.9	17.2	155.1	60.8	508.2	56,881	2.65	1.00	38	61¼ - 33¼	17.8	2.1
88	2,083.3	13.0	17.0	a146.8	83.7	727.0	53,105	a2.59	1.12	43	47¾ - 35¾	16.2	2.7
89	2,268.3	14.2	19.6	ab179.8	70.3	660.9	51,441	ab3.43	1.22	36	58⅜ - 42⅞	14.8	2.4

♦Long-Term Price Score — Short-Term Price Score; see page 4a. STATISTICS ARE AS ORIGINALLY REPORTED. Adjusted for 2-for-1 stock split, 11/83. a-Before a discontinued operations: 1988, cr$9.6 million ($0.17 a share); and 1989, cr$67.4 million ($1.28 a share). b-Incl. gain of $48.6 million on sale of a newspaper.

INCORPORATED:
August 31, 1976 — Fl.

PRINCIPAL OFFICE:
One Herald Plaza
Miami, FL 33132-1693
Tel.: (305) 376-3800

ANNUAL MEETING:
In May

NUMBER OF STOCKHOLDERS:
11,215

TRANSFER AGENT(S):
Manufacturers Hanover Trust Co.
New York, NY

REGISTRAR(S):
Manufacturers Hanover Trust & Co.
New York, NY

INSTITUTIONAL HOLDINGS:
No. of Institutions: 252
Shares Held: 29,297,992

OFFICERS:
Chairman & C.E.O.
A. J. K. Batten
President
P. A. Ridder
Sr. V.P. & C.F.O.
R. F. Singleton
Vice Pres. -Fin. & Treas.
L. A. Levine
Vice Pres. & Sec.
D. C. Harris

SOURCE: *Moody's Handbook of Widely Held Common Stocks,* Winter 1990–91. Reprinted by permission.

FIGURE 4.6 • A Sample Stock Report from *Value Line Investment Survey*

K MART CORP. NYSE-KM

RECENT PRICE **35** | P/E RATIO **10.4** (Trailing: 9.4 Median: 10.0) | RELATIVE P/E RATIO **0.75** | DIV'D YLD **5.1%** | VALUE LINE **1640**

TIMELINESS (Relative Price Performance Next 12 Mos.) **3** Average
SAFETY **2** Above Average
(Scale: 1 Highest to 5 Lowest)
BETA 1.15 (1.00 = Market)

	1979	1980	1981	1982	1983	1984	1985	1986	1987	1988	1989	1990
High:	19.1	19.9	15.9	18.2	26.2	25.1	27.7	38.3	48.4	39.8	44.9	37.3
Low:	15.0	10.3	10.3	10.3	14.5	17.8	20.4	22.4	21.6	29.0	32.5	23.4

1993-95 PROJECTIONS

	Price	Gain	Ann'l Total Return
High	80	(+130%)	*26%*
Low	60	(+70%)	*18%*

Insider Decisions

	M	J	J	A	S	O	N	D	J
to Buy	0	0	0	0	0	0	1	0	0
Options	0	1	2	0	0	0	0	0	1
to Sell	0	0	1	0	0	0	0	0	1

Institutional Decisions

	1Q'90	2Q'90	3Q'90
to Buy	132	149	132
to Sell	151	144	152
Hld's(000)	138171	145910	145920

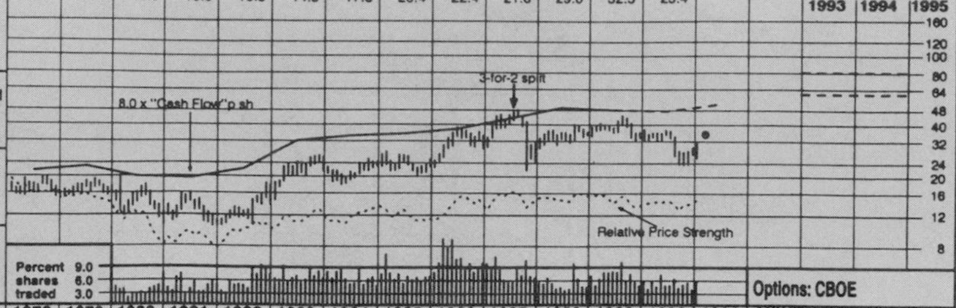

Target Price Range 1993 1994 1995

8.0 x "Cash Flow"p sh

3-for-2 split

Relative Price Strength

Percent shares traded 9.0 6.0 3.0

Options: CBOE

1974	1975	1976	1977	1978	1979	1980	1981	1982	1983	1984	1985	1986	1987	1988	1989	1990	1991	© VALUE LINE PUB., INC.	93-95
30.70	37.57	46.10	54.48	63.84	69.10	76.75	88.87	89.82	98.47	112.50	118.62	117.77	125.92	136.90	147.89	*160.50*	*175.00*	Sales per sh (A)	*224.00*
.80	1.40	1.77	2.03	2.68	2.84	2.48	2.42	2.75	4.01	4.28	4.40	4.68	5.37	6.22	6.04	*5.95*	*6.55*	"Cash Flow"per sh	*9.75*
.58	1.09	1.43	1.62	1.83	1.89	1.38	1.17	1.37	2.53	2.56	2.42	2.84	3.40	4.00	3.71	*3.50*	*3.85*	Earnings per sh (B)	*6.25*
.15	.16	.21	.37	.48	.56	.61	.64	.67	.72	.83	.93	.99	1.16	1.32	1.64	1.70	*1.78*	Div'ds Decl'd per sh (C)	*2.50*
5.64	6.62	7.93	9.25	10.46	11.86	12.66	13.20	13.93	15.57	17.24	17.32	19.48	21.66	25.12	24.90	*26.60*	*28.70*	Book Value per sh	*38.00*
180.36	180.93	181.81	182.47	183.21	184.25	185.07	185.96	186.74	188.87	187.53	189.00	202.18	203.51	199.43	199.69	*200.00*	*200.00*	Common Shs Outst'g (D)	*195.00*
32.8	18.3	17.6	12.2	9.2	8.9	10.1	10.8	9.9	8.8	8.4	9.6	11.3	11.2	8.7	10.1	*8.8*		Avg Ann'l P/E Ratio	*11.0*
4.59	2.44	2.25	1.60	1.25	1.29	1.34	1.31	1.09	.74	.78	.78	.77	.75	.72	.77	*.65*		Relative P/E Ratio	*.90*
.8%	.8%	.8%	1.9%	2.8%	3.3%	4.4%	5.1%	4.9%	3.2%	3.8%	4.0%	3.1%	3.1%	3.8%	4.4%	5.5%		Avg Ann'l Div'd Yield	*3.6%*
						14204	16527	16772	18598	21096	22420	23812	25626	27301	29533	*32100*	*35000*	Sales ($mill) (A)	*43700*
						28.1%	26.6%	28.2%	29.1%	29.1%	29.4%	29.1%	29.1%	28.7%	27.9%	*27.5%*	*27.5%*	Gross Margin	*28.0%*
						2403	2555	2569	2547	3520	3848	3782	3934	4082	4259	*4170*	*4395*	Number of Stores	*5150*
						260.5	220.3	261.8	492.3	499.1	471.0	570.0	692.0	803.0	745.2	*700*	*770*	Net Profit ($mill)	*1200*
						41.4%	33.2%	38.7%	42.9%	39.9%	37.7%	44.6%	40.9%	35.5%	35.5%	*35.5%*	*35.5%*	Income Tax Rate	*35.5%*
						1.8%	1.3%	1.6%	2.6%	2.4%	2.1%	2.4%	2.7%	2.9%	2.5%	*2.2%*	*2.2%*	Net Profit Margin	*2.7%*
						5.0	5.3	5.1	5.2	4.6	4.9	4.6	4.6	4.8	4.3	*4.3*	*4.3*	Inventory Turnover	*4.4*
						1526.5	1430.4	1827.2	2267.7	2421.7	2437.0	2533.0	3003.0	3654.0	3685.0	*3700*	*4100*	Working Cap'l ($mill)	*5200*
						2036.9	2167.0	2420.4	2533.5	2887.0	3169.0	2611.0	2748.0	2946.0	3029.0	*3250*	*3200*	Long-Term Debt ($mill)	*3000*
						2343.2	2455.6	2601.3	2940.1	3233.8	3273.0	3939.0	4409.0	5009.0	4972.0	*5320*	*5735*	Net Worth ($mill)	*7400*
						7.3%	6.9%	7.9%	11.4%	10.4%	9.8%	10.8%	11.5%	11.9%	10.3%	*10.0%*	*10.5%*	% Earned Total Cap'l	*13.0%*
						11.1%	9.0%	10.1%	16.7%	15.4%	14.4%	14.5%	15.7%	16.0%	15.0%	*13.0%*	*13.5%*	% Earned Net Worth	*16.0%*
						6.3%	4.2%	5.3%	12.2%	10.8%	9.2%	9.7%	10.6%	10.9%	8.7%	*6.5%*	*7.0%*	% Retained to Comm Eq	*9.5%*
						44%	53%	47%	27%	30%	36%	33%	33%	32%	42%	*49%*	*46%*	% All Div'ds to Net Prof	*47%*

CAPITAL STRUCTURE as of 10/31/90

Total Debt $4651 mill. **Due in 5 Yrs** $*1400* mill.
LT Debt $3059 mill. **LT Interest** $300.0 mill.

Incl. $1582 mill. capitalized leases.
(LT interest earned: 4.7x; total interest coverage: 4.0x) (38% of Cap'l)

Leases, Uncapitalized Annual rentals $497.0 mill.

Pension Liability None

Pfd Stock None

Common Stock 199,759,680 shs. (62% of Cap'l)

CURRENT POSITION ($MILL.)	1988	1989	10/31/90
Cash Assets	948.0	353.0	443.0
Receivables	527.0	698.0	811.0
Inventory (LIFO)	5671.0	6933.0	8250.0
Current Assets	7146.0	7984.0	9504.0
Accts Payable	2334.0	2319.0	3064.0
Debt Due	90.0	612.0	1592.0
Other	1068.0	1368.0	1414.0
Current Liab.	3492.0	4299.0	6070.0

ANNUAL RATES of change (per sh)	Past 10 Yrs.	Past 5 Yrs.	Est'd '87-'89 to '93-'95
Sales	8.0%	6.5%	*8.5%*
"Cash Flow"	9.0%	10.0%	*9.0%*
Earnings	7.5%	11.5%	*9.0%*
Dividends	11.5%	13.0%	*10.5%*
Book Value	8.5%	9.0%	*8.0%*

Fiscal Year Begins	QUARTERLY SALES ($ mill.)(A) Apr.Per	Jul.Per	Oct.Per	Jan.Per	Full Fiscal Year
1987	5594	6305	5973	7754	25626
1988	5842	6684	6358	8417	27301
1989	6068	7006	6707	9752	29533
1990	7044	7786	7493	*9777*	*32100*
1991	*7300*	*8200*	*7900*	*11600*	*35000*

Fiscal Year Begins	EARNINGS PER SHARE(A) (B) Apr.Per	Jul.Per	Oct.Per	Jan.Per	Full Fiscal Year
1987	.57	.71	.54	1.58	3.40
1988	.60	.81	.63	1.96	4.00
1989	.48	.73	.53	1.97	3.71
1990	.50	.74	.53	*1.73*	*3.50*
1991	*.40*	*.70*	*.60*	*2.15*	*3.85*

Cal-endar	QUARTERLY DIVIDENDS PAID(C) Mar.31	Jun.30	Sep.30	Dec.31	Full Year
1987	.247	.29	.29	.29	1.12
1988	.29	.33	.33	.33	1.28
1989	.33	.41	.41	.41	1.56
1990	.41	.43	.43	.43	1.70
1991					

BUSINESS: K mart Corp. is the 2nd largest retailer in the world. General merchandise division includes K mart discount stores, PACE Membership warehouse clubs, Jupiter/Kresge stores, and American Fare hypermarkets (51% owned). Specialty retail segment includes Waldenbooks, Pay Less Drug Stores, Builders Square home improvement centers, and Sports Authority stores. Owns 21% of Coles Myer, Australia's largest retailer, 22% of OfficeMax (office supplies and furniture), and 49% of Meldisco (footwear depts. in K mart stores). Labor costs: 15% of sales. Insiders own less than 1% of stock. Has 365,000 employees; 69,917 stkhldrs: Chmn., Pres., and C.E.O.: J. Antonini. Inc.: Mich. Address: 3100 W. Big Beaver Road, Troy, MI 48084. Tel.: 313-643-1000.

We think K mart will soon report that fiscal 1990 (ended January 30, 1991) earnings came in around $3.50 a share, about 5% lower than fiscal 1989 results. Sales and gross margins were soft throughout most of the year because of the weak consumer spending environment and the company's everyday-low-pricing-policy. Tight cost controls and benefits from computerization led to a better SG&A expense ratio, though, which helped stem the earnings shortfall.

We think K mart will earn about $3.85 a share in fiscal 1991. Because of recessionary conditions and low consumer confidence, we expect same-store sales growth to remain in the 2% area. Thanks to continued expansion of the specialty store concepts and the acquisition of Price Savers warehouse club stores, we think total sales will climb to the $35 billion mark. The gross margin will probably not change much because management is keeping a tight control over inventories. Factoring in benefits from automation and an increasing contribution from the low-expense-structured warehouse club business, we think K mart's share earnings will grow about 10% this year.

K mart common is ranked to match the market averages during the coming four quarters. Conservative investors should be attracted to the Above Average Safety rank, the high dividend yield, and the stock's low multiple to book value. Nevertheless, we'd hold off on purchases until the company posts improved earnings comparisons. Looking further out . . .

K mart stock offers good total return (includes dividends) potential over the 3- to 5-year pull. The company's strategy includes the continuation of its store expansion and modernization program, more aggressive pricing on commodity products, placing an increased emphasis on lifestyle departments (Apparel, Kitchen Korner, Sporting Goods, Automotive, Bed and Bath, etc.), increasing use of technology in order to lower costs, and aggressive expansion of its specialty retailing formats. The successful implementation of all of the above, combined with share repurchases, should lead to strong earnings growth and a higher relative price earnings ratio by 1993-95.

Bart Schneider *March 1, 1991*

(A) Fiscal year ends on last Wednesday in January of following calendar year. Sales do not include licensee fees and rental income. (B) Primary earnings. Excludes net nonrecurring gains (losses): '85,($1.27); '86,6¢; '89, ($2.10). Next earnings report due mid-March. (C) Next dividend meeting about April 24. Goes ex about May 11. Dividend payment dates: March 12, June 11, September 10, December 10. (D) In millions, adjusted for stock split.

Company's Financial Strength	A
Stock's Price Stability	75
Price Growth Persistence	75
Earnings Predictability	85

Factual material is obtained from sources believed to be reliable, but the publisher is not responsible for any errors or omissions contained herein.

SOURCE: *Value Line Investment Survey,* "Ratings and Reports," 46, *Value Line,* March 1, 1991, p. 1640.

• Investment Newsletter and Chart Services

About three hundred investment newsletters are published in the United States, with prices ranging from $100 to $300 a year. The newsletters offer advice based on a variety of approaches. An extreme example is the *Psychic Forecaster,* which relies on 10 psychics who predict natural disasters, political events, and economic trends. While it is difficult to assess the value of these newsletters to the investor, *Hulbert's Financial Digest* evaluates the annual financial performance of advice given in approximately one hundred newsletters. Hulbert assigns $10,000 to each newsletter at the beginning of the year and rates the newsletter's recommended portfolio on the basis of overall return and risk-adjusted return. Hulbert provides both short-term performance figures and cumulative averages. According to Hulbert, the top performers on a risk-adjusted basis over the period 1980–1990 were *Systems & Forecasts, The Mutual Fund Strategist, MPT Review, BI Research,* and *Fidelity Monitor.* Even assuming that Hulbert has interpreted the newsletters' advice correctly in forming the portfolios, there is no guarantee that the top-rated newsletters in the past will maintain their ratings in the future.

Some of the other more popular newsletters include *The Astute Investor, Dow Theory Letters, The Elliott Wave Theorist, The Holt Investment Advisory, The Independent Investor, The Professional Tape Reader, The Chartist, The Telephone Switch Newsletter, The Zweig Forecast,* and *The United and Babson Investment Report.* Advertisements for newsletters and other investment advisory services frequently appear in such publications as *Barron's* and *The Wall Street Journal.* Often these services offer inexpensive trial subscriptions.

For the technician who feels that insights into future price movements can be obtained from past price movements, there are a number of **chart services.** A few of the better-known services are *Daily Graphs, Technical Trends,* and Trendline's *Daily Action Charts.*

COMPUTERIZED DATA BASES

• Overview

In addition to the published financial information discussed in the preceding sections, a number of firms sell **computerized data bases.** Large data bases are available on tape and are processed on mainframe computers. Smaller data bases are available on floppy disks for the personal computer. Some sources provide both versions of the data. Large amounts of data are available on compact disk read-only memory (CD-ROM), which can be accessed by a personal computer with a CD reader. In addition, a growing number of real-time and on-line data resources are available to the investor with the appropriate personal computer setup. Because these information sources are so numerous, only the most widely used ones will be discussed in this section.

• Compustat

Compustat tapes are produced by Standard & Poor's Corporation. The magnetic tape files are segmented into industrials, OTC companies, banks, utilities, bankrupt companies, and Canadian companies. Data are provided in annual and quarterly formats. The 175-item annual and 100-item quarterly data tapes cover 20 years of company financial data as well as stock price and trading volume information on approximately 10,000 companies, including 6,400 actively traded companies on the OTC, regional, and national exchanges. The data are updated monthly. Compustat also produces a price-dividend-earnings (PDE) tape for over 5,700 stocks, beginning in 1962. Smaller versions of the Compustat tapes are available on floppy disk for the personal computer.

• CRSP

The Center for Research in Security Prices (CRSP) tape is produced by the University of Chicago. The CRSP magnetic tape files provide monthly stock price, dividend, and return information for every stock on the NYSE, from 1926 to the present. Daily tapes provide the same information from 1962 to the present. Tapes are also available for market indexes on a monthly and daily basis.

• ISL

The ISL magnetic computer tapes, produced quarterly by Interactive Data Corporation, provide daily price and volume data on all NYSE and AMEX stocks and some OTC stocks. Quarterly earnings and dividends are also included.

• Value Line Data Base

The Value Line Data Base on magnetic tape provides financial and market data, on an annual and quarterly basis, for the 1,700 companies covered by Value Line Investment Services. In addition to the historical data, the data base provides forecasts of various financial and market items for the coming year. Value Line also provides data disks for personal computers.

• Compact Disks

Over the past few years, advances in compact disk technology have significantly increased the availability of financial information. An enormous amount of information can be stored on a single disk. For example, a disk can house a 10-year history of all corporate earnings for every stock ever traded with room to spare. CD-ROMs boast not only vast data storage capabilities, but also a scanning speed of seconds. Data bases available in CD-ROM format range from bibliographic indexes with abstracts and source data bases containing full text (e.g., UMI's ABI/Inform and Business Periodicals' Ondisc data bases) to reference data bases (e.g., Disclosure and Value/Screen Plus). Many of the large reference data bases that have historically been processed on mainframe computers (e.g., Compustat) are available on CD-ROM.

Most individual investment portfolios are too small to warrant the hardware expenditures and annual costs associated with CD-ROM data bases. However, data from these sources can be retrieved at most university libraries and a number of business schools.

• On-Line Services

One of the first commercial uses of on-line services was for economic information. Economic information from government sources was collated, enhanced, and distributed via time-sharing systems. On-line services have expanded to the point where investors can use their personal computers to receive real-time stock prices and other financial information via FM radio waves and feed these data directly into a spreadsheet for modeling or portfolio updating, or as input for fundamental analysis software packages. The investor can then electronically transmit investment decisions to a brokerage house for execution.

The two basic types of on-line services are (1) those that provide current or historical price quotations and statistics and (2) those that offer news, research, and other descriptive information about investing. A leading on-line service is Dow Jones News/Retrieval Service. Many of the purveyers of CD-ROM data bases also offer on-line services, or their data bases can be accessed through on-line services. As with any of the sources of investment information, the investor must weigh the incremental costs of the information against the incremental expected returns.

MARKET INDEXES

"What did the market do today?" is possibly the question most frequently asked by investors. Why should investors be concerned with a market index or the aggregate movement of stock prices?

First, market indicators are used as a measure of performance. Investors use a market index as a base measure of how well their portfolio has performed. Since security prices tend to move together, investors feel that their portfolio should perform, on a risk-adjusted basis, at least as well as the market index.

Second, market indexes are used to determine if there is a relationship between historical price movements and economic variables. By analyzing market indexes and economic variables over time, the analyst can determine relationships between the market and such variables as interest rates, money supply, and GNP. The market index may be used for forecasting since it has been found to be a leading indicator of the economy.

Third, market indexes are used to estimate future price movements. Technical analysts believe that stock prices move in identifiable patterns. By identifying these patterns, technicians use past price movements to predict future movements in the stock market.

Finally, market indexes are used to determine systematic risk for individual securities and portfolios. Systematic risk measures the relationship between the security return and the market return. By regressing security or portfolio returns to market returns over a period of time, the analyst can determine an index of systematic risk, or beta, for the security or portfolio. This concept was introduced in Chapter 2 and is fully developed in Chapter 20.

Although market indicators tend to move up and down together, the magnitude of the movements may vary considerably. The way in which the indicators are constructed helps explain why their movements are different. Market indicators are affected by the population from which the indicator is drawn, the way in which the components of the indicator are weighted, and the method by which the indicator is computed.

Table 4.1 shows the major U.S. common stock market indicators. Foreign stock market indexes, bond indexes, and commodity indexes will be discussed in the chapters dealing with those investment alternatives.

• The Dow Jones Averages

The Dow Jones Industrial Average (DJIA) is the oldest and best-known market indicator. The answer to "What did the market do today?" is usually based on the change in the DJIA, or "the Dow." The present DJIA of 30 stocks began on October 1, 1928. The 30 companies comprising the DJIA change from time to time in response to shifts in the status and performance of the nation's biggest industrial companies and, also, to reflect the changing importance of particular industries in the economy. The latest change occurred in May 1991 when Walt Disney Company replaced USX Corporation, Caterpillar, Inc., replaced Navistar International Corporation, and J.P. Morgan & Company replaced Primerica Corporation. These were the first changes in the DJIA since March 1987. Of the original 30 stocks in the DJIA, only 8 remain today. The 30 stocks currently in the DJIA, shown in Table 4.2, represent large, well-known companies that are among the leaders of their respective industries.

The DJIA is a **price-weighted average** computed by adding the prices of the 30 stocks and dividing by a divisor that is adjusted for stock splits, stock dividends in excess of 10 percent, and the substitution of companies in the average. A simple example will help explain the divisor adjustment technique. Assume that each of the 30 stocks has a price of $2 per share. The average would have a value of 2 (60 ÷ 30). If one of the stocks splits two for one

TABLE 4.1 • Major U.S. Common Stock Indexes

Dow Jones Averages	**NASDAQ Indexes**
30 Industrials	OTC Composite
20 Transportation	Industrials
15 Utilities	Financial
65 Composite	Insurance
	Utilities
New York Stock Exchange Indexes	Banks
Composite	Transportation
Industrials	NMS Composite
Utilities	NMS Industrials
Transportation	NASDAQ-100
Financial	
	Others
Standard & Poor's Indexes	AMEX (American Stock Exchange)
500 Index	Value Line Index
400 Industrials	Wilshire 5000 Equity Index
20 Transportation	*The New York Times* Index
40 Utilities	*Barron's* 500 Stock Average
40 Financial	
400 MidCap	

TABLE 4.2 • The Thirty Dow Jones Industrial Stocks as of July 1991

Alcoa	International Paper
Allied-Signal	J.P. Morgan
American Express	McDonald's
AT&T	Merck & Co.
Bethlehem Steel	Minnesota Mining and Manufacturing
Boeing	Phillip Morris
Caterpillar	Procter & Gamble
Chevron	Sears Roebuck
Coca-Cola	Texaco
DuPont	Union Carbide
Eastman Kodak	United Technologies
Exxon	Walt Disney
General Electric	Westinghouse Electric
General Motors	Woolworth
Goodyear	
IBM	

SOURCE: *Barron's.*

(price decreases from \$2 per share to \$1 per share) and no other prices change, then the average should remain at 2. By adjusting the divisor from 30 to 29.5 ($59 \div X = 2$; $X = 29.5$), the average remains at 2. Since 1928, the divisor for the DJIA has decreased from 30 to approximately 0.5.

The method of calculating the average has resulted in several criticisms. First, high-priced stocks carry more weight than low-priced stocks in the average. As Table 4.3 shows, a 10 percent increase in Alpha common stock causes a 6.1 percent change in the average, but a 10 percent increase in the lower-priced Gamma stock results in only a 0.8 percent increase in the value of the average. Thus, price changes in high-priced stocks cause the average to move more than the overall market may have changed. In like manner, when high-priced stocks split, they create a downward bias in the average. Table 4.4 shows that when Alpha splits two for one, a new divisor must be calculated to keep the average constant. Now a 10 percent increase in Alpha increases the average by only 4.4 percent instead of the 6.1 percent in Table 4.3. It should be pointed out that the best-performing stocks rise in price over time and therefore have a high probability of splitting and causing a downward bias in the average.

Another criticism of the DJIA is that the divisor is not adjusted for stock dividends smaller than 10 percent. This also creates a downward bias in the value of the average since the numerator (price) is reduced by small stock dividends, with no corresponding adjustment in the divisor.

The final criticism is that the average includes only 30 large industrial stocks. Using only 30 stocks to represent the entire stock market is questionable. Since the average reflects the price changes of only large firms, some people claim that the DJIA is not representative of price movements in the broader market.

The Dow Jones Company also compiles the Dow Jones Transportation Average (DJTA), which is composed of 20 stocks in the transportation indus-

TABLE 4.3 • Effect on a Price-Weighted Average of a 10 Percent Change in the Value of a High-Priced Stock versus a Low-Priced Stock

	Original value	10% change in high-priced stock	10% change in low-priced stock
Alpha stock	\$160	\$176	\$160
Beta stock	80	80	80
Gamma stock	20	20	22
Sum	\$260	\$276	\$262
Divisor	3.0	3.0	3.0
Average	86.67	92.0	87.33
Percentage change		6.1%	0.8%

TABLE 4.4 • Effect on a Price-Weighted Average of a Two-for-One Stock Split

	Original value	After split	10% change in alpha value
Alpha stock	$160	$ 80	$ 88
Beta stock	80	80	80
Gamma stock	20	20	20
Sum	$260	$180	$188
Divisor	3.0	2.077	2.077
Average	86.67	86.67	90.52
Percentage change			4.4%

try; the Dow Jones Utility Average (DJUA), composed of 15 utility stocks; and a composite average of the 65 stocks. These averages are also price-weighted measures.

• Standard & Poor's Stock Indexes

Standard & Poor's Corporation computes six indexes: a 400-stock industrial index, a 40-stock utility index, a 20-stock transportation index, a 40-stock financial index, a 500-stock composite index, and a 400-stock index of medium-sized companies. This last index, MidCap, began on June 6, 1991. S&P must occasionally replace stocks in its indexes as is done in the Dow averages. As of April 6, 1988, S&P announced that it would vary the number of stocks included in the subindexes. This change will allow more "flexibility" in constructing the indexes.

The S&P indexes overcome many of the disadvantages of the Dow Jones averages. First, the S&P indexes are value weighted rather than price weighted. A **value-weighted index** is computed by summing the market value of all stocks in the index and dividing by the aggregate market value of the stocks in the base period. Market value (capitalization) is computed by multiplying the current price of the stock by the number of shares outstanding. The S&P 500 Index is calculated as shown in Equation 4.1. The base-period value for the index was initially set at 10; thus, the ratio of current market value to base-period market value is multiplied by 10.

$$\text{S\&P 500 Index} = \frac{\sum_{i=1}^{500} P_{ic} \times Q_{ic}}{\sum_{i=1}^{500} P_{io} \times Q_{io}} \times 10 \qquad (4.1)$$

where

$$P_{ic} = \text{current price of the } i\text{th stock}$$
$$Q_{ic} = \text{current number of shares outstanding for the } i\text{th stock}$$
$$P_{io} = \text{original price of the } i\text{th stock in the base period, 1941–1943}$$
$$Q_{io} = \text{original number of shares outstanding for the } i\text{th stock in the base period, 1941–1943}$$

An illustration of the computation of a three-stock, value-weighted index with a base-period value of 10 is shown in the upper part of Table 4.5.

The second advantage of a value-weighted index is that stock splits and dividends do not affect the index value since the adjusted price and the new number of shares outstanding are used in the calculations. This automatic adjustment is illustrated in the lower part of Table 4.5. A disadvantage of a value-weighted index is that high-capitalization stocks have a major influence on the index value. Thus, although the S&P indexes eliminate the small-

TABLE 4.5 • Calculation of a Value-Weighted Index

Base year

Stock	*Price*	*Number of shares outstanding (millions)*	*Total market value (capitalization in millions)*
Alpha	$160	1	$ 160
Beta	80	40	3,200
Gamma	20	20	400
			$3,760

$$\text{Base-period index} = \frac{\$3{,}760 \text{ million}}{\$3{,}760 \text{ million}} \times 10 = 10$$

One year later

Stock	*Price*	*Number of shares outstanding (millions)*	*Total market value (capitalization in millions)*
Alpha	$90	2	$ 180 (2-for-1 split)
Beta	75	40	3,000
Gamma	25	22	550 (10% stock dividend)
			$3,730

$$\text{Index one year later} = \frac{\$3{,}730 \text{ million}}{\$3{,}760 \text{ million}} \times 10 = .9920 \times 10 = 9.920$$

sample problem of the DJIA, they are still dominated by the larger firms. For example, in Table 4.5, both Alpha and Gamma increased in total market value, but the index declined to 9.92 from its base-period value of 10. This decline was caused by the decrease in Beta, a relatively high-capitalization stock. The new MidCap Index does not have this problem to the same extent as the S&P 500 Index since it contains stocks of comparable market value.

• New York Stock Exchange Indexes

In 1966, the New York Stock Exchange (NYSE) established the NYSE Common Stock Indexes. These indexes consist of a Composite Index, which includes *all* stocks listed on the NYSE, and four subindexes: Industrial, Transportation, Utility, and Financial. The base value of the index is 50 (the base year ended December 31, 1965). The NYSE indexes are value weighted and thus suffer from the effects of the price movements of large firms. However, the index is not subject to the small-sample criticism since it covers all stocks listed on the NYSE.

• American Stock Exchange Indexes

On September 4, 1973, the American Stock Exchange (AMEX) introduced a market value index that replaced a price change index used since April 1966. As of July 1983, the base level of the index was 50. The index is composed of common stocks, American Depository Receipts (ADRs), and warrants. The AMEX also computes 16 subindexes, including eight industrial and eight geographic groupings.

• NASDAQ Indexes

The National Association of Security Dealers produces 10 indexes. The NASDAQ/NMS Composite Index contains over 4,200 securities. The National Market System (NMS) was developed in 1979 and consists of large, actively traded issues with a number of market makers for each security. The other indexes include the OTC Composite, Industrial, Bank, Other Financial, Insurance, Utility, Transportation, NASDAQ/NMS Industrial, and NASDAQ-100. The indexes are computed in a manner similar to that of the S&P and NYSE indexes. The base-period value for the indexes is 100.

• Value Line Index

The *Value Line Investment Survey* began publishing its Composite Index in 1963. The index is an equally-weighted geometric average of stock prices. As discussed in Chapter 2, geometric averages have a downward bias relative to

TABLE 4.6 • Arithmetic versus Geometric Stock Averages

	Lower prices	Base-period prices	Higher prices
Alpha stock	$90	$100	$110
Beta stock	95	100	105
Gamma stock	85	100	118
Arithmetic average	$90	$100	$111
Percentage change from base period price (arithmetic)	−10.00%	—	+11.00%
Geometric average*	$89.87	$100	$110.82
Percentage change from base period price (geometric)	−10.13%	—	+10.82%

*Calculated as the third root of the product of the three stock prices, or $[(P_1)(P_2)(P_3)]^{.3333}$.

arithmetic averages. Therefore an index using a geometric average will rise more slowly and decrease more rapidly than an index that uses arithmetic averaging. However, because the index is geometric, low-priced stocks have the same effect as high-priced stocks on the index. Table 4.6 illustrates the differences between equally weighted arithmetic and geometric stock averages.

• The Wilshire 5000 Equity Index

The Wilshire 5000 Equity Index is a value-weighted index published by Wilshire Associates. The index represents the market value of all NYSE and AMEX stocks, as well as the most active OTC stocks.

COMPARISON OF MARKET INDEXES OVER TIME

Table 4.7 shows year-end values for five major stock indexes between 1972 and 1990. Table 4.8 lists the annual percentage change in the value of each of the indexes.

The correlation matrix at the bottom of Table 4.7 shows that the five market measures are highly correlated. The highest correlation, .994, is between the AMEX and NASDAQ composite indexes. The lowest correlation, .904, is between the AMEX and the DJIA.

As Table 4.8 shows, the market measures representing NYSE stocks have the lowest arithmetic and geometric mean percentage changes and lowest standard deviation when compared with the measures representing stocks on

TABLE 4.7 • Major Stock Indexes, 1972–1990

Year-end	S&P Composite	DJIA	NYSE Composite	AMEX	NASDAQ Composite
1990	330.22	2633.66	156.26	308	373.84
1989	353.4	2753.2	195.04	378	454.82
1988	277.72	2168.57	180.49	306	381.38
1987	247.08	1938.83	138.23	260	330.47
1986	242.17	1895.95	138.58	263	348.83
1985	211.28	1546.67	121.58	246	324.93
1984	167.24	1211.00	96.38	204	247.35
1983	165.34	1258.00	95.18	223	278.60
1982	141.24	1046.00	81.03	170	232.41
1981	122.30	875.00	71.11	160	195.84
1980	135.76	963.00	77.86	174	202.34
1979	107.94	838.00	61.95	123	150.83
1978	96.11	805.00	53.62	75	117.98
1977	95.10	831.00	52.50	64	105.05
1976	107.46	1004.00	57.88	55	97.88
1975	80.19	852.00	47.64	42	77.62
1974	68.56	616.00	36.13	30	59.82
1973	97.55	850.00	51.82	45	92.19
1972	118.05	1020.00	64.48	64	133.72

Correlation matrix

	S&P Composite	*DJIA*	*NYSE Composite*	*AMEX*	*NASDAQ Composite*
S&P Composite	1.000				
DJIA	0.991	1.000			
NYSE Composite	0.990	0.985	1.000		
AMEX	0.948	0.904	0.938	1.000	
NASDAQ Composite	0.959	0.920	0.949	0.994	1.000

the AMEX and OTC. This is to be expected since these NYSE measures are made up of larger, more mature companies.

The six-year percentage changes at the bottom of Table 4.8 indicate that in certain periods the larger, NYSE stocks are more in favor (or less out of favor) with investors than the smaller companies traded on the AMEX and OTC and vice versa. For example, over the 1984–1990 period, NYSE stocks appeared

TABLE 4.8 • Annual Percentage Change in Stock Indexes, 1972–1990

Year-end	S&P Composite	DJIA	NYSE Composite	AMEX	NASDAQ Composite
1990	− 6.56%	− 4.34%	−19.88%	−18.49%	−17.80%
1989	27.25	26.96	8.06	23.53	19.26
1988	12.40	11.85	30.57	17.70	15.41
1987	2.03	2.26	− 0.25	− 1.14	− 5.26
1986	14.62	22.58	13.98	6.96	7.36
1985	26.33	27.72	26.15	20.59	31.36
1984	1.15	− 3.74	1.26	− 8.52	−11.22
1983	17.06	20.27	17.46	31.18	19.87
1982	15.49	19.54	13.95	6.25	18.67
1981	− 9.91	− 9.14	− 8.67	− 8.05	− 3.21
1980	25.77	14.92	25.68	41.46	34.15
1979	12.31	4.10	15.54	64.00	27.84
1978	1.06	− 3.13	2.13	17.19	12.31
1977	−11.50	−17.23	− 9.30	16.36	7.33
1976	34.01	17.84	21.49	30.95	26.10
1975	16.96	38.31	31.86	40.00	29.76
1974	−29.72	−27.53	−30.28	−33.33	−35.11
1973	−17.37	−16.67	−19.63	−29.69	−31.06
1972	15.63	14.61	14.27	10.34	17.17
Arithmetic mean	7.74%	7.33%	7.07%	11.96%	8.57%
Geometric mean	6.37%	5.74%	5.51%	9.20%	6.45%
Standard deviation	16.49%	17.58%	17.58%	24.22%	20.10%
Six-Year Percentage Change					
1984–90	97.45%	117.48%	62.13%	51.03%	51.14%
1978–84	74.01%	50.43%	79.75%	172.00%	109.65%
1972–78	−18.59%	−21.08%	−16.84%	17.19%	−11.77%

to outperform their counterparts on the AMEX and OTC. The situation was reversed for both the 1972–1978 and 1978–1984 periods.

SUMMARY

This chapter discussed the major sources of investment information on the economy, industries, and individual firms.

The U.S. government is the primary source of information on economic activity. Two major sources of government information are the *Federal Reserve Bulletin* and the *Survey of Current Business*.

A number of sources provide information for evaluating specific industries. Various government publications provide aggregate information on industries. In addition, business and financial publications such as *The Wall Street Journal, Forbes,* and *Business Week* provide industry information. Trade journals are also excellent sources of information on industries. Financial services such as Value Line and Standard & Poor's provide information on industries and individual firms.

Corporate annual reports are an important source of information about individual firms. A variety of advisory services and newsletters also provide information on specific industries and firms. Moody's, Standard & Poor's, and Value Line are the major advisory services.

In addition to published financial information, a number of services provide computerized data bases. Data bases are available on tape for mainframes and on floppy disk and CDs for personal computers. Individual investors also have access to on-line financial services, such as the Dow Jones News/Retrieval Service, as well as to computer programs that assist in security analysis and portfolio management.

The chapter also examined market measures of performance, discussing how they are calculated and their strengths and weaknesses. Although these averages and indexes are calculated in different ways and are comprised of different securities, their movements tend to be highly correlated.

• KEY TERMS

Annual report
Chart services
Coincident indicators
Computerized data bases
Investment advisory services
Investment newsletters
Lagging indicators
Leading indicators
Price-weighted averages
Value-weighted indexes

• QUESTIONS

1. Explain what is meant by leading, coincident, and lagging economic indicators.
2. Where can you find information on leading, coincident, and lagging indicators of economic activity?
3. Why would an investor following a passive investment strategy have different information requirements than an investor with an active investment strategy?
4. What are the timeliness and safety of K Mart Corp. common stock according to Figure 4.6? Its estimated beta coefficient? Its projected price range for 1993–1995?
5. Which stock shown in Figure 4.3 has the highest ranking according to Standard & Poor's? When was its most recent dividend paid? Does the company have preferred stock?

6. Explain how the Dow Jones averages and the Standard & Poor's indexes are constructed. In what ways are the S&P indexes superior to the Dow Jones averages?
7. Explain how an average, constructed like the DJIA, would handle a two-for-one stock split and a 50 percent stock dividend.
8. Explain how an index, constructed like the S&P 500, would handle a two-for-one stock split and a 50 percent stock dividend.
9. Why is the divisor of the DJIA approximately 0.5?
10. In May 1991, three common stocks were replaced in the DJIA. Explain how this change in stocks might have affected the divisor.

• PROBLEM

Consider the information on Stocks A, B, and C:

Stock	*Number of shares*	*Price on 9/8/92*	*Price on 9/9/92*
A	200	$40	$42
B	400	30	30
C	800	10	12

a. Calculate a price-weighted average for the three stocks on 9/8/92 and 9/9/92.

b. What is the percentage change in the average between the two dates?

c. Calculate a value-weighted index using 9/8/92 as the base period, and assign a value of 50 for the base level. What is the value of the index on 9/9/92?

d. What is the percentage change in the index between the two dates?

e. Explain the difference in the percentage changes in parts (b) and (d).

• REFERENCES

Barron's. Dow Jones & Co., Inc., 200 Liberty St., New York, NY 10281.

Barron's Finance and Investment Handbook. Barron's Educational Services, Inc., 250 Wireless Blvd., Hauppauge, NY 11788.

Directory of Investment Advisors. McGraw-Hill Publishing, P.O. Box 1608, Charlottesville, VA 22901.

Economic Report of the President. Superintendent of Documents, U.S. Government Printing Office, Washington, D.C. 20402.

Encyclopedia of Business Information Services. Gale Research Company, Book Tower, Detroit, MI 48277.

Federal Reserve Bulletin. Division of Administration Services, Board of Governors of the Federal Reserve System, Washington, D.C. 20551.

Hulbert Financial Digest. 316 Commerce Street, Alexandria, VA 22314.

Moody's Handbook of Widely Held Common Stocks. Moody's Investor Services, Inc., 99 Church Street, New York, NY 10007.

Standard & Poor's Bond Guide. Standard & Poor's Corporation, 345 Hudson Street, New York, NY 10014.

Standard & Poor's Stock Guide. Standard & Poor's Corporation, 345 Hudson Street, New York, NY 10014.

Standard & Poor's Stock Reports. Standard & Poor's Corporation, 345 Hudson Street, New York, NY 10014.

Survey of Current Business. Superintendent of Documents, U.S. Government Printing Office, Washington, D.C. 20402.

Value Line Investment Survey. "Ratings and Reports," Value Line, Inc., 711 Third Ave., New York, NY 10017.

The Wall Street Journal. Dow Jones & Co., Inc., 1200 Liberty St., New York, NY 10281.

CHAPTER 5

Investing in Mutual Funds

The knowledge-level objectives of this chapter should enable the student to:

- Appreciate the growing importance of mutual funds in the investment environment faced by individual investors.
- Understand the differences and similarities between closed-end funds and mutual funds.
- Understand how holding period returns are calculated for mutual funds.
- Distinguish between load and no-load funds.
- Explain the key decision variables that investors should use in selecting a mutual fund.
- Compare and contrast active versus passive investment strategies using mutual funds.

INTRODUCTION

The purpose of this chapter is to provide an overview of investment companies. An *investment company* is simply a corporation that invests in marketable securities and other categories of investments such as real assets. Basically, it is a corporation that provides "collective" investing opportunities to individuals, businesses, and other types of investors. There are two primary forms of investment companies: open-end and closed-end companies. **Mutual funds,** the largest and most popular, are **open-end** investment companies because they stand ready to issue new shares or redeem outstanding shares on a continuous basis. The number of shares, therefore, fluctuates as investors purchase or redeem shares. A **closed-end** investment company is more like a traditional, publicly traded corporation, with a fixed number of shares of common stock outstanding.

Even though the chapter discusses several types of investment companies, its major emphasis is on mutual funds. Far more money is invested through mutual funds than through other types of investment companies, and these funds play an important role in the financial plans of many individuals.

Mutual funds are now the third largest financial intermediary in the United States, behind only commercial banks and life insurance companies. At the end of 1989, 52 percent of mutual fund accounts were owned by individuals between the ages of 18 and 44. An estimated 22.8 million households in the United States had invested in mutual funds; 56 percent of these households had incomes less than $50,000 per year. As these statistics indicate, mutual funds appeal to individuals in all age groups and income levels.

CLOSED-END COMPANIES

Although closed-end funds are the most popular form of closed-end investment company, several others exist. This section will examine closed-end funds and then will look briefly at other types of closed-end investment companies.

• Closed-End Funds

The share price of a closed-end fund is determined by supply and demand factors; its shares are traded on a stock exchange or the over-the-counter (OTC) market. Approximately 250 closed-end companies are publicly traded, but many of these are small in terms of assets. The shares of larger companies are traded on the New York Stock Exchange (NYSE) and American Stock Exchange (AMEX); the smaller companies are traded on the OTC market.[1] Table 5.1 provides information on the more actively traded closed-end funds.

---

[1] For information on the larger companies, see *Investment Companies* (New York: Wiesenberger Investment Companies Service, 1990).

TABLE 5.1 • Quotations for Closed-End Funds

INVESTMENT COMPANY INSTITUTE LIST

Friday, May 17, 1991

Fund Name	Stock Exch.	N.A. Value	Stock Price	% Diff.
Diversified Common Stock Funds				
Adams Express	NYSE	19.03	17	−10.67
Baker Fentress	NYSE	21.05	16⅞	−19.80
Blue Chip Value	NYSE	7.65	7⅛	− 6.86
Clemente Global Gro	NYSE	b10.99	9⅛	−16.97
Gemini II Capital	NYSE	15.27	12¾	−16.50
Gemini II Income	NYSE	9.43	12¾	+35.21
General Amer Invest	NYSE	25.70	22	−14.40
Growth Stock Outlook	NYSE	10.43	9⅞	− 5.32
Liberty All-Star Eqty	NYSE	10.06	9⅜	− 6.81
Niagara Share Corp.	NYSE	15.92	13½	−15.20
Nicholas-Applegate	NYSE	11.95	11⅞	− 0.63
Quest For Value Cap	NYSE	19.23	14	−27.20
Quest for Value Inco	NYSE	11.59	13½	+16.48
Royce Value Trust	NYSE	10.54	9⅞	− 6.31
Salomon Fd	NYSE	14.95	12⅝	−15.55
Source Capital	NYSE	40.43	42¾	+ 5.74
Tri-Continental Corp.	NYSE	27.35	24⅝	− 9.96
Worldwide Value	NYSE	16.64	14	−15.87
Zweig Fund	NYSE	11.17	12¼	+ 9.67
Closed End Bond Funds				
CIM High Yield Secs	AMEX	6.64	6⅜	− 3.99
Franklin Multi Inc Tr	NYSE	b8.77	8⅜	− 4.50
Franklin Prin Mat Tr	NYSE	b7.82	7⅝	− 2.49
Franklin Universal Tr	NYSE	b6.93	6½	− 6.20
Municipal High Inco	NYSE	a9.32	9¼	− 0.75
Zenix Income Fund	NYSE	a5.61	5¾	+ 2.50
Flexible Portfolio Funds				
America's All Seasn	OTC	5.75	4½	−21.74
European Warrant Fd	NYSE	9.71	7½	−22.76
Zweig Total Return Fd	NYSE	9.24	9¾	+ 5.52
Specialized Equity and Convertible Funds				
Alliance Global Env Fd	NYSE	13.62	12	−11.89
American Capital Conv	NYSE	20.13	17½	−13.07
ASA Ltd	NYSE	bcy42.87	45⅜	+ 5.84
Asia Pacific	NYSE	14.76	13¼	−10.23
Austria Fund	NYSE	11.62	9⅝	−17.17
Bancroft Convertible	AMEX	20.42	17⅞	−12.46
Bergstrom Capital	AMEX	80.35	81½	+ 1.43
BGR Precious Metals	TOR	be8.74	7¼	−17.05
Brazil	NYSE	11.59	13	+12.17
CNV Holdings Capital	NYSE	10.00	6	−40.00
CNV Holdings Income	NYSE	9.50	11	+15.79
Castle Convertible	AMEX	22.15	18¾	−15.35
Central Fund Canada	AMEX	b4.42	4 3/16	− 5.26
Central Securities	AMEX	11.39	9¼	−18.79
Chile Fund	NYSE	25.36	22⅛	−12.76
Couns Tandem Secs	NYSE	13.92	11⅞	−14.69
Cypress Fund	AMEX	5.82	4⅞	−16.24
Duff&Phelps Sel Utils	NYSE	8.50	8⅞	+ 4.41
Ellsw Conv Gr&Inc	AMEX	8.18	7⅛	−12.90
Emerging Ger Fd	NYSE	8.82	8⅛	− 7.88
Engex	AMEX	8.97	7⅝	− 14.99
Europe Fund	NYSE	13.11	11	− 16.09
1stAustralia	AMEX	10.16	9⅛	− 10.19
First Financial Fund	NYSE	6.87	7	+ 1.89
First Iberian	AMEX	9.50	8¾	− 7.89
First Philippine Fund	NYSE	10.55	7⅞	− 25.36
France Growth Fund	NYSE	10.23	8⅜	− 18.13
Future Germany Fund	NYSE	13.59	12¼	− 9.86
Gabelli Equity Trust	NYSE	11.38	11¼	− 1.14
Germany Fund	NYSE	10.62	11⅛	+ 4.76
Growth Fund Spain	NYSE	11.54	10⅛	− 12.26
GT Greater Europe Fd	NYSE	11.69	9¾	− 16.60
H&Q Healthcare Inv	NYSE	15.54	14¾	− 5.08
Hampton Utils Tr Cap	AMEX	b12.65	10⅞	− 14.03
Hampton Utils Tr Pref	AMEX	b49.57	49¾	+ 0.36
India Growth Fund	NYSE	f14.71	12⅝	− 14.17
Indonesia Fund	NYSE	10.79	10⅜	− 3.85
Inefficient Market Fund	AMEX	10.71	9	− 15.97
Irish Investment Fd	NYSE	9.30	7¾	− 16.67
Italy Fund	NYSE	11.51	9¾	− 15.29
Jakarta Growth Fd	NYSE	8.65	7⅞	− 8.96
Japan OTC Equity Fund	NYSE	12.09	11⅜	− 5.91
Korea Fund	NYSE	10.41	13¾	+ 32.08
Latin America Inv Fd	NYSE	19.79	17⅜	− 12.20
Malaysia Fund	NYSE	14.16	13	− 8.19
Mexico Equity Inc Fd	NYSE	13.78	11⅝	− 15.64
Mexico Fund	NYSE	b22.06	19⅞	− 9.90
Morgan Grenf SmCap	NYSE	10.95	11	+ 0.46
New Germany Fund	NYSE	12.05	10½	− 12.86
Pacific Eur Growth Fd	NYSE	10.62	9⅞	− 7.02
Patriot Prem Div Fd	NYSE	8.85	8⅞	+ 0.28
Patriot Prem Div Fd II	NYSE	10.47	10¼	− 2.10
Patriot Select Div Trust	NYSE	14.46	15	+ 3.73
Petrol & Resources	NYSE	29.69	27⅛	− 8.64
Pilgrim Regional	NYSE	9.25	9⅛	− 1.35
Portugal Fund	NYSE	10.90	9¾	− 10.55
Preferred Income Fd	NYSE	15.77	16	+ 1.46
Putnam Dividend Inco	NYSE	10.39	10⅜	− 0.14
RI Estate Sec Inco Fd	AMEX	7.23	7	− 3.18
ROC Taiwan Fund	NYSE	11.38	10¼	− 9.93
Scudder New Asia	NYSE	16.01	15¼	− 4.75
Scudder New Europe	NYSE	10.53	8⅞	− 15.72
SE Savings Inst Fd	OTC	b7.67	6¼	− 18.51
Singapore Fd	NYSE	b11.92	10	− 16.11
Spain Fund	NYSE	12.02	14¾	+ 22.71
Swiss Helvetia Fd	NYSE	13.16	12	− 8.81
Taiwan Fund	NYSE	b21.60	22⅞	+ 5.90
TCW Convertible Secs	NYSE	7.64	7⅞	+ 3.08
Templeton Em Mkts'	AMEX	b16.22	16⅜	+ 0.96
Templeton Global Util	AMEX	11.49	10⅞	− 5.35
Thai Capital Fund	NYSE	10.07	8⅜	− 16.83
Thai Fund	NYSE	16.68	17⅞	+ 7.16
Turkish Inv Fund	NYSE	7.69	7¾	+ 0.78
United Kingdom Fund	NYSE	11.37	9⅝	− 15.35
Z-Seven	OTC	15.77	16	+ 1.46

a-Ex-dividend. b-As of Thursday's close. c-Translated at Commercial Rand exchange rate. e-In Canadian Dollars. f-As of Wednesday's close. y—5—10,Nav:41.12; stck pr.46; % dif, + 11.87.

SOURCE: *Barron's,* May 20, 1991, p. 109.

While the number of closed-end funds is small relative to mutual funds, they offer investors certain unique characteristics. In particular, closed-end funds tend to sell at premiums or discounts from their **net asset value (NAV)**. NAV is simply the total market value of the securities owned, less any liabilities, divided by the number of shares outstanding. If the price of the shares is less than NAV, the investor can buy $1 worth of assets for less than $1. The discounts and premiums from NAV can be quite volatile. For example, the Gabelli Equity Trust went from a 4 percent premium in January 1990 to a 5 percent discount in June 1990. This move was in addition to a large decline in NAV.[2] The quotations in Table 5.1 indicate the percentage premium or discount on each fund.

Numerous studies have attempted to explain why closed-end fund shares usually have prices different from their NAVs. Popular explanations include the following: (1) the shares must be bought through a broker who may prefer to sell more traditional investments such as common stocks; (2) the funds do not have an active marketing campaign; (3) the market for the shares is "thin" because of the size of the companies and the lack of institutional investor interest; (4) actions taken by fund managers such as buying back shares or action by dissident shareholders may affect share prices; and (5) the market is inefficient in pricing the shares.

The idea that there may be some market inefficiencies in pricing the shares is of considerable interest to both financial researchers and investors. A study by Seth Anderson confirmed the results of earlier studies concerning the existence of possible market inefficiency.[3] Based on a sample of 17 closed-end equity funds over three different periods from January 1965 through August 1984, Anderson's findings supported conclusions by earlier researchers that market inefficiencies existed for closed-end shares. The inefficiencies were also of a magnitude and duration to allow investors to earn risk-adjusted excess returns from strategies based on the discounts and from buy-and-hold strategies. The study did not address the issue of why the inefficiencies exist, however.

A closed-end fund can operate as a diversified or a nondiversified fund. A *diversified* fund holds a large number of securities from different industries and thus provides the investor with diversification. In a *nondiversified* fund, the portfolio concentrates in specific industry segments such as petroleum resources or gold-mining issues. Some nondiversified funds also concentrate in specific types of securities such as junk bonds, convertible bonds, municipal bonds, real estate investment trusts (REITs), or preferred stock.

Many of the newly formed closed-end funds are international funds that invest in companies located in specific regions like the Europe Fund or Latin American Investment Fund. Other funds, known as **country funds,** invest only in securities of a particular country. Examples of country funds include

---

[2] Thomas J. Herzfeld, "Battered Beauties? Why Some Closed-Ends May Be Bargains," *Barron's*, August 13, 1990, pp. M27–M29.

[3] Seth Copeland Anderson, "Closed-End Funds versus Market Efficiency," *Journal of Portfolio Management* (Fall 1986): 63–65.

(1) the Austria Fund, (2) Brazil Fund, (3) Chile Fund, (4) France Growth Fund, and (5) Italy Fund. As will be discussed in Chapter 6, closed-end regional and country funds provide a practical way for individuals to make international investments. In addition to international closed-end funds, there are also a number of international mutual funds that will be discussed in Chapter 6.

• Other Types of Closed-End Companies

Individual investors should also be familiar with three other types of closed-end investment companies:

1. Unit trusts A **unit trust** is a special type of investment company. A "unit" or ownership interest in this type of portfolio typically sells for $1,000 and represents a claim to a *fixed* portfolio of securities. The securities in the portfolio are acquired before the units are offered to investors. No manager is needed for the trust once the securities are acquired because the composition of the portfolio does not change. After the initial public offering, the units are traded in the OTC market. The number of ownership units is fixed as in the case of a closed-end fund.

The portfolio of a unit trust normally consists of fixed-income securities that may be tax-exempt municipal bonds, corporate bonds, or government securities. All interest collected on the bonds is paid to the investors, usually on a monthly basis, by the trustee. When the bonds mature, the trustee distributes the principal, and the trust terminates. Information on unit trusts is available in Wiesenberger's *Investment Companies.*

2. Dual funds Another unique type of investment company is the closed-end **dual fund.** It is called a dual fund because it has two types of shares, income and capital. The income shareholder receives all interest and dividends, while the capital shareholder receives all capital gain distributions. This type of fund was popular in the 1970s and early 1980s, but is less popular today due to the elimination of preferential tax treatment for long-term capital gains under the Tax Reform Act of 1986.

3. Primes and scores Beginning in the early 1980s, a number of investment trusts were formed for the purpose of splitting blue-chip common stocks into conservative and speculative components.[4] A separate trust is created for each common stock, and the trust creates three different securities: trust units, primes, and scores. The **prime** (*p*rescribed *r*ight to *i*ncome and *m*aximum *e*quity) security is similar to preferred stock and is analogous to an income share in a dual fund. The **score** (*s*pecial *c*laim *o*n *r*esidual *e*quity) security entitles the holder to all the stock's price appreciation above a specified price when the trust is liquidated. The score is similar to a European warrant and resembles a capital share of a dual fund. The trust units (both a prime and a score), primes, and scores are traded on the AMEX.

---

[4] John Liscio, "Splitting Shares," *Barron's,* March 14, 1988, pp. 13, 72–73.

TABLE 5.2 • Balance Sheet and Income Statement of T. Rowe Price New Horizons Fund, June 30, 1990 (Amounts in Thousands)

Statement of net assets (balance sheet)		
Assets		
Short-term investments:		
Commercial paper	$107,525	
U.S. government obligations	3,063	
Total (cost = $110,588)		$ 110,588
Common stocks and warrants (cost = $668,111)		927,357
Convertible bonds (cost = $31,552)		32,379
Total assets		$1,070,324
Other assets less liabilities		(19,181)
Net assets consisting of:		
Accumulated undistributed net investment income	$ 3,913	
Accumulated undistributed net realized gains	54,791	
Unrealized appreciation of investments	260,609	
Paid-in capital applicable to 78,393,443 shares of $1.00 par value capital stock outstanding: 200,000,000 shares authorized	731,830	
Total Net Assets		$1,051,143
Net Asset Value per Share		$13.41

Studies have found that the combined price of the prime and score exceeds the stock price, often by a considerable amount.[5] This mispricing suggests a possible market inefficiency and offers the potential for arbitrage opportunities.

OVERVIEW OF MUTUAL FUNDS

Mutual funds hold cash, near-cash, stocks, bonds, other types of marketable securities, and, in some cases, real assets. The exact composition of the portfolio depends on the type of fund and the investment objective of the fund. A balance sheet and income statement for a typical mutual fund that stresses capital gains appear in Table 5.2. Mutual funds have very few liabilities

[5] For example, see Robert Jarrow and Maureen O'Hare, "Primes and Scores: An Essay on Market Imperfections," *Journal of Finance* (December 1989): 1263–87.

TABLE 5.2 • Balance Sheet and Income Statement of T. Rowe Price New Horizons Fund, June 30, 1990 (Amounts in Thousands) (*continued*)

Statement of changes in net assets (income statement)

	Six months ended June 30, 1990	Year ended December 31, 1989
Increase (Decrease) in Net Assets		
Operations		
Net investment income	$ 3,153	$ 5,491
Net realized gain on investments	58,552	103,962
Change in unrealized appreciation of investments	12,408	110,005
Increase in net assets from operations	74,113	219,458
Distributions to shareholders		
Net investment income	—	(4,945)
Net realized gain on investments	(3,285)	(71,350)
Decrease in net assets from distributions to shareholders	(3,285)	(76,295)
Capital share transactions		
Sold 10,728 and 20,560 shares	133,880	253,403
Distributions reinvested of 263 and 6,011 shares	3,049	71,889
Redeemed 16,523 and 27,832 shares	(199,735)	(339,904)
Decrease in net assets from capital share transactions	(62,806)	(14,612)
Total increase	8,022	128,551
Net Assets		
Beginning of period	1,043,121	914,570
End of period	$1,051,143	$1,043,121

SOURCE: Annual report (unaudited) provided to shareholders by T. Rowe Price New Horizons Fund. Reprinted by permission of T. Rowe Price Associates, Inc.

because of restrictions on the use of leverage imposed by the Investment Company Act of 1940.

Mutual funds operate like any other business, with a management staff, employees, and facilities. As corporations, they also have a board of directors. The key employees of a fund are the security analysts and portfolio managers, who develop investment strategies. Larger funds, such as T. Rowe Price and Fidelity Investments that offer a *family* or large number of individual funds, ordinarily have an agreement with an *investment adviser.* The investment adviser provides services to all the funds in the family on a fee basis and is responsible for research, security analysis, execution of security transactions, portfolio management, and (possibly) administrative duties. The fund may also contract with another firm to keep records of transfers of cash and securities and maintain shareholder records. A *custodian* may be employed to store and safeguard the securities. As an example, Fidelity Investments Freedom Fund has agreements with an investment adviser, Fidelity Management & Research Company; a servicing agent, Fidelity Service Company; and a custodian, Brown Brothers Harriman & Company. In addition, the fund conducts some of its security transactions through Fidelity Brokerage Services, Inc.

• Historical Development of Mutual Funds

The concept of an open-end investment company (mutual fund) originated in England and found its way to the United States in 1924. Both open-end and closed-end funds were organized in Boston, New York, and Philadelphia. The purpose of these original funds was essentially the same as today's: to offer investors a way to obtain professional investment management, along with diversification in terms of the number of securities in the portfolio.

The stock market crash of 1929 temporarily halted the growth of the investment company industry; in particular, many of the closed-end funds were severely hurt by the market collapse. Nevertheless, in 1940 the assets of closed-end funds were still larger than those of mutual funds. Over the next decades, however, mutual funds outpaced closed-end funds to become the dominant organizational form for investment companies (see Table 5.3). By the end of 1989, mutual fund assets exceeded $922.2 billion, while closed-end funds had grown to only $53.6 billion. (These figures were reported by Wiesenberger Financial Services, whose annual publication *Investment Companies* is an important source of information on investment companies. The 1990 edition contains data on more than 3,600 investment companies including mutual funds, closed-end funds, unit trusts, and variable annuity separate accounts.)

Other indications of the importance of mutual funds are the growth in the number of funds and the increase in the number of shareholders. In 1940, for example, there were 68 mutual funds, representing $448 million in assets and 296,000 shareholder accounts. At the end of 1989, more than 2,900 funds were in existence with 58.3 million shareholder accounts (see Figure 5.1).[6] A

[6] *Mutual Fund Fact Book* (Washington, D.C.: Investment Company Institute, 1990), pp. 78–79.

major development in the growth of the industry was the emergence of **money market** mutual funds, which were first offered in the early 1970s. Through these funds, small investors could invest in money market securities rather than being limited to the deposit accounts available at commercial banks or savings and loan associations. Since about 1978, money market and short-term municipal bond funds have been the most rapidly growing segments of the industry.

• Regulation of Mutual Funds

For all practical purposes, mutual funds and other types of investments were not regulated by the U.S. government prior to the market crash of 1929. In 1936, in the aftermath of the crash, Congress undertook a study of the investment company industry that resulted in the passage of the **Investment Company Act of 1940.**

The Investment Company Act of 1940, which is administered by the Securities and Exchange Commission (SEC), is designed to protect investors from the abuses that were common in the 1920s and to eliminate conflicts of interest for mutual fund managers. The act, however, avoids any attempt to control management's judgment or to offer an opinion on the soundness of funds.

Specifically, the act requires investment companies to (1) provide investors with complete and accurate information; (2) refrain from attempting to concentrate control by "pyramiding" companies or management; (3) use sound accounting practices; (4) allow shareholders to vote on major organizational or policy changes; (5) maintain adequate liquidity and reserves; (6) operate in the interest of shareholders; and (7) ensure that company securities contain adequate provisions to protect the preferences and privileges of shareholders.

The investment company industry often argues that it is the most closely regulated sector of the securities industry. In addition to the Investment Company Act of 1940, investment companies are regulated by a number of other statutes:

1. The individual state law under which the company is formed as a business entity.
2. The state law that governs the sale of securities or the activities of brokers and dealers within the state, often referred to as "blue sky" legislation.
3. The Federal Securities Act of 1933, which requires full financial disclosure through a prospectus.
4. The Federal Securities Exchange Act of 1934, which created the SEC.
5. The Federal Investment Company Amendments Act of 1970, which established standards of "reasonableness" for management fees and sales charges.[7]

[7] *Investment Companies*, p. 25.

TABLE 5.3 • Assets of Closed-End versus Open-End Investment Companies, 1940–1989

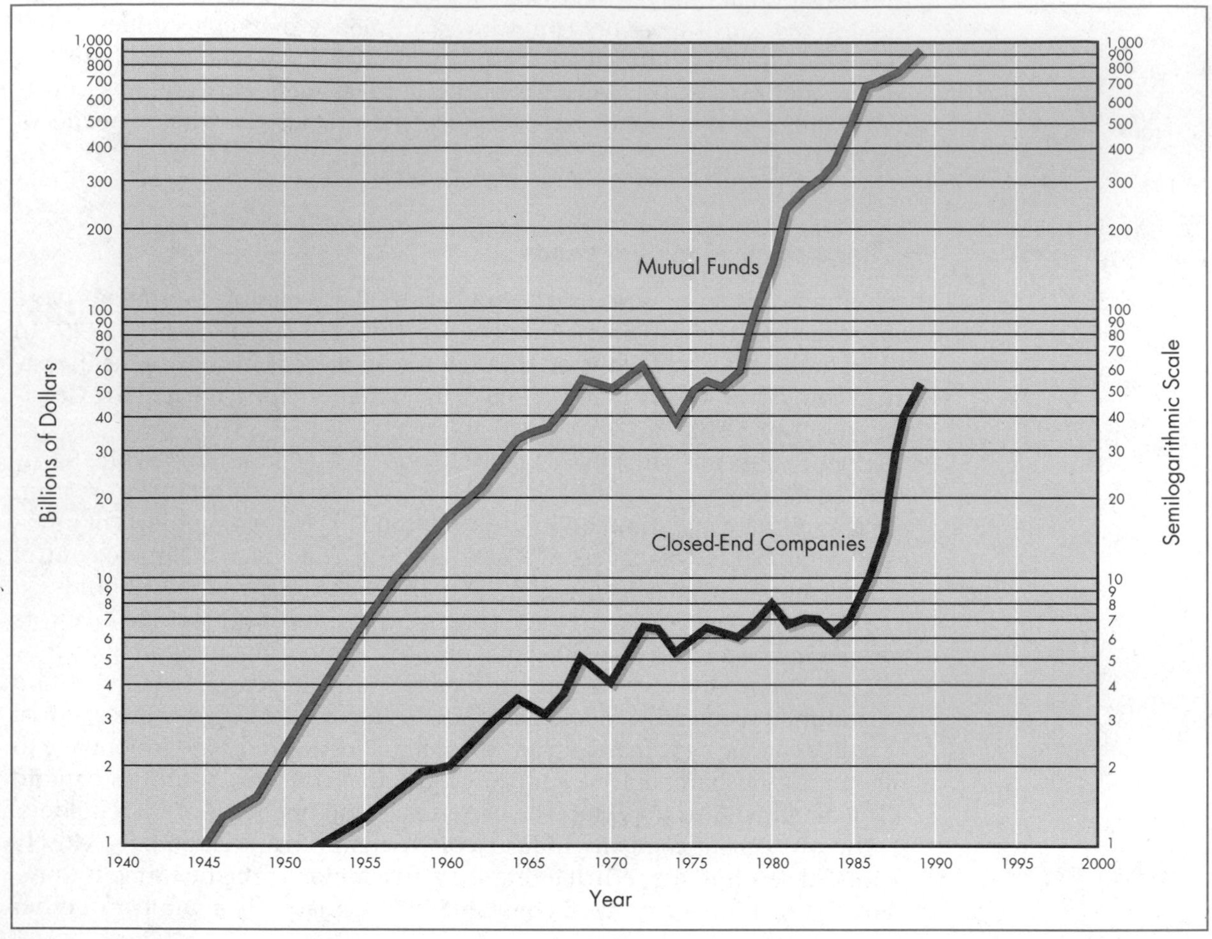

• Ex-Post Holding Period Return for Mutual Funds

As previously discussed, mutual funds issue and redeem shares based on their net asset value (NAV). The "price" of a share of a mutual fund is determined by the NAV of the portfolio of securities. An open-end company will issue or redeem shares at NAV, and in this sense NAV represents the price of the shares. However, some funds may charge fees for issuing or redeeming shares (this point is discussed later in the chapter). The NAV is used to calculate the holding period return (HPR) for an investor in a mutual fund:

$$HPR_t = \frac{NAV_{t+1} - NAV_t + CG_{t+1} + Div_{t+1}}{NAV_t} \quad (5.1)$$

TABLE 5.3 • Assets of Closed-End versus Open-End Investment Companies, 1940–1989 (continued)

Growth of investment company assets since 1940 (thousands of dollars)

Year	Mutual funds	Closed-end companies*	Total	Year	Mutual funds	Closed-end companies*	Total
1989	$922,208,200	$53,581,100	$975,789,300	1970	$50,645,900	$4,024,200	$54,679,100
1988	777,824,200	38,700,000	816,524,200	1969	52,621,400	4,743,700	57,365,100
1987	736,618,200	15,781,500	752,399,700	1968	56,953,600	5,170,800	62,124,400
1986	699,461,000	10,698,400	710,159,400	1967	44,701,302	3,777,100	48,478,402
1985	483,198,600	7,384,000	490,582,600	1966	36,294,600	3,162,900	39,457,500
1984	357,334,100	6,329,200	363,663,300	1964	30,370,300	3,523,413	33,893,713
1983	302,925,800	7,098,000	310,023,800	1962	22,408,900	2,783,219	25,192,119
1982	270,880,000	7,179,200	278,059,200	1960	17,383,300	2,083,898	19,467,198
1981	230,395,100	6,923,500	237,318,600	1958	13,242,388	1,931,402	15,173,790
1980	138,333,100	8,053,201	146,386,301	1956	9,046,431	1,525,748	10,572,179
1979	97,053,100	6,873,179	103,926,279	1954	6,109,290	1,246,351	7,355,641
1978	58,144,400	6,116,700	64,261,100	1952	3,931,407	1,011,089	4,942,496
1977	51,479,800	6,283,700	57,763,500	1950	2,530,563	871,962	3,402,525
1976	54,174,600	6,639,046	60,813,646	1948	1,505,762	767,028	2,272,790
1975	48,706,300	5,861,300	54,567,600	1946	1,311,108	851,409	2,162,517
1974	38,545,599	5,294,000	43,839,599	1944	882,191	739,021	1,621,212
1973	49,310,700	6,622,700	55,936,700	1942	486,850	557,264	1,044,114
1972	62,456,500	6,742,800	69,199,300	1940	447,959	613,589	1,061,548
1971	58,159,800	5,324,300	63,484,100				

OURCE: Sources of data: Open-end: Weisenberger Investment Companies Service, 1960–1989, Investment Company Institute, 940–1958 (data include ICI-member companies only). Closed-end: Weisenberger Investment Companies Service, 1948–1989, nvestment Company Institute. Reprinted from *Investment Companies* (New York: Weisenberger Investment Companies Service, 990), p. 12.

Includes funded debt bank loans.

The calculation of HPR for mutual funds includes the two types of distributions to shareholders: (1) capital gains (CG) and (2) dividends (Div). In addition to these two sources of income, the NAV itself can change over the holding period, causing capital gains or losses. This formula excludes sales or "load" fees that might be charged by the fund and therefore calculates a *gross HPR.*

To illustrate, assume that you purchased 100 shares of the International Stock Fund, offered by T. Rowe Price, for $10.24 per share on December 29, 1989. The fund paid $.16 per share in dividends and $.36 per share in capital gains during February 1990. The NAV of the fund on December 31, 1990, was $8.81. The HPR is

$$HPR_{1990} = \frac{\$8.81 - \$10.24 + \$.36 + \$.16}{\$10.24} \tag{5.2}$$

$$= -.0889 = -8.89\%$$

FIGURE 5.1
Mutual Fund Growth

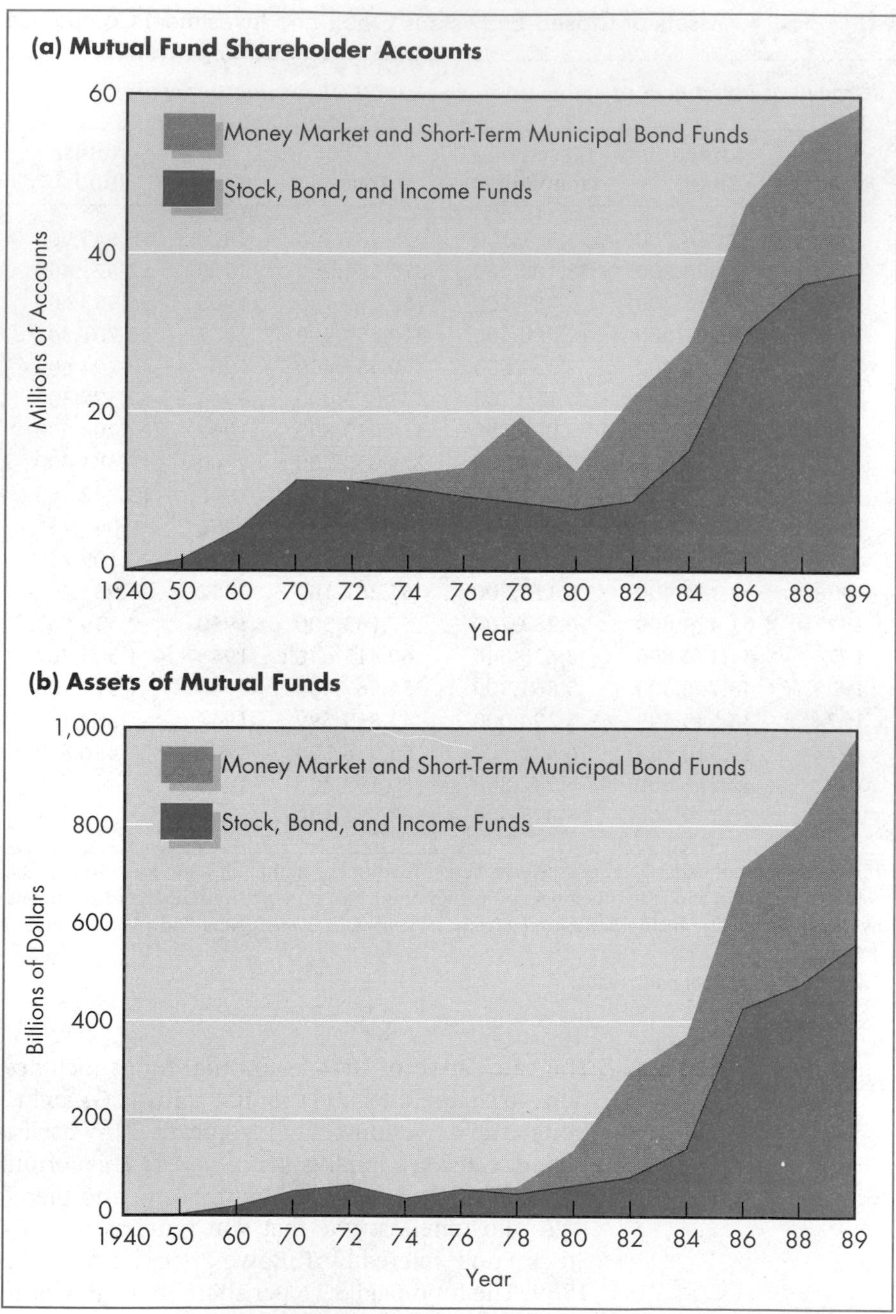

SOURCE: *Mutual Fund Fact Book* (Washington, D.C.: Investment Company Institute, 1990), p. 23.

The negative return of 8.89 percent reflects the change in the value of the dollar during 1990 as well as changes in the prices of the foreign stocks held by the fund.

Under a truth-in-advertising rule adopted by the SEC in 1988, mutual funds must report HPRs calculated using strict guidelines. If a fund advertises its historical return performance, it must provide 1-, 5-, and 10-year annual HPRs as well as the most recent 30-day current yield. The returns must also reflect both premiums and discounts from NAV. In addition, total expenses that investors will incur must be reported. These new regulations should help investors monitor historical HPRs.

MUTUAL FUND CHARACTERISTICS

Mutual funds can be analyzed in a number of ways. An individual investor who is considering investing in mutual funds should be aware of the differences between load and no-load funds, other fees that may be charged, and the variety of investment objectives that funds may pursue.

• Load versus No-Load Mutual Funds

A mutual fund can operate either as a load or a no-load fund. A **load fund** charges sales commissions on the purchase, and sometimes on the sale, of shares; there are no sales charges on a **no-load fund.**

Historically, the sales charge or load has been 8.5 percent, charged as a *front-end* fee. For example, on a $10,000 investment, a fee of $850 would be deducted, leaving $9,150 for the actual purchase of shares. Load funds are marketed through a commissioned sales force; the fee is used to compensate the salespersons. No-load funds are marketed directly, by mail or telephone, without a commissioned sales force. In 1989, of total sales of $120.7 billion of stock, bond, and income funds, 66.1 percent, or $79.8 billion, were by load funds; 33.9 percent, or $40.9 billion, by no-load funds.[8] The number of no-load funds is increasing rapidly, but load funds still outnumber no-load funds.

If a load fund charges the full 8.5 percent front-end load, the charge is substantially above the brokerage commission incurred on the purchase of a closed-end fund. However, the investor also pays a brokerage commission when the closed-end fund shares are sold, but does not pay a load fee on the sale of a front-end load fund. Load fees and brokerage commissions can be avoided entirely by investing in a no-load fund.

Studies that test for possible differences in the investment performances of load versus no-load funds generally find that, on average, investors realize higher *net* returns from no-load funds.[9] On the other hand, it appears that the

---

[8] *Mutual Fund Fact Book,* p. 87.

[9] For example, see E. Theodore Veit, John M. Cheney, Jeff Madura, and Mike Lucas, "Mutual Fund Returns and the Investment Horizon: Load versus No-Load Funds," *Akron Business and Economic Review* (Winter 1988): 104–18.

operating expenses of load funds (excluding load fees) are somewhat lower than those of no-load funds. Therefore, if an investor has a "long" investment horizon, it might be advantageous to incur an initial load fee in exchange for lower annual operating expenses.

Recently, a number of traditional no-load funds have begun to charge a load of 2 to 3 percent, creating a third class—**low-load** funds. For example, the industry or sector funds offered by Fidelity Investments charge a 3 percent load fee. Fidelity's Select Electric Utility Portfolio had an offering price of $12.05, with a NAV of $11.69, according to the May 24, 1991 *Wall Street Journal.* The difference of $.36 represents a 3 percent load, added to the NAV.

It is becoming increasingly difficult to determine the actual cost of investing in some mutual funds. The reason is that in addition to the traditional front-end loads, new funds may have *back-end* loads or exit fees plus other charges assessed as annual operating expenses. An investor should check the prospectus of mutual funds to determine the buying and selling fees.

• Other Types of Fees and Expenses

A mutual fund may charge several other fees as well. The more important are described in the following paragraphs.

DIRECT CHARGES AGAINST NET ASSET VALUE Both load and no-load funds incur operating expenses, including management fees, salaries, costs of office space and facilities, investment adviser fees, accountants' fees, postage, printing, and other expenses. Brokerage commissions, however, are included directly in the calculation of NAV and are not reflected in operating expenses. Publications that provide data on mutual funds now ordinarily include **expense ratios** for the funds, calculated as

$$\text{expense ratio} = \frac{\text{operating expenses (excluding brokerage cost)}}{\text{NAV}} \tag{5.3}$$

On an annual basis, the expense ratio may be as low as 0.2 of 1 percent (.002) or as large as 6 percent. Many funds, by provisions in the prospectus, limit expenses to 1 to 2 percent of NAV. Lipper Analytical Services has also reported that the trend in expenses is definitely upward, from 0.9 percent in 1980 to 1.2 percent in 1990. Expenses are also related to the type of fund. For 1990, expenses averaged 1.3 percent for diversified stock funds, 1.7 percent for specialty sector funds, 0.8 percent for bond funds, and 0.65 percent for money market funds. Funds with fewer assets also generally have higher expense

CHARGES FOR DISTRIBUTION SERVICES In 1980, in **Rule 12b–1** the SEC allowed funds to establish a *Distribution Service Agreement.* This agreement permits funds to charge distribution and marketing expenses, directly or indirectly, to NAV. Thus, Rule 12b–1 allows both load and no-load funds to

RESEARCH BOX

Brokerage Commissions and Mutual Funds

May 1, 1975, has historical significance for investors. The century-old fixed brokerage commission rate system ended on "Mayday." Individual and institutional investors were finally able to negotiate for the lowest brokerage rates, and brokerage firms were free to set their own rates. Full-service and full-fee brokerage firms were soon joined by reduced-service discount brokers.

Mutual funds, as one of the largest investors, should have benefited from Mayday. Their volume of trading should have enabled them to gain a favorable negotiating position with brokerage firms. If they could negotiate lower brokerage fees, their costs would decline, increasing their profits and thus the returns to their stockholders. Lower brokerage fees might also enable funds to achieve more complete diversification at lower costs by allowing them to increase the number of different stocks in their portfolio, thereby reducing its risk.

Kim and Wu examined the risk-return performance of a sample of 65 mutual funds before and after Mayday. The data they collected showed that for trades of 10,000 or more shares, the commission rate declined from 14 cents per share in 1975 to approximately 8 cents per share in 1984. For smaller trades of 200–299 shares, however, which individuals might make, the commission rate increased from 32 cents per share to slightly more than 40 cents per share. Despite the decline in the commission rate per share paid by institutional investors, the study concluded that "mutual funds have benefited only marginally from the reduction in commission rate." The study did find that funds reported slightly higher HPRs but the lower cost per transaction was offset by substantially more transactions. The lower brokerage costs seemed to encourage funds to trade more.

SOURCE: Moon K. Kim and Chunchi Wu, "Performance of Mutual Funds in the Pre versus Post-Mayday Periods," *Quarterly Journal of Business and Economics* (Spring 1989): 61–84.

charge for commissions or other distribution expenses and enables low-load and no-load funds to have load fees that are actually above the stated no-load or low-load fees. By most estimates over half of all funds now use 12b–1 plans. Critics of the industry contend that some funds use the 12b–1 rule to hide fees and that brokers and fund managements do not explain these charges to investors.[10] Obviously, investors should check the prospectus of a fund carefully to determine the actual charges and expenses.

The following example shows the importance of fees and expenses in fund selection:[11]

[10] Jack Willoughby, "Watch Out for the Fee Grabbers!" *Money,* May 1990, pp. 134–39.

[11] Gerald W. Perritt, "A Look behind the Bottom Line," *Barron's,* May 19, 1986, p. 53. Reprinted courtesy of *Barron's Weekly.*

Mutual Fund Expenses: A Sample Worksheet

Fund	Front-end load	Management fee	Expenses to NAV	12b–1 charges	Redemption fee	Transaction costs	Total annual expenses
Acorn	0.0%	0.6%	0.2%	0.00%	0.0%	1.3%	2.10%
Fidelity Magellan	3.1	0.8	0.3	0.00	1.0	5.0	10.20
Keystone S–3	0.0	0.7	0.3	1.25	4.0	5.5	11.75

The example was constructed assuming that the fund was held for one year and that the **portfolio turnover** rate was 0.4 times a year. The portfolio turnover rate indicates how much security trading takes place in the portfolio over a certain period of time. For mutual funds, it is usually calculated as the lesser of the value of security purchases or sales divided by average portfolio assets; higher ratios indicate more trading activity by the portfolio manager. This example shows that funds with no front-end load are not necessarily the cheapest funds to acquire. It should also be remembered that Rule 12b–1 charges, management fees, operating expenses, and transaction costs are incurred every year, while a front-end or redemption fee is assessed only once.

TAXES Mutual funds, as regulated investment companies under Subchapter M of the Internal Revenue Code, do not pay federal income taxes on the dividends, interest, and capital gains they earn. To receive this tax-exempt status, funds must distribute 90 percent or more of their income to their shareholders. After funds deduct their operating expenses and fees, most funds distribute the remaining income to their shareholders, who then incur the tax liability on both capital gains and income distributions. The shareholders have a tax liability whether the income is actually received or is reinvested in the fund (by the purchase of additional shares).

A 1976 change in the tax code allows mutual funds to invest in tax-free bonds (municipals). The interest received (or reinvested) by the shareholder is not subject to federal income tax. Capital gains on municipal bonds, however, represent taxable income to shareholders.

In summary, mutual fund investors should consider the impact of taxes when making investment decisions. For example, corporate bond funds or income stock funds are likely to distribute taxable income monthly to their shareholders. An "aggressive growth" common stock fund, however, may receive a limited amount of taxable dividends from its investments. The returns from this fund would be in the form of capital gains over a long period of time so that the tax liability is postponed until the gains are realized.

• Investment Objectives of Mutual Funds

In selecting mutual funds, investors need to be aware of the different investment objectives of the various funds and how these objectives may affect the choice of a fund.

CATEGORIES OF MUTUAL FUNDS Mutual funds differ greatly in their stated investment objectives and the portfolio strategies they have designed to achieve these objectives. Traditionally, funds could be neatly categorized into common stock or balanced funds. *Balanced* funds were designed to provide a "complete investment program" for shareholders; the fund's portfolio included common stocks, preferred stocks, and bonds. *Common stock* funds were not intended to offer a completely diversified portfolio since they consisted primarily of only one type of security—common stocks.

By 1975, there were 7 major categories of funds based on their stated investment objective. By the end of 1989, the categories had grown to 22. Today, the industry's slogan seems to be "There's a mutual fund to meet every investor's needs."

Mutual fund reporting services, such as Wiesenberger Investment Companies Service, use the stated investment objective to categorize each fund. Table 5.4 briefly describes the 22 categories. As the table indicates, balanced funds still cxist, but the traditional category of common stock funds has been expanded to four categories: aggressive growth, growth, growth and income, and income-equity. The traditional categories have been supplemented by bond funds and by specialized categories such as global equity, global bond, option/income, and flexible.

The number of funds and level of assets in each of the 22 categories are shown in Table 5.5. Money market funds are the most common type of fund with the highest level of assets. The 463 money market funds had assets of $358.7 billion in December 1989, representing a 31.7 percent increase from the 1988 year-end total of $272.3 billion.

USEFULNESS OF INVESTMENT OBJECTIVES TO INVESTORS The stated objective obviously provides a means of classifying a mutual fund. But once the fund is classified, is this information useful for investment decision making?

Numerous academic studies, dating back to the 1960s and continuing into the 1980s, have analyzed the relationship between investment performance and fund classification. Generally, these studies confirmed expectations that funds in a single category would display similar risk-return characteristics. For example, for the common stock categories (aggressive growth, growth, growth and income, and income-equity), the standard deviation (σ) of returns and beta (β) should be larger for the aggressive growth category than for the income-equity category. During a bull market, the holding period return (HPR) on the aggressive growth category should be greater than the HPR on the income-equity category. By following their stated investment objective,

TABLE 5.4 • Types of Mutual Funds

1. **Aggressive growth funds** seek maximum capital gains as their investment objective. Current income is not a significant factor. Some may invest in stocks of businesses that are somewhat out of the mainstream, such as fledgling companies, new industries, companies fallen on hard times, or industries temporarily out of favor. Some may also use specialized investment techniques such as option writing or short-term trading.
2. **Balanced funds** generally have a three-part investment objective: (1) to conserve the investor's principal; (2) to pay current income; and (3) to promote long-term growth of both principal and income. Balanced funds have a portfolio mix of bonds, preferred stocks, and common stocks.
3. **Corporate bond funds,** like income funds, seek a high level of income. They do so by buying bonds of corporations for the majority of the fund's portfolio. The rest of the portfolio may be in U.S. Treasury bonds or bonds issued by a federal agency.
4. **Flexible portfolio funds** may be 100 percent invested in stocks *or* bonds *or* money market instruments, depending on market conditions. These funds give the money managers the greatest flexibility in anticipating or responding to economic changes.
5. **GNMA or Ginnie Mae funds** invest in mortgage securities backed by the Government National Mortgage Association (GNMA). To qualify for this category, the majority of the portfolio must always be invested in mortgage-backed securities.
6. **Global bond funds** invest in the debt securities of companies and countries worldwide, including the United States.
7. **Global equity funds** invest in securities traded worldwide, including the United States. Compared to direct investments, global funds offer investors an easier avenue to investing abroad. The funds' professional money managers handle the trading and record-keeping details and deal with differences in currencies, languages, time zones, laws and regulations, and business customs and practices. In addition to another layer of diversification, global funds add another layer of risk—exchange-rate risk.
8. **Growth funds** invest in the common stock of well-established companies. Their primary aim is to produce an increase in the value of their investments (capital gains) rather than a flow of dividends. Investors who buy a growth fund are more interested in seeing the fund's share price rise than in receiving income from dividends.
9. **Growth and income funds** invest mainly in the common stock of companies that have an increasing share value but also a solid record of paying dividends. This type of fund attempts to combine long-term capital growth with a steady stream of income.
10. **High-yield bond funds** maintain at least two-thirds of their portfolios in lower-rated corporate bonds (Baa or lower by Moody's rating service and BBB or lower by Standard & Poor's rating service). In return for a generally higher yield, investors must bear a greater degree of risk than for higher-rated bonds.
11. **Income (bond) funds** seek a high level of current income for their shareholders by investing at all times in a mix of corporate and government bonds.

funds determine their risk-return characteristics. A word of warning: these generalizations are appropriate for mutual funds as a whole, but not for individual funds or for a small random sample of funds. Table 5.6, a good illustration of this point, shows that the mean annual gross HPR of the income-equity category was higher than that of the aggressive category over the period 1969–

TABLE 5.4 • Types of Mutual Funds (continued)

12. **Income (equity) funds** seek a high level of current income for their shareholders by investing primarily in equity securities of companies with good dividend-paying records.
13. **Income (mixed) funds** seek a high level of current income for their shareholders by investing in income-producing securities, including both equities and debt instruments.
14. **International funds** invest in equity securities of companies located outside the United States. Two-thirds of their portfolios must be so invested at all times for them to be classified as international funds.
15. **Long-term municipal bond funds** invest in bonds issued by states and municipalities to finance schools, highways, hospitals, airports, bridges, water and sewer works, and other public projects. In most cases, income earned on these securities is not taxed by the federal government, but may be taxed under state and local laws. For some taxpayers, portions of income earned on these securities may be subject to the federal alternative minimum tax.
16. **Money market mutual funds** invest in the short-term securities sold in the money market. These are generally the safest, most stable securities available, including Treasury bills, certificates of deposit of large banks, and commercial paper (the short-term IOUs of large U.S. corporations).
17. **Option/income funds** seek a high current return by investing primarily in dividend-paying common stocks on which call options are traded on national securities exchanges. Current return generally consists of dividends, premiums from writing options, net short-term gains from sales of portfolio securities on exercises of options or otherwise, and any profits from closing purchase transactions.
18. **Precious metals/gold funds** maintain two-thirds of their portfolios invested in securities associated with gold, silver, and other precious metals.
19. **Short-term municipal bond funds** invest in municipal securities with relatively short maturities. These are also known as tax-exempt money market funds. For some taxpayers, portions of income from these securities may be subject to the federal alternative minimum tax.
20. **State municipal bond funds—long term** work just like other long-term municipal bond funds (see above) except their portfolios contain the issues of only one state. A resident of that state has the advantage of receiving income free of both federal and state tax. For some taxpayers, portions of income from these securities may be subject to the federal alternative minimum tax.
21. **State municipal bond funds—short term** work just like other short-term municipal bond funds (see above) except their portfolios contain the issues of only one state. A resident of that state has the advantage of receiving income free of both federal and state tax. For some taxpayers, portions of income from these securities may be subject to the federal alternative minimum tax.
22. **U.S. government income funds** invest in a variety of government securities. These include U.S. Treasury bonds, federally guaranteed mortgage-backed securities, and other government notes.

SOURCE: *Mutual Fund Fact Book* (Washington, D.C.: Investment Company Institute, 1990), pp. 17–18.

1983. The standard deviation for the income-equity classification is larger than might be expected, however, relative to the growth category and the growth and income category.

Wiesenberger's *Investment Companies* is a good source of information about the volatility of mutual funds in bull and bear markets. A section in the

TABLE 5.5 • Mutual Funds by Investment Objective: Number of Funds and Year-End Assets (Billions of Dollars)

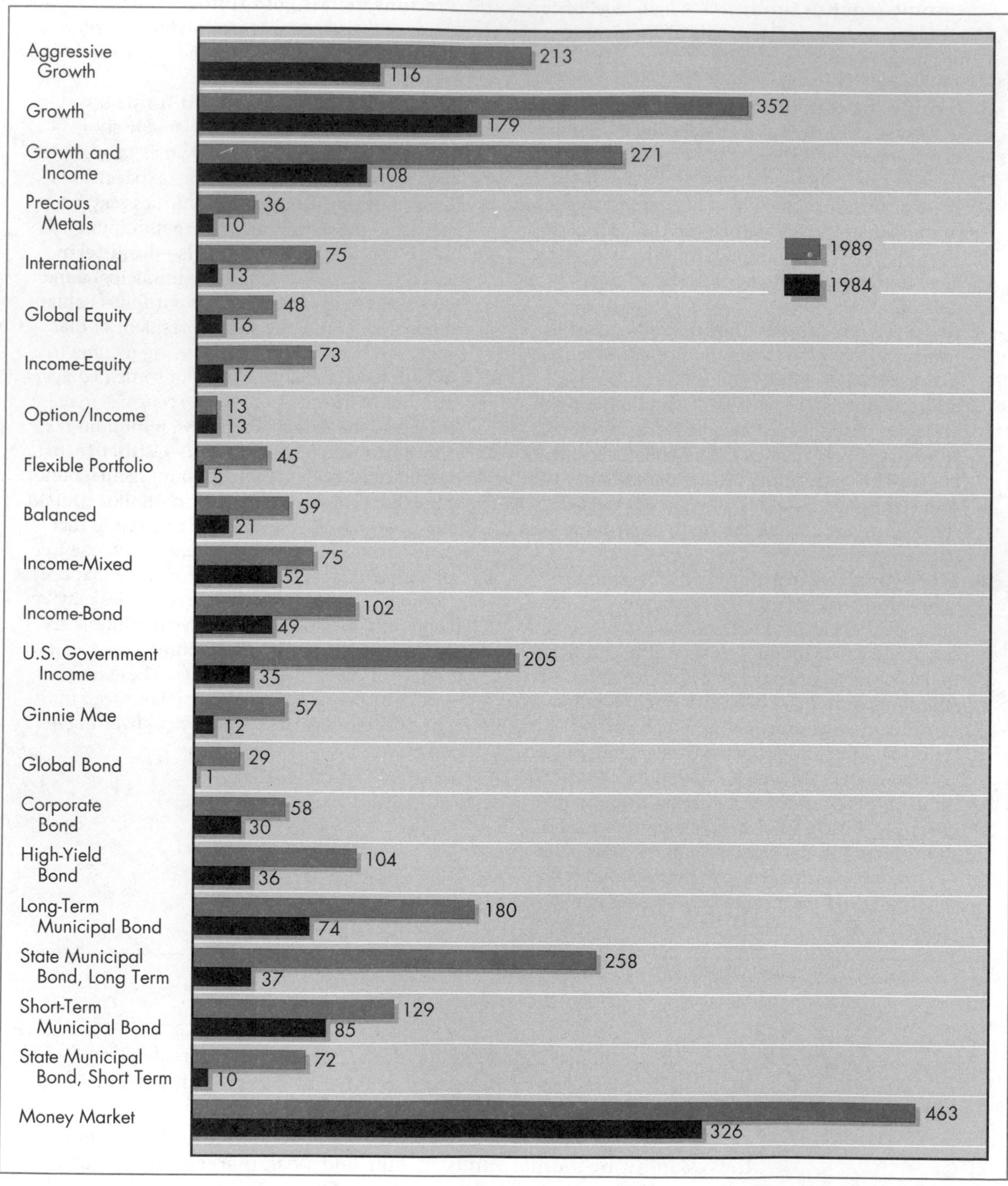

TABLE 5.5 • Mutual Funds by Investment Objective: Number of Funds and Year-End Assets (Billions of Dollars) (*continued*)

Mutual fund assets classified by investment objective, year-end (billions of dollars)

Investment objective	1988	1989	Percentage change
1. Aggressive growth	$ 29.5	$ 37.2	+26.1%
2. Growth	50.5	66.1	+30.9
3. Growth and income	70.9	91.4	+28.9
4. Precious metals	3.2	4.1	+28.1
5. International	6.8	9.9	+45.6
6. Global equity	11.1	13.7	+23.4
7. Income-equity	17.5	22.9	+30.9
8. Option/income	5.3	3.8	−28.3
9. Flexible portfolio	3.5	4.1	+17.1
10. Balanced	9.5	13.5	+42.1
11. Income-mixed	8.8	15.2	+72.7
12. Income-bond	10.7	13.4	+25.2
13. U.S. government income	82.7	81.4	− 1.6
14. Ginnie Mae	28.7	28.2	− 1.7
15. Global bond	3.0	3.1	+ 3.3
16. Corporate bond	10.5	11.7	+11.4
17. High-yield bond	33.4	28.5	−14.7
18. Long-term municipal bond	54.3	64.5	+18.8
19. State municipal bond, long term	32.4	41.2	+27.2
Total Long-Term Fund Assets	$472.3	$553.9	+17.3%
1. Short-term municipal bond	$ 54.5	$ 52.8	− 3.1
2. State municipal bond, short term	11.1	16.5	+48.6
3. Money market	272.3	358.7	+31.7
Total Short-Term Fund Assets	$337.9	$428.0	+26.7
Total Mutual Fund Assets	$810.2	$981.9	+21.2

SOURCE: *Mutual Fund Fact Book* (Washington, D.C.: Investment Company Institute, 1990), pp. 29, 44.

TABLE 5.6 • Risk and Return by Mutual Fund Classification, 1969–1983

Classification	Sample size	Standard deviation of return	Mean annual gross holding period return
Aggressive growth	12	2.98%	10.48%
Growth	21	2.39	10.45
Growth and income	20	2.31	10.95
Income-equity	10	2.74	11.38

SOURCE: Risk and return measures computed from data available in *Investment Companies.* Reprinted by permission of Wiesenberger Investment Companies Service, Division of Warren, Gorham & Lamont, Inc.

annual edition, entitled "Price Volatility of Mutual Fund Shares," provides the ratio of each mutual fund's percentage price change to the percentage change in the S&P 500 Index. The ratios are provided for each bull and bear market over approximately the last 10 years. For example, in the 1989 edition, Acorn Fund had a ratio of 0.88 for the bear market from August 31, 1987, to November 30, 1987, and a ratio of 1.03 for the bull market from November 30, 1987, to December 29, 1989.[12] Acorn Fund, with an objective of "maximum capital gains," declined only 0.88 times as much as the S&P 500 in the bear market but increased 1.03 times as much during the bull market. Acorn was, therefore, successful in adjusting to changing market conditions. These volatility ratios are provided for each mutual fund covered by Wiesenberger and are grouped by fund classifications. These ratios of volatility are useful to investors but should not be confused with the beta of a mutual fund.

INVESTING IN MUTUAL FUNDS

Investing in mutual funds can be a complex process in which the investor must consider a number of variables before making the investment decision. These variables as well as sources of information about them are examined in the following paragraphs.

• Sources of Information

As with any investment, an investor must obtain information in order to make informed investment decisions about mutual funds. Investment companies are required to furnish potential investors with a prospectus that pro-

[12] *Investment Companies,* p. 807.

• **INTEREST BOX**

Money Market Accounts versus Money Market Mutual Funds

Money market mutual funds (MMMFs) were introduced in the early 1970s. By the end of the decade, their assets had grown to $45.2 billion, which represented almost half of the total assets of all categories of mutual funds. MMMFs were developed to provide individual investors a practical avenue for investing in money market securities such as Treasury bills, negotiable certificates of deposit of large banks, and commercial paper issued by large U.S. corporations. Prior to this time, individuals typically used savings accounts (time deposits) at local banks or savings and loan associations to invest their short-term funds.

The immediate success and popularity of MMMFs prompted commercial banks to introduce money market deposit accounts (MMDAs) in 1982. These new deposit accounts were designed to offer interest rates competitive with MMMFs and are also federally insured. Many financial observers thought that MMMFs would virtually disappear with the introduction of MMDAs. Despite these forecasts, MMMFs experienced spectacular growth during the 1980s. At the end of 1989, the total investment in MMMFs reached $358.7 billion, or approximately 37 percent of the total assets of mutual funds.

Why did MMMFs continue to grow very rapidly in spite of the competition from MMDAs? In a study using national data through 1986, Cara Lown found that interest rates on MMMFs are always higher than those on MMDAs. Both types of investments continue to exist because they have unique characteristics that appeal to different types of investors. The data analyzed by Lown indicate that in the short run the typical investor is unlikely to move money from MMDAs to MMMFs to take advantage of the higher interest rates. In the long run, however, significant differences in the interest rates could result in mass movements of funds to MMMFs.

In May 1991, the interest rate on MMMFs was approximately 5.9 percent versus 5.2 percent on MMDAs. This information is available weekly in *Barron's*.

SOURCE: Cara S. Lown, "Money Market Deposit Accounts versus Money Market Mutual Funds," *Economic Review* (November 1987): 29–38.

vides detailed information about the shares. The prospectus provides the most complete and comprehensive source of information.

In addition, Wiesenberger Investment Companies Service provides detailed data about mutual funds and closed-end investment companies in four publications:

1. *Investment Companies* Published annually, *Investment Companies* is based on data compiled from the reports that various investment companies issue to their respective stockholders. Figure 5.2 is an example of the information provided for each fund.
2. *Mutual Funds Panorama* This annual publication "includes virtually all mutual funds registered for sale in the United States, regardless of size." *Mutual Funds Panorama* provides summary data on each fund, including the fund's objective, year organized, total net assets and per-

FIGURE 5.2 • Example of Mutual Fund Data

T. ROWE PRICE NEW HORIZONS FUND, INC.

The objective of the fund is long-term growth of capital through investment primarily in small growth companies which management believes have the potential to become major companies in the future. Investments are sought in such fields as science and technology, consumer and business services, retailing, entertainment and leisure, and energy, among others. The fund may also invest in larger companies which offer improved growth possibilities because of rejuvenated management, changes in product, or some other development that might stimulate earnings growth.

At the 1989 year-end, the fund had 90.2% of its assets in common stocks, of which a substantial proportion was in five industry groups: computer software & services (11.1% of assets); miscellaneous business services (10.4%); media & communications (10.2%); specialty merchandising (9.6%), and hospital supplies & management (9.3%). The major stock commitments were Home Depot (2.4%); Lin Broadcasting (2.3%); King World Productions (2.2%); Autodesk (2.1%), and Oracle Systems (1.8%). Turnover in the latest year was 45.1% of average assets. Unrealized appreciation in the portfolio at the year-end was 23.8% of total net assets.

Statistical History

	AT YEAR-ENDS				% of Assets in			ANNUAL DATA				
Year	Total Net Assets ($)	Number of Shareholders	Net Asset Value Per Share ($)	Yield (%)	Cash & Gov't	Bonds & Preferreds	Common Stocks	Income Dividends ($)	Capital Gains Distribution ($)	Expense Ratio (%)	Offering Price ($) High	Low
1989	1,043,120,750	57,085	12.43	0.5	8	2	90	0.07	1.01	0.79	14.30	10.69
1988	914,570,091	65,175	10.74	0.6	10	1	89	0.07	0.03	0.78	11.56	9.27
1987	855,460,756	73,130	9.51	0.5	11	1	88	0.06	1.93	0.78	15.69	9.35
1986	1,034,082,754	80,815	12.38	0.6	5	1	94	0.09	2.64	0.73	17.35	12.32
1985	1,474,740,973	96,075	15.13	0.9	6	1	93	0.14	0.52	0.70	15.23	12.32
1984	1,273,033,157	99,044	12.78	1.0	13	—	87	0.16	3.72*	0.71	18.56	11.81
1983	1,355,433,903	99,027	17.90	1.1	8	—	92	0.20	0.758	0.61	21.35	15.31
1982	1,198,534,092	64,309	15.90	1.9	9	—	91	0.35	2.61*	0.56	16.08	10.11
1981	875,770,863	45,855	16.06	2.5	15	—	85	0.321	1.678*	0.53	19.60	14.07
1980	970,826,261	35,649	19.53	1.2	11	—	89	0.232	0.368	0.54	19.94	10.62
1979	604,843,958	29,596	13.01	1.2	15	—	85	0.157	—	0.60	13.01	9.65

* Includes short-term capital gains of $0.17 in 1982; $0.13 in 1981; $0.29 in 1984.

An assumed investment of $10,000 in this fund, with capital gains accepted in shares and income dividends reinvested, is illustrated below. The explanation in the introduction to this section must be read in conjunction with this illustration.

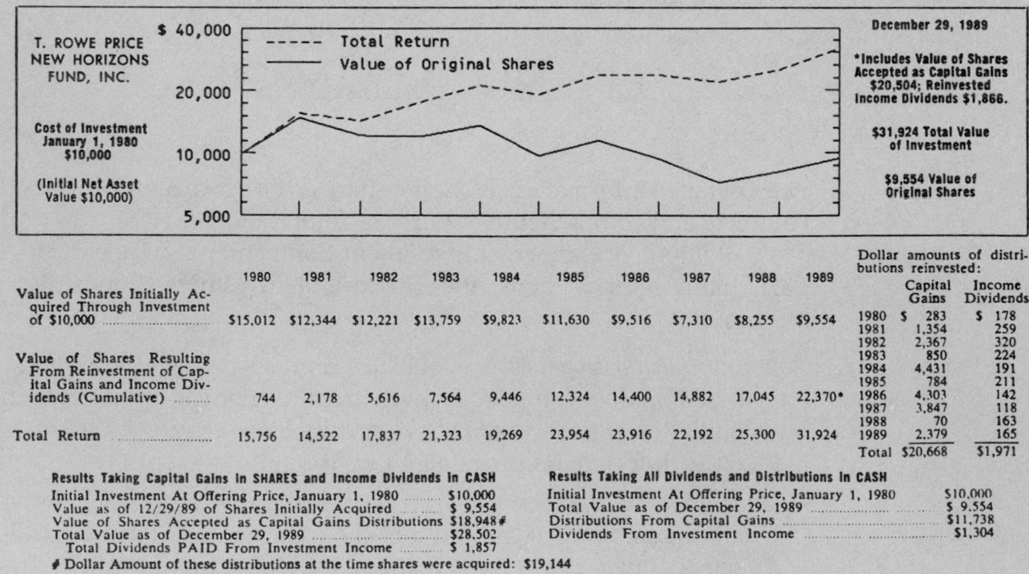

	1980	1981	1982	1983	1984	1985	1986	1987	1988	1989
Value of Shares Initially Acquired Through Investment of $10,000	$15,012	$12,344	$12,221	$13,759	$9,823	$11,630	$9,516	$7,310	$8,255	$9,554
Value of Shares Resulting From Reinvestment of Capital Gains and Income Dividends (Cumulative)	744	2,178	5,616	7,564	9,446	12,324	14,400	14,882	17,045	22,370*
Total Return	15,756	14,522	17,837	21,323	19,269	23,954	23,916	22,192	25,300	31,924

Dollar amounts of distributions reinvested:

	Capital Gains	Income Dividends
1980	$ 283	$ 178
1981	1,354	259
1982	2,367	320
1983	850	224
1984	4,431	191
1985	784	211
1986	4,303	142
1987	3,847	118
1988	70	163
1989	2,379	165
Total	$20,668	$1,971

Results Taking Capital Gains in SHARES and Income Dividends in CASH

Initial Investment At Offering Price, January 1, 1980	$10,000
Value as of 12/29/89 of Shares Initially Acquired	$ 9,554
Value of Shares Accepted as Capital Gains Distributions	$18,948#
Total Value as of December 29, 1989	$28,502
Total Dividends PAID From Investment Income	$ 1,857

\# Dollar Amount of these distributions at the time shares were acquired: $19,144

Results Taking All Dividends and Distributions in CASH

Initial Investment At Offering Price, January 1, 1980	$10,000
Total Value as of December 29, 1989	$ 9,554
Distributions From Capital Gains	$11,738
Dividends From Investment Income	$1,304

SOURCE: *Investment Companies* (New York: Wiesenberger Investment Company Service, 1990), p. 552.

share net asset value, dividend and capital gain distribution over the last 12 months, sales charges, and the expense ratio. A separate section also provides the addresses of the listed funds.

3. *Management Results* A monthly publication, *Management Results* reports the most current data on HPRs for individual funds. The most recent quarter's portfolio composition—in terms of cash and government securities, bonds and preferred stock, and common stock—is also provided.
4. *Current Dividend Record* A monthly publication, *Current Dividend Record* furnishes the most current data by fund on "investment income and capital gains distributions declared, and asset value changes during the preceding six and twelve months."

Barron's and the *Wall Street Journal* provide weekly and daily quotations on a large number of mutual funds. *Barron's* provides more detailed information, including the most recent and last 12-month dividend and capital gains distributions, along with the 52-week high and low quotations and the weekly high, low, close, and change in NAV. *Barron's* also publishes a quarterly report on performance.

With the growing popularity of mutual funds, a number of other publications have begun to report quarterly or semiannual performance data on the larger funds. *Money, Forbes, Consumer Reports,* and *Business Week* are four of the better known of these magazines. *Business Week* also offers the "Mutual Fund Scoreboard" on diskette, which provides raw data and "over 25 key performance factors and data fields on each fund."

In addition, some specialized publications, such as *Mutual Fund Forecaster* published by the Institute for Econometric Research, provide general information as well as specific buy-and-sell recommendations.

• Determining an Investment Objective

As a prerequisite to any investment decision, careful consideration should be given to formulating specific objectives. This step may appear obvious, but its importance should not be overlooked. The objective might be focused in terms of the appropriate risk-return trade-offs but should also include consideration of taxes, investment horizon, liquidity, and the costs of investing.

Once an individual has clearly formulated his or her investment objective, it can be matched with the 22 categories of funds previously discussed. For example, does the objective suggest an equity fund, which stresses long-term capital gains, or a fixed income fund, which provides price stability and current income?

• Services Provided by Mutual Funds

Most of the larger funds offer their shareholders a number of services that may be important in achieving a specific investment objective. The more common services include the following:

1. *Periodic Investment Plans* After an account is opened, for a minimum amount that can be as small as $1,000, additional investments can be made in amounts as small as $50. These additional investments can be on a *voluntary accumulation plan* or on a *fixed-amount/fixed-interval* basis using preauthorized checks drawn against the investor's checking account.

2. *Record Keeping* Mutual funds often provide cumulative monthly statements that help the investor track investment performance and maintain adequate tax records. Statements may also be issued after any transaction in the account.

3. *Distributions* Funds typically offer several options related to dividend and capital gains income. A *share option* automatically reinvests all dividend and capital gain distributions in additional shares or fractions of a share. (Typically, the fund calculates fractional shares to three decimal places.) A second choice is an *income-earned option* that reinvests capital gains and pays dividend income to the investor in cash. A third choice is the *cash option* that pays both dividends and capital gains in cash.

4. *Exchange Privileges* Funds offer telephone exchange privileges, with a toll-free number that is serviced by an account representative. In a no-load fund, no fees are charged for these exchanges, but the number of exchanges allowed during a calendar year may be restricted. Some load or low-load funds charge fees for the exchanges.

5. *Computerized account information and transactions* In addition to using an account representative, some larger funds now offer quotations and yields as well as specific account information by telephone, 24 hours a day, seven days a week. For example, "Tele*Access," offered by T. Rowe Price, provides a toll-free number; with a touch-tone phone and the appropriate codes, the investor can obtain specific information. The company's "Transaction-line" allows shareholders to exchange shares among the "family" of funds or to move money between the fund and the investor's checking account.

6. *Check-writing privileges* Many fixed-income and money market funds offer check-writing privileges with certain limitations. Often there is a minimum check amount, such as $500, and a limit on the number of checks that can be written each month. Any check is considered a withdrawal from the fund, executed at the prevailing NAV at the time of the transaction.

7. *Wire transfers* In addition to telephone, mail, and telegram exchange and transaction privileges, some funds offer electronic funds transfers. This service enables the investor to make a very rapid transfer to or from a fund.

• Key Decision Variables

In summary, investing in a mutual fund involves several logical steps:

1. Develop an appropriate investment objective.

2. Match the investment objective to a specific fund category.

3. Identify the types of services that may be useful or beneficial.

Finally, the investor obtains information on a number of specific funds, using the sources discussed previously, and selects one or more funds from this list. A major question that remains is, what are the key variables that should be considered in selecting a specific fund? The following factors are often cited in the investment literature as important in making a specific mutual fund investment decision.

CONSISTENCY OF PERFORMANCE The most popular variable used in mutual fund selection is ex-post returns, or HPRs. Wiesenberger's *Management Results* provides annual HPRs over the last 10 years for most funds. Other previously discussed publications, such as *Forbes, Barron's, Money,* and *Business Week,* also provide HPRs, which are used to rank funds. None of these rankings, however, are directly based on a risk-adjusted return basis. Research has indicated that very few funds have consistently beaten the market on a risk-return basis. (This will be discussed in detail in Chapter 21.) Investors should be very cautious in using historical returns to forecast ex-ante returns. It might be reasonable, however, to assume that superior ex-post return performances indicate that management has demonstrated the ability to perform successfully. A fund of this type would be a better selection than a fund that has never demonstrated superior return performance. However, many investment publications and advisers caution against using the most recent short-term performance in selecting a fund. A 1990 reader survey by *Money* magazine, however, found that 9 out of 10 investors cite long-term performance as the pivotal variable in selecting a fund.

A key to consistent performance is the portfolio manager. Under current SEC regulations, mutual funds do not have to notify investors if the portfolio manager or a key employee on the investment adviser team departs. Many investment advisers, however, recommend that mutual fund investors closely monitor any departure of a superlative fund manager. In March 1990, however, when Peter Lynch, the long-term and highly successful manager of the Magellan Fund, resigned, Fidelity reported shareholder redemptions of only one percent.[13]

EXPENSE RATIOS Other things being equal, investors benefit by investing in funds with low annual expense ratios. It is important to remember, however, that the type or classification of the fund and the size of the fund will

[13] Jerry Edgerton, "Should You Quit on the Magellan Fund?" *Money,* May 1990, pp. 82–83.

• INTEREST BOX

Mutual Fund Performance

Each year *Forbes* publishes an "honor roll" of 20 funds based on the following criteria:

1. The fund has roughly tripled an investor's money over the past three market cycles (approximately the last 10 years).

TABLE 1 • Funds on *Forbes* Honor Roll, 1990

Fund/distributor	Performance: *Up markets*	Performance: *Down markets*	Lead manager (years)	Average annual total return[a]	Hypothetical investment results[b]
Bergstrom Capital/ closed-end	C	A	Eric E. Bergstrom (14)	18.2%	$40,449
Dodge & Cox Stock Fund/ Dodge & Cox	A	B	Multiple managers (9)	16.3	33,410
Fidelity Destiny Portfolio I/ Fidelity Distributors	A	B	George Vanderheiden (10)	18.9	33,477
Franklin Growth Fund/ Franklin Distributors	B	B	Jerry Palmieri (25)	15.3	34,517
Guardian Park Ave Fund/ Guardian Investor Services	A	B	Charles Albers (18)	17.0	30,874
IAI Regional Fund/IAI Funds	A	B	Julian P. Carlin (10)	16.8	32,967
Investment Co. of America/ American Funds Group	B	A	Multiple managers (7)	16.7	30,626
Lindner Fund/Lindner Management	D	A+	Multiple managers (9)	18.8	38,621
Mutual Benefit Fund/Mutual Benefit Financial Services	A	B	Multiple managers (7)	17.0	32,871
New England Growth Fund/ New England Securities	A	B	G. Kenneth Heebner (14)	18.5	36,692
Nicholas Fund/Nicholas Co.	C	A	Albert O. Nicholas (21)	16.7	35,908
Phoenix Growth Fund/ Phoenix Equity Planning	B	A	Robert Chesck (10)	22.1	45,814
T. Rowe Price International Stock/T. Rowe Price Associates	B	B	Martin G. Wade (10)	18.0	37,536
Salomon Brothers Opportunity/Salomon Bros.	C	B	Irving Brilliant (11)	15.4	31,702
Selected American Shares/ Prescott, Ball & Turban	D	A	Donald A. Yacktman (7)	15.4	29,765
SLH Appreciation Fund/ Shearson Lehman Hutton	B	B	Harold A. Williamson (8)	15.9	34,432
SoGen International Fund/ SoGen Securities	C	A+	Jean-Marie Eveillard (12)	17.5	30,962
Source Capital/closed-end	D	A+	George H. Michaelis (18)	16.7	31,399
United Income Fund/ Waddell & Reed	A	A	Russell E. Thompson (11)	19.1	35,406
Washington Mutual Investors/American Funds Group	B	A	Multiple managers (9)	17.8	34,092

SOURCE: Spyros Manolatos, "Annual Fund Ratings: The Honor Roll," *Forbes*, September 3, 1990, pp. 126–27.

[a] From 11/30/80 through 6/30/90.

[b] Value on 6/30/90 of a $10,000 investment made on 11/30/80 considering load fees and taxes.

2. The fund has done well in bear markets, earning a grade of "B" or better.
3. The fund began operating before November 30, 1980.
4. The fund is not a specialized "sector" fund.
5. The fund has experienced continuity in management in terms of having the lead manager at the front for at least two market cycles (approximately seven years).
6. The fund is still open to new investors.

Table 1 provides data for the 20 open- and closed-end funds on the *Forbes* honor roll in 1990.

Net assets (millions)	Maximum load	Annual expenses per $100	Weighted average P/E	Assets in cash	Portfolio turnover	Minimum initial investment
$ 73	N/A	$0.97	28	5%	36%	None
157	None	0.65	15	5	4	$1,000
1,833	N/A	0.56	12	7	81	N/A
185	4.00%	0.72	15	11	2	100
253	4.50	0.68	13	7	47	1,000
191	None	1.00	18	27	116	5,000
5,874	5.75	0.52	15	20	18	250
716	None	0.62	9	26	19	2,000
38	4.75	1.45	16	16	14	250
640	6.50	1.22	11	10	203	1,000
1,520	None	0.82	15	9	21	500
756	6.90	1.04	15	13	180	500
1,163	None	1.05	N/A	14	48	2,500
108	None	1.26	16	17	8	1,000
412	None	1.08	16	8	46	1,000
1,121	5.00	0.89	17	13	24	500
195	3.75	1.38	15	26	31	1,000
311	N/A	0.96	12	21	36	N/A
1,742	8.50	0.69	14	3	61	500
5,349	5.75	0.69	13	5	7	250

influence this ratio. It is also critical to check for the existence of a 12b–1 plan that results in charges directly to NAV.

LOAD VERSUS NO-LOAD FUNDS If there are no differences in the risk and gross-return performances, no-load funds are generally a better choice for a "short" holding period. A load fund might be better, however, for a "long" holding period if the annual expenses and fees were lower than those of a comparable no-load fund.

PORTFOLIO TURNOVER Actively managed mutual funds make numerous portfolio revisions that result in large portfolio turnover ratios. The brokerage commissions and other costs associated with these transactions reduce the HPR, since they are reflected in NAV. High turnover ratios are acceptable to shareholders only if the portfolio manager has demonstrated skill in security selection and/or market timing, which is reflected in superior risk-return performance.

ASSET SIZE Marketing literature provided by large mutual funds often stresses their size, as indicated by total assets, as a desirable investment characteristic. Little in the academic literature, however, suggests that size influences risk-adjusted performance. Large funds may enjoy economies of scale in expenses and management fees but may also find it more difficult to find an adequate number of undervalued securities when their assets reach the billion-dollar-plus level.

CORRECT MARKET TIMING Successful mutual fund investing, like any other type of investing, depends to a large extent on buying the right fund at the right time. Before buying an aggressive equity fund, it is advisable to develop a realistic stock market forecast. A "bearish" forecast does not suggest an aggressive equity fund. A realistic interest rate forecast is also necessary before investing in a fixed-income or bond fund. Once the market forecast is made, the beta of the fund would be useful. Also, the historical performance during bull and bear markets indicates the ability of the fund's manager to take advantage of a bull market or to develop a defensive strategy for a bear market. Wiesenberger's "price volatility" ratios, which were discussed earlier, provide useful insights for this analysis.

Correct market timing, therefore, involves two aspects: (1) buying the right fund at the right time, and (2) finding a fund that may be expected to use market timing successfully in its portfolio management strategies. The use of mutual funds for market timing is discussed later in the chapter.

FUND GROWTH Are mutual funds that have shown rapid growth in assets better investments than slow growth funds? Previous research has shown a very weak relationship between growth and performance. The level of marketing expenses is more important in explaining growth than risk-adjusted performance.

INVESTMENT STRATEGIES FOR MUTUAL FUNDS

Investing in mutual funds has become increasingly complicated because of the rapid growth in the number of funds and the resulting proliferation of investment objectives and strategies. With over 3,000 funds in 1991, there are now far more mutual funds than common stocks listed on the NYSE. The following paragraphs present material that should help in developing a strategy that can be used to invest in mutual funds.

• Passive Strategies

Mutual funds offer several opportunities for investors who favor passive investment strategies (that is, strategies that emphasize buying and holding securities rather than market timing and active trading among investment alternatives).

BUY AND HOLD Traditionally, investment companies in general and mutual funds in particular were marketed as passive investments. Small investors, who typically lack the knowledge, time, or motivation, could depend on mutual funds for professional investment management, including security selection, market timing, and portfolio diversification. Mutual funds can still be used in this way, but there are several reasons why an investor should exercise caution in selecting individual funds:

1. Many new mutual funds are nondiversified; that is, they restrict investments to a specific industry or place other limitations on the portfolio's composition. Therefore, passive investors generally do not receive the benefits of diversification. Small, passive investors generally do not have other investments in stocks and bonds to provide personal portfolio diversification.

2. It is highly unlikely that an individual mutual fund can consistently beat the market on a risk-adjusted basis. To illustrate, in five of the last six years (1985–1990), the average fund had a return below the return on the S&P 500. The comprehensive review of studies dealing with mutual fund performance in Chapter 21 also supports this statement.

Norman Fosback, a recognized authority on funds and the editor of *Mutual Fund Forecaster,* offered some practical observations:

> In the aggregate, mutual funds cannot outperform the market because they are the market. Investors should formulate a realistic expectation of possible rewards or risks associated with any one fund. Then, to cope with the risks, buy several funds instead of just one.[14]

INDEX MUTUAL FUNDS A second passive mutual fund investment strategy uses **index** or *market* funds. Index funds form a portfolio that duplicates

[14] "What the Pros Say about Your Funds," *Money,* May 1987, pp. 44 and 46.

RESEARCH BOX

Mutual Fund Performance: Market Timing and Security Selection

According to Cheng-feu Lee and Shafiqur Rahman, the authors of a study of mutual fund performance:

> The investment performance of mutual fund managers has been extensively examined in the finance literature. It is apparent that superior performance of a mutual fund manager occurs because of his ability to "time" the market (market timing) and/or his ability to forecast the returns on individual assets (selection ability). Indeed, portfolio managers often characterize themselves as market timers and/or stock pickers.

This study used a random sample of 93 mutual funds over the 87 months from January 1977 through March 1984 to test for market timing and/or security selection success by the mutual fund manager. These 93 funds are listed in an appendix to the article, and tables provide measures of the timing and selection performance of each fund.

The empirical results from the study indicate that individual funds offer some evidence of superior timing and selection activity on the part of the fund manager. Of the 93 funds, 10 funds demonstrated both significant selection and timing skills; 4 had significant selection skill with no timing skill; and 5 funds had significant timing skill with no selection skill. The authors also note that their results are more favorable than previous research in terms of the timing and selection skills of mutual fund managers.

Mutual fund risk-return performance will be discussed in detail in Chapter 21. The chapter will present techniques that can measure the overall performance of funds as well as discuss methods of measuring specific aspects of performance, such as timing and selection.

SOURCE: Cheng-feu Lee and Shafiqur Rahman, "Market Timing, Selectivity, and Mutual Fund Performance: An Empirical Investigation," *Journal of Business* (April 1990): 261–78.

the performance of a market indicator portfolio like the S&P 500. This type of fund arose because of the implications of the efficient market hypothesis (EMH). A number of bank trust departments and insurance companies have also created index portfolios, and a growing number of pension funds use index portfolios. The largest index mutual fund is the Vanguard Index Trust-500 Portfolio, organized in 1976 as the First Index Investment Trust. There are now more than 20 index funds that are designed to mimic a variety of indexes including international stocks and various bond indexes. During the first half of 1990, over $100 million of individuals' money went into indexed funds.

The advantages of an index fund include broad diversification (in a common stock portfolio), low operating expenses, and limited brokerage fees. Index funds, by their very nature, do not require active portfolio management or the services of security analysts.

The Vanguard Index Trust-500 Portfolio illustrates this type of investment strategy. The fund describes its investment objective as follows:

> The fund seeks to provide investment results that correspond to the price and yield performance of publicly-traded common stocks, as represented by the Standard & Poor's 500 Corporate Stock Price Index. It attempts to duplicate the investment performance of the S&P Index by owning all of the 500 stocks contained in the Index, appropriately weighted. The trust will seek to be fully invested in common stocks at all times, owning no fewer than the 200 stocks having the largest weightings in the index.[15]

Key statistics for the fund for the period 1976–1989 appear in Table 5.7. In terms of net assets, the fund has grown rapidly—from $14.3 million in 1976 to $1,803.8 million in 1989. The annual HPRs of the fund are, as expected, closely correlated with the S&P 500. Notice also that the fund paid a constant dollar dividend of $.83 for 1980–1982, even though the dividend yield on the S&P 500 was not constant.

The lower portion of Table 5.7 provides Wiesenberger's price volatility ratios for eight bull and bear markets. The Vanguard Index Trust-500 Portfolio does not have a ratio of 1 as might be expected. For four of the eight periods it had ratios below 1. This would be a desirable characteristic during bear markets but not during bull markets. Fund expenses, brokerage costs, and dividend distributions that do not match the dividend yield on the S&P 500 cause Vanguard's price volatility to deviate from the expected value of 1. It is also interesting to note that the HPRs for the fund are both above and below those of the S&P 500.

The portfolio turnover rate for the Vanguard Index Trust-500 Portfolio was only 8 percent of average assets for 1989. Brokerage commissions were therefore small relative to other stock funds where turnover ratios may be over 100 percent.

Annual expense ratios, while somewhat high when the fund started, are now quite low compared to those of other common stock funds. The fund is a no-load fund but does have a 12b–1 plan that charges all marketing and promotional expenses directly to NAV. The expense ratios are therefore understated by the amount of those marketing and promotional expenses.

ASSET ALLOCATION FUNDS **Asset allocation funds** invest in different categories of securities such as money market securities, bonds, common stocks, and international stocks and bonds. The purpose of these funds is to provide an additional type of diversification within a single fund. Funds traditionally offered diversification in terms of a large number of securities of a single type. The new asset allocation funds also provide diversification by numbers but also by asset type or category. Thus, a small investor can benefit from asset allocation diversification without investing in a number of different mutual funds.

A number of mutual fund families have recently started asset allocation funds. For example, T. Rowe Price started the Spectrum Growth and Spectrum Income funds in 1990. Spectrum Growth invests in six existing T. Rowe

---

[15] *Investment Companies*, p. 685.

TABLE 5.7 • Vanguard Index Trust-500 Portfolio

Year	Total net assets (millions)	NAV	Expense ratio	Distribution		Holding period returns		Portfolio composition	
				Dividends	*Capital gains*	*Fund*	*S&P 500*	*Cash and equivalents*	*Common stock*
1989	$1,803.8	$33.64	0.21%	$1.20	$0.75	30.9%	31.6%	1%	99%
1988	1,055.1	27.18	0.22	1.10	0.32	16.0	16.5	5	95
1987	826.3	24.65	0.26	0.69	0.17	5.1	5.7	—	100
1986	485.1	24.27	0.28	0.89	2.02	18.2	18.1	(1)	101
1985	394.3	22.99	0.28	0.91	1.61	30.7	29.9	(2)	102
1984	289.7	19.52	0.27	0.88	0.48	6.0	4.1	2	98
1983	233.6	19.70	0.28	0.87	0.71	21.2	21.2	(1)	101
1982	110.0	17.56	0.39	0.83	0.25	20.1	22.2	1	99
1981	91.2	15.52	0.42	0.83	0.56	(5.2)	(4.8)	—	100
1980	98.8	17.84	0.35	0.83	0.53	31.2	34.1	(1)	101
1979	78.9	14.64	0.30	0.75	0.06	17.9	15.6	—	100
1978	66.2	13.11	0.36	0.65	—	5.8	8.5	—	100
1977	21.0	13.01	0.46	0.57	—	(4.6)	14.5	—	100
1976	14.3	14.72	NM	0.17	—	—	17.1	—	100

Wiesenberger's price volatility ratios

	Declining (bear) markets			Rising (bull) markets				
	11/28/80 to 7/30/82	*8/29/86 to 9/30/86*	*8/31/87 to 11/30/87*	*3/31/80 to 11/28/80*	*7/30/82 to 8/29/86*	*7/24/84 to 5/29/87*	*9/30/86 to 8/31/87*	*11/30/87 to 12/29/89*
NYSE Common Stock Index	1.00	1.00	1.00	1.00	1.00	1.00	1.00	1.00
Vanguard Index Trust-500 Portfolio	1.03	—	1.01	0.89	0.97	1.07	0.99	0.99

SOURCE: Data from *Investment Companies* (New York: Wiesenberger Investment Company Service, 1990), with HPRs calculated using Equation 5.1.

Price stock funds and a money market fund. Spectrum Income invests in certificates of deposit, U.S. Treasury notes, investment and junk grade bonds, foreign bonds, and high-dividend common stocks. These funds do not use aggressive market timing strategies but concentrate on long-term buy-and-hold investments. Both funds offer low minimun initial investments of $1,000 for IRA accounts.

Asset allocation funds can follow one of two strategies: a *variable* or a *fixed* mix of assets. Variable mix funds make frequent adjustments in the proportion of funds invested in each category. The fixed mix funds attempt to find an optimal mix and maintain the same proportions over time. As with any investment strategy, the investor should be sure that the returns of variable mix funds justify the additional brokerage commissions and expenses that occur.

• Active Strategies

Traditionally, because of the nature of mutual funds, investors did not attempt to use active strategies (market timing or switching between mutual funds) to obtain the best performance. Mutual fund managers selected individual securities for the fund and determined the appropriate diversification within the limitations of the stated investment objective. Funds were designed to be passive investments, were generally managed passively, and were viewed in this way by investors.

In recent years, however, several developments in the mutual fund industry have facilitated and encouraged active investment strategies. The introduction of money market funds within a family of funds has been a major factor. The proliferation of specialized sector or industry funds also offers more opportunities for active trading. The rapid growth of no-load funds has enabled many investors to eliminate brokerage costs when they make exchanges within a family of funds. Note, however, that some funds do charge fees for switching between family funds.

Due to these developments, mutual fund investors can now engage in the three major aspects of portfolio management: selection, market timing, and diversification. Although investors do not participate in decisions regarding individual securities, they can make selection decisions regarding specific industries. For example, as of December 1990, the Fidelity family of funds offered 29 select or industry-specific funds and 76 additional funds. A joke on Wall Street is, "When will an investment company offer the IBM common stock fund?" With the acceptance and rapid growth of the sector and specialized funds, it is not inconceivable that funds could be established to invest in a very limited number of securities. In fact, the AT&T Fund was started to "recreate" AT&T by holding only AT&T and the spin-off stocks.

Investors can pursue market timing by telephone exchanges and switching between money market, bond, common stock, and specialized funds within a single family of funds. On January 8, 1986, the DJIA lost 39 points—at that time a significant decline. One anonymous fund reported that its shareholders switched a net $27 million out of their equity funds between January 8 and 10,[16] an indication of how many mutual fund investors find the potential benefits of market timing attractive.

Telephone exchanges are common in sector funds, with over $1 billion exchanged since their introduction in the early 1980s. Is this timing strategy successful? One study indicated that the majority of investors using this strategy were unsuccessful.[17] It suggested that investors often move into specific sector funds when they are "hot," move out when they are "cold," and essentially "buy-high sell-low."

Telephone exchanges are being used so frequently by many investors, especially in volatile markets, that many funds are trying to curb switching. These funds argue that switching overburdens their service representatives, greatly increases the number of confirmation statements they must generate, and impacts the liquidity of the fund.[18]

The developments in the mutual fund industry also offer investors the opportunity to engage in diversification. It is no longer necessary for investors to rely on balanced funds for diversification among classes of securities. Specialized funds such as international stock funds and precious metal funds offer the opportunity to add very specialized diversification aspects to an individual's investment portfolio.

In summary, mutual funds are no longer regarded as passive investments where a professional portfolio manager makes all the decisions. Individual investors who are so inclined can pursue many active strategies that include aspects of selection, market timing, and diversification.

SUMMARY

The purpose of this chapter has been to provide an overview of mutual funds and other types of investment companies. It also examined factors to consider in making investment decisions in mutual funds and discussed various investment strategies.

The individual investor should be aware of major investment company characteristics such as the distinction between open- and closed-end funds and between load and no-load mutual funds. Tax implications and fees and expenses incurred by mutual funds are also important. Mutual fund investors should be aware of the operating expenses of funds in the same way that an investor in a common stock should be aware of the company's operating expenses.

---

[16] Kathleen Kerwin, "Dialing for Dollars: Switch Funds' Lure," *Barron's*, February 17, 1986, p. 56.

[17] Fred Norris, "Sector Funds: A Lot More Fumbles Than Touchdowns," *Barron's*, November 10, 1986.

[18] Werner Renberg, "Time Bombs? Why Funds Hate Frequent Switchers," *Barron's*, August 13, 1990.

• CONCEPT APPLICATIONS

Investment Concept	Concept Application
Closed-end fund	A type of investment company whose shares are traded on the NYSE, AMEX, or OTC market and can be bought or sold through a brokerage firm. Closed-end funds have a fixed number of shares of stock outstanding. The price of the common stock of closed-end funds is often substantially below (discount) or above (premium) the NAV per share. The movement of the discount and premium over time causes more variability in the HPRs of closed-end funds. Individuals may develop investment strategies based on the movement of the premium or discount and the NAV.
Mutual fund	The most popular and fastest growing type of investment company. The number of shares outstanding in a mutual fund varies with the purchase and redemption of shares by investors; hence, they are called open-end funds. With over 3,000 funds to choose from, many individuals feel mutual funds are the best way to invest in securities. However, selecting a fund is not an easy task. Individuals should match their objective for investing with a fund that has a compatible stated objective. Once the fund category is selected, the individual should analyze individual funds in terms of commission or load fees, consistency of investment performance, expense ratios, and possible success at timing and selection activities.
Index mutual fund	A specific category of funds that attempts to match the investment performance of an unmanaged index such as the S&P 500. These funds are designed to operate with limited expenses and consequently do not attempt active strategies. These funds appeal to investors with a passive strategy who do not want to attempt to "beat the market."
Active versus passive strategy	Individuals can use closed-end funds and mutual funds in an active or passive strategy. Fund managers may also pursue passive strategies while others use active strategies. The ability to switch between funds also gives flexibility to individuals who want to be "active" but yet leave most investment decisions up to the fund manager.

The possible variables to be considered in the decision to invest in an investment company include (1) consistency of performance, (2) expense ratios, (3) load fees, (4) turnover ratios, (5) asset size, (6) market timing, and (7) growth in assets. Which of these variables are most important will depend on the investor's objective.

Traditionally, investors in mutual funds followed essentially passive strategies since the portfolio manager made the decisions and investors often used a buy-and-hold strategy. Index funds, however, offer investors an even more passive strategy. The traditional job of the portfolio manager is eliminated; the only task of the manager is to make portfolio revisions so that the fund will mirror the performance of the index the fund is designed to match.

Recent developments in the mutual fund industry have greatly expanded the investment strategies available to individuals. Active strategies are now possible in which investors may manage their investments in mutual funds using many of the same strategies used for individual securities. These developments, while increasing the flexibility of strategies available to investors, also create potential pitfalls for the uninformed. The data suggest that the average active mutual fund investor is finding that market timing, selection, and diversification are very difficult and challenging activities in efficient capital markets.

• KEY TERMS

Asset allocation fund
Closed-end fund
Country fund
Dual fund
Expense ratio
Index fund
Investment Company Act of 1940
Load fund
Low-load fund
Money market fund
Mutual fund
Net asset value (NAV)
No-load fund
Open-end fund
Portfolio turnover
Prime
Rule 12b–1
Score
Unit trust

• QUESTIONS

1. Distinguish between an open- and a closed-end fund.
2. Distinguish between a load, a low-load, and a no-load mutual fund.
3. Compare and contrast a mutual fund with a unit investment trust.
4. Discuss the different types of fees and charges that might be incurred by a mutual fund investor.
5. Define the "investment objective" of a mutual fund. How can investors use the investment objective to identify a fund for a possible investment?
6. Identify and briefly discuss the services that mutual funds may offer their shareholders.
7. Mutual funds and other investment companies were traditionally regarded as appropriate investments for individuals pursuing a passive strategy. What recent developments suggest mutual funds may be appropriate for active strategies?
8. Assume that an individual investor is attempting to identify one or more mutual funds for a potential investment. Discuss the key decision variables that should be considered in identifying appropriate funds.
9. Suppose an investor is attempting to select between the following two mutual funds:

	Fund A	*Fund B*
Front-end load fee	0	6.0%
Annual management fee	0.4%	0.2%
Annual 12b–1 charges	1.0%	0
Rear-end load fee	0	0
Annual brokerage costs incurred by fund	2.0%	2.0%

If the investor thinks that there will be no difference in the gross HPRs (returns before expenses) and that the funds have equal risk:

a. Which fund would be better for a short holding period? Explain your answer.

b. Which fund would be better for a long holding period? Explain your answer.

10. Discuss the advantages and disadvantages of an index mutual fund versus an actively managed fund.

11. Explain how an open-end mutual fund calculates NAV. How is NAV used by the fund? What effect do income and capital gain distributions to shareholders have on NAV?

12. Explain the advantages and disadvantages of asset allocation funds.

13. Briefly define primes and scores and offer an explanation why they do not appear to be priced correctly relative to the underlying common stock.

14. Use the data on number of shares, assets, and liabilities in Table 5.2 to explain how the NAV per share of $13.41 was calculated.

• KEY TO THE INVESTMENT ANALYSIS SOFTWARE

Calculation	Appendix A-1 Page Reference	Access Procedure
Holding period return	A-8	BEGIN, STATISTICAL, HPR, ONE or MANY

• PROBLEMS

1. Consider the following data on an open-end mutual fund:

	NAV on January 1	Distribution at end of year	
		Dividends	*Capital gains*
1989	$10	$.75	$3
1990	15	.60	1
1991	12	—	—

a. Calculate the HPR for 1989.

b. Calculate the HPR for 1990.

2. Suppose that an individual invests $10,000 in an open-end mutual fund. The NAV is $48 and the offering price of the shares is $50. At the end of one year the investor receives $1 per share of dividends and sells the shares at a NAV of $51.

a. Calculate the HPR.

b. Assume that there is no load fee. Calculate the HPR.

3. Assume an individual invested $10,000 in a closed-end fund. The shares were trading at $50 per share and the stockbroker charged a 3 percent commission. At the end of one year, the investor received $1 per share of dividends and sold the shares at a price of $51 per share before the brokerage commission.

a. Calculate the HPR considering the brokerage commission.

b. Assume that there are no brokerage commissions. Calculate the HPR.

c. Compare your answers to Problems 2 and 3 in terms of the impact of load fees versus brokerage fees on HPRs.

4. Consider the following data on two mutual funds:

	Fund A	*Fund B*
Total net assets (assets less liabilities) at beginning of year	$1,000,000	$1,000,000
Number of shares outstanding at beginning of year	100,000	100,000
Annual operating expenses	$ 10,000	$ 12,000
Value of securities sold during year	$ 500,000	$ 800,000
Value of securities purchased during year	$ 400,000	$ 900,000
Brokerage fees for the year	$ 9,000	$ 17,000
Number of shares outstanding at end of year	110,000	100,000
Total net assets end of year	$1,100,000	$1,200,000

For each fund, calculate the following:

a. The NAVs per share at the beginning and end of the year. Assume that operating expenses and brokerage fees are reflected in the NAVs.

b. The expense ratios, using the NAVs at the beginning of the year.

c. The portfolio turnover ratios.

d. Do you think the higher operating expenses for Fund B are justified? Explain your answer.

e. Do you think the higher portfolio turnover ratio and brokerage fees for Fund B are justified? Explain your answer.

5. Assume that an investor is trying to decide between investing in a no-load fund with a 12b–1 plan or a fund with a front-end load:

	Fund X	*Fund Y*
Front-end load fee	0	4%
Annual 12b–1 charge	1%	0

The investor thinks that the risk and other characteristics of both funds are equal and that each fund will provide an annual HPR of 12% *before* considering the load fee and 12b–1 charge. Assume the investor has $10,000 to invest in either fund.

a. Calculate the anticipated dollar values of each investment after a three-year holding period. Assume annual compounding. Which fund appears to be the better alternative?
b. Answer part (a) assuming a six-year holding period.
c. Calculate the length of the holding period that would make the investor indifferent between the two funds.
d. Explain why the length of the anticipated holding period should be considered in comparing load fees with annual expenses such as 12b–1 charges.

• REFERENCES

Baldwin, William. "The Unload Funds." *Forbes,* September 5, 1988, pp. 158, 160.

———. "How to Choose a Fund." *Forbes,* September 3, 1990, pp. 122–24.

Bergeron, Woodrow J. "How to Figure Taxes on Your Fund Shares." *Barron's,* February 16, 1987, p. 68.

Brealey, Richard A. "How to Combine Active Management with Index Funds." *Journal of Portfolio Management* (Winter 1986): 4–10.

Carey, David, Michael K. Ozanian, Alexandra Ourusoff, and Alan Levine. "Mutual Funds 1990: Promises, Promises." *Financial World,* February 6, 1990, pp. 42–58.

Chambliss, Lauren. "Mutual Fund Watch: Show and Tell." *Financial World,* March 8, 1988, pp. 102–3.

Clements, Jonathan. "Be Stodgy and Make Money." *Forbes,* September 4, 1989, pp. 154–55.

Donovan, Kevin. "Careful, Conservative—That's What the SEC Wants Money Funds to Be." *Barron's,* August 13, 1990, pp. M25–M26.

Fabian, Douglas. "Asset Allocation Funds: Are They Overrated?" *Best's Review,* January 1989, pp. 88–89.

Friedman, Jon. "How the Fund Families Measure Up." *Business Week,* June 11, 1990, pp. 64–65.

Fritz, Michael, "Annual Fund Ratings: Tail End of Trend?" *Forbes,* September 3, 1990, p. 170.

Gage, Theodore Justin. "Controversy Returns to Indexed Funds after Market Crash." *Cash Flow,* March 1988, pp. 14–15.

Galant, Debbie. "Portfolio Strategy: Practicing What He Preached." *Institutional Investor,* June 1990, pp. 157–58.

Gregor, Anne. "The New Faces of Fees: More Fair, More Confusing." *Barron's,* November 13, 1989, p. 64.

Laderman, Jeffrey M. "How Mutual Funds Have Battled Back." *Business Week,* September 18, 1989, pp. 100–101.

———. "Want a Winner? Look Here First." *Business Week,* February 19, 1990, pp. 70–106.

Monks, Robert A. G., and Nell Minow. "Indexing Boosts Long-Term View." *Pensions and Investment Age,* January 11, 1988, pp. 16–17.

Nathans, Leah. "Allocating Your Assets: You May Not Need a Pro." *Business Week,* May 8, 1989, pp. 152–53.

Norris, Fred. "Closed-End Funds: The Riddle of Net Asset Value." *Barron's,* February 16, 1987, pp. 60–61.

Olin, Ronald G. "Never Buy at Retail." *Institutional Investor,* June 1990, p. 90.

Price, Margaret. "Fees Come under Scrutiny." *Pensions and Investments,* June 11, 1990, pp. 19, 22.

Savitz, Eric J. "The Schwab Advantage: Running Funds Could Pay Off Big for Discount Broker." *Barron's,* May 14, 1990, pp. M23–M24.

Scheibla, Shirley Hobbs. "Fee-ed Up: Why Investors Hate 12b–1s." *Barron's,* August 14, 1989, pp. 57–60.

Updegrave, Walter L. "Mutual Funds: Seven Tough Questions You Must Answer Now." *Money,* February 1988, pp. 134–42.

Updegrave, Walter L., and Leslie N. Vreeland. "The Smart Investor's Guide to Fund Families." *Money,* May 1988, pp. 73–78.

Walbert, Laura. "Shrinking Funds: Management Fees Tend to Take Bigger Bite as Mutual Funds' Assets Fall." *Financial World,* April 18, 1989, pp. 78–80.

Weiss, Gary. "Fixed-Income Funds: Where Safety Pays." *Business Week,* February 26, 1990, pp. 94, 109.

Willis, Clint. "Tax-Exempt Muni Funds Offer Zippy Yields—But Some May Zip Right Over a Cliff." *Money,* May 1990, pp. 37, 52.

CHAPTER 6

Investing Internationally

The knowledge-level objectives of this chapter should enable the student to:

- Describe the benefits and risks to an investor of investing internationally.
- Recognize the size and importance of international security markets.
- Differentiate the factors, particularly the degree of a country's market segmentation, that should be considered in diversifying internationally.
- Recognize that the risk-return relationships that made certain international investments attractive in the past will not necessarily hold into the future.
- Explain the impact of floating exchange rates on the risk of investing internationally.
- Describe the financial instruments, and the advantages and disadvantages of each, that individuals can use to invest internationally.

INTRODUCTION

Historically, many investors ignored international markets for two reasons: (1) they did not recognize the potential benefits from international diversification; and (2) the information and transaction costs associated with international investing were high. In recent years, international investing has become increasingly popular as investors recognize its potential benefits. In addition, information and transaction costs have been substantially reduced. This chapter first provides some background on international assets and markets. It then examines evidence on the potential gains from international diversification and the factors influencing these potential gains. Next, the methods that individuals can use to invest internationally are discussed. Finally, international money market diversification is considered.

INTERNATIONAL ASSETS AND MARKETS

Investors who have thought mainly in terms of U.S. investments are sometimes surprised at the size and diversity of overseas markets and companies. This section presents an overview of international assets and markets to help place them in perspective.

• The World Investable Market Portfolio

An estimate of *total world wealth* and *world investable wealth* as of 1984 has been made by Ibbotson, Siegel, and Love.[1] Total world wealth at that time was estimated at $27,681 billion, and as shown in Table 6.1, world investable wealth was estimated at $13,954 billion. The two figures differ largely because foreign real estate ($10,204 billion) and U.S. and foreign durables ($3,479 billion) are not included in the estimate of investable wealth. As the table shows, U.S. domestic bonds and equities constituted 26 percent of the world's total investable wealth. While these traditional investment alternatives in U.S. assets are sizable, a much broader universe of investments is available to the U.S. investor willing to consider the international markets.

• Background on Financial Markets

exchanges or resuscitating old markets. The total market value of securities traded (market capitalization) on the Tokyo Stock Exchange, the largest exchange in the world, surpassed that of the New York Stock Exchange in
traded (market capitalization) on the Tokyo Stock Exchange, the largest exchange in the world, surpassed that of the New York Stock Exchange in

[1] Roger G. Ibbotson, Laurence C. Siegel, and Kathryn S. Love, "World Wealth: Market Values and Returns," *Journal of Portfolio Management* (Fall 1985): 4–23.

TABLE 6.1 • World Investable Wealth, 1984

Asset	Amount (billions)	Percentage of total
U.S. cash	$ 673.2	4.8%
Foreign cash	103.6	0.7
Metals	932.0	6.7
Crossborders*	365.5	2.6
U.S. domestic bonds	1,773.6	12.7
Foreign domestic bonds	1,918.5	13.8
U.S. equities	1,862.2	13.3
European equities	489.4	3.5
Asian equities	669.8	4.8
Other equities	193.0	1.4
U.S. real estate		
Farm	689.8	4.9
Business	652.5	4.7
Residential	3,631.1	26.0
Total	$13,954.2	99.9%

SOURCE: Roger G. Ibbotson, Laurence B. Siegel, and Kathryn S. Love, "World Wealth: Market Values and Returns," *Journal of Portfolio Management* (Fall 1985): 6. This copyrighted material is reprinted with permission from Institutional Investor, Inc.

*Assets traded outside any given country's capital market.

1987. In 1989, the U.S. stock market represented only 29 percent of the total world market capitalization, compared to 66.3 percent in 1970. Portfolio managers are now becoming more familiar with foreign companies traded on local exchanges and on foreign exchanges. Consequently, professionally managed portfolios now contain a greater percentage of the stocks and bonds of foreign companies.

Table 6.2 presents the returns of a sample of foreign stock market indexes for 1990. In general, world stock markets performed poorly in 1990. In local currencies, only the Hong Kong index (Hang Seng) provided a positive return. When adjusted for exchange rates, however, several of the indexes showed a positive return as a result of the dollar's decline against their local currencies. The impact of exchange rate fluctuations on holding period returns is discussed later in the chapter.

The breadth, depth, and regulations of U.S. security markets have encouraged European, Japanese, and other overseas investors to trade securities in the United States. For the same reasons, many foreign companies have listed their stocks on U.S. exchanges. In addition, stocks of some very well-known companies have become globally accessible to investors. For example, Toyota Motor Corporation of Japan is listed on at least nine different stock exchanges around the world.

TABLE 6.2 • Returns on Foreign Stock Market Indexes, 1990

	In local currencies			In U.S. dollars[a]		
Index	*Percentage change*	*Value 12/31/90*	*52-week range*	*Percentage change*	*Value 12/31/90*	*52-week range*
The world	−23.0%	358.1	464.9−358.1	−18.7%	461.5	567.3−461.5
EAFE[b]	−31.0	470.1	681.1−470.1	−24.7	789.0	1047.9−789.0
Australia	−19.1	267.8	331.2−267.8	−21.0	184.6	233.6−184.6
Austria	−6.9	426.0	457.4−426.0	+5.2	1052.0	999.6−1052.0
Belgium	−25.4	351.6	471.2−351.6	−14.2	567.9	662.2−567.9
Canada	−15.2	366.8	432.5−366.8	−15.3	341.9	403.9−341.9
Denmark	−13.9	668.5	776.8−668.5	−2.0	867.5	885.4−867.5
Finland	−40.2	60.9	101.8−60.9	−33.3	66.3	99.3−66.3
France	−25.2	424.1	566.9−424.1	−15.2	461.0	543.9−461.0
Germany	−20.9	225.6	285.3−225.6	−10.8	550.7	617.2−550.7
Hong Kong	+3.6	2172.6	2096.9−2172.6	+3.7	1546.9	1492.0−1546.9
Italy	−29.4	370.9	525.6−370.9	−20.8	205.2	259.3−205.2
Japan	−39.6	994.1	1655.3−994.1	−36.4	2637.6	4149.2−2637.6
Netherlands	−17.4	277.0	335.2−277.0	−6.6	593.8	636.0−593.8
New Zealand	−39.6	59.4	98.3−59.4	−40.3	53.0	88.8−53.0
Norway	−11.4	738.7	833.6−738.7	−0.8	895.8	902.8−895.8
Singapore/Malaysia	−20.5	659.0	828.9−659.0	−13.1	1165.8	1341.7−1165.8
Spain	−27.6	180.3	248.8−180.3	−17.1	132.0	159.2−132.0
Sweden	−29.4	997.1	1413.0−997.1	−22.4	915.3	1179.8−915.3
Switzerland	−23.5	168.9	220.7−168.9	−7.8	567.2	615.1−567.2
United States	−5.6	306.9	325.0−306.9	−5.6	306.9	325.0−306.9
United Kingdom	−11.4	639.1	721.0−639.1	+6.0	513.6	484.6−513.6

SOURCE: *Barron's*, January 7, 1991, p. 56. Reprinted courtesy of Barron's Weekly.
[a] Adjusted for foreign exchange fluctuations relative to the U.S. dollar.
[b] Europe, Australia, Far East Index.

In October 1986, a computerized network resembling the NASDAQ over-the-counter system in the United States was created in London's International Stock Exchange. This event was referred to as the *Big Bang*. The system, called SEAQ (pronounced *see-yak*), allows international traders to trade by telephone and computer. In addition, the London exchange now allows investment firms that trade in the United States and Japan to trade in London, which was not allowed prior to the Big Bang. As a result of this deregulation, large investment firms that trade on the New York, London, and Tokyo exchanges have been able to create a near-24-hour market. They can use the New York Stock Exchange from 9:00 A.M. to 5:15 P.M. Eastern time, the Tokyo Stock Exchange from 7:00 P.M. to 1:00 A.M. Eastern time, and the London Stock Exchange from 4:00 A.M. to 10:30 A.M. Eastern time. Thus, shares

• **INTEREST BOX**

Features of Selected Foreign Stock Exchanges

The following descriptions provide a brief look at the characteristics of some of the more important foreign stock markets as of mid-1990:

- *France.* P/E 13 Yield 3% Market value: $358 billion

  Measured by its capitalization of $358 billion, the French stock market is the third largest European stock exchange. The French stock market underwent major reforms in 1988 as Bourse membership was transferred from individuals to firms. Other financial institutions and corporations, both French and foreign, may now invest in French brokerage houses.

- *Germany.* P/E 17 Yield 3% Market value: $369 billion

  The reunification of the two Germanys will not be without setbacks. A surge of East German immigrants is straining the West German economy. And rebuilding East Germany's infrastructure could cost an estimated $500 billion. Nevertheless, analysts expect West Germany's economy to continue to expand. West German firms like Volkswagen have already made deals with East Germany. Reflecting these prospects, the West German market's P/E is the second highest in Europe, after Austria.

- *Japan.* P/E 44 Yield 1% Market value: $3,428 billion

  And you think Wall Street is volatile! In December 1989, Japan's market capitalization reached $4.1 trillion, more than five times its value in December 1985, thanks in large part to the dollar's devaluation against the yen. Then in the first quarter of 1990, Japanese equities lost $1.2 trillion. Over the next months, it recouped 10 percent of its loss, but the Nikkei average (as of June 25, 1990) was still off 20 percent from its December 1989 peak.

- *Netherlands.* P/E 9 Yield 5% Market value: $120 billion

  The Netherlands market sells at the lowest P/E in Europe and has the third highest dividend yield, after Spain and the United Kingdom. The three largest Dutch firms (Royal Dutch/Shell, Unilever, Philips Group) are international powerhouses well known to U.S. investors.

- *Switzerland.* P/E 15 Yield 2% Market value: $211 billion

  Swiss stocks are not cheap: The least expensive share of the 18 largest, publicly traded companies in Switzerland is Swiss Bank Corporation at $226 per share. The most expensive is Sandoz Group, which sells for $8,141 per share.

- *United Kingdom.* P/E 12 Yield 5% Market value: $838 billion

  London's computerized International Stock Exchange trades more shares than any other in Europe.

SOURCE: Adapted from *Forbes*, July 23, 1990, pp. 313–44.

traded on these exchanges can be bought or sold at almost any time of the day. In the future, shares of most large companies are likely to be available on these three major exchanges. Globalization of the world's securities markets will continue at a rapid pace. For example, the European exchanges are currently discussing the creation of a pan-European stock market.

Although globalization of the world's financial markets has made significant strides over the last decade, international transactions still present some problems. Liquidation of holdings (settlement) is still difficult in a number of markets. For example, settling trades in Italy can take as long as 12 months. International settlements are complicated by time zones, exchange rates, overburdened foreign stock exchanges, the regulatory framework, and language differences. In addition, it is not uncommon for parties involved in an international transaction to fail to deliver securities by the effective settlement date. These "fails" are at least partially due to the fact that the securities must be delivered physically.

• Comparing Risk and Return

Table 6.3 compares the risks and returns for 16 investment categories with the rate of inflation for the 1980–1990, 1985–1990, and 1990 periods. Note,

TABLE 6.3 • A Comparison of Risk and Return

	Ten years		Five years		1990 annual return
	Annual return	*Risk*	*Annual return*	*Risk*	
EAFE (Europe, Australia, Far East Index)	15.1%	25.1%	17.5%	28.5%	−23.1%
Japanese stocks	14.9	21.7	11.2	29.8	−39.6
S&P 500	13.9	12.6	13.2	11.9	−3.2
U.S. government bonds	13.7	13.4	10.8	9.4	6.2
Art	13.0	14.9	20.7	16.9	−4.9
Foreign bonds	11.8	16.1	15.4	16.3	14.1
Commercial paper	9.4	2.7	7.7	0.9	8.3
Small stocks	9.3	18.0	0.6	15.5	−21.6
Commercial real estate	8.8	4.3	5.2	2.1	1.3
T-bills	8.5	2.5	6.8	1.1	7.8
Emerging market stocks	8.4	29.9	18.3	32.6	−28.4
Emerging growth stocks	8.3	13.4	7.9	11.1	3.5
Inflation	4.5	1.9	4.1	1.6	6.1
Residential housing	4.4	1.6	4.8	1.5	2.6
U.S. farmland	2.8	5.7	7.4	4.0	8.1
Gold	−1.9	15.2	3.7	14.7	−1.9
Venture capital	−2.4	17.9	−3.8	7.6	−12.7

SOURCE: Based on data from Morgan Stanley. *Barron's*, May 20, 1991, p. 12.

Note: Risk is measured by the standard deviation and annual returns include dividends, interest, and other distributions as appropriate.

however, that these results are not predictors of what will happen in the future. They are also very sensitive to the time periods selected to measure risk and return. Two examples will help illustrate this point. U.S. government bonds ranked as one of the top performers over the 10-year period ending in 1990. This strong performance was a result of the very high interest rates at the beginning of the 1980s. As interest rates declined from these relatively high rates, bonds provided high returns through an appreciation in price. Over the 5-year period, however, and, particularly, the 1-year period, the returns on U.S. government bonds have been moving toward their historical 50-year average of 4.5 percent.

Japanese stocks provide a second example of the sensitivity of the risk and return measures to the selected time period. With a negative 39.6 percent return in 1990, Japanese stocks had the worst one-year performance of the 16 investment alternatives. This poor performance in 1990 caused the 10-year and 5-year return results to be lower than the historical long-run average return of 15.7 percent on these stocks.

• Size of International Companies

Many investors may be surprised at the size of foreign companies relative to those in the United States. For example, when Nippon Telegraph and Telephone went public in February 1987, its market value of $330 billion was above the combined values of IBM, AT&T, General Electric, and General Motors. The 1990 market value of Japan's largest brokerage house, Nomura Securities, was approximately three times larger than Merrill Lynch's market value.

Table 6.4 lists the 30 largest, publicly traded companies in the world in 1989 ranked by sales and market value. The five companies with the largest sales are all Japanese, and they are all trading companies. As trading companies, their sales revenue represents value created by other companies. It is interesting to note that the highest ranked company, Sumitomo Corporation, had 13,000 employees in 1989. The highest ranked U.S. company, General Motors, had 775,000 employees.

It is also interesting to compare companies based on their market values. Note that there is very little correlation between the sales rankings and the market value rankings.

Comparing the 1989 revenues of the 500 largest, publicly traded foreign companies and the 500 largest publicly traded U.S. companies also proves interesting.[2] As the following statistics on page 169 indicate, the total revenues of the foreign companies are considerably larger, but the differences in total employees, net profits, and market values are not as significant. It is also important to remember that U.S.-based companies are being compared with com-

[2] "The Forbes Foreign Rankings," *Forbes*, July 23, 1990, 313–44.

TABLE 6.4 • Thirty Largest Publicly Owned Companies, 1989

Rank by sales	Company (business)	Country	Sales (millions)	Market value (millions)	Rank by market value
1	Sumitomo Corp. (trading)	Japan	$158.221	$ 9,331	23
2	C Itoh & Co., Ltd. (trading)	Japan	147,016	8,904	24
3	Mitsui & Co., Ltd. (trading)	Japan	136,578	10,455	22
4	Marukeni Corp. (trading)	Japan	131,419	8,256	25
5	Mitsubishi Corp. (trading)	Japan	129,689	16,719	19
6	General Motors (automobiles)	USA	126,932	28,675	12
7	Nissho Iwai Corp. (trading)	Japan	108,118	4,799	27
8	Ford Motor (automobiles)	USA	96,146	22,984	15
9	Exxon (oil and gas)	USA	96,076	58,398	4
10	Royal Dutch/Shell (oil and gas)	Holland	85,536	66,933	2
11	International Business Machines (computers)	USA	62,710	62,508	3
12	Toyota Motor Corp. (automobiles)	Japan	61,052	50,477	6
13	Mobil (oil and gas)	USA	56,656	25,443	14
14	General Electric (diversified)	USA	54,600	57,860	5
15	Sears, Roebuck (department stores)	USA	53,795	13,953	21
16	Hitachi, Ltd. (diversified)	Japan	49,557	33,066	9
17	British Petroleum Co. (oil and gas)	UK	48,602	29,495	11
18	Toyo Menka Kaisha (trading)	Japan	45,055	3,690	28
19	Phillip Morris (tobacco, food, and brewing)	USA	44,759	36,188	8
20	Nichimen Corp. (trading)	Japan	42,989	2,237	29
21	Nippon Telegraph & Telephone (communications)	Japan	42,166	118,881	1
22	Matsushita (consumer electronics)	Japan	42,030	29,655	10
23	Daimler-Benz (automobiles)	Germany	40,633	22,498	16
24	Nissan Motor Co., Ltd. (automobiles)	Japan	39,525	19,941	17
25	Kanematsu Corp. (trading)	Japan	39,219	1,312	30
26	Fiat Group (automobiles)	Italy	38,044	17,850	18
27	Citicorp (banking)	USA	37,970	7,709	26
28	American Telephone & Telegraph (telecommunications)	USA	36,112	44,904	7
29	E.I. du Pont (chemicals)	USA	35,991	27,455	13
30	Texaco (oil and gas)	USA	35,656	15,700	20

SOURCES: *Forbes*, July 23, 1990, pp. 313–44, and *Financial World*, May 1, 1990, pp. 36–39.

panies from the rest of the world. In addition, a number of large companies are not included because they are either government owned or privately held.

	500 largest foreign companies	500 largest U.S. companies
Total revenue	$5.2 trillion	$3.2 trillion
Total employees	19.8 million	19.0 million
Total net profits	$165 billion	$158 billion
Total market value	$3.4 trillion	$2.2 trillion

DIVERSIFYING INTERNATIONALLY

As we discussed in Chapter 2, a portfolio that includes securities that are not highly correlated with each other is beneficial to the investor. Combining securities that are less than perfectly, positively correlated helps to reduce the diversifiable risk and, thus, the total risk of the portfolio. Economic conditions will cause some securities in a portfolio to provide higher-than-normal returns, while other securities will simultaneously provide lower-than-normal returns. Under other economic conditions, the reverse would hold. This offsetting effect causes the overall portfolio returns to be less volatile over time. For those investors who use return volatility as a measure of risk, portfolio risk is reduced significantly when the portfolio includes securities that exhibit low or negative correlations with each other.

The degree to which investors can reduce the risk of a purely domestic portfolio is limited, however. Most corporations are affected by domestic economic conditions. Thus, the securities of these corporations will generate returns that often are highly correlated. Because the correlations between securities are never perfect (represented by a correlation of 1.0), portfolio risk can be reduced to some extent. However, the degree of risk reduction could be much greater if the portfolio contained securities whose returns were less highly correlated. To develop such a portfolio, many investment analysts and advisers suggest including foreign securities in a portfolio. Because these foreign securities represent foreign corporations, their returns should not move in perfect tandem with those of domestic securities.

• Evidence on the Benefits of Diversifying Internationally

Many studies have examined the role of international diversification in reducing portfolio risk. One of the first studies was conducted by Levy and Sarnat, who examined stock indexes of various countries.[3] The use of indexes rather

[3] Haim Levy and Marshall Sarnat, "International Diversification of Investment Portfolios," *American Economic Review* (September 1970): 668–75.

than individual stocks simplified the analysis. Levy and Sarnat found that stock indexes of various countries were not as highly correlated as one would expect the individual securities in a given country to be. Such results imply potential gains from international diversification. In particular, the indexes of the more industrialized countries were found to exhibit higher correlations. Perhaps this can be explained by the high degree of interaction among the more industrialized countries, which causes economic conditions in one country to influence conditions in others. In countries where international transactions are more restricted, the degree of interaction (and therefore influence) is reduced. Thus, such countries are more insulated, and economic conditions there should not be similar to economic conditions in other countries.

These findings suggest that securities of the less-industrialized countries should be included in a global portfolio in order to substantially reduce portfolio risk. To substantiate this implication, Levy and Sarnat used historical data to identify *efficient* portfolios. A portfolio is "efficient" if it represents the highest return for a given level of risk or, alternately, the lowest risk for a given level of return. Levy and Sarnat found that the less-industrialized stock indexes represented a large portion of many efficient portfolios.

The benefits of international diversification were also analyzed by Solnik.[4] First, he determined the average standard deviation of a randomly selected group of U.S. securities. He then randomly composed two-security portfolios (again using U.S. securities) and determined the average standard deviation of these portfolios. This process was repeated for three-security portfolios, four-security portfolios, and so on. This procedure simply examined how diversification among U.S. securities can reduce risk. The results are shown in Figure 6.1a. The variable on the vertical axis is the ratio of the average portfolio standard deviation to the average standard deviation of an individual security, $\bar{\sigma}_j$. As Figure 6.1a shows, this ratio decreases as the number of securities in the portfolio increases.

Solnik repeated the entire process to create international portfolios, using a sample of stocks from various countries. As Figure 6.1b shows, once again the ratio on the vertical axis decreases as the number of securities within the portfolio increases. However, the degree of reduction is significantly higher for the international portfolios. For a 20-security portfolio, international diversification yields an average risk level of about 50 percent of the average risk level of a domestic portfolio. This suggests that international diversification can reduce risk far beyond that which is possible domestically and that fewer stocks are needed to achieve this diversification.

Most researchers who have attempted to determine whether gains from international diversification are possible have based their findings on the relatively low correlations between stocks and stock indexes in the past. Yet the results from these studies do not guarantee gains from international diver-

---

[4] Bruno H. Solnik, "Why Not Diversify Internationally Rather than Domestically?" *Financial Analysts Journal* (July-August 1974): 48–54.

FIGURE 6.1
Diversification by Number of Securities in the Portfolio

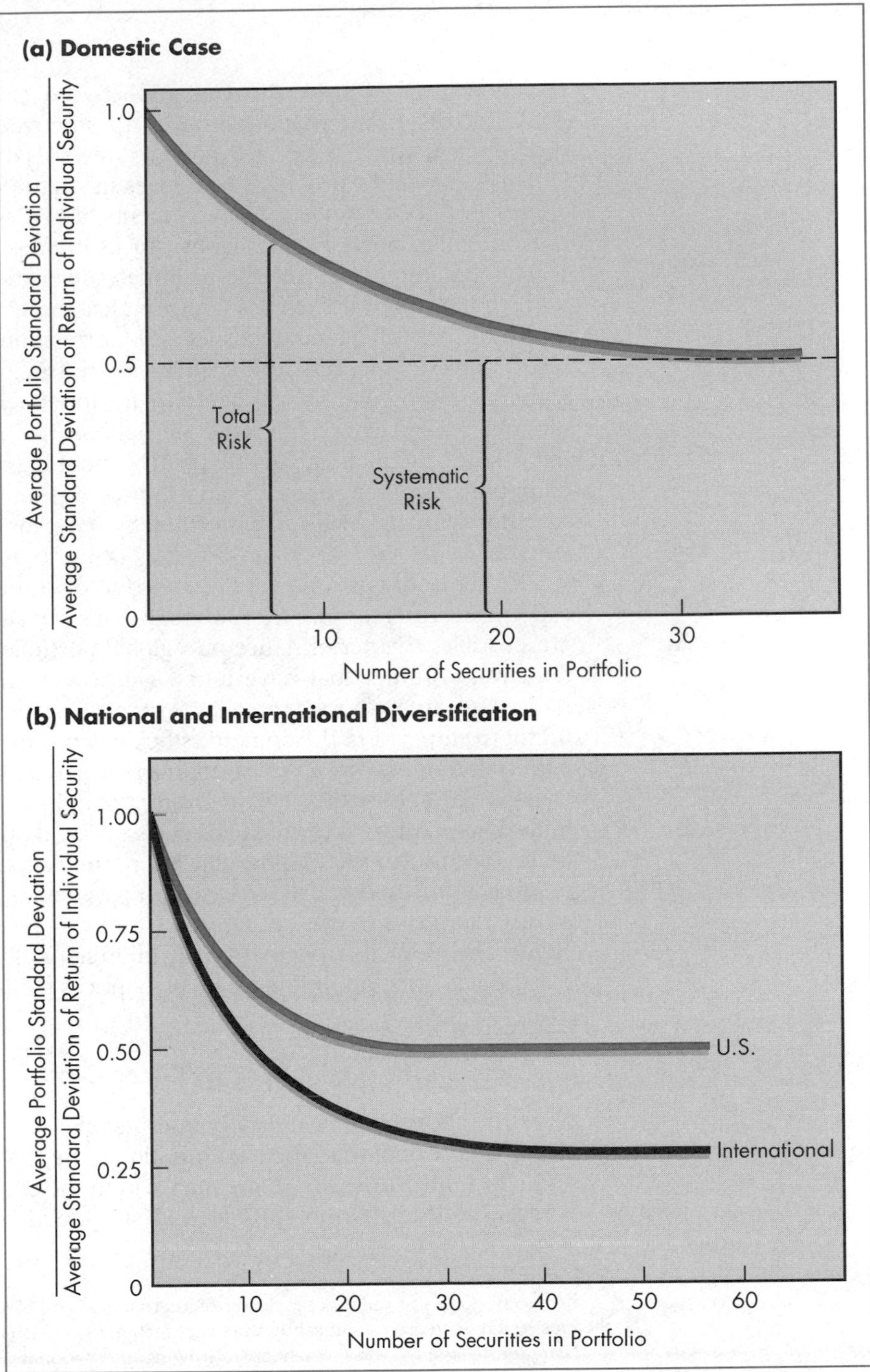

SOURCE: Adapted from Bruno H. Solnik. "Why Not Diversify Internationally Rather than Domestically?" *Financial Analysts Journal* (July-August 1974): 48–54. (Reprinted by permission.)

sification in the future. Correlations between stocks of different countries could increase if international transactions between countries increase. This development would lessen the potential rewards of global diversification.[5]

This is one of the problems with investing in the securities of less-developed countries (LDCs). Since the governments of LDCs often place severe restrictions on international transactions, stocks in these countries should serve as viable components of an internationally diversified portfolio. The problem with capitalizing on such a strategy is that the government restrictions that create the desirable characteristics (low correlations) of LDC stocks may also restrict investors' access to the stocks. As restrictions on international transactions are loosened, it will be easier for foreigners to purchase LDC stocks directly. Yet, once restrictions on international flows are lifted, interaction will increase. Consequently, the LDCs will be more highly influenced by economic conditions in other countries, and the correlation of LDC stocks with stocks of other countries will increase (thereby reducing the attractiveness of LDC stocks).

The above discussion is not intended to discourage international diversification, but rather to stress that although gains from international diversification are possible, the performance of a global portfolio depends on its composition. Most studies that have found gains from international diversification have used an ex-post approach, where the *ex-post efficient* portfolios were found to outperform the domestic stock index. Hence, the input used assumes perfect foresight. The ex-post approach is sufficient for demonstrating that gains were "achievable" over a given period, but efficient international portfolios for the future (referred to as *ex-ante efficient* portfolios) will not necessarily be identical to the ex-post efficient portfolios. Although one may attempt to forecast future correlations based on past data, it is virtually impossible for an investor consistently to construct a global portfolio that is ex-ante efficient.[6] Therefore, in order to diversify internationally, the investor must understand the factors that influence security prices globally.

• Factors Influencing Security Prices Globally

If, as the above studies indicate, international diversification can reduce the risk of a portfolio, then the next question to be answered is, Which countries and which industries and companies within the countries should be selected? A recent study by Grinold, Rudd, and Stefek addressed these questions.[7] The

---

[5] A recent study showed that the degree of international co-movements in major stock price indexes has increased significantly since the stock market crash of October 1987. See Jeon Bang Nam and George M. von Furstenberg, "Growing International Co-Movement in Stock Price Indexes," *Quarterly Review of Economics and Business* (Autumn 1990): 15–30.

[6] For an example of the use of ex-post data to project ex-ante efficient portfolios, see Jeff Madura and Gordon Abernathy, "Playing the International Stock Diversification Game with an Unmarked Deck," *Journal of Business Research* (December 1985): 465–71.

[7] Richard Grinold, Andrew Rudd, and Dan Stefek, "Global Factors: Fact or Fiction?" *Journal of Portfolio Management* (Fall 1989): 79–88.

authors examined the degree to which countries and companies within countries are related. If asset returns are closely related across countries, then the markets are **integrated,** and the impact from diversifying across countries is reduced. If, on the other hand, asset returns are not closely related across countries, then the markets are **segmented,** and diversification across countries can be beneficial to the investor.

Grinold, Rudd, and Stefek do not feel that the degree of market integration and segmentation can be accurately measured by using the stock indexes of various countries:

> The structure of global asset returns is also important for quantitative applications such as asset allocation and portfolio risk measurement and optimization. The covariance structure for asset allocation models is typically estimated from index returns. Index returns, however, are influenced by the transient behavior induced by unusual economic conditions that are unlikely to be repeated over any short period of time. For example, the Australian market is dominated by the resource companies, which will have a major impact on the Australian market index returns. The returns to resource companies will be more variable than the returns to the true underlying Australian market. Hence, correlations using market indexes are likely to be quite non-stationary because of the changing impact of the resource sector.[8]

Instead, the authors elected to isolate an asset's return relative to three factors: its local market return, its global industry membership, and the attributes of a particular company, such as its size, yield, and volatility. By examining asset returns in this way, the authors could isolate the factors affecting an asset's returns. Their empirical results indicated that, on average, the country impact is more important than the global industry to which a company belongs. However, "the most important industries are more important than the least important countries." They also found that company attributes can significantly impact returns.

One of the most interesting results of their study was the degree of market segmentation that they found for selected countries. Since the local market factor measures the return assigned to the country without any influence from the global industry or company attributes, this factor would be expected to perform in a manner similar to a market index for the country. As Table 6.5 shows, the correlations, as expected, are quite high. The United States has the lowest correlation coefficient (.70), and Mexico has the highest (.97). One interpretation of the correlations in Table 6.5 is that for the United States, 49 percent ($.70^2$) of the market index variance is explained by the local market factor whereas for Mexico, it is approximately 94 percent ($.97^2$). Thus, the U.S. market return is impacted *more* than Mexico by global factors. These results indicate that Mexico is a relatively segmented market whereas countries like the United States, Canada, Japan, the Netherlands, and the United Kingdom are more globally integrated.

---

[8] Ibid., p. 80.

TABLE 6.5 • Local Market Factor and Local Market Index Correlations

Country	Correlation	Rank	Country	Correlation	Rank
Australia	0.83	13	Malaysia	0.91	21
Austria	0.80	10	Mexico	0.97	24
Belgium	0.82	12	Netherlands	0.72	3
Canada	0.72	2	New Zealand	0.85	19
Denmark	0.79	8	Norway	0.83	15
Finland	0.85	17	Singapore	0.91	22
France	0.83	14	South Africa	0.74	6
Germany	0.79	9	Spain	0.86	20
Hong Kong	0.92	23	Sweden	0.80	11
Ireland	0.85	18	Switzerland	0.73	5
Italy	0.84	16	United Kingdom	0.75	7
Japan	0.72	4	United States	0.70	1

SOURCE: Richard Grinold, Andrew Rudd, and Dan Stefek, "Global Factors: Fact or Fiction?" *Journal of Portfolio Management* (Fall 1989): 85.

For the individual investor, the results of this study mean that an investor must be aware of company attributes, industry membership, and the country in which the company is located when making international portfolio selections. For example, an investor would not necessarily achieve significant diversification by investing in the automobile industry in both the United States and the United Kingdom.

• International Diversification with Floating Exchange Rates

The construction of a global portfolio becomes more complex when the impact of **floating exchange rates** is considered. This occurs because changes in the exchange rate affect the holding period return (HPR) on the security. The actual HPR, therefore, depends on two factors: (1) the performance of the security and (2) the exchange rates.

Consider a British investor who purchases 100 shares of a British stock on a British stock exchange. Assume that the stock was priced at 30 British pounds per share. Thus, the 100 shares would cost 3,000 pounds (assuming no transaction costs). Three years later, the investor sells the 100 shares for the current market price of 39 pounds per share. The HPR, assuming no cash dividends, is

$$\text{HPR} = \frac{\text{proceeds from stock sale} - \text{initial investment}}{\text{initial investment}} \tag{6.1}$$

$$= \frac{\pounds 3{,}900 - \pounds 3{,}000}{\pounds 3{,}000} = 30\%$$

This example reflects a British investor's perspective. If, instead, the British stock is purchased by a U.S. investor, an initial exchange of U.S. dollars for British pounds is necessary for the investor to purchase the stock. Assume that the value of a British pound is $1.90 at the purchase date. If the U.S. investor sells the British stock three years later at a price of 39 pounds per share, the British pounds received from the sale will be exchanged for U.S. dollars. Assume that the value of the British pound declines and is $1.45 at the selling date. The return to the U.S. investor, adjusted for the exchange rates (HPR_E), is determined as follows (assuming no transaction costs):

Step 1. Determine how many U.S. dollars will be needed for the £3,000 required to purchase 100 shares of the British stock:

$$\pounds 3{,}000 \times \$1.90 \text{ per pound} = \$5{,}700$$

Step 2. Determine the number of U.S. dollars to be received after selling the British stock and exchanging British pounds received from the sale for U.S. dollars:

$$\pounds 39 \text{ per share} \times 100 \text{ shares} = \pounds 3{,}900$$
$$\pounds 3{,}900 \times \$1.45 \text{ per pound} = \$5{,}655$$

Step 3. Determine the HPR_E as follows:

$$\text{HPR}_E = \frac{\begin{array}{l}\text{total} \\ \text{U.S. dollars} \\ \text{received after} \\ \text{selling British} \\ \text{stock}\end{array} - \begin{array}{l}\text{initial} \\ \text{investment of} \\ \text{U.S. dollars}\end{array}}{\text{initial investment of U.S. dollars}} \qquad (6.2)$$

$$= \frac{\$5{,}655 - \$5{,}700}{\$5{,}700} = -.7895\%$$

The HPR_E can also be calculated by first computing the HPR on the stock without adjusting for the fluctuation in exchange rates. Using Equation 6.1, the HPR was 30 percent. Then, compute the percentage change in the British pound's exchange rate over the holding period, E, as follows:

$$E = \frac{\begin{array}{l}\text{exchange rate at} \\ \text{end of period}\end{array} - \begin{array}{l}\text{exchange rate at} \\ \text{beginning of period}\end{array}}{\text{exchange rate at beginning of period}}$$

$$= \frac{\$1.45 - \$1.90}{\$1.90}$$

$$E = -23.6842\%$$

Now that values have been computed for the stock's rate of return *unadjusted* for the exchange rate fluctuation (HPR) and the percentage change in the exchange rate over the holding period (E), the stock's rate of return *adjusted* for the exchange rate fluctuation (HPR_E) is

$$\begin{aligned} HPR_E &= (1 + HPR)(1 + E) - 1 \\ &= (1 + .30)[1 + (-.236842)] - 1 \\ &= -.7895\% \end{aligned} \qquad \textbf{(6.3)}$$

This value for HPR_E coincides with value obtained from the alternative computation presented earlier. This second method is convenient in that it decomposes the HPR_E into the two factors (HPR and E) that influence it. Notice that in this example the depreciation of the British pound against the U.S. dollar more than offset the British stock's 30 percent appreciation. The British investor did not have to worry about the fluctuation of the pound's value against the dollar, while the U.S. investor's return was severely affected.

To illustrate the potential benefits from a change in the foreign currency's value, assume that the pound was worth $1.45 at the beginning of the holding period and $1.90 at the end of the holding period. The percentage change in the pound's exchange rate over the holding period (E), assuming no transaction costs, would be

$$\begin{aligned} E &= \frac{\$1.90 - \$1.45}{\$1.45} \\ &= 31.03\% \end{aligned}$$

Thus, from a U.S. investor's perspective, the return on the British stock adjusted for the exchange rate would be

$$\begin{aligned} HPR_E &= (1 + HPR)(1 + E) - 1 \\ &= (1 + .30)(1 + .3101) - 1 \\ &= 70.31\% \end{aligned}$$

The British pound's value actually depreciated more than 40 percent over the three-year period, 1981–1984, illustrating how an exchange rate fluctuation can hurt the U.S. investor in British stocks. On the other hand, the pound appreciated substantially against the U.S. dollar during the 1986–1987 period. This appreciation of the pound relative to the dollar benefited U.S. investors in British stocks. Between early 1988 and April 1991, the pound was rather stable against the dollar. Thus, exchange rate fluctuations between the two currencies have had very little impact on HPRs in recent years.

These examples demonstrate the degree to which exchange rate fluctuations can affect an investment in a foreign stock. The expectation that a foreign currency will strengthen will make stocks denominated in that currency more attractive to U.S. investors. Unfortunately, forecasting exchange rates is extremely difficult. With this limitation in mind, a portfolio manager should not make stock purchases based solely on exchange rate forecasts.

Because of the potentially large exposure of international portfolios to exchange rate fluctuations, some investors may think that international diversification is more risky than a purely domestic portfolio. However, one can reduce the exposure to the movements of any particular currency by diversifying among stocks denominated in different currencies. The degree to which such currency exposure can be reduced depends on the correlations among currency movements. For example, consider a U.S. investor who diversifies among stocks in France, the Netherlands, Switzerland, and Germany. The investor's currency exposure will be quite high, since all of these currencies move closely in tandem against the dollar. Thus, if any one of the currencies depreciates against the U.S. dollar, the other three currencies will probably depreciate as well and by about the same degree. Because movements in these currencies are highly correlated, diversifying among stocks denominated in these currencies is not much different from using stocks denominated in only one of these currencies. To reduce currency exposure substantially, an investor should assess the correlations of movements between currencies.

From the U.S. investor's perspective, some currencies are not highly correlated with each other. The Canadian dollar, for example, normally exhibits a low correlation with other currencies. The same holds for the Japanese yen. Furthermore, international portfolio managers should not automatically purchase stocks of a particular country simply because the currency denominating those stocks exhibits desirable characteristics. They must also consider the potential increase in the stock's value.

Like stock index co-movements, currency co-movements are unstable over time. Therefore, historical correlation coefficients of movements in currencies will not necessarily serve as accurate indicators of the future. However, the relative rankings of currency correlations have been somewhat stable; thus, it may at least be possible to determine which currency pairs will be less correlated on a relative basis.

Large investors who desire to avoid **exchange rate risk** may be able to **hedge** their positions in the forward exchange market.[9] For the widely used currencies, forward rates are commonly available for maturities such as 30 days, 90 days, 180 days, and one year. This means that an investor can buy or sell that currency forward for any of these maturities. Commercial banks offer this service; they are willing to deliver a currency or purchase a currency in the future and lock in the rate of exchange today. Regardless of how currency values move, the forward rate on the day the contract is established will serve as the rate of exchange on the settlement date. Because forward rates are offered only for large currency transactions, it is not practical for an individual to hedge using these contracts. Individuals, however, can hedge using futures on foreign currencies.

To illustrate how a hedge could work, assume that a U.S. investment firm has developed an international mutual fund with a portfolio partially composed of British stocks. If the British pound depreciates against the U.S. dollar, U.S. investors in the fund will be adversely affected. The mutual fund can

[9] Forward and futures markets for foreign currencies and currency options are discussed in Chapters 15 and 17.

RESEARCH BOX
Different Approaches to Currency Risk Exposure

A significant amount of recent research has been devoted to the problem of currency risk in an international portfolio. The three studies summarized here are indicative of the diverse approaches being used to examine currency risk.

Chamberlin, Cheung, and Kwan developed a simple portfolio model that explicitly recognized currency risk and return. The model requires only modest amounts of data and is computationally uncomplicated. The results of the study show that the currency factor is very important in asset allocation between securities denominated in U.S. dollars and those denominated in currencies that float against the dollar.

Black suggests a universal hedging formula that determines the percentage of a portfolio that should be hedged against currency risk. He believes that hedging currency exposure reduces risk, but that accepting some currency risk will add to the expected return of the portfolio. Black's formula indicates that the investor should hedge foreign equities, that equities should be hedged equally for all countries, and that less than 100 percent of foreign equities should be hedged.

A more radical approach for investors in the international fixed-income markets has been suggested by Lee. Observing that currency returns move relatively independently of local asset returns, Lee suggests that the asset investment decision should be made separately from the currency exposure decision. The results of a simulation over the 1971–1985 period for the U.S., Japanese, German, and U.K. bond markets using a naïve currency forecasting methodology indicate that separating the asset decision from the currency decision results in superior performance.

SOURCES: Trevor W. Chamberlin, C. Sherman Cheung, and Clarence C. Y. Kwan, "International Investment and Currency Risk," *Journal of Economics and Business* (May 1990): 141–52; Fischer Black, "Universal Hedging: Optimizing Currency Risk and Reward in International Equity Portfolios," *Financial Analysts Journal* (July-August 1989): 16–22; and Adrian F. Lee, "International Asset and Currency Allocation," *Journal of Portfolio Management* (Fall 1987): 68–73.

avoid this risk by "selling British pounds forward" for a particular date when it plans to liquidate British stocks. On that date, the firm will sell the stocks and exchange the pounds received from the sale for U.S. dollars, at the rate specified by the forward contract. If the firm decides not to sell the British stocks on this date, it can offset its "short" position in British pounds by purchasing pounds in the spot market at the spot exchange rate and selling them to fulfill its forward sale obligation. The gain (loss) from this strategy can offset most of the fund's loss (gain) due to fluctuations in the value of the British pound. If the investment firm expects the British pound to appreciate (strengthen), it may prefer not to hedge; the pound's appreciation will enhance the performance of the fund from the U.S. investor's perspective.

The majority of the foreign currency positions of international mutual funds are not hedged. Thus, the net asset values of most international mutual funds are highly susceptible to foreign currency movements against the U.S. dollar.

INTERNATIONAL INVESTMENTS FOR THE INDIVIDUAL INVESTOR

The performance of foreign markets relative to U.S. markets during the October 1987 crash increased investor awareness of international investing. For example, stock prices in Japan declined 5.9 percent on "Black Monday," compared to a 22.6 percent decline in the Dow Jones Industrial Average. In Hong Kong, however, stocks declined 45.0 percent; in Australia, 44.5 percent.

Individuals can use a number of methods to invest internationally: (1) direct foreign investments, (2) listed foreign stocks on a local stock exchange, (3) international mutual funds, (4) international closed-end funds, (5) American Depository Receipts (ADRs), and (6) multinational corporate stocks.

DIRECT FOREIGN INVESTMENTS Individual investors generally do not invest in foreign securities directly. In addition to high transaction costs, the difficulty of obtaining information on foreign firms, and problems with foreign currency transactions, investors may encounter vastly different trading rules and investment practices in foreign markets.

The Tokyo Stock Exchange (TSE) provides a good illustration of these differences. First, it is not uncommon for Japanese stocks to sell at 40 to 50 times their most recent 12-month earnings. By comparison, the average earnings multiple for U.S. stocks is in the range of 10 to 20. U.S. analysts using Western analytical methods are usually not successful at explaining these high multiples. Second, the Japanese government and private firms do not publish detailed economic and trade statistics. This limits the U.S. investor's ability to make the customary economic analysis and forecast. Third, security regulations in Japan do not require full financial disclosure by publicly traded firms. Fourth, Japanese regulations allow margin trading but prohibit selling short. Finally, price manipulation by brokerage firms and large investors is fairly common on the TSE. Because of these and other problems, it is probably not advisable for individuals to invest directly in foreign securities.

LISTED FOREIGN STOCKS ON A LOCAL EXCHANGE Some U.S. stock exchanges list foreign stocks. This allows a local investor easy access to such stocks and eliminates the necessity to exchange currencies. However, the number of foreign stocks listed on a local exchange is usually quite limited, providing investors with only a small sample of foreign stocks. Four of the largest and most actively traded foreign issues on the NYSE are (1) British Petroleum Company P.L.C. (United Kingdom), (2) Schlumberger Limited (Netherlands), (3) Royal Dutch Petroleum Company (Netherlands), and (4) Northern Telecom Limited (Canada).

INTERNATIONAL MUTUAL FUNDS **International mutual funds (IMFs)** are similar to domestic mutual funds in that they represent security portfolios constructed by an investment firm.[10] The composition of an IMF is determined by the fund's managers; therefore, investors in the fund rely on the management of the fund.

The IMFs exhibit characteristics similar to those of domestic mutual funds except that they include foreign securities (stocks, bonds, or both). An investor who purchases shares of an IMF is part owner of a portfolio containing international securities. Because each share represents ownership in the entire portfolio, mutual funds offer diversification to the small investor. In addition, because the volume of money in most funds is so large, far more diversification may be achieved than would be possible for an individual investor. This suggests that even if individual foreign securities could be purchased and sold easily by investors, the IMFs might still retain their popularity.

The shares of American IMFs are priced in U.S. dollars. Thus, the investor does not have to exchange dollars for other currencies. Nevertheless, the dollar value of securities of foreign countries is influenced by currency fluctuations. Thus, the market value of an IMF still reflects the foreign currency value of each security, translated into U.S. dollar terms. An IMF's value is determined not only by the value of each foreign security but also by the exchange rate of the currency denominating that security with respect to the U.S. dollar. In other words, an IMF's value is equal to the weighted sum of the values of its component securities adjusted for exchange rates.

Although most IMFs diversify their foreign security holdings across several countries, each fund usually concentrates its international investments on a specific region or continent. Some funds may purchase securities of mostly Far Eastern companies, while other funds may purchase mostly European stocks. Because each fund's foreign investments are typically concentrated in a specific geographic region, the full benefits of international diversification may not be realized. To grasp this concept, consider a fund composed of securities of companies based in several different European countries. Because of the intercountry influence in Europe, economic conditions may be somewhat similar in the various countries. A portfolio that includes securities from several continents is likely to be less exposed to any single economic event.

Even if individual IMFs are not as globally diversified as one might desire, an investor can invest in several different IMFs and create a portfolio of international security portfolios. To use such an approach, the investor must first identify the composition of each available IMF's foreign investments by country and then determine the appropriate mix of IMFs to achieve the desired global diversification. The asset composition of an IMF is identified in its prospectus.

---

[10] A complete description of the characteristics and types of mutual funds is presented in Chapter 5. Quite often a distinction is made between an international mutual fund and a global mutual fund. An international mutual fund usually has a portfolio made up of securities from outside the United States, while a global mutual fund contains a mix of U.S. and foreign securities. For the purposes of the discussion in this section, international and global mutual funds are not distinguished.

The number of IMFs increased from 17 funds in 1983 to approximately 100 funds in 1991. Reasons for this rapid growth include the recent performance of foreign securities and the decline in the value of the U.S. dollar. Table 6.6 provides basic information on 25 of the larger IMFs. As the table indicates, several of these funds have over a billion dollars under management. The average HPRs of these funds over periods of 1, 5, and 10 years were impressive.[11]

When evaluating performance, however, consideration must be given to the risk as well as the return achieved (see Chapter 21 for techniques used in evaluating portfolio performance). One study of nine U.S.-based IMFs for the period 1979–1983 concluded that "these funds have earned a rate of return that is consistent with the risk assumed. The funds, with the possible exception of Templeton Growth, do not reveal any superior ability in stock selection and market timing."[12] These results, while admittedly based on a small sample, indicate that IMFs are similar in their performance to mutual funds that invest in the U.S. equity markets. Nevertheless, this lack of superior performance by IMFs does not reduce their appeal as a means of diversifying an investor's portfolio internationally.

INTERNATIONAL CLOSED-END FUNDS Most **international closed-end funds** are nondiversified and concentrate their holdings in the securities of one country.[13] While these closed-end country funds provide a way for individual investors to internationalize their portfolios, they should be viewed as speculative, particularly when they are trading at large premiums relative to their net asset values (NAVs). To achieve appropriate international diversification using these country funds, the investor should buy several funds representing different countries or regions of the world.

In addition to currency risk, the prices of international closed-end funds that invest in companies located in one country or region react quite sharply to world events affecting that area. For example, when world stock markets surged at the news of the fall of the Berlin Wall in 1989, funds specializing in German companies moved up sharply. When Iraq invaded Kuwait and world stock markets declined by 20–30 percent, the funds investing in the countries most directly affected declined even further. Another example of price volatility is provided by the Spain Fund. In 1989, the fund moved from an 18 percent discount to a 165 percent premium over NAV in a matter of months. The dramatic increase in price was attributed to Japanese investors buying the fund. A more recent example involves the India Growth Fund. When Rajiv

---

[11] Recall from the earlier discussion that HPRs are sensitive to the time period selected. In this case, the ending date is 1989. If 1990 had been used as the ending date (see Table 6.2), the average HPRs would have been considerably lower than those shown in the table.

[12] Ramesh P. Rao and Raj Aggarwal, "Performance of U.S.-Based International Mutual Funds," *Akron Business and Economic Review* (Winter 1987): 106.

[13] A complete description of the characteristics and types of closed-end funds is provided in Chapter 5.

TABLE 6.6 • International Mutual Funds

	Total net assets, 12/31/89 (millions)	Holding period returns			Classification of assets (12/31/89)			
		Twelve months (1989)	*Five years (1985 to 12/31/89)*	*Ten years (1980 to 12/31/89)*	*Cash or govern-ment securities*	*Bonds or preferred stock*	*Common stock*	*Percentage yield last 12 months*
Alliance International Fund	$ 221.6	29.6%	280%		3%		97%	0.2%
Blanchard Strategic Growth Fund	253.8	15.7			18	24%	58	3.5
Dean Witter World Wide Investments	321.3		157		17	4	79	1.4
EuroPacific Growth Fund	405.2	24.2	205		26	3	71	1.7
Fidelity Overseas Fund	1,010.4	16.9	253		2	2	96	0.9
First Investors Global Fund	181.4	38.0	232		10	6	84	0.0
GT Pacific Growth Fund	169.9	48.1	258	540%	4	5	91	0.4
IDS International Fund	216.9	18.2	200		2		98	1.0
John Hancock Global Trust	110.9	17.6				7	93	0.8
Kemper International Fund	194.4	18.6	233		24		76	0.9
ML International Holdings	200.9	23.5	157		9		91	3.2

ML Pacific Fund	318.6	14.5	327	871	8		92	0.3
Oppenheimer Global Fund	566.8	35.0	102	75	2	4	94	0.3
Prudential-Bache Global Fund	405.1	12.0	174		2	5	93	2.4
Putnam International Equities Fund	534.3	24.6	231	451	4	1	95	1.6
Sci/Tech Holdings	146.8	11.5	88		11		89	0.6
Scudder International Fund	767.2	27.0	242	447	6	7	87	1.0
SoGen International Fund	162.3	17.2	152	503	31	14	55	3.6
T. Rowe Price International Stock	970.5	23.7	269		12	2	86	1.5
Templeton Foreign Fund	564.1	30.2	224		15		85	2.8
Templeton Global	896.8	17.9	108	259	10	1	89	2.3
Templeton Growth Fund	2,451.5	22.6	142	318	6	1	93	3.5
Templeton World Fund	4,714.9	22.6	134	361	1	3	96	3.1
Trustees' Commingled Fund-International	645.6	26.0	292		12	1	87	2.3
Vanguard World Fund–International Growth	685.2	24.8			7		93	1.2
TOTAL	$17,116.4							
Averages		23.3%	202.7%	425.0%	9.8%	3.6%	86.7%	1.6%

SOURCE: *Management Results* (New York: Wiesenberger Investment Companies Service, 1990).

Gandhi, former Prime Minister of India, was assassinated in a bomb blast in 1991, the fund declined $1\frac{5}{8}$ points to $11 per share.

AMERICAN DEPOSITORY RECEIPTS An **American Depository Receipt (ADR)** is a certificate issued by a major bank that represents ownership of a foreign security. Although most ADRs represent one share of stock, depending on the price of the foreign stock in U.S. dollars, an ADR can represent either multiple or fractional shares of the foreign stocks. ADRs can take two forms: *sponsored* and *unsponsored.* Sponsored ADRs are issued through banks by foreign corporations that have registered with the Securities and Exchange Commission (SEC) and qualify to trade on one of the exchanges. Unsponsored ADRs are issued by banks in response to investor demand; the corporation has not fully registered with the SEC. Unsponsored ADRs are traded in the over-the-counter market.

Because ADRs are traded on local stock exchanges or the over-the-counter market, they give local investors easy access to foreign securities. Local trading eliminates the need to exchange currencies, although the values of ADRs are influenced by exchange rate fluctuations. The issuing bank collects dividends and pays them to the ADR investor. About 800 companies trade in the United States in the form of ADRs, including such well-known companies as the Hard Rock Cafe, Sony, and Olivetti. Table 6.7 lists the 50 ADRs with the largest market value as of February 1990.

In addition to ADRs that represent shares of stock of foreign companies, there are also ADRs for debt. In September 1988, France listed two bonds, Obligations Assimilable du Tresor (OATS), on the New York Stock Exchange.

U.S. investors may purchase ADRs to capitalize on the potential benefits of international diversification. Information on the companies these ADRs represent is not as readily available as on domestic companies, however, and international mutual funds may serve as a more appropriate alternative.

Some people are predicting that ADRs may become extinct. The trend toward globalization of the world's capital markets, which made ADRs popular with investors, may also cause their demise. If financial markets become truly global, with an international custody and transfer network for shares, ADRs may no longer be attractive.[14]

MULTINATIONAL CORPORATE STOCKS A final method of investing internationally does not require the ownership of any foreign securities. Instead, an investor simply buys common stocks of U.S. **multinational corporations.** The logic behind such an approach is that the multinational corporation represents an international portfolio, containing subsidiaries based in foreign countries. Its overall value will be influenced not only by the economy of its headquarters country but also by the economies of all countries where it does business.

---

[14] Jeffrey E. Friedman, "The Last Days of the ADR," *Institutional Investor,* June 1990, p. 97.

Some research has been conducted to determine whether investment in multinational corporations can achieve the benefits available from other methods of international diversification. Jacquillat and Solnik found that the prices of multinational stocks moved in much the same way as the prices of purely domestic stocks.[15] This implies that investing in multinational stocks will not provide as much diversification in a portfolio as including foreign securities. A more recent study investigated whether investors recognized any increased value for firms involved in multinational manufacturing operations. The results indicated that investors did not place any premium on the value of the share prices of these firms.[16] This outcome is consistent with the earlier study by Jacquillat and Solnik in that investors do not appear to exhibit any additional demand for the shares of multinational firms in order to diversify internationally.

INTERNATIONAL MONEY MARKET INVESTMENTS

International investing is not confined to capital market instruments such as stocks and bonds. Large corporations often set up short-term (money market) deposits denominated in foreign currencies. In some cases, this is done to offset a future payable in that currency, but sometimes a foreign currency deposit is set up to capitalize on higher foreign interest rates. The arena for international short-term investing is known as the **Eurocurrency market.** It is made up of large banks (called Eurobanks) that are willing to accept large short-term deposits in foreign currencies and lend these deposits to corporations and governments in need of short-term funds.

Assume that you are the treasurer of a large U.S. corporation. One of your jobs is to manage a short-term portfolio. You must decide how to invest the funds for, say, a three-month period and must strive to meet specified goals related to high return and low risk. You may find that deposits denominated in French francs offer a higher quoted rate than U.S. dollar deposits. However, there is a risk that the French franc may depreciate during the life of the deposit. In this case, the deposit denominated in French francs may generate a return that is far lower than that of a deposit denominated in U.S. dollars. This **currency risk** is similar to the risk discussed in the section on international stock investing. One way to avoid this risk is to hedge your currency positions by selling forward the currencies on the date the deposit matures, when you plan to convert the currency held back to U.S. dollars. Unfortunately, the forward rate will typically contain a discount for currencies whose interest rates exceed those in the United States. The size of the discount will be directly related to the interest rate differential. This relationship is known as **interest**

[15] Bertrand Jacquillat and Bruno Solnik, "Multinationals Are Poor Tools for Diversification," *Journal of Portfolio Management* (Winter 1978): 8–12.

[16] Luc A. Soenen, "Stock Market Recognition of Multinationality: An Empirical Study of Markets," *Akron Business and Economic Review* (Winter 1990): 64–73.

TABLE 6.7 • The 50 Leading ADRs Based on Market Value, February 1990

Company (business)	Market value (millions)	Sales (millions)	Net income (millions)	Earnings per share	Stock price	Yield
Industrial Bank of Japan (banking)	$78,990	$ 15,588	$ 605	$ 2.57	$336	0.2%
Sumitomo Bank (banking)	61,002	24,740	1,579	5.27	204	0.3
Fuji Bank (banking)	60,290	20,739	1,356	4.92	219	0.3
Dai-Ichi Kangyo Bank (banking)	53,678	24,586	1,486	5.10	184	0.3
Mitsubishi Bank (banking)	49,267	20,076	1,237	4.52	180	0.3
Sanwa Bank (banking)	48,969	19,551	1,235	4.27	169	0.3
Toyota Motor (automobiles)	47,722	58,030	2,535	1.67	31	0.8
Royal Dutch Petrolem (integrated oil)	40,427	47,036	3,325	8.05	75	5.3
Nomura Securities (securities brokerage)	38,545	3,629	2,156	11.01	197	0.5
Hitachi (computers, electric machinery)	31,647	46,313	1,384	4.52	103	0.6
Mitsui Bank (banking)	30,861	13,686	567	3.02	165	0.3
British Telecom (telecommunications)	30,545	18,060	2,743	4.54	51	4.8
British Petroleum (integrated oil)	30,294	46,036	2,653	5.97	68	6.3
Matsushita Electronic Industrial (consumer electronics)	30,240	39,822	1,589	7.66	146	0.6
Tokai Bank (banking)	26,635	13,247	466	4.80	274	0.4
Shell Trans & Trad (integrated oil)	25,488	31,358	1,909	4.69	46	5.4
Daimler-Benz (automobiles)	23,743	40,968	1,458	31.28	510	2.2
Bank of Tokyo (banking)	22,200	12,546	457	2.29	112	0.5
Siemens (consumer electronics)	21,322	32,706	1,042	4.26	87	2.6
Nestlé (food processing)	21,241	29,545	1,247	1.76	30	2.0
Nissan Motor (automobiles)	21,180	34,811	838	0.67	17	1.1
Mitsubishi Trust (banking)	20,984	10,139	589	4.53	161	0.4
BAT Industries (tobacco, financial services)	20,259	20,480	1,876	1.23	13	5.1
NEC (computers, communications equipment)	19,432	22,303	520	1.72	64	0.5

Deutsche Bank (banking)	18,542	5,097	682	22.69	449	2.9
Sony (consumer electronics)	18,377	15,927	658	1.99	56	0.6
Tokio Fire & Marine (insurance)	18,077	6,040	320	1.09	61	0.4
Fujitsu (computers)	17,998	17,273	595	1.66	50	0.5
Japan Air Lines (airlines)	17,681	7,897	153	1.87	215	0.3
Glaxo Holdings (drugs)	17,660	4,192	1,124	1.51	24	3.3
Mitsubishi Estate (real estate leasing)	17,533	2,101	266	2.09	138	0.4
All Nippon Airways (airlines)	17,441	4,509	56	0.20	63	0.2
Daiwa Securities (securities brokerage)	16,780	3,111	1,089	8.37	129	0.7
Mitsubishi (trading)	16,392	113,179	402	2.58	105	0.5
Fiat (automobiles)	16,158	38,277	1,331	4.74	39	3.3
Kawasaki Steel (steel)	15,726	8,255	374	1.15	48	0.7
NKK (steel)	15,651	9,981	689	2.00	45	0.7
Nikko Securities (securities brokerage)	15,627	2,311	871	5.96	107	0.8
British Gas (natural gas utilities)	15,626	12,277	1,473	3.46	37	5.8
Asahi Glass (glass products)	15,414	7,692	363	3.11	132	0.4
Sumitomo Metal Industries (steel)	15,100	8,851	446	2.95	100	0.7
Mitsubishi Electric (electronics)	15,043	19,655	488	2.29	71	0.8
Hanson (diversified)	14,830	11,416	1,364	1.73	19	5.1
Nintendo (electronics)	13,325	2,107	248	9.45	508	0.2
Yamaichi Securities (securities brokerage)	13,074	2,204	742	6.17	109	0.8
Sharp (consumer electronics)	12,852	9,108	228	2.22	125	0.6
Yasuda Trust (banking)	12,617	7,978	447	4.29	121	0.4
Kyowa Bank (banking)	12,578	5,910	278	2.24	101	0.5
Kirin Brewery (brewing)	12,320	10,239	292	2.91	123	0.4
Imperial Chemical Industries (chemicals)	12,285	20.741	1,662	9.67	71	6.9

SOURCE: *Financial World*, May 1, 1990, p. 73.

rate parity. If interest rate parity exists, hedging a short-term deposit will result in a rate of return on the foreign deposit that is no higher than the return on a U.S. deposit. This does not mean that you cannot earn a higher return on foreign currency deposits, but it does imply that if you want to achieve higher gains than those possible domestically, you will have to remain unhedged (exposed to currency risk).

The first step in considering short-term deposits is to review all types of deposits and the rates they offer. The next step is to forecast the percentage change in the exchange rate of the currency denominating each deposit over the life of the planned investment. Then, the exchange-rate-adjusted yield on each deposit can be forecast. This return accounts for not only the interest rate offered on the deposit but also the anticipated exchange rate fluctuation. Table 6.8 provides an example of an assessment of four possible deposits, each denominated in a different currency. The anticipated yield adjusted for exchange rates that is shown in the final column of the table is computed as follows:

$$\begin{aligned}&\text{exchange-rate-adjusted yield on deposit} \\ &\quad = (1 + \text{quoted interest rate}) \\ &\quad\quad \times (1 + \Delta \text{ in exchange rate against U.S. dollar}) - 1\end{aligned} \tag{6.4}$$

Table 6.8 illustrates how much exchange rate fluctuations can affect the actual yield of foreign deposits. The French franc's quoted interest rate is the highest of all the currencies. Nevertheless, the British deposit is expected to earn the highest yield after accounting for the expected exchange rate fluctuations because the British pound is expected to appreciate relative to the U.S. dollar.

The appropriate selection of a foreign deposit depends on one's degree of risk aversion. An extremely risk-averse person would probably prefer the U.S. dollar investment because the 6 percent earnings are assured. Although the anticipated yield is higher for the other three deposits, the actual yield to be generated is uncertain. This uncertainty comes from the forecast of each currency's fluctuation against the U.S. dollar. A poor forecast could result in an

TABLE 6.8 • Computation of Anticipated Yield Adjusted for Exchange Rates

Currency denominating the deposit	Quoted interest rate offered on deposit	Anticipated change in exchange rate vs. the U.S. dollar	Anticipated rate of return
British pound	9%	4%	$(1 + .09)(1 + .04) - 1 = 13.36\%$
Canadian dollar	8	−1	$(1 + .08)(1 - .01) - 1 = 6.92$
French franc	10	−2	$(1 + .10)(1 - .02) - 1 = 7.80$
U.S. dollar	6	0	$(1 + .06)(1 + 0) - 1 = 6.00$

• **CONCEPT APPLICATIONS**

Investment Concept	Concept Application
International diversification	The investor should strive to create a portfolio that provides the highest level of expected return for a given level of risk. By including international securities in a portfolio, the investor can potentially reduce the risk of the portfolio without reducing the expected return.
Exchange rate risk	In investing internationally, the U.S. investor faces the risk of the individual asset as well as the risk of the movement of the foreign currency relative to the dollar. The investor can reduce exchange rate risk by diversifying across assets denominated in different foreign currencies.
Risks and problems of direct international investments	In addition to individual asset and exchange rate risks, the investor faces other problems in direct international investing. These problems include settling difficulties, "fails," price manipulations, and accurate financial disclosure. To avoid these problems, the investor may elect to invest internationally by buying international mutual funds and/or international closed-end funds.
Ex-post and ex-ante relationships	The research in international investing has demonstrated the benefits of including international securities in an investor's portfolio. However, these studies are based on factors that existed in the past. As the world's economy becomes more integrated, these factors will change, and the investor must be aware that these changes will affect the future performance of internationally diversified portfolios.

investment that generates a very low yield. A more detailed assessment of the risk of each deposit denominated in a foreign currency could be provided by creating a probability distribution for each currency's anticipated fluctuation. However, this risk assessment would be only as accurate as the probability distributions.

One way to reduce the currency risk on short-term deposits is to diversify the funds among several currencies (i.e., set up several different deposits, with each deposit denominated in a different currency). The degree to which currency risk is reduced depends on the co-movements of the currencies. If the currencies move in tandem against the U.S. dollar, such a portfolio will exhibit almost as much exposure as if all funds had been placed in a single deposit denominated in one of those foreign currencies. A more appropriate portfolio would contain currencies with low correlations.

SUMMARY

Over the last decade, major developments have encouraged international investing. Local exchanges are offering more foreign stocks, and ADRs, international mutual funds, and closed-end funds are increasing in number. Research has verified the potential benefits of international diversification At the same time, floating exchange rates may have an impact on the risk of international portfolios.

International diversification can improve portfolio performance. However, relationships that existed in the past will not necessarily hold into the future. The investor must recognize that increased interactions among countries are causing historically segmented markets to become more integrated. These changes will reduce, but not eliminate, the benefits of international diversification.

• KEY TERMS

American Depository Receipt (ADR)
Currency risk
Eurocurrency market
Exchange rate risk
Floating exchange rates
Hedging
Integrated markets
Interest rate parity
International closed-end funds
International mutual funds
Multinational corporations
Segmented markets

• QUESTIONS

1. Why would correlations between the returns of stocks issued in different countries change over time?
2. Why are historical data somewhat limited in their ability to identify appropriate global security portfolios in the future?
3. Assume that you are a portfolio manager. If your local currency is generally expected to appreciate against foreign currencies, should this increase or decrease your potential benefits from international diversification? How could you insulate your portfolio from such exchange rate risk?
4. Explain how an investor can invest internationally without purchasing foreign stocks directly on foreign stock exchanges.
5. Would you expect to achieve greater reduction in portfolio variability by including only securities from industrialized countries or by including securities from industrialized and less-developed countries? Why?
6. Explain some of the difficulties associated with direct foreign investments.
7. Explain what is meant by segmented and integrated markets, and describe the impact of integration and segmentation on international diversification.
8. If the governments of less-developed countries loosen their restrictions on international transactions, how might this affect the correlations of their securities' returns with those of other countries? Does this have any effect on the desirability of including such stocks in an international security portfolio?
9. Consider an investor who purchases an international mutual fund that is composed of over 20 stocks in each of several European countries. Is there

any reason for the investor to consider diversifying among other international mutual funds, or is the one fund sufficient to achieve maximum reduction in portfolio variability? Explain your answer.

10. During early 1991, the U.S. dollar declined in value relative to many other currencies. Assuming that the dollar will continue to decline, discuss several appropriate international investment strategies.

• KEY TO THE INVESTMENT ANALYSIS SOFTWARE

Calculation	Appendix A-1 Page Reference	Access Procedure
Holding period return	A-8	BEGIN, STATISTICAL, HPR, ONE or MANY

• PROBLEMS

1. One year ago a U.S. investor bought the common stock of a German company. At the time the stock was purchased, the German mark was trading at \$.5371 per mark. Today, the German mark is trading at \$.5905 per mark. If the price of the common stock of the German company appreciated by 20 percent during the year, what would be the HPR to the U.S. investor, adjusted for the exchange rate?

2. Assume that a British and a U.S. investor each purchased 100 shares of a British stock one year ago. At that time, the stock was worth 4 pounds per share. The exchange rate of the pound was \$2.00 at that time. Today, both investors sell their British stock for 5 pounds per share. The exchange rate of the pound today is \$2.10. (Ignore all transaction costs and dividends.)
   a. Calculate the HPR for the British investor.
   b. Calculate the HPR for the U.S. investor, considering the change in the exchange rate.
   c. Assume that the U.S. investor correctly forecast the number of pounds he would have at the end of one year and sold pounds one year forward to avoid the exchange rate risk. The forward rate at the time the contract was set up was \$2.02. Given this information, what was the return to the investor? Is the return to this investor higher or lower than it would have been if the currency exposure had not been hedged?

3. Assume that the treasurer of a U.S. corporation plans to invest \$1 million in a three-month deposit denominated in French francs. The quoted interest rate over the three-month period is 5 percent. The franc is expected to appreciate by 2 percent over this period. What is the anticipated rate of return on this three-month investment? What is the anticipated rate of return if the franc is expected to depreciate by 4 percent over this period?

4. Assume that a U.S. investor purchased 100 shares of common stock of the Hudson Bay Company, traded on the Toronto Stock Exchange, for $21 per share (Canadian). The investor exchanged U.S. dollars for Canadian dollars at an exchange rate of $.7918 U.S. dollars for each Canadian dollar. The stock appreciated to $22 per share (Canadian) and was sold. The Canadian dollars received from the sale were exchanged for U.S. dollars at an exchange rate of $.8123.
   a. Calculate the HPR on the stock investment, ignoring currency exchange rates.
   b. Calculate the HPR, considering changes in the stock price and in the currency exchange rate.
5. Assume you purchase 100 ADRs of the British firm, BAT Industries, for $13 per ADR. At the time you purchased the ADRs, the dollar price of the pound was $1.56. One year later, the dollar price of the pound is $1.50 and the price of the stock in pounds is £9. Ignoring commission costs and cash dividends:
   a. What is the one-year HPR for a U.S. investor and a British investor?
   b. If the dollar price of the pound is $1.60 rather than $1.50 one year later, what is the one-year HPR for a U.S. investor and a British investor?
   c. Explain the differences in your answers for parts (a) and (b).

• REFERENCES

Black, Fischer. "Universal Hedging: Optimizing Currency Risk and Reward in International Equity Portfolios." *Financial Analysts Journal* (July-August 1989): 16–22.

Chamberlin, Trevor W., C. Sherman Cheung, and Clarence C.Y. Kwan. "International Investment and Currency Risk." *Journal of Economics and Business* (May 1990): 141–52.

Errunza, Vihang R. "Gains from Portfolio Diversification into Less Developed Countries' Securities." *Journal of International Business Studies* (Fall-Winter 1977): 83–99.

Grinold, Richard, Andrew Rudd, and Dan Stefek. "Global Factors: Fact or Fiction?" *Journal of Portfolio Management* (Fall 1989): 79–88.

Haney, Richard L., Jr., and William P. Lloyd. "An Examination of the Stability of the Intertemporal Relationship among National Stock Market Indices." *Nebraska Journal of Economics and Business* (Spring 1978): 55–65.

Hardy, Daniel C. "Market Timing and International Diversification." *Journal of Portfolio Management* (Summer 1990): 23–27.

Hill, Joanne, and Thomas Schneeweis. "International Diversification of Equities and Fixed Income Securities." *Journal of Financial Research* (Winter 1983): 333–43.

Horn, Bernard. "International Investing Strategies." *American Association of Institutional Investors Journal* (November 1983): 11–19.

Hunter, John E., and T. Daniel Coggin. "An Analysis of the Diversification Benefit from International Equity Investment." *Journal of Portfolio Management* (Fall 1990): 33–36.

Ibbotson, Roger G., Laurence B. Siegel, and Kathryn S. Love. "World Wealth: Market Values and Returns." *Journal of Portfolio Management* (Fall 1985): 4–23.

Jacquillat, Bertrand, and Bruno Solnik. "Multinationals Are Poor Tools for Diversification." *Journal of Portfolio Management* (Winter 1978): 8–12.

Jeon, Bang Nam, and George M. von Furstenberg." Growing International Co-Movement in Stock Price Indexes." *Quarterly Review of Economics and Business* (Autumn 1990): 15–30.

Joy, O. Maurice, Don B. Panton, Frank K. Reilly, and Stanley A. Martin. "Comovements of Major International Equity Markets." *Financial Review* (1976): 1–20.

Lee, Adrian F. "International Asset and Currency Allocation." *Journal of Portfolio Management* (Fall 1987): 68–73.

Levy, Haim, and Zvi Jerman. "The Benefits of International Diversification in Bonds." *Financial Analysts Journal* (September-October 1988): 56–64.

Lloyd, William P., Steven J. Goldstein, and Robert B. Rogow. "International Portfolio Diversification of Real Assets: An Update." *Journal of Business, Finance, and Accounting* 8 (Spring 1981): 45–50.

Logue, Dennis E. "An Experiment in International Diversification." *Journal of Portfolio Management* (Fall 1982): 22–27.

Makin, Claire. "London: Bickering over a Eurobourse." *Institutional Investor,* July 1990, pp. 190–93.

Merjos, Anna. "The Lure of Faraway Places: ADRs Grow in Number and Popularity." *Barron's,* April 16, 1990, pp. 27–29, 31.

Micheli, Robin. "Best Ways to Buy Foreign Stocks." *Money,* May 1987, pp. 75–86.

Mikhail, Azmi D., and Hany A. Shawky. "Investment Performance of U.S.-Based Multinational Corporations." *Journal of International Business Studies* (Spring-Summer 1979): 53–66.

Officer, Dennis T., and J. Ronald Hoffmeister. "ADRs: A Substitute for the Real Thing?" *Journal of Portfolio Management* (Winter 1987): 61–65.

Powers, John G. "Global Investment in a Volatile World." *Intermarket* (March 1988): 10–12.

Rao, Ramesh P., and Raj Aggarwal. "Performance of U.S.-Based International Mutual Funds." *Akron Business and Economic Review* (Winter 1987): 96–107.

Schilfforth, Richard A. "The Three Cs of Global Investing." *Pension World* (January 1990): 50–51.

Senchack, Andrew J., Jr., and W.L. Beedles. "Is Indirect International Diversification Desirable?" *Journal of Portfolio Management* (Winter 1980): 49–57.

Williams, Fred. "ADR Use Increases in U.S. Acquisitions." *Pensions and Investment Age,* October 16, 1989, pp. 1, 67.

CHAPTER 7

Investment Strategies

The knowledge-level objectives of this chapter should enable the student to:

- Describe the different types of investment strategies and their importance in achieving an investor's financial objective(s).
- Understand the impact of taxes on investment decision making.
- Differentiate between speculative decisions and investment decisions.
- Comprehend the impact of trading strategies (e.g., margin trading and short selling) on risk.
- Differentiate between technical and fundamental analysis.
- Discuss the importance of the degree of market efficiency in selecting a passive or an active investment strategy.

INTRODUCTION

Investment decisions, like any other decision, are made on the basis of the individual's beliefs and attitudes. In Chapter 1 we discussed the importance of setting specific investment objective(s). The investment objective(s) is determined by the level of wealth the investor will need in the future and when the wealth will be needed. But selecting the objective does not answer the important question of *how* the investment objective(s) is going to be achieved.

The approach used to accomplish the investment objective(s) is called the investor's **investment strategy.** An investment strategy can be developed at a number of different levels, from the very specific to the very broad. A very specific strategy would be a decision on the part of an investor to invest only in specific types of assets, to never borrow money (margin trading) when buying securities, or to always engage in hedging activities to reduce the risk of a security position. Such strategies are called trading strategies.

On a broader level, investment strategies are related to the approaches used to analyze and select investment alternatives. The investor may elect to use *technical analysis,* which relies on historical patterns of price and volume data to estimate future values, *fundamental analysis,* which uses available financial information to estimate the value of a security, or a combination of the two approaches. These strategies are known as analysis strategies.

On an even broader level, the investor must decide how to approach the entire investment process. At one extreme, the investor may believe that because of certain personal attributes, such as superior analytical talents or informational advantages, he or she should personally make the investment decisions as to selection and timing. At the other extreme, the investor may conclude that the market is highly efficient and that there is no advantage to a do-it-yourself approach to investing. In this case, the investor would select a diversified portfolio with the appropriate risk and return characteristics and devote very little time and effort to security selection and market timing. These strategies can be classified as investment strategies in an efficient market.

The purpose of this chapter is to discuss the various types of investment strategies and the external factors, such as taxes, that may influence these strategies. The material on the investment strategies in an efficient market introduced in this chapter is developed in greater detail in the chapters that follow.

• Speculation versus Investing

The distinction between speculation and investing is often difficult to make. Generally, **speculation** involves more risk than *investing*. Another difference is the time horizon; speculation is typically associated with a short time horizon, while investing is for a longer period of time. A third criterion involves the amount of information available to the individual and the time he or she spends analyzing investment alternatives. In speculation, the individual usually makes a decision based on limited information and analysis.

The growing popularity of options (Chapter 15) and financial futures (Chapter 17), however, challenges the traditional distinction between speculation and investing. Individual positions in options and futures are risky relative to common stocks and bonds, and the investment horizon is often three months or less. Is an individual who purchases an option with a three-month maturity speculating or investing? Since the rate of return on an option can be −100 percent (total loss) or quite large (over 100 percent), the option has considerable risk. In terms of a portfolio, however, the option may reduce the overall risk since the option can be used to reduce the risk of the stock portfolio.

For each investment alternative covered in this book, techniques of investment analysis and investment strategies are presented. This approach emphasizes careful and informed investment decisions rather than speculative decisions.

• Taxes

All investment decisions should include a careful analysis of the tax consequences, both in terms of the initial investment and the investment returns. A major problem in tax analysis, however, is the tendency for the U.S. tax code to undergo frequent and numerous changes. For example, the Tax Reform Act of 1986 revised the tax code in ways that had major consequences for investment decisions. As a result of these changes, investment emphasis switched from sheltering income to generating income. This shift occurred because individual tax rates were lowered, allowing investors to retain more of their earnings, and many of the benefits accruing to tax-sheltered investments were removed.

One major change was the elimination of the favorable treatment given to long-term capital gains. Long-term capital gains are taxed like ordinary income, up to a maximum of 28 percent. Because of this change, individuals have less incentive to make investments that stress long-term gains over current income. Without the tax advantage, investments that produce current income, in the form of interest or dividends, have become relatively more popular than investments oriented toward capital gains. Capital gains, however, still retain the advantage of occurring at the investor's discretion, whereas dividend and interest payments are paid on a regular basis and are not controlled by the investor. Table 7.1 summarizes the tax rates for individuals and corporations for 1990.

Other major provisions of the 1986 act that affected investments were the elimination of the $100 dividend exclusion for individuals ($200 for married couples, filing jointly), restrictions on the deduction for investment interest, and more stringent requirements for tax shelters.

The Tax Reform Act of 1986 affected corporations as well as individuals. Effective July 1, 1987, the maximum tax rate for corporations was reduced to 34 percent from 46 percent. Nevertheless, because of the elimination of favorable tax treatment for long-term capital gains, less liberal depreciation allow-

TABLE 7.1 • Individual and Corporate Tax Rates, 1990

Married individuals, filing jointly		Unmarried individuals		Corporations	
Taxable income	*Rate*	*Taxable income*	*Rate*	*Taxable income*	*Rate*
$0–$32,450	15%	$0–$19,450	15%	$0–$50,000	15%
$32,450–$78,400	28	$19,450–$47,050	28	$50,000–$75,000	25
$78,400–$162,770	33[a]	$47,050–$97,620	33[a]	Over $75,000	34[c]
Over $162,770	28[b]	Over $97,620	28[b]		

[a]Reflects a 5% surtax.

[b]Plus lesser of (1) $574 times the number of personal and dependency exemptions or (2) 5% of taxable income less $162,770 for married filing jointly, or $97,620 for unmarried taxpayers.

[c]There is a 5% surcharge for corporate taxable income between $100,000 and $335,000.

ances, and the elimination of the investment tax credit, the new code resulted in higher taxes for many businesses.

The 1986 statute also affected investments in real property such as real estate. In addition to changing depreciation and limiting interest deductions, the act revised the definition of "passive losses" and the "at-risk" rules. These changes had repercussions for limited partnerships and investment trusts, which are often formed for the purpose of investing in real estate. For example, prior to the 1986 act, limited partners in highly leveraged real estate deals could benefit from very large tax write-offs generated through depreciation. These passive losses are no longer allowed as deductions.

This section has provided a very general overview of taxes. In the chapters that follow, specific tax aspects of each type of investment will be discussed.

TRADING STRATEGIES

A number of trading strategies are available to investors including short selling, margin trading, hedging, and arbitrage. All of these are examined in the next paragraphs.

• Long versus Short Position

The markets for most financial assets allow an investor to take a long or short position in the security. A **long position** is simply the purchase of a security. A **short position,** however, is the sale of a security that the investor does not currently own. The investor accomplishes this by borrowing the security from a brokerage firm. Since many investors who have long positions use the brokerage firm for registration and for safekeeping, brokerage firms have a large inventory of certificates. This practice is known as registering the securities in a "street name." For example, a brokerage firm may have thousands of shares of IBM common stock in its vault that actually are owned by the firm's customers but are registered in one street name. It is perfectly legal for the brokerage firm to allow another customer to borrow certificates that are needed for a short sale. The short seller must replace ("cover") the borrowed securities at a later date. The brokerage firm is protected, since the short seller has an established account with the firm and must keep the proceeds from the sale on deposit with the firm until the borrowed shares are replaced.

A long position in a security is appropriate in anticipation of a rising price. However, if an investor anticipates a decline in price, a *short* position is appropriate. By shorting the security, the investor hopes to make a profit by selling the stock now and buying it at a lower price later to replace the borrowed shares. The advantage of having the opportunity to take both long and short positions is that investors can earn returns in a rising or a declining market. It should be pointed out, however, that the New York Stock Exchange (NYSE) has an "up-tick" and "zero plus up-tick" rule for short sales; that is, the most recent trade on the stock that an investor wishes to sell short must have been at a price above the previous transaction, or if the price did not change on the previous trade, the trade prior to that transaction must have been on an up-tick. This rule helps stabilize the market. Without the up-tick rule, for example, the steep decline in the market on October 19, 1987, might have been even more severe.

The risks of long and short positions are quite different. A short position offers more risk than a long position in the same security. The reason is that the maximum loss on a long position is −100 percent, which would occur if the price declined to zero. Theoretically, however, there is no limit to the possible loss on a short position because there is no upper limit on the stock's price. If the price continues to rise, the short seller's potential loss grows because of the obligation to replace the borrowed shares. For example, if the price increases 200 percent, the loss to the short seller would be −200 percent (plus commissions) if the short seller purchased shares to cover the short position at that point.

Table 7.2 illustrates the rates of return (without considering trading commissions and taxes) that are possible on a long and a short position. A long position results in positive returns if the price of the stock increases, while negative returns occur for the short position.

Another important difference between long and short positions in common stocks is related to the cash dividends. The holder of a long position receives the cash dividends when they are paid by the company. On the other hand, the short seller must pay the amount of the dividends to the brokerage firm so that they can be credited to the account from which the shares were borrowed. However, the price of the stock is reduced by the amount of the dividends on the ex-dividend date.

It is also possible for an individual's portfolio to have both long and short positions at the same time. Long positions would be in securities that are expected to increase in price, while short positions would be in securities that are expected to decline in price.

TABLE 7.2 • Rates of Return on Long and Short Positions (Ignoring Commissions and Taxes)

Long position: Assume that 100 shares of common stock are purchased for $50 per share and sold one year later. Assume that no dividends are declared on the stock.

$$\text{Rate of return} = \frac{\text{ending price} - \text{beginning price}}{\text{beginning price}}$$

Ending price	*Beginning price*	*Rate of return*
$30	$50	−40%
40	50	−20
50	50	0
60	50	20
70	50	40

Short position: Assume that 100 shares of common stock are sold short for $50 per share, and the position is covered (shares purchased and returned to broker) one year later. Assume that no dividends are declared on the stock.

$$\text{Rate of return} = \frac{\text{beginning price} - \text{ending price}}{\text{beginning price}}$$

Ending price	*Beginning price*	*Rate of return*
$30	$50	40%
40	50	20
50	50	0
60	50	−20
70	50	−40

• Margin Trading

Margin trading allows investors to borrow part of the funds they need to take a position in a security. Currently, the maximum amount that can be borrowed for stock purchases is 50 percent. Under Regulation T, the Federal Reserve Board sets the margin requirement and has the authority to raise or lower the maximum percentage that can be borrowed. Historically, margin requirements have ranged from 40 to 100 percent. Setting higher margin requirements is a way of controlling speculation in the market. The higher the margin requirements, the more cash or other assets the customer's account must contain before he or she can undertake margin transactions. After the severe market declines in October 1987 and 1989, consideration was given to raising margin requirements above the 50 percent level. To date, the Federal Reserve has not taken any action to increase margin requirements.

The Federal Reserve requirement deals with the **initial margin** on the long position. Once the securities are purchased, however, the **maintenance margin** is regulated by the stock exchanges and individual brokerage firms. For example, if the price of the securities purchased on margin declines by a significant amount, the investor is required to maintain a minimum equity in the account. Since the decline in price has reduced the value of the equity, additional cash and/or securities must be deposited into the account with the brokerage firm.

The NYSE requires a minimum maintenance margin of 25 percent, but most brokerage firms usually require 30 percent. Maintenance margins allow for a decline in the value of securities before the brokerage firm is required to make a **maintenance call.** If the investor does not have the necessary cash and/or securities to meet the maintenance call, the broker is required to liquidate enough of the customer's holdings to provide the funds to meet the maintenance call.

It is important to realize that trading on margin significantly changes the risk-return characteristics of the investment. Margin trading is simply using *financial leverage* to purchase securities. The possibility of a maintenance call also increases uncertainty about future cash requirements.

Table 7.3 illustrates how to calculate the price that will trigger a maintenance call. In this example, the stock is purchased for $50 per share, using an initial margin of 50 percent. The remaining funds needed to purchase 100 shares are borrowed from the brokerage firm at a 10 percent annual interest rate. As the table indicates, with a maintenance margin of 30 percent, the price must fall below $35.71 before a maintenance call will occur.

The lower half of Table 7.3 illustrates the impact of margin trading on the possible rates of return from a long position. Notice that the rates of return with margin trading are significantly more volatile than the corresponding returns without borrowing. This volatility is due to the impact of leverage resulting from margin trading.

Margin is also used for short sales, but in this case, the investor does not have to make interest payments. Brokerage firms typically require a minimum deposit of $2,000 to open a margin account and require a higher maintenance margin for short positions. In a short sale on margin, maintenance calls occur if the stock price increases by a certain amount. Large amounts of additional assets might be needed because, theoretically, a stock's price has no upper limit. Table 7.4 illustrates the use of margin for short sales. Note that there is no interest expense in the return calculation in Table 7.4. There are no borrowed funds with margined short sales; the initial margin indicates the initial equity deposit made by the investor.

• Hedging

With **hedging** activities, the investor attempts to modify or eliminate risk by undertaking investment positions such that the gain on one investment counterbalances the loss on another. Chapter 6 described the use of the forward

TABLE 7.3 • Margin Trading for a Long Position

Purchase 100 shares on margin at $50 per share	$5,000
Initial margin (50%) required of investor	$2,500
Amount borrowed from brokerage firm at 10% interest per year	$2,500
Maintenance margin required by brokerage firm	30%

1. Price of stock that will trigger a maintenance call:

$$\text{Price of stock} = \frac{1 - \text{initial margin}}{1 - \text{maintenance margin}} \times \text{purchase price}$$

$$= \frac{1 - .5}{1 - .3} \times \$50 = \$35.71$$

Thus, if the price falls below $35.71, a maintanence call will be made.

2. Calculation of rate of return, based on the following ending stock prices, for margin trading versus no margin: Assume that the holding period is one year, with dividends, trading commissions, and taxes ignored. For purposes of illustrating the rate of return, the maintenance call requirement is ignored when the price declines below $35.71 per share.

$$\text{Rate of return without margin} = \frac{\text{ending price} - \text{beginning price}}{\text{beginning price}}$$

$$\text{Rate of return with margin} = \frac{\text{ending price} - \text{beginning price} - \text{interest expense per share}}{\text{beginning equity per share}}$$

Ending price	Beginning price	Beginning equity per share	Interest expense per share	Rate of return	
				Without margin	*With margin*
$20	$50	$25	$2.50	−60%	−130%
30	50	25	2.50	−40	− 90
40	50	25	2.50	−20	− 50
50	50	25	2.50	0	− 10
60	50	25	2.50	20	30
70	50	25	2.50	40	70
80	50	25	2.50	60	110

exchange market as a means of hedging exchange rate risk in international investments.

It is commonly believed that investments in real assets such as real estate can be used to hedge against unexpected inflation. This belief implies that real estate prices may increase rapidly during, or in anticipation of, inflationary periods, while financial assets may not. If this scenario occurs, the gains on the real asset portion of the portfolio may protect, or hedge, the portfolio against purchasing power risk. The empirical evidence concerning the ability of a class of investments to provide an inflation hedge is discussed in detail in

TABLE 7.4 • Margin Trading for a Short Position

Sold (shorted) 100 shares for $50 per share (proceeds from sale)	$5,000
Initial margin of 50% (equity deposit) required of investor	$2,500
Maintenance margin required by brokerage firm	35%

1. Price of stock that will trigger a maintenance call:

$$\text{Price of stock} = \frac{1 + \text{initial margin}}{1 + \text{maintenance margin}} \times \text{selling price}$$

$$= \frac{1 + .5}{1 + .35} \times \$50 = \$55.56$$

Thus, if the price increases above $55.56, a maintenance call will be made.

2. Calculation of rate of return, based on the following ending stock prices, for 50% initial margin versus 100% initial margin: Assume that the holding period is one year, with dividends, trading commissions, and taxes ignored. For purposes of illustrating the rate of return, the maintenance call requirement is ignored when the price exceeds $55.56 per share.

$$\text{Rate of return} = \frac{\text{Beginning price} - \text{ending price}}{\text{equity deposit}}$$

Ending price	Beginning price	Equity deposit (50% initial margin)	Equity deposit (100% initial margin)	Rate of return: *50% initial margin*	Rate of return: *100% initial margin*
$20	$50	$25	$50	120%	60%
30	50	25	50	80	40
40	50	25	50	40	20
50	50	25	50	0	0
60	50	25	50	− 40	−20
70	50	25	50	− 50	−40
80	50	25	50	−120	−60

the applicable chapters. For example, Chapter 18 discusses the hedging potential of real estate, and Chapter 17 reviews the evidence for commodities.

Hedging strategies can also be developed to protect an investment from possible downside price risk. As noted previously, a long position in common stock is appropriate in anticipation of a price increase. After the stock is purchased, however, the price may decline because of some unanticipated event or because the forecast was incorrect. The investor could form a hedge to protect against this possible price decline. One hedge would be to buy a put option on the stock. As explained in detail in Chapter 15, the put option allows the holder to sell the stock at a designated price. The price of the put would therefore increase if the price of the stock declined. The gain on the put would partially or completely offset the loss on the stock.

A hedge can also be used to protect a short position from a price increase. This risk can be hedged by purchasing a call option that allows the holder to purchase the stock at a specified price. If the stock price increases, the call can be used to cover the borrowed shares, or the profit on the call will offset some or all of the loss on the short position.

A final example of a hedge involves the use of stock index futures (see Chapter 17) in managing the market risk component of a portfolio. As discussed in Chapter 2, through appropriate diversification an investor can remove most of the firm-specific (diversifiable) risk from a stock portfolio. However, the market (nondiversifiable) risk component of the portfolio remains. The development of stock index futures has provided investors in stocks with a relatively inexpensive, new tool for hedging stock portfolios against adverse market movements.

One should remember, however, that hedging activities involve transaction and information costs. In addition, in many cases, the hedge may limit the upside potential of an investment in addition to protecting against downside risk. As is the case with other investment strategies, the investor should carefully weigh the costs and the benefits.

• Arbitrage

Another trading strategy that is discussed in various chapters of this book is **arbitrage** trading. An arbitrage strategy is designed to profit from imperfections in security markets. If markets are inefficient, a stock may sell simultaneously at different prices in different markets. An arbitrageur, spotting this inefficiency, would buy the stock in one market and immediately sell the same stock at a higher price in another market. This transaction is an example of risk-free arbitrage. The actions of arbitrageurs, however, tend to eliminate any price discrepancies such as the one described here.

A second type of arbitrage, which is not risk-free, attempts to exploit price differentials of companies involved in takeover efforts. For example, an arbitrageur may take a long position in the common stock of a firm being taken over and simultaneously short the common stock of the acquiring firm. This strategy is based on the expectation that the stock of the acquired firm will increase in price while the acquirer's stock will decrease in price. Such price movements often occur because the acquirer is usually forced to pay a "premium" to obtain the shares necessary to gain control.

ANALYSIS STRATEGIES

The purpose of this section is to introduce the two traditional analysis strategies—"technical" and "fundamental" analysis. The next section briefly introduces the efficient market hypothesis (EMH) and examines its implications for investment strategies.

• Technical Analysis

Technical analysis dates back to the 1800s. It attempts to resolve the *investment timing* issue by gaining insight into market behavior through analysis of historical price and volume data. Technical approaches analyze market prices, "breadth" of the market, general investor sentiment (both institutional and individual investors), and the price behavior of individual securities. Often technicians are referred to as chartists because much of their analysis takes the form of graphs or charts. Technicians believe that stock prices follow recurring patterns. Once these patterns are discovered, they can be used to forecast the direction and perhaps the magnitude of future price changes.

Technical analysis has become much more complex in recent years due to advances in communication technology and data processing. These technological developments allow technicians to obtain data almost instantaneously and to use a variety of procedures to analyze the data. Technical analysis of the market and individual stocks is discussed in Chapters 8 and 21, respectively.

• Fundamental Analysis

Fundamental analysis developed after the passage of the Securities Act of 1933 and the Securities Exchange Act of 1934. The primary purpose of these two laws was to require that publicly traded corporations provide "full disclosure" of financial and other information that could influence the price of their securities. Prior to this time, corporations were not required to provide a complete set of financial statements.

When detailed financial information became available, the techniques and procedures of fundamental analysis began to emerge. Benjamin Graham is recognized as the father of fundamental analysis. He and David L. Dodd published the first edition of their textbook *Security Analysis* in 1934. This text was widely used and entered its fourth edition in 1962. Graham also obtained considerable fame from the publication in 1948 of *The Intelligent Investor*, essentially a simpler version of the earlier text. The last edition of this book was published in 1974 prior to Graham's death in 1976.

Graham advocated the use of mathematics and quantitative procedures in the analysis of investments. This approach allowed him to estimate the **intrinsic value** of a stock, which is determined independently of the market price. Intrinsic value is the value that is justified by financial facts such as asset value, earnings, dividends, and other fundamentals. Graham's approach is known as fundamental analysis because it stresses the major (or fundamental) factors that determine a stock's value.

Many of the early techniques and procedures developed and advocated by Graham are still in use. The valuation analysis developed in later chapters of this book incorporates Graham's principles of fundamental analysis.

Despite the popularity and apparent success of Graham's approach, he constantly developed and tested new techniques and procedures. Graham

• INTEREST BOX

Investment Analysis and Artificial Intelligence

Peter Lynch, one of the best-known and most successful mutual fund managers, used a "hands-on" approach in guiding the Fidelity Magellan Fund during the 1970s and 1980s. His initial investment ideas often came as a result of his personal observations of products during shopping trips.

Brad Lewis, manager of Fidelity's Stock Selection and Disciplined Equity funds, takes an entirely different approach. He relies on the computer and sophisticated software called "artificial intelligence." The artificial intelligence software for investments is designed to mimic the analytic procedures of the financial analyst and the technician. Recommendations of when to buy and sell and at what price are generated by the software without the influence of human emotions or judgment.

Although a growing number of professional money managers, and some individual investors, are using the computer for investment decision making, the vast majority still rely ultimately on human judgment. The computer is used as an aid to initially identify (screen) companies that have the preferred financial characteristics or stock price patterns, and the decision to buy or sell is made by the individual. Used in this way, the computer generates a list of "candidates" for action, but the final decision is still made by humans.

SOURCE: Suzy Hagstrom, "More Brokers Investing Strictly by Numbers," *Orlando Sentinel,* May 26, 1991, pp. D1, D5.

recognized that techniques that have succeeded in the past may not work in the future. Prior to his death, Graham expressed the view that the markets were becoming more efficient, in the sense that it was difficult to identify undervalued securities. He believed that institutional investors dominated the market but concentrated their investments in the major issues on the NYSE and AMEX. A possible strategy, therefore, was to discover "pockets of inefficiency" in the smaller, less-analyzed companies.

INVESTMENT STRATEGIES IN AN EFFICIENT MARKET

Beginning in the 1950s, a number of empirical studies suggested that changes in stock prices appeared to be random. These early studies encouraged additional research that finally resulted in the "random walk" theory about stock price behavior. During the 1960s, additional empirical research indicated that stock prices adjust very rapidly to information and that professional investors, such as mutual fund managers, do not appear to outperform the market. The results from all these empirical tests form the foundation of the **efficient market hypothesis (EMH)**. The development of the EMH is discussed in detail in Chapter 21. For purposes of this chapter, however, a basic introduction to the EMH is sufficient.

The financial markets in the United States are extremely competitive, in the sense that many individual and institutional investors are attempting to maximize the performance of their portfolios. Exceptional performance for one investor, however, comes at the expense of other investors. To illustrate, assume that an investor earned risk-adjusted excess returns on a long position because the security was purchased at a price below its intrinsic value. The bargain purchase was possible because the seller did not realize that the security was undervalued. The success of the buyer therefore came at the expense of the seller.

Because of the competitiveness of the markets, naïve and uninformed investors eventually realize that they will not be able to earn risk-adjusted excess returns. They are at a competitive disadvantage. The remaining investors and traders represent the survival of the fittest and are likely to be the more knowledgeable and skilled players. In this type of market, security prices are likely to accurately reflect available information and to respond very rapidly to new information; prices reflect technical and fundamental factors and are unbiased indicators of intrinsic values.

Given this competitiveness and the resulting efficiency in correctly pricing securities, what investment strategies are appropriate? Is it reasonable to assume that strategies based on traditional technical and fundamental analyses can outperform the market on a risk-adjusted basis? If the market is perfectly efficient, then no strategy will be able to beat the market. If the market is less than perfectly efficient, some strategies may result in risk-adjusted excess returns. The critical question, therefore, is the *degree* of market efficiency.

The degree of market efficiency has been the subject of considerable debate. Academics tend to argue that markets are highly efficient, while practitioners tend to feel that there are inefficiencies. The evidence and debate are inconclusive since "the case for all forms of the EMH seems to us to be neither as strong as most academics assume nor as weak as most professional investors like to believe."[1]

The debate has resulted in two investment strategies: **passive strategies** and **active strategies.** Efficient markets suggest passive strategies, while market inefficiencies suggest active strategies.

• Passive Strategies

A passive strategy does not attempt to outperform the market or to earn risk-adjusted excess returns; the objective is to do as well as the market. At the extreme, stocks could be randomly selected since in a perfectly efficient market, the selected stocks would be correctly valued. To reduce the risk of possible unexpected company- or industry-specific developments (diversifiable risk), an adequate number of securities would be included in the portfolio.

---

[1] Bob L. Boldt and Hal L. Arbit, "Efficient Markets and the Professional Investor," *Financial Analysts Journal* (July-August 1984): 33.

The investment horizon would be long term, with little, if any, portfolio revisions because of security selection and market timing efforts. An advantage of passive management is that the transaction costs of the portfolio are minimized. The cost of trading or of acquiring and analyzing information is avoided. The task of the portfolio manager is limited to record keeping and tax planning.

Figure 7.1 provides some interesting statistics on the growth of passive equity investment funds that primarily manage retirement funds. These passive funds emerged during the early 1970s and by 1980 represented 7 percent of the $210 billion in retirement funds. By 1985, their share of the market had increased to 19 percent and was forecast to be 34 percent by 1990. The figure also suggests that a third category of funds may evolve that stresses "actively managed universes." This category would be a compromise between active and passive management since it would engage in market timing by shifting assets in response to forecasts of the investment environment.

Passive investment strategies include the following:

1. Indexing One approach to implementing a passive investment strategy is to invest in an indexed portfolio that is designed to duplicate precisely the performance of a market index such as the S&P 500. A growing number of pension funds are indexed portfolios. For example, the $54 billion California Public Employees' Retirement System is currently indexing about $17 billion of its $20 billion in domestic equity assets. The remaining $3 billion in equities is placed with external active managers. Individuals, however, must construct an indexed portfolio or invest in an indexed mutual fund. The advantages and disadvantages of indexed mutual funds were discussed in Chapter 5.

2. Combination strategy An alternative to a completely passive strategy such as indexing is to divide the portfolio into active and passive components. Indexed funds can be used for the passive component; selection and timing activities can be used for the active component. The division depends on the skill of the individual. An individual who can accurately forecast stock prices or identify other securities that offer abnormally high returns should exploit these opportunities by increasing the size of the active component of the portfolio.

In summary, efficient markets and high transaction costs suggest passive investment strategies. Evidence also indicates that passive strategies have become increasingly popular with both institutional and individual investors. In addition, many commentators have predicted that the popularity of passive strategies will continue to grow. These forecasts are often based on the feeling that active management is usually not successful.

• Active Strategies

Many of the techniques and procedures presented in this book can be used in active investment strategies. Since the book is oriented toward individual investors, its primary purpose is to provide information and procedures that can

FIGURE 7.1 • Active versus Passive Strategies

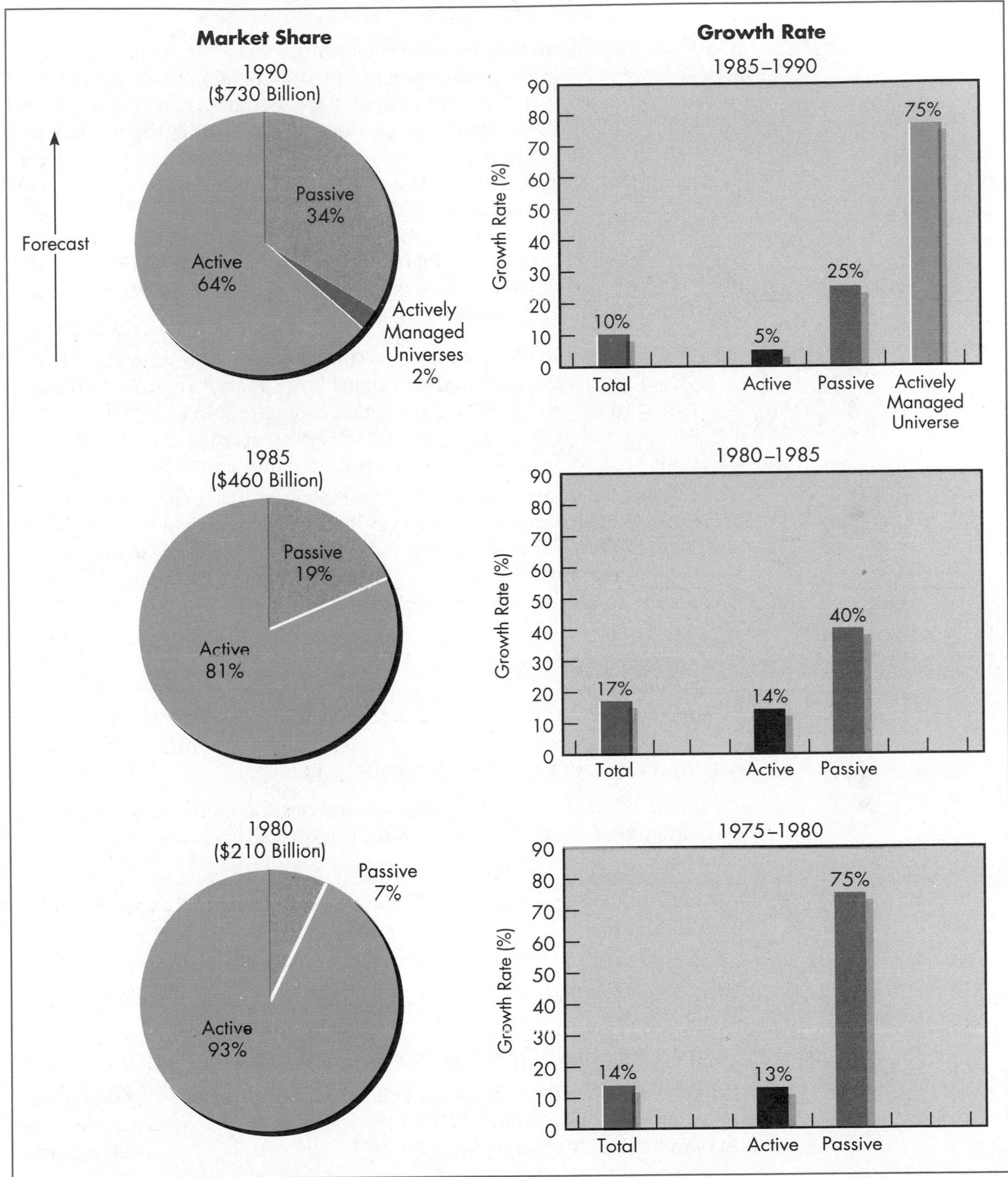

SOURCE: Walter R. Good, Roy W. Hermansen, and T. Kirkham Barneby. "Opportunity: Actively Managed Investment Universes," *Financial Analysts Journal* (January-February 1986): 50.

assist individuals in making informed investment decisions. As previously discussed, however, there is strong evidence that financial markets are efficient. Informed investors therefore should appreciate the pitfalls and complications that occur in pursuing an active investment strategy in an efficient market.

Although detailed discussions about efficient markets and their impact on investment strategies will occur throughout the book, some initial observations can be made concerning active strategies for individuals.

First, what are some basic arguments in support of the idea that market inefficiencies exist to the extent that an active strategy is rational? Essentially, this idea assumes that some investors have an advantage over others. The following are three possible areas of advantage:

1. *Timing* An investor who can accurately predict movements in individual securities or the market can achieve superior returns. As discussed in Chapter 1, however, market timing requires *consistently* accurate predictions. To be correct only 50 percent of the time will result in a performance that is inferior to a buy-and-hold strategy.
2. *Selection* In order to identify "undervalued" or "overvalued" securities or industry groups, the investor needs to gain insight that is superior to that of other investors. To do so, the investor must possess advantages in the quality and timeliness of information, the analytical approach employed, and/or judgment.
3. *Investment philosophy* Investment philosophy requires a commitment to a specific area or investment approach. For example, an area might include growth stocks in the high-technology field, and an investment approach might involve a concentration on analyzing assets or cash flows rather than earnings. In order to offer an advantage to the investor, an investment philosophy must be unique.

Another rationale supporting active strategies for individuals is that they have advantages over institutions and professional investors, including the following:

1. Individual investors engage in small trades that can be executed quickly.
2. Individuals have the flexibility to invest in small companies.
3. If they wish, individual investors can put all or most of their eggs in one basket.
4. Individuals have the flexibility to use short sales and margin trading.

These possible advantages and a belief that active strategies for individuals are justified are the premises behind the founding of the American Association of Individual Investors (AAII) in 1979.[2] The AAII is a nonprofit organiza-

[2] Additional information can be obtained by writing to the AAII at 625 N. Michigan Avenue, Chicago, IL 60611.

tion established to educate and encourage individuals to make their own investment decisions. By becoming a member, an individual can attend local chapter meetings in many cities in the United States, attend educational seminars, and receive educational materials including the *AAII Journal.* This journal provides practical information about developments in investment theory and research. The AAII advances the idea that individuals need to be knowledgeable in order to make rational investment decisions.

As discussed below, active investment strategies include doing it yourself and using an expert.

DO-IT-YOURSELF APPROACH FOR INDIVIDUAL INVESTORS Individuals who elect to pursue an active investment strategy can perform all the necessary tasks themselves. Essentially, these individuals are their own portfolio managers. Once this decision is made, the individual is faced with the task of identifying specific investment alternatives that can accomplish the objectives of the portfolio. Ways in which individual investors can undertake a do-it-yourself approach are discussed in detail throughout the book. As an introduction, however, the following tactics for common stocks have been suggested:

1. Invest in stocks selling below liquidation value.[3]
2. Invest in new issues of stocks or in stocks moving from the OTC to the NYSE.[4]
3. Form a portfolio of stocks selling for "low" P/E ratios.[5]
4. Invest in "small" companies.[6]
5. Buy stocks that have a high ratio of book value to stock price.[7]

Most of these tactics are based on *market anomalies* that may represent market inefficiencies and therefore provide risk-adjusted excess returns. These strategies are discussed in more detail in Chapter 21. In addition to these common stock tactics, each chapter on an investment alternative discusses active strategies that are appropriate for that particular alternative.

---

[3] Joel M. Greenblatt, Richard Pzena, and Bruce L. Newberg, "How the Small Investor Can Beat the Market," *Journal of Portfolio Management* (Summer 1981): 48–52.

[4] John J. McConnell and Gary C. Sanger, "A Trading Strategy for New Listings on the NYSE," *Financial Analysts Journal* (January-February 1984): 34–38; and Ben Branch, "Special Offerings and Market Efficiency," *Financial Review* (March 1984). 26–35.

[5] Clinton M. Bidwell III, "SUE/PE Revista," *Journal of Portfolio Management* (Winter 1981): 85–87; John W. Peavy III and David A. Goodman, "The Significance of P/Es for Portfolio Returns," *Journal of Portfolio Management* (Winter 1983): 43–47; and Stephen Kindel, "Outsmarting the Smart Money," *Financial World*, May 1, 1990, pp. 32–36.

[6] Marc R. Reinganum, "Portfolio Strategies for Small CAPs versus Large," *Journal of Portfolio Management* (Winter 1983): 29–36; and Andrew E. Serwer, "How to Profit in the Dicey World of Small Stocks," *Fortune*, January 15, 1990, pp. 25, 28.

[7] Barr Rosenberg, Kenneth Reid, and Ronald Lanstein, "Persuasive Evidence of Market Inefficiency," *Journal of Portfolio Management* (Spring 1985): 9–16.

• **INTEREST BOX**

Confessions of a Trader

On June 10, [1986] MCA, the huge movie and entertainment company, closed on the New York Stock Exchange at $46.50 a share. It was the stock's lowest close in many months, exactly 10 points below its April high of $56.50.

Yet despite this steep plunge, several sharp short-term insiders found the stock vastly appealing as the market prepared to open on June 11. Were they technical analysts who had stumbled upon an intriguing chart formation? Were they fundamentalists who had meticulously studied MCA's inner corporate working? Were they privy to a tidbit of highly positive inside information? No on all accounts. Actually, they liked MCA for four reasons: Robert Redford, Debra Winger, Darryl Hannah, and Ivan Reitman.

MCA's motion picture studio, Universal, had a new movie that was about 10 days from its nationwide opening. The film was *Legal Eagles* and it starred Redford, Winger, and Hannah. The director was Reitman, famed for the phenomenally successful *Ghostbusters.*

The traders figured that the *Legal Eagles* publicity campaign was about to hit and that anticipation of a possible blockbuster would give MCA stock a short-term boost.

They were right. Within a week, MCA was above $50 a share. Subsequently, *Legal Eagles* proved to be far less than a blockbuster, and the shares plummeted. But the traders didn't care. By then, they were long out of MCA and were focusing on other targets. . . .

If you find yourself tempted to stick a toe in the shark-infested waters of short-term trading, you'll be far better off with at least some semblance of a plan. Talk to enough habitual traders—and I'm speaking about the true lone wolves who rely on neither gurus nor supposedly insider tips—and you'll find that they all learned through costly personal experience. "I got my education, but I sure paid a lot of tuition," is how a veteran stock trader, who hangs out in a Miami Beach brokerage office, puts it. . . .

But for those who may possess the intelligence and steely spine necessary to trade successfully, I want to pass on some knowledge gleaned over a long period from people named Abe and Phil and Bill and The Horse, some of whom passed on after spending their last day on earth watching the tape. . . .

- Big primary factor. How do you look at life? If you see a new product that catches your eye, are you interested in seeing which company makes it? Do you care which movie company made the picture you saw last weekend?

Beyond the selection of alternative assets, individual investors should consider the asset composition of their overall portfolio. A popular term developed in the late 1980s for a portfolio management investment strategy is **asset allocation.** Asset allocation refers to the way investment dollars are divided among different types of investment vehicles, including (1) cash and cash equivalents, (2) fixed-income securities, (3) common stocks, (4) real estate, (5) natural resources, and (6) tangibles. Asset allocation strategies can be passive or active. An investor can decide, based on his or her risk-return preferences, on a fixed asset allocation scheme that requires only periodic adjustments. On the other hand, an asset allocation strategy can be an active strategy involving short-term adjustments in the portfolio's asset mix as the investor de-

Would you trade stocks just to make money or because you really enjoy the challenge and are curious about business events? My point here is that you have to think like a trader to have any chance of being a successful trader. You can pick up the knowledge and experience as you go, but you have got to start out with the right mental outlook. . . .

- So how does one get good at the trading game? I believe basically you must follow about 20 stocks very closely and really get to know what's going on with those companies. I don't mean giant firms such as IBM, Sears, and Exxon. They don't strike me as trading vehicles. Better suited to our purposes are well-established, easily understood, nonexotic companies with anywhere from three million to 50 million shares outstanding. Stocks that appear to trade within a fairly well-defined range are excellent, especially if they tend to move easily within that range. Unfortunately, the trend toward mergers and takeovers has removed some great trading stocks from the arena. . . .
- Which brings us to the essence of short-term trading—managing the risk/reward factor. It stands to reason that if you are trading for a limited objective, perhaps a quick 20 percent gain, you don't want to deal with the possibility of a major loss. Good traders are often buying stocks on weakness, sometimes accompanied by adverse news. You've got to know how to evaluate whether the bad news is transient or can really damage the company. Cancer litigation scares caused sharp drops in the tobacco stocks, but these declines turned out to be trading opportunities. E.F. Hutton's troubles with the law also created a buying situation. Bad news often leads to an overreaction by the market. A good trader profits by buying into other people's panics. . . .
- You've probably deduced from all this that being a sharp trader is almost a full-time job. I'd say 10 hours a week is minimum. I have no easy answers. There are excellent brokers that might do the legwork for you. If you find one, cherish that person. A broker with a keen eye for trading opportunities can be worth his or her weight in gold. . . .

You may never become a trader; you may never want to become one. But let's give these rugged individualists their due. They're willing to match their wits against the marketplace, and they more often than not come out ahead. That guy with the rolled-up newspaper and the beat-up chart book may not be the bum he appears to be. He may be a stock market genius.

SOURCE: Abstracted from Jerry Helzner, "Confessions of a Trader," *Barron's*, October 27, 1986, pp. 28, 30, 32.

termines that one of the categories is overvalued or undervalued in relation to the other categories. Professional money managers use computer-aided asset allocation models described by such terms as "tactical asset allocation" and "asset investment management."

USE AN EXPERT Rather than attempting a complete do-it-yourself approach, individuals may elect to use a professional for part or all of the portfolio tasks. For example, an individual may decide to rely on investment research performed by a brokerage firm or by an investment advisory service. There is evidence that some of this research can identify securities that can outperform the market.

An individual may also decide to invest in a mutual fund (see Chapter 5) that is actively managed. With the exception of indexed mutual funds, the majority of funds are actively managed. The task facing the individual is to select the mutual fund or funds with the appropriate objective that is most likely to achieve the best performance. Once the selection is made, the mutual fund manager performs the tasks of security selection, market timing, and diversification.

Another alternative in using professional help is to invest in one of the many new investment vehicles that are now offered by financial institutions such as insurance companies. Investing in new products such as universal life insurance or variable universal life insurance shifts the investment management decision to the company.

• Conclusions

The decision to pursue a passive or an active investment strategy in an efficient market is a key decision for individual investors. Much of this book is devoted to providing information that can be used to make this decision.

Once the passive-versus-active decision is made, a particular investment approach must be selected. It is important to realize that there is no optimal investment strategy and that risks and returns can vary widely from strategy to strategy.

Markets are also dynamic in the sense that new products are emerging and the important decision variables and relationships between variables are unstable. In a dynamic market, successful investors must also change; techniques and strategies that have been successful in the past may not be successful in the future. This dynamic environment increases the difficulty of making successful investment decisions but also provides a challenge to investors inclined to question the efficiency of the markets.

SUMMARY

This chapter has provided an introduction to investment strategies. This topic is a central theme that is discussed in detail throughout the book.

The beginning of the chapter stressed the different levels of investment strategies, from the narrow trading strategies to the broad-based approach of investment strategies in an efficient market. An attempt was also made to distinguish between speculation and investing. The distinction is difficult because of differences in the way individuals feel about the risk-return trade-offs and whether the alternatives are viewed independently or in the context of a portfolio. Certain alternatives are quite risky and may be considered speculative when they are viewed in isolation, but they can also reduce the risk of a portfolio. The orientation of this book is toward making investments rather than speculative decisions.

The strong evidence in support of the efficient market hypothesis (EMH) has generated considerable debate concerning the appropriateness of *active* versus *passive* investment strategies. If markets are highly or perfectly efficient, passive strategies are justified. Market inefficiencies, however, suggest that active strategies directed at exploiting the inefficiencies are justified. A key question facing investors is the *degree* of market efficiency.

The chapter concluded with a discussion of passive and active investment strategies in an efficient market. In a dynamic market, successful strategies are not likely to be stable. Strategies that have been successful in the past may not work in the future.

• KEY TERMS

Active strategies
Arbitrage
Asset allocation
Efficient market hypothesis (EMH)
Fundamental analysis
Hedging
Initial margin
Intrinsic value
Investment strategy
Long position
Maintenance call
Maintenance margin
Passive strategies
Short position
Speculation
Technical analysis

• QUESTIONS

1. Compare and contrast speculation and investing. Do all investors use the same criteria to classify an opportunity as a speculative opportunity versus an investment opportunity?
2. Compare and contrast technical analysis and fundamental analysis.
3. Describe the philosophy underlying the fundamental approach to investment analysis.
4. Individual investors may elect to pursue passive or active investment strategies. Discuss the advantages and disadvantages of these two approaches.
5. Explain why a short position in a common stock involves more risk than a long position in the same stock.
6. Explain why a margined common stock investment has the potential to provide higher returns but involves more risk than an unmargined position.
7. Distinguish between an initial margin and a maintenance margin.
8. How can hedging strategies be used to modify the risk-return characteristics of a portfolio?
9. In 1929, prior to regulation by the Federal Reserve, margin requirements were below 30 percent, and it has been estimated that individual investors borrowed in excess of $9 billion for margin trading. Explain how these factors contributed to the 1929 stock market crash.

10. Can arbitrage opportunities exist in an efficient market? In your opinion, should individual investors attempt to identify and exploit arbitrage opportunities?
11. Explain why the degree of market efficiency should be considered in comparing active and passive investment strategies.
12. It can be argued that individuals should not attempt active investment strategies unless certain criteria can be satisfied. Discuss the criteria or conditions that justify an active strategy.
13. Discuss the impact of taxes on an individual's investment strategy.

• PROBLEMS

1. An arbitrageur notices that XYZ common stock is selling for $29 per share on the NYSE and at $28 on the Philadelphia Stock Exchange. Assume that brokerage commissions are 2 percent on each transaction. Does this situation offer a profitable arbitrage opportunity?
2. Assume that an individual is considering an investment in the common stock of IBM Corporation. The common stock is currently selling for $115 per share with a $4.40 annual cash dividend. The investor anticipates a one-year holding period. Ignoring transaction costs and taxes:
   a. Calculate the annual rate of return on a long position in the stock for each of the following ending stock prices: $100, $110, $120, $130.
   b. Calculate the annual rate of return on a short position for each of the ending stock prices in part (a).
3. Consider the following information:

Stock price per share	$60
Margin requirement	50%
Interest rate on margin accounts	9%
Maintenance margin	30%

   Ignoring transaction costs and taxes:
   a. Assume that an investor takes a long position without using margin. Calculate the rate of return if the stock is sold for $70 per share after one year.
   b. Assume that an investor takes a long position using margin.
      (1) Calculate the stock price that will trigger a margin call.
      (2) Calculate the rate of return if the stock is sold for $70 per share after one year.
   c. Explain why the rate of return using margin is different from the rate of return without margin.
4. Consider the following information:

Stock price per share	$25
Margin requirement	50%
Maintenance margin	30%

Ignoring transaction costs and taxes:

a. Assume that an investor takes a short position with a cash deposit equal to 100 percent of the initial margin requirement. Calculate the rate of return if the investor covers (purchases) the stock at $20 after one year.

b. Assume that an investor takes a short position with a cash deposit equal to 50 percent of the initial margin requirement.
   (1) Calculate the stock price that will trigger a margin call.
   (2) Calculate the rate of return if the investor covers (purchases) the stock at $20 after one year.

c. Explain why the rates of return in parts (a) and (b) are different.

5. A portfolio manager forecasts the following rates of return for the next three years:

	One-year treasury bills	*Common stocks*
1992	9%	15%
1993	10	−20
1994	8	10

Assume that the portfolio manager is considering a passive versus an active investment strategy using Treasury bills and common stocks.

a. An example of a passive strategy would be to invest 50 percent of the portfolio funds in Treasury bills and 50 percent in common stock in each of the next three years. Calculate the annual rates of return for the portfolio.

b. An example of an active market timing strategy would be to shift funds between Treasury bills and common stocks. Assume that the portfolio manager has the flexibility to hold all Treasury bills (100 percent of funds in Treasury bills) or all common stocks.
   (1) Indicate the optimal proportion of portfolio funds that should be invested in Treasury bills and common stocks each year based on the forecast rates of return.
   (2) Calculate the expected annual rates of return for the portfolio using the portfolio proportions calculated in part b(1).

c. Discuss the advantages and disadvantages of the passive and active strategies described above. Describe the impact of transaction costs and income taxes on each of these strategies. In your opinion, which portfolio strategy involves more risk?

• REFERENCES

Bernstein, Peter L. "How Stable Are Successful Strategies?" *Journal of Portfolio Management* (Spring 1986): 1.

Block, Stanley B. "Efficient Markets: Buzz Word of the '60s Gets Stung." *AAII Journal* (September 1984): 9–13.

Boldt, Bob L., and Hal L. Arbit. "Efficient Markets and the Professional Investor." *Financial Analysts Journal* (July-August 1984): 22–34.

Curran, John J. "Why Investors Make the Wrong Choices." *Fortune,* Fall 1986, pp. 63–68.

Ellis, Charles D. *Investment Policy.* Homewood, Ill.: Dow-Jones-Irwin, 1985.

Ferguson, Robert. "An Efficient Stock Market? Ridiculous!" *Journal of Portfolio Management* (Summer 1983): 31–38.

Good, Walter R., Roy W. Hermansen, and T. Kirkham Barneby. "Opportunity: Actively Managed Investment Universes." *Financial Analysts Journal* (January-February 1986): 49–57.

Graham, Benjamin. *The Intelligent Investor,* 3d ed. New York: Harper & Row, 1959.

Graham, Benjamin, and David L. Dodd. *Security Analysis: Principles and Techniques,* 4th ed. New York: McGraw-Hill, 1974.

Grantham, Jeremy. "You Can't Fool All of the People All of the Time." *Journal of Portfolio Management* (Winter 1986): 11–15.

Grauer, Robert R., and Nils H. Hakansson. "Returns on Levered, Actively Managed Long-Run Portfolios of Stocks, Bonds and Bills, 1934–1983." *Financial Analysts Journal* (September-October 1985): 24–43.

Greenblatt, Joel M., Richard Pzena, and Bruce L. Newberg. "How the Small Investor Can Beat the Market." *Journal of Portfolio Management* (Summer 1981): 48–52.

Keane, Simon M. "The Efficient Market Hypothesis on Trial." *Financial Analysts Journal* (March-April 1986): 58–63.

Kindel, Stephen. "Outsmarting the Smart Money." *Financial World,* May 1, 1990, pp. 32–36.

Lee, Keun Chang, and Stephen P. D'Arcy. "The Optimal Investment Strategy through Variable Universal Life Insurance." *Journal of Risk and Insurance* (June 1989): 201–17.

Lerner, Eugene M., and Pochara Theerathorn. "The Returns of Different Investment Strategies." *Journal of Portfolio Management* (Summer 1983): 26–28.

Malkiel, Burton G. *A Random Walk down Wall Street,* 5th ed. New York: Norton, 1990.

McConnell, John J., and Gary C. Sanger. "A Trading Strategy for New Listings on the NYSE." *Financial Analysts Journal* (January-February 1984): 34–38.

Oppenheimer, Henry R. "A Test of Benjamin Graham's Stock Selection Criteria." *Financial Analysts Journal* (September-October 1984): 68–74.

Reinganum, Marc R. "Portfolio Strategies for Small CAPs versus Large." *Journal of Portfolio Management* (Winter 1983): 29–36.

Rosenberg, Barr, Kenneth Reid, and Ronald Lanstein. "Persuasive Evidence of Market Inefficiency." *Journal of Portfolio Management* (Spring 1985): 9–16.

Serwer, Andrew E. "How to Profit in the Dicey World of Small Stocks." *Fortune,* January 15, 1990, pp. 25, 28.

Sivy, Michael, Clint Willis, and Holly Wheelwright. "Prospering in Today's Manic Markets." *Money,* December 1989, pp. 72–87.

Sorensen, Roy A. "An Essential Reservation about the EMH." *Journal of Portfolio Management* (Summer 1983): 29–30.

Treynor, Jack L. "What Does It Take to Win the Trading Game?" *Financial Analysts Journal* (January-February 1981): 55–60.

Willis, Clint. "Beyond Dollar-Cost Averaging." *Money,* July 1988, pp. 105–9.

PART III

Valuation Concepts and Analysis

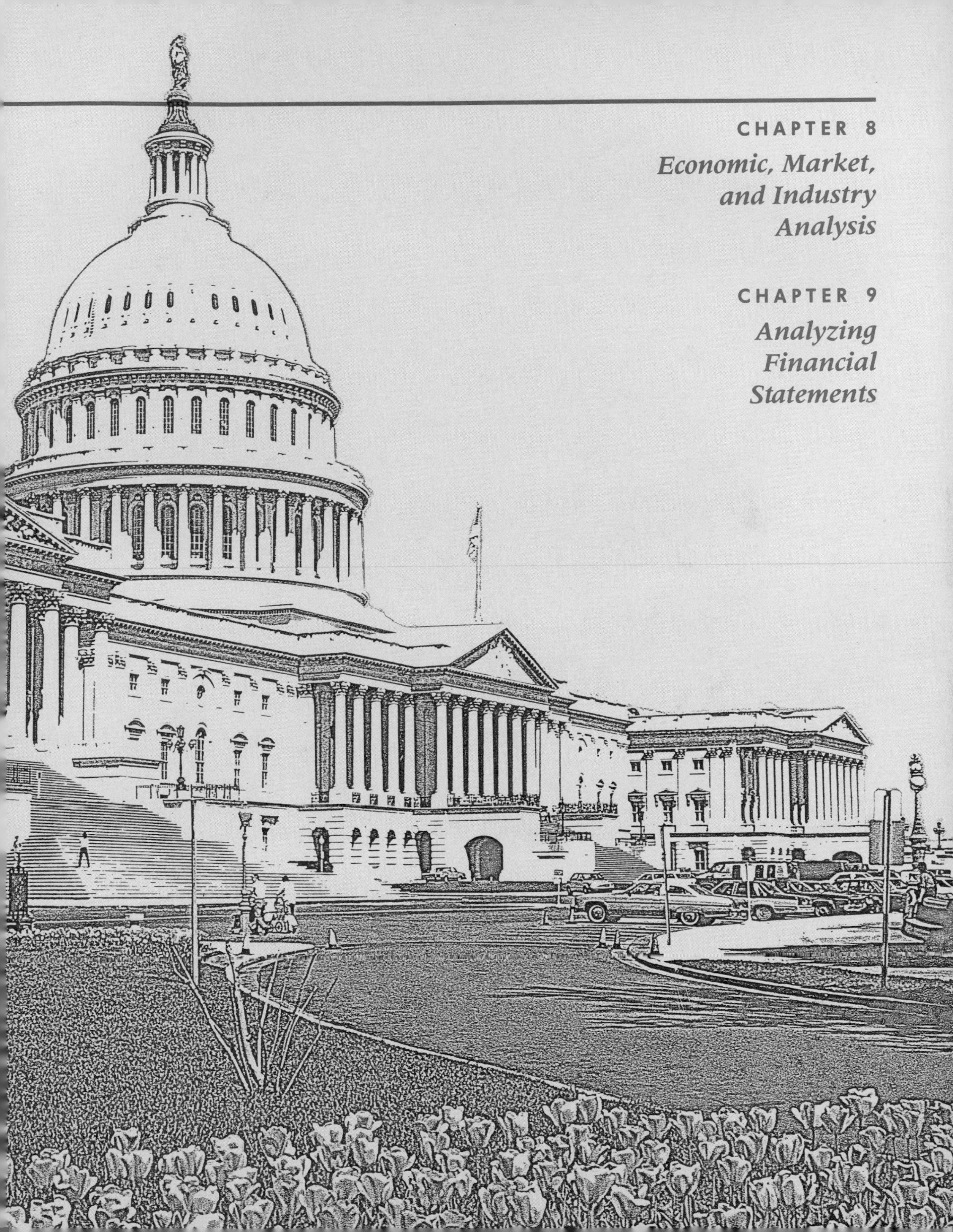

CHAPTER 8

Economic, Market, and Industry Analysis

CHAPTER 9

Analyzing Financial Statements

CHAPTER 8

Economic, Market, and Industry Analysis

The knowledge-level objectives of this chapter should enable the student to:

- Understand how forecasts for the economy, stock market, and specific industries are used in a traditional fundamental analysis approach to investing.
- Explain the key economic variables that influence economic activity and the stock market.
- Identify sources of professional economic forecasts and explain how the forecasts can be assessed for accuracy.
- Recognize some of the more popular technical indicators used in market timing.
- Describe how industries can be grouped and analyzed using the SIC codes.
- Explain key industry fundamentals that influence the performance of companies in the industry.
- Indicate techniques that can be used to identify industries that might provide superior investment performance.

INTRODUCTION

The first step in the traditional fundamental approach is an *economic analysis and forecast.* After completing an economic forecast and relating the forecast to common stocks in general, the next step is an *industry analysis.* The purpose of the industry analysis is to identify industries that can be expected to have the best relative investment performance over a particular horizon. For example, a pessimistic one-year economic forecast suggests an investigation of "defensive" industries; an optimistic forecast suggests "growth" industries.

The first part of the chapter discusses the economy, business cycles, and how economic activity influences industries and companies. Key economic variables are discussed, such as the composite economic indexes, interest rates, money supply, and deficits—trade and budget. Most individual investors do not attempt to do a formal economic analysis and forecast and often utilize professional forecasts instead. Accordingly, sources of professional forecasts are discussed in this section. Finally, the economic forecast is related to a stock market forecast.

Technical analysis is also used to provide clues about the direction the stock market may be taking. Some of the more popular indicators, such as the breadth of the market, confidence index, and put-call ratio, are briefly discussed and illustrated.

The last part of the chapter discusses the importance of industry analysis and suggests key variables that should be included in the analysis. It also discusses sources of information for the industry data needed for the analysis. The chapter concludes with techniques and criteria that can be used to identify industries with the potential for above-average performance. Appendix 8A presents a brief illustration of an industry analysis, using the automobile industry.

• Stock Prices and the Economy

Stock prices and economic activity are closely related. Eight business cycles occurred between 1948 and 1989, and in each case, the stock market declined significantly before the peak of the business cycle and rose significantly before the trough of the cycle. Thus, stock market changes lead economic activity. The relationship between the S&P 500 and economic activity is shown in Figure 8.1 where the shaded areas indicate the recessionary periods between 1961 and 1990.

Figure 8.1 also shows one of the problems in relating stock prices and business cycles. Stocks sometimes experience a significant decline that is not followed by a recession. The Wall Street adage that "the stock market has correctly forecast 15 of the last 8 recessions" refers to this problem. The market crash during October 1987 illustrates that factors other than economic events can greatly influence stock prices. Computerized program trading and speculation in stock-index futures are commonly cited reasons for "Black Monday." The economy, however, did not enter a recession in 1988 or 1989. The rate of economic growth declined, but the expansion that started in November 1982 continued after the October 1987 market collapse.

Although a significant bear market in stocks may not be followed by a recession, the stock market has never failed to forecast a postwar recession in the United States. For this reason, most fundamental analysts use an economic forecast in making investment decisions. The economic forecast is typically for a year or more, however, because the market *leads* economic activity.

During the period 1900–1979, the U.S. economy experienced 13 peacetime expansions. An analysis of this period indicates the following:

1. The average duration of a recession (contraction) in the economy is 18 months, and the average expansion lasts 27 months.

FIGURE 8.1 • Stock Prices and Economic Activity

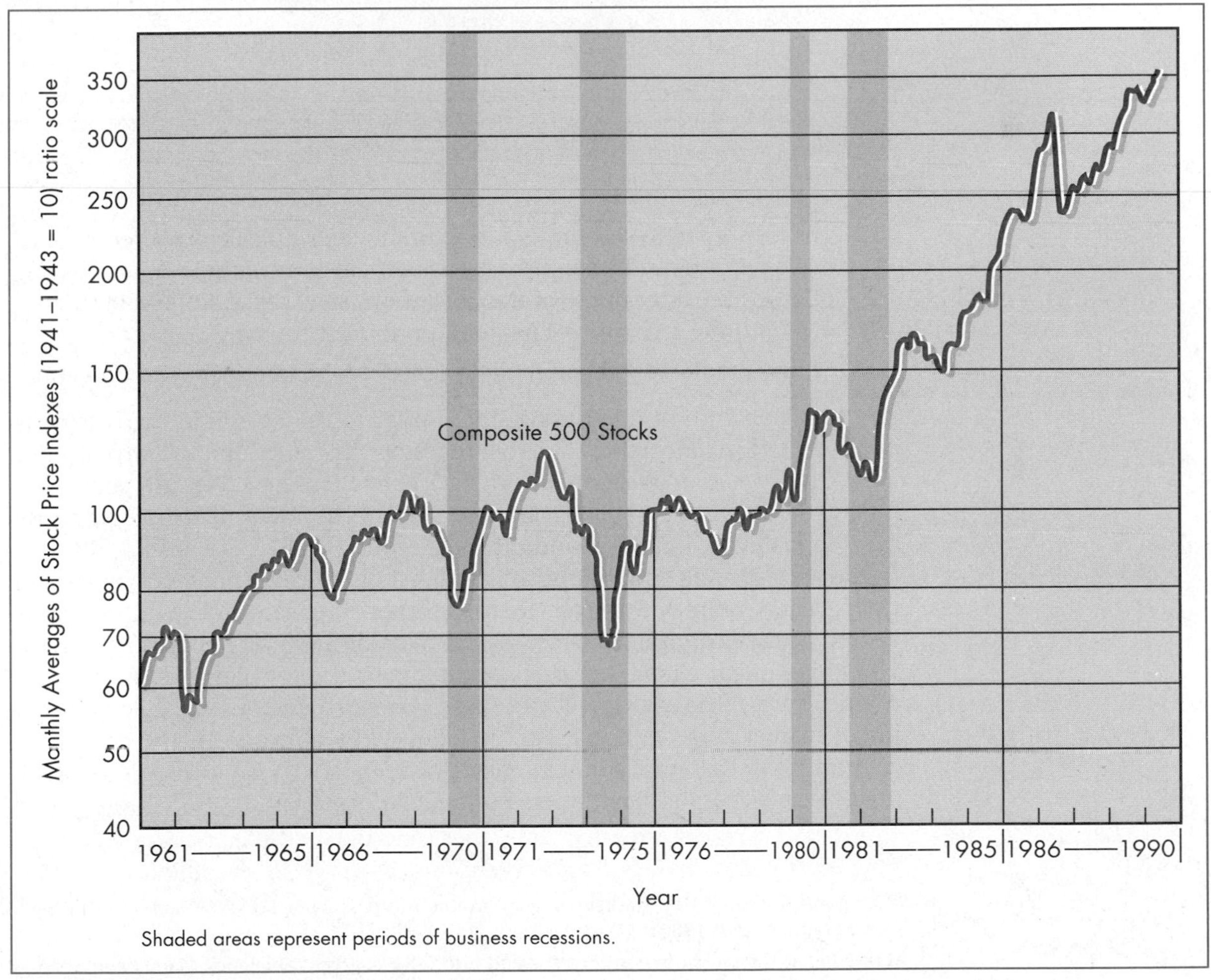

Shaded areas represent periods of business recessions.

SOURCE: *Analyst's Handbook* (Standard & Poor's, 1990), p. 193.

TABLE 8.1 • Percentage Changes in the Dow Jones Industrial Average during and after a Recession

Recessionary period	During recession	Twelve months after economic trough
1929–33	52.7%	61.7%
1937–38	40.3	− 3.8
1945	22.8	−12.7
1948–49	17.7	18.2
1953–54	37.1	33.6
1957–58	8.5	32.2
1960–61	16.9	6.1
1969–70	25.8	4.6
1973–75	36.2	23.9
1980	18.6	5.8
Average	27.8%	17.0%

SOURCE: Alfred L. Malabre, Jr., "Perverse Stocks: Just as the Economy May Be Recovering, Share Prices Wobble," *Wall Street Journal*, February 2, 1983, p. 1.

2. The ideal time to sell stocks is one to three months before a recession begins. However, because stocks usually do not continue to increase in price in the latter phase of the expansion, stocks should be sold up to eight months prior to the peak in economic activity.
3. Stocks should be purchased approximately six months into a recession.[1]

The importance of purchasing stocks prior to the trough in the **business cycle** is illustrated in Table 8.1. Note that stock prices exhibit the largest gains *during* the recession, with smaller gains occurring in the 12-month period following the economic trough. This pattern occurs because stock prices increase prior to the trough in the economic cycle.

Stock prices reflect the consensus forecast of future corporate earnings and the potential cash-flow stream. Future corporate earnings depend to a large degree on the economic environment and the future level of business activity. Therefore, major changes in stock prices may indicate changes in future economic activity.[2] As the October 1987 market crash demonstrated, however, a major market correction may not be followed by a recession. The consensus economic forecast implied by a market correction may be incorrect, or stock prices may be responding to noneconomic information.

[1] Raymond Piccini, "Stock Market Behavior around Business Cycle Peaks," *Financial Analysts Journal* (July-August 1980): 55–57.

[2] For additional discussions, see Joe Peek and Eric S. Rosengren, "The Stock Market and Economic Activity," *New England Economic Review* (May-June 1988): 39–50.

• The Business Cycle

The National Bureau of Economic Research identifies the specific months of the peak and trough of a business cycle. Officially, a downturn in economic activity is classified as a **recession** when *real GNP* (gross national product) has declined for two consecutive quarters. The economy, like the stock market, fluctuates from month to month, but minor fluctuations are not classified as a recession.

GNP is defined as the total final output of goods and services produced in the U.S. economy during a year. At the end of the third quarter of 1990, GNP was approximately \$5.51 trillion. One way to view or calculate GNP is to aggregate all expenditures by consumers, businesses, and governmental units plus the difference between imports and exports. For example, using data for the third quarter of 1990:

$$\begin{aligned} \text{GNP} &= \text{personal consumption} + \text{gross private investment} \\ &\quad + \text{governmental purchases} + \text{exports} - \text{imports} \\ &= \$3.70 + \$.76 + \$1.10 + \$.66 - \$.71 \\ &= \$5.51 \text{ trillion} \end{aligned} \tag{8.1}$$

Personal consumption expenditures for items such as food, clothing, services, and durable goods such as furniture and appliances represent approximately two-thirds of the total GNP as was the case in the third quarter of 1990. Gross private investments include expenditures for new homes, commercial buildings, machinery, equipment, and inventory changes. Investment expenditures are generally the most volatile of the major components of GNP. Governmental purchases include wages and salaries, purchases of goods and services, and expenditures on roads, bridges, and buildings. Finally, the difference between exports and imports has an impact on GNP. Since imports currently exceed exports, the **trade deficit** results in a reduction in GNP.

Real or **constant-dollar GNP** is calculated by adjusting **nominal GNP** for inflation. This adjustment is made using the *implicit price deflator,* which is a broad measure of inflation. For example, in the third quarter of 1990, real GNP was \$4.17 trillion based on 1982 dollars.

Because of the dollar magnitude of GNP, many economists concentrate on real rates of growth in GNP. For example, for the third quarter of 1990, nominal GNP increased at an annual rate of 5.5 percent. The annual rate of inflation as measured by the implicit price deflator, however, was 4 percent. Therefore, the annual rate of real GNP growth was

$$\begin{aligned} \text{real GNP growth} &= \frac{1 + \text{nominal GNP growth}}{1 + \text{inflation rate}} - 1 \\ &= \frac{1.055}{1.04} - 1 \\ &= 1.4\% \end{aligned} \tag{8.2}$$

The real GNP growth rate and the GNP deflator for the current quarter are published weekly in the "Market Laboratory/Economic Indicators" section of *Barron's*.

It is also important to understand that real GNP growth is much more significant than nominal growth in terms of the impact on stock prices. Studies have shown that stock prices are more closely related to future real economic growth.[3]

The U.S. economy, like the economies of other industrialized nations, experiences periods of recession and periods of real economic growth. Economists do not agree, however, about the causes of these cycles. Debate continues on the importance of such factors as monetary, fiscal, and trade policies. Often these arguments are supported by various economic theories, such as the Keynesian, monetarist, neo-Keynesian, supply-side, and rational expectations theories. No one theory or viewpoint appears to be able to explain consistently the level and direction of economic activity.

Most investors and financial analysts do not attempt to be experts at economic theory or economic forecasting. The relationship between the economic environment and stock prices, however, means that knowledgeable investors need a basic understanding of the business cycle. A sound and logical analysis of the causes of business cycles has been provided by Fischer Black.[4] His analysis indicates that cycles are caused by shifting supply and demand curves. These shifts occur because of changes in technology and consumer tastes. As a result of these changes, wage differentials develop between different sectors of the economy and lead to layoffs and unemployment. The peak of the cycle occurs when the demand for physical capital and the amount of capital available are closely matched. Troughs in the cycle occur when there is a poor match between the physical capital wanted and the amount available.

Black's analysis also suggests that the desire for rapid economic growth contributes to the severity of the cycle. If investments are limited to potentially high-growth alternatives, the recession will be more severe. Investing in both "high-growth" and "low-growth" sectors results in a more diversified economy that will be less subject to severe cycles. Investment in sectors that do not move together also improves economic diversification. Economic cycles occur, therefore, because of the trade-off that exists between the rate of economic growth and unemployment.

• Key Economic Variables

This section examines the key economic variables that are usually considered in an economic forecast oriented toward an analysis of common stocks.

---

[3] For example, see Peek and Rosengren, "The Stock Market and Economic Activity."

[4] Fischer Black, "The ABCs of Business Cycles," *Financial Analysts Journal* (November-December 1981): 75–80.

LEADING, COINCIDENT, AND LAGGING COMPOSITE INDEXES Perhaps the most widely followed and reported economic indicators are the leading, coincident, and lagging composite indexes, published on a monthly basis by the U.S. Department of Commerce in the *Survey of Current Business*. Table 8.2 lists the individual time-series components that are used to construct each of the three composite indexes.

The **leading composite index** consists of 11 key economic variables that lead economic activity. For the last seven recessions (1953–1989), the average lead time from the peak of the index to the peak in economic activity was 9.7 months. As Table 8.2 indicates, components of the composite index include stock prices, unemployment claims, money supply, and consumer expectations.

The **coincident composite index** is calculated using four economic variables that indicate the current phase of the business cycle. These four components are industrial production, manufacturing and trade sales, personal income, and the level of employment. Since GNP is estimated quarterly while the coincident index is estimated monthly, the coincident index provides more timely information about the current state of the economy. In the last seven recessions, the coincident composite index, on average, peaked 1.6 months prior to the peak in economic activity. On average, the index turned up just prior to the recovery in economic activity.

The **lagging composite index** uses seven variables to indicate where the economy has recently been. Typically, this index peaks after the peak in economic activity and only turns up after the economy begins to recover from a recession. The lagging index is useful because it *confirms* that a trough or peak in the economy has occurred. As Table 8.2 indicates, variables in the lagging index include the prime rate charged by banks, an inventory to sales ratio, the level of consumer installment credit outstanding relative to personal income, and the Consumer Price Index for Services.

The economic analysts at the Department of Commerce are constantly evaluating economic time series that might be used in one of the composite indexes. A desirable series should have several characteristics:

1. It should represent and accurately measure important economic variables or processes.
2. Over time, it should exhibit a consistent relationship with business-cycle movements and turns.
3. It should not be dominated by irregular and noncyclical movements.
4. It should be promptly and frequently reported.[5]

The 22 individual series that have been chosen for the three composite indexes satisfy these requirements.

---

[5] Ronald A. Ratti, "A Descriptive Analysis of Economic Indicators," *Review: Federal Reserve Bank of St. Louis* (January 1985): 14.

TABLE 8.2 • Components of the Leading, Coincident, and Lagging Composite Indexes

Leading Composite Index

1. Average weekly hours of production or nonsupervisory workers: manufacturing (hours)
2. Average weekly initial claims for unemployment insurance: state programs (thousands)
3. Manufacturers' new orders in 1982 dollars: consumer goods and materials industries (billions of dollars)
4. Vendor performance: slower deliveries diffusion index (percent)
5. Contracts and orders for plant and equipment in 1982 dollars (billions of dollars).
6. New private housing units authorized by local building permits (index: 1967 = 100)
7. Change in manufacturers' unfilled orders in 1982 dollars: durable goods industries, smoothed (billions of dollars)
8. Change in sensitive materials prices: smoothed (percent)
9. Stock prices: S&P 500 Index (index: 1941–1943 = 10)
10. Money supply: M2 in 1982 dollars (billions of dollars)
11. Consumer expectations: University of Michigan survey (index: 1966: 1 = 100)

Coincident Composite Index

1. Employees on nonagricultural payrolls (millions)
2. Personal income less transfer payments in 1982 dollars (annual rate, billions of dollars)
3. Industrial production (index: 1987 = 100)
4. Manufacturing and trade sales in 1982 dollars (billions of dollars)

Lagging Composite Index

1. Average duration of unemployment (weeks)
2. Ratio of manufacturing and trade inventories to sales in 1982 dollars (percent)
3. Change in index of labor cost per unit of output: manufacturing, smoothed (annual rate, percent)
4. Average prime rate charged by banks (percent)
5. Commercial and industrial loans outstanding in 1982 dollars (billions of dollars)
6. Ratio of consumer installment credit outstanding to personal income (percent)
7. Change in Consumer Price Index for Services: smoothed (annual rate, percent)

SOURCE: *Survey of Current Business* (Department of Commerce, Bureau of Economic Analysis, October 1990).

In 1989, the Bureau of Economic Analysis (BEA) revised the components and methodology used in constructing the composite indexes. The leading composite index dropped two components and added the series on changes in manufacturers' unfilled orders and consumer expectations. These and other changes are expected to improve the ability of the indexes to predict peaks and troughs in the business cycle.

A straightforward test of an economic indicator is to look at its past success in forecasting recessions. Figure 8.2 shows the movements of the three composite indexes from 1955 to late 1990; the dark vertical bars represent recessions. A casual analysis of the figure shows that all six recessions over the period were preceded by a significant decline in the Index of Leading Indicators. The downturn in the leading indicators in late 1990 forecast the recession in 1991. The Index of Coincident Indicators usually peaks at the beginning of a recession, and the Index of Lagging Indicators reaches a trough after the recession.

FIGURE 8.2 • Composite Indexes and the Business Cycle

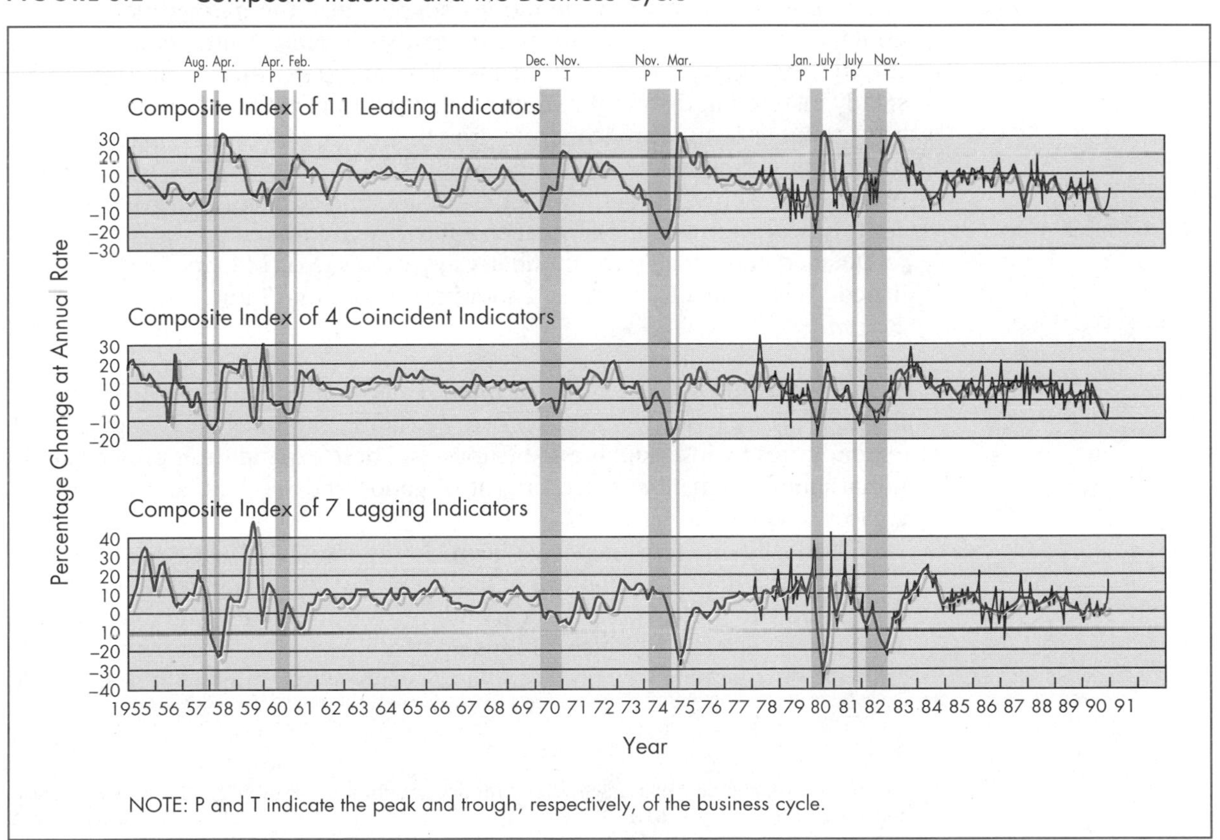

NOTE: P and T indicate the peak and trough, respectively, of the business cycle.

SOURCE: *Survey of Current Business* (Department of Commerce, Bureau of Economic Analysis, January 1991), p. C-8.

On occasion, the indexes issue false signals, such as when an index declines without being followed by a recession. For example, the leading indicators exhibited significant declines in 1966, 1984, and 1987, but no recession followed. This suggests that a recession is not imminent unless the leading indicators show three or four months of consecutive decline.

MONEY SUPPLY Milton Friedman is well known for his work on how the money supply and changes in the rate of growth in the money supply influence economic activity.[6] Beryl W. Sprinkel is also known for his studies relating the money supply to movements in stock prices.[7] Sprinkel's analysis indicates that a decline in the rate of monetary growth precedes bear markets by an average of nine months, while an increase in the monetary growth rate leads bull markets by an average of two months.

Many fundamental analysts consider the money supply in developing an economic forecast to be used in a stock market analysis. There is strong evidence that changes in the money supply influence nominal economic activity, but the effect of the money supply on real economic growth and stock prices is more hotly debated. In an efficient market, movements in stock prices would precede changes in the money supply since the market would likely anticipate money-supply changes. Monetarists usually recommend managing the money supply so as to avoid radical changes. In their view, a gradual, steady increase in the money supply will discourage inflationary expectations and promote long-term economic growth. To the extent this policy recommendation is implemented, changes in the money supply would be of limited use in forecasting stock movements. Unanticipated changes in the money supply, however, would likely cause a movement in stock prices.

Detailed data on all three monetary aggregates (M1, M2, and M3) are published weekly in the "Market Laboratory/Economic Indicators" section of *Barron's*.

INTEREST RATES The level of interest rates influences economic activity through the capital investment process because low rates encourage capital expenditures by individuals and businesses. These expenditures provide additional employment, increased output of goods and services, and overall increases in GNP.

Historically, interest rates have been closely correlated with economic activity because they usually move with the business cycle. Figure 8.3 illustrates this relationship for both long-term and short-term interest rates or yields on a variety of securities. If this relationship continues in the future, interest rate and GNP forecasts may be quite similar in terms of their implications for stock prices.

---

[6] Milton Friedman and Anna J. Schwartz, "Money and the Business Cycle," *Review of Economics and Statistics* (February 1963): 32–78.

[7] Beryl W. Sprinkel, *Money and Markets: A Monetarist View* (Homewood, Ill.: Richard D. Irwin, 1971).

FIGURE 8.3 • Interest Rates and Economic Activity

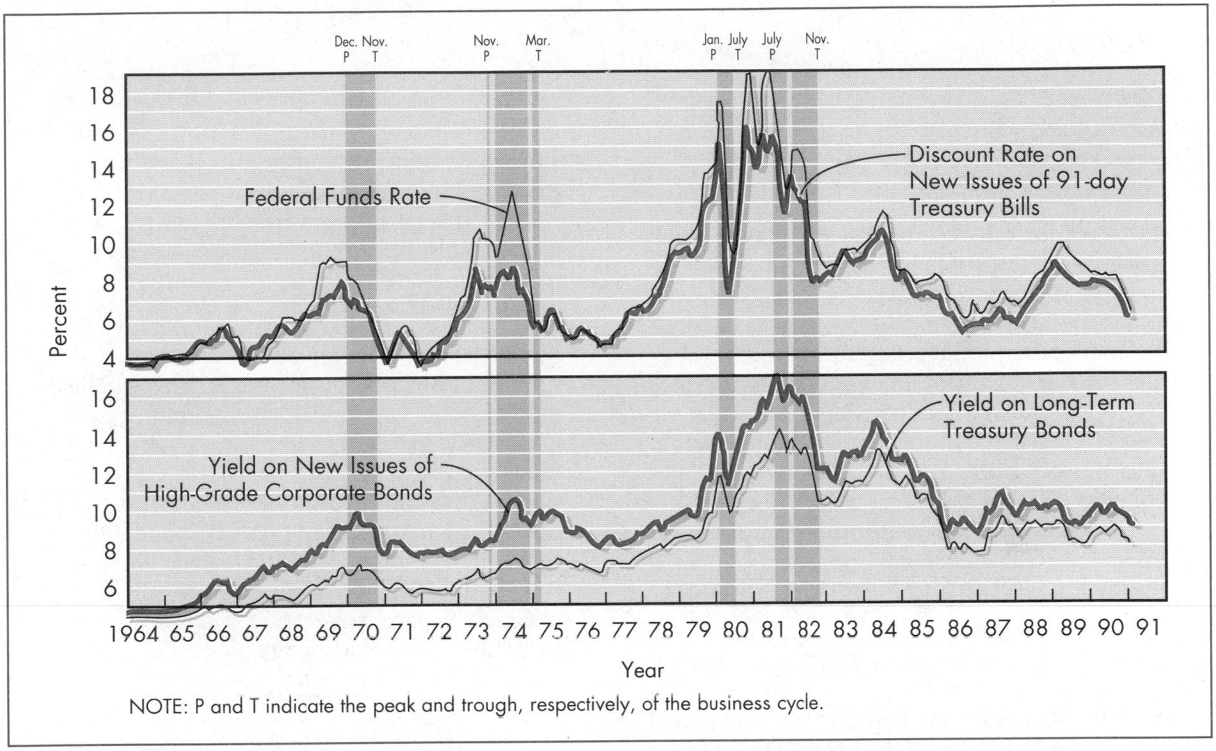

SOURCE: *Survey of Current Business* (Department of Commerce, Bureau of Economic Analysis, March 1991), p. C-21.

One alternative to actually forecasting interest rates is to use the observed yield differential between two types of securities. For example, the ratio of earnings per share to price or *earnings yield* on the S&P 500 could be compared to the yield on high-grade corporate bonds. An increasing or "large" difference between the yields is traditionally interpreted as a bullish signal for stocks.[8]

Another study based on yield differentials used the total return on the S&P Utility Index, less the yield on Treasury bills, to calculate a stock market risk premium.[9] Using the period 1964–1984, this study found five years (1968, 1969, 1972, 1975, and 1980) where the year-end risk premium was less than three percentage points. In four of the following five years, the holding period

[8] For example, see David A. Goodman and John W. Peavy III, "The Low Price Effect: Relationship with Other Stock Market Anomalies," *Review of Business and Economic Research* (Fall 1986): 18–37.

[9] Edward F. Renshaw, "A Risk Premium Model for Market Timing," *Journal of Portfolio Management* (Summer 1985): 33–35.

RESEARCH BOX
Interest Rates and Stock Price Volatility

A recent study examines the relationship between interest rates and stock price movements. The author, Peter Spiro, explains:

> Stock market critics claim that volatility in stock prices is evidence of fads exemplifying irrational trading. Such concerns have increased since the October 1987 stock market crash, especially among academic researchers. This article evaluates this question by building a model that explains stock price volatility in terms of fundamental economic factors. The model implies that the volatility of stock prices is attributable mainly to the volatility of interest rates (to which the stock market is perhaps excessively sensitive) rather than to unexplained irrational fads. This model should be useful in predicting longer-term trends in stock prices.

The empirical model presented in the article uses GNP and the real interest rate to forecast values of the S&P 500 Index. The model was tested over the 1982–1987 period using quarterly data. The real interest rate was measured as the yield on a three-month Treasury bill less the expected rate of inflation based on a survey conducted by the Federal Reserve Bank of Philadelphia. The results show that "we cannot precisely forecast every small movement of the stock index with just these two economic variables, but we can get a very good forecast of the major changes in direction."

Spiro concludes:

> My empirical investigation indicates that the significant movements in stock prices are explained by changes in two fundamental economic variables: GNP and the real interest rate. This latter is the factor responsible for most of the economic short-term volatility of stock price indexes. No one can claim to forecast precise turning points in the real interest rate, but fundamental analysis can contribute significantly to identifying its expected average value. Models of this type can be useful in setting asset mix policy and predicting broad trends in stock prices.

SOURCE: Peter S. Spiro, "The Impact of Interest Rate Changes on Stock Price Volatility," *Journal of Portfolio Management* (Winter 1990): 63–68. This copyrighted material is reprinted with permission from Institutional Investor, Inc.

return (HPR) on the S&P 500 was negative (1970 was the exception). Thus, "low" risk premium values suggest a bearish stock forecast.

Another recent study analyzed the difference between the yield to maturity on long-term Treasury bonds and the Federal Funds Rate.[10] The behavior of this spread or risk premium on Treasury bonds is related to future real economic growth and consequently to stock prices. The existence of a "low" premium also suggests a bearish stock forecast. This indicator seems to provide more reliable forecasts than the money supply and correctly predicted that there would not be a recession after the 1987 market crash.

FISCAL POLICY Tax policy and the state of the federal budget are often cited as key economic variables. Recent studies have also shown that fiscal policy seems to have more influence on the stock market than monetary pol-

[10] Robert D. Laurent, "Testing the 'Spread,'" *Economic Perspectives* (July-August 1989): 22–34.

icy. During the 1980s, attention focused on the historically large **budget deficit** and the inability of the president and Congress to agree on ways to reduce the deficit. Generally, the debate concerns the desirability of spending cuts versus tax increases as the primary methods to reduce the deficit. At one time, either method would have been considered bearish for stocks since corporate tax increases tend to lower earnings and spending cuts may reduce the overall level of economic activity. In recent years, the size of the present deficit and concern over the government's inability to reduce it have caused a reversal in this traditional thinking. Now political announcements of possible agreements on spending cuts and tax increases are often accompanied by increases in stock prices. Increases in federal taxes seem unlikely in the early 1990s, however, because of the weak economy in 1991.

Unfortunately, in recent years the United States has enjoyed few budget surpluses and more commonly has had budget deficits. Attempts to deal with surpluses, deficits, and fiscal policy in general can have a significant impact on the economy. But given the economic environment of the early 1990s, determining the impact of these activities on stock prices is difficult.

TRADE DEFICITS The large trade deficits incurred by the United States in the 1980s have been a significant economic and political problem. Rising imports have reduced domestic employment in many sectors of the economy, such as textiles, electronics, and automobiles. The impact of the deficit on the stock market has often been significant. For example, the announcement in December 1990 that the trade deficit for October was $11.61 billion—well above the September level of $9.33 billion—contributed to the decline in the value of the dollar and an overall weakness in corporate earnings and stock prices. This was the largest monthly trade deficit in more than two and a half years.

POLITICAL FACTORS The influence of politics on the economy, through fiscal and monetary policies, should not be underestimated. A realistic economic analysis and forecast should therefore include an assessment of the political environment.

Domestic **political risk** takes the form of changes in governmental regulations, subsidies, and tax policy. An increase in political risk can cause a downturn in the financial markets by reducing the expected cash flows from investments and/or raising the required rate of return, resulting in a decline in the value of securities. A more serious reaction would occur if investors liquidated their securities portfolios in favor of cash or real assets, such as gold or real estate.

The importance of political risk for financial markets can be demonstrated by studies that relate market cycles to political cycles. In an efficient market, the stock market should closely follow or lead political cycles that cause major changes in monetary and fiscal policies. Using the period 1926–1977, a study found evidence that supports a strong relationship between economic and political cycles.[11] This study found that some market cycles are closely associated with presidential election years. The evidence suggests a four-year cycle where stock prices peak in November of presidential election years. There also appears to be a two-year cycle where stock prices peak, on average, nine months following the election. The evidence supporting the two-year cycle, however, is not as strong as that for the four-year cycle. The implications of this study are that the period before an election is generally bullish whereas the period after the election tends to be bearish.

• Professional Economic Forecasts

Numerous economic forecasts are routinely published in business publications such as *Barron's*, the *Wall Street Journal*, *Fortune*, and *Business Week*. At the beginning of each year, these publications usually provide an economic forecast for the coming year. Often these forecasts are based on economic analyses developed by economists at large banks such as Manufacturers Hanover, Wells Fargo, and Morgan Guaranty Trust. Brokerage firms, insurance companies, universities, and mutual funds also provide economic forecasts that are often reported in business publications.

It is usually not feasible for individual investors to perform an economic analysis that can provide a forecast. A more practical approach is to rely on published forecasts prepared by professional economic forecasters. A major problem with this approach, however, is that economists are notorious for disagreeing about the outlook for the economy. One popular solution is to use a consensus forecast.

CONSENSUS ECONOMIC FORECAST A **consensus forecast** is simply an average of published forecasts. It does not represent a particular economic theory but instead uses forecasts that are prepared by monetarists, Keynesians, and supply-siders. Table 8.3 shows forecasts for 1990 from a number of banks, insurance companies, and security dealers/money managers, along with the average forecast for each group, an overall average, and the actual results for 1990.

The accuracy of each forecast and of the consensus forecast is measured as the absolute percentage deviation from the actual value. For example, a forecast of 1.9 percent for real GNP growth versus an actual growth rate of 0.96 percent is a 97.9 percent error [$|(1.9 - .96)/.96|$]. With absolute values, under- and overestimation errors are treated the same. While the forecasting errors look large, it should be pointed out that the forecasts are based on percentage changes. In terms of the accuracy of the individual forecasters, only 8 of the 22 forecasts of the growth rate in real GNP have errors equal to or smaller

[11] Anthony F. Herbst and Craig W. Slinkman, "Political-Economic Cycles in the U.S. Stock Market," *Financial Analysts Journal* (March-April 1984): 38–44.

than the errors for the overall consensus. For the civilian unemployment and Consumer Price Index forecasts, 14 and 9, respectively, of the 22 forecasters were more accurate than the overall consensus.

One of the most widely recognized consensus forecasts is provided by Blue Chip Economic Indicators. This organization publishes a newsletter based on a poll of an anonymous, fixed sample of economists. The average of their forecasts is published as a consensus economic forecast. The logic behind this approach is that few individual economists can consistently produce a more accurate forecast than the average forecast.

Studies of the accuracy of consensus forecasts generally conclude that the consensus is likely to be "less wrong" than the forecast of a single economist. Using data over the period 1980–1983, one study found an average error of only 1.1 percent between the actual real GNP and the forecast.[12] The consensus forecast usually predicts the direction of the economy but has occasionally missed an economic turning point, such as the recession in 1981. The evidence seems to indicate that the consensus forecasting approach is not as accurate as one might hope, but it does minimize the risk of relying on a single bad forecast.

THE PRESIDENT'S ECONOMIC REPORT In addition to the economic forecasts provided by private organizations, the U.S. government also develops a comprehensive economic forecast. The most widely known forecast is provided in the President's Economic Report, prepared by the **Council of Economic Advisers.** This annual report is often accused of making an overly optimistic forecast because of political considerations.

The report is typically presented to Congress in February each year and always includes an extensive set of statistical tables. The focus in recent years has been on tax reform, trade liberalization, and welfare reform. The Bush administration report presented in February 1991 stressed international trade and the movement toward a global economy.

AN EXAMPLE OF A PROFESSIONAL FORECAST An excellent example of a professional economic forecast, directed specifically toward the stock market, is an article written by William S. Gray.[13] This article provides an economic analysis and forecast based on key variables such as the growth rate in real GNP, expected inflation rate, and real stock returns. These estimates are then used to provide specific forecasts for the stock market (using the S&P 400) through 1992.

---

12 Peter L. Bernstein and Theodore H. Silbert, "Are Economic Forecasters Worth Listening To?" *Harvard Business Review* (September-October 1984): 38.

13 William S. Gray, "The Anatomy of a Stock Market Forecast," *Journal of Portfolio Management* (Fall 1989): 36–44.

TABLE 8.3 • Accuracy of Consensus Economic Forecast for 1990

	Forecast			Error of forecast (%)*		
Forecaster	*Percentage change in real GNP*	*Percentage change in civilian unemployment*	*Percentage change in consumer price index*	*Real GNP*	*Civilian unemployment*	*Consumer price index*
Banks						
1. Ameritrust	2.02%	−4.17%	3.12%	110.4%	210.6%	40.2%
2. Corestate Financial Corp.	1.77	−3.77	3.36	84.4	200.0	35.6
3. Fidelity Bank	1.32	5.26	2.92	37.5	39.5	44.1
4. First National of Chicago	1.87	2.00	3.91	94.8	46.9	25.1
5. Fleet National	2.52	3.45	3.06	162.5	8.5	41.4
6. First Interstate BanCorp	2.17	−5.17	3.21	126.0	237.1	38.5
7. Lasalle National	1.53	0.00	3.22	59.4	100.0	38.3
8. Manufacturers Hanover	2.46	−1.79	2.75	156.3	147.5	47.3
9. Marine Midland	1.85	3.70	4.07	92.7	1.9	22.0
10. Morgan Guaranty Trust	1.12	1.89	3.69	16.7	49.9	29.3
11. National City	1.88	−3.92	3.60	95.8	204.0	31.0
12. Shawmut of Boston	1.70	−5.36	2.74	77.1	242.2	47.5
13. Society National	1.36	3.64	3.06	41.7	3.4	41.4
14. Valley National	1.44	4.67	3.22	50.0	23.9	38.3
15. Wells Fargo	1.78	0.00	3.52	85.4	100.0	32.6
Consensus	1.79%	0.03%	3.30%	86.5%	99.2%	36.8%

Insurance Companies						
1. Equitable Life	1.52%	−3.57%	3.52%	58.3%	194.7%	32.6%
2. John Hancock	1.34	5.66	3.38	39.6	50.1	35.2
3. Metropolitan Life	0.21	3.57	3.29	78.1	5.3	37.0
Consensus	1.02%	1.89%	3.40%	6.3%	49.9%	34.9%
Security Dealers/Money Managers						
1. Brown Brothers Harriman	1.96%	0.00%	3.29%	104.2%	100.0%	37.0%
2. CM&M Asset Management	1.90	−7.84	4.61	97.9	308.0	11.7
3. Shearson Lehman	1.57	0.00	2.79	63.5	100.0	46.6
4. Paine Webber	1.65	0.00	3.15	79.1	100.0	39.7
Consensus	1.77%	−1.96%	3.46%	84.4%	152.0%	33.7%
Overall consensus for 22 forecasters	1.68%	−0.08%	3.34%	75.0%	102.1%	36.0%
Actual	.96%	3.77%	5.22%	—	—	—

SOURCES: Forecasts from *Journal of Business Forecasting* (Fall 1989): 37–39. Actual data from various issues of *Survey of Current Business* (Department of Commerce, Bureau of Economic Analysis).

*Calculated as the absolute value of |(forecast − actual)/actual| expressed as a percentage.

• **INTEREST BOX**

How Economists Make Forecasts

As this chapter has explained, economists use a number of economic theories and forecasting techniques to predict key economic variables such as the inflation rate, interest rates, employment level, and GNP. Various economists often arrive at quite different forecasts. For any given forecasting period, it is not unusual to find some economists forecasting a recession while others are predicting a strong, growing economy. Obviously, these divergent forecasts occur because of the difficulty of predicting the behavior of an economy as complex as that of the United States.

Another factor that may contribute to the divergent forecasts is the fact that different economists rely on different economic theories and forecasting techniques. A recent study reports the results of a mail survey of U.S. economic forecasters. The questionnaire asked economists to quantify the percentage weight they give to various economic theories and analytical techniques in preparing their forecasts. According to the survey, more economists use Keynesian theory than any other ideology. The most popular analytical technique is econometric model building. One somewhat surprising finding of the survey is that despite the popularity of Keynesianism and econometrics, most forecasters place more emphasis on their own judgment than on any formal modeling technique.

SOURCE: Roy Batchelor and Pami Dua, "Forecaster Ideology, Forecasting Technique, and the Accuracy of Economic Forecasts," *International Journal of Forecasting* (January 1990): 3–10.

• Relating an Economic Forecast to the Stock Market

Despite the use of economic forecasts in traditional fundamental analysis, debate continues about the usefulness and accuracy of this "top-down" decision-making process. Financial analysts generally agree that corporate earnings and the stock market are closely related. For example, one study, based on the period 1964–1983, found that changes in the yield to maturity on government bonds and in aggregate after-tax corporate profits explained over 50 percent of the changes in the S&P 500.[14] The changes in government bond yields and after-tax corporate profits were found to be almost equally important in explaining stock market cycles. On the other hand, approximately 50 percent of the changes in the S&P 500 were not explained by the model, suggesting that other variables are also important.

A second study analyzed the effect news announcements about key economic variables had on *hourly* stock prices and trading volume.[15] The study considered announcements about five variables:

[14] Steven E. Bolten and Susan W. Long, "A Note on Cyclical and Dynamic Aspects of Stock Market Price Cycles," *Financial Review* (February 1986): 145–49.

[15] Prem C. Jain, "Response of Hourly Stock Prices and Trading Volume to Economic News," *Journal of Business* (April 1988): 219–31.

1. Money supply
2. Consumer Price Index (CPI)
3. Producer Price Index (PPI)
4. Industrial production
5. Unemployment rate

The study used data over the period 1978–1984 and found that only two of the five variables were significantly related to short-term stock price changes. Announcements about the money supply and CPI had a significant effect on prices within one hour or so after the news was released.

Financial research and evidence from prior business cycles clearly demonstrate that the stock market reacts to economic developments. Investors, therefore, need to understand the key economic variables and their possible influence on the market over the investment horizon. An accurate economic forecast is essential in identifying appropriate industries for analysis and developing other aspects of an investment strategy.

TECHNICAL ANALYSIS

Technical analysis attempts to resolve the *investment timing* issuc by gaining insight into market behavior through a variety of techniques. Technicians or chartists, as they are sometimes called, use historical price and trading volume data to gain insight into future price trends or cycles. They generally are not as ambitious as fundamental analysts in that they do not estimate a specific future price.

Technicians are not concerned with economic analysis, balance sheets, income statements, or intrinsic values. Instead, they look for shifts in the underlying supply and demand factors for individual securities or for the overall market. The underlying premise of technical analysis is that significant shifts in supply and demand factors can be detected in order to forecast stock price movements. Using these data, technicians have developed a number of technical indicators that are used for market timing strategies.

• Breadth of the Market

The **breadth of the market** involves the relationship between the number of stocks with advancing versus declining prices. *Barron's* publishes this information in its "Market Laboratory/Stocks" section. The basic theory is that in a bona fide bull market, the majority of securities will be advancing in price; in a bear market, most securities will be declining. Technicians look carefully at the number of advancing versus declining issues and attempt to determine if they are behaving consistently with the market. For example, if a major market index should trend up for some time while the number of advancing stocks versus declining issues was declining, this inconsistency might suggest the possibility of a change in market direction.

One of the ways to analyze the relationship between advancing and declining issues is to maintain a running net cumulative sum of issues advancing versus issues declining, or

$$\text{sum} = \text{number of advancing issues} - \text{number of declining issues}$$

If the cumulative sum increases and the market is rising, the sum is confirming the bull market. If the cumulative sum declines in a rising market, then "nonconformance" is present, and concern about the continuation of the rising market may be justified.

• The Confidence Index

The **confidence index** originated in 1932 and is reported each week in the "Market Laboratory/Bonds" section of *Barron's*. This technical indicator compares the yield on high-grade bonds to the yield on medium-grade bonds. The underlying logic of this indicator is that when investors feel confident about the economy, they are willing to move funds from high- to medium-quality bonds. As this takes place, the yield on the lower-quality bonds tends to increase more slowly than the yield on high-quality bonds, causing the yield spread to narrow and the ratio to rise, implying market confidence. In recent years, however, this index has not been as reliable as it was earlier. One reason for this may be more aggressive management of monetary policy by the Federal Reserve.

• Mutual Funds' Cash Position

High liquidity by mutual funds signifies a large amount of investable funds. If mutual fund managers believe economic conditions are improving, they are likely to invest this money quickly in the market, with an attendant positive impact on security prices. On the other hand, if portfolio managers are generally optimistic, they tend to be fully invested, and their cash position is negligible; hence, mutual funds could be expected to provide little or no buying power to propel the market higher.

Because of changes in financial regulation, tax legislation, pension alternatives, and the like, it may be increasingly difficult to establish the extremes of cash positions; thus, care should be taken in interpreting this indicator. **Mutual funds' cash positions** in conjunction with other financial flow information, however, may improve some forecasts. As Chapter 5 pointed out, mutual fund assets have increased dramatically in recent years. Consequently, due to the increased importance of mutual funds in the market, extreme levels of cash positions could now be an even more important indicator. Monthly data on the cash position and liquid asset ratio of mutual funds are published in the "Mutual Fund Monthly Indicators" section of *Barron's*.

• Put-Call Ratio

With the advent of equity and index options, speculators (small and large) can now speculate or limit their losses by buying or "writing" (selling) contracts to buy or sell individual securities or indexes (see Chapters 15 and 17). An investor attempting to limit losses in a long position will purchase a *put* (the right to sell) if prices are expected to fall. A speculator who expects prices to increase will purchase a *call* (right to buy). Therefore, the relationship (ratio) of the number of puts to calls will give an indication of the bullish or bearish sentiment of option market participants. Typically, the **put-call ratio** is "low" during optimistic periods and "high" during pessimistic periods. Extreme readings of this ratio have been found in close proximity to major market reversals. This ratio is available weekly in the "Market Laboratory" section of *Barron's*.

• Short Interest

As discussed in Chapter 7, investors anticipating a decline in the price of a stock can sell the stock short. If their forecast proves correct and the price declines, the stock can be purchased to cover the short, and the investor realizes a profit. The **short interest** indicates the number of shares of stock that have been sold short during a particular time period. For example, the "Market Laboratory/Stocks" section of *Barron's* reports short sales for the week, previous week, and year-ago week for both the NYSE and AMEX. In addition to publishing total short sales, *Barron's* reports short sales by exchange members such as specialists and floor traders. This allows investors using this indicator to have an idea of what the "smart money" is doing relative to individuals.

Figure 8.4 illustrates some of the market timing technical indicators published in *Barron's*. Most technicians would not rely on a single indicator to make a forecast about the direction of the market. Instead, they would use several indicators, especially if a number of the indicators did not agree.

INDUSTRY ANALYSIS

In the broadest sense, an **industry** is a group of companies with common products and services. Analysts group companies into industries in an attempt to identify similar companies that can be analyzed without regard to differing industry factors. For example, the classification eliminates the problem of comparing a manufacturing firm with a financial services firm. The rationale behind this approach is that an **industry effect** may have a significant impact on an individual company's performance.

Industry classification schemes vary considerably in the criteria used to determine each classification. The following discussion briefly highlights some of the more widely used classification schemes.

FIGURE 8.4 • Some Technical Indicators Used for Market Timing

Market and Volume Reports

All numbers in thousands save percentages and ratios

New York Stock Exchange

	Week May 10	Prev. Week	Year-Ago Week
TOTAL VOLUME			
Weekly	792,013.8	880,960.7	827,324.5
Average Daily	158,402.8	176,192.1	165,464.9
MEMBER ACTIVITY			
Specialists Buys (#†)	76,135.9	85,047.3	74,667.6
Specialists Sales (#†)	74,473.2	87,413.2	77,059.5
Floor Traders Buys	120.6	213.2	0.0
Floor Traders Sales	127.0	235.2	5.0
Other Member Buys (#)	98,057.7	123,808.4	110,004.7
Other Member Sales (#)	114,573.5	116,237.7	113,568.3
Total Member Buys	174,314.1	209,069.0	184,672.3
Total Member Sales	189,173.7	203,886.1	190,632.9
Net Member Buy/Sell	−14,859.5	+5,182.9	−5,960.6
Member volume as % of total	22.95	23.44	22.68
SHORT SALES			
Total	72,410.0	83,167.9	79,512.8
Public	20,849.0	36,279.2	30,962.6
Members Total	51,561.0	46,888.7	48,550.2
Specialists	23,402.9	30,979.7	31,366.7
Floor Traders	49.9	107.3	5.0
Other Members	28,108.2	15,801.8	17,178.4
Specialists/Public Short Ratio	1.1	0.8	1.0
Members/Public Short Ratio	2.5	1.3	1.6

Customers Odd-Lot Activity

NYSE	Week May 10	Prev. Week	Year-Ago Week
Purchases, shares	3,206.6	3,560.5	2,363.7
Purchases $	142,136.8	159,397.7	101,533.6
Sales, shares	3,878.9	3,189.8	3,325.7
Sales $	150,724.9	122,056.6	132,080.5
Short Sales, shares	440.7	100.8	163.8
Short Sales $	18,830.6	4,561.3	8,019.3

Source: New York Stock Exchange, 11 Wall Street, New York, N.Y. Phone (212) 656-3000.

American Stock Exchange

	Week May 10	Prev. Week	Year-Ago Week
TOTAL VOLUME			
Weekly	55,387.6	61,604.4	69,421.8
Average Daily	11,077.5	12,320.9	13,884.4
MEMBER ACTIVITY			
Specialists Buys (#†)	6,692.6	7,146.8	6,681.6
Specialists Sales (#†)	6,744.2	6,949.1	6,917.6
Floor Traders Buys	83.9	67.0	145.8
Floor Traders Sales	80.8	59.4	99.5
Other Member Buys (#)	3,026.2	4,538.5	5,236.8
Other Member Sales (#)	3,057.8	4,829.4	6,186.8
Total Member Buys	9,802.7	11,752.3	12,064.2
Total Member Sales	9,882.8	11,837.9	13,203.9
Net Member Buy/Sell	−80.1	−85.6	−1,139.7
Member volume as % of total	17.77	19.15	18.20
SHORT SALES			
Total	1,054.0	1,639.6	2,322.4
Public	633.3	936.6	1,500.3
Member Total	420.7	703.0	822.1
Specialists	38.1	50.4	59.7
Floor Traders	24.9	22.4	42.6
Other Members	357.7	630.2	719.8
Specialists/Public Short Ratio	0.1	0.0	0.0
Members/Public Short Ratio	0.7	0.7	0.5

Customers Odd-Lot Activity

AMEX	Week May 10	Prev. Week	Year-Ago Week
Purchases, shares	54.8	55.8	56.4
Sales, shares	108.4	108.7	100.9

#Includes transactions effected by members acting as Registered Competitive Market-Makers. †Including offsetting round-lot transactions arising from odd-lot dealer activity by specialists and other members. w-Shares and warrants. Source: American Stock Exchange, 86 Trinity Place, New York, N.Y. Phone (212) 306-1000.

CBOE Put-Call Ratio

	Last Week Puts	Last Week Calls	Last Week's Ratio	Previous Week's Ratio
S&P 100	384,380	346,669	111/100	110/100
CBOE Equity	202,917	447,856	45/100	51/100

When the market is changing, a put-call ratio of 70 puts to every 100 calls on the Standard & Poor's 100 and 65 to every 100 calls on the CBOE Equity ratio is considered bullish.

Trading Diary

Market Advance/Decline Totals

Week ended last Friday compared to previous Friday

Weekly Comp.	NYSE	AMEX	NASDAQ
Total Issues	2,241	978	4,091
Advances	1,125	414	1,500
Declines	830	374	1,201
Unchanged	286	190	1,390
New Highs	181	42	265
New Lows	39	19	103

Weekly Bond Statistics

	Last Week	Prev. Week	Yr-Ago Week
New Offerings, (mil $) (v)			
Corporate	1,260	2,900	2,000
Municipal	2,600	2,800	1,750
Best Grade Bonds-y (Barron's index of 10 high-grade corporate bonds.)	8.73	8.76	9.35
Interm-Grade Bonds-y (Barron's index of 10 medium-grade corporate bonds.)	9.27	9.22	9.73
Confidence Index (High-grade index divided by intermediate-grade index; decline in latter vs. former generally indicates rising confidence, pointing to higher stocks.)	94.2	95.0	96.1

SOURCE: *Barron's*, May 27, 1991.

DOW JONES INDUSTRY GROUPS Dow Jones & Company publishes the closely watched Dow Jones Averages in the *Wall Street Journal.* These averages represent very broad "industry" indexes for only three categories: (1) industrials, (2) transportation, and (3) utilities. Figure 8.5 illustrates the price behavior of these three categories of stocks. A comparison of these indexes reveals very similar patterns of price movements. There are, however, some notable differences that suggest the importance of an industry effect.

Dow Jones also publishes indexes for a large number of industries in the *Wall Street Journal* and *Barron's.* The indexes are grouped into "leading" and "lagging" categories according to whether the industries are experiencing price increases or price decreases. A number of the strongest and weakest stocks in each category are also identified.

VALUE LINE INDUSTRY CLASSIFICATIONS The *Value Line Investment Survey* uses 94 industry classifications for the approximately 1,650 stocks that it analyzes. A two- to three-page industry analysis and forecast precedes the analyses of each individual company in the industry. Value Line also compiles price indexes for each of these 94 industries and ranks the industries by their probable price performance (timeliness rank) over the next six months.

STANDARD & POOR'S INDUSTRY CLASSIFICATIONS Standard & Poor's Corporation uses 92 industry classifications to compile and report industry data. Detailed industry data, analyses, and forecasts are given in Standard & Poor's *Industry Surveys.* This publication provides a "Current Analysis" for each industry, followed by a detailed "Basic Analysis" that can be 10 to 20 pages in length, depending on the industry. In addition, the "Earnings Supplement" section of the *Survey* lists each company in the industry and provides recent data on its revenues, income, and profitability. Each company is ranked on its performance in each of these three areas relative to other companies in the industry. These rankings are designed to highlight companies with superior performance within the industry.

The *Outlook,* also published by Standard & Poor's, provides economic, industry, and company analyses and forecasts. The industry analysis usually takes the form of a discussion of the "best and worst" industries based on past performance and makes recommendations for the following year. Individual companies in each of the recommended industries are also discussed. Table 8.4 provides information concerning companies in four of the industries recommended in May 1991. The industries were selected by Standard & Poor's analysts for investors seeking long-term capital appreciation or superior long-term total return.

STANDARD INDUSTRIAL CLASSIFICATIONS The most comprehensive and detailed system of industry classification is the **Standard Industrial Classification (SIC).** This system was developed by the federal government through the Office of Management and Budget. Definitions of each "industry" or classification, and types of businesses that meet these definitions, are given in the *Standard Industrial Classification Manual.*

FIGURE 8.5
Dow Jones Industrials, Transportation, and Utilities Averages

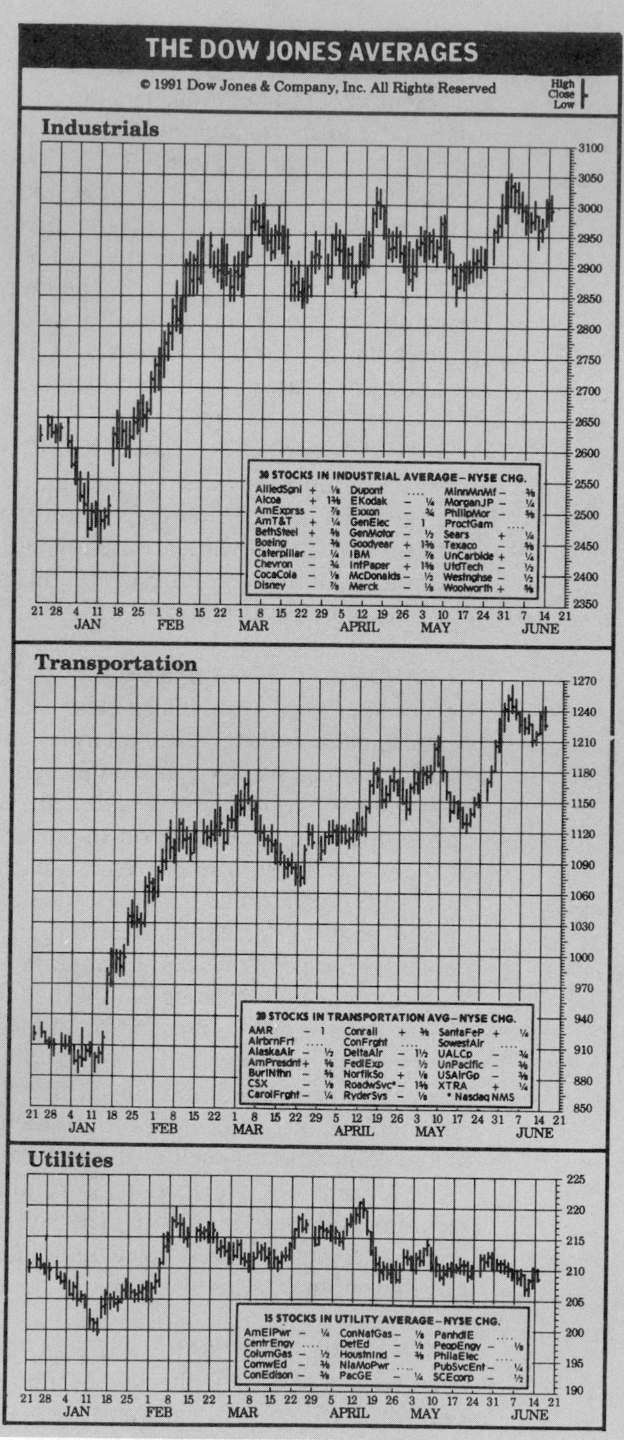

SOURCE: *Wall Street Journal,* June 18, 1991, p. C-3.

TABLE 8.4 • Standard & Poor's Industry and Company Recommendations: Master List of Recommended Issues

	Earnings per share								
	1990	*1991 (estimated)*	Indicated dividend	Stars*	Dividend yield	1990–1991 price range	Recent price	Quality rank	P/E ratio
Core Stocks for Long-Term Capital Appreciation									
Electrical equipment industry									
1. Emerson Electric	$2.75	$2.90	$1.32	4	2.9%	$47\frac{1}{4}$–$30\frac{3}{4}$	45	A+	15.5
2. General Electric	4.85	5.20	2.04	4	2.9	$75\frac{1}{2}$–50	70	A+	13.5
Foods industry									
1. ConAgra	2.15	2.55	0.69	4	1.6	$48\frac{3}{4}$–$22\frac{3}{4}$	42	A+	16.5
2. CPC International	4.83	5.40	2.20	3	2.5	89–62	89	A−	16.5
Health-care diversified industry									
1. Abbott Laboratories	2.22	2.55	1.00	4	2.0	54–$31\frac{1}{4}$	49	A+	19.2
2. Bristol-Myers Squibb	3.33	4.00	2.40	5	3.1	$81\frac{1}{4}$–$50\frac{1}{2}$	79	A+	19.8
Stocks for Superior Long-Term Total Return									
Telephone industry									
1. Ameritech	4.73	4.95	3.40	4	5.9	$69\frac{3}{4}$–$52\frac{1}{2}$	58	A−	11.7
2. Pacific Telesis	2.58	2.85	2.14	3	5.4	$51\frac{1}{2}$–$36\frac{1}{4}$	40	A−	14.0
3. Southwestern Bell	3.67	3.80	2.84	4	5.7	$64\frac{3}{4}$–$47\frac{1}{4}$	50	A−	13.2

SOURCE: Standard & Poor's *The Outlook,* May 22, 1991, p. 12.

*Stars represents a timeliness ranking with 5 being the highest ranking.

This system uses a four-digit numerical code to represent each industry. The first two digits of the code represent the "major" industry group. The following codes represent the major industries:

01 to 09	Agriculture, forestry, and fishing
10 to 14	Mining
15 to 27	Construction
28 to 39	Manufacturing
40 to 49	Transportation, communication, electric, gas, and sanitary services
50 to 59	Wholesale and retail trade
60 to 67	Finance, insurance, and real estate
70 to 89	Services
91 to 97	Government
99	Nonclassifiable

For example, a code 17-- represents one segment of the construction industry. The last two digits of the code provide more details about the industry. Thus, code 1711 is used for air conditioning, plumbing, and heating contractors. This system provides literally thousands of four-digit codes that can be used to classify any type of business or organization.

The SIC codes can be used in an industry analysis in several ways. First, an analyst who is interested in a particular industry can find the four-digit SIC code by consulting an alphabetical listing of the codes.[16] The code can then be used to obtain specific industry data from sources such as the *U.S. Industrial Outlook* published by the U.S. Department of Commerce.

Second, the codes can be used to identify all companies in a particular code. Publications such as Standard & Poor's *Corporate Records* and Moody's *Industrial Manual* list the SIC codes for companies in their manuals. Lists are then compiled that include all the companies in each four-digit SIC code.[17]

One problem with using the SIC codes is that many large publicly traded companies fall under a large number of codes. This occurs because the companies are diversified both vertically and horizontally, sometimes into areas not related to their principal business. Under the detailed criteria used by the SIC system, a single diversified company must be assigned multiple SIC codes. To analyze the company, therefore, the analyst must identify its principal industry or analyze each of the primary industries in which the company operates.

[16] For example, see Volume T–Z of Standard & Poor's *Corporate Records*.

[17] For example, see the "blue section" of Volume T–Z of Standard & Poor's *Corporate Records*.

• **INTEREST BOX**

Changes in the SIC Codes

The Standard Industrial Classification (SIC) codes were initially developed by the federal government in the 1930s to standardize reporting of statistical data at the company level. Despite the importance of the SIC codes to many financial and business researchers, the government revises the codes only infrequently. The codes need frequent revisions, however, as industries decline and disappear and new industries grow and develop. Surprising as it may seem, the SIC codes were not significantly revised between 1972 and 1987. Due to many complaints from code users, the Office of Management and Budget announced in 1984 that a revision was in process. The revision was completed in 1987.

The major changes in the 1987 revision are interesting because of what they tell us about the U.S. industrial structure. The 1987 revision deleted 78 industry classifications in areas such as forestry, mining and quarrying, and textile mill products. Types of businesses with a significant number of new and expanded codes include services, plastics, and computers. Among the new service industry codes are physical fitness facilities, videotape rentals, photocopying and duplicating services, and tax preparation services. The computer industry received new classifications for computer storage devices, computer terminals, and computer peripheral equipment.

SOURCES: Marydee Ojala, "SIC Codes Revisited: Dun's Goes Marching Two by Two," *Online*, November 1989, pp. 84–89; and Richard Kern, "At Long Last! Changes in the SIC System," *Sales and Marketing Management*, April 28, 1986, pp. 8–22, 24–26.

• Importance of Industry Analysis

The previous discussion and the traditionalist's viewpoint suggest that industry factors have a significant influence on the performance of an individual company. There have been numerous studies of the importance of this industry effect on individual stocks in the industry. Although the studies do not agree in all respects, the following observations can be made:

1. The industry effect is statistically significant in approximately two-thirds of all industries.
2. For industries with a significant industry effect, industry factors, on average, account for 18 percent of the variance of the return for individual stocks in the industry, but the importance varies greatly from industry to industry.
3. On average, the condition of the economy and of the overall stock market explains 23 percent of the variance of the returns for individual stocks.
4. Unique company and other factors, on average, explain 59 percent of the variance of individual stock returns.

Thus, these conclusions support the importance of the industry effect for the majority of industries and confirm the logic of performing an industry analysis as part of a security analysis. The conclusions also suggest that portfolios should be diversified by industry.

• Key Industry Fundamentals

This section briefly discusses the key fundamentals that are usually included in an industry analysis. Note, however, that the importance of each variable may vary from industry to industry and that unique variables may need to be considered for certain industries.

HISTORICAL FINANCIAL PERFORMANCE Historical industry financial information is available from a number of sources including *U.S. Industrial Outlook*, Standard & Poor's *Analyst's Handbook*, *Value Line Investment Survey*, and Standard & Poor's *Industry Surveys*. An example of the industry per-share data for automobiles provided by Standard & Poor's appears in Table 8.5.

TABLE 8.5 • Industry Financial Data: Automobiles

	1985	1986	1987	1988	1989
Sales	524.03	588.95	632.72	791.65	839.57
Operating income	54.30	57.48	66.61	201.58	144.10
Profit margin (%)	10.36	9.79	10.53	25.46	17.16
Depreciation	27.34	31.48	32.08	38.79	42.20
Taxes	10.56	7.20	11.53	18.35	14.78
Earnings	24.35	22.94	30.17	34.99	27.23
Dividends	6.40	7.48	8.48	9.46	11.80
Earnings/sales (%)	4.65	3.91	4.77	4.42	3.24
Dividends/earnings (%)	26.28	32.52	28.04	27.04	43.33
Price (1941–43 = 100):					
High	116.97	151.15	209.32	187.37	201.12
Low	94.46	110.95	128.95	140.82	160.96
Price-earnings ratio:					
High	4.80	6.59	6.94	5.35	7.39
Low	3.88	4.84	4.27	4.02	5.91
Dividend yield (%)					
High	6.78	6.72	6.56	6.72	7.33
Low	5.47	4.94	4.04	5.05	5.87
Book value	119.60	137.77	156.55	175.96	207.69
Return on book value (%)	20.36	16.65	19.27	19.89	13.11
Working capital	11.43	21.43	56.48	N/A	N/A
Capital expenditures	44.21	54.05	43.37	42.58	63.27

SOURCE: Standard & Poor's *Industry Surveys*, December 13, 1990, p. A98.

NOTE: The companies used for these per-share data are American Motors (delisted in 1987), Chrysler, Ford Motor, and General Motors.

Historical financial data can be analyzed using ratio analysis that assesses the industry's liquidity, financial leverage, profitability, and asset utilization characteristics. The ratios and analysis of the actual data can be used to identify significant trends or developments in the industry. Analysts often use the historical data to calculate growth rates in key variables such as sales and earnings.

RELATIONSHIP OF THE INDUSTRY TO THE ECONOMY The historical relationship between the industry and the economy can be useful in applying the economic forecast to a specific industry. For example, an examination of the industry's sales and profits during recessionary periods will indicate the impact of the business cycle on the industry.

Regression analysis of key economic and industry variables may also reveal interesting and useful relationships. For example, it may help explain how industry sales relate to GNP, aggregate consumer spending, or industrial output.

RELATIONSHIP OF THE INDUSTRY TO THE STOCK MARKET Industry stock prices may exhibit different patterns than do stocks in general because of unique industry factors. Figure 8.6 shows how a common stock price index for the automobile industry behaves relative to the S&P 400 Industrials. As expected, the two indexes are closely correlated, but the automobile index is much more volatile. Notice that the declines in the automobile index during the recessions of 1974 and 1982 are much more severe than the declines for industrials in general. The price behavior illustrated in Figure 8.6 suggests that the systematic (beta) and total (variance) risk of the automobile stocks are greater than the market's.

IMPORTS AND EXPORTS A key variable for many industries is their ability to compete in international markets. Often this involves the ability to compete against imports in the domestic market as well as the ability to penetrate foreign markets. For industries that depend on international trade, factors such as currency rates, trade policies, and economic conditions in other countries are important variables. For example, the automobile industry is significantly affected by imports from Japan and Germany.

REGULATORY ENVIRONMENT Many industries are subject to regulations imposed by local, state, and federal agencies. The regulations may deal with areas such as the environment, job safety, and restraint of trade. Many industries such as automobiles, mining, chemicals, and energy are significantly affected by these regulations.

LABOR ENVIRONMENT Manufacturing industries have historically had unionized workers; the status of wage contracts and the bargaining positions of labor and management can be significant factors in the industry analysis. An assessment of these factors may reveal the likelihood of a strike or of major wage concessions that can have a significant impact on the profitability of the industry.

INDUSTRY STRUCTURE Some industries have a few large firms, while others consist of numerous small firms. An analysis of the structure of the industry provides a basis for analyzing the competition among firms in the industry and their relative market shares. The structure may also indicate the life cycle of the products or services provided by the industry. From this, the analyst may predict the likelihood that new firms will enter the industry to exploit the early stages of a product's life cycle.

TECHNOLOGY AND INNOVATION Many new industries are highly dependent on technological innovations in engineering, computer science, or

FIGURE 8.6 • Automobile Industry and Industrial Stocks

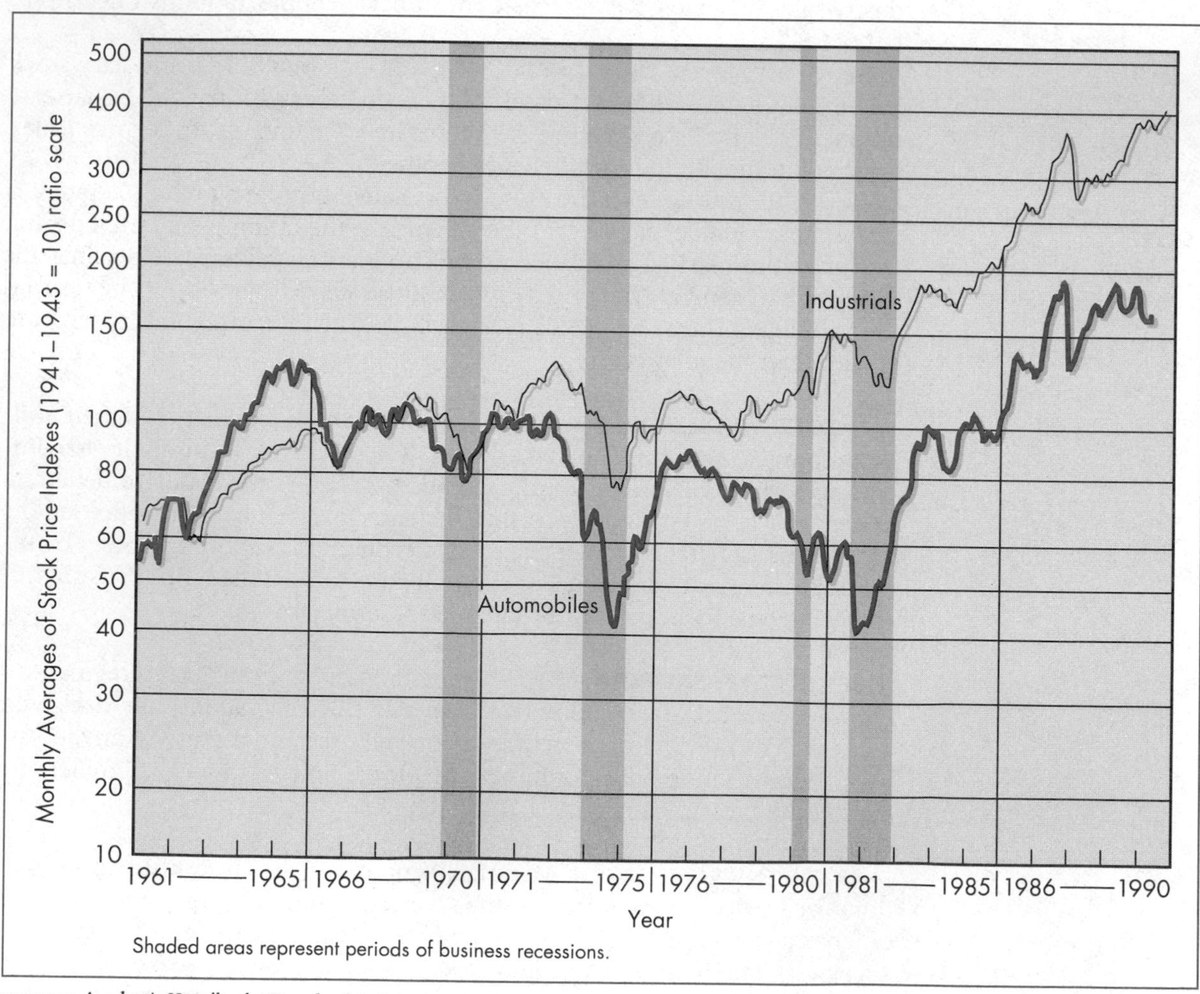

SOURCE: *Analyst's Handbook* (Standard & Poor's, 1990), p. 8.

health sciences. These "high-tech" industries require careful analysis because of rapidly changing technology.

• Industry Selection

Selecting industries that are expected to achieve above- or below-average performance is the ultimate objective of an industry analysis. The following are some of the techniques and procedures that might be used:

1. Relative strength Analysts have traditionally used **relative strength** measures to select industries and individual companies. One measure of relative strength for an industry is the ratio of industry stock prices to the prices of stocks in general. If the relative strength ratios are increasing, the industry stock prices are increasing at a faster rate than stocks in general. When analysts think the overall market is bullish, industries with the highest relative strength will be attractive. With a bearish forecast, low relative strength industries will be preferred. Figure 8.7 is a relative strength graph for the automobile and truck industry. The downward trend in the relative strength graph from 1989–1990 indicates that this industry was performing poorly relative to stocks in general.

FIGURE 8.7
Relative Strength Graph

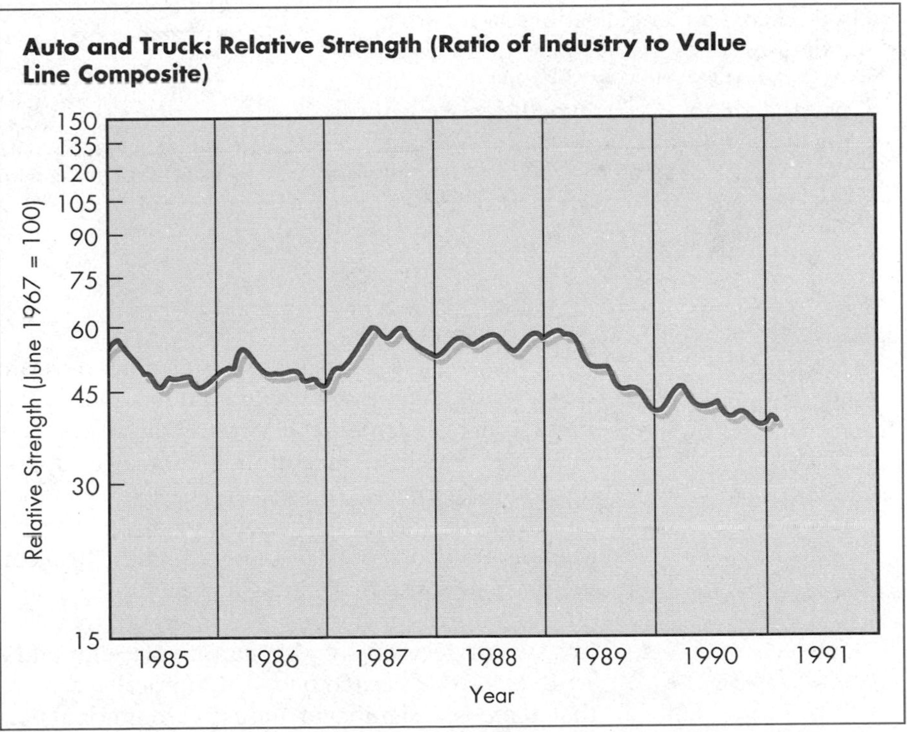

SOURCE: *Value Line Investment Survey,* March 22, 1991, p. 101. Copyright © 1991 by Value Line Publishing, Inc.; used by permission.

RESEARCH BOX

Using Industries to Hedge Inflation Risk

An industry analysis is typically done to identify industries that can be expected to achieve an above- or below-average performance. If the economic forecast indicates that the inflation rate is likely to increase, then the industry analysis should consider the impact of inflation on various industries. The overall stock market generally does not perform well in a period of "high" inflation rates. But do some industries have financial characteristics that enable them to perform well in an inflationary environment?

Ma and Ellis conducted a study to identify possible financial characteristics that an analyst can look for during the industry analysis. If such characteristics exist, then some industries might be identified that could be "inflation hedges." The empirical results presented in the study were based on data on 55 industries selected from Standard & Poor's *Industry Survey.* The researchers selected the period 1976–1982 as an inflationary period to test the hypothesis. The statistical analysis of the data indicates that four financial characteristics are significant in explaining performance during an inflationary period: (1) profitability, (2) financial leverage or debt financing, (3) the level of sales relative to total assets, and (4) the price of the common stock.

The authors concluded:

> In summary, the empirical evidence strongly suggests the existence of an industry effect in the stock market with respect to the ability to hedge unexpected inflation. Furthermore, the market return on industries with high debt level, low sales turnover, low price per share, and high profitability is more sensitive to unexpected inflation.

These results have practical implications for portfolio managers investing in periods of high inflation. Even in an overall depressed stock market, traders can use certain criteria for selecting industries that are better inflation hedges.

SOURCE: Christopher K. Ma and M.E. Ellis, "Selecting Industries as Inflation Hedges," *Journal of Portfolio Management* (Summer 1989): 45–48. This copyrighted material is reprinted with permission from Institutional Investor, Inc.

2. Industry beta A number of studies have shown that portfolio and **industry betas** are more stable than betas for individual securities. If the economic and overall market forecasts indicate a favorable environment for stocks, industries with betas greater than 1.0 may be appropriate. On the other hand, a pessimistic forecast suggests industries with low betas.

3. Published forecasts As previously discussed, both Value Line and Standard & Poor's publish industry ranks. Brokerage firms and other investment advisers also make industry recommendations. Depending on the confidence the investor has in these forecasts, they can be used directly to make investment decisions or as a starting place for additional analysis.

4. Industry diversification Empirical research supports the observation that there are significant industry commonalities. The magnitude of these commonalities, however, varies among industries and over time. One implication of this observation is that portfolios should have industry diversification.

The number of industries needed to eliminate diversifiable risk attributed to industry effects depends on the industries in the portfolio.

• Illustration of an Industry Analysis

Appendix 8A provides an illustration of a basic industry analysis, using the automobile industry. The procedures and techniques discussed in this section of the chapter are utilized in the illustration.

SUMMARY

This chapter has discussed the first two steps in a traditional fundamental analysis of common stocks: (1) economic and market analysis and (2) industry analysis. The final step is a company and stock analysis, which is presented in Chapters 9, 13, and 14.

As a practical matter, individual investors typically rely on widely published professional economic forecasts. Disagreements among economists concerning forecasts have encouraged the use of consensus forecasts. The investor can then use the economic forecast to develop a stock market forecast. Technical timing indicators may also be used in predicting the direction of the market.

The economic environment is likely to have an important effect on many industries and companies. The economic and market forecast should therefore be used to identify industries that might be expected to have the best relative performance. Once appropriate industries are identified, they can be analyzed using the key industry fundamentals discussed in the chapter.

• KEY TERMS

Breadth of the market
Budget deficit
Business cycle
Coincident composite index
Confidence index
Consensus economic forecast
Council of Economic Advisers
Industry
Industry beta
Industry effect
Lagging composite index
Leading composite index
Mutual funds' cash position
Nominal GNP
Political risk
Put-call ratio
Real (constant–dollar) GNP
Recession
Relative strength
Short interest
Standard Industrial Classification (SIC)
Technical analysis
Trade deficit

• CONCEPT APPLICATIONS

Investment Concept	Concept Application
Economic analysis	A traditional fundamental analysis requires an economic analysis and forecast as a first step. Historical data support the logic of this approach since the impact of previous recessions and periods of economic growth on stock prices is readily apparent. Making an accurate economic forecast, however, is quite difficult, and individuals often rely on forecasts made by professional economists. Due to frequent contradictions between published forecasts, the use of a consensus or average forecast may offer advantages.
Technical analysis	Fundamentalists use an economic forecast as a foundation for a stock market forecast. Technicians (and some fundamentalists) use market timing indicators such as the confidence index and mutual funds' cash position. When using this approach, it is advisable to use a number of indicators rather than rely on a single indicator.
Industry analysis	The second step in a traditional fundamental approach is an industry analysis. Key variables in an industry analysis include historical financial performance and the impact of economic and stock market developments on the industry. Other industry fundamentals such as imports/exports, regulatory and labor environments, and technology/innovation may also be important. If the industry analysis looks favorable, then individual stocks in the industry can be analyzed.

• QUESTIONS

1. Common stock price movements are widely recognized as a reliable leading indicator of economic activity. If stocks lead economic activity, why do most analysts use an economic forecast to estimate common stock values?
2. Common stocks often experience a significant price decline that is not followed by a recession in the economy. What are some possible reasons for this false recessionary signal?
3. Explain the justification for using a consensus economic forecast. What are the advantages and disadvantages of this approach?
4. What is meant by the leading, coincident, and lagging composite indexes? How can they be used in an economic analysis?
5. Briefly define an *industry*. Explain how industry classification procedures are used in a fundamental analysis of common stocks.
6. Briefly explain the SIC system. What problems are encountered when this system is applied to large diversified corporations?
7. Suppose a company you are analyzing has three SIC codes. What problems do these multiple classifications cause in the industry analysis? How would you solve these problems?

8. How can industry rankings such as those prepared by Value Line and Standard & Poor's be used as part of a fundamental approach to common stock valuation?
9. Briefly identify and discuss the "key industry fundamentals" that are commonly used in an industry analysis. Are these fundamentals equally important to all industries?
10. Explain the concept of "relative strength" as applied to industries.
11. Explain the similarities and differences between an industry's relative strength measure and its beta. Do you feel that industries with high relative strength measures have more systematic risk than the average industry?
12. Would a portfolio of 10 to 15 common stocks, all from the same industry, offer the same degree of diversification as a portfolio of 10 to 15 stocks from different industries? Explain.
13. Explain how technical market timing indicators can be used in a stock market forecast. Briefly discuss several of the more popular indicators.
14. The "Merrill Lynch Market Letter" for June 3, 1991, discussed the stock market rally that seemed to gain momentum after the Memorial Day holiday. The DJIA was pushing the 3000 level at that time. One factor the letter cited for the rally was that "investors have been willing to give the benefit of the doubt to recent economic data, hoping that a recovery isn't far off." Is this statement consistent with the lead/lag relationships between the economy and the stock market discussed in this chapter? Discuss.

• KEY TO THE INVESTMENT ANALYSIS SOFTWARE

Calculation	Appendix A-1 Page Reference	Access Procedure
Financial statement construction	A-8	BEGIN, FINANCIAL, FINANCIALS, INPUT or ADDFILES
Growth rate of key financial items	A-10	BEGIN, FINANCIAL, FINANCIALS, GROWTH
Ratio analysis	A-10	BEGIN, FINANCIAL, FINANCIALS, RATIOS
Income statement forecast	A-10	BEGIN, FINANCIAL, FINANCIALS, FORECAST
Required rate of return	A-12	BEGIN, CAPITAL, CAPM

• PROBLEMS

1. Assume that an individual investor collects the following information about the economic forecasts of four professional economists:

	Rate of real GNP growth	
Economist	*Forecast for next year*	*Last year's forecast*
1	2.0%	3.5%
2	−1.5	−2.0
3	2.5	3.2
4	3.5	4.1

 a. Calculate the consensus forecast for both years.

 b. Suppose last year's *actual* GNP growth was 2.75 percent. Calculate the accuracy of each economist's forecast for last year and the consensus forecast as the absolute percentage deviation from the actual value. Compare and contrast the accuracy of each forecast with the consensus forecast.

2. Assume that the yield on one-year Treasury bills is currently 8.3 percent and you estimate that the HPR on the S&P 500 will be 15 percent for next year. Use the capital asset pricing model (CAPM) to estimate the required return on the following industries:

Industry	*Industry beta*
1	1.3
2	0.8
3	1.1

3. Consider the following composite industry earnings per share (EPS) over the last five years:

Year	*Industry composite EPS*
1	$12.00
2	8.00
3	−2.00
4	10.00
5	15.00

 a. Calculate the annual compounded growth rate, using the first and last year's earnings.

 b. Calculate the growth rate in earnings for each year.

 c. Compare your results in parts (a) and (b).

4. In analyzing a particular industry and company, assume that you collect the following industry and market index values and common stock prices for the company:

Month	*Industry*	*S&P 500*	*Company*
1	110	260	$69
2	112	283	72
3	111	271	66
4	115	282	73
5	126	285	74
6	138	289	72

a. Calculate the monthly relative strength ratios for the industry and company using the S&P 500.

b. Based on the relative strength ratios, explain what is happening to the prices of the company and industry stocks versus stocks in general.

c. If the trend in the relative strength ratios continues, would this industry be attractive in a bull market? Would the company be attractive?

5. Consider the following composite per-share data on the aerospace/defense industry published by Standard & Poor's in its *Industry Survey* of June 21, 1990.

	1984	*1985*	*1986*	*1987*	*1988*
Sales	654.58	720.55	795.30	855.33	907.64
Operating income	60.12	68.83	62.43	74.50	78.70
Profit margin (%)	9.18	9.55	7.85	8.71	8.67
Depreciation	18.30	21.01	25.48	28.84	32.01
Taxes	14.53	20.71	16.73	18.64	14.38
Earnings	31.22	30.97	21.49	31.34	35.46
Dividends	6.90	7.57	8.15	9.19	9.82
Earnings/sales (%)	4.77	4.30	2.70	3.66	3.91
Dividends/earnings (%)	22.10	24.44	37.92	29.32	27.69
Price (1941–43 = 10)					
High	260.31	322.98	361.45	380.88	329.61
Low	194.44	250.55	290.63	244.06	262.75
Price-earnings ratio					
High	8.34	10.43	16.82	12.15	9.30
Low	6.23	8.09	13.52	7.79	7.41
Dividend yield (%)					
High	3.55	3.02	2.80	3.77	3.74
Low	2.65	2.34	2.25	2.41	2.98
Book value	141.92	151.27	161.47	180.50	229.00
Return on book value (%)	22.00	20.47	13.31	17.36	15.48
Working capital	60.85	54.89	60.60	66.61	78.83
Capital expenditures	31.34	38.99	39.98	39.57	41.56

Discuss the strengths and weaknesses of this industry's historical performance over the period 1984–1988.

• REFERENCES

Abken, Peter A., "Innovations in Modeling the Term Structure of Interest Rates." *Economic Review: Federal Reserve Bank of Atlanta* (July-August 1990): 2–27.

Bleiberg, Steven. "How Little We Know—About P/Es, but Also Perhaps More Than We Think." *Journal of Portfolio Management* (Summer 1989): 26–31.

Bohan, James. "Relative Strength: Further Positive Evidence." *Journal of Portfolio Management* (Fall 1981): 36–39.

Chatfield, Robert E., Scott E. Hein, and Charles R. Moyer. "Long-Term Earnings Forecasts in the Electric Utility Industry: Accuracy and Valuation Implications." *Financial Review* (August 1990): 421–39.

Christian, Robert J., and Lucinda S. Mezey. "Climate of the 1990s Looks Good for the Stock Market." *Trusts and Estates* (March 1990): 12–14, 72.

Cicarelli, James, and U. Jin Jhun. "Are the Leading Economic Indicators Really Leading?" *Journal of Business Forecasting* (Spring 1986): 18–19, 30.

Crum, Roy L., and Keqian Bi. "An Observation on Estimating the Systematic Risk of an Industry." *Financial Management* (Spring 1988): 60–62.

deLeeuw, Frank. "Leading Indicators and the 'Prime Mover' View." *Survey of Current Business* (August 1989): 23–29.

Eisner, Robert. "Debunking the Conventional Wisdom in Economic Policy." *Challenge* (May-June 1990): 4–11.

Henry, George B. "Wall Street Economists: Are They Worth Their Salt?" *Business Economics* (October 1989): 44–48.

Hertzberg, Marie P., and Barry A. Beckman. "Business Cycle Indicators: Revised Composite Indexes." *Survey of Current Business* (January 1989): 23–28.

Jacobs, Bruce I., and Kenneth N. Levy. "The Complexity of the Stock Market." *Journal of Portfolio Management* (Fall 1989): 19–27.

Kolman, Joe. "Grappling with Economic Forecasts." *Institutional Investor* (December 1986): 243–44.

Markese, John. "How P/E Ratios Can Lead You to the Best Buys." *Money,* March, 1990, pp. 159–60.

Paul, Duane A. "Does a Stock Market Meltdown Guarantee Economic Collapse?" *Business Forum* (Winter 1988): 30.

Renshaw, Edward. "Some Evidence in Support of Stock Market Bubbles." *Financial Analysts Journal* (March-April 1990): 71–73.

Roberds, William. "Forecast Accuracy and the Performance of Economic Policy: Is There a Connection?" *Economic Review: Federal Reserve Bank of Atlanta* (September-October 1988): 20–32.

Roley, V. Vance, and Lawrence D. Schall. "Federal Deficits and the Stock Market." *Economic Review: Federal Reserve Bank of Kansas City* (April 1988): 17–27.

Ross, Irwin. "Economic Statistics: Why They Often Lie." *Fortune,* April 28, 1986, pp. 58–60.

Rutledge, John. "The Great Capital Imbalance." *Business Forum* (Fall 1988–Winter 1989): 10–16.

Sinai, Allen. "The Crash of '87 and the Economy of '88." *Challenge* (January-February 1988): 11–21.

Updegrave, Walter L. "The Fine Art of Taking Profits." *Money,* August 1990, pp. 83–86.

———. "To Keep Profits on a Roll, Stay Tuned to the Business Cycle." *Money,* May 1989, pp. 169–72.

———. "Seven Signals That Help You Answer the Toughest Questions of All: When to Sell." *Money,* February 1989, pp. 123–24.

Vine, David. "EBB Offers Economic Information Online." *Link-up* (November-December 1989): 26.

Walter, John R. "Monetary Aggregates: A User's Guide." *Economic Review: Federal Reserve Bank of Richmond* (January-February 1989): 20–28.

Welling, Kathryn M. "Bears among the Bulls: They Think the Market's Living on Borrowed Time." *Barron's,* June 18, 1990, pp. 14–15, 39, 43.

Welsh, E. James. "Warning Signal: A Reliable Indicator Turns Bearish." *Barron's,* April 10, 1989, pp. 36, 45.

Wertheim, Paul. "Forecasting Cash Flow by Industry." *Journal of Business Forecasting* (Winter 1989-1990): 9–12.

APPENDIX 8A

Illustration of Basic Industry Analysis: Automobiles

Tables 8A.1, 8A.2, 8A.3, and 8A.4 present data on the automobile industry's historical performance (see also Table 8.5 and Figures 8.6 and 8.7), financial ratios, annual growth rates, and other industry fundamentals, respectively.[1]

INDUSTRY RECOMMENDATIONS

In 1990 and early 1991, consumers were concerned about the weakness of the U.S. economy and questioned the advisability of borrowing money to purchase an automobile. These consumer concerns contributed to the decline in industry production that began in 1988. The weak economic environment partly explains the unfavorable trends in the industry's financial performance such as profitability, liquidity, and financial leverage. The deteriorating financial performance has also caused significant price declines for the stocks of companies in this industry. Chrysler and General Motors drastically reduced dividends in early 1991, and it is likely that Ford will follow suit. Automobile stocks are cyclical relative to the economy, and the industry beta (Ford, Gen-

TABLE 8A.1 • Historical Performance

	Per-share data				
	1985	*1986*	*1987*	*1988*	*1989*
Sales	$524.03	$588.95	$632.72	$791.65	$839.57
Operating income	54.30	57.48	66.61	201.58	144.10
Depreciation	27.34	31.48	32.08	38.79	42.20
Taxes	10.56	7.20	11.53	18.35	14.78
Earnings	24.35	22.94	30.17	34.99	27.23
Dividends	6.40	7.48	8.48	9.46	11.80
Stock prices (1941–43 = 100)					
High	116.97	151.15	209.32	187.37	201.12
Low	94.46	110.95	128.95	140.82	160.96
P/E ratios					
High	4.80	6.59	6.94	5.35	7.39
Low	3.88	4.84	4.27	4.02	5.91

[1] This appendix is designed to illustrate the basic financial data impacting the industry. A comprehensive analysis would include other factors and estimates that influence industry performance. Sources of data include Standard & Poor's *Industry Surveys* and *Value Line Investment Survey;* used by permission.

TABLE 8A.2 • Financial Ratios

	1985	1986	1987	1988	1989
Operating profit margin	5.5%	4.77%	4.97%	4.17%	2.77%
Return on investment	10.17%	8.03%	7.70%	4.13%	1.87%
Return on equity	27.10%	21.13%	20.23%	18.30%	11.13%
Current ratio	1.10	1.13	1.23	1.28	1.28
Long-term debt to net working capital	241.93%	426.33%	85.10%	N/A	N/A
Long-term debt to assets	18.70%	20.73%	24.17%	57.63%	59.77%

TABLE 8A.3 • Annual Growth Rates

	1986	1987	1988	1989	1985–89
Sales	12.01%	7.80%	25.12%	6.05%	12.51%
Earnings	(5.79)	31.52	15.98	(22.18)	2.83

TABLE 8A.4 • Other Industry Fundamentals

	1987	1988	1989
U.S. passenger car production (thousands)	6,778.3	6,195.3	6,113.5
Import car sales to total domestic sales	39.3%	38.5%	37.3%
Total automobiles sold (thousands)	10,166	10,480	9,853
U.S. auto registrations (thousands)	136,246	140,155	143,249
Annual increases in new car prices	5.9%	5.9%	5.7%
Ratio of new to used car sales	0.93	0.97	N/A
Auto installment credit to disposable personal income	8.32%	8.18%	7.80%
Average maturity of new car loans (months)	53.5	56.2	54.3

eral Motors, and Chrysler) in early 1991 was 1.17. In addition to the weak economy, the industry faces increasing pressure from imports; increased governmental regulations dealing with safety, emissions, and fuel efficiency; and overcapacity. Even assuming the economy makes a quick recovery in 1991, it is unlikely that the automobile industry will perform as well as the average industry in 1991.

CHAPTER 9

Analyzing Financial Statements

The knowledge-level objectives of this chapter should enable the student to:

- Gain an understanding of the role financial statement analysis plays in the fundamental analysis process.
- Recognize the importance of approaching the analysis of financial statements in a meaningful, step-by-step manner.
- Analyze the strengths and weaknesses of a firm using its financial statements.
- Explain why recognizing the "flexibility" of accountants in applying generally accepted accounting principles is an important part of financial statement analysis and why this "flexibility" may require adjustments to the financial statements.
- Differentiate between the economic and accounting measurements of income.
- Recognize that financial statement analysis is an art, not a science.

INTRODUCTION

In order to analyze a company's financial condition and prepare a forecast of its earnings (see Chapter 13), an investor must be able to understand the company's financial statements and have the analytical tools necessary to assess the financial strengths and weaknesses of the company. This chapter focuses on the historical financial performance of the company as a basis for developing the foundation to perform a fundamental company analysis.

Financial analysis of a company plays a key role in the entire fundamental analysis process. Recall that in Chapter 8 we advocated a "top-down" approach that starts with a macro analysis of the economy and the industry before undertaking the company, or micro, analysis. Once this stage of the analysis is completed, valuation models (see Chapter 14) can be used to estimate the intrinsic or expected value of a security. Using the current value of the security and its expected value, it is possible to estimate the expected holding period return, *E*(HPR). Once the *E*(HPR) has been determined, it can be compared with an estimate of the required return for the security. Comparing the required return with the *E*(HPR) allows the investor to determine whether or not the security is under- or overvalued. Figure 9.1 depicts this fundamental analysis process.

An appropriate question at this point would be, If the financial markets are efficient, as discussed in Chapter 7, why bother with the fundamental analysis process? Answering this question requires some discussion of the evolution of fundamental security analysis. The "father" of fundamental security analysis was Benjamin Graham. He was the first to develop sophisticated techniques to analyze the firm's financial statements and make assessments based on certain financial ratios as to whether or not a stock was undervalued. His book *Security Analysis,* first published in 1934 with David Dodd, became the "bible" for other security analysts. It is reasonable to assume that so many investment professionals follow Graham's approach to fundamental analysis, many under- and overvalued investment opportunities have been eliminated.

The discussion of active investment strategies for the individual investor in Chapter 7 noted that some investors may have an advantage over others in terms of timing, selection, and investment philosophy. Individual investors may also have advantages over institutions and professional investors because small investors can execute small trades quickly, invest in small companies, consolidate their investments in one or two securities, and use the techniques of short selling and margin trading.

With the recent downsizing of many firms in the security industry, the number of financial analysts has decreased. This development increases the possibility of finding undervalued securities. However, it must be pointed out that for the individual investor, fundamental analysis is a time-consuming activity, and in this sense it has a cost. Thus, the investor must determine whether these additional costs will generate sufficient, incremental returns.

This chapter presents a systematic approach to financial statement analysis. Using return on equity as a focal point, ratio analysis is used as a tool to help

FIGURE 9.1
The Fundamental Analysis Process

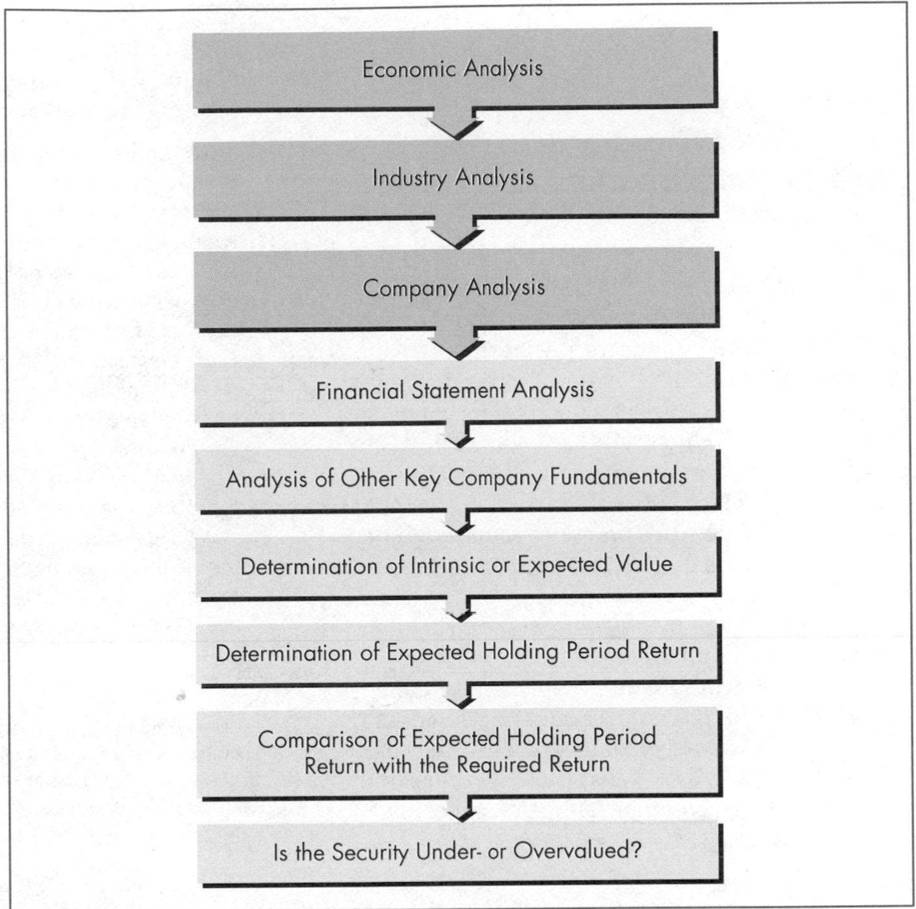

decipher the company's performance. In addition to the traditional liquidity, activity, profitability, and leverage ratios, market-based ratios are also examined.

In analyzing financial statements, it is important to recognize the quality of a company's earnings. The lives of financial analysts would be much easier if all companies used the same accounting practices or if the same company used consistent accounting practices from year to year. Unfortunately, this is not the case, and the difficulties associated with these inconsistencies are examined in the chapter.

In addition to an analysis of the financial statements, financial analysis includes consideration of nonquantifiable characteristics of a company, such as the quality of management, quality of employees, and corporate ethics. These issues, along with an illustration of the analysis of the financial statements of the Procter & Gamble Company, are also presented in the chapter.

• **INTEREST BOX**

Managing Reported Earnings: An Ethical Question

Reported earnings by corporations are subject to a number of possible manipulations by management, particularly in the short run. These manipulations can take a number of different forms, including changing accounting practices, understating costs, overstating revenues, and timing the sale of assets. Is this a common practice? Unfortunately, the answer appears to be yes. Do managers of publicly traded firms view this practice as ethical or unethical? Unfortunately, the answer seems to depend on whether the practice increases or decreases earnings and the means used in achieving the earnings manipulation.

In a 1990 study, William Burns and Kenneth Merchant sent out a questionnaire "describing 13 earnings-management situations" and received responses from 649 managers. The results of the survey are presented in Table 1 on page 269.

After reviewing the results of the questionnaire and interviewing a number of the respondents, the authors reached the following conclusion:

> Thus, in practice, it appears that a large majority of managers use at least some methods to manage short-term earnings. Although these methods are legal, they do not seem to be consistent with a strict ethical framework. While the manager's actions have the desired effect on reported earnings, the managers know there are no real positive economic benefits and the actions might actually be costly in the long run. These actions are at best questionable because they involve deceptions that are not disclosed. Most managers who manage earnings, however, do not believe they are doing anything wrong.
>
> We see two major problems. The most important is the generally high tolerance for operating manipulations. The other is the dispersion in managers' views about which practices are moral and ethical.

SOURCE: William J. Burns, Jr., and Kenneth A. Merchant, "The Dangerous Morality of Managing Earnings," *Management Accounting* (August 1990): 22–25; published by the Institute of Management Accountants (formerly the National Association of Accountants), Montvale, N.J.

THE FIRST STEPS IN COMPANY ANALYSIS

The first steps in company analysis involve simply deciding which company or companies to analyze and then obtaining information about the selected company or companies.

TABLE 1 • Earnings Manipulation

	Proportion of managers who judge the manipulation practice		
	Ethical	*Questionable or a minor infraction*	*Unethical or a serious infraction*
1. Managing short-term earnings by changing or manipulating operating decisions or procedures:			
When the result is to reduce earnings	79%	19%	2%
When the result is to increase earnings	57	31	12
2. Managing short-term earnings by changing or manipulating accounting methods:			
When the change in earnings is small	5	45	50
When the change in earnings is large	3	21	76
3. Managing short-term earnings by deferring discretionary expenditures into the next accounting period:			
To meet an interim quarterly budget target	47	41	12
To meet an annual budget target at year-end	41	35	24
4. Increasing short-term earnings to meet a budget target:			
By selling excess assets and realizing a profit	80	16	4
By ordering overtime work at year-end to ship as much as possible	74	21	5
By offering customers special credit terms to accept delivery without obligation to pay until the following year	43	42	15

• Selecting the Company for Analysis

Literally thousands of publicly traded companies are available for investment. Which company or companies should be selected for analysis? Using the "top-down" approach we have suggested, an investor may have identified several industries that are expected to perform well in the forecasted economic environment. Companies within these industries can be identified manually by examining such sources as Standard & Poor's *Corporate Record*, Moody's *Handbook of Widely Held Common Stocks*, or the *Value Line Investment Survey*. Alternatively, companies within an industry can be identified by searching a computerized data base, such as the Disclosure Database, by their Standard Industrial Classification (SIC) codes. The list of companies can be further reduced by identifying minimum financial criteria that a company must meet. This process is called **screening,** and the financial criteria are often called **filters.**

Assume that you have forecast an economic downturn and identified companies within certain industries that are considered to be countercyclical. The result may be a long list of companies. This list can be reduced by searching for companies that meet certain financial characteristics. These filters can include a wide variety of measures with minimum or maximum values. The initial screening may involve some minimum growth rate in earnings over the past five years, a maximum level of financial leverage as measured by the debt to equity ratio, and a minimum level of liquidity as measured by the current ratio. The more filters employed and the higher the standard set for each filter, the more the number of potential companies will be reduced. The screening process can be done in a few minutes by using a computerized data base with appropriate capabilities.

• Obtaining Company Information

Once the company or companies have been identified, the investor needs to gain access to information about them. An essential source of information for analysis is the financial statements of the firm. The investor can gain access to these financial statements in several ways. One way is to write or call the company directly and request the latest annual report, most recent quarterly report, and a copy of the company's report to the Securities and Exchange Commission (SEC) on form 10–K.

Other sources of company information include the investment advisory services and computerized data bases discussed in Chapter 4. These resources quite often include not only the historical (annual and quarterly) financial statements of a company, but also additional information such as earnings forecasts, historical growth rates in sales and earnings, financial ratios, and recent developments and prospects for the company.

ANALYSIS OF FINANCIAL STATEMENTS

Financial statement analysis is a complex process, but it can be approached systematically. Here the various elements of ratio analysis are presented in terms of the information they provide about return on equity.

• Return on Equity

The most important elements in the valuation of common stocks are the estimates of a company's future growth in earnings and dividends.[1] For example, the dividend discount model presented in Chapter 14 uses estimations of the growth in earnings and dividends as key elements in determining a stock's value. The estimate of a company's *earnings growth rate* (g) is a function of the *earnings retention rate* (b) and the **return on equity (ROE)** on new equity capital or

$$g = b \times \text{ROE} \tag{9.1}$$

As an example of Equation 9.1, assume that a company retains 60 percent of its earnings (i.e., $b = .60$) and therefore has a *dividend payout ratio* $(1 - b)$ of 40 percent. Assume further that the company is able to earn an 18 percent return on new investments; then the earnings growth rate can be estimated as

$$g = (.6)(.18) = 10.8\%$$

It is common for financial analysts to assume that a company will maintain a reasonably constant earnings retention rate or, conversely, a reasonably constant dividend payout ratio. Given this assumption, the growth rate in earnings and dividends is a function of ROE. It would only seem logical, therefore, for the analysis of financial statements to begin with the ROE measure.

• Ratio Analysis and Return on Equity

Return on equity can be defined as

$$\text{ROE} = \frac{\text{net income}}{\text{stockholders' equity}} \tag{9.2}$$

Defining ROE in this way, while correct, does not provide the analyst with a great deal of information. It is much more valuable to decompose the measure into three parts, which allows the analyst to examine measures of the firm's **asset utilization, profitability,** and **financial leverage.** Decomposing ROE in this manner results in the following expression:

$$\text{ROE} = \frac{\text{sales}}{\text{total assets}} \times \frac{\text{net income}}{\text{sales}} \times \frac{\text{total assets}}{\text{stockholders' equity}} \tag{9.3}$$

[1] An aid to the analysis of financial statements is provided in the Investment Analysis Software accompanying the text. Specific access reference to the software for analyzing financial statements is provided in the "Key to the Investment Analysis Software" section at the end of the chapter and in Appendix A-1.

The first term to the right of the equals sign (sales/total assets) is an aggregate measure of asset utilization by the firm in generating sales. The second term (net income/sales) measures the net profitability of the firm, and the third term (total assets/stockholders' equity) measures the amount of financial leverage employed by the firm.[2] Using algebra, it is easy to see that Equations 9.2 and 9.3 are equivalent expressions. This approach is often referred to as a modified DuPont system of analysis.

It is important to understand the influence of the firm's financing decisions on the return on equity measure. For a firm of a given size, the amount of financial leverage will not impact the asset utilization measure. The level of sales and assets is not affected by the means by which the assets are financed. However, both the profitability and leverage measures are sensitive to the amount of financial leverage employed by the firm. Clearly, the increased use of debt by a firm of a given size will cause the interest expenses to increase as well as the total assets to increase relative to stockholders' equity.

The impact of financial leverage on the firm's overall profitability is dependent upon the level of operating return the firm is able to earn on its assets (operating income/total assets). This measure is called **return on assets (ROA).** If the firm's ROA is greater than the cost of debt (favorable financial leverage), the overall profitability and return on equity will be higher as a result of the increased amounts of debt in the firm's capital structure. If the firm is unable to earn a ROA equal to the cost of debt (unfavorable financial leverage), the increased use of debt will have a negative impact on the overall profitability and return on equity measures. The increased use of debt will increase the financial leverage and, therefore, the financial risk of the firm.

Identifying the three components of return on equity is a critical first step in ratio analysis. The second step involves the further decomposition of these measures of asset utilization, profitability, and financial leverage. In a sense, the analyst is like a detective seeking to uncover the determinants of a firm's financial performance.

Literally hundreds of financial ratios can be constructed from data on the balance sheet and income statement. Table 9.1 illustrates the most commonly used ratios, categorized by the components of return on equity. Other ratios are often calculated, such as liquidity ratios and ratios expressed in terms of per share of common stock outstanding. These ratios are discussed in the next section.

Asset utilization ratios, also commonly called activity ratios, relate assets to sales or cost of goods sold. Since these ratios essentially measure the efficiency with which assets are being used, higher ratios are generally more desirable.

Profitability ratios indicate the relationships between measures of income and assets or sales. As Table 9.1 shows, these ratios are constructed for various measures of profitability. This allows the analyst to distinguish operat-

[2] This measure is equal to 1 + (debt/stockholders' equity).

TABLE 9.1 • Financial Ratios: Categorized by the Components of Return on Equity

Asset Utilization	=	Sales/Total Assets
1. Current asset turnover	=	Sales/current assets
a. Inventory turnover	=	Cost of goods sold/inventory
b. Accounts receivable turnover	=	Sales/accounts receivable
2. Fixed asset turnover	=	Sales/net fixed assets
Profitability	=	Net Income/Sales
1. Gross margin	=	(Sales − cost of goods sold)/sales
2. Operating margin	=	Operating income/sales
3. Nonoperating margin	=	Nonoperating income/sales
4. Return on assets	=	Operating income/total assets
5. Effective tax rate	=	Taxes/earnings before taxes
Financial Leverage	=	Total Assets/Stockholders' Equity
1. Debt ratio	=	Total liabilities/total assets
2. Debt to equity	=	Total liabilities/stockholders' equity
3. Long-term debt to total capitalization	=	Long-term debt/(long-term debt + stockholders' equity)
4. Times interest earned	=	Operating income/interest expenses

ing performance from other performance measures that are influenced by the firm's financing decisions or tax rates.

Financial leverage ratios measure the extent to which the firm is using debt financing and its ability to pay interest expenses from operating earnings. The importance of debt in the capital structure can be similarly measured by comparing total liabilities to total assets (debt ratio), total liabilities to stockholders' equity (debt to equity), long-term debt to total capitalization, or total assets to stockholders' equity. The firm's ability to meet its interest expense from operating income is reflected in the times-interest-earned ratio.

• Other Ratios

While return on equity and its decomposition are important first steps in the analysis of financial statements, financial analysts frequently examine other ratios as well.

LIQUIDITY RATIOS **Liquidity ratios** indicate the firm's ability to pay its short-term obligations. Typically, these ratios relate current assets to current liabilities. The most common liquidity ratios are the *current ratio* (current assets/current liabilities) and the more conservative *quick* or *acid test ratio* [(current assets − inventory)/current liabilities]. It is usually advisable to analyze individual current assets and liabilities in addition to the totals. For example, cash and near-cash items represent the most liquid asset of the firm. "Low" cash may indicate a significant liquidity problem, even though the relationship between current assets and current liabilities is acceptable. Further insight into a firm's liquidity can be gained by examining certain asset utilization ratios (e.g., inventory turnover and accounts receivable turnover) in order to better assess the true liquidity of these current assets.

Another approach to measuring liquidity is the *cash-flow liquidity ratio* (*CFL*):[3]

$$\text{CFL} = \frac{\text{cash and marketable securities} + \text{cash flow from operations}}{\text{current liabilities}} \tag{9.4}$$

The numerator approximates the cash available to the firm from cash and near-cash items and the cash flow generated from operations. Relating these cash resources to the firm's current liabilities is an excellent indicator of the firm's short-term liquidity.

PERCENTAGE FINANCIAL STATEMENTS It is common practice to convert balance sheets and income statements to percentages, with the income statement items expressed as a percentage of total sales and the balance sheet items expressed as a percentage of total assets. These statements are often referred to as **common size statements** since they remove the influence of the size, and the changes in size, of the firm.

PER-SHARE-BASED RATIOS Just as an almost unlimited number of ratios can be estimated from the financial statements, numerous ratios can also be expressed on the basis of a share of common stock outstanding. As is the case with other ratios, some of these **per-share-based ratios** are more revealing than others. Two frequently used per-share ratios are *earnings per share* and the *price-earnings ratio.* These two important ratios are discussed in detail in Chapters 13 and 14.

The *book value per share ratio* (stockholders' equity/number of common shares outstanding) expresses the relationship between the firm's net worth and the number of common shares outstanding. Quite often one hears that a certain stock is "selling at only 1.2 times book," which means that the common stock price per share is 1.2 times higher than its book value per share. Relating book value and price per share in this way is designed to signal some level of safety for the common stock price. This analysis is based on the premise that the closer the common stock price is to its book value, the less likely it is that the stock price will fall. For most firms, the book value and market

[3] For a complete discussion of this liquidity measure, see Chapter 5 of Lyn M. Fraser, *Understanding Financial Statements*, 2d ed. (Englewood Cliffs, N.J.: Prentice-Hall, 1988).

value of their assets are not highly correlated, and book value per share is not a reliable measure of stock price safety. Some of the reasons for the divergence between book value and market value per share will become clear when we draw a distinction between a firm's reported earnings and its economic earnings later on in this chapter.

Dividends per share is calculated by dividing the total cash dividends paid to the common stockholders by the number of common shares outstanding. Generally, this ratio is based on the annual cash dividends, not the quarterly dividends. The dividends per share figure can be used to calculate the *dividend yield* (dividend per share/price per share) and the *payout ratio* (dividend per share/earnings per share).

• Interpreting the Ratios

The interpretation of ratios can be undertaken in several different ways. Clearly, an individually calculated ratio or a combination of ratios contains useful information. A current ratio value of 2 indicates that the current assets, as reflected on the balance sheet of the firm, are two times greater then the current liabilities. The interpretation of ratios can be enhanced, however, if the analyst is able to compare specific ratios of a firm over time in order to detect trends in the ratios. The comparison of ratios for the same firm over time is called **time-series analysis.** Returning to the current ratio example, an analyst might interpret the calculated value of 2 for the firm's current ratio differently if the current ratio has steadily declined from a value of 3 over the past four years to its current value of 2.

Using the firm's historical financial statements to compare ratios over time is not always as straightforward as it appears on the surface, however. The analyst must be very careful to ensure that the observed changes in a particular ratio or group of ratios represent a trend and not a cyclical or irregular change. It is also important for the analyst to recognize that a firm's financial statements may not be prepared in a consistent manner over time. This occurs because **generally accepted accounting principles (GAAP)** allow for considerable flexibility in the treatment of certain transactions and reporting (or not reporting) of certain items.[4] Some of these differences in accounting practices are discussed in the next section on the quality of financial statements.

The interpretation of ratios can also be enhanced by comparing them at specific points in time with the ratios of other firms in the same industry. Comparing ratios of firms within the same industry is called **cross-sectional analysis.** Sources of information on industry norms were presented in Chapter 8.

Once norms are obtained, it is useful to compare the firm's ratios to the norms. It is usually not very helpful, however, to limit the analysis to observ-

---

[4] Examples of these problems in financial reporting can be found almost every week in Alan Abelson's column in *Barron's,* "Up and Down Wall Street."

ing which ratios are above or below the norm. Typically, most firms will have ratios both above and below the norms. If a particular ratio appears to be significantly different from the norm, the analyst should attempt to determine why. For example, is the asset turnover ratio relatively low because of an unusually high level of current or fixed assets or because of declining sales relative to the level of assets? A skilled analyst can often answer these questions by using several ratios.

There are also problems associated with applying cross-sectional analysis. First, the number of ratios provided and the formulas used to calculate the ratios vary from source to source. For example, the inventory turnover ratio may be calculated using sales or cost of goods sold in the numerator. The source of the industry norms should be consulted to determine the exact formula used in calculating the ratios. Further, the analyst should also make certain that the industry norms are for firms comparable in size to the one being analyzed.

Second, many companies are not what is called *pure plays;* that is, their sales and income may be generated from several different industry segments. In fact, it is very rare to find large, publicly traded companies that confine their business activities to only one industry. In order to undertake meaningful cross-sectional analysis, it is often necessary to compare the norms for several industries with the financial results, by business segment, for a particular company. The company will provide some financial information by business segment in its annual report and/or on the 10–K form filed with the SEC. However, this information is generally not as detailed as the company's consolidated financial statements.

Finally, the analyst should be aware that GAAP may also present problems when a firm's results are compared with an industry norm. Just as an individual firm may change its procedures for recognizing revenues and expenses over time, accounting practices may differ among firms within an industry. Financial analysts generally feel that GAAP need to be tightened so that financial statements are more consistent over time and between firms. Accountants argue, however, that flexibility is more important than consistency.

In using time-series and cross-sectional analysis to interpret the ratios, a useful first step is to identify the three components of return on equity (i.e., asset utilization, profitability, and financial leverage). By comparing these measures with the company's historical figures or industry averages, the analyst can begin the job of investigating the reasons for the changes in these ratios over time or why they diverge from the industry standards.

Figure 9.2 illustrates the suggested steps in ratio analysis. In the first step, the analyst identifies the three components of ROE: asset utilization, profitability, and financial leverage. Next, the analyst examines the ratios, which provide further insight into the three components of ROE. The final step employs additional ratios that will provide information about the firm's liquidity, remove the influence of size and change in size (percentage statements), and indicate the firm's performance on a per-share basis. These ratios can be compared over time for the firm (time-series analysis) and with industry standards (cross-sectional analysis).

FIGURE 9.2 • The Three Steps in Ratio Analysis

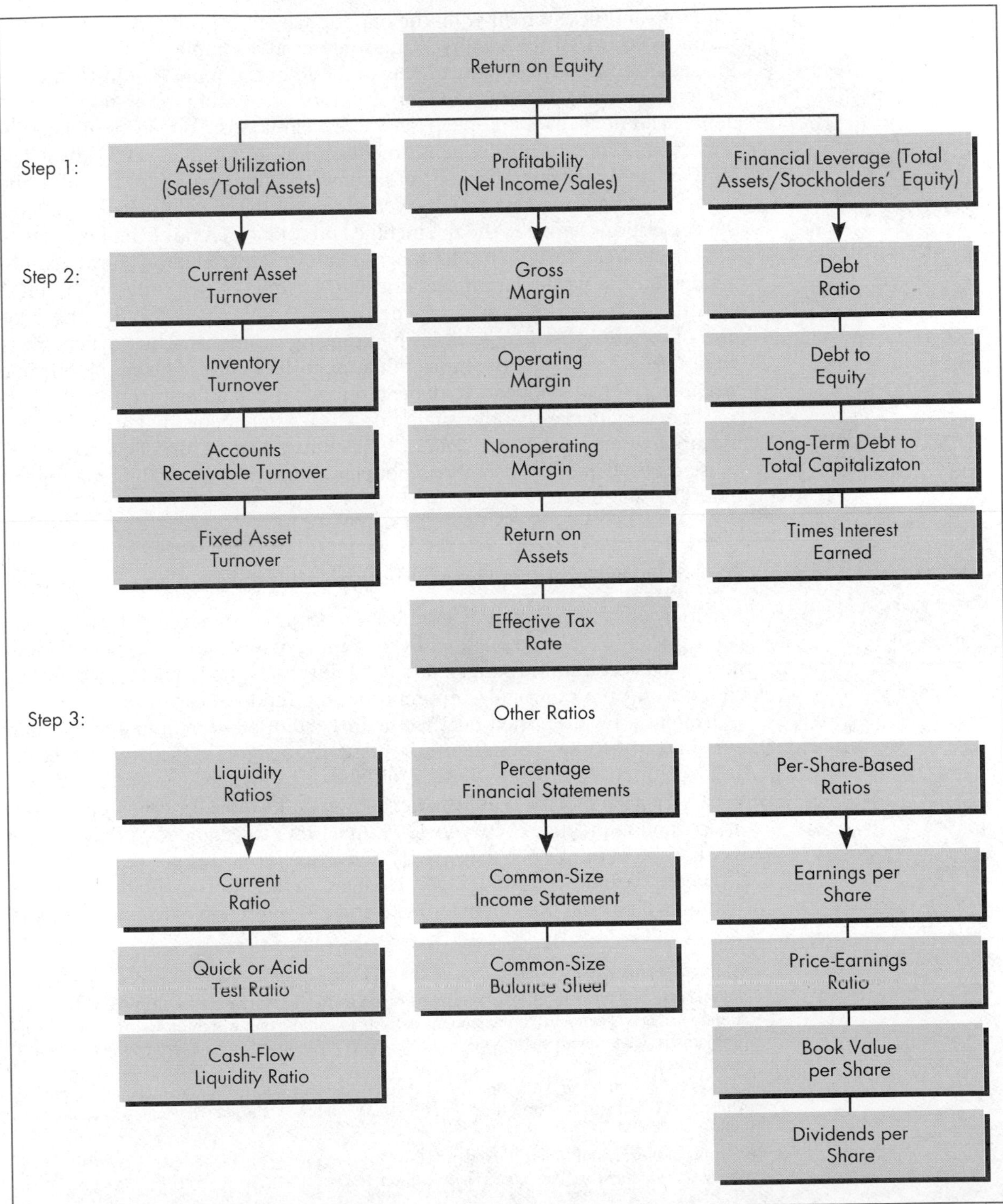

QUALITY OF FINANCIAL STATEMENTS

Opinions and research differ on the importance of "adjusting" financial statements to improve their quality.[5] One study used a sample of 96 firms to test the significance of these adjustments to the financial ratios.[6] Adjustments included converting all firms to FIFO inventory accounting, using tax-reported depreciation expenses and net asset values, eliminating the effect of deferred tax accounting, recognizing pension obligations as liabilities, and consolidating wholly owned subsidiaries. Net income and financial ratios based on the reported and adjusted statements were then compared. With few exceptions, the correlations between the net income and financial ratios from both sets of statements were very high. The magnitude of the correlations, however, depended on the particular adjustment. For example, based only on the FIFO adjustment, the correlation was 99 percent. The adjustment for the consolidation of wholly owned subsidiaries had the largest impact. Thus, when cross-sectional data are used, the impact of accounting adjustments on net income and financial ratios appears to depend on the type of adjustments made.

There is evidence that the quality of a firm's statements may vary depending upon whether they are quarterly or annual statements.[7] This occurs because external auditors usually do not play an important role in preparing the quarterly statements.

• The Impact of Accounting Changes

For individual firms, there is ample evidence that management can significantly increase reported earnings by the timing of revenue and expense recognition and accounting changes. Table 9.2 illustrates the impact of accounting changes on Union Carbide Corporation's 1980 reported earnings.

Union Carbide reported net income in 1980 of $890 million and earnings per share of $13.36. These figures represented a significant increase over the 1979 reported net income of $556 million and earnings per share of $8.47. When reported income is adjusted as shown in the table for the three changes in accounting practices between 1979 and 1980, the company's reported net income and earnings per share actually *decreased* over this period.

Union Carbide reported these changes in accounting practices in the "Notes to Financial Statements—1980 and 1979" section of its annual report.

---

[5] It is beyond the scope of this chapter to present an exhaustive examination of the accounting options that may have an effect on reported earnings. Several references at the end of this chapter can be very helpful to the student wishing to gain further insight into this topic. Specific problems associated with such issues as LIFO versus FIFO, inventory valuation, and inflation are discussed in Chapter 13.

[6] James P. Dawson, Peter M. Neupert, and Clyde P. Stickney, "Restating Financial Statements for Alternative GAAPs: Is It Worth the Effort?" *Financial Analysts Journal* (November-December 1980): 38–46.

[7] Frank J. Fabozzi and Robert Fonfeder, "Have You Seen Any Good Quarterly Statements Lately?" *Journal of Portfolio Management* (Winter 1983): 71–74.

RESEARCH BOX

Indicators of the Need to Adjust Financial Statements

Given the "flexibility" in applying accounting principles, the analyst should be aware of the most common areas where accounting changes may occur. The following are examples of situations or events that may serve as "red flags" indicating the need for possible adjustments in the financial statements, or at least an assessment of their quality:

1. A switching in the cost-flow assumptions of inventory from LIFO to FIFO, or vice versa.
2. Significant changes, relative to sales, in "discretionary" costs such as advertising, marketing, and research and development.
3. Significant changes, relative to sales, in the allowance for doubtful accounts.
4. Significant changes in depreciation expense, as well as amortization and depletion expenses, as a percentage of fixed assets.
5. Meaningful changes in the interest rate and mortality assumptions that will affect the annual pension expense and the degree of over- or underfunding of the pension account.
6. The recognition of nonoperating revenue and expense items such as gains (losses) from the sale of fixed assets (including whole divisions of a company) and interest income earned on temporary investments in marketable securities.
7. A change from the previous year in the accounting firm that performs the audit of the financial statements.
8. The auditors qualify a company's financial statement or do not give an opinion.

TABLE 9.2 • The Impact of Changes in Accounting Practices on Union Carbide's Reported Earnings

	Millions	Per share
1980 net income as reported	$890	$13.36
1. Change from deferred to flow-through method for investment tax credits		
Write off of investment tax credit for assets purchased prior to 1980	(217)	(3.28)
Use of new method in 1980	(24)	(.36)
2. Lengthening of depreciation period for machinery and equipment	(94)	(1.41)
3. Capitalization of interest per FASB Statement No. 34	(24)	(.36)
1980 net income as adjusted	$531	$ 7.95
1979 net income as reported	$556	$ 8.47

SOURCE: Lyn M. Fraser, *Understanding Financial Statements,* 2d ed. (Englewood Cliffs, N.J.: Prentice-Hall, 1988), p. 216. Reprinted by permission.

This example illustrates the importance of reading and understanding the notes to a company's financial statements. It also indicates that it may be a mistake to rely on unadjusted filters in the screening for initial company selection.

• Economic versus Accounting Measurement of Income

Accounting earnings are the reported earnings on a firm's income statement. **Economic earnings** are the real (adjusted for inflation) excess cash flows that a firm generates from a constant level of net assets. These are excess cash flows in that the firm does not need to reinvest these funds in order to maintain a constant level of real earnings. If these economic earnings are paid to stockholders in the form of cash dividends, the firm will have zero growth in earnings and be able to maintain these cash dividends indefinitely.

A simple example, using the accounting and economic definition of depreciation, can be used to illustrate the difference between accounting and economic measures of income. Assume you are analyzing a newly formed company called No-Grow, Inc. The company was initially financed through the issuance of common stock to the public. The name reflects the firm's policy of paying out 100 percent of its earnings in the form of cash dividends, or $b = 0$, and it will not make any new *net* investments in assets.

The assets of the firm consist of one machine costing $200,000, and the firm has elected to depreciate it over 10 years using the straight-line method. Depreciation on the machine will be $20,000 per year. The useful or *economic life* of the machine, however, is estimated to be 20 years, and the machine will be replaced at that time so that No-Grow can maintain a constant level of earnings and, thus, dividends. In order to simplify the example, assume that the expected rate of inflation is zero.

No-Grow applies accounting principles in such a way that, with the exception of depreciation, there is no reason to adjust the financial statements to more accurately reflect the earning power of its assets. Based on the difference between accounting and economic life depreciation, the accounting or reported earnings of the firm will be understated relative to economic earnings by $10,000 per year for the first 10 years ($20,000 per year accounting depreciation − $10,000 per year economic depreciation) and overstated by the same amount for the last 10 years of the life of the asset ($0 per year accounting depreciation − $10,000 per year economic depreciation).

How would you determine the intrinsic value of the stock of No-Grow? As will be discussed in Chapter 14, the analyst could elect to use the zero growth dividend discount model, or

$$V_0 = \frac{D}{K} \tag{9.5}$$

where V_0 is the intrinsic value of the stock, D is the constant, perpetual dividend, and K is the investor's required rate of return.

FIGURE 9.3
Ratio of Price per Share to Book Value per Share for the Standard & Poor's 500, 1946–1990.

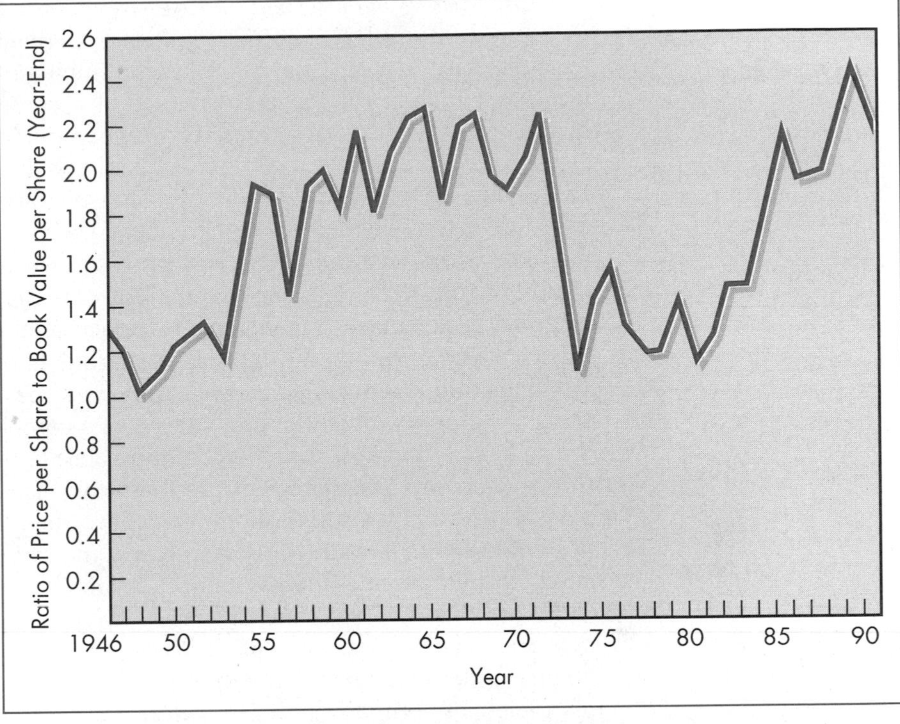

SOURCE: Data from Standard & Poor's *Statistical Service,* various issues.

If you use the accounting or reported earnings as the estimate of dividends in Equation 9.5 (recall the policy of the firm, $b = 0$), the intrinsic value estimate would be below the economic value of the firm. This is because the accounting earnings have understated the economic earnings by $10,000, the difference between the accounting and economic depreciation.

While this example uses depreciation to illustrate the difference between accounting and economic earnings, all factors materially affecting the quality of financial statements need to be considered in estimating earnings. As Figure 9.3 shows, the historical ratios of price per share to book value per share are quite different. The figure illustrates the point that the market (financial analysts) does not rely exclusively on reported earnings when undertaking security valuation. The published financial statements of a company and their accompanying notes represent only a beginning point for the analyst.

OTHER KEY FUNDAMENTALS IN COMPANY ANALYSIS

In addition to an analysis of financial statements, a traditional fundamental analysis includes a consideration of other company attributes. An assessment of these factors often requires subjective judgment.

1. Analysis of management The strengths and weaknesses of management are often reflected in the financial statements and can be revealed, at least partially, by ratio analysis. However, intangible factors can also have an important impact on the performance of a company. The commitment of management to the goal of maximizing shareholder wealth is important. Recently, considerable financial research has been directed at the *agency problem*. Essentially, this research looks at problems that arise because corporate managers are actually agents for stockholders. Do the managers or agents always make decisions that are in the best interest of stockholders? One solution to the problem is to try to make the interests of managers and stockholders correspond. For example, management compensation may be tied to the performance of the company through profit sharing, bonuses, or stock options.

Changes in key management personnel may have a significant impact on a company. For example, the past success of a company may have been due to the skill of certain key executives. But because of their skills, other firms may hire them away. On the other hand, a weak management team may be replaced, providing reason for optimism concerning the company's future prospects. Major changes in top management at Chrysler Corporation are often cited for the dramatic improvement in its performance.

Professional financial analysts often visit a company and confer with key managers. Such meetings enable the analysts to form opinions about the quality of the management team. These opinions can also be influenced by a discussion of company policies concerning such areas as product development, research and development, and financial planning.

2. Analysis of employees The real strength of many companies lies in their employees. Some companies, such as IBM, have historically stressed the importance of hiring and retaining excellent employees. Good employees are retained by competitive compensation packages and other benefits such as continued training and education, rapid advancement, and participation in management decisions, which fosters the development of a team spirit.

Unfortunately, other companies have a reputation for poor employee relations. This often results in rapid employee turnover and lack of commitment to the overall goals of the organization. Without dedicated employees with a long-term interest in the firm, it is unlikely the firm will be highly successful.

3. Analysis of other factors Other factors, such as customer relations, advertising, philosophy, corporate ethics, awareness of environmental concerns, and willingness to be a good corporate citizen, are intangible factors that may significantly influence the long-term success of a company.

ILLUSTRATION OF COMPANY FINANCIAL ANALYSIS: THE PROCTER & GAMBLE COMPANY

In this section, the methods of analysis presented earlier in the chapter will be applied to the analysis of the financial statements of one company. This illustration will follow the three-step process set out in Figure 9.2.

• Company Background

Procter & Gamble (P&G) is a worldwide leader in household and personal care products.[8] The company is committed to steadily expanding its product lines and gaining market share in the United States and abroad.

P&G dominates many personal care brand categories, often controlling more than 40 percent of the market. Personal care products, such as bar soaps (Ivory), paper tissue products (Charmin), disposable diapers (Pampers, Luvs), toothpaste (Crest), hair and skin care products (Pert, Oil of Olay, Cover Girl, Old Spice), and pharmaceuticals comprise P&G's largest product sector, accounting for about 48 percent of the approximately $24 billion in fiscal year 1990 sales.

Household and laundry products (Tide, Cheer, Bounce, Dawn, Cascade) contribute about 32 percent of sales, and foods (including such brands as Jif peanut butter, Folgers coffee, and Hawaiian Punch fruit drink) account for more than 13 percent.

P&G's sales and operating income by business segments for fiscal year 1990 were as follows:[9]

	Sales		Operating income	
Business segment	*Thousands*	*Percentage*	*Thousands*	*Percentage*
Laundry and cleaning	$ 7,942,000	32.2	$ 781,000	28.9
Personal care	11,767,000	47.7	1,314,000	48.6
Food and beverage	3,318,000	13.4	304,000	11.2
Pulp and chemicals	1,666,000	6.7	307,000	11.3

P&G is expanding vigorously in international markets, especially in Europe and the Far East. The company has dramatically increased foreign operations and is active in 46 countries. Strong expansion in overseas markets is likely to be a key factor in P&G's progress over the next few years. For example, disposable diapers are the company's largest single product with annual sales of more than $4.2 billion, about two-thirds of which is overseas.

• Analysis of Procter & Gamble's Financial Statements

P&G's income statements, balance sheets, and statement of cash flows for 1988–1990 appear in Tables 9.3, 9.4, and 9.5, respectively.[10] The Notes to the

[8]This background information on Procter & Gamble is adapted from a research report prepared by Merrill Lynch dated September 24, 1990.

[9]This information was taken from the "Notes to Consolidated Financial Statements" section of the Procter & Gamble Company and Subsidiaries 1990 *Annual Report*, p. 32. See Appendix 9A for more detailed segment information.

[10]This analysis does not include cross-sectional analysis because sufficient financial information was not available for the four business segments of P&G.

TABLE 9.3 • The Procter & Gamble Company and Subsidiaries Consolidated Statement of Earnings

	Procter & Gamble Company income statements ($000s) for fiscal years ending		
	6/30/90	*6/30/89*	*6/30/88*
Net sales	$24,081,000	$21,398,000	$19,336,000
Cost of goods	14,658,000	13,371,000	11,880,000
Gross profit	$ 9,423,000	$ 8,027,000	$ 7,456,000
Selling, general, & administrative expenses	7,121,000	5,988,000	5,660,000
Operating income	$ 2,302,000	$ 2,039,000	$ 1,796,000
Nonoperating income	561,000	291,000	155,000
Interest expense	442,000	391,000	321,000
Income before taxes	$ 2,421,000	$ 1,939,000	$ 1,630,000
Provision for income taxes	819,000	733,000	610,000
Net income	$ 1,602,000	$ 1,206,000	$ 1,020,000
Average outstanding shares of common stock (000,000)*	346.1	334.4	338.6
Preferred dividends	$ 47,000	$ 16,000	$ 11,000
Common dividends	$ 592,000	$ 504,000	$ 466,000

SOURCE: Disclosure Database.

*Adjusted for a two-for-one stock split effective October 20, 1989.

NOTE: See the accompanying Notes to Consolidated Financial Statements in Appendix 9A.

Consolidated Financial Statements are in Appendix 9A. The analysis of P&G's financial statements will follow the three steps outlined in Figure 9.2.

Step 1: ***Isolate the components of ROE.*** Using Equation 9.3, the asset utilization, profitability, and financial leverage components of ROE can be determined for P&G for 1990, 1989, and 1988.

	$\frac{\text{Sales}}{\text{Total assets}}$	×	$\frac{\text{Net income}}{\text{Sales}}$	×	$\frac{\text{Total assets}}{\text{Stockholders' equity}}$	= ROE
1990	1.3026	×	.0665	×	2.4590	= .2127
1989	1.3087	×	.0564	×	2.6309	= .1942
1988	1.3047	×	.0528	×	2.3386	= .1611

TABLE 9.4 • The Procter & Gamble Company and Subsidiaries Consolidated Balance Sheets

	Procter & Gamble Company balance sheets ($000s) as of fiscal years ending		
	6/30/90	*6/30/89*	*6/30/88*
Cash	$ 1,407,000	$ 1,587,000	$ 1,065,000
Receivables	2,647,000	2,090,000	1,759,000
Inventories	2,865,000	2,337,000	2,292,000
Other current assets	725,000	564,000	477,000
Total current assets	$ 7,644,000	$ 6,578,000	$ 5,593,000
Net property & equipment	7,436,000	6,793,000	6,778,000
Intangibles	2,594,000	2,305,000	1,944,000
Deposits & other assets	813,000	675,000	505,000
Total assets	$18,487,000	$16,351,000	$14,820,000
Accounts payable	$ 2,035,000	$ 1,669,000	$ 1,494,000
Current long-term debt	897,000	633,000	902,000
Accrued expenses	2,135,000	1,888,000	1,487,000
Other current liabilities	350,000	466,000	341,000
Total current liabilities	$ 5,417,000	$ 4,656,000	$ 4,224,000
Deferred charges/income	1,258,000	1,335,000	1,322,000
Long-term debt	3,588,000	3,698,000	2,462,000
Other long-term liabilities	706,000	447,000	475,000
Total liabilities	$10,969,000	$10,136,000	$ 8,483,000
Preferred stock	$ 1,000,000	$ 1,000,000	$ N/A
Common stock, net	346,000	162,000	169,000
Capital surplus	510,000	529,000	463,000
Retained earnings	6,581,000	5,587,000	5,688,000
Other liabilities*	(919,000)	(1,063,000)	17,000
Shareholder equity	$ 7,518,000	$ 6,215,000	$ 6,337,000
Total liabilities & equity	$18,487,000	$16,351,000	$14,820,000

SOURCE: Disclosure Database.

*Includes currency translation adjustments and reserve for employee stock ownership plan debt retirement.

NOTE: See the accompanying Notes to Consolidated Financial Statements in Appendix 9A.

TABLE 9.5 • The Procter & Gamble Company and Subsidiaries Consolidated Statement of Cash Flows

Procter & Gamble Company statement of cash flows ($000s)

Cash Flow Provided by Operating Activity	Fiscal year ending 6/30/90	6/30/89	6/30/88
Net income (loss)	$ 1,602,000	$ 1,206,000	$ 1,020,000
Depreciation/Amortization	859,000	767,000	697,000
Net increase (decrease) assets/liabilities	(455,000)	(229,000)	164,000
Other adjustments, net	NA	751,000	176,000
Net cash provided (used) by operations	$ 2,006,000	$ 2,495,000	$ 2,057,000

Cash Flow Provided by Investing Activity	Fiscal year ending 6/30/90	6/30/89	6/30/88
(Increase) decrease in property, plant	$ (1,300,000)	$ (1,029,000)	$ (1,018,000)
(Acquisition) disposal of subsidiaries, business	(484,000)	N/A	(399,000)
(Increase) decrease in securities investments	N/A	(506,000)	81,000
Other cash inflow (outflow)	263,000	98,000	N/A
Net cash provided (used) by investments	$ (1,521,000)	$ (1,437,000)	$ (1,336,000)

Cash Flow Provided by Financing Activity	Fiscal year ending 6/30/90	6/30/89	6/30/88
Issue (purchase) of equity	$ (179,000)	$ 206,000	$ (276,000)
Increase (decrease) in borrowing	153,000	(222,000)	356,000
Dividends, other distribution	(639,000)	(520,000)	(477,000)
Net cash provided (used) by financing	$ (665,000)	$ (536,000)	$ (397,000)
Increase (decrease) in cash and equivalents	$ (180,000)	$ 522,000	$ 324,000

SOURCE: Disclosure Database.

NOTE: See the accompanying Notes to Consolidated Financial Statements in Appendix 9A

Analysis: From 1988 through 1990, the ROE measure has shown a steady improvement. In each year, however, the major source of the increase came from a different component of ROE. In 1989, the increase in ROE over 1988 was due mainly to the increased use of financial leverage, with only slight improvements in asset utilization and profitability. In 1990, the increase in ROE over 1989 was due solely to the increased level of P&G's profitability.

Step 2: ***Analyze the components of ROE.*** While the information in Step 1 is revealing, additional analysis of the components of ROE provides insight into the changes in ROE. Using the ratios in Table 9.1, information about the sources of changes in asset utilization, profitability, and financial leverage can be uncovered.

	1990	1989	1988
Asset Utilization	1.3026×	1.3087×	1.3047×
Current asset turnover	3.1503×	3.2530×	3.4572×
Inventory turnover	5.1162×	5.7214×	5.1832×
Accounts receivable turnover	9.0975×	10.2382×	10.9926×
Fixed asset turnover	3.2384×	3.1500×	2.8528×

Analysis: While overall asset utilization did not change significantly over the 1988–1990 period, the turnover of current assets (particularly accounts receivable) decreased, but this was offset by an increase in the fixed asset turnover. An examination of the Notes to Consolidated Financial Statements (Appendix 9A) does not reveal any significant changes in inventory valuation procedures or depreciation/amortization schedules. The acquisition of Noxell Corporation in fiscal year 1990 did not appear to materially influence P&G's asset utilization measures.

	1990	1989	1988
Profitability	.0665	.0564	.0528
Gross margin	.3913	.3751	.3856
Operating margin	.0956	.0953	.0929
Nonoperating margin	.0233	.0136	.0080
Return on assets	.1245	.1247	.1212
Effective tax rate	.3383	.3780	.3742

Analysis: The overall profitability of P&G increased significantly over the 1988–1990 period. While increases in the gross and operating margins contributed to the improvement in overall profitability, the 1990 increase in deferred taxes of $116 million relative to 1989 and $305 million relative to 1988 (see Appendix 9A) reduced the effective tax rate and improved overall profitability. In addition, as indicated in Appendix 9A, a $125 million consent judgment and an after-tax gain of $91 million from the sale of the worldwide Crush soft drink business contributed to the overall profitability of P&G in 1990. Finally, a comparison of the interest rates on long-term debt contained in the Notes to Consolidated Financial Statements in Appendix 9A and the return on assets measure indicates that P&G is employing favorable financial leverage.

	1990	1989	1988
Financial leverage	2.4590	2.6309	2.3386
Debt ratio	.5933	.6199	.5724
Debt to equity	1.4590	1.6309	1.3386
Long-term debt to total capitalization	.3231	.3730	.2709
Times interest earned	5.2081×	5.2148×	5.5950×

Analysis: Over the 1988–1990 period, P&G has slightly increased its level of financial leverage. In 1988, total assets were approximately 2.34 times stockholders' equity. By 1990, total assets had risen to nearly 2.46 times stockholders' equity. The major portion of this increase came from the rise in long-term debt as indicated by the increase in the long-term debt to total capitalization ratio. P&G's ability to meet the interest payments, as measured by the times-interest-earned ratio, has declined slightly since 1988 but still represents a comfortable margin.

Step 3:* *Other ratios.

	1990	1989	1988
Liquidity			
Current	1.41×	1.41×	1.32×
Quick (acid test)	.88×	.91×	.78×
Cash-flow liquidity*	.63×	.88×	.74×

*The net cash flow from operating activities is provided in Table 9.5.

Percentage Statements	See Tables 9.6 and 9.7.		
	1990	**1989**	**1988**
Per Share Based[a]			
Book value	$21.71	$19.18	$18.71
Price (as of 6/30)	$87.13	$109.88	$76.25
Earnings	$4.49	$3.56	$2.98
Dividend[b]	$1.75	$1.50	$1.38
Dividend yield (%)[c]	2.01	1.37	1.81
Payout (%)[d]	39.0	42.1	46.3

[a] Where appropriate, per-share figures have been adjusted for a two-for-one stock split effective October 20, 1989.

[b] Based on the indicated annual dividend per share. The number of shares outstanding varies from quarter to quarter.

[c] Based on the June 30 stock price and indicated annual dividend rate per share.

[d] Dividend per share/earnings per share.

Analysis: Both the current ratio and the quick ratio increased over the 1988–1990 period, indicating a rise in liquidity. The cash-flow liquidity ratio, however, shows a decrease in short-run

TABLE 9.6 • The Procter & Gamble Company and Subsidiaries Common Size Statement of Earnings

	Procter & Gamble Company common size income statements (percent*) for fiscal years ending		
	6/30/90	*6/30/89*	*6/30/88*
Net sales	100.0%	100.0%	100.0%
Cost of goods	60.9	62.5	61.4
Gross profit	39.1	37.5	38.6
Selling, general, & administrative expenses	29.6	28.0	29.3
Operating income	9.5	9.5	9.3
Nonoperating income	2.3	1.4	.8
Interest expense	1.8	1.8	1.7
Income before tax	10.0	9.1	8.4
Provision for income taxes	3.4	3.4	3.2
Net income	6.6	5.6	5.3

*The percentages may not add because of rounding differences.

TABLE 9.7 • The Procter & Gamble Company and Subsidiaries Common Size Balance Sheets

	Procter & Gamble Company common size balance sheets (percent[a]) as of fiscal years ending		
	6/30/90	*6/30/89*	*6/30/88*
Cash	7.6%	9.7%	7.2%
Receivables	14.3	12.8	11.9
Inventories	15.5	14.3	15.5
Other current assets	3.9	3.4	3.2
Total current assets	41.3	40.2	37.7
Net property & equipment	40.2	41.5	45.7
Intangibles	14.0	14.1	13.1
Deposits & other assets	4.4	4.1	3.4
Total assets	100.0	100.0	100.0
Accounts payable	11.0	10.2	10.1
Current long-term debt	4.9	3.9	6.1
Accrued expenses	11.5	11.5	10.0
Other current liabilities	1.9	2.8	2.3
Total current liabilities	29.3	28.5	28.5
Deferred charges/income	6.8	8.2	8.9
Long-term debt	19.4	22.6	16.6
Other long-term liabilities	3.8	2.7	3.2
Total liabilities	59.3	62.0	57.2
Preferred stock	5.4	6.1	0.0
Common stock net	1.9	1.0	1.1
Capital surplus	2.8	3.2	3.1
Retained earnings	35.6	34.2	38.4
Other liabilities[b]	5.0	6.5	1.1
Shareholder equity	40.7	38.0	42.8
Total liabilities & equity	100.0	100.0	100.0

[a]The percentages may not add because of rounding differences.

[b]Includes currency translation adjustments and reserve for employee stock ownership plan debt retirement.

solvency. This divergence in liquidity measures can be partially explained by the $888 million increase in accounts receivable over the period. Accounts receivable are included in the numerator for both the current ratio and quick ratio calculations. Increases in accounts receivable are a use of funds, however, and therefore reduce the net cash flow from operating activities. The increase in accounts receivable relative to sales is reflected in the decrease in the accounts receivable turnover measure. Note also that in Table 9.7, accounts receivable have increased to 14.3 percent of total assets in 1990 from 11.9 percent in 1988.

It is also interesting to note the lack of relationship between book value per share and the market price per share. The market has drawn a distinction between reported earnings and economic earnings.

Finally, if P&G continues to retain 61 percent of its earnings and is able to earn the 1990 ROE of 21.27 percent on new investments, its earnings will grow at an estimated rate of approximately 13 percent ($g = b \times \text{ROE} = .61 \times .21271$).

SUMMARY

This chapter has presented the analytical tools necessary to assess the financial strengths and weaknesses of a company. Company analysis is an important element of the entire fundamental analysis process. The cornerstone of company analysis is an analysis of the financial statements.

The three-step approach suggested for financial statement analysis begins with an examination of ROE. By decomposing ROE into measures of asset utilization, profitability, and financial leverage, the analyst is able to gain valuable insights into the performance of the company. Liquidity ratios, percentage financial statements, and per-share-based ratios also assist the analyst in determining a company's financial strengths and weaknesses. Interpretation of the ratios is enhanced by using time-series and cross-sectional analysis.

Financial analysts also recognize that reported financial statements may not reflect an accurate picture of the firm. This occurs because GAAP allows for considerable flexibility in reporting financial performance. Differences in accounting and economic measures of income, as well as changes in accounting principles from one reporting period to the next, require adjustments by the financial analyst.

Factors other than the analysis of financial statements should be considered in company analysis. Analysis of a company is more than "number crunching." Intangibles such as the abilities and commitment of management and employees are also important.

The chapter concluded with an analysis of the financial statements of Procter & Gamble. The three-step approach for ratio analysis suggested in the chapter was demonstrated. The notes to the consolidated financial statements for P&G are included in Appendix 9A in order to underscore the importance of reading and understanding this information.

• CONCEPT APPLICATIONS

Investment Concept	Concept Application
Fundamental analysis	The fundamental analysis process has as its purpose an estimation of whether or not a security is under- or overvalued. The suggested approach for fundamental analysis is "top down." This entails an analysis of the economy, appropriate industry analysis, and individual company selection and analysis.
Financial statement analysis	Once a company or companies have been selected, detailed financial statement analysis is required. The approach to analyzing financial statements described in the chapter can guide the analyst through the process. The analyst must keep three elements in mind throughout the process. First, financial statements must be carefully examined (including the notes to the financial statements). GAAP provide flexibility, and the analyst must check for consistency from year to year. Second, in the short run, management can make operating and nonoperating decisions that can distort the financial statements. Third,there is a distinction between accounting and economic income. Simply "crunching" the numbers without understanding how the numbers are generated will lead to a poor financial analysis of the firm.
Efficient financial markets	In a perfectly efficient financial market, the individual investor would not benefit from financial analysis. However, because individual investors may have certain advantages, financial analysis may be worth the time (cost) the investor must spend.
Other key fundamentals in company analysis	While the ROE approach presented in the chapter can be very revealing, the analyst should not neglect other, less quantifiable factors. These factors include the quality of management, attitude and abilities of employees, and other intangible factors such as corporate ethics. These factors play an important role in a company's future success.

• KEY TERMS

Accounting earnings
Asset utilization ratios
Common size statements
Cross-sectional analysis
Economic earnings
Filters
Financial leverage ratios
Generally accepted accounting principles (GAAP)
Liquidity ratios
Per-share-based ratios
Profitability ratios
Return on assets (ROA)
Return on equity (ROE)
Screening
Time-series analysis

• QUESTIONS

1. If the stock market is considered to be at least moderately to strongly efficient, what justification is there for fundamental analysis?
2. What is the rationale for using a "top-down" approach in selecting companies for financial analysis?
3. Identify five filters you consider important in screening for company selection. Justify your selection of filters. What problems might you encounter in the screening process?
4. What sources of company financial information are available to an analyst?
5. What are the three components of ROE and why is it important to examine these component parts?
6. Discuss the influence of the firm's financing decision on its asset utilization, profitability, and financial leverage measures.
7. Describe how ROA and financial leverage can impact the firm's ROE.
8. Describe the logic underlying the cash-flow liquidity ratio. Why might the cash-flow liquidity ratio give a different indication of liquidity than the current or quick (acid test) ratio?
9. Does the relationship between book value per share and stock price indicate a level of safety for the common stock price? Why or why not?
10. Why is it important to use time-series analysis and cross-sectional analysis in interpreting ratios? What problems might the financial analyst encounter in using these comparative measures?
11. Table 9.2 illustrated the impact of changes in accounting principles on the 1980 reported earnings of Union Carbide. Do you think these changes, and the resulting increase in earnings, materially impacted Union Carbide's stock price?
12. Explain what is meant by the "quality of financial statements." What are some of the important factors that can be identified from financial statements and the accompanying notes that potentially reduce the "quality" of the statements?
13. Distinguish between economic and accounting measures of income. How can differences in economic and accounting measures of income affect the valuation of a firm's common stock?
14. Why was cross-sectional analysis not used in the financial analysis of Procter & Gamble?
15. Assume you are the regional sales manager of a large, publicly traded firm that sells personal computer clones to retailers. In the fourth quarter of the year, you realize that your region will not meet its sales and profitability quotas for the year. This failure to reach quotas will seriously impact your year-end bonus. What actions might you take to reach these quotas? Are the actions you describe in the best interests of the firm? The stockholders? Other stakeholders? Do you consider the actions you have described to be ethical?

• KEY TO THE INVESTMENT ANALYSIS SOFTWARE

Calculation	Appendix A-1 Page Reference	Access Procedure
Financial statement construction	A-8	BEGIN, FINANCIAL, FINANCIALS, INPUT or ADDFILES
Common size financial statement	A-10	BEGIN, FINANCIAL, FINANCIALS, COMMON
Growth rate of key financial items	A-10	BEGIN, FINANCIAL, FINANCIALS, GROWTH
Ratio analysis	A-10	BEGIN, FINANCIAL, FINANCIALS, RATIOS
Pro forma income statements	A-10	BEGIN, FINANCIAL, FINANCIALS, FORECAST

• PROBLEMS

1. Sunshine Corporation has a policy of paying out 70 percent of its earnings in dividends to its common stockholders. If the company is able to earn a 14 percent return on equity on new investments, what is the expected growth rate of Sunshine's earnings?

2. Consider the following financial information for Jeweler's, Inc., and Grocery, Inc.:

	Jeweler's, Inc.	*Grocery, Inc.*
Sales	$150,000,000	$200,000,000
Net income	9,000,000	4,000,000
Total assets	75,000,000	40,000,000
Stockholders' equity	50,000,000	22,222,000

a. Calculate the asset utilization, profitability, and financial leverage measures for Jeweler's, Inc., and Grocery, Inc.

b. Calculate the ROE for Jeweler's, Inc., and Grocery, Inc.

c. Which company is riskier? Why?

d. If the two companies had the same earnings per share and expected growth in earnings and dividends, which company would have a higher stock price? Why?

3. Consider the following information for JMI, Inc., and Candy, Inc. Both companies are in the same industry.

	JMI, Inc.	*Candy, Inc.*
Sales	$20,000,000	$15,000,000
Cost of goods sold	10,000,000	7,500,000
Current assets	6,000,000	3,500,000
Cash	1,000,000	500,000
Inventory	2,000,000	2,000,000
Accounts receivable	3,000,000	1,000,000
Net fixed assets	10,000,000	5,000,000

a. Calculate the overall asset utilization measure (sales/total assets) for the two companies.

b. Explain why the asset utilization measures are different for the two companies.

4. The following abbreviated income statements are for Laser, Inc., and Photo Optics, Inc. The two firms do not have any debt.

	Laser, Inc.	*Photo Optics, Inc.*
Sales	$25,000,000	$30,000,000
Cost of goods sold	12,000,000	15,000,000
Gross margin	$13,000,000	$15,000,000
Operating expenses	7,000,000	6,000,000
Operating income	$6,000,000	$9,000,000
Nonoperating income	500,000	—
Income before taxes	$6,500,000	$9,000,000
Taxes	2,210,000	1,800,000
Net income	$4,290,000	$7,200,000

a. Calculate the net profitability (net income/sales) for the two companies.

b. Explain why the net profitability of the two companies is different.

5. Assume that Pizza, Inc., and Mama's Pizza, Inc., have the same return on assets (ROA). However, Pizza, Inc., has a significantly higher return on equity (ROE) than its competitor. Explain how this could occur.

6. The Walt Disney Company has three major segments from which it generates sales and income: theme parks and resorts, filmed entertainment, and consumer products. Based on the financial information presented for Walt Disney in the following tables:

a. Calculate the ROE and the components of ROE for Walt Disney for 1990, 1989, and 1988. Discuss the contributions of the components to the overall ROE of Walt Disney.

b. Analyze the components of Walt Disney's ROE for each of the three years.

c. Calculate and analyze other ratios for Walt Disney for each of the three years.

d. Estimate Walt Disney's growth rate in earnings. Be specific about your assumptions.

e. What other information do you feel would be helpful in your analysis of Walt Disney?

Walt Disney Company
income statements (000s)
for fiscal years ending

	9/30/90	9/30/89	9/30/88
Net sales	$5,843,700	$4,594,300	$3,438,200
Cost of goods	4,418,200	3,365,300	2,553,400
Gross profit	$1,425,500	$1,229,000	$ 884,800
Selling, general, & administrative expenses	138,500	119,600	96,000
Operating income	$1,287,000	$1,109,400	$ 788,800
Nonoperating income	80,800	67,400	58,900
Interest expense	43,100	23,900	5,800
Income before taxes	$1,324,700	$1,152,900	$ 841,900
Provision for income taxes	500,700	449,600	319,900
Net income	$ 824,000	$ 703,300	$ 522,000
Average outstanding shares of common stock (000,000)	136.3	135.4	133.2
Common dividends	$ 74,100	$ 61,800	$ 50,500
Annual dividend rate per share	$ .56	$ .46	$ .38
Price per share as of 9/30	$ 90.38	$ 120.88	$ 64.88

Walt Disney Company
balance sheets (000s)
as of fiscal year ending

	9/30/90	9/30/89	9/30/88
Cash	$ 819,800	$ 380,800	$ 428,000
Marketable securities	588,100	662,300	668,600
Receivables	851,500	908,500	437,900
Inventories	269,200	264,300	159,900
Total current assets	$2,528,600	$2,175,900	$1,694,400
Net property & equipment	3,910,500	3,397,300	2,821,700
Deferred charges	641,000	443,300	211,000
Deposits & other assets	942,100	640,700	381,800
Total assets	$8,022,300	$6,657,200	$5,108,900

	9/30/90	9/30/89	9/30/88
Accounts payable	$1,158,100	$1,011,400	$ 698,700
Notes payable	N/A	N/A	435,500
Income taxes	200,300	250,900	204,300
Other current liabilities	841,900	912,700	823,300
Total current liabilities	$2,200,300	$2,175,000	$2,161,800
Deferred charges/income	748,800	577,600	587,800
Long-term debt	1,584,600	860,600	N/A
Total liabilities	$4,533,700	$3,613,200	$2,749,600
Common stock, net	$ 502,800	$ 392,800	$ 349,600
Retained earnings	3,401,100	2,651,200	2,009,700
Treasury stock	(483,000)	N/A	N/A
Other liabilities	67,700	N/A	N/A
Shareholder equity	$3,488,600	$3,044,000	$2,359,300
Total liabilities & equity	$8,022,300	$6,657,200	$5,108,900

Walt Disney Company
statement of cash flows (000s)

	Fiscal year ending		
Cash Flow Provided by Operating Activity	9/30/90	9/30/89	9/30/88
Net income (loss)	$ 1,324,700	$ 1,152,900	$ 841,900
Depreciation/Amortization	203,100	191,500	148,600
Net increase (decrease) assets/liabilities	(46,000)	48,200	145,100
Cash provided (used) by discontinued operations	N/A	N/A	1,163,900
Other adjustments, net	(122,900)	(117,000)	(60,200)
Net cash provided (used) by operations	$ 1,358,900	$ 1,275,600	$ 2,239,300

	Fiscal year ending		
Cash Flow Provided by Investing Activity	9/30/90	9/30/89	9/30/88
(Increase) decrease in property, plant	$ (716,300)	$ 749,600	$ (595,700)
(Acquisition) disposal of subsidiary, business	N/A	237,300	(221,700)
(Increase) decrease in securities investments	74,200	426,700	(658,500)
Other cash inflow (outflow)	(539,800)	315,600	(433,600)
Net cash provided (used) by investments	$ (1,181,900)	$ (1,729,200)	$ (1,909,500)

Cash Flow Provided by Financing Activity	Fiscal year ending 9/30/90	9/30/89	9/30/88
Issue (purchase) of equity	N/A	N/A	N/A
Increase (decrease) in borrowing	$ 336,100	$ 425,100	$ (237,700)
Dividends, other distribution	(74,100)	(61,800)	(50,500)
Other cash inflow (outflow)	N/A	43,100	75,400
Net cash provided (used) by financing	262,000	406,400	(245,800)
Effect of exchange rate on cash	N/A	(3,458,400)	N/A
Net change in cash or equivalents	$ 439,000	$ (47,200)	$ 84,000
Cash or equivalents at year-start	380,000	428,000	344,000
Cash or equivalents at year-end	$ 819,800	$ 380,800	$ 428,000

• REFERENCES

Berliner, Robert W. "Do Analysts Use Inflation-Adjusted Information? Results of a Survey." *Financial Analysts Journal* (March-April 1983): 65–72.

Black, Fischer. "The Magic in Earnings: Economic Earnings versus Accounting Earnings." *Financial Analysts Journal* (November-December 1980): 19–24.

Bowlin, Oswald D., John D. Martin, and David F. Scott, Jr. *Guide to Financial Analysis,* 2d ed. New York: McGraw-Hill Publishing Company, 1990.

Bromley, Michael. "The Efficient Market Hypothesis: Some Second Thoughts." *Management Accounting,* U.K. (May 1990): 36–38.

Brown, Philip, and Ray Ball. "Some Preliminary Findings on the Association between the Earnings of a Firm, Its Industry, and the Economy." *Journal of Accounting Research: Empirical Research in Accounting: Selected Studies* (1967): 55–77.

Clayman, Michelle. "In Search of Excellence: The Investor's Viewpoint." *Financial Analysts Journal* (May-June 1987): 54–63.

Dawson, James P., Peter M. Neupert, and Clyde P. Stickney. "Restating Financial Statements for Alternative GAAPs: Is It Worth the Effort?" *Financial Analysts Journal* (November-December 1980): 38–46.

Dopuch, Nicholas, and Morton Pincuo. "Evidence on the Choice of Inventory Valuation Methods: LIFO versus FIFO." *Journal of Accounting Research* (Spring 1988): 28–59.

Easton, Peter D., and Joseph Magliolo III. "Accounting Earnings and Security Valuation: Empirical Evidence of the Fundamental Links/Discussion." *Journal of Accounting Research* (Supplement 1985): 54–80.

Fabozzi, Frank J., and Robert Fonfeder. "Have You Seen Any Good Quarterly Statements Lately?" *Journal of Portfolio Management* (Winter 1983): 71–74.

Fraser, Lyn M. *Understanding Financial Statements,* 2d ed. Englewood Cliffs, N.J.: Prentice-Hall, 1988.

Gentry, James A., Paul Newbold, and David T. Whitford. "Profiles of Cash Flow Components." *Financial Analysts Journal* (July-August 1990): 41–48.

Gleckman, Howard. "Beware of Artificial Sweeteners in This Year's Earnings." *Business Week,* February 8, 1988, pp. 22–23.

Henke, Emerson O., and Charlene W. Spoede. "Annual Financial Reports: A User's Audit." *Baylor Business Review* (Summer 1990): 2–8.

Kamath, Ravindra. "How Useful Are Common Liquidity Measures?" *Journal of Cash Management* (January-February 1989): 24–28.

Kellogg, Irving, and Loren B. Kellogg. "Dig Beneath Gloss in Annual Reports." *Pensions & Investment Age,* June 13, 1988, pp. 13–14.

Nichols, Donald R. "A Study of the Market Valuation of Extraordinary Items Reported in Financial Statements." *Financial Review* (Fall 1977): 1–17.

Palmer, Jay. "Attractive Ratios: Companies with Below-Average Multiples of Earnings and Book." *Barron's,* November 5, 1990, pp. 18, 54.

———. "Hunting for Net-Nets: Screen Turns Up 34 of These Rare Birds." *Barron's,* March 14, 1988, p. 18.

———. "Shipshape Financials." *Barron's,* October 22, 1990, pp. 20, 22.

Siegel, Joel G. "The 'Quality of Earnings' Concept: A Survey." *Financial Analysts Journal* (March-April 1982): 60–68.

Stricharchuk, Gregory. "More Ailing Concerns Are Firing Auditors in Hopes of Keeping Bad News from Public." *Wall Street Journal,* May 12, 1983, p. 35.

Weiss, Gary. "Investing: Reading between the Lines of an Annual Report." *Business Week,* March 23, 1987, pp. 164–65.

APPENDIX 9A

The Procter & Gamble Company and Subsidiaries

Notes to Consolidated Financial Statements[1]

1. SUMMARY OF SIGNIFICANT ACCOUNTING POLICIES

Principles of Consolidation: The financial statements include the accounts of The Procter & Gamble Company and its majority-owned subsidiaries. Investments in 20% to 50% owned affiliates in which significant management control is exercised are included at original cost adjusted for the change in equity since acquisition. Other investments in affiliates are carried at cost.

Currency Translation: Assets and liabilities denominated in most foreign currencies are translated into U.S. dollars at year-end exchange rates and related gains and losses are reflected in shareholders' equity. Gains and losses from foreign currency transactions and translation of balance sheets in highly inflationary economies are included in earnings.

Cash Equivalents: Highly liquid investments with maturities of three months or less when purchased are considered to be cash equivalents.

Inventory Valuation: Inventories are valued at the lower of cost or market. Cost for inventories in the United States is primarily determined by the last-in, first-out method. Cost is determined by the average cost method for substantially all of the remaining inventories.

Futures contracts are purchased primarily to hedge certain agricultural commodity requirements. Gains and losses on these contracts are included in earnings when the related products are sold.

Goodwill and Other Intangible Assets: Intangible assets are amortized on a straight-line basis over periods not exceeding forty years.

Depreciation: For financial accounting purposes, depreciation is calculated on a straight-line basis over the estimated useful lives of the properties.

Other Expenses: Advertising and research and development costs are charged against earnings in the year incurred.

Income Taxes: Provision is made for the income tax effects of all transactions in the consolidated statement of earnings, including those for which actual tax payment or tax relief is deferred to future years. These deferrals result primarily from the use of shorter equipment lives and accelerated methods of depreciation for tax purposes.

Provision is made for all additional income taxes on dividends planned to be paid from accumulated international subsidiary earnings. No additional taxes are provided on the remaining $1,689 million of undistributed subsidiary earnings which are invested indefinitely in those subsidiaries.

[1] SOURCE: Procter & Gamble Company *1990 Annual Report*, pp. 26–33.

Statement of Financial Accounting Standards No. 96—Accounting for Income Taxes—will be adopted no later than 1993.

Net Earnings Per Common Share: Net earnings less preferred dividends (net of related tax benefits) is divided by the average number of common shares outstanding during the year to derive net earnings per common share. Net earnings per common share assuming full dilution is derived as follows: Net earnings are reduced by the difference between the preferred dividend paid and the common dividend that would have been paid if all of the preferred shares had been converted to common shares at the beginning of each period. This remainder is divided by the sum of the average number of common shares outstanding for the period plus the added common shares that would have been outstanding if: (1) all of the outstanding preferred shares had been converted into common shares at the beginning of the period and (2) all stock options granted that have economic value were exercised at the beginning of the period, and the related funds that would have been received by the Company upon such exercise were used to repurchase outstanding common shares.

2. ACQUISITIONS

In November 1989, Noxell Corporation was merged into the Company through the issuance by the Company of 22 million common shares. The merger was accounted for as a pooling of interests and the results of Noxell are included beginning July 1, 1989. Prior years have not been restated since the effect was not material.

Other acquisitions accounted for as purchases totaled, in millions, \$484, \$506 and \$408 in 1990, 1989 and 1988, respectively. The increase in goodwill and other intangible assets amounted, in millions, to \$347, \$442 and \$350 in those years. The pro forma full year effect of the acquisitions on consolidated earnings would not have been material in the respective years.

3. EARNINGS STATEMENT INFORMATION

Years Ended June 30 (Millions of Dollars)	**1990**	1989	1988
Research and Development Costs	**$ 693**	$ 628	$ 615
Capitalized Interest	**3**	7	11
Earnings Before Income Taxes			
U.S.	**1,897**	1,345	1,201
International	**524**	594	429
Income Taxes			
Current			
Federal	**691**	508	287
Foreign	**171**	196	125
Other	**86**	42	22
	948	746	434

Deferred			
Federal	**(132)**	(56)	113
Foreign and other	**3**	43	63
	(129)	(13)	176
Deferred tax components			
Depreciation	**67**	80	91
Provision for restructuring	**(58)**	60	122
Other	**(138)**	(153)	(37)
	(129)	(13)	176

Total Tax Expense

This expense includes income taxes identified separately on the consolidated statement of earnings as well as property, franchise, social security, and other taxes paid to federal, state and local governments throughout the world which are included in other cost and expense categories and amounted, in millions, to $1,261 in 1990, $1,120 in 1989 and $978 in 1988.

Effective Income Tax Rates

These rates were 33.8% in 1990, 37.8% in 1989 and 37.4% in 1988 compared to the U.S. statutory tax rate of 34%. In 1990, U.S. state and local income taxes increased the rate by 2.1%, which is offset by several factors including differences in taxes referable to foreign source income.

Changes in Currency Exchange Rates

Gains (losses) from changes in currency exchange rates which are included in net earnings amounted, in millions, to $(37) in 1990, $38 in 1989 and $1 in 1988.

Quarterly Results (Unaudited)
Millions of Dollars Except Per Share Amounts

		Quarter Ended				
		Sept. 30	Dec. 31	Mar. 31	Jun. 30	Total Year
1989–90	**Net sales**	**$5,717**	**$6,025**	**$6,123**	**$6,216**	**$24,081**
	Earnings before income taxes	**874**	**543**	**595**	**409**	**2,421**
	Net earnings	**564**	**350**	**404**	**284**	**1,602**
	Net earnings per common share assuming full dilution	**1.51**	**.93**	**1.08**	**.75**	**4.27**
1988–89	Net sales	5,267	5,268	5,430	5,433	21,398
	Earnings before income taxes	636	520	503	280	1,939
	Net earnings	400	325	310	171	1,206
	Net earnings per common share	1.18	.96	.92	.50	3.56
	Net earnings per common share assuming full dilution	1.17	.95	.89	.46	3.47

The quarter ended September 30, 1989 has been restated to include Noxell net sales of $142 million and net earnings of $13 million, and also includes the $125 million consent judgment from the favorable settlement of the litigation applicable to the Duncan Hines cookie business. Net earnings for the quarter ended December 31, 1989 include after-tax gain of $91 million from the sale of the worldwide Crush soft drink business and were reduced by a $174 million after-tax reserve to complete the consolidation of certain major worldwide manufacturing facilities. The quarter ended June 30, 1989 includes a $78 million after-tax provision for closing certain U.S. manufacturing facilities in connection with related production consolidations. Per share amounts have been adjusted for the two-for-one stock split effective October 20, 1989.

4. BALANCE SHEET INFORMATION

June 30 (Millions of Dollars)	**1990**	1989
Inventories		
Raw materials and supplies	**$ 1,179**	$ 944
Work in process	**250**	179
Finished products	**1,436**	1,214
	2,865	2,337
Replacement cost of LIFO inventories	**1,412**	1,214
Stated value of LIFO inventories	**1,219**	962
Excess of replacement cost over the stated value	**193**	252
Property, Plant, and Equipment		
Buildings	**1,862**	1,644
Machinery and equipment	**9,506**	8,529
Land	**203**	209
Timberlands, less depletion	**191**	164
	11,789	10,546
Less accumulated depreciation	**4,353**	3,753
	7,436	6,793
Goodwill	**2,099**	1,855
Other Intangible Assets	**840**	732
	2,939	2,587
Less accumulated amortization	**345**	282
	2,594	2,305
Accrued Liabilities		
Marketing expenses	**536**	391
Compensation expenses	**258**	232
Provision for restructuring	**196**	34
Other	**700**	708
	1,690	1,365

Long-Term Debt

8⅝% sinking fund debentures due 2016	**234**	234
9½% notes due 1998 (swapped for 7½% German DM obligation due 1998)	**200**	200
6% Japanese yen notes due 1991 (swapped for variable U.S. dollar obligation due 1991)	**193**	193
6⅝% Japanese yen notes due 1992 (swapped for 10.6% U.S. dollar obligation due 1992)	**193**	193
8¼% sinking fund debentures due 2005	**178**	178
9⅝% notes due 2001 (swapped for 7.8% German DM obligation due 2001)	**150**	155
10% notes due 1995 (a call option was sold, exercisable in 1992 which swaps from fixed to variable rate)	**150**	150
Variable rate notes due 1992 (swapped from Treasury-based to commercial paper–based variable rates)	**150**	—
8½% notes due 2009	**149**	—
8⅛% sinking fund debentures due 2017	**138**	138
5¾% Japanese yen notes due 1993 (coupons swapped for LIBOR-based variable rates)	**132**	140
11½% bonds due 1993	**125**	125
13% Italian lire notes due 1993 (swapped for U.S. dollar commercial paper–based, variable rate obligation due 1993)	**105**	—
11% Canadian dollar notes due 1992 (swapped for variable rate U.S. dollar obligation due 1992)	**103**	—
8% debentures due 2029 (coupons swapped for variable rate thru 1996. A swap option was sold allowing termination of the original swap in 1994)	**99**	—
9⅞% notes due 1992	**62**	151
10% notes due 1990	—	200
11% notes due 1989	—	150
10⅝% sinking fund debentures due 2015	—	131
*Other, due in varying amounts through 2019	**555**	622
7.78%–8.33% serial employee stock ownership plan notes due 1991–2004, guaranteed by the Company	**963**	1,000
	3,879	3,960
Less amounts included in debt due within one year	**291**	262
Total long-term debt	**3,588**	3,698

*Includes at June 30, 1990, $108 million of interest rate swaps referable to notes due through 2003.

The following payments, in millions, are required during the next five fiscal years: 1991—$291; 1992—$309; 1993—$511; 1994—$313; 1995—$84.

5. FINANCIAL INSTRUMENTS

In addition to the swaps and options mentioned in the Long-Term Debt table, the Company had foreign exchange forward contracts and other currency swaps, on hand at June 30, 1990, totalling $1,155 million, primarily to hedge transactions denominated in foreign currencies. These financial instruments are used by the Company to minimize exposure and to reduce risk from exchange rate and interest rate fluctuations in the regular course of its global business.

6. SHAREHOLDERS' EQUITY

Preferred Stock: Authorized Class A preferred stock is 600,000,000 shares without par value with stated value of $1 per share. Series A ESOP Convertible Class A Preferred Stock in the amount of 18,181,818 shares were issued to the employee stock ownership plan in March, 1989 at $55 per share, and were outstanding at June 30, 1990. Each issued share has a liquidation value of $55 and is convertible at the option of the holder into one share of the Company's common stock. The number of shares and per share amounts have been adjusted for the two-for-one stock split effective October 20, 1989.

Common Stock: Authorized common stock is 1,000,000,000 shares without par value with stated value of $1 per share. The number of shares and per share amounts have been adjusted for the two-for-one stock split effective October 20, 1989. Changes in outstanding shares for years ended June 30 are as follows:

	1990	1989	1988
Shares outstanding beginning of year (excludes 16,453,310, 854,966 and 1,124,400 treasury shares)	**323,980,816**	338,731,336	338,059,542
Purchased for treasury	**(2,857,669)**	(16,847,658)	(670,494)
Issued for option and remuneration plans (includes 965,151, 1,249,314 and 939,928 treasury shares)	**3,139,679**	2,097,138	1,342,288
Issued for Noxell merger	**22,031,333**	—	—
Shares outstanding end of year (excludes 18,345,828, 16,453,310 and 854,966 treasury shares)	**346,294,159**	323,980,816	338,731,336

Under the Company's stock option plans, options have been granted to key employees to purchase common shares of the Company at the market value on the dates of the grants. Activity for the year ended June 30, 1990, was as follows:

	Shares	Average Price
Outstanding at beginning of year	12,689,884	$37.72
Options granted	2,847,350	63.58
Options exercised	(2,803,917)	35.33
Options canceled	(212,202)	43.78
Outstanding at end of year	12,521,115	44.03

Options for 9,710,565 shares were exercisable at June 30, 1990. There were 10,558,060 shares available for the granting of options at that date.

Additional Paid-In Capital: Increases in additional paid-in capital resulted from the excess amount realized over the stated value of common shares issued pursuant to employee stock option and remuneration plans and, in millions, amounted to $124, $66, and $36 for the years ended June 30, 1990, 1989 and 1988, respectively. The Noxell merger increased additional paid-in capital by $23 million in 1990. The transfer to common shares and related expenses of the two-for-one stock split reduced additional paid-in capital by $166 million in 1990.

Currency Translation Adjustments credited to stockholders' equity, in million, amounted to $107, $(80) and $43 for the years ended June 30, 1990, 1989 and 1988, respectively.

Profit Sharing Plans: Most employees are covered by Company-funded, defined contribution profit sharing plans which provide retirement benefits. The Procter & Gamble Profit Sharing Trust and Employee Stock Ownership Plan is the largest and covers most employees in the United States. Participants' individual accounts in this plan are credited each year with amounts based on individual base salary and years of service. The total credited to all accounts does not exceed 15% of total salaries and wages of participants.

The credits to individual accounts in all plans come from two sources:

Years Ended June 30 (Millions of Dollars)	**1990**	1989	1988
Preferred shares of Procter & Gamble stock allocated at market value	**$102**	$ —	$ —
Company contributions	**127**	204	203
Benefits earned by participants	**229**	204	203

Within the largest plan, there is a leveraged employee stock ownership trust. This trust borrowed $1 billion in 1989 and the debt was guaranteed by the Company. The borrowed funds were used to buy a special class of Proctor & Gamble convertible preferred shares, some of which are allocated each year to individual accounts, as indicated above.

Principal and interest of $117 million on the borrowed funds is paid each year by the trust from dividends on preferred shares and cash payments from the Company. The 1990 payments were:

Millions of Dollars	Interest	Principal	Total
Dividends on preferred shares	$50	$24	$ 74
Payment from the Company	30	13	43
Total	80	37	117

Profit sharing expenses for all plans were $140 million in 1990, made up of the cash contributions of $127 million and the principal payment of $13 million on the loan. Profit sharing expenses in 1989 and 1988 were cash contributions of $204 million and $203 million.

Pension Plans: Other employees, primarily outside the U.S., are covered by local pension or retirement plans. Pension expense amounted to $60 million and $34 million in 1989 and 1988, respectively. The adoption of Statement of Financial Accounting Standards No. 87—Employers' Accounting for Pensions—was completed in 1990 and the effect was not material. Pension expense in 1990 includes:

Millions of Dollars	**1990**
Benefits earned by participants during the year	**$ 49**
Interest on projected benefit obligations	**53**
Return on plan assets	**(44)**
Net amortizations and other	**(4)**
Pension expense	**54**

At June 30, 1990 the accumulated benefit obligation was $568 million, including $513 million vested benefit obligation. The projected benefit obligation was $779 million and the market value of plan assets was $516 million. Net unrecognized transition obligations, gains and prior service costs were $7 million and accrued pension cost was $270 million. The projected benefit obligation is based on an average discount rate of 8%, long-term rate of return on plan assets of 9%, and rate of increase in compensation of 6%.

Other Retiree Benefits: Certain health care and life insurance benefits are provided for many retired employees. The cost of these benefits is charged against earnings in the year the claims and premiums are paid. This cost, in millions, amounted to $19 in 1990, $21 in 1989, and $16 in 1988.

8. SEGMENT INFORMATION

Sales between geographic areas and those between business segments, included in net sales below, are made at prices approximating market and are eliminated from total net sales. Corporate earnings include interest income and expense, and other general corporate income and expense. Corporate assets include primarily cash and cash equivalents.

Geographic Areas

Millions of Dollars		United States	International	Corporate	Total
Net Sales	1988	$12,423	$7,294	$ (381)	$19,336
	1989	13,312	8,529	(443)	21,398
	1990	**14,962**	**9,618**	**(499)**	**24,081**
Net Earnings	1988	864	305	(149)	1,020
	1989	927	417	(138)	1,206
	1990	**1,304**	**467**	**(169)**	**1,602**
Assets	1988	8,346	4,751	1,723	14,820
	1989	8,669	5,260	2,422	16,351
	1990	**9,742**	**6,516**	**2,229**	**18,487**

Business Segments: The Company's operations are characterized by interrelated raw materials and manufacturing facilities and centralized research and administrative staff functions, making any separate profit determination by product group dependent upon necessarily arbitrary assumptions as to allocations of common costs. Different assumptions or physical or organizational arrangements would produce different results.

		Product Groups					
Millions of Dollars		Laundry and Cleaning	Personal Care	Food and Beverage	Pulp and Chemicals	Corporate	Total
Net Sales	1988	$6,668	$ 8,676	$2,963	$1,532	$ (503)	$19,336
	1989	7,138	10,032	3,029	1,778	(579)	21,398
	1990	**7,942**	**11,767**	**3,318**	**1,666**	**(612)**	**24,081**
Earnings Before Income Taxes	1988	699	888	32	248	(237)	1,630
	1989*	754	1,031	(14)	362	(194)	1,939
	1990*	**781**	**1,314**	**304**	**307**	**(285)**	**2,421**
Assets	1988	2,852	7,114	1,721	1,410	1,723	14,820
	1989	2,964	7,511	2,023	1,431	2,422	16,351
	1990	**3,296**	**8,786**	**2,726**	**1,450**	**2,229**	**18,487**
Capital Expenditures	1988	285	483	120	117	13	1,018
	1989	273	510	101	138	7	1,029
	1990	**383**	**586**	**131**	**197**	**3**	**1,300**
Depreciation, Depletion and Amortization	1988	149	375	88	79	6	697
	1989	151	428	90	90	8	767
	1990	**170**	**464**	**117**	**101**	**7**	**859**

*Earnings before income taxes have been reduced by the establishment of reserves to consolidate manufacturing facilities as follows: Laundry and Cleaning Products: 1990—$131, 1989—$25; Personal Care Products: 1990—$87, 1989—$73; Food and Beverage Products: 1990—$34, 1989—$16; Pulp and Chemicals: 1990—$13, 1989—$5. Totals: 1990—$265, 1989—$119. Earnings of Food and Beverage Products have been increased in 1990 by $141 for gain on the sale of the Crush soft drink business and by $125 for favorable settlement of litigation applicable to the Duncan Hines cookies business.

Laundry and Cleaning Products include detergents, hard surface cleaners and fabric conditioners. Personal Care Products include personal cleansing products, deodorants, hair care products, skin care products, oral care products, paper tissue products, disposable diapers, digestive health products, cough and cold remedies and other pharmaceuticals. Sales of disposable diapers represented approximately 18%, 17% and 16% of consolidated sales in 1990, 1989 and 1988, respectively. Food and Beverage Products include shortening and oil, snacks, prepared baking mixes, peanut butter, coffee, soft drinks and citrus products. Products of the Laundry and Cleaning, Personal Care and Food and Beverage segments are distributed primarily through grocery stores and other retail outlets. Pulp and Chemicals are sold direct to customers and through jobbers. Net sales of Pulp and Chemicals include intersegment sales amounting, in millions, to $612 in 1990, $579 in 1989, and $503 in 1988.

PART IV

Fundamental Analysis of Bonds

CHAPTER 10

Bond Fundamentals

CHAPTER 11

Bond Analysis: Returns, Risk, and Strategies

Bond Fundamentals

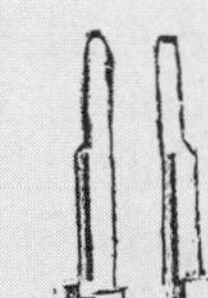

The knowledge-level objectives of this chapter should enable the student to:

- Explain how the risk-return characteristics of bonds and common stocks differ.
- Differentiate among the many different types of bonds including U.S. Treasury and agency securities, U.S. savings bonds, corporate bonds, and municipal bonds.
- Understand how the interest rate environment of the 1970s and 1980s changed investor attitudes toward bonds.
- Understand market quotations and the mechanics of bond trading.
- Identify bond rating categories and understand how ratings influence bond prices and yields.
- Distinguish between the primary and secondary bond markets.
- Identify the more important bond indexes and understand how they are used by individuals and bond portfolio managers.

INTRODUCTION

A **bond** is a type of fixed-income security issued by a borrowing entity in which the amount to be paid to the investor is specified in the investment contract or **indenture.** The inclusion of provisions specifying the amount of income is a major distinguishing characteristic of bonds. In contrast, the income from common stock—cash dividends—is determined periodically by the board of directors. A **trustee** (usually a large commercial bank) is appointed when the bond is issued to represent the collective interests of the investors. As this chapter will explain, there are many types of bonds.

As was briefly discussed in Chapter 1, the other major type of fixed-income security issued by corporations is preferred stock. Convertible bonds and convertible preferred stock are covered in Chapter 16.

It is important to remember that a bond represents a debt of the issuer. Essentially, the issuer has borrowed funds and agreed to make specified payments to the bondholders that represent periodic interest payments and ultimately the repayment of principal. Since a bond is a liability of the issuer, the bondholders receive priority over common stockholders in two important ways. First, they have priority in receiving interest income each period; the issuer has a contractual obligation to make these distributions, even if the issuer's income is not adequate for the period. Second, the bondholders have priority in the event the issuer's assets are liquidated; since bonds are liabilities, funds from a liquidation must be used to pay these claims before any distribution can be made to preferred or common stock investors.

COMPARING BONDS WITH OTHER TYPES OF INVESTMENTS

These two priorities (income and liquidation) mean that bonds, as a general class of security, are less risky than common stocks. "Less risky" in this sense refers to the greater likelihood of receiving income (interest or dividends) and repayment of principal. It should be noted, however, that when bonds and stocks of different corporations are compared, some individual bonds may have greater risk than some stocks. For example, most investors would view the bonds of a corporation with a significant probability of bankruptcy as considerably more risky than the common stock of a large successful firm like AT&T. In terms of the same corporation, however, bonds are always less risky than the common stock.

• Return Comparison: HPRs

One of the best ways to compare bonds with common stocks is to look at an example of ex-post return performance.[1] Table 10.1 provides graphs of the annual holding period returns (HPRs) for corporate bonds and common stocks. The returns for the bonds and common stocks are calculated as

[1] Details on calculating bond and stock returns are provided in Chapter 2.

$$\text{HPR}_t = \frac{P_{t+1} - P_t + I_t \text{ or } D_t}{P_t} \qquad (10.1)$$

where

P = the index value or price
I = the annual interest
D = the annual dividend

As would be expected, the returns varied considerably from year to year. In particular, bond prices and returns were very volatile over the period 1975–1990. In addition, notice that for a number of years the returns on corporate bonds were higher than those on common stocks. Such periods are

TABLE 10.1 • Annual Ex-Post Holding Period Returns

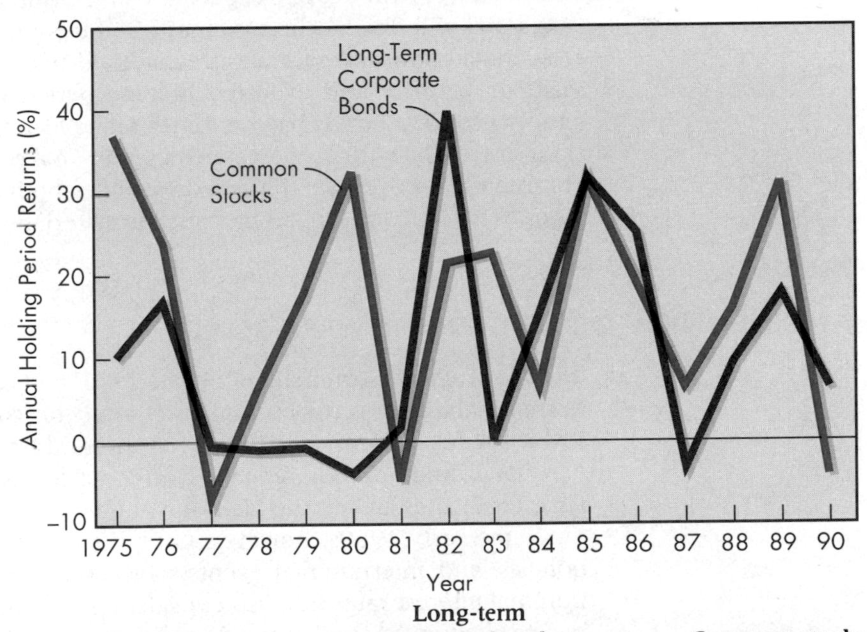

1975–1990	Long-term corporate bonds	Common stocks
Arithmetic mean	11.00%	16.09%
Standard deviation	13.24%	14.16%
Coefficient of variation	1.20	0.88

SOURCE: Graph constructed from data from Roger G. Ibbotson and Rex A. Sinquefield, *Stocks, Bonds, Bills, and Inflation (SBBI)* (Chicago: Ibbotson Associates, 1982), updated in *SBBI 1991 Yearbook.*

generally characterized by falling interest rates that produce large capital gains for bonds. The year 1982 was also highly unusual. It has been called a "once-in-a-lifetime" opportunity for bond investors because of the extraordinarily high capital gains that were realized.

• Risk Comparison

The summary statistics at the bottom of Table 10.1 illustrate that, on average for the period 1975–1990, the total risk of corporate bonds, as measured by the standard deviation, was almost as large as for common stocks. The coefficient of variation for bonds is also greater than the coefficient of variation for stocks over this period of time. A study by Sharpe showed that for longer periods (1938–1971 and 1946–1971) bonds offered less return and less risk.[2] Sharpe's research has been updated and expanded in a 1987 study.[3] This study, based on the period 1926–1985, found that the risk-adjusted returns from common stocks were superior to those from bonds during the post–World War II period, while bonds had higher risk-adjusted returns for the 20-year period prior to the war.

Chapter 11 will examine specific risk measures for bonds in considerable detail and will discuss the systematic and unsystematic components of bond risk. In addition, several measures of bond return will be presented such as yield to maturity and expected holding period return. For now, however, simply note that bonds have certain unique features that cause them to have their own risk-return characteristics and make them quite different from common stocks. These characteristics offer both advantages and disadvantages as will become apparent from the material that follows.

CHANGING INVESTOR ATTITUDES TOWARD BONDS

The economic environment of the late 1970s and early 1980s resulted in some dramatic changes in the bond market and, consequently, investors' attitudes toward bonds. Historically, investing in bonds was characterized as simply "buy and hold" or "clipping coupons"—a passive investment strategy (see Chapter 7) that lacked the glamour of investing in other types of securities. Since the early 1980s, however, double-digit inflation, monetary and fiscal policies, and international events have produced not only extremely high nominal interest rates but also considerable volatility in interest rates, which has resulted in fluctuating bond prices.

---

[2] W.F. Sharpe, "Bonds versus Stocks, Some Lessons from Capital Market Theory," *Financial Analysts Journal* (November-December 1973): 74–79.

[3] Meir Statman and Neal L. Ushman, "Bonds versus Stocks: Another Look," *Journal of Portfolio Management* (Winter 1987): 33–38.

FIGURE 10.1 • Moody's Corporate Bond Yields to Maturity by Ratings, 1929–1991

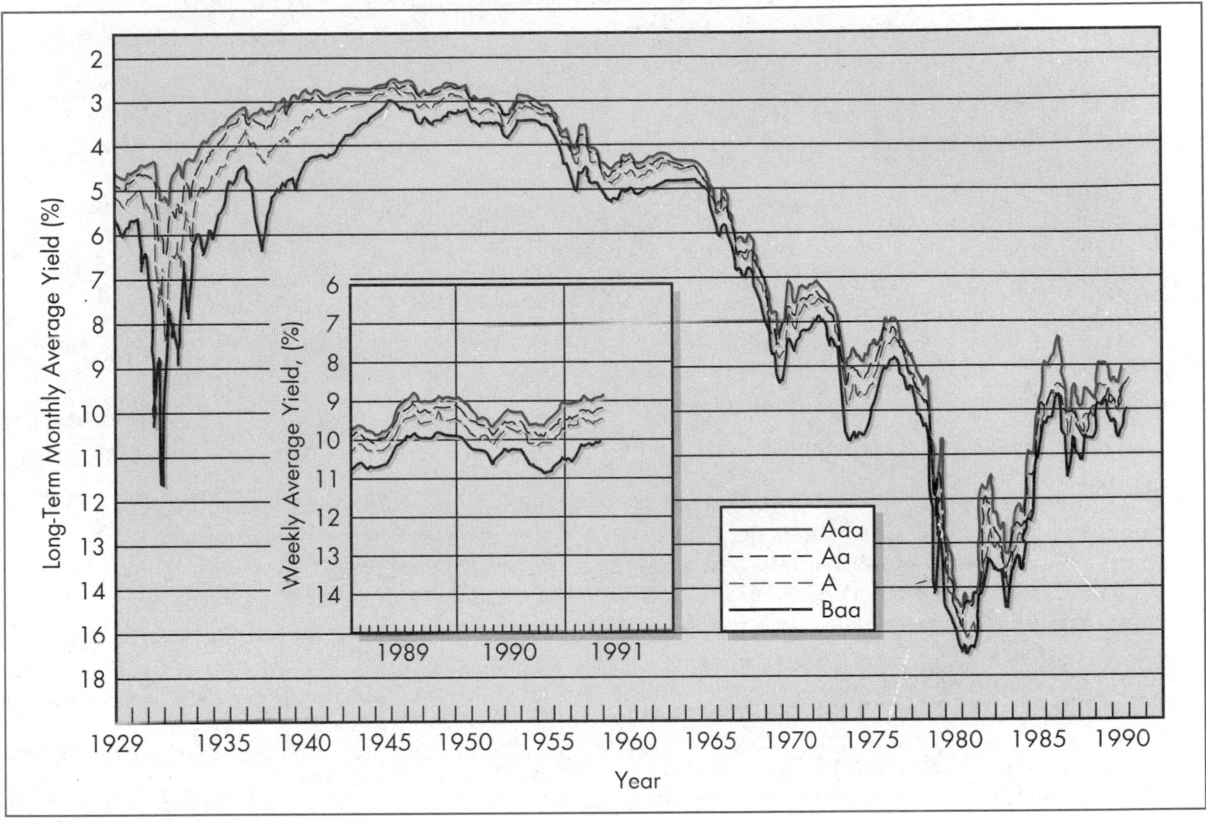

SOURCE: Moody's *Bond Record* (May 1991), p. 510. Reprinted by permission.

Figure 10.1 confirms these observations (notice the inverted scale on the yield axis). With the exceptions of the postdepression period and a small but persistent overall upward trend in yields, bond yields were reasonably stable until the late 1960s and 1980s. During the ensuing decades, yields reached all-time highs, and the distances between yield peaks and troughs increased. The implications of these developments for the risk return characteristics of bonds are quite apparent.

Edward H. Ladd, in an address to a seminar for Chartered Financial Analysts in 1983, made an interesting observation that illustrates the increase in yield volatility.[4] He noted that when he started his bond career in the early

[4] Edward H. Ladd, "The Changing Structures of the American Capital Market: The Past, the Present, and the Future," *The Revolution in Techniques for Managing Bond Portfolios* (Institute of Chartered Financial Analysts, 1983).

• **INTEREST BOX**

Advantages and Disadvantages of Bond Investing

Noting that investors have sometimes been reluctant to invest in bonds, Burton Malkiel has commented:

> Bonds are the Rodney Dangerfield of financial investments. They don't get much respect. They were defined in an early 1980s parody of the *Wall Street Journal* as "fixed-rate instruments designed to fall in price."
>
> The pessimistic view of bonds by many investors in the late 1980s is based on their performance during the 1960s and 1970s. Over the past 40 years, common stocks provided an annual compounded rate of return of approximately 10 percent while high-grade corporates returned approximately 5 percent. The poor performance of bonds is primarily due to *unexpected inflation* during the period 1950–1985. High and unexpected inflation rates cause interest rates to change and bond price volatility to increase. We have seen even safe Treasury bonds fall 2 to 3 points a day (that is, lose about 2% to 3% of their market value).

Despite the poor performance of bonds, Malkiel cautions that you should not "invest with a rear-view mirror." Investors and the bond markets have likely learned a hard lesson about underestimating the rate of inflation and the consequences to bond investors. Because investors are now extremely cautious about unexpected inflation, "bonds are priced more attractively than they were in the past."

Possible risk factors for bonds in the 1990s include having the bond called by the issuer if interest rates decline; possible default if a serious recession occurs; and the large federal budget deficit.

Despite these risk factors, Malkiel believes "bonds deserve a place in everyone's portfolio." In addition, he comments, "I still believe that bonds will provide reasonable generous real rates of return over the next decade—and with less risk than for roughly similar returns in stocks."

SOURCE: Burton G. Malkiel, "The Case for Bonds," *Forbes*, June 26, 1989, pp. 180–85.

1960s, technical analysis was a popular device for following and forecasting yields. He began charting the yield on long-term Treasury bonds. After two and a half years, the yield had fluctuated from 4.22 percent to 4.25 percent—a mere 3 "basis" points. By contrast, the yield on long-term Treasury bonds declined from 14.16 percent in January 1982 to 10.46 percent in November 1982—a decline of 370 basis points in less than a year.[5]

Investors in today's bond market are well aware of the changing bond environment. As a consequence, emphasis has shifted from "passive" to "active" bond portfolio management. In addition, bond issuers have responded to this new environment by offering bonds with features that are compatible with this market. Bonds without coupon payments (commonly called zeros), bonds with indexed interest rates, and bonds with options attached (such as

[5] Based on the yield to maturity of Moody's long-term "Government Bond Yield Averages" in Moody's *Municipal and Government Manual*, vol. 1 (Moody's Investor Services, 1984), p. a7.

warrants and "put" options) are attempts by issuers to modify the risk-return characteristics of bonds.

Predictably, there is considerable debate about the future bond environment. On the one hand, some analysts view the 1970s and 1980s as simply another page in history that will be remembered as unusual but not predictive; they believe the future will see a return to more passive bond portfolio management.[6] On the other hand, some analysts believe the period was a good indication of the future; they think that financial markets will continue to be volatile and that more active bond portfolio management strategies will be appropriate. Volatile markets encourage active management and call buy-and-hold strategies into question. Both viewpoints have some validity, and Chapter 11 will examine bond investing and portfolio management under both types of investment environments.

TYPES OF BONDS

Bonds can be categorized using several schemes. One possibility is to group bonds according to the issuer—the U.S. government, U.S. agencies, municipalities, and corporations. Another possibility is by term to maturity—"short" (less than one year), "intermediate" (one to ten years), "long" (over ten years). Another approach is to categorize bonds by the level of default risk, ranging from almost absolute security (U.S. government issues) to subordinated debentures.

The approach we have selected categorizes bonds according to their risk-return features. This approach has the advantage of relating basic bond characteristics to overall risk-return considerations. We will begin by discussing the bonds with the least risk and (in an efficient market) the lowest expected return and conclude with a discussion of bonds with the greatest risk and the highest return.

• U.S. Government Securities

The bonds with the least risk—and the lowest expected return—are securities issued by the U.S. government.

TREASURY BILLS **Treasury bills (T-bills)** are viewed as the safest of all fixed-income securities because of the lack of default risk and because the term to maturity is one year or less. The bills lack default risk because they are issued by the U.S. Treasury and are backed by the full credit of the U.S. government. Their short term to maturity also results in reasonably stable prices, even though short-term interest rates may fluctuate. In addition, an active secondary market for T-bills exists, providing the investor with considerable liquidity.

---

[6] Ladd, "Changing Structures."

T-bills have an interesting feature that sets them apart from other Treasury obligations: the investor does not receive interest payments. Rather, T-bills are sold at a discount from their maturity value, with the desired yield determining the size of the discount. This point is discussed in more detail in the next section.

TREASURY NOTES AND BONDS **Treasury notes** have maturities of ten years or less, while **Treasury bonds** have maturities over ten years. As a result of the longer term to maturity, both have more interest rate risk than T-bills. These securities also differ from T-bills in that interest is paid semiannually by the Treasury, and the investor does not depend entirely on the discount from par to achieve the appropriate yield.

Table 10.2 provides an example of the daily quotations on Treasury bills, bonds, and notes as they appear in the *Wall Street Journal.* The quotations are conveniently arranged by the term to maturity of the securities. Notice that the "bid" and "ask" quotations for T-bills are actually discounts rather than prices. The size of the discount determines the yield that is given in the last column. Bond and note prices are quoted for both the "bid" and "ask" and are in terms of "points" and $\frac{1}{32}$ of a point. For example, if the bid is given as 101.10, the price is \$1013.125, i.e., $[(101 + \frac{10}{32}) \times 10]$. These "point" values can be viewed as a percentage of face value; for a bond or note with a face value of \$1,000, each point is equivalent to \$10. The bond and note prices are also net of interest that has accrued since the last coupon payment. The accrued interest must be paid to the seller by the purchaser.

Notice also in Table 10.2 that the coupon rate, maturity date, bid change, and yield to maturity based on the "ask" quote are given for each bond and note. The influence of these factors on the risk-return characteristics of the securities will be discussed in Chapter 11. Information about the exact dates of interest payments and maturity, along with other features, can be found in publications such as *Moody's Municipal and Government Manual.*

• U.S. Savings Bonds

U.S. savings bonds are similar to other U.S. government securities in some ways, but they also exhibit some significant differences. First, they are not negotiable since no secondary market exists. They can be redeemed, however, at any bank without any fees or commission. Second, they do not pay interest directly to the investor but rather compound the interest semiannually.[7] This feature is similar to T-bills; the yield is determined by the discount from face value. The investor receives the accumulated interest as a lump sum when the bond is redeemed. Third, the **Series EE bonds,** introduced on November 1, 1982, have a market-based interest rate that is 85 percent of the market aver-

[7] Series HH bonds do pay interest semiannually. These bonds, however, are only available in exchange for Series E and EE bonds.

TABLE 10.2 • Quotations on Treasury Issues: Bills, Bonds, and Notes

Tuesday, May 28, 1991

Representative Over-the-Counter quotations based on transactions of $1 million or more.

Treasury bond, note and bill quotes are as of mid-afternoon. Colons in bid-and-asked quotes represent 32nds; 101:01 means 101 1/32. Net changes in 32nds. n-Treasury note. Treasury bill quotes in hundredths, quoted on terms of a rate of discount. Days to maturity calculated from settlement date. All yields are to maturity and based on the asked quote. For bonds callable prior to maturity, yields are computed to the earliest call date for issues quoted above par and to the maturity date for issues below par. *-When issued.

Source: Federal Reserve Bank of New York.

U.S. Treasury strips as of 3 p.m. Eastern time, also based on transactions of $1 million or more. Colons in bid-and-asked quotes represent 32nds; 101:01 means 101 1/32. Net changes in 32nds. Yields calculated on the bid quotation. ci-stripped coupon interest. bp-Treasury bond, stripped principal. np-Treasury note, stripped principal. For bonds callable prior to maturity, yields are computed to the earliest call date for issues quoted above par and to the maturity date for issues below par.

Source: Bear, Stearns & Co. via Street Software Technology Inc.

TREASURY BILLS

Maturity	Days to Mat.	Bid	Asked	Chg.	Ask Yld.
May 30 '91	0	5.55	5.45	+0.39	0.00
Jun 06 '91	7	5.32	5.22	+0.14	5.30
Jun 13 '91	14	5.32	5.22	+0.16	5.30
Jun 20 '91	21	5.36	5.26	+0.29	5.35
Jun 27 '91	28	4.42	4.32	−0.08	4.39
Jul 05 '91	36	5.30	5.26	+0.11	5.36
Jul 11 '91	42	5.22	5.18	+0.07	5.28
Jul 18 '91	49	5.21	5.17	+0.05	5.28
Jul 25 '91	56	5.24	5.20	+0.05	5.32
Aug 01 '91	63	5.32	5.30	+0.01	5.42
Aug 08 '91	70	5.33	5.31	+0.02	5.44
Aug 15 '91	77	5.36	5.34	−0.01	5.48
Aug 22 '91	84	5.40	5.38	....	5.52
Aug 29 '91	91	5.44	5.42	....	5.57
Sep 05 '91	98	5.44	5.42	....	5.59
Sep 12 '91	105	5.43	5.41	−0.01	5.59
Sep 19 '91	112	5.44	5.42	−0.01	5.60
Sep 26 '91	119	5.46	5.44	−0.01	5.62
Oct 03 '91	126	5.49	5.47	−0.01	5.67
Oct 10 '91	133	5.51	5.49	....	5.70
Oct 17 '91	140	5.52	5.50	−0.01	5.71
Oct 24 '91	147	5.53	5.51	....	5.72
Oct 31 '91	154	5.54	5.52	....	5.75
Nov 07 '91	161	5.57	5.55	....	5.79
Nov 14 '91	168	5.56	5.54	−0.01	5.78
Nov 21 '91	175	5.61	5.59	−0.01	5.83
Dec 19 '91	203	5.58	5.56	−0.01	5.80
Jan 16 '92	231	5.59	5.57	−0.01	5.82
Feb 13 '92	259	5.65	5.63	−0.02	5.90
Mar 12 '92	287	5.65	5.63	−0.03	5.93
Apr 09 '92	315	5.71	5.69	−0.01	6.01
Apr 23 '92	329	5.80	5.78	....	6.12
May 07 '92	343	5.74	5.72	....	6.06

GOVT. BONDS & NOTES

Rate	Maturity Mo/Yr	Bid	Asked	Chg.	Ask Yld.
8 3/4	May 91n	100:01	100:03	....	0.00
7 7/8	Jun 91n	100:09	100:11	....	3.73
8 1/4	Jun 91n	100:08	100:10	....	4.44
13 3/4	Jul 91n	101:02	101:04	− 2	4.61
7 3/4	Jul 91n	100:12	100:14	....	5.04
7 1/2	Aug 91n	100:12	100:14	....	5.31
8 3/4	Aug 91n	100:21	100:23	....	5.20
14 7/8	Aug 91n	101:31	102:01	− 2	5.01
8 1/4	Aug 91n	100:19	100:21	....	5.50
8 3/8	Sep 91n	100:28	100:30	....	5.46
9 1/8	Sep 91n	101:03	101:05	− 1	5.54
12 1/4	Oct 91n	102:13	102:15	− 1	5.48
7 5/8	Oct 91n	100:24	100:26	....	5.60
6 1/2	Nov 91n	100:08	100:10	....	5.79
8 1/2	Nov 91n	101:05	101:07	− 1	5.76
14 1/4	Nov 91n	103:25	103:27	....	5.63
7 3/4	Nov 91n	100:28	100:30	....	5.83
7 5/8	Dec 91n	100:31	101:01	....	5.81
8 1/4	Dec 91n	101:10	101:12	....	5.83
11 5/8	Jan 92n	103:15	103:17	....	5.82
8 1/8	Jan 92n	101:11	101:15	+ 1	5.87
6 5/8	Feb 92n	100:11	100:13	+ 1	6.04
9 1/8	Feb 92n	102:03	102:05	+ 1	6.00
14 5/8	Feb 92n	106:07	106:09	+ 2	5.54
8 1/2	Feb 92n	101:23	101:25	....	6.05
7 7/8	Mar 92n	101:13	101:15	+ 1	6.05
8 1/2	Mar 92n	101:28	101:30	....	6.09
11 3/4	Apr 92n	104:24	104:26	+ 1	6.04
8 7/8	Apr 92n	102:12	102:14	....	6.11
6 5/8	May 92n	100:13	100:15	....	6.11
9	May 92n	102:17	102:19	+ 1	6.18
13 3/4	May 92n	106:29	106:31	....	6.16
8 1/2	May 92n	102:04	102:06	+ 2	6.22
8 1/4	Jun 92n	102:01	102:03	+ 2	6.23
8 3/8	Jun 92n	102:04	102:06	+ 1	6.26
10 3/8	Jul 92n	104:09	104:11	+ 1	6.33
8	Jul 92n	101:25	101:27	+ 2	6.34
4 1/4	Aug 87-92	94:12	95:12	− 1	8.33
7 1/4	Aug 92	100:29	101:01	....	6.35
7 7/8	Aug 92n	101:19	101:21	+ 2	6.44
8 1/4	Aug 92n	102:01	102:03	+ 2	6.43
8 1/8	Aug 92n	101:31	102:01	+ 1	6.41
8 1/8	Sep 92n	102:01	102:03	+ 1	6.47
8 3/4	Sep 92n	102:26	102:28	+ 1	6.47
9 3/4	Oct 92n	104:04	104:06	+ 1	6.52
7 3/4	Oct 92n	101:17	101:19	+ 2	6.56
7 3/4	Nov 92n	101:18	101:20	+ 2	6.56
8 3/8	Nov 92n	102:14	102:16	+ 2	6.55
10 1/2	Nov 92n	105:11	105:13	+ 1	6.56
7 3/8	Nov 92n	101:03	101:05	+ 2	6.55
7 1/4	Dec 92n	100:28	100:30	+ 1	6.62
9 1/8	Dec 92n	103:21	103:23	+ 2	6.62
8 3/4	Jan 93n	103:04	103:06	....	6.65
7	Jan 93n	100:15	100:17	+ 3	6.66
4	Feb 88-93	93:30	94:30	....	7.19
6 3/4	Feb 93	100:02	100:10	+ 3	6.55
7 7/8	Feb 93	101:30	102:06	+ 2	6.51
8 1/4	Feb 93n	102:14	102:16	+ 1	6.68
8 3/8	Feb 93n	102:20	102:22	+ 1	6.69
10 7/8	Feb 93n	106:21	106:23	+ 2	6.66
6 3/4	Feb 93n	100:01	100:03	+ 2	6.69
7 1/8	Mar 93n	100:22	100:24	+ 3	6.68
9 5/8	Mar 93n	104:29	104:31	+ 1	6.71
7 3/8	Apr 93n	101:06	101:08	+ 2	6.66
7	Apr 93n	100:18	100:20	+ 2	6.65
7 5/8	May 93n	101:17	101:19	+ 2	6.74
8 5/8	May 93n	103:10	103:12	+ 2	6.76
10 1/8	May 93n	106:02	106:04	+ 2	6.74
6 3/4	May 93n*	100:05	100:06	+ 2	6.65
8 1/8	Jun 93n	102:17	102:19	+ 2	6.77
7 1/4	Jul 93n	100:27	100:29	+ 1	6.79
7 1/2	Aug 88-93	101:06	101:10	+ 2	6.85
8	Aug 93n	102:06	102:08	+ 1	6.89
8 5/8	Aug 93	103:17	103:21	+ 2	6.82
8 3/4	Aug 93n	103:23	103:25	+ 1	6.88
11 7/8	Aug 93n	110:02	110:04	+ 1	6.87
8 1/4	Sep 93n	102:27	102:29	+ 2	6.88
7 1/8	Oct 93n	100:14	100:16	+ 2	6.89
7 3/4	Nov 93n	101:23	101:25	+ 2	6.95
8 5/8	Nov 93	103:23	103:27	+ 2	6.90
9	Nov 93n	104:16	104:18	+ 2	6.95
11 3/4	Nov 93n	110:18	110:20	+ 1	6.97
7 5/8	Dec 93n	101:14	101:16	+ 2	6.98
7	Jan 94n	99:31	100:01	+ 2	6.99
6 7/8	Feb 94n	99:19	99:21	+ 1	7.02
8 7/8	Feb 94n	104:13	104:15	+ 2	7.04
9	Feb 94	104:23	104:27	+ 1	7.01
8 1/2	Mar 94n	103:19	103:21	+ 2	7.06
7	Apr 94n	99:27	99:29	+ 2	7.04
4 1/8	May 89-94	94:04	95:04	....	5.95
7	May 94n	99:27	99:29	+ 3	7.04
9 1/2	May 94n	106:06	106:08	....	7.12
13 1/8	May 94n	115:29	115:31	+ 1	7.05
8 1/2	Jun 94n	103:21	103:23	+ 2	7.14
8	Jul 94n	102:10	102:12	+ 1	7.14
8 5/8	Aug 94n	103:31	104:01	+ 1	7.20
8 3/4	Aug 94	104:13	104:17	+ 1	7.15
12 5/8	Aug 94n	115:09	115:11	+ 1	7.19
8 1/2	Sep 94n	103:20	103:22	+ 3	7.24
9 1/2	Oct 94n	106:15	106:17	+ 2	7.28
8 1/4	Nov 94n	102:27	102:29	+ 2	7.28
10 1/8	Nov 94	108:18	108:22	+ 2	7.24
11 5/8	Nov 94n	113:01	113:03	+ 2	7.28
7 5/8	Dec 94n	101:01	101:03	+ 2	7.27
8 5/8	Jan 95n	103:29	103:31	+ 1	7.36
3	Feb 95	92:31	93:31	....	4.79
7 3/4	Feb 95n	101:05	101:07	+ 2	7.37
10 1/2	Feb 95	109:28	110:00	− 1	7.37
11 1/4	Feb 95n	112:09	112:11	+ 1	7.39
8 3/8	Apr 95n	103:03	103:05	+ 2	7.42
8 1/2	May 95n	103:17	103:19	+ 2	7.44
10 3/8	May 95	109:25	109:29	+ 4	7.44
11 1/4	May 95n	112:22	112:24	+ 3	7.47
12 5/8	May 95	117:11	117:15	+ 3	7.45
8 7/8	Jul 95n	104:22	104:24	+ 2	7.52
8 1/2	Aug 95n	103:16	103:18	+ 6	7.50
10 1/2	Aug 95n	110:14	110:16	+ 4	7.55
8 5/8	Oct 95n	103:26	103:28	+ 4	7.57
8 1/2	Nov 95n	103:12	103:14	+ 3	7.58
9 1/2	Nov 95n	107:02	107:04	+ 4	7.59
11 1/2	Nov 95	114:14	114:18	+ 3	7.59
9 1/4	Jan 96n	106:04	106:06	+ 3	7.64
7 1/2	Jan 96n	99:19	99:21	+ 6	7.59
7 7/8	Feb 96n	100:28	100:30	+ 3	7.62
8 7/8	Feb 96n	104:25	104:27	+ 3	7.63
7 1/2	Feb 96n	99:15	99:17	+ 3	7.62
7 3/4	Mar 96n	100:10	100:12	+ 3	7.66
9 3/8	Apr 96n	106:22	106:24	+ 5	7.69
7 5/8	Apr 96n	99:25	99:27	+ 3	7.66
7 3/8	May 96n	98:22	98:24	+ 4	7.68
7 5/8	May 96n*	99:27	99:28	+ 3	7.66
7 7/8	Jul 96n	100:21	100:23	+ 5	7.70
8	Oct 96n	101:02	101:04	+ 5	7.74
7 1/4	Nov 96n	97:23	97:25	+ 5	7.76
8	Jan 97n	100:27	100:29	+ 5	7.80
8 1/2	Apr 97n	102:31	103:01	+ 5	7.85
8 1/2	May 97n	102:30	103:00	+ 5	7.86
8 1/2	Jul 97n	102:29	102:31	+ 6	7.88
8 5/8	Aug 97n	103:16	103:18	+ 7	7.89
8 3/4	Oct 97n	104:02	104:04	+ 6	7.91
8 7/8	Nov 97n	104:22	104:24	+ 6	7.92
7 7/8	Jan 98n	99:23	99:25	+ 7	7.92
8 1/8	Feb 98n	100:31	101:01	+ 6	7.92
7 7/8	Apr 98n	99:24	99:26	+ 6	7.91
7	May 93-98	94:31	95:07	+ 5	7.91
9	May 98n	105:11	105:13	+ 7	7.97
9 1/4	Aug 98n	106:21	106:23	+ 6	8.01
3 1/2	Nov 98	93:09	94:09	− 6	4.41
8 7/8	Nov 98n	104:22	104:24	+ 7	8.02
8 7/8	Feb 99n	104:23	104:25	+ 8	8.03
8 1/2	May 94-99	102:03	102:11	+ 6	7.60
9 1/8	May 99n	106:03	106:07	+ 7	8.05
8	Aug 99n	99:22	99:24	+ 7	8.04
7 7/8	Nov 99n	98:24	98:28	+ 7	8.06
7 7/8	Feb 95-00	98:21	98:25	+10	8.07
8 1/2	Feb 00n	102:12	102:14	+ 8	8.10
8 7/8	May 00n	104:22	104:24	+ 7	8.12
8 3/8	Aug 95-00	101:07	101:11	+ 3	7.99
8 3/4	Aug 00n	103:30	104:00	+ 7	8.12
8 1/2	Nov 00n	102:12	102:14	+ 7	8.13
7 3/4	Feb 01n	97:23	97:25	+ 8	8.08
11 3/4	Feb 01	123:29	124:05	+ 5	8.11
8	May 01n	99:18	99:20	+ 8	8.06
13 1/8	May 01	133:22	133:30	+10	8.10
8	Aug 96-01	99:14	99:22	+ 6	8.05
13 3/8	Aug 01	135:21	135:29	+ 6	8.13
15 3/4	Nov 01	152:26	153:02	....	8.12
14 1/4	Feb 02	142:25	143:01	+ 3	8.15
11 5/8	Nov 02	124:31	125:07	+ 7	8.19
10 3/4	Feb 03	118:16	118:24	+ 8	8.23
10 3/4	May 03	118:21	118:29	+ 9	8.24
11 1/8	Aug 03	121:18	121:26	+ 8	8.26
11 7/8	Nov 03	127:16	127:24	+ 9	8.27
12 3/8	May 04	131:29	132:05	+10	8.28
13 3/4	Aug 04	143:03	143:07	+ 9	8.30
11 5/8	Nov 04	126:09	126:13	+10	8.33
8 1/4	May 00-05	100:21	100:25	+18	8.13
12	May 05	129:23	129:27	+ 8	8.34
10 3/4	Aug 05	119:18	119:22	+10	8.36
9 3/8	Feb 06	109:05	109:09	+10	8.27
7 5/8	Feb 02-07	94:23	94:27	+10	8.22
7 7/8	Nov 02-07	96:25	96:29	+10	8.22
8 3/8	Aug 03-08	100:22	100:26	+ 9	8.27
8 3/4	Nov 03-08	103:07	103:11	+10	8.31
9 1/8	May 04-09	106:00	106:04	+10	8.34
10 3/8	Nov 04-09	115:11	115:15	+12	8.43
11 3/4	Feb 05-10	126:15	126:19	+11	8.44
10	May 05-10	113:00	113:04	+10	8.39
12 3/4	Nov 05-10	135:14	135:18	+10	8.44
13 7/8	May 06-11	145:17	145:21	+11	8.44
14	Nov 06-11	147:11	147:15	+12	8.44
10 3/8	Nov 07-12	116:22	116:26	+11	8.46
12	Aug 08-13	131:17	131:21	+12	8.47
13 1/4	May 09-14	143:21	143:25	+12	8.46
12 1/2	Aug 09-14	137:03	137:07	+13	8.46
11 3/4	Nov 09-14	130:19	130:23	+12	8.44
11 1/4	Feb 15	128:27	128:31	+11	8.41
10 5/8	Aug 15	122:20	122:24	+11	8.41
9 7/8	Nov 15	115:06	115:10	+11	8.39
9 1/4	Feb 16	108:23	108:27	+11	8.40
7 1/4	May 16	88:10	88:12	+10	8.37
7 1/2	Nov 16	90:25	90:27	+ 9	8.38
8 3/4	May 17	103:27	103:29	+11	8.38
8 7/8	Aug 17	105:04	105:06	+11	8.38
9 1/8	May 18	108:01	108:03	+10	8.36
9	Nov 18	106:27	106:29	+11	8.35
8 7/8	Feb 19	105:17	105:19	+11	8.35
8 1/8	Aug 19	97:19	97:21	+10	8.34
8 1/2	Feb 20	101:24	101:26	+11	8.33
8 3/4	May 20	104:24	104:26	+12	8.31
8 3/4	Aug 20	104:22	104:24	+11	8.31
7 7/8	Feb 21	95:09	95:11	+11	8.30
8 1/8	May 21	98:08	98:10	+ 8	8.28

SOURCE: *Wall Street Journal,* May 29, 1991, p. C15.

age for five-year Treasury securities.[8] Series EE bonds must be held at least five years to qualify for market-based rates. The current minimum yield on these bonds (held five years or longer) is 6 percent. Fourth, the initial price of the bond can be as little as $50 or as much as $10,000. The face value is al-

[8] Older Series E and EE bonds issued before November 1982 earn market-based interest rates, beginning with their first interest date on or after November 1, 1987.

ways twice the purchase price, but the investor may receive more or less than the face value, depending on the length of time the security is held. Another difference between savings bonds and other U.S. government securities is that savings bonds cannot be redeemed within six months after the initial purchase, except in an emergency. Finally, savings bonds offer less liquidity because interest is credited only semiannually; thus, an investor would lose interest if he or she redeemed the security prior to an interest payment date.[9]

U.S. savings bonds are similar to other government securities in that both are free of credit (default) risk. Income from both types of securities is exempt from state and local taxes but is subject to federal taxes. Savings bonds have two added tax advantages: (1) investors can defer the federal tax on the accrued interest until the bond is redeemed, and (2) interest is tax-free on Series EE bonds if they are used to pay for the cost of higher education. The first tax advantage may be an especially attractive feature to investors approaching retirement since their tax bracket may be considerably lower after retirement. Series EE bonds can be exchanged for **Series HH bonds** that pay semiannual interest. The Series HH bonds are designed to appeal to retired individuals who may need the semiannual coupons.

• Federal Agency and Miscellaneous Securities

Federal agency securities differ from Treasury securities in that they are not issued by the federal government. In one case (the Government National Mortgage Association), however, the securities are backed by the full credit of the U.S. government. With the exception of the guaranteed securities, these bonds have slightly more default risk and as a consequence offer slightly higher yields than Treasury securities.

Among the largest and fastest-growing groups of agency issues are **mortgage-backed** securities. These securities are collateralized by pools of mortgages. The major agencies that issue mortgage-backed securities are the **Federal National Mortgage Association** (**FNMA** or **"Fannie Mae"**), the **Government National Mortgage Association** (**GNMA** or **"Ginnie Mae"**), and the **Federal Home Loan Mortgage Corporation** (**FHLMC** or **"Freddie Mac"**). All three of these agencies were created by the federal government to increase available funds for mortgages.

Ginnie Mae is the largest of the three and is a government-owned corporation. Its mortgage-backed securities are known as Ginnie Maes and are backed by the full faith and credit of the U.S. government. The mortgages behind the Ginnie Maes are insured by the Federal Housing Administration (FHA) or the Veterans' Administration (VA). The minimum denomination of these securities is $25,000, and they pay interest and principal payments on a monthly basis.

---

[9] Additional facts are available in a brochure, "U.S. Savings Bonds: The Great American Investment," published by the Treasury. Current yields are available by calling 1-800-US-BONDS.

Freddie Mac is a federally chartered agency and guarantees the conventional mortgage pool through *participation certificates*. These securities, unlike those issued by Ginnie Mae, are not officially backed by the federal government. As a result, they have slightly more credit risk, but they are still considered extremely safe.

Fannie Mae, though federally chartered and sponsored, is a privately owned corporation; its common stock is traded on the New York Stock Exchange. While the corporation guarantees the conventional mortgage pool behind each note and bond, its securities are not backed by the U.S. government. Fannie Mae provides liquidity for mortgage-lending institutions by purchasing residential mortgages.

All of these securities are highly liquid and are considered quite safe, with Ginnie Maes having essentially no credit risk. All of them provide yields in excess of those on U.S. Treasury securities. One potential problem with these securities is the *pass-through* feature that allows the interest and principal from the mortgages to pass through (be paid) to the bond investors. The pass-through payments include a partial repayment of principal that can vary considerably from period to period. If the principal is repaid more quickly than anticipated, for example, the interest portion or coupon receipt declines. A mortgage may be paid off early or may be paid because the property is sold or damaged; in either case, the investor is subject to *prepayment risk*. The investor is usually unable to anticipate these prepayments and as a consequence will have uncertain cash flows. Typically, the principal prepayment rates are 6–10 percent per year.

Other popular agency securities that are either owned or sponsored by the federal government include the Federal Farm Credit Banks, Student Loan Marketing Association, World Bank, Federal Land Banks, and Federal Home Loan Banks. Quotations on these securities are given in the *Wall Street Journal* and *Barron's* on the same page and in the same format as the Treasury and agency issues.

• Municipal Securities

States, counties, cities, and other governmental units also issue bonds to finance public needs. These types of securities are classified under the general category of **municipals.** These securities have a greater risk of default than Treasury or agency securities and therefore offer higher after-tax yields.

One very attractive aspect of municipals is that their interest is generally exempt from federal income taxes, although any short-term or long-term capital gain (loss) realized on the security is subject to federal income taxes. The interest is also generally exempt from state and local taxes if the bond is issued by the investor's state of domicile. This favorable tax treatment makes municipals attractive to many individual investors.

Many investors have great confidence in the creditworthiness of municipal issuers. It should be pointed out, however, that there have been infrequent but very significant defaults and near-defaults on municipal securities. Two

• **INTEREST BOX**

How Bond Managers Adjust to a Changing Bond Market

Many bond managers are finding the bond market a different—and more challenging—place to work:

> Ah, the good old days. That pleasant time when a bond manager started his day taking down some new Treasuries at the opening, moving over to the mortgage desk to trade some Ginnie Maes, then maybe, after a call from the street, swapping two telephone bonds to pick up a few basis points. You had to use yield-curve judgment to control overall portfolio maturity, of course, and do a bit of credit work on some of the corporate names, but it was all pretty straightforward stuff.
>
> A far cry from the harried life of today's bond manager. He may have adjusted to the market's untoward volatility by now, but he certainly isn't used to event risk, as American industry turns itself upside down and inside out.

Another big problem for bond managers is all the new bond securities being created. "Wall Street bankers seem intent on collateralizing just about everything in sight and slicing and dicing bonds into strange securities that are horrendous to evaluate." New securities have surfaced in all types of bonds including the following:

1. Mortgage-backed bonds with prepayment possibilities, various cash-flow tranches, variable rate securities, and interest-and-principal-only securities.
2. Junk bonds, with event risk occurring because of takeovers and levereged buyouts, account for almost 30 percent of all corporate bonds traded.
3. Municipal bonds with nuclear decommissioning trusts.

Bond managers are coping with this more complex environment in several ways:

1. *Specializing.* Every bond firm cannot be a leader in every aspect of the bond market anymore.
2. *Improving their research.* Many firms are relying more on internal research than on street research.
3. *Adding in-house quantitative analysts.* "Quants," many of them fresh from academia, are in hot demand by many bond houses.
4. *Building proprietary models.* New computer models are needed to analyze many of the newer, more complex bond securities.

SOURCE: Adapted from Julie Rohrer, "Why Bond Managers Are Going Gray," *Institutional Investor,* May 1989, pp. 171–78.

of the most dramatic defaults were by New York City and the Washington Public Power Supply System (frequently referred to as WHOOPS rather than WPPSS).[10]

[10]For a discussion of the factors that determine the creditworthiness of municipals, see Jack L. Treynor, "On the Quality of Municipal Bonds," *Financial Analysts Journal* (May-June 1982): 25–30. For an analysis of the WPPSS crisis, see John W. Peavy III and George H. Hempel, "The Effect of the WPPSS Crisis on the Tax-exempt Bond Market," *Journal of Financial Research* (Fall 1987): 239–47.

Because of the defaults and near-defaults of the 1970s and 1980s, a number of private companies, like the Municipal Bond Insurance Association, insure municipal bonds. The insurance, obtained by the issuer, guarantees the payment of interest and principal to the investor. The insurance essentially eliminates the risk of default and causes a low-quality bond to be viewed as high quality. Since insured municipals are more attractive to investors, their liquidity is higher because the secondary market is more active.

Due to the favorable tax treatment and relatively low probability of default, many investors (primarily those in high tax brackets) devote part of their portfolios to municipals. Historically, most municipals were not registered (bearer bonds) and therefore required the investor to clip semiannually the coupons attached to the bond in order to receive the interest. Banks and other financial institutions usually accepted the coupons much as they would accept a check for deposit. Since 1981, however, new issues of municipals must be registered to receive tax-exempt status.

One potential problem for investors in municipals who follow a very passive or buy-and-hold strategy concerns the possibility of a *call* by the issuer. The call feature essentially allows the issuer to force the investor to sell the bond back at a predetermined price specified when the bond is initially sold. As some consolation to the investor, the price paid by the issuer is usually greater than the face value of the bond. This difference is referred to as the *call premium*. During the high interest rate period of 1981–1985, the vast majority of municipals issued allowed the issuer to call the bond before maturity.[11] During periods of falling interest rates, many states and municipalities may elect to exercise the call feature. Since the call premium declines over time, however, call risk exists even during periods of increasing interest rates.

Since most of the bonds issued before 1981 are unregistered, an issuer has no way to notify the investors directly when a call feature is exercised. Thus, most issuers resort to using some form of advertisement to advise investors of the redemptions. The advertisements often list the serial numbers of the affected bonds. Investors who do not follow the financial news closely are often unaware that their bonds have been called.[12] This can be costly to the investor, since the issuer stops paying interest on the called bonds. The call also denies the individual the opportunity to follow a buy-and-hold investment strategy since the proceeds from the call must be reinvested at rates that are often lower than the coupon rate on the called bonds.

There are two major types of municipal bonds: **general obligation** and **revenue:**

1. General obligation municipals This type of municipal bond is backed by the general or total taxing power of the municipality. They are also called

[11] One recent study found that 90 percent of a random sample of 160 municipals had a call feature.

[12] "Some Municipal Investors Get Nasty Surprises When the Bonds Are Called in Early by Issuers," *Wall Street Journal*, May 16, 1983, p. 58.

full-faith-and-credit bonds because all the taxing authority and tax revenues of the issuer can be used to satisfy the interest and principal payments.

2. Revenue bonds The funds used to pay the principal and interest of revenue bonds are derived from specific municipality-owned projects such as hospitals, waterworks, or sewerage systems. Only revenue from the specified project can be used to service the bonds. Revenue bonds are now the most commonly issued municipals. Because of their higher default risk, however, revenue bonds are more likely to be insured than general obligation municipals.

• Corporate Bonds

Bonds issued by corporations are often grouped under the general category of **corporates.** Corporates, as a general class of bonds, have more default risk than government agency or municipal bonds and therefore offer higher returns.

Most corporate bonds are traded in the over-the-counter (OTC) market, unless the issuing firm has its stock listed on the New York Stock Exchange (NYSE) or American Stock Exchange (AMEX). In these instances, the bonds are traded on the bond annex of the NYSE or the AMEX. An example of quotations from the *Wall Street Journal* appears in Table 10.3. In contrast to Treasury notes and bonds that are quoted in points and $\frac{1}{32}$ of a point, the prices for corporates are quoted in points and $\frac{1}{8}$ of a point. For example, consider the second Alabama Power (AlaP) bond in Table 10.3; its quote of $96\frac{3}{8}$ indicates a price of \$963.75, i.e., $[(96 + \frac{3}{8}) \times 10]$, since each point is \$10 for a bond with a face value of \$1,000.

Notice that the information in Table 10.3 gives the coupon rate and year of maturity directly after the abbreviated corporate name. Exact interest payment and maturity dates can be found in publications such as Moody's *Corporate Bond Manual*. The "cur yld," or *current yield*, is calculated by dividing the annual interest by the closing price. This represents only a "partial" rate of return, however, because any price change occurring after the bond's purchase is ignored. For the Alabama Power bond, the current yield is 8.8 percent. The "vol," or volume, indicates the number of bonds that were traded on the particular day, or a total of 5 for the Alabama Power bonds. Finally, the "net chg" represents the change in the "close" from the previous day. For the Alabama Power bond, the change from the previous day's close was $\frac{1}{8}$ or \$1.25.

• Comparison of Yields by Types of Bonds

Because of differences in risk and tax treatment of income, different categories of bonds should be priced to provide appropriate returns. This point is illustrated in Figure 10.2, which provides the yields over the period 1946–1991 for municipals, Treasuries, and corporate bonds. Notice the inverted scale on the yield axis. As expected, the yield on Treasuries is below the municipal

TABLE 10.3 • Quotations for New York Stock Exchange Bonds

CORPORATION BONDS
Volume, $42,920,000

Bonds	Cur Yld	Vol	Close	Net Chg.
AForP 5s30r	9.5	10	52½	+ 1¾
AL Lb 7¾14	cv	5	121⅞	– ⅛
AbbtL 9.2s99	9.1	6	101½	– 1
Advst 9s08	cv	15	75½	– 1½
AlaP 9s2000	9.0	20	100½	...
AlaP 8½s01	8.8	5	96⅜	+ ⅛
AlaP 9¾s04	9.5	10	103	+ ⅜
AlaP 8⅞s06	9.1	7	98	– 1½
AlskAr zr06	...	35	33½	+ ¼
AlldC zr98	...	60	53	– 1
AlldC zr2000	...	55	42⅞	– ⅛
AlldC zr9	...	10	84½	+ ¾
AlldC zr01	...	25	40½	+ 1½
AlldC zr03	...	5	31½	...
AlldC zr05	...	65	26¾	+ ¾
AlldC zr09	...	80	18¼	+ ¼
Amax 9.23s95	9.4	35	98⅝	+ ⅝
ABrnd 9⅛16	9.3	21	98	...
ATT 5⅝95	6.0	21	93	+ ¾
ATT 6s00	7.2	31	83¼	...
ATT 5⅛01	6.7	34	76⅞	+ ⅞
ATT 7s01	7.8	32	89⅜	+ ⅝
ATT 7⅛03	8.1	86	87⅞	+ ⅛
ATT 8.80s05	8.7	297	101¼	+ ⅛
ATT 8⅝s07	8.7	303	99⅜	+ ⅛
ATT 8¾00	8.6	161	101¾	– ¼
ATT 8⅝26	9.1	124	94⅜	+ ⅛
vjAmes 7½14f	cv	50	11	...
Amoco 9.2s04	9.2	19	100½	+ ⅜
Amoco 7⅞96	7.9	10	100	+ ⅝
Amoco 8⅝16	8.8	62	98⅛	+ ¼
AmocoCda 7⅜13	6.6	165	112	+ 1
Ancp 13⅞02f	cv	12	94	...
Andarko 6¼14	6.4	45	98	+ ½
Anhr 8s96	8.0	20	100⅝	+ ⅝
Anhr 8⅝16	9.1	15	94⅞	...
Apache 7½00	cv	1	102½	– ½
ArizP 10⅝00	10.3	1	102⅞	+ ¼
Arml 8½01	11.8	10	72⅛	– 1⅛
Arml 13½94	13.5	7	100	– ¾
AshO 6¾14	cv	10	87	...
ARich 7.7s00	8.1	5	95½	...
ARch 10⅜95	9.7	10	107½	– ½
ARch 10⅞05	9.5	10	115	– 3¼
ARch 9⅜96	9.2	10	102¾	– ¼
AubrnHl 15⅞20	23.2	676	68½	– ⅜
Avnet 8s13	cv	1	92	– 2
Avnet 6s12	cv	10	86	– ¾
BRE 9⅛08	cv	131	97⅛	– ⅞
Ballys 6s98f	cv	35	32⅝	...
Bally 10s06f	cv	204	39¼	+ ¾
BalGE 9⅛16	9.3	5	98⅜	+ ⅛
Banka 8⅞05	9.1	25	97⅛	...
Bkam 8.35s07	9.0	32	92½	+ ¼
Bkam zr92	...	48	90⅜	+ ¼
Bkam zr93	...	10	85⅞	+ ½
Barnt 8½99	9.1	31	93¼	+ 1⅛
BellPa 8⅝06	8.7	1	98¾	+ ⅛
BellPa 7⅛12	8.6	5	83¼	...
BellPa 9⅝14	9.3	30	103	...
BellPa 8¾15	8.8	5	99½	– ¾
BellPa 9⅛19	9.2	25	100½	+ ½
BenCp 8.3s03	9.0	10	92¼	– ⅝
BrkHa zr04	...	10	46¼	...
BethSt 9s00	10.0	69	90⅛	...
BethSt 8.45s05	10.5	64	80⅝	...
Bevrly 7⅝03	cv	18	78½	– ½
BlkD 8⅜97	9.4	20	89	– ⅞
BlkBst zr04	...	6	32⅜	+ ⅜
Boeing 8⅜96	8.3	20	101½	...
BoisC 7s16	cv	16	81½	+ 1
BwnSh 9¼05	cv	44	85	...
BwnFer 6¼12	cv	93	90¼	+ ½
BurNo 9s16	9.5	40	94½	+ 1⅞
CBS 10⅞95	10.4	35	104⅛	– ⅝
CIGNA 8.2s10	cv	129	98	– 1
CNA 8½95	8.6	10	99	+ ½
CSX 9½16	9.3	4	101⅝	– 1⅞
Carolco 14s93	19.5	81	71¾	+ 1¾
CaroFrt 6¼11	cv	4	69⅜	– ⅛
vjCarHaw 12½02f	...	69	17½	+ 1½
CtrlTel 8s96	8.2	5	98	...
CPoWV 9s15	9.2	20	97¾	– ½
Champ 6½11	cv	34	96½	+ 1¼
ChartC 12s99	12.9	2	93	...
ChsCp 8.20s99t	8.4	5	97⅝	– ⅜
ChsCp 7⅜94	7.6	5	96½	+ ¼
CPoM 8⅞09	9.0	5	99	– ½
Chvrn 8½95	8.4	48	101⅜	+ ¼
Chvrn 5¾92	5.8	25	99¼	+ ⅜
Chvrn 7s96	7.3	56	95⅜	– ⅝
Chvrn 8¾96	8.6	60	101⅞	...
Chvrn 9⅜16	9.2	10	101⅞	...
Chiquta 9⅛98	9.2	4	98⅞	+ 1⅜
Chiquta 11⅞03	11.7	145	101½	– ½
Chiquta 10½04	11.2	193	94	– 1⅞
Chiquta 10¼05	10.4	25	98¾	+ 1¾
ChryF 8.35s91	8.4	4	99⅞	+ ⅝
ChryF 9.30s94	10.3	108	90½	+ ½
ChryF 13¼99	13.3	70	99⅞	...
ChryF 12¾99	12.7	7	100¾	+ ¾
ChryF 12s92	11.9	190	100½	...
ChryF 7⅞91	7.9	87	99¼	...
ChryF 8⅜97	10.6	94	79	+ 1⅜
ChryF 8⅛94	9.0	129	90¼	...
Chryslr 12¾92	12.8	254	100	...
Chryslr 13s97	17.3	366	75	+ ½
Chryslr 12s15	18.6	1401	64⅝	+ 1⅝
Chryslr 9.6s94	12.6	302	76	...
Chryslr 10.95s17	18.4	133	59⅝	+ 1⅞
Chryslr 10.4s99	16.1	177	64¾	+ 1¾
ChvrnC 12s94	11.8	38	101¾	– ⅝
ChvrnC 10¾95	10.3	10	104	– 1
vjCircK 12¾97f	...	26	24	+ ¼
vjCircK 13s97f	...	100	6	...
CitiPP 12½96	cv	60	101	+ ¼
Citicp 8.45s07	9.4	34	90¼	– ¼
Citicp 8⅛07	9.3	122	87⅛	+ ⅜
Clmt zrD93	...	11	78	– 1¼
ClevEl 8¾05	9.3	12	94⅛	– ⅞
ClevEl 8¾11	9.1	8	91⅞	+ 2¼
ClevEl 8⅜12	9.4	10	89½	– 1⅛
Coastl 11¼96	10.7	10	105½	+ ¾
Coastl 11¾06	10.8	37	109	+ ½
ColuG 9⅛95	9.1	9	100⅛	+ ⅛
Cmdis 9.65s02	10.2	6	94¾	+ 1
CmwE 7⅝03F	8.5	1	89½	+ ¼
CmwE 8s03	8.6	25	92¾	+ ¼
CmwE 8¾05	8.9	25	98	+ ½
CmwE 9⅛08	9.0	3	100⅞	+ ⅞
CmwE 11¾15	10.6	5	110⅜	+ 1¼
ConrPer 6¾01	cv	116	94½	+ 1
Consec 12½96	12.5	40	99¾	– ¼
Consec 12¾97	13.2	175	96⅞	– ⅝
ConEd 9⅜00	9.2	55	102⅛	– ½
ConEd 7.9s02	8.5	35	93⅜	– ⅛
ConEd 8.4s03	8.6	11	97⅜	+ ⅛
ConEd 9⅛04	9.0	5	101½	+ ⅛
ConNG 7¼15	cv	50	98¼	+ ⅞
CnPw 6⅞98	7.7	5	89	– ⅞
CnPw 8⅛01	8.7	30	92⅞	+ ⅜
CtlOil 7½99	8.0	10	94¼	...
CoopCo 10⅝05	cv	20	75	+ ¼
CritAc 11½15	11.2	6	102½	– ½
CumE zr05	...	12	27½	...
Dana dc5⅞06	cv	1	73½	...
Datpnt 8⅞06	cv	44	33	+ 1
DeereCa 9.35s03	9.4	25	100	– 2
DetEd 6s96	6.6	5	90½	+ ½
DetEd 9.15s00	9.1	21	100¾	+ ¼
DetEd 8⅛01	8.6	20	94	+ ¾
DetEd 7⅜01	8.3	10	89	– 1
DetEd 7½03	8.6	2	87½	– 1
DetEd 9⅞04	9.6	6	103⅜	+ ½
Disney zr05	...	211	45	– ⅛
DmBk 7¾96	8.8	10	88½	+ 2½
Dow 8⅞2000	8.8	10	101	+ ⅞
Dow 8.92000	8.8	16	100¾	+ ⅛
Dow 7⅞07	8.7	25	90½	+ ¼
Dow 8⅝08	9.0	19	96⅛	...
duPnt 8.45s04	8.7	22	97½	...
duPnt 8½06	8.7	20	97¾	...
duPnt dc6s01	7.3	128	81¾	+ ½
duPnt 8½16	9.1	23	93¾	+ ¼
duPnt zr10	cv	54	24½	+ ¼
DukeP 7¾02	8.4	5	92¾	– ¼
DukeP 7⅜02	8.2	10	90⅜	...
DukeP 8⅛03	8.5	10	95⅝	+ 1⅛
DukeP 9⅜08	9.1	20	102¾	+ ¾
DukeP 10⅛09	9.6	10	105	– 1
EKod 8⅝16	9.3	48	93	+ ¼
EmbSuit 11s99	11.3	5	97½	+ ¼
Enron 10¾98	10.2	10	105½	– 1½
Ens 10s01	cv	28	102¼	– ¾
EnvSys 6¾11	cv	5	71	– 1
EqutR 9s96	9.0	5	99⅞	+ ⅜
vjEqutc 10s04	cv	1	2¾	– ¼
Exxon 6s97	6.7	15	89	– ¼
ExxP 8¼01	8.3	25	99¾	+ ¾
ExxP 6⅝98	7.1	5	93⅝	– ⅜
FMC 9½2000	9.6	12	99	...
vjFairfd 13⅛92	...	35	28	+ 1½
Fldcst 6s12	cv	115	45	– ¾
FleetFn 8½10	cv	15	125	+ 1
Flemg 6½96	cv	13	99¼	– ¾
Flwr 8¼05	cv	53	105	+ 1
FrdC 8.7s99	8.7	10	99½	– ⅛
FrdC 8⅜01	8.8	30	95¼	+ ⅝
FreptM 10⅞01	10.7	80	101½	– 1
Frpt dc6.55s01	cv	25	84	+ ½
Fuqua 9½98	10.9	24	87½	...
GMA 8s93M	8.0	58	100¼	+ ⅛
GMA 7¼95	7.5	15	97	+ ¼
GMA 7⅛92	7.1	135	99⅞	+ ⅛
GMA 7.85s98	8.3	35	94½	...
GMA 8⅞99	8.9	44	99⅝	– ½
GMA 8¾s00	8.8	28	99¼	...
GMA 8¾s01	8.9	150	98½	...
GMA 8⅛96	8.3	8	98⅜	– ⅛
GMA 8s07	8.9	2	90⅛	+ ⅝
GMA 8¼06	8.9	10	92¼	+ ⅜
GMA dc6s11	8.6	144	69¾	...
GMA zr15	...	8	105¾	– ¼
GMA 10⅜95	10.0	10	103½	+ ⅜
GMA 8⅞96	8.8	330	100⅝	+ ⅛
GMA 8¼16	9.3	65	88¼	+ ⅝
GMA 8s93J	8.0	54	100½	+ ⅛
GMA 8s93O	8.0	100	100⅝	+ ⅛
GMA 8s94	8.0	100	100¼	+ ⅛
GTE 9⅜99	9.1	9	103	– 1
GnCorp 12⅜03	13.1	66	94½	+ 1½
GnDyn 9s16	9.8	30	92¼	+ ¾
GnEl 7½96	7.6	15	99	+ 1¼
GnEl 8¼04	8.5	69	99¾	...
Gene dc9¾93	10.1	9	96⅞	...
Genrad 7¼11	cv	1	43¾	– ¼
GaGlf 15s00	13.7	79	109⅛	+ 1
GaPw 11⅝00	11.0	18	105⅝	– ⅝
GaPw 10½09	10.1	15	104	...
GaPw 11s09	10.8	115	102	+ ⅛
GaPw 10s16J	9.8	15	102½	– 1¼
GaPac 13½94	13.1	20	103	+ ⅝
GdNgF 13¼95	18.7	533	71	+ 2
Gdrch 8¼94	8.3	25	99½	...
Gdyr 8.6s95	8.9	13	96½	– 1½
Gdyr 7.35s97	8.4	23	88	...
Grace zr06	...	1	30¾	+ ¼
GreyF zr94	...	48	74½	– ⅛
Grumn 9¼96	9.6	10	99¼	+ 1
Grumn 10½11	10.7	68	97⅞	– ⅛
GlfRes 12½04	18.9	25	66	– 1½
HalIB 10.20s05	10.1	15	101¼	+ 1⅞
Hallb zr06	...	18	38⅜	+ ⅛
HalwdGp 13½09	...	15	82½	– ½
HarDav 7¼15	cv	45	109	...
HeclMn zr04	...	30	29⅛	+ ⅛
HmGrp 14⅞99	15.6	100	95½	– ½
HomFSD 6½11	cv	20	29½	– ½
HmeDep 6s97	cv	13	142½	+ ½
HousF 7¾99	8.4	36	91¾	+ ¼
HousF 9s00	9.2	36	98¼	...
HudFd 8s06	cv	6	74¾	– 5¼
HudFd 14s08	cv	35	107⅛	– 1⅛
Humn 10⅛91	10.1	38	100⅛	...
IICnt 15½94	15.4	10	100⅝	...
IllTWk zr05	cv	2	44	+ ½
Inco 12⅜10	11.9	3	104	+ ½
IndBel 8⅛11	8.7	38	93	+ ½
InldStl 8¾95	8.9	5	97⅞	– ⅛
InldStl 7.9s07	10.0	8	79	– ¾
InspRs 8½12	cv	25	65¼	+ ¼
InMin zr05	...	12	31½	...
Intlgc 11.99s96	29.6	6	40½	+ 1
IBM 9⅜04	9.1	46	102⅞	– ⅝
IBM 7⅞04	cv	179	101¼	– ½
IBM 10¼95	9.8	137	104½	– ½
IBM 9s98	8.6	10	104¼	+ ½
IPap 8.85s00	9.0	25	98⅝	– 1⅜
IPap dc5⅛12	...	57	60⅞	...
IntRec 9s10	cv	122	132	+ 6
IntJh 7¾11	cv	10	55	+ 5
Intnr 11s93	10.8	10	101⅝	+ ½
Jamswy 8s05	cv	60	58	...
K mart 8⅛97	8.2	35	99¼	+ ½
K mart 8⅜17	9.3	65	90½	+ ½
KaufBd zr04	...	14	31¼	...
KerrGl 13s96	13.8	23	93⅞	– ⅝
KogerP 9¼03	cv	4	64½	...
vjLTV 5s88mf	...	6	8	– 1
vjLTV 11s07f	...	15	8	– ½
vjLTV 15s00f	...	33	17¾	...
LoewCp zr04	...	6	41½	...
vjLomF zr01f	...	3	9	– ½
vjLomF 10¾93f	...	40	26⅞	+ ⅜
LglsLt 11½14	11.0	35	105	...
Lorilld 6⅞93	7.1	38	97½	+ ⅛
LouLE 8½00	cv	10	92½	– ½
MACOM 9¼06	cv	35	81½	...
MGMUA 12⅜93f	...	5	59	+ 9½
MGMUA 13s96f	...	258	36¼	– 1¼
MfrH 8⅛04	9.2	4	88	+ 1
Manvl zr03	...	140	53¾	+ ⅜
MarO 8½00	8.8	8	96¼	+ ¾
MarO 8.5s06	9.1	10	93	+ ½
MarO 9½94	9.3	789	102¼	...
MarO 9¾99	9.5	5	102⅝	– ⅜
Masco 5¼12	6.9	23	76½	+ ½
McCro 7½94	24.2	9	31	+ 1
McCro 7¾95	21.5	50	36	– 3
Mcdnl 9¾17	9.5	3	102⅜	...
MeYk 9.1s02	9.3	9	97¾	+ ⅛
Mead 6¾12	cv	10	90	...
MerLy zr06	...	2	31⅜	...
MesaCap 12s96	13.4	76	89¼	+ ¼
MichB 9.6s08	9.3	36	103¾	– ⅛
MichB 8⅛15	8.8	12	92½	– ½
MichB 9⅛18	9.0	46	101⅛	...
MidlBk 11.35s93	12.6	382	89¾	+ 4¼
MdlndAm 12¾03	11.6	10	109⅝	+ 1⅞
MPac 5s45f	...	38	51½	+ ½
Mobil 8½01	8.5	35	100	+ ¼
Mobil 7⅛92	7.1	100	100⅝	+ ⅛
Mobil 8⅜94	8.4	30	103	...
Mobil 8¾91	8.7	10	100¼	+ ¼
MobO 7⅜01	8.2	5	90¼	– ¾
Mons 9⅛00	9.0	4	101⅜	...
MorKnd zr05	...	10	36	– 1
Motrla zr09	...	82	36¼	...
MtSTI 9⅝15	9.4	45	102⅝	+ ⅜
NBD 7¼06	cv	29	102½	– 1
viNBI 8¼07f	cv	2	16	+ 1
NCNB 12⅝96	11.9	105	106¼	– 1¾
NJBTl 7¼11	8.5	8	85	+ ¼
NJBTl 8¼16	8.8	10	93¾	– ⅛
NJBTl 8¾18	8.8	10	98⅞	...
NRUt 9⅜95	9.2	10	101⅜	+ ¾
vjNaco 12s94f	...	100	60	+ 1½
vjNtGyp zr04	...	363	5⅜	+ ⅜
NtEdu 6½11	cv	25	55½	– ½
NMed zr04	...	1	53¾	+ ¼
NavFin 7½94	8.0	16	94	+ ¾
NavFin 11.95s95	11.9	15	100	...
Navstr 9s04	10.2	26	88⅜	– ¼
NYEG 9⅜05	9.4	5	100	...
NiMP 10.2s05	9.9	8	103½	+ ¼
NwnBl 8⅜12	9.1	10	95¼	...
NwnBl 9½16	9.4	65	101	...
Oakwd 6½12	cv	20	87½	+ 2
OcciP dc8.95s94	9.0	10	99⅞	...
OccP dc9.65s94	9.6	272	100⅜	– ¼
OccP 10½93x	10.4	20	101⅛	– ½
OcciP 10⅞96	10.4	20	104½	...
OcciP 11¾11	10.7	15	110¼	...
OcciP 11⅛19	10.3	9	107⅞	+ ¼
OcciP 9⅝99	9.5	345	101½	...
OcciP 10⅛09	9.8	8	103⅝	– ⅛
OcciP 10⅛01	9.7	45	104⅜	– ⅝
OhBIT 7⅞13	8.7	52	90⅝	+ 1¼
OhEd 9½06	9.4	4	101⅛	– ¼
Orion 11s98	35.5	292	31	– 2
Orion 10s99	33.3	74	30	– ⅝
Orion dc10s94	31.3	45	32	+ 2
Oryx 10⅜18	10.4	16	100⅛	– 2¼
Oryx 7½14	cv	85	101	+ ¼
OwCor 9½00	9.5	15	100	...
OxyOG 6⅝99	7.8	63	84¾	+ ⅜
vjPAA 11½94B f	...	33	100½	...
vjPAA dc13½03f	...	125	8	+ ⅛
vjPAA 15s04f	...	534	8⅞	+ ⅜
vjPAA 9s10f	cv	185	6	– 4

Quotations as of 4 p.m. Eastern Time
Tuesday, May 28, 1991

Volume $43,160,000

SALES SINCE JANUARY 1
(000 omitted)

1991	1990	1989
$5,976,882	$4,472,178	$3,005,788

	Domestic Tue.	Domestic Fri.	All Issues Tue.	All Issues Fri.
Issues traded	512	479	516	480
Advances	243	204	243	204
Declines	163	157	165	158
Unchanged	106	118	108	118
New highs	17	20	17	20
New lows	2	3	3	3

Dow Jones Bond Averages

–1990– High	–1990– Low	–1991– High	–1991– Low		–1991– Close	–1991– Chg.	–1991– %Yld	–1990– Close	–1990– Chg.
93.04	88.44	95.06	91.30	20 Bonds	94.97	+0.23	9.03	90.08	– 0.04
94.48	89.23	96.85	93.44	10 Utilities	96.55	+0.10	9.00	91.31	+ 0.01
91.60	86.43	93.40	89.06	10 Industrials	93.40	+0.36	9.05	88.85	– 0.09

EXPLANATORY NOTES
(For New York and American Bonds)

Yield is current yield.

cv-Convertible bond. cf-Certificates. dc-Deep discount. ec-European currency units. f-Dealt in flat. il-Italian lire. kd-Danish kroner. m-Matured bonds, negotiability impaired by maturity. na-No accrual. r-Registered. rp-Reduced principal. st-Stamped. t-Floating rate. wd-When distributed. ww-With warrants. x-Ex interest. xw-Without warrants. zr-Zero coupon.

vj-In bankruptcy or receivership or being reorganized under the Bankruptcy Act, or securities assumed by such companies.

SOURCE: *Wall Street Journal,* May 29, 1991, p. C14.

• **INTEREST BOX**

Takeovers and Buyouts and Corporate Bond Investors

Takeovers and leveraged buyouts (LBO) are having a marked impact on bonds, says one commentator:

> Not so long ago, blue-chip corporate bonds were considered ideal investments for widows and orphans. These days, bonds are so volatile that even sophisticated pros can lose billions on them—overnight. It can happen whenever a company gets caught up in a takeover or management-led buyout. The prospect that the company will have to take on more debt sends its bond prices plummeting. Look what happened last fall to the investment-grade bonds issued by RJR Nabisco, Inc. Their prices dropped a dizzying 20% after management proposed the largest LBO in history.
>
> A number of lawsuits have been filed against the managements of companies involved in takeovers and buyouts. The lawsuit against RJR Nabisco was filed by Metropolitan Life Insurance Company and Jefferson Pilot Life Insurance Company charging that management violated its fiduciary responsibilities to existing bondholders. Traditionally, managers are not fiduciaries for bondholders and are only expected to honor the covenants specified in the indenture or contract between the bondholders and the company.

Bondholders are fighting back in several ways:

1. *Stricter covenants.* New bonds are being issued with covenants that limit losses in any future restructurings. Recent bond issues by Harris Corporation, Northwest Pipeline, and Grumman Corporation have "poison puts" that force the corporation to buy the bonds back if certain events occur.
2. *Control.* Many bondholders are pushing to have more input into corporate decisions so they can share control with the stockholders.
3. *Litigation.* The numerous cases that have been filed by bondholders are aimed at preventing stockholders from gaining from a restructuring or buyout at the expense of bondholders.
4. *More careful analysis.* In addition to analyzing the creditworthiness of a corporation, many bond investors attempt to determine the likelihood that a company will be a takeover or restructuring candidate.

SOURCE: Adapted from Christopher Farrell, "Bondholders Are Mad as Hell—and They're Not Going to Take It Anymore," *Business Week*, February 6, 1989, pp. 82–83.

yields, with corporates providing the highest yields. The yield spreads between the three categories are not constant. The long-term upward trend in yields and the large cyclical swings in yields since the late 1960s are evident.

BASIC FEATURES OF BOND ISSUES AND INDIVIDUAL BONDS

All bond investors need a general understanding of the basic features and characteristics of individual securities and issuers. For new bond issues, the most comprehensive source of information is the *prospectus,* which can be obtained from the investment banker underwriting the issue or directly from the issuer. The Securities and Exchange Commission (SEC) requires the issuer to providc very detailed information about its financial condition and the char-

FIGURE 10.2 • Yields to Maturity on Municipal, Long-Term Treasury, and Corporate Bonds

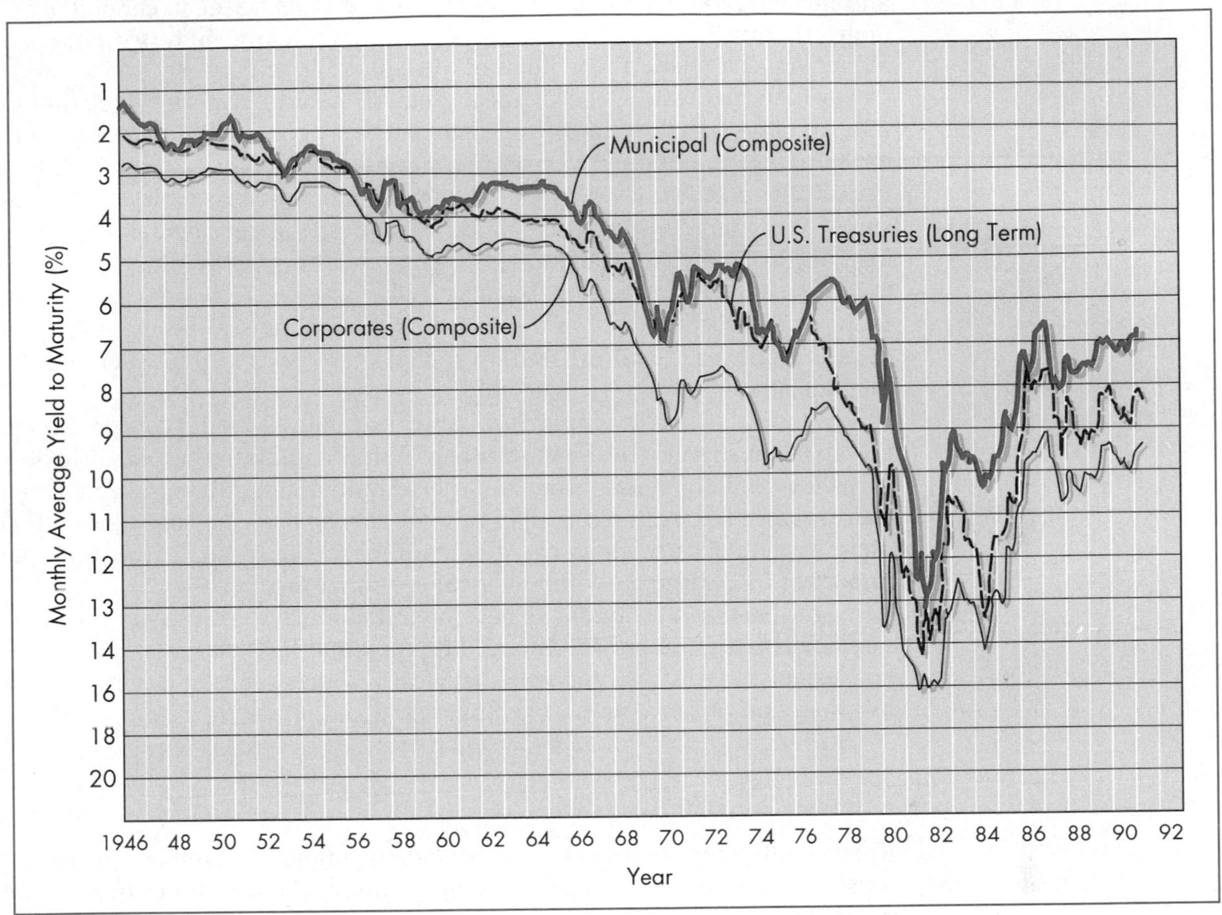

SOURCE: Moody's *Bond Record* (May 1991), p. 523.

acteristics of the particular security being offered. Essentially, any information that may be of interest to a potential investor can be found in the lengthy prospectus.

For bonds issued previously and traded in the secondary market, an investor can obtain detailed information from sources cited earlier such as Moody's *Bond Record* or Standard & Poor's *Bond Guide.* In addition, current financial information on the issuer can be found in sources such as Moody's *Industrial Manuals* or similar publications, depending on the classification of the issuer.

• Issuer Characteristics

A knowledgeable bond investor should be familiar with the characteristics of the bond issuer. For corporate and municipal issuers, the investor should perform an analysis comparable to the one performed before purchasing the stock of the firm. The main purpose of the analysis is to assess the business and financial condition of the issuer in order to estimate the likelihood of default. The investor may need to analyze economic and industry prospects along with the financial condition of the issuer.

For corporate issues, the financial analysis could begin by calculating financial ratios based on historical financial statements; these are designed to measure the firm's liquidity, asset utilization, leverage, and profitability. Particular attention would be paid to the operating and financial leverage measures. Many large institutional bond investors spend considerable time performing this analysis. Small individual bond investors, however, often rely on the judgment of a professional analyst, who assigns the bond a *rating*. The rating, which is discussed in the next section, attempts to assess the risk of default of the bond and is based on the characteristics of the issuer and the individual bond.

For general obligation municipal issues, the analysis would concentrate on the financial strength of the governmental unit issuing the security. The key variables would be the tax base and the amount of debt that has been issued on this base. For example, a ratio of total debt to the assessed value of real estate or net debt per capita could be used for this purpose. It would also be important to analyze local and regional economic factors.

Municipal revenue bonds can be analyzed in much the same way as corporate bonds since the project financed by the bond has estimates of revenues and expenses. This analysis would typically concentrate on the stability of revenues and the coverage of fixed operating and financing charges.

• Bond Characteristics

Bonds, unlike common stocks, can have many unique and important characteristics. Corporations typically have only one type of common stock; where more than one type does exist, it is usually because the voting rights differ. For example, General Motors has three classes of common stock with different voting rights. Corporations, municipalities, and governmental units, however, issue many different types of debt instruments, each with its own characteristics. Some of the more important characteristics are examined in the following paragraphs.

PRINCIPAL The face value, or *principal*, of a bond indicates the amount of money that must be repaid at maturity. It can be as low as $250 or as high as millions of dollars. Typically, the principal is $1,000.

MATURITY DATE All bonds, with the exception of *consols* or *perpetuities*, have a maturity date.[13] This provides the essential information that is neces-

[13] Consols or perpetuities are issued without a maturity date. Only a small number of these bonds are traded in the United States. The most actively traded issue is the Canadian Pacific Consols that were issued in 1921. These bonds are discussed in Chapter 11.

sary to calculate the *term to maturity* at the date of issue or at any time during the life of the bond. For example, if the bond has a maturity date of June 15, 2010, the term to maturity would be the time from the date of analysis to June 15, 2010. Term to maturity would be expressed in time units such as 19 years and six months (19.5) or 20 years and nine months (20.75). In some bond offerings, the maturities are staggered over a period of years, resulting in what is called a *serial issue*.

COUPON The **coupon** is established at the time the bond is issued and represents the nominal interest rate that will be paid. It is stated as an annual percentage rate, such as $7\frac{1}{2}$, which can be applied to the denomination or face value of the bond to calculate the dollar interest. Since interest is generally paid semiannually, the issuer pays only one-half of the coupon each semiannual period. For example, the investor would receive $37.50 semiannually for a $7\frac{1}{2}$ percent coupon bond with a $1,000 face value.

Traditionally, the coupon is constant over the life of the bond. Recently, however, some bonds have begun to "index" coupons to inflation or to market interest rates. These indexed bonds are much like an adjustable rate mortgage (ARM) on real estate, in that the interest rate on the mortgage or the coupon on the bond is adjusted for the rate of inflation. If the inflation rate is above a predetermined level, the rates (coupons) are adjusted upward.

At the other extreme, a number of corporate bonds offered in the early 1980s pay no coupon and are appropriately referred to as *zeros*. These bonds are sold at discounts from face value, much like Treasury bills. Zero corporate bonds are subject to federal income taxes on the "implied" interest income, while zeros issued by municipalities maintain their tax-exempt status. Examples of corporations that have issued zeros are American Medical International, Archer-Daniel-Midland, Barclays-American, and CIT Financial.

REGISTRATION Bonds can be either *registered* or *bearer* bonds for interest and/or principal payments. The issuer maintains records on the ownership of registered bonds, but the holder is assumed to be the owner of bearer bonds. Municipal bonds issued after 1981 must now be registered to be exempt from federal income taxes.

CALL FEATURE It is quite common for corporate, municipal, and some Treasury securities to be *callable* by the issuer. The earliest call date and call price are specified when the bonds are issued. The investor should always remember that the call feature is an advantage to the issuer and can be exercised at the issuer's discretion.

CONVERTIBILITY The **convertible** feature can be added to a bond as a "sweetener" to the investor. This feature may also be advantageous to the issuer: it improves the marketability of the bond and adds flexibility to the capital structure of the issuer. At the option of the investor, the bond can be exchanged for common stock, using a specified fixed conversion ratio or conversion price. For example, if the conversion ratio is 50, one bond can be exchanged for 50 shares of stock. The conversion price would be $20 since this would be the conversion value per share for a bond with a denomination of $1,000. Typically, only the more speculative bonds are offered with a convertible feature. This feature may provide considerable help in marketing the bond if the value of the firm's stock appears likely to increase above the conversion price. The issuer also commonly offers a lower coupon rate than would be the case for a "straight" (nonconvertible) bond with similar characteristics. Convertible bonds are discussed in detail in Chapter 16.

COLLATERAL The type of collateral is important for bonds that have some probability of default. Obviously, the investor should be concerned about the assets pledged as collateral in the event of default on interest or principal payments. Variations in collateral lead to several types of bonds:

1. *Secured* Bonds that have specific assets pledged as collateral are *secured* bonds. The collateral may be real assets such as real estate, in which case the bonds would be **mortgage** bonds. If stocks or bonds are given as collateral, the bonds are *collateral trust* bonds. For mortgage bonds, the bond contract or indenture can specify either a *closed-* or *open-ended* mortgage. A closed-end feature offers more security since additional bonds cannot be issued using the same collateral.
2. *Unsecured* Bonds without specific collateral are *unsecured* except for the general creditworthiness of the issuer. **Debentures** or subordinated debentures are examples of this type of security.
3. *Sinking fund* When investigating the provisions of a bond, it is advisable to know the details concerning any sinking fund requirements. When a **sinking fund** exists, the issuer must either periodically allocate funds to repay the principal or use the funds to purchase the bonds in the market and effectively retire them before maturity. Thus, a sinking fund is an advantage to the investor.

Table 10.4 summarizes the different types of bonds and their characteristics. As mentioned previously, the majority of bonds are traded in the OTC market by dealers and market makers. U.S. government securities, however, can also be purchased by individuals directly in the Treasury auction through a *noncompetitive tender.* Many corporate bonds are traded on the NYSE and AMEX. Bond markets are discussed in more detail in the last section of this chapter.

In addition to indicating where each type of bond is traded, Table 10.4 lists the denomination, frequency of coupon payments, maturity, security or collateral, and tax status for each type of bond.

• Bond Ratings

All of the features just described for both the issuer and the individual bond are considered by firms such as Standard & Poor's and Moody's when they assign a **rating** to a bond. The rating reflects the likelihood that the issuer will default on the payments of interest and/or principal. These firms employ professional analysts who evaluate the bond, using fairly standard financial analysis techniques. It should also be pointed out that the issuer must pay to have a rating assigned to a bond. Since many investors consider the rating essential information, it is uncommon for bonds not to be rated. One should realize, however, that a lack of a rating does not necessarily imply that a bond is of poor investment quality.[14]

Assigning a rating to a particular bond is an art rather than a science. In fact, the rating firms have always said that a mathematical model designed to assign a rating cannot duplicate the success of a team of skilled bond analysts. Standard & Poor's and Moody's also frequently disagree about the rating of a particular bond, resulting in a *split rating.* One study based on a sample of 218 bonds found that Moody's and Standard & Poor's disagreed 58 percent of the time, and that Moody's tends to rate bonds significantly lower than Standard & Poor's.[15]

In numerous instances, a corporation or municipality has experienced serious financial difficulties well in advance of a rating change. As a result, many investors have concluded that ratings are "sticky" and are not changed as frequently as they should be and are not as accurate as one might expect.

An interesting example of how ratings changed in response to a company's financial difficulties is provided by Braniff Airways. Table 10.5 lists information on a sinking fund debenture issued by Braniff in 1976 and on an index of yields for corporate bonds. The initial issue was for $50 million, with a coupon of 9.125 percent and a maturity date of January 1, 1997. Moody's assigned the bond a rating of Baa in 1979. Based on developments in the airline industry and particularly at Braniff, the rating was reduced one grade, to Ba, in 1980. As the table illustrates, the price of the bond began to decline significantly in early 1981; this decline reflected an increase in the overall yield to maturity on corporate bonds in general as well as the conditions in the industry and the company. Moody's changed the rating to B in April 1981. Due to the declines in the yield to maturity for bonds in general in the latter part of 1981, the price of the bond increased in December. However, Moody's lower rating of Caa in January 1982 was followed by dramatic price declines. The price reached $258.75 in early March 1982, several months before Moody's reduced the rating to Ca in May.

On May 13, 1982, Braniff filed for reorganization under Chapter 11 of the bankruptcy laws after suspending all service on May 12. Moody's recognized this development in its weekly *Bond Survey* of May 17 by announcing a rating change to Ca, effective May 13. The prices and ratings in Table 10.5 illustrate

---

[14] For details on these procedures, see Hugh C. Sherwood, *How Corporate and Municipal Debt Is Rated* (New York: John Wiley & Sons, 1976) and *Credit Overview: Corporate and International Ratings* (Standard & Poor's).

[15] Larry G. Perry, "The Effect of Bond Rating Agencies on Bond Rating Models," *Journal of Financial Research* (Winter 1985): 307–15. For a study of the impact of split ratings on yields, see Pu Liu and William T. Moore, "The Impact of Split Bond Ratings on Risk Premia," *Financial Review* (February 1987): 71–85.

TABLE 10.4 • Types and Characteristics of Bonds

	Market traded	Denomination or face value	Frequency of coupon payments	Maturity	Security or collateral	Tax status
U.S. Government Securities						
A. Treasury bills	Treasury auction/OTC	$10,000–$100,000 with increments of $5,000	No coupon (discounted)	13, 26, 52 weeks	Full backing of U.S. government	Subject to federal taxes; exempt from state and local taxes
B. Treasury notes	Treasury auction/OTC	$5,000 minimum with increments of $1,000	Semiannual	1–10 years	Full backing of U.S. government	Subject to federal taxes; exempt from state and local taxes
C. Treasury bonds	Treasury auction/OTC	$5,000 minimum with increments of $1,000	Semiannual	10–30 years	Full backing of U.S. government	Subject to federal taxes; exempt from state and local taxes
U.S. Savings Bonds						
A. Series EE bonds	Not marketable	$50–$10,000	No coupon (discounted)	Minimum of 5 years	Full backing of U.S. government	Federal taxes deferred until cashed or matures; exempt from state and local taxes
B. Series HH bonds	Not marketable	Multiples of $500	Semiannual	Minimum of 5 years	Full backing of U.S. Government	Interest received subject to federal taxes; exempt from state and local taxes

Federal Agency Bonds						
A. FHLMC	OTC	Minimum of $25,000	Monthly	1–30 years	Not guaranteed by U.S. government	Subject to federal, state, and local taxes
B. FNMA	OTC	Minimum of $25,000	Monthly	1–30 years	Not guaranteed by U.S. government	Subject to federal, state, and local taxes
C. GNMA	OTC	Minimum of $25,000	Monthly	1–30 years	Full backing of U.S. government	Subject to federal, state, and local taxes
Municipal Bonds						
A. General obligation bonds	OTC	$1,000 or more	Semiannual	5–30 years	Depends on issuer/insurance	Interest income exempt from federal taxes but capital gains taxable; exempt from state and local taxes if issued by state of domicile
B. Revenue bonds	OTC	$1,000 or more	Semiannual	5–30 years	Depends on issuer/insurance	Interest income exempt from federal taxes but capital gains taxable; exempt from state and local taxes if issued by state of domicile
Corporate Bonds	NYSE, AMEX, OTC	$250 or more, $1,000 standard	Semiannual	5–30 years	Depends on issuer/provisions of bond	Subject to federal, state, and local taxes

TABLE 10.5 • Rating Changes, Market Prices, and Yield to Maturity on Braniff Airways Sinking Fund Debenture Due in 1997 with a 9.125 Percent Coupon

			Yield to maturity	
Date	Moody's rating	Price	*Braniff bond*	*Standard & Poor's index of bonds rated BBB*
December 1980	Ba	$600.00	16.17%	14.36%
January 1981	Ba	580.00	16.73	13.92
February 1981	Ba	530.00	18.28	14.40
March 1981	Ba	558.75	17.38	14.55
April 1981	B	550.00	17.67	15.04
May 1981	B	510.00	19.01	15.99
August 1981	B	520.00	18.71	15.97
September 1981	B	440.00	21.93	16.95
October 1981	B	440.00	21.95	16.94
December 1981	B	480.00	20.27	15.72
January 1982	Caa	461.25	21.06	16.53
February 1982	Caa	450.00	21.85	16.67
March 1, 1982	Caa	400.00	23.95	16.29
March 8, 1982	Caa	258.75	35.93	16.03
March 15, 1982	Caa	330.00	28.63	16.14
March 22, 1982	Caa	333.75	28.33	16.08
March 29, 1982	Caa	355.00	26.76	16.35
April 5, 1982	Caa	347.50	27.29	16.26
April 12, 1982	Caa	348.75	27.20	16.27
April 19, 1982	Caa	352.50	26.94	16.02
April 26, 1982	Caa	360.00	26.41	16.02
May 3, 1982	Caa	355.00	26.76	16.06
May 10, 1982	Caa	358.75	26.50	15.74
May 17, 1982	Ca	328.75	Flat*	15.72
May 24, 1982	Ca	352.50	Flat*	15.85

SOURCE: Moody's *Bond Record*, Moody's *Bond Survey*, Standard & Poor's *Statistical Service*; all reprinted by permission.

*Bond is traded without interest.

that the bond market recognized the deteriorating condition of Braniff prior to and during the period of rating change announcements. The implication is that the market, in general, analyzes the credit condition of companies independently of the rating agencies.

Table 10.6 briefly summarizes the criteria for each rating category used by Moody's. Most investors view bonds rated Aaa–Baa as "investment" quality,

TABLE 10.6 • Definitions of Moody's Corporate Bond Ratings

Aaa

Bonds which are rated Aaa are judged to be of the best quality. They carry the smallest degree of investment risk and are generally referred to as "gilt edge." Interest payments are protected by a large or by an exceptionally stable margin and principal is secure. While the various protective elements are likely to change, such changes as can be visualized are most unlikely to impair the fundamentally strong position of such issues.

Aa

Bonds which are rated Aa are judged to be of high quality by all standards. Together with the Aaa group they comprise what are generally known as high grade bonds. They are rated lower than the best bonds because margins of protection may not be as large as in Aaa securities or fluctuation of protective elements may be of greater amplitude or there may be other elements present which make the long term risks appear somewhat larger than in Aaa securities.

A

Bonds which are rated A possess many favorable investment attributes and are to be considered as upper medium grade obligations. Factors giving security to principal and interest are considered adequate but elements may be present which suggest a susceptibility to impairment sometime in the future.

Baa

Bonds which are rated Baa are considered as medium grade obligations, i.e., they are neither highly protected nor poorly secured. Interest payments and principal security appear adequate for the present but certain protective elements may be lacking or may be characteristically unreliable over any great length of time. Such bonds lack outstanding investment characteristics and in fact have speculative characteristics as well.

Ba

Bonds which are rated Ba are judged to have speculative elements; their future cannot be considered as well assured. Often the protection of interest and principal payments may be very moderate and thereby not well safeguarded during other good and bad times over the future. Uncertainty of position characterizes bonds in this class.

B

Bonds which are rated B generally lack characteristics of the desirable investment. Assurance of interest and principal payments or of maintenance of other terms of the contract over any long period of time may be small.

(continued)

TABLE 10.6 • Definitions of Moody's Corporate Bond Ratings (continued)

Caa

Bonds which are rated Caa are of poor standing. Such issues may be in default or there may be present elements of danger with respect to principal or interest.

Ca

Bonds which are rated Ca represent obligations which are speculative in a high degree. Such issues are often in default or have other marked shortcomings.

C

Bonds which are rated C are the lowest rated class of bonds and issues so rated can be regarded as having extremely poor prospects of ever attaining any real investment standing.

Note: Moody's applies numerical modifiers, 1, 2 and 3 in each generic rating classification from Aa through B in its corporate bond rating system. The modifier 1 indicates that the security ranks in the higher end of its generic rating category; the modifier 2 indicates a mid-range ranking; and the modifier 3 indicates that the issue ranks in the lower end of its generic rating category.

SOURCE: Moody's *Bond Records* (May 1991), p. 3.

with ratings of Ba–B designating "speculative," "high-yield," or "junk" bonds. A rating of Caa–C warns that a bond is extremely risky and that the issuer may have already defaulted and be moving toward bankruptcy.

Chapter 11 provides additional information concerning ratings, including techniques that can be used independently to evaluate the safety of bonds. It also discusses how ratings can be employed in bond portfolio strategies.

BOND MARKETS

As for stocks, both primary and secondary markets exist for bonds. Despite certain similarities, however, bond trading differs from stock trading in several ways.

• Primary Market

Bonds, like stocks, are initially traded in the *primary market*, which entirely comprises new issues. This is the market where the underwriter or investment banker sells the bonds to initial investors—financial institutions or individuals. These transactions are between the underwriting syndicate or marketing group for the underwriter and the investor. Recall from Chapter 3 that the underwriter purchases the securities from the issuer and then resells them to investors. U.S. government securities are initially sold mainly to institutions and some individuals through auctions conducted by the Treasury. The auction procedures used by the Treasury are likely to be modified as a result of the revelations in September 1991 of abuses of the procedures by Salomon Brothers.

Potential investors learn of the new issue through the financial news and watch for offering announcements in the *Wall Street Journal* and other publications. *Barron's* also has weekly features entitled "Offerings in the Offing" and "Coming Financing." These features provide information on new issues of bonds, preferred stock, and common stock for the coming week and on new offerings filed with the SEC. Account executives at brokerage firms often call potential investors about new offerings. Upon learning of the new offering, the investor should request a copy of the prospectus giving the details of the offering. Announcements quite commonly "appear as a matter of record only." Such announcements usually indicate that a *direct placement* of the securities has been made and that they are therefore not offered to other investors.[16] These announcements simply provide advertising for the underwriting firm.

• Secondary Market

Once bonds have been placed through the primary market, they can be traded in the secondary market. For the majority of corporate bonds, this is the OTC market. For large firms, the bonds will be traded on the NYSE or AMEX if the company's stock is traded there.

• Quotations

Bond quotations are not as readily available as stock quotations because of the large number of outstanding bonds and infrequent trading in many of the smaller issues. Quotes can be obtained from brokerage houses or publications that specialize in bonds, such as Moody's *Bond Record.*

• Transaction Costs

Transaction costs, or brokerage fees, are quite nominal for bonds. There is no standard fee since brokerage fees can be negotiated, but it is not uncommon to pay as little as $3.50 to $4.50 per bond traded. No brokerage fees are

---

[16] For a study of direct placements of corporate bonds, including how prices are determined, see Nathaniel B. Cabanilla, "Directly-placed Bonds: A Test of Market Efficiency," *Journal of Portfolio Management* (Winter 1984): 72–74. For a study of municipals, see David S. Kidwell and Eric H. Sorensen, "Pricing of Municipal Bond Underwritings: It May Pay to Invest When Underwriters Don't," *Financial Analysts Journal* (March-April 1983): 58–64.

RESEARCH BOX
Bond Indexes

Bond portfolio managers use a number of comprehensive indexes that may include U.S. Treasury securities, corporate bonds, and mortgage-backed securities. Four indexes are used most frequently:

1. Merrill Lynch Domestic Government/Corporate Master Index, which includes 4,900 bonds.
2. Salomon Brothers Broad Investment Grade Index, which includes 4,500 bonds.
3. Shearson Lehman Government/Corporate Bond Index, which includes 6,000 bonds.
4. Ryan Financial Strategy Group Treasury Index, which includes 7 Treasuries.

The three comprehensive indexes are heavily weighted toward the government bond sector. The Shearson index has the largest percentage of government bonds with 73 percent while the Salomon index has the smallest percentage at 54 percent. All four of the indexes are designed to measure interest rate volatility since bond prices and the index values change as interest rates change.

Despite the differences in sample size and composition, all four indexes were almost perfectly correlated over the period 1980–1987. This extremely high correlation indicates there are only minor differences in the movements of the indexes over time.

Bond managers are not entirely satisfied with any of these four indexes. As one manager says, "There is no index which represents the fixed-income market. In equities you have about 5,000 stocks with 500 representing a fair weighting. The universe is fairly well defined. The fixed-income universe is a diverse and changing universe—with new sectors being created all the time."

The indexes are typically used as a benchmark to measure the performance of a fixed-income portfolio such as a mutual fund or pension portfolio. In selecting an appropriate index, one portfolio manager indicated that "we look at the objectives of the fund and use an appropriate index consistent with that."

SOURCE: Fred Williams and Margaret Price, "The World of Indexes Is Getting Bigger: High Correlation Exists among Bond Benchmarks; More Firms Vying in Global Areas," *Pensions & Investments*, May 1, 1989, pp. 3, 58.

charged for new issues. Many small bond issues, however, do not have the market liquidity that the common stocks of large firms offer. In addition, many bonds are often sold in "blocks," so that the purchase or sale of a denomination of $1,000 to $10,000 may be difficult. Institutional investors dominate the secondary bond market and typically trade in very large blocks.

• Indexes

Bond investors can follow general price and yield movements by watching numerous bond indexes in much the same way as stock prices can be followed using the Dow Jones Industrial Average or the Standard & Poor's 500

TABLE 10.7 • Example of Bond Yield Averages

Moody's Corporate Bond Yield Averages

	AV CORP.	CORPORATE BY RATINGS Aaa	Aa	A	Baa	CORPORATE BY GROUPS P.U.	IND.	R.R.	PUBLIC UTILITY BONDS Aaa	Aa	A	Baa	INDUSTRIAL BONDS Aaa	Aa	A	Baa	RAILROAD BONDS Aaa	Aa	A	Baa
1985																				
May	12.47	11.72	12.30	12.70	13.15	12.89	12.04	12.39	12.18	12.65	13.12	13.62	11.26	11.95	12.28	12.68	---	11.94	12.32	12.92
June	11.70	10.94	11.46	11.98	12.40	11.91	11.48	11.81	11.17	11.68	12.13	12.66	10.71	11.24	11.83	12.14	---	11.26	11.95	12.21
July	11.69	10.97	11.42	11.92	12.43	11.88	11.49	11.63	11.18	11.55	12.07	12.70	10.74	11.29	11.77	12.17	---	11.05	11.81	12.03
Aug.	11.76	11.05	11.47	12.00	12.50	11.93	11.57	11.56	11.23	11.65	12.13	12.73	10.87	11.29	11.87	12.27	---	11.22	11.62	11.85
Sept.	11.75	11.07	11.46	11.99	12.48	11.95	11.55	11.63	11.27	11.68	12.13	12.72	10.86	11.24	11.85	12.24	---	11.23	11.61	12.05
Oct.	11.69	11.02	11.45	11.94	12.36	11.84	11.53	11.54	11.23	11.61	12.01	12.52	10.80	11.29	11.85	12.20	---	11.17	11.58	11.86
Nov.	11.29	10.55	11.07	11.54	11.99	11.33	11.23	11.35	10.71	11.10	11.49	12.04	10.38	11.03	11.58	11.93	---	10.95	11.39	11.70
Dec.	10.89	10.16	10.63	11.19	11.58	10.82	10.96	11.18	10.24	10.57	10.97	11.48	10.08	10.69	11.39	11.67	---	10.75	11.25	11.53
1986																				
Jan.	10.75	10.05	10.46	11.04	11.44	10.66	10.83	10.86	10.14	10.44	10.79	11.24	9.95	10.47	11.27	11.63	---	10.45	10.88	11.24
Feb.	10.40	9.67	10.13	10.67	11.11	10.16	10.63	10.58	9.65	9.98	10.26	10.74	9.68	10.27	11.07	11.48	---	10.18	10.62	10.93
Mar.	9.79	9.00	9.49	10.15	10.49	9.33	10.24	10.05	8.75	9.16	9.48	9.91	9.23	9.82	10.81	11.07	---	9.74	9.98	10.42
Apr.	9.51	8.79	9.21	9.83	10.19	9.02	9.98	9.78	8.45	8.87	9.14	9.63	9.13	9.55	10.51	10.74	---	9.39	9.71	10.24
May	9.69	9.09	9.43	9.94	10.29	9.52	9.85	9.58	9.07	9.38	9.59	10.02	9.11	9.47	10.28	10.55	---	9.13	9.38	10.24
June	9.73	9.13	9.49	9.96	10.34	9.51	9.95	9.72	9.02	9.36	9.62	10.03	9.24	9.61	10.29	10.65	---	9.30	9.68	10.19
July	9.52	8.88	9.28	9.76	10.16	9.19	9.85	9.73	8.66	9.05	9.37	9.69	9.09	9.51	10.14	10.64	---	9.27	9.66	10.26
Aug.	9.44	8.72	9.22	9.64	10.18	9.15	9.73	9.69	8.59	9.03	9.29	9.70	8.85	9.41	9.97	10.66	---	9.24	9.70	10.13
Sept.	9.55	8.89	9.36	9.73	10.20	9.42	9.68	9.57	8.91	9.28	9.52	9.96	8.87	9.45	9.95	10.44	---	9.10	9.65	9.97
Oct.	9.54	8.86	9.33	9.72	10.24	9.39	9.68	9.65	8.84	9.24	9.52	9.95	8.88	9.42	9.91	10.51	---	9.26	9.67	10.01
Nov.	9.37	8.68	9.20	9.51	10.07	9.15	9.58	9.56	8.59	9.01	9.28	9.69	8.77	9.38	9.73	10.44	---	8.98	9.50	10.19
Dec	9.23	8.49	9.02	9.41	9.97	8.96	9.49	9.37	8.41	8.81	9.12	9.49	8.57	9.23	9.70	10.45	---	8.74	9.26	10.09
1987																				
Jan.	9.04	8.36	8.86	9.23	9.72	8.77	9.31	9.19	8.23	8.62	8.95	9.27	8.48	9.09	9.51	10.17	---	8.64	9.09	9.82
Feb.	9.03	8.38	8.88	9.20	9.65	8.81	9.25	9.22	8.29	8.69	9.00	9.24	8.47	9.06	9.39	10.06	---	8.63	9.08	9.95
Mar.	8.99	8.36	8.84	9.13	9.61	8.75	9.23	9.13	8.21	8.64	8.93	9.19	8.51	9.04	9.33	10.02	---	8.57	9.02	9.80
Apr.	9.35	8.85	9.15	9.36	10.04	9.30	9.40	9.30	8.83	9.15	9.38	9.85	8.87	9.15	9.34	10.24	---	8.76	9.07	10.06
May	9.82	9.33	9.59	9.83	10.51	9.82	9.81	9.53	9.34	9.63	9.91	10.40	9.31	9.56	9.73	10.62	---	8.95	9.46	10.17
June	9.87	9.32	9.65	9.98	10.52	9.87	9.87	9.56	9.37	9.61	10.02	10.46	9.26	9.69	9.93	10.58	---	8.75	9.74	10.19
July	9.92	9.42	9.64	10.00	10.61	10.01	9.82	9.52	9.56	9.70	10.15	10.62	9.26	9.58	9.86	10.59	---	8.71	9.68	10.18
Aug.	10.14	9.67	9.86	10.20	10.80	10.33	9.94	9.69	9.92	10.05	10.45	10.90	9.42	9.68	9.95	10.70	---	9.04	9.80	10.23
Sept.	10.64	10.18	10.35	10.72	11.31	11.00	10.28	9.96	10.53	10.66	11.22	11.58	9.83	10.03	10.22	11.04	---	9.37	10.10	10.42
Oct.	10.97	10.52	10.74	10.98	11.62	11.32	10.60	10.07	10.92	11.11	11.34	11.91	10.11	10.36	10.62	11.33	---	9.64	10.03	10.55
Nov.	10.54	10.01	10.27	10.63	11.23	10.82	10.25	10.30	10.43	10.62	10.82	11.40	9.59	9.91	10.43	11.05	---	10.00	10.18	10.71
Dec.	10.59	10.11	10.33	10.62	11.29	10.99	10.18	10.08	10.64	10.78	10.98	11.55	9.58	9.87	10.25	11.02	---	9.58	9.94	10.71
1988																				
Jan.	10.37	9.88	10.09	10.43	11.07	10.75	9.98	10.04	10.39	10.52	10.76	11.34	9.37	9.65	10.09	10.79	---	9.62	9.91	10.59
Feb.	9.89	9.40	9.60	9.94	10.62	10.11	9.67	9.85	9.77	9.91	10.10	10.65	9.02	9.29	9.79	10.59	---	9.58	9.72	10.24
Mar.	9.86	9.39	9.59	9.89	10.57	10.11	9.61	9.91	9.72	9.92	10.09	10.69	9.05	9.26	9.68	10.45	---	9.55	9.89	10.31
Apr.	10.15	9.67	9.86	10.17	10.90	10.53	9.76	10.08	10.07	10.29	10.54	11.23	9.27	9.41	9.81	10.56	---	9.54	10.02	10.68
May	10.37	9.90	10.10	10.41	11.04	10.75	9.97	10.03	10.29	10.53	10.81	11.38	9.51	9.66	10.00	10.71	---	9.45	9.97	10.66
June	10.36	9.86	10.13	10.42	11.00	10.71	9.99	10.04	10.27	10.52	10.79	11.27	9.43	9.75	10.05	10.74	---	9.66	9.95	10.59
July	10.47	9.96	10.26	10.55	11.11	10.96	9.98	10.06	10.50	10.76	11.04	11.52	9.42	9.76	10.05	10.70	---	9.57	10.00	10.60
Aug.	10.58	10.11	10.37	10.63	11.21	11.09	10.07	10.10	10.66	10.85	11.17	11.69	9.56	9.89	10.09	10.73	---	9.61	10.02	10.66
Sept.	10.28	9.82	10.06	10.34	10.90	10.56	10.00	10.12	10.15	10.34	10.61	11.13	9.49	9.78	10.06	10.66	---	9.72	10.02	10.63
Oct.	9.90	9.51	9.71	9.99	10.41	9.92	9.88	10.03	9.62	9.79	10.01	10.31	9.39	9.62	10.04	10.50	---	9.58	10.01	10.50
Nov.	9.91	9.45	9.72	9.97	10.48	9.89	9.93	10.00	9.52	9.80	9.90	10.35	9.38	9.64	10.09	10.60	---	9.39	10.11	10.50
Dec.	10.03	9.57	9.81	10.11	10.65	10.02	10.04	10.06	9.67	9.90	10.06	10.44	9.46	9.71	10.16	10.85	---	9.60	10.05	10.53
1989																				
Jan.	10.05	9.62	9.81	10.10	10.65	10.02	10.08	10.04	9.72	9.89	10.08	10.38	9.52	9.72	10.13	10.93	--	9.55	10.13	10.44
Feb.	10.05	9.64	9.83	10.13	10.61	10.02	10.08	10.05	9.71	9.93	10.07	10.38	9.55	9.73	10.18	10.84	---	9.68	10.13	10.34
Mar.	10.18	9.80	9.98	10.26	10.67	10.16	10.19	10.19	9.87	10.05	10.23	10.50	9.73	9.89	10.29	10.84	---	9.82	10.33	10.43
Apr.	10.14	9.79	9.94	10.20	10.61	10.14	10.13	10.27	9.88	10.02	10.18	10.49	9.70	9.86	10.22	10.73	---	9.77	10.31	10.74
May	9.95	9.57	9.75	10.00	10.46	9.92	9.97	10.31	9.60	9.79	9.99	10.29	9.54	9.71	10.00	10.63	---	9.94	10.24	10.73
June	9.50	9.10	9.29	9.59	10.03	9.49	9.51	10.17	9.13	9.37	9.64	9.80	9.06	9.20	9.52	10.26	---	9.90	10.09	10.52
July	9.34	8.93	9.14	9.42	9.87	9.34	9.34	10.05	8.98	9.23	9.50	9.64	8.88	9.05	9.34	10.10	---	9.89	10.01	10.26
Aug	9.36	8.96	9.14	9.45	9.88	9.37	9.35	---	9.02	9.27	9.52	9.64	8.89	9.01	9.38	10.11	---	---	---	---
Sept.	9.41	9.01	9.23	9.51	9.91	9.43	9.39	---	9.10	9.35	9.58	9.70	8.90	9.11	9.43	10.12	---	---	---	---
Oct.	9.34	8.92	9.19	9.44	9.81	9.37	9.31	---	9.01	9.28	9.54	9.64	8.83	9.09	9.34	9.98	---	---	---	---
Nov.	9.32	8.89	9.14	9.42	9.81	9.33	9.30	---	8.92	9.25	9.51	9.64	8.85	9.02	9.32	9.88	---	---	---	---
Dec.	9.30	8.86	9.11	9.39	9.82	9.31	9.28	---	8.92	9.26	9.44	9.60	8.79	8.96	9.33	10.03	---	---	---	---
1990																				
Jan.	9.43	8.99	9.27	9.54	9.94	9.44	9.42	---	9.08	9.39	9.56	9.74	8.90	9.14	9.51	10.14	---	---	---	---
Feb.	9.64	9.22	9.44	9.75	10.14	9.66	9.61	---	9.35	9.57	9.76	9.96	9.09	9.30	9.75	10.32	---	---	---	---
Mar.	9.73	9.37	9.51	9.82	10.21	9.75	9.70	---	9.48	9.60	9.85	10.06	9.26	9.41	9.80	10.35	---	---	---	---
Apr.	9.82	9.46	9.64	9.89	10.30	9.87	9.77	---	9.60	9.81	9.92	10.13	9.32	9.46	9.85	10.47	---	---	---	---
May	9.87	9.47	9.70	9.89	10.41	9.89	9.84	---	9.58	9.83	10.00	10.16	9.34	9.58	9.77	10.66	---	---	---	---
June	9.67	9.26	9.49	9.70	10.22	9.69	9.64	---	9.38	9.60	9.80	9.96	9.12	9.36	9.60	10.47	---	---	---	---
July	9.65	9.24	9.47	9.69	10.20	9.66	9.64	---	9.36	9.61	9.75	9.92	9.12	9.33	9.62	10.46	---	---	---	---
Aug.	9.84	9.41	9.63	9.89	10.41	9.84	9.83	---	9.54	9.78	9.97	10.12	9.28	9.48	9.86	10.69	---	---	---	---
Sept.	10.02	9.36	9.77	10.09	10.64	10.01	9.39	---	9.73	9.87	10.12	10.32	9.39	9.67	10.05	10.95	---	---	---	---
Oct.	10.03	9.53	9.77	10.06	10.74	9.94	10.11	---	9.66	9.77	10.05	10.28	9.39	9.77	10.07	11.19	---	---	---	---
Nov.	9.85	9.30	9.59	9.88	10.62	9.76	9.93	---	9.43	9.59	9.90	10.12	9.16	9.58	9.84	11.12	---	---	---	---
Dec.	9.63	9.05	9.39	9.64	10.43	9.57	9.68	---	9.18	9.42	9.73	9.96	8.92	9.36	9.54	10.90	---	---	---	---
1991																				
Jan.	9.62	9.04	9.37	9.61	10.45	9.56	9.68	---	9.17	9.39	9.71	9.96	8.92	9.35	9.50	10.94	---	---	---	---
Feb.	9.36	8.83	9.16	9.38	10.07	9.31	9.41	---	8.92	9.16	9.47	9.68	8.73	9.16	9.29	10.45	---	---	---	---
Mar.	9.43	8.93	9.21	9.50	10.09	9.39	9.47	---	9.04	9.23	9.55	9.74	8.82	9.19	9.44	10.43	---	---	---	---
Apr.	9.33	8.86	9.12	9.39	9.94	9.30	8.77	---	8.95	9.14	9.46	9.64	8.77	9.09	9.31	10.24	---	---	---	---

Notes: See Moody's Bond Survey for a brief description and the latest published list of bonds included in the averages. Because of the dearth of Aaa-rated railroad term bond issues Moody's Aaa railroad bond yield average was discontinued as of December 18, 1967. Moody's Aaa public utility average suspended from Jan. 1984 thru Sept. 1984. Oct. 1984 figure for last 14 business days only. The Railroad Bond Averages were discontinued as of July 17, 1989 because of insufficient frequently tradable bonds. The July figures were based on 8 business days.

SOURCE: Moody's *Bond Record* (May 1991), p. 83.

Index. There are many bond indexes, however, because of the many issuers and characteristics of bonds. Each index is constructed using a specific type of bond and can be based on yield to maturity, prices, or holding period returns (HPRs):

1. Yield indexes Some of the more common indexes based on yield to maturity are Moody's Corporate Bond Yield Averages, Moody's Government Bond Yield Averages, and Moody's Municipal Bond Yield Averages. Different indexes are constructed within each of these classifications to recognize differences in term to maturity and ratings. For example, Moody's has yield-to-maturity indexes for utilities, industrials, and railroads for rating classifications Baa–Aaa. Similar indexes are provided by Standard & Poor's Corporation. An example of Moody's indexes appears in Table 10.7.

2. Price indexes Several firms calculate and publish bond price indexes. These indexes are for a homogeneous sample of bonds with respect to classification, rating, and term to maturity. Examples include the Dow Jones Industrial and Utility Bond Averages.

3. Newer indexes The yield-to-maturity and price indexes have been criticized because they rely on small samples and do not use the most accurate price data for individual bonds. Several newer indexes developed by Salomon Brothers and BEA Associates are generally considered superior because of their larger samples, requirements concerning minimum dollar value, and the type of price data they use for individual bonds. Since many bonds trade infrequently and in large blocks, constructing a time series of yields or prices can be difficult. These newer indexes often use prices estimated by bond traders based on their knowledge of the market rather than actual transaction prices. These newer measures of bond prices and yields should aid bond investors and be useful in financial research.

Annual and monthly HPRs for long-term U.S. government and corporate bonds and for Treasury bills are available for the period 1926–1990.[17] These returns are widely used in financial research and investment performance evaluations.

SUMMARY

This chapter has provided the basic fundamentals of bond terminology, types of bonds, and characteristics important to investors. It also compared the risk-return characteristics of bonds with those of stocks.

Bonds can be classified using various procedures. This chapter used risk as the classification factor and therefore started with U.S. Treasury bills and ended with corporate bonds. Differences in risk are due primarily to higher default probabilities and term to maturity.

---

[17] *Stock, Bonds, Bills and Inflation 1991 Yearbook* (Chicago: Ibbotson Associates, 1991).

• CONCEPT APPLICATIONS

Investment Concept	Concept Application
Bond holding period return	The HPR for bonds includes price changes over the holding period and interest income. Bonds are traded with accrued interest; therefore, investors even with very short holding periods (a single day) should include interest in calculating the HPR.
Types of bonds	Major types of bonds include U.S. Treasury securities, U.S. savings bonds, federal agency issues, municipals, and corporate bonds. The risk and return characteristics vary among the various types or categories of bonds. Table 10.4 lists the characteristics of the five major types of bonds.
Individual bond characteristics	The most important characteristics include the principal or face value, maturity date or term, coupon, call feature, collateral, and tax status. The rating is important for municipal and corporate bonds. Table 10.4 lists the major characteristics of bonds in each of the five categories.
Bond markets	New issues of bonds are offered in the primary market with existing issues traded in the secondary markets.
Bond indexes	Indexes are available that measure yield and prices. Newer indexes are comprehensive in that they include different categories of bonds.
Bond ratings	The rating reflects the likelihood that the issuer will default on the payments of interest and/or principal. Table 10.6 provides definitions of Moody's corporate bond ratings.

The major types of bonds discussed in the chapter are U.S. government issues, U.S. savings bonds, federal agency securities, municipals, and corporate bonds. The order in which they are listed here corresponds to the risk-return trade-offs among these securities. The investor should note that there are hundreds of different types of fixed-income securities when differences in issuers and security characteristics are considered.

One very important feature of municipal and corporate securities is default risk and its impact on the bond's return. Traditionally, many investors have used bond ratings provided by Moody's or Standard & Poor's. Recently, more attention has been given to independent analysis of the credit risk of bonds by investors. One justification is that ratings seem to be "sticky"; bond prices often reflect major developments in a company that are not recognized until later by a rating change.

Like stocks, bonds are sold on both primary and secondary markets. These were examined, along with sources of information for current prices and typical transaction costs for trading in bonds. Bond indexes can be useful in following historical and current prices and yields.

This chapter has laid the foundation for the next chapter, which deals with bond risk-return analysis and investment strategies. Together these chapters should provide the investor with a clear understanding of the advantages and disadvantages of bond investing, along with the tools needed to analyze bonds and make intelligent bond investment decisions.

• KEY TERMS

Bond
Bond ratings
Convertible bond
Corporate bond
Coupon
Debenture
Federal Home Loan Mortgage Corporation (FHLMC or "Freddie Mac")
Federal National Mortgage Association (FNMA or "Fannie Mae")
General obligation municipals
Government National Mortgage Association (GNMA or "Ginnie Mae")
Indenture
Mortgage-backed bonds
Mortgage bond
Municipal bond
Revenue municipal bond
Series EE (savings) bond
Series HH (savings) bond
Sinking fund
Treasury bill (T–bill)
Treasury bond
Treasury note
Trustee

• QUESTIONS

1. Compare and contrast the risk-return characteristics of bonds and stocks.
2. The years 1980 and 1981–1982 were periods of recession in the United States. Using this knowledge, which of the two types of securities in Table 10.1 seems to offer the best returns during both recessions and periods of economic growth?
3. Figure 10.1 indicates that the yield to maturity on corporate bonds is influenced by agency ratings. Explain what the rating indicates about the bond and how the yield to maturity is affected by those ratings.
4. Based on this chapter and on your general knowledge, explain what developments in the economy and bond markets during the 1980's have caused a number of bond investors to reexamine their bond trading strategies. Do you think bonds are now more attractive to "speculators"? Why?
5. All common stocks involve more risk than bonds. Is this a true statement? Explain.
6. Assume you are interested in analyzing a particular corporate bond as a possible investment. What information would you like to have concerning both the issuer and the particular bond? Indicate sources where this information can be found.

7. There are major differences in the federal tax laws concerning income receipts from U.S. government securities, municipals, and corporate bonds. Explain these differences.
8. Explain why there may be significant differences in liquidity from the investor's viewpoint between corporate bonds and stocks.
9. Would you expect corporations with very strong financial positions to offer secured bonds? Explain.
10. Bond indexes are much more numerous than stock indexes. Why?

• KEY TO THE INVESTMENT ANALYSIS SOFTWARE

Calculation	Appendix A-1 Page Reference	Access Procedure
Holding period return	A-8	BEGIN, STATISTICAL, HPR

• PROBLEMS

1. Assume that you bought a corporate bond with a face value of $1,000 that pays an annual coupon of $75. You purchased the bond at a discount price of $900 and sold it one year later for $925. Calculate the annual HPR.
2. Suppose you are comparing a municipal and a corporate bond that are selling at face value. Both bonds have identical ratings and terms to maturity. The municipal is priced to provide a yield of 7 percent while the corporate provides a yield of 9 percent.
   a. If your marginal tax rate is 28 percent, calculate the after-tax yield on the corporate.
   b. Assuming the same tax rate of 28 percent, calculate the before-tax yield on the municipal.
   c. Assuming equal risk, which bond should be purchased?
3. Assume you found the following quotation for a Treasury bill in an issue of the *Wall Street Journal:*

Maturity	*Days to mat.*	*Bid*	*Ask*	*Change*	*Ask yld*
11/14/91	170	5.57	5.55	−0.03	5.79

   a. Explain the difference in the "bid" and "ask" quotes.
   b. Explain the "change" of −0.03.
   c. Notice that the bill matures in 170 days and has an "ask yield" of 5.79 percent. Is this a 170-day yield or an annualized yield?

4. A recent issue of the *Wall Street Journal* gave the following quote for a Treasury bond:

Rate	*Maturity Mo/Year*	*Bid*	*Ask*	*Change*	*Ask yld*
$9\frac{3}{8}$	Feb 06	106:26	106:30	−16	8.56

a. What is the dollar amount of the semiannual coupon that this bond pays?

b. What is the term to maturity of the bond from February 1992?

c. Convert the ask quote to a dollar price.

5. Consider the following quote from the *Wall Street Journal* on a corporate bond traded on the NYSE:

Bond	*Cur yld*	*Vol*	*Close*	*Net chg*
IBM 9s98	8.9	18	$101\frac{1}{2}$	$-\frac{1}{4}$

a. What is the dollar amount of the semiannual coupon that this bond pays?

b. If the bond pays the semiannual coupon on January 1 and July 1, calculate the accrued interest as of April 1.

c. Convert the "close" quote to a dollar price.

d. What year does the bond reach maturity?

• REFERENCES

Ahearn, Daniel S. "The Strategic Role of Fixed Income Securities." *Journal of Portfolio Management* (Spring 1975): 12–16.

Forsyth, Randall W. "Nuclear Meltdown: The Whoops Default and Fallout." *Barron's,* August 1, 1983, pp. 11, 32.

———. "Supporting Uncle: How to Buy Treasuries in One Easy Lesson." *Barron's,* June 25, 1984, p. 27.

Fortune, Peter. "An Assessment of Financial Market Volatility: Bills, Bonds, and Stocks." *New England Economic Review* (November-December 1989): 13–28.

Markese, John. "Buying Treasuries from the Factory." *Money,* December 1988, pp. 137–41.

Slater, Karen. "Before Selecting Municipal Bonds, Buyers Should Judge Issues' Future Marketability." *Wall Street Journal,* January 30, 1984, p. 35.

Updegrave, Walter L. "Riding the Wave of Long Bond Yields." *Money,* April 1989, pp. 100–11.

Bond Analysis: Returns, Risk, and Strategies

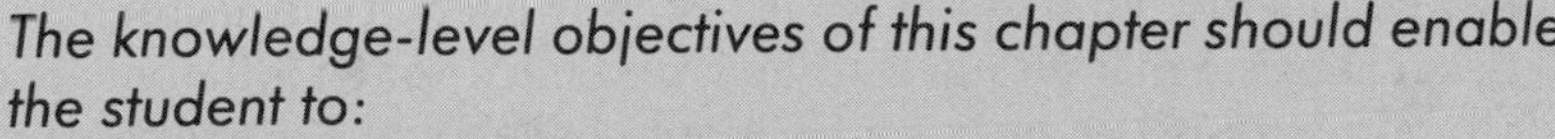

The knowledge-level objectives of this chapter should enable the student to:

- Calculate and interpret the major bond return measures including current yield, yield to maturity, yield to first call, holding period return, and expected holding period return.
- Understand the major types of risk for bonds including default risk, reinvestment rate risk, price risk, purchasing power risk, and call risk.
- Calculate and interpret the major bond risk measures including variance, standard deviation, and duration.
- Distinguish between passive and active bond investment strategies.
- Identify the strengths and weaknesses of active strategies including forecasting interest rates, adjusting maturities, riding the yield curve, and forecasting yield spreads.
- Understand why diversification in terms of the number of bonds in a portfolio reduces unsystematic risk.

BOND VALUATION

Bonds, like any other financial asset, can be valued by estimating the future cash flows and computing the total present value of these flows, using an appropriate discount rate. This approach is generally much easier to apply to fixed-income securities than to common stocks or other types of securities, since the bond indenture provides cash-flow information that can only be estimated for common stocks. The indenture indicates the interest or coupon rate and the frequency of payment, along with the maturity value and maturity date, key factors in determining value. This, of course, assumes that the issuer will be able to honor all of the contractual obligations in the indenture. If the issuer defaults on interest or principal payments, in either amount or timing, the value of the bond will be fundamentally changed.

The other variable that is needed to value a bond is the appropriate discount rate. This rate should represent the investor's required rate of return and include the risk-free rate of return plus a risk premium (see Chapter 2). The market consensus estimate of this rate can be observed at any time by examining the yield to maturity on a particular bond or by observing the yield to maturity on an appropriate bond index. This is in sharp contrast to a common stock where the investor is unable to determine the required rate of return because future cash flows are unknown and comparative required return estimates are not as readily available.

Bond valuation may initially appear to be fairly routine or mechanical, since the analyst is not forced to estimate many of the key variables that determine the value of the bond. As we will see, however, when factors such as default risk, changing market interest rates, and unexpected inflation are considered, bond analysis becomes much more challenging. In addition, if the analyst hopes to discover bonds that are currently over- or undervalued, estimates of future cash flows and the appropriate discount rate must be determined. This analysis must include a complete assessment of risk for the economy, the bond market, and the company over the analyst's investment horizon.

• Basic Equation

This section presents a basic **intrinsic valuation** equation that is commonly used in the analysis of bonds. For bonds with a stated coupon rate and maturity date, the equation is

$$V_0 = \frac{C_1}{(1+i)^1} + \frac{C_2}{(1+i)^2} + \ldots + \frac{C_N + M_N}{(1+i)^N} \qquad (11.1)$$

$$= \sum_{t=1}^{N} \frac{C_t}{(1+i)^t} + \frac{M_N}{(1+i)^N}$$

where

V_0 = intrinsic value of the bond
C_t = annual dollar coupon in period t

i = rate of discount or required rate of return
N = number of time periods remaining until the bond matures
M_N = maturity value of the bond

To calculate V_0, the analyst can use present value tables—present value of an annuity (PVIFA) and present value of a future sum (PVIF) tables are provided in Appendix A-4—bond valuation tables, or a financial calculator, or the bond value calculation in the Investment Analysis Software.

Equation 11.1 can be restated to facilitate computations with a calculator:

$$V_0 = C\left[\frac{1 - \frac{1}{(1+i)^N}}{i}\right] + \frac{M_N}{(1+i)^N} \tag{11.2}$$

Notice that the subscript t is not necessary for C because the equation assumes that the annual coupons are constant and therefore relies on the procedures for computing the present value of an annuity. For example, assume a bond has a stated annual coupon rate of 12 percent, a term to maturity of 20 years, a face value of $1,000, and a discount rate of 15 percent. Using Equation 11.2, the value of the bond is

$$\begin{aligned} V_0 &= .12(\$1{,}000)\left[\frac{1 - \frac{1}{(1.15)^{20}}}{.15}\right] + \frac{\$1{,}000}{(1.15)^{20}} \\ &= \$120(6.259) + \frac{\$1{,}000}{16.367} \\ &= \$751.08 + \$61.10 \\ &= \$812.18 \end{aligned}$$

Since the typical bond pays interest semiannually, Equation 11.2 can be modified to

$$V_0 = \frac{C}{2}\left[\frac{1 - \frac{1}{(1+i/2)^{2N}}}{i/2}\right] + \frac{M_N}{(1+i/2)^{2N}} \tag{11.3}$$

Using the same example, but assuming that the bond has a 12 percent coupon that is paid semiannually, the value is

$$\begin{aligned} V_0 &= \$120/2\left[\frac{1 - \frac{1}{(1+.15/2)^{40}}}{.15/2}\right] + \frac{\$1{,}000}{(1+.15/2)^{40}} \\ &= \$60(12.594) + \frac{\$1{,}000}{18.044} \\ &= \$755.64 + \$55.42 \\ &= \$811.06. \end{aligned}$$

Two factors cause the values of V_0 to differ ($812.18 versus $811.06). First, a bond paying interest semiannually is more valuable than one paying interest annually because cash flows are received earlier. Second, Equation 11.3 calculates a semiannual rate of discount as $i/2$, which in this case is $.15/2 = .075$. This semiannual rate results in an annual rate greater than .15, since $(1 + .075)^2 - 1 = .1556$. These two factors offset each other. Semiannual payment of interest increases V_0, while converting the annual discount rate to a semiannual rate by dividing by 2 lowers V_0. (You might like to convince yourself by recomputing V_0, using a semiannual rate that is equivalent to an effective annual rate of .15. This rate would be $\sqrt{1.15} - 1 = .0724$. Using this rate with Equation 11.3, the bond's value would be $839.20, which is greater than the value assuming annual coupons.)

Another factor that must frequently be considered when computing V_0 is that bonds are often bought or sold on dates other than the interest payment dates. The same problem for cash dividends on common stocks is handled by using ex-dividend dates, thereby avoiding the need to divide the dividend between the seller and buyer. This practice is not used for bonds because bonds are sold at prices that include interest accrued daily. For example, if a bond with interest payment dates of January 1 and July 1 is sold on April 1, the seller is due the interest that has accrued on the bond over the period from January through March. The buyer must pay the seller this amount since the *issuer* of the bond will pay the entire semiannual interest amount to the new owner on July 1.

• Consols, Zeros, OIDs, and LYONs

Although most bonds have finite maturity periods and fixed coupon payments, some bonds have infinite lives (theoretically), and some do not pay interest. A **consol** is a bond with an infinite term to maturity, while a bond that does not pay interest is commonly called a **zero.** The value of a consol can be computed as follows:

$$V_0 = \frac{C}{(1 + i)^1} + \frac{C}{(1 + i)^2} + \ldots + \frac{C}{(1 + i)^\infty} = \frac{C}{i} \qquad (11.4)$$

For example, assume annual interest of 12 percent and a face value of $1,000; the required rate of return is 15 percent. The value is simply (.12 × $1,000)/.15 = $800. This $800 value is the present value of an infinite stream of annual cash flows of $120, discounted at 15 percent.

For a zero, V_0 can be computed as

$$V_0 = \frac{0}{(1 + i)^1} + \frac{0}{(1 + i)^2} + \ldots + \frac{M_N}{(1 + i)^N} \qquad (11.5)$$

where M_N is the maturity value of the bond and N is the number of time periods remaining until maturity. For example, assume that a zero has a maturity value of $1,000 and a term to maturity of 25 years. If an investor requires a 15 percent annual rate of return, then $V_0 = \$1,000/(1 + .15)^{25} = \$1,000/32.919 = \$30.38$. This value may appear to be low, but with "high" values for N and i, the present value of M_N is smaller than might be expected. This feature is the reason zeros are often referred to as *multipliers*, since a $30.38 investment will "multiply" to $1,000 after 25 years at a 15 percent return.

Zeros are issued by corporations, municipalities, and the U.S. Treasury and are created by brokerage firms that have "stripped" the coupons and principal payments from U.S. Treasury notes and bonds. Stripped zeros have become so popular that in February 1985 the Treasury began stripping its own securities by offering "Separate Trading on Registered Interest and Principal Securities" or **STRIPS.** STRIPS are now actively traded with maturities of 1 to 30 years.

Another type of bond, similar to a zero, is an **original issue discount** bond or **OID.** The first OID was issued by Martin Marietta Corporation in March 1981 and was essentially a bond with a "low" coupon that initially sold at a sizable discount. Traditionally, corporate bonds were issued at prices at or near par, or face value, since the coupon rate was set at the yield to maturity for similar quality bonds. OIDs, however, are issued with coupons below prevailing market yields; thus, they must be sold at a discount. A zero is actually a special case of an OID.[1] The Tax Equity and Fiscal Responsibility Act (TEFRA) of 1982 eliminated the favorable tax treatment of zeros and OIDs for bonds issued after July 1, 1982. Zeros issued by municipalities, however, still receive favorable tax treatment.

Another unique type of zero is a **liquid yield option note (LYON),** first issued in 1985. This bond has a zero coupon, but is also convertible, callable, and puttable. The *put* feature allows the investor to sell the bond to the issuer at a predetermined price. The convertible and puttable features increase the value of the bond, but the callable feature lowers its value. The combined influence of these factors makes valuation of LYONs difficult.

Table 11.1 provides a sample of corporate zeros, OIDs, LYONs, and a consol. With the exception of the consol, all of the bonds were issued after 1980. Table 11.2 summarizes the characteristics of the LYON issued by Merrill Lynch. Notice that the prices specified for the put feature increase each year until 2005, when the put price reaches $960.20 versus the maturity value of $1,000 in 2006.

• Investment Decision Making

The basic concepts and valuation equations discussed earlier in the chapter provide the foundation for investment decisions concerning bonds. For a passive or buy-and-hold investor, the decision is straightforward. The investor

[1] For a discussion and analysis of OIDs, see Andrew J. Kalotay, "An Analysis of Original Issue Discount Bonds," *Financial Management* (Autumn 1984): 29–38; and Marcelle Arak, "Profit Opportunities with Old OIDs," *Journal of Portfolio Management* (Spring 1985): 63–66.

TABLE 11.1 • Examples of Zeros, OIDs, LYONs, and Consol

	Date issued	Coupon rate	Maturity date	Initial price*	Initial yield	Amount out-standing (millions)	Current price*	Current call price*	Yield to maturity
Zeros									
McDonald's	08/20/82	—	1994	25.00%	12.60%	$ 31.3	80.125%	100.0%	8.18%
Chase Manhattan Bank	04/29/82	—	1992	22.29	14.25	90.1	89.625	100.0	10.34
Conair Acquisitions	06/13/85	—	1994	29.64	—	34.9	36.000	100.0	Flat
Environdyne	07/31/89	—	1997	49.84	—	259.0	—	112.1	Flat
J. C. Penney	03/30/82	—	1992	25.00	13.50	150.0	87.375	100.0	8.03
OIDs									
Martin Marietta	03/10/81	7.00%	2011	53.83	13.25	96.2	79.375	100.0	9.28
Orion Pictures	01/27/84	10.00	1994	77.67	14.25	19.0	61.500	100.0	—
Owens-Illinois	05/21/87	15.00	2003	42.58	14.75	400.0	68.250	107.4	—
Philip Morris	11/17/81	6.00	1999	47.39	14.13	47.4	83.250	100.0	8.80
Transamerica	03/19/81	6.50	2011	48.07	13.80	98.4	73.750	100.0	9.43
LYONs									
Merrill Lynch	08/15/85	—	2006	20.00	—	222.8	30.875	104.0	—
National Medical	01/31/86	—	2004	25.00	—	284.0	57.000	367.9	—
Seagram (Joseph E.)	08/23/85	—	2006	20.00	—	310.3	43.000	104.0	—
Staley Continental	05/01/85	—	2001	24.12	—	110.0	44.125	103.6	—
Waste Management	04/22/85	—	2001	25.00	—	200.0	137.000	104.5	—
Consol									
Canadian Pacific	12/01/21	4.00	—	—	—	149.1	45.000	—	—

SOURCE: Moody's *Bond Record* (April 1991). Reprinted by permission.

*The price is expressed as a percentage of face value.

TABLE 11.2 • Characteristics of the Liquid Yield Option Note (LYON) Issued by Merrill Lynch & Company, Inc.

Denomination:	$1,000 and $5,000					
Callable feature:	Callable on or after August 15, 1987 at the following prices:					
	1987	108.00%	1992	104.00%		
	1988	107.20	1993	102.40		
	1989	106.40	1994	101.60		
	1990	105.60	1995	100.80		
	1991	104.80	1996 and after	100.00		
Put feature:	The investor (holder) can sell the LYON to Merrill Lynch on August 15, 1988, and each August thereafter at the following prices:					
	1988	$238.81	1994	$405.16	2000	$648.68
	1989	259.32	1995	438.22	2001	701.61
	1990	286.24	1996	473.98	2002	758.86
	1991	320.21	1997	512.66	2003	820.79
	1992	346.34	1998	554.49	2004	887.76
	1993	374.60	1999	599.74	2005	960.20
Convertible feature:	Convertible at any time into 5.31 shares of common stock.					

SOURCE: Moody's *Bank and Finance Manual*, vol. 2 (1990). Reprinted by permission.

may be quite willing to assume that the current market price of a bond (P_0) is a good indication of the bond's intrinsic value, which is essentially V_0, so that $P_0 = V_0$. This type of investor is not concerned with finding over- or undervalued bonds and essentially is willing to accept the general market consensus of the bond's value as indicated by P_0. If the issuer pays interest and principal according to the indenture provisions, the bond is held to maturity, and interest rates are constant, the annual rate of return to the investor will be the yield to maturity prevailing on the date the bond is purchased.

For individuals attempting to pursue a more active strategy, the possibility exists that $P_0 \lesseqgtr V_0$. In these instances, the bond would be overvalued ($P_0 > V_0$) or undervalued ($P_0 < V_0$), providing the investor with an opportunity to earn risk-adjusted excess returns. To pursue this strategy, the investor must compute V_0 using estimates of an appropriate discount rate (i) and, for a risky bond with default probabilities, must estimate the amount and timing of future cash flows. By using these individual estimates of the key variables that determine V_0, the investor may discover that the current value of the bond is different from the market's assessment, so that $V_0 \neq P_0$. Of course, if the investor is correct and the market is incorrect, excess returns will result if the price changes in the direction anticipated by the investor.

BOND RETURN MEASURES

This section discusses various rate of return measures for fixed-income securities and is closely related to the previous section on bond valuation. The previous section essentially assumed that the required rate of return is given and used this rate to compute value. This section assumes that the price or investment value of the bond is given and uses this value to compute a rate of return.

An example at the end of this section uses an actual corporate bond to show how an analyst might interpret and use each return measure.

• Current Yield

A bond return measure that is popular with investors and is provided on a daily basis in the *Wall Street Journal* is the **current** or **coupon yield.** As its name implies, this yield is based entirely on the relationship between the coupon rate and current price:

$$i_c = \frac{C}{P_0} \tag{11.6}$$

where

i_c = current or coupon yield
C = annual dollar coupon
P_0 = current market price

This return measure is only a partial indication of the return. First, the price of the bond will move toward face value as the bond approaches maturity, so that the actual return will be more or less than i_c, depending on whether the bond is purchased at a discount or premium price. Second, the price is likely to change over the holding period because of changes in market conditions. For investors who do not plan to hold the bond to maturity, the capital gains and losses resulting from price changes are ignored in calculating i_c. It is also easy to show that a bond currently selling at its face value will have a yield to maturity equal to the coupon rate, so that i_c is equal to the yield to maturity. At any other price, however, the current yield is different from the yield to maturity.

• Yield to Maturity

The **yield to maturity** of a bond represents the annual rate of return that will occur if certain conditions are satisfied. In computing the yield to maturity, several important assumptions are made:

1. The bond will be held to maturity.
2. All cash flows (interest and principal) will occur as indicated in the indenture (i.e., the issuer will not default on the contractual obligation).
3. The bond will not be called or redeemed by the issuer before the specified maturity date.
4. Coupon receipts will be reinvested at a rate of return equal to the yield to maturity.

Yield to maturity can be computed using Equations 11.2, 11.3, 11.4, or 11.5, depending on the characteristics of the bond. These equations all require that V_0 be equated with the current market price of the bond, P_0. By letting $V_0 = P_0$, the investor can determine what yield to maturity is implied by the current market price.

Unfortunately, calculating the yield to maturity can be quite time-consuming for bonds with a finite life and annual or semiannual coupon payments. The problem is that Equations 11.2 and 11.3 must be solved for i or the yield to maturity using a trial-and-error procedure.

To illustrate, using the simplified case of a zero, assume the current price is \$100, term to maturity is 25 years, and maturity value is \$1,000. Using Equation 11.5, the calculations are

$$V_0 = \frac{M_N}{(1+i)^N}$$

$$\$100 = \frac{\$1{,}000}{(1+i)^{25}}$$

$$(1+i)^{25} = \frac{\$1{,}000}{\$100}$$

$$1 + i = 10^{1/25}$$

$$1 + i = 1.0965$$

$$i = 9.65\%$$

Thus, if this zero is purchased for \$100 and held to maturity, and the issuer pays \$1,000 at maturity, then the yield to maturity is 9.65 percent, compounded annually.

A bond with a finite life and semiannual coupon payments requires a more difficult calculation, which cannot be solved explicitly using algebra. Without the benefit of a financial calculator, a trial-and-error procedure (with, possibly, the need for linear interpolation) must be used. Consider a corporate bond with a face value of \$1,000, a term to maturity of 25 years, a coupon rate of 12 percent paid semiannually, and a current market price of \$750 on an interest payment date. You might want to use a preprogrammed financial calculator or the yield-to-maturity calculation in the Investment Analysis Software to confirm that the yield to maturity on the bond is 16.75 percent.

• Yield To Maturity for Callable Bonds

Most bonds issued during the 1980s have a call feature that allows the issuer to redeem the bonds prior to maturity. Thus, the issuer can take advantage of lower yields by calling outstanding bonds and refinancing at lower rates. This possibility presents a problem in calculating the yield to maturity because yield to maturity is based on the full term of the bond.

To reflect the impact of a possible call on the yield, the **yield to first call** should be calculated in addition to the yield to maturity. Equation 11.3 can simply be modified as

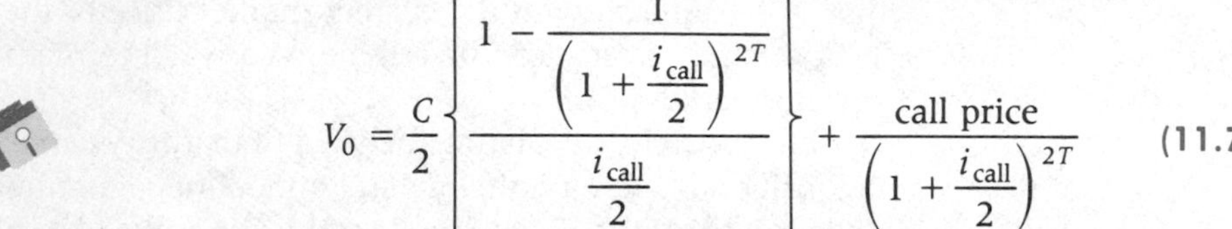

$$V_0 = \frac{C}{2}\left\{\frac{1 - \dfrac{1}{\left(1 + \dfrac{i_{\text{call}}}{2}\right)^{2T}}}{\dfrac{i_{\text{call}}}{2}}\right\} + \frac{\text{call price}}{\left(1 + \dfrac{i_{\text{call}}}{2}\right)^{2T}} \qquad (11.7)$$

Where the previous definitions given for Equation 11.3 apply and

i_{call} = yield to first call
T = length of time to first call date, in years
call price = price that issuer will pay at first call date

As with the yield to maturity, the equation can be solved using a financial calculator or the yield-to-first-call calculation in the Investment Analysis Software. Table 11.3 illustrates the calculation of the yield to first call. Notice that

TABLE 11.3 • Calculating the Yield to First Call

Characteristics of bond and current market information:

Face value	\$1,000
Coupon rate (paid semiannually)	12%
Term to maturity	5 years
Term to first call date	3 years
Current price	\$900
Yield to maturity	14.9% (calculated using Equation 11.3)
First call price	\$1,100

Yield to first call:

$$\$900 = \$60\left\{\frac{1 - \dfrac{1}{\left(1 + \dfrac{i_{\text{call}}}{2}\right)^{6}}}{\dfrac{i_{\text{call}}}{2}}\right\} + \frac{\$1{,}100}{\left(1 + \dfrac{i_{\text{call}}}{2}\right)^{6}}$$

Using a financial calculator, the i_{call} = 19.16%.

the yield to first call is significantly higher than the yield to maturity. This occurs, in part, because the call price of the bond is $1,100 versus a face value of $1,000.

The importance of yield to first call versus yield to maturity depends on the likelihood that the bond will be called. The probability of a call increases during periods of declining yields, especially when the yield to maturity declines below the coupon yield. The issuer also considers the relationship between the market and call prices when analyzing the feasibility of a call. In 1988, largely because of pressure from institutional investors, a number of corporations started to issue noncallable bonds named *Bullets*. They generally are offered at yields slightly below callable bonds and are long term. Major issuers include ITT, Dow Corning, Dayton-Hudson, Transamerica, and Eastman Kodak.

• Holding Period Return

Investors are often concerned about bond returns over a particular holding period. If the holding period was in the past, the return is a historical, or ex-post, measure. The investor concerned with a future holding period calculates the expected, or ex-ante, return. One of the major problems with yield to maturity is that it requires an assumption about the length of the holding period. The yield to maturity assumes the bond will be held until maturity, and the current yield ignores the term of the bond.

Recently, attention has moved from the traditional measures of bond returns to the **holding period return (HPR).** This shift is consistent with the idea that more active bond investment strategies may be desirable. These strategies may be for relatively short periods of time as opposed to long-term, buy-and-hold strategies. For example, a bond may be purchased and sold in a one-month period. The HPR represents an appropriate measure of the return for this type of strategy.

For bonds with coupons, the HPR can be calculated as

$$HPR_t = \frac{P_{t+1} - P_t + I_{t+1}}{P_t} \tag{11.8}$$

where

HPR_t = holding period return for period t
P_t = the beginning or purchase price of the bond
P_{t+1} = the ending or selling price of the bond
I_{t+1} = the coupon or interest received for period t

Notice that this equation assumes that interest will be received at the end of holding period t. This assumption is correct for bonds because they are sold with accrued interest due to the seller.

To illustrate, assume that a bond with a face value of $1,000 is purchased on January 1 for $800 and sold on July 1 for $850. The bond pays a 12 percent coupon semiannually on January 1 and July 1. The ex-post HPR is

$$\text{HPR}_t = \frac{\$850 - \$800 + \dfrac{.12(\$1{,}000)}{2}}{\$800}$$

$$= \frac{\$50}{\$800} + \frac{\$60}{\$800}$$

$$= .0625 + .075$$

$$= 13.75\%$$

Notice that the price appreciation represents a return of 6.25 percent, while the interest income represents a 7.50 percent return. It should also be recognized that the length of the holding period is six months, so the HPR is a semiannual return. Since returns are commonly stated on an annual basis, the semiannual return can be *annualized* as $(1 + .1375)^2 - 1 = .2939$, or 29.39 percent.

As was pointed out earlier, the HPR can be used to compute ex-ante or expected returns. To do this, the analyst estimates future interest income and selling price. The following section explains how to compute the expected rate of return for a bond.

• Expected Rate of Return

In analyzing various bonds for investment, the analyst must consider the **expected rate of return** that each bond can provide. For default-free bonds like U.S. Treasury securities that are held to maturity, the analyst may feel comfortable equating the yield to maturity of the bond to the expected rate of return. A more detailed analysis is needed when a bond has default probabilities, will not be held to maturity, and when yields in general may change over the holding period.

An example of an approach that can be used to analyze the influence of default risk on the expected rate of return appears in Table 11.4. The purpose of the analysis is to calculate the expected HPR or E(HPR). Part I of the table lists the basic characteristics of the bond, along with the current price and the resulting current yield and yield to maturity. The analyst also assumes that the bond will be held for one year and therefore, in Part II, estimates the economic environment for the coming year. For each of these states of nature, a probability, coupon, and end-of-year price for the bond must be estimated. If a recession occurs, the company will experience severe financial problems and will be unable to pay the coupon. As a result, the bond will be traded *flat*, or without interest; in that event, the price is expected to fall dramatically.

An HPR can be computed for each state of nature, using Equation 11.8, and the E(HPR) can be calculated as illustrated in Part III of Table 11.4. The E(HPR) of 7.86% should be compared to the yield to maturity of 14.96% and the current yield of 14.67%. This comparison is useful in illustrating why the yield to maturity or current yield should not be used as an indicator of the expected return for a bond with default probabilities that will not be held to

TABLE 11.4 • Calculating the Expected Rate of Return on a Risky Corporate Bond

I. Characteristics of the Bond and Current Market Information

Face value	\$1,000
Coupon rate (paid annually)	11%
Term to maturity	20 years
Rating by Moody's	B
Current price	\$750
Current yield	$\frac{(.11)(1{,}000)}{750} = 14.67\%$
Yield to maturity	14.96% (calculated using Equation 11.2)

II. Estimates by Analyst for Coming Year

State of Nature	*Probability*	*Coupon*	*Year-end price*
Recession	.1	\$ 0	\$400
No growth	.5	110	700
Moderate growth	.4	110	800

III. Calculations

State of nature	*Holding period return*
Recession	$\frac{400 - 750 + 0}{750} = -.4667$
No growth	$\frac{700 - 750 + 110}{750} = .0800$
Moderate growth	$\frac{800 - 750 + 110}{750} = .2133$

$$\text{Expected HPR} = E(\text{HPR}) = \sum_{i=1}^{n} (\text{probability})_i \times (\text{HPR})_i$$
$$= .1(-.4667) + .5(.08) + .4(.2133)$$
$$= -.0467 + .04 + .0853$$
$$= .0786 = 7.86\%.$$

maturity. For investment decision making, it is much more appropriate to think in terms of E(HPR) than in terms of the yield to maturity or current yield. Finally, the approach outlined in Table 11.4 can be expanded or developed in much greater detail by incorporating additional states of nature, holding periods longer than one year, and other factors such as the probability of a call.

• An Illustration and Comparison of Return Measures

Table 11.5 provides the characteristics, prices, coupon yields, yields to maturity, and HPRs for a debenture issued by AT&T. Notice that the coupon rate is below the yields to maturity because the bond is selling at a discount. The monthly HPRs were calculated using Equation 11.8 and recognizing that the

TABLE 11.5 • Rate of Return Measures for Debenture Issued by American Telephone and Telegraph (AT&T)

Characteristics of Debenture

Initial offering		$500.0 million		
Coupon rate		7.00%		
Maturity value		$1,000		
Maturity date		February 15, 2001		
Interest payment dates		February and August 15		
Amount outstanding		$104.6 million		
Traded on NYSE				
Call prices	1991	101.50%	1994	100.75%
	1992	101.25	1995	100.50
	1993	101.00	1996	100.25

Prices and Return Measures

		Month-end price	*Annual coupon yield*	*Yield to maturity*	*Monthly HPR*
1990	January	85.125%	8.22%	9.17%	—
	February	84.625	8.27	9.26	0.10%
	March	84.250	8.31	9.33	0.25
	April	82.000	8.54	9.73	−1.98
	May	85.125	8.22	9.21	4.52
	June	86.000	8.14	9.08	1.71
	July	86.000	8.14	9.09	0.68
	August	84.250	8.31	9.39	−1.36
	September	84.125	8.32	9.43	0.54
	October	84.500	8.28	9.38	1.14
	November	86.000	8.14	9.13	2.47
	December	85.500	8.19	9.23	0.10
1991	January	87.125	8.03	8.97	2.58
	February	88.625	7.90	8.73	2.39
	March	88.500	7.91	8.70	0.52

SOURCES: Prices and yields to maturity: Various issues of Moody's *Bond Record*. Reprinted by permission. Characteristics: Moody's *Public Utility Manual*, vol. 1 (1990). Reprinted by permission.

monthly interest is $5.83 [(.07)($1,000]/12. The variability and magnitude of the HPRs indicate that the realized or ex-post returns may be quite different from the coupon rate or yield to maturity for short holding periods. The volatility in the monthly prices also indicates that forecasting the ex-ante returns, or E(HPR), is a challenging problem. We will return to this example after bond risk analysis is introduced in the next section.

The bond in Table 11.5 is unlikely to be called in the immediate future because the coupon rate is below the yield to maturity. The call price of $1,015 for 1991 is also substantially above the March 1991 price of $885. If the analyst anticipates a longer holding period, however, the yield to first call should be calculated.

BOND RISK ANALYSIS

Bond valuation depends on the expected return and risk associated with the bond. The previous two sections presented some basic concepts of bond valuation and return measures. This section discusses some of the unique risk factors associated with bonds. It also looks at both traditional approaches to bond risk analysis and at more recent approaches that attempt to measure bond risk empirically. The section concludes with an illustration and comparison of risk measures.

• Systematic Sources of Bond Risk

One basic source of bond risk is the possibility that interest rates will change after a bond is purchased, thereby affecting the bond price and the reinvestment rate of return. Unanticipated inflation with the resulting loss in purchasing power is another important source of risk for fixed-income securities. These factors basically represent *systematic* or *nondiversifiable* risk for bonds since they generally have an impact on all bonds. There are three types of systematic risk: price risk, reinvestment risk, and purchasing power risk.

PRICE CHANGES RESULTING FROM CHANGES IN YIELDS Since the majority of bonds have fixed coupon and maturity values, any change in market interest rates will result in changes in bond prices. Coupon income will not increase if market interest rates increase, nor will the maturity value change. Therefore, for investors to receive the higher market rates on bonds currently outstanding, bond prices must decline. Conversely, if market interest rates decline, bond prices will increase. This inverse relationship between interest rates and prices represents the **price risk** of bonds.

Changes in market interest rates or yields cause all bond prices to change. The amount of change or price risk, however, depends on the characteristics of the bond. These relationships were formally specified by Burton G. Malkiel in 1961 and are referred to as theorems about bond price changes:

1. Prices and yields move inversely.
2. For a given change in yield, bonds with *longer* terms to maturity have greater percentage price changes, but these changes diminish as the term increases. For example, if bonds with terms of 5, 10, and 15 years are considered, the relative price changes of the 10-year bond and the 5-year bond will be greater than those between the 10- and 15-year bonds.
3. For a given change in yield, bonds with *lower* coupons have greater (percentage) price changes.
4. For a given price and equal increases or decreases in yields, the percentage increase in price resulting from a yield decline will be larger than the percentage decrease in price from an increase in yield.

REINVESTMENT RATE RISK Since the majority of bonds provide periodic income to the investor through coupon payments, a potential reinvestment problem can arise. **Reinvestment rate risk** results because of uncertainty about the rates of return that will be available when the coupons and principal are to be reinvested. As previously discussed, the yield to maturity implicitly assumes that coupons are reinvested at the yield to maturity that existed at the time the bond was purchased. Investors using other return measures such as the expected holding period return, E(HPR), and attempting to determine an appropriate holding period must also deal with reinvestment risk. For example, should a "low" or "high" coupon bond be purchased and should the holding period be "long" or "short"? If yields are expected to increase, and thereby provide higher reinvestment rates, the higher coupon bond may be preferred. In addition, a shorter maturity may be better since the principal can be received earlier and reinvested at a higher rate.

To illustrate the reinvestment rate problem and the impact of the coupon and term, consider an investor who is deciding between an 8 percent coupon bond with a two-year term (Bond A) versus a 12 percent coupon bond with a four-year term (Bond B). Both bonds are rated Aa by Moody's and pay interest annually. First, assume a constant yield to maturity over the two-year holding period. As Part I of Table 11.6 illustrates, if the investor purchases Bond A, the total value of the cash flows will be $1,168.80 at the end of year 2. This value is calculated by assuming the first coupon is received after one year and reinvested for one year at 11 percent, resulting in a terminal value at the end of year 2 of $88.80. The second coupon is received at the end of the second year, and since the holding period is assumed to be two years, the terminal value is simply $80. The last cash flow for Bond A is the maturity value of $1,000, which will be received at the end of year 2. The two-year HPR is 23.21 percent and the annualized HPR of 11 percent is identical to the original yield to maturity. For Bond B, the calculations assume that the bond is sold for its market value at the end of year 2. Since the yield to maturity is equal to the coupon rate and both are constant, the bond's price will not change. The two-year HPR is 25.44 percent and its annualized HPR is also

TABLE 11.6 • Illustrations of Reinvestment Rate Risk

I. HPRs if Coupons Are Reinvested at the Yield to Maturity (Yield to Maturity Remains Constant)

	Bond A	*Bond B*
Current yield to maturity	11%	12%
Current price	$948.62	$1,000
Assume a two-year holding period:		
Values of cash flows at end of year 2:		
Coupon for year 1	80(1.11) = $88.80	120(1.12) = $134.40
Coupon for year 2	80(1.0) = $80.00	120(1.0) = $120.00
Maturity value	$1,000.00	—
Price at end of year 2	—	$1,000.00
Total value at end of year 2	$1,168.80	$1,254.40

Annualized HPR:

Bond A: $\$1{,}168.80 = \$948.62(1 + r)^2$

$$1.2321 = (1 + r)^2$$

$$1 + r = \sqrt{1.2321}$$

$$r = 11\%$$

Bond B: $\$1{,}254.40 = 1{,}000(1 + r)^2$

$$1.2544 = (1 + r)^2$$

$$1 + r = \sqrt{1.2544}$$

$$r = 12\%$$

II. HPRs if Coupons Are Reinvested at a Rate *Lower* Than the Current Yield to Maturity

	Bond A	*Bond B*
Assumed reinvestment rate	8%	8%
Price at end of year 2	$1,000.00	$1,071.33
Total value of cash flows at end of year 2	$1,166.40	$1,320.93
Annualized HPR	10.89%	14.93%

III. HPRs if Coupons Are Reinvested at a Rate *Higher* Than the Current Yield to Maturity

	Bond A	*Bond B*
Assumed reinvestment rate	14%	14%
Price at end of year 2	$1,000.00	$967.06
Total value of cash flows at end of year 2	$1,171.20	$1,223.86
Annualized HPR	11.11%	10.54%

equal to the yield to maturity, or 12 percent. Comparing the results and assuming that yields do in fact remain constant, the investor would undoubtedly select Bond B based on its higher HPR.

Part II of Table 11.6 assumes that cash flows must be reinvested at the rate of 8 percent, which lowers the annualized HPR on Bond A to 10.89 percent. It should also be pointed out that the investor would not benefit from an increase in the price of Bond A due to the decline in yield because it is held to maturity. For Bond B, the decline in reinvestment income is more than offset by the price appreciation that results because the yield to maturity declined to 8 percent. The annualized HPR of 14.93 percent for Bond B is considerably higher than the yield to maturity of 12 percent. Again the results favor Bond B.

Assuming that cash flows are reinvested at *higher* rates, however, would make Bond A more attractive; Bond B would experience a price decline that would offset the higher reinvestment income. This is illustrated in Part III of Table 11.6.

If the holding period of two years is lengthened, however, and reinvestment rates increase, Bond A would be even more attractive since the maturity value of $1,000 could be reinvested after two years. If reinvestment rates *decrease,* however, Bond B would provide a higher HPR.

This example illustrates why bond investors should be concerned about reinvestment rate risk for both coupons and maturity values. It suggests several general conclusions:

1. If reinvestment rates of return are not equal to the yield to maturity, then the HPR will not equal the yield to maturity.
2. If the term and the desired holding period of a bond are equal (Bond A), the HPR and yield to maturity will still not be equal if yields change.
3. Anticipated higher reinvestment rates make high coupon and short-term bonds more attractive.
4. If yields decline, resulting in lower reinvestment rates, lower coupon and long-term bonds will experience larger price increases, which may offset the lower reinvestment income.

One of the major reasons investors have readily accepted newer bonds such as zeros is their ability to eliminate reinvestment rate risk. Since no coupons are received, the investor can simply purchase a zero with a term equal to the desired holding period. The disadvantage, however, is that rates may increase over the holding period, and the investor will not benefit from higher reinvestment income. Other factors that should be considered in the decision to purchase a zero or a coupon bond include tax considerations, call features, default risk, and the risk attitude of the investor.[2]

---

[2] A framework for this analysis is provided in James M. Johnson, "When Are Zero Coupon Bonds the Better Buy?" *Journal of Portfolio Management* (Spring 1984): 36–41.

PURCHASING POWER RISK Investors should always be concerned about after-tax returns rather than before-tax returns. They should also be concerned about *real* versus *nominal* rates of return. Real rates of return are adjusted for the impact of inflation and the resulting decline in purchasing power. **Purchasing power risk** results because general price increases over the holding period reduce the buying power of future coupon and principal receipts. Fixed-income securities are especially susceptible to purchasing power risk when inflation is unanticipated. For example, suppose bonds of a certain classification are priced to provide a nominal rate of return of r_n, which includes a real return, r_r, and an inflation premium, I_p:

$$r_n = r_r + I_p \tag{11.9}$$

If r_n is observed to be 12 percent and the desired real return is 5 percent, then the inflation premium would be 7 percent. If inflation is actually 7 percent, then the realized or ex-post value of r_r will be 5 percent. If, however, the rate of inflation is more or less than 7 percent, the real return will not be 5 percent.

A long-running debate, dating back to a 1930 study by Irving Fisher, concerns the ability of the market to correctly anticipate inflation and price financial assets to provide an inflation hedge. Empirical evidence for both fixed-income securities and common stocks, however, suggests that neither provide effective inflation hedges during periods of "high" inflation. This finding has naturally led to the suggestion that bonds are poor investments during inflationary periods.

Before discussing this point further, the procedures for adjusting nominal returns for inflation, or calculating real rates of return, should be considered. Assume that inflation will be measured by the Consumer Price Index (CPI) and that, for convenience, the value of this index is now 100. Also assume that you would like to earn a real rate of return of 8 percent on a $1,000 investment for one year and that you anticipate inflation will be 7 percent for the year (i.e., the CPI will increase to 107). What nominal rate of return must the investment provide? At first glance, you may think that 15 percent would be sufficient, as indicated by Equation 11.9. This rate, however, would *not* protect both your principal and income from the impact of inflation.

To illustrate, assume that you invest $1,000 today at 15 percent and receive $1,000(1.15) = $1,150 at the end of the year. Adjusting this value for the decline in purchasing power results in $1,150/1.07 = $1,074.77, providing a real rate of return of only ($1,074.77 − $1,000)/$1,000 = 7.48%.

This 7.48 percent is less than the desired real rate of return, 8 percent. The problem, of course, is that both income and principal are not protected against inflation. The following equation illustrates the correct procedure:

$$\begin{aligned} P_{t+1} + I_{t+1} &= P_t(1 + r_r)(1 + I_p) \\ &= P_t(1 + r_r + I_p + r_r I_p) \\ &= \$1{,}000[1 + .08 + .07 + (.08)(.07)] \\ &= \$1{,}000(1 + .1556) \\ &= \$1{,}155.60 \end{aligned} \tag{11.10}$$

Thus, you must receive cash flows of $1,155.60 at the end of the year, which would be a nominal holding period return of 15.56 percent. Assuming the bond's price is $1,000 ($P_{t+1}$) at the end of the year and the coupon or interest received (I_{t+1}) is $155.60, the real rate of return is

$$r_r = \frac{\dfrac{P_{t+1} + I_{t+1}}{(1 + I_p)} - P_t}{P_t} \tag{11.11}$$

$$= (\$1,155.60/1.07 - \$1,000)/\$1,000$$

$$= \frac{\$1,080 - \$1,000}{\$1,000}$$

$$= 8.0\%$$

Notice that both principal and interest income ($1,000 and $155.60) are protected against the loss in purchasing power. Equation 11.11 can be used to calculate the real rate of return. Compare it with Equation 11.8, which computes the nominal holding period return (HPR).

• Unsystematic Sources of Bond Risk

Interest rate changes and unanticipated inflation are major sources of systematic risk to bondholders. General economic conditions and specific developments in money and capital markets are responsible for these sources of risk. In addition, however, company and possibly industry developments must be considered when analyzing total risk. These factors can generally be classified as *unsystematic* or *diversifiable* risk because they do not influence the bond markets in general. The major source of unsystematic or diversifiable risk for bonds is the **risk of default.**

Unique company factors are only important to a bond investor if they are expected to have a major impact on the company's ability to meet the obligations detailed in the indenture. Essentially, the investor must assess the probability that the company will default on the indenture contract. For bonds that are generally viewed as default-free, such as U.S. Treasury securities, the probability of default is nil. Uninsured municipal and corporate debt always have the danger of default, so their probability of default is greater than zero.

The bond ratings assigned by the rating agencies are based on a financial analysis of the issuer and depend on the skills and judgment of the analysts. Studies have developed statistical models that are quite successful in predicting a bond's rating based on a fairly small number of financial variables.[3] Generally, these models correctly predicted two-thirds or more of the ratings. The models, of course, do not use any subjective, or judgmental, factors.

[3] For a discussion and comparison of the models, see Louis H. Ederington, "Classification Models and Bond Ratings," *Financial Review* (November 1985): 237–62.

RESEARCH BOX
Default Risk and Junk Bonds

The high-yield or junk bond market grew at a frenzied pace in the 1980s because of corporate restructuring, leveraged buyouts, and merger activities. Most of the growth came from new issues of bonds rather than from *fallen angels* that were issued as investment-grade bonds and declined to junk bonds because of a deteriorating financial condition.

Christopher Ma, Ramesh Rao, and Richard Peterson analyzed the junk bond market after the 1986 LTV bankruptcy, which at that time was the largest high-yield or junk bond default in history. The face value of the LTV bonds that defaulted was $1.766 billion. As might be expected, the study found that the LTV default had a dramatic negative effect on the junk bond market. In general, yields on junk bonds increased dramatically and bond prices declined. However, the study also found that the negative impact of the LTV default was transitory and lasted only approximately six months. After six months, the yield and prices on most junk bonds returned to their approximate levels before the LTV default. In the words of the authors of the study, "In contrast to previous conjectures, the high-yield bond market demonstrates surprisingly strong resiliency."

It should also be noted, however, that the study analyzed only one very large default. The market might not be so resilient if a number of major defaults occurred over a relatively short period of time.

SOURCE: Christopher K. Ma, Ramesh P. Rao, and Richard L. Peterson, "The Resiliency of the High-Yield Bond Market: The LTV Default," *Journal of Finance* (September 1989): 1085–97.

These models have identified the following variables as determinants of bond ratings:

1. Leverage as measured by the balance sheet.
2. Interest and fixed charge coverage.
3. Profitability.
4. Ratio of cash flow to long-term debt.
5. Firm size.
6. Subordination status.

In summary, bond ratings are important as measures of default risk. Ratings do contain additional information above and beyond the information available in accounting variables. Studies also indicate, however, that investors should depend on their own evaluations of creditworthiness.

• Empirical Measures of Bond Risk

Traditional bond risk measures include rating, coupon, and term. As discussed previously, rating indicates default risk, while coupon and term indicate price volatility and reinvestment rate risk. Since risk is often equated with the variability of price and the resulting HPRs, low-coupon and long-term bonds will experience larger price changes than high-coupon and short-term bonds. (See theorems 2 and 3 dealing with bond price changes presented earlier.)

TOTAL RISK A measure of the total risk of a bond is the *variance* or *standard deviation* of the various return measures such as coupon yield, yield to maturity, or HPR. The variance can be ex-post or ex-ante depending on whether historical or forecast returns are used. This measure of risk includes all variability in returns and, as a consequence, includes both systematic and unsystematic risk.

As an illustration, consider the analysis presented earlier in Table 11.4 showing an $E(\text{HPR})$ of 7.86 percent. The ex-ante variance and standard deviation associated with this estimate can be calculated as follows:

$$\sigma^2_{\text{HPR}} = \sum_{i=1}^{n} \text{probability}_i[\text{HPR}_i - E(\text{HPR})]^2 \tag{11.12}$$

where

$$\begin{aligned} \sigma^2_{\text{HPR}} &= \text{variance of holding period return} \\ i &= \text{states of nature, } i = 1 \ldots n \\ \text{HPR}_i &= \text{estimated holding period return for state of nature } i \\ E(\text{HPR}) &= \text{expected holding period return} \end{aligned}$$

The calculation is

$$\begin{aligned} \sigma^2_{\text{HPR}} &= .1(-.4667 - .0786)^2 + .5(.08 - .0786)^2 + .4(.2133 - .0786)^2 \\ &= .1(.2974) + .5(.000002) + .4(.0181) \\ &= .0297 + .000001 + .0072 \\ &= .0369 \\ \sigma_{\text{HPR}} &= \sqrt{.0369} = 19.21\% \end{aligned}$$

This value indicates that considerable total risk exists for this bond, primarily because of the possibility of a recession and the resulting low HPR for this state of nature.

SYSTEMATIC RISK Recent bond research has focused on other empirical risk measures that indicate the systematic risk of an individual bond or portfolio of bonds. Duration, a concept which was developed in the 1930s by Frederick Macaulay, has received considerable attention as a risk measurement and management tool. Duration originally was viewed as a measure of the "life" or "average" term of a bond that would be more useful to the analyst than the term of the bond. Since most bonds pay coupons, the investor receives income prior to the maturity date. Consequently, comparing bonds with different terms and coupons is difficult because their income streams will be quite different. **Duration** is defined as the weighted average number of years that cash flows occur. Cash flows include both coupon and principal payments. The weights are the present value of each cash flow as a percentage of the total present value of all cash flows. These weights are applied to the time period of the cash flow so that a weighted average time period or duration is computed. The resulting measure of duration, like the term of the bond, is expressed in units of time (e.g., 5.2 years). Duration (D) can be defined and calculated as

$$D = \frac{\sum_{t=1}^{N} \frac{tC_t}{(1+i)^t} + \frac{NM_N}{(1+i)^N}}{\sum_{t=1}^{N} \frac{C_t}{(1+i)^t} + \frac{M_N}{(1+i)^N}} \tag{11.13}$$

where

D = duration in time units
t = time period when cash flow is received, $t = 1 \ldots N$
N = term of the bond or number of time periods remaining until maturity
C_t = dollar coupon in period t
i = yield to maturity
M_N = maturity value of the bond

An examination of Equation 11.13 reveals that the denominator is simply the present value or price of the bond as previously defined in Equation 11.1. The numerator appears to be very similar to the denominator, but notice that t is multiplied by C_t for $t = 1 \ldots N$ and that M_N is multiplied by N. Table 11.7 illustrates how duration can be calculated using first a table format and then Equation 11.13.

Notice that the fourth column in Part I of Table 11.7 provides the present value of each cash flow and the sum of these present values. This value of \$828.39 is the denominator in Equation 11.13 and represents the current value of the bond. The fifth column indicates the proportion of each cash flow, in present value terms, to the total present value. The first coupon represents 9.53 percent of the total present value of the cash flows, while the last flow of \$1,090 represents 68.35 percent. Also, notice that the duration of 4.16 years is less than the term of 5 years. The duration for coupon-paying bonds will always be less than the term. For zeros, or bonds that do not pay a coupon, the duration and term are equal.

Part II of Table 11.7 is a vivid example of how tedious duration calculations with Equation 11.13 can be. This problem is magnified for bonds with long terms because the present value of each coupon must be calculated. Because

TABLE 11.7 • Calculating Duration

Assume that a bond provides a yield to maturity of 14 percent, has a face value of $1,000, pays a 9 percent coupon annually, and has 5 years remaining until maturity.

I. Table Format for Calculating Duration

(1) Time in years	*(2) Cash flow*	*(3) Present value factor, using yield to maturity of 14%*	*(4) Present value of cash flow*	*(5) Percentage of present value of each cash flow to total*	*(6) "Weights" multiplied by time period [(1) × (5)]*
1	$ 90	.8772	$ 78.95	.0953	.0953
2	90	.7695	69.25	.0836	.1672
3	90	.6750	60.75	.0733	.2199
4	90	.5921	53.29	.0643	.2572
5	1,090	.5194	566.15	.6835	3.4175
			$828.39	1.0000	Duration = 4.1571 years

II. Direct Calculation Using Equation 11.13

$$D = \frac{\frac{1(\$90)}{(1+.14)^1} + \frac{2(\$90)}{(1+.14)^2} + \frac{3(\$90)}{(1+.14)^3} + \frac{4(\$90)}{(1+.14)^4} + \frac{5(\$1{,}090)}{(1+.14)^5}}{\frac{\$90}{(1+.14)^1} + \frac{\$90}{(1+.14)^2} + \frac{\$90}{(1+.14)^3} + \frac{\$90}{(1+.14)^4} + \frac{\$1{,}090}{(1+.14)^5}}$$

$$D = \frac{\$3{,}443.60}{\$828.39} = 4.157 \text{ years}$$

the calculations are so tedious duration tables have been developed, and simplified equations have been derived.[4]

Another very important observation about duration is that it is a function of term, coupon, maturity value, and yield to maturity. Duration is directly related to term and inversely related to coupon and yield to maturity. Bonds with "low" coupons and "long" terms will have durations greater than bonds with "high" coupons and "short" terms. Also, as yield to maturity increases, duration will decrease. As these relationships suggest, duration is *directly* related to price volatility because bonds with a longer duration will experience more price volatility as interest rates change. Therefore, bond investors find it

[4] For example, see Jess H. Chua, "A Closed-Form Formula for Calculating Bond Duration," *Financial Analysts Journal* (May-June 1984): 76–78; and Gary A. Benesh and Stephen E. Celec, "A Simplified Approach for Calculating Bond Duration," *Financial Review* (November 1984): 394–96.

very helpful to know the duration of bonds. For example, an investor who expects interest rates to decline and is interested in capital gains should purchase bonds with longer durations.

The *approximate* relationship between duration and a bond's price change is

$$\Delta P_j = \frac{-D_j}{(1 + i_j)}\left(\frac{\Delta \text{ basis points}}{100}\right) \qquad (11.14)$$

where

ΔP_j = percentage change in price of bond j
D_j = duration of bond j
i_j = yield to maturity of bond j
Δ basis points = change in yield to maturity of bond j expressed in basis points where 1% = 100 basis points

Equation 11.14 indicates that duration and price volatility are closely related. Thus, bonds with long duration have more price risk than short-duration bonds. Equation 11.14 can be illustrated using the previous example of a bond with a duration of 4.16 years that is currently priced at $828.39. Suppose the yield to maturity declines from 14.0 percent to 12.0 percent, a decrease of 200 basis points. The price of the bond would increase approximately 7.30 percent to $888.86:

$$\Delta P_j = \frac{-4.16}{1.14}\left(\frac{-200}{100}\right) = 7.30\%$$

$$\$828.39(1 + .0730) = \$888.86$$

The actual price of the bond resulting from a 200 basis point decrease in yield to maturity would be $891.86 rather than the price of $888.86 estimated using Equation 11.14. Thus, Equation 11.14 is only an approximation of the actual relationship.

As mentioned earlier, duration is an indication of systematic risk for bonds. It is also useful in analyzing and managing the risk of bond portfolios. These points are discussed in Appendix 11B.

• An Illustration and Comparison of Risk Measures

Table 11.8 provides risk measures for the AT&T debenture that was used to illustrate return measures earlier in this chapter. The table includes price ranges for the years 1984–1990. Over the entire period, the debenture sold for a minimum price of $537.50 and a maximum price of $917.50. This wide range is yet another indication of the volatility of bond prices during this period.

Measures of total risk given in Table 11.8 include the standard deviation of monthly prices, yields to maturity, and HPRs using data in Table 11.5. As ex-

TABLE 11.8 • Risk Measures for a Debenture Issued by American Telephone & Telegraph (AT&T)

Price Ranges

	1984	*1985*	*1986*	*1987*	*1988*	*1989*	*1990*
High	$65\frac{5}{8}$	$77\frac{7}{8}$	90	$91\frac{3}{4}$	$87\frac{1}{4}$	$89\frac{1}{2}$	$88\frac{1}{4}$
Low	$53\frac{3}{4}$	$61\frac{7}{8}$	$74\frac{1}{4}$	$71\frac{1}{2}$	$80\frac{1}{2}$	$79\frac{2}{3}$	$81\frac{1}{4}$
Range	$11\frac{7}{8}$	16	$15\frac{3}{4}$	$20\frac{1}{4}$	$6\frac{3}{4}$	$9\frac{7}{8}$	7

Total Risk or Standard Deviation*

Standard deviation of monthly prices = 1.66%
Standard deviation of yield to maturity = 0.26%
Standard deviation of monthly HPRs = 1.62%

Systematic Risk

Duration in March 1991 = 7.04 years

Unsystematic Risk

Moody's rating in April 1991 = Aa3

SOURCE: Price ranges: Moody's *Bond Record* and *Public Utility Manual*, vol. 1 (1990). Reprinted by permission.

*Risk measures were calculated using monthly data in Table 11.5.

pected, the standard deviation of yield to maturity is relatively small compared to the variability in prices and HPRs.

The systematic risk measure for the debenture is duration. The debenture has a term of approximately 9.9 years from April 1991 and a duration of 7.04 years. Thus, using Equation 11.14, a decline in yield to maturity of 1 percentage point (i.e., 8.70 percent to 7.70 percent) will result in an increase of approximately 6.48 percent in the price of the debenture. Thus, because of its relatively long duration, this debenture has considerable price risk.

Finally, the unsystematic risk of the debentures is indicated by Moody's rating of Aa3. This relatively high rating indicates that the debenture does not have significant default risk.

BOND INVESTMENT STRATEGIES

There are many bond investment strategies. In very passive strategies, a diversified bond portfolio is assembled and held for a relatively long period, while very active strategies may involve same-day trading. This section examines passive, active, and combination strategies that arc appropriatc for bonds.

Before considering specific investment strategies and diversification methods, however, investors should establish their investment and portfolio *objectives*. As Chapter 7 pointed out, the objectives provide guidelines for identifying appropriate strategies. For fixed-income investing, important factors to be considered include annual income (cash flow) requirements, taxes, investment horizon, and risk-return preferences related to reinvestment rate, default, purchasing power, and price risk. The strategies discussed in this section differ greatly in their risk-return characteristics, and the investor should consider the specific objectives of the portfolio in evaluating the appropriateness of individual strategies.

• Passive Strategies

Traditionally, bond investments were viewed as conservative investments that typically involved a relatively long investment horizon. This strategy was appropriately labeled a *buy-and-hold strategy*. To implement such a strategy, the investor would simply select the type of bond that seemed most appropriate and form a portfolio of bonds of this type. For individuals in high marginal tax brackets, municipal securities were often appropriate. If the investor was conservative, often only the highest-quality municipals would be considered. The investor who was willing to tolerate additional default risk would consider lower-quality securities with their higher coupon yields and yields to maturity.

This passive strategy could also involve corporate, U.S. Treasury, or agency issues. Typically, the investor would be interested in securities with long terms to maturity since the securities were unlikely to be sold before maturity. Under this strategy, the investor accepted the market rate of return and made no attempt to outperform the market.

A passive strategy is most advantageous when interest rate risk is low; intervening price changes can be ignored and reinvestment risk minimized since yields are stable. In addition, purchasing power risk should be low. Given a well-diversified portfolio of high-quality securities, default risk would also be minor.[5] Thus, this strategy provided an acceptable real rate of return with relatively low risk over the period from 1925 to the mid-1960s.

Beginning in the late 1960s, however, the rate of inflation changed radically, as did the level and volatility of interest rates. Thus, the economic environment effectively eliminated some of the advantages of a passive strategy. Consequently, passive investors facing this type of environment may elect to abandon fixed-income investments or to change their investment strategies.

[5] The exception would be during the Great Depression when the number of bond defaults increased significantly. See W. Braddock Hickman, *Corporate Bond Quality and Investor Experience* (Princeton, N.J.: Princeton University Press, 1958).

• Active Strategies

Rather than following a strict buy-and-hold strategy, investors may decide to alter various aspects of the strategy to deal with an uncertain economic environment. One possibility would be to pursue a strategy based on **structuring maturities;** that is, to combine bonds with different maturities into a bond portfolio. This strategy does not require the investor to forecast interest rates.

A second type of active strategy is based on a forecast of the direction and magnitude of interest rate changes. These strategies are similar to active common stock strategies based on a forecast of overall stock price movements.

The final category of active strategies includes specific strategies based on possible bond **swaps.** These swaps may be based on perceived temporary yield differentials, tax considerations, and possible market pricing inefficiencies. Appendix 11A discusses bond swaps.

STRATEGIES BASED ON STRUCTURING MATURITIES Uncertainty about interest rate changes requires the investor to forecast these changes or attempt to eliminate part or all of the unfavorable consequences of these unknown changes. For example, a forecast of decreasing interest rates may suggest investing in bonds with long durations. If investors are unwilling or unable to make a specific forecast, they will need a strategy that allows for the possibility of both increases and decreases in rates.

1. Matching strategy An alternative to forecasting rates is to pursue a *matching* strategy. This strategy, which essentially ignores possible interest rate changes, involves two steps: (1) identifying an appropriate holding period or investment horizon and (2) forming a bond portfolio with a duration equal to the holding period. Thus, if the holding period is two years, a portfolio with a duration of two years is appropriate for a matching strategy. The details and the advantages and disadvantages of the strategy are discussed in Appendix 11B.

2. Laddered strategy In a *laddered* strategy, the investor forms a portfolio of bonds with various maturities. A ladder N years in length would be formed by using $1/N$ proportion of the available funds for each maturity, 1 through N. For example, a five-year laddered portfolio would include 20 percent of the funds in bonds with a one-year maturity, 20 percent in bonds with a two-year maturity, and so on. Essentially, this strategy invests equal dollar amounts in bonds with maturities staggered by one year.

3. Barbell strategy A *barbell* strategy is a modification of the laddered strategy. Rather than buying equal amounts of all maturities within the length of the ladder, the barbell strategy uses only short-term and long-term bonds. No intermediate-term bonds are included in the portfolio. This strategy is also referred to as the *dumbbell* strategy: a graph of portfolio values by maturity would show "bulges" or "bells" at either end of the maturity spectrum. This strategy is based on the assumption that intermediate-term bonds are not necessary in a portfolio because they have less liquidity than short-term bonds and

• INTEREST BOX

Active Management Using Maturity Structuring

As one analyst suggests, maturity structuring can be a way to protect against changes in interest rates:

> Given the Federal Reserve Board's concerted efforts to check inflation by reining in economic growth, analysts say rates will peak during the next six to twelve months. As the economy slows, 30-year Treasury yields could decline from 9.1% recently to 7.5% within two years. Prudent investors, therefore, should begin planning now to move at least some money into intermediate- and long-term bonds, thereby locking in today's lofty yields and simultaneously positioning themselves to reap impressive capital gains.

Investors may attempt to jump from short-term securities to long-term bonds exactly at the peak of the interest rate cycle. This strategy is risky to use, however, because identifying exactly when the peak in rates will occur is difficult. A more realistic and safe strategy is to move gradually into long-term bonds as interest rates continue to rise.

Investors who wish to switch from short-term to long-term securities can elect to switch all at once or gradually and can choose from at least six types of bond investments:

1. U.S. Treasury bonds
2. High-grade, long-term corporate bonds
3. High-grade, long-term municipal bonds
4. Long-term junk bonds
5. Closed-end bond funds
6. Long-term zero coupon bonds

Each of these types of bond investments offers advantages and disadvantages, and investors should carefully consider the pros and cons of each possibility.

SOURCE: Walter L. Updegrave, "Riding the Wave of Long Bond Yields," *Money*, April 1989, pp. 100–111.

lower yields than long-term bonds. The barbell portfolio obtains liquidity from the short-term maturities and return (yield) from the long-term maturities.

TESTS OF STRUCTURING MATURITY STRATEGIES By staggering the maturities of bonds in the portfolio, using a laddered or a barbell approach, the investor attempts to earn the average market return over the holding period and to eliminate some of the effects of interest rate movements on portfolio value and income. A number of studies of the risk-return characteristics of these strategies have been conducted and have reached the following conclusions:

1. On a return basis, no one strategy dominated any other strategy since the mean returns between strategies were not significantly different.
2. On a risk-adjusted performance basis, none of the strategies outperformed an investment in 90-day Treasury bills over the period 1969–1981. This result was due to the dramatic increase in interest rates between 1979 and 1981.
3. During the subperiods of increasing interest rates, all strategies had negative returns except the "short" (greater proportion of short-term bonds) barbell and matching strategies.

4. During the subperiods of decreasing interest rates, all strategies had positive returns, with the "long" (greater proportion of long-term bonds) barbell strategy providing the highest return and the "short" barbell strategy the lowest return. All strategies had returns above 90-day Treasury bills.
5. Over the period 1969–1981, the returns from all strategies compared favorably with the returns on six professionally managed bond mutual funds.

ACTIVE STRATEGIES BASED ON FORECASTING INTEREST RATE MOVEMENTS

Active strategies may require the investor to forecast interest rate movements. Interest rates can be forecast based on trend and cyclical analysis and yield curve analysis.

1. Trends and cycles A successful active strategy based on interest rate movements depends on an accurate interest rate forecast. The difficulty of this task should not be underestimated. Many economic analyses have been directed at simplifying interest rate forecasts, without much success. No one technique or procedure has been devised that correctly forecasts the level, or perhaps even the direction, of interest rate changes. In fact, there is considerable debate about which variables actually determine interest rates; current attention focuses on budget and trade deficits, inflation and inflationary expectations, the money supply, oil prices, and the real rate of interest.

Despite this somewhat pessimistic beginning, however, a general framework can be developed that will allow the analyst to attempt to forecast interest rates. Historically, a very close association has existed between economic turning points and peaks and troughs in interest rates. Interest rates and economic activity traditionally peak and trough at approximately the same time. Thus, an accurate economic forecast can be used as a basis for forecasting interest rates. The economic analysis material in Chapter 8 also applies to bond analysis. If the economic forecast can be used to forecast interest rate turning points accurately, then the investor can implement an active strategy of "buy low" (at the peak of the interest rate cycle) and "sell high" (at the trough of the interest rate cycle).

The impacts of inflation and expected inflation are critical factors in forecasting interest rates. In addition to the importance of the Fisher effect (as illustrated in Equation 11.9), studies indicate that both short- and long-term interest rates increase above their average levels during periods of inflation and deflation. During periods of high inflation, however, interest rates often lag behind the rate of inflation. For example, over the 189-year period 1791–1979, in only 14 of the 189 years were inflation rates greater than 9 percent, and the average yield on long-term bonds for these 14 years was approximately 6 percent. These observations suggest that the relationship between inflation and interest rates is complex and perhaps unstable over time. Despite these problems, an inflation forecast is an important element in forecasting interest rates.

• INTEREST BOX

Economic Factors and Interest Rates

Forecasting the level and direction of change in interest rates is a critical element in the success of many active bond market strategies. Before investors can accurately forecast interest rates, however, they must consider the many factors that influence rates, including the following:

1. Level of economic activity and vibrancy
2. Current rate of price increases (inflation)
3. What people expect to happen to price increases (expected inflation)
4. Real rate of interest
5. Federal Reserve System's fund rate
6. Supply and demand factors

Investors attempting to forecast rates need to understand how the real interest rate, the rate of inflation, and the nominal interest rate are related. A classic example of what happens when the relationships are not maintained in the market occurred in 1979. During 1979, the observed or nominal interest rate on one-year Treasury bills was 10 percent, but the actual inflation rate was above 13 percent. This situation obviously indicated that the nominal yield on Treasury bills was much too low and could be expected to increase dramatically.

SOURCE: Patricia M. Szymczak, "How Interest Rates Respond to Changing Economic Forces," *Futures: The Magazine of Commodities and Options*, January 1988, pp. 61–64.

2. *Structure of interest rates* Another tool considers how rates differ between short-term and long-term bonds. This analysis involves the *term structure* of interest rates; it relates term to maturity to yield to maturity and requires a homogeneous sample of bonds, so that all other factors that influence yield (except term) can be held constant. Since analysts commonly use U.S. government securities for the sample, differences in default risk, major tax implications, and industry factors are not a problem. In addition, the term structure is analyzed at one point in time, which may be the present or a point in the future.

Figure 11.1 illustrates the term structure of Treasury securities at three different points in time. These dates were selected to show the three major types of yield curves: increasing, decreasing, and flat. Thus, the relationship between term and yield to maturity is not necessarily stable. Most commonly, short-term securities have lower yields than long-term securities. At other times, however, the reverse is true. Short-term yields are also more volatile than long-term yields. Thus, most of the shifts in the yield curve occur for short-term securities. It should also be pointed out, however, that short-term bonds prices are more stable than long-term bond prices.

Considerable research has been directed toward explaining the shapes and movements of yield curves. Constructing yield curves is very easy, but explaining their shapes and movements has proved to be challenging and controversial. There are three main theories about the yield curve:

FIGURE 11.1 • Term Structure of U.S. Treasury Securities

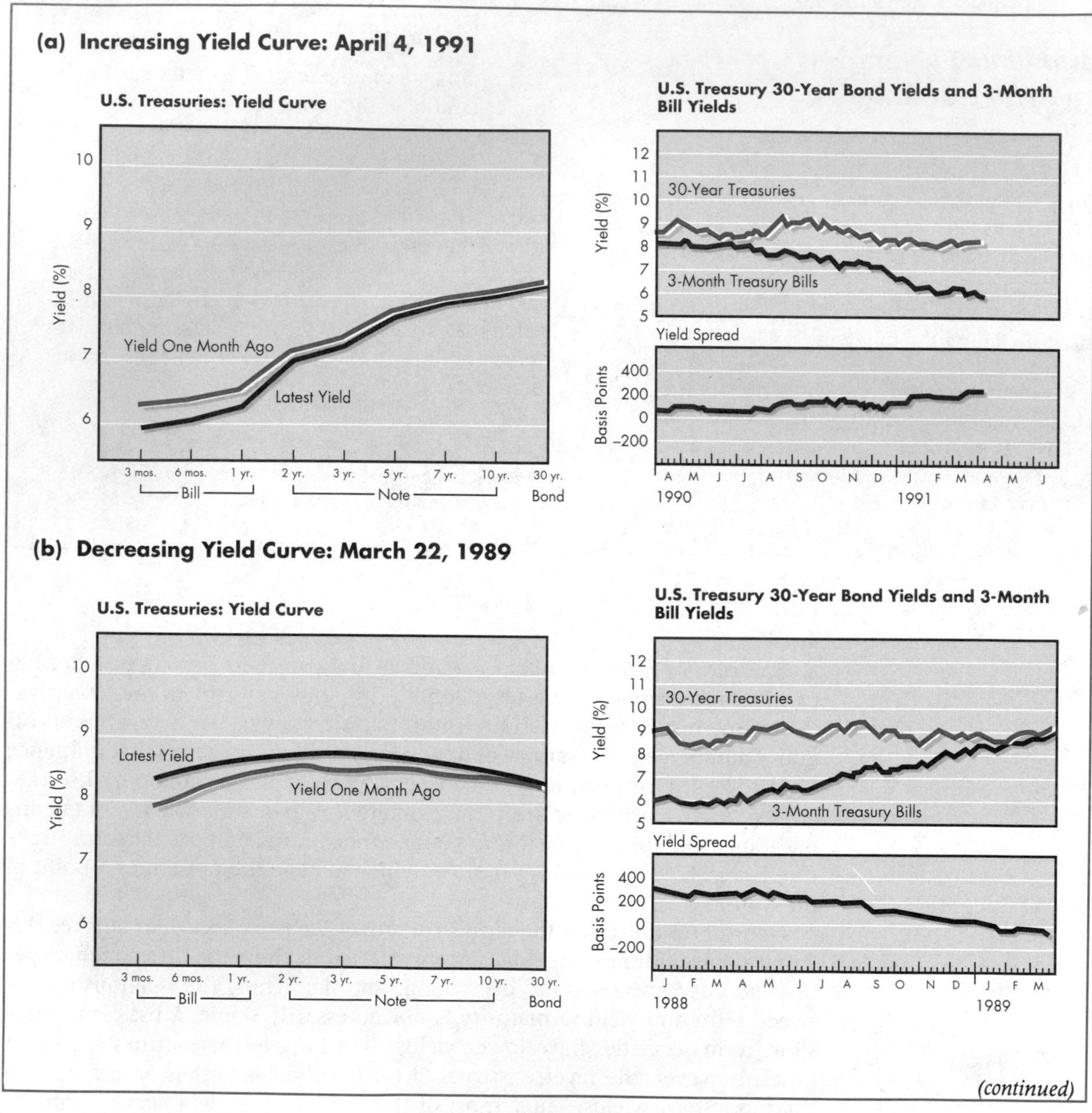

(continued)

SOURCE: Various issues of Moody's *Bond Survey*. Reprinted by permission.

FIGURE 11.1 • Term Structure of U.S. Treasury Securities (continued)

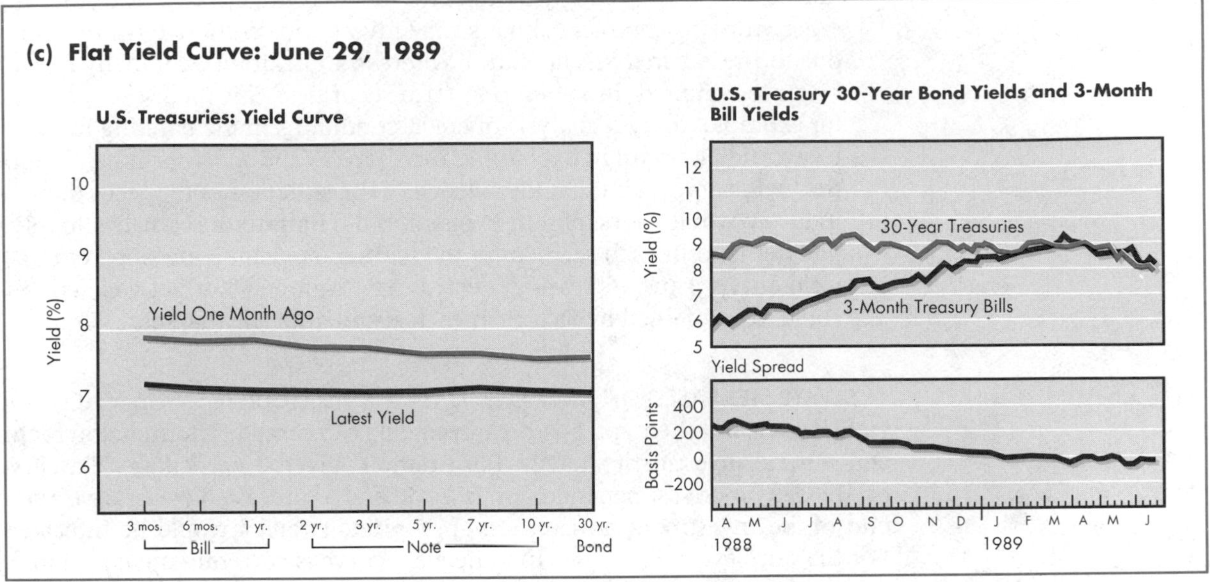

- *Expectations theory* This theory maintains that long-term yields are a function of the anticipated short-term rates that will prevail during the term of the long-term security. For example, assume that you have a five-year investment horizon and can invest in a bond with a five-year term or, sequentially, in five bonds, each with a one-year term. Thus, you could earn the yield to maturity on the five-year bond—or perhaps a higher yield on five one-year bonds if one-year yields increase over the five-year period. In the latter case, you could buy a one-year bond and then "roll over" into a second one-year bond at a higher rate. This scenario implies that an upward-sloping yield curve is explained by expectations of increasing yields. Thus, investors are purchasing short term rather than long term, with the hopes of favorably "rolling over." Conversely, a downward-sloping yield curve suggests expectations of declining yields.
- *Liquidity premium theory* This theory accepts the basic elements of the expectations theory but also maintains that short-term bonds have more stable prices and are more liquid than long-term bonds. This advantage (less risk) would indicate that the yields of short-term bonds should be lower than those of long-term bonds. This theory suggests that the yield curve should be upward sloping. The shape of the yield curve is therefore determined by expectations concerning future rates and by liquidity preferences.

- *Segmented market theory* Many investors, especially financial institutions, often view bonds with different terms as imperfect substitutes. In other words, a commercial bank may invest only in short-term securities due to the nature of its liabilities, whereas an insurance company may be quite willing to invest in long-term securities. This theory suggests, for example, that an analysis of credit conditions in the banking industry would be useful in explaining the shape of the short-term segment of the yield survey, and that knowledge of the situation in the insurance industry would be helpful in explaining the long-term segment. Supply and demand in each segment of the market determine the slope of the yield curve. Thus, increasing, decreasing, "humped," or flat yield curves could be explained by factors in each segment of the market.

STRATEGIES BASED ON AN ANALYSIS OF THE YIELD CURVE Understanding yield curves and their anticipated movements can provide a foundation for an active bond investment strategy. For example, given a particular yield curve on the date an investment decision is made and a forecasted yield curve at the end of the investment horizon, an appropriate strategy would be indicated. For the simplest case, assume that the yield curve is currently upward sloping and is expected to remain stable, both in shape and level of yields. In this scenario, the higher yields of long-term bonds would be attractive since interest rate risk is not anticipated to be a factor. This strategy is referred to as **riding the yield curve.**

Table 11.9 provides a simple illustration of riding the yield curve. The figure at the top of the table shows that the yield curve is currently upward sloping, with a one-year bond offering a 6 percent yield and a two-year bond a 7 percent yield. Given a one-year holding period, an investor might buy a one-year bond and hold it to maturity. A second strategy, however, would be to buy a two-year bond and sell it after one year. If the yield curve remains stable, the yield on a one-year bond one year from now would be 6 percent. The second strategy, therefore, "rides the curve" from point A to point B.

The HPRs at the bottom of Table 11.9 show that riding the yield curve (strategy 2) provides significantly higher returns when the yield curve is stable or declines over the holding period. If the yield curve shifts upward, strategy 2 still provides higher returns until the curve reaches the position shown by estimate 3. At this point, a one-year bond would be priced to yield 8 percent, resulting in an HPR for strategy 2 of 6.01 percent. If the yield curve shifts above the estimate 3 level, strategy 1 (buy and hold) would produce a higher HPR.

An investor (speculator) attempting to ride the yield curve would concentrate on the probability that the yield curve would shift upward to the extent that excess returns would be eliminated. In this example, the key estimate would be the probability that the yield on a one-year bond one year from now will be greater than or equal to 8 percent.

Success in riding the yield curve depends on the curve remaining stable or

TABLE 11.9 • Riding the Yield Curve

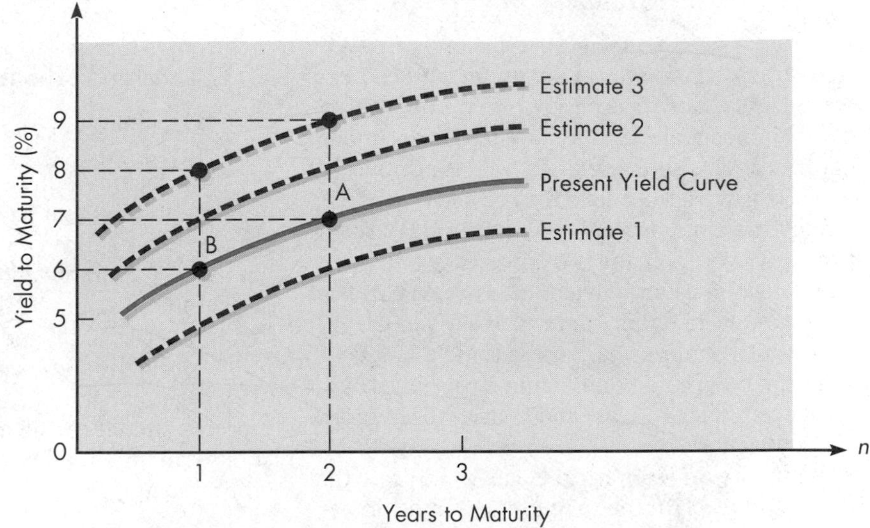

Assumptions:	Holding period is one year; pure discount bonds (no coupons); three estimates of yield curve one year from now.
Strategy 1:	Buy a bond priced at $943.40 with a one-year maturity and a yield of 6%.
Strategy 2:	Buy a bond priced at $873.44 with a two-year maturity and initial yield of 7%, and sell at the prevailing yield after one year.

Yield curve after one year	HPRs *Strategy 1*	HPRs *Strategy 2*	Additional return from riding the yield curve
No shifts, remains stationary	6.00%	8.01%	2.01%
Shifts to estimate 1	6.00	9.04	3.04
Shifts to estimate 2	6.00	7.00	1.00
Shifts to estimate 3	6.00	6.01	0.01

shifting downward. In addition, the market must forecast interest rates incorrectly. According to the expectations hypothesis, however, an upward-sloping curve implies that yields will increase. This theory indicates that the yield on a one-year bond one year from now would be 8 percent, which would eliminate the extra returns for riding the yield curve. Empirical studies using Treasury bills have generally found that riding the yield curve involved additional risk and provided only small incremental returns over a buy-and-hold strategy.

RESEARCH BOX

Active Management Using Intermarket Spreads

An example of an *intermarket spread* is the difference in yields between newly issued nongovernmental bonds and U.S. Treasury bonds of similar maturities. This spread will always be positive since Treasury bonds have lower yields than nongovernmental issues. The magnitude of the spread, however, changes over time.

Chris Dialynas has developed a new theoretical model and used empirical tests to explain the magnitude of intermarket spreads including conventional corporate bonds, municipal bonds, mortgage pass-throughs, and collateralized mortgage obligations.

The theory and empirical evidence indicate that two factors explain the magnitude of most intermarket spreads:

1. Actual and expected price volatility of bonds

2. Absolute level of interest rates

These factors capture the importance of traditional variables that have been cited as causing the spread such as credit cycles, imbalances between the supply and demand of a particular class of bonds, and changes in default probabilities in corporate and municipal bonds.

Accordingly, any investor employing an active strategy that attempts to exploit intermarket spreads should consider the price volatility of bonds and the level of interest rates in developing the strategy.

SOURCE: Chris P. Dialynas, "Bond Yield Spreads Revisited," *Journal of Portfolio Management* (Winter 1988): 57–62.

CONCLUSIONS ABOUT STRATEGIES BASED ON INTEREST RATE FORECASTS A forecast of declining yields suggests attractive opportunities for fixed-income investing. To maximize the HPR by earning capital gains, the investor should select securities that are expected to have the greatest increase in prices. Appropriate selections would be long-term, low-coupon, high-quality bonds—essentially, bonds with long durations and high agency ratings. The investor should be aware, however, that the probability of a call increases during periods of declining yields.

A forecast of increasing yields suggests a poor environment for fixed-income securities due to anticipated falling prices. If the investor still wishes to hold bonds for other reasons, as opposed to holding cash or other types of securities, then very short-term securities are appropriate. This would minimize price risk and also provide an opportunity to reduce the reinvestment rate risk since cash flows can be reinvested at the increasing short-term rates.

In addition to strategies based on forecasts of interest rate movements, numerous strategies are based on perceived inefficiencies in the bond market and for individual bonds. For example, two identical bonds may temporarily have unequal prices. An active bond investor may take the opportunity to purchase the undervalued bond, anticipating short-term capital gains when the market realizes that the bond is undervalued. Such strategies are often referred to as *bond swaps,* implying that an existing bond portfolio is actively managed for maximum return. Appendix 11A discusses various types of bond swap strategies.

BOND PORTFOLIO DIVERSIFICATION

Investors should appreciate the benefits of diversification in every investment portfolio. This appreciation may be based on the simple fact that there are real advantages to "not putting all your eggs in one basket." It may also be based on the knowledge that an adequately diversified portfolio offers the opportunity to reduce total risk by minimizing unsystematic risk, often without a significant reduction in portfolio returns. This section discusses a simple diversification technique that can be used for bond portfolios.

• Naïve Diversification

Studies on diversification for common stock portfolios indicate that, on average, a portfolio of 10 to 15 randomly selected stocks essentially eliminates most unsystematic or diversifiable risk. Is this also true for fixed-income security portfolios? This question has been addressed by studies that have investigated this and other issues concerning bond diversification.

Historically, many investors and analysts have thought that bonds, unlike common stocks, have a total risk that is essentially systematic rather than unsystematic. When interest rates and yields change, all bond prices and yields respond in essentially the same fashion. Since very few bonds exhibit independent price or yield movements, the amount of unsystematic risk appears to be limited. If this belief is true, diversification by numbers, or **naïve diversification,** would offer only a limited benefit.

Figure 11.2 contradicts this idea by showing that total portfolio risk (variance) is reduced dramatically as bonds are added to the portfolio. As with common stocks, the variances of returns of the bond portfolio decrease rapidly as bonds are added to the portfolio. As the lower limit of risk is approached, adding a bond to the portfolio has a minimal impact on portfolio risk. This optimal number occurs in the range of 8 to 16 bonds, depending on the agency rating. It appears that diversification by numbers is much more effective for bonds with lower ratings than for those judged to be higher-quality bonds.

The clear message from this study is that bond portfolios should be diversified, even by using naïve strategies (random selection). Portfolios with 8 to 16 bonds will have considerably less portfolio return variability than portfolios of 1 or 2 bonds. Increasing the number of bonds beyond 8 to 16 offers few added benefits, with the possible exception of portfolios of lower-rated corporate bonds.

FIGURE 11.2
Risk and Bond Portfolio Size

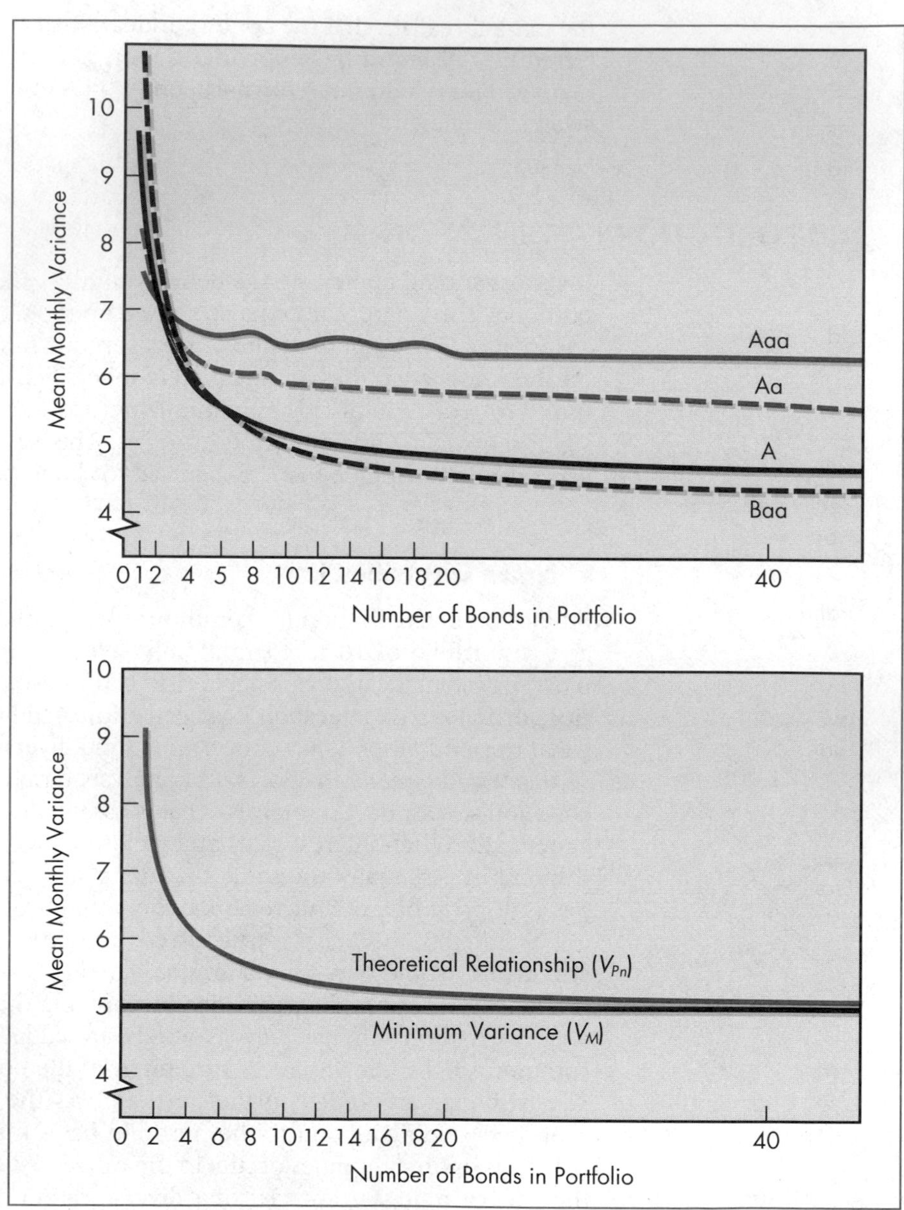

SOURCE: Richard W. McEnally and Calvin M. Boardman, "Aspects of Corporate Bond Portfolio Diversification," *Journal of Financial Research* (Spring 1979): 33 and 35. Reprinted by permission.

• CONCEPT APPLICATIONS

Investment Concept	Concept Application
Yield to maturity	The yield to maturity is a bond return measure that unrealistically assumes that coupons can be reinvested at the original yield on the bond. It also assumes that the issuer will not default and that the investor will hold the bond until maturity. The yield to maturity is a popular return measure, but investors should use it very cautiously.
Yield to first call	Most corporate bonds now have a call feature that the issuer can use to retire the bond. The yield to first call indicates the possible annual rate of return on the bond if it is called on the first call date. Investors should use caution in relying on this return measure, however, because it assumes coupons are reinvested at the original yield and that no default will occur.
Expected holding period return	The $E(\text{HPR})$ is the most useful return measure for individuals making bond investment decisions. It considers the length of the anticipated holding period, possible default, reinvestment rate risk, and price risk.
Duration	Duration is a very important systematic risk measure in bond analysis. Investors should consider the duration of bonds because it indicates the price volatility of the bond due to the coupon and term effects.
Active bond management strategy	Active management is a strategy that may involve forecasting interest rates, anticipating shifts in the yield curve, and engaging in bond swaps. The success of the strategy depends on the accuracy of the critical forecasts and therefore on the skill of the analyst.
Bond portfolio diversification	Investors should manage a bond portfolio to take advantage of diversification opportunities. This is especially important for default risk in lower-quality bonds.

SUMMARY

The primary purpose of this chapter has been to provide an overview of bond valuation, investment strategies, and diversification considerations. As is the case with most traditional security valuation techniques, bond valuation depends on the length, timing, and appropriately discounted future cash flows.

Bond return measures include both ex-post, or historical, measures and ex-ante, or expected, returns. These measures allow a bond investor to compute realized rates of return from previous investments and also to attempt to forecast the returns on investments that are being considered.

Risk analysis is also important for bond investors. Risk can be divided into two parts: unsystematic and systematic. Unsystematic risk is dependent on unique factors that may influence the bond issuer. Severe financial problems that may lead to default and bankruptcy are a major source of unsystematic risk. Price changes, due to changes in the general level of yields, unanticipated inflation, and fluctuating yields over the holding period, are major sources of systematic risk for bonds.

Bond strategies range from passive buy-and-hold strategies to very active strategies directed at "beating the market." A key ingredient in a successful active strategy is accurate interest rate forecasting. Forecasting interest rates was discussed in the context of trend and cyclical movements and yield curve analysis.

The unsystematic risk of a bond portfolio can be reduced by naïve diversification, which involves increasing the number of bonds in the portfolio. Empirical studies have shown that sizable benefits may be derived from naïve diversification, especially for lower-quality corporate bonds. This research indicates that 8 to 16 bonds are needed to eliminate most of the unsystematic or diversifiable risk. Adding bonds beyond this number to a portfolio provides only nominal additional reduction in unsystematic risk.

• KEY TERMS

Consol
Current (coupon) yield
Duration
Expected rate of return
Holding period return
Intrinsic valuation
Liquid yield option note (LYON)
Naïve diversification
Original issue discount bond (OID)
Price risk
Purchasing power risk
Reinvestment rate risk
Riding the yield curve
Risk of default
STRIPS
Structuring maturities
Swaps
Yield to first call
Yield to maturity
Zero

• QUESTIONS

1. Briefly describe the information you need to value a bond.
2. Bond valuation is mechanical. Discuss.
3. Explain how two bonds can have different coupon rates and yet provide identical yields to maturity.
4. Explain how bond valuation is influenced by the frequency of coupon payments.
5. Briefly compare and contrast zeros, OIDs, LYONs, and consols. Under what circumstances would these types of bonds be desirable investments?
6. Discuss the implicit assumptions of yield-to-maturity.

7. Will the yield to first call always be greater than the yield to maturity if the bond is called? In general, how will these two return measures be related for a single bond?
8. Is the holding period return an ex-post or an ex-ante return measure? Explain.
9. Explain what conditions are necessary such that the annualized HPR of a bond is equal to its yield to maturity.
10. Discuss how the coupon, term, and duration measures are related. Can two bonds with different coupons and terms have the same duration? Explain.
11. What are the advantages and disadvantages of using an agency rating as a measure of default risk?
12. Assume that a bond has the following risk values:

Duration	11.4 years
Rating	Baa

Explain what each measure indicates about the riskiness of the bond. Also, indicate how an investor can use each measure in an analysis of the bond.
13. Compare and contrast active and passive bond investment strategies.
14. What bond investment strategy is suggested by a period of stable yields? By a period of volatile yields?
15. Describe the dumbbell and laddered strategies. What type of risk are they designed to manage?
16. Is an economic forecast useful in forecasting interest rate movements? Discuss.
17. Assume that the yield curve is currently upward sloping. According to the expectations theory, what interest rate forecast does this imply?
18. Some evidence indicates that diversification by increasing the number of bonds in a portfolio is more beneficial for low-quality bonds than for high-quality bonds. What are some explanations of this evidence?
19. What type of risk is reduced as the number of bonds in a portfolio increases? What type of risk is not reduced? Why?
20. For each of the following forecasts, outline an appropriate bond investment strategy for an investor with a five-year investment horizon:
    a. Rapid increase in interest rates.
    b. Rapid decrease in interest rates.
    c. No clear interest rate forecast. Rates may increase or decrease.

• KEY TO THE INVESTMENT ANALYSIS SOFTWARE

Calculation	Appendix A-1 Page Reference	Access Procedure
Bond value	A-10	BEGIN, VALUATION, BONDS, VALUE
Duration	A-11	BEGIN, VALUATION, BONDS, DURATION
Holding period return	A-8	BEGIN, STATISTICAL, HPR
Yield to first call	A-11	BEGIN, VALUATION, BONDS, YIELD, CALL
Yield to maturity	A-11	BEGIN, VALUATION, BONDS, YIELD, ORDINARY or ZERO
Variance of holding period return	A-7	BEGIN, STATISTICAL, DISCRETE

• PROBLEMS

1. Find the value of a bond if its yield to maturity is 14 percent, its coupon is 10 percent, its face value is $1,000, and interest is paid annually. Assume the bond is purchased on an interest payment date and matures in 12 years.
2. Calculate V_0 for the bond described in Problem 1, but assume that interest is paid semiannually. Use a semiannual yield to maturity of 7 percent. Also calculate V_0 using the *effective* semiannual yield.
3. Find the yield to maturity on a zero that is currently priced at $400 and matures at $1,000 in eight years.
4. Calculate the value of a $1,000 face value consol that pays an annual coupon of 10 percent if the desired rate of return is 14 percent.
5. Find the yield to maturity of a $1,000 face value bond that pays interest semiannually based on a 12 percent coupon. Its current price is $900, and it matures in eight years.
6. Calculate the yield to first call on the bond described in Problem 5 if the bond is callable in three years at 110 percent of face value.
7. Assume that you bought a bond for $800 and sold it for $900. Calculate the annual HPR if the bond is held for one year, and $80 of interest is received the day the bond is sold.
8. Consider the following corporate bond characteristics and analysts' estimates. Calculate the $E(\text{HPR})$ and σ^2_{HPR}.

Face value	$1,000
Coupon rate (paid annually)	12%
Term to maturity	15 years
Current price	$400
Rating by Moody's	Caa

State of nature	*Probability*	*Coupon*	*Year-end price*
Recession	.2	0	$100
No economic growth	.6	0	300
Moderate economic growth	.2	$120	600

9. Consider the following information:

		Year-end	
Year	**CPI at beginning of year**	*Coupons*	*Capital gain*
1	100	$100	$500
2	110	150	300
3	114	125	800
4	122	—	—

Assume that you had invested $4,000 at the beginning of each of these years and earned the indicated coupon and capital gain income.

a. Calculate the inflation rate for each of the first three years.

b. Calculate for each of the first three years the nominal HPR.

c. Calculate for each of the first three years the real HPR.

10. Consider the following information on a corporate bond:

Face value	$1,000
Annual coupon rate	12%
Term	5 years
Yield to maturity	15%

Calculate the bond's duration assuming interest is paid annually.

11. Assume that the following yields will be available on three short-term bonds selling at par and on an intermediate-term bond. Calculate the annualized HPR using the three short-term bonds versus a buy-and-hold strategy using the intermediate-term bond. Assume that all income is reinvested at the available yield and that your investment horizon is three years. Discuss the risk and return characteristics of the two strategies.

One-year bonds			Intermediate-term bond
Year	*Yield*	*Maturity*	(term = 3 years)
1	12%	1 year	Current price = $1,000
2	14	1 year	Face value = $1,000
3	11	1 year	Coupon rate = 13%

12. Consider the following yields and terms to maturity on U.S. government securities:

Security	*Term (years)*	*Yield*
1	1	10.4%
2	2	11.6
3	4	12.4
4	8	14.2
5	16	14.0

a. Use these data to construct a yield curve.

b. Does the yield curve indicate any inefficiencies in the market? Explain.

c. Do you observe any pricing inefficiencies that might provide profit opportunities? Explain.

13. Consider the following two bonds:

	Bond A	*Bond B*
Current price	\$900	\$950
Term	4 years	6 years
Coupon (paid annually)	10%	12%
Face value	\$1,000	\$1,000

a. Calculate the yield to maturity for both bonds.

b. Calculate the duration for both bonds.

c. What investment horizons would be necessary so that each bond individually could be used in a matching strategy?

14. Assume that you would like to have \$30,000 in three years to buy your "dream" car and that you have the following two investment options available today:

	Option 1	*Option 2*
Security	U.S. Treasury note	Corporate bond
Term	3 years	4 years
Yield to maturity	12%	15%
Coupon (paid semiannually)	10%	10%

a. Calculate the amount you must invest in each option today to have \$30,000 in three years. Assume a rate of return equal to the yield to maturity on each security.

b. Discuss which strategy you would follow, and the advantages and disadvantages of each, in your quest for a "dream" car.

15. A friend asks you to evaluate her bond portfolio and supplies the following information:

Security	Face value	Market value	Term (years)	Coupon (paid semi-annually)	Yield to maturity	Duration (years)
U.S. Treasury bill	$10,000	$ 9,091	1	0%	10.00%	1.00
U.S. Treasury note	20,000	19,500	5	10	10.67	4.16
Corporate bond, Ba rated	15,000	12,000	10	12	16.16	5.90
Corporate bond, Aa rated	10,000	11,000	5	15	12.21	3.91

a. Calculate the annual cash flow for the next year. What is the coupon yield of the portfolio?

b. Suppose your friend has an investment horizon of three years and plans to liquidate the portfolio at that time. Would you make any recommendations for a portfolio revision? Specifically, what are your recommendations?

c. Is default risk a major concern for this portfolio?

d. Does the portfolio provide liquidity in case your friend needs cash? Explain.

e. Do you think that the portfolio has adequate diversification in terms of the number and types of bonds? Explain.

f. Suppose your friend thinks that interest rates are likely to *increase* dramatically during the coming year. What recommendation would you make?

g. Answer part (f) assuming she expects rates to dramatically decline.

• REFERENCES

Altman, Edward I., and Scott A. Nammacher. "The Default Rate Experience on High-Yield Corporate Debt." *Financial Analysts Journal* (July-August 1985): 25–41.

Barnes, Tom, Keith Johnson, and Don Shannon. "A Test of Fixed-Income Strategies." *Journal of Portfolio Management* (Winter 1984): 60–65.

Becketti, Jean. "The Role of Stripped Securities in Portfolio Management." *Economic Review of the Federal Reserve Bank of Kansas City* (May 1988): 20–31.

Dyl, Edward A., and Michael D. Joehnk. "Riding the Yield Curve: Does It Work?" *Journal of Portfolio Management* (Spring 1981): 13–17.

Hickman, W. Braddock. *Corporate Bond Quality and Investor Experience.* Princeton, N.J.: Princeton University Press, 1958.

Ibbotson, Roger G., and Rex A. Sinquefield. "Stocks, Bonds, Bills, and Inflation: Year-by-Year Historical Returns (1926–1974)." *Journal of Business* (January 1976): 11–47.

———. "Stocks, Bonds, Bills, and Inflation: Simulation of the Future (1976–2000)." *Journal of Business* (July 1976): 313–37.

Kharabe, Prakash S., and P.R. Chandy. "A Note on the Relationship among Yield-to-Maturity, Expected Return and Risk-Free Rate for Corporate Bonds." *Engineering Economist* (Winter 1990): 149–58.

Lewis, Janet. "How Good Is Junk-Bond Research?" *Institutional Investor,* July 1989, pp. 53–55.

Ma, Christopher K., and Garry M. Weed. "Fact and Fancy of Takeover Junk Bonds." *Journal of Portfolio Management* (Fall 1986): 34–47.

Maloney, Kevin J., and Jess B. Yawitz. "Interest Rate Risk, Immunization, and Duration." *Journal of Portfolio Management* (Spring 1986): 41–49.

Retkwa, Rosalyn. "The Treasury Strip: Zero Treasury Bonds Have Become Big Business." *Financial Planning* (June 1985): 42, 44.

Walbert, Laura. "Confessions of a Junk Bond Fanatic." *Financial World* (November 1989): 86, 88.

Weinstein, Mark I. "A Curmudgeon's View of Junk Bonds." *Journal of Portfolio Management* (Spring 1987): 76–80.

APPENDIX 11A

Bond Swaps

An active bond portfolio strategy may often involve frequent transactions in which current bonds are replaced with new bonds. Such strategies are commonly called *bond swaps.* The motivation is to earn short-term gains by exploiting perceived inefficiencies in the bond markets. The most frequently used swaps are substitution, yield pickup, tax, and rate anticipation swaps.

1. Substitution swap A *substitution swap* is designed to take advantage of a perceived temporary yield differential between bonds that are similar with respect to coupons, ratings, maturities, and industry. As an illustration of this type of swap, Table 11A.1 provides data on two similar utility bonds that have a yield-to-maturity spread of 14 basis points. The price of the Duke Power Company bond is 91.50 percent ($915), and the Commonwealth Edison bond's price is 90.50 percent ($905). If the bond portfolio currently contains the Duke Power bonds, a substitution swap may be feasible; a similar bond can be purchased for $10 less than the bond currently in the portfolio. In this transaction, the investor simply sells an overvalued bond and replaces it with an undervalued bond. The underlying assumption is that one or both of the bonds are incorrectly priced, based on the slight difference in their prices.

2. Yield pickup swap A second type of swap is the *yield pickup swap,* which is designed to change the cash flow of the portfolio by exchanging similar bonds that have different coupon rates. For example, if additional cash flow is desired, an existing "low" coupon bond in the portfolio could be swapped for a similar "high" coupon bond. Table 11A.2 illustrates two likely candidates for a yield pickup swap. Notice that the two bonds are similar except for their coupon rates. If a bond portfolio currently contained the Philadelphia Electric bond, it might be feasible to swap for the Consumer Power bond, with a resulting increase in coupon income. Notice that the yields to maturity are similar, but the Philadelphia Electric bond is selling at a larger discount because of its relatively low coupon. Thus, a large portion of the yield to maturity is based on the assumed increase in price over the life of the bond to the maturity value of $1,000. On the other hand, a large portion of the yield to maturity of the Consumer Power bond is based on its higher coupon since the bond is selling for a price close to its face value.

The proposed swap would therefore result in an exchange of potential returns: capital gains for coupon income. Thus, the investor would obtain higher coupon income and a small increase in the overall yield to maturity of the portfolio.

TABLE 11A.1 • Bond Substitution Swap

	Duke Power Company	Commonwealth Edison
Moody's rating (April 1991)	Aa2	A3
Standard & Poor's rating (April 1991)	AA−	A−
Coupon rate	$8\frac{1}{8}$%	$8\frac{1}{8}$%
Maturity date	7/1/2007	1/15/2007
Interest payment dates	1/1 and 7/1	1/15 and 7/15
Current call price	104.03%	104.21%
Amount outstanding (millions)	$119.5	$180.0
Price at end of March 1991	91.50%	90.50%
Yield to maturity at end of March 1991	9.13%	9.27%

SOURCES: Moody's *Bond Record* (April 1991). Standard & Poor's *Bond Guide* (April 1991). Reprinted by permission.

TABLE 11A.2 • Bond Yield Pickup Swap

	Philadelphia Electric	Consumer Power Company
Moody's rating (April 1991)	Baa2	Baa3
Standard & Poor's rating (April 1991)	BBB	BBB−
Coupon rate	$7\frac{3}{4}$%	$8\frac{5}{8}$%
Maturity date	12/15/2000	7/1/2000
Interest payment dates	6/15 and 12/15	1/1 and 7/1
Current call price	102.50%	102.93%
Amount outstanding (millions)	$6.8	$50.0
Price at end of March 1991	91.125%	95.50%
Yield to maturity at end of March 1991	9.14%	9.34%
Current or coupon yield at end of March 1991	8.50%	9.03%

SOURCES: Moody's *Bond Record* (April 1991). Standard & Poor's *Bond Guide* (April 1991). Reprinted by permission.

The yield pickup swap can also be based on a desire to change the yield to maturity of the portfolio rather than the coupon yield. In this case, an investor with the Philadelphia Electric bond might consider a *yield-to-maturity pickup* swap, swapping for the Consumer Power bond with its slightly higher yield to maturity.

3. Tax swap Another important type of bond swap is the *tax swap*. As its name implies, this swap is made for tax purposes. Many types of swaps can have a favorable impact on taxes. One very effective swap involves selling a bond at a loss so that a book loss can be converted to an actual loss, which will offset capital gains from other transactions. The proceeds from the sale can be used to acquire a similar bond so that the overall characteristics of the portfolio are not changed. One restriction imposed by the Internal Revenue Code is that the bond that was sold cannot be repurchased. Such a transaction would be classified as a *wash sale,* and the loss would not be recognized for tax purposes.

A second type of tax swap involves the exchange of bonds that receive different tax treatments. For example, corporate bonds may be exchanged for municipals if the marginal tax rate of the investor and the intermarket yield spread between the two will provide a higher after-tax return. Again, any risk difference must be carefully considered.

4. Rate anticipation swap Other swap strategies, called *rate anticipation swaps,* are based on forecasts of general interest rate changes. For example, a forecast of increasing yields may motivate a swap of long-term for short-term securities so that price declines are minimized. In this case, the securities may have significant differences in coupons, ratings, durations, or other important characteristics.

APPENDIX 11B

Immunization

This appendix deals with techniques that can be used to manage the systematic risk of a bond portfolio. As the chapter pointed out, naïve diversification reduces the unsystematic risk of a bond portfolio. It is also desirable, however, to reduce the total risk in a bond portfolio, which includes both systematic and unsystematic risk.

CLASSICAL IMMUNIZATION

One diversification technique, called *classical immunization*, is designed to "immunize" a bond portfolio from interest rate risk, including both price risk and reinvestment rate risk. Immunization involves the formation of a bond portfolio, including bonds of various coupons and terms to maturity, that will provide a specified HPR.

This technique requires that the investor specify the desired length of the holding period. Once this is done, the key to the immunization strategy is to *match* the duration of the portfolio to the desired holding period. If the desired holding period or investment horizon is five years, a bond portfolio with a duration of five years will be constructed.

To illustrate this concept for a single bond, assume that the desired holding period is three years. Thus, a bond with a duration equal to three years must be purchased. Assume that a corporate bond that is currently selling for $900 has a 12 percent coupon paid annually and a term to maturity of four years. You should be able to verify that the yield to maturity for this bond is 15.54 percent and that the duration is approximately three years. This bond could therefore immunize the investor against interest rate risk, so that even if yields and (therefore) prices change over the three-year horizon, the HPR will be equal to the yield to maturity. Table 11B.1 illustrates this technique.

Notice from Part I of Table 11B.1 that the terminal value of the three coupons is calculated using an assumed yield to maturity of 13 percent. The yield to maturity dropped one year after the bond was purchased, from 15.54 percent to 13 percent. Also, since the bond has a term to maturity of four years, its price will not be the face value after three years since the coupon rate is 12 percent and the yield to maturity is 13 percent. Thus, the value of the bond, or selling price, must be calculated. This calculation indicates that the bond will be selling at $991.15 at the end of the investor's desired holding period. Combining the terminal value of the coupons with the selling price indicates that the investor will have a total terminal value of $1,399.98, based

TABLE 11B.1 • Illustration of the Classical Immunization Technique for a Corporate Bond

I. Immunization

Desired holding period	3 years
Characteristics of an available corporate bond:	
Duration	3 years
Term to maturity	4 years
Coupon (paid annually)	12%
Current price	$900
Yield to maturity when bond was purchased	15.54%

Assume that *one* year after the bond is purchased, the yield to maturity declines to 13%. Thus, coupons must be reinvested at lower rates, and the price of the bond will also change.

Calculation of the annualized HPR:

Terminal value of first coupon: $\$120(1 + .13)^2$	=	$153.23
Terminal value of second coupon: $\$120(1 + .13)^1$	=	135.60
Terminal value of third coupon: $\$120(1 + .13)^0$	=	120.00
Total terminal value of coupons		$408.83

Value of bond at end of three years with yield to maturity of 13%:

$$P_0 = \frac{\$120}{(1 + .13)} + \frac{\$1{,}000}{(1 + 13)} = \$991.15$$

Therefore the total terminal value is $408.83 + $991.15 = $1,399.98, and the annualized HPR is

$$\begin{aligned} \$1{,}399.98 &= \$900(1 + r)^3 \\ 1.5555 &= (1 + r)^3 \\ \sqrt[3]{1.5555} &= 1 + r \\ 1.1586 &= 1 + r \\ r &= .1586 = 15.86\% \end{aligned}$$

II. Calculation of Annualized HPR Assuming Yields Do Not Change

Terminal value of first coupon:	$\$120(1 + .1554)^2 =$	$160.19
Terminal value of second coupon:	$\$120(1 + .1554)^1 =$	138.65
Terminal value of third coupon:	$\$120(1 + .1554)^0 =$	120.00
Total terminal value of coupons		$418.84

Value of bond at end of three years with yield to maturity of 15.54%:

$$P_0 = \frac{\$120}{(1 + .1554)} + \frac{1000}{(1 + .1554)} = \$969.36$$

Annualized HPR:

$$\begin{aligned} \$418.84 + \$969.36 &= \$900(1 + r)^3 \\ 1.5424 &= (1 + r)^3 \\ r &= .1554 = 15.54\% \end{aligned}$$

on a $900 investment three years earlier. The annualized HPR of 15.86 percent is approximately equal to the initial yield to maturity of 15.54 percent. The slight difference occurs because the duration of the bond is not exactly three years; its actual duration is 3.37 years.

Part II of Table 11B.1 calculates the annualized HPR, assuming that yields do not change after the bond is purchased. As the calculations indicate, the annualized HPR is 15.54 percent, or the yield to maturity when the bond was purchased.

The major purpose of this example is to show how duration can be used to immunize a bond portfolio. Classical immunization works because price risk and reinvestment rate risk are exactly offset when the holding period equals duration. Notice in the example that income from reinvesting the coupons was less than anticipated because the yield to maturity declined from 15.54 to 13 percent. This decline was offset by the price appreciation resulting from the decline in yield. To illustrate, if the yield to maturity had remained at 15.54 percent, the bond's price would have been $P_0 = \$1{,}120/(1 + .1554) = \$969.36$, rather than $991.15. If yields had increased, the higher income from reinvestment returns would also have offset the price decline exactly. It should also be pointed out that if more than one yield change had occurred, the portfolio would no longer be immunized. It would be necessary to *rebalance* the portfolio by equating duration to the remaining length of the holding period.

Since a portfolio should include more than one bond, the concept of immunization should be viewed in a portfolio context. Doing this is quite easy since duration, like beta, is additive; the duration of a portfolio (D_p) can be defined as

$$D_p = \sum_{j=1}^{n} X_j D_j \tag{11B.1}$$

where X_j is the proportion of funds invested in bond j, and D_j is the duration of bond j. The portfolio can be immunized if its duration is equal to the investor's desired holding period.

The duration measure that we have been discussing is called the classical or single-factor model. When used to immunize a bond portfolio, this model assumes that the term structure is flat and subject only to parallel shifts. These assumptions can present problems for investors attempting to immunize; the portfolio must be rebalanced to reflect changes in yields, price, and term to maturity. That is, the duration of the portfolio must always equal the investment horizon. If an investor started with a five-year horizon, the initial portfolio's duration must also be five years. After one year, however, the remaining horizon is only four years, and the portfolio must be rebalanced or revised so that its duration is also four years. The investor should also recognize that the change in term of the portfolio is unlikely to equal the change in duration. For example, if the term declines from five to four years, the duration of the portfolio will not necessarily be four years. This suggests that transaction costs may be significant, and gains or losses may occur during the process of rebalancing.

CONTINGENT IMMUNIZATION

Attempts have been made to develop other measures of duration that do not require an assumption of a flat yield curve limited to parallel shifts. Efforts have also been directed at improving the classical immunization strategy so that the portfolio will not only provide a minimum return but will also have the potential to generate a higher return.

In this approach, called *contingent immunization*, the bond portfolio is actively managed in an attempt to earn at least a specified minimum rate of return, with the possibility that the return can be higher. The portfolio is therefore immunized against downside risk but allows for upside potential. To follow this strategy, the specified minimum rate must be set below the prevailing market yield, and the investment horizon may need to be shortened or lengthened, depending on yield movements.

As a simple example of contingent immunization, assume that an investor is considering a long-term bond portfolio. The investor is unsure about future yield movements but thinks that both increases and decreases are possible. Rather than initially forming a portfolio with a duration equal to the holding period, the investor may simply purchase bonds with maturities longer than the anticipated investment horizon. If yields decline, the portfolio will increase in value, providing an HPR above the minimum. If yields increase to a certain level, however, the investor will immediately rebalance the portfolio so that duration equals the desired holding period. The rebalancing will require selling existing bonds and purchasing new bonds to achieve the desired portfolio duration.

Contingent immunization allows active management prior to the time that the portfolio needs to be immunized. For example, the investor may trade in bonds that are perceived to be over- or undervalued. If losses occur to the extent that the specified minimum HPR is threatened, then active trading will cease, and the portfolio will be immunized to guarantee the desired minimum HPR.

PART V

Fundamental Analysis of Preferred and Common Stocks

CHAPTER 12

Preferred and Common Stock Basics

CHAPTER 13

Analyzing and Forecasting Company Earnings

CHAPTER 14

Preferred and Common Stock Valuation

CHAPTER 12

Preferred and Common Stock Basics

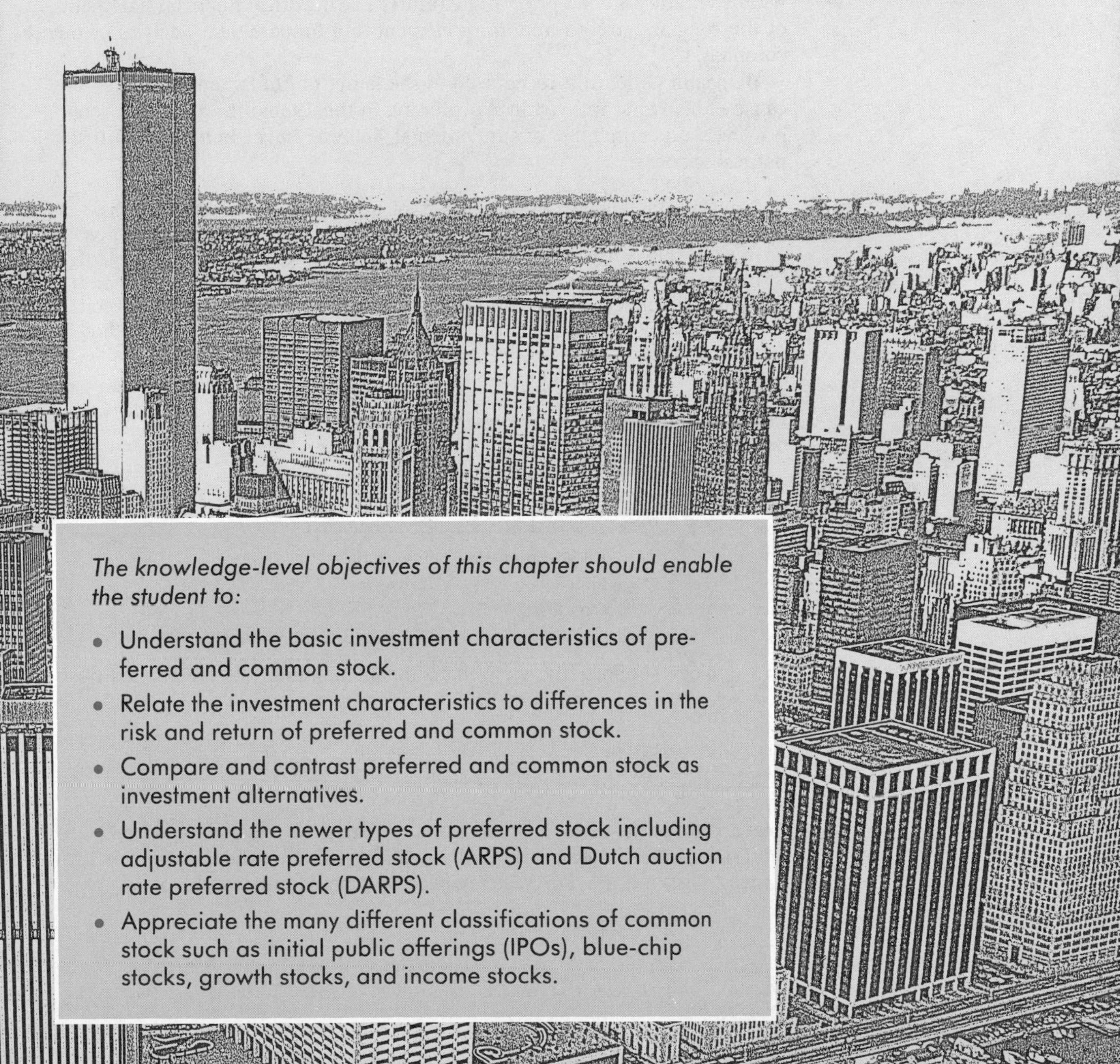

The knowledge-level objectives of this chapter should enable the student to:

- Understand the basic investment characteristics of preferred and common stock.
- Relate the investment characteristics to differences in the risk and return of preferred and common stock.
- Compare and contrast preferred and common stock as investment alternatives.
- Understand the newer types of preferred stock including adjustable rate preferred stock (ARPS) and Dutch auction rate preferred stock (DARPS).
- Appreciate the many different classifications of common stock such as initial public offerings (IPOs), blue-chip stocks, growth stocks, and income stocks.

INTRODUCTION

As was pointed out in Chapters 8 and 9, *fundamental analysis* comprises analyses of the economy, the industry, and the company. Essentially, this is a "top-down" approach that starts with a macro analysis of the economy and the industry before undertaking the company, or micro, analysis. This method centers on an identification and estimate of the "fundamental" factors that will determine a stock's price in the future. The historical financial statements of the company are an important element in a fundamental analysis of the company.

Benjamin Graham is recognized as the father of fundamental analysis because of his work and writings beginning in the 1930s.[1] In a broader sense, however, the principles of fundamental analysis have their origins in the natural sciences:

> Fundamental analysis is a method of systematically modeling facts—economic and industry statistics, financial ratios, et al.—in order to derive in a logically coherent manner an explanation, hence an understanding, of observed phenomena. We employ this understanding to pass judgment and ultimately influence behavior. This is procedurally congruent to the method articulated by Darwin with respect to the natural sciences; both his method and explanations provide the theoretical foundation for modern scientific, economic, and social thought and, yes, even fundamental analysis.[2]

Developing the analogy further, the three steps of fundamental analysis can be related to Darwin's work as follows:[3]

Darwin	Fundamental analysis
Environment	Economy
Species	Industries
Organisms	Firms

This analogy supports the view that fundamental analysts are applied business scientists.

PREFERRED STOCK

Preferred stock, though not as popular with investors as bonds and common stock, offers unique features that make it attractive under certain circumstances. First, it is a *hybrid* security because it has characteristics of two types

[1] Benjamin Graham and David Dodd, *Security Analysis* (New York: McGraw-Hill, 1934).

[2] Malvin C. Spooner, "Origin of Fundamental Analysis," *Financial Analysts Journal* (July-August 1984): 79–80.

[3] Ibid., p. 79.

TABLE 12.1 • New Issues of Bonds, Preferred Stock, and Common Stock, 1984–October 1990

	Corporate bonds[a]		Preferred stock[b]		Common stock	
	Millions of dollars	*Percentage of total*	*Millions of dollars*	*Percentage of total*	*Millions of dollars*	*Percentage of total*
1984	$133,113	85.47%	$ 4,118	2.64%	$18,510	11.89%
1985	203,500	85.14	6,505	2.72	29,010	12.14
1986	355,293	85.18	11.514	2.76	50,316	12.06
1987	325,753	85.93	10,123	2.67	43,225	11.40
1988	352,912	89.26	6,544	1.66	35,911	9.08
1989	318,300	90.81	6,194	1.77	26,030	7.42
1990						
January	9,849	79.38	269	2.17	2,290	18.45
February	10,892	78.86	167	1.21	2,752	19.93
March	17,405	82.10	1,028	4.85	2,767	13.05
April	13,590	88.55	193	1.26	1,564	10.19
May	22,853	90.67	665	2.64	1,686	6.69
June	26,027	90.06	310	1.07	2,563	8.87
July	17,728	88.75	350	1.75	1,897	9.50
August	12,942	94.12	145	1.05	663	4.83
September	14,109	97.07	100	0.69	326	2.24
October	18,300	95.01	550	2.86	412	2.13

SOURCE: Board of Governors of the Federal Reserve System, *Federal Reserve Bulletin*, various issues.

[a]Includes convertible bonds and private placements.

[b]Includes convertible preferred stock.

of securities: debt and common stock. Second, it is essentially a fixed-income security—preferred stock investors typically receive a fixed dollar dividend.

The dollar amounts of new issues of corporate bonds, preferred stock, and common stock from 1984 through October 1990 are listed in Table 12.1. New issues of convertible bonds and convertible preferred stock are included in the figures. Notice that the percentage of new issues of preferred stock is considerably below those for common stock and corporate bonds. The value of new issues of convertible preferred stock exceeds the value of new issues of "straight" (nonconvertible) preferred stock.

• Debt or Equity?

As a hybrid security, preferred stock has characteristics of both debt and equity. Legally, however, preferred stockholders are considered owners rather than creditors. Corporate balance sheets, therefore, show preferred stock in the equity section. The legal classification of preferred stock as equity has important implications for stockholders' voting rights, their right to receive income, and their rights in liquidation.

Although preferred stock represents equity, which suggests control, it is uncommon for the preferred stock in publicly traded firms to have significant voting rights. Typically, when voting rights exist, the preferred stockholders are only allowed to vote in the election of corporate directors and only if preferred dividends have not been paid over a designated number of periods. If dividends are in arrears, the preferred stockholders may be allowed to vote for a minority of the directors to be elected. Unlike preferred stockholders, common stockholders usually have voting control.

Preferred stockholders receive dividend income declared by the board of directors. Since dividends represent income distributions to owners rather than to creditors, preferred stockholders have no legal right to receive dividends. Bondholders, as creditors, do have legal rights to force interest payments or to force the corporation into bankruptcy, reorganization, or liquidation. Legally, however, preferred stockholders are entitled to receive dividends before any distribution can be made to common stockholders.

In a corporate liquidation, preferred shareholders' claims are subordinated to those of bondholders and other creditors. In other words, proceeds must be paid first to creditors and bondholders, and all liabilities must be satisfied before any distributions can be made to preferred stockholders. The preferred stockholders are entitled to receive distributions prior to common stockholders, however.

In summary, preferred stockholders have a "preferred" claim relative to common stockholders in terms of receiving income and in the event of liquidation. Unlike common stockholders, however, they can exercise little if any control through their voting rights. In comparison to bondholders, preferred stockholders have a secondary claim on income and liquidation proceeds. Thus, for a single corporation, preferred stock is less risky than common stock, but more risky than bonds.

• Dividends

Dividends on preferred stock are generally fixed. The dividend will be stated as a dollar amount or as a percentage of par value; for example, $2 paid quarterly ($8 per year), or 8 percent per year, based on $100 par value. Since 1982, a number of preferred stocks have been issued with adjustable dividend rates. This feature is discussed later in the chapter.

Historically, some corporations issued **participating preferred stock** that allowed the holder to participate with the common stockholders in receiving income above a certain level of earnings. Currently, very few participating preferred stocks are outstanding and publicly traded. An exception, however, is a participating preferred stock issued on Janaury 3, 1989, by the Federal Home Loan Mortgage Corporation (Freddie Mac).[4] This preferred

[4] Leland Brendsel, "Freddie Mac Is the New Kid on the Street," *Bottomline* (January 1989): 38–40.

RESEARCH BOX

Do Existing Common Stockholders Gain or Lose When New Preferred Stock Is Issued?

When corporations wish to obtain additional long-term financing, they may elect to issue bonds, preferred stock, or common stock. For established corporations, the new issue may be in addition to bonds or stocks that have been issued previously. Existing common stockholders may view a new issue of preferred stock positively or negatively. Their reaction will likely depend on the type and characteristics of the preferred stock and the effect the issue will have on the risk-return characteristics of the common stock.

Linn and Pinegar analyzed the reaction of common stock investors to all new issues of preferred stock between 1962 and 1984. The final sample consisted of 308 preferred stock offerings. One interesting finding of the study is that the industry of the issuing firm is important in explaining the reaction of the common stock price to the offering. The empirical results indicate that when utilities issue new preferred stock, the price of their common stock does not change significantly. The common stock of financial issues reacts *positively,* and that of industrial companies reacts *negatively.* Consequently, common stockholders in financial firms that issue new preferred are likely to see the price of their stock increase whereas investors in industrial firms are likely to see a decrease in the value of their common stock.

Corporations and investors should therefore be aware that a new issue of preferred stock may have an impact on existing common stockholders.

SOURCE: Scott C. Linn and Michael J. Pinegar, "The Effect of Issuing Preferred Stock on Common and Preferred Stockholder Wealth," *Journal of Financial Economics* (October 1988): 155–84.

stock allows investors to participate in the extraordinary earnings performance of Freddie Mac. If savings and loan associations purchase the preferred stock, they can use it as collateral for cash advances from a Federal Reserve district bank.

In the vast majority of new issues, the preferred stock has a **cumulative dividend** feature rather than a participating feature. The cumulative feature provides that any omitted dividends accrue to the preferred stockholders and must be paid in full before any dividends can be paid on the common stock. The cumulative feature also allows the corporation to pay the accrued dividends to the current stockholder rather than to the stockholders who owned the stock when the dividend was skipped. Cumulative preferred stock is therefore traded with the right to receive accrued dividends when and if they are paid.

• Taxes

There are advantages and disadvantages in the tax treatment of preferred stock dividends. The major disadvantage is that the issuing corporation must pay the preferred dividend from after-tax income. This unfavorable tax treatment is one reason corporations that have a tax liability consider preferred stock an unattractive financing alternative. Consequently, most new issues of preferred stock are from utilities (because of their regulations on return on equity) or are issued in connection with corporate takeovers or buyouts.

The major tax advantage is that corporations that *receive* common or preferred dividends from a nonaffiliated corporation are allowed to exclude a portion of the dividends from taxable income. Prior to January 1, 1987, corporations were allowed to exclude 85 percent of these dividends. Tax reform, however, reduced the exclusion to 55 percent but also reduced the maximum marginal corporate tax rate to 34 percent. The maximum effective tax rate on dividend income for a corporation is now 15.3 percent [(1 − .55)(.34)].

The tax code creates an unusual yield relationship between bonds and preferred stock. As previously noted, bonds have less risk than preferred stock and therefore should offer lower yields. However, the *before-tax* yield (BTY) on bonds is almost always above the BTY on preferred stock. This occurs because the favorable tax treatment of preferred dividends for corporate investors causes the *after-tax* yield (ATY) on preferred stock to exceed the ATY of bonds. Corporations that are seeking income therefore have a tax incentive to invest in preferred stock while noncorporate investors do not enjoy this tax advantage. This feature of preferred stock is discussed in more detail in chapter 14.

• Call Feature

Traditionally, most preferred stock was not callable and was issued without a maturity date. Now, the vast majority of new preferred stock issues are redeemable and have a **sinking fund.** The sinking fund can be used to buy the stock directly in the market and thus improve the marketability of the issue for investors. Studies have also found that yields may be lower for sinking fund preferreds. More commonly, the stock has a *call feature* that allows the issuer to redeem the shares at predetermined prices. The sinking fund is then used to pay the investors for the called shares. The call price places an upper limit on the market price of the preferred stock.

• Convertibility

Preferred stock may be issued with a convertible feature that can be exercised at the option of the investor. Typically, preferred stock that has a convertible feature will not have a cumulative dividend. The dividend rate on a **convertible preferred** is also usually below the rate on a similar "straight" or nonconvertible preferred. If the preferred is both convertible and callable, the investor still has the option of converting the stock between the call announcement date and the call date. For example, Masco Industries announced that its preferred stock would be redeemed on September 28, 1987, for $27.03 plus accrued dividends of $.28. A share of preferred stock was convertible into two shares of common stock through September 25, 1987. Since the common stock was trading between $16 and $17 per share during mid-September, making the conversion value $32 to $34 per share, investors should have converted prior to September 25 rather than have their shares called.

Historically, many issues of convertible preferred stock have been by industrial companies. The company typically uses the issue to finance an acquisition or merger by exchanging the new preferred stock for the common stock of the acquired or merged firm. Due to the lack of financial strength of the issuer and the characteristics of the convertible preferred, these securities usually have high risk and often provide low realized returns.[5]

• Adjustable Dividend Rates

Traditionally, preferred stock was issued with a fixed dividend and was therefore subject to a considerable degree of *price risk*. That is, as market yields increased because of inflation pressures or other factors, the prices of preferred stock fell.

The volatility of market interest rates and yields in the 1980s, however, provided an incentive to offer **adjustable rate preferred stock (ARPS),** which adjusts the dividend to provide market yields. ARPS was first issued in 1982 by Chase Manhattan Corporation and Manufacturers Hanover Trust Company.[6] These issues provided a fixed yield spread between the preferred yield and the highest of the yields on short-, intermediate-, or long-term U.S. Treasury bonds. The quarterly preferred dividend adjustments were designed to keep the preferred price relatively constant, thereby eliminating price risk from changing interest rates.

Most of the initial ARPS issues were by banks or bank holding companies. But problems in the banking industry in 1983–1984, such as losses on loans to less-developed countries, reduced the creditworthiness of many of the multinational banks and therefore lessened the popularity of ARPS. For example, approximately $8–$10 billion of ARPS was issued over the period 1982–1984, but less than $1 billion was issued in 1985.[7]

To deal with both interest and credit risk problems, **Dutch auction rate preferred stock (DARPS)** was introduced in August 1984; approximately $10 billion had been issued through 1986.[8] The yield on DARPS is adjusted by auction every seven weeks instead of quarterly. The rate is set by a Dutch auction procedure where bidding occurs between both current and potential investors. The bids naturally incorporate market yield changes and an assess-

---

[5] For a discussion of convertible preferred, see Monther Nijim and Glenn V. Henderson, Jr., "Volume and Performance of Merger-Related Convertible Preferred," *Review of Business and Economic-Research* (Spring 1989): 13–26.

[6] For a discussion of the history of ARPS, see Michael J. Alderson, Keith C. Brown, and Scott L. Lummer, "Dutch Auction Rate Preferred Stock," *Financial Management* (Summer 1987): 68–73.

[7] Ibid., p. 69.

[8] Ibid., p. 70.

• **INTEREST BOX**

ARPS versus DARPS

ARPS and DARPS differ in several important respects. First, the yield on ARPS is adjusted quarterly to the "reset" rate measured by the yield on short-, intermediate-, or long-term Treasury securities. The yield on DARPS is determined by auction every 49 days. Second, the yield on ARPS reflects only credit market conditions because the yields are set according to Treasury yields. The yield on DARPS reflects credit market conditions and the credit risk of the issuer. For example, if the financial condition of the issuer declines and credit risk increases, the yield set by the auction procedure for DARPS will reflect this additional risk. The ARPS yield, however, will not reflect the increased credit risk. Third, an active secondary market now exists for DARPS, providing liquidity to investors.

ARPS and DARPS also are similar in certain ways, including their tax treatment. The issuer must pay the preferred dividend from after-tax income—it is not a tax deductible expense. Corporate investors that hold the security for a minimum of 46 days can exclude 55 percent of the dividend income from taxable income. This favorable tax treatment has made ARPS and DARPS attractive primarily to corporate investors. Finally, corporate investors use both types of preferred stocks as short-term investments for cash management purposes. Traditional preferred stock was not appropriate as a short-term investment because of price risk.

SOURCES: Paul R. Allen, "Auction Advantages," *Secondary Mortgage Markets* (Spring 1988): 7–11; and Carl R. Chen and Bernard J. Winger, "Adjustable Rate Preferred Stocks: A New Short-Term Investment," *Journal of Cash Management* (March-April 1987): 42–46.

ment of the creditworthiness of the issuer. Since the price of DARPS is essentially fixed at par by the auction procedure, both price and credit risks are eliminated. Therefore, DARPS yields for creditworthy issuers are close to those on money market securities.

In late 1990, the auction for one of Citicorp's outstanding DARPS resulted in an unprecedented high yield of 12.5 percent. This yield resulted from investor concerns about bank losses tied to risky lending portfolios. As a $100 million issue, the new yield would cost Citicorp approximately $12.5 million in preferred stock dividends per year. Because Citicorp had approximately $950 million of DARPS and ARPS outstanding, it announced a plan to redeem $275 million of its preferred stock. This announcement indicated the bank was unwilling to pay such a high yield, which was well above the rate it was paying on other short-term borrowings. The redemption announcement also resulted in a lower yield for Citicorp from an auction on a similar issue of ARPS.

• Marketability

While preferred stock is usually marketable, investors should recognize that the market may be "thin," even though the company's common stock is actively traded. This thin market occurs because preferred stock issues are often small relative to the size of the common stock issues and companies may have multiple issues of preferred stock. Also, the typical preferred stock generates less investor interest and is traded less frequently than the typical common stock.

A thin market for a specific issue of preferred stock may limit its marketability and increase the "spread" or difference between the bid and ask prices. Table 12.2 provides a selected sample of trading activity for the common and preferred stock of five corporations traded on the NYSE. Notice the differences in the trading volume, relative to the shares outstanding, for the preferred and common stock.

Despite the typically thin market for preferred stock, trading occurs on the NYSE, AMEX, and OTC market. The preferred stock is generally traded on the same market as the company's common stock with the quotation for the preferred stock appearing after the quotation for the common stock. An example of a recent quotation from the NYSE appears in Table 12.3. Notice that Adobe Resources (Adobe Res) common stock has a single line, followed by quotations for two different issues of preferred stock. The preferred stock is indicated by "pf" after the company name. The "pf" indication is also used in quotations on the AMEX and OTC market. The other information provided in the quotations in Table 12.3 is discussed in the common stock section of this chapter.

COMMON STOCK

This section of the chapter discusses the characteristics and the various ways of expressing values of **common stock.** Common stock represents an ownership interest in a corporation. As owners, common stockholders are entitled to certain rights and privileges, which are described in the following paragraphs.

• Control

Common stock has voting rights that can be used to elect corporate directors who, in turn, appoint the corporate officers. Generally, stockholders also have the right to vote on (1) any issue that will have a material effect on the corporation; (2) any proposal that will change their individual percentage ownership; and (3) any significant contract or financial arrangement. The extent of control depends on the voting rights specified in the corporate charter, the number of shares held relative to the total shares outstanding, the method of voting, and the stock ownership of the officers and their representation on the board of directors.

Members of the board of directors are elected by two methods: **straight voting** and **cumulative voting.** Straight voting is essentially one vote per share for each director. If the shares allow cumulative voting, however, a stockholder can use all his or her votes for a *single* candidate. For example, if a stockholder has 100 shares and five directors are to be elected, the stock-

TABLE 12.2 • Trading Volume of Selected Issues of Preferred and Common Stock

	Shares outstanding, December 1990 (thousands)	Shares traded in December (thousands)					
		1984	*1985*	*1986*	*1987*	*1988*	*1989*
Commonwealth Edison							
Common stock	212,099	16,511	20,921	28,771	23,790	13,468	17,104
Preferred stock ($1.90 cumulative)	4,250	127	116	180	130	54	45
General Motors							
Common stock	600,071	11,334	16,259	25,046	18,180	14,531	17,315
Preferred stock ($5.00 cumulative)	1,530	75	42	122	32	34	9
Goodrich (B.F.)							
Common stock	25,381	711	990	1,264	5,529	3,203	2,920
Preferred stock ($7.85 cumulative)	150	1	—	17	—	37	0.2
McDermott International							
Common stock	44,058	2,008	3,733	4,616	21,974	3,975	3,167
Preferred stock ($2.60 cumulative B)	3,725	174	82	196	320	29	173
Tenneco, Inc.							
Common stock	123,483	5,312	5,256	8,737	11,589	8,249	4,968
Preferred stock ($7.40 cumulative)	1,814	52	30	19	26	235	0.7

SOURCE: Various issues of Standard & Poor's *Stock Guide*. Reprinted by permission.

TABLE 12.3 • Example of Quotations for Preferred Stock Traded on the New York Stock Exchange

Quotations as of 5 p.m. Eastern Time
Monday, July 1, 1991

52 Weeks Hi	Lo	Stock	Sym	Div	Yld %	PE	Vol 100s	Hi	Lo	Close	Net Chg
		-A-A-A-									
24⅛	9⅛	AAR	AIR	.48	3.2	16	381	15¼	14⅞	14⅞	– ⅝
11⅝	8¾	ACM Gvt Fd	ACG	1.26	11.6	...	1429	11	10⅞	10⅞	...
9¾	7¾	ACM OppFd	AOF	1.01e	11.2	...	247	9	8⅞	9	+ ⅛
11	8⅝	ACM SecFd	GSF	1.26	12.3	...	1672	10⅜	10¼	10¼	...
9¼	7¼	ACM SpctmFd	SI	1.01	11.1	...	706	9¼	9	9⅛	...
n 8⅜	6½	ACM MgdIncFd	AMF	1.01	12.2	...	261	8¼	8⅛	8¼	...
12⅞	10¾	ACM MgdMultFd	MMF	1.50	12.4	...	235	12⅛	12	12⅛	+ ⅛
18¾	**11¼**	**AL Labs A**	**BMD**	**.16**	**1.0**	**18**	**551**	**15⅞**	**15**	**15⅞**	**+ ⅞**
2⅝	1	AM Int	AM		...	...	28	1½	1½	1½	...
12¾	4⅝	AM Int pf		2.00	22.9	...	51	8⅞	8⅝	8¾	...
11	8¾	AMEV Sec	AMV	1.08	9.8	...	58	11	10¾	11	+ ¼
68⅝	39¾	AMR	AMR		...	...	3544	62⅞	61½	62¾	+2
27¼	25	ANR pf		2.67	10.3	...	1	25⅞	25⅞	25⅞	+ ½
44¼	29¾	ARCO Chm	RCM	2.50	6.3	14	127	40	39¾	39⅞	+ ⅛
3⅝	1¼	ARX	ARX		...	...	14	1½	1½	1½	...
56¼	38¼	ASA	ASA	3.00	5.7	...	2341	53½	52	52⅜	– ⅛
5⅞	1⅞	ATT Cap yen wt			...	...	330	5⅞	5⅝	5⅞	...
54	34½	AbbotLab	ABT	1.00	1.9	23	6314	52½	51¾	52½	+ ¾
14½	9⅞	Abitibi g	ABY	.50	3.7	...	12	13⅝	13⅝	13⅝	...
8⅝	**3½**	**AcmeElec**	**ACE**		**...**	**...**	**30**	**4⅛**	**4**	**4**	**+ ¼**
8⅞	4½	AcmeCleve	AMT	.40	6.5	15	89	6⅛	6	6⅛	+ ⅛
s 40	22	Acuson	ACN		...	21	4679	30¼	29½	29⅞	+ ¾
18½	14⅛	AdamsExp	ADX	1.72e	9.7	...	183	17⅞	17¾	17¾	+ ⅛
14½	6¾	AdobeRes	ADB		...	...	150	7⅜	7⅛	7¼	...
21¼	18	AdobeRes pf		2.40	12.9	...	17	18¾	18⅝	18⅝	– ⅛
19¾	14¼	AdobeRes pf		1.84	12.1	...	37	15½	15¼	15¼	...
14¼	3⅝	AdvMicro	AMD		...	...	4980	12⅝	12¼	12⅜	+ ⅜
38⅜	13	AdvMicro pf		3.00	8.5	...	21	35¼	34¾	35¼	+ ¾
5⅛	1⅝	Advest	ADV		...	...	93	4⅜	4⅜	4⅜	+ ⅛
53⅞	29	AetnaLife	AET	2.76	6.6	8	2351	42⅝	41⅜	42⅛	+ ¾
10⅞	6¼	AffilPub	AFP	.24	2.7	36	1687	9¼	9	9	– ⅛
22¼	10⅝	Ahmanson	AHM	.88	4.9	12	809	18⅜	18	18⅛	...
▲ 10⅝	**2⅛**	**Alleen**	**AEE**		**...**	**14**	**1020**	**10¾**	**9¾**	**10⅝**	**+1**
74⅛	42⅞	AirProduct	APD	1.56	2.2	16	1538	70⅛	67⅜	70	+2⅝
27	13½	AirbornFrght	ABF	.30	1.2	15	1204	24¾	24¼	24¾	+ ¾
20	11¼	Airgas	ARG		...	16	8	14⅞	14⅝	14⅝	– ⅛
19⅛	10	Airlease	FLY	1.60	12.8	7	24	12⅝	12½	12½	...
25½	21	AlaPwr pf		2.01e	8.2	...	62	24½	24⅜	24½	...
10¼	9	AlaPwr pf		.87	8.8	...	10	10	9⅞	9⅞	+ ⅛
102½	90	AlaPwr pf		9.00	9.0	...	z100	99½	99½	99½	+1
104½	94⅛	AlaPwr pf		9.44	9.3	...	z230	101½	101	101	–1
25⅜	13⅞	AlaskaAir	ALK	.20	.9	135	615	21⅝	21⅜	21⅝	+ ⅛
▲ 17¾	8	AlbanyInt	AIN	.35	1.9	90	79	18	17⅞	18	+ ¼
34¼	19⅛	AlbertoCl	ACV	.22	.9	17	110	23½	22½	23½	+1
24⅞	15⅛	AlbertoCl A	ACVA	.22	1.2	14	106	19¼	18¾	18⅞	...
51⅜	28	Albertsons	ABS	.56	1.4	23	1445	41½	40⅞	41⅜	+ ⅜
24½	16⅝	Alcan	AL	1.12	5.5	13	2467	21	20⅜	20⅜	– ⅜
37⅞	27⅝	AlcoStd	ASN	.88	2.7	14	580	32⅜	31⅜	32⅜	+ ⅞
27⅝	16⅛	Alex&Alex	AAL	1.00	4.4	17	823	22¾	22¼	22⅝	+ ⅛
41	19¾	Alexanders	ALX		...	...	39	36	35¼	35⅞	+ ⅛
101¾	73	AlleghanyCp	Y	1.86t	1.9	11	81	99	98¾	99	+ ¼
34¼	18⅛	AllegLud	ALS	.88	3.4	15	316	25⅞	25⅛	25⅞	+ ¾
39⅞	34	AlleyPw	AYP	3.10	8.2	11	1173	30¾	30½	30¾	+ ⅛
20	9¾	AllenGp	ALN		...	9	39	13¾	13⅜	13¾	+ ⅜
21¾	14¼	AllenGp pf		1.75	9.3	...	25	19	18¾	18¾	...
25½	12½	Allergan	AGN	.32	1.7	15	1519	19⅛	18⅞	19	+ ¼
▲ 28⅞	11½	AllncCapMgt	AC	1.84e	6.3	20	589	30½	28⅞	29	+ ⅛
14⅜	8⅝	AllncGlblEnv	AEF	.34e	3.0	...	117	11⅜	11¼	11⅜	+ ¼
n 28¼	8⅝	AlliantTech	ATK		...	10	508	26¾	25¾	26⅝	+ ⅛
25¼	15¾	AlldIrishBk pf		2.97	12.6	...	141	23¾	23⅜	23½	– ¼
8½	3	AlliedPdts	ADP		...	8	47	6½	6⅜	6½	...
36¾	24⅞	AlliedSgnl	ALD	1.80	5.3	12	5460	34⅛	32¾	34⅛	+1⅛
10⅝	9⅜	AllmonTr	GSO	.61e	6.2	...	280	9⅞	9¾	9⅞	...

NYSE EXTENDED TRADING

July 1, 1991

	Total Volume	Market Value
First crossing session	158,400	b-$5,292,994
Second session (baskets)	418,600	$17,865,325

MOST ACTIVE ISSUES

(First session)

Issue	Sym.	a-Volume 100s	NYSE Close	Comp. Close
Acuson Corp	ACN	107	29⅞	29⅞
Putnam Prem	PPT	102	7⅝	7⅝
Kemper Tr sbl	KMM	83	9½	9½
Boeing Co	BA	79	46	46
IBM	IBM	76	98⅜	98⅜
Philip Morris	MO	57	65⅛	65⅛
Putnam Inco	PMT	50	8	8
BankAmerica	BAC	40	35⅝	35⅝
Citicorp	CCI	36	14¾	14¾
Nuveen NY Inv	NQN	33	15⅝	15⅝

a-From 4:15 p.m. to 5:00 p.m. Eastern time, NYSE only. b-WSJ calculation, estimate.

52 Weeks Hi	Lo	Stock	Sym	Div	Yld %	PE	Vol 100s	Hi	Lo	Close	Net Chg
40½	19	BancOne	ONE	1.16	3.0	14	3977	39⅜	38⅝	38⅞	+ ⅝
13/16	**⅛**	**BancTexas**	**BTX**		**...**	**...**	**51**	**⅜**	**⅜**	**⅜**	**– 1/32**
25½	18	BancoCentrl	BCM	.99e	5.4	6	13	18⅜	18¼	18⅜	+ ⅛
55⅞	37½	BancoSantdr	STD	2.15e	4.7	8	16	45⅝	45½	45⅝	...
s 66½	59⅝	BcpHawii	BOH	1.64	2.7	11	517	60¼	59¾	60	+ ⅛
105¼	66	Bandag	BDG	1.10	1.1	19	44	103¾	102¼	102⅞	– ⅛
12⅝	**3**	**BankBost**	**BKB**	**.40**	**5.4**	**...**	**4511**	**7⅜**	**6⅞**	**7⅜**	**+ ½**
30½	11¼	BankBost pfA		3.51e	13.5	...	48	26	25	26	+1
28½	10¾	BankBost pfB		3.39e	13.2	...	58	25¾	25	25⅝	+1⅛
51	16	BankBost pfC		6.15	13.4	...	z1800	46	43½	46	+2⅛
34⅝	13¼	BankNY	BK	1.52	5.4	18	1913	28½	27½	28⅛	+ ¾
40⅜	17½	BankAmer	BAC	1.20	3.4	9	6397	36⅞	35⅝	35⅝	– ⅝
40	30½	BankAmer pfA		3.40e	8.7	...	29	39¼	39	39¼	– ⅛
68⅝	55¼	BankAmer pfB		6.00	9.1	...	3	66	65⅝	65⅝	+ ⅜
26½	25	BankAmer pfF		2.41	9.5	...	361	25¾	25⅜	25½	– ¼
52	47½	BankAmer pfG		3.25	6.8	...	145	49	48	48	–1
57	28½	BankTrst	BT	2.54	5.1	7	1856	50¼	49¼	50	+1⅝
n 14⅛	6¾	BannerAero	BAR		...	8	98	8⅞	8⅝	8⅝	– ¼
n 1⅝	5/16	BanyanMtg	VMLPZ		...	...	74	9/16	½	½	...
25⅝	21	Barclays pr		2.78	11.1	...	98	25¼	25	25⅛	...
25½	20⅝	Barclays prB		2.72	11.2	...	191	24½	24⅛	24⅜	...
25¾	21	Barclays pfC		1.90e	7.5	...	29	25⅜	25⅛	25⅜	...
26⅛	24¾	Barclays pfD		.51e	2.0	...	116	26	25⅝	25⅝	...
▲ 28¼	13	Bard CR	BCR	.44	1.6	33	1462	28½	28	28⅜	+ ¼
34⅛	23⅞	BarnesGp	B	1.40	4.2	14	24	33¾	33½	33⅝	+ ⅛
33	14⅛	BarnettBks	BBI	1.32	4.7	17	2190	28¼	27⅞	27⅞	+1⅛
66¾	52¼	BarnettBks pf			...	...	16	61	60¼	60½	+1½
n 9	4¾	BaroidCp	BRC	.20	3.1	21	428	6⅝	6¼	6½	+ ⅛
n 21⅜	15	Bass	BAS	.71e	4.7	9	84	15	15	15	...
13⅞	5½	BattleMtn	BMG	.10	1.0	56	4947	10⅛	9¾	10⅛	+ ⅜
s 44¾	27⅜	BauschLomb	BOL		...	18	2139	41⅜	40½	40⅞	+ ⅛
37⅛	21½	BaxterInt	BAX	.74	2.3	18	13044	32¾	32¼	32¾	+ ½
44⅛	35	BaxterInt pfA		3.55e	8.6	...	29	41½	41⅛	41½	+ ¼
21⅝	18	BayStGas	BGC	1.34	6.7	13	62	20¼	20	20	+ ⅛
15¾	7⅛	BearStearns	BSC	.60b	4.3	12	1577	14⅛	13¾	14	+ ⅜
23¾	13⅜	BearingsInc	BER	.64	2.8	55	51	23¼	23	23¼	+ ¼
13¾	4¾	Beazer	BZR	.77e	13.4	3	4685	5⅞	5⅝	5¾	...
20	11⅞	BeckmanInstr	BEC	.28	1.5	15	366	18⅝	18⅛	18½	+ ⅜
81½	60⅝	BectonDksn	BDX	1.16	1.5	16	1140	75⅛	74¼	75⅛	+ ¾
30¼	15¾	BeldenHem	BHY	.64	3.8	43	42	17⅛	17	17	...
56¼	39½	BellAtlantic	BEL	2.52	5.1	14	5025	49	47¾	49	+1¾

SOURCE: *Wall Street Journal*, July 2, 1991, p. C3.

holder can cast a total of 500 votes for one or more of the directors. The majority of states now require or permit cumulative voting, with the intent of increasing the voting power of minority stockholders.

Rather than actually attending the annual stockholders' meeting to vote, stockholders may use a *proxy* that temporarily transfers their voting rights to another individual, such as a corporate officer, a member of the board of directors, or an individual trying to gain control of the corporation. Proxy battles in which two or more groups try to obtain proxies are not unusual. Due to the economic significance of voting control, the Securities and Exchange Commission (SEC) regulates and supervises proxy procedures.

In some cases, a corporation may have more than one category or class of common stock that provide different voting rights. For example, Class A may be nonvoting, while Class B has voting rights. The Toronto Stock Exchange, the AMEX, and the OTC market allow trading in shares with restricted voting rights. The NYSE, beginning in the 1920s, did not allow listings for firms that issued multiple classes of shares with different voting rights; this prohibition was lifted in 1986. Congress has considered measures that would prohibit all U.S. exchanges and markets from trading dual voting class common stock.

A study of voting and nonvoting common stock traded on the Toronto Stock Exchange provides evidence of the importance that some investors place on voting rights.[9] The study analyzed companies that issued both voting and nonvoting shares to existing stockholders in exchange for the original voting stock. (This procedure is similar to a stock split, except that the new shares differ in their voting rights.) The restricted-voting shares declined in price, and the superior voting shares increased in price, providing a "positive premium of roughly 7 percent." The evidence also suggests that some investors reacted by selling the restricted-voting shares in favor of alternative investments.

• Preemptive Right

A **preemptive right** gives existing stockholders the first option to purchase a proportionate interest in a new issue of a corporation's stock. The purpose of this provision is to protect stockholders against a loss of voting control and a dilution in the value of their shares. The preemptive right is usually satisfied by the use of a *rights offering* (discussed in detail in the appendix to chapter 16).

• Liquidation Rights

As owners rather than creditors, common stockholders receive no priority in the distribution of assets resulting from a liquidation of the corporation. Typi-

---

[9] Vijay M. Jog and Allan L. Riding, "Price Effects of Dual-Class Shares," *Financial Analysts Journal* (January-February 1986): 58–67.

cally, after assets are sold and liabilities and preferred stockholders are satisfied, little if any cash will be available for common stockholders.

• Right to Income and Distribution of Additional Shares

Common stockholders have no legal right to receive income distributions from the corporation. As a practical matter, however, the board of directors may declare *cash dividends* to stockholders, provided the financial resources are available, even for periods when the corporation has experienced a loss.

Because of tax code changes in 1981, many large corporations now allow shareholders to elect to have cash dividends automatically reinvested into additional shares of common stock. These **dividend reinvestment plans** avoid brokerage fees that would result if the stockholder received the dividends and used the cash to purchase additional shares. The dividends, however, are taxable income to investors whether they are received as cash or reinvested in new shares. To encourage stockholders to use these reinvestment plans, some companies sell the stock at discounts of 3 to 5 percent below the current market price and are also willing to credit fractional shares to individual accounts.

In lieu of or in conjunction with a cash dividend, the board of directors may declare a **stock dividend.** In an efficient market, the economic significance of a stock dividend should be negligible because the price of the stock will decline to reflect the additional shares.

For example, a 4 percent stock dividend declared on a stock selling for $26 should result in a new price of $25 ($26/1.04). Assuming an investor previously held 100 shares, the new price of $25 would keep the total value of the investment at $2,600 ($25 × 104). Thus, the investor neither gains nor loses as a result of the stock dividend. Unlike cash dividends, stock dividends are not taxable income to investors.

A **stock split** is similar to but usually larger than a stock dividend, and the two transactions are handled differently on the balance sheet. A stock split results in a reduction in the par value of the stock and a corresponding increase in the number of shares outstanding. In a stock dividend, the corporation adjusts the balance sheet by transferring an amount equal to the market value of the stock dividend from the retained earnings account to the paid-in-capital and common stock accounts.

Generally, a stock dividend of 25 percent or greater is essentially a stock split. The NYSE uses 25 percent as the dividing line between dividends and splits for stocks listed on the exchange. In effect, a 25 percent stock dividend is equivalent to a five-for-four stock split.

Corporations that declare stock dividends and splits offer a variety of justifications for their actions including the following:

1. Investor psychology—investors prefer stocks that are not too expensive and trade in a "desirable" price range.

RESEARCH BOX

Financial Engineering: Puttable Common Stock

Once a corporation issues common stock, it has no obligation to redeem the stock by purchasing it from the investor. Essentially, common stock is issued with a perpetual life. The investor, however, will likely be able to sell the stock in the secondary market to another investor.

One potential problem for an investor in a new company that may be making its initial offering of common stock is how the stock will ultimately be valued by the secondary market. The possibility that the secondary market price may be significantly below the offering price in the primary market may limit the investor's interest in buying the new offering.

In the late 1980s, in an example of financial engineering, investment bankers devised an innovation that would solve this problem by making the common stock puttable. In other words, an investor who purchases a new offering receives the right to sell (or put) the stock back to the issuing corporation. If the price of the stock increases above the offering price in the primary market, the investor will not use the put feature. If, however, the stock does not do well on the secondary market, the investor can elect to "put" the stock back to the issuer. Thus, the put feature provides downside risk protection to the investor but maintains the upside price appreciation potential.

One disadvantage of puttable common stock, however, is that the issuer normally has several options in paying the investor for the stock. The payoff can be in cash, notes, preferred stock, or some combination of these. Thus, investors may not be able to get their initial cash investment back by electing to "put" the stock. The put guarantee, therefore, is only as sound as the issuing corporation.

SOURCE: Andrew H. Chen and John W. Kensinger, "Puttable Stock: A New Innovation in Equity Financing," *Financial Management* (Spring 1988): 27–37.

2. Trading volume—the increased number of shares leads to more trading and improves liquidity.
3. Signaling to investors—a decision to split or declare a stock dividend indicates that management and the directors are bullish about the stock.
4. Attention—the announced split results in increased publicity for the firm and draws additional investor attention.
5. Naïve investors—the feeling that some shareholders equate cash and stock dividends and do not realize that stock dividends and splits may have little economic significance.[10]

[10]For a typical discussion, see Lawrence Ingrassia, "Recent Increase in Share Prices Has Led to Flurry of Stock Splits, Stock Dividends," *Wall Street Journal*, January 27, 1983, p. 56. For a discussion of management's reasons for paying stock dividends, see Peter C. Eisemann and Edward A. Moses, "Stock Dividends: Management's View," *Financial Analysts Journal* (July-August 1978): 77–80.

Numerous empirical studies have examined the possible economic significance of stock dividends and stock splits.[11] Surprisingly, some of these studies indicate that stockholder wealth does increase prior to the announcement of a stock dividend or split. The reason for this, however, appears to be that stockholders view a stock dividend or split as a favorable message or *signal* from management that it is optimistic about the prospects of the company. Thus, the increase in stockholder wealth occurs because of the signal and not because of the stock dividend or split.

• Common Stock Values

Terms that are frequently used to refer to common stock values include *par value, book value,* and *market value.* These terms are quite different, and in most cases, the dollar amounts of these values are not related for an individual stock.

PAR VALUE The face value of the stock, established at the time the stock is initially issued, is the par value. Without a stock split or other action by the board of directors, the par value of the stock does not change. For new issues, popular par values are $1 or $.01 per share, but the directors are free to select any value that seems appropriate. Stock is often issued without a par value.

BOOK VALUE **Book value per share** is calculated by dividing the total common equity on the balance sheet (book) by the number of common shares outstanding. This figure represents the asset value per share after deducting liabilities and preferred stock. Typically, common stock in a profitable corporation will be valued based on *earning power* and will sell at prices significantly greater than book value. (For a comparison of price per share to book value per share for the Standard & Poor's 500 from 1946 through 1990, see Figure 9.3 on page 281). Likewise, common stock in unprofitable companies and companies experiencing financial distress will be valued based on *liquidation* or book value and will sell at prices close to or below book value. Traditionally, fundamental analysts often compare market and book values because a stock price below book value may be an indication that the stock is undervalued.

MARKET VALUE Market value in the secondary markets is determined by supply and demand factors and reflects the consensus opinion of investors

---

[11] For example, see E. Fama et al., "The Adjustment of Stock Prices to New Information," *International Economic Review* (February 1969): 1–21; M. Grinblatt, R. Masulis, and S. Titman, "The Valuation Effects of Stock Splits and Stock Dividends," *Journal of Financial Economics* (December 1984): 461–90; R. Spudeck and R. Moyer, "Reverse Splits and Shareholder Wealth: The Impact of Commissions," *Financial Management* (Winter 1985): 52–56; and L. S. Klein and D. R. Peterson, "Earnings Forecast Revisions Associated with Stock Split Announcements," *Journal of Financial Research* (Winter 1989): 319–28.

and traders concerning the "value" of the stock. As the following chapters indicate, market value is influenced by many factors including economic and industry conditions, expected earnings and dividends, and market and company risk considerations.

• Quotations

Table 12.4 provides examples of common stock quotations for the NYSE, AMEX, and national OTC markets. As the table illustrates, the quotations for the NYSE, AMEX, and "NASDAQ National Market Issues" on the OTC have identical formats. Each Monday's edition of the *Wall Street Journal* provides the "NASDAQ Weekly Bid & Asked Quotations" for many small, thinly traded common stock issues. However, the quotations for the "NASDAQ Bid & Ask Quotation" consist only of "bid" and "asked" prices, volume, and change. Prices for stocks are quoted in dollars and increments of dollars. For example, the closing price of Abbott Lab in the NYSE quotations is $52.50.

TABLE 12.4 • Examples of Quotations for Common Stocks Traded on the NYSE, AMEX, and OTC Markets

NYSE

Quotations as of 4:30 p.m. Eastern Time
Thursday, May 30, 1991

52 Weeks Hi	Lo	Stock	Sym	Div	Yld %	PE	Vol 100s	Hi	Lo	Close	Net Chg
		-A-A-A-									
24¼	9⅛	AAR	AIR	.48	3.5	13	2180	13⅞	12⅞	13¾	+ ⅛
11½	8¾	ACM Gvt Fd	ACG	1.26	11.1	...	2104	11½	11¼	11⅜	+ ⅛
9¾	7¾	ACM OppFd	AOF	1.01e	10.9	...	384	9½	9¼	9¼	− ⅛
11	8⅝	ACM SecFd	GSF	1.26	11.5	...	1816	11	10¾	11	+ ¼
9¼	7¼	ACM SpctmFd	SI	1.01	10.9	...	518	9¼	9⅛	9¼	...
n 8¼	6½	ACM MgdIncFd	AMF	1.01	12.4	...	681	8¼	8⅛	8⅛	...
12⅞	10⅝	ACM MgdMultFd	MMF	1.50	11.9	...	720	12¾	12⅝	12⅝	− ⅛
x 18¾	11¼	AL Labs A	BMD	.16	1.0	19	x2328	16¾	16⅜	16¾	+ ¼
2⅞	1	AM Int	AM		...	...	383	1⅝	1⅜	1½	...
13	4⅝	AM Int pf		2.00	18.8	...	11	10⅝	10½	10⅝	+ ⅛
10⅞	8⅝	AMEV Sec	AMV	1.08	10.4	...	42	10½	10⅜	10⅜	− ⅛
70¼	39¾	AMR	AMR		...	...	5856	65⅜	62¾	65¼	+2¼
24⅝	22¼	ANR pf		2.12	8.8	...	1	24	24	24	...
44¼	29¾	ARCO Chm	RCM	2.50	6.1	14	387	40¾	39⅝	40¾	+1
3⅝	1¼	ARX	ARX		...	...	7	1⅝	1⅝	1⅝	...
56¼	38¼	ASA	ASA	3.00	6.1	...	1721	49	47¼	48⅞	+1⅜
5⅛	1⅞	ATT Cap yen wt	·		...	...	55	4¼	4⅛	4¼	+ ¼
54	34½	AbbotLab	ABT	1.00	1.9	23	9556	53½	51⅞	52½	− ½
14	9⅞	Abitibi g	ABY	.50	3.6	...	33	13¾	13⅝	13¾	+ ¼
9⅛	3½	AcmeElec	ACE		...	...	22	4	3⅞	3⅞	+ ⅛
9⅜	4½	AcmeCleve	AMT	.40	6.2	15	68	6½	6⅜	6½	...
s 40	22	Acuson	ACN		...	24	1847	34¾	33¾	34¼	− ⅛
▲ 18⅛	14⅛	AdamsExp	ADX	1.72e	9.4	...	216	18⅜	18	18¼	+ ¼
14½	7	AdobeRes	ADB		...	...	150	8⅛	8	8	− ⅛
19⅞	16	AdobeRes pf		1.84	10.8	...	32	17	17	17	...
14¼	3⅝	AdvMicro	AMD		...	...	9536	13⅜	12⅞	13¼	+ ⅜
▲ 36	13	AdvMicro pf		3.00	8.2	...	174	36¾	35⅝	36¾	+1¼
5¼	1⅝	Advest	ADV		...	...	177	4⅜	4⅛	4⅜	+ ⅛
54⅜	29	AetnaLife	AET	2.76	6.6	8	2289	41⅞	41⅛	41¾	+ ¾
10⅞	6¼	AffilPub	AFP	.24	2.7	36	2120	9	8⅝	8⅞	...
22½	10⅝	Ahmanson	AHM	.88	4.6	12	7041	19¼	18¼	19¼	+ ⅞
8½	2⅛	Aileen	AEE		...	13	223	8	7½	8	+ ⅛
▲ 70⅜	42⅞	AirProduct	APD	1.44	2.0	16	1433	70½	68⅝	70½	+1⅝
27	13½	AirbornFrght	ABF	.30	1.2	16	940	25⅛	24½	24⅞	+ ⅜

AMEX

Quotations as of 4:30 p.m. Eastern Time
Thursday, May 30, 1991

52 Weeks Hi	Lo	Stock	Sym	Div	Yld %	PE	Vol 100s	Hi	Lo	Close	Net Chg
		-A-A-A-									
9¾	7½	AIM StratFd	AST	.84	10.0	...	31	8½	8⅜	8⅜	− ⅛
9⅝	3	AMC Entn	AEN		...	...	85	6⅜	6	6⅜	+ ½
2¼	5/16	AOI Coal	AOI		...	...	167	5/16	5/16	5/16	− 1/16
▼ 25⅞	1½	AT&E	ATW		...	...	1165	1¾	1⅜	1½	− ⅛
58½	45¾	AT&T Fund	ATF	2.53e	4.9	...	87	51⅜	50	51⅛	+1⅛
13½	2⅝	ATI Med	ATI		...	12	35	3⅜	3¼	3¼	+ ⅛
12¾	5	Abiomed	ABD		...	...	34	8¾	8⅜	8½	...
5	2⅛	AckrlyComm	AK		...	...	42	3⅛	3	3	...
7⅞	4⅞	AcmeUtd	ACU	.20e	4.0	13	80	5	5	5	...
5¾	2	ActionInd	ACX		...	...	185	4⅞	4⅝	4⅞	+ ⅛
12⅜	3⅝	ActonCp	ATN		...	...	8	5	4⅞	4⅞	− ⅛
25	15½	Acton pf		3.75	21.4	...	1	17½	17½	17½	+ ½
2	⅞	AdamsRes	AE		...	8	22	1½	1⅜	1½	+ ⅛
13	6¼	AdvMed	AMA		...	...	242	10	9⅝	9⅞	...
16⅝	6	AdvMed pf		1.00	12.7	...	3	7⅞	7⅞	7⅞	− ⅛
38⅝	11¾	AirWaterTech	AWT		...	53	3542	19½	17⅞	19¼	+1⅜
▲ 27⅞	10¾	AirExprss	AEX		...	12	224	28⅝	28	28½	+ ⅝
7¾	1⅝	AircoaHotel	AHT		...	...	40	2¼	2	2¼	+ ¼
2¾	¾	Alfin	AFN		...	...	132	1	1	1	...
▲ 4⅝	1¾	AllouHlth	ALU		...	8	102	4½	4¼	4½	+ ¼
1¾	¼	AllouHlth wt			...	...	70	1¼	1¼	1¼	...
4¼	2¾	AlphaInd	AHA		...	20	10	3⅝	3⅝	3⅝	...
5⅝	1	AlpineGp	AGI		...	...	103	4⅞	4½	4⅞	+ ¼
50	40⅝	Alcoa pf		3.75	7.6	...	z650	49½	49½	49½	− ½
68⅝	36⅛	Alza	AZA		...	86	923	65	64¼	64¾	+ ½
47¾	24⅝	Alza wt			...	...	76	42⅛	41⅛	41½	...
18⅞	10	Amdahl	AMH	.10	.6	11	2265	16½	16⅛	16⅜	+ ⅛
13/16	1/16	Amerhlth	AHH		...	...	40	9/16	9/16	9/16	+ ⅛
14⅜	11	AmFPrepFd2	PF	1.67	12.0	...	27	14	13¾	13⅞	− ⅛
18⅜	40¾	AmBkCT	BKC	1.32	8.1	7	5	16⅜	16⅜	16⅜	+ ¼
⅜	⅛	AmCapital	ACC		...	...	1	3/16	3/16	3/16	− 1/16
4⅝	2¾	AmExplor	AX		...	43	448	3	2⅞	3	...
2½	13/16	AmExplor wt			...	...	52	13/16	13/16	13/16	− 1/16
26	19⅛	AmFructse A	AFCA	.40	1.9	9	77	21⅜	21¼	21¼	− ¼

NATIONAL OTC

Quotations as of 4:00 p.m. Eastern Time
Thursday, May 30, 1991

52 Weeks Hi	Lo	Stock	Sym	Div	Yld %	PE	Vol 100s	Hi	Lo	Close	Net Chg
		-A-A-A-									
37¾	20	A&W Brands	SODA	.10e	.3	25	133	34¾	34	34¼	− ¼
8½	5⅛	ABS Ind	ABSI	.32	4.9	20	5	6½	6½	6½	...
14¾	4⅛	ACC	ACCC	.16	1.4	22	314	11½	11	11¼	− ¼
▲ 37¾	15¼	ADC Tel	ADCT		...	21	2854	40½	38	39¾	+2
31⅝	11⅜	ADT	ADTLY	t	...	4	9377	13⅛	12⅝	13⅛	+ ½
7¼	4	AEL Ind A	AELNA		...	14	157	6¼	5⅞	6	− ⅛
16¼	7	AEP Ind	AEPI		...	23	339	13¾	13	13¾	+ ¼
10¼	4	ASK Cptr	ASKI		...	23	198	8⅛	7¾	7¾	− ⅜
s 32¾	7⅜	AST Rsrch	ASTA		...	11	8938	24¼	22¾	23½	− ⅜
10½	6½	AaronRents	ARON	.10	1.2	36	45	8½	8¼	8¼	+ ⅛
13	6⅝	AccelInt	ACLE	.24	2.3	7	111	10½	10⅜	10½	+ ½
16	3	AcclmEntn	AKLM		...	9	427	3 5/16	3⅛	3¼	...
14⅝	10¼	Aceto	ACET	.28	2.4	10	67	12¼	11¾	11⅞	− ⅜
14¼	10¼	Acmat	ACMT		...	17	10	11¼	10¾	11¼	+ ½
11	5	Acmat A	ACMTA		...	...	393	6⅞	6	6⅞	+ ⅞
17¼	10¾	AcmeSteel	ACME		...	19	34	13⅝	13½	13½	...
8	⅛	ActnAutRnt	AXXN		...	...	150	1⅛	1 1/16	1 1/16	+ 1/16
▼ 22¾	10¼	Acxiom	ACXM		...	14	35	11	10	11	+ ½
2⅝	11/16	AdacLabs	ADAC		...	24	548	2¼	2⅛	2⅛	− 1/16
▲ 1 13/16	⅝	Adage	ADGE		...	18	765	1⅞	1⅜	1⅝	+ 3/16
23½	8½	Adaptec	ADPT		...	11	1916	13¼	12¾	13	+ ⅛
s 20¾	7¼	AddintnRes	ADDR		...	...	54	7¾	7½	7½	− ¼
25¾	14½	AdiaSvcs	ADIA	.16	.8	18	11	20¼	20¼	20¼	...
63	17	AdobeSys	ADBE	.32	.6	25	4515	52	50¼	50⅞	− ⅞
3 13/16	2	Adtec	JAIL		...	...	50	2⅜	2¼	2 5/16	...
12	8¼	AdvRoss	AROS		...	6	43	9½	8¾	8¾	− ¾
s 11⅛	4⅜	AdvCircuit	ADVC		...	7	386	10¼	9¾	9¾	− ⅛
20¾	4½	AdvLogicRsrch	AALR		...	9	1001	13	12½	13	...
29¼	9	AdvMagnet	ADMG		...	32	14	21	19½	21	...
6¼	1	AdvMktg	ADMS		...	...	402	2¾	2½	2¾	+ ¼
7¼	2	AdvPolymer	APOS		...	...	718	3⅞	3⅝	3¾	+ ⅛
24¼	13½	AdvTelecom	ATEL		...	15	128	23¼	23	23	...
20½	8	Advanta	ADVN	.20	1.1	11	16	18¾	18¼	18¾	...

SOURCE: *Wall Street Journal,* May 31, 1991, pp. C3, C6, and C10.

Each stock is assigned a trading symbol. For example, the trading symbol for Abbott Lab is ABT. The dividend yield, "Yld Div %," is calculated by dividing the *annual* cash dividends, based on the last quarter, semiannual, or annual declaration, by the closing price. The price-earnings ratio or "PE" is calculated by dividing the closing price by the most recent four-quarter earnings per share (EPS). EPS excludes extraordinary items and is generally defined as "primary" earnings. The 52-week "Hi" and "Lo" prices are adjusted to reflect stock dividends or splits of more than one percent. The trading volume, "vol 100s," gives the number of shares traded for the day. "Net Chg" indicates the change in price from the *previous* day's close.

The quotations also include other letters or symbols. These include "pf," a preferred stock; "wt," a warrant; "rt," rights; and "vj," a company in bankruptcy or receivership or being reorganized under the Bankruptcy Code. An underlined quotation indicates the stock had a large change in trading volume. Detailed explanations of all the letters and symbols used in the quotation appear in the "Explanatory Notes" published in the *Wall Street Journal.*

For the OTC daily and weekly quotes, the **bid** represents the price the dealer is willing to pay to buy the security, and the **asked** is the price at which the dealer is willing to sell. The difference between the bid and asked prices represents the **spread** and indicates the dealer's markup. Widely traded secondary issues tend to have smaller spreads than thinly traded issues. The size of the spread is one indication of a security's marketability. Other factors that influence the spread include beta, price level, and market characteristics.[12]

CLASSIFICATIONS OF COMMON STOCK

As opposed to fixed-income securities, common stock is often viewed as a homogeneous type of security. The majority of common stocks have similar voting, income, and liquidation rights. Nevertheless, despite the homogeneous nature of common stock, it is important to realize that the risk-return characteristics of stocks can vary significantly. Indeed, stocks are often classified on the basis of these characteristics.

• Blue-Chip Stocks

Stocks of very large, firmly established corporations, such as General Motors, IBM, and Xerox, are often referred to as **blue chips.** Many of these are included in the 30 stocks that comprise the Dow Jones Industrial Average. Because of their dominant industry positions, strong balance sheets, and size, these stocks are often viewed as conservative investments. Blue chips become more popular with some investors during periods of slow or declining eco-

[12] Frank J. Fabozzi, "Bid-Ask Spreads for Over-the-Counter Stocks," *Journal of Economics and Business* (Fall 1979): 56–65.

nomic activity because such companies are not likely to experience severe financial problems. Blue chips, however, can also be classified in other categories. For example, General Motors is dominant in the car and truck industry and it can therefore be considered a cyclical company.

• Growth Stocks

Investors often try to identify stocks that are likely to experience above-average price appreciation. Accomplishing this may be a more difficult task than it first appears to be, however. First, the business may be successful in increasing revenues by increasing its market share or developing new markets. This revenue growth, however, may not necessarily increase EPS and the stock price. Thus, the company may be a *growth company,* but its stock is not a **growth stock.** Second, other more skilled investors may already have recognized the growth prospects, so that these expectations are currently reflected in the stock's price. Unusual growth will not, therefore, result in a further increase in the stock's price. Finally, it may be very difficult to distinguish between "superficial" or "transitory" growth and "sustainable" growth.[13] Only sustainable growth should cause an increase in the stock's price. For example, an observed significant increase in EPS that results from an increase in financial leverage would not be a reason to expect sustainable growth. This point is discussed in detail in the next chapter.

• Income Stocks

Stocks that have a long-term record of stable cash dividends are often referred to as **income stocks.** For example, utilities are noted for their stable cash dividends. Their stock prices, however, can be quite volatile depending on economic and market cycles. Other companies, because of perceived growth opportunities and/or lack of profitable operations, do not pay cash dividends on a regular basis. Investors with a preference for income will be attracted to companies that stress cash dividends rather than companies primarily motivated by the desire to increase their stock's price. There have been numerous cases where investors did not select individual stocks or investment advisers that matched their expectation of income, as opposed to capital gains.[14]

Financial research has also identified a dividend *clientele effect.* Essentially, investors who stress income are attracted to dividend-paying stocks, and they expect the established dividend policy to continue. The board of directors, therefore, is expected to cater to its clientele of stockholders.

---

[13] Meir Statman, "Growth Opportunities vs. Growth Stocks," *Journal of Portfolio Management* (Spring 1984): 70–74.

[14] For example, see R. Foster Winans, "Investors Sue an Advisory Firm in Boston, Charging Loss of Millions on AZL Stock," *Wall Street Journal,* May 18, 1983, p. 60.

• INTEREST BOX

IPOs: Speculating or Investing?

"For those interested in prospecting for sunken treasure, Treasure Quest is an initial public offering (IPO) that proposes to do just that. In November 1988, Lombard Street Securities Corp. will issue, on a 'best efforts, minimum-maximum' basis, between 75,000 and 200,000 units at $10 apiece. Each unit consists of 40 shares of common stock and 40 Class A warrants, exercisable within 18 months of the final prospectus date, for the purchase of one share of common stock and one Class B share at a combined price of 35 cents. Each Class B warrant entitles the holder to purchase one share of common stock for 60 cents within 2 years of the prospectus date, unless the company redeems the warrants. Treasure Quest plans to use the funds to search and salvage known shipwrecks and to purchase and market recovered relics. To date, the company has almost no revenues, a loss of $136,826, no business activity, and an absence of full-time management. Although Treasure Quest has assembled an impressive advisory board, the prospectus contains 27 caveats."

SOURCE: Lauren R. Rublin, "Plumbing the Depths: An IPO Wants to Look for Sunken Treasure," *Barron's*, October 24, 1988, pp. 26–30.

• Cyclical and Defensive Stocks

Most stocks are influenced by economic and industry cycles. For example, companies in the homebuilding and machine-tool manufacturing industries are affected by recessions and periods of economic growth and are therefore known as **cyclical stocks.** Other types of industries and companies, however, are viewed as **defensive.** These industries and companies appear to be less susceptible to economic cycles. For example, stocks in gold-mining companies are commonly viewed as defensive or possibly even countercyclical because they tend to do well in periods of adverse economic developments.

• Speculative Stocks

The distinction between **speculative** and *investment-quality* stocks is difficult to quantify. Clearly, an **initial public offering (IPO)** of a relatively new company without a successful track record would be viewed by most investors as a highly risky and consequently a speculative issue. However, large established companies that are experiencing financial difficulties may also be speculative investments. Essentially, the classification of a stock as speculative or investment quality depends on the way the investor feels about risk. A stock that is classified as speculative by one investor may be viewed as less speculative by another investor.

• Small Stocks

There is no standard definition of how "small" a company must be to be a **small stock.** A NYSE-traded company with a total capitalization of less than $500 million may be considered small in relation to blue-chip stocks. An OTC-traded stock, however, may have a total capitalization of less than $50 million. These "small-caps" or "secondaries" may be a new initial public offering with few shares offered or an established firm with many shares of stock outstanding that is experiencing financial difficulties and consequently has a low stock price.

There is some empirical evidence that "small" stocks outperform "large" stocks in terms of risk-adjusted excess returns. Often small stocks are popular during periods of economic stability and growth. In the economic environment of 1990, however, small stocks were not popular with individual investors.

• Treasury Stock

Corporations have authorized, issued, outstanding, and treasury stock. If a corporation decides to buy back its own stock, the acquired stock is called **treasury stock** and appears as a reduction in stockholders' equity on the balance sheet. Treasury stock is stock that has been issued but is not outstanding. Consequently, it does not maintain voting rights and is not entitled to dividends.

The corporation may elect to buy its own stock for a number of reasons:

1. Undervalued—the company may feel the stock is a good investment because it is undervalued.

2. Stock dividends—treasury stock can be used to pay stock dividends.

3. Mergers and acquisitions—treasury stock can be reissued and used to finance a merger or acquisition.

4. Stock options—treasury stock can be used to award stock options to management or other key employees.

5. Control—since the treasury stock cannot be voted, it may help the company maintain control by making a hostile takeover more difficult.

For these and other reasons, a number of corporations frequently buy back their own shares. Studies have shown that both the corporation and its shareholders may receive tangible advantages from these buy-backs.

• Quality Ratings

Investment organizations such as Standard & Poor's Corporation assign **quality ratings** to common stocks that reflect a number of the classifications discussed above. The ratings are similar to bond ratings and are designated as

• INTEREST BOX

Financial Engineering: Unbundled Stock Units

In late 1988, a number of major U.S. corporations introduced unbundled stock units (USUs). The idea for USUs was developed by Shearson Lehman Hutton and was tried by Dow Chemical, Sara Lee, Pfizer, and American Express, among others. Essentially, these corporations offered to exchange USUs for their outstanding common stock. USUs consist of three separate securities: (1) a 30-year bond that pays interest at the stock's current dividend rate; (2) a share of preferred stock that initially pays no dividend but receives all dividend increases on the company's common stock during the 30 years; and (3) an equity appreciation certificate, resembling a stock warrant, that allows investors to profit if the price of the company's stock rises over the 30-year period.

The issuing company would benefit if investors agreed to the exchange since its current cash payout from dividends on the existing common stock would be the same as the payout on the USUs. There would be a big tax advantage, however, because the payout on the USUs would be classified as interest payments and would therefore be deductible for tax purposes. Investors who agreed to the exchange might also benefit if the total value of the three new securities created by the exchange was greater than the value of the common stock. However, investors would also lose voting power because, unlike common stock, the USUs do not have voting rights.

Because of numerous accounting, tax, and other problems, USUs are an example of financial engineering that failed. The idea was not popular with investors. It is likely, however, that many other attempts at financial engineering will be tested on Wall Street in the future.

SOURCES: Phyllis Feinberg, "Discovering the Break-up Value of a Share of Stock," *Corporate Cashflow* (March 1989): 50, 53; Julian Walmsley, "Unbundling the World?" *Intermarket* (August 1989): 48–49; Robert Willens, "Corporate Finance Vehicles: Unbundled Stock Units," *Journal of Taxation of Investments* (Summer 1989): 332–37.

A+, A, A−, B+, and so on. The stock ratings are designed to indicate likely long-term risk-return performance. Empirical studies have shown that the ratings are closely related to risk measures, such as beta and earnings variability, and to fundamentals, such as firm size and financial leverage.[15] These studies suggest that the ratings are useful proxies for risk measures and are useful in common stock analysis.

SUMMARY

This chapter has discussed the major investment characteristics of preferred and common stocks. An understanding of these characteristics is essential in differentiating between the risk-return aspects of these two types of invest-

[15] For example, see Frederick L. Muller and Bruce D. Fielitz, "Standard & Poor's Quality Rankings Revisited," *Journal of Portfolio Management* (Spring 1987): 64–68.

• CONCEPT APPLICATIONS

Investment Concept	Concept Application
Preferred stock	Preferred stock has less risk than common stock but more risk than bonds issued by the same corporation. The favorable tax treatment of dividend income received by corporations makes preferred stock more popular with corporate investors than with individuals. The newer types of preferred stock—DARPS and ARPS—are suitable as short-term or money market types of investments for corporate investors.
Common stock	Common stock is more risky than the bonds and preferred stock issued by the same corporation. Although all common stock has certain similar characteristics, risk can vary dramatically for different categories of stock. At one extreme is an initial public offering (IPO) and at the other a blue-chip stock. Before investing in common stocks, an investor should understand their risk-return characteristics. Chapters 13 and 14 provide techniques and procedures that investors can use to analyze and consequently make investment decisions about individual common stocks.
Fundamental analysis	A traditional way to analyze preferred and common stocks is the economic-industry-company or fundamental analysis approach. This approach is discussed in detail in Chapters 8, 9, 13, and 14.
Quotations	Individual investors can obtain current prices, trading volume, dividends, and earnings from many financial newspapers such as the *Wall Street Journal*. Stocks are quoted using dollars and fractions. For example, a quote of $15\frac{5}{8}$ is \$15.625.

ments. This material also provides a foundation for the valuation of preferred and common stock presented in Chapter 14.

Preferred stock represents an important but relatively minor source of equity financing for utilities and other industries. Because corporations may exclude 55 percent of preferred dividends received, preferred stock is much more popular with corporate investors than with individuals. Because of fixed dividends and credit risk, many new issues of preferred have adjustable dividends (ARPS). A new type of ARPS is DARPS where the dividend is set by a Dutch auction.

Because common stockholders have low priority in receiving dividends or distributions in a potential liquidation, common stocks have more risk than preferred stock. However, voting rights give common shareholders control that preferred shareholders do not enjoy. Traditionally, each corporation issued one type of common stock with voting rights. Now a number of corporations have two classes of stock: voting and nonvoting. Despite the fairly homogeneous nature of common stocks, they can differ significantly in their risk-return characteristics. Stocks can be classified into categories such as blue chip, growth, income, small, cyclical, and so forth on the basis of their different risk-return characteristics.

• KEY TERMS

Adjustable rate preferred stock (ARPS)
Bid-ask spread
Blue-chip stock
Book value per share
Common stock
Convertible preferred stock
Cumulative preferred dividend
Cumulative voting
Cyclical stock
Defensive stock
Dividend reinvestment plan
Dutch auction rate preferred stock (DARPS)
Growth stock
Income stock
Initial public offering (IPO)
Participating preferred stock
Preemptive right
Preferred stock
Quality ratings
Sinking fund
Small stock
Speculative stock
Stock dividend
Stock split
Straight voting
Treasury stock

• QUESTIONS

1. Does preferred stock represent debt or equity to the issuing corporation?
2. Does an adjustable rate preferred stock have less price risk than a fixed dividend preferred stock with the same degree of credit risk?
3. Explain why preferred stocks are less actively traded than common stocks.
4. Compare and contrast adjustable rate preferred stock (ARPS) and Dutch auction rate preferred stock (DARPS).
5. Explain why the credit risk for preferred stock is less than for common stock but greater than for bonds for securities issued by the same corporation.
6. Compare and contrast blue-chip, speculative, and small common stocks.
7. Briefly explain the top-down or three-step procedure that fundamental analysts use to analyze preferred and common stocks. In your opinion, what are the strengths and weaknesses of this approach?
8. Explain how a stock dividend or split may influence a fundamental analysis of the common stock. Is the possibility of a stock dividend or split an advantage or disadvantage in holding a particular stock?
9. Compare and contrast the book and market values for a share of common stock. In your opinion, is the book value of the stock a major determinant of its market value?
10. Would you expect a company that has a high dividend payout ratio to be a growth company? Would its stock be likely to be a growth stock?

11. Can a company be a growth company without its stock experiencing growth? Explain.

12. Is investing in initial public offerings (IPOs) investing or speculating? Discuss.

13. Discuss the advantages and disadvantages of a dividend reinvestment plan.

14. Cite two examples of financial engineering by Wall Street that are presented in the Research and Interest Boxes in the chapter. Explain how financial engineering by adding, changing, or modifying traditional characteristics of preferred or common stocks can change their risk-return trade-offs.

• PROBLEMS

1. Assume you found the following quotation for a preferred stock in the *Wall Street Journal:*

52 weeks				Yld			Vol				Net
Hi	*Lo*	Stock	Sym	*Div*	%	PE	100s	Hi	Lo	Close	chg
32	$26\frac{1}{8}$	ComwEd pf	—	2.87	9.4	—	9	$30\frac{5}{8}$	$29\frac{3}{4}$	$30\frac{5}{8}$	$+\frac{7}{8}$

a. Use the "net chg" and "close" to determine the close for the previous day.

b. The 52-week high and low prices indicate that the price of the preferred stock changed significantly over the previous year. Since the preferred stock has a fixed dividend of $2.87, what factors likely caused the price changes?

c. Explain how the "div yld %" of 9.4 percent is calculated. Is the dividend yield on a preferred stock constant over time?

d. How many shares of the Commonwealth Edison preferred stock traded on the day of the quotation?

2. Assume you found the following quotation for a common stock in the *Wall Street Journal:*

52 weeks				Yld			Vol				Net
Hi	*Lo*	Stock	Sym	*Div*	%	PE	100s	Hi	Lo	Close	chg
40	$27\frac{1}{4}$	ComwEd	CWE	3.00	8.1	—	8690	$37\frac{1}{2}$	$36\frac{7}{8}$	$36\frac{7}{8}$	$-\frac{1}{4}$

a. How many shares of the Commonwealth Edison common stock traded on the day of the quotation?

b. Give several reasons why the volume of trading for the common stock is much higher than for the preferred stock in Problem 1.

c. The range of the 52-week high and low prices for the common stock is much greater than the range for the preferred stock in Problem 1. What characteristics of the preferred stock would account for it having less price volatility than the common stock?

d. Why do you think a price-earnings ratio (PE) is not provided in the quotation?

3. Consider the following quotations from the *Wall Street Journal* on two preferred stocks issued by Chase Manhattan Bank:

52 weeks				Yld			Vol				Net
Hi	*Lo*	Stock	Sym	*Div*	%	PE	100s	Hi	Lo	Close	chg
$25\frac{1}{4}$	$15\frac{1}{4}$	Chasemanh PfH	—	2.44	10.2	—	43	$23\frac{7}{8}$	$23\frac{3}{4}$	$23\frac{7}{8}$	—
26	$25\frac{1}{8}$	Chasemanh PfI	—	2.71	10.7	—	410	$25\frac{1}{2}$	$25\frac{1}{8}$	$25\frac{3}{8}$	$+\frac{1}{8}$

a. The first preferred stock quoted has a closing price of $23.875 versus $25.375 for the second stock. Using the characteristics of each preferred stock provided in the quotations, explain why the stocks have different prices.

b. The 52-week high and low prices indicate the first stock is quite volatile while the second stock had almost no price volatility. What characteristic could the second preferred stock have that would keep its price almost constant?

c. Explain which, if either, of the two preferred stocks would be appropriate investments for the following:
   (1) An individual investor.
   (2) A corporation interested in making a long-term investment to produce dividend income.
   (3) A corporation interested in a short-term investment similar to a money market instrument.

4. The XYZ Corporation announced a three-for-two stock split. Prior to the announcement, the stock's closing price was $29\frac{3}{4}$.

a. Assume you currently own 100 shares of this stock. How many shares will you own after the split?

b. What will be the price of the stock after the split, assuming the market places no value on the split?

c. The company is currently paying dividends of $1 per share (DPS). Assume the company does not want to increase its cash dividend payout after the split. Calculate the DPS after the split.

d. Assume that in the split announcement, the company indicates that DPS will remain at $1 after the split. Would you expect to see a positive stock price adjustment because of the split and dividend announcements? Explain.

5. ABC Corporation announced that instead of the normal cash dividend of $2 per share, a 25 percent stock dividend would be paid. Before the announcement, the stock had a closing price of $49\frac{3}{4}$.

a. Assume you currently own 100 shares of this stock. How many shares will you own after the stock dividend?

b. What will be the price of the stock after the stock dividend, ignoring the possible negative reaction to the cash dividend announcement. Also assume the market places no value on the stock dividend.

c. As a stockholder, would you be indifferent between the customary cash dividend of $2 and the 25 percent stock dividend? Explain.

• REFERENCES

Atchison, Michael D., and John L. Kling. "How Good Are Preferred Dividend Capture Plans?" *Journal of Cash Management* (November-December 1988): 71–74.

Baker, Marci. "Industries, Utilities Try Dutch Preferred." *Pensions & Investment Age,* February 17, 1986, pp. 53, 56.

Baskin, Jonathan. "Dividend Policy and the Volatility of Common Stocks." *Journal of Portfolio Management* (Spring 1989): 19–25.

Cabot, Walter M., Jr. "Auction Rate Preferred." *Cash Flow* (September 1987): 34, 36.

Cochran, Thomas N. "What's New in New Issues? Long-Dormant IPOs Show Signs of Life." *Barron's,* July 24, 1989, pp. 16, 48.

Dierson, Dennis A. "Keeping Corporate Distributions of Stock and Stock Rights Nontaxable." *Taxation for Accountants* (April 1989): 202–5.

Dodge, Peter M. "Increase Your Returns with an ARP Fund." *Cash Flow* (December 1985): 43–44.

Fooladi, Iraj, and Gordon S. Roberts. "On Preferred Stock." *Journal of Financial Research* (Winter 1986): 319–24.

Hetherington, Norriss. "High Return and Low Risk in Called Preferreds." *Journal of Portfolio Management* (Spring 1987): 81–82.

Kichen, Steve. "Unpopular Stocks." *Forbes,* January 22, 1990, pp. 140–43.

Laderman, Jeffrey M. "New Kids on the Block Have Won the Street's Heart." *Business Week,* July 9, 1990, p. 64.

Mahar, Maggie. "No Class Act—Resort B Shares Are More Equal Than Resort A Shares." *Barron's,* December 15, 1986, p. 18.

Mamis, Robert A. "All Shares Are Not Created Equal." *INC.* (March 1987): 99–102.

———. "The World According to ARPS." *INC.* (December 1986): 129–30.

Mavrides, Lazaros P. "Development of the Variable Rate Preferred Stock Market." *European Journal of Operational Research* (June 1987): 6–12.

Scharf, Jeffrey R. "Question of Preference: How Preferred Stocks Stack Up vs. Bonds." *Barron's,* September 8, 1986, p. 71.

Scholl, Jaye. "Will It Play in Peoria? Mel Brooks Gets Ready for His Wall Street." *Barron's,* January 15, 1990, p. 22.

Schultz, John W. "Second Wind? Small-CAPS May Be Poised for Comeback." *Barron's,* July 2, 1990, pp. 16, 30.

Wansley, James W., Fayez A. Elayan, and Brian A. Maris. "Preferred Stock Returns, Creditwatch, and Preferred Stock Rating." *Financial Review* (May 1990): 265–85.

Weberman, Ben, and Jason Zweig. "The Mixed Bag." *Forbes,* June 27, 1988, pp. 222–23.

Winger, Bernard J., Carl R. Chen, John D. Martin, William J. Petty, and Steven C. Hayden. "Adjustable Rate Preferred Stock." *Financial Management* (Spring 1986): 48–57.

Wise, Richard M. "Through the Preferred Shares Maze." *CA Magazine* (June 1986): 81–83.

Worndl, Barbara, and David Malach. "Taxation: Waltzing through the Preferred Share Maze." *CA Magazine* (July 1988): 47–52.

Zweig, Jason. "Let 'Em Eat Stock." *Forbes*, May 16, 1988, pp. 44, 46.

CHAPTER 13

Analyzing and Forecasting Company Earnings

The knowledge-level objectives of this chapter should enable the student to:

- Understand the importance of earnings per share (EPS) forecasts for the valuation of common stock.
- Explain how EPS is calculated and differentiate between simple, primary, and fully diluted EPS.
- Know the primary sources of EPS forecasts and the pros and cons of using a professional forecast.
- Understand the major techniques that can be used to forecast EPS.
- Distinguish between expected and unexpected EPS.

INTRODUCTION

The purpose of this chapter is to explain why *earnings per share* (*EPS*) are important to common stock values. The material presented here provides the foundation for Chapter 14, which deals with common stock valuation. Accurate forecasts of EPS and unexpected changes in EPS can be used to earn risk-adjusted excess returns, but as this chapter stresses, making accurate forecasts of EPS is extremely difficult. Because of this difficulty, the market rewards analysts and investors who can make accurate forecasts.

Investors may be willing to rely on EPS forecasts made by professional security analysts, management, and many investment publications. The advantages and disadvantages of these professional earnings forecasts as well as their accuracy are discussed in the chapter.

Rather than using published EPS forecasts, individual investors may elect to formulate their own estimates of EPS for individual companies. A number of techniques that can be used to forecast EPS are presented here.

Finally, an analysis and forecast of EPS for Procter & Gamble Company are presented. This example illustrates the forecasting techniques developed in the chapter.

DEFINITIONS OF EARNINGS PER SHARE

Earnings per share (EPS) are the per-share profits after taxes and after preferred stock dividends that are available to the common stockholders. EPS can be calculated quarterly and for a full year. These calculations may become complicated, however, because most large, publicly traded corporations experience frequent changes in the actual or potential number of common stock shares outstanding. As a result, three different definitions of EPS are used:

1. Simple EPS **Simple EPS** is calculated in a straightforward way:

$$\text{EPS} = \frac{\text{profits after taxes} - \text{preferred stock dividends}}{\text{number of shares of common stock outstanding}} \tag{13.1}$$

This calculation would be appropriate if the number of shares of common stock outstanding was constant over the period in which the profits occurred. For some companies, however, the number of shares outstanding is not constant even for a single quarter. The number of shares outstanding may change for a variety of reasons including the following:

- New shares are issued to provide additional equity financing.
- The company purchases its own stock, creating treasury stock, which is classified as issued but not outstanding stock.
- Previously purchased treasury stock is sold.

- Options and warrants issued by the company are exercised, or convertible bonds and preferred stocks are converted to common stock.

2. Primary EPS Whenever actual or potential changes in the number of shares of stock outstanding may occur, the Accounting Principles Board (APB) Opinion Number 15 requires that the company report **primary EPS,** in which profits after taxes and the number of shares outstanding are adjusted. This calculation of EPS includes **common stock equivalents,** which are options and warrants that can be used to purchase common stock from the company and certain convertible securities. Profits after taxes are restated to reflect the impact of the common stock equivalents. In addition, primary EPS must be calculated using the weighted average number of shares outstanding over the period. The weights are based on the amount of time the shares are outstanding. Primary EPS is calculated as

$$\text{primary EPS} = \frac{\begin{matrix}\text{profits after taxes} \\ \text{reflecting common stock} \\ \text{equivalents}\end{matrix} - \begin{matrix}\text{preferred stock} \\ \text{dividends}\end{matrix}}{\begin{matrix}\text{weighted average number of shares} \\ \text{of common stock outstanding}\end{matrix}} \tag{13.2}$$

Equation 13.2 can be illustrated using the Procter & Gamble data in Chapter 9. For the year ending June 30, 1990, Procter & Gamble's profit after taxes reflecting common stock equivalents was $1,602 million with preferred stock dividends of $47 million. The number of shares of common stock at the beginning of the year was 324.0 million versus 346.3 million at the end of the year. The weighted average number of shares outstanding for the year was 346.1 million. Therefore the primary EPS for 1990 as reported by Procter & Gamble was

$$\frac{\$1{,}602 - \$47}{346.1} = \$4.49$$

The procedures and rules outlined in APB Opinion Number 15 are quite complex and are best left to accountants. Financial analysts and investors, however, typically use primary EPS when analyzing a company's earnings. Consequently, when EPS is discussed in this chapter, the reference is to primary EPS.

3. Fully diluted EPS APB Opinion Number 15 also requires that firms report **fully diluted EPS** under certain conditions. Fully diluted EPS assumes that all options and warrants are exercised and all convertible securities are converted. Appropriate changes are made in profits after taxes and in the number of shares outstanding. Fully diluted EPS is a very conservative estimate and is typically below the primary EPS. For example, in 1990 Procter & Gamble reported primary EPS of $4.49 and fully diluted EPS of $4.27. Most of the time, analysts do not use fully diluted EPS.

• INTEREST BOX

Problems with How EPS Is Calculated

Accountants, through the Accounting Principles Board (APB), develop policies and procedures that are referred to as generally accepted accounting principles (GAAP). Accountants use APB Opinion 15 to guide them in the calculation and reporting requirements for EPS.

Opinion 15 is often criticized by accountants, financial analysts, and investors. The most basic criticism is that few people understand the EPS rules specified in the opinion. As a result, EPS is frequently misinterpreted or misused. A second criticism is that fully diluted EPS is usually understated because of the way common stock equivalents are defined. Opponents of the opinion argue that the rules used to determine whether convertible securities, options, and warrants are common stock equivalents are arbitrary. In addition, the rules do not predict which securities will be converted into common stock. Furthermore, comparisons of fully diluted EPS between companies are often unreliable because some convertible securities may be classified as common stock equivalents by one company and not by another.

Because of these and other problems with Opinion 15, it has been suggested that a new measure, called "adjusted EPS," should replace fully diluted EPS. Adjusted EPS would only increase the number of shares of common stock outstanding by those securities whose market price at the date of the financial statements indicates that they are likely to be converted in the near future.

SOURCES: Eugene J. Laughlin and Kenneth L. Fox, "Taking the ESP out of EPS," *Woman CPA* (January 1989): 4–8; and Lola Woodward Dudley, "A Critical Look at EPS," *Journal of Accountancy* (August 1985): 102–11.

EARNINGS FORECASTS

Accurate earnings forecasts are extremely useful for investors, but also extremely difficult to prepare. Investors may elect to use forecasts prepared by professionals or to prepare their own. No matter which option they choose, investors will need to assess the accuracy of the forecasts.

• Difficulty of Forecasting Earnings

Despite the significant risk-adjusted excess returns that are possible with superior earnings forecasting skills, the difficulty of making an accurate forecast should not be underestimated. A number of studies of historical earnings suggest that the year-to-year changes are random. To the extent that this is true for a particular company, a simple extrapolation of historical earnings will not provide an accurate forecast.

Table 13.1 presents the reported earnings for a sample of companies over the period 1980–1990. These companies were selected to illustrate the potential variability of earnings from year to year. The amount of variability, however, is different from company to company. Because of economic, industry,

TABLE 13.1 • Sample of Reported EPS, 1980–1990

Year	American Express	American Home Products	Bank-America	Boston Edison	Chrysler	Liz Claiborne	TECO Energy
1980	$1.32	$1.42	$4.39	$1.88	$(11.56)	$0.08	$1.56
1981	1.40	1.59	3.02	2.08	(3.19)	0.13	1.50
1982	1.51	1.80	2.60	1.59	(0.57)	0.17	1.25
1983	1.27	2.00	2.18	1.80	1.91	0.27	1.57
1984	1.40	2.13	1.77	2.43	5.22	0.50	1.86
1985	1.78	2.35	(4.26)	2.52	6.25	0.71	1.79
1986	2.27	2.54	(3.74)	2.58	6.31	1.00	1.73
1987	0.87	2.87	(6.43)	1.97	5.90	1.32	1.95
1988	2.43	3.19	2.77	1.86	5.08	1.26	2.13
1989	2.70	3.54	3.74	1.90	1.36	1.87	2.36
1990	2.12	3.69	3.84	1.60	0.30	2.37	2.45
Beta	1.35	1.00	1.10	0.70	1.35	1.55	0.60
Market traded	NYSE	NYSE	NYSE	NYSE	NYSE	NYSE	NYSE

SOURCE: *Value Line Investment Survey* (Value Line, Inc., 1991). Copyright © 1991 by Value Line Publishing, Inc.; used by permission.

and company factors, some companies have more stable patterns of earnings than others. This implies that historical earnings may be more useful in predicting earnings for some companies than for others.

As Table 13.1 shows, the earnings of BankAmerica, Chrysler, and Liz Claiborne vary considerably from year to year. American Home Products and TECO Energy, however, have much more stable earnings with what appears to be a somewhat predictable upward trend. Note that the betas at the bottom of the table also are related to earnings volatility. The companies with volatile earnings generally have larger betas than those with more stable earnings.

Analysts and investors may be tempted to select companies that appear to have more stable earnings since preparing earnings forecasts for them may be easier than for companies with volatile earnings. However, research has shown that risk-adjusted excess returns are proportionate to the magnitude of the difference between forecast and reported earnings.[1] The rewards for accurate forecasts are therefore much greater for companies with significant variability in reported earnings.

[1] For example, see Gary A. Benesh and Pamela P. Peterson, "On the Relationship between Earnings, Changes, Analysts' Forecasts and Stock Price Fluctuations," *Financial Analysts Journal* (November-December 1986): 29, 39, 55.

• Professional Earnings Forecasts

Investors always have the option of using earnings forecasts made by professional security analysts, company management, and many investment publications.

SECURITY ANALYSTS Thousands of professional security analysts are employed by brokerage firms, financial institutions, and mutual funds. Often the analysts specialize in a single industry or even a specific company. Essentially, their job is to be aware of all publicly available information that will have an impact on the industry and company.

Security analysts' reports that include earnings estimates are available from large brokerage firms and other organizations that employ analysts. Forecasts and recommendations from many analysts on approximately 4,000 companies are available in data bases such as the Institutional Brokers Estimate System (IBES), maintained by the brokerage firm of Lynch, Jones & Ryan. A second large data base of earnings forecasts is available from Zacks Investment Research.

MANAGEMENT FORECASTS Under Securities and Exchange Commission (SEC) regulations, many companies publish earnings estimates by top management. Companies, however, are not required to publish forecasts, and the SEC does not regulate how the forecasts are made or the "quality" of the forecasts. These forecasts are made available in a number of ways, including stockholder reports, stockholder meetings, press releases, and management interviews.

Recent studies have shown that voluntary management forecasts of earnings provide useful information to analysts and investors. In fact, statistical evidence shows that unexpected (favorable or unfavorable) earnings forecasts by management are quickly incorporated into revised earnings estimates by analysts. These studies illustrate the importance that professional analysts place on management forecasts of earnings. In addition, stock prices usually adjust rapidly to any unexpected earnings announcements by management. The stock price adjustments also usually precede publication of the revised analysts' forecasts.[2]

INVESTMENT PUBLICATIONS Many investment publications provide both short- and long-term earnings forecasts. Some of the better known publications are *Value Line Investment Survey* and Standard & Poor's *Earnings Forecaster.*

---

[2] For a discussion of the history and empirical tests of management forecasts, see Stephen P. Baginski and John M. Hassell, "The Market Interpretation of Management Earnings Forecasts as a Predictor of Subsequent Financial Analyst Forecast Revision," *Accounting Review* (January 1990): 175–90; Jerry C.Y. Han, John J. Wild, and K. Ramesh, "Managers' Earnings Forecast and Intra-Industry Information Transfers," *Journal of Accounting and Economics* (February 1989): 3–33; and Robert Jennings, "Unsystematic Security Price Movements, Management Earnings Forecasts, and Revision in Consensus Analyst Earnings Forecast," *Journal of Accounting Research* (Spring 1987): 90–110.

• INTEREST BOX

An Investment Strategy Using the IBES Data Base

Many uninformed investors use the ratio of the current stock price to reported EPS—the P/E ratio—in forming an opinion about whether the stock is over- or undervalued. The problem with this practice is that it uses the current or historical EPS. Future or forecasted EPS are much more important in explaining the current stock price than historical earnings.

One way to make the P/E ratio more useful is to calculate an estimated P/E ratio using a forecast of EPS in the denominator. One source of EPS forecasts is the Institutional Brokers Estimate System (IBES). A recent article describes how a P/E ratio "screen" was developed to identify currently "unpopular" stocks. For each of the approximately 4,000 companies included in the IBES file, the estimated P/E ratio was compared to the five-year average actual P/E ratio. An unpopular stock was defined as one where the 1990 estimated P/E ratio was no higher than 75 percent of the five-year average historical P/E ratio. This screening device resulted in a list of 145 unpopular stocks that may be undervalued.

The next step in this strategy involved trying to identify "which stocks deserve to be cheap and which do not." The article suggests using several factors available on the IBES file to identify the stocks on the list that are most likely to be currently undervalued.

SOURCE: Steve Kitchen, "Unpopular Stocks," *Forbes*, January 22, 1990, pp. 140–43.

CONSENSUS FORECAST As the economic forecasting section of Chapter 8 pointed out, investors and analysts are using consensus forecasts more and more frequently. **Consensus EPS forecasts** for individual companies are reported in IBES and Zacks Investment Research.

• Accuracy of Earnings Forecasts

A number of studies have compared the accuracy of earnings forecasts made by different groups using different forecasting methods.[3] For example, a study might compare the accuracy of forecasts made by security analysts, management, and statistical estimates.

The studies have reached different conclusions concerning the accuracy of forecasts. A 1982 study by Imhoff and Pare compared the accuracy of forecasts prepared by security analysts, by management, and by using statistical procedures.[4] Four earnings estimates were made, using various statistical pro-

[3] For examples of discussions of security analysts' forecasts, see Werner F.M. DeBondt and Richard H. Thaler, "Do Security Analysts Overreact?" *American Economic Review* (May 1990): 52–57; Jong H. Kim, Robert K. Su, and Eugene Sauls, "Measuring Market Forecasts of Earnings," *Journal of Business Forecasting* (Spring 1990): 20–26; and William Kross, Byung Ro, and Douglas Schroeder, "Earnings Expectations: The Analysts' Informational Advantages," *Accounting Review* (April 1990): 461–76.

[4] Eugene A. Imhoff and Paul V. Pare, "Analysis and Comparison of Earnings Forecast Agents," *Journal of Accounting Research* (Autumn 1982): 429–39.

cedures and historical data. Thus, the study actually compared six (security analysts, management, and four statistical) earnings estimates. The empirical evidence in the study indicated that the estimates were not statistically independent and that the six forecasts differed very little.

A 1984 study concluded that earnings forecasts made by financial analysts are "significantly more accurate" than statistical model predictions that extrapolate from past earnings trends.[5] This study also found that analysts' forecasts incorporate historical trends and are reasonable proxies of consensus earnings. The study also observed that a large difference between forecasts can be useful information since it represents a risk proxy. A measure of the dispersion of analysts' forecasts is a measure of the uncertainty associated with predicting the earnings of a company; thus, it represents a risk measure.

A third study was less complimentary toward security analysts' earnings forecasts.[6] This study found that the forecasts of different analysts were closely related: "strong trends prevail among analysts' forecasts." In this study, the consensus forecast of earnings was used to select stocks whose predicted earnings were expected to be revised the most over the following nine-month period. Portfolios formed from the 20 percent of the sample of 240 firms with the largest revised earnings during a three-month period produced risk-adjusted excess returns over the following nine-month period. This study suggested that revisions of earnings forecast by analysts are predictable and can be used to predict the direction of the change in the forecast, thus generating forecasts that are more accurate than the consensus.

Several recent studies have tried to explain why security analysts' earnings forecasts may not be accurate. One of the many hazards faced by analysts is the flexibility in financial reporting that accountants are allowed under generally accepted accounting practices (GAAP). Essentially, the analysts must attempt to forecast accounting changes and their likely impact on reported EPS.

A 1988 study found that many NYSE- and AMEX-traded companies shift to last in, first out (LIFO) inventory accounting procedures during periods of high inflation.[7] The LIFO method increases the cost of goods sold and reduces taxable income, thereby generating tax savings for these firms. In addition, this study found that analysts "systematically overestimate" earnings for firms adopting LIFO. This implies that analysts may have difficulty in forecasting and adjusting for accounting policy changes.

A recent study used a sample of 500 firms that made 612 accounting changes over the period 1976–1984.[8] A variety of changes were analyzed

---

[5] Dan Givoly and Josef Lakonishok, "The Quality of Analysts' Forecasts of Earnings," *Financial Analysts Journal* (September-October 1984): 40–47.

[6] Thomas J. Kerrigan, "When Forecasting Earnings, It Pays to Watch Forecasts," *Journal of Portfolio Management* (Summer 1984): 19–26.

[7] Gary C. Biddle and William E. Ricks, "Analyst Forecast Errors and Stock Price Behavior near Earnings Announcement Dates of LIFO Adopters," *Journal of Accounting Research* (Autumn 1988): 169–94.

[8] John A. Elliott and Donna R. Philbrick, "Accounting Changes and Earnings Predictability," *Accounting Review* (January 1990): 157–74.

along with the information about the changes provided in the notes to the financial statements. Analysts' forecasts of EPS for these 500 firms were compared to the actual reported EPS. The comparisons were made both in years where accounting changes occurred and in years where no changes were made.

The empirical results confirmed previous research that found that analysts' earnings forecasts are more dispersed and less accurate in years with accounting changes. This evidence suggests analysts have difficulty anticipating accounting changes and incorporating the impact of the changes into their EPS forecasts.

A 1990 study examined analysts' forecasts for firms experiencing financial difficulty.[9] Based on a sample of firms from 1977 through 1985, this study found that the forecasts were of "poorer quality" than forecasts for healthy firms. This implies that analysts do not adequately adjust earnings estimates for firms with a deteriorating financial position.

• Methods of Forecasting Earnings

This section discusses some of the more widely used techniques and procedures used to forecast earnings. In many cases, analysts do not rely on a single technique and make several independent estimates.

STATISTICAL METHOD Historical earnings can be used to develop a regression model that can be used to forecast earnings.[10] Table 13.2 illustrates this procedure. Many software packages and financial calculators can quickly perform the regression analysis. Notice that there is a trend in EPS over the 10-year period. The regression estimates confirm the existence of a significant trend. The *coefficient of determination* (R^2) is simply the square of the correlation coefficient between time and EPS. The R^2 of .8257 given in the table indicates that 82.57 percent of the changes in EPS is explained by the trend. The regression intercept ($\hat{a}$) and slope ($\hat{b}$) indicate the statistical relationship between time and EPS. By using these estimates along with the value for the next year, EPS is estimated for year 11 as $2.14. This technique is further illustrated for Procter & Gamble later in the chapter.

RETURN ON EQUITY AND DIVIDEND POLICY METHOD As Chapter 9 explained, a company's earnings growth rate can be defined as

$$g = b \times \text{ROE} \quad (13.3)$$

where b is the earnings retention rate and ROE is the return on new equity capital. To use this technique to forecast g, estimates of b and ROE are needed.

---

[9] Moses O. Douglas, "On Analysts' Earnings Forecast for Failing Firms," *Journal of Business Finance and Accounting* (Spring 1990): 101–18.

[10] Appendix A-2 at the end of the book provides an explanation and illustration of simple regression analysis.

TABLE 13.2 • Regression Estimates of Earnings

Year	EPS
1	$ .50
2	.45
3	.56
4	.80
5	.75
6	.90
7	1.10
8	1.30
9	1.80
10	2.50

Linear Regression Estimates

$$EPS_t = \hat{a} + \hat{b}(\text{time})_t + e_t$$

$$\hat{a} = -.0073,\ \hat{b} = .1952,\ R^2 = .8257$$

Using the Regression Estimates to Forecast Earnings

Estimate of year 11 earnings = −.0073 + .1952(11) = $2.14

Using historical values for *b* and ROE assumes that the firm's dividend policy, asset utilization, profitability, and financial leverage will not change over the estimation period. Since these are unrealistic assumptions, care should be exercised in using historical values of *b* and especially of ROE to estimate *g*. A more realistic approach would be to estimate *b* and ROE based on the financial analysis techniques discussed in Chapter 9. This technique is illustrated for Procter & Gamble later in the chapter.

PRO FORMA INCOME STATEMENT METHOD A popular procedure for estimating earnings is to construct a **pro forma income statement** over the investment horizon. This approach lets the analyst develop individual forecasts of the key variables that determine earnings, such as sales, cost of goods, operating expenses, interest expense, taxes, and the number of shares of common stock outstanding. Considerable effort may go into estimating each of these key variables. For example, a regression model may be developed to estimate sales. Many corporate finance texts devote at least one chapter to financial forecasting. These texts develop in detail methods that can be used to forecast earnings, including the percentage of sales method, simulation, leverage analysis, and break-even analysis. These texts can be consulted for details concerning these methods. An illustration of this technique using Procter & Gamble is presented later in the chapter.

ADJUSTMENTS FOR INFLATION The high rates of inflation during the late 1970s and early 1980s generated considerable discussion and research on the implications of inflation for accounting statements, earnings estimates, and stock prices.[11] In general, it appears that stock prices have not provided an adequate inflation hedge during periods of high, unexpected inflation. This suggests that the stock market realized that the inflated earnings of many companies did not reflect real earnings growth. Stock prices, therefore, did not increase for companies that reported inflated earnings because of the rapid inflation rate. This research suggests that earnings estimates should be adjusted for inflation or stated in *real* rather than *nominal* dollars.

Since inflation may have a different impact on the revenues and costs of a particular firm, a pro forma statement can be used to adjust for these possible differences. Essentially, both revenues and costs can be forecast in nominal dollars and then adjusted, using the appropriate rates of inflation. This procedure results in an estimate of EPS in real or constant dollars.

GROWTH RATE METHOD Analysts often estimate the growth rate for earnings rather than estimating dollar earnings directly. This approach is useful because many valuation models require an estimate of earnings or dividend growth. As with estimates of earnings, growth estimates should be adjusted for inflation or factors that may overstate the true growth rate. This technique is illustrated for Procter & Gamble later in the chapter.

CASH FLOW PER SHARE

As previously discussed, many financial analysts are not happy with the accountants' definition of EPS. Generally accepted accounting principles require that a company report primary EPS, which considers common stock equivalents and the weighted average number of shares of stock outstanding. In addition, different depreciation techniques and changes in depreciation policies over time can distort the reported earnings. Because of these and other problems with primary EPS, analysts often calculate cash flow per share. In its simplest form, **cash flow per share (CFPS)** is calculated by adding noncash expenses such as depreciation and amortization to profits after taxes as follows:

---

[11] For example, see Russell J. Fuller and Glenn H. Petry, "Inflation, Return on Equity, and Stock Prices," *Journal of Portfolio Management* (Summer 1981): 19–25; Ahmet Tezel, "The Effect of Inflation on Common Stock Values," *Journal of Financial Research* (Spring 1982): 17–25; David C. Leonard and Michael E. Solt, "Stock Market Signals of Changes in Expected Inflation," *Journal of Financial Research* (Spring 1987): 57–63; Rene M. Stulz, "Asset Pricing and Expected Inflation," *Journal of Finance* (March 1986): 209–23; and Jean C.H. Loo, "Common Stock Returns, Expected Inflation, and the Rational Expectations Hypothesis," *Journal of Financial Research* (Summer 1988): 165–71.

$$\text{CFPS} = \frac{\begin{array}{c}\text{profits}\\\text{after}\\\text{taxes}\end{array} + \begin{array}{c}\text{depreciation}\\\text{and}\\\text{amortization}\end{array} - \begin{array}{c}\text{preferred}\\\text{stock}\\\text{dividends}\end{array}}{\begin{array}{c}\text{weighted average number of shares}\\\text{of common stock outstanding}\end{array}} \tag{13.4}$$

An example of the use of CFPS appears in Table 13.3, which shows how EPS and CFPS are related to the stock price of Procter & Gamble. Notice that CFPS is much larger than EPS although both are closely correlated with the stock price.

UNEXPECTED EARNINGS

Common stock prices typically reflect the consensus forecast of EPS. An active common stock investment strategy, therefore, could not use a consensus forecast of earnings to earn risk-adjusted excess returns. A successful strategy would need to be based on a more accurate estimate of earnings or on discovering companies that may have *unexpected earnings announcements.* These announcements are unexpected because the earnings differ significantly from the consensus forecast.

TABLE 13.3 • EPS, Cash Flow per Share and Stock Price for Procter & Gamble

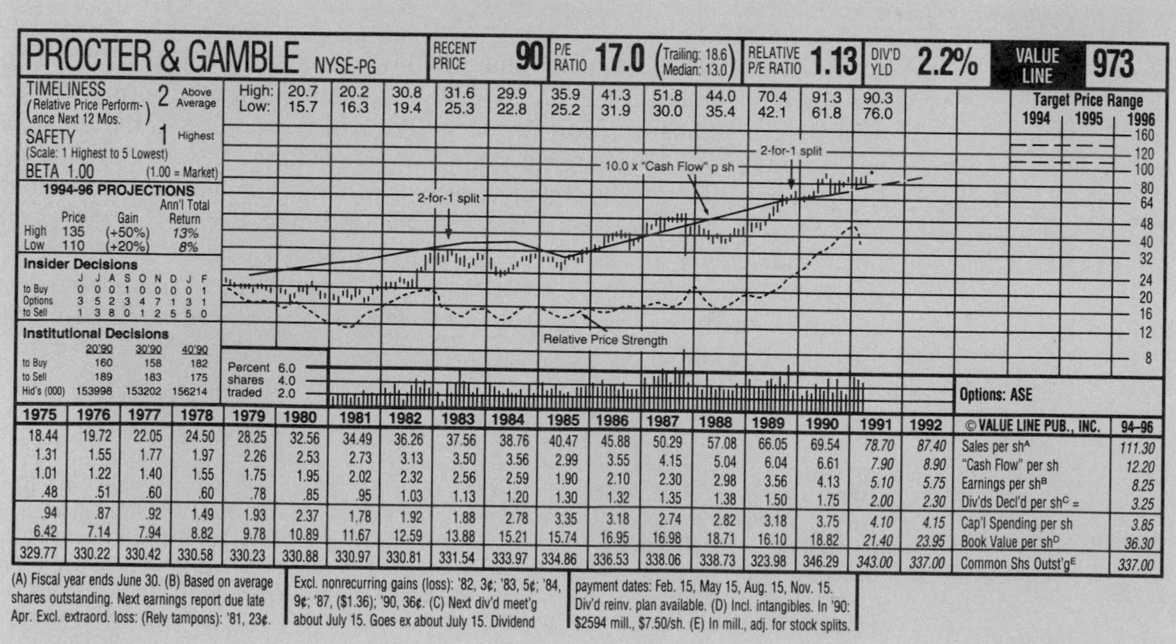

PROCTER & GAMBLE NYSE-PG | RECENT PRICE 90 | P/E RATIO 17.0 (Trailing: 18.6, Median: 13.0) | RELATIVE P/E RATIO 1.13 | DIV'D YLD 2.2% | VALUE LINE 973

TIMELINESS 2 Above Average (Relative Price Performance Next 12 Mos.)
SAFETY 1 Highest (Scale: 1 Highest to 5 Lowest)
BETA 1.00 (1.00 = Market)

1994-96 PROJECTIONS

	Price	Gain	Ann'l Total Return
High	135	(+50%)	13%
Low	110	(+20%)	8%

Insider Decisions

	J	J	A	S	O	N	D	J	F
to Buy	0	0	0	1	0	0	0	0	1
Options	3	5	2	3	4	7	1	3	1
to Sell	1	3	8	0	1	2	5	5	0

Institutional Decisions

	2Q'90	3Q'90	4Q'90
to Buy	160	158	182
to Sell	189	183	175
Hld's (000)	153998	153202	156214

	1975	1976	1977	1978	1979	1980	1981	1982	1983	1984	1985	1986	1987	1988	1989	1990	1991	1992	© VALUE LINE PUB., INC.	94–96
High:						20.7	20.2	30.8	31.6	29.9	35.9	41.3	51.8	44.0	70.4	91.3	90.3			
Low:						15.7	16.3	19.4	25.3	22.8	25.2	31.9	30.0	35.4	42.1	61.8	76.0			
	18.44	19.72	22.05	24.50	28.25	32.56	34.49	36.26	37.56	38.76	40.47	45.88	50.29	57.08	66.05	69.54	78.70	87.40	Sales per sh[A]	111.30
	1.31	1.55	1.77	1.97	2.26	2.53	2.73	3.13	3.50	3.56	2.99	3.55	4.15	5.04	6.04	6.61	7.90	8.90	"Cash Flow" per sh	12.20
	1.01	1.22	1.40	1.55	1.75	1.95	2.02	2.32	2.56	2.59	1.90	2.10	2.30	2.98	3.56	4.13	5.10	5.75	Earnings per sh[B]	8.25
	.48	.51	.60	.60	.78	.85	.95	1.03	1.13	1.20	1.30	1.32	1.35	1.38	1.50	1.75	2.00	2.30	Div'ds Decl'd per sh[C] =	3.25
	.94	.87	.92	1.49	1.93	2.37	1.78	1.92	1.88	2.78	3.35	3.18	2.74	2.82	3.18	3.75	4.10	4.15	Cap'l Spending per sh	3.85
	6.42	7.14	7.94	8.82	9.78	10.89	11.67	12.59	13.88	15.21	15.74	16.95	16.98	18.71	16.10	18.82	21.40	23.95	Book Value per sh[D]	36.30
	329.77	330.22	330.42	330.58	330.23	330.88	330.97	330.81	331.54	333.97	334.86	336.53	338.06	338.73	323.98	346.29	343.00	337.00	Common Shs Outst'g[E]	337.00

(A) Fiscal year ends June 30. (B) Based on average shares outstanding. Next earnings report due late Apr. Excl. extraord. loss: (Rely tampons): '81, 23¢. Excl. nonrecurring gains (loss): '82, 3¢; '83, 5¢; '84, 9¢; '87, ($1.36); '90, 36¢. (C) Next div'd meet'g about July 15. Goes ex about July 15. Dividend payment dates: Feb. 15, May 15, Aug. 15, Nov. 15. Div'd reinv. plan available. (D) Incl. intangibles. In '90: $2594 mill., $7.50/sh. (E) In mill., adj. for stock splits.

SOURCE: *Value Line Investment Survey,* April 26, 1991, p. 513. Copyright © 1991 by Value Line Publishing, Inc.; used by permission.

The research dealing with unexpected earnings announcements strongly supports the importance of earnings changes. One recent study found that "'approximately' 15 to 20 percent of the variation in individual security returns is explained by either actual or unexpected earnings changes."[12]

For empirical research purposes, **unexpected earnings** are usually defined as the difference between actual (reported) earnings and expected earnings. Studies use both quarterly and annual reported earnings in analyzing unexpected earnings. Several different procedures have been used to measure expected earnings. One approach is to estimate expected earnings using a regression trend line of historical earnings in the same way that earnings are forecast (refer back to Table 13.2):[13]

$$EPS_t = \hat{a} + \hat{b}(\text{time})_t + e_t \qquad (13.5)$$

where

EPS_t = reported earnings per share for period t
time_t = index variable representing time

For example, assume that the data consisted of reported EPS for the period 1981–1991. The index variable for time could be 1 for 1981, 2 for 1982, and so forth. Given the regression constants $\hat{a}$ and $\hat{b}$, the expected EPS for 1992 (the twelfth time period) could be calculated as

$$E(EPS_{1992}) - \hat{a} + \hat{b}(12) \qquad (13.6)$$

Table 13.4 illustrates one way to estimate expected and unexpected EPS using six years of EPS data. The EPS are very unpredictable from year to year with a standard deviation of $.49. This variability results in considerable scatter around the regression line. The coefficient of determination of 16.17 percent is therefore low for the trend line. The estimate of EPS for year 7 of $1.97 is below the actual announced earnings of $2.25, resulting in unexpected earnings of $.28. If the market has not anticipated the unexpected favorable earnings of $.28, the stock price is likely to rise. Since EPS were quite volatile in the past, however, unexpected earnings of $.28 may not cause a large increase in the stock price. In other words, the announced earnings of $2.25 may be within the "range" of earnings anticipated by the market since the standard deviation of historical earnings is $.49.

Estimates of expected earnings can also be obtained by using published forecasts of EPS made by security analysts. As noted earlier, a number of pri-

---

[12] Benesh and Peterson, "Earnings, Changes, Analysts' Forecasts and Stock Price Fluctuations," p. 35.

[13] This approach is used in Henry A. Latane and Charles P. Jones, "Standardized Unexpected Earnings—1971–77," *Journal of Finance* (June 1979): 717–24; and Charles P. Jones, Richard J. Rendleman, Jr., and Henry A. Latane, "Earnings Announcements Pre-and-Post Responses," *Journal of Portfolio Management* (Spring 1985): 28–32.

TABLE 13.4 • Actual, Expected, and Unexpected Earnings

Year	Actual EPS
1	\$1.20
2	1.80
3	1.00
4	1.40
5	2.50
6	1.50

Linear Regression Estimates

$$EPS_t = \hat{a} + \hat{b}(\text{time})_t + e_t$$

Regression estimates: $\hat{a} = 1.1667$, $\hat{b} = .1143$, $R^2 = .1617$

Forecast of Expected Earnings

Expected earnings for year 7 = $E(EPS_7) = 1.1667 + .1143(7) = \$1.97$

Calculation of Unexpected Earnings

If actual earnings for year 7 are \$2.25,

$$\text{Unexpected earnings for year 7} = EPS_7 - E(EPS_7) = \$2.25 - \$1.97 = \$.28$$

vate firms publish earnings forecasts. The IBES monitors earnings estimates for over 4,000 companies, and Standard & Poor's publishes its *Earnings Forecasts* monthly. Using this method, unexpected earnings are calculated as the difference between reported earnings and the consensus earnings forecast made by analysts.

Most of the studies of unexpected earnings announcements (including those previously cited) conclude that significant stock price adjustments occur for firms that report earnings significantly different from expected earnings. Based on historical or ex-post data, portfolios formed from stocks reporting the largest positive unexpected earnings also appear to offer risk-adjusted excess returns for the months immediately following the period of unexpected earnings. However, there is also evidence that stock prices adjust prior to the announcement of unexpected earnings. This suggests that additional risk-adjusted excess returns are possible if unexpected earnings can be forecast prior to the earnings announcement date. Thus, the market offers a "reward"—excess returns—for investors who can accurately forecast earnings.

RESEARCH BOX

An Active Common Stock Strategy: Unexpected EPS

Despite numerous previous studies of the market reaction to unexpected earnings announcements, two 1989 studies provide useful additional information. A study by Alexander, Peterson, and Goff analyzed the actual holding period returns (HPRs) calculated to reflect transaction costs of a strategy that invests in stocks prior to the announcement of unexpected earnings. In addition, the study used a more recent period of time and analyzed the HPRs over 30 sample quarters. The evidence suggests that larger excess returns occurred earlier in the 30-quarter sample period but that the profitability of the strategy declined over the period. The decline in profitability suggests more individuals may be attempting to use the strategy. This influx of investors would cause stock prices to increase prior to the announcement, with the result that the strategy would become less effective.

A study by Davis investigated the question of whether firm size might affect the magnitude of price adjustments to unexpected earnings announcements. Using a sample of 374 firms, the study found that the market values announcements by "small" firms more highly than those of "large" firms. This suggests that an unexpected EPS strategy may still be effective if "small" rather than "large" firms are used.

SOURCES: John C. Alexander, Pamela P. Peterson, and Delbert Goff, "Profitability of a Trading Strategy Based on Unexpected Earnings," *Financial Analysts Journal* (July-August 1989): 67–71; and Henry H. Davis, "Firm Size: A Determinant of Differential Market Reaction to Earnings Releases," *Review of Business and Economic Research* (Spring 1989): 43–58.

AN ILLUSTRATION OF ANALYZING AND FORECASTING EPS

Table 13.5 provides data over the period 1986–1990 on profits after taxes, shares of common stock outstanding, and primary EPS for Procter & Gamble. This information, along with the detailed financial data and analysis for the company presented in Chapter 9, can be used to forecast EPS for the company.

Notice that the reported primary EPS in Table 13.5 are fairly stable from year to year but with a definite upward trend. The three professional forecasts in Part I of Table 13.6 are quite similar, but the four forecasts in Part II of the table are more varied. Notice that the estimates of EPS range from $4.90 to $5.43. The trend line regression estimate provides the lowest estimate of $4.90. This estimate should probably be discarded since it treats each of the five historical EPS equally. It does not give more weight to recent developments at Procter & Gamble such as the November 1989 acquisition of Noxell Corporation (see Appendix 9A) or the marked improvement in ROE in 1989 and 1990 (see the ROE analysis in Chapter 9).

The historical earnings growth rate method provides the highest estimate of $5.43. The estimate is high because the five-year annual earnings growth rate

TABLE 13.5 • Data for EPS Analysis of Procter & Gamble, 1986–1990

For year ending June 30	Profit after taxes (thousands)	Number of shares of common stock outstanding (thousands)	Reported primary EPS
1986	$ 709,000	336,500*	$2.10*
1987	786,000	338,100*	2.30*
1988	1,020,000	338,600*	2.98*
1989	1,206,000	334,400	3.56
1990	1,602,000	346,100	4.49

SOURCE: Disclosure and recent edition of *Value Line Investment Survey.*

*Adjusted for a two-for-one stock split in 1989 by multiplying the shares outstanding by a factor of 2. The reported EPS, therefore, are reduced by 50 percent.

TABLE 13.6 • EPS Forecasts for Procter & Gamble for Year Ending June 30, 1991

I. Professional Forecasts

A. Merrill Lynch (9/24/90)	$5.25
B. Zacks consensus forecast (Disclosure 8/10/90)	5.34
C. *Value Line Investment Survey* (8/31/90)	5.25
D. Management forecast	(Not provided by management)

II. Forecasts by Various Methods

A. Statistical method:

$$EPS_t = \hat{a} + \hat{b}(\text{time})_t + e_t$$

Regression estimates: $\hat{a} = 1.274$, $\hat{b} = .604$, $R^2 = .961$, $\sigma_{EPS} = \$.871$

Forecast: $EPS_{1991} = 1.274 + .604(6) = \$4.90$

Year	*EPS*
1	$2.10
2	2.30
3	2.98
4	3.56
5	4.49

B. Return on equity and dividend policy method:

ROE for 1990[a] = 21.27%

Earnings retention rate for 1990[a] = 61%

$g = b \times \text{ROE} = .61 \times .2127 = 13\%$

$EPS_{1991} = EPS_{1990}(1 + g) = \$4.49(1 + .13) = \$5.07$

TABLE 13.6 • EPS Forecasts for Procter & Gamble for Year Ending June 30, 1991 (continued)

	1991 (millions)
C. Pro forma income statement method:	
Sales (Value Line estimate on 8/31/90)	$26,500
Cost of goods (60.9%[b])	16,138
Gross profit	$10,362
Selling, general, and administrative expenses (29.6%[b])	7,844
Operating income	$ 2,518
Nonoperating income (2.3%[b])	610
Interest expense[c]	442
Income before taxes	$ 2,686
Provision for taxes (1990 average tax rate = 33.83%)	909
Net income	$ 1,777
Preferred stock dividends[c]	47
Earnings available to common stockholders	$ 1,730
Average share outstanding (Value Line estimate on 8/31/90)	347
EPS estimate	$4.99

D. Historical earnings growth rate method:
Historical growth rate calculation:

$$\bar{g} = \sqrt[n]{\frac{\text{EPS}_n}{\text{EPS}_0}} - 1 = \sqrt[4]{\frac{4.49}{2.10}} - 1 = \left(\frac{4.49}{2.10}\right)^{.25} - 1 = .2092$$

Forecast:

$$\text{EPS}_{1991} = \text{EPS}_{1990}(1 + \bar{g}) = \$4.49(1 + .2092) = \$5.43$$

[a] See the financial analysis for Procter & Gamble in Chapter 9, p. 284.
[b] See Table 9.6 for 1990 cost percentages relative to sales, p. 289.
[c] See Table 9.3, p. 284—same as 1990.

of 20.92 percent is used. The weak economic environment in late 1990 and early 1991 (see Chapter 8) suggests that earnings growth rates for 1991 for many corporations may be below their historical average. Remember that the last recession in the United States ended in November 1982 and the period 1983–1989 represented a strong economy.

The ROE and dividend policy method estimates EPS for 1991 of $5.07. It uses a more conservative estimate of earnings growth of 13 percent. This growth rate, however, assumes that Procter & Gamble's ROE and earnings retention rate will remain at their 1990 levels. Due to the rapid sales growth and aggressive acquisition program that Procter & Gamble is pursuing, it is likely that a larger proportion of earnings will be retained in the future. As Chapter 9 illustrated, the retention rate increased from 53.7 percent in 1988 to

61.0 percent in 1990. An increase in the retention rate in 1991 would result in an increase in the estimated growth rate of 13 percent. Based on this reasoning, the EPS estimate of $5.07 for 1991 is probably too conservative.

The estimate of $4.99 provided by the pro forma income statement method suffers from the same problems as the ROE and dividend policy method. It assumes that cost of goods and selling, general, and administrative expenses in 1991 will be the same percentage of sales as in 1990; thus, it assumes no improvements in the gross or operating profit margins. It is also possible that the sales estimate of $26,500 million for 1991 is too low in light of the acquisition in 1989 of Noxell Corporation and the announcement in early 1991 that Procter & Gamble had reached an agreement to buy Revlon's Max Factor Cosmetic unit.

Based on this analysis of the forecasts, it seems logical to conclude that the EPS for Procter & Gamble for 1991 will likely be in the range of $5.20 to $5.40. An alternative to this procedure is to compute the consensus (average) of two or more of the seven estimates. The overall average, using all seven estimates, is $5.18. Another alternative is to select a single estimate as the most likely.

This example illustrates the difficulty that an analyst has in estimating EPS for a company. As previously discussed, fundamental analysis is more of an art than a science. An analyst must be familiar with procedures and techniques, but the final estimate depends on the insights and judgments that the analyst must make.

If the analyst is able to make a more accurate forecast than the consensus, then excess returns may be possible. This would be the case if Procter & Gamble's reported 1991 EPS were significantly below or above the consensus forecast. The *magnitude* of the price adjustment, however, would depend on the difference between reported and consensus earnings or on the size of the unexpected earnings. The *pattern* of the price adjustment would depend on when the market began to recognize the possibility of unexpected earnings. If the market begins to anticipate the unexpected earnings, then the price may adjust gradually so that by the time actual EPS for 1991 are announced, little or no additional price movements will occur.

SUMMARY

Timely and accurate estimates of future earnings and dividends are crucial to a fundamental analysis of common stocks. Numerous studies have demonstrated the importance of earnings and changes in earnings to common stock value. Individual investors can formulate their own estimates of earnings using the techniques discussed in the chapter. An alternative is to rely on estimates published by professional analysts or by company managements.

Despite the numerous earnings forecasting techniques, the success and accuracy of the forecast depend essentially on the experience and skill of the analyst. All forecasts depend on the same set of publicly available informa-

• CONCEPT APPLICATIONS

Investment Concept	Concept Application
Earnings per share	EPS is probably the single most important variable that determines a stock's value. Investors buy stocks for their anticipated future income stream that results from earnings that are paid as dividends or retained and reinvested, producing higher earnings in the future. Forecasts of EPS are provided by brokerage firms, investment publications, and sometimes management of the company. Investors can also develop their own EPS forecast using techniques discussed in the chapter.
Cash flow per share	CFPS is calculated like EPS but noncash expenses, such as depreciation and amortization, are added to profits after taxes. Some analysts like to use CFPS rather than EPS because accounting adjustments, such as changes in the depreciation technique, have less influence on CFPS. Generally, the stock price is highly correlated with both EPS and CFPS.
Unexpected earnings	Unexpected EPS announcements can cause significant changes in a stock's price. Stock prices reflect the consensus forecast of EPS, and unexpected EPS are significantly different from the consensus forecast. An active common stock strategy would involve a more accurate forecast of EPS that may be able to identify firms that will report unexpectedly good or bad earnings. Taking a long or short position in these stocks before the market recognizes the unexpected earnings may result in excess returns.

tion. The ability to use this information in unique ways to discover information that is not generally known or to draw conclusions based on many factors may result in more accurate estimates. Making or using an average or consensus forecast of earnings is therefore unlikely to result in risk-adjusted excess returns.

• KEY TERMS

Cash flow per share (CFPS)
Common stock equivalents
Consensus EPS forecast
Earnings per share (EPS)
Fully diluted EPS
Primary EPS
Pro forma income statement
Simple EPS
Unexpected earnings

• QUESTIONS

1. Explain how a pro forma income statement can be used to forecast company earnings.

2. Compare and contrast primary and fully diluted EPS. Which estimate of earnings is likely to be more useful to a stock analyst? Explain.
3. Clearly distinguish between expected and unexpected earnings. How can unexpected earnings be measured? In terms of an active investment strategy, would expected or unexpected earnings be more valuable in attempting to "beat the market"? Explain.
4. Using the sample of companies in Table 13.1, comment on the apparent difficulty or ease of forecasting future earnings based on historical earnings. Which of the companies would most likely report unexpected earnings? Explain.
5. Discuss the advantages and disadvantages of using a consensus approach to forecasting a company's earnings.
6. Describe the Institutional Brokers Estimate System (IBES). How has this data base been used in investment research? Can the data base be used in an active investment strategy?
7. Define cash flow per share. What are some of the advantages and disadvantages of using cash flow per share versus reported earnings in a company analysis?
8. Are management forecasts of earnings useful to security analysts? Explain. Are they useful to individual investors?
9. Do you feel the *Value Line Investment Survey* provides accurate earnings estimates for the companies it analyzes? Would you be willing to use its forecast in an active investment strategy designed to "beat the market"?
10. Describe how a simple linear regression model can be used to forecast earnings. Do you feel this statistical technique provides more accurate estimates than those provided by professional analysts? Explain.

• KEY TO THE INVESTMENT ANALYSIS SOFTWARE

Calculation	Appendix A-1 Page Reference	Access Procedure
Pro forma income statement	A-10	BEGIN, FINANCIAL, FINANCIALS, FORECAST
Growth rate in key financial variables	A-10	BEGIN, FINANCIAL, FINANCIALS, GROWTH
Regression analysis	A-7	BEGIN, STATISTICAL, REGRESS

• PROBLEMS

1. In 1990, Procter & Gamble reported \$4.49 primary EPS and \$4.27 fully diluted EPS. Explain why these two earnings figures are different. (*Hint:* See Appendix 9A.)

2. Boston Edison reported the following primary EPS:

1980	\$1.88
1981	2.08
1982	1.59
1983	1.80
1984	2.43
1985	2.52
1986	2.58
1987	1.97
1988	1.86
1989	1.90

   a. Estimate the EPS for 1990 using a regression trend line. Also calculate the coefficient of determination for the regression.
   b. Given that Boston Edison reported EPS of \$1.60 for 1990, calculate the unexpected earnings for 1990 using your estimate from part (a).
   c. Based on your analysis, do you think that the stock likely had a significant price adjustment because of the announced earnings of \$1.60 for 1990? Explain.

3. Liz Claiborne reported the following primary EPS:

1984	\$0.50
1985	0.71
1986	1.00
1987	1.32
1988	1.26
1989	1.87
1990	2.37

   a. Calculate the six annual rates of growth in EPS.
   b. Calculate the annual rate of growth in EPS using only the first and last earnings. Be sure to consider the compounding effect.
   c. Estimate the EPS for 1991 using your answer to part (b). How much confidence would you have in this estimate? Would you use this estimate in making an investment decision about this stock? Explain.

4. Consider the following income statement data on Chrysler Corporation (in millions):

	1986	1987	1988	1989	1990
Net sales	$22,586.3	$29,257.9	$34.067.0	$34,602.0	$29,797.0
Cost of goods	18,635.2	21,531.6	26,155.0	26,849.0	23,395.0
Gross profits	$ 3,951.1	$ 7,726.3	$ 7,912.0	$ 7,753.0	$ 6,402.0
General and administrative expenses	1,613.1	2.585.2	2,971.0	3,154.0	3,323.0
Depreciation and amortization	543.6	899.5	629.0	726.0	781.0
Operating income	$ 1,794.4	$ 4,241.6	$ 4,312.0	$ 3,873.0	$ 2,298.0
Nonoperating income	563.6	0.0	(251.0)	(464.0)	307.0
Interest expense	32.7	2,061.9	2,440.0	2,844.0	2,458.0
Earnings before taxes	$ 2,325.3	$ 2,179.7	$ 1,621.0	$ 565.0	$ 147.0
Taxes	921.7	890.0	612.0	242.0	79.0
Net income	$ 1,403.6	$ 1,289.7	$ 1,009.0	$ 323.0	$ 68.0

a. Assume sales are likely to be $28,307 million in 1991. Use the five years of historical data and the percentage of sales method to estimate net income for 1991.

b. What are the strengths and weaknesses of this estimation technique?

c. Would you use this net income estimate to make an investment decision about this stock? Explain.

5. Procter & Gamble reports the following information:

	1988	1989	1990
Sales (millions)	$19,336	$21,398	$24,081
Depreciation (millions)	$697	$767	$859
Profit after taxes (thousands)	$1,020,000	$1,206,000	$1,602,000
Preferred stock dividends (thousands)	$11,000	$16,000	$47,000
Average outstanding shares (thousands)	338,600	334,400	346,100

a. Calculate the primary EPS for each year.

b. Calculate the cash flow per share for each year.

• REFERENCES

Abbott, Joseph. "Corporate Earnings Outlook—A Consensus Forecast." *Journal of Business Forecasting* (Summer 1989): 42–44.

Baginski, Stephen P. "Management Forecast and Release—Specific Directional Information Transfer." *Quarterly Review of Economics and Business* (Winter 1989): 49–62.

Baginski, Stephen P., and John M. Hassell. "The Market Interpretation of Management Earnings Forecasts as a Predictor of Subsequent Financial Analyst Forecast Revision." *Accounting Review* (January 1990): 175–90.

Bauman, W. Scott, and Richard Dowen. "Growth Projections and Common Stock Returns." *Financial Analysts Journal* (July-August 1988): 79–80.

Bierman, Harold, Jr. "Common Stock Equivalents, Earnings per Share, and Stock Valuation." *Journal of Accounting, Auditing and Finance* (Winter 1986): 62–70.

Bowen, Robert M., Marilyn F. Johnson, and Terry Shevlin. "Informational Efficiency and the Information Content of Earnings during the Market Crash of October 1987." *Journal of Accounting and Economics* (July 1989): 225–54.

Chang, S.J., and Son-Nan Chen. "Stock Price Adjustment to Earnings and Dividend Surprises." *Quarterly Review of Economics and Business* (Spring 1989): 68–81.

Chatfield, Robert E., Charles R. Moyer, and Phillip M. Sisneros. "The Accuracy of Long-Term Earnings Forecasts for Industrial Firms." *Quarterly Journal of Business and Economics* (Summer 1989): 91–104.

DeBondt, Werner F.M., and Richard H. Thaler. "Do Security Analysts Overreact?" *American Economic Review* (May 1990): 52–57.

Easton, S.A., and N.A. Sinclair. "The Impact of Unexpected Earnings and Dividends on Abnormal Returns to Equity." *Accounting and Finance* (May 1989): 1–19.

Farrell, Christopher, and Robert Mims. "Before You Leap, Look at the Numbers That Count; Investment Outlook Scoreboard." *Business Week,* December 26, 1988, pp. 187–232.

Guerard, John B., Jr. "Combining Time-Series Model Forecasts and Analysts' Forecasts for Superior Forecasts of Annual Earnings." *Financial Analysts Journal* (January-February 1989): 69–71.

Johnson, Lewis D. "Growth Prospects and Share Prices: A Systematic View." *Journal of Portfolio Management* (Winter 1987): 58–60.

Kim, Jong H., Robert K. Su, and Eugene Sauls. "Measuring Market Forecasts of Earnings." *Journal of Business Forecasting* (Spring 1990): 20–26.

Millar, James A., Thakol Nunthirapakorn, and Steve Courtenay. "A Note on the Information Content of Primary and Fully Diluted Earnings per Share." *Financial Analysts Journal* (September-October 1987): 77–79.

Ozanian, Michael. "Is the Consensus Always Wrong?" *Forbes,* December 2, 1985, pp. 254–58.

Peavy, John W. III, and David A. Goodman. "How Inflation, Risk and Corporate Profitability Affect Common Stock Returns." *Financial Analysts Journal* (September-October 1985): 59–65.

Rendleman, Richard J., Jr., Charles P. Jones, and Henry A. Latane. "Further Insight into the Standardized Unexpected Earnings Anomaly: Size and Serial Correlation Effects." *Financial Review* (February 1987): 131–44.

CHAPTER 14

Preferred and Common Stock Valuation

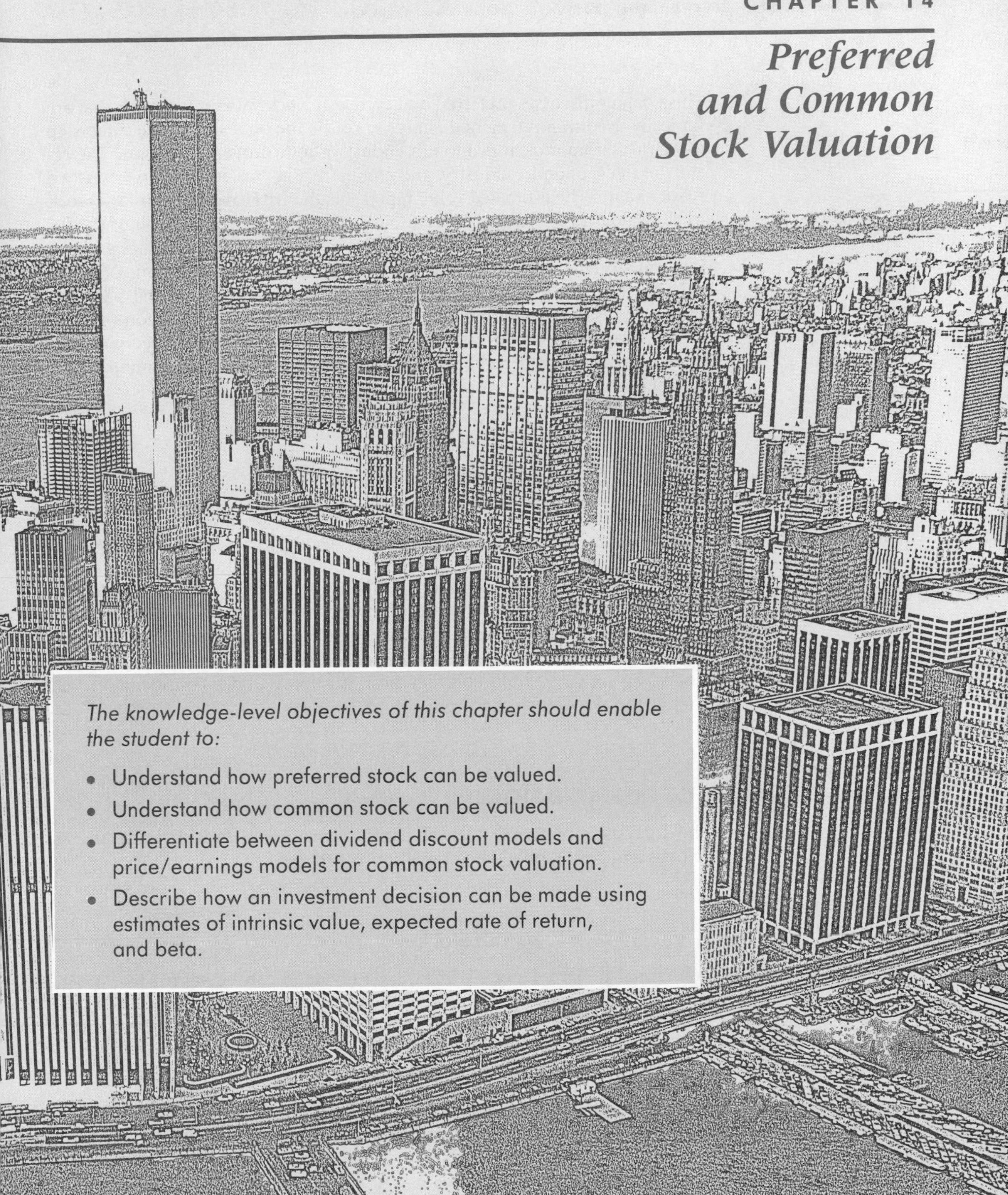

The knowledge-level objectives of this chapter should enable the student to:

- Understand how preferred stock can be valued.
- Understand how common stock can be valued.
- Differentiate between dividend discount models and price/earnings models for common stock valuation.
- Describe how an investment decision can be made using estimates of intrinsic value, expected rate of return, and beta.

INTRODUCTION

This chapter discusses preferred and common stock valuation models that are typically used in fundamental analysis. This is the final step in the three-step fundamental approach: economic, industry, and company analyses. The results of the economic, industry, and company analyses are used to estimate a stock's value. The estimated value represents the **intrinsic value** of the stock or the value that is suggested by the fundamentals. A comparison of the intrinsic value with the current market price of the stock provides a basis for the investment decision. The analyst attempts to answer the question, Does the existing stock price provide the opportunity to earn excess returns, based on the estimates of risk and intrinsic value over the investment horizon?

The chapter concludes with a discussion of the investment decision suggested by the fundamental approach. The investor must choose among three basic possibilities:

1. Purchase the stock by taking a long position.
2. Sell the stock now by taking a short position.
3. Do not take a long or short position in the stock.

These possibilities assume that the investor does not have a position in the stock at the present time. The analysis may also be used to recommend strategies involving options, financial futures, or options on futures. These strategies are discussed in Chapters 15 and 17. The basic decision possibilities also assume that in making the final decision, the investor will consider the risk-return relationships between an existing portfolio and the stocks under consideration. In other words, if the investor already has a portfolio of common stocks, he or she should consider how the stock under consideration will change the risk-return characteristics of the portfolio.

INVESTMENT ANALYSIS OF PREFERRED STOCK

The analysis of preferred stock involves calculating its intrinsic value and its returns and considering the various sources of risk.

• Valuation of Preferred Stock

Traditional preferred stock with a fixed dividend can be valued like a perpetuity. This approach assumes that the dividends will be received each year from now to infinity. The present value or intrinsic value of all these future dividends can be calculated as follows:

$$V_0 = \frac{D_0}{R_I} \tag{14.1}$$

where

V_0 = current intrinsic value of preferred stock
D_0 = current annual cash dividend
R_I = investor's required rate of return

The valuation of newer types of preferred stock, such as ARPS and DARPS discussed in Chapter 12, must consider the fact that dividends are adjusted periodically to reflect market yields. The dividend adjustments and auction procedures, however, result in very stable if not constant prices for these newer types of preferred stock.

• Calculating Returns for Preferred Stock

Two measures of return can be used in an investment analysis of preferred stock: (1) the dividend or current yield and (2) the holding period return.

The **dividend yield** is calculated as

$$Y_{PS} = \frac{D_0}{P_0} \tag{14.2}$$

where

Y_{PS} = dividend yield on preferred stock
D_0 = current annual cash dividend
P_0 = current price of the preferred stock

The dividend yields for preferred stocks are listed in the *Wall Street Journal* and other sources of market quotations.

The dividend yield is only a partial indication of the return, however, because it ignores capital gains or losses. The holding period return (HPR) considers dividends and price changes:

$$\text{HPR}_{PS,t} = \frac{P_{t+1} - P_t + D_{t+1}}{P_t} \tag{14.3}$$

where

$\text{HPR}_{PS,t}$ = holding period return on a share of preferred stock for period t
P_{t+1} = price of the preferred stock at the end of the holding period
P_t = price at the beginning of the holding period
D_{t+1} = cash dividend received during the holding period

Since dividends are typically paid quarterly, the HPR for a specific month may not include a dividend; preferred stock is traded with ex-dividend dates.

Equation 14.3 should be used in an investment analysis of preferred stock. The equation can be used to calculate both the historical or ex-post HPR and the expected or ex-ante HPR, $E(\text{HPR})$. Calculation of the expected HPR requires the analyst to estimate the future price, $E(P_{t+1})$, and dividend, $E(D_{t+1})$. These estimates are then used as follows:

$$E(\text{HPR}_{\text{PS},t}) = \frac{E(P_{t+1}) - P_t + E(D_{t+1})}{P_t} \qquad (14.4)$$

• Traditional Risk Analysis for Preferred Stock

A traditional risk analysis for preferred stock would consider two sources of risk: interest rate risk and credit risk. With regard to *interest rate risk,* the lack of a maturity date can cause the price of a preferred stock to be very sensitive to changes in the market's required rate of return.

Table 14.1 demonstrates this interest rate risk for a preferred stock. The required rate of return under present market conditions is 8 percent for the preferred stock. The example then assumes that market conditions change so that the market's required rate of return increases by 20 percent, from 8 percent to 9.6 percent. The values of the preferred stock are calculated using Equation 14.1.

Table 14.1 shows that an increase of 20 percent in the market's required rate of return causes the value of the preferred stock to *decline* from \$62.50 to \$52.08, or by 16.67 percent. As this example illustrates, changes in the market's required rate of return can cause preferred stock prices to be very volatile.

A second type of risk exhibited by preferred stock is *credit risk,* which essentially refers to the business and financial risk of the issuer. Credit analysis

TABLE 14.1 • Interest Rate Risk for a Preferred Stock

Term to maturity	∞
Annual dividend, D_0	\$5
Market's required rate of return, R_M	8%
Current value[a]	\$62.50
Market's new required rate of return	8%(1.2) = 9.60%
New value[b]	\$52.08
Percentage change in value	(\$52.08 − \$62.50)/\$62.50 = −16.67%

[a]Current value calculation: preferred stock value $= \dfrac{D_0}{R_M} = \dfrac{\$5}{.08} = \$62.50$

[b]New value calculation: preferred stock value $= \dfrac{\$5}{.0960} = \$52.08$

RESEARCH BOX

Credit Risk and Preferred Stock

In November 1981, Standard & Poor's Corporation (S&P) created a *CreditWatch* list. The list is published weekly and includes firms that have had a "significant development" that may affect their bond and stock ratings. The development may be either positive or negative. The inclusion of a firm on the CreditWatch list indicates that S&P is considering changing the quality ratings on the securities. The firm is removed from the list when the ratings are changed or when S&P decides that the development does not justify a rating change.

A study by Wansley, Elayan, and Maris identified 125 firms that were placed on the CreditWatch list from November 1981 through September 1987. These 125 firms had 151 issues of preferred stock whose ratings could have been raised, lowered, or confirmed after being placed on the CreditWatch list.

One interesting finding of the study is that 123 of the 151 issues of preferred stock were placed on the CreditWatch list for negative developments. Of these 123, however, only 65, or 53 percent, had their rating lowered. Fifty-four, or 44 percent, had their rating affirmed, and 4, or 3 percent, had a rating increase.

The empirical evidence shows that preferred stocks placed on the list because of negative developments suffer a significant price decline. The price adjustments occur one day before and one day after the announcement. The empirical evidence also shows that there is little price reaction to the subsequent reratings of the stock. The authors conclude: "The results indicate that CreditWatch provides useful information to market participants and has reduced the surprise associated with subsequent reratings."

SOURCE: James W. Wansley, Fayez A. Elayan, and Brian A. Maris, "Preferred Stock Returns, CreditWatch, and Preferred Stock Ratings," *Financial Review* (May 1990): 265–85.

measures the company's ability to make the preferred dividend payment. A traditional credit analysis would use financial ratios that measure the liquidity, financial leverage, and profitability of the issuer. The techniques presented in Chapter 9 can be used for this analysis.

Independent agencies like Moody's and Standard & Poor's provide preferred stock ratings, which reflect the safety of the preferred dividend and provide an indication of credit risk. These ratings are similar to the bond ratings discussed in Chapter 10.

• Systematic and Nonsystematic Risk for Preferred Stock

The market model, or CAPM, has been applied to the analysis of preferred stock.[1] One question raised by this research is, What is the appropriate bench-

[1] For example, see John S. Bildersee, "Some Aspects of the Performance of Nonconvertible Preferred Stocks," *Journal of Finance* (December 1973): 1187–201; and Robert M. Soldofsky, "Risk and Return for Long-Term Securities: 1971–1982," *Journal of Portfolio Management* (Fall 1984): 57–64.

mark or market portfolio to use in estimating the beta of a preferred stock? Preferred stock has characteristics of both common stocks and bonds. Therefore, should a stock, bond, or some combination index be used as a proxy for the market portfolio? The introduction to capital market theory in Chapter 2 indicated that the market portfolio should include a composite of all risky assets. Since data on such a portfolio do not exist, proxies such as the Dow Jones Industrial Average and S&P 500 Index are typically used.

Researchers have found a relationship between the quality ratings and the betas for preferred stock. Lower-quality preferred stocks have more systematic risk than higher-quality preferred stocks, which indicates that the betas also reflect credit, or unsystematic risk. When the S&P 500 is used as the proxy for the market index, preferred stock betas are greater than or approximately equal to the betas for U.S. government bonds and high-quality (Aaa-rated) corporate bonds. Betas for preferred stocks are also smaller than the betas for the common stock of the *same* company.

INVESTMENT STRATEGIES FOR PREFERRED STOCK

Using the information obtained from the investment analysis, the investor can determine whether preferred stocks fit into the chosen investment strategy. Individual investors are likely to find that preferred stocks are more attractive alternatives for active strategies than for passive strategies.

• Passive Strategies

Table 14.2 provides yields on market indexes of preferred stocks and bonds. The key point of this table is that before-tax preferred yields are almost always *lower* than before-tax yields on bonds. Thus, an investor who holds a preferred stock strictly for the dividend income will earn a lower return but incur *more* risk than an investor who holds bonds. The before-tax yields on preferred stock are below those of bonds because of the favorable tax treatment accorded corporate investors. As one commentator has said, ". . . where comparable preferred stocks and bonds are available, the noncorporate investor should keep one phrase in mind: Ladies and gentlemen prefer bonds."[2]

Table 14.3 illustrates the difference in after-tax yields (ATYs) for preferred stocks and bonds from the standpoint of a corporate and an individual investor. Notice that the before-tax yield (BTY) on the bond is larger than the BTY on the preferred stock (9.20 percent versus 8.66 percent). For a corporate investor, however, the ATY on the preferred stock is greater than the ATY on the bond (7.335 percent versus 6.072 percent); the reverse is true for the individual investor. Ignoring the differences in credit risk (bond versus preferred

---

[2] Jeffrey R. Scharf, "Question of Preference: How Preferred Stocks Stack Up vs. Bonds," *Barron's,* September 8, 1986, p. 71.

TABLE 14.2 • Yields on Preferred Stocks and Corporate Bonds

	Yields		
	New issues of investment-grade bonds	*Medium-grade industrial preferred stock*	*Yield spread*
1975	9.42%	8.18%	1.24%
1976	8.72	7.81	0.91
1977	8.32	7.44	0.88
1978	9.17	8.12	1.05
1979	10.30	9.16	1.14
1980	12.60	10.63	1.97
1981	15.26	13.07	2.19
1982	14.23	14.04	0.19
1983	12.20	11.71	0.49
1984	13.05	12.14	0.91
1985	11.71	11.04	0.67
1986	9.42	9.23	0.19
1987	9.51	9.34	0.17
1988	10.02	9.51	0.51
1989	9.39	9.53	(0.14)

SOURCE: Moody's *Industrial Manual,* Vol. 1 (1990), pp. a39, a51.

stock), and possible price changes, the corporate investor should purchase the preferred stock, the individual investor the bond.

In addition to the tax treatment, preferred stocks are not good passive investments for individuals because transaction costs are high. Brokerage fees are higher for preferred stocks than for bonds.

• Active Strategies

Nonconvertible preferred stock has some characteristics that may make it a favorable investment alternative for individuals using an active investment strategy. Since preferred stock has considerable interest rate risk, it may be an attractive investment prior to a general decline in interest rates and yields that would cause a decline in the market's required rate of return. This price volatility was illustrated in Table 14.1. It is important to remember, however, that this strategy can backfire if the market's required rate of return increases.

A limited number of studies have analyzed the market's efficiency at pricing preferred stock. If market inefficiencies can be discovered, they may indicate active strategies that can be used in an attempt to "beat the market."

TABLE 14.3 • After-Tax Yields for Preferred Stocks versus Bonds

Investment alternatives		Corporate investor[a] Before-tax yield	Corporate investor[a] After-tax yield	Individual investor[b] Before-tax yield	Individual investor[b] After-tax yield
Duke Power preferred stock					
Dividend:	$8.70	BTY = $8.70/$100.50	ATY = BTY(1 − marginal tax rate)	BTY = 8.66%	ATY = 8.66%(1 − .28)
Price:	$100.50	= 8.66%	= 8.66%[1 − (1 − .55)(.34)]		= 6.235%
			= 7.335%		
Duke Power bond					
Coupon:	9.75%	BTY = $97.50/$1,060	ATY = 9.20%(1 − .34)	BTY = 9.20%	ATY = 9.20%(1 −.28)
Maturity date:	2004	= 9.20%	= 6.072%		= 6.624%
Price:	$1,060				

SOURCE: Price data from *Wall Street Journal,* June 4, 1991.

[a] Assumes that the corporate investor's marginal tax rate is 34%, and that it is entitled to the 55% dividend income exclusion.

[b] Assumes that the individual marginal tax rate is 28%.

Stevenson and Rozeff examined returns and risk from a strategy that involved buying preferred stock with dividends in arrears.[3] A company that has not been paying preferred dividends is likely to be having severe financial problems, and the preferred stock price should reflect this credit risk. Is it possible to buy the stock while the price is depressed in the hope that the company will recover and eventually pay the skipped dividends? The study concluded that after adjusting for risk, the market was efficient in pricing these preferred shares. There was no evidence that this strategy could be used to "beat the market."

A study by Hetherington that assessed the strategy of buying preferred stock after a call announcement did detect market inefficiencies.[4] One of his examples concerned Nevada Power Preferred C shares that were called at \$21.48 (including accrued dividends). For several weeks after the call announcement, Hetherington noted, the preferred stock traded as low as \$21.00 and as high as \$22.75. His strategy would be to buy at any price less than the call price of \$21.48, and sell when the price exceeded \$21.48. The annualized HPR on this transaction would obviously be very high. Hetherington argued that these small dollar trading opportunities could be profitably exploited by using a discount broker (lower commission) and, possibly, a favorable margin transaction. Buying the stock on margin would increase the HPR if the rate of interest charged on the margin account was less than the HPR on the investment. He concluded: "Trading in called preferred presents attractive opportunities for investors and furnishes a simple and decisive example for academics of a less than efficient market."[5]

INVESTMENT ANALYSIS OF COMMON STOCK

A common stock valuation model attempts to develop a mathematical formulation of the variables (and their relationships) that determine value. It is important to recognize that these models grossly oversimplify the valuation process. In reality, many factors determine the market price of a common stock. These factors may change, and the relationships between factors may change. No model can consider all the complexities of the "real-world" process. The models, however, can provide a useful framework for the analysis.

Mathematical models imply precision and accuracy, and the valuation models in this chapter may give the impression that valuation is essentially a quantitative procedure. In reality, however, common stock valuation is an *art*. Models are useful to the analyst but are not substitutes for judgment and com-

[3] Richard A. Stevenson and Michael S. Rozeff, "Are the Backwaters of the Market Efficient?" *Journal of Portfolio Management* (Spring 1979): 31–34.

[4] Norriss Hetherington, "High Returns and Low Risk in Called Preferreds," *Journal of Portfolio Management* (Spring 1987): 81–82.

[5] Ibid., p. 82.

• **INTEREST BOX**

An Active Preferred Stock Strategy: Dividend Capture Plans

Atchison and Kling have investigated an active preferred stock strategy designed to capture dividends. As they explain:

> Corporate cash managers traditionally invest idle cash balances in money market instruments such as commercial paper, Treasury bills, and certificates of deposit. These securities have the desirable properties of safety, liquidity, and a commensurate rate of return. Today, however, research shows cash managers can use preferred stock to earn an even higher rate of return on idle balances. With a strategy commonly referred to as a *dividend roll,* cash managers buy a dividend-paying stock just prior to its ex-dividend date and sell the stock on or shortly after the ex-dividend date. This strategy supposedly earns superior returns due to the preferential tax treatment that corporations enjoy on dividends received from other corporations.

The dividend roll strategy can use traditional preferred stock, adjustable rate preferred stock (ARPS) or Dutch auction rate preferred stock (DARPS). This study collected daily price data on all ARPS issued between December 1, 1982, and July 18, 1984, and between July 19, 1984, and September 30, 1986. Price data on 17 issues of traditional preferred stock and on Treasury bills over the same two time periods were also collected. All of the issues of preferred stock were traded on the NYSE. The daily price data on the preferred stock and Treasury bill yields were used to calculate the HPRs and variance of HPRs on various strategies for several short-term holding periods. Then the risk-return profiles of the various strategies were compared. The comparisons showed that strategies using "ARPS can always be dominated, in a risk-return context, by some combination of Treasury bills and traditional preferred stock."

The authors concluded: "The results of this study show that an investor investing in preferred dividend rolls would be better off using traditional preferred stock as opposed to ARPS."

SOURCE: Michael D. Atchison and John L. Kling, "How Good Are Preferred Dividend Capture Plans?" *Journal of Cash Management* (November-December 1988): 71–74. Reprinted with permission.

mon sense. A skilled analyst may find a model helpful in making accurate forecasts, but the same model may not improve the forecasts of an unskilled analyst. Models should therefore be viewed as tools for decision making and not as the decision maker.

Finance theory indicates that the value of a common stock is essentially a function of the future income the stock can provide and the riskiness of the income stream. Valuation models, therefore, generally take the form

$$V_n = f(\text{income, risk}) \tag{14.5}$$

where V_n represents the intrinsic value of the common stock in period n. For example, if the analyst has a one-year investment horizon, the value of the stock one year from now, V_1, would be estimated. In other words, the estimate of V_n will indicate the likely selling price one year from today.

Given an estimate of the cash dividends that the stock might pay the next year, D_1, the expected one-year holding period return could be calculated as

$$E(\text{HPR}_1) = \frac{V_1 - P_0 + D_1}{P_0} \tag{14.6}$$

The analyst must also estimate the risk of the stock over the investment horizon. The risk estimate may simply be a historical or ex-post risk measure such as the stock's beta, variance, or standard deviation. This approach assumes that risk will remain constant over the investment horizon. Alternatively, an ex-ante risk estimate may be made by calculating the variance or the standard deviation for the estimated probability distribution associated with $E(\text{HPR})$.

Once estimates of $E(\text{HPR})$ and risk are made, the analyst can compare the stock to other stocks or to the estimated risk-return relationship for stocks in general. This procedure is discussed at the end of this chapter. Portfolio considerations should also be included in the final recommendation.

DIVIDEND DISCOUNT MODEL

One of the most widely used common stock valuation models is the **dividend discount model (DDM)**. As its name implies, the DDM defines the intrinsic value of a share as the present value of future dividends. Despite its simplicity, the DDM is a useful tool in fundamental analysis. This section illustrates basic DDMs and a more complex DDM.

• Basic Models

There are several variations of the basic DDM because different assumptions can be made about the growth rate of dividends and its relationship to the discount rate used to calculate present values.

ZERO GROWTH DDM The most basic of all the DDMs is the **zero growth** model. This model assumes that dividends will be constant over time—so growth is zero—and that the investor's required rate of return is constant. This model is

$$V_0 = \frac{D_1}{(1+K)^1} + \frac{D_2}{(1+K)^2} + \frac{D_3}{(1+K)^3} + \cdots + \frac{D_\infty}{(1+K)^\infty} \tag{14.7}$$

where

V_0 = intrinsic value of stock today or at time period 0
D_t = dividends per share in period t
K = investor's required rate of return

Since $D_1 = D_2 = D_3 = \ldots = D_\infty$ by assumption, the time subscript can be dropped. The dividend income stream is essentially a perpetuity, and as with preferred stock, the value can be calculated simply as

$$V_0 = \frac{D}{K} \tag{14.8}$$

For example, assume that the dividends per share are estimated to be $2 per year indefinitely, and the investor requires a 16 percent rate of return. The intrinsic value of the common stock is $2/.16 = $12.50.

The constant dividend assumption makes this model more appropriate for an analysis of preferred stock than for common stock.

CONSTANT GROWTH DDM It is unlikely that many common stocks will pay a constant dividend. A more realistic assumption is that dividends will change. The simplest assumption assumes a *constant* rate of change. If an analyst forecasts that dividends will grow by g percent per year, then

$$\begin{aligned} D_1 &= D_0(1 + g) \\ D_2 &= D_0(1 + g)^2 \\ &\vdots \\ D_n &= D_0(1 + g)^n \end{aligned}$$

For example, assume D_0 = \$2 and g = 6 percent, or .06:

$$\begin{aligned} D_1 &= \$2(1 + .06) &&= \$2.1200 \\ D_2 &= \$2(1 + .06)^2 &&= \$2.2472 \\ &\vdots && \vdots \\ D_{10} &= \$2(1 + .06)^{10} &&= \$3.5817 \end{aligned}$$

Notice that this procedure assumes that dividends are growing at a rate of 6 percent per year compounded annually. Assuming a constant required rate of return, the intrinsic value of the stock can be calculated as

$$V_0 = \frac{D_0(1 + g)}{(1 + K)^1} + \frac{D_0(1 + g)^2}{(1 + K)^2} + \cdots + \frac{D_0(1 + g)^\infty}{(1 + K)^\infty} \tag{14.9}$$

If one assumes that the growth rate is less than the investor's required rate of return ($g < k$), Equation 14.9 simplifies to

$$V_0 = \frac{D_0(1 + g)}{K - g} = \frac{D_1}{K - g} \tag{14.10}$$

• INTEREST BOX

Institutional Investors and the DDM

Sanford C. Bernstein & Company is a successful money management firm that has both institutional and individual accounts. As of 1989, the company had $17 billion of assets under management. The firm was founded in 1967 as a brokerage house that also provided money management services, primarily to individuals. In the early 1980s, the company developed a "value approach" to investing that is very systematic. The approach is based on the dividend discount model (DDM).

The Bernstein approach stresses a buy-and-hold strategy rather than short-term trading. Their typical holding period for a stock is three years, which is long by Wall Street standards. The foundation of their strategy is a fundamental analysis of over 500 common stocks. The Bernstein analysts use the DDM "by estimating a company's ability to pay dividends in the future (i.e., its underlying earning power), which is then discounted to ascertain its securities' present worth." Before the analysts' estimates are plugged into the DDM, however, an effort is made to identify forecasts that are "vulnerable" to exaggeration. This is accomplished through what is essentially a quality-control process that includes devices that can spot forecasts that are illogical or out of line with historical data.

Once the forecasts are screened, they are used in the DDM to calculate the intrinsic value of each stock. The expected holding period return is then calculated, and the 500 stocks are ranked. According to Bernstein's rule, "the 100 stocks in the top 20 percent of their universe are buy candidates. Those that drop below that level are sell candidates, and if they fall into the bottom 40 percent, they must be sold."

The "Bernstein Formula," according to a recent article," beat the S&P seven out of ten years, or 70 percent of the time, even though a strategy may take three years to play out."

SOURCE: Adapted from Julie Rohrer, "The Bernstein Formula," *Institutional Investor* (November 1989): 86–94.

Equation 14.10 is a widely used DDM. Sometimes it is referred to as the *Gordon model* or the **constant growth model.**

To illustrate, assume that $g = .06$, $k = .16$, and $D_0 = \$2$:

$$V_0 = \frac{\$2(1 + .06)^1}{(1 + .16)^1} + \frac{\$2(1 + .06)^2}{(1 + .16)^2} + \cdots + \frac{\$2(1 + .06)^\infty}{(1 + .16)^\infty} \qquad (14.11)$$

$$= \frac{\$2.12}{.16 - .06} = \$21.20$$

Additional insights concerning a stock's intrinsic value, as indicated by the constant growth model, can be obtained by relating dividends to earnings, and growth to dividend policy and the rate of return the firm earns on its equity capital. If E_t represents earnings per share (EPS) in period t and b is the *earnings retention rate* for the firm,

$$D_0 = E_0(1 - b)$$

For example, assume the firm has a current EPS of \$5 and that the directors decide to retain 60 percent of earnings for reinvestment in the firm. Dividends per share are

$$D_0 = \$5(1 - .6) = \$2$$

Next, assume that the firm's retention rate, b, is constant and that the after-tax rate of *return on equity* capital, ROE, is constant. Under these very restrictive assumptions, it can be shown that the firm's earnings and dividends will grow at a constant rate:

$$g = b \times \text{ROE} = br \tag{14.12}$$

For example, if the firm retains 60 percent of its profits and earns 10 percent after taxes on its equity:

$$g = (.6)(10\%) = 6\%$$

These relationships can be incorporated into the constant growth model:

$$\begin{aligned} V_0 &= \frac{E_0(1 - b)(1 + br)}{(1 + K)^1} + \frac{E_0(1 - b)(1 + br)^2}{(1 + K)^2} \\ &\quad + \cdots + \frac{E_0(1 - b)(1 + br)^\infty}{(1 + K)^\infty} \\ &= \frac{E_0(1 - b)(1 + br)}{K - br} \end{aligned} \tag{14.13}$$

Equation 14.13 indicates that the intrinsic value of the stock depends on the company's earnings, its dividend policy, the profitability of the firm as measured by the return on equity, and the investor's required rate of return.

As an illustration of Equation 14.13, assume $E_0 = \$5$, $b = .6$, $r = .1$, and $K = .16$:

$$V_0 = \frac{\$5(1 - .6)[1 + (.6)(.1)]}{.16 - (.6)(.1)} = \frac{\$2.12}{.1} = \$21.20$$

SENSITIVITY OF THE MODEL TO ESTIMATES Table 14.4 provides five cases that illustrate the sensitivity of the basic DDMs to estimates of K and g. In Cases 1 and 2, an increase in K from 16 percent to 20 percent results in a 20 percent reduction in V_0. Cases 3 and 4 show that increasing the assumed growth rate from a "normal" rate of 6 percent to a "rapid" rate of 12 percent increases V_0 from \$21.20 to \$56.00, or 164 percent. Finally, Case 5 considers

TABLE 14.4 • Illustration of the Basic Dividend Discount Model's Sensitivity to *K* and *g*

Case 1 = no growth	Case 2 = no growth	Case 3 = normal growth	Case 4 = rapid growth	Case 5 = declining growth
$D_0 = \$2$	$D_0 = \$2$	$D_0 = \$2$	$D_0 = \$2$	$D_0 = \$2$
$K = 16\%$	$K = 20\%$	$K = 16\%$	$K = 16\%$	$K = 16\%$
$g = 0$	$g = 0$	$g = 6\%$	$g = 12\%$	$g = -6\%$
$V_0 = \frac{D}{K}$	$V_0 = \frac{D}{K}$	$V_0 = \frac{D_1}{K - g}$	$V_0 = \frac{D_1}{K - g}$	$V_0 = \frac{D_1}{K - g}$
$V_0 = \frac{\$2}{.16} = \$12.50$	$V_0 = \frac{\$2}{.20} = \$10.00$	$V_0 = \frac{\$2(1 + .06)}{.16 - .06} = \$21.20$	$V_0 = \frac{\$2(1 + .12)}{.16 - .12} = \$56.00$	$V_0 = \frac{\$2(1 - .06)}{.16 - (-.06)} = \$8.55$

the impact of a negative or declining growth rate. Using a negative 6 percent growth rate, V_0 is \$8.55 in Case 5, compared to $V_0 = \$21.20$ in Case 3 where a positive 6 percent growth rate is assumed. This change in g causes a decline in V_0 of 60 percent. As this example demonstrates, an analyst should be extremely careful in estimating the variables used in the DDM.

FINITE HOLDING PERIOD The basic DDMs can be modified to reflect a specific investment horizon. For example, assume that the investment horizon is one year:

$$V_0 = \frac{D_0(1 + g)}{(1 + K)} + \frac{P_1}{(1 + K)} \tag{14.14}$$

In this case, the analyst must estimate the dividend for the next year and the likely price of the stock at the end of one year, P_1. A two-year horizon model would be

$$V_0 = \frac{D_0(1 + g)}{(1 + K)} + \frac{D_0(1 + g)^2}{(1 + K)^2} + \frac{P_2}{(1 + K)^2} \tag{14.15}$$

In this case, the analyst assumes that dividends will increase by rate g for the next two years. The appropriate model for P_2 is either Equation 14.8 or 14.10, depending on the assumed dividend growth rate starting in year 3.

• H-Model

One of the obvious problems with the basic DDMs is the restrictive assumptions that the models require, such as a constant growth rate, constant required rate of return, and that $g < K$. Removing these restrictive assumptions, and thereby providing a more flexible model, results in more complex DDMs. Moreover, there is evidence that more complex DDMs improve the accuracy of the forecasts and therefore their usefulness in selecting stocks.

Fuller and Hsia have developed a DDM model that allows for multiple growth rates over specified periods of time.[6] The model, which is called the **H-model,** allows for three growth phases: rapid growth, transition growth, and steady-state growth. These three growth phases are illustrated in Figure 14.1. This model also allows the growth rate for phase one, g_1, to be greater than the required rate of return (K). The growth rate for phase three, g_2, however, must be less than K. The H-model is

$$V_0 = \frac{D_0}{K - g_2}\left[(1 + g_2) + \frac{A + B}{2}(g_1 - g_2)\right] \tag{14.16}$$

[6] Russell J. Fuller and Chi-Cheng Hsia, "A Simplified Common Stock Valuation Model," *Financial Analysts Journal* (September-October 1984): 49–56.

FIGURE 14.1
H-Model Growth Rates

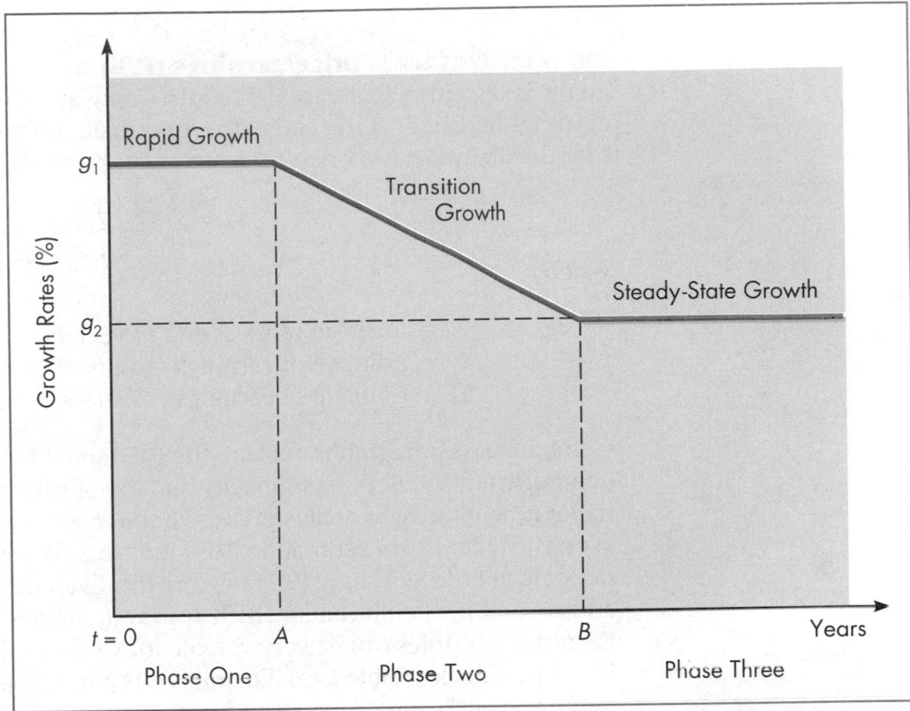

where A is the number of years to the beginning of phase two and B is the number of years until the beginning of phase three (see Figure 14.1). The term $(A + B)/2$ is therefore the midpoint or halfway (H) point of phase two. An illustration of the H-model appears in Table 14.5.

TABLE 14.5 • Illustration of the H-Model

Assumptions: $D_0 = \$2$ $\quad g_2 = 10\%$
$K = 16\%$ $\quad A = 4$ years
$g_1 = 20\%$ $\quad B = 9$ years

Phase two assumes that the growth rate declines in a linear fashion from 20% to 10% over a 5-year period or by 2% per year. In other words, the growth rate for years 1–4 = 20%, year 5 = 18%, year 6 = 16%, year 7 = 14%, year 8 = 12%, and years 9–∞ = 10%.

H-model calculations:

$$V_0 = \frac{\$2}{.16 - .10}\left[(1 + .1) + \frac{4 + 9}{2}(.2 - .1)\right] = \$33.33(1.75) = \$58.33$$

PRICE/EARNINGS MODEL

Many analysts use a **price/earnings (P/E) model** as part of a fundamental analysis. Essentially, the model requires only an estimate of the P/E ratio and earnings per share at the end of the investment horizon. For example, assume that the analyst has a one-year investment horizon. The model would be

$$V_1 = (M_1)(E_1) \tag{14.17}$$

where

V_1 = intrinsic value at end of year 1
M_1 = estimate of earnings multiplier or P/E ratio at end of year 1
E_1 = estimate of earnings per share at end of year 1

As the next paragraphs explain, the P/E model is closely related to the dividend discount models. Its simplicity and use of earnings rather than dividends make it popular with analysts. Despite the model's apparent simplicity, however, the difficulty of estimating P/E ratios should not be underestimated. The major factors determining P/E ratios are the dividend payout, earnings growth, and earnings volatility, all of which appear in models for estimating P/E ratios. Earnings multiples can be very volatile for stocks in general and especially for individual stocks. Table 14.6 illustrates this point by providing a sample of P/E ratios and betas for a number of companies and the S&P 500 over the period 1980–1990. Estimating a future P/E ratio by extrapolating from historical ratios does not appear to be advisable.

• Basic Models

This section develops some of the more popular models used to estimate a future P/E ratio. Most of these models define the P/E ratio using the same variables as in the DDMs.

ZERO GROWTH MODEL A P/E ratio for a company that distributes all earnings as dividends and has no earnings growth is

$$M = \frac{1}{K} \tag{14.18}$$

For example, assume that the investor's required rate of return is 16 percent, indicating a P/E ratio of 6.25. If K is constant, then the multiplier will also be a constant.

If the company retains earnings by reducing dividends, however, so that $b > 0$, and these retained earnings do not lead to earnings growth, the multiplier should decline. If the dividend payout rate is defined as D/E, and $D/E < 1$, the multiplier becomes

$$M = \frac{D/E}{K} \tag{14.19}$$

TABLE 14.6 • Sample of P/E Ratios for Individual Common Stocks and the S&P 500

Year	American Express	American Home Products	Bank-America	Boston Edison	Chrysler	Liz Claiborne	TECO Energy	Texaco	S&P 500
1980	6.4	9.6	5.7	5.7	d	NMF	5.4	4.6	8.1
1981	8.0	10.3	8.2	5.2	d	NMF	6.4	4.1	8.2
1982	8.0	10.9	7.3	7.1	d	NMF	7.9	5.5	9.7
1983	15.5	11.8	9.8	7.6	5.8	13.1	7.4	7.2	11.1
1984	11.3	12.1	10.5	5.9	2.4	10.0	7.1	8.9	9.6
1985	12.5	12.7	d	7.8	2.6	14.2	8.9	7.7	12.9
1986	13.3	15.7	d	9.8	4.0	19.7	12.8	12.7	15.8
1987	37.9	14.5	d	11.4	5.8	21.2	11.6	22.2	14.1
1988	11.0	12.2	4.7	8.5	4.8	12.9	10.9	11.3	11.7
1989	12.5	13.5	7.1	9.3	17.9	11.9	10.7	12.2	15.5
1990	12.5	13.6	6.7	11.7	NMF	11.3	11.9	11.0	15.4
Beta	1.35	1.00	1.10	0.70	1.35	1.55	0.60	0.70	1.00

SOURCE: *Value Line Investment Survey,* Value Line Publishing, Inc., various issues; Standard & Poor's *Analyst's Handbook* (1990); and *Monthly Supplement* (April 1991); used by permission.

NOTE: d = negative EPS; NMF = not meaningful figure because EPS is close to zero.

For example, if $K = 16$ percent and $D/E = .5$, then $M = .5/.16 = 3.125$. If the company distributes all earnings as dividends, M would be 6.25. Earnings should be retained only if they can be used to produce earnings growth.

The **zero growth P/E model** and the DDM arrive at identical valuation estimates as shown below. Assume $K = .16$, $E = \$4$, and all earnings are distributed as dividends. Both models find the same value:

$$\text{DDM:} \quad V_0 = D/K = \$4/.16 = \$25$$
$$\text{P/E model:} \quad V_0 = ME = (1/K)E = (1/.16)(\$4) = \$25$$

Suppose the company retains 50 percent of earnings with zero earnings growth:

$$\text{DDM:} \quad V_0 = \frac{E(1 - b)}{K} = \frac{\$4(1 - .5)}{.16} = \$12.50$$
$$\text{P/E model:} \quad V_0 = [(D/E)/K]E = (.5/.16)\$4 = \$12.50$$

CONSTANT GROWTH MODEL If the company retains earnings that result in earnings growth, the multiplier can be calculated as

$$M = \frac{(D/E)(1 + g)}{K - g} \tag{14.20}$$

For example, assume $g = 10$ percent and $K = 16$ percent and the firm retains 50 percent of the earnings. The multiplier would be

$$M = \frac{(.5)(1 + .1)}{.16 - .1} = 9.17$$

The similarity of the constant growth DDM and the **constant growth P/E model** can be shown using the same example of $E = \$4$, $K = .16$, $D/E = .5$, and $g = .1$:

$$\text{DDM:} \quad V_0 = \frac{E(1 - b)(1 + g)}{K - g} = \frac{\$4(1 - .5)(1 + .1)}{.16 - .1} = \$36.67$$

$$\text{P/E model:} \quad V_0 = \left[\frac{(D/E)(1 + g)}{K - g}\right]E = \left[\frac{(.5)(1 + .1)}{.16 - .1}\right]\$4 = \$36.67$$

• Whitbeck-Kisor Model

One of the first and best-known attempts at developing an econometric model of theoretical P/E ratios was made by Whitbeck and Kisor.[7] This study used a sample of 135 NYSE stocks to estimate the following regression model:

[7] V.S. Whitbeck and M. Kisor, "A New Tool in Investment Decision-Making," *Financial Analysts Journal* (May-June 1963): 55–62.

RESEARCH BOX

An Active Common Stock Strategy: Low P/E Stocks

A traditional active strategy for common stocks is to buy stocks that have a low price relative to their earnings per share. The P/E ratio is typically calculated by dividing the current stock price by the most recent four-quarters EPS. This strategy assumes that stocks with low P/E ratios are undervalued and may provide high returns when their prices increase.

The P/E strategy has been the subject of numerous empirical research studies published in financial journals. A number of studies in the late 1970s and early 1980s found that the risk-adjusted rates of return of "low" P/E stocks exceeded those of "high" P/E stocks. More recent studies, however, found the opposite—"low" P/E stocks earned lower risk-adjusted returns.

A 1989 study by Johnson, Fiore, and Zuber used monthly data on 1,168 NYSE-traded stocks for the period January 1979 to January 1985 to test the strategy. The P/E ratio for each of the 1,168 stocks was calculated in January, and the stocks were ranked by their ratios. Based on the rankings, the 20 percent of the stocks with the lowest P/Es were placed in a portfolio. The 20 percent of the stocks with the next lowest P/Es were used to form a second portfolio. Using this procedure, five equal-size portfolios of approximately 234 stocks were created. The return and risk of each portfolio were then calculated for the year. The same procedure was then followed for each successive year.

Based on an analysis of the risk-return performance, the authors state: "For the period from 1979 through 1984, we conclude that there were some moderate excess rates of return earned by selecting stocks based on their P/E ratios but that these excess rates were *not* obtained from investing in low P/E stocks."

SOURCE: R. Stafford Johnson, Lyle C. Fiore, and Richard Zuber, "The Investment Performance of Common Stocks in Relation to Their Earnings Ratios: An Update of the Basu Study," *Financial Review* (August 1989): 499–505.

$$(\mathrm{P/E})_j = \hat{a}_0 + \hat{a}_1 g_j + \hat{a}_2 (D/E)_j + \hat{a}_3 \sigma_j + e_j \qquad \mathbf{(14.21)}$$

where

$(\mathrm{P/E})_j$ = price-earnings ratio for firm j
$\hat{a}_0 - \hat{a}_3$ = regression constants
g_j = historical earnings growth for firm j
$(D/E)_j$ = historical dividend payout ratio for firm j
σ_j = standard deviation of the past earnings growth rate around the earnings trend line
e_j = random disturbance term

The results of their regression:

$$\mathrm{P/E} = 8.2 + 1.5g + 6.7(D/E) - .2\sigma \qquad \mathbf{(14.22)}$$

Although the **Whitbeck-Kisor model** was reasonably accurate in estimating the theoretical P/E ratios for stocks in the early 1960s, its validity for the

1990s is questionable. The regression equation would need to be reestimated, using more recent data and possibly new or different independent variables. The model does illustrate, however, that econometric models of P/E ratios may provide valuable insights into the analysis of common stocks.

RECENT DEVELOPMENTS IN COMMON STOCK VALUATION MODELS

The preceding discussion of the basic DDM and P/E models observed that the DDMs and the P/E models utilize the same estimates. The key variables are dividend policy, growth prospects, the profitability of the firm, and the investor's required rate of return.

In reality, however, the relationships among these key variables and their role in determining value are complex. A number of recently published articles provide some practical guidelines that can be used to incorporate these key variables and their relationships into the basic models.

Two articles by Merrett and Newbould address the relationship between dividend policy, growth, and the valuation models.[8] Their analysis suggests a procedure that can be used to estimate the impact of dividend policy and the firm's profitability on future earnings. The major insight provided by their model involves replacing the traditional estimate of earnings with an estimate of *corrected earnings per share* (*CEPS*). Their model is called the **CEPS model,** and the name is protected by trademark registration. The DDM form of their model is

$$V_0 = \frac{\text{CEPS}(1 + g_{\text{CEPS}})}{K - g_{\text{CEPS}}} \tag{14.23}$$

Notice that the traditional measure of dividends is replaced by CEPS and that g is replaced by a growth estimate based on CEPS.

This model recognizes the fact that corporations can achieve higher EPS simply by retaining earnings. Part of this apparent growth is "illusory," however, if the company reinvests the retained earnings at a rate of return equal to or below the stockholders' required rate of return. Part I in Table 14.7 is adopted from the 1982 Merrett and Newbould article and demonstrates this illusory growth. Notice that the EPS, the DPS, and the stock's value are growing at 9 percent per year because the company is retaining 50 percent of its earnings and reinvesting the earnings at the stockholders' 18 percent required rate of return. If the company elected to distribute all earnings, the growth rate would be zero, but the shareholders would be just as well off. Notice that by using the constant growth DDM, the stock's value increases each year.

---

[8] A.J. Merrett and Gerald D. Newbould, "CEPS: The Illusion of Corporate Growth," *Journal of Portfolio Management* (Fall 1982): 5–10; and "Integrating Financial Performance and Stock Valuation," *Journal of Portfolio Management* (Fall 1983): 27–32.

TABLE 14.7 • Illustration of the CEPS Model

I. Illusory Growth

Assumptions: Annual EPS growth of 9% resulting from retaining 50% of earnings. The firm's return on equity capital and the stockholders' required rate of return are both 18%.

	Year				
	1	*2*	*3*	*4*	*5*
EPS	$ 2.00	$ 2.18	$ 2.38	$ 2.59	$ 2.82
DPS	1.00	1.09	1.19	1.29	1.41
Retention	1.00	1.09	1.19	1.30	1.41
Stock value[a]	12.11	13.22	14.33	15.67	17.08

II. CEPS Model

	Year				
	1	*2*	*3*	*4*	*5*
Reported EPS	$ 2.00	$ 2.18	$ 2.38	$ 2.59	$ 2.82
Retention	1.00	1.09	1.19	1.30	1.41
Returns on retention[b]	—	.18	.38	.59	.82
CEPS[c]	2.00	2.00	2.00	2.00	2.00
CDPS	1.00	1.00	1.00	1.00	1.00
Stock value[d]	11.11	11.11	11.11	11.11	11.11

[a] Calculated using the constant growth DDM (Equation 14.10).

[b] Calculated as the cumulative retentions per share times the shareholders' required rate of return of 18%. For year 2, the returns on retentions are $1(.18) = $.18; for year 3, they are ($1 + $1.09)(.18) = .38, and so on.

[c] Calculated as reported EPS minus returns on retention.

[d] Calculated using Equation 14.23 where $g_{CEPS} = 0$.

Part II of Table 14.7 calculates CEPS by removing the portion of earnings due to the reinvestment of earnings at a rate of return of 18 percent. Notice that the annual returns on the retentions must consider the fact that returns on retained earnings are cumulative. The CEPS and corrected DPS (CDPS) are constant, indicating $g_{CEPS} = 0$, and consequently, the stock's intrinsic value is constant. In effect, the company has no economic growth in earnings.

In summary, the CEPS for a company will always be less than reported EPS if the company retains part of its earnings. It is also possible that CEPS will increase, representing growth that occurs because the company is able to reinvest earnings at a rate greater than the stockholders' required rate of return. Essentially, the analyst should calculate the marginal after-tax rate of return on additions to retained earnings and compare this rate to the stockholders' required rate of return. If the comparison is favorable, then the company can experience real economic growth by retaining earnings and reinvesting in the company at a favorable rate.

INVESTMENT DECISION

After the traditional fundamental analysis is completed, the investor must finally make a decision about the common stock under consideration. This section presents a procedure that can be used to determine what recommendation should be made relative to other stocks under consideration or to stocks in general.

• Estimate of Expected and Required Holding Period Returns

The expected HPR over a one-year holding period can be calculated as

$$E(\text{HPR}_1) = \frac{V_1 - P_0 + D_1}{P_0} \tag{14.24}$$

For example, assume that the fundamental analysis indicates that the stock should be selling for \$22 within one year, V_1, and is currently selling for \$20. Dividends for the next year are estimated to be \$3.

$$E(\text{HPR}_1) = \frac{\$22 - \$20 + \$3}{\$20} = 25\%$$

This estimate indicates that the stock will provide a 25 percent return over the next year. Is this return adequate to justify a long position? The $E(\text{HPR})$ can be compared to the return suggested by the CAPM:

$$E(R_j) = R_f + \beta_j[E(R_M) - R_f] \tag{14.25}$$

Based on the economic analysis, assume that the expected market return for the next year, $E(R_M)$, is 15 percent and the yield to maturity on one-year Treasury bills is currently 9 percent. If the beta for the stock is 1.3, the CAPM suggests the stock should provide a return of

$$E(R_j) = 9\% + 1.3(15\% - 9\%) = 16.8\%$$

The analyst can now compare $E(\text{HPR})$ and $E(R_j)$ and conclude that the stock appears to be undervalued. The present price of \$20 suggests that the stock may appreciate over the next year and provide an HPR of 25 percent. Stocks

FIGURE 14.2
The Security Market Line and an Analyst's Estimate of Expected HPR

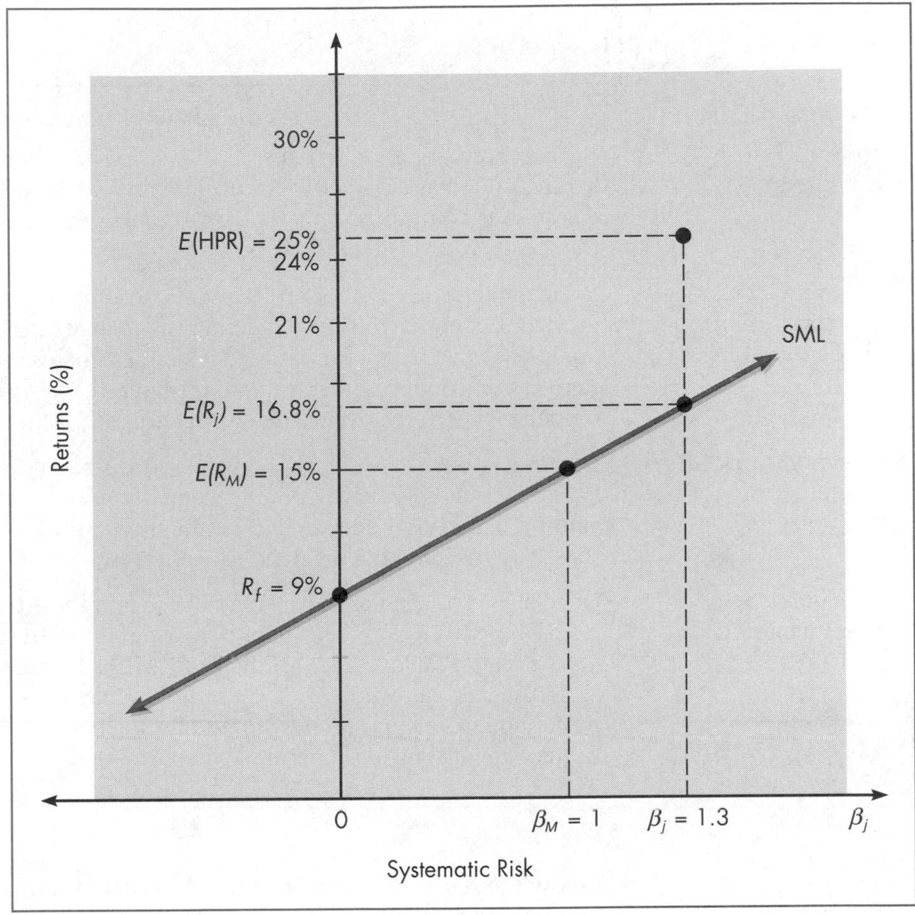

with the same degree of systematic risk are expected to provide a return of only 16.8 percent. Figure 14.2 illustrates this relationship.

Stocks that plot above the security market line (SML) offer higher returns than their systematic risk suggests. Thus, they are *undervalued,* and a long position is appropriate. Stocks that plot below the SML are *overvalued,* and a short position may be justified. Stocks that plot on the SML are correctly valued.

A variation of this approach, called the **market plane approach,** was developed by Wells Fargo Bank. This approach requires that E(HPR) be available for a number of stocks. These expected returns are then plotted against the betas for each stock. A regression or best-fit line is then estimated using these points. Stocks that plot above the regression line offer high expected returns relative to their betas and may therefore be undervalued. Stocks plotting

• CONCEPT APPLICATIONS

Investment Concept	Concept Application
Preferred stock valuation	Because traditional preferred stock has a constant dividend and infinite life, it can be valued as a perpetuity. Since the annual dividend is specified, the variables that must be estimated are the investor's required rate of return and the credit worthiness of the issue.
Common stock valuation using dividend models	Basic models include the zero growth, constant growth, and three-phase growth. Depending on the dividend growth characteristics of the stock, the analyst selects the appropriate model and estimates the needed variables. Remember, common stock valuation is an art! The values produced by the model are very sensitive to the estimates used for the key variables.
Common stock valuation using P/E models	Common stocks may be valued using models based on dividends or P/E ratios. P/E models are popular with many practitioners. But, with properly defined variables, the P/E models arrive at valuation estimates that are identical to those produced by the dividend models.
Common stock investment decision	Once a common stock has been analyzed and the *E*(HPR) has been calculated, the *E*(HPR) should be compared to the return suggested by the SML. Stocks plotting above the SML have an *E*(HPR) greater than the equilibrium return suggested by the SML. These stocks may be undervalued, and a long position may be appropriate. Stocks plotting below the SMLs may be overvalued, and a short position may be appropriate.

below the regression line offer small expected returns relative to their systematic risk and may be overvalued. The market plane approach eliminates the need to estimate the expected return for the market.[9]

SUMMARY

This chapter has presented a traditional fundamental analysis approach to preferred and common stock valuations. The key variable in valuation is the estimate of future earnings and dividends. Dividend discount models (DDMs) and price/earnings (P/E) models are the traditional common stock valuation models. They are quite similar in terms of the variables they use.

[9] For more details, see Robert Ferguson and Richard Lynn, "A Security Market Plane Approach to Stock Selection," *Financial Analysts Journal* (September-October 1984): 75–80; and James L. Farrell, Jr., "The Dividend Discount Model: A Primer," *Financial Analysts Journal* (November-December 1985): 16–25.

Despite the availability of numerous models, common stock valuation is essentially an art, not a science. The success of the valuation depends on the analyst's ability to make accurate forecasts and select an appropriate model.

The final investment decision should be made by comparing the expected HPR to the expected return on other stocks with the same degree of risk. Through this procedure, the investor hopes to identify over- and undervalued stocks.

• KEY TERMS

CEPS model
Constant growth DDM
Constant growth P/E model
Dividend discount model (DDM)
Dividend yield
H-model
Intrinsic value
Market plane approach
Price/earnings (P/E) model
Whitbeck-Kisor model
Zero growth DDM
Zero growth P/E model

• QUESTIONS

1. Explain why preferred stocks are generally not attractive to individuals pursuing a passive investment strategy.
2. Explain why preferred stocks may be attractive to individuals pursuing an active strategy.
3. Discuss the causes of systematic and unsystematic risk for preferred stock.
4. Explain how fundamental analysts use an estimate of a stock's intrinsic value to make an investment recommendation.
5. Discuss the pros and cons of viewing common stock valuation as an art rather than a scientific procedure.
6. Compare and contrast the constant growth dividend discount model with the equivalent P/E model. Discuss the advantages and disadvantages of both models.
7. Why do many analysts use the P/E approach rather than DDM in valuing common stock?
8. Explain the concept of corrected earnings per share (CEPS). How does this approach measure earnings growth compared to the growth rate in reported earnings?
9. In your opinion, is it appropriate to assume that the required rate of return on a particular stock will be constant over time? What factors may cause the required rate of return to change? How would a change in the required rate of return influence the intrinsic value of a particular stock?
10. Indicate how the CAPM and SML can be used to make an investment recommendation concerning a particular stock.

• KEY TO THE INVESTMENT ANALYSIS SOFTWARE

Calculation	Appendix A-1 Page Reference	Access Procedure
Holding period return	A-8	BEGIN, STATISTICAL, HPR, ONE or MANY
Value of zero growth stock	A-11	BEGIN, VALUATION, STOCKS, NONE
Value of constant growth stock	A-11	BEGIN, VALUATION, STOCKS, CONSTANT
Stock value using the H-model	A-11	BEGIN, VALUATION, STOCKS, THREE
Value of stock using CEPS	A-11	BEGIN, VALUATION, STOCKS, EPSCORRECT
Security market line (SML) and required rate of return	A-12	BEGIN, CAPITAL, CAPM

• PROBLEMS

1. Consider the following data on a preferred stock:

Face value	$100
Price on January 1, 1990	$80
Price on January 1, 1991	$70
Dividend rate	7%

a. Calculate the dividend yield on January 1, 1990, and on January 1, 1991.

b. Calculate the holding period return for 1990.

2. Assume that a preferred stock is currently priced to provide a 12 percent required rate of return and pays a $6 dividend.

a. Calculate the intrinsic value of the stock.

b. Assume that the required rate of return declines to 11 percent. Calculate the new intrinsic value for the stock.

c. Calculate the holding period return, assuming that you purchased the preferred stock when it was priced to provide a 12 percent required rate of return and sold when the required rate of return reached 11 percent. Also assume that you held the stock long enough to receive an annual dividend.

3. Assume that a preferred stock is currently priced to provide a yield of 10 percent and a bond provides an 11 percent yield.

a. Calculate the after-tax yields for the preferred stock and bond for a corporate investor with a marginal tax rate of 34 percent.
b. Calculate the after-tax yields for the preferred stock and bond for an individual investor with a marginal tax rate of 28 percent.
c. Ignoring risk considerations, indicate which of the two securities is more desirable for corporate and individual investors pursuing a passive investment strategy.

4. According to the *Wall Street Journal*, on June 4, 1991, the $5 cumulative preferred stock of General Motors was priced at $60\frac{5}{8}$. Calculate the dividend yield. The 52-week high and low were 61 and 55, respectively. Calculate the dividend yield for the high and the low price.

5. Consider the following information on a share of common stock:

Current dividend per share	$2.50
Investor's required rate of return	16%

a. Calculate the intrinsic value of the stock, assuming that the dividend will remain at $2.50 indefinitely.
b. Calculate the intrinsic value, assuming that the dividend will increase by 8 percent per year indefinitely.
c. Calculate the intrinsic value, assuming that the dividend will increase at a rate of 5 percent per year for the next three years and then will remain at the third year level indefinitely.

6. A fundamental analysis of DSK, Inc., produced the following:

Stock's current price	$18.00
Estimate of stock's price in one year	$20.00
Estimate of dividends for next year	$2.50
Present yield on one-year Treasury bill	8.62%
Beta	1.50
Estimate of HPR on S&P 500 for next year	14.00%

a. Calculate the stock's expected one-year HPR.
b. Use the CAPM to calculate the required rate of return for the stock.
c. Does the stock appear to be priced to offer a risk-adjusted excess return for next year? Explain.
d. Based on this analysis, would you recommend a long, short, or no position in the stock?

7. Suppose the DPS for a particular stock increased from $1.00 in 1980 to $2.25 in 1990. The required rate of return on the stock is 15 percent. Calculate the intrinsic value of the stock on January 1, 1991, assuming that dividends will continue to grow at the same rate as they did over the period 1980–1990.

8. PIL, Inc., distributes 40 percent of earnings to stockholders in the form of cash dividends. Based on a fundamental analysis, you estimate next year's earnings at $3.29 and expect earnings to increase by 8 percent per year.

Given a required rate of return of 15 percent, calculate the intrinsic value of the stock.

9. EAM, Inc., retains 70 percent of its earnings to finance the rapid sales growth it has been experiencing. An analysis of the company indicates that, on average, it earns a 14 percent rate of return on incremental equity capital. Based on the business and financial risk of the company, you conclude that a required rate of return on the common stock is 16 percent.
   a. Calculate the likely reported growth rate in earnings and dividends.
   b. If current earnings are $3.86 per share, use your answer to part (a) to calculate the stock's value.
   c. Suppose the company changes its dividend policy, so that 40 percent of earnings are retained. Calculate the stock's value.
   d. What dividend policy would you recommend to maximize the value of the stock?

10. Kevin O'Hare, a local stockbroker, indicates that Holiday, Inc., is currently undervalued and recommends that you buy 100 shares of the stock. His opinion is based on a projected 20 percent increase in EPS for next year, combined with an optimistic market forecast that indicates an increase of 5 percent in the P/E ratio for stocks in general.
    a. Assume that the stock of Holiday, Inc., is currently priced at $8\frac{1}{4}$ with EPS of $1.37. Calculate the P/E ratio.
    b. Suppose that the EPS and the P/E ratio increase at the rates suggested by Kevin. Calculate the value of the stock one year from now.
    c. Assuming the company will not pay any cash dividends, calculate the expected HPR based on your answer to part (b).
    d. If you think a required rate of return of 18 percent is appropriate, should you follow Kevin's recommendation?

11. A company you are analyzing currently has EPS of $2.29 and distributes 60 percent of earnings in the form of cash dividends to shareholders. Assume that the required rate of return is 14 percent and that this is also the rate the firm earns on its equity capital.
    a. Calculate an appropriate theoretical multiplier for this stock.
    b. If the stock is currently selling for $19\frac{1}{2}$ per share, would you recommend a long position? Would you recommend a short position?
    c. Assume a short position is taken at the current price. Calculate the expected HPR if the stock is purchased at the end of the year to cover the short position. Base your calculations on the assumption that the P/E ratio will decline to its theoretical value by the end of the year. Also remember that dividends represent a cash *outflow* to a short seller. Does this analysis indicate that a short position is desirable?

12. Hanna, Inc., currently has EPS of $3.69. An analysis indicates that it earns approximately 15 percent on equity capital. Its beta and current market

conditions indicate that a 14 percent required rate of return on the stock is appropriate.

a. Calculate the theoretical multiplier for the company, assuming it distributes all earnings to stockholders.

b. Calculate the theoretical multiplier, assuming the company distributes 60 percent of its earnings to stockholders.

c. Suppose Hanna, Inc., distributes 60 percent of its earnings and uses the retained profits to acquire a small company that produces no additional earnings for Hanna, Inc. Calculate its theoretical multiplier.

13. Growth, Inc., is currently being recommended by several investment advisory services. The stock is priced at $118 per share with current dividends of $3 per share. Analysts are optimistic about the stock's prospects because earnings are expected to grow at 25 percent per year for the next five years. The growth rate will decline, however, from 25 percent to 10 percent over a three-year transition period. Thus, the growth rate will be 25 percent for years 1–5 and 10 percent starting in year 9. Years 6–8 represent the transition period for the growth rate. Calculate the value of the stock using the H-model and indicate whether a long position is appropriate.

14. Suppose Illusory, Inc., has current earnings of $3 per share and distributes 40 percent of its earnings as dividends. The appropriate required rate of return on the stock is 18 percent. Assume the firm reinvests retained profits at a rate of return of 18 percent.

a. Calculate the intrinsic value of the stock using the constant growth DDM.

b. Calculate the growth rate based on corrected earnings per share (CEPS).

c. Calculate the intrinsic value of the stock using the CEPS model.

d. Suppose the company is able to reinvest retained profits at a rate of return of 20 percent but maintains the same dividend policy. Calculate the impact this will have on CEPS and the CEPS growth rate. Calculate the intrinsic value of the stock using the CEPS model.

• REFERENCES

Bauman, W. Scott, and Richard Dowen. "Growth Projections and Common Stock Returns." *Financial Analysts Journal* (July-August 1988): 79–80.

Benesh, Gary A., and Pamela P. Peterson. "On the Relationship between Earnings, Changes, Analysts' Forecast and Stock Price Fluctuation." *Financial Analysts Journal* (November-December 1986): 29–39.

Clemente, Holly A. "What Wall Street Sees When It Looks at Your P/E Ratio." *Financial Executive* (May-June 1990): 40–44.

Elayan, Fayez A., Brian A. Maris, and Jo-Mae B. Maris. "Common Stock Response to False Signals from CreditWatch Placement." *Quarterly Journal of Business and Economics* (Summer 1990): 16–35.

Estep, Preston W. "A New Method for Valuing Common Stocks." *Financial Analysts Journal* (November-December 1985): 26–33.

Fielitz, Bruce D., and Frederick L. Muller. "A Simplified Approach to Common Stock Valuation." *Financial Analysts Journal* (November-December 1985): 35–41.

Fogler, H. Russell. "Common Stock Management in the 1990s." *Journal of Portfolio Management* (Winter 1990): 26–35.

Fuller, Russel J., and G. Wenchi Wong. "Traditional versus Theoretical Risk Measures." *Financial Analysts Journal* (March-April 1988): 52–57, 67.

Gentry, James A., Paul Newbold, and David T. Whitford. "Predicting Bankruptcy: If Cash Flow's Not the Bottom Line, What Is?" *Financial Analysts Journal* (September-October 1985): 47–56.

Good, Walter R. "Bias in Stock Market Valuation." *Financial Analysts Journal* (September-October 1989): 6–7.

Harris, Robert S. "Using Analysts' Growth Forecasts to Estimate Shareholder Required Rates of Return." *Financial Management* (Spring 1986): 58–67.

Jahnke, Gregg, Stephen J. Klaffke, and Henry R. Oppenheimer. "Price-Earnings Ratios and Security Performance." *Journal of Portfolio Management* (Fall 1987): 39–46.

Johnson, Lewis D. "Dividends and Share Value: Graham and Dodd Revisited, Again." *Financial Analysts Journal* (September-October 1985): 79–80.

———. "Growth Prospects and Share Prices: A Systematic View." *Journal of Portfolio Management* (Winter 1987): 58–60.

Jones, Charles P., and Jack W. Wilson. "Stocks, Bonds, Paper, and Inflation: 1870–1985." *Journal of Portfolio Management* (Fall 1987): 20–24.

Markese, John. "How P/E Ratios Can Lead You to the Best Buys." *Money*, March 1990, pp. 159–60.

Nagorniak, John J. "Thoughts on Using Dividend Discount Models." *Financial Analysts Journal* (November-December 1985): 13–15.

Oppenheimer, Henry R. "Ben Graham's Net Current Asset Values: A Performance Update." *Financial Analysts Journal* (November-December 1986): 40–47.

Palmer, Jay. "Low Debt, Low P/E." *Barron's*, November 6, 1989, p. 18.

Pari, Robert, Steven Carvell, and Timothy Sullivan. "Analyst Forecasts and Price/Earnings Ratios." *Financial Analysts Journal* (March-April 1989): 60–62.

Rappaport, Alfred. "The Affordable Dividend Approach to Equity Valuation." *Financial Analysts Journal* (July-August 1986): 52–58.

Rie, Daniel. "How Trustworthy Is Your Valuation Model?" *Financial Analysts Journal* (November-December 1985): 42–48.

Rozeff, Michael S. "The Three-Phase Dividend Discount Model and the ROPE Model." *Journal of Portfolio Management* (Winter 1990): 36–42.

Sorensen, Eric H., and David A. Williamson. "Some Evidence on the Value of Dividend Discount Models." *Financial Analysts Journal* (November-December 1985): 60–69.

Timme, Stephen G., and Peter C. Eisemann. "On the Use of Consensus Forecast of Growth in the Constant Growth Model: The Case of Electric Utilities." *Financial Management* (Winter 1989): 23–35.

PART VI

Analysis of Alternative Investments

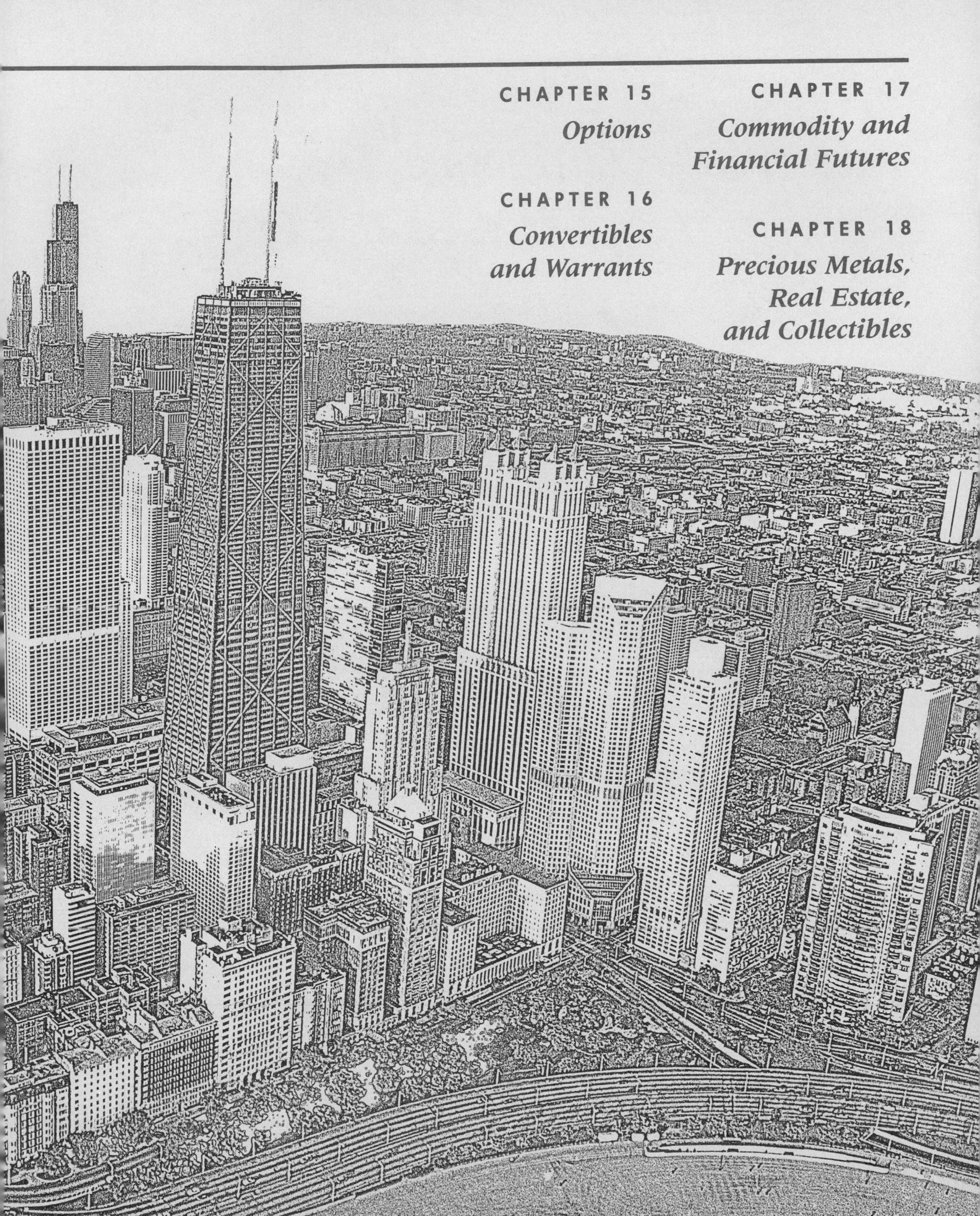

CHAPTER 15
Options

CHAPTER 16
Convertibles and Warrants

CHAPTER 17
Commodity and Financial Futures

CHAPTER 18
Precious Metals, Real Estate, and Collectibles

CHAPTER 15

Options

The knowledge-level objectives of this chapter should enable the student to:

- Discuss the characteristics of the different types of options including equity, index, interest rate, currency, and commodity options.
- Compare and contrast the risk-return characteristics of long versus short positions in options.
- Describe how put and call options can be used to hedge a portfolio.
- Identify the key variables and describe their influence on option values.
- Discuss hedging and speculative strategies using options.

INTRODUCTION

This chapter deals with options, which are also called **derivative securities** because their value depends on an underlying asset or security such as common stock. An **option** is a legal contract that gives the holder the right to buy or sell a specified amount of the underlying asset at a fixed price within a specified period of time. The underlying asset may be an individual common stock, stock index, U.S. government debt, commodity, or foreign currency. Due to the large number of underlying assets that options can be issued against, the number of traded options is very large. For example, *Value Line* typically monitors over 10,000 options.

Traditionally, options were traded in the OTC market through individual brokerage firms. Because of this somewhat informal market structure, options were not widely traded. In 1973, however, the *Chicago Board Options Exchange* (*CBOE*) was established. As a result, investor interest increased dramatically because the more formal market structure provided increased liquidity. In addition to the CBOE, options are now traded on the NYSE, AMEX, and Philadelphia (PHLX) and Pacific (PSE) exchanges and on a number of foreign exchanges.

In addition to the formalization of the markets, the volatility of the financial and commodity markets during the 1970s and 1980s increased investor interest in options. Volatile markets make options more attractive because they can be used to reduce the volatility of a portfolio or to speculate on future price movements of the underlying asset. These uses of options are discussed in detail in the chapter. Trading volume in options declined significantly, however, immediately after the stock market collapse on October 19, 1987.

PUT AND CALL EQUITY OPTIONS

Equity options, where the underlying asset is a specific common stock, are very actively traded options. The exchanges where these options are traded are listed in Table 15.1 along with the other five types of options. (The other types of options are discussed later in this chapter.)

Development of the **Options Clearing Corporations** (**OCC**) facilitated and improved option trading.[1] The OCC is owned by the stock exchanges and the National Association of Securities Dealers (OTC market) that trade options and is regulated by the Securities and Exchange Commission (SEC). The OCC guarantees the provisions specified in the option contract since it acts as an intermediary between the buyer and writer. The OCC actually issues **standardized options,** so that the buyer relies on the OCC rather than the individual writer to fulfill the obligations of the option. Likewise, the option writer has an obligation to the OCC rather than to any particular buyer. No

[1] Details about the OCC and the options markets are available in a booklet entitled *Characteristics and Risks of Standardized Options*, published by the OCC.

TABLE 15.1 • Types of Options and Trading Exchanges

1. Equity options on individual stocks	NYSE CBOE AMEX PHLX PSE
2. Equity index options	
a. S&P 100	CBOE
b. S&P 500	CBOE
c. NYSE Composite Index	NYSE
d. Major Market Index	AMEX
e. Oil Stock Index	AMEX
f. Institutional Index	AMEX
g. Japan Index	AMEX
h. Value Line Index	PHLX
i. NYSE Beta Index	NYSE
3. Foreign currency options	PHLX
4. Gold/silver index options	PHLX
5. Interest rate options	
a. Short-term rates	CBOE
b. Long-term rates	CBOE
6. Options on futures	
a. Crude oil	New York Mercantile Exchange
b. Heating oil	New York Mercantile Exchange
c. Unleaded gasoline	New York Mercantile Exchange
d. Gold	New York Commodity Exchange
e. Copper	New York Commodity Exchange
f. S&P 500	Chicago Mercantile Exchange
g. Foreign currencies	Chicago Mercantile Exchange
h. Treasury notes and bonds	Chicago Board of Trade
i. Agricultural	Chicago Board of Trade; Coffee, Sugar, Cocoa Exchange; New York Cotton Exchange
j. Mortgage-backed bonds	Chicago Board of Trade
k. Municipal bonds	Chicago Board of Trade
l. Livestock	Chicago Mercantile Exchange

physical certificate is created when options are written; instead, all transactions are simply bookkeeping entries maintained by the OCC. The obligations of the individual writers and buyers are guaranteed to the OCC by *clearing members*, the brokerage firms representing the individuals. The clearing members provide the OCC with the margin required of option traders and also contribute funds to ensure that the OCC can fulfill its obligations.

• Characteristics of Equity Options

Most securities, such as common stocks and bonds, are created or issued by a corporation. Option contracts, however, are created by option writers that can be individuals or institutions, but do not involve the corporation that issued the underlying stock. A **call** contract (or simply a call) grants the holder the right to buy, while a **put** contract (a put) gives the right to sell. For example, an investor who *purchases* a put or call is buying the right to sell or purchase 100 shares of the underlying stock, at a specified price, within a specified period of time. The *seller,* or *writer,* of the put or call has the opposite legal obligation. The writer of the call promises to sell the stock; the writer of a put promises to buy the stock. The option buyer has the right to exercise the option, sell it in the secondary market, or let it expire. The option writer, however, cannot force the option holder to exercise the option.

The differences between calls and puts and the relationship between the purchaser and writer can be summarized as follows:

	Purchaser (long position)	Writer (short position)
Call	Right to buy stock	Obligation to sell stock
Put	Right to sell stock	Obligation to buy stock

An option purchaser has a long position since he or she actually owns the option and can use it to buy (call) or sell (put) the stock. The option writer has a short position since he or she issued or wrote the option. At the discretion of the purchaser, the writer can be forced to sell (call) or buy (put) the stock.

Standardized options have specified expiration dates and exercise prices. The maximum life of most options on individual stocks is nine months. The **expiration date** falls on the Saturday following the third Friday of the expiration month. Three life cycles are used for options, one of which is assigned to each stock by the exchange:

- January, April, July, and October
- February, May, August, and November
- March, June, September, and December

At any point in time, however, the exchange may allow options to be traded with expiration dates for successive months. For example, in September, options with expiration months of September, October, November, and December could be available, depending on investor interest.

Standardized options also have uniform **exercise** or **striking prices** in increments of $2.50 or $5, depending on the price of the underlying common stock. The striking price is the price at which the stock may be acquired or sold if the investor exercises the option. For example, options on a particular stock might have striking prices of $65, $70, $75, or $80. Striking price intervals of $2.50 are used for stock priced below $25. Generally, striking prices will be both above and below the market price of the underlying common stock; as the price of the common stock moves up or down, additional options can be issued with striking prices that reflect these price changes.

A comparison of the striking price and the actual market price of the underlying stock indicates whether an option is in-the-money, out-of-the-money, or at-the-money. For example, the following two call options were available on Exxon common stock with a July 1991 expiration:

Option	Striking price	Exxon's common stock price	Call option price	Classification
1	$50	$51\frac{5}{8}$	$3\frac{3}{4}$	In-the-money
2	$55	$51\frac{5}{8}$	$1\frac{3}{8}$	Out-of-the money

Option 1 is *in-the-money* since the striking price is below the common stock price. Option 2 is *out-of-the-money* since the striking price is above the common stock price. If the striking price is equal to the stock price, the option is *at-the-money.* For *put* options, the classifications for in- and out-of-the-money options are simply reversed.

In this example, option 1 has value because it allows the holder to acquire a stock selling for $51\frac{5}{8}$ for the striking price of $50. This $1\frac{5}{8}$ difference is called the **intrinsic value** of the option. Except in the case of mispricing, the actual price of the call option is always equal to or greater than the intrinsic value. Since the price of $3\frac{3}{4}$ is above the intrinsic value, this additional amount, $2\frac{1}{8}$, is the **time value** of the option. The time value depends on expectations of future stock price increases and the length of time before the expiration date. Options with a longer time period before expiration have a larger time value. Option 2 does not have intrinsic value because it is out-of-the-money. Since its price cannot be negative or zero, however, it will be priced to reflect time value.

The following chart indicates how the market prices of the two call options can be divided between intrinsic and time value:

	Option 1	Option 2
Intrinsic value	$51\frac{5}{8} - 50 = 1\frac{5}{8}$	0
Time value	$3\frac{3}{4} - 1\frac{5}{8} = 2\frac{1}{8}$	$1\frac{3}{8}$
Price of option	$3\frac{3}{4}$	$1\frac{3}{8}$

Although the holder of an option has the right to exercise before expiration, the vast majority of investors do not exercise options because they do not want a position in the underlying stock. Instead, most investors make a *closing transaction*, which effectively cancels the position; for example, the buyer of an option would write (sell) an identical option as a closing transaction, while the option writer would cancel by purchasing an identical option. The transaction costs for closing transactions are generally lower than the cost of exercising the option.

When an option holder elects to exercise the option, the OCC randomly assigns the *exercise notice* to an option writer. Typically, the writer is the brokerage firm that represents the individual investor. The brokerage firm then receives the exercise notice and must randomly assign it to one or more of its customers who wrote the specific option. Once the exercise has been assigned to a particular writer, the position cannot be canceled by using a closing transaction. Thus, one of the risks of writing options is that the investor may be randomly assigned an exercise notice at any time during the life of the option. Since less than 5 percent of the options are exercised, however, the likelihood of being assigned an exercise notice is small.

Options can be either **American-style** or **European-style** options. The difference is related to the terms of exercising the option. An American option may be exercised by the holder at any time after it is purchased until it expires. A European option may be exercised only during a specified period, which may end on the expiration date or be for a designated period prior to the expiration date. Historically, options traded in the United States were American-style, but since 1985, some European-style options have been traded, and it is likely that others may be introduced in the future. American-style options provide the holder more flexibility in designing option strategies. For the typical investor, however, the distinction between an American- and European-style option is immaterial because an option with some time remaining before expiration is likely to have time value. Therefore, a rational investor would not exercise an American-style option and lose the time value. Rather, the option would either be sold or exercised at the expiration date if the stock price was above the exercise price.

Option writers must meet applicable *margin requirements*. There is, however, a major difference between the margin requirements on stocks or bonds and those on options. A margin requirement on a stock or bond purchase is a required down payment, and the remaining funds are borrowed from the brokerage firm. Options cannot be bought on credit; when options are purchased, the full price must be paid at the time of purchase. When an option is written without an existing position in the underlying stock, the *issuer* must deposit cash or U.S. Treasury bills with the broker as collateral—usually called a margin but actually a type of performance bond. The option writer may also have to meet margin calls if the underlying stock moves in an unfavorable direction. If an option is written against an existing position in the common stock, the common stock must be on deposit with the brokerage firm and serves as the margin.

Margin requirements for option writers without a position in the underlying stock vary, depending on the brokerage firm, the price of the underlying stock, the price of the option, and whether the option is a put or a call. As a general rule, initial margins are at least 30 percent of the stock price when the option is written, plus the intrinsic value of the option. The amount of the margin influences the degree of *financial leverage* the investor has and consequently the returns and risk on the position.

• Quotations on Put and Call Equity Options

As previously discussed, equity options are traded on the NYSE, AMEX, Philadelphia and Pacific exchanges, and the CBOE. Table 15.2 provides a sample of quotations for put and call options on individual common stocks

TABLE 15.2 • Quotations on CBOE Put and Call Equity Options

Expire date Strike price	Sales	Open Int.	Week's High	Week's Low	Price	Net Chg.	N.Y. Close
Citicp Aug15 p	1025	2361	1 7-16	13-16	1⅜	+ ⅛	14⅛
Citicp Oct12½.	225	497	2⅝	2¼	2 5-16	−3-16	14⅛
Citicp Oct12½ p	598	5200	⅝	⅜	½	......	14⅛
Citicp Oct15.	809	3411	1 3-16	⅞	1	......	14⅛
Citicp Oct15 p	1639	14993	1¾	1 3-16	1 11-16	+5-16	14⅛
Citicp Oct17½.	371	7883	7-16	¼	¼	− ⅛	14⅛
Citicp Oct17½ p	106	4043	3½	3	3⅜	+ ⅛	14⅛
Citicp Jan12½ p	158	483	¾	⅝	¾	......	14⅛
Citicp Jan15.	300	1191	1 9-16	1 5-16	1½	+1-16	14⅛
Citicp Jan15 p	314	2478	2	1¾	1⅞	......	14⅛
Coke Jul50.	115	450	6	5⅝	6	+ 2⅛	55¾
Coke Jul50 p	110	223	⅛	1-16	1-16	− ⅛	55¾
Coke Jul55.	1008	2487	1⅞	1 3-16	1¾	+ ¾	55¾
Coke Jul55 p	913	2614	1 5-16	⅝	⅝	− ⅞	55¾
Coke Jul60 p	531	219	5⅜	4½	4½	− 1	55¾
Coke Aug50 p	125	2152	7-16	⅜	7-16	− ⅛	55¾
Coke Aug55.	348	3596	2¾	2	2¼	+ ⅜	55¾
Coke Aug55 p	549	1866	1⅞	1⅜	1½	− 1	55¾
Coke Aug60.	143	2310	⅝	⅜	⅝	+ ¼	55¾
Coke Nov55.	200	2186	4⅛	3⅜	3¾	+ ¾	55¾
Coke Nov55 p	150	1327	3¼	2½	2½	− 1	55¾
Coke Nov60.	114	802	1 15-16	1½	1⅝	+ ⅛	55¾
ColgPl Aug35 p	154	532	9-16	½	9-16	+3-16	37⅜
ColgPl Aug37½.	119	708	1⅛	1	1	− ⅛	37⅜
CmpAsc Jul10.	603	6651	⅝	¼	7-16	−1-16	10
CmpAsc Jul12½.	250	1831	1-16	1-16	1-16	......	10
CmpAsc Oct10.	373	1901	1¼	1	1⅛	− ⅛	10
Corng Jul65.	116	127	2	⅞	1¾	+ 1⅛	65⅜
Corng Aug65.	478	547	3	1 13-16	2½	+ ¾	65⅜
CrCare Aug35.	104	182	1⅛	1	1	− ⅜	33
CypSem Sep20.	129	845	1¾	1½	1¾	+ ¾	18⅞
Delta Jul70.	244		3½	1½	3¼	+ 1½	71⅞
Delta Jul70 p	256	857	2¼	⅜	⅜	− 2⅜	71⅞
Delta Jul75.	193		13-16	⅜	½	+3-16	71⅞
Delta Aug70 p	127	158	3⅛	1¾	1⅞	− 1¾	71⅞
Delta Aug75.	130	146	1 13-16	1 5-16	1 13-16	+15-16	71⅞
Delta Oct65 p	234	510	2⅛	1⅜	1 11-16	−5-16	71⅞
DiaSrk Oct25.	150	337	⅜	¼	¼	−1-16	21½
Dow Ch Jul55.	459		⅞	½	¾	......	53⅝
Dow Ch Aug55 p	120	160	3⅜	2⅝	2⅝	− ⅜	53⅝
Dow Ch Sep55.	327		2⅝	2	2½	+ ⅛	53⅝
Dow Ch Sep60.	304		13-16	⅝	¾	+1-16	53⅝
Dow Ch Dec45 p	105	190	1⅛	1	1	+ ⅛	53⅝
EKodak Jul35 p	205	829	⅛	1-16	1-16	−1-16	39
EKodak Jul40.	1184	4017	⅞	⅜	⅜	−3-16	39
EKodak Jul40 p	483	3385	1⅜	⅜	1¼	− ¼	39
EKodak Jul45.	392	8591	1-16	1-16	1-16	......	39
EKodak Aug40.	264	256	1¾	1	1⅛	− ⅛	39
EKodak Aug40 p	365	424	1⅞	1½	1¾	− ¼	39
EKodak Aug45.	191	167	¼	¼	¼	......	39
EKodak Oct35 p	654	680	11-16	½	11-16	+1-16	39
EKodak Oct40.	474	1203	2¼	1¾	1⅞	− ⅛	39
EKodak Oct40 p	262	1551	2¾	2⅛	2½	− ¼	39
EKodak Oct45.	508	3436	¾	9-16	9-16	−1-16	39
EKodak Oct50.	743	1841	3-16	⅛	3-16	−1-16	39
EKodak Jan50.	828	1959	¾	½	⅝	−1-16	39
EKodak Jan40.	107	712	3	2½	2½	− ⅛	39
EKodak Jan40 p	103	274	3¼	3	3⅛	− ⅜	39
EKodak Jan45.	246	2126	1½	1⅛	1⅛	− ⅛	39
Exxon Jul55.	708	5879	5	2½	2⅞	− ¾	57½
Exxon Jul60.	960	9020	13-16	⅛	⅛	− ⅜	57½
Exxon Jul60 p	285	2439	2 15-16	⅞	2 15-16	+1 1-16	57½
Exxon Jul65 p	450	115	7⅝	6	7⅝	+ 1	57½
Exxon Aug55.	186	239	5⅛	3	3⅜	− 1⅛	57½
Exxon Aug60.	662	737	1¼	7-16	½	− ¼	57½
Exxon Oct55.	129	2567	5¾	3⅜	4	− 1⅜	57½
Exxon Oct55 p	200	1189	1 3-16	13-16	1 3-16	+3-16	57½
Exxon Oct60.	419	4389	2 7-16	1¼	1½	−1-16	57½
Exxon Oct60 p	220	1630	4	2¼	4	+ ⅜	57½
G M Dec45.	164	2372	2½	2⅛	2⅜	+ ½	42½
GtLCh Sep90.	133	182	1⅝	1⅜	1⅜	− 1	82¼
Halbtn Aug35 p	349	424	1¾	1¼	1¾	+ ¼	35¼
Halbtn Oct35.	103	149	4⅛	2½	2½	− 2⅛	35¼
Hanson Sep17½.	106	333	¾	⅝	⅝	+1-16	16¾
Heinz Aug40.	250		11-16	⅜	½	+ ⅛	38
Heinz Sep40.	158		1	11-16	1	+ ¼	38
Heinz Sep45.	276		⅜	¼	⅜	+3-16	38
Heinz Dec45.	269		⅝	½	⅝	+1-16	38
Hewlet Jul50.	370	2056	3⅜	1⅞	2	......	50¾
Hewlet Jul50 p	365	2121	15-16	9-16	¾	− ⅜	50¾
Hewlet Jul55.	308		9-16	⅛	⅛	−3-16	50¾
Hewlet Aug45.	250	1098	7⅞	7	7	+ ¼	50¾
Hewlet Aug50.	601		4⅛	2 11-16	2⅞	− ⅛	50¾
Hewlet Aug50 p	253	1286	2	1⅛	1¾	− ¼	50¾
Hewlet Aug55.	589		1 9-16	13-16	1	......	50¾
Hewlet Nov45 p	124	604	1½	1	1½	......	50¾
Hewlet Nov50.	125		5	5	5	+ ⅛	50¾
Hewlet Nov55.	205	1381	3⅜	2¾	2⅞	+ ⅛	50¾
Hitachi Jul80.	140		4⅛	2¼	3½	+ 2	82⅜
Homstk Jul15.	1505		3⅜	2 1-16	3⅜	+ 1⅝	18⅜
Homstk Jul17½.	4395		1⅛	½	1⅛	+ ¾	18⅜
Homstk Jul17½ p	1141	1311	15-16	3-16	¼	−13-16	18⅜
Homstk Jul20.	280		3-16	1-16	3-16	+ ⅛	18⅜
Homstk Jul20 p	365	145	2⅞	1⅝	2	− 1⅜	18⅜
Homstk Aug15 p	112	71	¼	⅛	⅛	− ¼	18⅜
Homstk Aug17½.	2098		1 11-16	⅞	1½	+13-16	18⅜
Homstk Aug17½ p	440	296	1 1-16	½	⅝	+ ⅝	18⅜
Homstk Aug20.	244		9-16	¼	9-16	+9-16	18⅜
Homstk Aug20 p	167	125	2¾	2 3-16	2 3-16	+2 3-16	18⅜
Homstk Oct15.	423		4	3	4	+ 1½	18⅜
Homstk Oct15 p	197	1298	¾	⅜	½	−5-16	18⅜
Homstk Oct17½.	1874		2¼	1⅜	2 1-16	+15-16	18⅜
Homstk Oct17½ p	133	217	1½	1⅛	1⅛	− ¾	18⅜
Homstk Oct20.	1632		1 3-16	⅝	1 1-16	+7-16	18⅜
Homstk Jan15.	106		4½	3⅜	4½	+ 1⅜	18⅜
Homstk Jan15 p	163	166	15-16	⅝	13-16	−7-16	18⅜
Homstk Jan17½.	445		2¾	2 3-16	2¾	+ ¾	18⅜
Homstk Jan20.	263		1 15-16	1⅛	1 11-16	+1 11-16	18⅜
I B M Jul95.	798		5	3¾	4½	+ ¾	90⅝
I B M Jul95 p	3392	8133	1 1-16	⅜	9-16	−11-16	98⅝
I B M Jul100.	8162		1 9-16	15-16	1 3-16	+1-16	98⅝
I B M Jul100 p	3506	11430	3⅜	2	2⅜	− 1⅜	98⅝
I B M Jul105.	3016		½	¼	5-16	−1-16	98⅝
I B M Jul105 p	1593	4881	7⅝	5¾	6⅜	− 1⅝	98⅝
I B M Jul110.	2047		3-16	⅛	⅛	−1-16	98⅝
I B M Jul115.	919		⅛	1-16	1-16	......	98⅝
I B M Jul125.	188		1-16	1-16	1-16	......	98⅝
I B M Jul125 p	202	22	26⅜	26¼	26⅜	− ⅞	98⅝
I B M Aug95.	369		5¾	5	5½	+ ⅝	98⅝
I B M Aug95 p	1144	1180	2 7-16	1½	1¾	− ⅞	98⅝
I B M Aug100.	2442		2 11-16	2⅛	2 7-16	+3-16	98⅝
I B M Aug100 p	655	1089	4⅞	3½	3⅞	− 1⅜	98⅝
I B M Aug105.	1810		1	¾	⅞	......	98⅝
I B M Aug105 p	933	642	8⅛	7⅛	7⅜	− 1½	98⅝
I B M Oct95.	474		7¼	6¾	7	+ ⅜	98⅝
I B M Oct95 p	1504	3974	3½	2 11-16	2⅞	− 1	98⅝
I B M Oct100.	1012		4⅝	4	4¼	+ ¼	98⅝
I B M Oct100 p	649	3474	6	4¾	5⅜	− 1	98⅝
I B M Oct105.	2449		2⅝	2 5-16	2½	+3-16	98⅝
I B M Oct105 p	193	2541	8⅞	8	8⅜	− 1⅛	98⅝
I B M Oct110.	2758		1 7-16	1 1-16	1⅜	+ ⅛	98⅝
I B M Oct115.	1880		13-16	⅝	13-16	+ ⅛	98⅝
I B M Oct120.	786		½	⅜	½	+1-16	98⅝
I B M Oct125.	321		⅜	5-16	5-16	......	98⅝
I B M Oct135.	135	1807	3-16	3-16	3-16	−1-16	98⅝
I B M Jan95 p	123	565	5¼	4¼	4½	− 1	98⅝
I B M Jan100.	375		6½	6	6½	+ ⅝	98⅝
I B M Jan105.	262		4⅜	4⅛	4⅜	+ ¼	98⅝
Merck Oct105 p	257	1655	1⅝	1 5-16	1½	− ½	117⅝
Merck Oct110 p	259	777	2¾	2 5-16	2 11-16	−5-16	117⅝
Merck Oct115.	135	927	9⅛	7½	8	− ¼	117⅝
Merck Oct120.	190	1415	6¼	4¾	5⅜	+ ⅜	117⅝
Merck Oct120 p	138	420	7⅛	6¼	6¾	− 1⅛	117⅝
Merck Oct125.	245	1030	4	3⅛	3⅛	+ ⅛	117⅝
M M M Jul80 p	110	391	3-16	1-16	3-16	+1-16	90¾
M M M Jul90.	174	1884	5¼	2¼	2⅝	− 1¾	90¾
M M M Jul90 p	592	1095	1½	7-16	1⅛	+ ½	90¾
M M M Jul95.	421	2520	1½	7-16	½	−1 1-16	90¾
M M M Jul95 p	158	742	4⅜	2⅛	4	+ 1¾	90¾
M M M Jul100 p	488	1272	9⅛	6⅝	9⅛	+ 3⅛	90¾
M M M Aug90 p	190	240	2¼	1 3-16	2⅛	+ ⅞	90¾
MIPS Jul17½ p	152	894	2 15-16	2¾	2⅞	+ ⅞	15
Mobil Jul65.	350	681	1 11-16	½	½	− ½	63¾
Mobil Jul65 p	148	360	1⅝	15-16	1⅝	−3-16	63¾
Mobil Jul70 p	215	125	6¼	4¼	6	+ ¼	63¾
Mobil Aug60.	160	634	6⅛	4¾	4⅞	+ ¼	63¾
Monsan Jul60.	259	390	9	7⅛	9	+ 2⅝	69
Monsan Jul65.	118	627	4½	3	4½	+ 1½	69
Monsan Jul65 p	116	525	⅞	⅜	⅜	− ½	69
Monsan Jul70.	513	1080	1 3-16	½	1⅛	+ ⅝	69
Monsan Aug65.	102	102	4⅛	3½	4⅛	+ 4⅛	69
Monsan Oct55.	150	403	13¾	13¾	13¾	+ 1¾	69
Monsan Oct70.	116	379	3½	2 7-16	3½	+1 7-16	69
N C R Jul100.	410	3653	8½	7¾	8⅜	+ 1⅜	108¼
N C R Jul100 p	505	3880	3-16	⅛	⅛	−1-16	108¼
N C R Jul105.	159	2096	3	2⅝	3	+ ⅜	108¼
N C R Jul110.	200	1349	¼	3-16	3-16	−1-16	108¼
N C R Aug110.	1920	2884	1	11-16	11-16	−3-16	108¼
N C R Sep80 p	283	2199	5-16	5-16	5-16	+1-16	108¼
N C R Sep90.	2192	5614	19½	18⅞	19½	+ ⅞	108¼
N C R Sep90 p	2222	5655	½	⅜	⅜	−1-16	108¼
N C R Sep95 p	102	6146	⅞	9-16	11-16	−1-16	108¼
N C R Sep100.	599	18799	10½	9⅞	10½	+ ⅞	108¼
N C R Sep100 p	431	11609	1¼	1	1	−3-16	108¼
N C R Sep105.	2961	31740	6⅛	5¼	6⅛	+ ⅞	108¼
N C R Sep105 p	1077	10447	1¾	1⅜	1⅜	− ⅝	108¼
N C R Sep110.	7394	18826	2¼	1½	2	+ ⅛	108¼
N C R Dec100.	302	922	13½	12¾	13½	+ 1¼	108¼
N C R Dec100 p	103	1436	2⅞	2⅝	2¾	− ¼	108¼
N C R Dec105.	464	887	9⅝	9	9	+ ¼	108¼
N C R Dec105 p	313	1556	4⅛	3¾	3¾	− ¼	108¼
N C R Dec110.	769	2283	6⅛	5½	6	+ ¾	108¼
N Semi Aug7½.	238	3407	⅛	1-16	1-16	......	5¾
Occi Jul20.	109	586	1¾	1 7-16	1½	+1-16	21½
Occi Jul22½.	930	4342	5-16	⅛	⅛	− ⅛	21½
Occi Aug20.	320	5554	2¼	1¾	1¾	− ½	21½
Occi Aug22½.	699	7590	⅝	⅜	7-16	−3-16	21½
Occi Nov22½.	298	3923	1 1-16	⅞	1	−1-16	21½
Oracle Jul7½.	243	622	1¼	⅞	15-16	− ⅜	8⅛
Oracle Jul10.	300	3891	3-16	⅛	⅛	......	8⅛
Oracle Jul10 p	554	525	1 15-16	1½	1⅞	+ ¼	8⅛
Oracle Sep10.	217	3145	¾	½	½	− ⅛	8⅛
Oracle Sep12½.	129	1323	¼	⅛	3-16	......	8⅛
Oracle Dec7½.	101	1390	2¼	1¾	1¾	− ⅜	8⅛
OutbdM Sep20.	240	332	7-16	7-16	7-16	+1-16	15¾
OutbdM Sep20 p	242	1716	4¾	4¼	4¾	+ 1	15¾
ParaCm Jul40.	823	2582	2¾	1¼	1 13-16	+ ⅜	41¼
ParaCm Jul40 p	352	872	1	⅜	½	− 1⅛	41¼
ParaCm Jul45.	1647	4148	9-16	¼	5-16	−1-16	41¼
ParaCm Jul45 p	344	250	5	3⅜	3¾	− 1¾	41¼
ParaCm Jul50.	389	1327	3-16	⅛	⅛	......	41¼
ParaCm Aug45.	769	441	1 3-16	⅝	¾	− ⅛	41¼
ParaCm Sep35.	156	1272	7½	6½	7	+ 1⅛	41¼
ParaCm Sep40.	411	3220	4	2 13-16	3½	+ ½	41¼
ParaCm Sep45.	456	3610	1⅞	1¼	1½	+3-16	41¼
ParaCm Sep50.	338	2955	⅞	⅝	11-16	+1-16	41¼
ParaCm Dec40.	118	653	5⅜	4¼	4¾	+ ½	41¼

SOURCE: *Barron's*, July 8, 1991. Reprinted courtesy of *Barron's Weekly*.

traded on the CBOE. Notice that put contracts are indicated by "*p*" immediately following the striking price. The quoted price, which is usually called the **premium,** is the price for the right to buy or sell one share of the underlying stock. Since an option contract is for 100 shares, the indicated price must be multiplied by 100 to determine the price of the contract.

Notice that both the "sales" and "open int." are given for each contract in Table 15.2. The *sales* figure is the number of options traded during the week; the *open interest* is the total number of contracts outstanding at the end of the week.

Some basic pricing relationships are evident in Table 15.2. The more distant the expiration date and the lower the striking price, the higher the price of a call option. For put options, however, a lower striking price reduces the price of the option. Notice also that many options that are out-of-the-money have significant value because of the time value of the option. These relationships are explained in detail later in the chapter.

• Tax Considerations

The tax treatment of gains and losses on option transactions can be quite complicated. The tax rules are different for the major types of options. The tax liability also depends on whether the option was exercised or was closed and whether the option was covered or uncovered. (With a **covered** option, the writer has a position in the underlying common stock, while the writer of an **uncovered** or **naked** option has no position in the underlying stock.) Most of the option markets and brokerage firms that trade in options have publications that deal with specific tax aspects of options.

In very general terms, the Tax Reform Act of 1986 effectively eliminated the favorable tax treatment for long-term capital gains. As of January 1, 1987, all profits on option transactions are taxed at the maximum rate of 28 percent, regardless of the length of the holding period. The actual tax rate depends on the investor's marginal rate. If an option is exercised and therefore used to acquire or sell a stock, the premium or price of the option is included in the tax basis for the stock and influences the ultimate capital gain or loss on the stock. If an individual writes an option, the premiums or proceeds are not recognized as income until the position is terminated, by expiration, delivery of the underlying stock, or a closing transaction.

• Risk and Return on Equity Options

This section discusses the risks and returns associated with writing or buying call and put options on individual common stocks. To simplify the examples, several assumptions are made. First, as previously discussed, the options will not be exercised before the expiration date. Second, the option positions are uncovered or naked since hedging (strategies involving covered options) is discussed later in the chapter. Finally, brokerage commissions and taxes are ignored in calculating gains and losses. Brokerage fees on options can be negotiated but generally involve a minimum charge of $20–$50 for small trades under $1,000, or 2–3 percent of the value for larger trades. Brokerage fees are assessed on the initial trade and when the option is sold or a reversing transaction is made. Consideration of brokerage fees and taxes would obviously reduce the gains and increase the losses in the examples.

CALL OPTIONS Table 15.3 provides an illustration of possible profits and losses on an in-the-money call option on IBM's common stock. On January 2, 1991, investor A writes the call, while investor B takes a long position. Investor A earns a profit of $1,050 if the stock price remains constant or declines because the option will not be exercised. This profit is the proceeds or **premium** received from writing the option. If the stock price increases, investor A's profit declines until it reaches zero when the stock price is at $120.50. At stock prices above $120.50, the option writer loses money because the option will be exercised or, more commonly, the writer will make a reversing transaction. Theoretically, there is no limit to A's losses if the stock price continues to increase and the writer does not make a closing transaction by purchasing an identical call.

Investor B has exactly the opposite situation. Losses occur until the stock price reaches $120.50 because the option cannot be profitably exercised. For stock prices between $110 and $120.50, losses can be reduced by selling the option for its intrinsic value or exercising the option. Profits only occur when the stock price is above $120.50. There is no upper limit on the profits if the stock price continues to increase. The maximum loss, however, is the initial premium, or $1,050.

As this example illustrates, an investor who thinks that IBM's common stock will be above $120.50 at the expiration date should go long or buy a call option. An investor who thinks that the stock price will remain constant or decline should go short or write a call option. The risk of the two positions is quite different, however, since the short position is subject to unlimited losses while the long-position loss is limited to $1,050. Based on the actual quotation for the IBM call quoted on July 8, 1991 in Table 15.2, which investor (A or B) will have a profit on the call option?

The **leverage effect** also influences the returns and risks. Essentially, the price or premium on an option is a fraction of the cost of a position in the underlying common stock. If an option is traded at its intrinsic value, however, the dollar losses and gains on the option approximately match the losses and gains on the underlying stock. Thus, a "small" dollar investment in options can result in extremely large positive or negative HPRs. For example, if IBM's price at expiration was $130, the HPR over the 7.5 months for the option purchaser (investor B) would be 90.48 percent ($950/$1,050). If the actual stock was purchased in January for $113.375 and sold for $130, the HPR would be 14.66 percent ($16.625/$113.375). The leverage effect can increase HPRs, but it also increases the risk when the stock price declines.

TABLE 15.3 • Illustration of Profits and Losses on Call Options

Contract:	Call on IBM common stock
	Expiration month: July 1991
	Striking price: $110
	Price of option: $10\frac{1}{2}$ on January 2, 1991
	Price of common stock: $113\frac{3}{8}$ on January 2, 1991
Investor A:	Writes one contract and receives $1,050 ($10.50 × 100)
Investor B:	Buys one contract for $1,050

Possible prices of IBM stock on last trading date before expiration (7/19/91)	*Investor A (writer) profit (loss)*	*Investor B (purchaser) profit (loss)*
$ 90.00	$1,050	$(1,050)
100.00	1,050	(1,050)
110.00	1,050	(1,050)
120.00	500	(500)
120.50	0	0
130.00	(950)	950
140.00	(1,950)	1,950

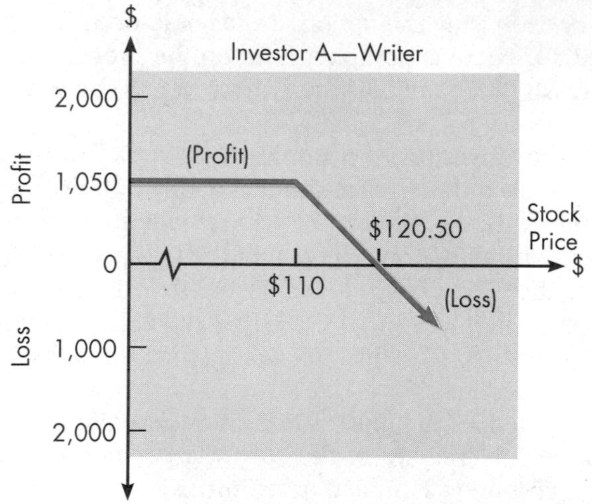

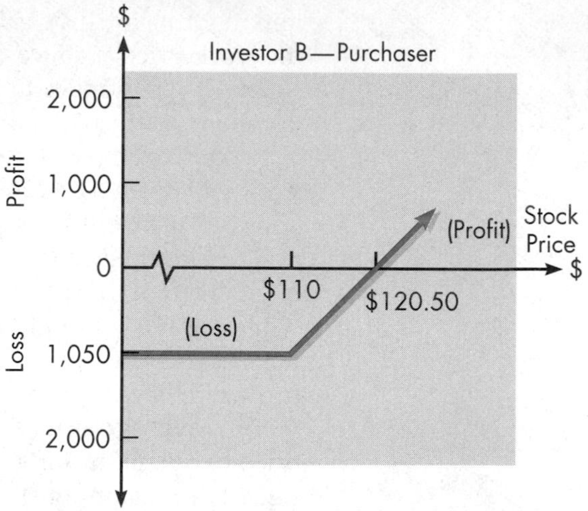

PUT OPTIONS Table 15.4 illustrates a long and a short position in an IBM put. On January 2, 1991, investor A writes a put; investor B buys the put. The writer earns a profit if the stock price is above $101.125 at the expiration date. Losses occur at prices below $101.125 and can theoretically reach $10,012.50 [$(0 - 105 + 4\frac{7}{8}) \times 100$] if the stock price declines to zero.

TABLE 15.4 • Illustration of Profits and Losses on Put Options

Contract:	Put on IBM common stock Expiration month: July 1991 Striking price: \$105 Price of option: $4\frac{7}{8}$ on January 2, 1991 Price of common stock: $113\frac{3}{8}$ on January 2, 1991
Investor A:	Writes one contract and receives \$487.50 (\$4.875 × 100)
Investor B:	Buys one contract for \$487.50

Possible prices of IBM stock on last trading date before expiration (7/19/91)	*Investor A (writer) profit (loss)*	*Investor B (purchaser) profit (loss)*
\$ 80.000	(\$2,012.50)	\$2,012.50
90.000	(1,012.50)	1,012.50
100.000	(12.50)	12.50
101.125	0	0
105.000	487.50	(487.50)
120.000	487.50	(487.50)

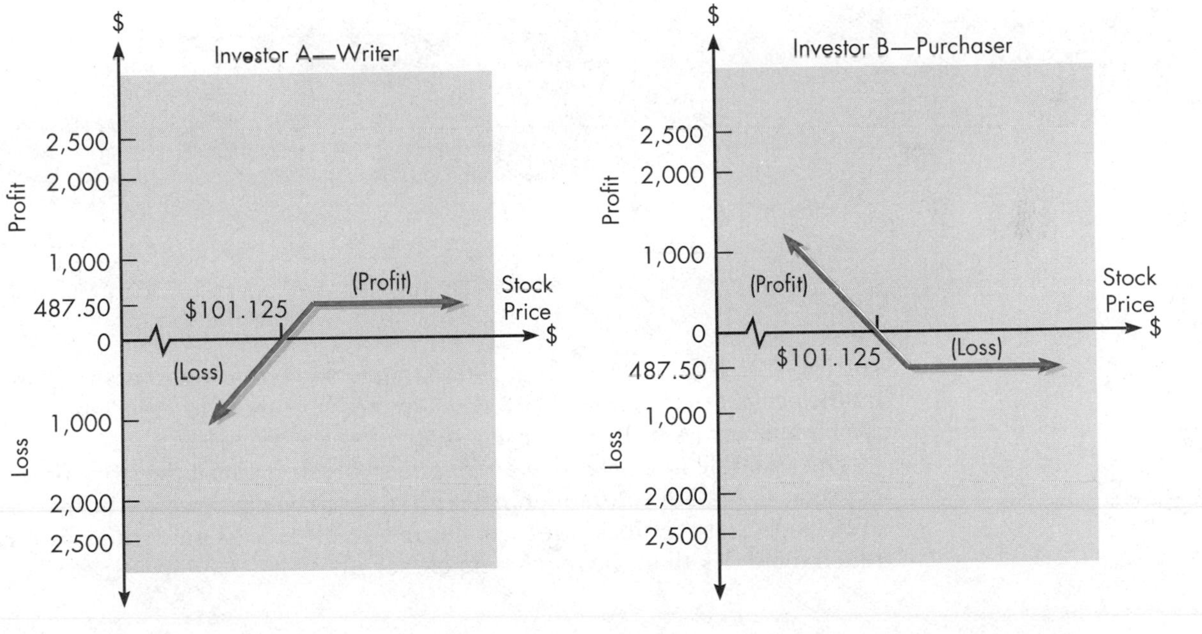

The maximum loss to the put purchaser is \$487.50, the premium paid for the option. The maximum loss occurs if the stock price at the expiration date is \$105 or greater. Profits occur if the stock price is below \$101.125 and can

TABLE 15.5 • Hedging Using Call and Put Options

I. Short the Stock and Buy a Call

Stock: $100 per share, 100 shares
Call option: $500 per contract (100 shares), striking price $100

Stock price at expiration	*Stock position gain (loss)*	*Option position gain (loss)*	*Total gain or (loss) on hedged position*
$ 80	$2,000	$ (500)	$1,500
90	1,000	(500)	500
95	500	(500)	0
100	0	(500)	(500)
110	(1,000)	500	(500)
120	(2,000)	1,500	(500)

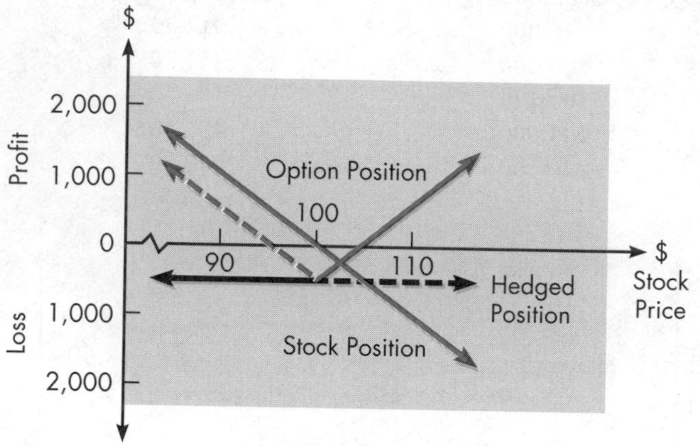

(continued)

reach $10,012.50 [(105 − $4\frac{7}{8}$) × 100] if the stock price declines to zero. Based on the actual quotation for the IBM put quoted on July 8, 1991 in Table 15.2, which investor (A or B) will have a profit on the put option?

This example illustrates that an investor will write puts if the stock price is expected to remain constant or increase. Puts will be purchased if the investor anticipates that the stock price will decline. As with calls, put writers assume much more risk than the purchasers of the put.

• Hedging Using Call and Put Options

Hedging is a strategy designed to limit losses in one position by simultaneously taking a second offsetting position in the same or a different security. In

TABLE 15.5 • Hedging Using Call and Put Options (continued)

II. Buy the Stock and a Put

Stock: $100 per share, 100 shares

Put option: $500 per contract (100 shares), striking price $100

Stock price at expiration	*Stock position gain (loss)*	*Option position gain (loss)*	*Total gain or (loss) on hedged position*
$ 80	$(2,000)	$1,500	$ (500)
90	(1,000)	500	(500)
100	0	(500)	(500)
95	500	(500)	0
110	1,000	(500)	500
120	2,000	(500)	1,500

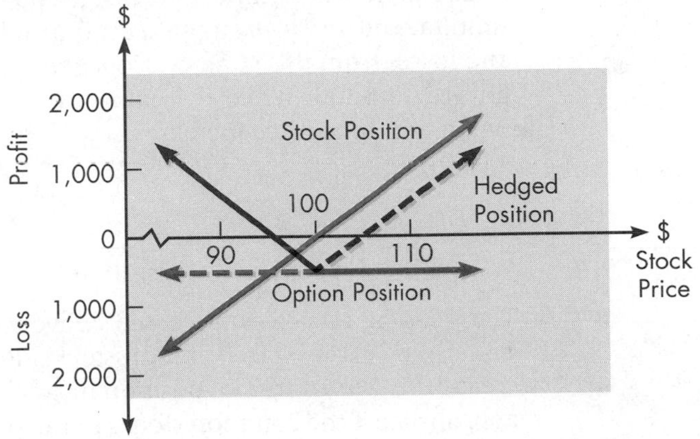

$
2,000
1,000
0
1,000
2,000
Profit
Loss
Stock Position
100
Hedged Position
90
110
Option Position
$ Stock Price

most cases, hedges are not perfect; they cannot eliminate all losses. Typically, a hedge strategy attempts to eliminate large losses without significantly reducing gains.

Equity options are often used to hedge a long or short position in the underlying common stock; in this case, they are covered options. When options are used to hedge an investment in individual stocks or a portfolio of stocks, they reduce risk. A correctly hedged portfolio of common stocks and options, therefore, has less risk than a portfolio without options.

HEDGING A SHORT POSITION IN STOCK A short seller of stock anticipates that the stock will decline in price. By selling or shorting the stock now and buying it at a lower price in the future, the short seller earns a profit. The losses from this strategy can be large if the price increases, however, because the short seller has an obligation to purchase the stock in the future. A hedge would be designed to minimize this risk. One hedge would be to short the stock and simultaneously *buy* a call with a striking price equal to or close to the selling price of the stock. The call option could be used to acquire the stock in the event the stock increases in price. If the stock price declines as expected, however, the option will be worthless, and this loss will reduce the gain on the short position.

Part I of Table 15.5 illustrates the short hedge. Notice that losses occur in the hedged position until the stock price falls below $95. However, the maximum loss on the hedged position is $500. Therefore, the hedge is not perfect in the sense that it does not eliminate all possible losses. The "cost" of forming the hedge is the price for the call, which will be lost if the stock price declines.

HEDGING A LONG POSITION IN STOCK An investor who buys common stock anticipates the stock will increase in value. The risk, of course, is that the stock's price will decline. One hedge could be formed by buying the stock and simultaneously *buying* a put. Part II of Table 15.5 illustrates the possible gains and losses from this strategy. Notice that the losses on the hedged position are limited to $500, while the gains are reduced by the cost of the put option when the stock price increases.

• Writing Covered Calls and Puts

The hedging strategies discussed above were designed to limit the *risk* of an underlying position in common stocks. Puts and calls can also be used to increase the *returns* from a position in stocks. This strategy may be particularly appropriate if the common stocks in the portfolio are not expected to undergo significant short-term price changes. For example, an investor may think that stocks are good long-term investments (short position in an expected down market or a long position in an expected rising market), but expects short-term price changes to be small. By *writing covered options,* the investor can increase the short-term returns of the portfolio. The investor will not benefit if large stock price changes occur because the option will be exercised or the investor (writer) will need to make a reversing transaction. Writing covered options is a very conservative strategy for both individual and institutional investors. Table 15.6 illustrates the possible gains and losses from a strategy of writing a call against a long position in the stock.

As the secondary market for options developed during the 1970s, institutional investors frequently wrote call options against long positions in stocks. Research based on data for the 1970s found that writing covered call options was an effective strategy since the investors realized risk-adjusted excess returns. This finding suggests that call options may have been overpriced during this period.

TABLE 15.6 • Writing Covered Calls

Long position: Purchase 100 shares of stock for $50, for long-term price appreciation

Short position: Write one call contract with striking price of $50, for $400

Stock price at expiration	*Stock position gain (loss)*	*Option position gain (loss)*	*Combined positions gain (loss)*
$45	$(500)	$400	$(100)
46	(400)	400	0
47	(300)	400	100
48	(200)	400	200
49	(100)	400	300
50	0	400	400
51	100	300	400
52	200	200	400
53	300	100	400

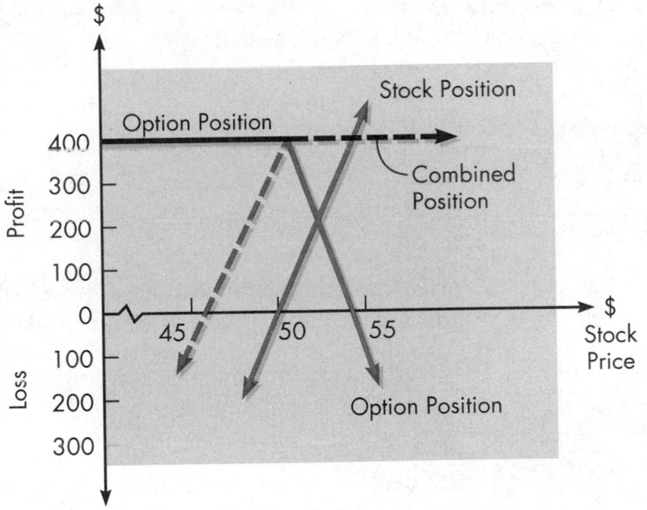

OTHER OPTION STRATEGIES USING PUTS AND CALLS

Investors may also use a number of other strategies involving options. As discussed below, several popular strategies combine positions in puts and calls. Hundreds of option strategies become possible when *combinations* are used. For example, an investor may simultaneously take a put and a call position on the same common stock or take several call positions at different striking

RESEARCH BOX

Hedging Strategies Using Derivative Securities

A recent research paper examined hedging strategies employing stock options, index options, options on index futures, and index futures contracts. The first three of these derivative securities are discussed in this chapter, and index futures contracts are discussed in Chapter 17. Essentially, the paper analyzed the circumstances or conditions that should exist before a portfolio manager should use these securities to hedge a portfolio.

To test the various strategies, historical data on 20 individual stocks over a 155-month period were used. Average returns, correlations, and standard deviations were calculated for each of the stocks. The data were then used in a numerical simulation procedure.

The strategies tested included writing covered calls on the underlying stock positions, buying put options on the underlying stock positions, and selling financial futures. A large number of strategies were tested that varied by the hedging technique and by the percentage of the portfolio that was hedged. For each strategy, the mean, standard deviation, beta, and a third measure of risk were computed. The advantages and disadvantages of each strategy were then analyzed using the return and risk measures. In general, as might be expected, when a larger percentage of the portfolio was hedged, risk and returns declined. By making certain assumptions about the risk preferences of the portfolio manager, however, the results also showed that index options appear to be preferable hedging techniques compared to writing covered calls or taking a long position in puts.

SOURCE: Robert Brooks, "Investment Decision Making with Derivative Securities," *Financial Review* (November 1989): 511–27.

prices and/or expiration dates. The most common of these combination strategies are straddles, spreads, strips, and straps.

STRADDLES In a **straddle,** the investor simultaneously takes a position in a put and a call on the same underlying security, with the same striking price and expiration date. The put and call will be *purchased* (long straddle) if the investor thinks the underlying stock is likely to have a *large* price movement but is uncertain of the direction of the price change. For example, if a company is a likely takeover candidate, its stock price might be bid up, and the call would increase in value. If the speculation was incorrect, however, and no takeover attempt occurs, the stock price would decrease, and the put would increase in value.

A *short straddle* position is appropriate if the investor thinks that the underlying stock price is *unlikely* to move significantly up or down. As long as the stock price remains relatively constant, the writer benefits from the premiums received from writing the put and call. When writing both a put and call, however, large losses can occur if the stock price moves significantly in either direction.

SPREADS A **spread** is a more general type of straddle; the put and call may have different striking prices and/or expiration dates. An investor who creates a *long spread* is motivated by the expectation that the underlying stock will experience a *large* price change. The purchase prices for the call and put options are likely to be lower for a spread than for a straddle. To form a long spread, "cheap" puts and calls that are out-of-the-money and have only time value are purchased. The price change of the stock must be larger for the spread than for the straddle before profits occur.

A *short spread* strategy involves writing both puts and calls under the assumption that the price of the underlying stock will *not* move significantly. Writing a put with a striking price below that of the call increases the range of the stock price where profits occur. The premium income will also be lower, however, than with a straddle strategy.

There are many more spread than straddle strategies—for example, bullish, bearish, and neutral spread strategies, in addition to calendar (different expiration dates), vertical (different striking prices), or combination (different expiration dates and striking prices) strategies.

STRIPS AND STRAPS The strip and the strap strategies are special cases of a straddle. In a straddle, the striking price and expiration date are the same for the put and the call. This is also the case for the strip and strap strategies. A *strip*, however, involves two puts and one call, while a *strap* involves two calls and one put. In both cases, an investor can take a short (write) or long (buy) position.

In a strip strategy, a long position is appropriate if a *large* stock price change is anticipated. Because the investor buys two puts and one call, however, the profit will occur sooner and be larger if the stock price *declines* rather than increases. In this case, the buyer is uncertain about the direction of the stock price movement but is more confident of a decline than an increase. If the investor thinks that a large price *increase* is more likely, the appropriate strategy would be a long strap, involving two calls and one put.

A *short strip* or *strap* strategy is appropriate if the stock price is *not* expected to change significantly. In writing two puts and one call (strip), the profit potential is greater in the case of a stock price increase. The reverse is true for a short strap strategy.

OPTION PRICING

This section presents three techniques or models for determining the value of options: a generalized graphic model that establishes upper and lower limits to an option's value and identifies the key variables that influence value; the Black-Scholes call option model; and the put-call parity principle, which can be used to value puts.

FIGURE 15.1
Call and Put Values

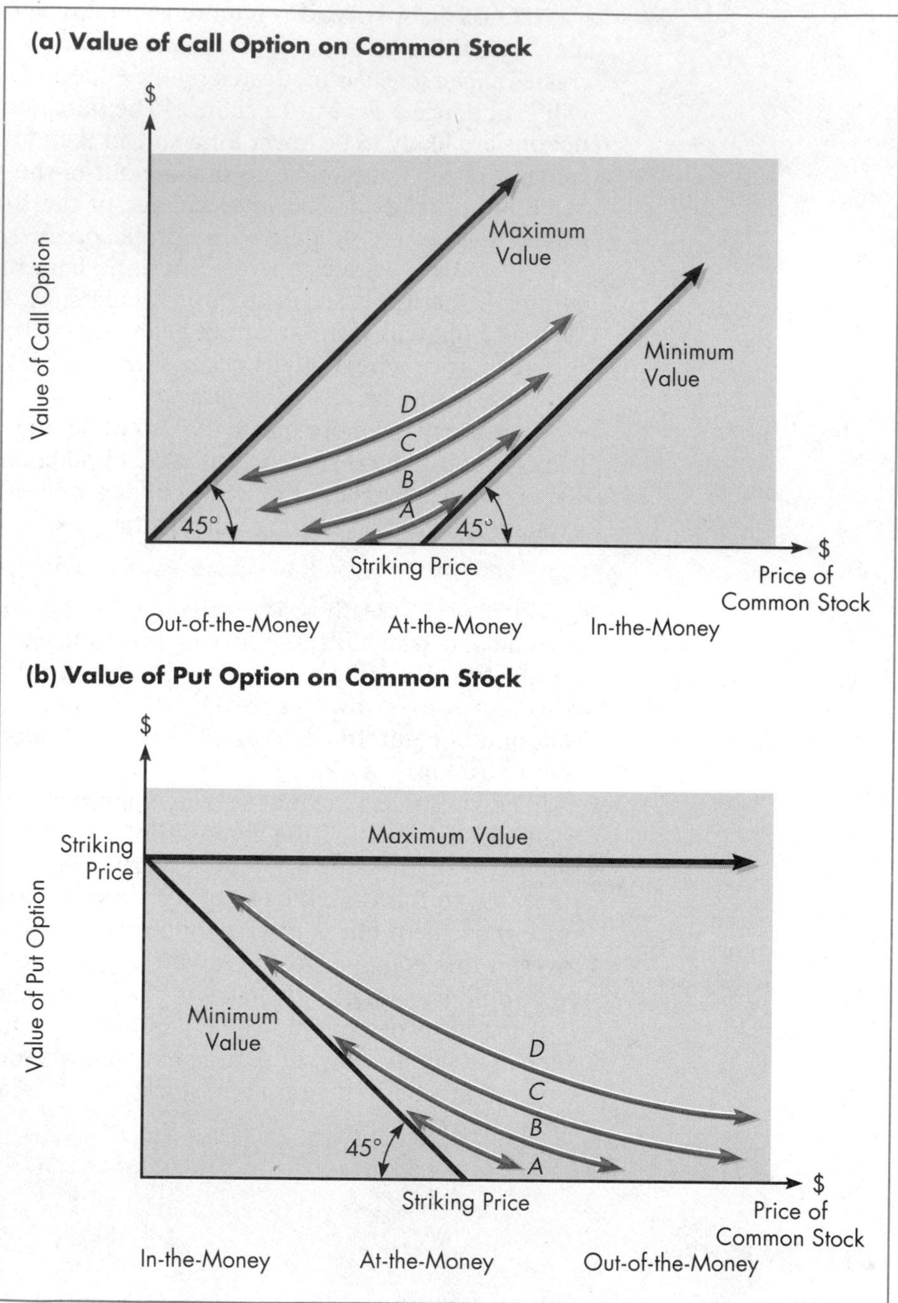

GRAPHIC ANALYSIS OF CALL AND PUT VALUES Figure 15.1 provides a graphic analysis of call and put values on an individual common stock. The major variable that determines an option's value is the price of the underlying common stock. This price is shown on the horizontal axis in the figures. Panel (a) of Figure 15.1 illustrates a call option. The call cannot have a value (V_c) above the value of the stock (V_s) because of the striking price, or $V_c \leq V_s$. The *maximum value* line is therefore drawn as a 45-degree line from the origin. The call option cannot have a value less than its intrinsic value, or $V_c \geq V_s - S$ where S is the striking price and $V_s - S$ is the intrinsic value of the option. This relationship defines the *minimum value* line, drawn at a 45-degree angle from the striking price. The call option, therefore, must have a value on or above the minimum value function (intrinsic value). For example, assume a call option has a striking price of $25 and that the common stock is currently selling for $28. The maximum value of the call option is $28. Since the option is in-the-money, its price cannot be less than $3, its intrinsic value. If the stock price increases to $29, the minimum value of the option will increase to $4. Thus, the slope of the minimum value function is 1, and it is therefore drawn with a 45-degree angle from the striking price on the horizontal axis.

The functions labeled A, B, C, and D represent hypothetical values for identical call options with different times before expiration. Function A represents the possible values for the option with the shortest time before expiration. These functions indicate that options with longer lives will have higher time values than options with short lives. The curvature of the function indicates that in-the-money call options will have greater values than out-of-the-money options, but the relationship is not linear. The out-of-the-money call options have *time* value because of expectations about future increases in the stock price. The value of the in-the-money options includes both intrinsic and time value. The key to option valuation is the correct estimate of the time value.

Panel (b) of Figure 15.1 deals with a put option. The minimum value function for puts is drawn from the striking price on the horizontal axis to an equal value point on the vertical axis. For example, assume the stock price is $0 and that the striking price is $30. The put option will have a minimum value equal to its intrinsic value, or the striking price of $30, as shown on the vertical axis. If the stock price increases to $15, the minimum value of the option will decrease to $15. When the stock price and striking price are equal, the minimum value of the put will be $0.

The put cannot have a value greater than the striking price since the stock price cannot be negative. The maximum value function is therefore drawn as a horizontal line originating from a point equal to the striking price on the vertical axis. A put's value must be on or above the minimum value function and on or below the maximum value function.

In-the-money puts have value because of their intrinsic value and time value. Thus, in-the-money puts will have higher values than out-of-the-money puts, but the relationship is not linear. Functions labeled A–D in Figure 15.1b represent hypothetical values for puts. They differ only in respect to the length of time before expiration. As with calls, puts with longer lives have greater value.

From this discussion and Figure 15.1, we can identify the following as the key variables that influence an option's value:

1. Value of underlying common stock.
2. Striking price.
3. Length of time before expiration.

Other variables that have been identified and, in some cases, incorporated into option pricing models include the following:

1. Price volatility of the underlying common stock.
2. Risk-free rate of return over the same period as the option's life.
3. Cash dividends on the common stock.
4. Market imperfections.

The discussion that follows will explain how these variables influence option values.

THE BLACK-SCHOLES OPTION PRICING MODEL In 1973 a paper was published that represented the first rigorous effort toward developing a mathematical model for valuing European-type calls on stocks that do not pay cash dividends.[2] The model also assumes that the call is used to form a perfect hedge for a stock portfolio; thus, the return on the hedged portfolio should be the risk-free rate of return. The **Black-Scholes option pricing model:**

$$V_c = P_s N(d_1) - Se^{-rt} N(d_2) \qquad (15.1)$$

where

V_c = value of the call option
P_s = current stock price
S = striking or exercise price
t = length of time before expiration, expressed as a fraction of one year
e = base e antilog = 2.7183 . . .
r = risk-free rate of return for one year

$N(d_1)$ and $N(d_2)$ are probabilities from a standard normal cumulative probability table evaluated at d_1 and d_2:

$$d_1 = \frac{\ln (P_s/S) + (r + .5\sigma^2)t}{\sigma t^{.5}} \qquad (15.2)$$

$$d_2 = d_1 - \sigma t^{.5} \qquad (15.3)$$

[2] Fischer Black and Myron Scholes, "The Pricing of Options and Corporate Liabilities," *Journal of Political Economy* (May-June 1973): 637–54.

where

$\ln(P_s/S)$ = natural logarithm (base e logs) of P_s/S
σ^2 = variance of stock's continuously compounded rate of return
σ = standard deviation of stock's continuously compounded rate of return

An inspection of Equations 15.1 and 15.2 indicates that the value of a call option is a function of the current stock price, striking price, length of time before expiration, risk-free rate of return, and variance of the stock return. These variables and their influence on call option values can be summarized as follows:

1. *Current stock price* The most important variable influencing an option's value is the price of the underlying stock. Other things being equal, higher stock prices result in higher option prices because higher priced stocks are likely to experience larger dollar price changes that are magnified in terms of their influence on the option's value.
2. *Striking price* Other things being equal, a higher striking price reduces the value of the option because the higher the striking price, the lower the probability the call will be exercised.
3. *Length of time before expiration* Other things being equal, options with longer lives have higher values because of the greater probability that a significant change will occur in the stock's price. Thus, the time value of the option is directly related to the option's life.
4. *Risk-free rate of return* The risk-free rate of return is used to calculate the present value of the striking price (Se^{-rt}). Therefore, higher values for the risk-free rate reduce the present value of the striking price and *increase* the option's value. Since the Black-Scholes model assumes that call options are written to create a riskless hedge, the value of the options must increase as the risk-free rate increases in order to provide a higher risk-free return on the hedged portfolio.
5. *Variance of the stock's return* Other things being equal, options on stocks with volatile prices (returns) will be more valuable than options on stocks with stable prices (returns). The higher volatility increases the probability that a significant change will occur in the stock's price.

Table 15.7 provides an illustration of the Black-Scholes model. Using this model, the calculated value for the option can be compared to its actual market price. If the value is higher than the market price, the option is considered to be undervalued. The opposite assessment is made if the market price is higher than the calculated value.

A major problem in using the Black-Scholes model is determining the variance of the stock's return. As Equation 15.1 indicates, the other variables can easily be determined. Typically, historical stock prices are used to calculate an estimate of the stock's return variance. There is debate, however, over the cor-

TABLE 15.7 • Illustration of the Black-Scholes Model

Stock price = P_s = \$50

Striking price = S = \$45

Length of time before expiration = t = 3 months = .25

Risk-free rate of return = r = 10% per year = .1

Variance of stock's return = σ^2 = .16

Standard deviation of stock's return = σ = .4

$$d_1 = \frac{\ln(50/45) + [.1 + .5(.16)].25}{(.4)(.25)^{.5}}$$

$$= (.1054 + .0450)/.2 = .7520$$

$$d_2 = .7520 - .4(.25)^{.5} = .5520$$

$N(d_1) \sim .7742$ (interpolation estimate from the cumulative normal distribution table in Appendix A-5)

$N(d_2) \sim .7095$ (interpolation estimate from the cumulative normal distribution table in Appendix A-5)

$$V_c = 50(.7742) - 45e^{-(.1)(.25)}(.7095)$$

$$= 38.71 - (43.89)(.7095)$$

$$= 38.71 - 31.14$$

$$V_c = \$7.57$$

rect length of the historical period and the interval of time between the observed stock prices used to calculate the variance.

Table 15.8 demonstrates the sensitivity of a call option's value to several of the variables used in the Black-Scholes model. Part I of the table provides option values for various stock prices and striking prices. Notice that changes in the stock's price have a significant impact on the option's value, but the relationship is not linear or one-for-one. Part II of the table illustrates the influence of the risk-free return and the variance of returns on option values. Notice that changes in the variance have a major effect on the option values.

An interesting aspect of the Black-Scholes model is that $N(d_1)$ is the **hedge ratio,** or the number of shares of stock relative to one option contract needed in order to form a risk-free hedged position. In Table 15.7, the value of $N(d_1)$ is given as .7742. Thus, 77.42 shares of stock along with one call option are needed to form a riskless hedge. Essentially, $N(d_1)$ represents how the option's price will change relative to a change in the stock price. For *small* changes in the stock's price, the change in the option's value would be

$$\Delta V_c = (\Delta P_s) N(d_1) \tag{15.4}$$

TABLE 15.8 • Sensitivity of Call Option Values to Key Variables

I. Sensitivity to Stock Price and Striking Price

Length of time before expiration = t = 3 months = .25

Risk-free rate of return = r = 10% per year = .1

Variance of stock's return = σ^2 = .16

Option values for combinations of stock and striking prices

Stock price	Striking price *$35*	*$40*	*$45*	*$50*
$35	$ 3.21	$1.37	$0.51	$0.17
40	6.77	3.67	1.75	0.75
45	11.17	7.16	4.12	2.15

II. Sensitivity to Risk-Free Rate of Return and Variance

Length of time before expiration = t = 3 months = .25

Stock price = P_S = $50

Striking price = S = $45

Option values for combinations of risk-free rate of return and variance

Annual risk-free return	Variance of stock's return *.08*	*.16*	*.24*	*.32*
.06	$6.40	$7.25	$8.06	$8.60
.08	6.53	7.40	8.20	8.69
.10	6.75	7.57	8.35	8.99

For example, if the stock's price increased from its current level of $50 to $51, the value of the option would increase by $.7742. Thus, the portfolio would not be completely hedged if one option was held for each 100 shares of stocks. The perfect or riskless hedge would require 1.2917 (1/.7742) options for each 100 shares of stock. Since $N(d_1)$ is calculated using the current stock price, however, the hedge ratio changes as the price of the stock changes.

One problem with the Black-Scholes model is the influence of cash dividends on the value of the option; cash dividends influence the stock's price and the variance of the stock's return and thus influence the option's value. The price of the stock will decline by the approximate value of the dividend

• INTEREST BOX

The Idea behind the Black-Scholes Model

Recently, Fischer Black described how he and Myron Scholes developed the logic underlying their option pricing model:

> My paper with Myron Scholes giving the derivation of our option formula appeared in the Spring of 1973. We had published a paper on the results of some empirical tests of the formula, however, in the Spring of 1972. The work that led to the formula started in the Spring of 1969, and the background research started in 1965. Here is the story of how the formula and the papers describing it came to be.
>
> Before I describe the events surrounding our discovery of the formula, here is the idea behind the formula.
>
> Suppose there is a formula that tells how the value of a call option depends on the price of the underlying stock, the volatility of the stock, the exercise price and maturity of the option, and the interest rate.
>
> Such a formula will tell us, among other things, how much the option value will change when the stock price changes by a small amount within a short time. Suppose that the option goes up about \$.50 when the stock goes up \$1.00, and down about \$.50 when the stock goes down \$1.00. Then you can create a hedged position by going short two options contracts and long one round lot of stocks.
>
> Such a position will be close to riskless. For small moves in the stock in the short run, your losses on one side will be mostly offset by gains on the other side. If the stock goes up, you will lose on the option but make it up on the stock. If the stock goes down, you will lose on the stock but make it up on the option.
>
> At first, you create a hedged position by going short two options and long one stock. As the stock price changes, and as the option approaches maturity, the ratio of option to stock needed to maintain a close-to-riskless hedge will change. To maintain a neutral hedge, you will have to change your position in the stock, your position in the option, or both.
>
> As the hedged position will be close to riskless, it should return an amount equal to the short-term interest rate on close-to-riskless securities. This one principle gives us the option formula! It turns out that there is only one formula for the value of an option that has the property that the return on a hedged position of option and stock is always equal to the short-term interest rate.

SOURCE: Adapted from Fischer Black, "How We Came Up with the Option Formula," *Journal of Portfolio Management* (Winter 1989): 4–8. Reprinted with permission from Institutional Investor, Inc.

on the ex-dividend date. This decline in the stock's value will cause a decline in the value of the call.

In order to analyze options on dividend-paying stocks, the present value of the estimated future dividends must be subtracted from the value of the stock. Using the example in Table 15.7, the indicated option value of \$7.57 is correct, assuming no cash dividends. If the analyst expects a \$1 dividend to be paid in three months and the risk-free rate of return is 10 percent, then \$.98 [\$1/(1 + .025)] should be subtracted from the current stock price of \$50, and the value of the option should be recalculated. This results in a dividend-adjusted option value of \$6.82.

Many empirical tests of the Black-Scholes model have been conducted. Essentially, these tests have concluded that the model provides reasonably accurate estimates of an option's value. Problems occur, however, in valuing options on dividend-paying stocks, options that are out-of-the-money, and options on stocks with "high" or "low" variances. Consequently, there is an ongoing research effort directed at improving and expanding the Black-Scholes model.

PUT-CALL PARITY The Black-Scholes model can be used to value put options based on the principle of **put-call parity.** To illustrate this approach, assume an investor forms a portfolio by (1) writing one call option, (2) buying one put with the same striking price and time to expiration as the call option, and (3) purchasing one share of the underlying stock. Thus, price changes in the stock will be exactly offset by changes in the option values. This portfolio should provide a risk-free return so that

$$V_p - V_c + P_s = P_t e^{-rt} \tag{15.5}$$

where

V_p = value of the put option
V_c = value of the call option
P_s = current stock price
P_t = value of the portfolio, which is the striking price of the options
e = base e antilog = 2.7183 . . .
t = length of time before expiration, expressed as a fraction of one year
r = risk-free rate of return for one year

Equation 15.5 can be solved for the put's value:

$$V_p = P_t e^{-rt} + V_c - P_s \tag{15.6}$$

Using the example in Table 15.7, the value of the put is

$$\begin{aligned} V_p &= \$45e^{-(.1)(.25)} + \$7.57 - \$50 \\ &= \frac{\$45}{1.0253} + \$7.57 - \$50 \\ &= \$1.46 \end{aligned}$$

INDEX, INTEREST RATE, CURRENCY, AND COMMODITY OPTIONS

Beginning in 1982, options began to be written against many more types of underlying assets. This section briefly discusses these newer types of options.

• Equity Index Options

The first options contract against an index of common stocks began trading on March 11, 1983, on the CBOE. The underlying index for this initial contract was the S&P 100. The CBOE also introduced options on the S&P 500 Index. These **equity index options** proved so popular that the AMEX and NYSE quickly started trading them. The AMEX introduced options on the Major Markets Index (MMI) in April 1983. This index is designed to be very similar to the Dow Jones Industrial Average (DJIA). In September 1983, the NYSE began trading options on the NYSE Composite Index. These first contracts were issued on *broad-based* indexes. Equity index options are now also written against *narrow-based* indexes such as the Oil Stock Index and the Institutional Index and are traded on the AMEX. The AMEX also recently introduced options on the Japanese stock market, as represented by the Nikkei Average. Two regional exchanges, Philadelphia and Pacific, offer options against the Value Line Index and the Financial News Composite Index.

CHARACTERISTICS OF INDEX OPTIONS As the name implies, equity index options are written against an underlying index of common stocks. Since the value of the option depends on the value and changes in value of the underlying index, it is important to understand how the index is calculated (see Chapter 4). Indexes can be calculated in a number of different ways. For example, some indexes are simple price-weighted indexes, such as the MMI, while others are value-weighted indexes like the S&P 100 and S&P 500. Each index is designed to represent a different segment of the stock market.

Unlike options on individual stocks, index options are not written against a particular number of shares. The size of the contract is determined by the *multiplier.* The quoted price for the option is multiplied by the multiplier to determine the total value of the contract. For example, the multiplier for the S&P 100, MMI, and NYSE Composite is 100. If the quoted option price is 18¼, the total contract value is $1,825.

Index options are exercised in essentially the same way as equity options except that index options must be *settled by cash* since there is no underlying deliverable asset. The cash settlement amount is calculated as the difference between the index value and the exercise price, times the applicable multiplier. Because of the cash settlement requirement, call writers cannot completely hedge by taking a position in the underlying asset. Instead, the hedge must be formed by taking a position (either long or short) in an actual portfolio of stocks that is identical to the stocks included in the index. This is not practical for most investors.

In April 1986, the CBOE introduced a modified S&P 500 option contract that is a European-style contract that cannot be exercised until maturity. The new contract also has a much wider range of expiration cycles and dates. Some contracts now offer expiration dates over two years away.[3]

---

[3] For more details, see Trudy Ring, "S&P Contracts a Hit," *Pensions and Investments,* June 25, 1990, pp. 3, 48.

GAINS AND LOSSES Profits and losses on a long position in a call on an equity index option are computed as the difference between the actual value of the underlying index and the exercise price less the cost of the option. For example, assume you purchased a call on the S&P 100 on December 15, 1990, for $15 with an exercise price of $285. Since the closing value of the S&P 100 Index on December 31, 1990, was 309.44, your profit is

Actual S&P 100 Index value	309.44
Exercise price on call	285.00
Difference	24.44
Less original cost of call	15.00
Net difference	9.44
Times multiplier	100
Profit	$944.00

RISK FACTORS Unlike equity options, equity index options are subject to *timing risk*. Option writers face this risk because there is a delay between the exercise date and the time when they receive a notice of exercise. The writer may not be informed of the exercise until a minimum of one day after the exercise. In the meantime, the value of the index may change substantially. This is not a problem with an equity option if the writer has a position in the underlying stock since the exercise can be covered by delivery; with an index option, however, the writer must make a cash settlement. Even if the writer attempts to hedge by holding a position in a stock portfolio similar to the index, timing risk cannot be eliminated; the stocks will also change in value without the writer realizing the option has been exercised.

Another risk factor for equity index options is the influence of dividends. As we noted in the discussion of equity options, cash dividends present problems in analyzing American options using the Black-Scholes model. The situation is even more complex for equity index options because the stocks in the index have different dividend rates and ex-dividend dates. Also, many of the companies composing the index are likely to change their dividends, thus increasing the uncertainty of the dividend stream. The dividend problem therefore complicates the valuation of equity index options and influences possible trading strategies.

QUOTATIONS Table 15.9 provides an example of quotations on some of the more actively traded equity index options. Notice that options are available with expiration dates every month rather than on a three-month cycle like equity options. Also notice the volume of trading (sales) that many of these contracts enjoy; index option contracts are heavily traded. For example, the weekly volume of put and call equity index options on the S&P 100 contract traded on the CBOE for the week ending July 5, 1991, was 592,865 contracts, compared to a total volume of 444,514 contracts for puts and calls on CBOE individual stocks.

TABLE 15.9 • Quotations on Equity Index Options

CHICAGO BOARD

S&P 100 INDEX OEX

Index	Expire date Strike price	Sales	Open Int.	Week's High	Low	Price	Net Chg.	N.Y. Close
SP100	Jul375.	14318	17775	¾	3-16	5-16	−1-16	355.67
SP100	Jul380.	7446	15136	⅜	⅛	⅛	−1-16	355.67
SP100	Jul385.	2800	13825	3-16	1-16	1-16	......	355.67
SP100	Jul330.	1451	16803	30¾	27⅞	27⅞	+3⅛	355.67
SP100	Jul330 p	10024	20845	⅝	5-16	7-16	−9-16	355.67
SP100	Jul340.	121	1736	19½	16	17¾	+2	355.67
SP100	Jul340 p	29624	29450	1⅝	⅝	15-16	−1¼	355.67
SP100	Jul350.	10783	18954	12½	7¾	8⅞	+1⅜	355.67
SP100	Jul350 p	56145	42898	3½	1¾	2⅝	−2⅛	355.67
SP100	Jul360.	75882	51041	5⅜	2 11-16	3	+¼	355.67
SP100	Jul360 p	51526	36346	8⅜	4¾	6⅞	−3¼	355.67
SP100	Jul370.	27309	29574	1½	9-16	11-16	−1-16	355.67
SP100	Jul370 p	419	1584	16¾	11½	15	−2½	355.67
SP100	Aug335.	575	554	24⅛	23	24⅛	+24⅛	355.67
SP100	Aug335 p	3695	2775	3¼	2	2 11-16	−11-16	355.67
SP100	Aug340 p	2168	6267	4⅛	2 9-16	3⅜	−¾	355.67
SP100	Aug345 p	2885	5672	5⅜	3⅜	4⅞	−¾	355.67
SP100	Aug350.	299	5335	15	11½	12¼	+1½	355.67
SP100	Aug350 p	4551	10081	7⅛	4½	6¼	−1⅜	355.67
SP100	Aug355.	3697	4774	11⅝	8¼	9½	+1⅝	355.67
SP100	Aug355 p	7064	6533	9	6⅛	8¼	−1⅝	355.67
SP100	Aug360.	5384	11689	8½	5⅝	6¾	+1¼	355.67
SP100	Aug360 p	5491	10703	11⅞	8	10⅜	−1⅞	355.67
SP100	Aug365.	4239	11572	6	4	4⅝	+⅞	355.67
SP100	Aug365 p	175	809	15	10¾	13⅜	−2⅜	355.67
SP100	Aug370.	2630	6780	4	2½	2 15-16	+½	355.67
SP100	Aug375.	2437	8824	2 9-16	1 9-16	1 13-16	+3-16	355.67
SP100	Aug380.	2211	10199	1 9-16	15-16	1 1-16	+1-16	355.67
SP100	Aug385.	632	2774	15-16	9-16	⅝	+1-16	355.67
SP100	Sep335 p	1849	1813	5½	4	5	−¾	355.67
SP100	Sep340 p	705	2434	7	4⅞	5⅞	−1⅛	355.67
SP100	Sep345 p	682	3875	8⅛	6	7	−1⅜	355.67
SP100	Sep350 p	1780	2040	9¾	7¼	9	−¾	355.67

S&P 500 INDEX SPX

Index	Expire date Strike price	Sales	Open Int.	Week's High	Low	Price	Net Chg.	N.Y. Close
SP500	Jul345 p	555	2107	½	¼	⅜	−7-16	374.07
SP500	Jul350.	1515	10754	28	24½	24½	−1	374.07
SP500	Jul350 p	215	2106	11-16	7-16	11-16	−11-16	374.07
SP500	Jul355.	776	7652	24	20½	20½	+4⅛	374.07
SP500	Jul355 p	649	8694	1⅛	½	11-16	−13-16	374.07
SP500	Jul360.	327	1570	19½	14½	17⅜	+4¼	374.07
SP500	Jul360 p	4884	3082	1⅝	13-16	1	−1⅜	374.07
SP500	Jul365.	210	810	15	10⅜	11⅜	+2	374.07
SP500	Jul365 p	1288	5041	2⅝	1¼	2	−1¾	374.07
SP500	Jul370.	2182	12596	11	6¾	7⅝	+1⅝	374.07
SP500	Jul370 p	2084	9922	4¼	2 3-16	3	−2½	374.07
SP500	Jul375.	1769	16539	7½	3⅞	4½	+⅝	374.07
SP500	Jul375 p	2464	12210	6¼	3½	5¼	−3⅛	374.07
SP500	Jul380.	2547	7878	4¾	2	2½	+¼	374.07
SP500	Jul380 p	876	5003	9⅜	5½	8	−3¼	374.07
SP500	Jul385.	1660	5591	2 9-16	1	1 3-16	+1-16	374.07
SP500	Jul385 p	182	700	13	8½	13	−2	374.07
SP500	Jul390.	1654	8811	1¼	7-16	½	−1-16	374.07
SP500	Jul395.	1091	1615	11-16	¼	¼	−⅛	374.07
SP500	Aug350 p	252	1388	2½	1¾	2 5-16	−1 1-16	374.07
SP500	Aug355.	250	250	25⅝	25⅝	25⅝	+25⅝	374.07
SP500	Aug355 p	460	388	3¼	2¼	3⅛	+½	374.07
SP500	Aug360 p	547	686	4¾	2⅞	4	−⅞	374.07
SP500	Aug365 p	2131	2228	6⅜	4½	5⅝	−⅞	374.07
SP500	Aug370 p	1480	3333	7½	5	6⅜	−1¾	374.07
SP500	Aug380.	1258	1526	8	5¾	6	+1⅛	374.07
SP500	Aug380 p	1127	916	12¼	8⅝	12¼	+12¼	374.07
SP500	Aug390.	1201	942	3⅞	2⅜	3	+15-16	374.07
SP500	Sep405.	230	3063	2⅞	1⅞	2⅜	+5-16	374.07
SP500	Sep410.	235	1538	1¾	1¾	1¾	+¾	374.07
SP500	Sep250 p	324	11271	⅛	⅛	⅛	−⅛	374.07
SP500	Sep300 p	555	7315	⅝	9-16	⅝	......	374.07
SP500	Sep325 p	510	7646	2	1⅜	1⅞	−⅛	374.07
SP500	Sep345 p	1232	12223	3¾	3	3⅝	−¾	374.07
SP500	Sep350 p	2463	13482	5	3½	4¼	−⅝	374.07
SP500	Sep355.	1417	1391	29⅜	25	26½	+2⅝	374.07
SP500	Sep355 p	198	3270	6⅜	4¼	5⅝	+⅞	374.07
SP500	Sep360 p	888	12119	7½	5¼	6⅜	−1	374.07
SP500	Sep365 p	625	8966	8¾	6½	7⅜	−1⅜	374.07
SP500	Sep370.	4043	6204	18	15	15⅞	+2⅜	374.07

AMERICAN EXCHANGE

MAJOR MARKET INDEX XMI

Index	Expire date Strike price	Sales	Open Int.	Week's High	Low	Price	Net Chg.	N.Y. Close
MMIdx	Jul540 p	263	2343	3-16	⅛	3-16	−⅛	618.33
MMIdx	Jul550 p	192	2399	¼	3-16	¼	−3-16	618.33
MMIdx	Jul560 p	120	530	7-16	¼	¼	−9-16	618.33
MMIdx	Jul570 p	226	585	¾	7-16	9-16	−7-16	618.33
MMIdx	Jul580 p	639	1662	1¼	9-16	¾	−1	618.33
MMIdx	Jul590 p	1391	3287	2⅛	15-16	1⅜	−1¾	618.33
MMIdx	Jul600.	316	1203	24¼	20¾	22	+2½	618.33
MMIdx	Jul600 p	4777	4469	3⅜	1 11-16	2½	−2⅝	618.33
MMIdx	Jul605 p	511	681	4¼	2 3-16	3⅛	−3⅛	618.33
MMIdx	Jul610 p	4001	1870	6⅛	3	4½	−3⅜	618.33
MMIdx	Jul615.	910	440	16	9⅞	10¾	+1⅝	618.33
MMIdx	Jul615 p	1111	717	8¼	4	6¼	−3½	618.33
MMIdx	Jul620.	2486	2058	12⅞	6⅜	7¾	+⅝	618.33
MMIdx	Jul620 p	3101	1992	10½	5⅜	8¼	−4⅛	618.33
MMIdx	Jul625.	3655	1338	9½	4⅝	5⅜	+⅜	618.33
MMIdx	Jul625 p	698	542	12¾	7¼	11	−4¼	618.33
MMIdx	Jul630.	2538	2333	6⅞	2⅞	3⅝	+¼	618.33
MMIdx	Jul630 p	265	391	15¼	9½	14¼	−3⅝	618.33
MMIdx	Jul635.	1852	1299	4¾	2 1-16	2 7-16	+1-16	618.33
MMIdx	Jul640.	1998	2310	3¼	1 5-16	1½	−1-16	618.33
MMIdx	Jul645.	799	746	2	⅞	1	−3-16	618.33
MMIdx	Jul650.	1758	2091	1¼	7-16	½	−1-16	618.33
MMIdx	Jul655.	189	548	¾	5-16	5-16	−⅛	618.33
MMIdx	Jul660.	145	1753	7-16	3-16	3-16	−1-16	618.33
MMIdx	Aug560 p	110	548	2½	2	2½	+¼	618.33
MMIdx	Aug600 p	335	747	8¾	5½	8¾	−1¼	618.33
MMIdx	Aug605 p	325	599	7⅞	7⅜	7⅜	−4½	618.33
MMIdx	Aug610 p	423	387	12	8	11¾	−2½	618.33
MMIdx	Aug625.	336	275	15	10½	10½	+⅛	618.33
MMIdx	Sep600 p	105	326	10⅝	10⅜	10⅜	−2⅜	618.33
MMIdx	Sep625.	130	140	20¾	17⅛	20¾	+6⅛	618.33
MMIdx	Sep650 p	780	854	39	30¾	37	+1¼	618.33
MMIdx	Sep680.	200	400	2⅛	2⅛	2⅛	+⅜	618.33

OIL INDEX XOI

Index	Expire date Strike price	Sales	Open Int.	Week's High	Low	Price	Net Chg.	N.Y. Close
Oil Idx	Jul240 p	125	67	5½	2⅞	5½	......	236.19

INSTITUTIONAL INDEX XII

Index	Expire date Strike price	Sales	Open Int.	Week's High	Low	Price	Net Chg.	N.Y. Close
InstIdx	Jul290.	125	295	5⅜	3⅝	3⅝	......	387.91
InstIdx	Jul290 p	400	580	7	4⅝	5¾	−3¼	387.91
InstIdx	Jul375 p	475	260	2	1⅛	1¼	−1⅜	387.91
InstIdx	Jul380.	200	155	13⅜	10⅝	10¾	−3	387.91
InstIdx	Jul380 p	575	145	3¼	1¾	2¼	−2⅛	387.91
InstIdx	Jul385.	220	174	10⅞	6⅝	7⅝	+1	387.91
InstIdx	Jul385 p	1127	908	4⅞	3	3¾	−2¼	387.91
InstIdx	Jul395.	357	784	4⅝	2 1-16	2 5-16	......	387.91
InstIdx	Jul395 p	500	695	10¼	6	8½	−3⅜	387.91
InstIdx	Jul400.	220	476	2 7-16	1⅛	1 3-16	+1-16	387.91
InstIdx	Jul400 p	475	707	13¾	9⅛	12	−1⅜	387.91
InstIdx	Aug200.	225	225				......	387.91
InstIdx	Aug200 p	225	225	⅛	1-16	1-16	......	387.91
InstIdx	Aug290.	125	125	8¾	8	8¾	......	387.91
InstIdx	Aug330 p	150	100	9-16	½	9-16	+9-16	387.91
InstIdx	Aug360 p	110	1000	2¼	1 15-16	2¼	−¾	387.91
InstIdx	Aug375 p	260	300	4⅞	4⅛	4⅞	+⅛	387.91
InstIdx	Aug385 p	223	160	8⅛	5¾	6⅞	+¼	387.91
InstIdx	Aug410.	105	750	2	1 13-16	1 13-16	+¼	387.91
InstIdx	Aug415.	260	645	1⅝	1⅛	1⅛	......	387.91
InstIdx	Aug450.	225	240	⅛	1-16	1-16	......	387.91
InstIdx	Aug450 p	225	225	61	58	61	+1¾	387.91
InstIdx	Sep425.	548	2224	1¾	1⅝	1⅝	+⅝	387.91
InstIdx	Sep300.	112	1164	94⅜	93¾	93¾	+6¼	387.91
InstIdx	Sep350 p	500	750	2½	2½	2½	−¼	387.91
InstIdx	Sep400.	400	6745	9⅛	9⅛	9⅛	+2⅞	387.91
InstIdx	Sep405.	155	155	7⅜	5½	5¾	+1	387.91
InstIdx	Sep415.	200	1100	3⅞	2¾	2¾	+11-16	387.91
InstIdx	Sep420.	143	200	2⅝	2	2⅝	+⅝	387.91

PACIFIC EXCHANGE

FINANCIAL NEWS INDEX FNC

Index	Expire date Strike price	Sales	Open Int.	Week's High	Low	Price	Net Chg.	N.Y. Close
FinIdx	Jul255 p	143	50	5⅛	3¼	4½	−½	253.38

SOURCE: *Barron's*, July 8, 1991. Reprinted courtesy of *Barron's Weekly*.

INVESTMENT STRATEGIES Like equity options, index options may be used to speculate or hedge. The major difference is that the speculating or hedging is on stocks in general or a major segment of the market rather than on an individual stock. The investor in a long or short position in an option on an individual stock is subject to *company-* or *non-market-related* risk. Equity index options do not have company-related risk since the underlying asset is an index representing many different stocks. Equity index options only have market risk, although narrow-based index options also involve *industry* or *specific-sector* risk.

1. Hedging Investors can use equity index options to hedge a long or short position in common stocks. The hedge for a long position in stocks is designed to eliminate some of the losses that would occur if stocks in the portfolio declined in price. A hedge can be formed by going long in a put on an appropriate index. For example, assuming the stocks in the portfolio are all blue-chip issues and their prices are closely correlated with the DJIA, an appropriate option would be the MMI index option, traded on the AMEX. The price of the index put option will increase if the MMI declines. The profits on the long position in the put would therefore offset some of the losses on the common stock portfolio.

2. Speculating Equity index options can also be used to speculate about movements in stocks in general. A bullish forecast for stocks indicates a long position in a call index option, while a bearish forecast indicates a long position in a put index option. Uncovered short positions would be appropriate if stocks were not expected to undergo a significant price change *and* if the speculator was willing to assume the risk of large losses.

• Interest Rate Options

Interest rate options are now available on indexes of short-term and long-term interest rates. They are not written against a specific security, and exercise is handled by cash settlement. These options are traded on the CBOE.

Trading activity in interest rate options has been relatively minor since their introduction. Activity is much greater for options on futures, where the futures contract represents a position in Treasury securities, mortgage-backed bonds, or municipal bonds. Options on financial futures are discussed in Chapter 17.

• Currency Options

Foreign **currency options** were first traded on the Philadelphia Stock Exchange (PHLX) in December 1982. The first currency traded was the British pound, but options are now traded on the Austrian dollar, Canadian dollar, Japanese yen, Swiss franc, and German mark. The majority of the traded options are American style, but European-style options are also traded.

• **INTEREST BOX**

Life of an Index Option Trader

During the years prior to October 19, 1987, "Black Monday," many individual investors and professional money managers earned significant returns in the securities markets. As the stock market continued to rise, many investors abandoned their normal trading strategies and began to engage in more risky investments such as options. The following story reveals how one index option trader fared on the day the stock market declined more than 20 percent:

> Rolling into last year's fateful week of Oct. 19, Bob McNally (only the name is fictitious in deference to the trader code of secrecy and his family's suburban respectability) had ample reason to be smug. Though his trading year had two and a half months yet to run, he'd made more than $7 million between his trading profits as a Chicago Board Options Exchange market maker and market appreciation on a large position in a technology issue he owned.
>
> With his keen mathematical skills, McNally was deft at being able to lay off his risk almost immediately in esoteric combination of puts and calls with different expirations and exercise prices, or in futures. He even employed three clerks not only to track his positions during the day but also to engage in endless computer number-crunching to uncover profitable price disparities among the profusion of option classes and series.
>
> For McNally, Black Monday, Oct. 19, began like so many other trading days. He arrived about a half hour early and soon pushed his way to his accustomed spot in the teeming S&P 100 pit. There's always a certain amount of chatter and badinage before the 8:30 (CST) market opening. It helps release the tension. On this day, talk revolved around Sunday's Bears game and the frenzied trading the previous Friday when the Dow dropped a then-unprecedented 108 points.
>
> But for all his seeming nonchalance, McNally was worried. For the previous Friday, he'd closed out a major short position in the S&P 100 Index when the October options on the index expired at the CBOE. At the same time, however, he'd violated his normal practice by neglecting to either hedge or take off the other side of his spread position. Thus, he was stuck with a large long position in the S&P 500 futures market at the Chicago Mercantile Exchange and short puts at the CBOE. In other words, he was massively exposed were the stock market to resume its steep decline of the previous week.
>
> The ensuing firestorm of selling on Black Monday made short work of both McNally's composure and his net worth. First, he dumped his 250 futures contracts using the special firm order phone on the floor. He got out 40 points below the Friday close. His loss on the position—250 times 40 times 500 = $5 million. He then bought in puts at drastically higher prices, incurring an additional $700,000 loss. He dumped his position in the high-tech stock at fire-sale prices, taking another big hit.
>
> The whole thing was incredible. He'd lost more than $9 million in less than an hour and wiped out a dozen years of successful trading.

SOURCE: Adapted from Jonathan R. Laing, "In the Pits: How One Option Dealer Blew $9 Million," *Barron's*, October 17, 1988, pp. 22, 24, 26.

All of the options traded on the PHLX are options to purchase or sell foreign currencies for U.S. dollars. The exercise price and quoted prices are therefore stated in terms of U.S. dollars and cents. For example, a December 1991 call on Canadian dollars with an exercise price of $.86 allows the holder the right to buy a Canadian dollar for $.86. The contract size is different for each currency and may range from 31,250 British pounds to 6.25 million Japanese yen. The total price of the contract is, therefore, determined by multiplying the per-unit option price by the size of the contract. Contracts can be settled by cash or the actual delivery of the currency.

A valuation of a particular currency option depends on an analysis of the U.S. dollar and the specific foreign currency. Together, these two values determine the *exchange rate* (see Chapter 6) for the currency. This complicates the analysis, since most other types of options are written against a single underlying asset. For currency options, however, changes in the value of the U.S. dollar and changes in the foreign currency both influence the value of the option.

Under a floating exchange rate system, each currency's value is determined by supply and demand factors. It is common, however, for foreign governments to use market intervention and/or regulatory controls to increase or decrease the value of their currency relative to another currency; these efforts pose a unique type of risk for currency options.

If a foreign currency decreases in value relative to the U.S. dollar (exchange rate decline), call prices will decrease, and put prices will increase. On the other hand, if a foreign currency increases relative to the U.S. dollar, call prices will increase, and put prices will decrease. For example, if an investor expects the yen to increase in value relative to the dollar, an appropriate strategy would be to purchase calls and/or write puts.

• Commodity Options

Options written against commodity and financial future contracts are one of the fastest-growing segments of the option market. The underlying asset for these options is a futures contract that allows the investor to buy or sell the underlying commodity or financial asset at a fixed price. Chapter 17 deals with commodity and financial futures. A discussion of options on financial futures appears at the end of Chapter 17.

SUMMARY

This chapter has discussed equity, index, currency, and commodity options. All of these options derive their value from the value of the underlying asset; in this sense, they are similar types of securities that exhibit common risk-return characteristics. Each type of option can be used to speculate in price changes of the underlying asset or to hedge or reduce the risk of a portfolio. Due to the increased volatility of the financial and commodity markets during the 1980s, speculator and investor interest in these derivative securities has grown dramatically. Because of this increased interest, the trading volume of these markets is likely to continue to grow. In the future, a number of new financial products will probably be introduced, and some existing products

• CONCEPT APPLICATIONS

Investment Concept	Concept Application
Hedging with puts and calls	A short position in a stock can be hedged by a long position in a call. If the stock price increases, the gain on the option will at least partially offset the loss on the stock. The option could also be exercised to acquire the stock to cover the short. A long position in the stock can be hedged by buying a put.
Speculating with puts and calls	Calls can be written or purchased to speculate about price movements in the underlying stock. A speculator with a forecast of a declining stock price could go long in a put or write a call. A forecast of an increasing stock price suggests writing a put or going long in a call. Remember, however, that writing or going short is always more risky than going long.
Valuing options	The Black-Scholes model can be used to value call options. The principle of put-call parity can then be used to value a put. Because the Black-Scholes model is so widely used by option traders, market prices are close to the estimates of value obtained from the model.
Hedging or speculating in other types of options	Options are now traded with a wide variety of underlying assets. For example, options are available on stock indexes, interest rates, foreign currencies, and commodities. These options can be used to hedge a position in the underlying asset or speculate about price movements.

may disappear. For this reason, interested investors should follow market developments closely, especially in the area of options on financial futures.

• KEY TERMS

American-style option
Black-Scholes option pricing model
Call
Commodity option
Covered option
Currency option
Derivative security
Equity index option
Equity option
European-style option
Exercise (striking) price
Expiration date
Hedge ratio
Hedging
Interest rate option
Intrinsic value
Leverage effect
Option
Options Clearing Corporation (OCC)
Premium
Put
Put-call parity
Spread
Standardized options
Straddle
Time value
Uncovered ("naked") option

• QUESTIONS

1. Options are sometimes called derivative securities. Explain this terminology.
2. Compare and contrast put and call equity options.
3. Briefly define the following terms as they apply to options:
   a. Standardized options
   b. Options Clearing Corporation
   c. Expiration date
   d. Exercise price
   e. Clearing members
4. Striking prices on options are often compared to the price of the underlying stock using the following terminology: out-of-the-money, at-the-money, and in-the-money. Briefly define each of these terms for both call and put equity options.
5. Compare and contrast the intrinsic value and time value of an option. Can an option that is out-of-the-money have intrinsic value? Can an out-of-the-money option have time value?
6. Explain the differences between a European-style call option and an American-style call option.
7. An investor who purchases calls that are not covered by the underlying stock has limited risk exposure, while an investor who writes uncovered calls has unlimited risk exposure. Explain this statement.
8. Explain the leverage effect in option investing.
9. Explain why the potential losses from writing uncovered puts are much larger than the possible losses from buying uncovered puts.
10. Explain the justification for a hedge that consists of a long position in a call and a short position in the underlying stock. Does this hedge eliminate the possibilities of both large losses and large gains?
11. Explain the justification for a hedge that consists of a long position in a put and in the underlying stock. Does this hedge eliminate the possibilities of both large losses and large gains?
12. Discuss the risk-return characteristics of a strategy of writing covered calls.
13. Compare and contrast straddle and spread strategies using options.
14. Compare and contrast strip and strap strategies using options.
15. Discuss the key variables that determine an option's value. Also indicate if the variable has a positive or negative influence on the option's value.
16. How do equity index options differ from options on individual common stocks?
17. Explain the put-call parity relationship, and indicate how it can be used to value a put.

• KEY TO THE INVESTMENT ANALYSIS SOFTWARE

Calculation	Appendix A-1 Page Reference	Access Procedure
Value of call	A-13	BEGIN, OPTIONS
Hedge ratio	A-13	BEGIN, OPTIONS
Value of put	A-13	BEGIN, OPTIONS

• PROBLEMS

1. Consider the following three call options:

Option	*Striking price*	*Common stock price*	*Option price*
1	$60	$50	$ 2
2	50	50	$ 6
3	40	50	$15

a. Indicate which option is in-the-money and which is out-of-the-money.

b. Calculate the intrinsic value of each option.

c. Calculate the time value of each option.

2. Consider the following three put options:

Option	*Striking price*	*Common stock price*	*Option price*
1	$40	$50	$ 2
2	50	50	6
3	60	50	15

a. Indicate which option is in-the-money and which is out-of-the-money.

b. Calculate the intrinsic value of each option.

c. Calculate the time value of each option.

3. Assume an investor *purchases* five call options for $5,000. The options have a striking price of $100 per share. Calculate the profits and losses on the options for each of the following stock prices:

Stock price
$ 80
90
100
110
120

4. Assume that an investor purchases five put options for $5,000. Use the striking price and stock prices in Problem 3 to calculate the profits and losses on the put options for each of the stock prices.

5. Answer Problem 3, assuming that the investor writes five call options.

6. Answer Problem 4, assuming that the investor writes five put options.

7. Consider an investor who purchases 100 shares of XYZ common stock at $50 per share and buys a put on the stock for $300 with a striking price of $45.

a. Calculate the gain or loss if both positions are liquidated when the stock price is $60.

b. Calculate the gain or loss if both positions are liquidated when the stock price is $40.

c. Calculate the maximum dollar *loss* that can occur for this strategy.

d. Is there a maximum dollar gain for this strategy?

8. Consider an investor who shorts 100 shares of XYZ common stock at $50 per share and buys a call on the stock for $300 with a striking price of $45.

a. Calculate the gain or loss if both positions are liquidated when the stock price is $60.

b. Calculate the gain or loss if both positions are liquidated when the stock price is $40.

c. Calculate the maximum dollar *loss* that can occur for this strategy.

d. Is there a maximum dollar gain for this strategy?

9. Assume that an investor with a long position of 100 shares of common stock purchased for $50 per share writes a call option with a striking price of $48, for $600.

a. Calculate the maximum possible dollar *gain* for this strategy.

b. Calculate the minimum possible dollar *loss* for this strategy.

c. Compare your answers to parts (a) and (b) with the maximum and minimum possible gains from the stock position only.

10. Consider the following data on a common stock and a call option on the stock:

Stock price:	$50
Striking price:	$48
Time to expiration:	3 months
Risk-free rate of return:	8% per year
Variance of stock's return:	.25

a. Calculate the value of the option, using the Black-Scholes model.

b. If the option is priced at $6, what investment strategy is suggested?

c. Use your answer to part (a) to calculate the value of a put with the same time to expiration and striking price.

• REFERENCES

Andresky, Jill. "Poor Man's Arbitrage." *Financial World,* February 21, 1989, pp. 63–65.

Auster, Rolf. "Investment Strategies Involving Convertibles and Options." *Practical Accountant* (August 1988): 60–70.

Baldo, Anthony. "Stock Option Roulette." *Financial World,* August 23, 1988, pp. 37–38.

Block, Stanley B., and Timothy J. Gallagher. "How Much Do Bank Trust Departments Use Derivatives?" *Journal of Portfolio Management* (Fall 1988): 12–15.

Brennan, William G. "Stay 'Put' during Bearish Market." *Small Business Reports* (April 1990): 75–78.

Brenner, Menachem, and Dan Galai. "New Financial Instruments for Hedging Changes in Volatility." *Financial Analysts Journal* (July-August 1989): 61–65.

Brill, Susan L., and Susan Jayson. "Pricing American Options: Managing Risk with Early Exercise." *Financial Analysts Journal* (November-December 1986): 48–55.

Chance, Don M., and Randall S. Billingsley. "Managing Your Portfolio with Index Options." *Futures: The Magazine of Commodities and Options* (September 1985): 70–74.

Chang, Jack S.K., and Latha Shanker. "Hedging Effectiveness of Currency Options and Currency Futures." *Journal of Futures Market* (Summer 1986): 289–305.

Commins, Kevin. "Risk Management: The Eight Best Hedges." *Intermarket* (August 1987): 17–23.

———. "The Whirlwinds of OTC Option Applications." *Intermarket* (April 1987): 12–14, 18–24.

Dattatreya, Ravi E., and Frank J. Fabozzi. "A Simplified Model for Valuing Debt Options." *Journal of Portfolio Management* (Spring 1989): 64–72.

Dinn, Jennifer. "Downturn Protection." *Financial World,* September 22, 1987, pp. 60–61.

Dubashi, Jagannath. "Futures and Options." *Financial World,* August 12, 1988, pp. 24–30.

Duggan, Patrice. "International Investing: Purchasing Power Insurance." *Forbes,* June 25, 1990, pp. 194–98.

Eaton, Leslie. "If You're Bearish on Japan—A Novel Way to Short the Nikkei." *Barron's,* February 27, 1989, pp. 13, 18.

Epstein, Lee. "Hedge Your Bets with Futures and Options." *Cash Flow* (April 1988): 50–51.

Ferguson, Robert, and Roken Ahmed. "Technical Notes: How to Get Rich Quick (Without Losing Sleep)." *Financial Analysts Journal* (July-August 1988): 68–75.

Figlewski, Stephen. "What Does an Option Pricing Model Tell Us about Option Prices?" *Financial Analysts Journal* (September-October 1989): 12–15.

Frank, John N. "This Triple Witching Hour Could Last All Day." *Business Week,* June 22, 1987, pp. 126, 128.

Friedman, Amy. "An Options Primer." *Financial World,* March 24, 1987, pp. 39–42, 103.

Hardy, Steve. "Index Options versus Stock Options." *Intermarket* (October 1986): 70–71.

Hayre, Lakhbir S. "Understanding Option-Adjusted Spreads and Their Use." *Journal of Portfolio Management* (Summer 1990): 68–69.

Henriques, Diana. "The $900,000 Lesson: Educators Learn about Index Options." *Barron's,* September 7, 1987, pp. 14, 71–72.

Heston, Clark. "Can Little Players Compete in Index Arbitrage Trading?" *Futures: The Magazine of Commodities and Options* (December 1986): 49–51.

Kling, Arnold. "How the Stock Market Can Learn to Live with Index Futures and Options." *Financial Analysts Journal* (September-October 1987): 33–39.

Krause, David S. "The Covered Call Dividend Capture Strategy." *Journal of Cash Management* (March-April 1988): 22–25.

Labuszewski, John. "Playing the Odds with Options." *Futures: The Magazine of Commodities and Options* (March 1987): 68, 70.

Levy, Haim, and James A. Yoder. "Applying the Black-Scholes Model after Large Market Shocks." *Journal of Portfolio Management* (Fall 1989): 103–6.

Muscovitz, Steven D. "A Viable Option: The Case for Writing Covered Calls." *Barron's,* August 21, 1989, pp. 20–21.

O'Brien, Thomas J. "The Mechanics of Portfolio Insurance." *Journal of Portfolio Management* (Spring 1988): 40–47.

Pettit, R. Richardson, and Ronald F. Singer. "Instant Option Betas." *Financial Analysts Journal* (September-October 1986): 51–62.

Reddy, Girish V., and John W. O'Brien. "Different Options Abroad: Systematic Risk Management in International Markets." *Institutional Investor* (June 1990): 95.

Ring, Trudy. "Derivatives Making Waves." *Pensions and Investments,* April 30, 1990, pp. 21, 28.

———. "Supporters Rally behind Dynamic Hedging." *Pensions and Investments,* June 25, 1990, p. 19.

Sloan, Allan, and Richard L. Stern. "How the Formula Led to Black Monday." *Forbes,* January 25, 1988, pp. 55–59.

Smith, Clifford W., Jr., Charles W. Smithson, and D. Sykes Wilford. "Building Blocks: Forwards, Futures, Swaps, Options, and Hybrids." *Intermarket* (June 1989): 32–37.

Thayer, Peter W. "Seven Reasons to Choose Index Options." *Pension World* (October 1985): 34–36, 50.

Thompson, Thomas G. "Handy Hedges." *Secondary Mortgage Markets* (Winter 1989-1990): 22–26.

Walmsley, Julian. "Covering the Nakedness." *Intermarket* (November 1989): 52–53.

Weiss, Stuart. "Beating Swords into Stock Shares." *CFO: The Magazine for Chief Financial Officers* (August 1990): 45–46.

Wyatt, Edward. "The Action in Options—It's Still Conspicuous by Its Absence." *Barron's*, May 15, 1989, pp. 40, 124.

———. "Nixing the Nikkei: There Are More Ways to Short Tokyo." *Barron's*, March 26, 1990, pp. 20, 22.

Yates, James W., Jr., and Robert W. Kopprasch, Jr. "Writing Covered Call Options: Profits and Risks." *Journal of Portfolio Management* (Fall 1980): 74–79.

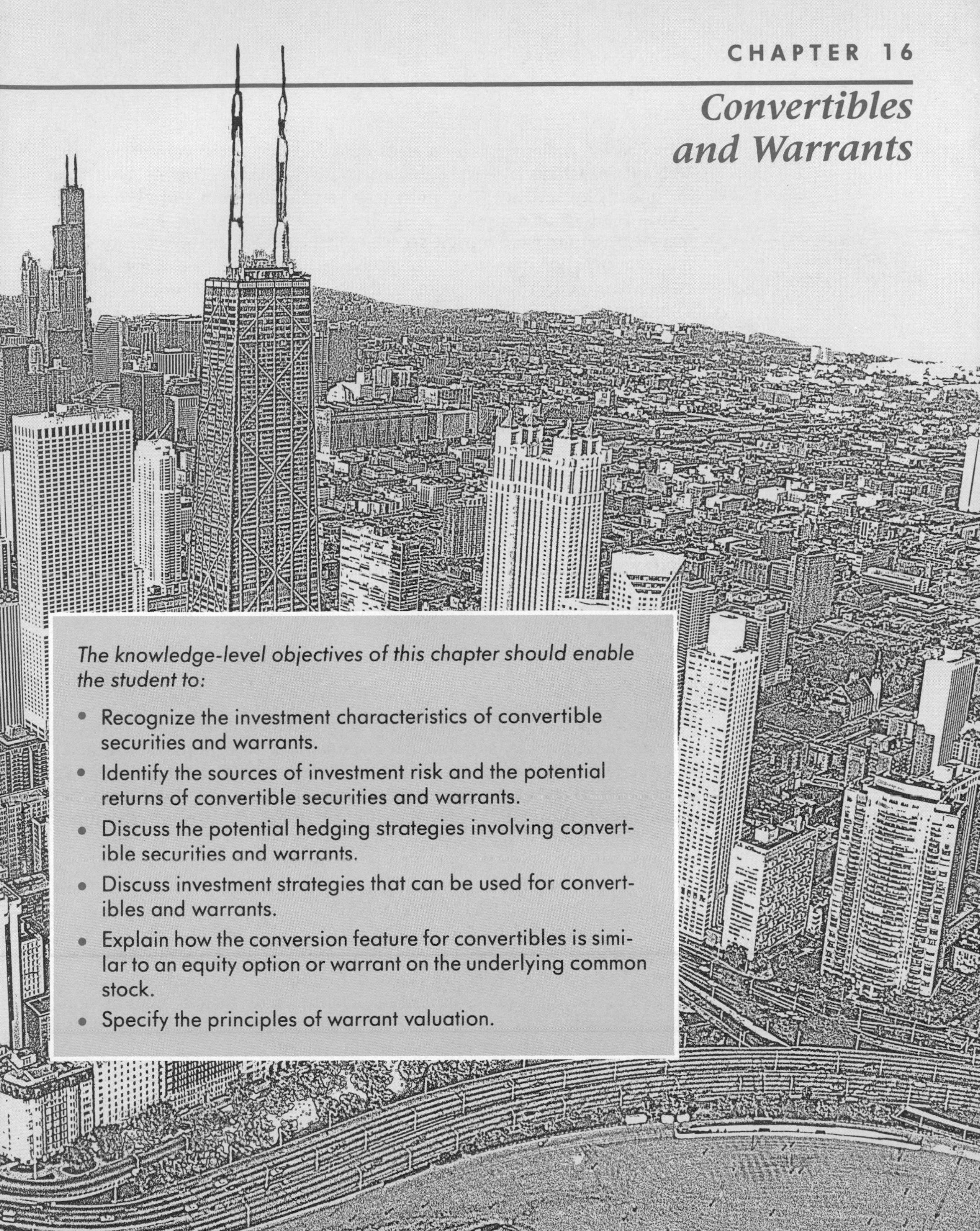

CHAPTER 16

Convertibles and Warrants

The knowledge-level objectives of this chapter should enable the student to:

- Recognize the investment characteristics of convertible securities and warrants.
- Identify the sources of investment risk and the potential returns of convertible securities and warrants.
- Discuss the potential hedging strategies involving convertible securities and warrants.
- Discuss investment strategies that can be used for convertibles and warrants.
- Explain how the conversion feature for convertibles is similar to an equity option or warrant on the underlying common stock.
- Specify the principles of warrant valuation.

INTRODUCTION

This chapter examines two types of derivative securities: convertibles and warrants. As Chapter 15 explained, a derivative security derives its value from an underlying security. The underlying security for both convertibles and warrants is the common stock of the firm. *Convertible securities* (bonds or preferred stocks) are fixed-income securities that can be exchanged for the issuing company's common stock. Convertibles are often described as *hybrid* securities because they resemble both fixed-income and common stock securities. The convertible feature creates unique investment characteristics: the securities must be analyzed as both fixed-income and equity securities.

The last part of the chapter discusses warrants. *Warrants* are essentially a call option and can be defined as a contract issued by a corporation that grants the holder the option to purchase that corporation's common stock, at a stated price, within a stated time. They differ from call options in one respect, however; warrants are issued by the corporation whereas individual investors or institutions issue options.

The appendix to the chapter discusses stock rights. *Rights* are securities issued by a corporation that give existing common stock shareholders the opportunity to acquire a proportionate share of a new issue of common stock. Stockholders who receive rights may sell them in the secondary market or use them to acquire additional shares of common stock. Rights, therefore, have characteristics that make them similar to convertibles and warrants.

CONVERTIBLE SECURITIES

Convertible securities are considered an alternative investment. Although they are not as popular as traditional investments in straight (nonconvertible) bonds and common stocks, their unique features may make them attractive alternatives in an active investment strategy. The volatility of the bond and stock markets during the 1980s and early 1990s has increased investor interest in convertibles. In late 1989, the total market value of all outstanding convertibles was around $50–$60 billion.

The stock market collapse during 1987 also affected convertibles. Their price decline, however, was considerably smaller than the decline in common stocks. For example, the NASDAQ composite index fell 11.6 percent from January through November 1987, while the Value Line Convertible Index declined 7.9 percent. Convertible prices did not decline as much as common stocks because their value, in part, is determined by their straight or nonconvertible value. The strong stock and bond markets during early 1990 also generated considerable investor interest in convertibles.[1]

---

[1] For example, see Randall W. Forsyth, "It's Convertible Weather," *Barron's*, June 11, 1990, p. 53.

Corporate investors receive favorable tax treatment on dividend income from common and preferred stock (see Chapter 14), but this favorable treatment is not available to individual investors. For this reason, corporate investors prefer **convertible preferred stock** while individual investors prefer **convertible bonds.** This chapter focuses on convertible bonds, but with the expection of the tax treatment, the analysis also applies to convertible preferred stocks.

As with all securities, convertibles exist because they offer advantages to both the issuer and the investor. This part of the chapter examines specific characteristics of convertibles and provides several approaches for investment analysis. Finally, a number of investment strategies for convertibles are presented.

• Characteristics of Convertibles

Because they combine features of both fixed-income and common stock securities, convertibles have several unique characteristics. Their hybrid nature offers investors several advantages and disadvantages.

CONVERSION RATIO The **conversion ratio** indicates the number of shares of common stock that will be received at conversion. For example, a conversion ratio of 25 to 1 indicates that 25 shares of common stock would be received for each convertible bond (or preferred stock). The conversion ratio is specified at the time the security is initially issued and is protected from dilution caused by stock splits and large stock dividends. If the conversion ratio is 25 to 1 and the stock has a two-for-one split, the conversion ratio would automatically become 50 to 1.

CONVERSION PRICE A **conversion price** rather than a conversion ratio may be specified in the bond indenture. The conversion price represents the price per share at which the convertible can be exchanged for common stock. The conversion price can be calculated as

$$CP = \frac{\text{face value}}{CR} \tag{16.1}$$

where

$$\begin{aligned} CP &= \text{conversion price} \\ \text{face value} &= \text{face or maturity value of bond (usually \$1,000)} \\ CR &= \text{conversion ratio} \end{aligned}$$

For example, a convertible bond with a face value of $1,000 and conversion ratio of 25 shares has a conversion price of $40 per share. The conversion price of $40 is therefore equivalent to a conversion ratio of 25 to 1.

CONVERSION VALUE The **conversion value** represents the total *market* value of the common stock received at conversion and can be calculated as

$$CV = (P_s)(CR) \tag{16.2}$$

where

CV = conversion value
P_s = market price of common stock
CR = conversion ratio

For example, if the conversion ratio was 25 (indicating a conversion price of $40) and the stock was selling for $50 per share, the conversion value for the 25 shares would be $1,250 ($50 × 25).

STRAIGHT VALUE The analysis of a convertible requires a determination of the value of a *straight* or nonconvertible bond or preferred stock that is identical to the convertible in all other characteristics. Assume you are analyzing a convertible bond with an 8 percent coupon and 20 years to maturity. Because of the bond's characteristics and convertible features, the bond is selling for $1,200. What would be the price of an "identical" nonconvertible bond? Assume that these nonconvertible bonds are selling for $900. The $1,200 price of the convertible can therefore be divided into two parts: the value due to bond characteristics or the **straight value** ($900) and the value of the convertible feature ($300). The value of the convertible feature essentially represents the value of an implied call option (see Chapter 15) or warrant on the common stock.

COUPON OR CURRENT YIELD Convertible bonds are initially offered with a coupon yield lower than the yield on a similar straight bond. In exchange for the lower interest cost to the issuer, the investor receives the conversion feature. The yield on the convertible, however, will be above the dividend yield on the common stock.

Recent innovations from Wall Street include the introduction of **zero-coupon** convertible bonds, **adjustable rate** or **resettable** convertible bonds, and convertibles that allow the investor to select cash, notes, or the traditional common stock when the bond is converted.[2] Examples of companies that issued these nontraditional convertibles in 1990 include Carnival Cruise Line, Inc., and Illinois Tool, Inc.

MINIMUM VALUE A convertible security will not sell for a price below the higher of the conversion value or straight value:

$$MV = \max(CV, P_b) \tag{16.3}$$

[2] Marcia Parker, "New Convertibles Drawing Issuers, Investors," *Pensions & Investments,* July 9, 1990, pp. 3, 32.

• INTEREST BOX

Zero-Coupon Convertible Bonds

Zero-coupon bonds were discussed in Chapter 11 along with liquid yield option notes (LYONs) and other types of bonds. A recent article points out a number of reasons why zero-coupon convertible bonds are becoming more attractive to investors and corporations that need additional financing:

> Convertible bonds offer corporations a way to achieve equity financing with a premium over their current stock price. In the past 2 years, the zero-coupon convertible bond has accounted for 40% of domestic convertible new issuance. Investors who buy stocks receive 100% of the stock's upside appreciation and are exposed to 100% of the downside risk. However, investors who buy zero-coupon convertible bonds receive, on average, 85% of the equity's appreciation and are exposed to none of the downside risk over time.
>
> Companies issue zero-coupon convertibles because the premium they receive generally is 15% above the price of the common stock. In addition, zeros require no periodic cash payments of either dividends or interest. There are cash flow benefits as well. Interest is accrued but not paid until zeros mature at par value or are put back to the company at the specified put date. At maturity, if the stock has appreciated in value by an amount that exceeds the initial premium and the implied yield, conversion will occur and no cash payments will be required.

SOURCE: Adapted from Lee R. Cole, "Consider the Convertible: Zero-Coupon Convertible Bonds Are the Vehicle of Choice for Many Issuers," *Institutional Investor* (June 1990): 96.

where

$$\begin{aligned} MV &= \text{minimum value} \\ CV &= \text{conversion value} \\ P_b &= \text{price of a straight bond or preferred stock} \end{aligned}$$

The **minimum value** therefore represents a *floor* or lower limit for the market value. If the conversion price is substantially above the market price of the stock, the convertible security will be priced ignoring the convertible feature. For example, if the conversion price is $40 and the market price of the common stock is $20, the minimum value will be the straight value. In Wall Street terminology, this security would be called a **busted** bond or busted preferred stock. If the conversion price is below the market value of the common stock, the convertible's price will reflect the conversion feature. For example, if the conversion price is $40 and the market price of the common stock is $60, the minimum value then becomes the conversion value. These securities would be referred to as *in-the-money* convertibles.

PREMIUM The **premium** on a convertible represents the difference between market price and the conversion value (or straight value for a busted convertible). The premium is usually expressed as a percentage of conversion value (or straight value for a busted convertible). The premium for an in-the-money convertible is

$$\text{premium} = \frac{P_c - \text{CV}}{\text{CV}} \tag{16.4}$$

where

P_c = market price of the convertible
CV = conversion value of the convertible

For example, assume that a convertible bond is selling for $1,200 and has a conversion ratio of 20. If the stock price is $50, the conversion value is $1,000 and the premium is $200, or 20 percent.

CALL FEATURE Almost all bonds, including convertibles, are issued with a call feature and are therefore subject to **call risk.** Typically, the bonds cannot be called until several years after they are issued, and initial call prices are set above the original offering price. For example, a convertible bond issued on January 1, 1991, might have a call provision permitting a first call on January 1, 1994. The call price might be 110 ($1,100) in 1994 and decline to 100 ($1,000) by 1998.

The issuer of the convertible can use the call provision to force conversion when the conversion value exceeds the call price. In this case, the investor would elect conversion because the value of the stock received would be greater than the amount of cash received from the call. Commonly, however, issuers do not call a convertible the moment the conversion value exceeds the call price. The call may be delayed because of expectations of declining interest rates, refunding and other costs associated with the call, and capital structure considerations. The possibility of a call, however, reduces the premium on the convertible because the investor faces a call risk.

RATINGS Moody's and Standard & Poor's rate convertibles, using the same rating categories used for straight debt and preferred stock. The rating definitions used by Moody's were given in Chapter 10. Approximately two-thirds of all outstanding convertibles do not have investment-grade ratings (Aaa–Baa) because of two factors. First, many issuers of convertibles are small, rapidly growing companies with weak balance sheets that do not justify an investment-grade rating for the bonds. Because of the corporation's financial condition, investors may not be interested in a new offering of straight debt. The firm, however, may attract more investor interest by adding a "sweetener" like the conversion feature to a new bond issue. Second, many convertible bonds are subordinated to straight bonds and would have a lower priority in a corporate bankruptcy. **Credit risk,** therefore, can be an important part of an investment analysis of convertibles. The techniques of company analysis dealing with leverage and liquidity discussed in Chapter 9 can be used to assess the credit risk for convertibles.

As the sample of seven corporations in Table 16.1 shows, different bond issues of a corporation may be assigned different ratings due to subordination

TABLE 16.1 • Sample of Straight and Convertible Bonds

Issuer	Security	Maturity date	Coupon	Rating	Amount outstanding (millions)
Ashland Oil, Inc.	Sinking fund debenture	1992	6.150%	A3	$ 16.8
	Convertible subordinated debenture	2015	6.750	Baa1	200.0
CBS, Inc.	Debenture	2001	7.850	Baa1	29.8
	Eurodollar convertible subordinated debenture	2002	5.000	Baa2	400.0
W.R. Grace	Sinking fund debenture	2008	11.750	Baa3	100.0
	Convertible subordinated debenture	1996	6.500	Ba2	2.2
I.B.M.	Debenture	2004	9.375	Aaa	404.0
	Convertible subordinated debenture	2004	7.875	Aa1	1,285.0
Pan American World	Senior debenture	2003	13.500	Caa	87.0
	Convertible senior subordinated debenture	2010	9.000	Ca	165.0
USX Corporation	Sinking fund debenture	2001	7.750	Baa3	83.0
	Convertible subordinated debenture	2001	5.750	Ba2	215.9
Western Union	Subordinated debenture	1997	10.750	C	25.1
	Convertible subordinated debenture	1997	5.250	C	27.7

SOURCE: Moody's *Bond Record* (January 1991). Reprinted by permission.

• **INTEREST BOX**

Resettable Convertibles and Leveraged Buyouts: The Case of RJR Nabisco

A recent innovation in preferred stock and debt financing involves adjusting the dividend or coupon periodically to keep the security trading at a price close to face or par value. As Chapter 12 explained, adjustable rate preferred stock (ARPS) and Dutch auction rate preferred stock (DARPS) are examples of this type of financial engineering. "Resettable" bonds or "resets" have a provision that requires the issuer to raise or lower the coupon to keep the bond price fairly stable. This provision, in theory at least, is designed to reduce or eliminate price risk and credit risk on the bond. What happens, however, when the financial condition of the issuer deteriorates to the point that coupons would need to be increased to 20 percent or more per year to keep the bonds trading at par? Could the financially weak firm afford this level of interest payments?

In 1989, Kohlberg Kravis Roberts and Company (KKR) used a leveraged buyout to acquire RJR Nabisco, Inc. (RJR). At that time, it was the second largest leveraged buyout in history. A large part of the capital needed for the buyout was obtained by two issues of resettable convertible bonds. By early 1990, however, investors had begun to worry about the junk bonds of the debt-laden company, and one issue of the resets was trading at approximately 73 percent of face value. Fortunately, RJR was not required to adjust the coupon until mid-1991. At a price of 73 percent of face value, it was estimated that RJR would have to reset the issue's coupon at 20 percent to 25 percent. Coupons of that magnitude would likely cause additional cash-flow problems, further reducing the company's financial condition and possibly leading to a higher reset to keep the bonds' value at par.

In April 1990, KKR and RJR were considering their options well before the 1991 reset date. Under one plan, the company might sell some major parts of the business, such as the Planters/Life Savers units or its 20 percent stake in the ESPN cable network, and use the money to buy the bonds back from investors. However, the company would need to obtain permission from its banks and other creditors before it could sell major assets.

SOURCE: Adapted from Judith H. Dobrzynski, "Would $2 Billion Buy Faith in RJR Nabisco?" *Business Week,* April 9, 1990, pp. 70–71.

provisions. If the company is in financial distress (e.g., Western Union), however, the subordination provisions will not make a difference in the ratings.

TAXES Prior to the Tax Reform Act of 1986, favorable capital gain tax rates were available for investors who received long-term profits from converting or selling the convertible for a price above cost. The tax reform, however, eliminated the capital gain exclusion for individuals and corporations and taxes capital gains as ordinary income. Some analysts think that the tax reform will make convertible securities more attractive since it favors investments that pay dividends and interest and reduces the incentive to buy common stocks to obtain long-term capital gains.[3]

[3] See, for example, "A Connoisseur of Convertibles," *Fortune,* September 29, 1987, p. 157.

PUT FEATURE Some convertibles (and nonconvertibles) are now issued with a **put feature** that allows the investor to "put" or sell the security back to the issuer at a specified price. For example, in 1984 Ohio Edison issued a convertible preferred stock with a put feature; the put allows investors to exchange the convertible for cash or common stock at a fixed value and therefore establishes a floor or minimum value. Many of the recently issued zero-coupon convertibles also have a put provision. Normally, after three years, the investor has the option of selling the convertible to the issuer for the fixed value plus the implied interest earned to date.

QUOTATIONS Convertible bonds are quoted on all the major exchanges and the OTC market. They can be distinguished from straight bonds in the quotations because the current yield provided for straight bonds is replaced with "CV." An example of quotations for straight and convertible bonds from the NYSE appears in Table 16.2.

Convertible preferred stocks are also quoted on all the major exchanges and the OTC market. Preferred stocks are identified in the quotations with "Pf" after the abbreviated company name. The quotations, however, do not distinguish between straight and convertible preferred stocks. Publications such as Standard & Poor's *Stock Guide* can be used to identify preferred stocks with the conversion feature.

INVESTMENT ANALYSIS OF CONVERTIBLES

Convertibles can be analyzed in several ways. Here three methods are examined: the graphic approach, the option pricing approach, and an approach based on the capital asset pricing model (CAPM).

• Graphic Approach

Figure 16.1 illustrates the various factors that influence the value of a hypothetical convertible bond over its life. The figure assumes that the convertible was sold at face value with a delayed call date. The convertible feature allows the corporation to offer a coupon yield below that required for a similar straight bond. As the figure illustrates, a straight bond with the same coupon yield would be initially valued at a discount relative to the convertible. The value of the straight bond will move toward face value as it matures. Note that in indicating the behavior of the straight bond's value, the figure *assumes* that market yields are constant over the life of the bond.

Notice that the convertible is initially offered at a price substantially above its conversion value. Recent new issues of convertibles have usually had an initial offering premium of 20 to 30 percent. The initial premium on new zero-coupon convertibles is usually smaller with a range of 10 to 20 percent. The zero-coupon convertibles have a lower initial premium to make them more attractive to investors.

TABLE 16.2 • Quotations on Straight and Convertible Bonds

NEW YORK EXCHANGE BONDS

CORPORATION BONDS
Volume, $29,800,000

Bonds	Cur Yld	Vol	Close	Net Chg.
AForP 5s30r	10.0	5	50	− 2½
AL Lb 7¾14	cv	5	117	...
AMR zr06	...	35	41⅝	+ ⅞
Advst 9s08	cv	40	70	+ 2
AlaP 9s2000	9.0	4	100½	− 1
AlaP 8⅞s03	9.1	5	97⅞	− ¼
AlaP 9¾s04	9.5	17	102⅝	...
AlaP 8¾07	8.9	8	98⅜	+ 1¼
AlaP 9¼07	9.1	15	101½	+ ½
AlaP 9½08	9.2	20	103	+ ½
AlskAr 6⅞14	cv	34	85	...
AlskAr zr06	...	4	32	− ¾
AlldC zr98	...	7	51¼	...
AlldC zr92	...	8	90⅝	+ ⅛
AlldC zr95	...	35	69¾	− ¾
AlldC zr01	...	10	40¼	− ¾
AlldC zr03	...	10	31	+ ¾
AlldC zr07	...	30	21	...
AlldC zr09	...	25	18⅛	+ ⅝
AMAX 9.23s95	9.5	45	97⅝	− ⅜
viAmdur 5½93	cv	30	16	+ 1
AmGn 9⅜08	9.3	25	100⅝	+ ⅝
ATT 6s00	7.3	34	82	− ½
ATT 5⅛01	6.8	5	75⅜	− 1⅛
ATT 7s01	7.9	156	88¼	− ⅛
ATT 7⅛03	8.1	141	87¾	+ ¼
ATT 8.80s05	8.7	94	101¼	+ ⅛
ATT 8⅝s07	8.8	58	98½	+ ¾
ATT 8¾00	8.6	164	101⅝	+ ¼
ATT 8⅝26	9.2	175	94¼	+ ¼
viAmes 7½14f	cv	30	12	...
Amoco 8⅜05	8.6	10	97⅝	+ ⅛
Amoco 7⅞96	7.9	10	99⅝	− ⅛
Amoco 8⅝16	8.8	50	97⅞	+ ⅝
AmocoCda 7⅜13	6.7	54	110¾	+ 1¾
Ancp 13⅞02f	cv	10	90	...
Andarko 6¼14	6.6	16	94½	− ½
Anhr 6s92	6.1	24	99	...
Anhr 8s96	8.0	160	99¾	...
Anhr 8⅝16	9.2	5	94	+ ½
Apache 7½00	cv	10	100	+ ½
Arml 9.2s00	11.6	5	79	+ 3⅝
Arml 13½94	13.5	25	100	+ ½
Asar 9¾2000	9.8	30	99	− 1
ARich 8⅝00	8.7	5	99½	− ⅝
ARch 10⅜95	9.7	20	107⅜	+ 1
ARch 10⅞05	9.5	7	114	+ 1⅜
ARch 10½95	10.0	43	104½	− ⅛
ARch 9½96	9.2	90	103	+ ½
AubrnHl 15⅞20	21.2	351	75	+ ¼
Avnet 8s13	cv	10	91	− ½
BRE 9½08	cv	56	101½	+ 1
BakrHgh 9½06	cv	10	101½	...
BakrHgh 9s08	9.3	9	97	...
Ballys 6s98f	cv	3	35	+ ½
Bally 10s06f	cv	28	38	+ 1
BalGE 9⅜08	9.3	42	101	+ ⅜
BalGE 9⅛16	9.1	10	99⅞	+ 1
BncFla 9s03	cv	15	53	− 3
Banka 8⅞05	9.4	15	94⅞	+ ½
Bkam 8.35s07	9.3	89	90	...
Bkam zr92	...	12	90	...
Bkam zr93	...	78	85⅝	− ½
BnkTr 8⅝02	8.9	6	97⅜	...
Barnt 8½99	9.2	30	92¼	+ ½
BellPa 8⅝06	8.7	30	99	+ ⅛
BellPa 7⅛12	8.7	12	82¼	+ ½
BellPa 9¼19	9.1	10	101⅛	+ ⅛
BenCp 8.4s07	9.2	5	91	+ ½
BethSt 9s00	10.0	21	89⅝	− ⅛
BethSt 8.45s05	10.4	22	80⅞	+ ⅝
BethSt 8⅜01	10.1	3	83	...
Bevrly 7⅝03	cv	51	79⅝	+ ⅝
BlkD 8⅜97	9.0	60	93	+ ½
BlkBst zr04	...	10	30½	− 1
Boeing 8⅜96	8.3	35	100⅝	+ ⅛
BoisC 7s16	cv	80	83¼	+ ½
BoltBer 6s12	cv	5	60½	+ ¼
BrkUn 9⅛95	9.0	5	101	...
BrkUn 8¾99	8.8	15	99	+ ⅛
BrnGp 9⅞00	9.8	2	100½	− ½
BwnFer 6¼12	cv	210	88¼	+ ½
BusInd 5½07	cv	25	32¾	+ ¼
CBS 10⅞95	10.5	78	103⅜	+ ⅞
CIGNA 8.2s10	cv	187	96	+ 1½
CIT 9⅝09	9.6	5	100½	...
CSX 9½16	9.5	50	100½	− 1½
CUC zr96	cv	20	111¼	+ ¾

Bonds	Cur Yld	Vol	Close	Net Chg.
CPc4s perp	9.4	15	42½	...
Carolco 14s93	16.8	173	83½	+ ½
CaroFrt 6¼11	cv	5	68½	− ½
CPoV 7¼12	8.7	5	83½	+ 1
CPoV 8⅝09	9.0	5	96¼	+ ¼
CPoV 9½19	9.2	10	103½	+ 1
Champ 6½11	cv	62	97¼	− ¼
ChartC 12s99	12.7	5	94¾	+ ⅜
ChmWst zr10	...	36	31⅞	+ ⅛
Chvrn 8½95	8.4	65	100⅝	+ ⅜
Chvrn 7s96	7.3	52	95¾	− ⅛
Chvrn 8¾05	8.8	1	99⅞	+ 1⅞
Chvrn 9⅜16	9.3	25	101	...
Chiquta 11⅞03	11.6	58	102¾	+ 1⅛
Chiquta 10½04	10.8	39	97	+ ⅞
Chiquta 10¼05	10.5	10	97⅝	...
ChNY 8.4s99	9.4	12	89½	− ¾
ChckFul 7s12	cv	5	86	− ⅛
ChryF 9.30s94	10.3	4	90	+ ⅛
ChryF 13¼99	13.4	15	99¼	− ⅝
ChryF 12s92	11.9	336	100 23/32	+ 5/32
ChryF 8.95s97t	9.8	50	91½	+ ⅝
ChryF 7⅞91	7.9	30	99½	+ ⅛
ChryF 8⅜97	10.7	20	78½	...
ChryF 8⅛94	9.3	5	87⅝	+ ½
ChryF 7⅝92	7.7	3	98 15/32	+ 1/16
Chryslr 12¾92	12.7	425	100½	+ 3/32
Chryslr 13s97	16.6	413	78¼	+ ⅝
Chryslr 12s15	17.7	342	67⅝	+ ⅛
Chryslr 9.6s94	12.0	420	79⅞	+ ¼
Chryslr 10.95s17	17.0	94	64⅜	− ⅛
Chryslr 10.4s99	15.8	66	66	...
ChvrnC 12s94	11.8	60	101½	...
ChvrnC 7⅞97	8.2	30	96⅝	− ⅞
vjCircK 12¾97f	...	30	21⅞	+ ¾
vjCircK 7¼06f	cv	10	8¼	...
vjCircK 13s97f	...	25	6½	...
CitiPP 12½96	cv	31	100	...
Citicp 8.45s07	9.6	105	88⅛	+ ⅛
Citicp 8⅛07	9.7	101	83¾	− ¼
Clmt zrD96	...	9	59⅛	− 2⅛
Clmt zrD01	...	5	33⅛	+ ⅛
Clmt zrD02	...	4	30⅛	+ 1⅛
ClayHm 7¾03	cv	25	116½	− ½
ClevEl 8⅜11	9.3	20	90	+ 1¼
Coastl 11¼96	10.8	15	103⅞	− ⅛
Coastl 11¾06	10.8	13	108¾	+ 1¼
Coastl 11⅛98	10.6	23	104½	+ 1
ColuG 9s94	10.1	52	89½	− ¼
ColuG 8¾95	10.0	153	87½	− ½
ColuG 9⅛95	10.2	52	89⅜	+ ⅜
ColuG 8¼96	9.7	10	85¼	− 2
ColuG 10⅛95	10.9	11	93	...
ColuG 9⅛96	10.5	7	87	+ 1
ColuG 10¼99	11.4	8	90	...
ColuG 9s93	9.8	40	92¼	+ ¼
ColuG 10¼11	11.5	75	89	− 2
ColuG 10½12	11.3	5	93	+ 2⅜
CmwE 8¾05	9.1	10	96⅜	+ ½
CmwE 9⅜04	9.3	55	100⅝	− ⅛
CmwE 8¼07	9.0	18	91½	+ ¼
CmwE 9⅛08	9.3	65	98⅝	+ ⅞
ConrPer 6¾01	cv	336	86	+ 2¼
Consec 12½96	12.6	50	99	+ ¼
Consec 12¾97	13.1	148	97⅛	...
ConEd 7.9s01	8.4	22	93¾	+ 1½
ConEd 7¾03	8.5	8	91⅜	+ ⅝
ConEd 9⅛04	9.0	5	101	+ ¼
CnNG 6⅛92	6.3	7	97¼	− 1¼
CnNG 7¾94	7.9	5	98	− 1
CnNG 9s95	8.9	4	101	+ ¼
ConNG 7¼15	cv	8	98	...
CnPw 7½01	8.5	10	88	...
CnPw 9¾06	9.7	20	101	+ ¾
CnPw 9s06	9.3	22	97¼	− ½
CtlDat 8½11	cv	21	81½	− ½
CoopCo 10⅝05	cv	3	76½	+ 1
Crane 7s94	7.3	6	95⅜	+ ¼
CrayRs 6⅛11	cv	1	75	+ 2½
DatGen 8⅜02	11.2	6	75	− 4
DataGn 01	cv	5	102	+ 2¾
Datpnt 8⅞06	cv	50	35	...
DaytP 8⅞16	9.4	25	94⅛	− 1½
DetEd 9s99	9.0	16	100	+ 1
DetEd 9.15s00	9.2	25	99⅛	− 1⅛
DetEd 8.15s00	8.6	3	95	...
DetEd 7⅜01	8.4	13	87⅞	− ⅛
DetEd 7½03	8.6	60	87⅝	+ ¼
DetEd 11⅞00	11.1	12	107	+ ¼
Disney zr05	...	190	42½	...

SOURCE: *Wall Street Journal*, July 2, 1991, p. C14. Reprinted by permission.

FIGURE 16.1
Graphic Analysis of a Convertible Bond

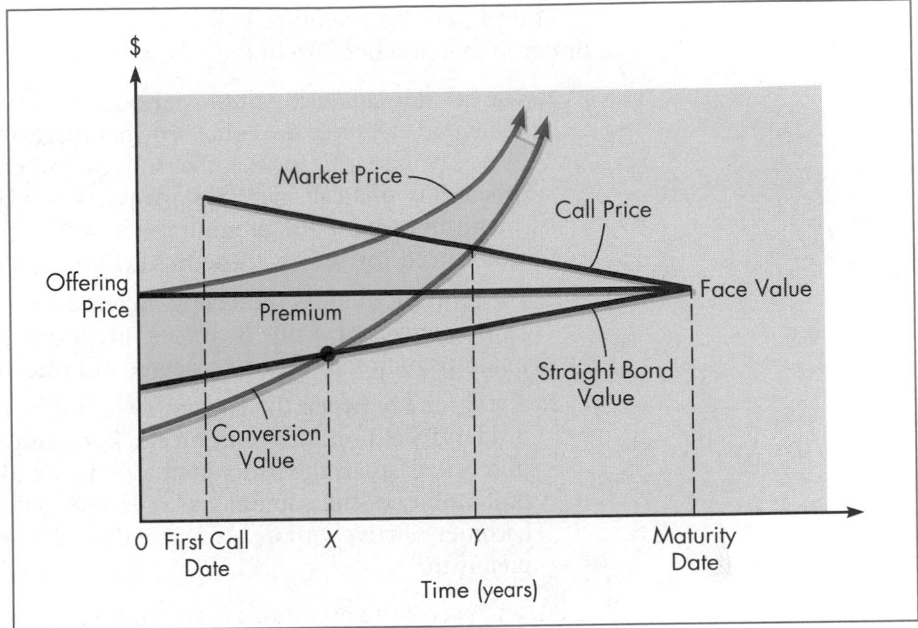

Figure 16.1 assumes that the common stock price begins to increase at a constant rate shortly after the convertible bond is issued. This is illustrated by the exponential upward-sloping conversion value function. Initially, the *floor* or *minimum value* of the convertible is the value of the straight bond. After X years (see the figure), however, the conversion value equals the straight bond value. Additional increases in the common stock price cause the conversion value to exceed the straight bond value. The floor then becomes the conversion value.

The function indicating the market price of the convertible is drawn so that a sizable initial premium exists. Why would a premium exist and behave in the fashion indicated in the figure? The premium exists because of the following factors:

1. Expectations that the stock price will increase, causing the convertible's price to rise.
2. Reduction of downside risk because if the stock price declines substantially, the convertible will sell at a price reflecting its straight bond value.

Thus, the floor makes the convertible less risky than the common stock but does not substantially reduce the upside price potential. The convertible investor benefits from increases in the stock price in approximately the same fashion as a stockholder but is protected to a certain degree from declines in the stock price.

The size of the premium will decline, even though the stock price continues to increase because of the following factors:

1. The bond is callable. At time period *Y* in Figure 16.1, the conversion value and call price are equal. Further increases in the stock price would allow the issuer to force conversion by calling the bond. Since the probability of a call increases, investors will be unwilling to pay a large premium because the premium would disappear when the call was announced (or before, if the market anticipates the call).
2. The amount of "loss protection" offered by the straight value decreases as the conversion value increases. Investors therefore reduce the premium to maintain the same degree of protection.
3. The spread between the current yield on the convertible bond and the dividend yield on the common stock is likely to decline as the stock price increases. If the issuer increases dividends because of the increased profitability of the company as reflected in the stock price, the stock becomes relatively more attractive than the bond, resulting in a smaller premium.

An analysis of the premiums is an important part of an investment analysis of convertibles. Why the premium exists and why it behaves in the manner suggested have been debated in the finance literature. The downside risk protection, or "insurance," provided by the floor has a limited influence in determining the premium if interest rates increase. If interest rates are stable or decline, as during the 1990–91 recession, the floor can provide downside protection.

Table 16.3 provides a numerical illustration of a convertible bond analysis based on the graphic analysis. The analysis uses common stock prices both below and above the current price of $39.50. At the time of the analysis, the convertible bond has a market price of $1,012.50, which reflects the conversion value and a 16 percent premium. The behavior of the premium for different stock prices is consistent with the graphic analysis. Obviously, the estimates of likely premiums are a key factor in the analysis.

• Option Pricing Model

The *option pricing approach* to analyzing the premium on a convertible was initially developed by Ingersoll and by Brennan and Schwartz.[4] These studies analyzed the premium by applying the framework of the Black-Scholes call option pricing model, which was discussed in Chapter 15 as part of the analysis of call options. It is important to realize that the convertible feature is essentially a call option (or warrant) issued by the corporation. The convertible

---

[4] Jonathan Ingersoll, "An Examination of Corporate Call Policies on Convertible Securities," *Journal of Finance* (May 1977): 463–78; and M.J. Brennan and E.S. Schwartz, "Convertible Bonds: Valuation and Optimal Strategies for Call and Conversion," *Journal of Finance* (December 1977): 1699–715.

TABLE 16.3 • Numerical Illustration of Convertible Bond Analysis

Data

Kerr-McGee Corporation

Common stock: Market price = $39½

Convertible subordinated debenture: Market price = $101¼; coupon = 7.25%; maturity date = 2012; conversion price = $45.30; conversion ratio = 22.08; call price = $1,050

Convertible Analysis

Stock price	*Conversion value*[a]	*Straight value*[b]	*Minimum value*[c]	*Premium*[d]	*Market value*[e]
$30.00	$ 662.40	$845.20	$ 845.20	0%	$ 845.20
35.00	772.80	845.20	845.20	6	895.91
39.50	872.16	845.20	872.16	16	1,012.50
45.00	993.60	845.20	993.60	21	1,202.26
50.00	1,104.00	845.20	1,104.00	20	1,324.80
55.00	1,214.40	845.20	1,214.40	18	1,432.99

SOURCES: Moody's *Bond Record* (June 1991); and *Barron's*, June 23, 1991.

[a] Calculated as (stock price) × (conversion ratio).

[b] Estimate based on a sample of prices for six straight debentures with similar coupon rates, maturity dates, and ratings. Assumes market yield will not change even if stock price changes.

[c] Defined as the higher of the conversion value or straight value.

[d] Premium is defined as the difference between market value and minimum value expressed as a percentage of minimum value. At current prices of $39.50 for the common stock and $1,012.50 for the bond, the actual premium is 16%. The premiums for the other stock prices are estimates.

[e] For stock prices other than the actual price of $39.50, the market values are estimated by increasing the minimum value by the premium percentage.

feature does not expire like a call option, but unlike a call option, it can be effectively canceled if the corporation calls the bonds.

The following conclusions result from an analysis of the convertible premium using an option pricing model.

1. Higher common stock prices generally *increase* the premium because the market price of the convertible increases relative to the conversion value.
2. The lack of a call provision or a long period before the first call date *increases* the premium.
3. Premiums on convertible bonds and preferred stocks are *larger* if the underlying common stock has significant price volatility, indicated by a high beta.
4. Cash dividends paid on the common stock *reduce* the premium because of their influence on the stock price and dividend yield.
5. Similar to the relationship between the risk-free rate of return and the value of an option, higher risk-free rates of return *increase* the premium.

RESEARCH BOX

Conversion Ratio: A Signal from Management?

As previously discussed, new convertible bonds are typically issued with an offering premium of 20 to 30 percent. In other words, the offering price of the bond is 20 to 30 percent above conversion value. Since the common stock is currently outstanding, its price is determined by the market. Management, therefore, sets the conversion value by adjusting the conversion ratio. With a high conversion ratio, a "small" offering premium (20 percent) results, while a low conversion ratio leads to a "larger" offering premium (30 percent). Thus, management controls the size of the initial premium by adjusting the number of shares of common stock that will be received at conversion. Is it possible that investors could use the announcement of the conversion ratio as a "signal" from management? If management is optimistic about the future earnings of the firm and the stock price, it might select a "low" conversion ratio. A "high" conversion ratio announcement might imply a negative signal from management.

In a recent article examining the conversion ratio issue, the author describes a model and the results as follows:

> The paper uses a signalling equilibrium (model) to explain the market's reaction to the announcement of a firm's financing decision. In our model, a firm can issue one of the following securities: convertible debt with a different conversion ratio, straight debt, and stock. We identify conditions under which the conversion ratio of a convertible debt issue serves as a credible signal of a firm's private information, given the continuous distribution of attributes (information) across firms. In this signalling equilibrium, we find that the lower the expected future earnings, the higher the conversion ratio of a convertible debt issue. At the limit, firms that expect the highest earnings will use straight debt financing, and firms that expect the lowest earnings will use equity financing. Based on the signalling equilibrium, we predict that at announcement of a convertible debt issue, negative abnormal common stock return increases in absolute value with the conversion ratio.

The model developed in the paper is theoretical and has not been empirically tested with actual data. Assuming the model and its conclusions are accurate, however, the article provides some useful information to investors in new or recently issued convertibles. A convertible that is offered with a "high" conversion ratio and consequently "low" offering premiums may not be a bargain after all. The low offering premium may be a subtle or unintended signal from management that it is somewhat pessimistic about the earnings prospects of the firm. Following this reasoning, an investor pursuing an active strategy involving new or recently issued convertibles may be better off investing in securities with a *high* premium (low conversion ratio).

SOURCE: Yong O. Kim, "Informative Conversion Ratios: A Signalling Approach," *Journal of Financial and Quantitative Analysis* (June 1990): 229–43.

Raymond King used the option pricing model to analyze convertible bonds.[5] Using a sample of 103 convertible bonds, he tested the model by determining the theoretical prices for the bonds and comparing them to actual market

[5] Raymond King, "Convertible Bond Valuation: An Empirical Test," *Journal of Financial Research* (Spring 1986): 53–69.

prices. King concluded that "90 percent of the model predictions are within 10 percent of market values."[6] Thus, the option pricing approach appears to model accurately the market's analysis of the premiums.

• Capital Asset Pricing Model

Convertibles have also been analyzed using the market model or CAPM. Using the S&P 500, the common stock betas are larger than the convertible bond betas when compared on a company-by-company basis. Research also shows evidence of considerable nonstationarity in the convertible betas.[7] This would be expected since the convertible would behave like the common stock when the conversion value was high and like a bond when the conversion value was low. The results from previous studies suggest that there are major problems in using the CAPM as a foundation for a convertible analysis. Essentially, a convertible beta will be useful only when the convertible is in-the-money or when it is selling to reflect the conversion feature. During these periods, the convertible price can be expected to behave like that of the underlying common stock. Using the beta for the underlying common stock may therefore be more appropriate during these periods than trying to estimate a beta directly for the convertible.

INVESTMENT STRATEGIES FOR CONVERTIBLES

As a general rule, convertible securities should not be used in a buy-and-hold or passive investment strategy (see Chapter 7). Convertibles, because of their hybrid nature, require careful analysis. The potential for rapid change in the premium also means that the investor must monitor investment developments closely and not buy convertibles and "forget" about them.

However, a number of active investment approaches can be used for convertibles. These approaches involve market timing (when to buy convertibles) and selection (which convertibles should be bought).

• Fundamental Analysis

Convertibles, like straight bonds, preferred stocks, and common stocks, can be analyzed using a fundamental analysis approach consisting of economic, industry, and company analyses. An analysis of the creditworthiness of the issuer (see Chapters 9 and 10) is important because of default risk on the bond

---

[6] Ibid., p. 53.

[7] For example, see Randolph P. Beatty, Cheng F. Lee, and K.C. Chen, "On the Nonstationarity of Convertible Bond Betas: Theory and Evidence," *Quarterly Review of Economics and Business* (Autumn 1988): 15–27.

or preferred stock component of the convertible. An analysis of the company's profitability and earning growth prospects (see Chapters 9 and 13) is useful in the analysis of the common stock component of the convertible.

• Traditional Premium Analysis

A successful active convertible strategy depends essentially on the correct analysis of the premium. A basic and traditional strategy is to invest in convertibles when the premium is below 20 percent, provided the security offers a reasonable yield.[8] If the premium is too high, the investor will not benefit as much from an upward movement in the stock price. The 20 percent cutoff is commonly cited in the popular literature, but there is little evidence to support the idea that this is the optimal cutoff value.

• Payback Analysis

Another strategy frequently cited in the popular literature uses a *payback analysis* of the premium.[9] The **payback period** for an in-the-money convertible can be calculated as

$$PP = \frac{\dfrac{P_c - CV}{CV}}{Y_c - Y_s} = \frac{\text{premium}}{\text{yield spread}} \tag{16.5}$$

where

PP = payback period in years
P_c = market price of the convertible
CV = conversion value of the convertible
Y_c = coupon yield on the convertible
Y_s = dividend yield on the underlying common stock

To illustrate Equation 16.5, assume that the common stock dividend yield is 4 percent; the convertible bond coupon yield is 9 percent; and the premium on the convertible is 25 percent. The premium would be recovered in 5 years [25%/(9% − 4%)]. According to this strategy, convertibles with shorter payback periods are more attractive investments than convertibles with long payback periods.

There are some basic problems with this strategy. First, the payback calculation ignores the time value of money. This is important because the pre-

---

[8] For example, see Steven D. Moscovitz, "Hedging Your Bets: Several Strategies to Consider," *Barron's*, April 7, 1986, p. 36.

[9] For example, see Randall W. Forsyth, "Flashy Convertibles: Why They're an Attractive Investment Vehicle," *Barron's*, August 20, 1984, pp. 28, 31.

mium is paid immediately when the convertible is purchased, but the interest income is received in the future. Second, what is the appropriate critical value for the payback? Is a convertible with a payback of five years a "good" investment, or should the payback be no more than three years? Finally, how can the possibility of a call be incorporated into the analysis?

• Market Timing

Traditionally, convertibles are often recommended when there is considerable uncertainty about the outlook for bonds and common stocks.[10] Since a convertible is a hybrid, it may offer a strategy for investors who are unable to decide between bonds and common stocks. The danger of this strategy, however, is that the convertible will *not* provide a hedge if interest rates increase and stock prices decline. The increase in interest rates reduces the value of bonds and lowers the floor for the convertible. The premium on the convertible is also likely to decline because of the declining stock price. The hedge will work if the stock price increases and interest rates remain constant or decline. Depending on the size of the premium when the convertible is purchased, the convertible's price will not necessarily match the gain on the common stock. It also may not match the gain in the bond market caused by declining interest rates.

• Busted Convertibles

As discussed earlier, if the conversion price is substantially above the market price of the common stock, the convertible is referred to as a busted or broken bond (or preferred stock). The convertible's price will not reflect the conversion feature but will be based on the straight bond's value. Several studies have analyzed an investment strategy based on busted convertible bonds.[11] The studies used various definitions of "busted" or "deep discount" to identify a sample of convertibles for analysis. One selection screen would classify a convertible as busted if its coupon yield exceeded the yield on the Moody's AAA utility bond index by a certain percent. Another screen would require the bond to be selling for a price below $700 or some other price substantially below face value.

Generally, these studies concluded that busted or deep discount convertibles appear to be underpriced and offer excess returns even after adjusting for risk. Typically, a CAPM methodology was used to adjust for risk, and the results applied to portfolios of convertible bonds, not to individual bonds in the

---

[10] For example, see Ben Weberman, "Fence-Sitter Bonds," *Forbes,* February 9, 1987, p. 143; and Forsyth, "It's Convertible Weather," p. 53.

[11] For an illustration, see Randall W. Forsyth, "Mutual Bonds: Heavy Lifting," *Barron's,* June 18, 1990, p. 45.

RESEARCH BOX

Risk and Returns for Convertibles

Portions of a recent article describing the return and risk characteristics of convertible bonds are presented here. Of particular interest are the default loss characteristics of convertibles compared to straight debt.

Convertible bonds made up about 6 percent of the almost $700 billion total corporate domestic debt market at the end of 1987. Non-investment-grade (high-yield) convertible debt accounted for 67 percent of the rated convertible debt issued that year, but only 48 percent of the market in dollar terms. The high-yield convertibles overall were not as high-yielding as their straight debt counterparts; companies issuing convertibles obviously pay a lower interest rate in exchange for the conversion sweetener.

Convertibles provided a fairly good return to investors over the 1983–1987 period—slightly above the returns on the S&P 500 and NYSE and slightly below those on high-yield straight debt and long-term governments. The strong correlation between convertible returns and stock returns was reflected in the exceptional performance of convertible bond funds over the 1978–1987 period, when they almost doubled the performance of high-yield straight debt and long-term government funds. They did less well, however, over the more recent three- and five-year subperiods.

In the case of default, convertible bonds, like straight debt, sell at significant discounts from par value. Over the 1980–1987 period, total convertibles, including both high and low grades, had an average default rate of 1.24 percent per year (including Texaco's massive Eurobond default) versus 0.32 percent for total straight debt. The recovery rate after default was also lower for convertibles than for straight debt (36.4 percent of par versus 43.2 percent). The average annual loss on the total convertible debt market was thus higher than that on the total straight debt market (0.69 percent versus 0.16 percent). The average annual default loss on high-yield convertibles, however, was 1.75 percent (versus 1.17 percent for high-yield straight debt).

Our results are based on a particular sample period; one cannot necessarily expect that the same return comparisons will continue in the future. But the high correlation between convertible returns and stock market returns suggests that convertible performance will depend in large part on future stock market activity. And longer-term measures of performance, such as ten-year mutual fund returns, suggest that convertibles are likely to outperform all other fixed-income funds.

The default loss data on convertibles should be considered seriously by investors and regulators. Institutional investors in convertible debt could very well benefit from a careful analysis of historical loss rates in determining loss reserves. Default loss experience affects net returns as well as stock market performance.

Finally, more research needs to be devoted to convertible debt issuers. Our empirical results indicate that the default loss risk is greater for high-yield convertible issuers than for straight debt borrowers in the high-yield segment. Can this be explained by an in-depth analysis of the fundamental risk characteristics of the issuing firms, or are there other reasons for this phenomenon?

SOURCE: Adapted from Edward I. Altman, "The Convertible Debt Market: Are Returns Worth the Risk?", *Financial Analysts Journal* (July-August 1989): 23–31.

sample. This risk-adjustment methodology is questionable, however, because, as noted previously, the CAPM cannot easily be applied to convertibles. Do the busted convertibles offer risk-adjusted excess returns because the market is not efficient? An alternative interpretation would be that the market correctly prices the bonds and that the risk-adjustment methodology is incorrect. The observed risk-adjusted excess return is simply additional return to compensate for the additional risk not detected by the CAPM methodology.

• Takeover Convertibles

The wave of corporate takeovers and leveraged buyouts in the 1980s created new opportunities and hazards for convertible investors. In many takeovers and buyouts, the convertible holder is forced to convert, thereby losing the existing conversion premium. If the conversion is not forced, the investor may be able to convert, but the conversion will be to the common stock of the privately held or highly leveraged company that emerged from the takeover or buyout. Two classic examples of these hazards are the leveraged buyout in 1989 of RJR Nabisco, Inc., by Kohlberg, Kravis, Roberts and Company, and the "successful" takeover defense mounted by Harcourt, Brace, Jovanovich, Inc.

• Mutual Funds

The number of mutual funds specializing in convertible securities has increased significantly over the past few years. Table 16.4 provides *Money* magazine's ranking of the top performing convertible mutual funds as of January 1, 1991. The ranking is based on a five-year performance. It is interesting to note that the "Money risk-adjusted grade" column uses the Sharpe portfolio performance technique (see Chapter 21) to assign a grade. Funds ranked in the top 20 percent in a group received an A, the next 20 percent a B, and so on. The "Lipper market-phase rating" column compares a fund's return with that of its competition during the current period as well as the most recent up and down phase for both stocks and bonds. The growing number of specialized convertible funds provides additional opportunities for a convertible investment strategy.

WARRANTS

Warrants are essentially a call option; they are a contract issued by a corporation granting the holder the option to purchase that corporation's common stock, at a stated price, within a stated time. Warrants are most often used as a *sweetener* in a new bond issue (or, less often, a preferred stock issue) to enhance its marketability and/or lower the interest or dividend rate. Warrants are also issued in corporate reorganizations or mergers. Warrants are traded on the organized exchanges and the OTC market and are designated in the quotations by "wt" after the company name.

Warrants have historically been issued mainly by small, growing corporations. When initially issued, the exercise price is usually 15 to 20 percent above the current market price of the common stock, so that as a firm prospers and its stock price rises above the exercise price, the warrant can be exer-

TABLE 16.4 • The *Money* Ranking of Convertible Mutual Funds

	Money risk-adjusted grade	Percentage gain (loss) to January 1, 1991				Percentage compound annual return		Five-year analysis		Lipper market-phase rating			Net assets (millions)
		One year	*Three years*	*Five years*	*Ten years*	*Five years*	*Ten years*	*Best quarter*	*Worst quarter*	*Current*	*Prior up*	*Prior down*	
Category average		(7.7%)	21.6%	39.9%	217.3%	6.8%	12.1%						
1. Phoenix Convertible	A	4.1	30.7	69.3	304.6	11.1	15.0	12.8%	(8.3%)	B	C	A	$143.3
2. American Capital Harbor	D	(1.2)	39.1	52.2	212.1	8.8	12.1	13.5	(20.4)	C	A	A	324.2
3. Dreyfus Convertible Securities	D	(16.7)	17.8	43.4	175.1	7.5	10.7	12.6	(20.0)	E	A	E	194.3
4. Value Line Convertible	E	(3.7)	23.7	35.0	—	6.2	—	13.5	(18.1)	B	B	C	33.1
5. Putnam Convertible Income & Growth	E	(10.0)	17.6	28.7	177.4	5.2	10.7	12.1	(19.3)	B	C	D	528.9

TABLE 16.4 • The *Money* Ranking of Convertible Mutual Funds (continued)

	Portfolio analysis				
	Percentage yield	*P/E ratio*	*Percentage cash*	Largest sector (percentage of assets)	Senior fund manager, age (years managing fund)
Category average	6.5%				
1. Phoenix Convertible	5.8	N/A	15.0%	Pollution control (11.7)	John Martin, 51 (9)
2. American Capital Harbor	6.7	N/A	1.6	Domestic oil (8.1)	James Behmann, 47 (8)
3. Dreyfus Convertible Securities	6.6	N/A	17.0	Communications (11.8)	Kathryn Jacobson, N/A (1)
4. Value Line Convertible	6.6	N/A	28.0	Government securities (12.2)	Committee management
5. Putnam Convertible Income & Growth	7.9	N/A	8.1	Consumer goods (7.3)	Anthony Kriesel, N/A (1)

	Expense analysis					
	Percentage turnover	*Percentage maximum initial sales charge*	*Annual expenses (percentage of assets)*	*Five-year projection*	Minimum initial investment	Telephone
1. Phoenix Convertible	214%	6.9%	1.03%	$122	$ 500	800-243-4361
2. American Capital Harbor	94	5.75	0.76	102	500	800-421-5666
3. Dreyfus Convertible Securities	66	None	1.05	60	2,500	800-782-6620
4. Value Line Convertible	105	None	1.05	58	1,000	800-223-0818
5. Putnam Convertible Income & Growth	49	5.75	0.93	119	500	800-225-1581

SOURCE: *Money,* February 1991, pp. 122–23.

cised. When the warrants are exercised, the firm benefits by receiving the exercise price in cash.

Warrants may also be *callable* by the issuing corporation. The call feature may allow the corporation to force the holder to exercise the warrant. Research has shown that investors pay lower prices for warrants that are callable. It has also been found, however, that many companies may not call a warrant even though the exercise price is below the current stock price.

The exercise price on warrants is stated when the warrants are issued. It is fairly common, however, for a warrant to have an increasing exercise price over its life. The exercise price is adjusted downward for stock dividends or splits that reduce the price of the common stock. This *dilution clause* protects the warrant holder. Warrants are usually issued with expiration dates three to five years in the future. In some cases, however, the warrant is issued without an expiration date; for example, Atlas Corporation's warrant, traded on the AMEX, does not have an expiration date and is a *perpetual warrant*. The issuing corporation may also extend the life of a warrant.

Another interesting characteristic of warrants is that in some cases the exercise "price" can be paid by surrendering a bond or preferred stock, usually at par, rather than cash. Since the market price of the bond or preferred stock is likely to change over the life of the warrant, the effective exercise price also changes.

These characteristics suggest that warrants have less risk than call options but more risk than the underlying common stock. The longer lives of warrants relative to call options reduce their risk. Thus, in an efficient market, the holding period returns (HPRs) on warrants should be greater than the HPRs on the underlying common stock, but below the HPRs on call options.

• Valuation of Warrants

The valuation of warrants is somewhat more complicated than the valuation of options. One complicating factor is that the issuing corporation is likely to receive cash when the warrants are exercised. This may well change the value of the underlying common stock and therefore the value of the warrant. A second factor is the potential **dilution** of earnings per share caused by the increased number of shares outstanding when the warrants are exercised. Thus, the difficulty in valuing warrants is due to the warrants' influence on the price of the common stock. This problem does not arise with options because they do not directly influence the underlying common stock.

Ignoring the possible influence on the value of the underlying common stock, determining the value of a warrant is a simple matter. Since the warrant is essentially a call option, it can be valued using a variation of the Black-Scholes model. The valuation variables are

$$V_w = f(\text{EP}, T_n, P_0, D_1, P_c) \tag{16.6}$$

where

V_w = value of the warrant
EP = exercise price
T_n = time remaining before the warrant's expiration date
P_0 = current price of the common stock
D_1 = potential dilution of earnings
P_c = expected future common stock price

In addition to the variables in Equation 16.6, a warrant's price is influenced by other factors, including (1) the dividend yield on the common stock, (2) the exchange listing, (3) the number of warrants outstanding for a particular issue, and (4) the "effective" cost of exercising the warrant. The identified variables not only are determinants in themselves, but they also have combined effects. The current price of the common stock (P_0) is a function of the possible dilution of earnings (D_1). Also, the expected future common stock price (P_c) is a function not only of D_1 but also of T_n, the remaining life of the warrant.

Investors need an estimate of the value of a warrant that can be compared to the price of the warrant, which is determined by supply and demand factors. The value of a warrant consists of two parts: *intrinsic* value and *time* value. The intrinsic or *minimum value* of a warrant is determined as

$$MV_w = (P_0 - EP)N \tag{16.7}$$

where

MV_w = intrinsic or minimum value of a warrant
P_0 = current market price of the common stock
EP = exercise price
N = number of warrants needed to purchase one share (usually a one-to-one relationship)

If the actual price of the warrant was less than MV_w, then arbitrage activities would be possible—buying the warrant and using it to acquire the common stock at a cost below its market value. It can also be seen that if P_0 is greater than EP and P_0 increases, the value of the warrant will increase. If the price of the common stock is less than the exercise price, $P_0 < EP$, the intrinsic value will not be negative, even though the value according to Equation 16.7 is less than 0, because the minimum value cannot be negative. It is common for warrants to sell above their minimum value, primarily because of the call option characteristics of the warrant and the expectation that the price of the common stock will increase before the warrant expires. This additional value represents the *time* value of the warrant.

• Other Factors That Influence a Warrant's Price

The difference between market value and minimum value is defined as the *time value*, which depends on several interrelated factors: (1) the time remaining before expiration, (2) the volatility of the stock price, and (3) the leverage of the warrant contract.

TIME The time value declines as the time remaining until expiration decreases. From Equation 16.7, it is easy to see that as the underlying stock price rises, the warrant will also increase in value. Time value will likely exist if the stock price has a significant probability of rising above the exercise price before expiration.

PRICE VOLATILITY OF THE UNDERLYING STOCK As with any option type of contract, the volatility of the underlying stock is a major consideration. The more volatile the stock, the higher the value of the warrant because of the increased probability that the price of the stock will move to a higher level. For example, if a $10 stock has a 25 percent chance of falling to $8, a 50 percent chance of staying the same, and a 25 percent chance of moving to $12, then the expected stock price, $E(P_S)$, is $10, computed as follows:

Probability	Price	Probability × Price
.25	$ 8	$ 2
.50	10	5
.25	12	3
Expected stock price = $E(P_S)$ =		$10

If the expected stock price is $10 and the exercise price is also $10, Equation 16.7 indicates that the minimum value of the warrant will be $0. This would be the case only if the stock price is $8 or $10. If the stock price is $12, the minimum value of the warrant will be ($12 − $10), or $2. The expected minimum value of the warrant can be calculated as

$$E(V_W) = .25(0) + .50(0) + .25(\$2) = \$.50$$

Since the value of the warrant will increase as the stock price increases, a warrant on a more volatile stock will have a greater value than a warrant on a less volatile stock. This can easily be shown by increasing the maximum possible stock price of $12 in the preceding example.

LEVERAGE The third reason that a warrant might sell for more than its minimum or intrinsic value is due to the speculative appeal of warrants. They give an investor the possibility of very large HPRs because their market prices are low relative to the underlying common stock.

For example, suppose XYZ, Inc., warrants are priced above their intrinsic value and an investor is debating purchasing the common stock or the warrant. The common stock is currently selling for $25, the warrant for $3. The exercise price on the warrant is also $25, indicating its intrinsic value is 0. If the investor buys the stock and it goes to $50, the HPR is 100 percent. However, if the investor had bought the warrant at $3 instead, the HPR would be a minimum of 733 percent [($25 − $3)/$3].

The possibility of large capital appreciation, combined with the loss limitation, clearly has value to some investors. The exact determination of their worth, however, is a function of supply and demand forces in the market.

WARRANTS AND FINANCIAL ENGINEERING

Like many traditional securities, warrants are being modified and new features are being added. Historically, investor interest and trading in warrants have been limited simply because only a few companies issued warrants. The problem of a limited supply, however, has recently been alleviated with the introduction of **covered equity warrants.** These are issued by companies (usually investment or financial institutions) *other* than the company that issued the underlying stock. The company that issues the warrant simply has a position in the underlying common stock (a covered position) and issues warrants against these shares.

SWORDS (an acronym for *s*tock *w*arrants of an *o*ff-balance-sheet *r*esearch and *d*evelopment *s*ubsidary) are a variation of the new covered equity warrants. For example, Immunex Corporation, the biotechnology company, formed a new company in 1990 by selling common stock in the new company with attached warrants. The new company, Receptech Corporation, is primarily a research and development company and, as an initial public offering (IPO), is very risky. The warrants issued by Immunex, however, allow the holder to acquire stock in the less risky parent firm, Immunex. Because of the success of this innovation or financial engineering, a number of other firms have also issued SWORDS.

A third innovation is the **currency exchange warrant (CEW).** These warrants allow the holder to acquire a fixed amount of foreign currency from the issuer. CEWs have characteristics similar to the foreign currency options discussed in Chapter 15. The CEW typically has a maturity of up to five years. The major issuers of CEWs in the United States have been the credit subsidiaries of major corporations that have a position in the foreign currency.

With the recent development of SWORDS and CEWs, the traditional underlying common stock is not the only type of asset that can be acquired by exercising a warrant. These recent examples of financial engineering also suggest that investors may expect to see many new types of warrants.

• CONCEPT APPLICATIONS

Investment Concept	Concept Application
Convertible security valuation	An analysis of a convertible bond or preferred stock requires an assessment of both the convertible feature and the "straight" or nonconvertible feature. Analysis of the premium is the key to the valuation. The premium can be viewed and valued much like a long-term call option on the company's stock. Understanding option valuation, therefore, is essential in understanding the behavior of the premium.
Warrant valuation	Warrants are like a long-term call option written against the company's common stock. Unlike a call option, however, warrants are issued by the corporation. The exercise of a warrant, therefore, directly affects the corporation since it receives cash and the number of shares of stock increases. The dilution effect from exercise and the impact of cash dividends should be considered in the valuation of warrants.
Investment strategies for convertibles	The majority of convertible bonds are "junk" bonds since they do not have an investment-grade rating. Credit risk analysis is, therefore, an essential part of a convertibles strategy. If new or recently issued convertibles are considered, it might be better to select those with high premiums. This would be true if the size of the initial premium is a signal from management about earnings prospects. Other possible strategies for convertibles trading in the secondary market include payback analysis of the premium, hedging, investing in busted convertibles, and investing in convertible mutual funds. Risk and return analysis for convertibles over the period 1983–1987 indicates a diversified portfolio (to reduce credit risk) of convertibles provided a slightly higher return than for common stocks in general. Since the performance of convertibles is highly correlated with the stock market, their future performance is directly tied to future stock market activity.
Investment strategies for warrants	Warrants are very risky investments because they have volatile prices and become worthless at expiration. Because of their longer lives, however, they are less risky than call options written against the same underlying common stock. Investors can use warrants for hedging or for speculation in much the same way options can be used. There are many recent financial innovations (engineering) involving warrants. New strategies involving covered equity warrants, SWORDS, and CEWs are now possible.

SUMMARY

Convertibles may be bonds or preferred stock. Investment analysis of convertibles is complicated by the fact that as hybrid securities, they must be analyzed as both fixed-income and equity securities. Approaches that can be used to analyze convertibles include a graphic approach, an option pricing framework, and a CAPM framework. Studies indicate that an option pricing model, such as the Black-Scholes model, provides the best framework for an analysis of the premium on a convertible.

Traditional strategies for convertible investors include simple selection screens to determine if the premium is too low (underpriced) or too high (overpriced). The simple payback analysis from capital budgeting can also be used. Other strategies suggest using convertibles as hedges, buying deep discount or busted convertibles, and investing in mutual funds that specialize in convertibles.

Warrants are similar to call options and to convertibles since they are derivative securities. Warrants can be valued like options, but adjustments must be made for the dilution effect and for cash dividends. Warrants can be used to hedge an underlying portfolio of stocks or to speculate about future stock price movements. Many new features and types of warrants have recently been introduced into the financial markets, suggesting warrants will receive more attention from investors in the future.

• KEY TERMS

Busted convertible
Call risk
Conversion price
Conversion ratio
Conversion value
Convertible bond
Convertible preferred stock
Covered equity warrants
Credit risk
Currency exchange warrant (CEW)
Dilution
Minimum value
Payback period
Premium
Put feature
Resettable (adjustable rate) convertible bond
Straight value
Warrants
Zero-coupon convertible bond

• QUESTIONS

1. Explain why many convertible securities are issued with a call feature.
2. Discuss the characteristics of convertibles that cause them to be classified as hybrid securities.
3. Define the conversion value and straight value of a convertible security, and indicate how these values determine the floor or minimum value.
4. Explain why the call price limits the premium on a convertible.
5. Why might a company delay the call of a convertible even though the conversion value exceeds the call price?
6. Explain the likely behavior of the premium on a convertible bond as the bond approaches maturity.
7. Explain why the premium is likely to be larger on convertibles where the underlying common stock has a high beta.
8. Define a "busted" convertible, and discuss the risk-return characteristics of an investment strategy using busted convertibles.

9. Explain why the conversion feature of a convertible security is similar to a call option for common stock. Also explain the differences.
10. Explain why the conversion feature of a convertible security is similar to a warrant for the common stock. Also explain the differences.
11. Investing in convertibles is often referred to as a market timing strategy. Explain how investing in convertibles may (or may not) be appropriate under the following conditions:
    a. Interest rates and common stock prices are expected to *decline.*
    b. Interest rates are expected to remain *stable,* common stock prices to *increase.*
    c. Interest rates and common stock prices are expected to *increase.*
    d. The investor is uncertain about the future direction of interest rates and common stock prices.
12. Explain how payback analysis is used to identify under- and overvalued convertibles. Discuss the weaknesses of this approach.
13. Discuss the potential problems that have been identified in applying the CAPM to convertibles. Does this research indicate that a convertible's beta would be useful in an investment analysis?
14. Discuss the advantages and disadvantages of investing in a mutual fund that specializes in convertibles rather than investing directly in convertibles.
15. Compare and contrast equity call options with warrants.
16. Explain why the Black-Scholes model must be modified before it can be used to value warrants.
17. Discuss three recent examples of financial engineering that involve warrants.

• KEY TO THE INVESTMENT ANALYSIS SOFTWARE

Calculation	Appendix A-1 Page Reference	Access Procedure
Value of convertible bond	A-12	BEGIN, VALUATION, CONVERTIBLES, DEBS
Value of convertible preferred stock	A-12	BEGIN, VALUATION, CONVERTIBLES, PFD
Convertible payback period for premium	A-12	BEGIN, VALUATION, CONVERTIBLES, DEBS or PFD
Premium on convertible bond or preferred stock	A-12	BEGIN, VALUATION, CONVERTIBLES, DEBS or PFD
Minimum value for a convertible	A-12	BEGIN, VALUATION, CONVERTIBLES, DEBS or PFD

• PROBLEMS

1. The common stock of IBM is selling for 98\frac{5}{8}$, and its $1,000 face value, 7.875 percent coupon convertible subordinated bond is priced at 101. The conversion ratio is 6.51, and the bond matures in 2004. The current call price is 103.5.
   a. Calculate the conversion price.
   b. Calculate the conversion value.
   c. Calculate the premium.
   d. Assuming that similar straight bonds are selling at 89, calculate the minimum value for the convertible.
   e. Briefly discuss the factors that explain the size of the premium for the IBM convertible bond.
2. Assume that the dividend yield on the common stock of IBM is 4.1 percent. Use the information and your answers to Problem 1 to calculate the payback period for the premium on the convertible bond. In your opinion, does the payback period indicate the convertible is correctly valued, overvalued, or undervalued?
3. Chock Full O'Nuts Corporation has a convertible subordinated bond with a coupon yield of 8.0 percent and a Moody's rating of B2; it matures in 2006. The convertible is priced at 90, and the common stock is currently trading at a price of 7\frac{1}{2}$. The conversion ratio is 110.49; the convertible is callable at 104.80.
   a. Calculate the conversion price.
   b. Calculate the conversion value.
   c. Calculate the premium.
   d. Is the convertible priced to reflect its conversion value or its straight value?
   e. Does this bond appear to be suitable for a "busted convertible" strategy? Explain.
4. Wild Bill, Inc., has a convertible subordinated bond with a coupon yield of 6.0 percent and a Moody's rating of B3; it matures in 2011. The convertible is priced at 32, the common stock at 1\frac{3}{8}$. The conversion price is $46.25; the convertible is callable at 105$\frac{3}{8}$.
   a. Calculate the percentage price increase in the common stock that will be necessary for the conversion value to equal the current market price of the convertible.
   b. Does this bond appear to be suitable for a "busted convertible" strategy? Explain.
5. Use Moody's *Bond Record,* Standard & Poor's *Bond Guide,* or other appropriate sources to obtain the necessary data to analyze the 8.50 percent convertible subordinated bonds issued by Humana, Inc.

• REFERENCES

Auster, Rolf. "Investment Strategies Involving Convertibles and Options." *Practical Accountant* (August 1988): 60–70.

Calamos, John P. "Investment Opportunities in New-Issue Convertible Bonds." *Cash Flow* (February 1987): 35–37.

Clark, Heston. "How to Get Stocks and Bonds in One Package." *Futures: The Magazine of Commodities and Options* (September 1986): 50–51.

Coletti, Richard J. "Mutual Fund Watch: Hedging His Bets." *Financial World*, August 21, 1990, pp. 68–70.

Curran, John J., and Ellen Schultz. "Investment Strategy and Vehicles." *Fortune*, Fall 1989, pp. 22–25.

Dubroff, Henry. "Warrants: An Equity Kicker for All Occasions." *CFO: The Magazine for Chief Financial Officers* (September 1987): 57–58.

"Fence-Straddling with Convertible Bond Funds." *Fortune*, August 4, 1986, p. 220.

Ferri, Michael G., Scott B. Moore, and David C. Schirm. "Investor Expectations about Callable Warrants." *Journal of Portfolio Management* (Spring 1988): 84–86.

Fisher, Kenneth L. "15% with Little Risk." *Forbes*, May 18, 1987, p. 256.

Hitchings, Bradley. "Bonds That Can Bring You The Best of Two Worlds." *Business Week*, September 22, 1986, pp. 98–99.

Janus, Richard, and Tim Ringler. "Five Questions to Ask When Choosing a Convertibles Manager." *Pension World* (June 1986): 47–48.

Kuntz, Mary. "Old Money in New Bottles." *Forbes*, October 6, 1986, p. 194.

Lewis, Julian. "Why Warrants Could Oust Equities." *Euromoney* (November 1989): 43–56.

Liscio, John. "The Worst of Both Worlds: What's Wrong with Convertible Securities?" *Barron's*, May 16, 1988, pp. 16–18, 22.

———. "The Best of All Worlds: Convertibles Never Had It So Good." *Barron's*, August 7, 1989, pp. 16, 25.

Luxenberg, Stan. "Metamorphosis: The Lure of Convertible Debentures." *CFO: The Magazine for Chief Financial Officers* (March 1987): 65–66.

Morrison, Tex. "A Note of Caution on the Rush to Convertibles." *Business Week*, May 18, 1987, p. 158.

Moscovitz, Steven D. "They Warrant a Look: How Warrants Work as Hedging Devices." *Barron's*, December 21, 1987, pp. 28–29.

O'Neal, Jason. "The Chameleon in Your Portfolio: Calculating the Break-Even Period for Convertible Bonds." *CFO: The Magazine for Chief Financial Officers* (October 1989): 52–55.

Pakkala, A.L. "There Is a Free Lunch." *Financial Analysts Journal* (September-October 1988): 83–87.

Parker, Marcia. "Convertible Investors Fight Losses." *Pensions & Investment Age*, July 27, 1987, pp. 1, 51.

———. "Convertibles Revived: Investors Embrace Flood of New Issues." *Pensions & Investment Age*, May 29, 1989, pp. 21–22.

———. "Index Warrant Use Grows." *Pensions & Investments*, April 2, 1990, p. 10.

Rohrer, Julie. "Portfolio Strategy: Conquering Convertibles." *Institutional Investor* (October 1989): 301–10.

Rudin, Brad. "Foreign Currency Warrants Blast Off." *Pensions & Investment Age,* July 13, 1987, pp. 17, 20.

Sachar, Laura. "Balancing Act." *Financial World,* November 25, 1986, pp. 118–19.

Weberman, Ben, and Jason Zweig. "The Mixed Bag." *Forbes,* June 27, 1988, pp. 222–23.

Whitfield, Heidi, Merry L. Mosbacher, and Daniel A. Burkhardt. "Convertible Bonds: The Best of Both Worlds." *Public Utilities Fortnightly,* August 3, 1989, pp. 30–35.

APPENDIX 16A

Stock Rights

RIGHTS

Rights allow existing common stock shareholders to acquire a proportionate share of a new issue of common stock. If stockholders are protected with a *preemptive right,* a rights offering satisfies this requirement. The use of rights may also benefit the corporation because of the ease of distributing the new stock issue and lower flotation costs. Rights are usually transferable or marketable; the stockholder who receives the rights can either exercise them or sell them. Rights are therefore traded along with the common stock on the stock exchanges and the OTC market.

• Characteristics of Stock Rights

For common stocks with a preemptive right, normally a stockholder receives one right for each share of common stock when the company issues additional shares of common stock. To determine how many rights are needed to keep proportionate control, the following calculations can be made:

$$\text{number of rights needed} = \frac{\text{number of shares outstanding}}{\text{number of new shares to be issued}} \quad (16A.1)$$

For example, if the company is offering 1 million new shares of common stock and you now own 10 percent of the 9 million shares outstanding, or 900,000 shares, you would need to purchase 10 percent of the new shares, or 100,000 shares, to maintain proportionate control. Thus, the company would specify that nine rights are needed to acquire one additional share of stock:

$$\frac{9{,}000{,}000}{1{,}000{,}000} = 9 \quad (16A.2)$$

These nine rights, plus a *subscription price* per share, would be needed to purchase each new share of stock. The subscription price is generally set lower than the current market price of the stock to persuade the existing stockholders to purchase the new shares.

• Value of Stock Rights

The exercise period or life of a right can be divided into two periods—the rights-on period and the rights-off period—as follows:

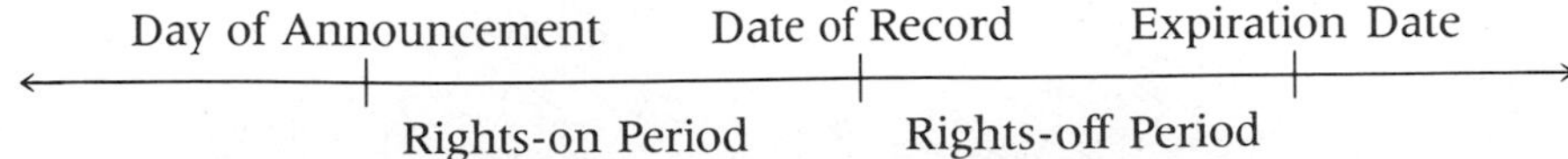

From the day that the board of directors announces the rights offering until approximately four days prior to the date of record, the rights are traded with the shares of stock, or *rights-on.*

VALUE WITH RIGHTS ON During the rights-on period, rights are included when the stock is traded, so their value is reflected in the market price of the stock. The value of the right can be calculated as

$$V_{on} = \frac{M_1 - S}{N + 1} \quad \textbf{(16A.3)}$$

where

V_{on} = value of right, rights-on
M_1 = market price of the stock with rights
S = subscription price per share for new shares of stock
N = number of rights needed to purchase one new share of stock

VALUE WITH RIGHTS OFF When the stock begins trading *rights-off,* the owner has a two-part investment: (1) one share of stock and (2) the rights. The rights are then traded in the same market as the common stock. Unless other factors change the market price of the stock, the two should theoretically add to the value of the stock rights-on. The new price of the *stock* can be calculated as

$$M_{off} = \frac{M_1 N + S}{N + 1} \quad \textbf{(16A.4)}$$

or

$$M_{off} = M_1 - V_{on}$$

The theoretical value of the right in the rights-off period can be calculated as

$$V_{off} = \frac{M_{off} - S}{N} \quad \textbf{(16A.5)}$$

Continuing with the example where $N = 9$, assume $S = \$30$, and $M_1 = \$40$; then the value of the right can be calculated as

$$V_{on} = \frac{\$40 - \$30}{9 + 1} = \$1$$

The value of the stock rights-off can be calculated as

$$M_{\text{off}} = \frac{40(9) + 30}{9 + 1} = \frac{390}{10} = \$39$$

or as

$$\begin{aligned} M_{\text{off}} &= M_1 - V_{\text{on}} \\ &= \$40 - \$1 \\ &= \$39 \end{aligned}$$

The value of M_{off} can then be used to calculate V_{off}:

$$V_{\text{off}} = \frac{\$39 - \$30}{\$9} = \$1$$

Notice the value of the right did not change in this example between rights-on and rights-off: $V_{\text{on}} = V_{\text{off}}$. The value of the right plus the share of stock (V_t) is

$$\begin{aligned} V_t &= M_{\text{off}} + V_{\text{off}} \\ &= \$39 + \$1 = \$40 \end{aligned} \quad \textbf{(16A.6)}$$

When the right is separated from the stock, the value of the stock should always decrease by the value of the right.

VALUING A RIGHT AS A CALL OPTION Traditionally, the theoretical or intrinsic value of a right has been determined as in the preceding section. However, a right can also be valued as a call option, using a variation of the Black-Scholes option pricing model. This approach is superior to the traditional approach because it recognizes the right's additional value due to possible increases in the common stock price. An estimate of the future common stock price is not needed, however, to value the right using the call option approach.

BASIC INVESTMENT STRATEGIES

Subsequent to the effective date of record (when the books are closed as to ownership of the stock), an investor has three possible courses of action with respect to rights:

1. Exercise the rights.
2. Sell the rights.
3. Do nothing—let the rights expire.

Continuing with the previous example, but assume you only own 9 shares of stock on the date of record and the subscription price was set at $30 per share. The 9 shares entitle you to receive 9 rights that can be used to purchase

1 additional share. Also assume that you have an initial cash balance of \$30. As previously indicated, the stock value was \$40 prior to the day of announcement (M_1 = \$40), and the value of the right is \$1, or $V_{on} = V_{off}$ = \$1. The following table sets out the three possible courses of action and the ending portfolio values:

Beginning portfolio value:		
9 shares @ \$39/share	\$351	
9 rights @ \$1/right	9	
Cash	30	
	\$390	
1. Exercise:	Ending portfolio value:	
	10 shares @ \$39/share	\$390
2. Sell rights:	Ending portfolio value:	
	9 shares @ \$39/share	\$351
	Cash (\$30 + \$9)	39
		\$390
3. Do nothing:	Ending portfolio value:	
	9 shares @ \$39	\$351
	Cash	30
		\$381

As the "do nothing" option indicates, the value of the portfolio declines by the value of the rights that were allowed to expire. Obviously, this third alternative is not a good course of action.

Stock price volatility and its impact on the return from owning rights can easily be demonstrated. Continuing with the previous example, suppose you could buy a share of the stock at \$39 or a right for \$1. Which is the better strategy if the stock price increases to \$45 per share?

Holding period return on stock strategy (assuming no cash dividends):

$$\text{HPR}_s = \frac{\$45 - \$39}{\$39} = 15.38\%$$

Holding period return on rights strategy:

$$V_{off} = \frac{\$45 - \$30}{9} = \$1.67$$

$$\text{HPR}_r = \frac{\$1.67 - \$1.00}{\$1.00} = 67.0\%$$

These HPR calculations illustrate the *leverage* effect of trading (speculating) in stock rights. Also, in terms of dollar profits, assume you buy 39 rights, since this is the amount of the investment one share of stock would require. Your profit on the stock investment is \$6, but your profit on the rights investment is \$26.13 (\$.67 × 39). Given a volatile stock price, the dollar profit and HPR resulting from an increase in the value of the rights could far exceed that of the stock. A decline in the stock price, however, has the opposite effect: the dollar and HPR losses will be significantly larger than the losses associated with owning the stock.

An additional risk factor is that the right has an expiration date. At expiration, the right has no value, but it is unlikely that the stock's price would decline to zero. If the right is purchased in anticipation of stock price increases, the HPR on the right might be as low as −100 percent if the right cannot be sold or exercised profitably before expiration.

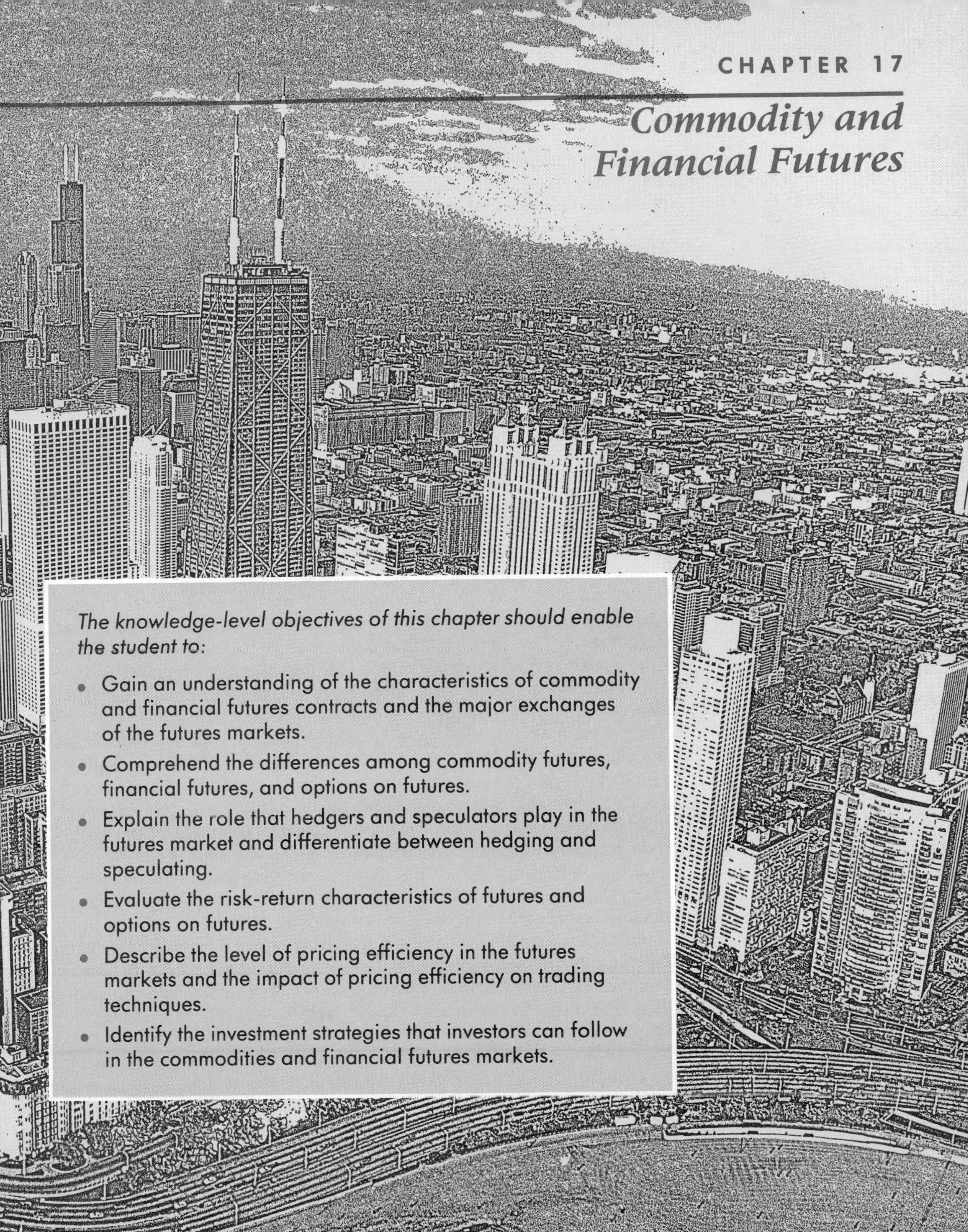

CHAPTER 17

Commodity and Financial Futures

The knowledge-level objectives of this chapter should enable the student to:

- Gain an understanding of the characteristics of commodity and financial futures contracts and the major exchanges of the futures markets.
- Comprehend the differences among commodity futures, financial futures, and options on futures.
- Explain the role that hedgers and speculators play in the futures market and differentiate between hedging and speculating.
- Evaluate the risk-return characteristics of futures and options on futures.
- Describe the level of pricing efficiency in the futures markets and the impact of pricing efficiency on trading techniques.
- Identify the investment strategies that investors can follow in the commodities and financial futures markets.

INTRODUCTION

Imagine, for a moment, that you are a corn farmer and you have planted your corn for the season. If you wait to sell the corn when it is harvested, revenues will depend entirely on the price of corn at harvest time. To protect against this pricing uncertainty, you can enter into a forward contract with a buyer of corn. A **forward contract** is a formal agreement between a buyer and seller in which the buyer agrees to accept delivery of a specified quantity of a commodity, on a specific date, at a fixed price. The seller agrees to make delivery according to the specified terms. Forward contracts between buyers and sellers of commodities have existed for centuries. The forward contract removes the future price uncertainty for both the producer and the buyer of the commodity. One problem with forward contracts, however, is that performance is uncertain in that either the buyer or the seller may fail to fulfill the contract obligations. If one party to the contract defaults, the other party suffers the loss or sues for damages.

To overcome this and other problems with forward contracts, the Chicago Board of Trade (CBOT) began trading *future contracts* in the 1860s. The CBOT established a **clearing corporation** that acts as an intermediary for each contract; the clearing corporation actually guarantees the performance of all participants in the market.

Both the buyer and writer of future contracts are free to transfer their interest in the contract to another party, so that the contracts are essentially marketable financial instruments. Either party can also liquidate his or her position by initiating a *reversing* trade. For example, the original buyer can sell (write) an identical contract at a later date, effectively canceling the original contract.

The prices for commodity contracts, like other securities, are determined by supply and demand factors. Brokers at commodity exchanges negotiate the highest price for the seller and the lowest price for the buyer. Future contracts are traded on organized exchanges that are similar to a stock exchange. The contracts are also *standardized* by the exchanges; the quantity and quality of the particular commodity are specified.

In actual trading of commodities, few contracts are held to the delivery or maturity date. Typically, less than 5 percent of commodity contracts will be settled by the delivery of the specified commodity. However, if a buyer holds the contract on the maturity date, it is settled by having the title or ownership interest in the specified commodity transferred from the seller to the buyer.

The initial purpose of commodity markets was to provide a mechanism for farmers or commodity producers to hedge against a future decline in the commodity's price. Manufacturers or users of a particular commodity could also buy a contract to hedge against future price increases. Traders or speculators were also attracted to the market because they were willing to assume the price risk in anticipation of trading profits. Thus, in a traditional commodity market, hedgers (actual producers and users of commodities) attempt to reduce or eliminate price risk, and speculators seek trading profits by eliminating imbalances in trading between the hedgers. Because very few contracts are actually settled by delivery, speculators play a very important role as both writers and buyers of contracts. Under a basic speculative strategy, a speculator would write a contract when the commodity's price was expected to decline and buy a contract when the price was expected to increase.

For years, future contracts were limited to commodity contracts on real assets such as agricultural products, metals, and petroleum products. As a result of the changing economic environment in the 1970s, in particular, fluctuating interest rates, growing government debt, and increased international trade, investors began to look for ways to hedge the risks associated with investments in fixed-income securities, common stocks, foreign currencies, and other financial instruments. Just as future contracts in real assets emerged to provide farmers and users of commodities with a way to hedge against price fluctuations in real assets, contracts on **financial futures** and *options on financial futures* were developed to provide a hedge for financial instruments. Today, the volume in contracts for financial futures and options on financial futures far exceeds the volume of commodity futures contracts on real assets. This chapter discusses commodity futures on real assets and financial futures as well as options on financial futures.

• Commodity Markets

Commodity futures in the United States are traded exclusively on organized exchanges that must be licensed by the federal government through the Commodity Futures Trading Commission (CFTC). There is no over-the-counter market for futures contracts similar to that which exists for common stocks. The largest and best-known exchanges are the Chicago Board of Trade, Chicago Mercantile Exchange, New York Mercantile Exchange, and New York Commodity Exchange. Table 17.1 lists eight major commodity exchanges and the contracts that each exchange trades. In addition to futures on real assets, exchanges may also trade financial futures and options on futures. For example, the Chicago Mercantile Exchange trades index futures on the S&P 500 and the Nikkei 225. It also trades options on such financial and commodity futures as the S&P 500, Nikkei 225, currencies, Treasury bills, cattle, hogs, and lumber.

Commodity markets operate in much the same fashion as stock markets. Trading is accomplished by *floor brokers,* who use an auction procedure to execute buy and sell orders in the *trading pit.* For example, on the trading floor at the CBOT, traders are required to use "open outcry" in trading. Hand signals are used to clarify the verbal trades. Unlike the stock markets, however, the commodity markets do not have specialists. Copies of the actual commodity contract are not delivered to the buyer and seller since transactions result only in bookkeeping entries. Sample contracts, however, are available from each exchange and provide prospective traders with the specific details of trading for each commodity.

• INTEREST BOX

Screen Trading in Futures and Options

The open outcry auction process, accompanied by hand signals, has historically provided the liquidity and capital necessary for trading futures contracts and options on futures. With the globalization of the financial markets and advances in electronic technology, the process is changing.

As the partial list of contracts traded electronically around the world indicates (see Table 1 on the facing page), commodity and option exchanges worldwide have begun to use computer networks to match buyers and sellers of futures and options. Thus, the name *screen trading.* On some exchanges (e.g., the London International Financial Futures Exchange), the open outcry process is used during regular trading hours, and screen trading is used for after-hours trading. On other exchanges (e.g., the Tokyo International Financial Futures Exchange), screen trading is used exclusively. The computer trading systems developed overseas are not integrated systems, but are tied to a single exchange.

Screen trading has been rather slow in developing in the United States. Some blame the lack of progress on floor traders who have a vested interest in keeping trading activities in the trading pits and off computer screens. Similarly, some argue that specialists have been influential in slowing the automation process on the New York Stock Exchange.

In 1987, the Chicago Mercantile Exchange and Reuters Holding PLC proposed Globex, a screen-trading system designed to provide trading for futures contracts from around the world on a 24-hour basis. In 1990, the Chicago Board of Trade abandoned development of its rival trading system, Aurora, and joined in the development of Globex. This international, interactive trading system is scheduled to become operational in late 1991 or early 1992. In March 1991, the New York Mercantile Exchange announced a joint agreement with American Telephone & Telegraph Company and Task Management to develop an automated system for after-hours trading on the exchange.

SOURCE: Stanley W. Angrist, "Futures Traders Wait Quietly for Globex," *The Wall Street Journal,* May 21, 1991, pp. C1, C9.

TABLE 1 • Volume of Screen Trading Overseas (thousands of contracts)

	1990	January-March 1991
London Futures and Options Exchange		
White sugar	347	90
Deutsche Terminboerse		
German government bond	60[b]	262
London International Financial Futures Exchange		
Long gilt (open outcry[a])	5,426	1,267
Long gilt (screen[a])	217	53
German government bond (open outcry[a])	9,582	2,638
German government bond (screen[a])	402	101
Sydney Futures Exchange		
Australian 90-day bank bills (open outcry[a])	5,015	1,038
Australian 90-day bank bills (screen[a])	66	18
Swiss Options and Financial Futures Exchange		
Swiss market index option	4,655	1,489
Tokyo International Financial Futures Exchange		
Three-month Euroyen	14,414	3,165
Tokyo Stock Exchange		
Japanese government bond	16,307	3,506
By comparison . . .		
Chicago Board of Trade		
U.S. Treasury bond	75,499	17,180

SOURCES: Futures Industry Association and the exchanges.

[a]Traded by open outcry during regular hours, on computer screens after hours.

[b]Trading began in late November 1990.

TABLE 17.1 • Major Commodity Exchanges and Contracts Traded

Exchange	Contracts traded
1. Chicago Board of Trade	Wheat, corn, oats, soybeans, soybean oil, soybean meal, silver
2. Kansas City Board of Trade	Wheat
3. Chicago Mercantile Exchange	Cattle, feeder cattle, hogs, pork bellies, lumber
4. New York Cotton Exchange	Cotton, orange juice
5. New York Commodity Exchange	Gold, silver, copper
6. New York Mercantile Exchange	Crude oil, heating oil, unleaded gasoline, natural gas, platinum, palladium
7. New York Coffee, Sugar, Cocoa Exchange	Sugar-World 11, sugar 14, coffee C, cocoa
8. Mid-America Commodity Exchange (Chicago)	Cattle, corn, gold, hogs, oats, silver, soybeans, sugar, wheat

The clearing corporation uses the fees it collects on transactions to provide the necessary funds to guarantee each contract. Buyers and sellers are also required to deposit an **initial margin** on the contract—typically, 5 to 10 percent of the contract's value. The exact amount of the margin is set by the exchange and the clearing corporation. The margin is actually a *performance* bond rather than a down payment on the contract; thus it differs from the margin required to purchase stocks. The margin requirement serves to reduce the loss to the clearing corporation from a possible default by the buyer or seller. Additional factors that are used to determine the margin are the underlying commodity's price volatility, the daily price moves (limits) permitted for the contract, and the time required to collect position losses from customers. Keeping the margin low encourages active trading and increases the leverage effect on returns.

The use of an initial margin means that investors are required to pay for only a small portion of the cost of the contract at the time of purchase. For example, on February 8, 1991, a 10 percent initial margin on a New York Commodity Exchange gold contract was $4,071. The contract represents 100 troy ounces of gold for December 1991 delivery at $407.10 per ounce. This provides considerable leverage to an investor/speculator: a 1 percent increase (decrease) in the price of gold results in a 10 percent increase (decrease) in the wealth of the investor.

After the initial margin is deposited, either in cash or U.S. Treasury bills, a change in the price of the contract causes a change in the percentage relationship between the margin and the contract value. The customer is therefore required to ensure a **maintenance** or **variation margin** on a day-by-day basis. Typically, the maintenance margin is 75 percent of the initial margin. At the close of each day's trading, the clearing house credits each customer's account with the gains or losses due to price changes. Losses and gains are netted against the initial margin. This process is called **marking to market.** If the net gains and losses cause the initial margin to decline below the required maintenance margin, the customer receives a **margin call** and is required to deposit additional cash or U.S. Treasury bills. If the customer cannot meet the margin call, the contract position is liquidated, and any remaining margin is distributed to the customer. Daily marking to market is one reason the initial margin is low on commodity contracts relative to common stocks. The initial margin needs to be only large enough to cover one day's price change.

To illustrate, assume that a December-delivery wheat contract is purchased, for 5,000 bushels, at $2.50 per bushel, with a 10 percent initial margin. The contract value is $12,500, indicating a $1,250 initial margin. If the maintenance margin is 75 percent of the initial margin, a minimum of $937.50 (.75 × $1,250) must be maintained. Therefore, if the price declines by more than 6.25 cents per bushel [($1,250 − $937.50)/5,000], an additional deposit to the margin account is required. If the price increases by 6.25 cents per bushel, however, $312.50 ($.0625 × 5,000) can be withdrawn from the account.

The daily marking-to-market practice of the clearing corporation results in daily debits and credits to each customer's account, based on the change in the contract price. If a customer has purchased a contract, price increases in the contract will result in additional cash being credited to the account. The contract writer, however, will have cash deducted from his or her account. Since cash flows occur daily, many traders deposit additional funds above the required minimum with their brokers to avoid having to meet frequent margin calls. Since the gains and losses are recognized on a daily basis, the required cash settlement when the contract is traded will be small relative to the possible overall price change over the holding period. The clearing corporation also benefits because it can maintain a net zero position on a day-by-day basis since each credit to a margin account is offset by a debit to another trader's margin account.

Another difference between the margin requirements for commodities and those for stocks and bonds is that the initial margin on commodities can be paid with U.S. Treasury bills rather than cash. The investor is entitled to any interest income received on the Treasury bills. Therefore, if an investor already has a large portfolio of Treasury bills, the incremental investment in a commodity contract can be essentially zero.

• Commodity Contracts and Quotations

Commodity contracts are available on many types of assets, such as wheat, soybeans, cotton, sugar, coffee, unleaded gasoline, orange juice, hogs, cattle, gold, and silver. Each contract specifies both the quality and quantity of the asset (e.g., 5,000 bushels of winter wheat, grade 2).

• **INTEREST BOX**

The Role of Commodity Futures at Nestlé

Nestlé is one multinational giant that's literally a household name. One of the 100 largest companies in the world, its market capitalization is some $13 billion. In 1988, it had sales of 40.7 billion Swiss francs ($26.1 billion), producing net profits of 2.04 billion francs ($1.3 billion).

Nestlé manufactures in 59 countries and is a raw materials producer and grower in many of them. The company is a sprawling agglomeration, owning about 430 factories and employing almost 200,000 people around the world.

The Swiss company's size and products have made Nestlé familiar to consumers around the world. Its enormous buying power has also made Nestlé a formidable name in the commodity markets, particularly coffee and cocoa. The company is the world's largest buyer of green coffee and one of the three largest buyers of cocoa. It also is among the world's largest buyers of sugar, cereals, and many other commodities. . . .

None of the commodities used by Nestlé is bought centrally. Instead, commodity buying is decentralized, and each of the company's operating divisions or subsidiaries is responsible for getting its own raw materials.

However, that does not mean the divisions have a free rein as far as commodity buying goes. The divisions operate within guidelines set by the purchasing department in the company's headquarters in Vevay, a small Swiss town on the northern shore of Lake Geneva.

The big questions commodity traders ask include how strict are the guidelines and how much control is exerted by Vevay? The answer is not easy to determine.

Like all Swiss companies, Nestlé is secretive. It also knows the benefits of keeping commodity markets in the dark. What is clear is that Gordon Gillett, the man in charge of day-to-day purchasing department operations, and the executive management panel exert more control over commodity buying than many suspect.

Gillett, from Britain, has spent most of his career at Nestlé. He has worked in most areas of its commodity operations in various parts of the world, so he should know the ins and outs of commodity buying.

So, what guidelines does he lay down to his commodity buyers?

Assurance of supply—supply of the right quality—is the most important parameter for the buyers, he says.

"Above all else, we are quality buyers of growth and grade. The next most important parameter is the assurance of price," Gillett says.

The company does not see itself as a commodity trader.

"Our business is to take raw materials at attractive prices and convert them into value-added customer goods," Gillett says.

That might seem like a pointless reiteration of the blindingly obvious. However, it is an important guide to the company's attitude to risk, commodity price risk, in particular.

That doesn't mean the company won't trade in and out of commodity markets. It does. But in general terms, Nestlé is a hedger, albeit an aggressive (or at least active) one.

In coffee and cocoa, Nestlé uses all major futures markets for price risk management: New York's Coffee, Sugar, and Cocoa Exchange, the London Futures and Options Exchange, and the Paris Bourse.

The company's decentralized commodity buying means each of the 15 main coffee and cocoa buyers around the world are responsible for their own futures market activity, including the choice of broker or commission house used for the trade.

SOURCE: Paul Dickins, "Nestlé Makes the Very Best of Market Opportunities," *Futures: The Magazine of Commodities & Options*, December 1989, pp. 54–56.

Obviously, not all commodities are traded on exchanges. Generally, in order for a commodity to be traded, it must be storable and in high demand. It should also be capable of being classified into clearly identifiable grades or categories. Each commodity must be approved for trading by the exchange and the CFTC. The CFTC also controls contract provisions and trading procedures.

Typically, commodity contracts for agricultural products are issued with a delivery or maturity date of less than one year. Due to the seasonal nature of some agricultural commodities, contracts with delivery dates in some months are not available. For precious metals, contracts that mature every month for the next two years may be available.

Types of orders used for futures contracts are very similar to those for common stocks. The most common are the market, limit, and stop orders. These orders were described in Chapter 3, and the definitions apply to both common stocks and futures contracts.

In terms of the value of the contract, commissions on trading commodity contracts are lower than commissions on common stock trades. For example, as of March 1, 1991, Merrill Lynch charged a $100 round-turn fee to write (buy) and close a position with a reversing trade. For a contract such as gold, this fee represented approximately 0.2 percent of the contract's value as of March 1991. For a wheat contract on the CBOT, however, the $100 fee represented 0.7 percent of the contract's value. In either case, the brokerage fee is lower than that for a common stock transaction of equal dollar value.

Table 17.2 provides a sample of quotations for various commodities on several of the commodity exchanges. Notice that the "prices" are in different units of measurement, such as dollars per bushel or cents per pound, depending on the commodity. The amount or volume of the commodity for each contract is given directly below the contract's name. Also, notice that there is not always a clear relationship between the price and the length of the contract. For example, the "price" of the corn contracts on the CBOT increases as the delivery period lengthens, but prices for feeder cattle on the Chicago Mercantile Exchange decrease as the delivery period increases. The reasons for these differences are discussed later in the chapter. These variations in price are in contrast to put and call options on common stocks, where the price increases with the term to expiration.

The July 1991 wheat contract on the CBOT in Table 17.2 illustrates the contract and quotation system used with commodities. The contract specifications for wheat futures traded on the CBOT are shown in Table 17.3. Wheat contracts are for 5,000 bushels, and the pricing unit is in dollars per bushel. As Table 17.2 shows, the season's high and low prices for July wheat ranged from $3.63 per bushel to $2.62. For the week ending February 8, 1991, July wheat traded at a high of $2.80 per bushel and at a low of $2.6825. The last price for the week, also known as the **settle price,** was $2.7275. The net change for the week was a decrease of 7.25 cents per bushel.

Another important item of information is the **open interest,** the total number of contracts outstanding at a given point in time. The quotations indicate the total number of contracts for each delivery month and the total num-

TABLE 17.2 • Quotations on Commodity Futures

Chicago Board of Trade

Season's High	Season's Low		Week's High	Week's Low	Sett	Net Chg	Open Int.
WHEAT							
5,000 bu minimum; dollars per bushel							
3.85	2.44½	Mar	2.62½	2.48	2.52¾	−.09½	17,190
3.73	2.54¼	May	2.71¼	2.58½	2.62½	−.07½	12,344
3.63	2.62	Jul	2.80	2.68¼	2.72¾	−.07¼	16,352
3.26	2.69½	Sep	2.86¾	2.75½	2.79½	−.07½	1,864
3.17	2.81½	Dec	2.99	2.88½	2.92½	−.07	2,095
3.70¾	2.89¼	Mar	3.00	2.97	3.00	−.06	176
Fri. to Thurs. sales 42,061.							
Total open interest 50,021.							
CORN							
5,000 bu minimum; dollars per bushel							
3.02½	2.27¼	Mar	2.45¼	2.38¾	2.40¼	−.03¾	66,182
3.06½	2.35	May	2.53¼	2.47	2.49	−.03	51,157
3.08¼	2.41½	Jul	2.59¼	2.53	2.55	−.03	61,286
2.87½	2.40¼	Sep	2.59½	2.53¾	2.55¾	−.03¼	9,329
2.75	2.42½	Dec	2.60¾	2.55	2.58	−.02¾	28,766
2.70	2.49	Mar	2.67	2.61¾	2.64½	−.02¾	1,922
2.72	2.58¼	May	2.69½	2.67¼	2.68¾	−.02	57
Fri. to Thurs. sales 169,558.							
Total open interest 218,699.							
OATS							
5,000 bu minimum; dollars per bushel							
2.01	1.05¼	Mar	1.11	1.07½	1.11	+.02	6,244
1.83¾	1.11¼	May	1.17¼	1.13½	1.17¼	+.02¼	3,458
1.63½	1.17	Jul	1.23½	1.19½	1.23½	+.02¾	2,549
1.52½	1.22½	Sep	1.28	1.25	1.28	+.02	144
1.49	1.31	Dec	1.36	1.33	1.36	+.02	126
Fri. to Thurs. sales 2,879.							
Total open interest 12,521.							
SOYBEANS							
5,000 bu minimum; dollars per bushel							
7.03	5.49½	Mar	5.75¾	5.63	5.68¾	+.01¾	36,917
7.11	5.61	May	5.89½	5.77¼	5.82½	+.01¼	25,841
7.18	5.76	Jul	6.02¼	5.89½	5.95½	+.01¾	25,228
6.95	5.82	Aug	6.06	5.93¾	6.00¾	+.03¼	3,969
6.54	5.83½	Sep	6.08½	5.96¼	6.04¾	+.05¾	3,870
6.74	5.90½	Nov	6.17	6.03	6.14¾	+.08½	12,056
6.42½	6.02½	Jan	6.28	6.16½	6.26½	+.07¼	567
6.54	6.11⅜	Mar	6.39½	6.30	6.39	+.07½	165
6.48	6.39½	May	6.48	6.39½	6.48½	+.08	4
Fri. to Thurs. sales 134,704.							
Total open interest 108,617.							
SOYBEAN OIL							
60,000 lbs; dollars per 100 lbs.							
25.61	19.82	Mar	22.11	21.27	21.47	−.13	23,621
25.55	20.15	May	22.43	21.65	21.78	−.18	24,191
25.60	20.85	Jul	22.65	21.91	22.03	−.19	13,511
25.50	20.90	Aug	22.58	21.95	22.05	−.16	3,903
25.10	21.00	Sep	22.50	22.07	22.07	−.08	2,320
24.90	21.08	Oct	22.42	22.05	22.05	......	1,795
24.00	21.17	Dec	22.60	21.90	22.30	+.05	4,490
22.95	21.00	Jan	.....	.....	22.15	+.05	296
22.95	20.10	Mar	22.55	22.55	22.40	+.25	3
.....	.....	May	.....	.....	22.30	+.15	1
Fri. to Thurs. sales 68,271.							
Total open interest 74,131.							

Chicago Mercantile Exchange

Season's High	Season's Low		Week's High	Week's Low	Sett	Net Chg	Open Int.
CATTLE							
40,000 lbs.; cents per lb.							
79.15	72.50	Feb	79.15	78.42	78.47	−.20	6,843
78.17	74.15	Apr	78.17	76.85	77.17	−.20	36,447
75.62	72.15	Jun	75.62	74.45	74.80	+.05	17,087
74.02	70.35	Aug	74.02	73.40	73.57	+.10	12,494
74.10	70.70	Oct	74.10	73.40	73.77	+.25	6,240
74.62	71.75	Dec	74.62	73.85	74.05	+.13	1,641
74.50	72.80	Feb	74.50	73.90	74.00	+.15	84
Fri. to Thurs. sales 75,861.							
Total open interest 80,836.							
FEEDER CATTLE							
44,000 lbs.; cents per lb.							
89.15	80.90	Mar	89.15	87.40	88.47	+.85	4,847
86.65	81.20	Apr	86.65	85.40	86.05	+.45	3,117
85.00	80.20	May	85.00	84.00	84.40	+.30	3,523
85.20	80.20	Aug	85.20	84.00	84.70	+.53	1,266
84.50	79.75	Sep	84.50	83.70	84.20	+.35	211
84.25	80.20	Oct	84.25	83.35	84.00	+.30	249
84.50	81.20	Nov	84.50	83.75	84.20	+.30	68
84.35	84.00	Jan	84.35	84.00	84.35	......	18
Fri. to Thurs. sales 9,636.							
Total open interest 13,299.							
HOGS							
30,000 lbs.; cents per lb.							
54.45	45.25	Feb	53.70	51.65	52.57	−.15	4,028
51.80	43.60	Apr	51.75	49.17	49.55	−1.10	12,678
56.10	47.70	Jun	55.62	53.95	54.42	−.20	5,187
55.95	48.30	Jul	55.30	53.85	54.40	−.05	1,835
53.50	46.90	Aug	52.87	51.65	51.87	−.43	1,115
48.20	42.90	Oct	47.50	46.85	46.85	−.40	197
48.50	44.50	Dec	47.60	47.00	47.15	−.22	82
48.25	44.50	Feb	.....	.....	47.25	−.30	5
Fri. to Thurs. sales 46,561.							
Total open interest 25,127.							
PORK BELLIES							
40,000 lbs.; cents per lb.							
73.80	48.07	Feb	68.40	63.17	63.92	−2.78	1,169
73.45	49.20	Mar	67.40	62.55	63.30	−2.35	4,116
73.12	49.50	May	66.55	62.80	63.45	−1.25	3,403
72.80	50.75	Jul	65.25	62.00	62.32	−.93	1,074
70.05	51.60	Aug	63.50	60.45	60.25	−1.50	281
63.00	58.75	Feb	62.50	58.75	58.60	−3.40	7
61.00	61.00	Mar	.....	.....	59.00	−2.90	......
Fri. to Thurs. sales 29,133.							
Total open interest 10,050.							
LUMBER							
150,000 bd. ft.; $ per 1,000 bd. ft.							
206.10	156.50	Mar	173.30	163.80	172.80	+9.30	1,031
206.70	159.10	May	178.60	166.70	178.60	+12.50	706
189.20	171.50	Jul	189.20	175.50	189.10	+14.70	118
184.40	171.30	Sep	184.40	176.50	187.30	+15.20	46
181.90	165.50	Nov	181.90	172.50	182.00	+14.00	6
179.50	167.00	Jan	179.50	175.90	180.50	+8.00	1
Fri. to Thurs. sales 3,883.							
Total open interest 1,908.							

Coffee Sugar Cocoa Exchange

Season's High	Season's Low		Week's High	Week's Low	Sett	Net Chg	Open Int.
SUGAR-WORLD 11							
112,000 lbs.; cents per lb.							
15.22	8.47	Mar	9.06	8.47	8.54	−.46	49,769
15.05	8.54	May	9.06	8.54	8.55	−.47	31,697
14.90	8.55	Jul	9.08	8.55	8.57	−.48	24,186
14.40	8.58	Oct	9.17	8.58	8.59	−.50	21,805
10.14	8.80	Mar	9.25	8.80	8.80	−.44	6,207
9.77	8.92	May	8.95	8.95	8.84	−.48	61
.....	.....	Jul	.....	.....	8.94	......	......
Fri. to Thurs. sales 110,108.							
Total open interest 133,725.							
SUGAR 14							
112,000 lbs.; cents per lb.							
23.35	21.31	Mar	21.55	21.31	21.32	−.05	1,298
23.41	21.34	May	21.55	21.34	21.35	−.06	3,918
23.41	21.55	Jul	21.70	21.55	21.58	−.02	2,819
23.35	21.60	Sep	21.70	21.60	21.63	+.02	2,631
23.17	21.85	Nov	21.99	21.85	21.89	+.02	2,467
23.01	22.00	Jan	22.05	22.05	22.10	+.04	365
22.80	22.04	Mar	22.12	22.05	22.13	+.09	702
22.30	22.05	May	22.15	22.10	22.13	+.08	194
22.19	22.10	Jul	22.19	22.10	22.18	......	10
Fri. to Thurs. sales 3,305.							
Total open interest 14,404.							
COFFEE C							
37,500 lbs.; cents per lb.							
116.75	81.75	Mar	87.40	81.75	87.25	+4.95	18,159
123.00	84.35	May	89.70	84.35	89.35	+4.50	17,939
111.50	86.90	Jul	92.20	86.90	91.85	+4.50	5,791
113.50	89.50	Sep	94.00	89.50	94.00	+4.25	3,430
116.00	92.50	Dec	96.80	92.50	96.80	+4.20	1,334
107.50	95.50	Mar	98.00	95.50	98.00	+2.45	176
103.00	99.00	May	99.00	99.00	100.50	+3.30	6
.....	.....	Jul	.....	.....	102.50	......	......
Fri. to Thurs. sales 38,367.							
Total open interest 46,835.							
COCOA							
10 metric tons; $ per ton							
1581	607	Mar	1159	1123	1132	+1	9,487
1572	1000	May	1192	1151	1159	−10	10,362
1590	1060	Jul	1228	1191	1193	−13	9,299
1515	1230	Sep	1263	1232	1228	−13	4,518
1535	1276	Dec	1308	1283	1276	−16	3,917
1538	1325	Mar	1350	1325	1318	−16	1,950
1385	1350	May	1350	1350	1350	−15	405
....	.....	Jul	.....	.....	1380	......	100
Fri. to Thurs. sales 21,157.							
Total open interest 40,038.							

SOURCE: *Barron's,* February 11, 1991. Reprinted courtesy of *Barron's Weekly.*

ber of contracts for all delivery months. The open-interest figures should not be confused with the volume or number of contracts traded during the day or week. When an investor/speculator writes a contract that is purchased by a buyer, the open interest increases by one. When trading initially starts on a contract, the open interest is typically low, but it increases over the life of the contract, depending on investor interest. Since over 95 percent of all contracts are canceled by reversing trades prior to delivery, there may be many more contracts outstanding than the actual supply of the commodity. As the delivery date approaches, however, the open interest declines to a level indicating the number of contracts that will be settled by delivery. For July wheat, the open interest on February 8, 1991, was 16,352 contracts.

TABLE 17.3 • CBOT Wheat Futures Contract Specifications

Trading unit	5,000 bushels
Deliverable grades	No. 1 Northern Spring wheat at par and No. 2 Soft Red, No. 2 Hard Red Winter, No. 2 Dark Northern Spring and substitutions at differentials established by the exchange.
Price quotation	Cents and quarter-cents per bushel
Tick size	One-quarter ($\frac{1}{4}$) cent per bushel ($12.50 per contract)
Daily price limit	20 cents per bushel ($1,000 per contract) above or below the previous day's settlement price (expandable to 30 cents per bushel). No limit in the spot month (limits are lifted two business days before the spot month begins).
Contract months	March, May, July, September, and December
Contract year	Starts in July and ends in May
Last trading day	Seventh business day preceding the last business day of the delivery month
Last delivery day	Last business day of the delivery month
Trading hours	9:30 A.M. to 1:15 P.M. (Chicago time), Monday through Friday. On thc last trading day of an cxpiring contract, trading in that contract closes at noon.
Ticker symbol	W

SOURCE: *Contract Specifications 1991* (Chicago Board of Trade), p. 34.

PRICE AND RETURN CHARACTERISTICS OF COMMODITY FUTURES

This section discusses the price and return characteristics of commodity contracts. The discussion covers the behavior of futures prices relative to cash or spot prices as well as the behavior of futures prices in the same or related commodities. Three hypotheses that attempt to explain the relationship between futures prices and expected spot prices are examined. Ex-post holding period returns (HPRs) and risk measures for commodity contracts are also discussed.

• Price Limits

In a completely free or unregulated market, prices are determined by supply and demand and fluctuate as market conditions change. For example, assume that a severe and unexpected freeze damages the orange crop in Florida. Because of the freeze, the future supply of fresh and frozen orange juice concentrate is likely to be significantly reduced unless there is a large inventory of frozen concentrate or unless the supply from other sources, such as Brazil, can be increased. The freeze is likely to be immediately reflected in spot market prices. The full impact will not be felt at once, however, because the commodity exchange imposes maximum **price limit** changes. Orange juice futures are traded on the New York Cotton Exchange; a contract represents 15,000 pounds of frozen concentrate. The exchange limits the daily price change to 5 cents per pound (either up or down) or $750 (15,000 × $.05) per contract. The price *range* during the day is limited to 10 cents per pound. Bid and ask prices outside these limits are not allowed. Thus, the necessary adjustment to the futures prices due to a freeze may not take place within a single trading day because of the price limit.

These restrictions obviously reduce the potential price volatility of futures contracts in the short run. Over a longer period, however, prices reflect the underlying supply and demand conditions. Although the purpose of the price limits is to ensure a viable and orderly market, they may favor the hedger at the expense of speculators who hope for large excess returns in a short time. In comparison, the stock markets have no price limits. Prices are free to fluctuate to the extent that buyers and sellers, often through the help of specialists, are able to execute transactions. On rare occasions, trading may be temporarily suspended in a particular stock because of a potentially large price change.

• Basis

The vast majority of commodities are actually bought and sold in the *cash* or *spot* market at price P_S rather than in the futures market. The *futures price* (P_F) represents the price of the commodity at some future point in time. The difference between the futures price and the current spot price is called the **basis (*B*)**:

$$B = P_F - P_S \tag{17.1}$$

Ignoring market pricing inefficiencies, the basis on most agricultural commodities will usually be positive, indicating that the futures price (P_F) is greater than the current spot price (P_S). The basis will be positive because of the **carrying costs** associated with a particular commodity: storage costs, insurance, financing expense, and other costs incurred to keep the commodity in inventory until its delivery date. Typically, the longer the time before delivery, the greater the carrying costs. As the delivery month approaches, the basis will decline until the spot and futures prices are approximately equal. This price behavior is known as **convergence.**

Figure 17.1 illustrates the behavior of the basis for a CBOT #2 yellow corn contract. Notice that the basis is initially positive but narrows considerably as the contract approaches the delivery date. Prices are low during and following the harvest, but tend to increase as the inventory of corn declines during the year. Thus, corn prices exhibit significant seasonal patterns. In addition to the seasonal pattern shown in the figure, both cash and futures prices exhibit significant volatility, and the two prices are highly correlated.

Commodity contracts can also have a negative basis. This may occur because the particular commodity is currently in short supply in the cash market, causing upward pressure on prices. If the future supply is expected to increase (because of a good harvest), future prices can be below spot prices, creating a negative basis.

• Spreads

In the discussion of option strategies using puts and calls in Chapter 15, we described a combination strategy called a **spread.** A spread in options involves simultaneously taking a position in a put and a call in the same underlying security. The put and call may have different striking prices and/or expiration dates. The same concept can be employed in commodity futures.

FIGURE 17.1 • Cash versus Futures Price of #2 Yellow Corn

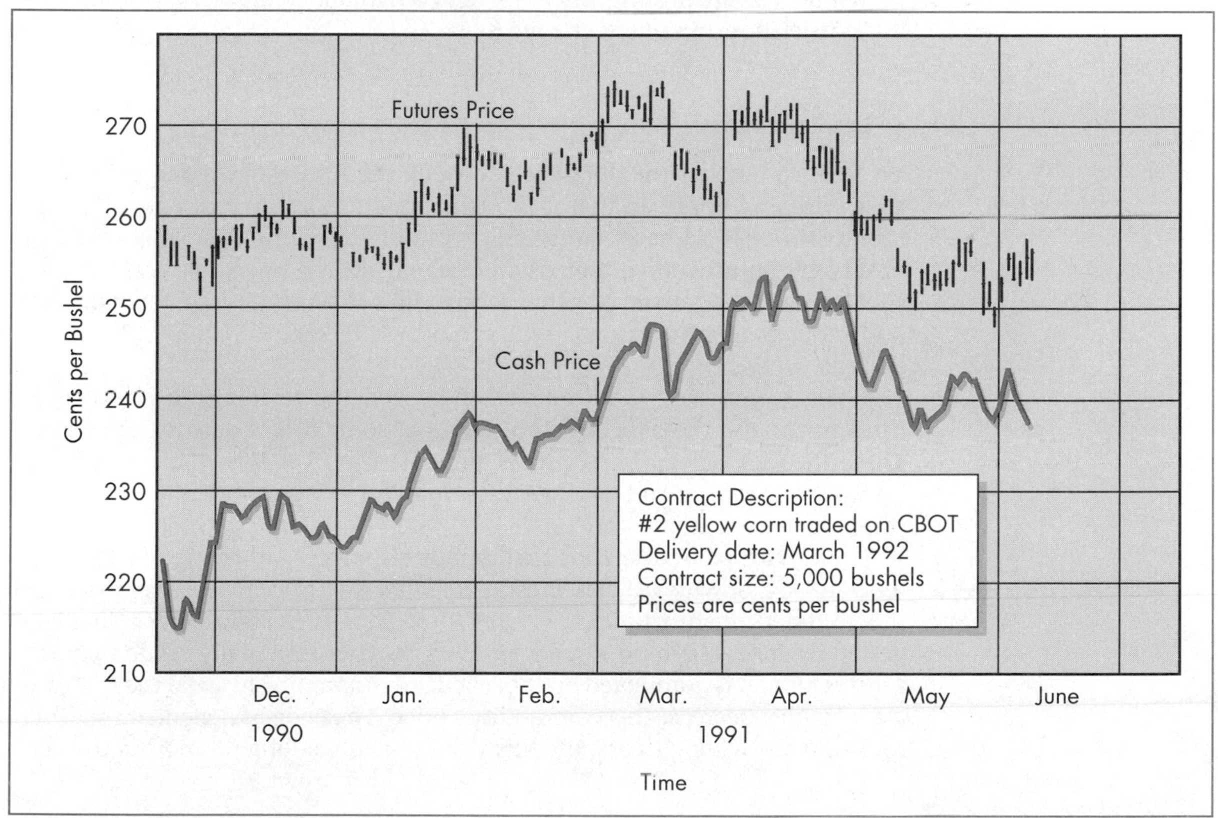

SOURCE: *Futures Chart Service* (Commodity Research Bureau). Reprinted with permission. © 1991 Commodity Research Bureau, 30 S. Wacker Drive, Chicago, IL 60606.

An example of a spread in commodity futures would be a trader simultaneously taking a long position in a futures contract and a short position in a futures contract in the same commodity. The two contracts would differ only in their delivery dates. This type of spread is known as a *time spread.* For example, if the trader believes that the basis (carrying costs) is too large for the contract with the later delivery date relative to the basis for the contract with the shorter delivery date, the distant futures contract will be shorted, and a long position will be taken in the near futures contract. The trader is not concerned with the price level changes in the underlying commodity, but rather with a relative change in the basis of the two contracts.

Spreads in commodity futures are not limited to taking long and short positions in the same commodity. Spreads may be undertaken in different commodities that are related in some way. For example, since soybean oil is a derivative of soybeans, a trader may observe an opportunity to undertake a spread in these two commodities. Another spread might involve the crude oil–gasoline–heating oil relationship. This relationship is called the *crack spread* and might be expressed as 5–3–2, reflecting the fact that five barrels of crude produce about three barrels of gasoline and two barrels of heating oil. In winter, when heating oil is in heavy demand relative to gasoline, the 5–3–2 relationship might change to 3–2–1.

• Expected Basis

We defined basis as the difference between the futures price and the current spot price and observed that it is attributable to the carrying cost of a commodity. In a world of certainty and without considering carrying costs, the observable futures price today would equal the unobservable but expected spot price in the future. In other words, in a market without carrying costs and other inefficiencies, but with certainty, the *expected basis,* $E(B)$, would be zero.

When uncertainty is introduced, however, the relationship between futures prices and the expected spot prices at some future date is not so clear. Three theories or hypotheses have attempted to explain $E(B)$: *normal backwardation, contango,* and the *expectation hypothesis.* Figure 17.2 illustrates these three theories of futures prices.

The **normal backwardation** hypothesis suggests that the "future price tends to be a downward biased estimate of its spot price in the cash market at the contract's maturity date,"[1] or $E(B) < 0$. This hypothesis was first suggested by John Maynard Keynes in 1924. Keynes essentially argued that the futures market is dominated by short hedgers attempting to avoid the risk associated with a decrease in a commodity's price. The hedgers depend on speculators who are willing to assume this risk by taking a long position in the con-

[1] Zvi Bodie and Victor I. Rosansky, "Risk and Return in Commodity Futures," *Financial Analysts Journal* (May-June 1980): 27–39.

FIGURE 17.2
Futures Prices through Time, Assuming a Constant Spot Price

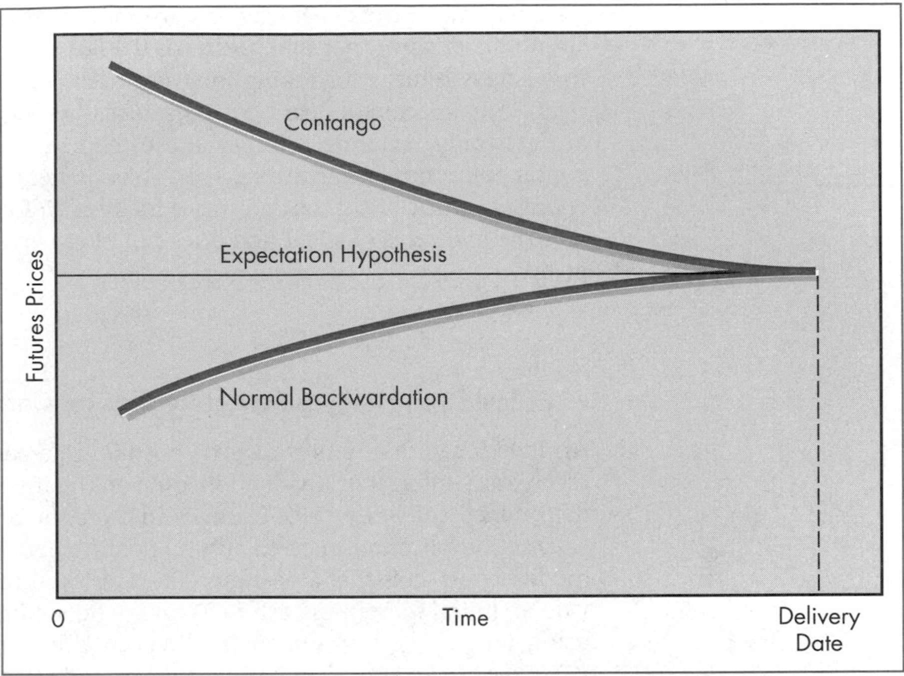

tract. The hedgers must therefore write contracts at prices below the expected spot price to compensate the speculator for assuming the risk. The expected basis is therefore negative. This theory assumes that hedgers usually write (net short) contracts and that speculators usually buy (net long) contracts.

The second hypothesis is that $E(B) > 0$.[2] This hypothesis suggests that speculators, because of market inefficiencies or because of their particular skill and knowledge about the futures market, are more than willing to assume the price risk in anticipation of earning profits. Because of these anticipated profits, speculators bid up the prices of commodity contracts so that the expected basis is positive. Speculators earn their anticipated profit only if they are net short and the futures price declines. This price behavior—with the initial price of the futures contract above the spot price and the futures price declining over time—is known as **contango.** This theory assumes that hedgers generally purchase contracts (net long) and that speculators generally write contracts (net short).

The third theory, the **expectation hypothesis,** is that $E(B) = 0$, as would be the case in an efficient market. Essentially, this view argues that futures prices are unbiased estimates of expected futures spot prices. The market, therefore, does not provide excess returns to hedgers or to speculators.

[2] C.O. Hardy and L.S. Lyon, "The Theory of Hedging," *Journal of Political Economy* (April 1923): 276–87.

In summary, the debate centers around whether the expected basis, $E(B)$, should be positive, negative, or zero. If $E(B) < 0$, the market offers speculators excess returns for taking long positions and assuming the price risk. If $E(B) > 0$, speculators earn excess returns by being net short while hedgers are generally net long. Both of these theories (normal backwardation and contango) assume that the net positions of hedgers and speculators do not change over the life of the contract. Finally, if $E(B) = 0$ (expectation hypothesis), the market is efficient and does not offer excess returns on short or long positions.

• Calculating Holding Period Returns on Commodity Contracts

An investor with a long (or short) position in a commodity contract will not receive any interest or dividend income on the investment. Gains or losses are determined solely by price changes in the contract over the holding period.

One complication in calculating a holding period return (HPR) for a commodity contract is that a position (short or long) requires the investor to provide an initial margin in cash or Treasury bills. Should the HPR be calculated using only the initial margin (equity) as the initial investment? Typically, HPRs for stocks are calculated as unleveraged returns, even if margin trading is used. If the HPRs on commodities and stock are to be compared, the influence of leverage should be removed. One approach is to calculate the HPR on the commodity as

$$\text{HPR}_t = \frac{P_1 - P_0}{P_0} \tag{17.2}$$

where P_0 is the beginning price of the contract rather than the amount of the initial margin required of the investor, and P_1 is the ending price of the contract. This procedure ignores the leverage effect.

The impact of leverage on returns can be measured by defining the HPR as

$$\text{HPR}_t = \frac{P_1 - P_0}{mP_0} \tag{17.3}$$

where m is the margin requirement in decimal form. Since m is usually 10 percent or less, the HPR will be magnified, or leveraged, if the price changes over the holding period of the contract.

An alternative calculation reflects the fact that the initial margin may be in Treasury bills where the investor is entitled to any interest income from the bills. This interest income can be considered in calculating the HPR. Because of the practice of marking to market every day, the investor may be required to post additional margin or be able to remove funds for other purposes. These daily cash inflows and outflows change the margin and therefore influence the HPR.

If Treasury bills are used for the initial margin, the HPR is

$$HPR_t = \frac{P_1 - P_0}{P_0} + R_{F,0} \qquad (17.4)$$

where $R_{F,0}$ is the yield to maturity or HPR on a U.S. Treasury bill of the same maturity as the holding period on the commodity contract. Equation 17.4 ignores the leverage effect and the daily inflows and outflows of cash that may occur because of marking to market. Table 17.4 presents a simple illustration of alternative HPR calculations for commodities contracts. Notice the large impact that leverage has on the HPRs.

TABLE 17.4 • Calculating HPRs on Commodity Contracts

Data

Contract: Gold, traded on New York Commodity Exchange
One contract represents 100 troy ounces of gold.
Delivery month is February 1991.
Initial margin requirement is 10 percent of contract value.

Date	*Closing price of commodity contract (dollars per troy oz.)*	*Initial margin on contract (10%)*	*Quarterly yields to maturity on 90-day U.S. treasury bills*
October 2, 1989	$402.50	$4,025	1.98%
January 2, 1990	434.50	4,345	1.89
April 2, 1990	393.90	3,939	1.95
July 2, 1990	373.00	3,730	1.94
October 1, 1990	412.60	4,126	1.79
December 30, 1990	385.70	3,857	—

Holding Period Returns (HPRs)

Period	*Calculated from price changes (Equation 17.2)*	*Calculated considering leverage (Equation 17.3)*	*Calculated considering interest income (Equation 17.4)*
1989 fourth quarter	7.95%	79.50%	9.93%
1990 first quarter	−9.34	−93.44	−7.45
1990 second quarter	−5.31	−53.06	−3.36
1990 third quarter	10.62	106.17	12.56
1990 fourth quarter	−6.52	−65.20	−4.73

SOURCE: Prices and Treasury bill yields are from the *Wall Street Journal*, various issues.

TABLE 17.5 • Historical Real Rates of Returns and Standard Deviations on U.S. Treasury Bills and Bonds, Stocks, and Commodities and the Rate of Inflation, 1953–1981

Year	U.S. Treasury bills	U.S. Treasury bonds	S&P 500	Commodity futures	Rate of inflation (CPI)
1953	1.19%	2.99%	− 1.60%	− 3.46%	0.62%
1954	1.37	7.73	53.39	13.23	−0.50
1955	1.20	− 1.66	31.08	− 7.63	0.37
1956	−0.39	− 8.22	3.60	12.38	2.86
1957	0.12	4.30	−13.40	− 5.04	3.02
1958	0.22	− 7.72	40.88	− 3.47	1.76
1959	1.43	− 3.70	10.30	− 2.84	1.50
1960	1.16	12.12	− 1.00	− 3.93	1.48
1961	1.45	0.30	26.05	0.02	0.67
1962	1.50	5.60	− 9.83	− 2.40	1.22
1963	1.45	− 0.43	20.81	16.32	1.65
1964	2.32	2.29	15.11	4.54	1.19
1965	1.97	− 1.18	10.33	5.13	1.92
1966	1.36	− 0.29	−12.98	9.70	3.35
1967	1.34	−11.87	20.32	− 0.06	3.04
1968	0.47	− 4.76	6.05	− 2.18	4.72
1969	0.44	−10.55	−13.77	12.20	6.11
1970	0.99	6.27	− 1.40	− 1.62	5.49
1971	1.00	9.55	10.59	− 1.65	3.36
1972	0.42	2.20	15.06	29.35	3.41
1973	−1.72	− 9.11	−21.56	72.69	8.80
1974	−3.74	− 7.00	−34.47	17.97	12.20
1975	−1.13	2.04	28.21	−10.03	7.01
1976	0.26	11.39	18.16	5.30	4.81
1977	−1.55	− 6.92	−13.07	− 4.90	6.77
1978	−1.83	− 7.34	− 2.42	18.60	9.03
1979	−2.59	−12.82	4.53	15.91	13.31
1980	−1.79	−15.80	17.44	5.24	12.41
1981	4.35	− 6.47	−12.68	−33.08	8.90
Mean	0.37	− 1.65	6.68	5.69	4.50
Standard deviation	1.68	7.43	19.48	17.36	3.86

SOURCE: Zvi Bodie, "Commodity Futures as a Hedge against Inflation," *Journal of Portfolio Management* (Spring 1983): 13. Reprinted with permission from Institutional Investor, Inc.

• Ex-Post Returns and Risk on Commodity Contracts

Table 17.5 provides historical *real* HPRs (HPR less the rate of inflation) on Treasury bills and bonds, common stocks, and commodity futures. The returns are adjusted for the rate of inflation, using the Consumer Price Index (CPI). The commodity returns for the years 1953–1963 are based on a portfolio composed of 13 commodities. As new commodity contracts were introduced for trading over the 1964–1981 period, they were added to the portfolio. In the more recent years (1964–1981), the number of commodities in the portfolio varied from 18 to 22. The real HPRs for commodities, based on price changes, do *not* reflect the impact of leverage (Equation 17.3) or of using U.S. Treasury bills for the margin (Equation 17.4). The returns on bonds and stocks, however, reflect price changes and interest and dividend income.

Several interesting observations can be made from the data in Table 17.5. First, the real HPRs from the commodities portfolio ranged from −33.08 percent in 1981 to 72.69 percent in 1973, while the real HPRs on common stocks ranged from −34.47 percent in 1974 to 53.39 percent in 1954. Despite the larger HPR range for commodities, the standard deviation for the stock returns (19.48 percent) is larger than the standard deviation for commodities (17.36 percent). The arithmetic mean return for stocks is also larger than the mean for the commodities portfolio (6.68 percent versus 5.69 percent). The coefficient of variation (see Chapter 2) for stocks is 2.92, compared to 3.05 for commodities. The coefficient of variation indicates that the relative risk of stocks is less than that of commodities. Second, notice that for the years with relatively high rates of inflation (1969, 1973–1975, and 1978–1981), the real HPRs for commodities were usually quite favorable, compared to generally negative real HPRs for common stocks and U.S. Treasury bills and bonds.

Table 17.6 provides the correlation coefficients between the real HPRs for U.S. Treasury bills and bonds, common stocks, commodity futures, and the

TABLE 17.6 • Correlation Coefficients between Real Rates of Return on U.S. Treasury Bills and Bonds, Commodities, Stocks, and Inflation, 1953–1981

	Treasury bills	Treasury bonds	Commodities	Common stocks	Inflation rate (CPI)
Treasury bills	1.000				
Treasury bonds	0.430	1.000			
Commodities	−0.512	−0.230	1.000		
Common stocks	0.252	0.187	−0.210	1.000	
Inflation rate (CPI)	−0.673	−0.579	0.247	−0.467	1.000

SOURCE: Zvi Bodie, "Commodity Futures as a Hedge against Inflation," *Journal of Portfolio Management* (Spring 1983): 13. Reprinted with permission from Institutional Investor, Inc.

rate of inflation. The real returns on commodity futures are positively correlated with inflation (+.247), whereas bills (−.673), bonds (−.579), and common stock (−.467) are negatively correlated. This suggests that commodity returns may provide an inflation hedge. The negative correlation between commodity real returns and the returns on financial assets suggests that diversification benefits may result from including commodities in an investment portfolio.

INVESTMENT ANALYSIS OF COMMODITY CONTRACTS

It is unlikely that most individuals trade in commodities to hedge. This is because individuals (excluding farmers) are typically not commodity producers, nor do they have a large inventory of a commodity. Their motivation, therefore, is likely to be speculation. Individuals may be attracted to commodity trading because of its large and rapid price changes and the possibility of using small initial margins to take trading positions. It is quite possible that the HPR on a commodity contract will be over 100 percent, given a 10 percent change in the spot price of the commodity. On the other hand, the loss is also quite likely to be more than 100 percent if the initial margin is totally lost and additional margin is used to maintain the position.

A number of studies have shown that hedgers in commodity markets have been able to purchase their "insurance" very cheaply since, as a general rule, futures prices contain a very small risk premium. This suggests that, on average, a speculator should expect a loss or very low returns on the majority of trades. It is possible, however, that the current futures price does not accurately reflect the commodity's price in the future. This possibility provides the speculator's motivation. As a word of warning, however, it should be noted that "analyses of the returns to speculators have shown that speculation should be regarded as a skilled occupation, not merely as risk-bearing; returns vary greatly with the ability and knowledge of the speculators."[3]

• Demand and Supply Analysis

A fundamental approach to speculation in commodity futures requires a demand and supply analysis of the underlying commodity. Demand for agricultural commodities is somewhat stable and predictable since many of these commodities are food staples. The supply of agricultural commodities can be very volatile, however, because of uncertain harvests due to unpredictable weather conditions, crop diseases, and other factors. The impact of the drought during the summer of 1988 is a recent example of how weather can affect commodity prices.

---

[3] Avraham Kamara, "The Behavior of Futures Prices: A Review of Theory and Evidence," *Financial Analysts Journal* (July-August 1984): 70.

Much of the information needed for a demand and supply analysis is developed and reported by the U.S. Department of Agriculture (USDA). The USDA collects data through regional field offices that monitor local growing conditions and take crop samples to forecast the harvest. The individual speculator can obtain information directly from the USDA or through commodity research organizations and brokerage firms.

• Systematic and Unsystematic Risk

A number of studies have attempted to apply the CAPM to agricultural commodity contracts. Generally, these studies (using a combination of the S&P 500 and the Dow Jones Cash Commodity Index as the market proxy) have concluded that the systematic risk in agricultural futures contracts is insignificant. Factors unique to agricultural commodities, such as wheat, corn, and soybeans, appear to be primarily responsible for price changes and the resulting return on the commodity contracts. Thus, systematic risk estimates (beta) for agricultural futures contracts do not appear to be useful in an investment analysis.

A recent study of metals (copper, platinum, and silver), however, found significant systematic risk in these futures contracts over the 1978–1983 period.[4] The authors determined that metal futures have above-average total risk when compared to common stocks and that the return per unit of total risk was less than that of common stocks. They also found that beta estimates for metal futures ranged from .731 to 1.054 and that the market compensated for the systematic risk (i.e., the futures contracts did not provide any excess returns). The results of this study indicate that there are market-related risks in metal futures and that these risks cannot be eliminated by combining metal futures with a portfolio comprised of other assets.

INVESTMENT STRATEGIES FOR COMMODITY FUTURES CONTRACTS

Speculators use a variety of strategies for commodity futures contracts. This section examines several possibilities including using commodity futures contracts as an inflation hedge, investing in publicly traded commodity funds, and using commodity futures to increase portfolio diversification.

• Commodity Futures Contracts as an Inflation Hedge

Can commodity contracts be used to provide an inflation hedge? Surprisingly, the answer to this question is not clear because various studies have produced contradictory empirical results. For example, as Table 17.6 showed, the study

[4] Eric C. Chang, Chao Chen, and Son-Nan Chen, "Risk and Return in Copper, Platinum, and Silver Futures," *Journal of Futures Markets* (February 1990): 29–39.

by Bodie over the 1953–1981 period concluded that commodity futures correlated relatively well with the rate of inflation (CPI) and consequently provided an effective hedge. A more recent study, using data for 14 agricultural and two metals contracts over the 1967–1982 period, reached a different conclusion.[5] The study tested whether portfolios of common stocks and commodity futures contracts provided an inflation hedge against *unexpected inflation* in the cost of consumer goods, shelter, and transportation. The empirical results suggested that hedging was possible but that "commodity futures contracts contributed nothing to hedging effectiveness."[6] Essentially, the hedging strategy worked because of the performance of the common stocks in the portfolio.

In summary, the empirical tests indicate that returns on a portfolio of commodity contracts are usually above the observed rate of inflation and consequently provide a positive real return. It is also generally recognized that common stocks, and particularly long-term bonds, do not provide adequate real rates of return during periods of high inflation. In terms of unexpected inflation, common stocks rather than commodities appear to provide a hedge against cost increases in specific items such as food, shelter, and transportation.

• Market Inefficiencies

Numerous studies have tested for nonrandom price movements and other types of market inefficiencies in commodity prices. If nonrandom patterns of sufficient magnitude can be discovered, then trading rules or strategies can be developed to earn excess returns. Despite some evidence of seasonality and serial correlation in futures prices, the evidence is not very compelling. This suggests that "the mere existence of some nonrandom components is not sufficient evidence against the random walk hypotheses; they must present unexploited opportunities for above-average profits."[7] This conclusion tends to discount the usefulness of technical analysis in identifying speculative trading opportunities in commodity futures.

• Publicly Traded Commodity Funds

Table 17.7 summarizes the characteristics of publicly traded **commodity funds.** A 1990 study analyzed the investment performance of such funds over the period 1980 through 1988.[8] Table 17.8 summarizes the risk and re-

[5] Victor L. Bernard and Thomas J. Frecka, "Commodity Contracts and Common Stocks as Hedges against Relative Consumer Price Risk," *Journal of Financial and Quantitative Analysis* (June 1987): 169–88.

[6] Ibid., pp. 185–86.

[7] Kamara, "The Behavior of Futures Prices," p. 71.

[8] Edwin J. Elton, Martin J. Gruber, and Joel Rentzler, "The Performance of Publicly Offered Commodity Funds," *Financial Analysts Journal* (July-August 1990): 23–30.

TABLE 17.7 • Characteristics of Publicly Traded Commodity Funds

Publicly offered commodity funds are professionally managed limited partnerships, offered to investors by prospectus, that buy and sell futures contracts. While individual funds may differ, the typical fund has the following characteristics:

1. Most funds have the ability to trade (and do trade) in many futures and forward contracts on financial instruments, foreign currencies, and commodities. In addition, they frequently hold financial instruments directly (using them for margin against their futures transactions). Most fund prospectuses stress diversification and the ability to take long as well as short positions in commodities (i.e., to buy or sell futures contracts).
2. Most funds can only be purchased for a short time after the initial prospectus, but allow investors to liquidate their position at net asset value at monthly (sometimes quarterly) intervals. A monthly rate of return can, however, be computed.
3. Most funds use technical and trend-following systems to decide whether to take a long or short position with respect to any commodity (futures contract).
4. Most funds incur high management fees and transaction costs relative to other types of asset management such as mutual funds. Management fees usually exceed 5 percent of capital a year, while the sum of management fees and transaction costs exceeds 19 percent of capital per year.
5. Most fund prospectuses contain a clause that calls for the fund to dissolve if either the net asset value per share falls below a predetermined level (most often 25 to 30 percent of the initial capital an investor pays in) or the total size of the fund (assets under management) falls below a specific level.

Prior to 1978, there were only three publicly offered commodity funds, but their number has grown rapidly in recent years—from 94 funds with $600 million under management in 1985 to 130 funds with over $2 billion under management in 1988. Their popularity has continued despite two apparent handicaps—extremely high management fees and transaction costs and almost exclusive reliance on technical analysis.

SOURCE: Edwin J. Elton, Martin J. Gruber, and Joel Rentzler, "The Performance of Publicly Offered Commodity Funds," *Financial Analysts Journal* (July-August 1990): 23–24.

turn measures for the funds and for other categories of financial assets. Part I of the table provides the monthly standard deviations and annual returns of the commodity funds. In both columns, the annual return is a continuously compounded rate of return. Returns in the "All" column are based on all funds that existed at any time during the year. The "Beginning Year" returns are based on funds that existed at the beginning of a year. If a fund that was in existence at the beginning of a year dissolved during the year, it was assumed that the proceeds from the dissolution were invested in Treasury bills for the remainder of the year. The "Beginning Year" returns were slightly higher than

TABLE 17.8 • Performance of Publicly Traded Commodity Funds

I. Risk and Return for Commodity Funds, 1980–1988

Year	Monthly standard deviation	Annual Return: *All*	Annual Return: *Beginning year*
1980	12.6%*	5.8980%	2.0748%
1981	10.0	0.5452	4.0716
1982	10.1	0.4944	− 0.0864
1983	11.7	−16.1568	−15.0768
1984	10.6	7.0620	7.6656
1985	8.7	10.5096	10.8840
1986	10.4	−17.3916	−17.1588
1987	8.7	27.8676	28.3200
1988	10.4	0.4962	0.5568
	10.4%	2.2565%	2.3612%

II. Comparison of Commodity Funds to Other Financial Assets, 1980–1988

	Yearly return	*Standard deviation of monthly return*
Common stocks	14.88%	4.91%
Long-term corporate bonds	11.80	3.83
Long-term government bonds	11.40	4.17
Shearson Lehman Bond Index	11.40	2.38
Treasury bills	8.64	0.25

SOURCE: Edwin J. Elton, Martin J. Gruber, and Joel Rentzler, "The Performance of Publicly Offered Commodity Funds," *Financial Analysts Journal* (July-August 1990): 25.
*This number excludes the firm with the highest standard deviation.

the "All" returns because the Treasury bill rates over the period were higher than the commodity fund returns.

Part II of Table 17.8 shows the performance of stocks, bonds, and bills over the 1980–1988 period. Comparing the performance of the commodity funds in Part I with the performance of the alternative investments in Part II shows that the funds had the lowest average annual return but the highest standard deviation of monthly returns. These results indicate that investments in commodity funds, on average, have not historically proved worthwhile.

The study also examined indicators of the predictability of future fund returns. One conclusion was that prior fund performance was not a good indicator of future performance. The authors of the study also used information contained in the fund prospectus to predict future fund performance. The items examined included the offering size of a fund, the amount of experience of the general partners of the fund, and the past performance of other funds managed by the general partners. Although the sample was small, the authors concluded that funds with general partners who had above-average prior performance with funds were more likely to outperform funds managed by partners with below-average prior experience. The size and amount-of-experience variables were not found to be good predictors of future fund performance.

• Portfolio Considerations

Commodity speculators, because of their investment philosophy and motivation, are not interested in reducing risk at the expense of returns. Typically, a small individual speculator actively trades in only one or a few specific types of futures contracts because obtaining and analyzing demand and supply factors for many commodities can be very difficult. Since it has been shown that the risk of agricultural commodity contracts is unsystematic, an overall economic or market analysis is generally not useful. Unique supply and demand factors must be individually analyzed for these types of commodities. Metal futures, however, do appear to have significant systematic risk.

Investment advisers and brokerage houses often recommend that individuals segregate funds for commodity speculation from other investment funds. In this sense, commodity speculation is not viewed in a portfolio context. This practice is designed to limit the risk exposure from commodity speculation so that if the entire amount is lost, it will represent only a small portion of the individual's total wealth. As this chapter indicates, commodity investing is *very risky*. In a portfolio context, however, there is some evidence that commodity futures returns are negatively correlated with bond and stock returns (see Table 17.6). This suggests that the risk of a securities portfolio may be reduced by adding commodity futures.

INTRODUCTION TO FINANCIAL FUTURES

Many individual and institutional investors that traditionally concentrated their investments in stocks and bonds have readily accepted the introduction of financial futures. As the previous sections indicated, investing in commodity futures requires an analysis of the underlying real asset, which may be an agricultural commodity or a precious metal. Typically, few stock and bond investors have the necessary understanding of the supply and demand factors for commodities. Their expertise is analysis of financial assets, such as stocks and bonds.

The first financial future came into existence in the United States in 1972 with the introduction of **currency futures** by the International Monetary Market (IMM), a division of the Chicago Mercantile Exchange. Contracts on

TABLE 17.9 • Major Types of Financial Futures and U.S. Trading Markets

Chicago Board of Trade

1. Ten-year Treasury notes
2. Five-year Treasury notes
3. Two-year Treasury notes
4. U.S. Treasury bonds
5. 30-day interest rate
6. Municipal bond index
7. Mortgage-backed (GNMA)
8. Major Market Index
9. CBOT Tokyo Stock Index
10. CBOT long-term Japanese government bond

Chicago Mercantile Exchange

1. U.S. Treasury bills
2. S&P 500
3. Nikkei 225 Average
4. Eurodollars
5. British pound
6. Canadian dollar
7. French franc
8. German mark
9. Japanese yen
10. Swiss franc
11. Australian dollar

New York Cotton Exchange

1. European currency units
2. U.S. dollar
3. Five-year Treasury notes

Kansas City Board of Trade

1. Value Line Stock Index
2. Mini Value Line Stock Index
3. Value Line Stock Index

New York Futures Exchange

1. NYSE Composite
2. Russell 2000
3. Russell 3000

Treasury securities were introduced by the IMM in 1976. Stock index futures were first offered in 1982 by the Kansas City Board of Trade. When investors accepted these futures enthusiastically, other exchanges began to offer financial futures.

Table 17.9 lists five major U.S. markets and the types of financial futures traded on each market. In addition, markets such as the Toronto Stock Exchange, Winnipeg Commodity Exchange, London International Futures Exchange, and Tokyo International Financial Futures Exchange trade financial futures.

U.S. exchanges are also constantly seeking to add new types of contracts. Before a new type of contract can be introduced, however, it must be approved by the CFTC. Considering the rapid developments since financial futures were introduced, investors have apparently recognized the advantages of these new products and markets. Today, financial futures and options on financial futures are an important part of the investment portfolios of many institutions and individuals. In the last decade, U.S. volume in financial futures and options has increased dramatically. During 1989, over 50 percent of the 267 million futures contracts traded were financial futures.

The market collapse in October 1987, however, has raised some serious concerns about the role and regulation of the options and financial futures markets. Congressional investigations and studies by the Securities and Exchange Commission (SEC), the exchanges, and a presidential commission have made numerous recommendations: (1) increasing the required margins on options and financial futures; (2) reducing the daily price change limits on futures contracts; (3) regulating arbitrage trading involving index options, financial futures, and common stocks; and (4) changing the regulatory functions of the SEC, Federal Reserve, and CFTC. The proposed regulatory reforms revolve around the question of who should regulate the financial futures industry. One suggestion has been to merge the SEC and the CFTC, so they would function as separate divisions under an umbrella organization. Any transfer of regulatory authority will require legislation by Congress.

The mechanics of trading, contract characteristics, and institutional arrangements for financial futures are essentially the same as for commodity futures. Consequently, much of the previous discussion of commodity futures applies to financial futures as well. There are, however, three major differences between commodity and financial futures:

1. Certain financial futures have no underlying real asset; in this sense, they are *derivative securities* in that their value is determined by the price movements of the assets they represent. In some instances, the assets they represent do not actually exist. For example, a futures contract on the S&P 500 Index represents a hypothetical common stock portfolio and cannot be settled by the delivery of the underlying assets. Thus, stock index futures must be settled for *cash* on the delivery date while other futures can be settled by the delivery of the securities or commodities.

2. Contract maturity dates are standardized for financial futures; many of these contracts are available with maturities in March, June, September, and December. Maturity months for commodity contracts vary from commodity to commodity, depending on the characteristics of the commodity.

3. Financial futures are generally available with longer lives than agricultural commodity futures. For example, contracts on U.S. Treasury bonds are traded with settlement dates over two years away. Agricultural contracts are usually for 90 days or less and generally cannot exceed a year.

In the following sections, we will discuss interest rate futures, stock index futures, and foreign currency futures. The chapter will conclude with a discussion of options on financial futures.

INTEREST RATE FUTURES

Interest rate futures are available on debt securities and interest rates such as U.S. Treasury bills, notes, and bonds; 30-day interest rates; Eurodollar deposits; and municipal bonds. These contracts represent a promise to buy or sell a specified amount of the fixed-income security at some future time. For example, a contract on Treasury bills represents $1 million. The contract writer (short position) promises to deliver, and the buyer (long position) promises to accept delivery. The motivation of both the buyer and seller is to hedge or to speculate on interest rate changes over the life of the contract. For example, the contract writer may be trying to hedge against the impact of increases in interest rates to protect a long position in Treasury bills.

Rather than hedging, the writer may be speculating that Treasury bills will be less valuable in the future because of increases in interest rates. In this instance, the seller will not actually have a long position in Treasury bills. In general, a trader who expects interest rates to *increase* will write a contract (short position), while a trader who expects rates to *decrease* will buy a contract (long position).

Table 17.10 provides an example of the quotations on six interest rate futures. The contracts for the Treasury bill futures are traded on the Chicago Mercantile Exchange using a price index. The price index is derived by subtracting the annualized yield on Treasury bills from 100.00:

$$\text{price index} = 100.00 - \text{Treasury bill annualized yield} \quad \textbf{(17.5)}$$

For example, the December 1991 contract is quoted at 93.98. This price index of 93.98 indicates an annualized yield of 6.02 percent (100.00 − 93.98). Therefore, as yields on Treasury bills increase, the index price of the futures contract will decline.

Because each futures contract in Treasury bills has a delivery value of $1 million, each basis point (.01 percent) of price change represents a $25 change in contract value:

$$\begin{pmatrix}\text{basis-point}\\ \text{change}\end{pmatrix}\left(\frac{\text{days to maturity}}{\text{360 days}}\right)\begin{pmatrix}\text{delivery value}\\ \text{of contract}\end{pmatrix} = \begin{matrix}\text{change}\\ \text{in value}\end{matrix} \quad \textbf{(17.6)}$$

Using the futures contract for December 1991 90-day bills in Table 17.10, a 1-basis-point (.01 percent) change in its price represents a $25 increase in the value of the contract:

$$(.0001)(90/360)(\$1{,}000{,}000) = \$25$$

The actual value of the 90-day bills represented in the December 1991 futures contract can be calculated as

$$\begin{aligned}\begin{matrix}\text{actual value}\\ \text{of bills}\end{matrix} &= \left[1.0 - \frac{\begin{pmatrix}\text{days to}\\ \text{maturity}\end{pmatrix} \times \left(1 - \begin{matrix}\text{quoted}\\ \text{contract price}\end{matrix}\right)}{360}\right]\begin{matrix}\text{delivery value}\\ \text{of contract}\end{matrix}\\ &= \left[1.0 - \frac{90 \times (1.0 - .9398)}{360}\right]\$1{,}000{,}000\\ &= \$984{,}950 \qquad \textbf{(17.7)}\end{aligned}$$

Therefore, the reported futures prices for Treasury bill contracts do not represent the dollar value of the Treasury bills represented by the contract.

TABLE 17.10 • Quotations on Interest Rate Futures

Season's High	Season's Low		Week's High	Week's Low	Sett	Net Chg	Open Int.
Chicago Mercantile Exchange							
US T. BILLS							
$1 million; pts of 100 pct.							
94.55	91.60	Sep	94.49	94.36	94.37	−.11	46,263
94.16	92.24	Dec	94.10	93.96	93.98	−.12	8,617
94.03	93.42	Mar	93.87	93.86	93.85	−.15	894
93.52	93.15	Jun	93.52	93.52	93.47	+.10	148
.....	.....	Sep	.....	.....	93.14	......	1
Fri. to Thurs. sales 39,766.							
Total open interest 55,923.							
Chicago Board of Trade							
10 YR. TREASURY							
$100,000 prin; pts & 32nds of 100 pct							
100-1	96-1	Sep	97-20	96-26	96-28	− 20	82,664
98-12	95-15	Dec	96-29	96-6	96-7	− 20	952
97-5	95-8	Mar	.....	.....	95-22	− 21	1
Fri. to Thurs. sales 62,735.							
Total open interest 83,617.							
5 YR. TREASURY							
$100,000 prin; pts & 32nds of 100 pct							
100.230	98.275	Sep	99.280	99.100	99.115	−.135	69,895
99.010	98.190	Dec	99.010	99.000	98.250	−.820	705
Fri. to Thurs. sales 34,301.							
Total open interest 70,600.							
US TREASURY BONDS							
(8 pct-$100,000;pts & 32nds of 100 pct)							
99-5	85-29	Sep	93-27	92-22	92-25	− 27	237,113
98-20	85-19	Dec	93-1	92	92-2	− 27	8,744
98-13	85-14	Mar	92-13	91-15	91-15	− 26	3,732
97-19	85-3	Jun	91-27	90-29	90-29	− 26	3,872
95-0	07-14	Sep	91-11	90-13	90-13	− 26	712
94-11	85-6	Dec	90-23	90-19	90	− 25	199
Fri. to Thurs. sales 813,665.							
Total open interest 254,372.							
MUNICIPAL BONDS							
$1000x index;pts & 32nds of 100 pct							
92-11	84-7	Sep	91-17	90-16	90-17	− 19	5,950
91-11	88-16	Dec	.....	.....	89-19	− 19	27
89-17	88	Mar	.....	.....	88-25	− 19	6
Last index 92-7 , off 27.							
Fri. to Thurs. sales 5,559.							
Total open interest 5,983.							
30 DAY INTEREST RATE							
$5 million; points of 100 pct.							
94.28	93.65	Jul	94.15	94.10	94.14	−.05	1,658
94.24	93.58	Aug	94.11	94.07	94.11	−.03	1,044
94.18	93.40	Sep	94.02	94.00	94.00	−.06	1,128
94.13	93.69	Oct	93.94	93.[illegible]4	93.93	−.04	497
94.06	93.70	Nov	.....	.....	93.84	−.04	374
93.85	93.35	Dec	93.56	93.54	93.55	−.05	368
93.52	93.52	Jan	93.52	93.52	93.51	−.06	7
Last index 5.77, off .14.							
Fri. to Thurs. sales 1,105.							
Total open interest 5,076.							

SOURCE: *Barron's*, July 8, 1991. Courtesy of *Barron's Weekly*.

Assume that a speculator buys the December contract at the quoted price of 93.98 and that market yields do, in fact, immediately decline. Because of the yield decline, the future's price will increase. The profit to the speculator from a 10-basis-point yield decline can be calculated as

$$\text{(basis-point change)}(\$25) = \text{profit} \tag{17.8}$$
$$(10)(\$25) = \$250$$

Another way to calculate the profit to the speculator is to compute the new value of the Treasury bills using Equation 17.7 (note that the quoted contract price of 94.08 reflects the 10-basis-point yield decline):

$$\left[1.0 - \frac{90 \times (1.0 - .9408)}{360}\right]\$1{,}000{,}000 = \$985{,}200 \quad \textbf{(17.9)}$$

The profit represents the $250 increase in the value of the bills ($985,200 − $984,950). The easiest way to calculate profit and loss for a Treasury bill future is to use the formula that a 1-basis-point change in the contract's price equals $25 of gain or loss to the trader.

• Hedging Using Treasury Bill Futures

Two basic hedging strategies can be used for Treasury bills—a short hedge and a long hedge:

1. Short hedges A short hedge, used by the investor with a long position in Treasury bills, is designed to protect the long position from increases in yields that might occur before the bills mature or are sold. Ideally, the hedger *writes* (shorts) a futures contract with a face value equal to the value of the long position. If interest rates increase, the values of the long position and the futures contract will decline. Since the hedger is short in the futures contract, however, the position can be closed by buying an identical contract (a reversing trade), at a price below the issue price. The difference will be a gain that offsets at least a portion of the loss on the long position.

Considerable research has been directed toward determining the optimal *hedge ratio:* the number of futures contracts needed to hedge a long position in the underlying asset. Usually, it is not possible to form a perfect hedge where all risk is eliminated; futures contracts are not available for all maturities of Treasury bills, and futures contracts are available only for a fixed amount of $1 million. For example, suppose a trader had a long position in 90-day Treasury bills with a $1.5 million maturity value. Should one or two futures contracts be issued?

2. Long hedges A long hedge is used if the investor does not currently have a position in Treasury bills but anticipates going long at some time in the immediate future. For example, the hedger may anticipate a large cash inflow within a short period of time and expects yields to decline prior to buying Treasury bills. How can the hedger "lock in" the higher yields today? The correct strategy is to buy a futures contract immediately. If yields do decline, the value of the long position in the futures contract will increase. This profit will then offset the lower yield that will be earned when the Treasury bills are actually purchased in the future.

• Speculating with Treasury Bill Futures

Speculators can also take a short or a long position in Treasury bill futures in anticipation of yield changes. These strategies are illustrated in Table 17.11.

TABLE 17.11 • Speculative Strategies for Treasury Bill Futures (Without Considering Commission Costs)

I. Gain on Short Position Strategy

Sell a Treasury bill futures contract at 93.75 with an initial margin of $2,500. Assume that the yield on Treasury bills *increases* by 20 basis points in one month.

Gain on contract (Equation 17.8):	(20)($25) = $500
HPR considering leverage:	$500/$2,500 = 20%
Annualized HPR:	$(1 + .2)^{12} - 1 = 791.61\%$

II. Gain on Long Position Strategy

Purchase a Treasury bill futures contract at 93.75 with an initial margin of $2,500. Assume that the yield on Treasury bills *decreases* by 20 basis points in one month.

Gain on contract (Equation 17.8):	(20)($25) = $500
HPR considering leverage:	$500/$2,500 = 20%
Annualized HPR:	$(1 + .2)^{12} - 1 = 791.61\%$

III. Loss on Long Position Strategy

Purchase a Treasury bill futures contract at 93.75 with an initial margin of $2,500. Assume that the investor thought that yields would decrease, but they actually *increased* by 20 basis ponts in one month. The investor closed the position when the minimum maintenance margin was reached ($2,000). Thus, no additional margin was required.

Loss on contract (Equation 17.8):	(20)($25) = ($500)
HPR considering leverage:	($500)/$2,500 = −20%
Annualized HPR:	$(1 - .2)^{12} - 1 = -93.13\%$

1. Short positions A short position should be taken if the speculator anticipates that yields will increase during the life of the contract. Because of low commission costs (approximately $50 per trade) and the relatively low initial margins (0.25 percent, or .0025 times the face value of the contract), large gains can result from small increases in yields. The speculator will essentially be (a) selling the contract at a "high" price and (b) buying an identical contract at a "low" price (to cancel the short position).

2. Long positions A long position is appropriate for speculators who anticipate yield decreases. The speculator buys a contract (long position) and profits from the increase in the contract's price as the yield declines. Part III of Table 17.11 illustrates the large losses that can occur for speculators in Treasury bill futures if interest rates do not move in the anticipated direction.

• Futures on Notes and Bonds

Contracts are also available on two-year, five-year, and ten-year Treasury notes, long-term Treasury bonds, mortgage-backed securities (Government National Mortgage Association mortgage pools or GNMAs), and municipal bonds. The exchanges where these contracts are traded are shown in Table 17.9, and examples of price quotations appear in Table 17.10. The "price" quotations for the note and bond futures in Table 17.10 are in "points" and $\frac{1}{32}$s of a point. For example, a quote of 92-25 for a Treasury bond future is equivalent to 92.78125 percent ($\frac{25}{32}$ = .78125) of the face value of $100,000. The contract also specifies that the coupon on the underlying Treasury bond is 8 percent. Table 17.12 provides the contract specifications for U.S. Treasury bond futures traded on the CBOT.

TABLE 17.12 • CBOT U.S. Treasury Bond Futures Contract Specifications

Trading unit	One U.S. Treasury bond having a face value at maturity of $100,000 or a multiple thereof.
Deliverable grades	U.S. Treasury bonds that, if callable, are not callable for at least 15 years from the first day of the delivery month or, if not callable, have a maturity of at least 15 years from the first business day of the delivery month. The invoice price equals the futures settlement price times a conversion factor plus accrued interest. The conversion factor is the price of the delivered bond ($1 par value) to yield 8 percent.
Price quotation	Points ($1,000) and $\frac{1}{32}$s of a point; for example, 80-16 equals 80$\frac{16}{32}$.
Tick size	One thirty-second ($\frac{1}{32}$) of a point ($31.25 per contract); par is on the basis of 100 points.
Daily price limit	Three points ($3,000 per contract) above or below the previous day's settlement price (expandable to 4$\frac{1}{2}$ points). Limits are lifted the second business day preceding the first day of the delivery month.
Contract months	March, June, September, and December
Delivery method	Federal Reserve book-entry wire-transfer system
Last trading day	Seventh business day preceding the last business day of the delivery month
Last delivery day	Last business day of the delivery month
Trading hours	7:20 A.M. to 2:00 P.M. (Chicago time), Monday through Friday. Evening trading hours are 5:00 to 8:30 P.M. (central standard time) or 6:00 to 9:30 P.M. (central daylight saving time), Sunday through Thursday. On the last trading day of an expiring contract, trading in that contract closes at noon.
Ticker symbol	US

SOURCE: *Contract Specifications 1991* (Chicago Board of Trade), pp. 53–54.

Another interesting aspect of Treasury bond futures is that the contract writer (short position) can settle the contract by actual delivery of the bonds (see the Deliverable Grades section of Table 17.12). Actually delivering the bonds presents something of a problem, however, because only 8 percent coupon bonds with a maturity of 15 years or longer can be delivered, whereas many of these long-term bonds do not have an 8 percent coupon. To resolve this difficulty, a complex adjustment procedure allows the delivery of bonds with different coupons and maturity date.

Treasury bill futures, as well as note and bond futures, have some characteristics that are important to both hedgers and speculators:

1. Price volatility The price of a futures contract is closely correlated with the price of the underlying security or index. Long-term bond prices are more volatile than short-term bond prices. Therefore, prices for futures on long-term bonds are *more* volatile than Treasury bill futures prices. Essentially, the price risk or duration of a bond future is directly related to the duration of the underlying bond.

2. Basis risk Bond futures are also subject to basis risk. As previously discussed, the basis is the difference between the futures price and the cash or spot price. The basis can increase or decrease during the life of the contract but approaches zero on the delivery date. A change in the basis during the life of the contract represents gains or losses to the trader.

3. Leverage Positions in interest rate futures can be obtained by making the relatively small initial margin deposit and maintaining the margin. The low margin requirement and the resulting high degree of leverage cause HPRs on futures contracts to be very sensitive to changes in market yields.

4. Liquidity Because the clearing corporation marks to market on a daily basis, traders must maintain adequate liquidity to cover margin calls. Since long-term bond prices are more volatile than short-term bond prices, greater liquidity is required for trading in Treasury note and bond futures than in Treasury bill futures.

• Market Efficiency of Interest Rate Futures

Numerous studies have analyzed the efficiency of the interest rate futures market, especially that for Treasury bills. Generally, these studies have examined the relationship between the spot or cash price and the futures price. Surprisingly, the extent of market efficiency remains unresolved because the empirical tests have produced conflicting results. Some studies concluded that the market was efficient, while other studies found arbitrage opportunities that suggested inefficiencies.

The evidence indicates that some speculators may earn excess returns in the Treasury bill market. The magnitude of these excess returns, however, is likely to be very small. In fact, annualized excess returns may be less than 30 basis points, which, while statistically significant, will not represent large dollar profits unless large sums are invested.

STOCK INDEX FUTURES

Stock index futures are available on five major stock market indexes: (1) S&P 500, (2) NYSE Composite, (3) Value Line Composite Average, (4) Nikkei 225, and (5) Major Market Index. The first three are relatively well known. The Nikkei 225 is an index for the Tokyo Stock Exchange, and the Major Market Index consists of a portfolio of 20 of the largest companies traded on the NYSE. This latter index was developed because Dow Jones & Company refused to allow a futures contract on the Dow Jones Industrial Average.

Table 17.13 provides quotations for the five major stock index futures. The "prices" in Table 17.13 are in terms of "points" that represent the level of the index. For example, the close for the September 1991 S&P 500 contract is 376.20. The dollar value of this contract is determined by multiplying the quoted "price" by \$500, or $376.20 \times \$500 = \$188{,}100$. Thus, a 1-point change in the "price" of the contract represents \$500. The \$500 constant is also used for the NYSE Composite and Value Line contracts. The Major Market Index uses a constant of \$250, and the Nikkei 225 uses a constant of \$5.

Stock index futures are similar in many respects to other financial futures, but also exhibit some important differences. First, as mentioned earlier, delivery is not an option for a stock index future since there is no deliverable instrument; therefore all delivery settlements are made in cash. Second, stock prices are generally more volatile than bond prices; since futures prices closely follow the prices of the underlying asset, stock index futures prices are more volatile than prices on interest rate futures. Third, the prices of stock index futures are more volatile than the underlying indexes. Fourth, the basis risk on stock index futures is greater than that on interest rate futures. Finally, the five major stock index futures have different levels of risk. One reason for this is that stocks are not as homogeneous as bonds. Thus, stock indexes constructed from different types of stocks do not have equal risk. For example, the S&P 500 includes stocks from the NYSE, AMEX, and OTC markets; the NYSE Composite includes only stocks traded on that exchange.

• Speculating in Stock Index Futures

Speculating in stock index futures, as opposed to hedging, primarily involves anticipating a short-term market movement without having an underlying position in common stocks. A speculator who is bullish about stocks in general buys (long position) a stock index future. A futures position has several advantages over a long position in stocks including lower transaction costs and a lower initial margin. A third advantage is that the speculator does not have to select individual stocks. Thus, the possibility of being correct on the market's direction but incorrect on individual stocks is eliminated.

A speculator who is bearish on stocks can take a short position. Rather than shorting individual stocks, however, the speculator can *short the market* by writing a stock index future.

TABLE 17.13 • Quotations on Five Major Stock Index Futures

INDEX FUTURES

N.Y. Futures Exchange

NYSE Composite

Season's High	Season's Low		Week's High	Week's Low	Sett	Net Chg	Oper Int.
points and cents							
216.40	173.10	Sep	208.50	204.60	205.65	+1.75	4,317
217.60	175.50	Dec	209.85	206.00	207.10	+2.10	259
217.90	207.20	Mar	210.95	209.20	208.60	−.95	87
.....	.....	Jun	.....	.....	210.10	......	......

Last index 204.92, up 1.45.
Fri. to Thurs. sales 23,161.
Total open interest 4,663.

Chicago Mercantile Exchange

S&P 500

Season's High	Season's Low		Week's High	Week's Low	Sett	Net Chg	Oper Int.
points and cents							
396.05	304.00	Sep	380.90	374.00	376.20	+3.95	135,065
399.05	321.75	Dec	383.70	377.10	379.10	+4.05	4,646
401.05	380.00	Mar	.....	.....	382.30	+.90	191
.....	.....	Jun	.....	.....	385.60	......	......

Last index 374.08, up 2.92.
Fri. to Thurs. sales 161,942.
Total open interest 139,902.

Nikkei 225

Season's High	Season's Low		Week's High	Week's Low	Sett	Net Chg	Oper Int.
$5 x nsa							
28200	23290	Sep	24505	23290	23345	−260	8,558
28525	24900	Dec	25065	24900	23905	−260	287
25125	25125	Mar	.....	.....	24505	−260	......

Fri. to Thurs. sales 2,667.
Total open interest 8,845.

Chicago Board of Trade

Major Market Maxi Index

Season's High	Season's Low		Week's High	Week's Low	Sett	Net Chg	Oper Int.
mmi+250 x index							
645.40	610.50	Jul	627.50	615.50	618.60	+4.30	4,492
642.95	612.20	Aug	627.30	617.15	618.95	+4.25	183
638.00	619.50	Sep	628.20	619.75	620.40	+4.15	112

Last index 618.33, up 4.17.
Fri. to Thurs. sales 8,062.
Total open interest 4,787.

Kansas City Board of Trade

Value Line

Season's High	Season's Low		Week's High	Week's Low	Sett	Net Chg	Oper Int.
points and cents							
318.95	255.30	Sep	305.45	299.00	300.75	+1.75	1,762
319.20	250.00	Dec	305.00	305.00	303.15	+2.65	16
323.50	323.50	Mar	.....	.....	305.65	+2.65	2

Last index 303.39, up .85.
Fri. to Thurs. sales 183.
Total open interest 1,780.

SOURCE: *Barron's,* July 8, 1991. Courtesy of *Barron's Weekly.*

• Hedging Using Stock Index Futures

Many institutional and individual investors use stock index futures to hedge positions in common stocks. The rapid growth in stock index futures trading is primarily a result of this hedging process. This growth suggests that investors are aware of the advantages of using stock index futures in portfolio management decisions.

Before the introduction of index futures in 1982, only limited portfolio management techniques were available to deal with nondiversifiable or systematic risk. Diversifiable or nonsystematic risk could essentially be eliminated by adding enough stocks to the portfolio. The beta of the portfolio, however, could be managed only by changing the mix of cash, bonds, or stocks in the portfolio and by adding "low" or "high" beta stocks to the portfolio. The introduction of index futures, however, has provided new ways of managing systematic risk.

To illustrate, assume that a common stock portfolio manager is bearish about stocks in the short run. This suggests that the beta of the portfolio should be reduced. Traditionally, this could be accomplished by selling stocks and investing the proceeds in near-cash or bonds and by selling stocks with high betas. Because of transaction costs and possible institutional restrictions, the portfolio manager had limited flexibility in attempting to hedge against a short-run decline in stock prices. Today, however, the manager can construct a hedge by writing index futures. If stocks do in fact decline, the profit on the futures position will offset some or all of the losses on the long stock position. Essentially, by writing the index future, the manager has added a *negative beta security* to the existing portfolio. The overall beta of the portfolio is therefore reduced. The success of the strategy in reducing losses depends on the ability of the portfolio manager in structuring the hedge. However, it is unlikely that a perfect hedge can be constructed.

PROGRAM TRADING Stock index futures are used in **program trading** strategies employed by pension funds, mutual funds, brokerage firms, and other institutional investors. Program trading is the simultaneous trading of large blocks of common stocks and opposing positions in stock index futures and/or index options to earn a riskless profit. This process is called **index arbitrage.** For example, if index futures or options are priced "high" relative to the underlying stocks, arbitrageurs will write index futures or options and simultaneously buy the common stocks in the underlying index.

Program trading is also referred to as *computerized trading* since actual trades can be executed by computers. The NYSE's Designated Order Turnaround (DOT) system executes orders for trades of 2,000 shares or less within three minutes. Larger orders are not guaranteed such quick execution but are generally executed very rapidly. A program trader can therefore enter the desired trades in the computer in advance and then transmit the entire order at the appropriate time.

Program trading helps to coordinate or link the futures and stock markets by eliminating any price discrepancies. In this sense, it improves the pricing efficiency in the markets. Since the market crash of October 19, 1987, however, program trading has come under attack. Many critics have blamed program trading for starting the panic that caused the crash. For example, the SEC estimates that 30–68 percent of the trading volume on the NYSE during critical hours on October 19 was due to 12 to 15 program traders.

PORTFOLIO INSURANCE An active hedging strategy that has been accused of contributing to increased market volatility is *dynamic hedging* or **portfolio insurance.** This technique is designed to protect or insure an underlying stock or bond portfolio against price declines. For example, if common stocks are expected to decline in price, the insurer writes stock index futures. The profit on the futures from the decline in common stocks offsets part or all of the loss on the underlying long position in stocks. During the October crash, portfolio insurers were forced to continue writing futures contracts in an attempt to offset losses on their stock portfolios. Because the Chicago Mercantile Exchange was forced to suspend trading in the S&P 500 futures contracts, the portfolio insurance strategy did not work as expected, and many insurers resorted to selling the stocks in their portfolios, which intensified the market collapse.

• Market Efficiency of Stock Index Futures

Studies of the efficiency of the stock index futures market have been limited because of the lack of a price history, since trading only began on February 24, 1982. Several early empirical studies noted that it was common for the futures price (P_F) to be below the spot price (P_S), causing a negative basis. This relationship is contrary to finance theory; it suggests that index futures are biased estimates of future stock prices and implies that futures are undervalued.

One major difference between a position in index futures and a long position in stocks is that no dividends are received or paid on an index futures investment. This suggests that because of ex-dividend price adjustments, $P_F < P_S$ and results in a negative basis. To the extent that this is true, the basis can be negative without implying market inefficiencies. Overall, the evidence indicates that the stock index futures market is reasonably efficient.

FOREIGN CURRENCY FUTURES

Foreign currency futures were the first financial commodity to be actively traded through a futures market. The Chicago Mercantile Exchange is now the largest currency futures market. Table 17.14 provides an example of quotations for the most actively traded currency futures. The prices for the Canadian dollar contract in Table 17.14 represent the number of U.S. dollars relative to one Canadian dollar. For example, the December 1991 close shows a price of \$.8654; the reciprocal, \$1.1555, is the number of Canadian dollars per U.S. dollar.

TABLE 17.14 • Quotations on Currency Futures

Chicago Mercantile Exchange

Season's High	Season's Low		Week's High	Week's Low	Sett	Net Chg	Open Int.
EURODOLLARS							
$1 million;pts of 100 pct.							
93.77	90.04	Sep	93.62	93.49	93.51	−.08	257,077
93.33	90.04	Dec	93.06	92.90	92.91	−.11	166,637
93.17	90.09	Mar	92.94	92.77	92.78	−.13	112,850
92.77	90.35	Jun	92.54	92.34	92.34	−.17	54,124
92.44	90.32	Sep	92.13	91.93	91.93	−.18	41,627
92.10	90.24	Dec	91.80	91.59	91.59	−.19	33,777
92.03	90.28	Mar	91.80	91.61	91.61	−.17	29,257
91.89	90.27	Jun	91.61	91.42	91.42	−.17	20,721
91.81	90.27	Sep	91.41	91.23	91.24	−.16	16,501
91.66	90.22	Dec	91.19	91.00	91.02	−.15	11,340
91.66	90.24	Mar	91.19	91.05	91.03	−.14	9,622
91.57	90.40	Jun	91.08	90.96	90.94	−.14	7,494
91.52	90.36	Sep	91.00	90.92	90.88	−.12	5,194
91.44	90.71	Dec	90.85	90.75	90.74	−.11	5,186
91.09	90.75	Mar	90.86	90.78	90.75	−.10	3,746
90.91	90.73	Jun	90.82	90.74	90.70	−.10	1,182
Fri. to Thurs. sales 533,386.							
Total open interest 776,335.							
BRITISH POUND							
$ per pound; 1 point equals $0.0001							
1.9340	1.5824	Sep	1.6102	1.5824	1.6024	−18	29,320
1.7900	1.5670	Dec	1.5960	1.5670	1.5872	−14	1,292
1.6000	1.5670	Mar	1.5700	1.5670	1.5756	−10	85
Last spot 1.6175, off 40.							
Fri. to Thurs. sales 54,512.							
Total open interest 30,697.							
CANADIAN DOLLAR							
$ per dlr; 1 point equals $0.0001							
.8718	.7985	Sep	.8715	.8684	.8701	−11	24,642
.8667	.8175	Dec	.8667	.8649	.8654	−11	803
.8630	.8268	Mar	.8625	.8600	.8615	−11	1,587
.8585	.8330	Jun	.8580	.8573	.8576	−9	160
.8480	.8420	Sep	.....	.....	.8540	−9	2
Last spot .8746, off 15.							
Fri. to Thurs. sales 13,183.							
Total open interest 27,194.							
FRENCH FRANC							
$ per franc; 1 point equals $0.00001							
No open contracts.							
GERMAN MARK							
$ per mark; 1 point equals $0.0001							
.6810	.5401	Sep	.5495	.5401	.5444	−38	69,236
.6770	.5365	Dec	.5456	.5365	.5406	−38	1,653
.5840	.5353	Mar	.5380	.5353	.5378	−38	58
Last spot .5479, off 41.							
Fri. to Thurs. sales 167,080.							
Total open interest 70,947.							
JAPANESE YEN							
$ per yen; 1 point equals $0.000001							
.007870	.007003	Sep	.007235	.007141	.007215	−32	41,286
.007559	.006997	Dec	.007212	.007128	.007198	−30	1,986
.007302	.007000	Mar	.007120	.007120	.007196	−28	1,245
.007220	.007150	Jun	......	......	.007199	−25	1,490
Last spot .007236, off 37.							
Fri. to Thurs. sales 84,568.							
Total open interest 46,007.							
SWISS FRANC							
$ per franc; 1 point equals $0.0001							
.8055	.6277	Sep	.6426	.6277	.6317	−106	36,812
.8090	.6261	Dec	.6395	.6261	.6297	−104	676
.6995	.6267	Mar	.6270	.6267	.6288	−104	74
Last spot .6353, off 82.							
Fri. to Thurs. sales 86,612.							
Total open interest 37,562.							
AUSTRAL. DOLLAR							
$ per dlr; 1 point equals $0.0001							
.7725	.7418	Sep	.7608	.7570	.7596	−3	1,819
.7528	.7520	Dec	.7520	.7520	.7526	−3	2
Last spot .7625, off 40.							
Fri. to Thurs. sales 668.							
Total open interest 1,821.							

SOURCE: *Barron's*, July 8, 1991. Reprinted courtesy of *Barron's Weekly*.

Currency futures, in addition to the forward markets, provide a way to eliminate *currency exchange risk* in international trade and investing (see Chapter 6). For example, a U.S. investor who wants to invest directly in Japanese stocks must convert dollars to yen to purchase the stocks and then convert yen to dollars after the stocks are sold. Since the exchange rate between the two currencies is likely to change, the investor faces currency exchange risk. If the investor expects the dollar to fall relative to the yen after the stocks are purchased, no hedging strategy is needed since the investor will benefit. If the dollar is expected to increase in value relative to the yen, however, a currency future can be used to hedge against this risk.

Large international businesses also use currency futures to hedge against exchange risk. For example, a survey of Fortune 500 companies found that approximately 20 percent of the responding companies used futures and options to hedge against exchange risk.[9]

Speculators also trade in currency futures. The recent rapid and large changes in the value of the U.S. dollar relative to other currencies have caused large changes in the prices of currency futures. Because of arbitrage activities, currency futures markets are expected to be efficient. A 1986 study, however, found that currency *forward* prices are biased estimates of future spot rates, indicating that the forward market may not be efficient.[10]

OPTIONS ON COMMODITY AND FINANCIAL FUTURES

Beginning in 1982, the CFTC allowed the futures and stock exchanges to trade options on futures. Since that time, the number of options on commodity and financial futures has continued to grow. Table 17.15 lists options on commodity and financial futures that were actively traded as of June 1991. The exchanges where these options are traded were listed in Chapter 15.

Futures options, as they are called, have the same characteristics as the more traditional call and put equity options discussed in Chapter 15. They have specified exercise or striking prices, expiration dates, and the same quotation system. The motivation, strategies, and profit and loss profiles for buyers and writers of futures options are the same as those for the buyers and writers of equity options. The value of these derivative securities depends on the value of the underlying futures contract.

The 1991 CBOT contract specifications for options on wheat futures and U.S. Treasury bond futures both appear in Table 17.16, providing a comparison of the specifications for options on commodity futures and financial futures. (The wheat futures and U.S. Treasury bond futures contract specifica-

---

[9] Stanley B. Block and Timothy J. Gallagher, "The Use of Interest Rate Futures and Options by Corporate Financial Managers," *Financial Management* (Autumn 1986): 73–78.

[10] Thomas C. Chiang, "Empirical Analysis on the Predictors of Futures Spot Rates," *Journal of Financial Research* (Summer 1986): 153–62.

TABLE 17.15 • Actively Traded Options on Commodity and Financial Futures

Commodities	Financial Futures
Broilers	Australian dollar
Cocoa	British pound
Coffee "C"	Canadian dollar
Copper	Deutschemark
Corn	Eurodollar
Cotton	Japanese yen
Crude oil	Libor
Feeder cattle	Municipal bond index
Gold	NYSE Composite Index
Heating oil	Nikkei 225 Average
Live cattle	S&P 500 Stock Index
Live hogs	Swiss franc
Oats	Treasury bills
Orange juice	Treasury bonds
Platinum	Treasury notes
Pork bellies	5-year Treasury notes
Random-length lumber	U.S. dollar index
Silver	
Soybeans	
Soybean meal	
Soybean oil	
Sugar 11	
Unleaded gasoline	
Wheat	

TABLE 17.16 • CBOT Contract Specifications for Options on Wheat Futures and U.S. Treasury Bond Futures

Specification	Options on wheat futures	Options on U.S. Treasury bond futures
Trading unit	One CBOT wheat futures contract (of a specified contract month) of 5,000 bushels	One CBOT U.S. Treasury bond futures contract (of a specified delivery month) having a face value at maturity of $100,000 or a multiple thereof
Tick size	One-eighth ($\frac{1}{8}$) cent per bushel ($6.25 per contract)	One sixty-fourth ($\frac{1}{64}$) of a point ($15.625 per contract), rounded up to the nearest cent per contract
Strike prices	10 cents per bushel	Two points per T-bond futures contract to bracket the current T-bond futures price. For example, if T-bond futures are at 86-00, strike prices may be set at 80, 82, 84, 86, 88, 92, and so on.
Daily price limit	20 cents per bushel ($1,000 per contract) above or below the previous day's settlement premium (expandable to 30 cents per bushel). Limits are lifted on the last trading day.	Three points ($3,000 per contract) above or below the previous day's settlement premium (expandable to $4\frac{1}{2}$ points). Limits are lifted on the last trading day.

(continued)

TABLE 17.16 • CBOT Contract Specifications (continued)

Specification	Options on wheat futures	Options on U.S. Treasury bond futures
Contract months	March, May, July, September, and December	The front month of the current quarter plus the next three contracts of the regular quarterly cycle (March, June, September, and December). If the front month is a quarterly contract month, no monthly contract will be listed. The monthly options contract exercises into the current quarterly futures contract. For example, a July T-bond option will exercise into a September futures position.
Contract year	Starts in July and ends in May	
Last trading day	The last Friday preceding the first notice day of the corresponding wheat futures contract by at least five business days	Options cease trading in the month prior to the delivery month of the underlying futures contract. For example, the last trading day for December 1991 T-bond options is November 15, 1991. Options cease trading at noon on the last Friday preceding by at least five business days the last business day of the month preceding the option contract month.
Exercise	The buyer of a futures option may exercise the option on any business day prior to expiration by giving notice to the Board of Trade Clearing Corporation by 6:00 P.M. (Chicago time). Option exercise results in an underlying futures market position. Options at least 20 cents per bushel in-the-money on the last day of trading are automatically exercised.	The buyer of a futures option may exercise the option on any business day prior to expiration by giving notice to the Board of Trade Clearing Corporation by 6:00 P.M. (Chicago time). Options at least two points in-the-money on the last day of trading are automatically exercised.
Expiration	Unexercised options expire at 10:00 A.M. (Chicago time) on the first Saturday following the last day of trading.	Unexercised options expire 10:00 A.M. (Chicago time) on the first Saturday following the last day of trading.
Trading hours	9:30 A.M. to 1:15 P.M. (Chicago time), Monday through Friday. On the last trading day of an expiring contract, trading in that contract closes at noon.	7:20 A.M. to 2:00 P.M. (Chicago time), Monday through Friday. Evening trading hours are 5:00 to 8:30 P.M. (central standard time) or 6:00 to 9:30 P.M. (central daylight saving time), Sunday through Thursday. On the last trading day of an expiring contract, trading in that contract closes at noon.
Ticker symbols	WY for call options WZ for put options	CG for call options PG for put options

SOURCE: *Contract Specifications 1991* (Chicago Board of Trade), pp. 35–36, 55–56.

tions appeared in Tables 17.3 and 17.12, respectively.) The tick size (minimum price movement), strike prices, daily price limit, and exercise in-the-money designations for the two contracts reflect the price quotations for the underlying futures contracts. Wheat futures are quoted in cents and quarter-cents per bushel, and Treasury bond futures are quoted in points and $\frac{1}{32}$s of a point. Since wheat is a commodity, a contract year is designated, whereas the financial future does not have a contract year designation. Finally, the contract months and trading hours for the options are consistent with the underlying futures contracts.

Based on empirical tests to date, it appears that the market for options on financial futures is efficient, in the sense that arbitrage profits are not available. The investor should realize that options on commodity and financial futures are highly leveraged investments and, therefore, very volatile. Even using futures options as a hedge against a position or anticipated position in equities, debt securities, currencies, or commodities requires a high degree of sophistication on the part of the investor.

SUMMARY

The financial markets developed commodity and financial futures to meet the needs of hedgers in physical commodities and financial assets. Future contracts in commodities began trading in the 1860s to overcome the problems associated with potential defaults by individual buyers and sellers. Using basically the same market structure as the commodity futures market, the financial futures market developed to cope with the rapid changes of a technologically linked global economy.

Commodity futures markets have unique characteristics and differ in many respects from stock markets. These differences are significant and should be understood by the investor. For example, initial margins are required for both futures and common stocks. However, a margin in stocks represents a down payment of approximately 50 percent of the value of the stock whereas a margin of 5 to 10 percent in futures represents a performance bond. Other differences in stocks and futures trading practices include commission costs, price limits, the use of specialists, length of holding periods, units of trading, and regulatory authorities, to name just a few.

Investors should realize that investing in commodity futures and options on commodity futures is *very* risky relative to traditional investments in stocks and bonds. The investment performance of publicly traded commodity funds attests to the difficulty of achieving acceptable levels of risk-adjusted returns. However, commodity futures may offer an inflation hedge and may reduce the risk of a securities portfolio.

The financial futures market has enjoyed remarkable growth since its inception in the early 1970s. The real growth in financial futures began with the introduction of stock index futures in 1982. There are also active markets for interest rate futures, foreign currency futures, and options on financial futures.

• CONCEPT APPLICATIONS

Investment Concept	Concept Application
Commodity and financial futures	The individual investor can use these assets to hedge a position or speculate on future price movements. Because of the financial leverage involved in these contracts, the returns can be very volatile. Adding commodity futures to a portfolio of stocks and bonds may reduce the risk of the portfolio. The markets in both commodity and financial futures are generally considered to be efficient.
Options on commodity and financial futures	Futures options, like options on common stocks, are very volatile. Investors can lose 100 percent of their investment or make significant positive returns. The markets for futures options appear to be efficient.
Speculating in commodity and financial futures	Because of the risk, it is recommended that individual investors not speculate in these markets unless they have special expertise.
Hedging in commodity and financial futures	An individual investor ordinarily would not have a long position in a commodity and would not be a hedger in the commodity futures markets. However, an individual may desire to hedge positions in financial assets using financial futures.
Publicly traded commodity funds	Historically, these funds have not provided returns commensurate with their risk. However, using these funds in combination with a stock and bond portfolio may reduce the overall risk of the investor's portfolio.

Like investors in the commodities futures market, investors in financial futures may be motivated by speculative or hedging objectives. Speculators are attracted to the low margins and volatile short-term price changes of the futures markets. Hedgers can use futures to reduce the risk of a long position or a short position. Speculating in futures is extremely risky; hedging with futures is viewed as a risk-reducing activity.

New futures products are constantly being introduced or considered for introduction to meet the needs of the market. For example, the CBOT has designed futures contracts for group health, personal automobile collision damage, homeowners' property damage, and commercial property damage insurance. These futures contracts are designed to provide insurers with a hedge against rising reinsurance costs and to control volatility. Other new or proposed contracts include a macroeconomic index contract based on the CPI, futures on an expanding number of Japanese securities, and futures on semiconductor chips. In order for futures contracts to be successful, traders must be able to understand the contracts easily, and all the following must exist: a demand to hedge the underlying asset, low competition from existing contracts, a very volatile underlying asset, and a cash or spot market for the asset.

Along with the new products, international futures and option exchanges have grown rapidly. Futures markets in such locations as London, Paris,

Tokyo, Hong Kong, and Singapore are offering new products and expanding their market share. The number of futures and options exchanges worldwide has grown from 52 in 1985 to 72 in 1989. In 1985, U.S. exchanges enjoyed a 91 percent share of global futures trading; by 1989 this share had fallen to 75 percent. The long awaited introduction of Globex, a screen-trading system designed to provide trading for futures contracts from around the world on a 24-hour basis, should help the U.S. exchanges recapture some of this global futures trading business.

Throughout the chapter, the question of market efficiency in the futures markets has been examined. The results of empirical research indicate that the futures markets are reasonably efficient. If risk-adjusted excess returns are possible in the futures markets, they appear to be quite small.

• KEY TERMS

Basis
Carrying cost
Clearing corporation
Commodity fund
Commodity future
Contango
Convergence
Currency future
Expectation hypothesis
Financial future
Forward contract
Futures option
Index arbitrage
Initial margin
Interest rate future
Maintenance (variation) margin
Margin call
Marking to market
Normal backwardation
Open interest
Portfolio insurance
Price limit
Program trading
Settle price
Spread
Stock index future

• QUESTIONS

1. Define the following terms dealing with commodity futures:
   a. Reversing trade
   b. Marking to market
   c. Price limits
   d. Initial margin
   e. Maintenance margin
   f. Open interest
   g. Hedging
   h. Speculating
   i. Options
2. Compare and contrast a forward contract and a futures contract.
3. Explain the concept of basis. Why is the analysis of basis an important aspect of investing in futures?

4. Assume that the spot or cash price for feeder cattle is $.7765 per pound and the futures price for a feeder cattle contract with three months until delivery is $.7820 per pound.
   a. Explain why the basis for this commodity is positive.
   b. Does the value of the basis support the normal backwardation hypothesis? Explain.
   c. Suppose the spot price was $.7820 and the futures price was $.7765. How could this relationship between the two prices be explained?
5. The correlation coefficients in Table 17.6 indicate that the real HPRs on commodities are negatively correlated with the real HPRs on common stocks and Treasury bills and bonds. Discuss the investment implications of these negative correlation coefficients.
6. Discuss the appropriateness of using the CAPM to analyze agricultural and metal futures.
7. What role, if any, should commodity futures have for the individual investor?
8. Explain why the financial futures markets developed in the United States.
9. Discuss the logic and mechanics of long and short hedges for Treasury bills, using financial futures. Can all interest rate risk be eliminated by using a hedge?
10. Explain the concept of "leverage" as it applies to the HPRs for speculators in financial futures.
11. Explain the relationship between Treasury bill yields and prices and a futures contract on Treasury bills. Do the prices of Treasury bills and futures on bills move in the same or opposite direction as yields change?
12. Discuss how stock index futures can be used to hedge a long position in stocks. Also explain how they can be used to hedge a short position in stocks.
13. Explain how currency futures can be used to hedge against currency exchange risk.
14. Speculators in currency futures must be aware of potential price changes in two underlying assets. Explain the logic of this statement.
15. Are futures options more or less risky than stock options? Why or why not?

• KEY TO THE INVESTMENT ANALYSIS SOFTWARE

Calculation	Appendix A-1 Page Reference	Access Procedure
Holding period return	A-8	BEGIN, STATISTICAL, HPR

• PROBLEMS

1. Jack Thrifts bought three May 5,000-bushel oats futures contracts at $1.17 per bushel. The initial margin requirement is 8 percent, and the maintenance margin requirement is 75 percent of the initial margin requirement.
   a. What is Jack's initial margin requirement?
   b. If the May price of oats rises to $1.23, how much equity does Jack have in his account?
   c. If the May price of oats falls to $1.00, what alternative actions could Jack have taken?
2. Assume that the price of gold based on a commodity contract increased from $360 per ounce on January 1, 1991, to $390 on April 1, 1991. The quarterly yield on Treasury bills was 2 percent on January 1, 1991. Suppose an investor took a *long* position on January 1 with a 10 percent initial margin and closed the position on April 1.
   a. Calculate the quarterly and annualized HPR, based only on the commodity price change.
   b. Calculate the quarterly and annualized HPR, based on the price change and leverage.
   c. Calculate the quarterly and annualized HPR, assuming that Treasury bills were used for the margin. Ignore the influence of leverage.
3. A long position in a silver contract was taken at a price of $6.50 per troy ounce; three months later the position was closed at $6.75 per troy ounce.
   a. Ignoring leverage and transaction costs, calculate the quarterly HPR.
   b. Use the quarterly HPR calculated in part (a) to calculate the annualized HPR. Assume quarterly compounding.
   c. Assume that the CPI increased from 300 to 325 during the year. Did the silver commodity investment provide an inflation hedge?
4. A futures contract for Treasury bills is quoted at 92.50.
   a. What is the change in price for the futures contract for each basis-point change?
   b. Calculate the actual price of the bills represented by the futures contract.
5. A futures contract on Treasury bills is available for 96.00.
   a. Assume that a speculator takes a *short* position in the futures contract with an initial margin of $2,500. Ignoring potential margin calls, calculate the HPRs for each of the following basis-point changes in yields:

Basis-point change
−10
−5
0
+5
+10

   b. Assume that a speculator takes a *long* position in the futures contract with an initial margin of $2,500. Ignoring potential margin calls, calculate the HPRs for each of the above basis-point changes in yields.

6. A futures contract on the S&P 500 is available for 300.00.

   a. Assume that a speculator takes a *short* position in the futures contract with an initial margin of $7,500. Ignoring any potential margin calls, calculate the HPRs for each of the following point changes in the contract price:

Point change
−10
−5
0
+5
+10

   b. Assume that a speculator takes a *long* position in the futures contract with an initial margin of $7,500. Ignoring any potential margin calls, calculate the HPRs for each of the point changes in the contract price.

7. A futures contract on Canadian dollars closed at .7882.

   a. Explain this price.

   b. How many Canadian dollars can be purchased by one U.S. dollar, based on the futures price?

• REFERENCES

Block, Stanley B., and Timothy J. Gallagher. "The Use of Interest Rate Futures and Options by Corporate Financial Managers." *Financial Management* (Autumn 1986): 73–78.

Bodie, Zvi, and Victor I. Rosansky. "Risk and Return in Commodity Futures." *Financial Analysts Journal* (May-June 1980): 27–39.

Bodie, Zvi. "Commodity Futures as a Hedge against Inflation." *Journal of Portfolio Management* (Spring 1983): 12–17.

Borsen, B. Wade, and Louis P. Lukac. "Optimal Portfolios for Commodity Futures Funds." *Journal of Futures Markets* (June 1990): 247–58.

Chang, Eric C., Chao Chen, and Son-Nan Chen. "Risk and Return in Copper, Platinum, and Silver Futures." *Journal of Futures Markets* (February 1990): 29–39.

Edwards, Franklin R. "Futures Trading and Cash Market Volatility: Stock Index and Interest Futures." *Journal of Futures Markets* (August 1988): 421–39.

Elton, Edwin J., Martin J. Gruber, and Joel C. Rentzler. "Professionally Managed, Publicly Traded Commodity Funds." *Journal of Business* (April 1987): 175–99.

———. "The Performance of Publicly Offered Commodity Funds." *Financial Analysts Journal* (July-August 1990): 23–30.

Fama, Eugene F., and Kenneth R. French. "Commodity Futures Prices: Some Evidence on Forecast Power, Premiums, and the Theory of Storage." *Journal of Business* (January 1987): 55–73.

Gastineau, Gary, and Albert Madansky. "S&P 500 Stock Index Futures Evaluation Tables." *Financial Analysts Journal* (November-December 1983): 68–76.

Gay, Gerald D., and Robert W. Kolb. "Interest Rate Futures as a Tool for Immunization." *Journal of Portfolio Management* (Fall 1983): 65–70.

Gendreau, Brian C. "Carrying Costs and Treasury Bill Futures." *Journal of Portfolio Management* (Fall 1985): 58–64.

Hill, Joanne M., and Thomas Schneeweis. "Reducing Volatility with Financial Futures." *Financial Analysts Journal* (November-December 1984): 34–40.

Kamara, Avraham. "The Behavior of Futures Prices: A Review of Theory and Evidence." *Financial Analysts Journal* (July-August 1984): pp. 68–75.

Kao, Duen-Li. "The Strategies and Risks of Synthetic Short-Term Instruments." *Journal of Cash Management* (May-June 1990): 56, 58.

Kolb, Robert W., Gerald D. Gay, and William C. Hunter. "Liquidity Requirements for Financial Futures Investments." *Financial Analysts Journal* (May-June 1985): 60–68.

Koppenhaver, G. D. "Futures Market Regulation." *Economic Perspectives* (January-February 1987): 3–15.

Luke, David. "Japanese Futures: Index Trading Sets Amazing Pace." *Asian Finance* (April 15, 1990): 43–44.

Modest, David M. "On the Pricing of Stock Index Futures." *Journal of Portfolio Management* (Summer 1984): 51–57.

Morris, Charles S. "Managing Stock Market Risk with Stock Index Futures." *Economic Review* (June 1989): 3–16.

Niederhoffer, Victor, and Richard Zeckhauser. "Market Index Futures Contracts." *Financial Analysts Journal* (January-February 1980): 49–55.

Nordhauser, Fred. "Using Stock Index Futures to Reduce Market Risk." *Journal of Portfolio Management* (Spring 1984): 56–62.

Peters, Ed. "The Growing Efficiency of Index-Futures Markets." *Journal of Portfolio Management* (Summer 1985): 52–56.

Phillips, Susan M., and Paula A. Tosini. "A Comparison of Margin Requirements for Options and Futures." *Financial Analysts Journal* (November-December 1982): 54–58.

Pierog, Karen, and Jon Stein. "New Contracts: What Makes Them Fly or Fail?" *Futures: The Magazine of Commodities & Options* (September 1989): 50–54.

Saunders, Edward M., and Arvind Mahajan. "An Empirical Examination of Composite Stock Index Future Pricing." *Journal of Futures Markets* (April 1988): 211–28.

Smith, Donald J., and Robert A. Taggart, Jr. "Bond Market Innovations and Financial Intermediation." *Business Horizons* (November-December 1989): 24–33.

Trainer, Francis H., Jr. "The Uses of Treasury Bond Futures in Fixed-Income Portfolio Management." *Financial Analysts Journal* (January-February 1983): 27–34.

Zeckhauser, Richard, and Victor Niederhoffer. "The Performance of Market Index Futures Contracts." *Financial Analysts Journal* (January-February 1983): 59–65.

CHAPTER 18

Precious Metals, Real Estate, and Collectibles

The knowledge-level objectives of this chapter should enable the student to:

- Demonstrate an understanding of the investment characteristics of three types of popular real assets: precious metals, real estate, and collectibles.
- Explain the potential contribution of real assets to an investor's portfolio.
- Specify appropriate investment strategies for precious metals, real estate, and collectibles.
- Recognize that investing in real assets, like financial assets, requires significant expertise on the part of the investor.
- Discuss the many factors impacting the prices of real assets and understand that these factors may not influence real asset prices in the future as they have in the past.

INTRODUCTION

Traditionally, investment analysis and portfolio management dealt almost exclusively with financial assets. Numerous valuation and portfolio management techniques are available for bonds, common stocks, options, futures, and other types of financial assets. Since the late 1970s, however, interest has been growing in extending traditional investment analysis to include **real** or **tangible assets** such as real estate, precious metals, and collectibles.

Several developments have encouraged the inclusion of real assets in the investment analysis process. First, the historically high inflation of the late 1970s and early 1980s increased interest in investments that might provide better hedges against inflation. Bond returns during much of this period were below the rate of inflation, resulting in a negative real rate of return. The return on common stocks was also low relative to the rate of inflation. During this period, however, gold, silver, real estate, and other real asset prices increased dramatically. Do real assets provide an effective hedge against inflation? If the average investor accepts this hypothesis and buys real assets prior to or during inflationary periods, the prophecy will be self-fulfilling: real asset prices will increase rapidly before and during an inflationary period.

The second development that has increased investor interest in real assets is the application of modern portfolio management techniques to these investment alternatives. In a portfolio analysis framework, potential investments are viewed in terms of their impact on the portfolio. A growing body of empirical evidence indicates that real assets can have a very positive impact on a portfolio of financial assets.

Should real assets be included in an investment portfolio? Portfolio theory indicates that if the investments are not perfectly correlated, adding them to the portfolio reduces risk. In a practical sense, however, there are costs associated with adding assets to a portfolio. The real question is, Do the benefits from adding real assets to a portfolio exceed the cost?

The purpose of this chapter is to discuss the investment characteristics of three popular real assets: precious metals (particularly, gold and silver), real estate, and collectibles. Investment characteristics, investment strategies, and portfolio considerations will be presented for each.

GOLD, SILVER, AND OTHER PRECIOUS METALS

Precious metals are a widely discussed—and at times popular and glamorous—alternative investment. The most popular metals for investment purposes are gold and silver. However, other metals—such as copper, aluminum, platinum, and palladium—attract some attention, primarily through trading in commodity futures. Because gold is the most familiar and popular precious metal, this section will primarily concentrate on gold with an occasional reference to silver. Most of the discussion of gold also applies to silver.

Gold has an interesting investment history. It has served as a medium of exchange and as a store of wealth since the early civilizations of Egypt and Rome. Beginning in the 1800s, industrialized nations used gold reserves to back their currencies and adopted the *gold standard.* The gold standard established a fixed value for an ounce of gold relative to a currency. The gold standard was strengthened at the Bretton Woods Conference in 1944 when the United States accepted a *gold exchange standard* that fixed the value of gold at $35 per ounce and agreed to redeem dollars for gold at that price. The official value of an ounce of gold in the United States was raised to $38 in 1971 and to $42.22 in 1973. Beginning in 1968, individuals other than U.S. investors were allowed to buy bullion at a free market price. On January 1, 1975, the restrictions that prevented U.S. investors from buying and holding gold were lifted.

Because gold has had a remarkable history of preserving its value during periods of economic and political turmoil, investors seeking to protect their wealth have traditionally regarded it as an alternative investment. Historically, gold has been viewed as an **inflation hedge.** As Figure 18.1 demonstrates,

FIGURE 18.1 • Bull Markets in Gold Bullion

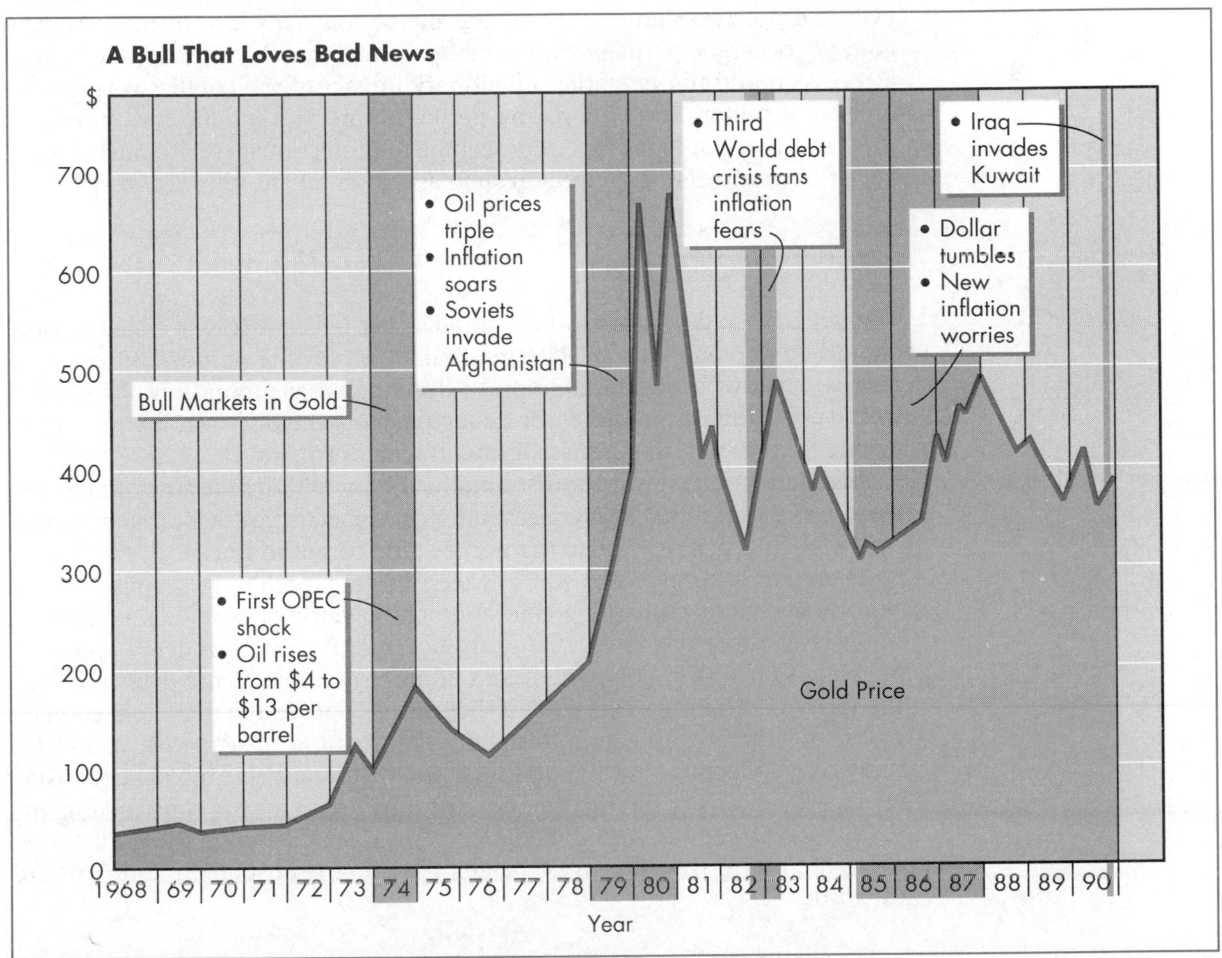

SOURCE: Susan E. Kuhn, "Is Gold Still the Best Bet for Troubled Times?" *Fortune,* September 24, 1990, p. 25.

there have been four major "bull" markets in gold bullion since 1968. Each of these bull markets was caused by a combination of political and inflationary uncertainties. For example, the 1979–1980 rise in gold bullion prices has been attributed to the uncertainty created by the Soviet Union's invasion of Afghanistan and inflationary fears caused by OPEC tripling the price of oil from $13 to $39 per barrel.

From 1982 to 1991, the price of gold fluctuated between $300 and $500 per ounce. Many gold "bugs" were surprised and possibly disappointed by gold's price behavior after the stock market collapse on October 19, 1987. On October 19, the price of gold increased by $10.10 to $481.75 per troy ounce but fell to $463.20 by the end of the next day.

The Persian Gulf crisis in late 1990 and the first three months of 1991 provided the key ingredients for a possible surge in gold prices. In addition to the political turmoil created by the crisis, the supply of oil from the region was threatened, creating the possibility of increased inflation. Gold prices, however, did not rise significantly during the period. This lack of movement in gold prices can be partially explained by the fact that the United States was in a recession and the potential inflationary impact of the conflict was considered to be minor. In addition, and perhaps more importantly for future gold price movements, today investors seeking to protect their wealth have a number of alternatives to gold bullion such as real estate or other real assets.

• Ways to Invest in Gold

The price of gold appears to be unpredictable because it is so volatile. Gold should be purchased as an investment and not for the purpose of seeking a fast, speculative profit. In addition to deciding what proportion of the portfolio should consist of gold (or other precious metals), the investor must decide from whom to purchase it and in what form.

Investors in precious metals should deal only with a seller they know and trust. Cases of fraudulent practices in precious metals transactions are numerous, particularly in low price (penny) mining common stocks.

There are a number of ways to invest in gold, including the purchase of numismatic coins containing gold and gold jewelry. These two mediums, as opposed to those discussed below, are not traditionally considered appropriate ways to invest in gold. The prices of numismatic coins are determined by the rarity, condition, and beauty of the coins as opposed to their gold content. Consequently, investing in numismatic coins requires the expertise associated with coin collecting, not the ability to forecast gold price movements. Gold jewelry is not a very liquid asset, and the buyer pays for the construction and design costs in addition to the gold content. Even excluding these mediums, there are many ways to invest in gold, ranging from bullion coins to mutual funds.

BULLION COINS Readily available and popular coins include the Canadian Maple Leaf, Mexican Peso, Austrian Crown, and American Eagle. Gold

TABLE 18.1 • Price Quotations and Premiums on Gold Coins

Coins	Price	Premium*	
		Dollar Value	*Percentage*
Krugerrand	$374.78	$ 5	1.35%
Maple Leaf	381.75	12	3.25
Mexican Peso	460.20	12	3.25
Austrian Crown	371.80	2	0.54
U.S. Eagle	381.75	12	3.25

SOURCE: *Barron's,* February 11, 1991, p. 134. Reprinted courtesy of *Barron's Weekly.*

*The premium is the difference in the price and the value of the gold content in the coin. The dollar values are rounded to the nearest whole dollar.

NOTE: The Mocatta Metals Corporation spot gold price was $369.70.

coins have been so popular and successful that many other countries have introduced coins; these include Australia's Nugget, Britain's Britannia, Belgium's Ecu, China's Panda, and Japan's Hirohito, Historically, the South African Krugerrand was also a popular coin. Because of the government's apartheid policies, however, some investors have refused to invest in these gold coins. **Bullion coin** prices are regularly published in publications such as *Barron's.* Table 18.1 provides a sample of price quotations that include the dollar and percentage premiums of the coins over their gold value. Gold coins trade at modest premiums over their gold value, reflecting minting and distribution costs as well as supply and demand.

BULLION **Bullion,** in the form of gold bars, can be bought through gold dealers and brokerage firms. The investor has the choice of having the bars delivered or leaving them with the dealer or broker for storage. If the dealer or broker stores the bars, the investor must pay additional charges for storage and insurance.

If the investor takes physical possession of the gold, he or she will have to store it in a safe place. In addition, the investor will have to have the bullion assayed to verify its gold content prior to selling it. Assaying adds to the cost of buying gold in this form, but it also protects the buyer against fraud.

Historically, a disadvantage of investing in gold coins and bullion was the relatively high transaction costs. Now, however, a number of discount brokers offer precious metals through brokerage accounts. For example, as of June, 1991 Fidelity Investments Brokerage Services, Inc., handled minimum trades of $2,500 for a commission of 2.9 percent that declines to 0.99 percent for trades over $100,000. The Securities Investor Protection Corporation (SIPC) does not insure precious metals purchased through a brokerage account. Precious metals cannot be bought on margin, and transactions must be settled in two business days.

GOLD CERTIFICATES **Gold certificates** are issued by financial institutions that have bullion in storage as collateral for the certificates. Gold certificates can be purchased through a bank or broker and represent a specific quantity of gold. The advantage of gold certificates over gold bullion is that the investor does not incur the additional expense associated with taking delivery of the underlying asset. Another advantage of gold certificates over gold coins and bullion is that the investor does not have to pay state sales tax on the purchase.

COMMON STOCK OF GOLD-MINING COMPANIES There are a number of publicly traded gold-mining companies that operate primarily in North America. In addition, a number of **gold-mining stocks** are traded on the Johannesburg Stock Exchange in South Africa. As one would expect, common stock prices of gold-mining companies are closely correlated with the price of gold.

There is limited evidence that gold shares are superior investments to bullion for U.S. investors.[1] Gold-mining companies typically have high degrees of operating and financial leverage. In addition, their P/E ratios often reach very high levels prior to and during periods when gold prices are increasing. One advantage of common stocks of gold-mining companies over coins, bullion, and gold certificates is that these common stocks may provide dividend income, which is not possible from the other forms of gold ownership.

FUTURES AND OPTIONS **Gold futures** are actively traded on the New York Commodity Exchange. A gold futures contract represents 100 troy ounces of gold. The issuer of the contract promises to deliver 100 troy ounces of gold, at a specified price, at some time in the future. The contract buyer agrees to a price today for delivery of the gold in the future. Call and put **options on gold futures** are traded on the New York Comex. (See Chapters 15 and 17 for a discussion of commodity futures and options on futures.)

COMMODITY-BACKED BONDS A limited number of corporations have issued bonds whose coupons and/or maturity values are indexed to the price of specific commodities such as gold or silver. For example, Sunshine Mining Company's **commodity-backed bond** has a maturity value of $1,000 *or* the market price of 50 troy ounces of silver, whichever is higher.

MUTUAL FUNDS A number of **tangible asset mutual funds** specialize in gold and other precious metals. There are also mutual funds that combine debt and dividend-paying equity securities for income with precious-metal stocks for inflation protection. The primary advantage of these mutual funds is the diversification they provide the investor. These funds offer the investor an alternative way to invest in gold, silver, and other precious metals and can be used in a passive investment strategy.

---

[1] Kevin J. Carter, John F. Affleck-Graves, and Arthur H. Money, "Are Gold Shares Better Than Gold for Diversification?" *Journal of Portfolio Management* (Fall 1982): 52–55.

• Investment Characteristics of Gold and Silver

Since the commodities gold and silver are not income-producing investments, the holding period return (HPR) consists only of capital gains or losses. If, on the other hand, the investment takes the form of common stock of gold- or silver-mining companies that may pay a cash dividend, the HPR may include dividends as well as capital gains.

Table 18.2 provides the annual HPRs, arithmetic and geometric means, standard deviations, and coefficients of variation for gold, silver, and the S&P 500 over the period 1978–1990. The HPRs for the precious metals are more closely correlated with each other than they are with the S&P 500. Also, notice the large differences in the arithmetic and geometric means for the metals, caused by their very volatile HPRs. Gold and silver were much more volatile over this 13-year period than were equities as measured by the S&P 500. Finally, note that most of the positive return for the metals can be attributed to 1979. The average return for gold, excluding 1979, would have been slightly less than 2 percent, and the return on silver would have been negative.

TABLE 18.2 • Returns and Risk for Gold, Silver, and Common Stocks

	Holding period returns		
	Gold	*Silver*	*S&P 500**
1978	33.3%	27.0%	6.4%
1979	126.5	361.3	18.0
1980	14.5	−44.1	31.5
1981	−31.6	−47.3	−4.8
1982	13.9	32.1	20.3
1983	−16.5	17.9	22.3
1984	−19.2	−28.9	6.0
1985	6.9	−8.3	31.4
1986	20.4	−7.9	18.4
1987	21.9	24.6	5.7
1988	−13.6	−10.0	16.6
1989	−0.8	−8.3	31.1
1990	−6.4	−24.9	−3.2
Arithmetic mean	11.5%	19.0%	15.4%
Geometric mean	6.6%	−1.1%	14.7%
Standard deviation	37.8%	101.7%	12.0%
Coefficient of variation	3.3	5.3	.8

SOURCE: Return measures for gold and silver calculated on per-troy-ounce base prices reported by Handy and Harman.

*Includes dividends.

Herbst found that for the period 1952–1976, the *real* or inflation-adjusted annual HPRs for gold and common stocks were almost equal—2.28 and 2.58 percent, respectively.[2] The historical record indicates that the annualized HPR for gold, calculated over a relatively long period, is below the HPR for common stocks, in both nominal and real terms. For shorter periods, however, gold returns can be much higher or lower than stock returns. For example, during the inflationary period 1971–1976, the annualized *real* HPR on gold was 16.82 percent, compared to 10.46 percent for common stocks.

Herbst also found that the beta for gold was very unstable. The betas were calculated using *real* HPRs, with the Dow Jones Industrial Average representing the market proxy. Herbst examined 33 five-year time spans from 1940 through 1976 and found that the beta for gold was negative for 6 of the 33 periods. The betas ranged from −1.283 (1972–1976) to 1.097 (1966–1970). The results from the study should be used cautiously, however, because of the market proxy problem discussed in Chapter 20.

• Reasons for Investing in Gold and Silver

Because gold and silver have essentially the same investment characteristics, the same investment strategies can be applied to both. One major difference, however, is relative value; silver prices are much lower than gold prices. Consequently, traders often watch the ratio of gold to silver prices as a possible indication of over- or underpricing of one metal relative to the other. The main arguments that have been cited for including these metals in investment portfolios are examined in the following paragraphs.

INFLATION HEDGE Over short periods, gold provides an alternative to financial assets because it may increase in value faster than the rate of inflation. As noted previously, this was the case during the period 1971–1976. Over a longer time, however, "the historical evidence simply does not support the conclusion that, over the long run, gold is superior to common stocks as an inflation hedge."[3]

CONFIDENCE HEDGE Gold is often viewed as an "insurance" investment that will "pay off" if the international monetary system ever collapses (in other words, it serves as a **confidence hedge**). Fortunately, there has never been a test of this hypothesis in the United States. Investment advisers often recommend that some percentage of a portfolio's assets be invested in gold as "insurance." The percentage may vary from 5 to 50 percent, depending on the confidence the adviser has in the health of the international economic and monetary system.

---

[2] Anthony F. Herbst, "Gold versus U.S. Common Stocks: Some Evidence on Inflation Hedge Performance and Cyclical Behavior," *Financial Analysts Journal* (January-February 1983): 66–74.

[3] Ibid., p. 72.

SPECULATION The extreme short-term price variability of gold relative to financial assets provides opportunities for market timing. To be successful, however, an investor must correctly forecast the rate of inflation, changes in the value of the U.S. dollar, and investor confidence in the world economy. These factors are generally cited as being the important influences on the demand for gold, and consequently they have a major impact on prices. An analysis of supply factors is usually not as extensive because the supply of gold is relatively constant. The supply is primarily controlled by five gold-producing nations: South Africa, the Soviet Union, Canada, the United States, and Australia. These nations usually time their sales of newly mined gold to exploit short-term price movements.

Countries producing and hoarding gold may not always be able to time their sale of gold to exploit price movements, however. For example, the current political and economic turmoil in the Soviet Union may cause the price of gold to fluctuate with the level of grain production. If bad weather and disruption in the distribution system force the Soviet Union to buy more foreign grain than anticipated, the Soviets will have to sell gold to raise cash for these increased imports. This will add to the supply of gold traded in the world market and have a negative impact on gold prices.

Some evidence in the literature also suggests that some form of technical analysis or time-series analysis may be appropriate in addition to a macroeconomic demand analysis. For example, a study of daily prices of gold over the period from February 5, 1969, through March 31, 1980, found "persistent dependence" in the time series that was both statistically and economically significant.[4] This finding suggests that a historical cyclical analysis may be helpful in developing timing strategies.

Short-term market timing may be accomplished through the use of gold futures contracts. Contracts are available with delivery dates up to two years. Despite their relatively short lives, gold contracts require a small margin relative to the value of the contract (100 troy ounces) and therefore offer considerable leverage. Call and put options on gold futures are available as well as futures contracts and options on other precious metals, such as silver and platinum.

PORTFOLIO CONSIDERATIONS Any investment strategy should be considered in terms of its impact on the overall portfolio. From this viewpoint, gold is often recommended as a valuable addition to a portfolio of stocks and bonds. Its contribution to a portfolio of financial assets is potentially valuable if it improves returns and reduces risk. A study by Sherman found that over the period 1977–1981, gold proved to be an "effective diversifier" and improved portfolio returns in almost all types of environments.[5] Alternatively,

[4] G. Geoffrey Booth, Fred R. Kean, and Peter E. Koveos, "Persistent Dependence in Gold Prices," *Journal of Financial Research* (Spring 1982): 85–93.

[5] Eugene J. Sherman, "Gold: A Conservative Prudent Diversifier," *Journal of Portfolio Management* (Spring 1982): 21–27.

however, one might argue that economic conditions during the late 1970s and early 1980s were unique and are not likely to be repeated. Without this unique environment, gold is unlikely to provide significant benefits to a portfolio.

A number of factors reduce the attractiveness of gold. First, its liquidity is less than that of other investments, such as stocks and bonds, since it is not traded on an organized exchange like the NYSE. Liquidity should not be confused with marketability. Gold, especially bullion coins, is very marketable, but the problem is the price at which the gold can be sold. Second, transaction costs for precious metals are generally higher than those for financial assets. Finally, delivery, storage, and safekeeping costs can be significant.

REAL ESTATE

It is difficult to assess the total dollar value of real estate in the United States. Estimates for 1988 ranged from $1,295 billion to $9,994 billion.[6] Others have estimated that the value of real estate represents 50 percent of the total value of the portfolio comprising U.S. assets and 33 percent of the portfolio comprising all assets.[7] As an investment, real estate has characteristics of both fixed-income and equity securities. Rental income provides a yield similar to the coupon yield on a bond, while changes in the value of the property provide capital gains or losses similar to those on common stock.

Traditionally, real estate has not been viewed as a viable investment by portfolio managers who deal primarily in financial assets such as stocks and bonds. One explanation for the exclusion of real estate is that "there seems to be a cultural gap between people who understand real estate and the stock and bond people."[8]

This situation is slowly changing. Real estate investment funds have increased their public accessibility by taking the form of marketable securities. As a result, real estate markets are becoming *institutionalized* as mutual funds, real estate investment trusts, and limited partnerships provide increased opportunities for individual investors in real estate. These institutions are playing a larger role in real estate markets in much the same way that financial institutions have greatly influenced the bond and stock markets. "Institutionalization" should increase investment opportunities for individual investors.

In view of the growing empirical evidence that real estate can be a valuable addition to a portfolio, this section of the chapter discusses the investment characteristics of real estate and suggests some strategies for individual investors.

---

[6] Mike Miles, "What Is the Value of All U.S. Real Estate?" *Real Estate Review* (Summer 1990): 69–77.

[7] James R. Webb and Jack H. Rubens, "How Much in Real Estate? A Surprising Answer," *Journal of Portfolio Management* (Spring 1987): 10.

[8] Ibid., p. 14.

• Ways to Invest in Real Estate

Traditionally, individuals made direct investments in real estate by buying specific properties, including personal residences.[9] Of course, this avenue is still available and will be discussed in the next section, but because of the institutionalization of the real estate market, other ways to invest are now available.

LIMITED PARTNERSHIPS Real estate syndications have traditionally taken the form of **limited partnerships.** This form of organization allows revenues and expenses to be "passed through" to individual investors for tax purposes. The investors, who are limited partners as opposed to the general partner, have limited liability. A limited partnership interest is typically sold in units of $5,000 to $10,000. Syndicators may be brokerage firms, specialized real estate companies operating on a national scale, or even individuals.

Besides offering the small investor an opportunity to invest in real estate, limited partnerships were once marketed as excellent tax shelters. Through accelerated depreciation, interest expense, and operating expense deductions, limited partners could be provided with tax-deductible losses of $2 to $4 for each $1 invested. The tax reforms of 1976, 1981, 1984, and 1986, however, have essentially eliminated these "abusive" shelters. Limited partnerships are now marketed for their potential returns rather than strictly as tax shelters. Many investment advisers recommend limited partnerships in real estate as appropriate IRA investments. Since an IRA enables the investor to defer taxes on investment income, potential returns dominate the investment decision.

Traditionally, one major disadvantage of a limited partnership interest has been that it has little if any marketability since there is usually no secondary market for these investments. The investor is generally forced to hold the investment until the partnership is liquidated by a sale of the real estate. This may take 7 to 12 years, or even longer. One reason for the lack of a secondary market is that the fair market value of the partnership is difficult to determine; the value of the partnership interest depends on the value of the underlying real estate, and an individual investor cannot easily determine the market value of the real estate until the property is actually sold. Recently, however, some larger partnerships are providing a secondary market.

Another major disadvantage of a limited partnership is the fee of the syndicator and/or general partner. Investors in limited partnerships commonly

---

[9] Home ownership is clearly an investment, and for many people it represents the largest single asset in a portfolio. Analyzing home ownership involves both qualitative and quantitative forms of analysis. On the qualitative side, there is the psychic income associated with owning a home. On the quantitative side, an investor can compare the cost of home ownership with the alternative of renting. Data required in this type of analysis include the cost of the home, down payment, interest and principal payments on the mortgage, expected annual appreciation in the value of the home, realtor's commission, property taxes, marginal tax rate, and the cost differentials between renting and buying for utilities, insurance, and maintenance. The Investment Analysis Software (described in Appendix A-1) has a program for the analysis of the rent-versus-buy decision.

• INTEREST BOX

Evaluating a Real Estate Limited Partnership

The Financial Products Standards Board, Inc., has developed a set of standards that can be used in the evaluation of real estate limited partnerships. Using a question-and-answer format, these standards identify the appropriate questions to ask and potential problem areas. The areas a potential investor should investigate include the following:

1. The partnership's business plan.
2. The economic soundness of the investment.
3. The background of the people involved.
4. Whether any conflicts of interest exist.
5. Disclosures related to the risk of the investment.
6. Tax opinions.
7. The reasonableness of the financial forecasts and projections.
8. The performance of other, related projects.
9. The reporting requirements and other communications with the limited partners.
10. The partnership agreement.

SOURCE: Adapted from Barry L. Cliff, "How to Evaluate a Real Estate Investment," *Journal of Financial Planning* (April 1990): 58–61. Reprinted with permission from the *Journal of Financial Planning* published by the Institute of Certified Financial Planners.

incur sales charges of 7 to 10 percent in addition to the syndicator's fee, for a total cost of 15–25 percent. These costs are much higher than transaction costs for stock and bond investments. Any publicly offered partnership must be registered with the Securities and Exchange Commission (SEC), and potential investors must be given a prospectus, which should be reviewed carefully. The sales charges and other fees are often concealed in the prospectus and can only be discovered by careful analysis.

REAL ESTATE INVESTMENT TRUSTS **Real estate investment trusts (REITs)** had their beginning in legislation enacted in 1960 that provided a corporate income tax exemption for qualified trusts investing in real estate. Income is distributed to the stockholders with the trust incurring no tax liability. Thus, the dividend payout percentages of REITs are higher than those of typical common stocks. REITs may invest in real estate in several ways, including lending funds for construction purposes, providing intermediate- and long-term mortgages on properties, buying equity positions in property, and combinations of these activities. They may also restrict investments to specific purposes, such as investing in rundown shopping malls or developing and managing mini-warehouses.

One major advantage of REITs is liquidity; their stocks are traded on the organized exchanges or the OTC market. This provides investors with liquidity that may not be available in a direct investment in real estate. A second advantage is that REITs can provide the investor with access to quality commercial real estate managed by professionals.

Despite the fact that REITs invest in real estate, their stocks can be quite risky because of high degrees of financial and operating leverage and major cycles in the overall real estate market. For example, during the recession of 1974–1975, many REITs experienced severe financial problems, and a number declared bankruptcy.

Even with these earlier problems and significant tax changes in 1984 and 1986, REITs are gaining in popularity with investors and provide a viable investment opportunity. They are available in several types including equity REITs, mortgage REITs, and hybrid REITs that combine the investment strategies of equity and mortgage REITs. Table 18.3 provides financial information on a sample of REITs traded on the NYSE and AMEX. This sample includes some of the largest companies, but there are many other publicly traded REITs, including those traded in the OTC market.

MUTUAL FUNDS There are a growing number of public, open-ended mutual funds concentrating in real estate securities. These open-ended funds provide liquidity for the investor. Examples of these mutual funds include the U.S. Real Estate Fund, National Securities & Research Corporation's National Real Estate Stock Fund and National Real Estate Income Fund, and Fidelity Investment's Real Estate Investment Portfolio. These funds differ in their investment objectives and the portfolio strategies designed to achieve these objectives. While some of these funds limit their investments to REITs, others may engage in a variety of real estate–related investments. For example, the National Real Estate Stock Fund attempts to time the real estate cycle. De-

TABLE 18.3 • Sample of Real Estate Investment Trusts (REITs)

	1988			1989			1990		
	Earnings per share	*P/E ratio*	*Dividend yield*	*Earnings per share*	*P/E ratio*	*Dividend yield*	*Earnings per share*	*P/E ratio*	*Dividend yield*
BRE Properties	$1.87	15.6	8.3%	$2.03	14.8	8.0%	$3.74	7.5	8.5%
Federal Realty	0.68	30.5	6.1	0.82	30.5	5.9	0.35	28.6	7.7
First Union	1.25	15.5	7.5	1.63	11.0	8.0	1.14	12.1	7.9
HRE Properties	1.06	21.6	7.9	1.57	14.9	7.7	0.70	25.1	9.1
L&N Housing	d1.08	NMF	7.8	0.17	NMF	11.7	d0.64	NMF	13.6
L&N Mortgage	2.54	8.1	15.2	0.28	NMF	11.8	d2.26	NMF	11.0
MGI Properties	1.64	11.5	8.5	0.83	16.9	8.9	0.66	16.1	9.1
New Plan Realty	0.88	16.2	6.2	0.95	17.0	6.0	1.01	17.0	0.1
Property Capital	2.07	9.4	8.2	1.83	10.9	11.0	2.02	6.6	16.3
Santa Anita Realty	1.56	19.6	6.7	1.61	19.1	6.8	1.41	18.0	8.2
Washington REIT	0.84	19.8	5.7	0.96	20.8	5.1	1.04	16.2	6.5

SOURCE: *Value Line Investment Survey*, February 12, 1991. Copyright © 1991 by Value Line Publishing, Inc.; used by permission.
NOTE: d = deficit or negative earnings per share; NMF = not meaningful figure.

pending on the cycle, the fund may emphasize nonvolatile areas like REITs or more volatile stocks like homebuilders and real estate finance companies.

Other larger mutual funds offer real estate portfolios in their "family" of funds. In 1985, T. Rowe Price offered the Realty Income Fund I, which was organized as a limited partnership. This offering was unique; no sales fee was charged, and no leverage (borrowing) was used to purchase the real estate. These characteristics qualify the partnership as an IRA investment. As with most limited partnerships, however, the secondary market for the partnership interests is very limited. Based on the success of the first two offerings, T. Rowe Price completed the sale of Realty Income Fund III in 1987.

COLLATERALIZED MORTGAGE OBLIGATIONS The characteristics of *mortgage-backed securities* were discussed in Chapter 10. These are securities that are collateralized by pools of mortgages and are issued by federal agencies. **Collateralized mortgage obligations (CMOs)** are similar to those offered by the Government National Mortgage Association ("Ginnie Mae"), but they offer a range of maturities, more predictable cash flows, and monthly interest income. They generally require a minimum initial investment of $25,000 with investment increments of $1,000 thereafter. In addition to the range of maturities, which allows an investor to select an appropriate holding period for the investment portfolio, CMOs attempt to overcome the pass-through problem in which early repayment of principal results in uncertain cash flows. Assumptions about repayment of principal are based on the interest rates of the underlying mortgages, past experiences with prepayment, the age of the underlying mortgages, and economic projections. Because of the active secondary market in CMOs, they are liquid investments.

• Investment Analysis of Direct Real Estate Investments

An individual investor who is interested in direct investment in real estate can analyze income-producing real estate using many of the tools and techniques previously discussed in this text. This section briefly examines two discounted cash-flow techniques. In addition to these two techniques, real estate appraisers use a variety of other models and procedures that are beyond the scope of this text.

NET PRESENT VALUE TECHNIQUE The net present value approach compares the present value of the annual after-tax cash flows and reversion value, using the investor's after-tax required rate of return, to the initial equity interest in the property. Typically, real estate is financed with both debt and equity capital, but the after-tax cash flows are usually used to calculate the investment value of the equity. Thus, the cash flows are reduced by the interest expenses and principal repayments associated with the debt.

The after-tax cash flow for period t (CF_t) is defined as

$$CF_t = NOI_t - DS_t - T_t \tag{18.1}$$

where

NOI_t = net operating income for period t
DS_t = debt service for period t including interest expense and amortization of principal
T_t = tax liability in period t

The estimate of NOI over the life of the investment includes all revenue and expenses for the property, such as rent income, maintenance, and management fees. NOI is calculated, however, before debt service and taxes. In calculating the income tax liability, the principal payments on debt are not tax deductible, but interest expense and depreciation charges are deductible.

The **reversion value (RV),** or expected selling price at the end of the investment holding period, is estimated because most investors do not anticipate holding the real estate indefinitely. RV is defined as

$$RV_n = SP_n - E_n - D_n - T_n \tag{18.2}$$

where

RV_n = reversion value at period n
SP_n = selling price at period n
E_n = expenses incurred when the property is sold, such as brokerage fees
D_n = remaining mortgage or debt at time of sale
T_n = taxes incurred as a result of the sale

Combining the after-tax cash flow and reversion value, the **investment value of the equity interest (V_E)** can be defined as

$$V_E = \sum_{t=1}^{n} \frac{CF_t}{(1 + K_e)^t} + \frac{RV_n}{(1 + K_e)^n} \tag{18.3}$$

where

V_E = investment value of the equity interest
K_e = investor's after-tax required rate of return on equity
CF_t = after-tax cash flow for period t
RV_n = after-tax reversion value at period n

Equation 18.3 is very similar to the bond valuation models presented in Chapter 11. The estimates of CF_t and RV_n are more uncertain than their equivalents in the bond valuation models, however. The required rate of return (K_e) should be based on an estimate of the rate of return expected by an investor for equivalent-risk investments traded in the capital market.

The estimate of the equity value (V_E), determined by Equation 18.3, can be used to compute the net present value (NPV) of the real estate investment:

$$NPV = V_E - EI_0 \tag{18.4}$$

where

EI_0 is the initial equity interest in the property.

If NPV > 0, the property appears to be undervalued and may be an attractive investment. If NPV ≤ 0, the property is correctly valued or overvalued according to the analysis.

INTERNAL RATE OF RETURN TECHNIQUE An alternative or supplement to the NPV calculation is the internal rate of return (IRR). This approach finds the discount rate that equates the investment value of the equity interest with the initial equity interest in the property:

$$EI_0 = \sum_{t=1}^{n} \frac{CF_t}{(1 + IRR_e)^t} + \frac{RV_n}{(1 + IRR_e)^n} \quad (18.5)$$

Once Equation 18.5 is solved for IRR_e, an investment decision is made by comparing IRR_e and K_e. If $IRR_e > K_e$, the property is undervalued and may be a good investment alternative. If $IRR_e \leq K_e$, the property is correctly valued or overvalued according to the analysis.

Table 18.4 presents a simple illustration of the NPV and IRR techniques applied to real estate. In this particular example, NPV > 0, and $IRR_e > 12$ percent, the after-tax required rate of return on equity, so the commercial office building appears to be undervalued.

• Investment Characteristics of Real Estate

A number of studies have examined the historical holding period returns on real estate. A major problem with these studies, however, is that there is no national real estate market that generates transaction prices on a continuous basis. Without prices at regular intervals, HPRs cannot be accurately calculated. Although REITs are traded on a regular basis in the stock market, they represent only a particular segment of the market for real estate. Studies often use proxies for price or yield data from a specific geographical location. Because of these problems, the following summary of investment characteristics should be viewed with caution.

Research into the investment characteristics of real estate yields the following conclusions:

1. Holding period returns A comparison of real estate returns to the HPRs on corporate securities, such as common stocks and bonds, indicates that real estate returns compare quite favorably with corporate securities. Results from a study by Webb and Rubens, shown in Table 18.5, provide a comparison of historical mean returns of real estate and three major categories of financial assets.

Table 18.5 also provides the correlation coefficient matrix for the six categories of investments. Notice that the correlations are low for the three catego-

TABLE 18.4 • Illustration of Real Estate Investment Analysis

Data

Property description:	Small commercial office building
Initial equity interest:	$5,000,000
Holding period:	5 years
Estimate of annual net operating income:	$500,000
Annual debt service:	$100,000
Estimated annual tax liability:	$135,000
Estimate of after-tax reversion value:	$7,500,000
After-tax required rate of return on equity:	12%

Annual Cash Flow

$$\begin{aligned} CF_t &= NOI_t - DS_t - T_t \\ &= \$500{,}000 - \$100{,}000 - \$135{,}000 = \$265{,}000 \end{aligned}$$

Investment Value of the Equity Interest

$$\begin{aligned} V_E &= \frac{\$265{,}000}{(1+.12)} + \frac{\$265{,}000}{(1+.12)^2} + \cdots + \frac{\$265{,}000}{(1+.12)^5} + \frac{\$7{,}500{,}000}{(1+.12)^5} \\ &= \$265{,}000\left[\frac{1 - \dfrac{1}{(1+.12)^5}}{.12}\right] + \frac{\$7{,}500{,}000}{(1+.12)^5} \\ &= \$265{,}000(3.6048) + \frac{\$7{,}500{,}000}{1.7623} \\ &= \$955{,}272 + \$4{,}255{,}802 \\ &= \$5{,}211{,}074 \end{aligned}$$

Net Present Value

$$\begin{aligned} NPV &= \$5{,}211{,}074 - \$5{,}000{,}000 \\ &= \$211{,}074 \end{aligned}$$

Internal Rate of Return

$$\$5{,}000{,}000 = \$265{,}000\left[\frac{1 - \dfrac{1}{(1+IRR_e)^5}}{IRR_e}\right] + \frac{\$7{,}500{,}000}{(1+IRR_e)^5}$$

By trial and error or calculator: IRR = 13.01%.

TABLE 18.5 • Returns and Risk on Real Estate and Financial Assets, 1973–1984

	Arithmetic mean HPR	Standard deviation of HPR	Coefficient of variation
Residential real estate	10.53%	4.44%	.42
Farmland	14.03	11.06	.79
Business real estate	10.78	2.77	.26
Common stocks	9.62	19.71	2.05
Corporate bonds	7.51	13.92	1.85
Small stocks	21.96	28.11	1.28

Correlation Coefficient Matrix

	Residential real estate	*Farm-land*	*Business real estate*	*Common stocks*	*Corporate bonds*	*Small stocks*
Residential real estate	1.00					
Farmland	0.15	1.00				
Business real estate	0.11	−0.56	1.00			
Common stocks	0.23	−0.31	0.31	1.00		
Corporate bonds	−0.25	−0.37	−0.24	0.39	1.00	
Small stocks	0.33	−0.39	0.35	0.85	0.21	1.00

SOURCE: James R. Webb and Jack H. Rubens, "How Much in Real Estate? A Surprising Answer," *Journal of Portfolio Management* (Spring 1987): 10–13. This copyrighted material is reprinted with permission from Institutional Investor, Inc.

ries of real estate and, in one case, are negative. Real estate returns also appear to be negatively correlated with corporate bond returns. It should be emphasized that these comparative return and correlation results will vary with the time period selected for study.

2. Risk Most empirical studies conclude that the risk of real estate returns, as measured by the standard deviation or coefficient of variation, is lower than for corporate securities. As Table 18.5 shows, real estate was less risky than the three categories of financial assets over the 1973–1984 time period. Caution should be used, however, when interpreting risk measures for real estate. Quite often real estate returns are reported on appraised values rather than transaction prices, and these values tend to "smooth" the returns.

A number of studies have attempted to calculate betas for real estate, but selecting a proper proxy for the market portfolio can be difficult. A number of different market proxies have been used, including the S&P 500, GNP, and a portfolio consisting of real estate. The results of these studies suggest that systematic risk is a relatively small part of the total risk of real estate.

• Reasons for Investing in Real Estate

Because of the lack of liquidity and high transaction costs, direct investment in real estate has traditionally been regarded as a long-term investment. This viewpoint would suggest that direct real estate investment strategies should be passive rather than active. The following discussion supports this view.

INFLATION HEDGE Considerable research has empirically tested the hypothesis that real estate provides an inflation hedge. The results from these studies are somewhat contradictory. Several studies conclude that some types of real estate are an effective hedge against expected inflation, but not *unexpected inflation.* Expected inflation is often measured by the observed yield on bonds; investor expectations of inflation are reflected in the inflation yield premium included in the overall yield. Unexpected inflation is not reflected in market yields on bonds. Other studies conclude that some types of real estate are an effective hedge against both expected and unexpected inflation.

One possible explanation for the contradictory results is that the studies were based on different time periods. Studies that use data from the 1970s generally conclude that real estate is one of the few assets that provides an effective hedge against inflation. A study by Fogler of the 1915–1978 period found that real estate was an effective hedge during the inflationary periods of the 1960s and 1970s, but not during earlier inflationary periods.[10]

Another possible explanation of the contradictory results is that studies generally use data from a specific geographic area. Real estate markets are highly segmented or regionalized. For example, one area of the country may be experiencing a real estate boom while prices are depressed or even declining in another area. A study based on data from Florida, which enjoyed a booming real estate market during the 1980s, might reach very different conclusions from a study based on data from a "rust-belt" area. Real estate may be a good hedge against inflation during a given period of time for a certain location, but not for all locations.

Real estate investments are not homogeneous. There are many different types of real estate, including unimproved or "raw" land, farms, residential, and retail office buildings. Studies of real estate as an inflation hedge have found that the type of property influences the conclusions. For example, office properties may provide a better or worse hedge than retail properties in certain markets. After reviewing a number of studies, Sirmans and Sirmans concluded that "taken together, the studies seem to indicate that real estate served as a better inflation hedge over the time periods studied than common stocks and corporate or government bonds."[11]

---

[10] H. Russell Fogler, "20% in Real Estate: Can Theory Justify It?" *Journal of Portfolio Management* (Winter 1984): 6–13.

[11] G. Stacy Sirmans and C.F. Sirmans, "The Historical Perspective of Real Estate Returns," *Journal of Portfolio Management* (Spring 1987): 31.

Empirical evidence suggests that real estate should be included in an investment portfolio to protect against purchasing power loss during inflationary periods. Evidence also suggests that the proportion of the portfolio devoted to real estate should increase before or during periods of high inflation.

MARKET TIMING Is it possible to buy real estate "low" and sell it "high"? Doing so would be similar to forecasting bull and bear stock markets and trading accordingly. Fogler argues that because real estate is illiquid, it is not possible to use short-term timing strategies.[12] For example, if an investor anticipates a decline in the real estate market and decides to sell a real estate investment, it may take many months to find a buyer. Likewise, it may be difficult to find and close on an appropriate property in a short time period prior to a favorable market.

MARKET INEFFICIENCIES Is it possible to find real estate that is under- or overvalued? If so, the real estate market would be inefficient in correctly valuing some properties.[13] A "weak form" test of market efficiency would involve evaluating whether past price information in real estate markets can be utilized to predict future prices. If the market is "weakly" efficient, then all information contained in past price movements is fully reflected in current prices. An analysis of the trends or cycles in historical prices in a "weakly" efficient market therefore cannot be successfully used to forecast future price movements.

A "semistrong form" test of market efficiency would be to measure the speed with which real estate prices adjust to new publicly available information. For example, what price adjustment patterns could be observed in real estate prices resulting from announced government policy changes or interest rate movements? According to the semistrong form of the efficient market hypothesis, prices reflect all publicly available information, and any significant new public information should immediately be reflected in real estate prices.

Two studies using time-series prices on real estate from a major Canadian metropolitan area concluded that the market was both "weakly" efficient and "semistrong" efficient.[14] In other words, no model using sophisticated statistical techniques had any forecasting ability, and real estate investors cannot use publicly available information to earn excess returns on a risk-adjusted

---

[12] Fogler, "20% in Real Estate," p. 12.

[13] Analysis of market efficiency in real estate is an extension of the efficient market hypothesis developed for the stock and bond markets. Chapter 21 provides a complete discussion of the efficient market hypothesis.

[14] George W. Gau, "Weak Form Tests of the Efficiency of Real Estate Investment Markets," *Financial Review* (November 1984): 301–20; and "Public Information and Abnormal Returns in Real Estate Investment," *AREUEA Journal* (Spring 1985): 15–31.

basis. Other studies are needed, however, before conclusions can be reached about the efficiency of real estate markets.

PORTFOLIO CONSIDERATIONS There is growing empirical evidence that real estate can make a very valuable contribution to a portfolio:

1. Portfolios of stocks, bonds and real estate As Table 18.5 illustrates, the returns on real estate may be higher than those on financial assets, and the total risk of real estate, measured by the standard deviation or coefficient of variation, may be lower. Also, real estate returns may be negatively correlated with bond returns. The results in Table 18.5 reflect the ex-post period 1973–1984. Thus, there is no guarantee that the returns, risks, and correlations will be similarly related in the future. Nevertheless, these characteristics suggest that adding real estate to a portfolio of stocks and bonds can improve the risk-return performance of the portfolio.

Using historical returns, what proportion of a portfolio's funds should be invested in real estate? Fogler's 1984 study suggested that 15–20 percent of a portfolio's funds would be appropriate.[15] The 1987 study by Webb and Rubens reached the surprising conclusion that the majority of a portfolio's funds should be invested in real estate.[16] According to the authors, the return and risk characteristics of residential, farmland, and business real estate were much better than those of common stocks, corporate bonds, and small stocks. These favorable characteristics existed for three different time periods: 1947–1959, 1960–1972, and 1973–1984.

2. Diversification by number of properties in a portfolio Another portfolio consideration is the number of properties needed to eliminate unsystematic or diversifiable risk. Studies of common stocks generally conclude that, on average, 10 to 15 randomly selected stocks essentially eliminate the unsystematic risk of the portfolio. Studies of real estate also show large potential gains from diversification by increasing the number of properties in the portfolio. These benefits occur because much of the variability in real estate returns is unsystematic. These studies generally find that, on average, fewer than 10 properties in a real estate portfolio essentially eliminate all of the unsystematic risk.

3. Diversification by property type and location Would it be equally effective to invest in a portfolio consisting of 10 office buildings or a portfolio of 10 different types of real estate in several geographic locations? Empirical evidence suggests that the correlation coefficients between the returns on different types of real estate are quite low and in some cases may be negative. This suggests that real estate portfolios should be diversified by types of property and, as indicated earlier, by geographic location.

---

[15] Scott H. Irwin and Diego Landa reached the same conclusion for low-risk portfolios in "Real Estate, Futures, and Gold as Portfolio Assets," *Journal of Portfolio Management* (Fall 1987): 29–34.

[16] Webb and Rubens, "How Much in Real Estate?"

COLLECTIBLES

A number of other tangible or real assets are sometimes viewed as investments; these include diamonds, paintings, prints, stamps, antiques, and numismatic coins. This view was strengthened by the high rates of inflation during the late 1970s and early 1980s. Many individuals thought that any type of real asset provided a better hedge against inflation than financial assets—and also provided intangible benefits and aesthetic value.

Applying traditional techniques of investment analysis to **collectibles** is difficult because time-series price data are lacking and the objects all have unique characteristics. Consequently, few academic or rigorous investment studies have been conducted.[17]

This section of the chapter provides a brief discussion of the more traditional types of collectibles: diamonds, fine art, and numismatic coins.

• Diamonds

The peak of the diamond craze occurred in 1980. The price of a "D flawless" one-carat diamond increased from approximately $1,500 in 1970 to a high of $65,000 in 1980. This represents an annual compounded HPR of 45.77 percent. Many "investors" were convinced that inflation would continue to increase at a rapid rate and that the price of diamonds would continue to rise. However, the peak occurred in 1980, with the price of the benchmark diamond (D flawless) declining by 75 percent within a few months. The spectacular price cycle has been attributed to speculation by investors attempting to identify and take advantage of inflation hedges.

Because of their value, portability, and aesthetic appeal, diamonds have traditionally been viewed as an attractive medium for personal investment. If an individual is inclined to view diamonds as investments, the following factors should be considered:

1. *Diamonds lack liquidity* There is no national market where diamonds can easily be bought and sold.
2. *Diamonds are not homogeneous* Diamonds are graded by color, clarity, weight, and proportion. No two diamonds are exactly alike, and prices of one-carat diamonds can vary considerably because of their grade. Grading is an art that requires considerable experience, and individuals without extensive training will have difficulty determining the quality of a stone. The current grading standards and certificates of the Gemological Institute of America (GIA) are accepted through-

[17] For an example of an analysis of the investment performance of collectibles, see Stephen P. Ferris and Anil K. Makhija, "Tangible Assets as Investments: A Risk and Return Analysis," *Akron Business and Economic Review* (Fall 1987): 115–28.

• **INTEREST BOX**

The List of Collectibles Gets Larger

George Lois created the advertising slogan, "I want my MTV." He and his wife, Rosemary, are collectors of African, Oceanic, and Eskimo art. The estimated value of their collection is $20 million. In 1967, the Loises paid $40,000 for a carved skeletal figure exported from Easter Island by Captain James Cook in the eighteenth century. The figure is currently worth $1 million.

The investor should remember it is very easy to make a costly mistake in acquiring collectibles. It is important to gain expertise, as the Loises did, before acquiring collectible assets. While some collectibles are well known, such as the baseball card collection that our mothers threw away when we left for college, the types of assets investors are collecting are expanding rapidly. The following list provides a sample of some lesser known collectibles that have been discussed in popular business magazines and newspapers over the past several years:

Aborigine paintings ("dreamings")
African, Oceanic, and Eskimo art
American pocket watches
Architectural drawings
Automobiles (classics, special interest, muscle, and antiques)
Cartoon art (original)
Colored gems
Decorative glass
Guns
Mexican art (contemporary)
Music boxes
Old bond and share certificates
Oriental ceramics
Photographic prints (master photographers)
Postcards
Rugs (oriental and antique)
Swords (samurai)
Wines

SOURCES: Christie Brown, "They Pump, They Ooze, They Reek!" *Forbes*, February 19, 1990, pp. 172–75. Various issues of *Forbes*, *Barron's*, and *Business Week*.

out the diamond industry. No diamond should be purchased as an investment unless it is accompanied by a grading certificate issued by the GIA.

3. *Transaction costs are high* Retail markups on diamonds can be as high as 100 percent, with wholesale markups of 15 percent on large quantities of quality stones. Investment returns on diamonds must be considerable to cover these very high transaction costs.
4. *The market is closely controlled* It has been estimated that the South African De Beers cartel controls 85 percent of the world's supply of uncut stones. This degree of control by a single supplier may not be advantageous to buyers.

• Fine Art

Fine art investments include paintings, sculptures, antiques, and many other items. The value of individual works of art is primarily determined by the artist's reputation, the rarity of the work, its condition, and its popularity with other collectors and investors. Most experts advise collectors to value an item on the basis of aesthetics rather than potential profits. Investors and speculators are often advised to avoid buying items unless they are familiar with the particular type of art. Some dealers actually discourage individuals from regarding fine art as an investment.

Fine art must be appraised by an expert to determine its authenticity, condition, and value. Due to the uniqueness of most art objects, however, an auction is the only way to establish value firmly. There are many dealers and appraisers of fine art and professional associations such as the International Society of Appraisers and the International Society of Fine Art Appraisers. The better-known auction houses, which also offer appraisal services, are Christie's and Sotheby's, both located in New York City.

Small investors/speculators may be attracted to the work of "up-and-coming young artists." Buying new works of art is very risky; most will never become collectors items. Essentially, this is similar to buying the stock of a new, unproved corporation in its initial public offering.

Transaction costs are also a disadvantage of fine art investing. Auction houses typically charge a commission of 10 percent; dealers, who often sell items on a consignment basis, can charge a 10 to 25 percent commission, based on the selling price.

• Numismatic Coins

The American Numismatic Association estimates that approximately 500,000 Americans are serious coin collectors and that another 2.5 million are casual collectors, compared to approximately 9 million who trade in coins as investors or speculators. The interest of investors and speculators has grown partly because of the HPRs that coins have provided. Salomon Brothers estimates that over the 15-year period, 1973–1987, coins achieved a compounded annual rate of return of 18.8 percent. The performance of coins over this period may explain why Kidder Peabody started the $42 million Rare Coin Fund limited partnership and why Merrill Lynch filed, in April 1990, a public limited partnership prospectus to sell $50 million to $75 million of rare coins to investors.

One major disadvantage of investing in coins is that their value is greatly influenced by their condition and rarity. Consequently, it is usually necessary to have coins *graded* by a professional service like the Numismatic Guarantee Corporation of America, the Professional Coin Grading Service, or the American Numismatic Association's Certification Service. The time and cost associated with grading reduce the liquidity and return of coin investments.

The value of numismatic coins does not depend on the value of the metal in the coin or its bullion value. Thus, their prices do not respond to changes in the price of gold and silver. In addition to condition and rarity, the value of numismatic coins depends primarily on collector or speculator demand for a particular coin. Before buying coins, the investor or speculator should become knowledgeable about rare coins, find a reputable coin dealer, study the price history of coins, avoid esoteric coins, and acquire a safe location to store any purchases.

SUMMARY

This chapter has presented empirical evidence suggesting that HPRs on real assets during some time periods are often much larger than HPRs on financial assets. There is also evidence that risk for some types of real assets may be below that of common stocks and, in some cases, bonds. To the extent that these observations are correct, investors' portfolios should include real assets.

• CONCEPT APPLICATIONS

Investment Concept	Concept Application
Precious metals	Precious metals, particularly gold, traditionally have been considered valuable assets for a portfolio. Reasons cited for including precious metals in a portfolio include their ability to serve as an inflation hedge, a confidence hedge, and an effective diversifier. Some evidence suggests that precious metals may not prove to be as attractive an addition to portfolios in the future as they have been in the past.
Real estate	Investment in real estate can take many forms, ranging in liquidity from direct investment in real estate to publicly traded REITs and mutual funds. Historically, real estate has provided relatively higher returns and lower risk than alternative investments such as common stocks and corporate bonds. In addition, real estate's historical negative or low correlation of returns with other investment alternatives has made it an attractive addition to an investor's portfolio. As evidenced by the declining real estate market in 1991, these historical relationships may not hold in the 1990s.
Collectibles	Collectibles range from traditional assets such as diamonds, art, and numismatic coins to less well known items such as pocket watches and samurai swords. In addition to problems of liquidity, collectibles require that the investor develop an in-depth knowledge of the collectible under consideration. Even so-called experts have been victims of fraudulent practices in the acquisition of collectibles.

There is also evidence that the correlation coefficients between the returns on real assets and financial assets are low and, in some cases, negative. This provides further evidence that real assets should be included in portfolios.

As with virtually all investment research, these observations are based on historical or ex-post return data. If history repeats itself, then real assets should indeed be seriously considered for diversified portfolios.

• KEY TERMS

Bullion
Bullion coin
Collateralized mortgage obligation (CMO)
Collectibles
Commodity-backed bond
Confidence hedge
Gold certificate
Gold futures
Gold- and silver-mining stocks
Inflation hedge
Investment value of the equity interest (real estate)
Options on gold futures
Precious metals
Real estate investment trust (REIT)
Real estate limited partnership
Real or tangible asset
Reversion value (RV)
Tangible asset mutual fund

• QUESTIONS

1. Clearly differentiate between *real* and *financial* assets, and cite several examples of each.
2. Compare and contrast numismatic coins with bullion coins. In your opinion, which type of coin has greater investment risk? Justify your opinion.
3. Explain why a commodity-backed bond may provide a better inflation hedge than a traditional bond.
4. Compare an inflation hedge with a confidence hedge.
5. Compare the advantages and disadvantages of owning gold by purchasing bullion and gold certificates.
6. Discuss the four ways individuals can invest in real estate in addition to direct investment.
7. Discuss the investment characteristics of gold.
8. Discuss the possible reasons for including real assets in a portfolio.
9. Discuss the pros and cons of considering collectibles as investments.
10. "The benefits of including real assets in a portfolio are based on studies of historical (ex-post) relationships." Explain this statement and its implications for portfolio construction.

• KEY TO THE INVESTMENT ANALYSIS SOFTWARE

Calculation	Appendix A-1 Page Reference	Access Procedure
Holding period return	A-8	BEGIN, STATISTICAL, HPR, ONE or MANY
Real estate analysis (rent versus buy)	A-14	BEGIN, PERSONAL, REALESTATE

• PROBLEMS

1. Consider the following information on three investment alternatives:

	Cost	*Selling price*	*Income over holding period*	*Transaction costs**	*Storage costs*
Blue-chip common stock	$ 20	$ 25	$1.00	2%	—
REIT common stock	10	12	1.20	2	—
Gold coin	400	500	—	8	5%

*Transaction costs occur when the asset is bought and sold.

a. Calculate the gross HPRs for each investment alternative (i.e., ignore transaction costs and storage costs).

b. Calculate the net HPRs for each investment alternative.

c. Discuss the impact of transaction and storage costs on the assets' net HPRs.

2. Assume that a gold coin increased in value from $100 to $160 over a six-year period and that the Consumer Price Index increased from 100 to 140 over the same period.

a. Calculate the annualized HPR for the gold coin and the annualized rate of inflation.

b. Calculate the annualized *real* HPR for the gold coin.

c. Did the gold coin provide an inflation hedge? Explain.

3. Consider the following potential real estate investments:

	Cost	*Commission expense to purchase*	*Annual income*	*Initial syndication fee*	*Value after one year*
Limited partnership interest	$10,000	10%	$1000	5%	$11,500
100 shares of REIT common stock	10,000	2	1000	—	11,500

a. Calculate the gross (before expenses and fees) HPRs for each investment alternative.

b. Calculate the *net* HPR for each investment alternative.

c. Can an investor actually realize these expected HPRs by selling the investments after one year? Explain.

4. Consider the following potential real estate investment:

Year	*After-tax cash flow*	*After-tax reversion value*
0	$(100,000)	
1	15,000	
2	60,000	
3	30,000	$115,000

a. Assume an after-tax required rate of return on equity of 12 percent. Calculate the net present value and indicate whether the real estate appears to be an acceptable investment.

b. Calculate the internal rate of return and indicate whether the real estate appears to be an acceptable investment.

5. Consider the following information on a small apartment complex that is being evaluated as a potential investment:

Initial equity interest	$1,000,000
Holding period	3 years
Estimate of annual net operating income	$150,000
Annual debt service	$50,000
Estimated annual tax liability	$40,000
Estimate of after-tax reversion value	$1,200,000
After-tax required rate of return on equity	13%

a. Calculate the annual after-tax cash flow.

b. Calculate the net present value and indicate whether the property is an acceptable investment based on this analysis.

c. Calculate the internal rate of return and indicate whether the property is an acceptable investment based on this analysis.

d. Discuss other factors that would need to be analyzed before a final investment decision is made.

• REFERENCES

Aggarwal, Raj, and P.S. Sundaranaghavan. "Efficiency of the Silver Futures Market: An Empirical Study Using Daily Data." *Journal of Banking and Finance* (March 1987): 49–64.

Baker, Stephen A., and Roger C. Van Tassel. "Forecasting the Price of Gold: A Fundamentalist Approach." *Atlantic Economic Journal* (December 1985): 43–51.

Booth, G. Geoffrey, Fred R. Kean, and Peter E. Koveos. "Persistent Dependence in Gold Prices." *Journal of Financial Research* (Spring 1982): 85–93.

Brown, Christie. "Collectibles: Welcome, Suckers!" *Forbes*, June 25, 1990, pp. 282–85.

Carter, Kevin J., John F. Affleck-Graves, and Arthur H. Money. "Are Gold Shares Better Than Gold for Diversification?" *Journal of Portfolio Management* (Fall 1982): 52–55.

Chan, M.W. Luke, and Dean C. Mountain. "The Interactive and Causal Relationships Involving Precious Metal Movements: An Analysis of the Gold and Silver Markets." *Journal of Business and Economic Statistics* (January 1988): 69–77.

Corcoran, Patrick J. "Explaining the Commercial Real Estate Market." *Journal of Portfolio Management* (Spring 1987): 15–21.

Curran, John J. "How Good a Hedge Is Gold?" *Fortune*, June 22, 1987, pp. 169–70.

Ferris, Stephen P., and Anil K. Makhija. "Tangible Assets as Investments: A Risk and Return Analysis." *Akron Business and Economic Review* (Fall 1987): 115–28.

Froland, Charles. "What Determines Cap Rates on Real Estate?" *Journal of Portfolio Management* (Summer 1987): 77–82.

Grissom, Terry V., James L. Kuhle, and Carl H. Walther. "Diversification Works in Real Estate, Too." *Journal of Portfolio Management* (Winter 1987): 66–71.

Herbst, Anthony F. "Gold versus U.S. Common Stocks: Some Evidence on Inflation Hedge Performance and Cyclical Behavior." *Financial Analysts Journal* (January-February 1983): 66–74.

Irwin, Scott H., and Diego Landa. "Real Estate, Futures, and Gold as Portfolio Assets." *Journal of Portfolio Management* (Fall 1987): 29–34.

Jaffe, Jeffrey E. "Gold and Gold Stocks as Investments for Institutional Portfolios." *Financial Analysts Journal* (March-April 1989): 53–59.

Kehrer, Daniel M. "Gold for Armchair Investors." *Fact: The Money Management Magazine* (October 1986): 35–37.

Kuhn, Susan E. "Is Gold Still the Best Bet for Troubled Times?" *Fortune*, September 24, 1990, pp. 25–28.

Kuntz, Mary. "A Realty Fund Primer." *Forbes*, March 9, 1987, pp. 162–63.

Ma, Christopher K. "A Further Investigation of the Day-of-the-Week Effect in the Gold Market." *Journal of Futures Markets* (Fall 1986): 409–19.

Meyer, Marsha. "The Right and Wrong Ways to Buy Gold." *Money*, August 1987, pp. 47–54.

Miles, Mike, and Tom McCue. "Diversification in the Real Estate Portfolio." *Journal of Financial Research* (Spring 1984): 57–68.

Renshaw, Anthony, and Edward F. Renshaw. "Does Gold Have a Role in Investment Portfolios?" *Journal of Portfolio Management* (Spring 1982): 28–31.

Schubert, Todd S. "Publicly Traded Real Estate and the Myth of Inherent Appreciation." *Real Estate Finance* (Fall 1990): 53–59.

Smith, Maurice. "Diamonds: An Investor's Best Friend." *Small Business Reports* (September 1989): 76–79.

Webb, James R., and C.F. Sirmans. "Yields and Risk Measures for Real Estate, 1966–77." *Journal of Portfolio Management* (Fall 1980): 14–19.

Webb, James R., and Jack H. Rubens. "How Much in Real Estate? A Surprising Answer." *Journal of Portfolio Management* (Spring 1987): 10–14.

Wofford, Larry E., and Edward A. Moses. "The Relationship between Capital Markets and Real Estate Investment Yields: Theory and Application." *Real Estate Appraiser and Analyst* (November-December 1978): 51–61.

Wofford, Larry E., Edward A. Moses, and John M. Cheney. "Using Capital Market Theory in Real Estate Appraisal: Evidence from the Securities Markets." *Real Estate Appraiser and Analyst* (Fall 1982): 34–39.

Zigas, David. "Trade Metals! Little Money Down! Lose a Bundle Quick!" *Business Week* (Industrial/Technology Edition), January 29, 1990, pp. 87–88.

PART VII

Portfolio Theory and Analysis

CHAPTER 19

Portfolio Theory

CHAPTER 20

Capital Market and Arbitrage Pricing Theories

CHAPTER 21

Analysis of Portfolio Performance and Market Efficiency

CHAPTER 19

Portfolio Theory

The knowledge-level objectives of this chapter should enable the student to:

- Assess the impact of portfolio diversification on risk and return.
- Recognize that investors should attempt to maximize expected return at a given level of risk and minimize risk at a given level of expected return.
- Comprehend that investors have different preferences for risk and return and that these preferences can be expressed through each investor's set of indifference curves.
- Differentiate between efficient and inefficient portfolios.
- Explain what is meant by a risk-free asset and understand the role the risk-free asset plays in extending portfolio theory.
- Describe how an investor can combine efficient portfoli[illegible] with his or her preferences for risk and return in order [illegible] select the optimal portfolio.

INTRODUCTION

utility

When investment risk and return were introduced in Chapter 2, the benefits of diversification were discussed. This chapter develops the concepts and the logic underlying portfolio theory and highlights the importance of diversification. An appreciation of the theory will provide the investor with a better understanding of how risk is measured in a portfolio context and the relationship between expected return and risk.

Portfolio theory was originally proposed by Harry M. Markowitz in 1952.[1] The theory is concerned with the selection of an optimal portfolio by a risk-averse investor. A **risk-averse investor** is an investor who selects a portfolio that maximizes expected return for any given level of risk or minimizes risk for any given level of expected return. That is, a risk-averse investor will select only **efficient portfolios.**

Once an investor has selected securities to be considered for inclusion in a portfolio, portfolio theory can be used to determine the combination of these securities that will create the set of efficient portfolios. But determining the efficient portfolios only solves a portion of the selection problem. The investor must then choose from the set of efficient portfolios the portfolio that is the **optimal portfolio** for that particular investor. The selection of the optimal portfolio depends on the investor's preferences for risk and return. The investor's risk-return preferences can be represented by **indifference curves.** By combining the efficient portfolios with the investor's indifference curves, the optimal portfolio can be determined. These concepts are fully developed in ...pter.

... Risk and Return

... *averse investor* will prefer less risk to more risk.
..., the value or **utility** of a given expected re-
...n investor to determine the various combina-
...isks that provide a constant utility. For ex-
...ave been determined to have the given risk

...Risk	Expected return
...ow)	?
	?
	?
	?
...high)	?

...tion," *Journal of Finance* (March 1952): 77–91.

FIGURE 19.1
Indifference Curves for Four Investors

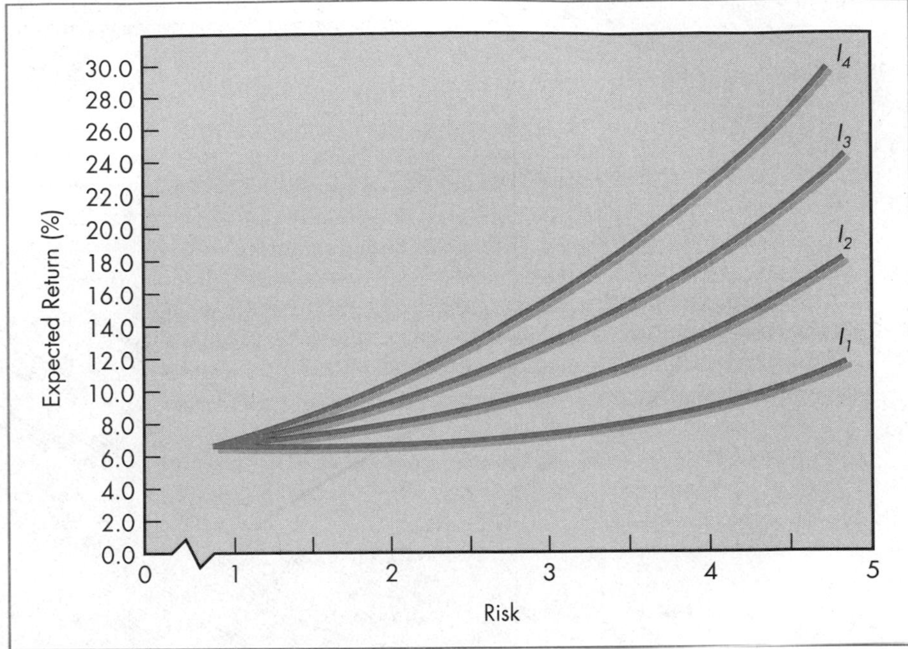

Suppose that four different investors are asked to fill in the expected return column such that each investor maintains a constant utility for each portfolio. In other words, by inserting the expected returns such that an investor would be indifferent among the portfolios with lower risk and higher risk, points on each investor's *indifference curve* can be located. Figure 19.1 illustrates the hypothetical indifference curves for the four investors. The investor whose indifference curve is represented by I_1 has a very high tolerance for risk. This investor's expected or required return does not rise substantially with increasing levels or risk. On the other hand, the investor represented by indifference curve I_4 has a relatively high aversion to risk. In order for this investor to remain indifferent (utility remains constant) among investment alternatives of increasing risk, the expected returns on the higher-risk portfolios must increase substantially.

All of the indifference curves in Figure 19.1 show that as risk increases, the expected return rises. This assumes that these investors are risk-averse. It is hard to imagine that any investor would be **"risk-neutral"** (i.e., willing to accept equal levels of expected return for higher levels of risk) or a **"risk-taker"** (i.e., willing to accept lower levels of expected return for higher levels of risk). If "risk-neutral" or "risk-taker" investors exist, the actions of the risk-averse individuals should offset their influence in pricing financial assets.

Each investor's attitude toward risk can be represented by a set of indifference curves. For example, in Figure 19.2, the indifference curve for investor 2 from the previous example is shown as I_B. The investor would find port-

FIGURE 19.2
Investor 2's Set of Indifference Curves

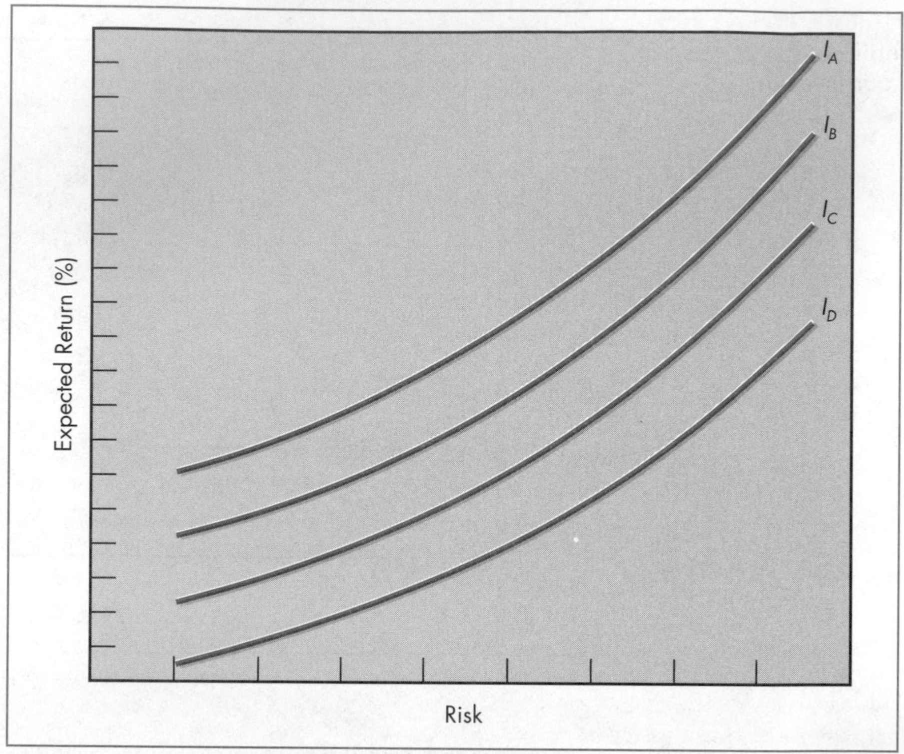

folios H, I, J, K, and L with the assigned risk and expected returns equally desirable. By creating other examples of portfolio risk and return, additional indifference curves for investor 2, such as I_A, I_C, and I_D can be created. In fact, it is theoretically possible to create an infinite number of nonintersecting indifference curves for each investor.

Other things being equal, investors prefer more return to less return. Returning to Figure 19.2, this would mean investor 2 would prefer to be on indifference curve I_A since for any given level of risk, the expected return is highest for I_A relative to I_B, I_C, and I_D. Since investors are also assumed to be risk-averse, other things being equal, less risk is preferred to more risk. For this reason the investor would also prefer I_A over I_B, I_C, and I_D *since for any given level of expected return, risk is lowest for* I_A relative to I_B, I_C, and I_D. In summary, to achieve maximum utility, investor 2 prefers to be on the indifference curve in Figure 19.2 that is the highest and farthest to the left.

The investor should select the portfolio providing the highest utility. Not every portfolio is a candidate for selection; only those portfolios that are efficient in a risk-return sense should be considered. The determination of efficient portfolios and the selection of the optimal portfolio by the investor are developed in the following sections of the chapter.

PORTFOLIO THEORY ASSUMPTIONS

Investors often think of their investment portfolio as consisting only of common stocks, bonds, and other marketable securities. Also, investment portfolios are generally created piece by piece. The investor buys a home, acquires collectibles such as coins and stamps, and purchases common stocks, bonds, and other marketable securities. He or she treats these assets as separate investments, giving little consideration to the interaction of these assets within the portfolio.

Portfolio theory warns us that thinking of an investment portfolio only in terms of marketable securities is wrong. Further, deciding to add or delete an asset solely on the basis of the individual asset's expected return and risk characteristics will result in a less than optimum portfolio. Each asset's expected return and risk, along with the expected return and risk for other assets and their interrelationships, are important inputs in portfolio selection. Using these inputs, *efficient portfolios,* defined as portfolios that maximize the expected return at any given level of risk, can be identified. These portfolios *dominate* all other portfolios with the same level of expected risk. In order to construct efficient portfolios, the investor must be able to quantify the portfolios' expected return and risk. Markowitz developed the basic model, which defines the expected return of a portfolio as a weighted average of the expected returns of the individual assets in the portfolio.[2] The weights are defined as the portion of the investor's wealth invested in a particular asset.

Markowitz used the variance of return as the measure of risk. The risk of the portfolio is not the weighted average of the variances of the expected returns of the individual assets in the portfolio, however. Estimating portfolio risk in this way would obscure the effect of combining assets with different return patterns in a portfolio. Portfolio expected return and risk will be explained and illustrated in the next two sections.

The portfolio model developed by Markowitz is based on the following reasonable assumptions:

1. The expected return from an asset is the mean value of a probability distribution of future returns over some holding period.

2. The risk of an individual asset or portfolio is based on the variability of returns (i.e., the standard deviation or variance).

3. Investors depend solely on their estimates of return and risk in making their investment decisions. This means that an investor's utility (indifference) curves are only a function of expected return and risk.

4. Investors adhere to the **dominance principle.** That is, for any given level of risk, investors prefer assets with a higher expected return to

[2] Markowitz, "Portfolio Selection," pp. 77–91; and *Portfolio Selection* (New York: John Wiley & Sons, 1959).

assets with a lower expected return; for assets with the same expected return, investors prefer lower to higher risk.

PORTFOLIO EXPECTED RETURN

The single-period expected return or holding period return, $E(\text{HPR})$, is defined as

$$E(\text{HPR}) = \frac{(\text{expected ending price} - \text{beginning price}) + \text{expected cash receipts}}{\text{beginning price}}$$

For a share of common stock, this measure of return can be expressed as

$$E(\text{HPR}) = \frac{E(P_{t+1}) - P_t + E(D_{t+1})}{P_t} \qquad (19.1)$$

where

P_t and $E(P_{t+1})$ = price per share at the beginning and end of the period, respectively
$E(D_{t+1})$ = expected cash dividends per share paid over the time interval t to $t + 1$

Equation 19.1 expresses the return in terms of the total return per dollar invested at the beginning of the period.

The expected **return of a portfolio** is the weighted average of the expected returns of the individual assets in the portfolio. The weights are the proportion of the investor's wealth invested in each asset (X_j), and the sum of the weights must equal 1 (i.e., $\Sigma_{j=1}^{n} X_j = 1$). Table 19.1 illustrates this idea for a two-asset portfolio.

In this example, 30 percent of the portfolio's value is invested in asset 1, and 70 percent in asset 2. The expected returns for assets 1 and 2 are 12 percent

TABLE 19.1 • Portfolio Expected Return

Asset	Asset weight, X_j	Asset expected return, $E(\text{HPR}_j)$	Portfolio expected return $E(\text{HPR}_p) = \sum_{j=1}^{n} X_j E(\text{HPR}_j)$
1	30%	12%	3.6%
2	70	15	10.5
			$E(\text{HPR}_p)$ = 14.1%

and 15 percent, respectively. The expected return of the portfolio, $E(\text{HPR}_p)$, is calculated as follows:

$$E(\text{HPR}_p) = \sum_{j=1}^{n} X_j E(\text{HPR}_j) \qquad (19.2)$$
$$= (.30)(.12) + (.70)(.15)$$
$$= 14.1\%$$

Equation 19.2 holds for any number (n) of assets in a portfolio.

PORTFOLIO RISK[3]

The calculation of a **portfolio's risk** is not as straightforward as the calculation of a portfolio's expected return. In order to calculate the risk of a portfolio, consideration must be given not only to the risk of the individual assets in the portfolio and their relative weights but also to the extent to which the assets' returns move together. We measure the risk of an individual asset by the variance of returns or its square root, the standard deviation. The degree to which the assets' returns move together is measured by the **covariance** or **correlation coefficient.** By combining the measures of individual asset risk (variance or standard deviation), relative asset weights, and the co-movement of assets' returns (covariance or correlation), the risk of the portfolio can be estimated.

• Variance and Standard Deviation

The variance of an asset's returns around its expected value or its square root, the standard deviation, is used to define an asset's risk. The use of these measures is based on the assumption that the risk of an asset is a function of the degree to which the future return may deviate from its expected return. Equation 19.3 defines the variance of an asset's HPR (σ_j^2) as follows:

$$\sigma_j^2 = \sum_{j=1}^{n} (P_j)[(\text{HPR}_j - E(\text{HPR}_j)^2] \qquad (19.3)$$

where

HPR_j = a possible HPR
P_j = the probability of the possible HPR
$E(\text{HPR}_j)$ = the expected return

[3]A review of the statistical procedures presented in this section can be found in Appendix A-2, Review of Analytical Techniques.

The square root of the variance or the standard deviation (σ_j) is defined as

$$\sigma_j = \sqrt{\sigma_j^2} \tag{19.4}$$

As Equations 19.3 and 19.4 show, the computation of the variance and standard deviation requires an estimation of the asset's future possible returns and the probability associated with each of these returns. Since risk has been defined as the dispersion of future returns, this approach to measuring risk is appropriate.

Although we are interested in ex-ante or future uncertainty, as a practical matter risk or variance can be calculated using historical HPRs:

$$\sigma_j^2 = \frac{1}{n}\sum_{t=1}^{n}(\text{HPR}_t - \overline{\text{HPR}}_j)^2 \tag{19.5}$$

where

n = the number of historically observed returns, HPR_t
$\overline{\text{HPR}}_j$ = the mean of the historical returns

Using Equation 19.5 to estimate an ex-ante measure of risk is appropriate when it is likely that the ex-post or historical volatility of return accurately reflects ex-ante uncertainty. It has been shown that in most cases asset return volatility changes quite slowly.[4] If there is reason to believe that the historical return pattern will not reflect the future (e.g., a company has changed its business operations as a result of a major acquisition or has undergone a change in leverage), then Equation 19.3 may be more appropriate to estimate ex-ante risk.

• Covariance and Correlation

According to portfolio theory, consideration must be given not only to the risk of the individual assets in the portfolio but also to the degree to which the returns of the assets covary or move together. Consider the return patterns shown in Figure 19.3. In part (a), the returns on assets A and B appear to move in opposite directions each month. That is, in a particular month, if asset A's return is up from the previous month, asset B's return is down, and vice versa. This pattern indicates a negative covariance (and correlation coefficient) of returns between assets A and B. Assets A and B are similar in their return patterns to the Red Ink Company and Black Ink Company discussed in Chapter 2.

In contrast, assets C and D in Figure 19.3b exhibit a different pattern of returns. The returns move together from month to month, indicating a positive covariance (correlation coefficient) of returns.

---

[4] Marshall Blume, "On the Assessment of Risk," *Journal of Finance* (March 1971): 1–10.

FIGURE 19.3
Return Patterns

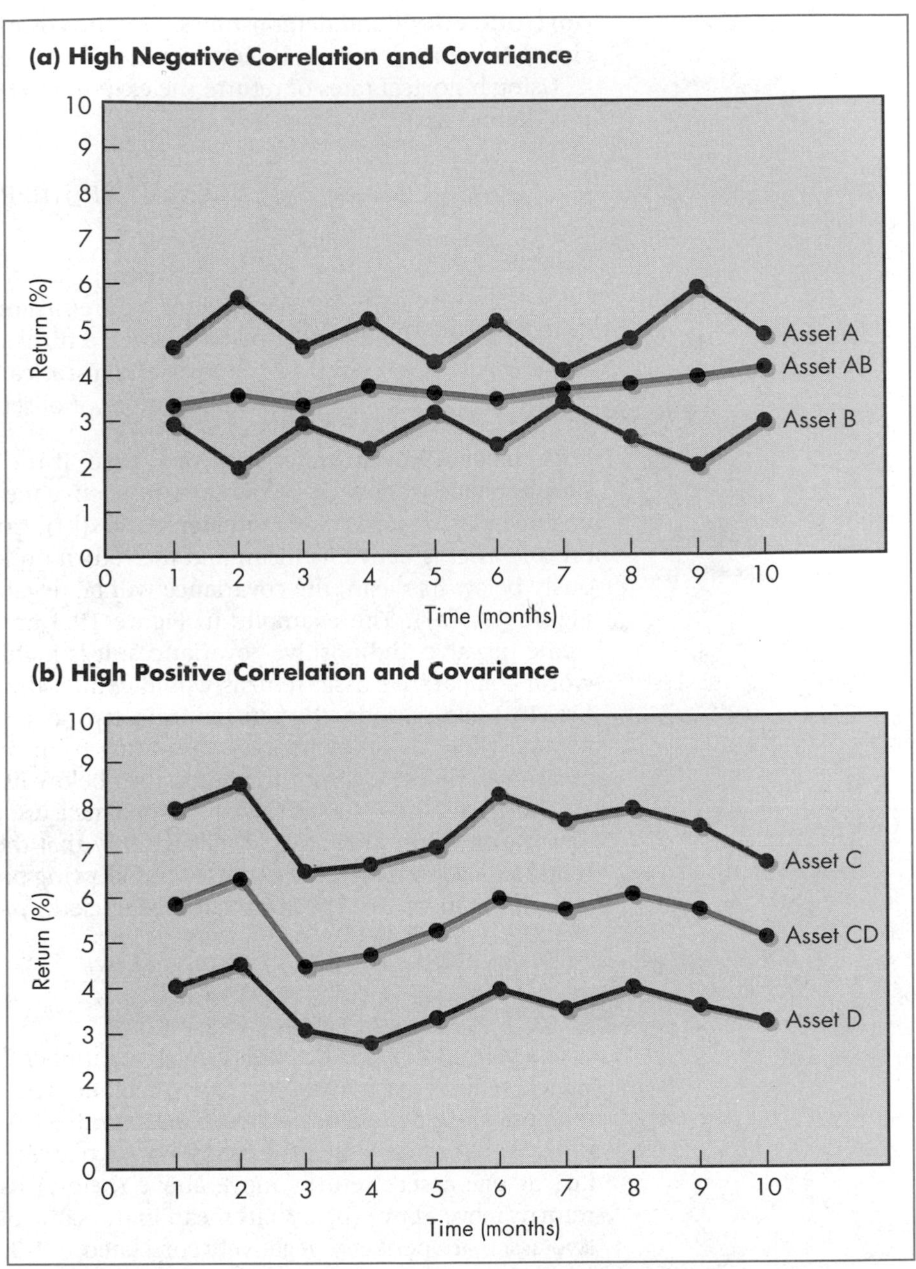

When assets A and B are combined in a portfolio, the volatility of the returns of portfolio AB is reduced relative to the volatility in returns of the individual assets A and B. On the other hand, combining assets C and D does not significantly reduce the volatility of the returns of portfolio CD relative to the volatility of the individual assets. Figure 19.3 illustrates what is called the

portfolio effect and demonstrates why the covariance or correlation coefficient between assets must be considered in determining the risk of a portfolio.

Using historical rates of return, the ex-post covariance for two assets, i and j, is defined as

$$\text{Cov}_{ij} = \frac{1}{n} \sum_{t=1}^{n} (\text{HPR}_{it} - \overline{\text{HPR}}_i)(\text{HPR}_{jt} - \overline{\text{HPR}}_j) \tag{19.6}$$

where

HPR_{it} and HPR_{jt} = the rates of return on the two assets
$\overline{\text{HPR}}_i$ and $\overline{\text{HPR}}_j$ = the average returns of assets A and B over the historical period
n = the number of observations

Equation 19.6 illustrates that, over time, if the returns on two assets are simultaneously above or below their respective means, the covariance will be positive (e.g., assets C and D in Figure 19.3(b)). Conversely, when the return on one asset is above its mean and the return on another asset is simultaneously below its mean, the covariance will be negative (e.g., assets A and B in Figure 19.3(a)). The examples in Figure 19.3 are designed to illustrate extreme negative and positive covariances. It is highly unlikely that in the real world comparative asset returns would exhibit the patterns shown in the figure. In some periods, the returns from two assets may both be above their means, while in other periods the return from one asset may be above its mean and the return from the other asset below its mean.

The calculated value of the covariance measure is not easily interpreted. A covariance value such as +30 tells us only that the returns of the two assets tend to move together. We can use the following procedure to standardize the covariance measure. The correlation coefficient (ρ_{ij}) is defined as

$$\rho_{ij} = \frac{\text{Cov}_{ij}}{\sigma_i \sigma_j} \tag{19.7}$$

The correlation coefficient is a relative number that measures the degree to which returns on two assets move together. The correlation coefficient can take on a range of values between +1.0 and −1.0. Perfectly positive correlation, +1.0, indicates that the returns on two assets move together perfectly—i.e., as one asset's returns move above (below) its mean, the second asset's returns move above (below) its mean in the same proportion. If the returns on two assets are perfectly negatively correlated, −1.0, then as one asset's returns move above (below) its mean, the returns of the second asset move below (above) its mean. A correlation statistic of 0.0 indicates that there is no consistent relationship between the movements of the two asset's returns.

Rewriting Equation 19.7, the covariance can be expressed in terms of the correlation coefficient and the standard deviations of the individual assets:

$$\text{Cov}_{ij} = \rho_{ij} \sigma_i \sigma_j \tag{19.8}$$

• Portfolio Standard Deviation

Earlier we pointed out that the risk of the portfolio must consider not only the risk of the individual assets in the portfolio but their covariance (correlation coefficient). Portfolio risk is measured as

$$\sigma_p^2 = \sum_{i=1}^{n} \sum_{j=1}^{n} X_i X_j \text{Cov}_{ij} \tag{19.9}$$

Taking the square root of both sides of Equation 19.9 and substituting Equation 19.8 for the covariance measure allows us to express the risk of the portfolio in terms of its standard deviation, σ_p:

$$\sigma_p = \sqrt{\sum_{i=1}^{n} \sum_{j=1}^{n} X_i X_j \rho_{ij} \sigma_i \sigma_j} \tag{19.10}$$

$$= \left[\sum_{i=1}^{n} \sum_{j=1}^{n} X_i X_j \rho_{ij} \sigma_i \sigma_j \right]^{1/2} \tag{19.10a}$$

Equations 19.9, 19.10, and 19.10a contain double summations (i.e., $\Sigma\Sigma$). It is a relatively easy task to perform the double summation calculation. Assume that there are three securities in the portfolio and, therefore, $n = 3$. Initially set the i value at 1, and perform the summation for j by allowing it to go from 1 to 3. Once the first summation for j is completed, increase the i value to 2, and perform the summation for j by allowing it to go again from 1 to 3. Finally, increase the i value to 3, and perform the summation for j a final time by allowing it to go from 1 to 3. Performing the double summation on Equation 19.10a for three securities results in the following:

$$\begin{aligned}
\sigma_p &= \left(\sum_{j=1}^{3} X_1 X_j \rho_{1j} \sigma_1 \sigma_j + \sum_{j=1}^{3} X_2 X_j \rho_{2j} \sigma_2 \sigma_j + \sum_{j=1}^{3} X_3 X_j \rho_{3j} \sigma_3 \sigma_j \right)^{1/2} \\
&= (X_1 X_1 \rho_{11} \sigma_1 \sigma_1 + X_1 X_2 \rho_{12} \sigma_1 \sigma_2 + X_1 X_3 \rho_{13} \sigma_1 \sigma_3 \\
&\quad + X_2 X_1 \rho_{21} \sigma_2 \sigma_1 + X_2 X_2 \rho_{22} \sigma_2 \sigma_2 + X_2 X_3 \rho_{23} \sigma_2 \sigma_3 \\
&\quad + X_3 X_1 \rho_{31} \sigma_3 \sigma_1 + X_3 X_2 \rho_{32} \sigma_3 \sigma_2 + X_3 X_3 \rho_{33} \sigma_3 \sigma_3)^{1/2}
\end{aligned}$$

Reviewing the results of the double summation leads to several observations:

1. Performing the double summation for three securities results in nine terms being added together. This relationship can be generalized as follows: the double summation of n terms results in n^2 terms that must be added together. It is easy to see that calculating the risk of a portfolio with a large number of securities would be very difficult to do without a computer.

2. An examination of the nine terms reveals that each term involves the product of the weight of two securities and their covariance. Because of the double summation process, all the subscripts in three of the nine terms are for the same security.

3. When the weights are for the same security (e.g., the first term, X_1), the result is the weight squared (e.g., $X_1X_1 = X_1^2$). Similarly, when the standard deviations are for the same security (e.g., the first term, σ_1), the result is the standard deviation squared or variance (e.g., $\sigma_1\sigma_1 = \sigma_1^2$).
4. When the subscripts for the correlation coefficient are for the same security, the correlation coefficient is equal to +1. This is a logical result since a security's return must be perfectly correlated with itself.
5. Terms that have the same subscripts for the weights, standard deviations, and correlation coefficients can be added together. It is not necessary for the order of the subscripts to be the same (e.g., $X_1X_3\rho_{13}\sigma_1\sigma_3 = X_3X_1\rho_{31}\sigma_3\sigma_1$).

Applying these observations to the terms in the double summation performed above, and slightly changing the order of the terms so that like terms are together, results in the following:

$$\sigma_p = (X_1^2\sigma_1^2 + X_2^2\sigma_2^2 + X_3^2\sigma_3^2 + 2X_1X_2\rho_{12}\sigma_1\sigma_2 + 2X_2X_3\rho_{23}\sigma_2\sigma_3 + 2X_1X_3\rho_{13}\sigma_1\sigma_3)^{1/2}$$

• Portfolio Risk: An Example

Equation 19.10 measures the risk of a portfolio with n assets. It is useful to illustrate this calculation for a portfolio comprising two assets rather than a large number of assets. The use of two assets not only simplifies the example, but the two-asset portfolio also plays a central role in capital market theory, which will be discussed in Chapter 20.

THE TWO-ASSET CASE Table 19.2 uses historical returns for assets A and B [columns (2) and (3)] to illustrate the calculation of each asset's mean return ($\overline{\text{HPR}}$), variance (σ^2), standard deviation (σ), the covariance of assets A and B (Cov_{AB}), and the correlation coefficient (ρ_{AB}) between the returns of assets A and B. Historical returns are used because it is assumed that the ex-post return volatility of assets A and B is a good estimate of ex-ante return volatility.

The value of the correlation coefficient in Table 19.2 is .1321, reasonably close to 0. This would indicate that the relationship between the returns of assets A and B is not very strong. The importance of this relatively low correlation between the returns of assets A and B will become evident when the risk of the portfolio containing these two assets is estimated.

Suppose that assets A and B are combined in equal proportions to form a portfolio. That is, 50 percent of the portfolio's value is invested in asset A, and

50 percent in asset B. Given this assumption, the weights of asset A (X_A) and asset B (X_B) are both equal to 50 percent. With this additional information, it is possible to calculate the total risk of the portfolio.

Recall from Equation 19.10 that the risk of a portfolio can be estimated as

$$\sigma_p = \sqrt{\sum_{i=1}^{n} \sum_{j=1}^{n} X_i X_j \rho_{ij} \sigma_i \sigma_j}$$

Performing the double summation procedure described earlier for a two-asset portfolio comprised of assets A and B, Equation 19.10 can be rewritten as

$$\sigma_p = \sqrt{X_A^2 \sigma_A^2 + X_B^2 \sigma_B^2 + 2X_A X_B \rho_{AB} \sigma_A \sigma_B} \qquad \textbf{(19.11)}$$

Given the equal weights assigned to assets A and B and the information from Table 19.2, we can calculate the risk of the portfolio (σ_p) as follows:

$$\begin{aligned} \sigma_p &= \sqrt{(.5)^2(5.62)^2 + (.5)^2(6.33)^2 + 2(.5)(.5)(.1321)(5.62)(6.33)} \\ &= \sqrt{7.90 + 10.02 + 2.35} \\ &= \sqrt{20.27} \\ &= 4.50\% \end{aligned}$$

It is important to note that the expected risk of the portfolio ($\sigma_p = 4.50\%$) is *less* than the expected risk of either asset A (5.62%) or asset B (6.33%). This reduction in risk illustrates the portfolio effect of combining assets that are less than perfectly correlated (i.e., the correlation between the returns of the two assets is less than +1.0). The higher the correlation between two assets, the lower the impact on portfolio risk of combining them in a portfolio.

Breaking the right side of Equation 19.11 into its parts illustrates the portfolio effect. The first two terms ($X_A^2 \sigma_A^2 + X_B^2 \sigma_B^2$) are very similar to a portfolio's expected return (Equation 19.2) calculation. Rather than using the weighted average of the assets' expected returns, the weighted average of the assets' variances are used. The last term in Equation 19.11 considers the degree to which the two assets move together. The lower the correlation coefficient, the lower the risk of the portfolio. Thus, it is clear from the equation that combining two assets with negative correlation ($\rho_{AB} < 0$) will significantly reduce the risk of the portfolio. Portfolio risk will be reduced whenever the correlation coefficient is less than +1.0.

THE THREE-ASSET CASE Suppose a third asset, C, with the following expected characteristics, is included in the portfolio:

$$\overline{\text{HPR}}_C = 16\% \qquad \rho_{AC} = .1500$$
$$\sigma_C = 7.50\% \qquad \rho_{BC} = .2000$$

Note that the addition of asset C requires the calculation of three correlation coefficients (ρ_{AB}, ρ_{AC}, and ρ_{BC}) as opposed to one in the two-asset case. The

TABLE 19.2 • Expected Return, Variance, Standard Deviation, Covariance, and Correlation Coefficient Calculation

Year (1)	Asset *A* returns, HPR_A (2)	Asset *B* returns, HPR_B (3)	$(HPR_{At} - \overline{HPR}_A)^2$ (4)	$(HPR_{Bt} - \overline{HPR}_B)^2$ (5)	$(HPR_{At} - \overline{HPR}_A)(HPR_{Bt} - \overline{HPR}_B)$ (6)
1981	16%	12%	129.96	12.25	39.90
1982	5	(2)	0.16	110.25	−4.20
1983	5	10	0.16	2.25	0.60
1984	6	6	1.96	6.25	−3.50
1985	(4)	11	73.96	6.25	−21.50
1986	6	3	1.96	30.25	−7.70
1987	0	(1)	21.16	90.25	43.70
1988	3	16	2.56	56.25	−12.00
1989	(2)	14	43.56	30.25	−36.30
1990	11	16	40.96	56.25	48.00
Total	46%	85%	316.40	400.50	47.00

Statistics

1. Mean:

$$\overline{HPR} = \frac{1}{n} \sum_{t=1}^{n} (HPR_{jt})$$

$$\overline{HPR}_A = \frac{1}{10}(46\%) = 4.60\%$$

$$\overline{HPR}_B = \frac{1}{10}(85\%) = 8.50\%$$

2. Variance:

$$\sigma_j^2 = \frac{1}{n} \sum_{t=1}^{n} (\text{HPR}_{jt} - \overline{\text{HPR}}_j)^2$$

$$\sigma_A^2 = \frac{1}{10}(316.40) = 31.64$$

$$\sigma_B^2 = \frac{1}{10}(400.50) = 40.05$$

3. Standard deviation:

$$\sigma = \sqrt{\sigma^2}$$

$$\sigma_A = \sqrt{31.64} = 5.62\%$$

$$\sigma_B = \sqrt{40.05} = 6.33\%$$

4. Covariance:

$$\text{Cov}_{AB} = \frac{1}{n} \sum_{t=1}^{n} (\text{HPR}_{At} - \overline{\text{HPR}}_A)(\text{HPR}_{Bt} - \overline{\text{HPR}}_B)$$

$$\text{Cov}_{AB} = \frac{1}{10}(47.00) = 4.70$$

5. Correlation coefficient:

$$\rho_{AB} = \frac{\text{Cov}_{AB}}{\sigma_A \sigma_B}$$

$$\rho_{AB} = \frac{4.70}{(5.62)(6.33)} = .1321$$

addition of assets under consideration for a portfolio adds to the complexity of the calculations.

Using Equation 19.10 where $n = 3$ and assuming the three assets are combined in approximately equal proportions (i.e., $X_A = .33$, $X_B = .33$, and $X_C = .34$), the variance of the portfolio can be estimated as follows:

$$\begin{aligned}\sigma_p^2 &= (X_A^2)(\sigma_A^2) + (X_B^2)(\sigma_B^2) + (X_C^2)(\sigma_C^2) + 2X_AX_B\rho_{AB}\sigma_A\sigma_B \\ &\quad + 2X_BX_C\rho_{BC}\sigma_B\sigma_C + 2X_AX_C\rho_{AC}\sigma_A\sigma_C \\ &= (.33)^2(5.62)^2 + (.33)^2(6.33)^2 + (.34)^2(7.50)^2 \\ &\quad + 2(.33)(.33)(.1321)(5.62)(6.33) + 2(.33)(.34)(.2000)(6.33)(7.50) \\ &\quad + 2(.33)(.34)(.1500)(5.62)(7.50) \\ &= 3.44 + 4.36 + 6.50 + 1.02 + 2.13 + 1.42 \\ &= 18.87\end{aligned}$$

The standard deviation can be estimated as

$$\begin{aligned}\sigma_p &= \sqrt{\sigma_p^2} = \sqrt{18.87} \\ &= 4.34\%\end{aligned}$$

The risk of this three-asset portfolio, 4.34 percent, is less than the risk of the three individual assets in the portfolio. This occurs because in this case the correlations between assets A and B, B and C, and A and C are all substantially less than +1.0. Also, the fact that the risk of the three-asset portfolio (4.34 percent) is less than the risk of the two-asset portfolio (4.50 percent) illustrates the impact of portfolio diversification. This reduction in risk occurred even though the expected return of 9.76 percent for the three-asset portfolio [i.e., (.33)(4.60%) + (.33)(8.50%) + (.34)(16.00%)] is greater than the 6.55 percent return estimated for the two-asset portfolio [i.e., (.5)(4.60%) + (.5)(8.50%)].

CORRELATION COEFFICIENT AND PORTFOLIO RISK In order to assess the impact of the correlation coefficient on portfolio risk, assume that the correlation coefficients for assets A and B in Table 19.2 have the following values rather than the calculated value of .1321:

$$\begin{aligned}&\text{Case 1:} \quad \rho_{AB} = 1.00 \\ &\text{Case 2:} \quad \rho_{AB} = 0.00 \\ &\text{Case 3:} \quad \rho_{AB} = -1.00\end{aligned}$$

Also, assume the weights (X_j) of assets A and B in the portfolio are allowed to have values ranging between 0 and 100 percent. This assumption rules out the possibility of taking a short position in either asset A or B. Table 19.3 shows the portfolio's expected return and risk for varying weights for each of the three correlation coefficients.

TABLE 19.3 • Correlation Coefficient and Portfolio Risk

Case 1

$\rho_{AB} = 1.00$, $\overline{\text{HPR}}_A = 4.60\%$, $\overline{\text{HPR}}_B = 8.50\%$, $\sigma_A = 5.62\%$, $\sigma_B = 6.33\%$

X_A	X_B	σ_p	$E(R_p)$
100%	0%	5.62%	4.60%
75	25	5.80	5.58
50	50	5.98	6.55
25	75	6.15	7.52
0	100	6.33	8.50

Case 2

$\rho_{AB} = 0.00$, $\overline{\text{HPR}}_A = 4.60\%$, $\overline{\text{HPR}}_B = 8.50\%$, $\sigma_A = 5.62\%$, $\sigma_B = 6.33\%$

X_A	X_B	σ_p	$E(R_p)$
100%	0%	5.62%	4.60%
75	25	4.50	5.58
50	50	4.24	6.55
25	75	4.95	7.52
0	100	6.33	8.50

Case 3

$\rho_{AB} = -1.00$, $\overline{\text{HPR}}_A = 4.60\%$, $\overline{\text{HPR}}_B = 8.50\%$, $\sigma_A = 5.62\%$, $\sigma_B = 6.33\%$

X_A	X_B	σ_p	$E(R_p)$
100%	0%	5.62%	4.60%
75	25	2.63	5.58
50	50	0.46	6.55
25	75	3.34	7.52
0	100	6.33	8.50

Figures 19.4, 19.5, and 19.6 are plots of the information from Table 19.3. The points in the figures are connected on the assumption that the proportion invested in each asset (X_j) can vary in much smaller increments than those shown in Table 19.3.

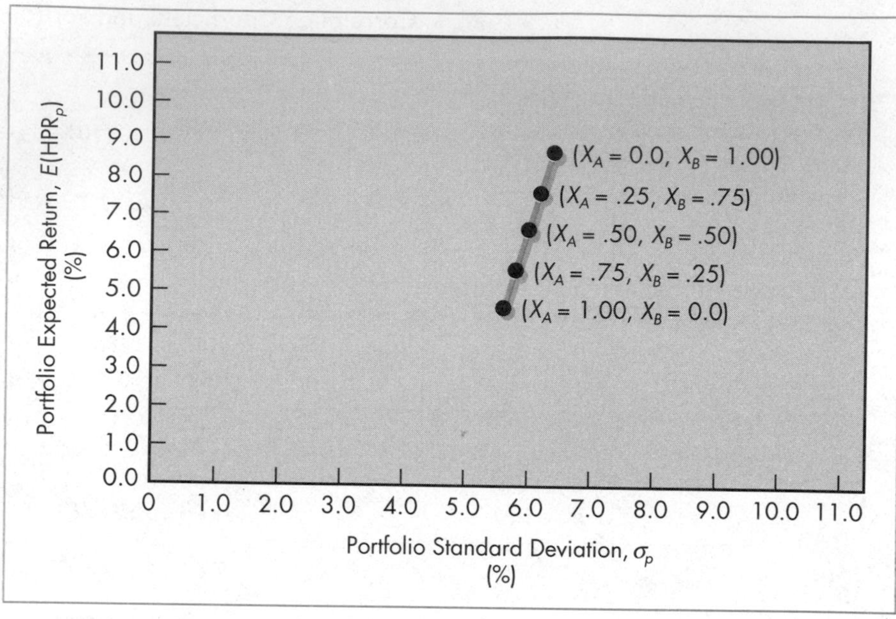

FIGURE 19.4
Plot of Risk and Return for Perfectly Positively Correlated Assets ($\rho = 1.00$)

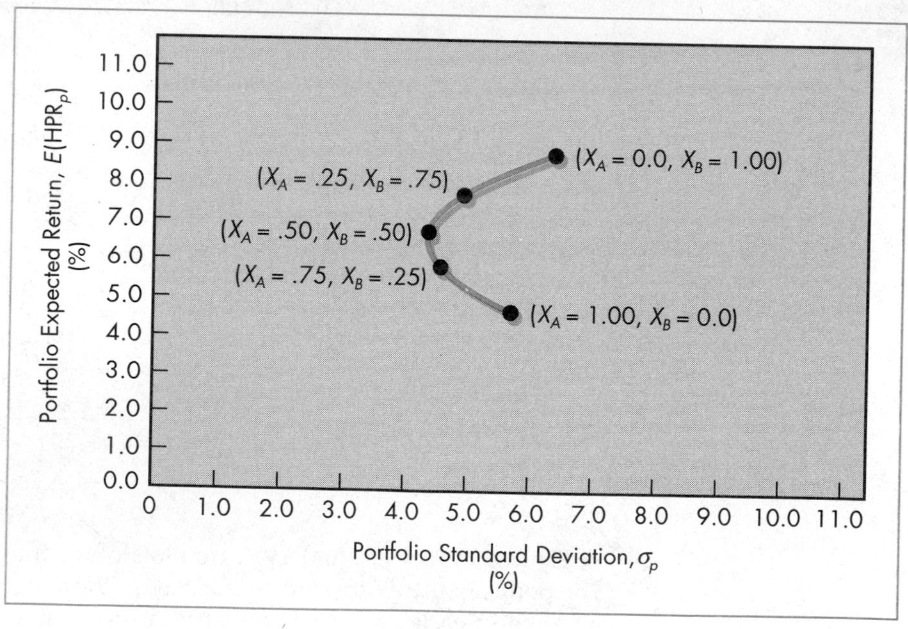

FIGURE 19.5
Plot of Risk and Return for Zero-Correlated Assets ($\rho = 0.00$)

FIGURE 19.6
Plot of Risk and Return for Perfectly Negatively Correlated Assets ($\rho = -1.00$)

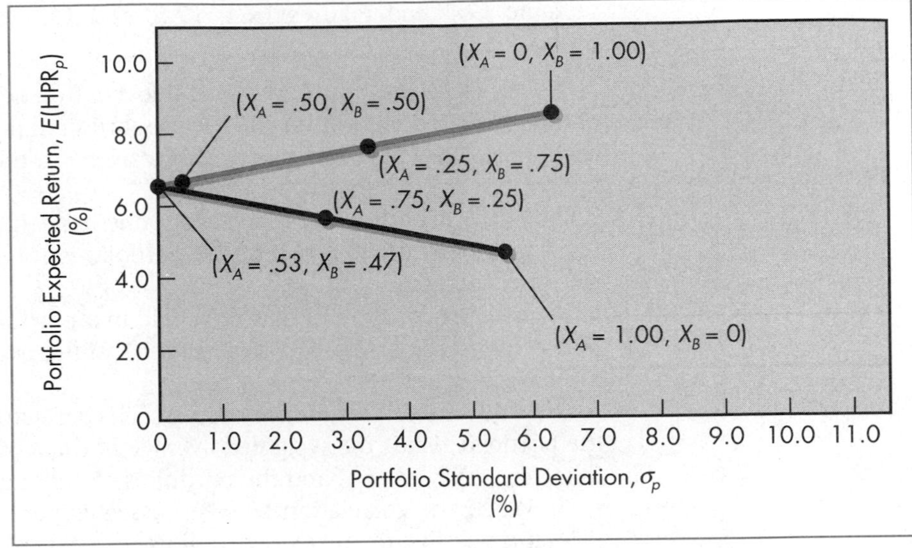

Figure 19.6 contains one more point estimate than was provided in Table 19.3. This portfolio (with $X_A = .53$, $X_B = .47$, and $\rho_{AB} = -1.00$) has an expected return of 6.43 percent and risk of zero.[5]

[5]When the correlation between two assets is -1, it is possible to calculate the asset weights that will produce zero risk ($\sigma_p = 0$). The derivation is based on algebra. Since the sum of the weights is equal to 1, then $X_B = 1 - X_A$. From Equation 19.9, for $n = 2$ and substituting Equation 19.8 for the covariance measure, we know the variance of the portfolio is

$$\begin{aligned}\sigma_p^2 &= X_A^2\sigma_A^2 + (1 - X_A)^2\sigma_B^2 + 2X_A(1 - X_A)\rho_{AB}\sigma_A\sigma_B \\ &= X_A^2\sigma_A^2 + \sigma_B^2 - 2X_A\sigma_B^2 + X_A^2\sigma_B^2 + 2X_A\rho_{AB}\sigma_A\sigma_B - 2X_A^2\rho_{AB}\sigma_A\sigma_B\end{aligned}$$

If $\rho_{AB} = -1$, the equation can be rearranged as

$$\begin{aligned}\sigma_p^2 &= X_A^2(\sigma_A^2 + 2\sigma_A\sigma_B + \sigma_B^2) - 2X_A(\sigma_B^2 + \sigma_A\sigma_B) + \sigma_B^2 \\ &= X_A^2(\sigma_A + \sigma_B)^2 - 2X_A\sigma_B(\sigma_A + \sigma_B) + \sigma_B^2 \\ &= [X_A(\sigma_A + \sigma_B) - \sigma_B]^2 \\ \sigma_p &= X_A(\sigma_A + \sigma_B) - \sigma_B\end{aligned}$$

Since the standard deviation (risk) equals 0, the appropriate weights for the two assets in the portfolio can be estimated as

$$X_A(\sigma_A + \sigma_B) - \sigma_B = 0$$

$$X_A = \frac{\sigma_B}{\sigma_A + \sigma_B} = \frac{6.33\%}{5.62\% + 6.33\%} = .53$$

and

$$X_B = 1 - X_A = \frac{\sigma_A}{\sigma_A + \sigma_B} = \frac{5.62\%}{5.62\% + 6.33\%} = .47$$

Table 19.3 and Figures 19.4, 19.5, and 19.6 allow us to make several observations:

1. The expected return of a portfolio is a function of the expected returns of the assets in the portfolio and the proportion of the portfolio represented by each asset. The correlation between the assets in the portfolio does not affect the expected return of the portfolio.

2. When a portfolio contains only one asset (i.e., $X_A = 100$ percent, or $X_B = 100$ percent), the risk of the portfolio is the standard deviation of the return of the asset.

3. When more than one asset is held in a portfolio, the lower the correlation between the assets, the lower the risk of the portfolio for any given set of asset weights.

4. When the correlation between assets is perfectly positive (i.e., $\rho_{AB} = +1$), the portfolio risk is the weighted average of the risk of the assets in the portfolio ($\sigma_p = \Sigma_{j=1}^{n} X_j \sigma_j$), and the portfolios plot along a straight line.

5. When the correlation between assets is perfectly negative (i.e., $\rho_{AB} = -1$), it is possible to create a portfolio with zero risk.

6. Some portfolios dominate other portfolios (e.g., for a given level of risk, the expected return of one portfolio is greater than the expected return of another portfolio), and the dominant portfolio would be preferred by the investor. For example, in the case where the correlation coefficient equals 0, the risk of a portfolio with asset *A* representing 36 percent of the portfolio and asset *B* the remaining 64 percent is approximately 4.5 percent $\{[(.36)^2(5.62)^2 + (.64)^2(6.33)^2]^{1/2}\}$. This is the same risk level as a portfolio consisting of 75 percent of asset *A* and 25 percent of asset *B* (Table 19.3). However, the portfolio with $X_A = 36$ percent and $X_B = 64$ percent has an expected return of 7.1 percent $[(.36)(4.60) + (.64)(8.50)]$, whereas the portfolio with $X_A = 75$ percent and $X_B = 25$ percent has an expected return of only 5.58 percent. Thus, the portfolio with $X_A = 36$ percent and $X_B = 64$ percent dominates the portfolio with $X_A = 75$ percent and $X_B = 25$ percent.

7. Significant insight can be gained by combining Figures 19.4, 19.5, and 19.6 as shown in Figure 19.7. The straight lines in Figure 19.7 represent the upper and lower limits of risk that can be incurred with portfolios consisting of assets *A* and *B*. The straight line connecting points *A* and *B* (from Figure 19.4) represents the maximum possible level of risk for portfolios composed of assets *A* and *B*. This is the case because the line was generated under the assumption that the correlation coefficient was equal to 1. Under this assumption, the standard deviation of the portfolio is equal to the weighted average of the standard deviation of the two assets. There is no portfolio effect.

On the other hand, the minimum level of risk is represented by the lines from point *A* to 6.43 percent on the Portfolio Expected Return axis and then to point *B* (from Figure 19.6). No portfolio composed of assets *A* and *B* can have less risk than that represented by these line segments because they were generated under the assumption that the correlation coefficient of *A* and *B* was -1. This assumption represents the maximum portfolio effect.

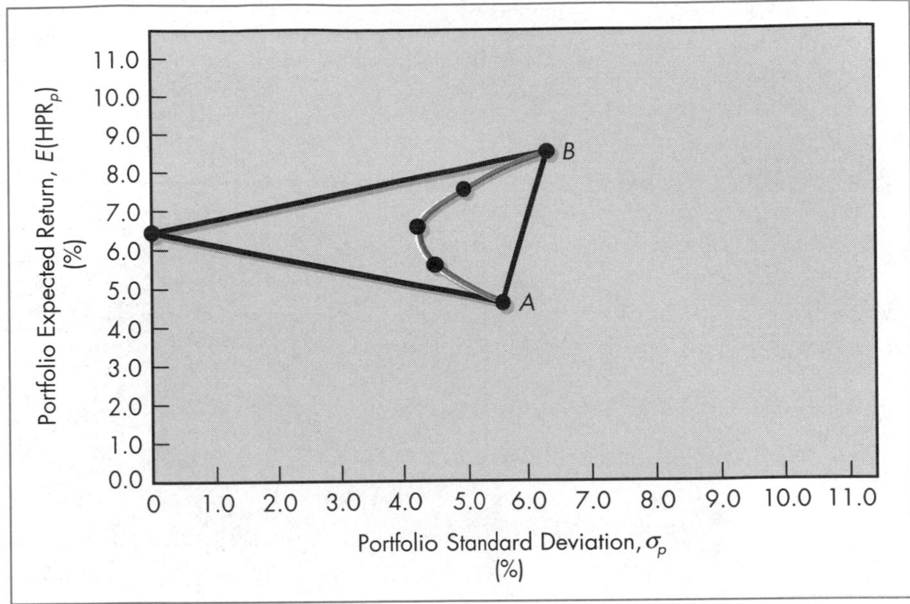

FIGURE 19.7
Minimum and Maximum Levels of Risk Demonstrated by Combining Figures 19.4, 19.5, and 19.6.

The curved line from *A* to *B* (from Figure 19.5) represents one set of possible portfolios. It reflects the risk and return of combining *A* and *B* in varying proportions when the correlation coefficient between *A* and *B* equals 0. If the correlation coefficient was less than 0, the curved line would be to the left of the one shown, and if the correlation coefficient was greater than 0, it would be to the right. The curved line will have the same general shape regardless of the number of assets under consideration since the correlation coefficients between the assets range between +1 and −1. The middle section of the curve will always be *concave* as opposed to the indifference curves discussed earlier, which are *convex*. The importance of these shapes will become apparent as we discuss the concepts of the efficient frontier and the investor's optimal portfolio in the following sections of the chapter.

THE EFFICIENT FRONTIER

To this point we have dealt with portfolios containing only one, two, or three assets. Figures 19.4, 19.5, and 19.6 demonstrated that with only two assets being considered for inclusion in the portfolio, a large number of potential portfolios can be generated by simply varying the proportion of the total portfolio invested in each asset.

If *n* assets are considered (where *n* can take on values of 5, 10, 100, 500, 1,000, and so on), the number of potential portfolios is even larger. If potential portfolios are plotted in risk-return space, as shown by the dots in Figure 19.8, it is apparent that certain portfolios are preferred over others.

FIGURE 19.8
The Attainable Set and Efficient Frontier

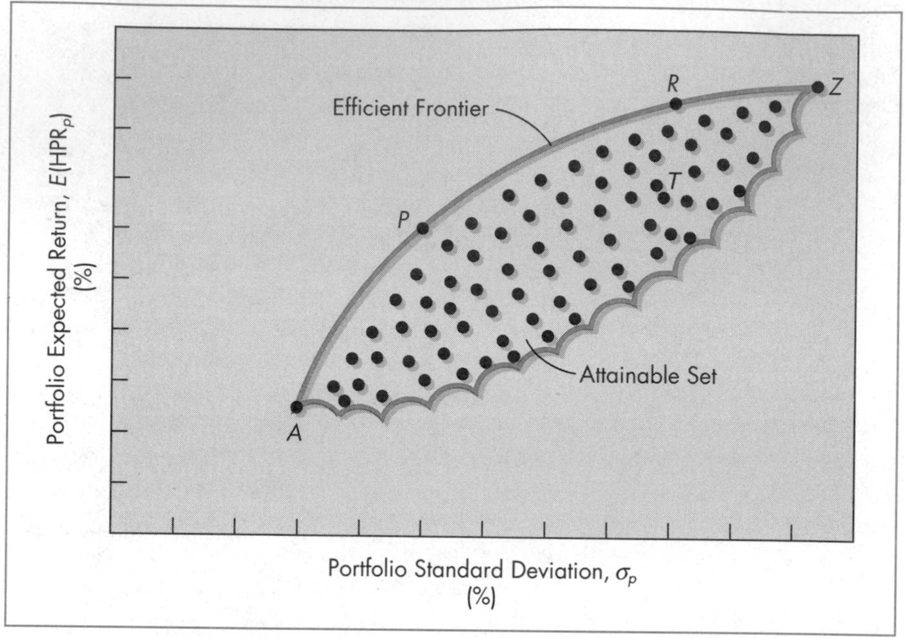

You will recall that we defined a risk-averse investor as one who attempts to maximize expected return for any given level of risk and minimize risk for any given level of expected return. Thus, in Figure 19.8, portfolio R is preferred by risk-averse investors to portfolio T, since at the given level of risk, the expected return for portfolio R is greater than the expected return for portfolio T. Portfolio P is also preferred to portfolio T since portfolios P and T have the same level of expected return but portfolio P has a lower level of risk.

All possible portfolios comprise what is called the **attainable set** of investment opportunities. At any given level of risk (expected return), however, there is one portfolio that provides the highest (lowest) level of expected return (risk). This set of portfolios that dominate all other portfolios in the attainable set is referred to as the **efficient frontier.** With the possible exception of portfolios A and Z, portfolios on the efficient frontier will contain more than one asset, because of the portfolio effect of combining assets with returns that are less than perfectly correlated ($\rho < +1.0$). Note that the shape of the efficient frontier is concave, similar to a portion of the curved line in Figure 19.7.

The attainable set and the efficient frontier shown in Figure 19.8 can be constructed from the assets being analyzed by the investor. Once the investor has determined the expected returns and standard deviations for each of the assets and the correlation coefficients between the assets, then the portfolios on the efficient frontier can be identified. Estimation of the efficient frontier requires quadratic programming that will simultaneously estimate the minimum portfolio risk at each level of expected return. Since the advent of the personal computer and the development of appropriate software, individual investors can undertake this estimation.[6] Software for portfolio analysis, along with other investment analysis programs, is sold commercially by a number of vendors. When a large number of assets are being considered, the computational requirements, even with a computer, are quite demanding.

Construction of the "true" efficient frontier requires that we consider the risk and return statistics for *all* assets. But even if it were possible to get return and risk data for all assets, the information and computation costs would be formidable. Even if the assets to be considered in the estimation of the efficient frontier were limited to common stocks traded in the United States, thousands of issues would be involved, and the information and computation costs would be prohibitive.

Research has shown that when only common stocks are considered as components of portfolios on the efficient frontier, a sample size of several hundred randomly selected securities will provide an estimate of the efficient frontier not significantly different from the frontier obtained by using the entire universe of common stocks.[7] In other words, increasing the number of securities beyond several hundred only marginally improves the expected return at any given level of risk. One reason the necessary number of securities can be limited is that a certain portion of the returns on common stocks is due to the co-movement of their returns with "market forces." The impact of the market on individual security returns is the subject of the next chapter on capital market theory.

THE OPTIMAL PORTFOLIO

Estimation of the efficient frontier still requires the investor to select one of the many portfolios on the efficient frontier. The selection of the appropriate (optimal) portfolio is determined by superimposing the investor's set of indifference curves on the efficient frontier, as shown in Figure 19.9. Recall from the earlier discussion that each investor has a set of indifference curves, and the preferred indifference curve maximizes a particular investor's utility. In Figure 19.9, the point of tangency between indifference curve I_C and the efficient frontier—portfolio S—maximizes the investor's utility. Portfolios on indifference curve I_D would not be selected because investor utility is higher for portfolios on indifference curve I_C than for those on I_D. Portfolios on indifference curves I_A and I_B, which have even higher utility, are not attainable.

[6] The program DOMINANT in the Investment Analysis Software accompanying this text is not a Markowitz-based analysis using quadratic programming. The program simply identifies investments (single securities or portfolios) that dominate other investments, as determined by the risk and return measures of the investments entered as data.

[7] See, for example, Robert A. Olsen, "Sample Size and Markowitz Diversification," *Journal of Portfolio Management* (Fall 1983): 18–22.

FIGURE 19.9
Optimal Portfolio Selection

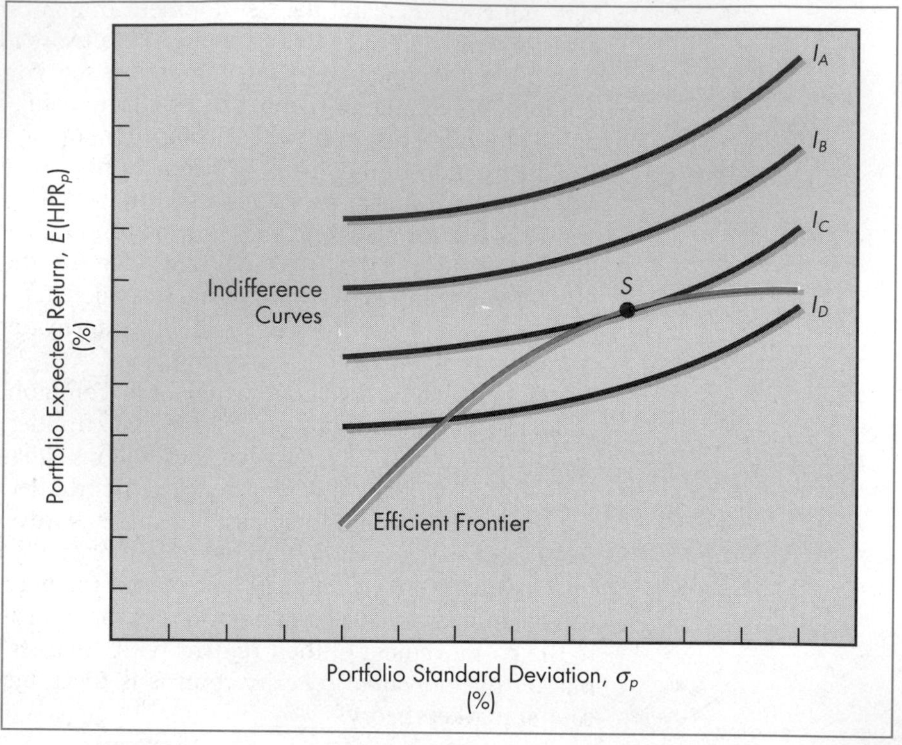

Thus, portfolio S is optimal for an investor with the set of indifference curves shown in Figure 19.9.[8]

Unless their risk-return preferences are identical, investors will select different portfolios on the efficient frontier. A more risk-averse investor than the one whose indifference curves are shown in Figure 19.9 will have an indifference curve with a tangency point to the left of portfolio S on the efficient frontier (i.e., the investor will select a portfolio with lower expected return and risk). An investor with a very high tolerance for risk will have a set of indifference curves that indicate the selection of a portfolio on the efficient frontier to the right of portfolio S. In sum, the selection of the optimal portfolio will depend on the individual investor's risk-return preferences.

[8] Assume investor 2, whose set of indifference curves were shown in Figure 19.2, identified the portfolios on the efficient frontier in Figure 19.8. Then portfolio S would represent the optimal portfolio for investor 2.

EXTENDING PORTFOLIO THEORY

The approach to selecting the optimal portfolio we have just described applies to a specific holding period. That is, the investor makes the investment decision based on a predetermined holding period of a particular length of time. This holding period can be for three months, six months, one year, or longer. Also, the approach has only considered portfolios of risky assets. Suppose that a "riskless" asset exists and that investors can borrow or lend in unlimited amounts at the **risk-free rate (R_f)** represented by this **risk-free asset.** What would be the impact on the efficient frontier and the investor's optimal portfolio? This section will address this question.

• Risk-Free Asset

In order for an asset to be classified as riskless, its future rate of return must be known with certainty. In other words, there is no deviation around the expected return; thus, the standard deviation (σ_f) is equal to 0. The yield on U.S. Treasury bills is often used as a proxy for the risk-free rate. Because of their relatively short maturity and backing by the U.S. government, Treasury bills have relatively stable returns, and the risk of default is nil.

One more element is needed to classify Treasury bills as riskless, however. The length of maturity of the bill must be equal to the holding period of the portfolio. If this is not the case, the investor will face both **interest rate risk** and **reinvestment rate risk.** Interest rate risk, which can also be called price risk, occurs when the length of maturity of the bill is greater than the holding period of the portfolio. Assume that the investor's holding period is six months and Treasury bills with a maturity of one year are purchased. At the end of the six-month holding period, the value of the Treasury bill may be greater or less than anticipated at the time of purchase. If interest rates have risen over the six-month period, the Treasury bill will have a lower value than anticipated. If interest rates have declined, the Treasury bill will have a greater value than anticipated. Thus, the rate of return on the Treasury bill is uncertain, and it cannot be considered a riskless asset.

Reinvestment rate risk occurs when the length of maturity of the Treasury bill is less than the holding period of the portfolio. Again, assume the investor's holding period is six months, but the investor purchases Treasury bills with a maturity of three months. At the end of three months, the investor will have to reinvest the proceeds of the maturing Treasury bills for an additional three months. What rate of return will the investor receive on the Treasury bills for the last three months? The rate could be higher or lower than the original three-month investment. Thus, the investor faces reinvestment rate risk, and the Treasury bill cannot be considered a risk-free asset.

In order to avoid the risks associated with interest rate changes, the maturity of the Treasury bill must be the same as the holding period of the portfolio of risky assets. If the investor's holding period is greater than one year, other

U.S. government securities with corresponding maturity dates, such as Treasury notes and bonds, can be considered proxies for the risk-free asset.

• Risk-Free Lending

The existence of a risk-free asset means that investors can allocate (lend) a portion of their investment wealth to the risk-free asset and the remaining portion to a portfolio on the efficient frontier. In many respects, this resembles the two-asset case examined earlier in the chapter. The expected return on this **lending portfolio** will be the weighted average of the expected returns on the risk-free asset and the portfolio. The weights are the proportions of the investor's wealth invested in each asset. Since we know that the sum of the weights (X_j) must equal 1, the expected return of the portfolio, $E(\text{HPR}_p)$, can be expressed as

$$E(\text{HPR}_p) = \sum_{j=1}^{n} X_j E(\text{HPR}_j) \qquad \textbf{(19.12)}$$
$$= X_f R_f + (1 - X_f) E(\text{HPR}_j)$$

where

X_f = proportion invested in the risk-free asset
R_f = rate of return on the risk-free asset
$E(\text{HPR}_j)$ = expected return of the portfolio on the efficient frontier

The equation for the risk of this two-asset portfolio can be derived starting with Equation 19.11 as follows:

$$\sigma_p = \sqrt{X_A^2\sigma_A^2 + X_B^2\sigma_B^2 + 2X_A X_B \rho_{AB}\sigma_A\sigma_B}$$
$$= \sqrt{X_f^2\sigma_f^2 + (1 - X_f)^2\sigma_j^2 + 2X_f(1 - X_f)\rho_{fj}\sigma_f\sigma_j}$$

Since the variance (σ_f^2) of the risk-free asset is, by definition, 0 and the correlation (and covariance) of returns between the risk-free asset and the portfolio on the efficient frontier (ρ_{fj}) is also 0, then

$$\sigma_p = \sqrt{0 + (1 - X_f)^2\sigma_j^2 + 2X_f(1 - X_f)(0)(0)(\sigma_j)} \qquad \textbf{(19.13)}$$
$$= \sqrt{(1 - X_f)^2\sigma_j^2}$$
$$= (1 - X_f)\sigma_j$$

where σ_j is the standard deviation of the risky portfolio on the efficient frontier.

Figure 19.10 shows several possible portfolios—A, B, C, E, and G—that can be constructed by combining the risk-free asset with a portfolio on the efficient frontier. For example, portfolios B and E are formed by combining the risk-free asset with portfolio H on the efficient frontier. Portfolio B contains a higher proportion of the risk-free asset than does portfolio E.

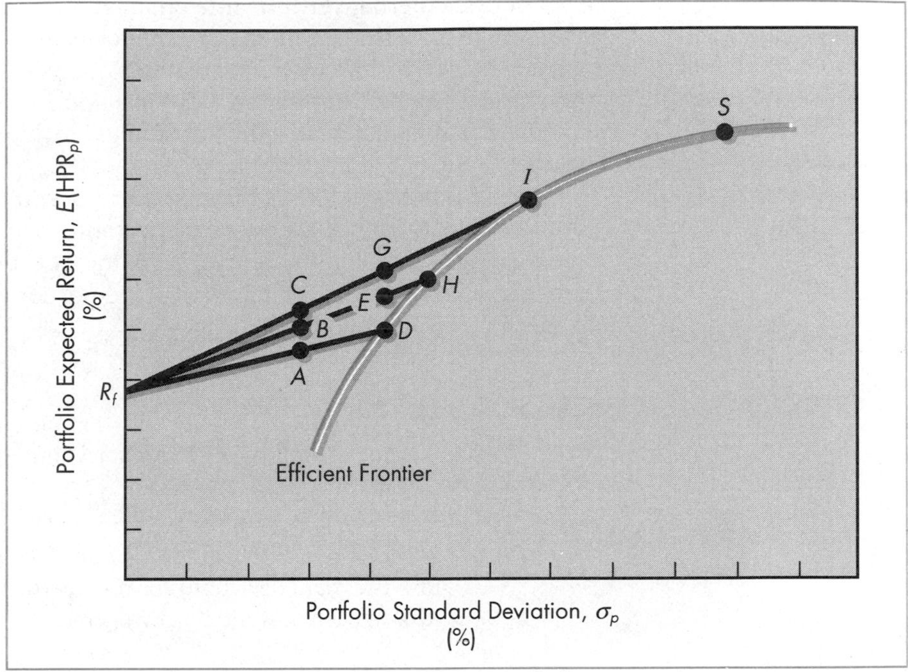

FIGURE 19.10
Portfolios Formed by Combining Portfolios on the Efficient Frontier with the Risk-Free Asset

Equations 19.12 and 19.13 indicate that the portfolio expected return and risk are linear functions of the proportion invested in the risk-free asset (X_f). Thus, as shown in Figure 19.10, portfolios composed of the risk-free asset and a single portfolio on the efficient frontier will plot as a straight line, with the intercept equal to the return on the risk-free asset. The portfolio's expected return and risk will vary directly with the proportion invested in the risk-free asset.

Assuming that investors are risk-averse, then from Figure 19.10, portfolio C is preferred to portfolio B, and portfolio B is preferred to portfolio A. In other words, portfolio C dominates portfolios A and B. Using the same logic, portfolio G dominates portfolios E and D.

The number of lines emanating from R_f to the efficient frontier is limited only by the number of portfolios on the efficient frontier.[9] The risk-return characteristics of these alternative portfolios are a function of the proportion of the portfolio invested in the risk-free asset.

The line emanating from R_f to the efficient frontier with the greatest slope will contain portfolios that have the highest expected return for any given

[9] Many additional portfolios could be constructed by combining the risk-free asset with portfolios in the attainable set. However, since it has been shown that portfolios on the efficient frontier dominate all other portfolios in the attainable set, a risk-averse investor would not consider these alternative portfolios.

level of risk. Alternatively, the line emanating from R_f to the efficient frontier with the greatest slope will contain the lowest risk for any given level of expected return. The line with the greatest slope will have a tangency point with the efficient frontier. In Figure 19.10, it is line R_fI. Every portfolio alternative on line R_fI dominates all other portfolios, including those on the efficient frontier to the left of portfolio I.

Since portfolios on line R_fI dominate all portfolios to the left of portfolio I on the efficient frontier, a new efficient frontier can be constructed with risk-free lending. As shown in Figure 19.10, the new efficient frontier, with risk-free lending, is the R_fI line *and* the curved portion of the old efficient frontier to the right of portfolio I.

TABLE 19.4 • Rates of Return and Risk for Lending and Borrowing Portfolios*

Expected rate of return for risky portfolio I	16%
Risk (standard deviation) for risky portfolio I	5%
Risk-free lending and borrowing rate	7%

I. Rates of Return and Risk for Lending Portfolios

Portfolio	*Proportion invested in the risk-free asset, X_f*	*Portfolio expected return, $E(HPR_p)$*	*Portfolio standard deviation, σ_p*
A	10%	15.1%	4.5%
B	20	14.2	4.0
C	30	13.3	3.5
D	50	11.5	2.5
E	70	9.7	1.5

II. Rates of Return and Risk for Borrowing Portfolios

Portfolio	*Proportion borrowed at the risk-free rate, X_f*	*Portfolio expected return, $E(HPR_p)$*	*Portfolio standard deviation, σ_p*
K	−10%	16.9%	5.5%
L	−20	17.8	6.0
M	−30	18.7	6.5
N	−50	20.5	7.5
O	−70	22.3	8.5

*The rates of return and risk are calculated using Equations 19.12 and 19.13, respectively.

• Risk-Free Borrowing

Earlier it was assumed that investors could lend *or* borrov
Borrowing in this sense is similar to margin trading. T
part of the funds needed to take a position in a security
culation of the expected return and risk of the portfolio with borrowed
is identical to the procedure used in Equations 19.12 and 19.13 for lending portfolios. The only difference is that for **borrowing portfolios,** the proportion invested in the risk-free asset (X_f) will be negative. Since the sum of the weights (X_j) must equal 1, the proportion invested in the risky portfolio must be greater than 1. Table 19.4 provides an illustration of the impact on portfolio expected return and risk for both lending and borrowing portfolios. The table is constructed assuming that I is the risky portfolio and that varying proportions of investable dollars are being invested in the risk-free asset (Part I) or borrowed at the risk-free rate (Part II) to buy more of portfolio I.

Notice in Part I that as the proportion of funds invested in the risk-free asset increases (lending portfolios), the expected return and risk decrease. This is consistent with Figure 19.10. In Part II, the reverse occurs. As more dollars are borrowed at the risk-free rate and invested in risky portfolio I (borrowing portfolios), the expected return and risk increase.

In Figure 19.11, the borrowing portfolios have been added to the lending portfolios in Figure 19.10. Since portfolios on the straight line to the right of portfolio I dominate all portfolios on the curved portion of the efficient frontier to the right of I, the straight line represented by the borrowing portfolios

FIGURE 19.11
The Efficient Frontier with Unlimited Borrowing and Lending at the Risk-Free Rate

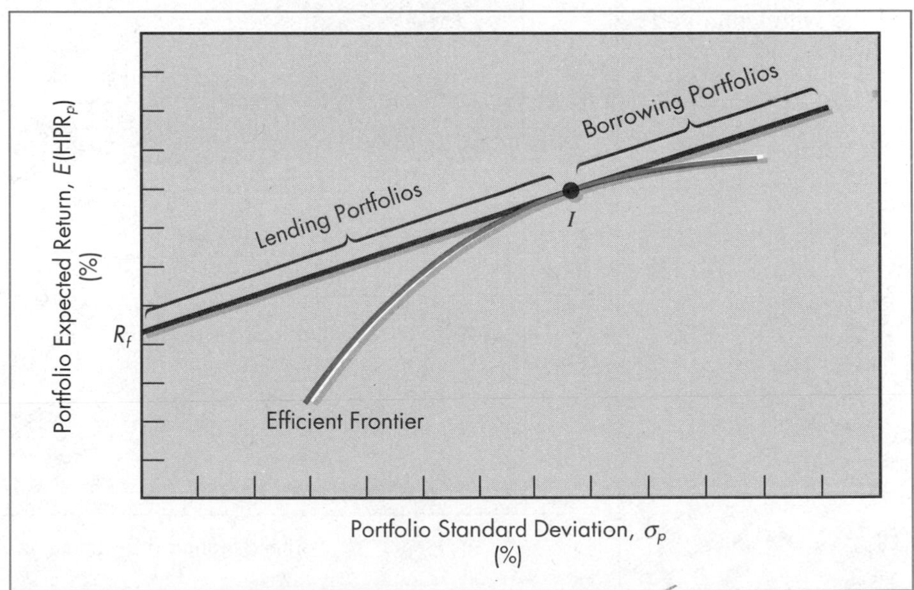

becomes the new efficient frontier to the right of portfolio I. Combining the lending and borrowing portfolios shifts the entire efficient frontier from the curved line to the straight line from R_f through portfolio I.

Figure 19.11 allows us to make several observations:

1. The lending and borrowing portfolios dominate all other portfolios and are thus preferred to all portfolios on the old efficient frontier, except portfolio I.
2. The new efficient frontier is a straight line consisting of various combinations of portfolio I and the risk-free asset.
3. Recall from Figure 19.4 that two assets that are perfectly positively correlated plot as a straight line in risk-return space as the weights of the assets in the portfolios vary. The portfolios on the new efficient frontier consisting of a combination of portfolio I and the risk-free asset are perfectly positively correlated. This is a logical conclusion since, from Equation 19.13, the standard deviation of a portfolio on the new efficient frontier is a function of the volatility of only one portfolio, portfolio I.

• The New Optimal Portfolio

By combining the new, linear efficient frontier with the investor's set of indifference curves, a new optimal portfolio can be identified. In Figure 19.12,

FIGURE 19.12
The New Optimal Portfolio with Unlimited Borrowing and Lending

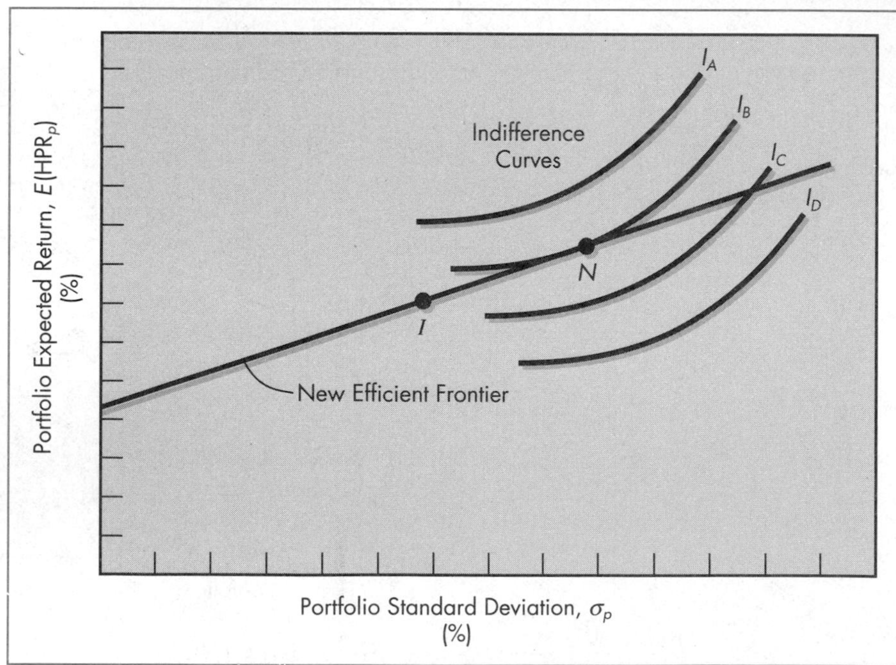

borrowing portfolio N is the investor's optimal portfolio
tainable indifference curve is tangent to the new efficient
On the other hand, if an investor is more risk-averse, th
lower and to the left of those shown in the figure. In th
averse investor would have an optimal portfolio with a
and risk than portfolio N.

SUMMARY

This chapter has presented portfolio theory and its extension created by the assumption of a risk-free asset. The theory is concerned with risk-averse investors; that is, investors who desire the highest level of expected return for

• CONCEPT APPLICATIONS

Investment Concept	Concept Application
Indifference curve	Each investor's attitude toward risk and return can be represented by a set of indifference curves. In order to achieve maximum utility, the investor should select the portfolio lying on the highest possible indifference curve.
Portfolio expected return and risk	Estimates of expected return and risk are important inputs in portfolio selection. Expected return can be estimated as the weighted average of the expected returns of the individual assets. In addition to the risks of the individual assets, portfolio risk calculation must take into consideration the degree to which the returns of the assets covary or move together.
Dominance principle	Risk-averse investors are assumed to adhere to the dominance principle. That is, for any given level of risk, investors will prefer a portfolio with a higher expected return to a portfolio with a lower expected return; for portfolios with the same expected return, investors prefer lower to higher risk.
Markowitz efficient frontier	All possible portfolios comprise the attainable set. According to the dominance principle, there is a set of portfolios that is preferred to all others, and this set of portfolios lies on the concave, Markowitz efficient frontier. The computational requirements for identifying the "true" Markowitz efficient frontier are significant. The investor's optimal portfolio is the point of tangency between the investor's highest indifference curve and the Markowitz efficient frontier.
Linear efficient frontier	By introducing the concept of a risk-free asset and assuming the ability to borrow and lend at this rate, the linear efficient frontier dominates the Markowitz efficient frontier. As will be shown in Chapter 20, the linear efficient frontier reduces the investor's computational requirements. The optimal portfolio is the point of tangency between the investor's highest indifference curve and the linear efficient frontier.

any given level of risk and the lowest level of risk for any given level of expected return.

Through an examination of portfolio selection as prescribed by Markowitz, the concave efficient frontier was developed. Portfolios on the efficient frontier dominate all other assets or portfolios in the attainable set. Thus, risk-averse investors will prefer the portfolios on the efficient frontier to all other investment opportunities. By combining the investor's risk and return preferences (indifference curves) with the efficient frontier, the investor's optimal portfolio can be identified.

Introducing borrowing and lending at the risk-free rate creates a second, linear efficient frontier that dominates the original, concave efficient frontier. The linear efficient frontier consists of some combination of a risky portfolio on the concave efficient frontier and the risk-free asset. The risky portfolio is the portfolio that lies on a point of tangency of a line emanating from the risk-free return to the concave efficient frontier.

Given the composition of portfolios on the linear efficient frontier, it can be shown that these portfolios are perfectly positively correlated with each other. By combining this efficient frontier with an investor's set of indifference curves, the investor's optimal portfolio can be selected.

Investors should only be interested in investing in assets and portfolios that lie on the "true" efficient frontier. However, most assets (and portfolios) do not lie on this efficient frontier. In the next chapter, we will introduce *capital market theory* and *arbitrage pricing theory* and examine their applications for portfolio construction as well as individual asset valuation.

• KEY TERMS

Attainable set
Borrowing portfolio
Correlation coefficient
Covariance
Dominance principle
Efficient frontier
Efficient portfolio
Indifference curve
Interest rate risk
Lending portfolio
Optimal portfolio
Portfolio effect
Portfolio return
Portfolio risk
Reinvestment rate risk
Risk-averse investor
Risk-free asset
Risk-free rate (R_f)
"Risk-neutral"
"Risk-taker"
Utility

• QUESTIONS

1. From an investment perspective, explain what is meant by the term "risk aversion."

2. Figure 19.1 shows four indifference curves. Match each of the following individuals with what might be their appropriate indifference curve and explain your selection.
   a. Retired college professor, 65 years old, living on Social Security and income from the college's retirement plan.
   b. Young professional, unmarried and living in an apartment.
   c. Middle-aged executive with a spouse and two high-school-age children.
   d. Young executive with a working spouse and no children.
3. Define what is meant by the "dominance principle," and explain the role of this principle in portfolio theory.
4. Explain how a portfolio's return is calculated from the assets' returns. How are the weights assigned to the assets in the portfolio?
5. What are the dangers associated with using historical return variability to make estimates of future risk?
6. Describe what is meant by the "portfolio effect." Why is this concept important in measuring portfolio risk?
7. Interpret a correlation coefficient of +1, 0, and −1.
8. Explain how it is possible for the risk of a portfolio, as measured by its standard deviation, to be less than the standard deviation of any of the assets in the portfolio.
9. Without considering a risk-free asset, the shape of the efficient frontier is concave. Explain why this is so.
10. What are the characteristics of assets that lie on the Markowitz efficient frontier? What is the difference between the efficient frontier and the attainable set of investment opportunities? What role does the dominance principle play in this difference?
11. Would two risk-averse investors necessarily select the same optimal portfolio? Why or why not?
12. What role does the individual's set of indifference curves play in the selection of the optimal portfolio?
13. What is meant by a risk-free asset? What are its characteristics?
14. Why is it important for the maturity date of the risk-free asset to correspond to the investor's holding period?
15. Explain the role of the risk-free asset in the construction of the linear efficient frontier.
16. Explain what is meant by interest rate risk and reinvestment rate risk.
17. How are borrowing and lending portfolios created? Explain why a borrowing portfolio will be more risky than a lending portfolio.
18. Compare and contrast the linear efficient frontier and the Markowitz efficient frontier. What portfolio will lie on both efficient frontiers?

• KEY TO THE INVESTMENT ANALYSIS SOFTWARE

Calculation	Appendix A-1 Page Reference	Access Procedure
Correlation coefficient	A-7	BEGIN, STATISTICAL, CORR
Covariance	A-7	BEGIN, STATISTICAL, CORR
Dominant portfolios	A-13	BEGIN, CAPITAL, DOMINANT
Holding period return	A-8	BEGIN, STATISTICAL, HPR
Variance	A-7	BEGIN, STATISTICAL, DESCRIP or DISCREET
Standard deviation	A-7	BEGIN, STATISTICAL, DESCRIP or DISCREET
Weighted average portfolio return	A-7	BEGIN, STATISTICAL, PORT

• PROBLEMS

1. An investor purchased a share of common stock for $45 one year ago. During the year, the stock paid a cash dividend of $2.25. The stock is currently selling for $51.25. What is the investor's holding period return?

2. You are anticipating investing 60 percent of your investable funds equally in three common stocks. The remaining 40 percent of your funds will remain in Treasury bills earning 6 percent interest. If the expected returns on the three stocks are 12 percent, 10 percent, and 15 percent, respectively, what is the expected return for your portfolio?

Use the following quarterly holding period returns for Problems 3 through 7.

	Stock 1	*Stock 2*	*Stock 3*
1986			
1	7.2%	0.6%	16.2%
2	12.9	6.0	−12.7
3	7.4	0.6	16.4
4	−2.1	9.7	−11.5
1987			
1	4.0	−18.0	−10.7
2	6.9	6.1	−0.6
3	−8.4	−1.8	3.4
4	1.3	6.5	−3.4

(continued)

	Stock 1	*Stock 2*	*Stock 3*
1988			
1	−5.6	−10.3	−8.8
2	0.1	12.0	26.9
3	20.2	0.8	6.8
4	−3.7	−0.3	9.2
1989			
1	9.2	−14.6	−7.4
2	3.8	1.2	2.8
3	1.2	3.2	−8.7
4	5.1	−0.7	−8.8
1990			
1	7.2	−8.2	0.4
2	16.7	23.0	8.2
3	7.4	1.7	13.6
4	17.2	−0.9	0.1

3. Calculate the mean return and standard deviation for the three stocks.

4. Calculate the correlation coefficients for stocks 1 and 2, 1 and 3, and 2 and 3.

5. Assume that you invested 50 percent of your investable funds in stock 1 and 50 percent in stock 2. Using the historical information, what are the expected quarterly return and risk (standard deviation) of your portfolio? How does the risk of your portfolio compare with the individual risks of stocks 1 and 2?

6. Assuming $X_1 = .33$, $X_2 = .33$, and $X_3 = .34$, what are the expected quarterly return and risk of the portfolio? How do the expected return and risk of this portfolio compare with these same measures for the two-asset portfolios calculated in Problem 5? Explain the differences.

7. Suppose that a risk-free asset exists with a quarterly rate of return of 2 percent.

a. Calculate the risk and expected return of a portfolio consisting of 10 percent of the risk-free asset and 90 percent of the portfolio constructed in Problem 6.

b. Calculate the risk and expected return of a portfolio consisting of 20 percent of the risk-free asset and 80 percent of the portfolio constructed in Problem 6.

c. Calculate the risk and expected return of a portfolio consisting of 70 percent of the risk-free asset and 30 percent of the portfolio constructed in Problem 6.

d. Graph in risk-return space the results of your calculations in parts (a), (b), and (c). Interpret the graph.

8. Given the following information for an individual investor:

Portfolio	*Expected return*	*Standard deviation*	*Investor utility*
A	6%	2%	5
B	7	5	5
C	10	10	5
D	15	15	5
E	12	2	10
F	13	5	10
G	16	10	10
H	21	15	10
I	18	2	15
J	19	5	15
K	22	10	15
L	27	15	15

a. Graph the investor's indifference curves.

b. Would you classify this investor as risk-averse, "risk-neutral," or "risk-taker"? Explain your answer.

9. Given the following information about assets G and H:

$$\overline{HPR}_G = 6.0\% \qquad \sigma_G = 3.0\%$$
$$\overline{HPR}_H = 9.0\% \qquad \sigma_H = 5.0\%$$
$$\rho_{GH} = -.2$$

a. Plot in risk-return space the portfolios with the following proportions of G and H.

	X_G	X_H
Portfolio A	100%	0%
Portfolio B	20	80
Portfolio C	50	50
Portfolio D	80	20
Portfolio E	0	100

b. Is it possible to connect the portfolios plotted in part (a) with a line through the portfolios? Why or why not?

c. Provide an explanation for the shape of the line connecting the portfolios.

10. (Library project) Calculate the quarterly holding period returns from 1986 through 1990 for the following common stocks: American Express (stock 1), Procter & Gamble (stock 2), and Westinghouse (stock 3). Answer Problems 3 through 7 above, based on the quarterly holding period returns for these three stocks.

• REFERENCES

Babcock, Guilford C. "The Roots of Risk and Return." *Financial Analysts Journal* (January-February 1980): 56–63.

Bernstein, Peter L. "Markowitz Marked To Market." *Financial Analysts Journal* (January-February 1983): 18–22.

Blume, Marshall. "On the Assessment of Risk." *Journal of Finance* (March 1971): 1–10.

Brennan, Peter J. "Portfolio Management: Software Choices Rise to the Surface." *Wall Street Computer Review* (March 1990): 24–30, 78.

Burgess, Richard C., and Roger P. Bey. "Optimal Portfolios: Markowitz Full Covariance versus Simple Selection Rules." *Journal of Financial Research* (Summer 1988): 153–63.

Chen, Son-Nan. "Simple Optimal Asset Allocation under Uncertainty." *Journal of Portfolio Management* (Summer 1987): 69–76.

Hudson-Wilson, Susan. "New Trends in Portfolio Theory." *Journal of Property Management* (May-June 1990): 57–58.

Irwin, Scott H. "Diversification Dampens Volatility to Your 'Satisfaction' Level." *Futures: The Magazine of Commodities and Options* (April 1987): 45–47.

Jenkins, James W. "Allocating Assets: A New Look at Principles and Guidelines." *Journal of Financial Planning* (October 1989): 201–10.

Markowitz, Harry M. "Portfolio Selection." *Journal of Finance* (March 1952): 77–91.

———. *Portfolio Selection.* New York: John Wiley & Sons, 1959.

Michaud, Richard O. "The Markowitz Optimization Enigma: Is 'Optimized' Optimal?" *Financial Analysts Journal* (January-February 1989): 31–42.

Schmerken, Ivy. "Optimization Package Draws on Modern Portfolio Theory." *Wall Street Computer Review* (January 1987): 8–14.

Tobin, James. "Liquidity Preference as Behavior towards Risk." *Review of Economic Studies* (February 1958): 65–86.

CHAPTER 20

Capital Market and Arbitrage Pricing Theories

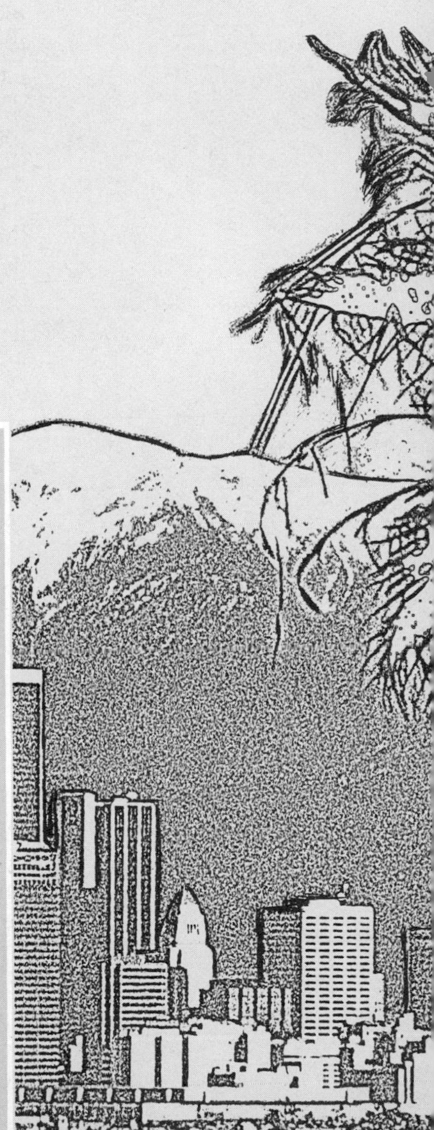

The knowledge-level objectives of this chapter should enable the student to:

- Recognize that even though the capital asset pricing model has a number of seemingly restrictive assumptions, these assumptions do not necessarily invalidate its usefulness in describing the asset pricing process.
- Distinguish between risk that is rewardable (systematic risk) and nonrewardable (unsystematic risk).
- Recognize the importance of diversification in portfolio construction.
- Explain why only perfectly diversified portfolios are on the capital market line whereas all assets and portfolios are on the security market line.
- Define the meaning of beta and describe its role in determining the expected return of an asset.
- Compare and contrast the capital asset pricing model and the arbitrage pricing theory.

INTRODUCTION

In Chapter 19 we examined portfolio risk and return and established that rational investors should be interested in investing only in portfolios that lie on the efficient frontier. Using the original approach suggested by Markowitz, a concave efficient frontier was derived from which the investor selected the optimal portfolio. This optimal portfolio was based on the risk and return preferences reflected by the investor's set of indifference curves.

Introducing the concepts of the risk-free asset and lending and borrowing portfolios allowed us to extend portfolio theory. As a result, the efficient frontier became linear as opposed to concave. The optimal portfolio then became the point of tangency of one of the investor's indifference curves with the linear efficient frontier.

To this point we have been considering the optimizing decisions of individual investors. Suppose *all* investors operate in this manner. What will be the implications for the pricing for all assets? **Capital market theory** provides us with a framework for determining these implications. Whereas portfolio theory deals with the selection of optimal portfolios, capital market theory deals with an **equilibrium** model of asset prices. Specifically, capital market theory postulates the ex-ante risk-return relationship of individual assets as well as portfolios under equilibrium conditions.

An example may help illustrate these pricing implications. In Chapter 14, we presented various techniques for valuing common stock. One basic technique is the dividend discount model:

$$V_0 = \frac{D_1}{(1 + K)^1} + \frac{D_2}{(1 + K)^2} + \frac{D_3}{(1 + K)^3} + \cdots + \frac{D_\infty}{(1 + K)^\infty} \quad \textbf{(20.1)}$$

where

V_0 = intrinsic value of stock today or at time period 0
D_t = dividends per share in period t
K = investor's required rate of return

Using capital market theory, the investor can estimate the required rate of return (K) for the stock. The intrinsic value of the stock (V_0) is inversely related to K. The higher K is, other things remaining unchanged, the lower V_0. Thus, capital market theory has pricing implications for common stocks, which helps explain why its derivative returns model is called the **capital asset pricing model (CAPM).**

Like capital market theory, the **arbitrage pricing theory (APT)** is an equilibrium theory of expected return. Whereas CAPM traditionally uses one systematic factor—the relationship of an asset's return to the return of the **market portfolio**—to estimate the asset's expected return, the central thesis of the APT is that more than one systematic factor may affect the long-term average returns on financial assets. Since the CAPM uses one factor and the

APT uses one or more factors, CAPM can be seen as a special case of the APT.

ASSUMPTIONS OF THE CAPITAL ASSET PRICING MODEL

Capital market theory (CMT) uses portfolio theory as its starting point; thus, the assumptions underlying portfolio theory also pertain to the CAPM. The additional assumptions underlying CMT and the CAPM appear less realistic than the portfolio theory assumptions. The impact of relaxing these assumptions on CMT is discussed in the appendix to this chapter. The assumptions of CMT are as follows:

1. All investors are risk-averse. Thus, all investors seek to be on the efficient frontier.
2. There are no constraints on the amount of money that can be borrowed or lent. Borrowing and lending occur at the identical risk-free rate, R_f.
3. All investors have identical beliefs about the expected returns and risks of assets and portfolios; that is, all investors have homogeneous expectations.
4. All investors have a common investment horizon, whether it be one month, three months, one year, or whatever.
5. All investments are infinitely divisible and marketable; that is, it is possible to buy or sell any portion of an asset or portfolio.
6. Taxes and transaction costs do not exist. That is, there are no tax effects, costs of acquiring information, or transaction costs associated with buying or selling securities. These are often referred to as perfect market assumptions. Markets are assumed to be competitive; therefore, the same investment opportunities are available to all investors.
7. There are no unanticipated changes in inflation or interest rates.
8. The capital markets are in a state of equilibrium or striving toward equilibrium. There are no underpriced or overpriced securities; if underpricing or overpricing exists, the prices will move to correct this disequilibrium situation.

THE CAPITAL MARKET LINE

Recall from Chapter 19 that the introduction of a risk-free asset and lending and borrowing portfolios allows us to derive a linear efficient frontier that is tangent to the curved, Markowitz efficient frontier. As Equation 19.12 showed, the expected return of a portfolio on the linear efficient frontier is equal to

$$E(\text{HPR}_p) = \sum_{j=1}^{n} X_j E(\text{HPR}_j)$$
$$= X_f R_f + (1 - X_f) E(\text{HPR}_j)$$

where

X_f = proportion invested in the risk-free asset
R_f = rate of return on the risk-free asset
$E(\text{HPR}_j)$ = expected return of the tangent portfolio on the efficient frontier

Similarly, Equation 19.13 showed that the risk of the portfolio on the linear efficient frontier is equal to

$$\sigma_p = \sqrt{(1 - X_f)^2 \sigma_j^2}$$
$$= (1 - X_f)\sigma_j$$

where σ_j is the standard deviation of the tangent portfolio.

Figure 20.1 shows the linear efficient frontier for an investor. Based on the risky assets being considered by the investor, portfolio I is the optimal risky portfolio. The investor indicates where he or she wishes to be on the efficient frontier by the amount of lending or borrowing undertaken at the risk-free rate. In effect, the selection of a risk level (amount of lending or borrowing) is separated from the problem of choosing risky assets to be included in the portfolio. This important distinction is known as the **separation theorem.**[1]

[1] James Tobin, "Liquidity Preference as Behavior towards Risk," *Review of Economic Studies* (February 1958): 65–86.

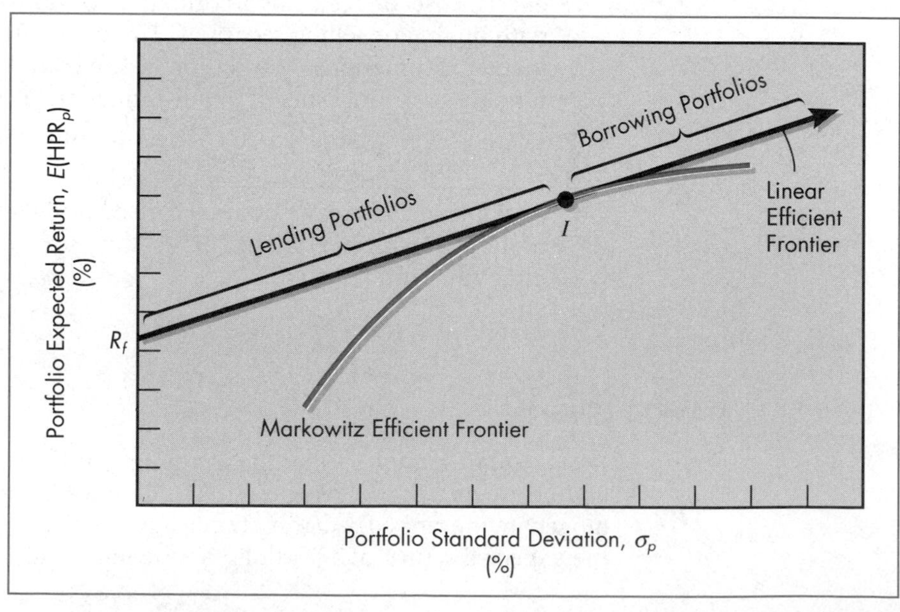

FIGURE 20.1
Portfolios Formed by Combining Portfolios on the Investor's Efficient Frontier with the Risk-Free Asset

Given the assumptions of CMT (particularly assumption 3 about homogeneous expectations), every investor will choose the same tangent portfolio of risky assets. If the investment holdings of all investors willing to face some level of risk contain the same risky portfolio, then this portfolio must be very large and consist of all risky assets, including domestic and international financial securities, precious metals, real estate, and collectibles. Given that the capital markets are in equilibrium (assumption 8), this common, risky portfolio is constructed in such a way that each risky asset is represented in the portfolio in proportion to its value relative to the value of all risky assets:

$$X_j = \frac{\text{total value of risky asset } j}{\text{total value of all risky assets}} \tag{20.2}$$

This portfolio (M) is called the *market portfolio.*[2] Individual risky portfolios—for example, portfolio I referred to earlier—are no longer on the efficient frontier and will not be selected by investors. The new efficient frontier with portfolio M is shown in Figure 20.2. This new efficient frontier is known as the **capital market line (CML).** As before, investors wishing to face less risk will combine an investment in portfolio M with an investment in the risk-free asset. Investors willing to face higher risk than that offered by portfolio M will borrow at the risk-free rate and will buy portfolio M with their investable funds as well as with funds borrowed at the risk-free rate.

[2] Eugene F. Fama, "Risk, Return and Equilibrium: Some Clarifying Comments," *Journal of Finance* (March 1968): 32–33.

FIGURE 20.2
The Capital Market Line with Unlimited Borrowing and Lending at the Risk-Free Rate

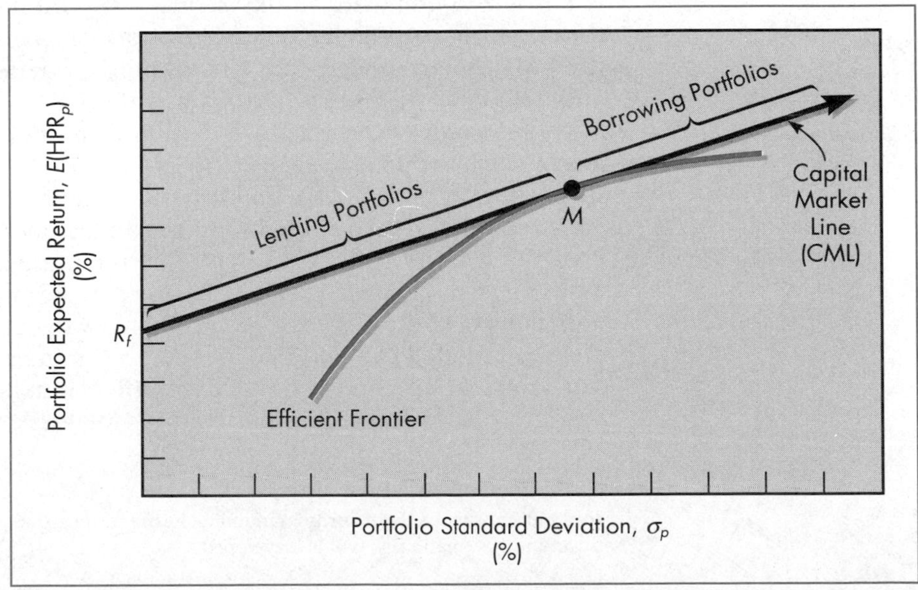

The separation theorem allows for a distinction to be drawn between the traditional technique of portfolio selection and the technique suggested by capital market theory. Traditionally, risky portfolios were "customized" for the investor based on the investor's risk-return preferences. A highly risk-averse investor would have a portfolio that would reflect his or her level of risk aversion. For example, the common stock portion of the portfolio might consist of only blue-chip stocks. The investor with less risk aversion would have common stocks of higher-risk companies in the portfolio. With CMT, all risk-seeking investors hold the same risky portfolio, portfolio M, and adjust for risk through lending and borrowing at the risk-free rate.

MARKET PORTFOLIO RISK

Since the market portfolio contains all risky assets in proportion to their market value, it is, by definition, a perfectly diversified portfolio. The market portfolio (or any of the portfolios on the CML) is, therefore, subject only to **systematic** or **nondiversifiable risk.** The volatility of the market portfolio is due to macroeconomic factors that affect all risky assets (e.g., changes in expected rates of inflation, interest rates, and the like) and not to company- or industry-specific factors (i.e., a change in sales expectations for a particular product, pollution laws, and the like). Volatility in returns created by unique company- or industry-specific factors is called **unsystematic** or **diversifiable risk;** this risk can be diversified away by adding risky assets to a portfolio.[3]

A portfolio's (or a single asset's) total risk is equal to the sum of its systematic risk and unsystematic risk. In the case of the market portfolio, there is no unsystematic or diversifiable risk, and total risk equals systematic risk. Since it is possible to eliminate all unsystematic risk through perfect diversification, the capital markets do not reward investors for facing unsystematic risk. Thus, the CML shown in Figure 20.2 holds only for perfectly diversified portfolios and not for portfolios that have diversifiable or unsystematic risk.

To this point, we have defined the market portfolio as consisting of all risky assets, combined in proportion to their market value, but realistic measures of such a market portfolio are impractical to estimate. Therefore, proxies for the market portfolio, such as the Dow Jones Industrial Average or the Standard & Poor's Composite 500 Stocks Index, are often used. When these proxies are used, the market portfolio can be regarded as a composite of common stocks.

A number of studies have been conducted to determine how many stocks must be included in a portfolio in order to eliminate diversifiable risk. That is, using random selection or **naïve diversification,** how many stocks, on average, must be included in a portfolio for total risk to equal systematic risk?

[3] In the discussion of the security market line in the next section, the actual measures of systematic and unsystematic risk will be developed.

FIGURE 20.3
Naïve Diversification and Portfolio Unsystematic Risk

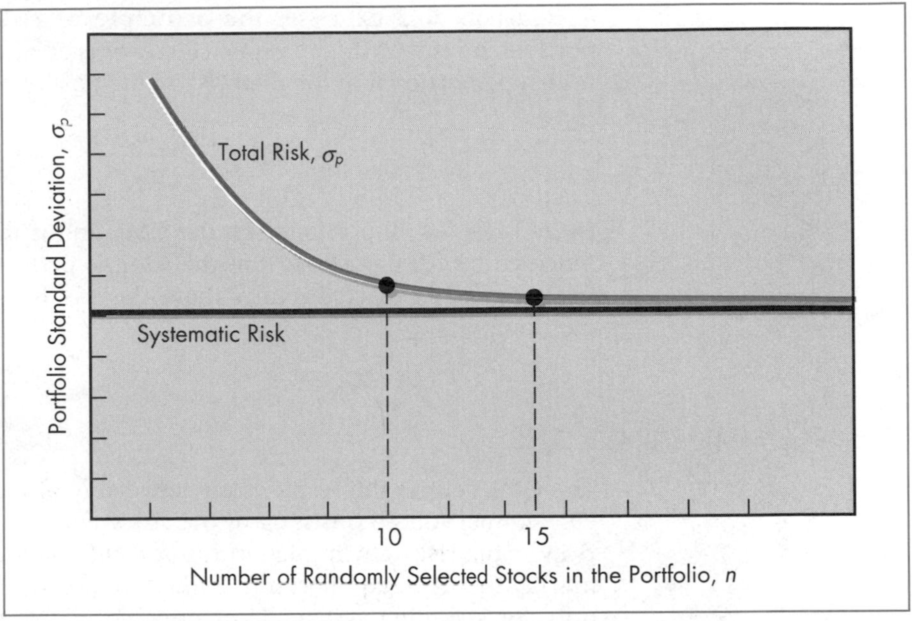

Studies have shown that between 10 to 15 stocks will remove most of the unsystematic or diversifiable risk of the portfolio and that additional stocks beyond this number only marginally reduce the unsystematic risk of the portfolio. Figure 20.3 illustrates the impact of naïvely diversifying a portfolio by adding randomly selected securities. As Figure 20.3 illustrates, after about 10 stocks, the impact of additional stocks in reducing total risk to the systematic level is quite small.

• The Principle of Risk Compensation

In Figure 20.2, the CML goes through the point of the market portfolio's expected return, $E(R_M)$, and risk, σ_M, and the intercept of the CML is the risk-free rate, R_f. The equation for the CML can thus be expressed as

$$E(R_p) = R_f + \left[\frac{E(R_M) - R_f}{\sigma_M}\right]\sigma_p \qquad \textbf{(20.3)}$$

where $E(R_p)$ and σ_p are the expected return and standard deviation of a portfolio on the CML, respectively. Given that the capital markets are in equilibrium or striving toward equilibrium, the expected return can be considered the return investors *require*. In order to make this distinction, expected return required by investors will now be expressed as $E(R)$.

Equation 20.3 expresses the **principle of risk compensation.**[4] For a portfolio on the CML, the expected return is equal to the risk-free rate plus a return proportional to the total risk of the portfolio. The slope of the CML

$$\frac{E(R_M) - R_f}{\sigma_M}$$

is the same for all portfolios on the CML and is the **market price of risk.** Since each of the portfolios on the CML is perfectly diversified, these portfolios have an expected return above the risk-free rate proportional to their own total risk.

THE SECURITY MARKET LINE

The CML defines the relationship between total risk and expected return for efficient portfolios consisting of the risk-free asset and the market portfolio. How is the risk-return relationship for *individual* assets defined in a capital market that is in equilibrium? Earlier we noted that investors are rewarded only for assuming systematic or nondiversifiable risk. This section will examine the relationship between an asset's systematic risk and the expected rate of return.

• Systematic and Unsystematic Risk

Recall from Equation 19.9 that the risk of a portfolio is a function of the covariance of the individual assets in the portfolio or

$$\sigma_p^2 = \sum_{i=1}^{n} \sum_{j=1}^{n} X_i X_j \mathrm{Cov}_{ij}$$

The higher the covariance between the assets, the higher the risk. From CMT, we know that the investment holdings of all investors willing to face some level of risk will contain some proportion of the market portfolio. Individual assets or portfolios that have a high covariance of returns with the market portfolio will not significantly reduce the risk of the portfolio; thus, their prices will reflect this lack of popularity. Since the income-generating ability of these assets is unaffected by their covariance with the market portfolio, the lower their prices, the higher their expected returns. The opposite relationship will exist for assets with low covariances of returns with the market portfolio. They will be actively sought by investors, with resultant price increases and lower expected returns.

Following this line of reasoning, the relationship between the expected (re-

4 For an excellent discussion of this principle, see Oldrich A. Vasicek and John A. McQuown, "The Efficient Market Model," *Financial Analysts Journal* (September-October 1972): 71–84.

quired) rate of return for *any* asset or portfolio, $E(R_j)$, and its covariance with the market portfolio can be expressed as

$$E(R_j) = R_f + (P)\text{Cov}_{jM} \tag{20.4}$$

where

Cov_{jM} = covariance of the asset or portfolio j with the market portfolio
P = constant of proportionality

Since Equation 20.4 holds for any asset or portfolio of assets, the expected return of the market portfolio, $E(R_M)$, is

$$E(R_M) = R_f + (P)\text{Cov}_{MM}$$

The covariance of any asset's return with itself is the variance of the asset's return; thus, the expected return of the market portfolio is

$$E(R_M) = R_f + (P)\sigma_M^2 \tag{20.5}$$

Solving for P in Equation 20.5 $\{P = [E(R_M) - R_f]/\sigma_M^2\}$ and substituting this expression for P in Equation 20.4 allows us to express the expected return for any asset or portfolio as

$$E(R_j) = R_f + \left[\frac{E(R_M) - R_f}{\sigma_M^2}\right]\text{Cov}_{jM} \tag{20.6}$$

$$= R_f + \left[\frac{E(R_M) - R_f}{\sigma_M}\right]\left[\frac{\text{Cov}_{jM}}{\sigma_M}\right] \tag{20.7}$$

Comparing Equation 20.7, which holds for any asset or portfolio, with Equation 20.3, which holds for perfectly diversified portfolios on the CML, illustrates that investors are compensated only for the covariance of the return of an asset with the return of the market portfolio. In order for an asset to lie on the CML, the total risk of the asset (σ_j) must equal its systematic risk, or the risk due to its covariance with the market portfolio.

Systematic risk of asset j is defined as Cov_{jM}/σ_M. Assets with systematic risk less than total risk will fall below the CML, and only a portion of their risk is "rewarded." The unrewarded portion of the risk is unsystematic or diversifiable risk. This risk is eliminated in perfectly diversified portfolios (i.e., when $\sigma_j = \text{Cov}_{jM}/\sigma_M$).

Since the total risk of the asset or portfolio equals the sum of systematic and unsystematic risk,

$$\sigma_j = \frac{\text{Cov}_{jM}}{\sigma_M} + \text{unsystematic risk} \tag{20.8}$$

and recalling from Equation 19.8 that $\text{Cov}_{jM} = \rho_{jM}\sigma_j\sigma_M$, then rearranging Equation 20.8 results in unsystematic risk being defined as

$$\begin{aligned}\text{unsystematic risk} &= \sigma_j - \frac{\text{Cov}_{jM}}{\sigma_M} \\ &= \sigma_j - \frac{\rho_{jM}\sigma_j\sigma_M}{\sigma_M} \\ &= \sigma_j - \rho_{jM}\sigma_j \\ &= \sigma_j(1 - \rho_{jM})\end{aligned} \tag{20.9}$$

Thus, total asset or portfolio risk can be defined as

$$\text{total risk} = \text{systematic risk} + \text{unsystematic risk} \tag{20.10}$$

$$\sigma_j = \frac{\text{Cov}_{jM}}{\sigma_M} + \sigma_j(1 - \rho_{jM})$$

Equation 20.10 makes it clear that the risk of an asset or portfolio consists of two parts: the systematic risk, which is due to the correlation (covariance) of the asset or portfolio with the market, and the unsystematic risk, which is caused by unique company- or industry-specific factors and is not related to market movements. The lower the asset's correlation with the market, the higher the proportion of unsystematic risk to total risk, and vice versa.

• Beta and Equilibrium Expected Return

Equation 20.6 can be rearranged as

$$E(R_j) = R_f + [E(R_M) - R_f]\frac{\text{Cov}_{jM}}{\sigma_M^2} \tag{20.11}$$

The term $\text{Cov}_{jM}/\sigma_M^2$ is the **beta** of asset j (β_j). Note that the beta of an asset is its systematic risk (Cov_{jM}/σ_M), expressed in units of market risk (σ_M). Thus, beta is *not* a measure of the systematic risk of a security or portfolio. Rather, it is more like an index of systematic risk. Since the only difference between the actual measure of systematic risk and beta is the divisor σ_M, which is common to all assets and portfolios, beta provides a relative ranking of the level of systematic risk for assets and portfolios. Using β_j, Equation 20.11 can be rewritten as

$$E(R_j) = R_f + [E(R_M) - R_f]\beta_j \tag{20.12}$$

Equation 20.12 is the CAPM and the equation for the **security market line (SML).** The SML is illustrated in Figure 20.4. Figure 20.4 shows the relationship between the relative level of systematic risk (β_j) and the expected return of an asset. In Figure 20.4, $\beta_M = 1$. This is true by definition since $\text{Cov}_{MM} = \sigma_M^2$ and thus $\beta_M = \sigma_M^2/\sigma_M^2 = 1$.

From the equation for the SML, the expected return of an asset is a function of the return on the risk-free asset, the **risk premium** in the market $[E(R_M) - R_f]$, and the asset's β_j. Only the last measure, β_j, is asset-specific; thus, an asset's expected return will be higher or lower than other assets' expected returns based upon its relative level of covariance with the market.

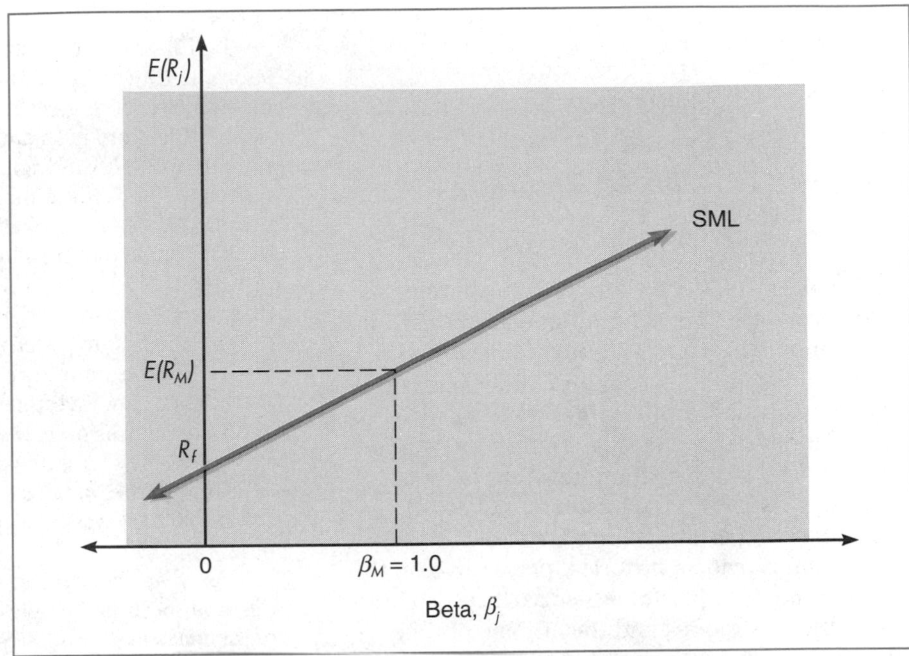

FIGURE 20.4
The Security Market Line

For example, assume the risk-free rate is 8 percent, the expected return on the market portfolio is 16 percent, the beta of asset A is 1.2, and the beta of asset B is 0.6. Then the expected return from Equation 20.12 for these two assets would be

$$E(R_A) = .08 + (.16 - .08)(1.2) = 17.6\%$$
$$E(R_B) = .08 + (.16 - .08)(.6) = 12.8\%$$

• Estimating Beta

Since beta, $\text{Cov}_{jM}/\sigma_M^2$, reflects the relationship between an asset's return and those of the market portfolio, it is possible to estimate this relationship, using a simple linear regression model:

$$R_{jt} = \hat{\alpha}_j + \hat{\beta}_{jt} R_{Mt} + e_{jt} \qquad (20.13)$$

where

$\hat{\alpha}_j$ = intercept estimate of the regression
$\hat{\beta}_j$ = slope estimate for the regression line, which is the estimate of beta ($\text{Cov}_{jM}/\sigma_M^2$)
R_{Mt} = return of the market in time period t
R_{jt} = return of asset j in time period t
e_{jt} = random error term for asset j around the regression line in time period t

• **INTEREST BOX**

Markowitz and Sharpe Receive the Nobel Memorial Prize in Economic Science

In 1990, Harry Markowitz, William Sharpe, and Merton Miller received the Nobel Memorial Prize in Economic Science. Although Miller's contributions (along with those of his colleague, Franco Modigliani) were no less important to the development of finance theory than those of Markowitz and Sharpe, the contributions of the latter are directly related to this chapter and Chapter 19. The following excerpts from an article by Peter Bernstein provide a historical perspective on the birth of modern portfolio theory. They also illustrate the frustrations and the amount of time required for new theories to be accepted by academicians and practitioners.

> When Harry Markowitz, Merton Miller and William Sharpe take off for Europe early next month to receive the 1990 Nobel Memorial Prize in Economic Science, their trip will be the culmination of a long, lonely and arduous journey that began more than 30 years ago. . . .
>
> The story begins at a time when the interest in a theory of investments was just about nil. It was a rare portfolio that had less than two thirds of its assets in bonds. Finance and investment courses in the 1950s concerned themselves with accounting procedures, rules of thumb and old saws. The investment course at Harvard Business School was so unpopular that it was denied prime-time classroom space and was held at noon—hence the nickname taken from the title of Arthur Koestler's gloomy novel: "Darkness at Noon." Between 1951 and 1955, fewer than 4 percent of the graduates of the business school went to Wall Street; even the huge bull market in the second half of the decade raised that ratio to only 6.6 percent. An index of the *Financial Analysts Journal* from 1945 to 1966 does not even give the subject of portfolio management its own references; under that listing, it recommends, "See Investing."
>
> When Harry Markowitz began his graduate studies at the University of Chicago in the early 1950s, he did not choose investments as a field of study—he stumbled into it. In addition to economics, his primary interest was in operations research and related methods for minimizing inputs while maximizing outputs. He looked into investing partly at the suggestion of a stockbroker he met outside a professor's office and partly at the suggestion of that same professor. His single indoctrination in the subject was one afternoon in the university library reading John Burr William's classic work on the theory of investment value.
>
> Markowitz was only 25 years old and did not even have his doctorate when "Portfolio Selection" appeared in the March 1952 issue of the *Journal of Finance,* which was itself only six years old at the time. . . .
>
> Three years later, when Markowitz defended the doctoral thesis he had developed as an elaboration of the ideas in "Portfolio Selection," he had to sweat his way through the afternoon. Milton Friedman, the star of the Chicago economics faculty, was on the committee and gave him a hard time from the outset. The subject matter was too novel. "Harry," he remonstrated, "this isn't a dissertation in economics, and we can't give you a Ph.D. in economics for a dissertation that's not economics. It's not math, it's not economics, it's not even business administration." After the ordeal was over, Markowitz spent a lonely and agitated few minutes until he was certain that other members of the committee had for once persuaded Friedman to change his mind and approve the degree.
>
> Despite the importance of what Markowitz had to say, few people were listening. From 1952 to 1960, fewer than twenty citations to him appear in the academic literature. The world was not yet ready to view investing as a fertile field for theoretical analysis.
>
> Furthermore, although the Markowitz paradigm for portfolio selection was unquestionably one of the great innovations in financial theory, it left the investor with awesome obstacles to its practical application. The identification of efficient portfolios from a universe of only 50 securities involves a total of 1,225 calculations: 50 expected returns,

50 variances and 1,125 covariances between each pair of securities; for 500 stocks, the calculations run up to nearly 125,000. On a state-of-the-art IBM computer of the late 1950s, the identification of the efficient frontier from a universe of just 100 securities took 33 minutes and, in 1990 dollars, cost at least $300 in computer time.

Markowitz's dissertation, which appeared as a book published in 1959, has a brief footnote that suggests a way around the complexity of calculating how each stock will behave relative to each of the others in the universe. Again in language that sounds picturesque to us, Markowitz declares:

> The returns on most securities are correlated. If the Standard & Poor's Index rose substantially, we would expect United States Steel (Common) to rise. If the Standard & Poor's Index rose substantially, we would also expect Sweets Company of America (Common) to rise. For this reason, it is more than likely that United States Steel will do well when Sweets Company does well.

The full development of Markowitz's intuition and the exploration into its deeper meaning was achieved by his protégé, William Sharpe, who is seven years his junior. Yet Sharpe's interest in investments was just as much a coincidence as Markowitz's had been. After studying economics at the University of California at Berkeley, Sharpe went on to do graduate work at the University of California at Los Angeles and part-time work at Rand Corp., the local think tank. As it happened, Markowitz was also at Rand, having moved there from Chicago to develop linear-programming applications for industrial firms. . . .

The collaboration blossomed rapidly. Sharpe was permitted to pursue his graduate studies under Markowitz, even though Markowitz was not on the UCLA faculty. He soon took the Sweets Company idea to its fruition in what he called the diagonal model and is now generally known as the single-index model—"the assumption that the returns of various securities are related only through common relationships with some basic underlying factor . . . the factor thought to be the most important single influence on the return from securities."

Now portfolio selection no longer demanded the endless calculation of covariances between every pair of securities. The covariance with "the most important single influence"—the market itself—was all that was necessary. In addition, Sharpe, who has always described himself as a "computer nerd," was able to program the diagonal model for a computer and to reduce the 33-minute stint to 30 seconds while expanding the computer's capacity to handle the problem from 249 securities to 2,000. The capital asset pricing model for valuing securities was a direct outgrowth of the diagonal model for composing efficient portfolios. . . .

Sharpe drafted "Capital Asset Prices: A Theory of Market Equilibrium under Conditions of Risk" in 1961 and sent it to the *Journal of Finance*, whose editor promptly rejected it. Three years of painful revisions and sheer patience had to pass before the paper achieved final acceptance and publication. And, as with Markowitz's work, the world did not rush to shout its enthusiasm. Sharpe thought at the time that the article was "the best thing I would ever do—the phone would start ringing any moment." Nevertheless, after one year, "total silence."

Sharpe's paper subsequently generated more than 2,000 citations in the academic literature, but it met the most stubborn and intense resistance among practitioners. Its ideas were not only unorthodox and unfamiliar, they were threatening to security analysts and portfolio managers alike. As late as 1977, an article in this magazine quoted one of the most respected directors of research on Wall Street—a man still revered as a guru among institutional investors—as saying, "I think it's just a lot of baloney."

To its credit, this magazine had more foresight. The article concluded that, as the influence of the new theory took hold, "as like hybrid seed corn it must, the investment management business seems destined for what can be considered a revolution."

SOURCE: Peter L. Bernstein, "The Vindication of the Professors," *Institutional Investor* (November 1990): 81–87.

FIGURE 20.5
Plot of Martin Marietta and Standard & Poor's 500 Returns and the Characteristic Line

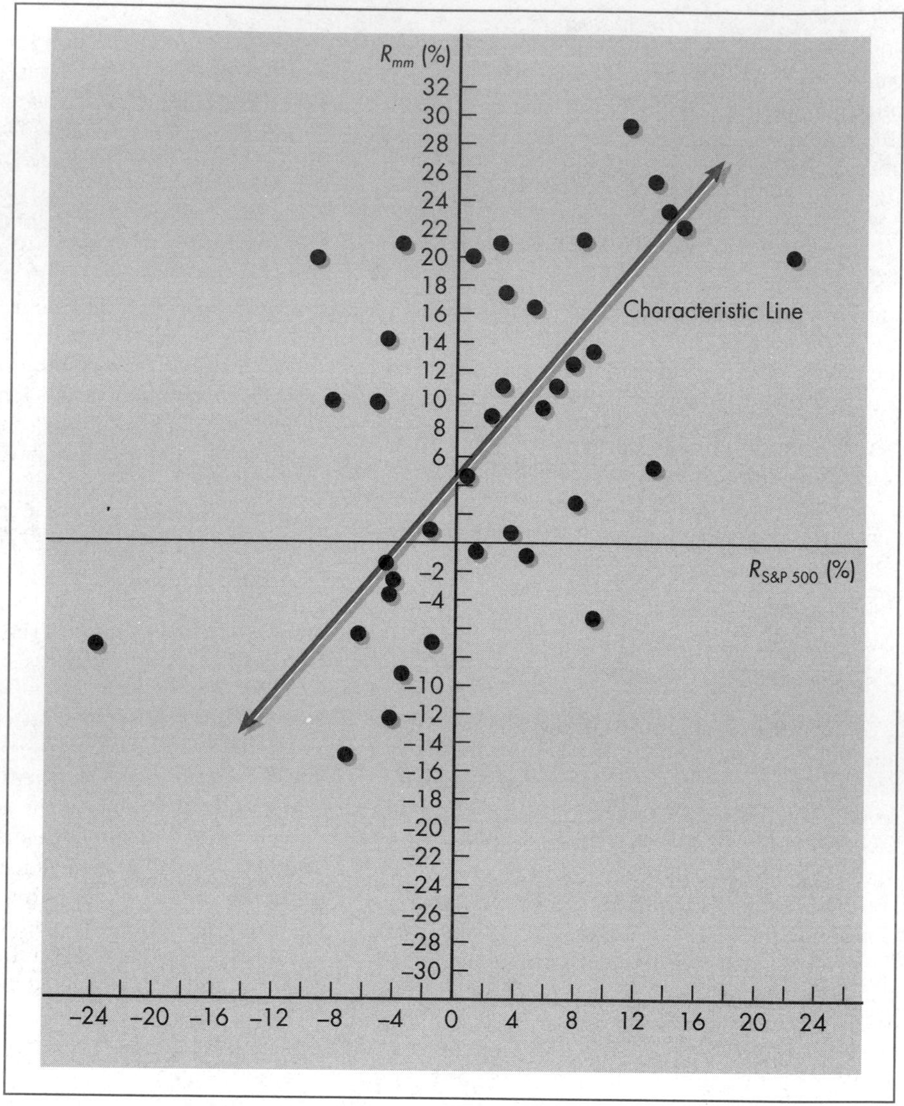

The linear regression model shown in Equation 20.13 is the line of best fit and is called the **characteristic line** for the security. Figure 20.5 shows a scatter diagram of the returns of the market as represented by the Standard & Poor's 500, the quarterly returns over 10 years for the common stock of Martin Marietta, and the characteristic line for Martin Marietta (see Table 20.1 for the data). The statistics from the return data are as follows:

TABLE 20.1 • Quarterly Returns for Martin Marietta and the Standard & Poor's 500

Year	Quarter	Martin Marietta HPR	S&P 500 HPR	Year	Quarter	Martin Marietta HPR	S&P 500 HPR
1	1	21.727%	9.699%	6	1	25.846	12.874
	2	4.311	0.165		2	20.994	2.384
	3	−2.209	−0.589		3	−0.625	1.844
	4	−1.687	4.594		4	11.064	3.072
2	1	9.441	5.758	7	1	−6.893	−7.438
	2	−7.931	0.651		2	17.989	3.201
	3	0.759	3.901		3	−10.000	−2.812
	4	−2.994	7.497		4	0.615	−0.271
3	1	−1.800	−4.859	8	1	14.093	−4.932
	2	−12.897	−5.788		2	9.862	8.461
	3	15.565	4.784		3	9.106	8.652
	4	−17.447	−9.255		4	−3.715	−5.034
4	1	21.404	−2.778	9	1	10.250	7.054
	2	−7.059	−7.560		2	8.812	2.613
	3	−6.935	−25.072		3	12.500	7.568
	4	−4.779	9.317		4	20.013	0.030
5	1	21.524	22.926	10	1	−3.458	−4.076
	2	22.080	15.305		2	5.864	13.384
	3	20.260	−10.917		3	29.793	11.150
	4	13.333	8.632		4	23.899	12.952

	Martin Marietta	S&P 500
Variance of returns (σ^2)	141.70	73.50
Standard deviation of returns (σ)	11.9%	8.6%
Mean return ($\overline{HPR}$)	7.0%	2.4%

The correlation coefficient (ρ_{jM}) derived from the regression is .533. With this information, the slope of the characteristic line or beta (β_j) and the intercept (α_j) can be calculated.[5]

[5] For Martin Marietta, the dispersion of the quarterly returns around the mean return (7 percent) is the variance of returns (141.70). The square root of the variance (standard deviation) is 11.9 percent. This total risk can be divided into its systematic and unsystematic components. In *(continued)*

$$\beta_j = \frac{\text{Cov}_{jM}}{\sigma_M^2} = \frac{\rho_{jM}\sigma_j\sigma_M}{\sigma_M^2}$$

$$= [(.532)(11.9)(8.6)]/73.50$$

$$= .741$$

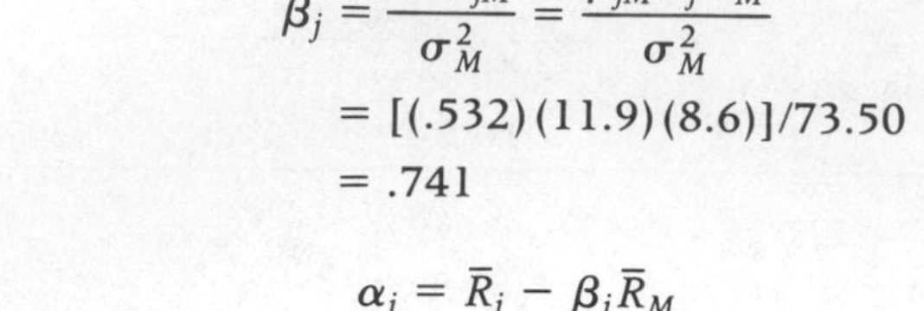

$$\alpha_j = \bar{R}_j - \beta_j\bar{R}_M \tag{20.14}$$

$$= .07 - (.741)(.024)$$

$$= .07 - .0178$$

$$= 5.22\%$$

This method of calculating beta coefficients can also be applied to a portfolio. Rather than regressing the returns of an individual asset against the returns of the market portfolio, the returns of the portfolio are regressed against the market returns. If the individual betas of the stocks in a portfolio are known, the portfolio's beta (β_p) can be calculated as the weighted average of the individual betas:

$$\beta_p = \sum_{j=1}^{n} X_j\beta_j \tag{20.15}$$

Some observations about the slope coefficient, or beta, are in order. These observations hold whether the beta is calculated as shown above or is obtained from such sources as Value Line or Merrill Lynch. Beta values are rarely negative. They generally range between +.5 and 2.0. This reflects the fact that the returns for most securities are positively related, in varying degrees, to the overall return in the market. Stocks or portfolios with betas above 1.0 are classified as "aggressive" since they are expected to have more volatile returns than the market. Stocks or portfolios with betas less than 1.0 are classified as "defensive" since their returns are less volatile than that of the market.

(continued from previous page)
Equation 20.10, it was shown that total risk can be defined as the sum of systematic risk plus unsystematic risk:

$$\sigma_j = \frac{\text{Cov}_{jM}}{\sigma_M} + \sigma_j(1 - \rho_{jM})$$

Recalling that $\text{Cov}_{jM} = \rho_{jM}\sigma_j\sigma_M$, then Martin Marietta's total risk can be separated into its systematic and unsystematic risk components as follows:

$$\sigma_j = \frac{(.532)(11.9)(8.6)}{8.6} + (11.9)(1 - .532)$$

$$= 6.33 + 5.57$$

$$= 11.90\%$$

For Martin Marietta over this 10-year period, systematic risk accounted for approximately 53 percent of total risk (6.33/11.9), unsystematic risk for 47 percent (5.57/11.9).

Beta estimates are based on historical information, and it is assumed that this historical relationship with the market will remain constant. Many articles have examined the stationarity of beta and have compared the estimates of the CAPM with actual or ex-post risk and return. The results of this research are examined in the next section.

TESTS OF THE CAPITAL ASSET PRICING MODEL

CMT is a theory of asset pricing. As such, it is based on assumptions that are not totally realistic. Although the assumptions of CMT can be relaxed to reflect the real world more closely (see Appendix 20A), the question naturally arises whether the original version of the model accurately reflects the relationship between the measures of risk and expected return in the real world. The appeal of the CAPM is its rather simple expression of the relationship between risk and expected return. However, if its original form does not reasonably reflect this relationship, its usefulness in assessing security risk, portfolio construction, and portfolio performance evaluation is questionable.

• Is the CAPM Testable?

In addressing this question, it is important to distinguish Markowitz's portfolio theory from CMT. Markowitz suggested a *normative* approach to portfolio management in which the return of an individual security is a function of its contribution to a portfolio's risk. This analysis requires the estimation of the expected return, variance of returns, and the correlation of return between each pair of securities being considered for the portfolio. For a portfolio manager considering a significant number of securities, the calculation of all possible correlation coefficients is a difficult task. Recognizing this difficulty, Markowitz suggested that an **index model** be developed that could explain the correlation among the returns of the securities under consideration.[6] The index model is also referred to as the *single-index model* and the *market model.*

This normative theory did not identify the market portfolio as such. Nor did it have the restrictive assumptions associated with CMT. The *positive* CMT was developed later, and as Markowitz suggests,

> Tobin, Sharpe, and Lintner knew, as well as you and I do, that investors have different beliefs, that borrowing rates are typically higher than lending rates, and that there are credit restrictions on the amount that one can bor-

[6] For a discussion of the distinction between Markowitz's theory and the index model, see Harry M. Markowitz, "The 'Two Beta' Trap," *Journal of Portfolio Management* (Fall 1984): 12–20; and Barr Rosenberg, "The Capital Asset Pricing Model and the Market Model," *Journal of Portfolio Management* (Winter 1981): 5–16.

row. They chose these assumptions to have a theory with neat, quantitative implications. They left it to empirical research to see whether the conclusions deduced from these idealized assumptions fit aggregate economic data.[7]

Empirical research on the CAPM has been considerable. Researchers have been concerned about the single-index or market model's ability to capture total systematic risk, the stationarity of beta, and its ability to explain differences in observed and expected returns. These issues and empirical tests will be examined in the next section.

The empirical tests of the CAPM have relied on proxies for the market portfolio. Recall that the market portfolio is defined as a portfolio consisting of all risky assets combined in proportion to their market values. There is no quantifiable measure of the market portfolio, and researchers have generally substituted a capitalization-weighted index, such as the S&P 500 or the NYSE Index, for the market index. The assumption is that the proxy index is a "good" substitute for the market portfolio.

Richard Roll contends that proxies for the market portfolio may not be efficient, in the sense that they would not lie on the efficient frontier.[8] This assertion has serious implications for CMT's ability to accurately reflect the relationship between risk and expected return, for empirical tests of CMT, and for portfolio evaluation techniques using CMT (see Chapter 21).

• Results of Empirical Tests of the CAPM

According to Roll, misspecification of the market portfolio raises serious doubts about empirical tests of the CAPM.[9] Nevertheless, numerous studies, both prior and subsequent to Roll's articles, have tested the stationarity of beta values and undertaken tests of the theory itself.

TESTS OF THE CAPM: INDIVIDUAL SECURITIES The CAPM is stated in terms of investor expectations, yet tests of the CAPM are stated in terms of realized or ex-post HPRs. The difference between realized and expected returns is the residual term, which, if the model is correctly specified, should be zero on average.

Figure 20.6 illustrates the test for the CAPM based on individual securities. Each point represents a security's actual return versus its estimated beta. If the CAPM is correct, the regression of returns against beta should result in a posi-

[7] Markowitz, "The 'Two Beta' Trap," p. 13.

[8] Richard Roll, "A Critique of the Asset Pricing Theory's Tests," *Journal of Financial Economics* (March 1977): 129–76; and "Ambiguity When Performance Is Measured by the Security Market Line," *Journal of Finance* (September 1978): 1051–69.

[9] This section draws heavily on the presentation of earlier studies in Franco Modigliani and Gerald A. Pogue, "An Introduction to Risk and Return (Part II)," *Financial Analysts Journal* (May-June 1974): 69–86.

FIGURE 20.6
Relationship between the Average Security Return and Security Beta

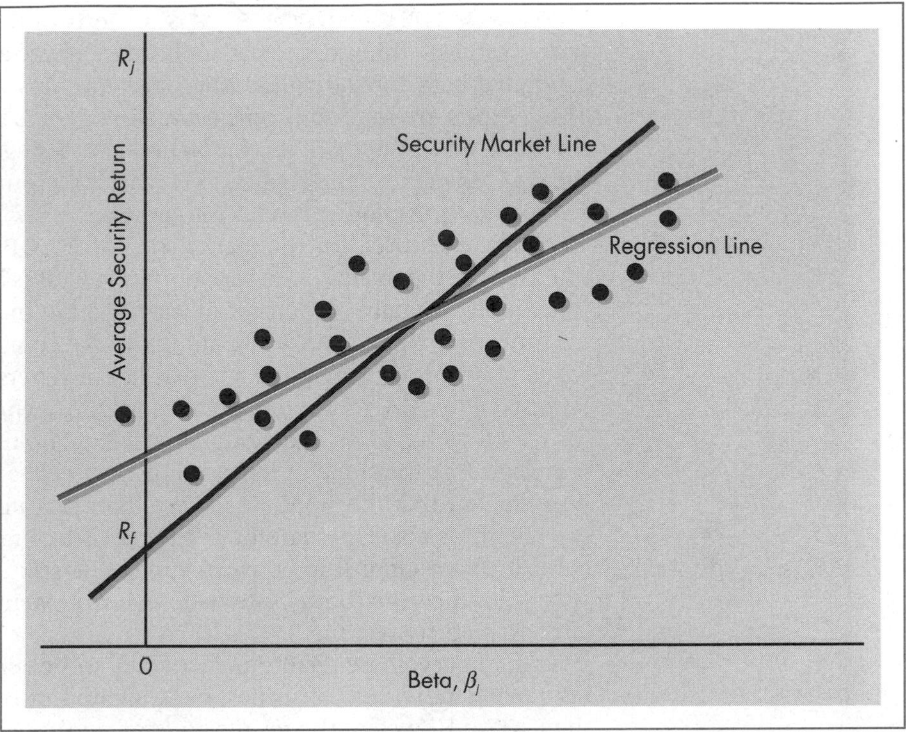

tive slope equal to the average market risk premium $(R_M - R_f)$ and should have an intercept on the vertical axis at the average risk-free rate (R_f).

The results of empirical tests based on individual securities are mixed. Some tests show that, on average, securities with larger betas have higher rates of return and that the relationship between beta and the returns was linear.[10] Other studies however, found that the slope of the regression line between beta and the returns was somewhat lower than predicted and that the intercept was somewhat higher than the average risk-free rate.[11] This empirical relationship between beta and the returns and the SML is shown in Figure 20.6.

[10] See, for example, Nancy Jacob, "The Measurement of Systematic Risk for Securities and Portfolios: Some Empirical Results," *Journal of Financial and Quantitative Analysis* (March 1971): 815–34; and Merton H. Miller and Myron Scholes, "Rates of Return in Relation to Risk: A Reexamination of Some Recent Findings," in *Studies in the Theory of Capital Markets,* ed. Michael Jensen (New York: Praeger, 1972), pp. 47–48.

[11] For example, see Irwin Friend and Marshall E. Blume, "Measurement of Portfolio Performance under Uncertainty," *American Economic Review* (September 1970): 561–75; and Fischer Black, Michael C. Jensen, and Myron Scholes, "The Capital Asset Pricing Model: Some Empirical Tests," in *Studies in The Theory of Capital Markets,* ed. Michael C. Jensen (New York: Praeger, 1972), pp. 79–121.

TESTS OF THE CAPM: PORTFOLIOS Tests of the CAPM based on individual securities, while somewhat supportive, have several drawbacks. First, the estimated beta for individual securities contains some measurement errors. These errors are random: some estimates of betas for individual securities are too high, and others are too low. Therefore, using estimated betas in tests of the CAPM weakens the results. This type of measurement error can be greatly reduced by grouping securities into portfolios.

The proxies used for the market (e.g., the S&P 500) explain, on average, only about 30 percent of the variation in the HPRs of individual stocks. Therefore, approximately 70 percent of the variation in the HPRs is residual variation, or diversifiable (unsystematic) risk. By combining securities into portfolios, much of this unsystematic risk can be diversified away.

Tests of the CAPM conducted on portfolios generally have taken the same form as tests based on individual securities. The results of the tests generally indicated that the slope of the relationship between beta and the returns was positive, but that the slope was lower than that indicated by the CAPM. The intercept was also less than the average risk-free rate. The empirical tests also confirmed a relationship between systematic risk and the returns. There was some evidence that both systematic and unsystematic risk are positively related to security returns.

In summary, these results are generally more supportive of the CAPM than tests using individual securities, but they do not constitute empirical *proof* of the CAPM. However, the results do confirm that beta is a useful, though perhaps not a complete, indicator of risk.

BETA STATIONARITY The calculation of beta values for securities and portfolios is a relatively straightforward procedure. These calculated betas based on historical HPRs are useful for investment decisions, however, only if they provide information about the future relationships between security or portfolio returns and market returns. The empirical results indicate that the stationarity of beta estimates is directly related to (1) the number of securities in the portfolio, (2) the length of the period used to estimate beta, (3) the length of the holding period for estimating returns (e.g., returns may be estimated over daily, weekly, monthly, or annual intervals), (4) the level of the beta estimate, (5) structural variations in the market, and (6) changes in certain company-specific attributes.

Robert Levy addressed a number of these issues in a 1971 study.[12] Levy used the *weekly* returns of 500 stocks over the 20-week period from December 30, 1960, through December 18, 1970. His proxy for the market portfolio was the S&P 500. He developed betas for all nonoverlapping 51-week periods (500 betas), 26-week periods (1,000 betas), and 13-week periods (2,000

[12] Robert A. Levy, "On the Short-Term Stationarity of Beta Coefficients," *Financial Analysts Journal* (November-December 1971): 55–62.

betas) by regressing the weekly HPRs of the securities upon the appropriate HPRs for the S&P 500.

The more significant results of Levy's study of betas can be summarized as follows:

1. "Over the entire 10-year period the average beta was 1.043, the median was .976, and the first and ninth decile points respectively were 0.400 and 1.756. For investors searching for high beta stocks, it is worth noting that in no 52-week period were there as many as 10 percent of the stocks with betas of 2.0 or greater. Conversely for those investors seeking stocks which have moved counter to the market, only 1.7 percent of the companies qualify."[13]
2. Betas are reasonably predictable for large portfolios, less predictable for smaller portfolios, and quite unpredictable for individual securities.
3. Forecasts of beta are clearly better the longer the estimation period (e.g., a 52-week estimation period versus a 13-week period).
4. Reversals in the market occurring near the forecast date do not diminish the degree of predictability of beta.
5. The predicted betas of the portfolios with the lowest betas tended to be underestimated, and the predicted betas of the portfolios with the highest betas tended to be overestimated.

Fundamental economic and financial variables influence betas for individual securities. For example, Beaver, Kettler, and Scholes found that betas are related to the firm's dividend payout ratio, growth rate in assets, and variability in earnings.[14] Essentially, firms with high levels of business and financial risk should have higher betas than firms with lower levels of business and financial risk. It also follows that firms experiencing significant changes in business and financial risk would have unstable betas. For example, if a firm experiences an improved bond rating, the beta for its common stock may decline, reflecting the lower level of default risk.[15]

An article by McDonald suggests that nonstationarity in individual stock betas may be due to structural variations in the market resulting from major political and economic shocks such as the Arab oil embargo, hostilities in the Middle East, the financial stability of Mexico, and the like.[16] McDonald found that the 1958–1972 period (the period of Levy's study) was relatively stable,

---

[13] Ibid., pp. 56–57.

[14] William Beaver, Paul Kettler, and Myron Scholes, "The Association between Market Determined and Accounting Determined Risk Measures," *Accounting Review* (October 1970): 654–82.

[15] See, for example, Naval K. Modani and William P. Lloyd, "Bond Rating Changes and Behavior of Risk Proxies," *Akron Business and Economic Review* (Spring 1984): 46–49.

[16] Bill McDonald, "Making Sense Out of Unstable Alphas and Betas," *Journal of Portfolio Management* (Winter 1985): 19–22.

but that the years 1974–1975 should be avoided because of evidence of structural shifts in the economy. McDonald was careful to point out that large fluctuations in the market index (e.g., October 19, 1987) do not necessarily reflect structural shifts.

Robert Levy's study was based on weekly HPRs. Haim Levy contends that the estimate of a security's beta is a function of the length of the period used for estimating the security and market returns.[17] Haim Levy shows that for aggressive stocks (beta greater than 1), systematic risk increases as the return estimating period (investment horizon) lengthens and that with defensive stocks (beta less than 1), systematic risk decreases as the estimating period increases. These results indicate that the selection of different estimating intervals will result in different beta estimates for securities and that the selection of the investment horizon is crucial in performance evaluations based on the CAPM or in empirical research on the validity of the CAPM. These conclusions are directly related to assumption 4 of CMT—that all investors have a common investment horizon.

If betas calculated on the relationship between the HPRs on individual securities and the market are unstable over time, are there ways to produce more predictable future betas? A number of approaches to improving beta predictability have been suggested. For example, Steven Carvell and Paul Strebel suggest that beta estimates for small firms, not regularly followed by a large number of analysts, can be improved by combining the traditional beta estimation procedure with a second "beta" based on the standard deviation of the analysts' forecasts.[18]

Barr Rosenberg has combined industry and company fundamental factors with historical stock price movements to improve beta predictability. According to Rosenberg, his "BARRA El" predictive beta improves the predictive power of beta by more than a factor of 1.6.[19]

George M. Frankfurter and Herbert E. Phillips have employed traditional beta calculation techniques, factor and statistical cluster analysis, and fundamental security analysis to improve risk-adjusted portfolio returns.[20] A final example is provided by Dan French, John Groth, and James Kolari who claim to have produced superior estimates of future betas by using variances estimated from the Black-Scholes option pricing model (see Chapter 15) and combining it with betas estimated from historical data.[21]

---

[17] Haim Levy, "The CAPM and the Investment Horizon," *Journal of Portfolio Management* (Winter 1981): 32–40.

[18] Steven Carvell and Paul Strebel, "A New Beta Incorporating Analysts' Forecasts," *Journal of Portfolio Management* (Fall 1984): 81–85.

[19] Barr Rosenberg, "Prediction of Common Stock Betas," *Journal of Portfolio Management* (Winter 1985): 5–14.

[20] George M. Frankfurter and Herbert E. Phillips, "MPT Plus Security Analysis for Better Performance," *Journal of Portfolio Management* (Summer 1982): 29–36.

[21] Dan W. French, John C. Groth, and James W. Kolari, "Current Investor Expectations and Better Betas," *Journal of Portfolio Management* (Fall 1983): 12–17.

• Conclusions about Tests of Capital Market Theory

The results of tests of capital market theory suggest that security returns do conform to the general precept of the CAPM: the higher the level of systematic risk, the higher the level of expected return. When the results of specific tests of the CAPM are examined, it is possible to conclude that the CAPM is correct in a general sense, but that its reliability is suspect for individual assets or portfolios. It should be remembered, however, that tests of the CAPM are based on the use of historical (ex-post) information to form expectations about ex-ante risk and return.

The CAPM does not suggest that historical information can be used to accurately forecast future levels of risk and return. In fact, it would be surprising if a firm's attributes (e.g., levels of business and financial risk) remained constant over time. Thus, tests of the CAPM using historical information as a basis for analysis require the bold assumption that past return patterns are accurate predictors of future returns. Thus, these results cannot be used to conclude that the CAPM equilibrium pricing model is invalid. A second theory related to asset pricing is discussed in the next section.

ARBITRAGE PRICING THEORY

Like capital market theory, the *arbitrage pricing theory (APT)* developed by Stephen Ross is an equilibrium theory of expected return.[22] The central thesis of the APT is that more than one systematic factor affects the long-term average returns on financial assets. While some assumptions of the APT are less restrictive than those of the CAPM (e.g., the existence of a market portfolio and riskless borrowing and lending rates), the APT does share with the CAPM assumptions related to perfect capital markets and common investment horizons of investors. Additionally, the APT assumes the arbitrage portfolio (explained below) can be achieved with no money invested, a rather unrealistic assumption for the majority of investors. However, it is important to consider that only a few investors (arbitrageurs) are needed to bring expected return and risk for assets into proper proportion.

• Factor Models

Factor models have been used in finance for a long time. Initially, they were known as *index models.* The change in terminology occurred as analysts began to use *factor analysis* to identify the major forces that influence the returns on a large number of securities. As Sharpe points out:

[22] Stephen A. Ross, "The Arbitrage Theory of Capital Asset Pricing," *Journal of Economic Theory* (December 1976): 341–60.

• INTEREST BOX

Is Beta Dead?

In an *Institutional Investor* article, Anise Wallace asked the question, "Is beta dead?" Peter Bernstein responded with the following editorial in the *Journal of Portfolio Management:*

> The question is ridiculous. As long as individual securities continue to move up and down in sympathy with—or as part of—broad market movements, portfolio managers must be concerned about the sensitivity of their portfolios to the general market, the stability of that relationship, and the accuracy of the measurement tools that they employ.
>
> Is the capital asset pricing model dead? This question is also ridiculous. As long as we have free markets in which investors are risk averse rather than risk-seekers, they will tend to price securities so that the riskier asset classes will have higher expected returns than the less risky classes.
>
> Is modern portfolio theory dead? How ridiculous can you get? As long as the interaction of individual securities within a portfolio produces results that are different from the performance of a single security, the art of composing a portfolio will remain a different art from the skills employed in security selection as such.
>
> Are the tools that we use to measure the sensitivity of individual securities to the general market, their sensitivity to one another, or the degree of rationality in investor expectations alive and well? Ah, there's the rub!
>
> While the special series of articles in this issue provides strong evidence that beta, the CAPM, and modern portfolio theory are robust descriptions of how free markets work under conditions of uncertainty and how investors can expect their portfolios to perform under those conditions, the authors do raise a whole set of important questions about the quantitative concepts that we use to put theory into practice. Nevertheless, the thrust of the entire discussion is that these quantitative concepts readily lend themselves to improvement and revision.
>
> There is nothing here to justify doubts about the ability of valid measurement techniques to enhance the value of the theoretical structure for the active portfolio manager. On the contrary, active management can be far more effective with than without the use of these tools.

Dead or alive, there is no question that the CAPM has provided us with a vocabulary and perspective that are valuable and insightful. The concepts of the market portfolio, systematic (rewardable) risk, and unsystematic (nonrewardable) risk are important and useful constructs of modern portfolio theory. Additionally, no one questions the important insights provided by Markowitz's portfolio theory in which the expected return of an individual security is related to its contribution to portfolio risk rather than to the variability of its own expected return.

SOURCES: Anise Wallace, "Is Beta Dead?" *Institutional Investor* (July 1980): 23–30; and Peter L. Bernstein, "Dead—or Alive and Well?" *Journal of Portfolio Management* (Winter 1981): 4. This copyrighted material is reprinted with permission from Institutional Investor Inc.

As a practical matter one must employ a factor model, either explicitly or implicitly. It is impossible to think separately about the interrelationship of every security with every other. Abstraction is essential. Good investment managers identify important factors in the economy and marketplace and assess the extent to which different securities will respond to changes in these factors. Passive managers attempt to assess the market's predictions about the risks and returns associated with the factors and security-specific returns. Active managers also attempt to outguess the market on likely outcomes for factors and/or stocks.

There is no reason to assume or believe that a good factor model for one period will be a good one for the next period; key factors change—remember OPEC! So do the risks and returns associated with various factors and the sensitivities of securities to factors. Causes of changes include mergers, new lines of business, changes in leverage, etc.[23]

A factor model can take the following general form:

$$\tilde{R}_i = a_i + b_{i1}\tilde{F}_1 + b_{i2}\tilde{F}_2 + \cdots + b_{im}\tilde{F}_m + \tilde{e}_i \quad \textbf{(20.16)}$$

where the tildes are placed over variables not known in advance. $\tilde{R}_i$ is the return on security i; $\tilde{F}_1$ is the value of the first factor; $\tilde{F}_2$ is the value of the second factor, and so on; b_{ij} is the sensitivity of security i's returns to movements in the factor (factor loadings); and $\tilde{e}_i$ is the variation in return unexplained by the factors. The $\tilde{e}_i$ term is called the *security-specific return* or, more commonly, security i's *idiosyncratic return*. The $\tilde{e}_i$ values for securities are assumed to be uncorrelated.

As indicated earlier in the discussion of portfolio theory, the use of a factor model is a practical necessity for portfolio managers considering a large number of securities for a portfolio. It is virtually impossible for the portfolio manager to identify the interrelationships among many pairs of securities. Markowitz suggested an index model; Sharpe is credited with being among the first to develop the single-index model, using the market as the factor; and Kalman Cohen and Gerald Pogue were among the first researchers to employ multifactor models.[24]

• The Elements of the APT

The APT is an ex-ante and an ex-post model in its specification of returns (R_i), as shown in the following equation:

$$R_i = E_i + b_{i1}\delta_1 + b_{i2}\delta_2 + \cdots + b_{ij}\delta_j + e_i \quad \textbf{(20.17)}$$

---

[23] William F. Sharpe, "Factor Models, CAPMs, and the APT," *Journal of Portfolio Management* (Fall 1984): 21–25.

[24] Harry M. Markowitz, *Portfolio Selection: Efficient Diversification of Investments* (New York: John Wiley & Sons, 1959); William F. Sharpe, "A Simplified Model for Portfolio Analysis," *Management Science* (January 1963): 277–93; and Kalman J. Cohen and Gerald A. Pogue, "An Empirical Evaluation of Alternative Portfolio Selection Models," *Journal of Business* (April 1967): 166–93. A number of researchers have identified relevant factors: Benjamin F. King, "Market and Industry Factors in Stock Price Behavior," *Journal of Business* (January 1966): 139–90; Edwin J. Elton and Martin J. Gruber, "Estimating the Dependence Structure of Share Prices—Implications for Portfolio Selection," *Journal of Finance* (December 1973): 1203–32; and Eugene F. Fama and James MacBeth, "Risk, Return and Equilibrium: Empirical Tests," *Journal of Political Economy* (May-June 1973): 607–36.

where

E_i = ex-ante expected return of asset i
δ_i = ex-post sample factor, systematic in that it influences the return of all assets and is uncorrelated with other factors
b_{ij} = sensitivity of the returns of asset i to the movements of factor j
e_i = idiosyncratic return (residual) of asset i's return, having an expected value of 0 and no correlation with idiosyncratic returns of other assets

According to the APT, asset returns covary with the movement of the factors and are thus the sources of systematic risk. It would logically follow then that these factors and an asset's sensitivity to these factors would determine the *expected* and *actual* returns. Given this relationship, expected return (E_i from Equation 20.17) can be expressed as

$$E_i = \lambda_0 + \lambda_1 b_{i1} + \lambda_2 b_{i2} + \cdots + \lambda_j b_{ij} \qquad \textbf{(20.18)}$$

where

λ_0 = return on a risk-free asset
λ_j = market price of risk related to the jth factor

If there was only one factor, the market, then λ_1 would equal $E(R_m) - R_f$, and Equation 20.18 would be similar to the equation for the security market line. Thus, the CAPM can be seen as a special case of the APT.

The λ's in Equation 20.18 represent ex-ante required premiums for anticipated changes, while the δ's in Equation 20.17 represent ex-post unanticipated changes. Thus, if unanticipated changes for all factors are 0, the asset will simply achieve its expected return, E_i.

An example may help explain the difference between anticipated and unanticipated changes in the factors. Assume that there are four factors that affect securities' returns and that the unanticipated change in factors 1, 3, and 4 is 0. The return, R_i, on the asset is shown in Figure 20.7, which shows the straight-line relationship between the actual returns for asset i and the return (movement) in factor 2. The slope of the line is a function of the sensitivity of asset i's return to factor 2, b_i. If the b_i value is larger (smaller) than shown, the slope of the line will be higher (lower). The value for b_i can be negative, indicating that an unanticipated increase in the factor would cause a decrease in the asset's return. Note that if the unanticipated return of factor 2 were 0, the return on asset i would not be 0, but its expected return, E_i.

• Arbitrage

The APT is based on the reasonable and straightforward intuition that in efficient capital markets, assets with similar risk must have similar expected rates of return. For example, suppose that two bonds with the same maturity and

FIGURE 20.7
Factor and Asset Return

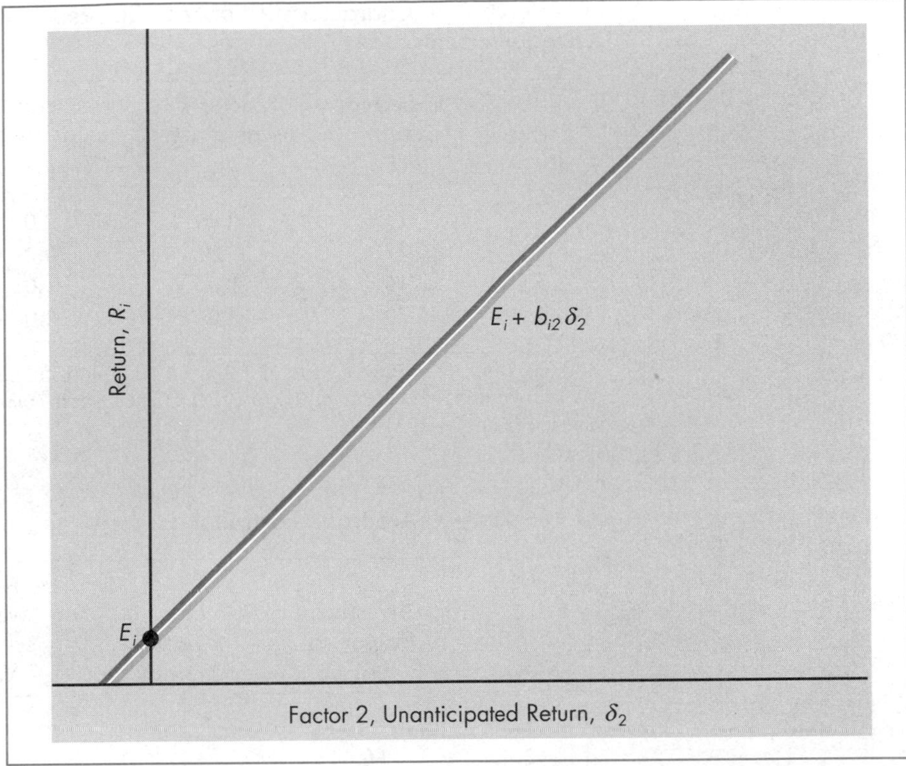

the same risk sold at different yields. Once investors spotted this opportunity, arbitrageurs would enter the market by selling short the lower-yielding bond and buying the higher-yielding bond until the yields were equal. In terms of the APT, assets with the same sensitivity (b_i) to identified factors in the economy must have the same expected return. In more general terms, if the situation permits investors to add to their wealth without investing dollars or facing risk, they will continue to take advantage of this opportunity until it no longer exists.

Consider the characteristics of the four stocks in Table 20.2, and assume that the idiosyncratic return (residual risk) has been diversified away through other investments.[25] For purposes of this example, only two factors are considered to be statistically significant. Additional factors could be considered, but this would only complicate the example. Could the situation in Table 20.2 exist in an efficient capital market? The answer is no, because an opportunity for positive risk-free returns exists. Arbitrageurs would enter the market and create an **arbitrage** portfolio like the one shown in Table 20.3.

[25]This example is from Dorothy H. Bower, Richard S. Bower, and Dennis E. Logue, "A Primer on Arbitrage Pricing Theory," *Midland Corporate Finance Journal* (Fall 1984): 31–40.

TABLE 20.2 • Characteristics of Four Stocks: Disequilibrium

Stock	Expected return, $E(R_i)$	Factor 1 sensitivity, b_{i1}	Factor 2 sensitivity, b_{i2}
1	13%	0.2	2.0
2	27	3.0	0.2
3	16	1.0	1.0
4	20	2.0	2.0

SOURCE: Dorothy H. Bower, Richard S. Bower, and Dennis E. Logue, "A Primer on Arbitrage Pricing Theory," *Midland Corporate Finance Journal* (Fall 1984): 31–40.

TABLE 20.3 • Arbitrage Portfolio

Stock	Investment proportion, X_i	Expected return, $X_i \times E(R_i)$	Factor 1 weighted sensitivity, $X_i \times b_{i1}$	Factor 2 weighted sensitivity, $X_i \times b_{i2}$
1	+1.000	+13.000%	+0.200	+2.000
2	+0.643	+17.361	+1.929	+0.129
3	−1.157	−18.512	−1.157	−1.157
4	−0.486	− 9.720	−0.972	−0.972
Portfolio	0.000	+ 2.129%	0.000	0.000

SOURCE: Dorothy H. Bower, Richard S. Bower, and Dennis E. Logue, "A Primer on Arbitrage Pricing Theory," *Midland Corporate Finance Journal* (Fall 1984): 31–40.

The investment weights (X_i, in Table 20.3) are determined as a result of an arbitrage portfolio having zero investment (some stocks are sold short) and zero factor risk. In this example, these requirements can be expressed as

$$\begin{aligned} X_1 + X_2 + X_3 + X_4 &= 0 && \text{(0 investment)} \\ X_1 b_{11} + X_2 b_{12} + X_3 b_{13} + X_4 b_{14} &= 0 && \text{(0 factor 1 risk)} \\ X_1 b_{21} + X_2 b_{22} + X_3 b_{23} + X_4 b_{24} &= 0 && \text{(0 factor 2 risk)} \end{aligned}$$

To solve for the proportion invested in each of the four stocks (X_i), as shown in Table 20.3, a fourth equation can be created by setting the investment in one of the stocks equal to 1 and then solving for the remaining proportions in the other stocks. For example, if the investment in the first stock is set at, $X_1 = 1$, then based on the arbitrage requirements and the information from Table 20.2

$$X_2 + X_3 + X_4 = -1 \quad (20.19)$$

$$X_2(3.0) + X_3(1.0) + X_4(2.0) = -.2 \quad (20.20)$$

$$X_2(.2) + X_3(1.0) + X_4(2.0) = -2 \quad (20.21)$$

Subtracting Equation 20.21 from Equation 20.20 gives .643 for X_2, the proportional investment in stock 2 ($2.8X_2 = 1.8$; $X_2 = .643$). Subtracting Equation 20.20 from Equation 20.19 and substituting .643 for X_2 results in X_4 being equal to $-.486$ [$-2X_2 - X_4 = -.8$; $-2(.643) - X_4 = -.8$; $X_4 = -.486$]. Substituting the solved values for X_2 and X_4 in Equation 20.19 gives -1.157 as the proportional investment in stock 3 ($.643 + X_3 - .486 = -1$; $X_3 = -1.157$).

Thus, when the investment weights are as shown in Table 20.3, the total investment in the arbitrage portfolio is zero, and a positive, risk-free return of 2.129% is available. As a result of this action by arbitrageurs, the expected returns of stocks 1 and 2 will be lower than those of stocks 3 and 4. This relative change results because stocks 1 and 2 are being bought (their prices rise and expected returns decrease) while stocks 3 and 4 are being sold (their prices decline and expected returns increase).

• Empirical Tests of the APT and Factors

In an initial empirical test of the APT, Stephen Ross and Richard Roll used factor analysis to analyze 1,260 NYSE stocks over the period 1962 through 1972.[26] The stocks were divided into groups of 30 stocks each. First, the factor coefficients and expected returns were estimated from the daily returns of each stock. Next, the sensitivity of the security's returns to movements in the factor (b_{ij}) was used as the independent variable in cross-sectional regression analysis to estimate the factor's risk premium (λ_j). The authors hypothesized that one or more of the coefficients (λ_j) should be nonzero constants. In several different tests, they found that between two and four factors were significantly different from 0. That is, these factors were "priced," in the sense that they affected the expected returns of the stocks.

Additional research has indicated that more than four factors are priced.[27] Others contend that the number of securities in the portfolios determines the number of factors that are priced.[28] A recent article, however, concludes that

> APT provides a powerful and appealing framework to consider security returns. Its acceptance, in both the academic and business community, is con-

[26] Richard Roll and Stephen A. Ross, "An Empirical Investigation of the Arbitrage Pricing Theory," *Journal of Finance* (December 1980): 1073–1103.

[27] D. C. Cho, Edwin J. Elton, and Martin J. Gruber, "On the Robustness of the Roll and Ross Arbitrage Pricing Theory," *Journal of Financial and Quantitative Analysis* (March 1984): 1–10.

[28] Phoebus J. Dhrymes, Irwin Friend, and N. Balent Gultekin, "A Critical Reexamination of the Empirical Evidence on the Arbitrage Pricing Theory," *Journal of Finance* (June 1984): 323–46.

> tingent upon supportive empirical tests of the theory. The standard empirical methodology is inadequate because inappropriate tests for the sufficient number of factors are being employed and because the standard tests fail to determine if the estimate model satisfies equilibrium conditions.[29]

The lack of agreement about the appropriate number of factors is not as important as the fact that more than one factor has been found to be statistically significant in pricing assets. This raises serious questions about the traditional CAPM, which depends on one factor, the market portfolio.

Another question has been raised concerning the APT: If statistically significant factors can be identified from security return data, what are the economic variables that these factors represent? Progress is being made in this area. Roll and Ross, based on their research with Nai-fu Chen, suggest that the following four economic factors are related to unanticipated returns on large portfolios:[30]

1. Unanticipated changes in inflation.
2. Unanticipated changes in industrial production.
3. Unanticipated changes in risk premiums (as measured by the spread between low-grade and high-grade bonds).
4. Unanticipated changes in the slope of the term structure of interest rates.

Currently, there is considerable debate in the literature about the correctness and relevancy of the CAPM and APT. One issue is the "testability" of the APT. Essentially, questions similar to those raised about the empirical tests of the CAPM have been extended to the tests of the APT. A second issue is whether the APT is more robust and appropriate than the CAPM. A possible solution is to recognize that both models have strengths and weaknesses, but that the combined models may provide more guidance for investment decision making than either model alone.

The APT does not overcome all the shortcomings of the CAPM. Both theories of asset pricing will continue to undergo empirical tests. The multifactor model of the APT is quite appealing, but its application in risk analysis awaits further empirical testing.

SUMMARY

This chapter has presented capital asset pricing model and arbitrage pricing theories, both of which are equilibrium theories of expected return. The efficient frontier according to CMT—the capital market line (CML)—consists of

[29] Michael C. Ehrhardt, "Arbitrage Pricing Models: The Sufficient Number of Factors and Equilibrium Conditions," *Journal of Financial Research* (Summer 1987): 111–20.

[30] N. F. Chen, "Some Empirical Tests of the Theory of Arbitrage Pricing," *Journal of Finance* (December 1983): 1394–1414; and Richard Roll and Stephen A. Ross, "The Arbitrage Pricing Theory Approach to Strategic Portfolio Planning," *Financial Analysts Journal* (May-June 1984): 14–26.

• CONCEPT APPLICATIONS

Investment Concept	Concept Application
Market portfolio	The market portfolio is a theoretical portfolio constructed in such a way that each risky asset is represented in the portfolio in proportion to its value relative to the value of all risky assets. Investors use a proxy for the market portfolio, such as the S&P 500.
Separation theorem	The theorem states that the selection of an individual investor's desired risk level is separate from the problem of selecting the assets to be included in the portfolio. If a market portfolio existed, investors would determine their desired risk levels by selecting the proportion of their investable funds they would put in the market portfolio and in the risk-free asset.
Capital market line	The CML describes the relationship between the total risk and expected return for perfectly diversified portfolios. This concept is only valid for pricing portfolios that are perfectly diversified. Individual assets will not lie on the CML.
Security market line	The SML describes the relationship between an asset's systematic risk and expected return. Therefore, all assets and portfolios lie on the SML. An investor can use the SML to estimate an asset's expected (required) return and compare this return to his or her estimate of the asset's return that is actually expected. This comparison can be helpful in making buy and sell decisions.
Systematic and unsystematic risk	Total risk can be separated into its systematic (market-related) risk and unsystematic (company- and industry-specific) risk. The investor should strive to eliminate all or most of the unsystematic risk from the portfolio through proper diversification. The market does not provide compensation in the form of increased return for facing unsystematic risk.
Beta	The beta coefficient is an index of systematic (rewardable) risk. Assets or portfolios with a beta greater than 1 are considered to be aggressive (more risky than the market), and assets or portfolios with a beta less than 1 are considered to be defensive (less risky than the market). Investors can use the beta measure to assess the risk level of the portfolio.
Arbitrage pricing theory	The central thesis of the APT is that more than one systematic factor affects the returns on financial assets. While the APT is appealing, its application for the individual investor awaits further development.

some combination of the market portfolio and the risk-free asset. Given this composition of the portfolios on the CML, it can be shown that all the portfolios on the CML are perfectly positively correlated.

The CML consists of perfectly diversified portfolios; that is, they contain no diversifiable or unsystematic risk. Therefore, for portfolios on the CML, total risk is equal to systematic risk. In order to estimate the expected return for less than perfectly diversified portfolios or individual assets, the relationship between systematic risk and expected return must be understood. This relationship is expressed by the security market line (SML), and the index of systematic risk is known as beta.

Important concepts developed in the chapter include the impact of diversification on risk and the fact that the market will reward investors only for nondiversifiable or systematic risk. This latter concept has pricing implications for assets. The CMT has applications not only for portfolio construction but also for common stock valuation (Chapter 14) and the analysis of portfolio performance (Chapter 21).

While the assumptions of CMT are restrictive, the test of the theory is its ability to fit economic data. Numerous empirical tests of beta stationarity indicate that betas for individual stocks are not stationary, but that betas for large portfolios of securities remain relatively stable from period to period. Tests of the CAPM using individual securities and portfolios of securities have been somewhat supportive of the theory. However, differences from the expected relationship between risk and return have been observed. Since these results are based on historical information, however, they cannot be used to conclude that the CAPM is invalid.

Some researchers have asked whether the CAPM is even testable. Richard Roll contends that proxies for the market portfolio used in the tests of the CAPM are not Markowitz-efficient and thus cannot be used in the empirical testing of the model.

The one-factor or market model of the CAPM has been challenged by Richard Roll and Stephen Ross. Ross developed a multifactor model—arbitrage pricing theory—in which the CAPM is a special case that uses one factor. The APT poses a serious challenge to the CAPM's preeminence in explaining the expected relationship between risk and return. While much developmental work and empirical investigation of the APT have been undertaken, much remains to be done. In particular, the actual economic factors that relate to unanticipated returns on large portfolios need to be identified.

• KEY TERMS

- Arbitrage
- Arbitrage pricing theory (APT)
- Beta
- Capital asset pricing model (CAPM)
- Capital market line (CML)
- Capital market theory
- Characteristic line
- Equilibrium
- Factor model
- Index model
- Market portfolio
- Market price of risk
- Naïve diversification
- Principle of risk compensation
- Risk premium
- Security market line (SML)
- Separation theorem
- Systematic (nondiversifiable) risk
- Unsystematic (diversifiable) risk

• QUESTIONS

1. Are the terms *rewardable, systematic,* and *nondiversifiable risk* interchangeable? Explain.
2. Are the terms *nonrewardable, unsystematic,* and *diversifiable risk* interchangeable? Explain.
3. What is meant by a "risk-free" asset? What are its characteristics?
4. Explain the role of the risk-free asset in the construction of the CML.
5. How are borrowing and lending portfolios created in CMT? Explain why a borrowing portfolio will be more risky than a lending portfolio.
6. Define what is meant by the market portfolio, and describe how it is constructed.
7. A portfolio's total risk can be divided into systematic risk and unsystematic risk. For which part of total risk can the investor expect to receive a return? Why?
8. Explain what is meant by the "market price of risk."
9. Compare and contrast the CML with the SML, including a discussion of the type of assets that will be on both lines and how risk is measured for each.
10. What does a beta coefficient measure? How is it calculated for an individual asset? For a portfolio of assets?
11. In terms of a beta coefficient, explain what is meant by an "aggressive" and "defensive" security or portfolio.
12. Explain how the CAPM might be used to estimate the cost of equity capital for a firm.
13. Are betas for individual securities stationary over time? If they are not stationary, what factors might contribute to this lack of stationarity?
14. Using the latest issue of the *Value Line Investment Survey* in the library, find the beta coefficient for General Motors, American Telephone and Telegraph, Chrysler Corporation, Homestake Mining, and Anheuser-Busch, Inc. What explanations can you offer for the differences in the beta coefficients?
15. Using the separation theorem, explain why the traditional approach to portfolio construction differs from the approach suggested by CMT.
16. Explain how the use of a proxy market portfolio can influence the empirical tests of the CAPM.
17. Compare and contrast the CAPM and APT.
18. Compare the "market" factor with "economic" factors that have been identified by the APT. Are all APT factors aggregate economic factors? Do you think it would be appropriate to consider industry factors as part of an APT model for an individual security?
19. Briefly discuss the empirical problems that have been encountered in testing the CAPM.
20. Empirical tests of the CAPM are generally supportive of the theory. However, the actual risk-return relationship prescribed by the CAPM is not consistent with the empirical tests. Does this invalidate the CAPM? Discuss.

• KEY TO THE INVESTMENT ANALYSIS SOFTWARE

Calculation	Appendix A-1 Page Reference	Access Procedure
Alpha	A-12	BEGIN, CAPITAL, CAPM
Beta	A-12	BEGIN, CAPITAL, CAPM
Capital market line	A-12	BEGIN, CAPITAL, CAPM
Characteristic line	A-12 or A-7	BEGIN, CAPITAL, CAPM (and CHAR for graph); or BEGIN, STATISTICAL, REGRESS
Security market line	A-12	BEGIN, CAPITAL, CAPM (and SML for graph)

• PROBLEMS

1. The expected return of the market portfolio is 16 percent, the risk-free rate is 8 percent, and the standard deviation of return of the market portfolio is 9 percent.

a. Draw a graph of the CML.

b. What is the market price of risk?

c. If you borrow an amount equal to 30 percent of your investable funds at the risk-free rate and invest it along with all your investable funds in the market portfolio, what are the expected return and risk of your portfolio?

2. Given the following information:

Risk-free rate	6%
Expected return of the market portfolio	11%
Standard deviation of the market portfolio	11%
Correlation coefficient of asset A and the market portfolio	+.80
Standard deviation of the return of asset A	9%

a. Calculate the beta coefficient for asset A. Is asset A classified as an aggressive or defensive asset? Why?

b. Draw the SML and locate asset A on it.

c. What is the expected return for asset A?

d. Suppose that you have independently estimated that the expected return for asset A is 15 percent. Is asset A underpriced or overpriced? In a market that is striving toward equilibrium, what would happen to the price of asset A?

e. Calculate the systematic and unsystematic risk for asset A. Interpret your answer.

3. Assume two common stocks have the following betas:

$$\beta_1 = 1.2 \qquad \beta_2 = 0.9$$

a. Calculate the beta for a portfolio consisting of equal dollar investments in each stock.

b. If an investor thought that a portfolio beta of 1.1 was appropriate, indicate the proportion of funds that could be invested in *both* stocks to form this portfolio.

4. Consider the following information on three common stocks:

Stock	*Beta*	*Correlation of HPRs with market portfolio HPRs*
Alpha	1.2	1.0
Delta	−0.8	−0.8
Gamma	1.6	0.3

a. Indicate the stock(s) with no unsystematic risk.

b. Based on the CAPM, which stock would have the highest expected return? The lowest expected return?

5. The following are the quarterly HPRs for common stock XYZ and the S&P 500:

Year	*Quarter*	*Common stock XYZ HPR*	*S&P 500 HPR*
1	1	9.7%	10.0%
	2	28.4	11.0
	3	3.7	−0.2
	4	−13.1	.4
2	1	−5.7	−2.4
	2	−1.2	−2.6
	3	16.7	9.6
	4	18.8	1.8
3	1	16.5	9.2
	2	9.2	7.3
	3	−10.1	−4.1
	4	7.5	17.1
4	1	22.8	14.0
	2	0.0	5.8
	3	−9.9	−7.0
	4	0.6	5.6

a. Calculate the expected return, based on the historical data, of common stock XYZ and the S&P 500.

b. Calculate the standard deviations of the historical returns of common stock XYZ and the S&P 500.

c. Calculate the covariance and the correlation coefficient of the returns of common stock XYZ and the S&P 500.

d. What is the estimated beta for common stock XYZ?

e. Identify the systematic and unsystematic components of total risk for common stock XYZ.

6. You are given the following information:

Security	*Beta*
A	1.40
B	1.20
C	.90
D	.80

The risk-free rate is 8 percent, and the expected return on the market portfolio is 15 percent.

a. Draw the SML.

b. What is the expected return of securities A, B, C, and D?

c. Locate securities A, B, C, and D on the SML.

7. Suppose you are attempting to estimate an appropriate expected return for a particular common stock. Assume the risk-free return is 8 percent.

a. If the expected return on the market is 15 percent and the stock's beta is 1.2, use the CAPM to calculate the expected return.

b. Using an APT approach, the following factors and sensitivity indexes have been identified:

Factor	*Market price of risk*	*Sensitivity index*
Unanticipated changes in inflation	6.0%	1.1
Unanticipated changes in industrial production	2.0	0.8
Unanticipated changes in risk premiums	3.0	1.0
Unanticipated changes in term structure	4.0	−0.9

Use an appropriate APT model to calculate the expected return.

c. What explanations can you offer to account for the difference in the two estimates of expected return?

• REFERENCES

Abell, John D., and Thomas M. Krueger. "Macroeconomic Influences on Beta." *Journal of Economics and Business* (May 1989): 185–93.

Arnott, Robert D. "What Hath MPT Wrought: Which Risks Reap Rewards?" *Journal of Portfolio Management* (Fall 1983): 5–11.

Barry, Michael A., Edwin Burmeister, and Marjorie B. McElroy. "Sorting Out Risks Using Known APT Factors." *Financial Analysts Journal* (March-April 1988): 29–42.

Beaver, William, Paul Kettler, and Myron Scholes. "The Association between Market Determined and Accounting Determined Risk Measures." *Accounting Review* (October 1970): 654–82.

Bernstein, Peter L. "Dead—or Alive and Well?" *Journal of Portfolio Management* (Winter 1981): 4.

Black, Fischer, Michael C. Jensen, and Myron S. Scholes. "The Capital Asset Pricing Model: Some Empirical Tests." In *Studies in the Theory of Capital Markets,* edited by Michael Jensen, pp. 79–121. New York: Praeger, 1972.

Blume, Marshall E. "On the Assessment of Risk." *Journal of Finance* (March 1971): 1–10.

———. "Betas and Their Regression Tendencies." *Journal of Finance* (June 1975): 785–95.

———. "Betas and Their Regression Tendencies: Some Further Evidence." *Journal of Finance* (March 1979): 265–67.

Blume, Marshall E., and Irwin Friend. "A New Look at The Capital Asset Pricing Model." *Journal of Finance* (March 1973): 19–33.

Bower, Dorothy H., Richard S. Bower, and Dennis E. Logue. "A Primer on Arbitrage Pricing Theory." *Midland Corporate Financial Journal* (Fall 1984): 31–40.

Carvell, Steven, and Paul Strebel. "A New Beta Incorporating Analysts' Forecasts." *Journal of Portfolio Management* (Fall 1984): 81–85.

Chatterjee, Sangit, and Robert A. Pari. "Bootstrapping the Number of Factors in the Arbitrage Pricing Theory." *Journal of Financial Research* (Spring 1990): 15–21.

Cohen, Kalman J., and Gerald A. Pogue. "An Empirical Evaluation of Alternative Portfolio Selection Models." *Journal of Business* (April 1967): 166–93.

Dhrymes, Phoebus J., Irwin Friend, and N. Balent Gultekin. "Arbitrage Pricing Theory." *Journal of Portfolio Management* (Summer 1984): 35–44.

Dybvig, Philip H., and Stephen A. Ross. "Yes, The APT Is Testable." *Journal of Finance* (September 1985): 1173–88.

Elton, Edwin J., and Martin J. Gruber. "Estimating the Dependence Structure of Share Prices—Implications for Portfolio Selection." *Journal of Finance* (December 1973): 1203–32.

Fama, Eugene F., and James D. MacBeth. "Risk Return and Equilibrium: Empirical Tests." *Journal of Political Economy* (May-June 1973): 607–36.

Findlay, M. Chapman III, and Edward E. Williams. "Better Betas Didn't Help the Boat People." *Journal of Portfolio Management* (Fall 1986): 4–9.

Fogler, Russell H. "Common Stock Management in the 1990s." *Journal of Portfolio Management* (Winter 1990): 26–35.

Frankfurter, George M., and Herbert E. Phillips. "MPT Plus Security Analysis for Better Performance." *Journal of Portfolio Management* (Summer 1982): 29–36.

French, Dan W., John C. Groth, and James W. Kolari. "Current Investor Expectations and Better Betas." *Journal of Portfolio Management* (Fall 1983): 12–17.

Hill, Ned C., and Bernell K. Stone. "Accounting Betas, Systematic Operating Risk, and Financial Leverage: A Risk-Composition Approach to the Determinants of Systematic Risk." *Journal of Financial and Quantitative Analysis* (September 1980): 595–637.

Jones, Robert C. "Designing Factor Models for Different Types of Stock: What's Good for the Goose Ain't Always Good for the Gander." *Financial Analysts Journal* (March-April 1990): 25–30, 50.

King, Benjamin F. "Market and Industry Factors in Stock Price Behavior." *Journal of Business* (January 1966): 139–90.

Kolb, Robert W., and Ricardo J. Rodriguez. "The Regression Tendencies of Betas: A Reappraisal." *Financial Review* (May 1989): 319–34.

Lee, Cheng F., Paul Newbold, Joseph E. Finnerty, and Chen-Chin Chu. "On Accounting-Based, Market-Based and Composite-Based Beta Predictions: Methods and Implications." *Financial Review* (February 1986): 51–68.

Levy, Haim. "The CAPM and the Investment Horizon." *Journal of Portfolio Management* (Winter 1981): 32–40.

Levy, Robert A. "On the Short-Term Stationarity of Beta Coefficients." *Financial Analysts Journal* (November-December 1971): 55–62.

Lintner, John. "Security Prices, Risk, and Maximal Gain from Diversification." *Journal of Finance* (December 1965): 587–615.

———. "The Aggregation of Investor's Diverse Judgments and Preferences in Purely Competitive Security Markets." *Journal of Financial and Quantitative Analysis* (December 1969): 347–400.

Lloyd, William P., and Naval K. Modani. "Stocks, Bonds, Bills, and Time Diversification." *Journal of Portfolio Management* (Spring 1983): 7–11.

Markowitz, Harry M. *Portfolio Selection: Efficient Diversification of Investments.* New York: John Wiley & Sons, 1959.

———. "The 'Two Beta' Trap." *Journal of Portfolio Management* (Fall 1984): 12–20.

McDonald, Bill. "Making Sense Out of Unstable Alphas and Betas." *Journal of Portfolio Management* (Winter 1985): 19–22.

Miller, Merton H., and Myron Scholes. "Rates of Return in Relation to Risk: A Reexamination of Some Recent Findings." In *Studies in the Theory of Capital Markets,* edited by Michael Jensen, pp. 47–78. New York: Praeger, 1972.

Modani, Naval K., William P. Lloyd, and John H. Hand. "Behavior of Risk Proxies and Merger Activity." *Review of Business and Economic Research* (Spring 1984): 81–89.

———. "Bond Rating Changes and Behavior of Risk Proxies." *Akron Business and Economic Review* (Spring 1984): 46–49.

Modigliani, Franco, and Gerald A. Pogue. "An Introduction to Risk and Return (Part II)." *Financial Analysts Journal* (May-June 1974): 69–86.

Reilly, Frank K., and David J. Wright. "A Comparison of Published Betas." *Journal of Portfolio Management* (Spring 1988): 64–69.

Reinganum, Marc R. "Abnormal Returns in Small Firm Portfolios." *Financial Analysts Journal* (March-April 1981): 52–57.

Roll, Richard. "A Critique of the Asset Pricing Theory's Tests." *Journal of Financial Economics* (March 1977): 129–76.

———. "Ambiguity When Performance Is Measured by the Security Market Line." *Journal of Finance* (September 1978): 1051–69.

Roll, Richard, and Stephen A. Ross. "An Empirical Investigation of the Arbitrage Pricing Theory." *Journal of Finance* (December 1980): 1073–1103.

———. "The Arbitrage Pricing Theory Approach to Strategic Portfolio Planning." *Financial Analysts Journal* (May-June 1984): 14–26.

Rosenberg, Barr. "Prediction of Common Stock Betas." *Journal of Portfolio Management* (Winter 1985): 5–14.

Ross, Stephen A. "The Arbitrage Theory of Capital Asset Pricing." *Journal of Economic Theory* (December 1976): 341–60.

———. "A Reply to Dhrymes: APT Is Empirically Relevant." *Journal of Portfolio Management* (Fall 1984): 54–56.

Schmerken, Ivy. "Making Risk Analysis Easy as Alpha, Beta." *Wall Street Computer Review* (January 1988): 81–12.

Sharpe, William F. "A Simplified Model for Portfolio Analysis." *Management Science* (January 1963): 277–93.

———. "Factor Models, CAPMs, and the APT." *Journal of Portfolio Management* (Fall 1984): 21–25.

Statman, Meir. "Betas Compared: Merrill Lynch vs. Value Line." *Journal of Portfolio Management* (Winter 1981): 41–44.

Tallman, Ellis W. "Financial Asset Pricing Theory: A Review of Recent Developments." *Economic Review* (Federal Reserve Bank of Atlanta) (November-December 1989): 26–41.

Tole, Thomas M. "You Can't Diversify without Diversifying." *Journal of Portfolio Management* (Winter 1982): 5–11.

Vasicek, Oldrich A., and John A. McQuown. "The Efficient Market Model." *Financial Analysts Journal* (September-October 1972): 71–84.

Wagner, Wayne H., and S. C. Laer. "The Effect of Diversification on Risk." *Financial Analysts Journal* (November-December 1971): 48–53.

Wallace, Anise. "Is Beta Dead?" *Institutional Investor* (July 1980): 23–30.

Willis, Clint. "Managing Your Portfolio like a Pro." *Money,* May 1986, pp. 152–56.

APPENDIX 20A

Relaxing the Assumptions:

The Impact on CMT

The assumptions underlying CMT are less realistic than portfolio theory assumptions. If CMT assumptions reflected the "real world," each investor would hold only the market portfolio since any other portfolio would contain some diversifiable risk. Further, investors would price each asset with respect to its covariance with the market portfolio, as indicated in the equation for the security market line. Relaxing the assumptions of CMT changes this "idealized" world.

THE EFFICIENT FRONTIER, HOMOGENEOUS EXPECTATIONS, AND COMMON INVESTMENT HORIZON

Assumptions 1, 3, and 4 of CMT assume that all investors seek to be on the efficient frontier, have homogeneous expectations about the risk and return of assets, and share a common investment horizon. If these assumptions were true in an absolute sense, there would be no need for active portfolio management. With homogeneous expectations and the ability to identify, ex-ante, the efficient frontier, all investors would hold some combination of the market portfolio and the risk-free asset.

Investors have different horizons and diverse expectations about the risk and return of individual assets. Thus, a unique, ex-ante market portfolio identifiable by all investors cannot exist. Rather, each investor creates a portfolio that is efficient in terms of his or her own expectations and investment horizon. These portfolios are not necessarily efficient as defined by CMT.

Does the existence of these "inefficient" portfolios held by investors make CMT an invalid concept? The answer is no, if one is willing to accept Lintner's argument that the market clearing process does not reflect homogeneous expectations of market participants but rather a "consensus expectation" of market participants.[31] The impact of these heterogeneous expectations is such that rather than only one portfolio—the market portfolio—being on the CML, a number of portfolios would be on the CML.

Defining equilibrium in the capital market in terms of consensus expectations does not invalidate the concepts of rewardable (systematic) and nonrewardable (unsystematic) risk. It simply means that rather than one SML defin-

---

[31] John Lintner, "The Aggregation of Investor's Diverse Judgments and Preferences in Purely Competitive Security Markets," *Journal of Financial and Quantitative Analysis* (December 1969): 347–400. See also, Joseph T. Williams, "Capital Asset Prices with Heterogeneous Beliefs," *Journal of Financial Economics* (November 1977): 219–39.

ing the risk-return trade-off, there may be multiple SMLs, reflecting differing expectations and investment horizons.

UNLIMITED BORROWING AND LENDING AT THE RISK-FREE RATE AND CERTAINTY OF INTEREST RATES AND INFLATION

Relaxing assumption 2 of CMT means that all borrowing and lending may not occur at the identical risk-free rate. This has important implications for the shape of the CML. Recall that the CML was constructed assuming lending and borrowing at the risk-free rate (R_f). A more reasonable assumption is that investors can lend at a risk-free rate (e.g., buying Treasury bills), but they cannot borrow at a rate this low. In other words, the borrowing rate (R_B) is expected to be higher than R_f.

Differentiating between lending and borrowing rates creates two tangency portfolios, as shown in Figure 20A.1, compared to the one tangency portfolio in Figure 20.2. Lending portfolios will be located along the line segment R_fS, according to the investor's risk-return preference. Borrowing portfolios will be located on line segment *VX*, again depending on the investor's risk-return preference.

FIGURE 20A.1
The Capital Market Line with Different Borrowing and Lending Rates

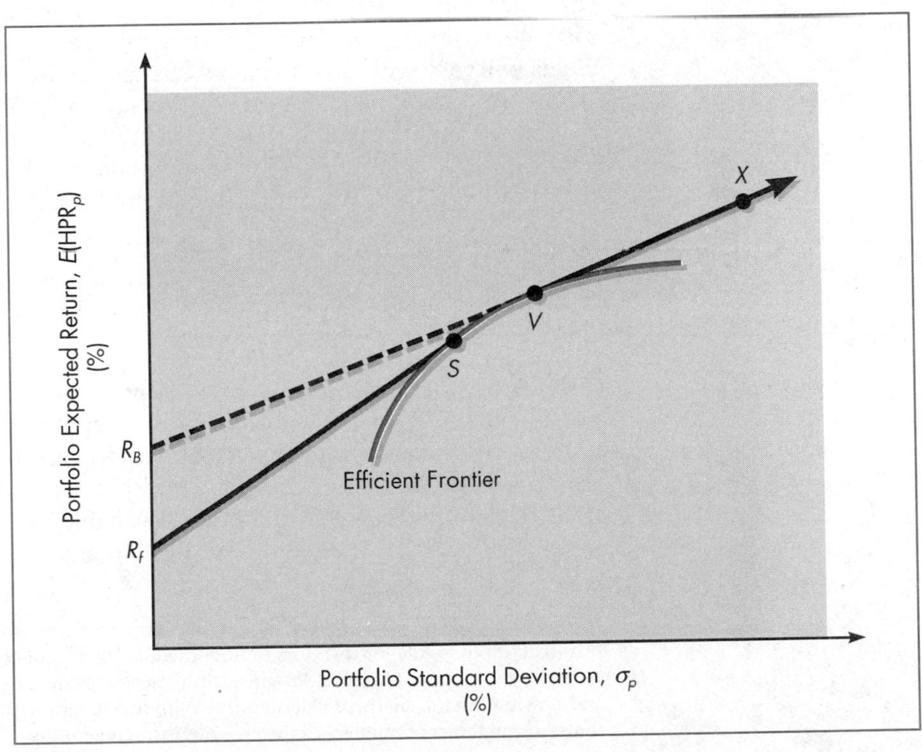

The dashed portion of the R_BX line in Figure 20A.1, which is not a part of the "new" efficient frontier when differential borrowing and lending rates exist, indicates that the slope of the R_BX line is less than the slope of the R_fS line. Recall that the market price of risk is the slope of the CML. Under assumption 2 of CMT, the borrowing and lending rate is R_f, and the slope of the CML is

$$\text{slope} = \frac{E(R_M) - R_f}{\sigma_M}. \tag{20A.1}$$

Since R_B is assumed to be greater than R_f, compensation per unit of total risk will be less with borrowing portfolios than with lending portfolios:

$$\frac{E(R_M) - R_B}{\sigma_M} < \frac{E(R_M) - R_f}{\sigma_M} \tag{20A.2}$$

Empirical tests of the CAPM have indicated that the relationship between the expected return and the measure of systematic risk is linear, with a positive intercept. However, the slope of the SML is less than that predicted by the CAPM; this may very well be due to the unrealistic assumption that investors can borrow at the risk-free rate.

Relaxing assumption 7, which assumes no unanticipated changes in inflation or interest rates, raises doubts about whether a "true" risk-free rate exists. Yields on Treasury bills have been suggested as a proxy for the risk-free rate; nevertheless, although Treasury bills contain no default risk, their real yields will vary with unanticipated changes in the rate of inflation. Thus, there is some variance in the return on Treasury bills, which is related directly to macroeconomic variables; thus, Treasury bills are not "risk-free." This problem of yield variance can be partially addressed by matching the maturity of the Treasury security with the investment horizon of the portfolio.

INVESTMENT DIVISIBILITY

The impact on CAPM of relaxing assumption 5, which maintains that it is possible to buy or sell any portion of an asset or portfolio, is rather minor. The SML would be represented by discrete or discontinous segments rather than a continuous or solid line segment. Thus, portfolios with all possible combinations of risk and return would not be available.[32]

[32] In fact, it is possible for investors to buy fractional shares of common stocks. For example, Merrill Lynch has a "Blueprint Program" in which investors can invest in stocks, mutual funds, and precious metals by the dollar amount. With this program, investors can acquire fractions of shares or, in the case of metals, ounces—not just whole units.

TAXES, TRANSACTION AND INFORMATION COSTS, AND MARKET EQUILIBRIUM

The Tax Reform Act of 1986 eliminated the favorable treatment given long-term capital gains; the tax rates on capital gains and ordinary income are equal. Nevertheless, the investor still has more control over the timing of taxes on capital gains. Ordinary income—for example, cash dividends—is generally not controlled by the investor. On the other hand, the investor can decide when capital gains will be taken and thus when the taxes associated with the capital gains will be paid. In addition, a tax effect manifests itself not only in the differential rates of taxation among individual investors but also in the applicability of the tax law to types of investors and investment instruments. For example, municipal bonds, which are tax-exempt are held by taxable investors, not by investors who are tax-exempt. Further, the vast majority of preferred stock shares are held by corporations because they can exclude a portion of the dividends of preferred stock from taxes.

Clearly, investors will hold the types of investments that provide the largest tax advantage. Thus, on an after-tax basis, investors will have different perspectives on what comprises an efficient portfolio, resulting in more individualized SMLs.

Removing the assumption of no transaction and information costs creates a range of possible SMLs, as shown in Figure 20A.2. Because of the existence

FIGURE 20A.2
Impact of Transaction and Information Costs on the Security Market Line

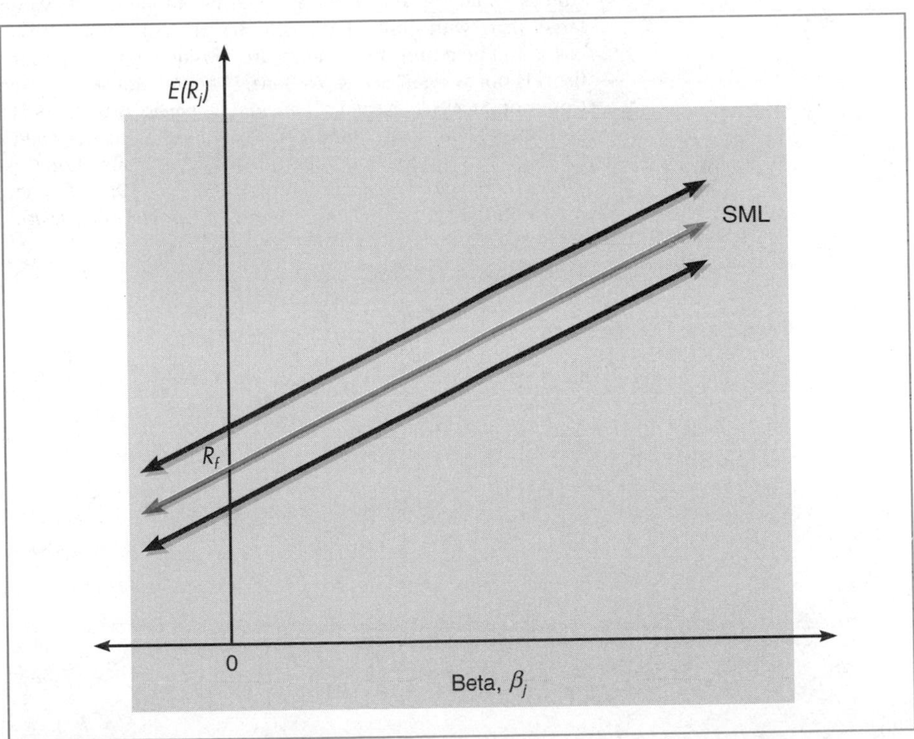

of transaction costs, a certain degree of disequilibrium in the capital markets will be allowed. That is, the increase in expected return from discovering an undervalued security may not be large enough to compensate for the transaction costs associated with taking advantage of the undervalued situation. The width of the band around the SML will therefore be a function of the size of the transaction costs. Given that (1) a large proportion of all security transactions are undertaken by institutions that have very low transaction costs, (2) commissions on transactions have been negotiable since May 1, 1975, and (3) the number of discount brokerage houses has increased, the size of the band around the SML is relatively narrow.

The same logic that created a range of SMLs for transaction costs also applies to information costs. The cost of acquiring information and research must be weighed against the possible increased returns from using this information. For example, discount brokerage firms have lower commission costs but do not provide research services for their clients. To acquire this information, the investor must trade with the source of the information, the nondiscount broker, at a higher transaction cost. At some point, the increased expected return will be offset by higher transaction costs, and thus a disequilibrium situation will be allowed to exist.[33]

---

[33] Studies of the effect of firm size on return illustrate the impact of transaction and information costs. Leaving aside the question of whether the CAPM properly specifies expected return, these studies found that smaller firms, in terms of total market value, provided higher returns than larger firms with similar levels of systematic risk. When the costs of transactions, information costs, and premiums for liquidity are considered, the superiority of the net returns for the small firms is not as clear. See R. W. Banz, "The Relationship between Return and Market Value of Common Stocks," *Journal of Financial Economics* (March 1981): 3–18; Marc R. Reinganum, "Abnormal Returns in Small Firm Portfolios," *Financial Analysts Journal* (March-April 1981): 52–57; Hans R. Stoll and Robert E. Whaley, "Transaction Costs and the Small Firm Effect," *Journal of Financial Economics* (June 1983): 57–80; and Avner Arbel and Paul Strebel, "Pay Attention to Neglected Firms!" *Journal of Portfolio Management* (Winter 1983): 37–42.

CHAPTER 21

Analysis of Portfolio Performance and Market Efficiency

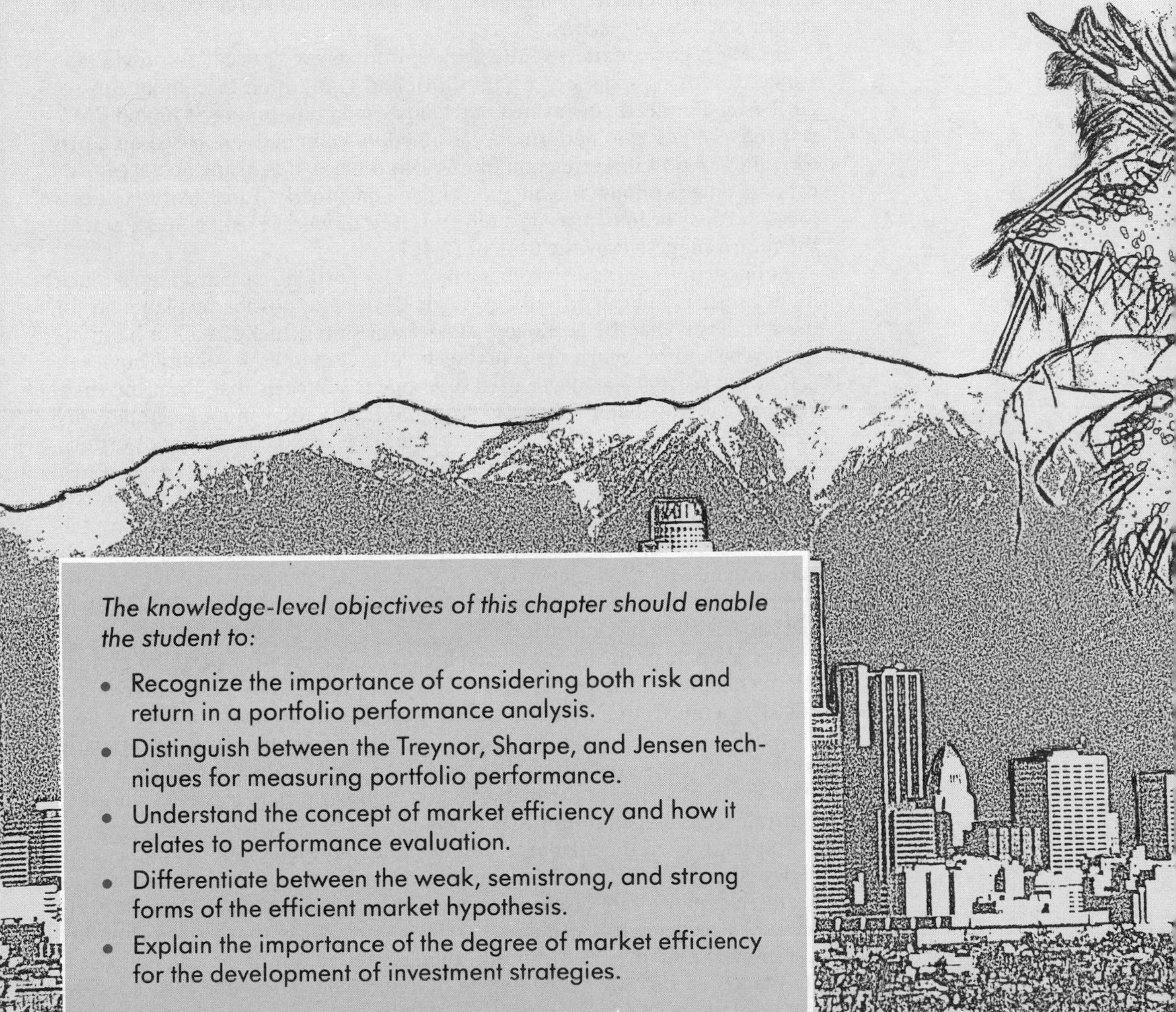

The knowledge-level objectives of this chapter should enable the student to:

- Recognize the importance of considering both risk and return in a portfolio performance analysis.
- Distinguish between the Treynor, Sharpe, and Jensen techniques for measuring portfolio performance.
- Understand the concept of market efficiency and how it relates to performance evaluation.
- Differentiate between the weak, semistrong, and strong forms of the efficient market hypothesis.
- Explain the importance of the degree of market efficiency for the development of investment strategies.

INTRODUCTION

This chapter discusses portfolio performance evaluation based on techniques developed from capital market theory (CMT), presented in Chapters 2 and 20. As CMT indicates, the returns earned by a portfolio should be related to the risk taken by the portfolio. The security market line (SML) indicates how the expected returns on securities or portfolios should be related to their systematic risk or betas. The capital market line (CML) indicates how the expected returns of perfectly diversified portfolios should be related to their total risk or standard deviations.

If CMT is correct and securities and portfolios are "priced" to provide the expected returns suggested by the SML and CML, then in equilibrium securities and perfectly diversified portfolios would plot on the SML and CML, respectively. Portfolio performance evaluation techniques are based on a historical or ex-post interpretation of CMT. In other words, using actual historical data on a portfolio and an appropriate benchmark or market proxy portfolio, did the portfolio provide a return (given its level of risk) consistent with the return suggested by the SML or CML?

Suppose initially, however, that a particular portfolio earned a return much higher than is indicated by the SML or CML. One possible explanation for these results is that the portfolio manager was simply lucky in his or her market timing and/or security selection techniques. Another possibility, however, is that the portfolio manager used investment strategies that "beat the market." A final possibility is that the "true" SML or CML cannot be empirically estimated. For example, an inefficient market proxy or benchmark portfolio may have been used rather than the "true" market portfolio as defined by CMT.

As this discussion indicates, portfolio performance evaluation and market efficiency are closely related. If a significant number of portfolios can consistently achieve superior performance based on evaluation techniques developed from CMT, then maybe capital markets are not very efficient. On the other hand, if few portfolios consistently achieve superior performance, then market efficiency is confirmed.

The first part of this chapter examines three widely used portfolio evaluation techniques, using actual data from two mutual funds. Next, the chapter discusses a number of empirical studies dealing with the performance of professionally managed portfolios, such as mutual funds and insurance company portfolios. These studies show that, on average, professionally managed portfolios are unable to beat the market when their performance is assessed using techniques developed from CMT.

The last half of the chapter continues to explore the issue of market efficiency. The studies of portfolio performance and other studies of various investment strategies are discussed in terms of their implications for market efficiency. Based on this evidence, the key question is the *degree* of market efficiency. If markets are inefficient, then strategies can be developed to beat the market. A high or strong degree of market efficiency, however, suggests that no strategy can consistently beat the market.

OVERVIEW OF PORTFOLIO PERFORMANCE EVALUATION

One important aspect of investment decision making is the historical or ex-post analysis of a portfolio's performance. The analysis of historical performance is an indication of the success of the portfolio's investment strategy and the skill of the portfolio's manager. The results of the performance analysis may suggest the need for portfolio revisions, modification of the investment strategy, or even a change in the portfolio manager.

As a simple illustration, assume that two highly diversified common stock portfolios earned the following holding period returns (HPRs) for 1990:

Portfolio	HPR
A	15%
B	20

These returns are computed as net of transactions cost and expenses incurred in managing the portfolio. Would it be correct to conclude that the performance of portfolio B was superior to portfolio A's? The correct answer, of course, is no, since a valid performance analysis should consider both returns and *risk*. It is quite possible that the risk of portfolio B is substantially above that of portfolio A even though both portfolios contain only common stocks. If the risk of both portfolios is equal, however, then portfolio B would be judged to have outperformed portfolio A.

• Calculating Ex-Post Returns for Performance Analysis

In analyzing a portfolio's performance, the HPR on the portfolio needs to be correctly calculated over the period of the evaluation. For a single holding period, the ex-post HPR of the portfolio can be calculated as

$$\text{HPR}_{p,t} = \frac{V_{t+1} - V_t + I_t}{V_t} \tag{21.1}$$

where

V_{t+1} = market value of the portfolio at the end of the holding period

V_t = market value of the portfolio at the beginning of the holding period

I_t = income that was *distributed* by the portfolio during the period of the evaluation

As an illustration, assume that on January 1, 1990, the market value of the portfolio was \$10,000. By December 31, 1990, the market value had in-

TABLE 21.1 • Measures of Risk and Return for Selected Mutual Funds, the S&P 500, and One-Year Treasury Bills, 1980–1989

	Fidelity Magellan Fund		T. Rowe Price New Horizons Fund, Inc.		S&P 500		One-year Treasury bill	
	HPR	*End-of-year value*	*HPR*	*End-of-year value*	*HPR*	*End-of-year value*	*HPR*	*End-of-year value*
1980	76.5%	$ 17,650	57.6%	$15,760	34.1%	$13,410	12.06%	$11,206
1981	12.1	19,786	(7.8)	14,531	(4.8)	12,766	14.08	12,784
1982	48.1	29,303	22.8	17,844	22.2	15,600	14.32	14,614
1983	38.6	40,613	19.5	21,323	21.3	18,923	8.62	15,874
1984	2.0	41,426	(9.6)	19,276	4.1	19,699	9.90	17,446
1985	43.1	59,280	24.3	23,960	29.9	25,589	9.33	19,073
1986	23.8	73,389	(0.1)	23,936	18.1	30,221	7.06	20,420
1987	2.4	75,150	(7.1)	22,237	5.7	31,943	5.60	21,564
1988	22.8	92,284	14.0	25,350	16.5	37,214	6.74	23,017
1989	34.6	124,215	26.2	31,992	31.6	48,974	8.45	24,962
Average annual HPR	30.40%		13.98%		17.87%		9.62%	
Geometric average annual HPR	28.65%		12.33%		17.22%		9.58%	
Standard deviation	22.88%		20.92%		12.83%		3.01%	
Correlation with S&P 500	0.84		0.88		1.00		—	
Beta	1.50		1.44		1.00		—	

SOURCE: Data to calculate the HPRs were obtained from Wiesenberger Financial Services, *Investment Companies* (1989) and *Management Results* (March 1990); *Federal Reserve Bulletin*, various issues; and Standard & Poor's Statistical Service. Reprinted by permission.

creased to $11,000 *after* a distribution of income (dividends and interest) of $1,000 to the portfolio's owner. The HPR for 1990 would be

$$HPR_{p,1990} = \frac{\$11{,}000 - \$10{,}000 + \$1{,}000}{\$10{,}000} = 20\% \qquad (21.2)$$

Table 21.1 provides annual HPRs over the 1980–1989 period for a sample of two mutual funds, the S&P 500, and one-year Treasury bills. The HPRs were calculated using Equation 21.1.[1] The income distributions (I) used in

[1] The HPRs do not reflect the initial investment fee or "load" charge. The Fidelity Magellan Fund charges a fee of 3 percent, while the New Horizons Fund does not charge a fee. The importance of fees for mutual fund investing was discussed in Chapter 5.

calculating the HPRs include both capital gains and dividend distributions made by the funds. The second column under each fund ("End-of-Year Value") is calculated by assuming that an initial investment of \$10,000 was made on January 1, 1980. It is also assumed that the distributions (capital gains and dividends) were reinvested in new shares.

For example, a \$10,000 investment in the Fidelity Magellan Fund on January 1, 1980, would have grown to \$124,215 by December 31, 1989, assuming all distributions were reinvested. The geometric average annual HPR for the Fidelity Magellan Fund can be calculated as

$$\overline{\text{HPR}}_g = [(1.765)(1.121)\ldots(1.346)]^{1/10} - 1 = 28.65\% \quad (21.3)$$

Alternatively, the geometric average annual HPR could be calculated, using the initial investment of \$10,000 and the 1989 ending portfolio value:

$$\$124{,}215 = \$10{,}000(1 + \overline{\text{HPR}}_g)^{10}$$
$$\overline{\text{HPR}}_g = 28.65\%$$

• Analysis of Risk in Performance Analysis

The two mutual funds in Table 21.1 are both common stock funds with an investment objective of "growth" and an emphasis on "maximum capital gains." Since the two funds have the same investment objectives and invest almost exclusively in common stocks, is the risk of the funds equal? As would be expected, because of the investment objective, both betas are significantly greater than 1. In addition, the funds' standard deviations and correlation coefficients with the S&P 500 also exhibit some differences. These differences, along with CMT as discussed in Chapter 20, suggest that any performance analysis of the two funds should consider *both* HPRs and risk.

Given that risk should be considered in any analysis of portfolio performance, how should risk be measured? Several measures are available, including beta and the standard deviation. The correlation coefficient may also need to be considered since it provides an indication of the diversification of a portfolio relative to some benchmark portfolio. The next section presents a number of techniques based on CMT that can be used in a risk-adjusted performance analysis both to rank portfolios and to compare their performances to a benchmark portfolio.

TECHNIQUES FOR MEASURING PORTFOLIO PERFORMANCE

The development of portfolio theory—specifically, CMT and the capital asset pricing model (CAPM)—provided the foundation for risk-adjusted performance analysis. These developments provided empirical risk measures that could be used in conjunction with return measures.

• The Treynor Portfolio Performance Technique

In an article in the *Harvard Business Review* in 1965, Jack L. Treynor presented the first formal technique that combined risk and returns in a single performance measure.[2] His technique used the systematic or nondiversifiable risk of the portfolio as the appropriate measure of risk. Treynor argued that the HPRs of the portfolio that deviate from the characteristic line of the portfolio represent unsystematic or diversifiable risk. The portfolio manager, through adequate diversification, should be able to reduce these deviations so that they are relatively unimportant in the analysis. The appropriate measure of risk then becomes beta or the systematic risk of the portfolio.

Treynor's technique used the ratio of the **risk premium** of the portfolio divided by the beta:

$$T_p = \frac{\overline{\text{HPR}}_p - \bar{R}_f}{\beta_p} \tag{21.4}$$

where

T_p = Treynor's portfolio performance measure
$\overline{\text{HPR}}_p$ = average holding period return on the portfolio over the evaluation period
$\bar{R}_f$ = average risk-free return over the evaluation period
β_p = beta of the portfolio over the evaluation period

Since T_p is a ratio of excess return, or the risk premium divided by a measure of the portfolio's systematic risk, larger ratios indicate superior performance. T_p can be viewed essentially as excess return per unit of systematic risk. Portfolios can consequently be ranked by T_p.

Using Treynor's technique, a similar measure for the benchmark or market portfolio can be calculated:

$$T_m = \frac{\overline{\text{HPR}}_m - \bar{R}_f}{\beta_m} \tag{21.5}$$

where

T_m = Treynor's performance measure for the market portfolio
$\overline{\text{HPR}}_m$ = average holding period return on the market portfolio over the evaluation period
$\bar{R}_f$ = average risk-free return over the evaluation period
β_m = beta of the market portfolio

Since, by definition, the beta of the market portfolio (β_m) is 1, T_m reduces to $\overline{\text{HPR}}_m - \bar{R}_f$. If $T_p > T_m$, then according to Treynor's technique, the portfolio outperformed the market. If $T_p \leq T_m$, then the market did as well or better than the portfolio.

[2] Jack L. Treynor, "How to Rate Management of Investment Funds," *Harvard Business Review* (January-February 1965): 63–75.

The data on the mutual funds and S&P 500 in Table 21.1 can be used to illustrate the Treynor technique:

$$\text{Magellan Fund:} \quad T_p = \frac{28.65\% - 9.58\%}{1.50} = 12.71\%$$

$$\text{New Horizons Fund:} \quad T_p = \frac{12.33\% - 9.58\%}{1.44} = 1.91\%$$

$$\text{S\&P 500:} \quad T_m = 17.22\% - 9.58\% = 7.64\%$$

Notice that the geometric average HPRs are used rather than the simple average. The Magellan Fund clearly had the best performance. Magellan outperformed the market over the period, while the New Horizons Fund underperformed the market.

A SML based on the data in Table 21.1 appears in Figure 21.1. It also shows the two mutual funds relative to the SML. The graph illustrates that T_m

FIGURE 21.1
SML and Treynor's Performance Measure, 1980–1989

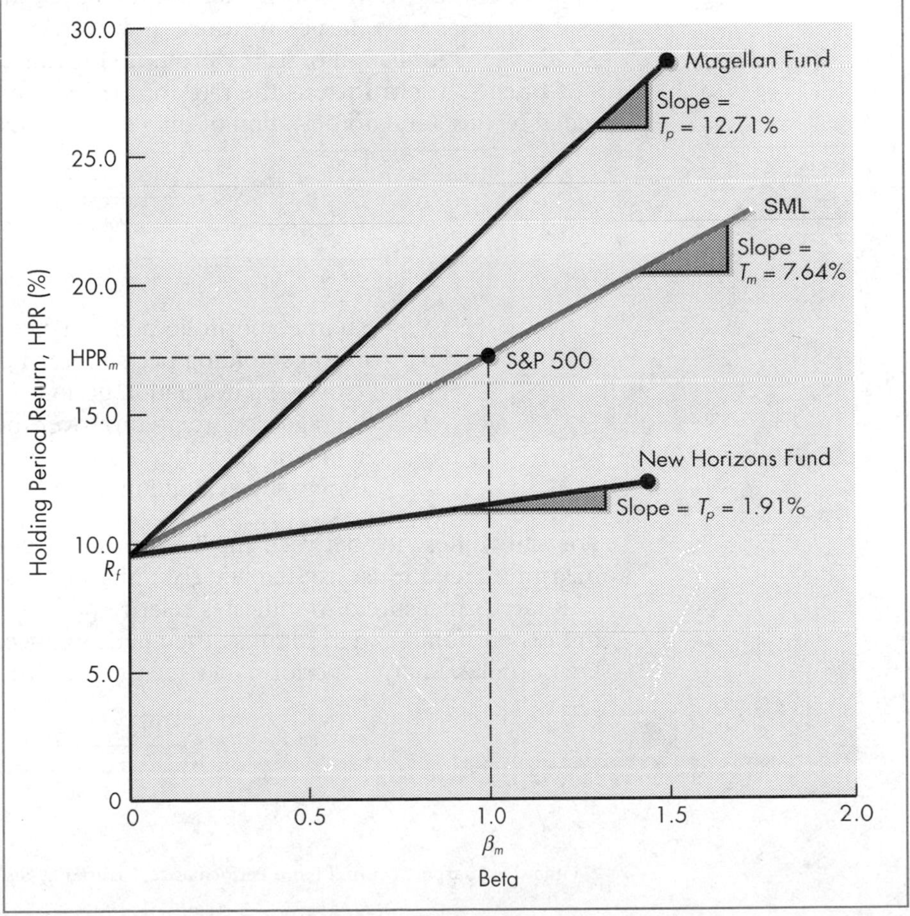

is simply the slope of the SML (7.64 percent in this case). The T_p measure may be viewed as the slope of a risk-return line drawn from R_f through the geometric average HPR of the portfolio. These risk-return lines are also shown in Figure 21.1. The slope of these risk-return lines is simply the Treynor performance measure for each fund. If the slope or T_p is less than the slope of the SML or T_m, then the market's performance is superior to the portfolio's performance. In summary, Treynor's technique indicates the performance of a portfolio relative to other portfolios or to a benchmark portfolio.

• The Sharpe Portfolio Performance Technique

Shortly after Treynor's technique was published in 1965, William F. Sharpe introduced an alternative technique for performance evaluation, which he illustrated by evaluating the performance of a large number of mutual funds.[3] Sharpe's technique used total risk, as indicated by the standard deviation of the HPRs over the evaluation period, as the appropriate risk measure. This was surprising because Sharpe was known for his contribution to the development of the CAPM, which suggests the importance and usefulness of beta as a risk measure. Sharpe's measure, however, uses the CML rather than the SML as the foundation of its performance measure.

Sharpe's technique is the ratio of the risk premium of the portfolio divided by the standard deviation of the portfolio's return:

$$S_p = \frac{\overline{\text{HPR}}_p - \overline{R}_f}{\sigma_p} \tag{21.6}$$

where

S_p = Sharpe's portfolio performance measure
$\overline{\text{HPR}}_p$ = average holding period return of the portfolio over the evaluation period
$\overline{R}_f$ = average risk-free return over the evaluation period
σ_p = standard deviation of the portfolio's HPRs calculated over the evaluation period

The only difference between the Treynor and Sharpe techniques is the risk measure: Treynor uses systematic risk; Sharpe uses total risk.

Sharpe's measure also indicates relative performance, since it can be used to rank portfolios and to compare their performance to the benchmark or market portfolio. Sharpe's performance measure for the market is calculated as

$$S_m = \frac{\overline{\text{HPR}}_m - \overline{R}_f}{\sigma_m} \tag{21.7}$$

[3] William F. Sharpe, "Mutual Fund Performance," *Journal of Business* (January 1966): 119–38.

If $S_p > S_m$, the portfolio outperformed the market. If $S_p \leq S_m$, the portfolio did as well as or underperformed the market.

Again, the data for the two mutual funds and S&P 500 in Table 21.1 can be used to illustrate Sharpe's measure:

$$\text{Fidelity Magellan Fund:} \quad S_p = \frac{28.65\% - 9.58\%}{22.88\%} = 0.83$$

$$\text{New Horizons Fund:} \quad S_p = \frac{12.33\% - 9.58\%}{20.92\%} = 0.13$$

$$\text{S\&P 500:} \quad S_m = \frac{17.22\% - 9.58\%}{12.83\%} = 0.60$$

Notice that as a ratio of the risk premium, expressed as a percentage return divided by the standard deviation in percentage units, S_p is an index number that is not expressed in percentage units. It is simply the ratio of the portfolio's excess return per unit of portfolio total risk. Magellan Fund again shows superior performance compared to the New Horizons Fund and to the market.

The CML in Figure 21.2 is based on the data in Table 21.1 and illustrates the ex-post performance analysis of the two mutual funds. Like the Treynor measure, Sharpe's measure can also be regarded as the slope of a risk-return line drawn between the risk-free rate and the geometric average HPR of the portfolio. These risk-return lines for the two mutual funds are shown in Figure 21.2.

If a portfolio plots above the CML, then Sharpe's measure indicates superior performance. For the Treynor technique, if the fund plots above the SML, its performance is better than the market on a risk-adjusted basis.

• The Jensen Portfolio Performance Technique

Following Treynor and Sharpe, Michael C. Jensen developed a third measurement technique.[4] Like Treynor's technique, **Jensen's technique** is based on the CAPM. The basic equation for the CAPM is

$$E(R_j) = R_f + \beta_j[E(R_m) - R_f] \tag{21.8}$$

where

$E(R_j)$ = expected return on security j
R_f = risk-free rate of return
β_j = systematic risk of security j
$E(R_m)$ = expected return on the market portfolio

[4] Michael C. Jensen, "The Performance of Mutual Funds in the Period 1945–1964," *Journal of Finance* (May 1968): 389–416.

FIGURE 21.2
CML and Sharpe's Performance Measure, 1980–1989

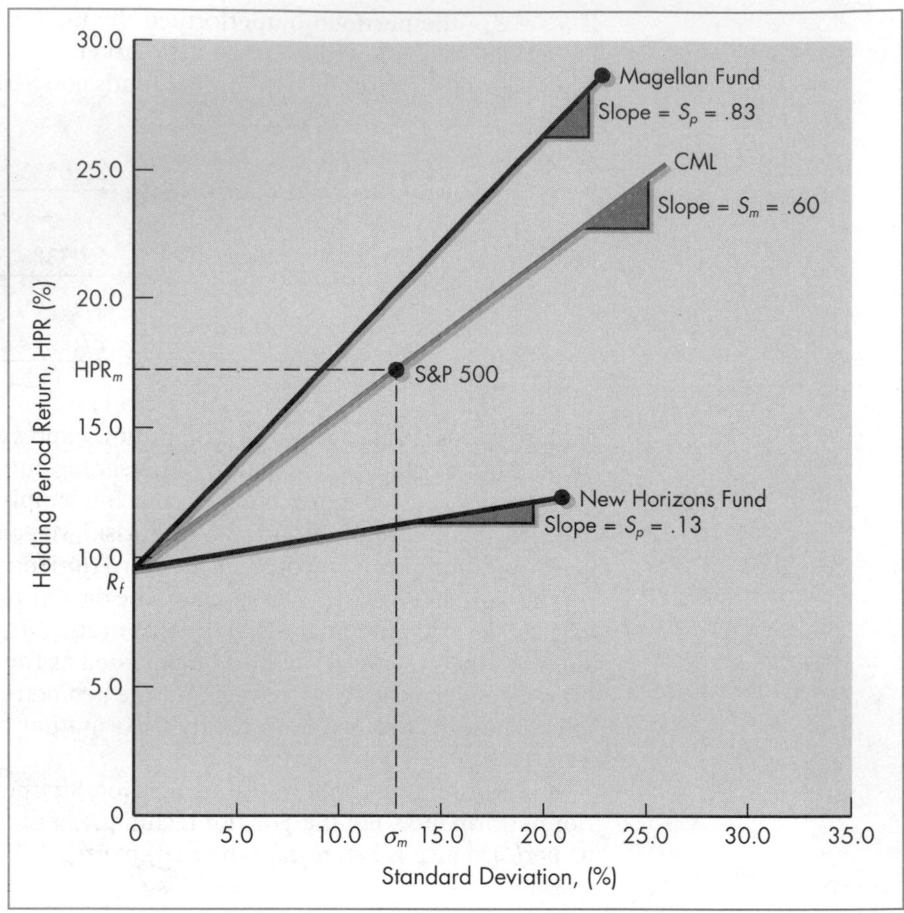

Although the CAPM describes how risk and expected returns are related, empirical tests of the model typically use ex-post or historical data. The ex-post HPRs are calculated for an individual security (R_{jt}), the risk-free rate (R_{ft}), and a proxy of the market portfolio (R_{mt}). These time-series returns can then be used in a regression that represents the *market model:*

$$R_{jt} - R_{ft} = \hat{\alpha}_j + \hat{\beta}_j(R_{mt} - R_{ft}) + e_{jt} \tag{21.9}$$

The dependent and independent variables are the *risk premiums*. The risk premium is simply the difference between the security or portfolio return and the risk-free rate for each period. The risk premium on the market proxy is simply the difference between the market return and the risk-free rate for each period. Notice that the risk-free rate (R_f) is not a constant but has a different value for each time period. Treasury bill yields are usually used to represent R_f. The maturity of the bill should match the holding period used to calculate returns. For example, if annual HPRs are calculated for a fund, then the yield on a Treasury bill with a one-year maturity should be used. The *y* intercept of the regression, $\hat{\alpha}_j$, is the estimate of **alpha** for the security or portfolio while the slope of the regression, β_j, is an estimate of the beta. The deviations or errors around the regression line are represented by e_{jt}.

Jensen argued that $\hat{\alpha}_j$ or the average risk-adjusted excess HPR is an indication of a portfolio's performance. It can be measured as the regression intercept using risk premiums. Essentially, if $\hat{\alpha}_j > 0$ and is significantly different from zero in a statistical test, then the portfolio exhibited superior performance. If $\hat{\alpha}_j < 0$ and is statistically significant, then the portfolio demonstrated poor performance. Finally, if $\hat{\alpha}_j$ is not statistically different from zero, the portfolio did not provide a risk-adjusted excess HPR. Jensen's *alpha* can be interpreted simply as the average incremental HPR (positive or negative) earned by the portfolio after adjusting for systematic risk.

Jensen's technique is applied to Magellan in Table 21.2 and Figure 21.3. The HPRs from Table 21.1 were used to calculate the risk premium each year for the fund and the S&P 500. A regression equation was estimated using the formula in Equation 21.9. The regression or market model line parameters are given in Table 21.2. Magellan's beta based on risk premiums is 1.30 versus 1.50 based on HPRs (see Table 21.1). The correlation coefficient between the fund and the S&P 500 using risk premiums is 0.79. Thus, 62.4 percent of the variability of the fund's risk premiums is explained by the variability in the market's risk premiums.

TABLE 21.2 • Jensen's Portfolio Performance Measure: Fidelity Magellan Fund, 1980–1989

	Holding period returns			Risk premiums	
	Fidelity Magellan	*S&P 500*	*Risk-free rate*	*Fidelity Magellan*	*S&P 500*
1980	76.5%	34.1%	12.1%	64.4%	22.0%
1981	12.1	(4.8)	14.1	(2.0)	(18.9)
1982	48.1	22.2	14.3	33.8	7.9
1983	38.6	21.3	8.6	30.0	12.7
1984	2.0	4.1	9.9	(7.9)	(5.8)
1985	43.1	29.9	9.3	33.8	20.6
1986	23.8	18.1	7.1	16.7	11.0
1987	2.4	5.7	5.6	(3.2)	0.1
1988	22.8	16.5	6.7	16.1	9.8
1989	34.6	31.6	8.5	26.1	23.1

Geometric mean of risk premiums:

Fidelity Magellan = 19.04%

S&P 500 = 7.46%

Standard deviation of risk premiums:

Fidelity Magellan = 20.76%

S&P 500 = 12.62%

Market model line parameters based on risk premiums:

Alpha = 10.04%

Beta = 1.30

Correlation coefficient = .79

FIGURE 21.3
Scatter Diagram and Market Model Line: Fidelity Magellan Fund, 1980–1989

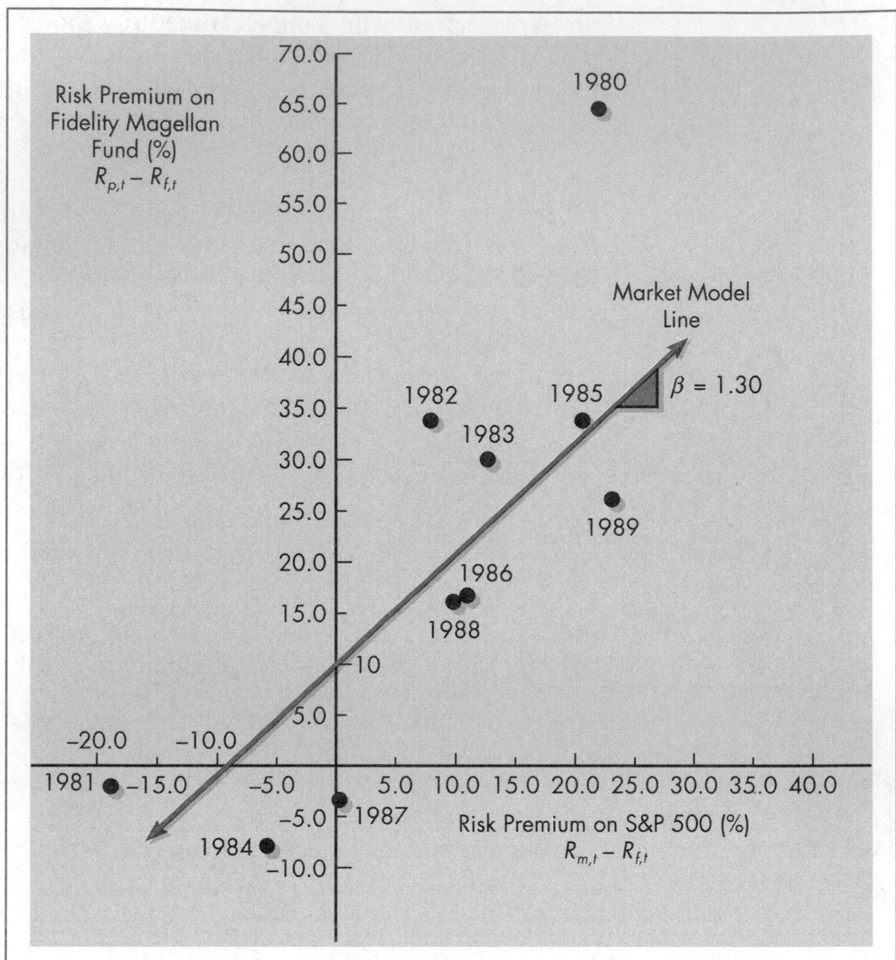

The alpha of 10.04 percent in Table 21.2 indicates the excess HPR the fund earned after allowing for the systematic risk of the portfolio. Figure 21.3 provides a scatter diagram and market model regression line for the fund. The *y* intercept of 10.04 percent is Jensen's alpha, and it is statistically significant.

Jensen's technique was also applied to New Horizons:

$$\text{New Horizons Fund:} \quad \hat{\alpha}_j = -6.43\%$$

The α_j for the New Horizons is negative and statistically different from zero. This fund's performance, therefore, is inferior to the S&P 500's on a risk-adjusted basis. In summary, Jensen's technique provides an indication of the relative and absolute performance of a portfolio.

• Summary of Results from Performance Examples

Three different evaluation techniques have been used to analyze the performance of the two mutual funds over the 1980–1989 period. The results can be summarized as follows:

	Treynor, T_p	Sharpe, S_p	Jensen, $\hat{\alpha}_j$
Fidelity Magellan Fund	12.71%	0.83	10.04%
New Horizons Fund	1.91	0.13	−6.43
S&P 500	7.64	0.60	0.00

The three performance measures produce identical rankings, with Magellan as the best performer. All three techniques also indicate that Magellan outperformed the market, while the New Horizons Fund underperformed the market.

Generally, the three techniques will agree on the assessment of performance. Despite this general agreement, however, it is usually a good idea to use all three techniques for the following reasons. First, the Treynor and Jensen techniques use beta, or a systematic risk measure, while Sharpe's technique uses standard deviation, or a measure of total risk. Consequently, if a portfolio is poorly diversified with a large standard deviation, the Treynor and Jensen measures may not uncover this aspect of poor performance. Second, the Jensen technique provides an indication of the average risk-adjusted excess return earned by the portfolio. It is, therefore, intuitively appealing because it provides an indication of how much, in terms of an incremental positive or negative HPR, the portfolio manager was able to earn. Jensen's alpha can also be tested statistically to see if it is significantly different from zero. Finally, in some cases, the three techniques may produce different portfolio rankings or reach different conclusions about whether the portfolio outperformed or underperformed the market on a risk-adjusted basis. This possibility can be checked by using all three techniques.

STUDIES OF PROFESSIONALLY MANAGED PORTFOLIOS

Numerous studies have examined the ex-post, risk-adjusted return performance of professionally managed portfolios. Mutual funds are studied most frequently because they are publicly traded and data are readily available. However, there are some studies of other professionally managed portfolios, such as those of pension funds, commercial banks, and life insurance companies. This section briefly summarizes the conclusions reached by these studies.

• Mutual Funds

Mutual funds have been evaluated according to several standards: overall performance, security selection, and market timing.

• **INTEREST BOX**

Peter Lynch Resigns at Fidelity Magellan Fund

Will there ever be another Peter Lynch? A stock picker so dazzling that he could juggle a $13 billion mutual fund portfolio—double what most other leading money managers would dare handle—and still lead the field? An old-fashioned sort who scorned the crapshoots of options trading and market timing and sought only solid long-term growth? A public figure so full of straight talk and common sense that a million small investors were convinced he was the one who could make them rich? Another Lynch? Not likely?

Consider the record. Since taking over Magellan in 1977, Lynch has achieved a total return of 2,541 percent—about five times the gains of the Standard & Poor's Index of 500 stocks. No other fund came close. His five-year gain through 1989, 195.5 percent, placed him first among diversified equity funds in *Money*'s most recent fund rankings. And his superb 1989 return of 34.6 percent, compared with 31.6 percent for the S&P 500, put Magellan in the top 12 percent of stock funds for the year.

All that is over now, as many fund investors already know. On May 31, burned out by 80-hour weeks that left him too little time for his wife and three daughters, and chilled by the fact that at 46 he is exactly as old as his own father was when he died of cancer, Lynch will turn over his fund to Morris Smith, age 32.

The question of the moment: Should you follow Lynch off the good ship Magellan, or should you give Smith a chance to prove himself as captain?

To decide you'll need to know more about young Mr. Smith. Like Lynch, he is an intense, enthusiastic, home-grown Fidelity fund manager who relentlessly researches individual companies. He's also off to a strong start.

So far, so good. But Smith is taking over a unique superfund nearly 20 times the size of the $700 million OTC portfolio and holding almost four times as many stocks. "At Magellan's size, it's tougher to find attractive stocks that you can buy in sufficient quantity to make a difference in your portfolio," says Kenneth Heebner, a rival Boston money manager who has posted a star-quality record with his New England Growth Fund. "I am managing $2 billion, and I wouldn't want much more."

What comforts some knowledgeable Magellan fans is the help Smith will be getting. Fidelity's stock-evaluation system, starting with 72 industry analysts, serves all its funds and feeds Magellan's top man alone at least 40 fresh ideas a week. "I didn't just find all these stocks by myself," says Lynch.

So far, investors seem willing to give Smith a chance. A week after Lynch announced his departure in late March, shareholders had removed less than 1 percent of the fund's assets, or $130 million, not as much as Fidelity executives feared. That compares with a net inflow the previous week. Lynch had quietly built up an unusually high 13 percent cash position, partly to cushion against possible redemptions because of his announcement.

SOURCE: Adapted from Jerry Edgerton, "Should You Quit on the Magellan Fund?" *Money*, May 1990, pp. 82–83.

OVERALL PERFORMANCE Beginning with the classical studies of Treynor, Sharpe, and Jensen in the mid to late 1960s, the performance of mutual funds has been a very popular research topic. The general conclusion reached by these studies is that when expenses are considered, mutual funds do not consistently beat the market and typically underperform the market. For example, Jensen concluded that his sample of funds earned "about 1.1 percent less per year (compounded continuously) than they should have earned given their level of systematic risk."[5]

In a more recent study, Shawky analyzed the performance of all mutual funds (255) from January 1973 through December 1977. His analysis included the traditional Treynor, Sharpe, and Jensen measures. In addition, he also provided an analysis of diversification and performance during bull and bear markets. Shawky concluded that "the performance of the mutual fund industry in the 1970s seems to be better than what has been reported earlier for the 1950s and 1960s. Specifically, funds seem to earn a return that is generally commensurate with their systematic risk."[6] He also concluded that the diversification efforts had improved over early years, with a 75 percent coefficient of determination (R^2) for all funds.

ANALYSIS OF SECURITY SELECTION A number of studies have specifically analyzed the security selection success of mutual funds. Jensen conducted the initial study in this area in 1968. A 1986 study of 43 mutual funds provided some interesting results that conflict, to a certain degree, with the earlier studies.[7] Using an improved methodology, the study found that 30 percent of the funds (13 of the 43 funds) demonstrated statistically significant security selection performance. The results of the empirical tests led the authors to conclude that some mutual funds had the ability to select undervalued securities. Earlier studies had generally concluded that, on average, funds showed little if any ability in security selection.

ANALYSIS OF MARKET TIMING One of the classic articles on mutual fund timing activity is a 1979 study by Fabozzi and Francis.[8] They tested for a nonlinear relationship in the market model lines estimated for a sample of 85 mutual funds. Specifically, a quadratic term was added to the simple linear regression equation usually used to estimate the market model line. If the quadratic term was statistically significant, this would be evidence that mutual funds increased their betas in bull markets and reduced them in bear markets. The study found no evidence of curvilinear market model lines for the sample of funds.

In addition to testing for changes in the fund's beta, the asset composition of the mutual fund's portfolio can be analyzed. A 1983 study analyzed the balance sheet proportions of funds in terms of cash, fixed-income securities,

---

[5] Ibid., p. 405.

[6] Hany A. Shawky, "An Update on Mutual Funds: Better Grades," *Journal of Portfolio Management* (Winter 1982): 29–34.

[7] Carl R. Chen and Steve Stockum, "Selectivity, Market Timing, and Random Beta Behavior of Mutual Funds: A Generalized Model," *Journal of Financial Research* (Spring 1986): 87–96.

[8] Frank Fabozzi and Jack Francis, "Mutual Fund Systematic Risk for Bull and Bear Markets," *Journal of Finance* (December 1979): 1243–50.

and stocks.[9] If funds increased the proportion of stocks during bull markets and increased the cash proportion during bear markets, such shifts would be evidence of successful timing activity. The analysis detected statistically significant but relatively small shifts in the asset compositions. The significant shifts, however, were almost always incorrect. Funds tended to shift into cash prior to bull markets and into stock prior to bear markets—evidence of *incorrect* timing decisions.

Regardless of methodology, time period, or sample, there appears to be no evidence that mutual funds can successfully time the market; the evidence suggests that some funds do attempt market timing but are usually unsuccessful.

ADVANTAGES OF MUTUAL FUND INVESTING The previous discussion has been generally unfavorable in terms of mutual funds outperforming the market on a risk-adjusted basis. Some funds appear to be able to select securities successfully, but few, if any, demonstrate expertise in market timing. However, studies do find that mutual funds provide adequate diversification, follow their stated investment objectives, and generally maintain relatively low expenses. These positive factors indicate that mutual funds serve an important function for many investors. On the other hand, the evidence suggests that investors in mutual funds should *not* expect to beat the market consistently on a risk-adjusted basis. Chapter 5 provided a detailed discussion of mutual fund investing.

• Performance of Other Types of Portfolios

A limited number of studies have analyzed the risk-adjusted return performance of commercial banks, insurance companies, and pension fund portfolios. A 1980 study compared the performances of mutual funds, commercial banks, insurance companies, and investment counselors.[10] This study covered the 10-year period ending December 31, 1977, and included HPRs on approximately 1,738 portfolios. The results indicated that mutual funds had the best performance, followed (in order) by investment counselors, insurance companies, and commercial banks. The results of this study, when combined with the results from the studies previously discussed, suggest that *no* group of professionally managed portfolios can consistently beat the market on a risk-adjusted basis.

The conclusions from studies of professionally managed portfolios suggest that beating the market on a risk-adjusted basis may be very difficult. This would be the case if markets were efficient or correct in pricing securities to

---

[9] John M. Cheney and E. Theodore Veit, "Evidence of Shifts in Portfolio Asset Composition as a Market Timing Tool," *Financial Review* (February 1983): 56–78.

[10] John C. Bogle and Jan M. Twardowski, "Institutional Investment Performance Compared: Banks, Investment Counselors, Insurance Companies, and Mutual Funds," *Financial Analysts Journal* (January-February 1980): 33–41.

RESEARCH BOX

The Relationship between Incentive Compensation and Performance of Mutual Fund Managers

It is quite common for corporate executives' compensation to be based on performance. If the executive accomplishes some predetermined goals and/or causes the stock price to increase, his or her compensation increases. This is typically accomplished through employee stock options issued by the corporation to the executive. Performance- or incentive-based compensation is uncommon for portfolio managers of mutual funds, however. Is it possible that the few mutual fund managers who are compensated based on the investment performance of the fund outperform managers who do not receive performance compensation?

A recent study looked at a sample of 387 mutual funds over the period January 1, 1982, through December 31, 1987. Of these 387 funds, however, only 29 funds used incentive compensation during the period, and 2 began operation in 1984 and consequently did not have data for the entire period. Each of the 27 funds with data for the entire period was matched with a fund with risk characteristics very close to the incentive fund. The funds were then divided into three groups: (1) the total sample of 387 funds, (2) the 27 funds with incentive compensation, and (3) the 27 "matched" funds that did not have incentive compensation. Jensen's performance measure was calculated for each of the 387 funds.

Based on an analysis of the data, the author reached the following observations:

1. Based on the Jensen alphas, the incentive funds outperformed (had higher alphas) than the nonincentive funds.
2. The incentive funds had higher average betas and standard deviations than the averages for the total sample of 387 funds.
3. Larger funds, based on asset size, seemed more inclined to use incentive compensation.
4. Funds that were part of a "family" of funds were more likely to use incentive compensation.

In conclusion, the author stated, "Incentive fees appear to improve the relative performance of mutual fund managers."

SOURCE: Adapted from Joseph H. Golec, "Do Mutual Fund Managers Who Use Incentive Compensation Outperform Those Who Don't?" *Financial Analysts Journal* (November-December 1988): 75–78.

reflect their risk. Correct or efficient pricing eliminates the opportunity to find undervalued or overvalued securities. The next section of the chapter further explores the question of the degree of market efficiency.

MARKET EFFICIENCY

One of the most profound but controversial theories of stock market behavior and its implications for investment decision making is the **efficient market hypothesis (EMH).** This theory deals with the *degree* of capital market efficiency. **Market efficiency** in this context refers to the market's ability to price securities correctly and instantaneously change security prices to reflect new information. In other words, does the market price of a security reflect its investment value, or are market prices poor indicators of investment value? In an efficient market, a security's price would correctly reflect the important variables for that security and would represent an unbiased estimate of its investment value. Market efficiency also implies that as new information becomes available, it is quickly analyzed by the market, and any necessary price adjustments occur rapidly.

The degree of market efficiency has important implications for the economy and for investment decision makers. In an economic sense, it is important that security prices provide accurate signals that can be used to allocate capital resources correctly. Mispriced securities would result in incorrect allocations of capital. Although efficient markets may be important and desirable from an economic perspective, they present a dilemma to investors in terms of an appropriate investment strategy.

• Brief Overview and History of the EMH

Prior to the 1950s, it was generally believed that the traditional technical and fundamental approaches could be used to beat the market. During the 1950s, however, two important empirical studies of security prices provided the initial evidence against the traditional view.[11] These early studies analyzed *changes* in both British and U.S. stock prices and concluded that the patterns of changes were indistinguishable from patterns generated by a series of random numbers.

These two early studies provided the basis for a number of additional studies during the 1960s that also analyzed patterns of stock price changes but, more importantly, began to develop a theory to explain the apparently random behavior. Thus, the early empirical work was used to develop a theory—rather than the normal procedure of developing and then empirically testing a theory. These studies provided the basis for the **random walk** or **fair game** theory of market efficiency. The fair game theory suggests that there is a 50 percent chance of earning a return above or below the expected return. It also suggests that the next price change in a security has an equal probability of being an increase or a decrease regardless of the previous price change. The price changes are therefore random and do not reflect any distinguishable pattern. The random walk theory is associated with the **weak form** of market efficiency.

Other studies analyzed the pattern and speed of stock price adjustments to specific types of new information that reaches the market. Two of the more important early studies considered how stock prices react to stock splits and

[11] Maurice G. Kendall, "The Analysis of Economic Time-Series, Part I: Prices," *Journal of the Royal Statistical Society* (1953): 11–25; Harry V. Roberts, "Stock Market 'Patterns' and Financial Analysis: Methodological Suggestions," *Journal of Finance* (March 1959): 1–10.

annual unexpected earnings announcements.[12] Surprisingly, the study of stock splits found that generally the stock price correctly adjusted to the split *prior* to the actual announcement date, and that little adjustment occurred after the announcement date. Stock split announcements are generally viewed as positive events because many firms also increase cash dividends at the same time the split is announced. The earnings announcement study also found that the market generally anticipated the increased or decreased earnings, with little price adjustment occurring at or before the announcement date.

Such studies, which are generally called **event studies,** provide the empirical evidence for the **semistrong form** of market efficiency. Essentially, this theory holds that security prices reflect all publicly available information.

A third group of studies analyzed the actual investment behavior of various groups of investors that might be expected to beat the market. As previously discussed, many studies have analyzed the investment performance of mutual funds. The mutual fund studies found evidence that after considering risk and expenses, mutual funds, on average, did not outperform the market. Other studies looked at *corporate insiders*—that is, officers, directors, owners of 10 percent or more of the stock, or persons who fit some combination of these criteria. The results from these studies are inconclusive. Generally, "insider buyers" outperformed "insider sellers," and knowledge of buyer actions may be useful in making investment decisions.

The results of these studies are used to support the **strong form** of market efficiency. This hypothesis suggests that all available information (public or private) is fully reflected in the security's price. The empirical evidence supporting this hypothesis is mixed. It appears that mutual funds, with the benefit of professional analysts and portfolio managers, are unable to outperform the market consistently. The theory suggests that their skills and access to information are not in themselves advantages that can produce superior investment performance. In the case of corporate insiders and specialists on the NYSE, the evidence suggests that nonpublic information available to them can be used to outperform the market.

In summary, empirical studies that began in the 1950s provided the foundation for a theory of stock market behavior that has become known as the EMH. Based on the early studies and numerous more recent studies, there appears to be little doubt that capital markets are efficient. The controversial and unresolved issue, however, is the degree of market efficiency.

Table 21.3 briefly summarizes the three forms of the EMH, each of which proposes a different degree of market efficiency. The weak form holds that security prices reflect all historical market data. Market data are essentially se-

---

[12] Eugene F. Fama, Lawrence Fisher, Michael Jensen, and Richard Roll, "The Adjustment of Stock Prices to New Information," *International Economic Review* (February 1969): 1–21; Ray Ball and Philip Brown, "An Empirical Evaluation of Accounting Income Numbers," *Journal of Accounting Research* (Autumn 1968): 159–78.

TABLE 21.3 • Summary of the Three Degrees of the EMH

Degree of efficiency	Definition
Weak	Security price changes are random and do not reflect any distinguishable pattern. Current prices also reflect all information contained in historical prices and trading volume data.
Semistrong	Security prices reflect all publicly available information and adjust rapidly to any new information.
Strong	Security prices reflect all public and private information and adjust rapidly to any new information.

curity prices and information on trading volume. The weak form of market efficiency can be directly related to the premise underlying technical analysis.

The semistrong form holds that all publicly available information is reflected in prices. This information includes market data and all information typically analyzed by fundamentalists dealing with the economy, industry, and company.

The strong form suggests that all information is reflected in security prices. This includes not only information on fundamental valuation factors typically found in financial statements, but also information that may be known to only a few people and is therefore not public.

The remainder of this chapter examines each degree of market efficiency in more detail. Empirical tests are discussed, as are the implications for investment decision making.

THE WEAK FORM OF THE EFFICIENT MARKET HYPOTHESIS

The initial efforts in developing the EMH concerned the historical behavior of common stock price changes observed over relatively short periods of time, such as a day or week. As discussed in Chapter 7, traditional technical analysis deals with the behavior of historical prices and trading volume. The basic assumption of technical analysis is that there are recurring and therefore predictable patterns of price behavior. An analysis of historical prices can consequently be used to forecast the direction and level of prices.

The weak-form hypothesis holds that past prices do not provide information that can be used to outperform the market. Essentially, if short-run price changes follow a "random walk," then an analysis of a historical time series cannot provide any useful information about future price changes.

• **INTEREST BOX**

A Review of Capital Market Efficiency

A recent article by Stephen LeRoy reviewed much of the research published since Eugene Fama's 1970 article on market efficiency. LeRoy analyzed the October 1987 market crash and overall market volatility and considered their implications for market efficiency. He also reviewed the research on asset pricing anomalies. The following are some of his conclusions:

Economist 1: "That looks like a $100 bill over there on the sidewalk."
Economist 2: "Don't bother going over to check it out. If it were genuine, someone would have picked it up already."

The theory of efficient capital markets says, most simply, that the prices of financial assets equal the discounted value of the expected cash flows these assets generate. In the context of the stock market, efficiency implies that stock prices equal the discounted value of expected future dividends. Investors are not assumed to form perfectly accurate forecasts of future dividends, but they are assumed to make effective use of whatever information they have. If capital markets are efficient in this sense, changes in stock prices should be associated exclusively with new information leading to revisions in expected future dividends: when dividend prospects improve, stock prices rise, and conversely.

Moreover, since all relevant, publicly available information is discounted in asset prices as soon as it becomes available, investors cannot construct systematically profitable trading rules based only on this information. Thus, in an efficient market, there is no motive to buy stock based on favorable information; if the information is in fact favorable, the market already has discounted it. In other words, the $100 bill above could not be genuine; otherwise, it would have been picked up already.

Statistical evidence accumulated in the 20 years following Eugene Fama's (1970) survey raises questions about his conclusions that capital markets are efficient. Stock price volatility has been shown to exceed the volatility consistent with capital market efficiency. Other evidence—for example, the small-firm effect, the January effect, and other calendar-based anomalies of stock prices—points in the same direction. Finally, analysts find it difficult to explain stock prices even after the fact using realized values of variables which, according to efficient capital markets theory, should account for stock price changes.

The evidence reviewed here suggests, rather, that economists ought to be aware that the evidence in favor of their way of thinking about the economy is far from clear-cut.

SOURCE: Adapted from Stephen F. LeRoy, "Capital Market Efficiency: An Update," *Federal Reserve Bank of San Francisco Economic Review* (Spring 1990): 29–40.

• Empirical Tests of the Random Walk Model

Many of the statistical tests of the random walk model have analyzed the independence of successive price changes. Various methodologies have been used, including *serial correlations, runs tests, filter rules,* and *relative strength* measures.

SERIAL CORRELATIONS The correlation coefficient, defined and illustrated in Chapter 2, is essentially a measure of how two variables are related.

A **serial correlation** coefficient indicates how a variable is related to lagged values. For example, in calculating a serial correlation for stock *j*'s price, the two variables would be as follows:

Week	Observed price	Lagged price
1	\$10	\$11
2	11	9
3	9	12
4	12	.
.	.	.
.	.	.
.	.	.

If the serial correlation coefficient calculated using the observed and lagged prices is significantly different from zero, then successive weekly price changes for stock *j* are related. This finding would contradict the random walk hypothesis. On the other hand, a finding that the serial correlation coefficient is essentially zero would support the random walk hypothesis.

Researchers have analyzed serial correlation coefficients, using samples of common stocks and stock indexes. Some evidence indicates that smaller, less actively traded stocks do tend to have slightly larger coefficients, but their magnitude does not offer much hope in forecasting future price changes using historical price changes. Thus, the results of the serial correlation tests generally support the random walk hypothesis.

RUNS TESTS A **runs test** is a statistical test that can be used to test for dependence in successive price changes. Instead of the actual numerical values for the price changes, the sign (positive or negative) of the price change is used. A *run* is simply a sequence of price changes with the same sign. If price changes were dependent, then there would be "long" runs of positive or negative signs. Tables are available to test for the statistical significance of runs of a certain length.

The results of many studies using runs tests support the random walk hypothesis. These studies indicate that successive price changes are generally independent.

FILTER RULES A third test of the dependence of successive price changes, **filter rules,** involves developing mechanical trading rules based on price changes that can be used to simulate buying and selling individual securities. Filter rules that produce risk-adjusted returns greater than returns from a buy-and-hold strategy would be evidence against the random walk hypothesis. For example, a simple filter rule would be to buy the stock the day after the price increased by *X* percent and sell (or short) the stock the day after the price declined by *Y* percent. Because they test actual investment strategies that are based on the existence of dependent prices, filter rules are a more direct test of price-change dependency then serial correlations and runs tests.

Many tests of various filter rules have been conducted for filters ranging from 0.5 percent to 50 percent that were applied to the DJIA and to individual common stocks. Essentially, the studies concluded that after taking into account transaction costs, no filter rule could be devised that outperformed a naïve buy-and-hold strategy.

RELATIVE STRENGTH The fourth methodology used to test the random walk hypothesis involves trading rules based on **relative strength** measures. As discussed in Chapter 8, relative strength relates the price for the security to an index or some other variable. For example, a relative strength ratio may be calculated by dividing the price of a stock by the value of an index of stocks in the same industry. Analysis of the ratios over time indicates how the stock price changes relative to the index.

Empirical studies have found that after adjusting for risk and considering transaction costs, relative strength trading rules do not outperform a buy-and-hold strategy.

• Implications for Technical Analysis

The empirical tests discussed above provide very strong support for the random walk hypothesis. Short-term stock price changes are essentially independent, and trading rules based on historical changes should not be successful in outperforming a buy-and-hold strategy. The small degree of observed dependence is not significant enough to offset the transaction costs involved in applying the trading rules.

These results raise a major question about the implications of the random walk hypothesis for technical analysis (see Chapter 7 for an overview of technical analysis and Chapter 8 for a discussion of how technical indicators are used in market timing decisions). If technical analysis is defined simply as a mechanical analysis of past prices, volume, and/or relative strength measures, then the random walk hypothesis indicates that these approaches are doomed to failure. If, on the other hand, technical analysis is more broadly defined, the implications are not so clear.

Considering recent advances in communications and data processing technology, it is apparent that modern technical analysis involves much more than a simple analysis of past prices. The methodology of technical analysis is constantly being refined and expanded to adapt to a dynamic and changing market environment in the same way techniques of fundamental analysis are being expanded. It should also be noted that many analysts and investors believe in the validity of technical analysis. Are all of these individuals incorrect? It appears that additional empirical research needs to be undertaken to test the validity of specific techniques of modern technical analysis.

THE SEMISTRONG FORM OF THE EFFICIENT MARKET HYPOTHESIS

Based on the results of empirical tests of the weak form of the EMH conducted during the 1950s and 1960s, research turned toward other degrees of market efficiency. These tests measured the speed with which stock prices adjusted to new, publicly available information. For example, what price adjustment patterns could be observed for companies announcing stock splits, significant changes in dividend policies, or unexpected large or small earnings per share? The weak form of the EMH postulates that future prices reflect all information contained in past prices. The *semistrong* form holds that prices reflect all publicly available information. Thus, any significant new public information should immediately be reflected in the stock price. Furthermore, no lag should exist between the time the information becomes available and the adjustment of the stock price.

Figure 21.4 illustrates the price adjustment patterns that might occur in inefficient and efficient markets. Panel (a) shows a stock price that appears to be following a random walk prior to period $t = 0$. At period $t = 0$, however, significant new information relative to the stock is made available to the market. Investors, reacting to the new information, cause the stock price to increase for a number of periods until it finally reaches a new price equilibrium at time period $t = n$; at this point, it resumes a random walk. This price adjustment pattern would not occur in a semistrong efficient market because of the period of time ($t = 0$ to $t = n$) required before the price fully reflects the new information.

FIGURE 21.4 • Price Adjustment Patterns for Inefficient and Efficient Markets

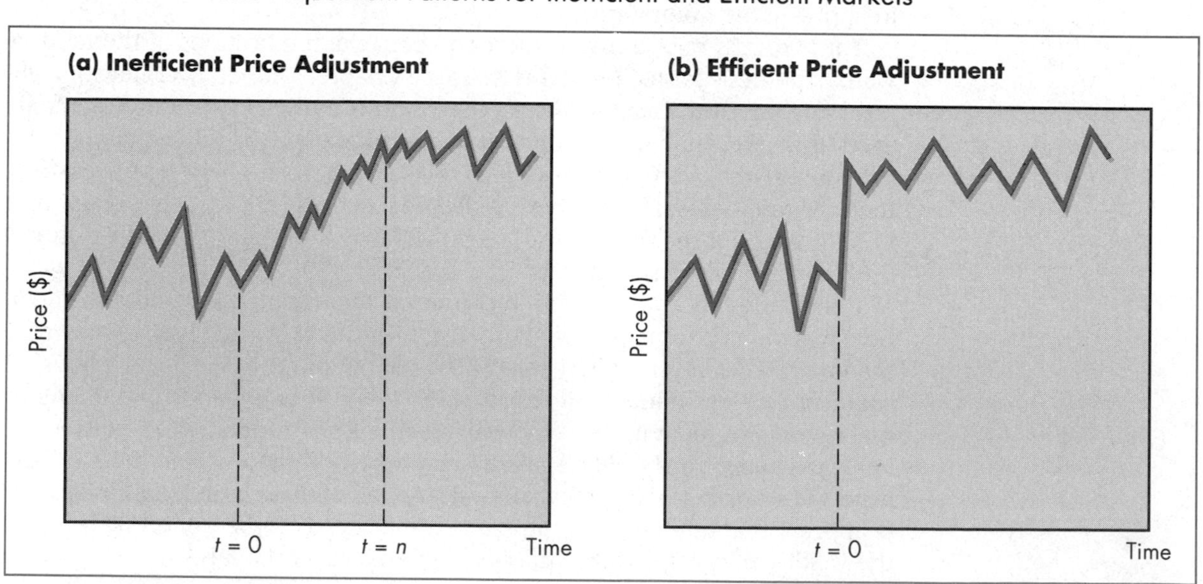

Panel (b) of Figure 21.4 illustrates the pattern of price adjustment suggested by the semistrong form of the EMH. Notice that the stock price instantaneously reflects the new information at time period $t = 0$. Essentially, no time elapses between the date the new information is available and the date the new equilibrium price is established. The market immediately obtains the new information, correctly analyzes its significance for the price, and incorporates the new information into the price.

• Event Studies

Numerous *event studies* provide insights concerning semistrong market efficiency. As the name implies, these studies identify a specific development or event that is expected to influence stock prices and examine a sample of companies where the "event" has occurred. Previously studied events include stock splits, earnings announcements, acquisitions and divestitures, and financial distress. Once the event and sample of firms are identified, HPRs are calculated, usually on a daily or weekly basis, for periods both before and after the event.

STOCK SPLITS A 1969 study developed the methodology for event studies and provided a very interesting analysis of stock splits.[13] The empirical analysis was based on a sample of all 940 stock splits that occurred on the NYSE from 1927 to 1959. The purpose of the study was to see if any unusual price behavior occurred before or after the split date. The split itself is an event that should not impact the wealth of the stockholder. For example, when a company has a two-for-one split, the price of the stock should decrease by 50 percent, and the stockholder will have double the number of original shares. It is possible, however, that the change in cash dividends may not match the terms of the split. The company may use the split to increase or decrease dividends. For example, assume that prior to the two-for-one split, the company was paying $1 per share. Effective with the date of the split, the dividend will be $.60 per share, which represents a 20 percent increase in dividends. In an efficient market, the stock price should increase before or on the split date to reflect the increase in dividends. The authors, based on the empirical results, argued that the market appears to anticipate splits and the likely impact of dividend changes correctly. The prices of stocks that split and increased dividends rose above those associated with stocks that decreased dividends.

EARNINGS ANNOUNCEMENTS Other important event studies have analyzed how the market reacts to unexpected earnings announcements (see Chapter 13). Large samples of stocks were tested for the market reactions to

[13] Fama, Fisher, Jensen, and Roll, "The Adjustment of Stock Prices to New Information," pp. 1–21.

favorable or unfavorable unexpected earnings announcements. The announced earnings were classified as favorable if they were above the consensus forecast of earnings and unfavorable if they were below the consensus forecast.

The results of these studies tend to support the semistrong form of the EMH since the market quickly adjusted to the unexpected earnings announcements. In other words, stock prices declined quickly after the announcement of unfavorable earnings and increased rapidly for favorable announcements.

OTHER EVENT STUDIES Since the initial event studies were published in the late 1960s, many additional studies have been conducted. This section briefly describes some of the different "events" that have been analyzed but is by no means a complete summary.

Many investors rely on the *Wall Street Journal* and similar publications to follow economic and financial developments in general as well as specific company information. Do stock prices change significantly before or after important public announcements, such as information about new products, new contracts, or an acquisition? A 1984 study found that significant price changes occurred, along with unusual trading volume, *prior* to the publication of the new information in the *Wall Street Journal.*[14] This finding supports market efficiency and argues against an investment strategy based on trading securities on days when new information appears in the *Wall Street Journal.*

A number of studies have analyzed the investment success of corporate insiders (some of these studies will be reviewed later in the chapter). A related issue is how the market reacts to *announcements* about insider trading. By law, corporate insiders must report their transactions to the Securities and Exchange Commission (SEC) by the tenth of the month following the trade. Once this information is published by the SEC or by an investment advisory letter, can the information be used to outperform the market? A recent study found that price adjustments occurred up to four months *prior* to publication of the information and that "moderate" excess returns occurred in the 12 months after the published information appeared.

Individual stocks often have "extreme" daily price changes. This is to be expected in an efficient market since no time lag should occur between the arrival of new information to the market and the appropriate stock price adjustment. Would it be possible, however, either to buy or sell (short) stocks on the day after an "extreme" price change with the expectation that additional price adjustments would occur? A 1982 study concluded that the market was efficient in making rapid and complete price adjustments, since no effective investment strategy could be found based on extreme price changes.[15]

---

[14] Dale Morse, "Wall Street Journal Announcements and the Securities Markets," *Financial Analysts Journal* (March-April 1982): 69–76.

[15] Avner Arbel and Bikki Jaggi, "Market Information Assimilation Related to Extreme Daily Price Jumps," *Financial Analysts Journal* (November-December 1982): 60–66.

RESEARCH BOX

An Unusual Event Study: Accidental Death of CEOs

One problem with event studies is dealing with the stock market's anticipation of the event. The market may anticipate a favorable earnings announcement or a stock split announcement, and the stock's price may consequently increase prior to the day of the announcement. One type of event that would avoid the anticipation or prior price adjustment problem would be a totally unpredictable event—the sudden death of a chief executive officer (CEO).

Using the obituaries listed in the *Wall Street Journal Index*, a 1987 event study collected data on an initial sample of 110 CEO deaths over the period January 1, 1972, through December 31, 1982. Deaths that were not sudden or for which the cause or date were not given were eliminated from the initial sample of 110. A final sample of 48 resulted that included deaths of 30 CEOs and 18 presidents. The causes of death were classified into three groups: heart attacks; accidental deaths, such as those resulting from automobile or plane crashes; and suicides.

The data were analyzed in terms of the following questions:

1. Did the sudden death of a CEO have any effect on the common stock returns?
2. Was the effect on the common stock returns different if the chairman of the board died versus the president?
3. Did the common stock returns adjust differently to the three causes of death?

The authors concluded:

> The results indicate that an immediate decline in the price of the stock occurs on the days of the deaths, but that subsequent stock return behavior depends partly upon the type of officer dying and the cause of death.
>
> There are a number of implications for investors arising from these findings. First, the sudden death of a chief executive officer initially presents an opportunity to go short in the stocks of the affected firms, but the short position must be closed rapidly because the negative response seems to last only one day.

SOURCE: Adapted from Ahmad Etebari, James O. Horrigan, and Jan L. Landwehr, "To Be or Not to Be—Reaction of Stock Returns to Sudden Deaths of Corporate Chief Executive Officers," *Journal of Business Finance and Accounting* (Summer 1987): 255–78.

The majority of event studies report results that support the semistrong form of the EMH. A limited number of studies report results contrary to the hypothesis, however; two examples are analysts' recommendations and financial distress. Studies of these two events found evidence of inefficient price adjustments based on subsequent events.

SUMMARY OF EVENT STUDIES Based on the evidence from many event studies, it appears that the market is efficient in the sense suggested by the semistrong form of the EMH. One should not conclude from these studies, however, that the market is efficient in reacting to every possible event. Not all events have been studied, and not all possible investment strategies based on events have been analyzed.

There is also evidence that the results of some event studies may be biased in cases where the beta is nonstationary (see Chapter 20) around the event date. The event study methodology calculates the beta based on data prior to the event and then uses the beta and market model to estimate returns. This implies beta stationarity.

• Anomalies

In addition to event studies, other types of research have tested the semistrong form of the EMH. These studies test whether various investment strategies based on publicly available information outperform the market. If no strategy can be found, it is likely that the market is efficient. Successful strategies, however, indicate that the market may be inefficient in discovering and incorporating certain types of information into prices.

Beginning in the late 1970s, a number of studies reported evidence that suggested market inefficiencies. This section reports the results of some of these studies based on strategies dealing with firm size, the level of P/E ratios, recurring daily or weekly price patterns, neglected firms, and other possible strategies. These studies attempt to identify *anomalies* or possible market inefficiencies that can be used in an active investment strategy.

SIZE EFFECT Beginning in the early 1980s, a number of studies noted that, after adjusting for risk, small firms appeared to offer significantly larger returns than large firms. Size is usually measured by the capitalization of the firm, which is the total market value of the firm's outstanding stock. Typically, these studies rank stocks by size and form a portfolio of the smallest stocks. The actual returns on the portfolio are then compared to the returns estimated by the CAPM. In a 1981 study, Reinganum found that the risk-adjusted excess return (actual returns less the CAPM estimated return or Jensen's alpha) was approximately 18 percent per year for the decile consisting of the smallest firms.[16] Clearly, this level of excess return is significant.

Debate followed about whether the findings indicated market inefficiency or whether the CAPM methodology was flawed. Essentially, do small firms have greater risk than large firms, and is this difference not reflected in their betas? Reinganum concluded that the CAPM was not appropriate in analyzing the risk of small firms. A study by Roll also indicated that beta did not adequately measure the risk of small firms and that infrequent trading in these stocks may have influenced the empirical results.[17]

One study argues that small firms are actually "neglected" firms that do not receive the degree of investment research and analysis that large firms

---

[16] Marc R. Reinganum, "Misspecification of Capital Asset Pricing: Empirical Anomalies Based on Earnings' Yield and Market Values," *Journal of Financial Economics* (March 1981): 19–46.

[17] Richard Roll, "A Possible Explanation of the Small Firm Effect," *Journal of Finance* (September 1981): 879–88.

do.[18] Thus, the observed excess returns are due partly to the "neglect effect" rather than to the **size effect.** This finding suggests that excess returns may be available on small firms that receive limited investor attention.

Additional studies have noted that the stocks of small firms have more *unsystematic* risk than large firms. Investors who purchase stocks of small companies should therefore adequately diversify the number of small stocks in the portfolio. With adequate diversification, the unsystematic risk of the portfolio can essentially be eliminated.

Another factor that has been offered in an attempt to explain the small firm effect is the influence of industry classification. Since some industries include many small firms while others consist of a few large firms, the observed small firm effect may actually be an industry effect. Thus, buying small firms may result in concentrating investments in certain industries that outperform industries dominated by large firms. The conclusion reached by a 1986 study, however, indicated that the small firm effect still existed after removing the possible industry effect.[19]

As this discussion indicates, the small firm effect and its implications for the EMH remain controversial. The small firm effect cannot be fully explained by problems with the CAPM, neglect, industry influence, or unsystematic risk.

JANUARY EFFECT A second possible market anomaly deals with apparent recurring patterns in stock returns. This evidence has implications for both the weak and semistrong forms of the EMH. The **January effect** essentially finds that stock returns appear to be higher in January than in other months of the year. The January effect may also be related to the size effect since stocks of small companies outperform stocks of large companies in the month of January.[20]

Other evidence suggests there may be daily patterns in stock returns.[21] Based on daily stock prices over the period 1963–1985 for a large sample of NYSE and AMEX issues, it appears that daily returns are higher on Fridays and weaker on Mondays. This pattern also exists in January and is related to the size effect since stocks of small firms demonstrate higher returns on Friday.

P/E EFFECT Traditionally, fundamentalists like Benjamin Graham have recommended using the P/E ratio in selecting stocks (see Chapters 7 and 14). Basically, the **P/E effect** suggests that stocks should be purchased when their P/E ratios are "low" and sold (shorted) when they are "high." Using a CAPM

---

[18] Avner Arbel and Paul Strebel, "The Neglected and Small Firm Effects," *Financial Review* (November 1982): 201–18.

[19] Willard T. Carleton and Josef Lakonishok, "The Size Anomaly: Does Industry Group Matter?" *Journal of Portfolio Management* (Spring 1986): 36–40.

[20] Richard J. Rogalski and Seha M. Tinic, "The January Size Effect: Anomaly or Risk Measurement?" *Financial Analysts Journal* (November-December 1986): 63–70.

[21] Donald B. Keim, "Daily Returns and Size-Related Premiums: One More Time," *Journal of Portfolio Management* (Winter 1987): 41–47.

methodology to adjust for risk, a number of empirical studies have reported that portfolios of stocks with low P/E ratios outperformed portfolios formed with high P/E ratio stocks. Other studies suggest that this apparent market inefficiency is due to problems with the CAPM and a failure to deal with transaction costs adequately.

It should also be noted that the P/E effect and size effect are probably related. The P/E ratio is highly correlated with the stock price, which is usually used to calculate the size variable. Buying stocks with low P/E ratios may be essentially equivalent to buying stock in small companies.

OTHER POSSIBLE MARKET ANOMALIES Many additional studies appear to suggest market inefficiencies. Briefly, some of these studies indicate that using variables such as book value or presidential elections and investing in special offerings or new issues may help in developing an investment strategy that generates risk-adjusted excess returns.

• Implications for Fundamental Analysis

Fundamental analysis assumes that public information can be used to develop superior investment strategies. Event studies, however, have shown that the market reacts quickly to new information and that appropriate changes in stock prices occur rapidly. In many cases, the market actually anticipates the information. Recently, a number of studies have reported on what appear to be market anomalies. Portfolios formed with stocks of small companies, stocks with "low" P/E ratios, or stocks of firms experiencing financial distress are examples of strategies that provide excess returns. Based on the empirical research to date, what conclusions are appropriate in terms of the usefulness of fundamental analysis? The following quotation effectively summarizes the key issue:[22]

> There can be little dispute that the accumulated empirical evidence is inconsistent with any view other than that the market is a highly efficient information processor. What is in dispute is the degree of efficiency—whether there is sufficient deviant price behavior to make it worthwhile for the ordinary investor to seek out opportunities for abnormal gain, or whether the reasonable policy for most investors is simply to buy and hold an internationally diversified portfolio.

Investors using fundamental analysis should recognize that the markets are efficient to the extent that it is unlikely that naïve strategies can beat the market consistently. On the other hand, there is evidence that market inefficiencies exist. One view that seems reasonable is that some investment strategies are superior to others and that it is possible to develop anomaly-based strategies that will outperform random selection strategies.

---

[22] Simon M. Keane, "The Efficient Market Hypothesis on Trial," *Financial Analysts Journal* (March-April 1986): 63.

Another interesting aspect about the debate concerning the degree of market efficiency is that many analysts do not believe in market efficiency. This belief justifies their active investment strategies that attempt to beat the market. Their efforts, however, increase market efficiency, since they are always seeking and analyzing information in making investment decisions. If most investors think that the market is inefficient, it is likely to be efficient because of these activities directed at obtaining and analyzing new information.

THE STRONG FORM OF THE EFFICIENT MARKET HYPOTHESIS

The *strong form* of the EMH hypothesizes that *all* information is reflected in stock prices. "Information" includes both public and private information. Private information implies that certain individuals or organizations, such as corporate insiders or trading specialists, may have monopolistic access to information. According to the strong form of market efficiency, however, the availability of private information is limited and is not a significant factor in security prices.

Fama, in suggesting the strong form of market efficiency, recognized that it is an "extreme null hypothesis" and that "we do not expect it to be literally true." It seems obvious that if an investor has significant monopolistic information, it can be used profitably. The theory does not dispute this possibility. Rather, the theory argues that it is unlikely that monopolistic information is available to any significant extent. The information that may initially be private or secret will quickly be discovered by the market and reflected in the stock's price.

The strong form of the EMH is equivalent to perfect markets in that the market correctly prices securities at all times. Prices adjust quickly to new information, public and private.

• Empirical Tests of Strong Form Efficiency

Two studies from the late 1960s dealing with specialists on the stock exchanges and corporate insiders are recognized as important initial tests of strong-form efficiency.[23] Both studies found evidence that private information available to these two groups could be used to earn risk-adjusted excess returns. The empirical results showed that specialists had monopolistic access to information concerning unexecuted limit orders. This information allowed the specialists to earn trading profits. Other studies have examined corporate insiders and the performance of professionally managed portfolios:

---

[23] Victor Niederhoffer and M.F.M. Osborne, "Market Making and Reversal of the Stock Exchange," *Journal of the American Statistical Association* (December 1966): 897–916; and Myron Scholes, "A Test of the Competitive Hypothesis: The Market for New Issues and Secondary Offerings" (Ph.D. diss., Graduate School of Business, University of Chicago, 1969).

1. Corporate insiders A number of studies have analyzed the investment success of corporate insiders. These studies deal with legal trading activities rather than illegal insider trading. Generally, a corporate insider can make legal trades as long as privately available information is not used and the trade is reported to the SEC. Although laws and regulations attempt to distinguish between legal and illegal insider trading, the line separating the two activities is often very fine. Some people have argued that the SEC defines illegal activities too broadly, with the result that market efficiency is reduced.

Some studies on the performance of corporate insider trading find evidence of risk-adjusted excess returns. There is also evidence that some corporate insiders are more successful than others. For example, a 1983 study found that CEOs and directors had better performance than vice presidents and beneficial owners.[24] Somewhat surprising, however, is the finding that aggregate trading by corporate insiders is not an effective overall market timing indicator. The empirical evidence indicated that there was a tendency for the stock to rise after "intensive" insider buying *and* selling.[25]

2. Performance of professionally managed portfolios A second previously discussed test of strong-form efficiency involves the performances of mutual funds and other professionally managed portfolios. Since these portfolios employ skilled analysts and forecasters, it can be argued that these individuals should be able to discover information that may not be reflected in stock prices. For example, an analyst may make a personal visit to a company and discover information that is not publicly known. Given this information and the expertise of the analyst, superior performance of the portfolio would be an indication of market inefficiency.

As we have seen, however, mutual funds and other professionally managed portfolios, on average, do not earn risk-adjusted excess returns. This finding supports the strong form of the EMH.

• Implications for Investors

The evidence supporting the strong form of market efficiency is not as convincing as the evidence supporting the weak and semistrong forms. There appear to be groups of investors, such as corporate insiders and specialists, who have information that can be used to beat the market. In a broader sense, however, there is evidence that professional investors like mutual funds have difficulty discovering information that can be used to outperform the market consistently. This suggests that the availability of monopolistic information is limited.

---

[24] Kenneth P. Nunn, Jr., Gerald P. Madden, and Michael J. Gombola, "Are Some Insiders More 'Inside' than Others?" *Journal of Portfolio Management* (Spring 1983): 18–22.

[25] Wayne Y. Lee and Michael E. Solt, "Insider Trading: A Poor Guide to Market Timing," *Journal of Portfolio Management* (Summer 1986): 65–71.

A logical conclusion seems to be that if significant private information can be discovered, it can be used profitably. Thus, investors have an incentive to discover information that is not generally known. The possibility of profiting from such information also suggests, however, that access to monopolistic information should be closely regulated and controlled. Investors should support the SEC and other regulatory agencies in assuring that the markets remain competitive and that no individuals or groups are allowed to profit by using illegally acquired information.

• Market Mechanisms versus Pricing Efficiency

In addition to pricing securities correctly and instantaneously changing prices to reflect new information, market efficiency involves *institutional* or *trading procedure efficiency.* Clearly, the U.S. financial markets are highly efficient in terms of the speed and costs associated with transactions. This efficiency is due to information processing and communications technology. The markets therefore provide an environment that promotes pricing efficiency.

Trading procedures also ensure that prices can fluctuate and that pricing information is provided to market participants on a timely basis. Competition and the regulatory environment also increase pricing efficiency. Because of the influence of regulations on market efficiency, many investors and industry leaders are recommending that trading procedures and regulations be carefully reviewed in light of what appears to be increased market volatility.

• Investing in Efficient Markets

The degree of market efficiency remains a hotly debated issue. There is no debate, however, about the significance of the issue for an appropriate investment strategy. In light of the debate, is it rational for individual investors to pursue strategies that attempt to beat the market? Unfortunately, there is no simple answer to this question. Each investor must reach his or her own conclusion.

For investors who conclude that it is worthwhile to pursue a course of active management, the following strategies appear to be reasonable and logical:

1. Anomaly-based strategies Empirical evidence suggests that portfolios consisting of small firms, firms with low P/E ratios, or initial public offerings may offer risk-adjusted excess returns. The January effect may also be significant.

2. Fundamental analysis There is evidence that some investment firms using fundamental analysis have developed techniques or models that can beat the market. While these firms do not usually reveal the details of their techniques, investors may benefit by relying on their recommendations. The apparent success of some fundamental approaches indicates the possibility of discovering techniques that can earn risk-adjusted excess returns.

3. Unique and innovative uses of fundamental and technical analysis A number of research articles have described successful investment strategies based on unique or innovative uses of traditional fundamental and technical analysis.

As an example, one study reported that portfolios formed using both P/E and unexpected earnings announcement criteria provided risk-adjusted excess returns.[26] Using data for the period November 1976 to February 1979, this study found that stocks reporting unexpected good earnings and a "low" P/E ratio outperformed other stocks in the sample. The use of the "dual screening" procedure, a somewhat unusual approach, appears to offer excess returns.

The combined use of the familiar relative strength measure employed by technicians and the CAPM has also been suggested as a viable strategy. Using data on over 300 stocks over an 18-year period, a study found that the strategy resulted in an annual compounded rate of return after transaction costs of 15.2 percent versus 5.9 percent for the S&P 500.[27] Essentially, the strategy ranked stocks on a beta-adjusted recent price momentum basis and formed a portfolio of the stocks in the top decile.

A third example of a possible successful strategy used the ratio of book value per share to price.[28] The strategy involved buying stocks with a high ratio on the ground that they might be undervalued relative to their asset value.

As a final example, a study reported excess returns based on a strategy using P/E ratios and book value per share.[29] The authors argued that the strategy was successful because it provided a *highly disciplined approach* that avoided decisions based on market emotions. The model, described in detail in the article, utilized P/E and book value ratios as dual screening variables.

SUMMARY

This chapter has had two major purposes: (1) to present techniques that can be used to analyze the ex-post performance of portfolios on a risk-adjusted basis and (2) to discuss the degree of market efficiency and the resulting implications for investors.

Based on the development of CMT and, specifically, the CAPM, formal techniques have been devised that combine return and risk into a single per-

[26] Clinton M. Bidwell III, "SUE/PE Revista," *Journal of Portfolio Management* (Winter 1981): 85–88.

[27] John S. Brush and Keith E. Boles, "The Predictive Power in Relative Strength & CAPM," *Journal of Portfolio Management* (Summer 1983): 20–23.

[28] Barr Rosenberg, Kenneth Reid, and Ronald Lanstein, "Persuasive Evidence of Market Inefficiency," *Journal of Portfolio Management* (Spring 1985): 9–16.

[29] Robert F. Vandell and Robert Parrino, "A Purposeful Stride down Wall Street," *Journal of Portfolio Management* (Winter 1986): 31–39.

• CONCEPT APPLICATIONS

Investment Concept	Concept Application
Portfolio performance evaluation	An analysis of the historical investment performance of a portfolio should consider both returns and risk. The Treynor, Sharpe, and Jensen techniques can be used to analyze a portfolio and the benchmark. The performance analysis can be used to test the skill of the portfolio manager and/or the investment strategies or techniques used in managing the portfolio.
Market efficiency	The concept of market efficiency refers to the type of information that is reflected in security prices and the speed with which new information is incorporated into prices. The major issue in the debate is the *degree* of market efficiency. The major implication of the debate is the impact of market efficiency on investment strategies. Inefficient or weakly efficient markets suggest active strategies while efficient markets indicate passive strategies. Individual investors should determine how efficient they believe the markets are and develop appropriate strategies.
Anomalies	Investment strategies that appear to or actually earn risk-adjusted excess returns are called anomalies. They are anomalies because they are exceptions to the EMH. Examples of strategies that have been tested and reported in the investment literature include investing in small firms, taking a long position in stocks in the month of January, and buying stocks that have low P/E ratios. If these strategies are actual anomalies, then they can be successfully used in an active investment strategy.

formance measure. Treynor, Sharpe, and Jensen all have developed such techniques.

Using these and other techniques, numerous studies have examined the performance of professionally managed portfolios. Due to the availability of data, the majority of these studies have dealt with mutual funds. Earlier studies conducted in the late 1960s generally concluded that, on average, mutual funds do not beat the market on a risk-adjusted basis. More recent studies suggest that the funds' performance has improved, but that only a small percentage seem to be able to beat the market.

The last part of the chapter traced the development of the EMH from its beginning in the late 1950s through the many empirical tests that continue to the present. The key question for investors is the *degree* of market efficiency. In terms of theory, the three degrees of efficiency are represented by the weak, semistrong, and strong forms of the EMH.

The empirical studies reviewed in this chapter lead to the conclusion that investment strategies based on a naïve use of technical or fundamental analysis are highly unlikely to beat the market. Security prices reflect publicly available information and react quickly to new information. Advances in communication and data processing technology are improving market efficiency.

A growing number of studies, however, appear to have discovered market anomalies that constitute evidence against the EMH. Studies have also demonstrated that investment strategies based on the anomalies, or on unique and innovative approaches, may provide risk-adjusted excess returns.

Individual investors should carefully consider the arguments and evidence both for and against the EMH. The decision to be a passive or an active investor depends on the individual's conclusion concerning the degree of market efficiency.

• KEY TERMS

Alpha
Efficient market hypothesis (EMH)
Event study
Filter rule
January effect
Jensen's technique
Market efficiency
P/E effect
Random walk (fair game)
Relative strength
Risk premium
Runs test
Semistrong form of the EMH
Serial correlation
Sharpe's technique
Size effect
Strong form of the EMH
Treynor's technique
Weak form of the EMH

• QUESTIONS

1. Explain why an analysis of portfolio performance should consider both return and risk.
2. Discuss how portfolio ex-post returns should be calculated for a performance analysis.
3. The two mutual funds analyzed in the chapter (Fidelity Magellan Fund and T. Rowe Price New Horizons Fund) are common stock funds with an investment objective of "growth." What are some problems that might occur if a fund with a different investment objective was included in the performance analysis?
4. Briefly describe Treynor's portfolio performance technique. Do larger or smaller values indicate better performance? Explain how a portfolio can be compared to the market portfolio using this technique.
5. Assume that a portfolio had a low correlation with the S&P 500 over the last 10 years. Does the Treynor technique consider the level of unsystematic risk implied by the correlation coefficient?

6. Can the Treynor performance measure for a portfolio be a negative number? Under what conditions could this occur?
7. Briefly describe Sharpe's portfolio performance technique. Explain how a portfolio can be compared to the market portfolio using this technique.
8. Consider the following performance information on three portfolios:

	Treynor, T_p	*Sharpe,* S_p	*Jensen,* $\hat{\alpha}_i$
Portfolio A	−4%	−.5%	−5%
Portfolio B	8	1.2	3
Portfolio C	4	.3	0
S&P 500	5	.6	0

   a. Rank the portfolios using each of the performance measures. Are the rankings consistent among the three techniques?
   b. Compare each portfolio's performance to the market's performance. Are the comparisons consistent among the three techniques?
9. The performance techniques of Treynor, Sharpe, and Jensen assume that the risk of the portfolio remained constant over the evaluation period. Discuss the implications of this assumption for the performance evaluation.
10. Empirical studies of mutual funds' performances generally conclude that, on average, funds do not outperform the market on a risk-adjusted basis. Despite this evidence, explain why mutual funds are popular and viable investments for many individuals.
11. Briefly describe the three forms of the efficient market hypothesis. Why is the *degree* of market efficiency an important issue for investors who might pursue an active strategy?
12. Compare and contrast the "size" and "January" effects. Do studies of these possible anomalies indicate that risk-adjusted excess returns are available to investors?
13. Can knowledge concerning the trading activity of insiders be used to earn risk-adjusted excess returns?
14. One form of market efficiency suggests that the speed of price adjustments to new information is an indication of efficiency. Do you think that the 508-point drop in the DJIA on October 19, 1987, was a sign of market efficiency or inefficiency?
15. Based on the discussion and review of efficient market studies in this chapter, do you think that a passive or active investment strategy is appropriate for individual investors?

• KEY TO THE INVESTMENT ANALYSIS SOFTWARE

Calculation	Appendix A-1 Page Reference	Access Procedure
Holding period return	A-8	BEGIN, STATISTICAL, HPR, ONE or MANY
Arithmetic mean holding period return	A-8	BEGIN, STATISTICAL, HPR, MANY
Geometric mean holding period return	A-8	BEGIN, STATISTICAL, GEOM
Sharpe performance measure for portfolio or benchmark	A-7	BEGIN, CAPITAL, PERFORM, SHARPE
Jensen performance measure for portfolio or benchmark	A-13	BEGIN, CAPITAL, PERFORM, JENSEN
Treynor performance measure for portfolio or benchmark	A-13	BEGIN, CAPITAL, PERFORM, TREYNOR
Variance and standard deviation	A-7	BEGIN, STATISTICAL, DESCRIP
Beta	A-12	BEGIN, CAPITAL, CAPM

• PROBLEMS

1. A portfolio's market value increased from $10 to $11 million during the year. In addition, the portfolio distributed $500,000 to its investors at the end of the year. Calculate the holding period return (HPR).

2. Consider the following data on a portfolio's performance:

	Market value	*Income distribution*
January 1, 1989	$10,000	—
December 31, 1989	8,000	$1,000
December 31, 1990	11,000	1,500

a. Calculate the HPRs for 1989 and 1990.

b. Calculate the simple or arithmetic mean HPR over the two-year period.

c. Calculate the geometric mean HPR over the two-year period.

d. Explain any difference in the arithmetic and geometric means.

3. The ex-post return and risk measures for two mutual funds and a benchmark portfolio over the period 1981–1990 are as follows:

	Fund A	*Fund B*	*Benchmark*
Geometric mean annual HPR	18.0%	12.0%	15.0%
Standard deviation	9.0%	6.0%	7.0%
Beta	1.2	0.8	1.0
Geometric mean of annual risk premiums	10.0%	4.0%	7.0%

The geometric mean risk-free return over the period was 8 percent.

a. Calculate the Treynor and Sharpe performance measures for both funds and the benchmark portfolio.

b. Rank the funds, using each performance measure.

c. Compare each fund's performance to the benchmark portfolio, using the two performance measures.

4. Consider the following annual HPRs for two portfolios, a benchmark portfolio, and one-year Treasury bills:

	Portfolio X	*Portfolio Y*	*Benchmark*	*Treasury bills*
1987	20%	15%	12%	8%
1988	25	5	2	6
1989	18	12	10	7
1990	4	3	5	6
1991	30	20	15	8

a. Calculate the arithmetic and geometric means for portfolios X and Y, the benchmark portfolio, and Treasury bills.

b. Calculate the standard deviations for portfolios X and Y, the benchmark portfolio, and Treasury bills.

c. Calculate the correlation coefficient for each portfolio with the benchmark portfolio.

d. Calculate the betas for each portfolio.

e. Calculate the Treynor, Sharpe, and Jensen performance measures for portfolios X and Y and the benchmark portfolio. Rank the two portfolios using the three performance measures.

• REFERENCES

Addis, Ronit, and John Heins. "Annual Fund Ratings: Dog Funds; Betting on the House," *Forbes,* September 4, 1989, pp. 176–81.

Anderson, Seth Copeland. "Closed-End Funds versus Market Efficiency." *Journal of Portfolio Management* (Fall 1986): 63–65.

Arnott, Robert D., and Stephen J. Vincent. "S&P Additions and Deletions: A Market Anomaly." *Journal of Portfolio Management* (Fall 1986): 29–33.

Barrett, Amy. "Mutual Fund First-Quarter Review." *Financial World*, May 15, 1990, pp. 84–92.

Bloch, Howard, and Roger Pupp. "The January Barometer Revisited and Rejected." *Journal of Portfolio Management* (Winter 1983): 48–50.

Bower, Richard S., and Dorothy H. Bower. "The Salomon Brothers Electric Utility Model: Another Challenge to Market Efficiency." *Financial Analysts Journal* (September-October 1984): 57–67.

Brown, Keith C., and C.V. Harlow. "Market Overreaction: Magnitude and Intensity." *Journal of Portfolio Management* (Winter 1988): 6–13.

Carleton, Willard T., and Josef Lakonishok. "The Size Anomaly: Does Industry Group Matter?" *Journal of Portfolio Management* (Spring 1986): 36–40.

Dowen, Richard J., and W. Scott Bauman. "The Relative Importance of Size, P/E, and Neglect." *Journal of Portfolio Management* (Spring 1986): 30–34.

Eaton, Leslie. "Rewards of Risk: Swinging Funds Race Ahead of the Pack." *Barron's*, April 10, 1989, pp. 38–39.

Ferguson, Robert. "The Trouble with Performance Measurement." *Journal of Portfolio Management* (Spring 1986): 4–9.

Fraser, Donald R., and R. Malcolm Richards. "The Penn Square Bank Failure and the Inefficient Market." *Journal of Portfolio Management* (Spring 1985): 34–36.

French, Dan W., and Glenn V. Henderson, Jr. "How Well Does Performance Evaluation Perform?" *Journal of Portfolio Management* (Winter 1985): 15–22.

Goodman, David A., and John W. Peavy. "The Risk Universal Nature of the P/E Effect." *Journal of Portfolio Management* (Summer 1985): 14–16.

Huang, Roger D. "Common Stock Returns and Presidential Elections." *Financial Analysts Journal* (March-April 1985): 58–61.

Ippolito, Richard A., and John A. Turner. "Turnover, Fees and Pension Plan Performance." *Financial Analysts Journal* (November-December 1987): 16–26.

Jacobs, Bruce I., and Kenneth N. Levy. "Forecasting the Size Effect." *Financial Analysts Journal* (May-June 1989): 38–54.

Joy, O. Maurice, and Charles P. Jones. "Should We Believe the Tests of Market Efficiency?" *Journal of Portfolio Management* (Summer 1986): 49–54.

Keane, Simon M. "The Efficient Market Hypothesis on Trial." *Financial Analysts Journal* (March-April 1986): 58–63.

Keim, Donald B. "Dividend Yields and the January Effect." *Journal of Portfolio Management* (Winter 1986): 54–59.

Kritzman, Mark. "How to Detect Skill in Management Performance." *Journal of Portfolio Management* (Winter 1986): 16–20.

Lakonishok, Josef, and Seymour Smidt. "Trading Bargains in Small Firms at Year-End." *Journal of Portfolio Management* (Spring 1986): 24–29.

Malkiel, Burton G. *A Random Walk down Wall Street,* 5th ed. New York: W. W. Norton, 1991.

Reinganum, Marc R. "The Anatomy of a Stock Market Winner." *Financial Analysts Journal* (March-April 1988): 16–28.

Rosenberg, Barr, Kenneth Reid, and Ronald Lanstein. "Persuasive Evidence of Market Inefficiency." *Journal of Portfolio Management* (Spring 1985): 9–16.

Treynor, Jack L. "Market Efficiency and the Bean Jar Experiment." *Financial Analysts Journal* (May-June 1987): 50–53.

Vandell, Robert F., and Robert Parrino. "A Purposeful Stride down Wall Street." *Journal of Portfolio Management* (Winter 1986): 31–39.

Zarowin, Paul. "Short-Run Market Overreaction: Size and Seasonality Effects." *Journal of Portfolio Management* (Spring 1989): 26–29.

PART VIII

Individual Investment Decision Making

CHAPTER 22

Personal Investment Management

CHAPTER 22

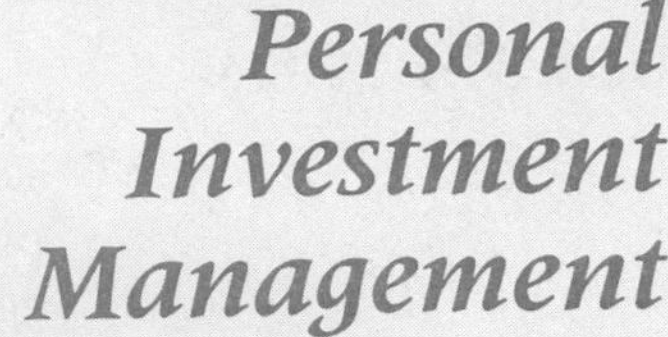

Personal Investment Management

The knowledge-level objectives of this chapter should enable the student to:

- Recognize the importance of developing a personal financial plan.
- Understand how investment analysis and management are used to accomplish the goals of a personal financial plan.
- Distinguish among the many different types of insurance products such as term, whole life, endowment life, universal life, and variable life.
- Assess the importance of developing a tax-sheltered retirement plan as part of the overall financial plan.
- Discuss the three major professional designations for financial planners and investment advisers.

INTRODUCTION

The purpose of this chapter is to integrate much of the material that has been presented previously and show how it applies to personal investment management. Throughout the book, information has been presented from the perspective of individual investors and the major financial decisions they face including the following:

1. Identifying personal goals.
2. Developing investment objectives to achieve the goals.
3. Developing financial plans for each goal.
4. Developing appropriate investment strategies for each goal.
5. Monitoring the performance of the portfolios and changing their composition as needed.
6. Monitoring the financial plans and revising them when necessary.

This chapter will not attempt to repeat or summarize the discussions that have been presented concerning most of these decisions. Rather, the chapter will look at the broader issue of personal investment management. Life insurance and other insurance products are discussed as a part of the overall financial plan as is planning for retirement. An illustration of financial planning is provided for the Stanton family whom we met in Chapter 1. The chapter concludes with a discussion of the financial services industry and the professional designations that can be earned by financial planners and investment counselors. This material is relevant to individuals who are interested in pursuing careers in these areas. The discussion may also help individuals who decide to seek professional advice in formulating their investment strategies and developing an overall financial plan.

PERSONAL FINANCIAL PLANNING

Financial planning is the process of identifying lifetime goals and determining the level and proper management of financial resources needed to accomplish those goals. As this very broad definition indicates, financial resources are essential to accomplishing many of the goals individuals may have, such as completing college, starting their own business, becoming wealthy, or retiring early. Once the goals are identified and formalized, the investment objective(s) indicates when they are achievable and how much money will be required. Specific financial plans and strategies can then be developed to accumulate and manage the financial resources that will be needed.

Figure 22.1 provides a simple illustration of the personal financial planning process. Notice that the individual identified three goals to be achieved over the next decades. Then the investment objective for each goal is identified followed by the appropriate financial plans and investment strategies. It is important to realize that each goal may require different investment strategies.

FIGURE 22.1 • The Personal Financial Planning Process

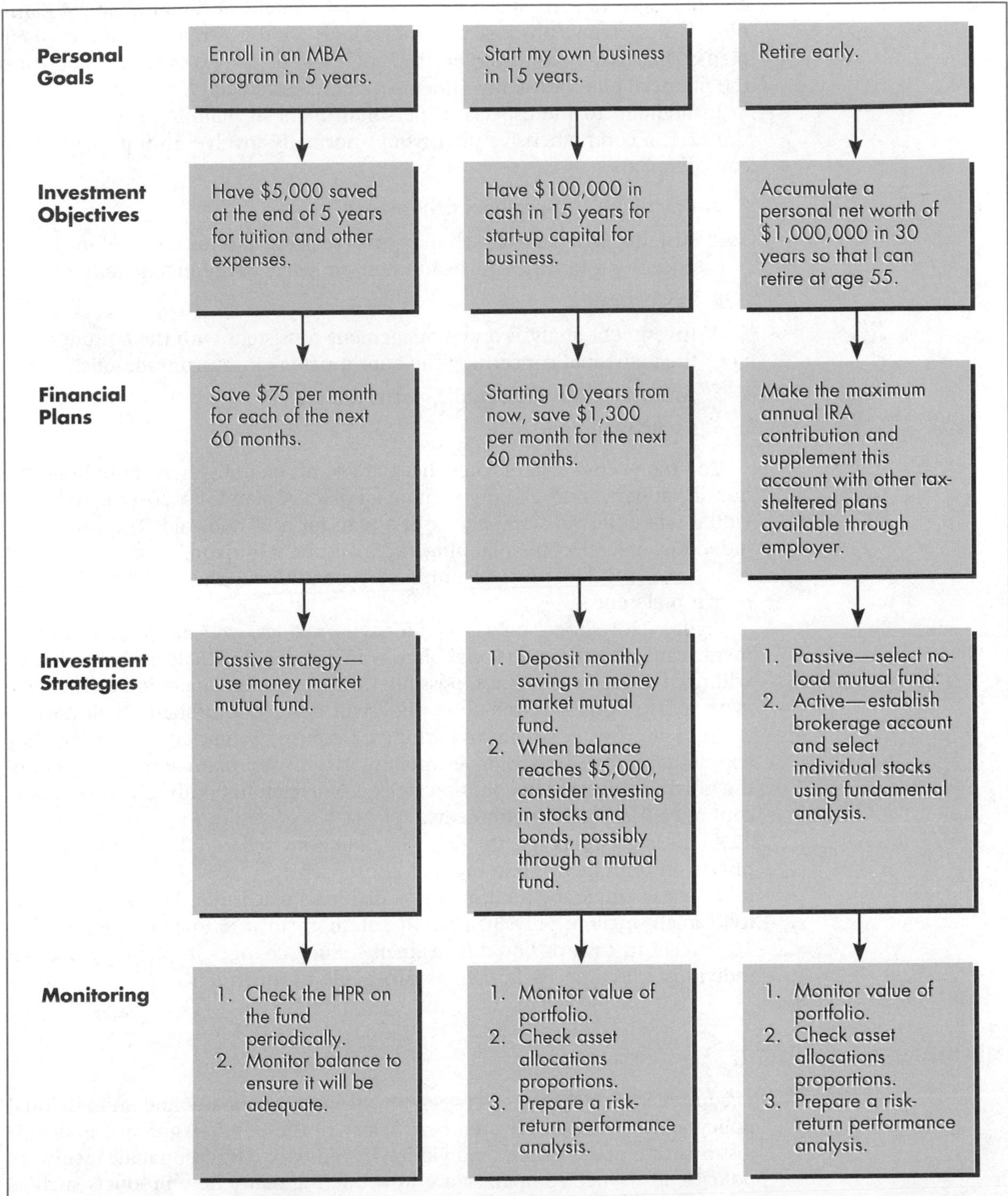

Thus, an individual may have a number of separate portfolios, each formed and managed to accomplish a specific goal. Finally, personal financial planning is a dynamic process, and individuals should carefully monitor their plans. They may need to add or drop goals and objectives or simply fine-tune the financial plan or the investment strategies developed for the plan.

In addition to the aspects of personal financial planning shown in Figure 22.1, a comprehensive plan would normally involve a number of other considerations:

1. Cash-flow and personal debt management.

2. Risk management, which may involve using various forms of insurance to protect the life, health, and property of the individual.

3. Tax planning.

4. Investment analysis and management consistent with the attitudes of the individual concerning the appropriate risk-return trade-offs.

5. Analysis of buying a home versus renting.

6. Estate planning.

Common sense also dictates that the age of the individual should play an important part in developing a financial plan. A plan for a 20-year-old individual will differ substantially from a plan for a 60 year old. The age of the individual will affect the planning and investment horizon, the type and level of income, the level of consumption expenditures, and possibly the risk-return preferences.

Figure 22.2 shows how age, life-style, savings, and appropriate investments can influence a financial plan. Notice that individuals in their mid-20s will need disciplined savings, possibly through automatic payroll deductions. With a fast, aggressive life-style, they will need, and probably will have, a steady but growing stream of earnings. Because of their age, however, they should have an aggressive investment plan with approximately 70 percent of the portfolio invested in common stock, 25 percent in bonds, and only 5 percent in cash or liquid investments.

As the individuals age, the financial plan is revised to reflect a growing emphasis on retirement planning and consequently a more conservative portfolio. For example, by the time the individuals reach their late 60s, the portfolio might include only 30 percent common stock, 60 percent bonds, and 10 percent in cash or liquid investments. Such changes in planning over an individual's lifetime are known as **life-cycle planning.**

INSURANCE PRODUCTS

Life insurance is a contract between an insurance company and an individual policyholder that provides the beneficiary of the policy a guarantee against loss by death of the insured individual. In addition to traditional life insurance policies, insurance companies are now offering many new products such as universal and variable life policies.

FIGURE 22.2 • Life-Cycle Financial Planning

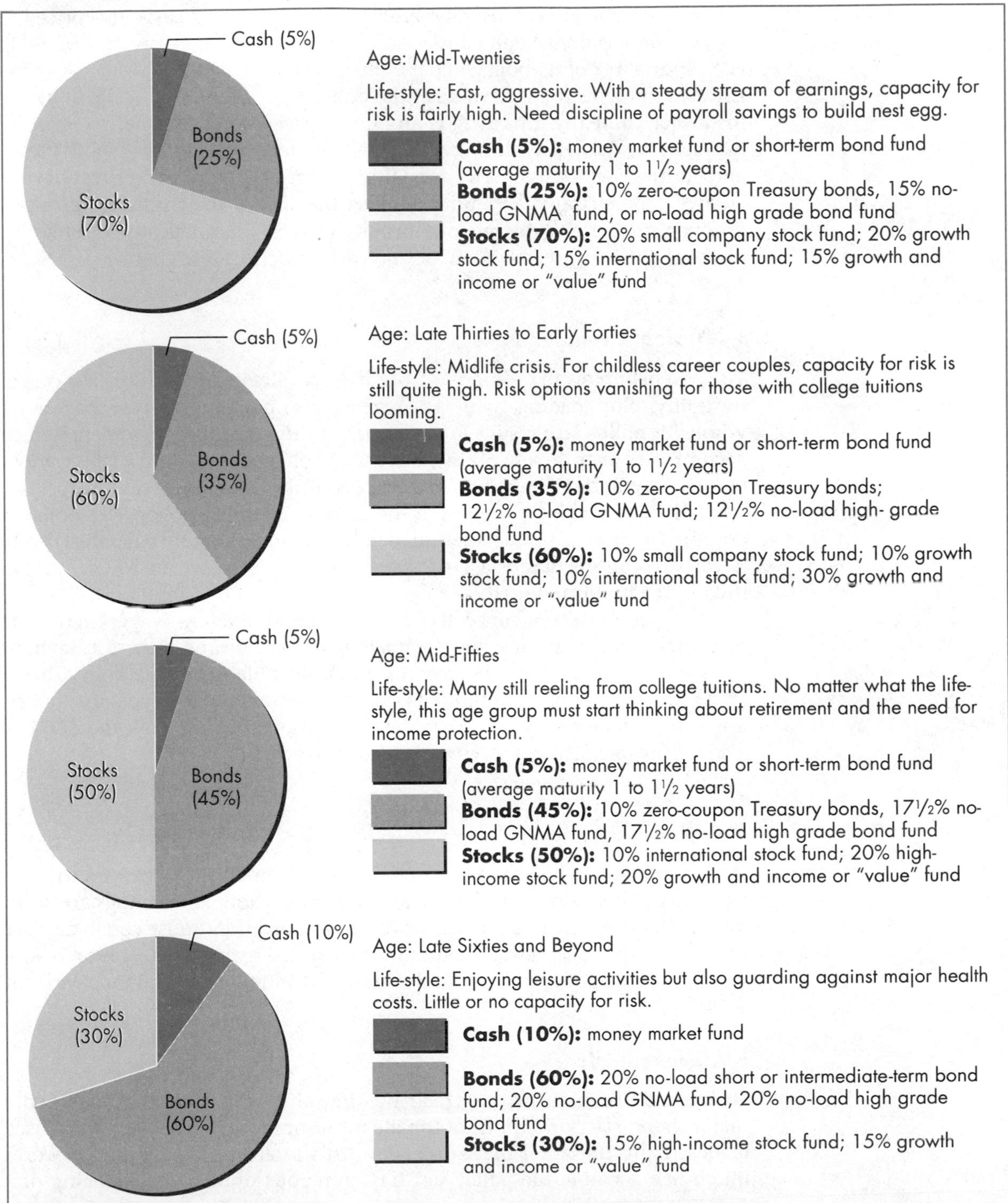

SOURCE: Reproduced from Burton G. Malkiel, *A Random Walk down Wall Street,* 5th ed. (New York: W.W. Norton, 1991), p. 358. Used by permission of W.W. Norton & Company, Inc. Copyright © 1990, 1985, 1981, 1975, 1973 by W.W. Norton & Company, Inc.

• Term Life

Term life insurance is usually purchased on an annual basis. It is priced to provide the insurance company with funds to cover the yearly cost of dying (i.e., mortality) of its policyholders, plus loading. The *cost of dying,* or **mortality,** represents the face value of the policy that will be paid at death by the insurance company. **Loading** is an all-inclusive expression that includes all expenses associated with marketing and servicing the product, plus profits and contingency charges. The annual premium on a one-year term policy increases geometrically over time because the size of the insurance group is growing smaller and the rate of mortality increases dramatically for older individuals. The insured accumulates no cash value in a term policy.

• Ordinary Whole Life

The cost of buying an ordinary **whole life** contract includes the yearly cost of mortality, plus loading, with an increasing annual mortality exposure. A whole life policy also results in an annual **savings/reserve** increment, which accumulates over the life of the policy. The policyholder accumulates savings because the annual premium is in excess of the amount needed to pay for mortality and loading expenses in the early years of the policy. This policy is designed to provide protection until death, and premiums are paid until death. A variation of this plan is a *single-premium whole life policy,* in which only an initial premium is required.

The savings/reserve concept is used in several different ways. One of the most important is to provide *nonforfeiture options;* at any time, the savings/reserve in the policy may be used to purchase a life insurance policy that is "paid up" and therefore nonforfeitable. The face value of the "paid up" policy, however, will be below the face value of the original policy. Policyholders can also borrow against their savings/reserve balances.

• Endowment Life

Endowment life policies are priced to cover the mortality factor for the policy period, plus loading, in the same manner as whole life. Savings are accumulated at a much faster rate, however, because they must equal the face value of the policy in a specified number of years—such as 10, 15, or 20—at which time the policy matures and requires no additional premium payments.

• Universal Life

Universal life insurance, which was introduced in 1979, has captured a major share (over one-third) of the life insurance market. The key word used in describing universal life is *flexibility.* This interest-sensitive policy works much like a whole life policy but has numerous options for changing pre-

FIGURE 22.3
A Universal Life Policy

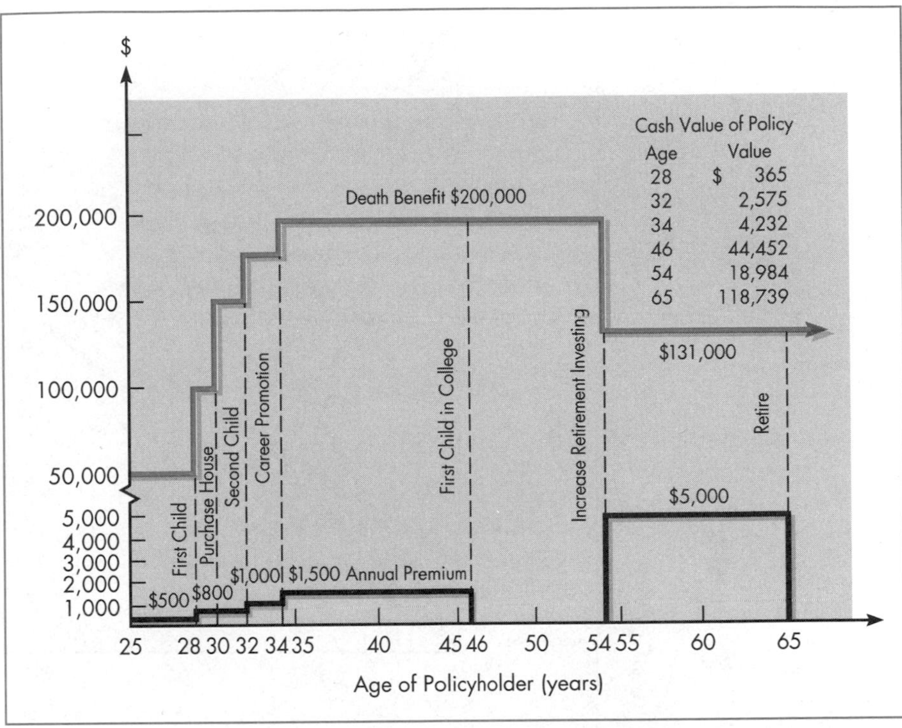

SOURCE: Adapted from Robert Runde, "At Last an Almost Ideal Policy," *Money,* July 1981, p. 88. Reprinted by permission.

miums, cash values, and death benefits. Figure 22.3 shows how the premium, death benefit, and cash value can fluctuate over the lifetime of a policyholder.

• Variable Life

If the key word describing universal life is flexibility, the key phrase for a **variable life** policy is *separate account.* Unlike other insurance policies, variable life policies are regulated by federal and state securities laws. A variable life contract consists of two parts: (1) a whole life policy and (2) a separate *investment account,* which can be invested in common stocks, bonds, and other types of investments that meet state regulations. The whole life part of the contract guarantees a minimum death benefit, and the investment account reflects the return on the underlying instruments, with their associated risk. *Barron's* publishes the *unit values* for a number of variable life accounts each week.

• Comparison of Policies

The abbreviated descriptions in the preceding sections were not intended to provide a detailed working knowledge of the five basic types of life insurance policies, but simply to provide sufficient background about these policies so

FIGURE 22.4
Savings/Reserve on Four Types of Life Insurance Policies

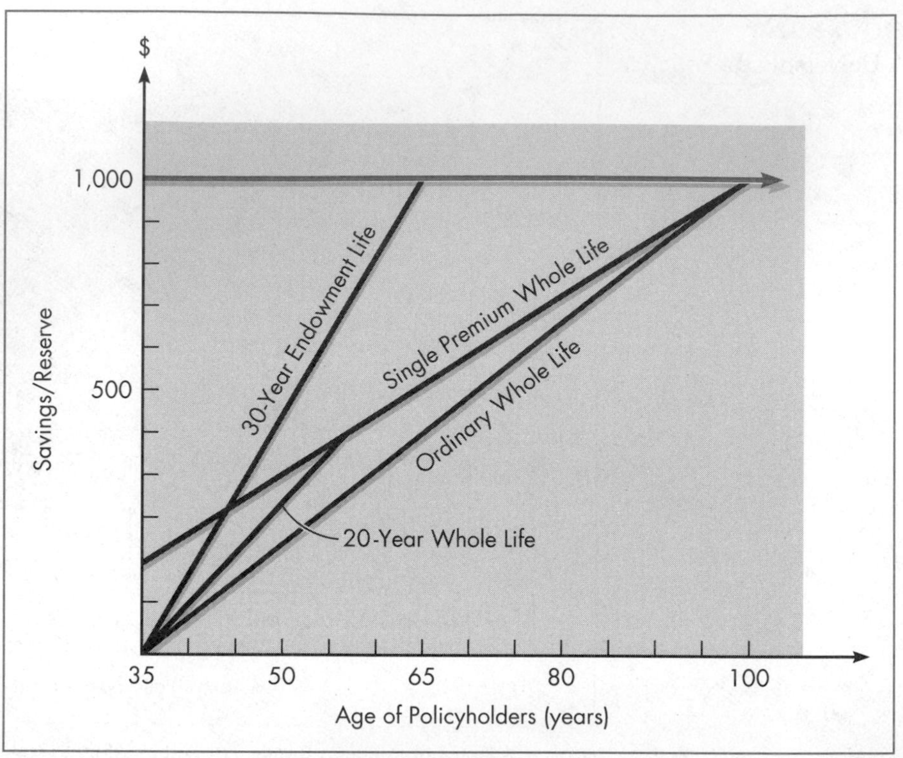

that they can be considered in the financial planning process. Figure 22.4 compares four types of life insurance policies: (1) ordinary whole life, (2) whole life with premium paid in 20 years, (3) single-premium whole life, and (4) endowment life. The savings/reserve of each policy over time is shown on the vertical axis. The savings/reserve value is calculated by subtracting the mortality and load factors from the premiums. The savings/ reserve is also credited with interest income over the life of the policy. For example, for an ordinary whole life policy with face value of $1,000 purchased at age 35, the savings/reserve would be $300 at age 55; the insurer would have a net outflow of cash of $700 after considering the savings/reserve balance of $300. Notice that the single-premium whole life policy has an *initial* savings/reserve balance because the premium is above the amount necessary to cover the mortality and loading costs.

By their very nature, ordinary life and endowment contracts are designed for the long run. Any product making promises about long-term interest rates (perhaps for 30 or more years) must be conservative. The policyholder is subject to limited risk since the guarantees provide interest rate floors, such as 5 percent. Actual returns on the savings/reserve balances may be higher, however. This possibility, coupled with legislated restrictions on investment alternatives for insurance companies, results in modest but low-risk returns. When one examines the actual return on the savings/reserve element, a modest rate of return is indeed what is found. However, certain tax advantages accrue to these policies that are not available in other investments. Despite the tax advantages, the older, nonparticipating policies have experienced considerable **disintermediation** from policyholders canceling their policies and receiving the cash reserve. The disintermediation is attributed to the lack of investment competitiveness of older policies, compared with the new interest-sensitive products.

The flexibility of a universal life policy enables it to respond to the changing financial circumstances of the policyholder. Neither the premium nor the death benefit is fixed as they are with ordinary whole life and endowment policies. Most companies, however, limit the timing and the number of changes permitted. In general, loading and mortality charges are deducted from the annual premium. The difference—the savings/reserve element—is then credited with a *current* market rate of interest. The older whole life and endowment policies do not credit interest at prevailing market rates. Universal life policies also give the policyholder the option of paying no premium in a given year as long as the savings/reserve is sufficient to carry the mortality and loading charges. In addition, the policyholder may withdraw a portion of the savings/reserve. Later, premium payments may be voluntarily increased, with the goal of increasing retirement savings.

Competition has forced companies to lower loading factors for universal life policies. In addition, current mortality rates are below those used in older type policies. Both of these changes have reduced the cost of these products to the policyholder. At least once a year, the policyholder is provided with a statement, showing the breakdown of premiums, mortality and loading factors, interest credited, and total savings/reserve. Universal life policies can offer policyholders low-cost life insurance coverage and flexibility, but note that they do not provide the built-in discipline of policies with fixed annual premiums.

The key characteristics of variable life policies include a separate investment account and the necessity for regulation by the Securities and Exchange Commission (SEC). Most firms offer a variety of investment options, including common stocks, bonds, and money market securities. After mortality and loading expenses are paid, the balance of the premiums is invested at the direction of the policyholder, who then assumes the risk of the investments. Since no guarantees are made on the savings/reserve portion, however, its value could fall to zero if the investments perform poorly.

Another critical factor that must be considered with these new policies is how much one-year term insurance is needed to provide the desired face value, or death benefit, at any given time. Better investment results cause the savings/reserve to increase more rapidly, resulting in smaller annual mortality charges. There is one major problem, however. Suppose a policyholder pursuing a high-risk investment program suddenly, at age 55, finds that equity values in the policy have fallen by one-half or more. Will the annual savings increment be enough to keep the plan at the targeted death benefit? Considering the high cost of pure mortality protection (one-year term policy) during the remaining years of life, the plan could fail by a considerable margin to provide the desired death benefit.

• Tax Implications

Life insurance proceeds payable to a named beneficiary are exempt from federal income tax. Settlement options and loan provisions also provide further tax advantages, but it is beyond the scope of this text to discuss these complicated income and estate tax planning problems. Many currently available life insurance products are designed to solve these and other personal investment management problems.

• Stability of the Insurance Industry

As noted earlier, the insurance industry has responded to the problems created by the decline in the popularity of whole life policies. New products have attempted to combine insurance and investments. It should be remembered, however, that the insurance industry is very cyclical. Its revenues and profitability are highly dependent on the performance of the financial and real estate markets because the premiums collected from policyholders are largely invested in those markets. The investment income is then used to pay policy claims and provide reserves for future claims.

Therefore, individuals who elect to invest in the newer products offered by the insurance industry should be concerned about the financial health of the specific company and the industry. In 1991, several large insurance companies were in financial difficulty because of the depressed real estate market. It is always a good idea to check the "Best Rating" of a company before buying a policy. These ratings, which are similar to bond ratings, provide an indication of the financial health of the company.

INVESTING FOR RETIREMENT

The importance of developing investment objectives has been stressed throughout this book. An individual investor may have a number of different goals—for example, to start a new business, to purchase a home, and to provide retirement income. Each of these goals may require different investment strategies.

This section of the chapter discusses investment strategies that are appropriate for retirement investing. Generally, these strategies involve a long investment horizon, are designed to take advantage of favorable tax treatments, and should be somewhat conservative in terms of their risk-return trade-offs.

• Tax-Sheltered Retirement Plans

The tax laws provide several significant tax benefits for retirement investments. Most importantly, an individual is allowed to make contributions to a retirement plan on a before-tax basis and to defer taxes on the investment returns until retirement. These tax breaks are so significant that most individu-

• INTEREST BOX

Retirement Planning for Baby Boomers

Many individuals, including baby boomers who may have only recently started their professional careers, dream about early retirement. The "ultimate" dream is not only to retire early but also to have the financial resources to have a life-style that only the very rich can enjoy. Is it possible for baby boomers to realize their early retirement dreams?

A recent survey of insurance company actuaries suggests the answer to this question is "no." The actuaries feel that only about half of the baby boomers will find retirement affordable at the normal retirement age of 65. Furthermore, few of those who can afford to retire at age 65 will have accumulated the financial resources that will support the life-style they are dreaming about.

The actuaries cited several factors that contribute to this gloomy forecast:

1. Baby boomers and most individuals wait far too long to start a financial plan for retirement. Baby boomers need to start saving *now* for retirement.
2. Tax incentives are inadequate to encourage retirement savings through employer-sponsored pension plans and personal savings.
3. Social Security benefits will be inadequate because not enough workers will be paying Social Security to support the enormous number of baby boomers who will reach the retirement age of 65 between 2010 and 2028.

SOURCE: Adapted from Richard Donahue, "Baby Boomers Can Ill Afford Retirement," *National Underwriter*, Property & Casualty edition, November 27, 1989, pp. 16–17.

als should use tax-sheltered plans to the fullest extent possible before considering other plans. All of the following plans offer favorable tax treatment to individual investors:

1. Individual retirement account Probably, the most popular and best known of the retirement plans is the **individual retirement account (IRA).** This plan allows an individual to contribute up to $2,000 per year to the account or $2,250 for a spousal IRA if the spouse does not work. Beginning in 1987, the full $2,000 contribution is tax deductible if the individual is not covered by an employer-maintained retirement plan. If the individual is covered by a pension plan, the full deduction is still allowed if his or her annual income is less than $25,000 ($40,000 for joint income). Partial deductions are allowed for incomes between $25,000 and $35,000 ($40,000 and $50,000 for joint income), but no deductions are allowed for incomes above $35,000 ($50,000 for joint income). Although tax reform eliminated the tax deductibility of IRA contributions for some individuals, the tax liability on IRA earnings can still be deferred.

2. Keogh plans Keogh plans are attractive to self-employed individuals. A **Keogh plan** is essentially a profit-sharing plan that can be used to shelter self-employment income. If the business has employees in addition to the owner, they must be included in the plan. The annual contribution limit to the plan is 15 percent of self-employment net income, up to a maximum of $30,000. The larger deductible annual contributions make Keogh plans more attractive than IRAs for higher-income individuals. Individuals who are employed but who also have their own business can have an employer-sponsored pension plan and a Keogh plan for their self-employment income.

3. 401(k) plans A **401(k) plan** differs from an IRA or Keogh plan in that it allows annual contributions from both the employee and the employer. Contributions by the employee are made on a before-tax basis, and employer contributions are tax deductible. In one sense, a 401(k) plan is basically a deferred compensation plan for employees. As of 1991, annual employee contributions are limited to $8,475 per year and are further reduced by any amount contributed to an IRA. Individuals may use a "catch-up" provision that allows contributions of up to $15,000 per year if the maximum allowable annual contribution has not been made in the past.

PENSION PLANS

A **pension fund** or **pension plan** is an investment portfolio that is established to provide retirement benefits to employees of an organization. Pension funds, insurance products, and tax-sheltered retirement plans are all important to individuals' overall financial planning and, specifically, to their retirement planning.

As employees, most individual investors do not have direct control of their pension plan and historically have not been able to influence its investment policies. Control is exercised by the employer, which may be a small privately held business, a publicly traded corporation, or a governmental unit or agency. However, employees should be aware of the various types of pension plans and the specific characteristics of the plans in which they have an interest. This information is essential in planning for retirement and formulating strategies for the overall personal financial plan.

Pension plans may be funded or sponsored by business (private plans) or by government units or agencies (public plans). Pension funds are very large investors in common stocks and fixed-income securities. The investments and investment strategies of pension funds vary according to the type of plan and the risk-return attitudes of the pension fund's sponsor and manager.

• How Pension Funds Operate

A pension fund is a separate organization from its sponsor. This arrangement protects the employees and permits the fund to receive funding from the sponsor for investment purposes. Contributions (funding) by the sponsor and investment income are used to provide income to retired employees or lump-sum benefits to employees who leave the organization.

Before an employee becomes eligible for pension benefits, certain requirements must be met. Historically, employees became **vested** or entitled to benefits after completing 10 years of employment with the sponsoring organization. Under the Tax Reform Act of 1986, however, plans are required to reduce the vesting period. Beginning January 1, 1989, plans have two options: 100 percent vesting after five years of service, or 20 percent vesting after three years of service, rising in 20 percent increments to full vesting after seven years.

Once vested, an employee may leave the organization before retiring and retain his or her benefits. Typically, the pension fund maintains the accrued benefits in escrow until the former worker reaches retirement age; then benefits are paid out monthly. A second option distributes accrued benefits as a lump sum upon the employee's leaving the organization. Because of possible tax consequences, the recipient of a lump-sum distribution should consider "rolling over" the distribution into another retirement fund.

Details about vesting and distribution options for employees are provided in the **summary plan description** that pension funds are required to furnish to plan participants. The summary plan description also explains other important characteristics of a plan, including whether it is a defined benefit or defined contribution plan.

• Defined Benefit Plan

The **defined benefit plan (DBP)** is the oldest and most common type of pension plan and, as the name implies, specifies the benefits that will be received at retirement. The plan sponsor (employer) makes specified contributions to each employee's account; the employee's account is then used to provide the defined benefit at retirement.

The amount of the benefit depends on a number of factors, including length of employment and level of income. Typically, DBP benefits are larger for employees with greater longevity and higher salaries: a typical benefit formula uses a percentage of the average of the last five years' salary, adjusted for length of employment, to determine monthly retirement benefits. Benefits do not depend on the investment performance of the fund.

• Defined Contribution Plan

The other major type of pension plan is the **defined contribution plan (DCP).** This plan specifies the contribution that employers (and/or employees) will make to the plan, rather than stating pension benefits. A DCP may take a number of forms, including a profit-sharing plan, employee stock option plan (ESOP), 401(k) savings plan, and money-purchase pension plan.

One advantage of a DCP employee account is that after vesting, it is considered the property of the employee and can easily be transferred. Another advantage is that this plan often allows employees to match the contributions of

RESEARCH BOX

Defined Benefits versus Defined Contribution Pension Plans

Defined benefit plans (DBPs) are older than defined contribution plans (DCPs). Since they are older, they are also much larger and more numerous than DCPs. For example, in 1990, 81.4 percent of the assets of the 200 largest pension plans in the United States were in DBPs. The assets in DBPs of the 200 largest plans reached $1.164 trillion in 1990.

Despite the size and importance of DBPs, however, DCPs are becoming much more popular. The decline in the use of DBPs and the increasing popularity of DCPs can be explained by the following factors:

1. New regulations that have reduced the pension benefits available to senior managers.
2. Increased administrative cost of DBPs versus DCPs.
3. Risk of penalties and severe sanctions imposed on overfunded DBPs.
4. Likelihood of increased government scrutiny.

DBPs and DCPs are likely to differ in their investment strategies. Since DCPs often have options that allow plan participants to select the type of investment vehicle they prefer, many select conservative investments such as bonds. In fact, the largest asset of DCPs is fixed-income securities. On the other hand, DBPs may invest in common stocks, real estate, international investments, and a variety of other assets including fixed-income securities.

Finally, individuals will be relying more heavily in the future on income from pension plans than they have in the past. DCPs usually offer improved flexibility and more encouragement for individuals to make contributions to their own plans.

SOURCE: Arnold J. Chassen, "Whatever Happened to Defined Benefit Plans?" *Management Accounting* (July 1990): 18–19; and Curtis Vosti, "Markets Fuel 18% Asset Gain," *Pension and Investments*, January 22, 1990, pp. 1, 81.

the employer; all contributions and earnings are tax-free until retirement distributions begin.

A disadvantage of a DCP is that the level of retirement benefits depends to a great extent on the investment performance of the plan; the employee does not know the value of his or her share in the plan until retirement. At that point, however, the funds may be used to purchase some type of annuity contract that will provide a defined benefit for a specified period of time.

• Pension Fund Risk

A pension fund, like any other investment portfolio, can have varying degrees of risk. Prior to 1974, the rules and regulations governing funding and other aspects of pension plans were lax. The *Employee Retirement Income Security Act* (*ERISA*) of 1974 and the *Pension Benefit Guaranty Corporation* (*PBGC*) that was created by ERISA have improved the financial health of many pension plans.

Despite increased regulation and control, there is growing concern about the financial soundness of many privately funded plans. This concern has developed, in part, because of the bankruptcy of such well-known firms as LTV Corporation, Allis-Chalmers, and Wheeling-Pittsburgh Steel. The failure of the funding corporations results in the termination of retirement benefits for underfunded plans. Large and widespread bankruptcies could also drain the financial resources of the PBGC. Individuals should, therefore, be aware of the financial strength of the funding corporation and of their pension fund.

ILLUSTRATION OF PERSONAL FINANCIAL PLANNING

This section provides a basic illustration of financial planning using the Stanton family. As discussed in Chapter 1, the Stantons have three major goals: (1) having enough money to pay for college for their three children; (2) accumulating enough wealth to retire early; and (3) maintaining their standard of living.

The following is a brief summary of the information about the Stantons presented in Chapter 1:

- Ages: Bill = 49; Martha = 49; Roger = 20; Sarah = 17; Tim = 15.
- Roger is a senior finance major; Sarah and Tim plan to attend college after high school.
- Current family earnings: $68,000 per year from family-owned carpet business.
- Major assets: home with fair market value of $130,000 and fixed-rate mortgage balance of $83,000; savings account balance of $62,000; 50 percent ownership of common stock of retail carpet business.
- Annual savings: $6,000.

Roger, the oldest child, wanted to help his parents analyze their present financial situation and began to develop a plan that could be used to accomplish their goals. Roger had recently completed an investments course at the university and wanted to apply some of the things he had learned. His parents, though initially skeptical, agreed to let Roger analyze their situation and recommend a course of action.

Roger prepared the analysis presented in Table 22.1. This analysis projects the family's income and expenses over the next 10 years and assumes his parents will retire at age 60. Since his father and mother do not have a pension plan through the business, Roger realized that the first priority was to establish a plan to take advantage of the favorable tax laws. His plan assumes that a 401(k) plan, funded by contributions from the carpet business, would be appropriate. Because the business does not have any significant earnings after paying salaries, Roger assumed that his father would reduce his salary by $6,000 per year and have the business contribute this amount to the 401(k) plan. This contribution would not have an impact on the taxes or cash flows of the business. His father, however, would benefit because he would be saving $6,000 before taxes rather than the $6,000 currently saved from after-tax income.

TABLE 22.1 • A Financial Plan for the Stantons

	Current year	Remaining working years			
		1	*2*	*3*	*4*
After-tax earnings[a]	$68,000	$62,000	$65,100	$68,355	$71,773
Expenses[b]	62,000	62,000	64,480	67,059	69,742
Savings	$ 6,000	$ 0	$ 620	$ 1,296	$ 2,031
College expenses[c]					
Roger	$ 7,000				
Sarah		$ 7,560	$ 8,165	$ 8,818	$ 9,523
Tim				8,818	9,523
Total	$ 7,000	$7,560	$ 8,165	$17,636	$19,046
Savings					
Beginning of year	$62,000	$68,930	$70,186	$71,618	$64,438
College expenses	(7,000)	(7,560)	(8,165)	(17,636)	(19,046)
Annual savings (withdrawal)	6,000	—	620	1,296	2,031
Investment income[d]	7,930	8,816	8,977	9,160	8,242
End of year	$68,930	$70,186	$71,618	$64,438	$55,665
401(k) retirement plan					
Beginning of year	—	—	$ 6,000	$12,776	$20,429
Annual contributions (withdrawal)	—	$ 6,000	6,000	6,000	6,000
Investment income[e]	—	—	776	1,653	2,643
End of year	—	$ 6,000	$12,776	$20,429	$29,072

[a] Assumes an annual growth rate of 5%.
[b] Assumes an annual growth rate of 4%.
[c] Assumes college costs will increase 8% per year.

From his investments class, Roger was convinced that the financial markets are efficient and that investors are unlikely to earn risk-adjusted excess returns. Using historical rates of return, he decided to use these average holding period returns (HPRs) as a reasonable estimate of future returns. Since his parents' savings will be needed to pay for college expenses, he decided a conservative portfolio with liquidity was appropriate. Based on his economic forecast and the investment environment, he decided to invest 50 percent of the funds in a money market mutual fund at a 9.88 percent yield. Roger realized that this historical yield was above the current yield for money market funds, but his economic forecast indicated a rising rate of inflation. The remaining 50 percent will be invested in a common stock index mutual fund that attempts to match the performance of the S&P 500. According to historical data Roger found, the average annual HPR on the S&P 500 had been 15.69 percent. Thus, the savings balance will be invested in a portfolio expected to provide a return of 12.79 percent [.5(9.88%) + .5(15.69%)].

Remaining working years						Retirement years	
5	6	7	8	9	10	11	12
$75,361	$79,129	$83,086	$87,240	$91,602	$ 96,182	$ 65,404	$ 68,674
72,531	75,432	78,450	81,588	84,851	88,245	65,404	68,674
$ 2,830	$ 3,697	$ 4,636	$ 5,652	$ 6,751	$ 7,937	—	—
$10,285	$11,108						
$10,285	$11,108						
$55,665	$55,330	$54,996	$66,666	$80,845	$ 97,936	$118,399	$116,900
(10,285)	(11,108)	—	—	—	—	—	—
2,830	3,697	4,636	5,652	6,751	7,937	(16,642)	(16,642)
7,120	7,077	7,034	8,527	10,340	12,526	15,143	14,952
$55,330	$54,996	$66,666	$80,845	$97,936	$118,399	$116,900	$115,210
$29,072	$38,834	$49,859	$62,311	$76,374	$ 92,257	$110,195	$108,824
6,000	6,000	6,000	6,000	6,000	6,000	(15,630)	(15,630)
3,762	5,025	6,452	8,063	9,883	11,938	14,259	14,082
$38,834	$49,859	$62,311	$76,374	$92,257	$110,195	$108,824	$107,276

[d]Before-tax rate of return assumed to be 12.79% earned on beginning-of-year balance. The rate is not adjusted for taxes since 401(k) contributions will offset most of the additional taxes on the additional income from savings.

[e]Before-tax rate of return assumed to be 12.94% earned on beginning-of-year balance. No annual tax liability since the income is through a tax-sheltered retirement plan.

Roger decided that the funds for the 401(k) plan should also be conservatively invested. Because of the longer investment horizon and his economic forecast, he decided that 20 percent of the funds should be in a money market mutual fund, 30 percent in an international common stock mutual fund, and 50 percent in a corporate bond fund. Using historical data, he estimated the HPR on this portfolio as

$$E(R_p) = .2(9.88\%) + .3(20.32\%) + .5(9.73\%) = 12.94\%$$

Roger used these estimated rates of return to calculate the amount his parents should have in their savings and retirement accounts at age 60.

Using the most recent estimates of the percentage of preretirement income that will be needed during retirement, Roger calculated that his parents would need a minimum of 68 percent of their preretirement income. Applying this percentage to his estimate of earnings for the year before retirement ($96,182) indicated income needs of $65,404.

If his parents' savings account equals \$118,399 at retirement, as indicated for year 11 in Table 22.1, they should be able to withdraw a maximum of \$16,642 per year for 20 years, using a present value annuity procedure:

$$\$118{,}399 = A\left[\frac{1 - \dfrac{1}{(1.1279)^{20}}}{.1279}\right]$$

$$A = \$16{,}642$$

The \$16,642 annual withdrawal would be essentially tax-free since it represents principal, and taxes have already been paid each year on the investment income from the savings plan. A similar calculation for the 401(k) retirement plan beginning balance of \$110,195 (year 11) results in a maximum possible annual before-tax withdrawal of \$15,630. In addition, all of the withdrawals from the 401(k) would be taxed at his parents' marginal tax rate that existed in the year of the withdrawal.

Because both his parents contributed to Social Security, their combined benefits with a reduction for early retirement would be approximately \$12,000 per year. His parents' before-tax retirement income would be

Social Security	\$12,000	27.1%
401(k) withdrawals	15,630	35.3
Savings withdrawals	16,642	37.6
Total	\$44,272	100.0%

Using data published by the Social Security Administration, Roger compared his plan with the following sources of retirement income for someone currently retiring with at least \$20,000 of annual income:

Pensions	19%
Social Security	21
Investments savings	34
Earned income	24
Other benefits	2
	100%

Based on this analysis, Roger concluded that his plan would not allow his parents to retire early with the level of income they are likely to need, and they may have to consider delaying their retirement so that they would be entitled to full Social Security benefits. There is also the possibility that they could sell their ownership interest in the business at their retirement. Roger recalculated Table 22.1 based on the possibility of Sarah and Tim paying their own college expenses by working part-time and going to school. Without the college expenses for the two children, the parents' savings account would equal $279,033 at retirement. They would then be able to withdraw a maximum of $39,221 per year for 20 years. This amount, along with their Social Security and 401(k) withdrawals, would provide them with a before-tax retirement income of $66,851. This amount exceeded Roger's estimated income needs of $65,404. Roger decided to discuss the analysis with his parents without Sarah and Tim being present.

Roger realized that his plan did not answer all of the questions raised by his parents and that additional work, possibly with a professional planner, was needed.

FINANCIAL SERVICES INDUSTRY

The financial services industry has undergone significant changes since the early 1970s. Prior to this time, the functions provided by the industry were available from a diverse group of professionals such as tax attorneys, CPAs, insurance agents, and stockbrokers. Advice from these professionals is still available, but many financial services firms now provide all of these services within a single organization. These firms offer a comprehensive list of services, including tax planning, legal advice, investment and financial research, and brokerage services, in addition to other products.

Individuals acting as investment advisers and/or financial planners must register with the SEC under the Investment Advisors Act of 1940. This act requires each adviser to inform the SEC of his or her experience, education, type of advice, and fees for services. Because of the broad definition of "investment adviser," however, many individuals act as advisers without registering. In 1987 the SEC issued an opinion that clarifies the relationship between a financial planner and investment adviser. A financial planner is considered an adviser if he or she (1) gives clients advice about securities, (2) gencrates investment newsletters or reports on a regular basis, and (3) is compensated for providing investment advice.

Because of the increasing complexity of investment products, the investment environment, and tax laws, the investment advisory industry is likely to continue its rapid growth. Many individual investors may decide that they do not have the time or expertise to manage their portfolio effectively and will seek professional help. If these trends continue, the industry will offer an increasing number of jobs to individuals who have the necessary knowledge and skills.

Investment advisers and financial planners may charge a fee or receive their compensation in commissions on products or services that they sell. The fee can be based on a percentage of the market value of the portfolio that is being managed. Typically, a fee would be 1–2 percent per year for portfolios $100,000 or larger. Many established money managers will not accept a client unless the portfolio is at least $100,000. A second alternative is to base the fee on the time devoted to the client. Fees for established advisers and planners often exceed $100 per hour.

The majority of financial planners receive their compensation from commissions on products. This practice, while common in the industry, raises the issue of the objectivity of the planner in making recommendations. The client may wonder whether the adviser is suggesting a particular product or service because of the potential commission or because the planner thinks the product or service is best for the client.

An individual who is interested in using an adviser or planner should inquire about charges and fees. In certain cases, especially for individuals with small portfolios, it might be appropriate to seek an adviser/planner who bases compensation on commissions. In other cases, a fee arrangement may be more appropriate. Recognizing this possibility, some advisers/planners use a combination of fees and commissions. In addition to charges, a potential client should carefully check the training and experience of the adviser/planner. The following section briefly discusses three widely recognized professional designations that can be achieved by financial analysts and advisers/planners.

PROFESSIONAL INVESTMENT PLANNING AND COUNSELING

Many individuals claim to be experts in financial planning and investment management. Unfortunately, some of these individuals earn more money by selling advice than by following their own recommendations. The purpose of this section is to discuss three professional designations for individuals offering financial planning and investment counseling. That an individual possesses one of these designations, however, is no guarantee that his or her advice and recommendations are always correct. Rather, the designation indicates that the individual has met certain standards and is knowledgeable about financial planning, investment selection, and investment management. Knowledge of these professional designations may be useful for individuals considering a career in investments and personal financial planning or for individuals attempting to select an investment planner or adviser.

• Chartered Financial Analyst

The professional designation of **Chartered Financial Analyst (CFA)** was first offered in the early 1960s by the Institute of Chartered Financial Analysts (ICFA). The CFA designation is considered the most prestigious and the most difficult designation to obtain.

The idea of developing a certification process for financial analysts was first proposed by Benjamin Graham in the 1920s. Graham thought that an accreditation program was needed because financial analysts were not regulated by law or by the industry. Due to his efforts, a committee was formed in 1959 to develop an accreditation program. The committee contacted Professor Ezra Solomon, who developed the basic requirements for what is now the CFA designation.

The early organization continued to grow, and the ICFA was incorporated in Virginia in January 1962. The ICFA first offered an examination for the CFA designation in 1963. In 1990, over 11,300 candidates were enrolled for the 1990 examinations. More than 12,000 individuals have earned the CFA designation since 1963.[1] In January 1990, the Association for Investment Management and Research (AIMR) was formed by a merger of the ICFA and Financial Analysts Federation (FAF). The AIMR now has a membership of over 20,000 investment professionals.

REQUIREMENTS FOR THE CFA The process leading to the CFA designation takes a minimum of three years but varies with the background of the individual. A CFA candidate must meet four requirements:

1. Hold a bachelor's degree or the equivalent in professional work experience.
2. Provide three acceptable character references.
3. Complete and return the registration and enrollment form for the current year.
4. Pay the indicated fee for the Level I Examination (approximately $450).

Once an individual is admitted as a CFA candidate, he or she must meet four requirements before the CFA designation can be awarded:

1. Have at least three years' experience in investment-related work.
2. Comply with the Code of Ethics and Standards of Professional Conduct of the AIMR.
3. Pass the Level I, II, and III examinations.
4. Apply for membership or be a member of the FAF.

Candidates prepare for the three written examinations largely through a program of self-study, using materials provided by the AIMR. The three examinations are progressively more complex and cover several major topics:

- Ethical and professional standards
- Financial accounting
- Quantitative analysis
- Economics
- Fixed-income securities
- Equity securities analysis
- Portfolio management

[1] *The CFA Candidate Program* (Charlottesville, Va.: Association for Investment Management and Research, 1990), p. 1.

Only one exam can be taken each year, and the exams must be taken and passed in order (i.e., Level I, Level II, Level III). Therefore, it takes a minimum of three years to complete the examination requirements. The following statistics apply to the June 1990 examinations:[2]

	Exam level			
	I	*II*	*III*	All exams
Candidates taking exam	4,415	2,522	1,823	8,760
Pass rate	60%	63%	75%	64%
1989–1990 average pass rate	59%	68%	75%	65%

Additional information and application forms are available from the ICFA at the following address:

Association for Investment Management and Research
Post Office Box 3668
Charlottesville, Virginia 22903
Telephone: (804) 977-6600

• Chartered Financial Consultant

A second professional designation that indicates training and knowledge in the area of investments and financial planning is the **Chartered Financial Consultant (ChFC).** This program is available through the American College, located in Bryn Mawr, Pennsylvania. This program traditionally offered training to individuals in the insurance industry but recently has been expanded to include all aspects of personal financial planning.

The ChFC program is more general than the CFA program and prepares candidates to provide financial counseling and financial services management to clients. The ChFC designation has been awarded to over 22,000 individuals.

Candidates must complete eight required courses and two elective courses in the following areas:

Required:

1. Fundamentals of Financial Planning

2. Income Taxation

3. Individual Life and Health Insurance

[2] *1990 Annual Report* (Charlottesville, Va.: Association for Investment Management and Research, 1990), p. 11.

4. Investments
5. Fundamentals of Estate Planning I
6. Wealth Accumulation Planning
7. Financial Planning Applications
8. Financial Decision Making at Retirement

Any two of the following electives:

1. Personal Risk Management and Insurance I
2. The Financial System in the Economy
3. Planning for Business Owners and Professionals
4. Fundamentals of Estate Planning II
5. Business Taxation and Planning

In addition to passing these 10 courses, candidates must have three years of business experience and comply with the college's Code of Ethics. Depending on the background of the candidate, the program can be completed in two to five years. Additional information can be obtained from the American College at the following address:

The American College
270 Bryn Mawr Avenue
Bryn Mawr, Pennsylvania 19010-2196
Telephone: (215) 526-1490

• Certified Financial Planner

A third professional designation, **Certified Financial Planner (CFP),** is offered by the International Board of Standards and Practices For Certified Financial Planners (IBCFP) in Denver, Colorado. The objectives of this program are to (1) advance the knowledge of individuals in the financial planning and counseling field; (2) provide learning opportunities through programs of study; (3) develop and administer examinations for candidates; (4) improve and maintain a uniform code of ethics and uniform practice standards; (5) establish, conduct, and enforce investigatory and disciplinary procedures to regulate the professional conduct of CFPs; and (6) promote public awareness and understudy of the CFP designation.

An individual interested in becoming a CFP must enroll in an approved financial planning course of study that involves 180 hours of classroom instruction. Approved universities and schools around the country offer the program of study. In addition, the IBCFP offers a self-study program. The program also requires work experience in a financial planning–related position for a period of time that depends on the educational background of the individual. Candidates without a college degree must have five years of work experience while persons with graduate education may need only one year of work experience.

Once the approved program of study is completed, the candidate must pass six comprehensive three-hour examinations over the following topics:

1. Financial planning
2. Risk management
3. Investments
4. Tax planning and management
5. Retirement planning and employee benefits
6. Estate planning

On average, the program requires two years to complete. As of June 1, 1990, 19,350 individuals had earned the CFP designation. Additional information about the CFP designation is available from the IBCFP at the following address:

The International Board of Standards and Practices for CFPs
1660 Lincoln Street
Suite 3050
Denver, Colorado 80264
Telephone: (303) 830-7543

The CFA, ChFC, and CFP designations are similar in some ways but different in others. The CFA is considered the most specialized and rigorous of the programs and is highly regarded in the business and academic communities. The CFP is also becoming a prestigious designation and is earning credibility in the financial planning industry. The majority of individuals who have earned the ChFC designation are involved with the insurance industry and often hold other designations such as Chartered Life Underwriter (CLU).

Individuals who are considering hiring an investment adviser or financial planner should research the credentials of the individual. In addition to professional designations, the education, experience, specialization, and reputation of the adviser should be investigated.

SUMMARY

This chapter has provided some additional insights into personal investment management. A personal financial plan should be comprehensive and should be adapted to the life cycle of the individual. Insurance products and retirement planning will play an important part in most individuals' financial planning. As the simple financial plan for the Stanton family illustrated, financial planning involves many considerations.

• CONCEPT APPLICATIONS

Investment Concept	Concept Application
Financial planning	Individuals should identify lifetime goals and develop financial plans to accomplish their goals. An investment plan with strategies is part of an overall financial plan. Individuals may want to consider using a professional financial planner or investment adviser for this important task.
Insurance	Various insurance products usually play an important role in a financial plan where they protect the life, health, and property of the individual. Newer products such as universal and variable life have investment characteristics and may receive favorable tax treatment.
Tax-sheltered investing	Many tax breaks are available to individuals who are saving and investing for retirement. IRAs, Keogh plans, and 401(k) plans offer favorable tax breaks: contributions are made with before-tax dollars, and all investment income accumulates tax-free. Generally, individuals should maximize their contributions to tax-sheltered plans before utilizing other methods of saving for retirement.
Professional financial planners	Professionals in the field include individuals with the CFA, CFP, and ChFC designations. Financial planners/advisers may offer planning and investment advice on a fee or commission basis. Good planners/advisers could be well worth the costs for individuals unwilling or unable to perform their own personal financial planning.

Many individuals rely on professional financial counselors. In selecting a counselor, it is important to consider how his or her compensation is determined and the counselor's professional qualifications. The three major professional designations for advisers/planners are the Chartered Financial Analyst (CFA), Chartered Financial Consultant (ChFC), and Certified Financial Planner (CFP). These designations do not guarantee that the adviser's advice will always be correct, but they do indicate that the adviser has had a minimum level of training and experience. Individuals contemplating a career as an investment analyst/counselor should consider earning one of these professional designations.

• KEY TERMS

Certified Financial Planner (CFP)
Chartered Financial Analyst (CFA)
Chartered Financial Consultant (ChFC)
Defined benefit plan (DBP)
Defined contribution plan (DCP)
Disintermediation
Endowment life insurance

Financial planning
401(k) plan
Individual retirement account (IRA)
Keogh plan
Life-cycle planning
Loading
Mortality (cost of dying)
Pension fund
Savings/reserve
Summary plan description
Term life insurance
Universal life insurance
Variable life insurance
Vested
Whole life insurance

• QUESTIONS

1. Compare and contrast IRAs, Keogh plans, and 401(k) plans. Discuss the two major tax advantages that make these plans attractive for retirement investing.
2. Compare and contrast defined benefit and defined contribution pension plans.
3. Suppose you are attempting to determine the benefits that will be provided by your company's pension plan. Explain how the retirement benefits can be estimated if the plan is a defined benefit plan and if the plan is a defined contribution plan.
4. Suppose your company's pension plan is a defined contribution plan and you are concerned about the investment performance of the plan. Should this concern influence how you manage your own personal retirement savings?
5. Compare and contrast term life, ordinary whole life, endowment life, universal life, and variable life insurance policies.
6. Explain how insurance companies are able to offer an ordinary whole life policy with a death benefit (face value) far in excess of the initial premium cost.
7. In your opinion, should insurance products be viewed as an investment alternative? Explain.
8. Do you think that all individuals need life insurance coverage, regardless of their personal financial circumstances?
9. Discuss the similarities and differences in the CFA, CFP, and ChFC designations. Which professional designation appears to be most difficult to obtain? If an individual is interested in becoming a security analyst, which professional designation would be most appropriate?
10. Define the financial services industry. What trends appear to be emerging in this industry?
11. What recommendations would you make to improve the financial plan presented in Table 22.1?

• KEY TO THE INVESTMENT ANALYSIS SOFTWARE

Calculation	Appendix A-1 Page Reference	Access Procedure
Personal portfolio management	A-14	BEGIN, PERSONAL, PORTFOLIO
Personal financial statements	A-14	BEGIN, PERSONAL, STATEMENTS, NETWORTH or INCOME
Real estate analysis (rent versus buy)	A-14	BEGIN, PERSONAL, REALESTATE

• PROBLEMS

1. Assume one of your goals is to start your own business. Suppose you believe the minimum start-up capital that will be needed is $75,000. Calculate the monthly savings that will be necessary to accumulate the start-up capital over the next 10 years. Also assume that your savings will be invested in a money market mutual fund that has a yield of 7.5 percent per year compounded monthly.
2. Suppose you want to retire early and you are now 20 years old. You have decided that you would take early retirement at age 50 if you had $1,000,000 in retirement savings. Anticipating conservative management of the retirement portfolio, you estimate an annual rate of return of 8 percent per year compounded annually.
   a. Calculate the monthly contribution that will be needed to accumulate the $1,000,000. Assume you will start contributions this month and thus make 360 equal monthly contributions.
   b. Assume you accumulate $1,000,000 by age 50. Calculate the maximum monthly withdrawals that can be made so that all of your retirement funds are exhausted in 20 years or by the time you reach age 70.
   c. Suppose you anticipate that the inflation rate will average 4 percent per year over the next 50 years. Using the other information provided in part (b), calculate the real or inflation-adjusted value of your monthly retirement benefits.
3. Use the Investment Analysis Software to create your own personal financial statements including a statement of net worth and a statement of past and forecasted income. Do you feel the "available for savings" figure provided on the personal income statement will be adequate for your personal financial goals?
4. Use the Investment Analysis Software to analyze whether you should purchase or rent a home. If you don't currently own a home, estimate some realistic data to use in the analysis. If you own a home, use the data on your current home for the analysis and estimate the costs of renting.

5. Prepare a new financial plan for the Stantons assuming the yield on a money market mutual fund will be 7.5 percent as opposed to 9.88 percent and that the Stantons will pay the children's college expenses. Comment on the importance of the assumed yield on investments in preparing a financial plan.

• REFERENCES

American College. *Action Information.* Bryn Mawr, Pa.: 1990.

Association of Investment Management and Research. *Annual Report.* Charlottesville, Va.: 1990.

Benari, Yoav. "An Asset Allocation Paradigm." *Journal of Portfolio Management* (Winter 1988): 47–51.

Bzik, Debra R., and Thomas J. Bzik. "Winning with IRAs, SEPs, and 401(k)s." *Tax Adviser* (February 1990): 96–98.

Cohen, Edwin R. "So You Want to be a Financial Planner?" *Mid-America Insurance* (December 1989): 15–19.

Crosson, Cynthia. "Financial Planning: In Danger of Unraveling?" *National Underwriter,* August 6, 1990, pp. 1, 38.

Feldman, Saul. "Winning Strategies for Personal Investment." *Personal Computing,* July 27, 1990, pp. 100–108.

Fritz, Michael. "Do-It-Yourself IRAs." *Forbes,* June 25, 1990, pp. 206–7.

Gahin, Fikry. "When and Where to Invest in Tax-Deferred Saving Plans." *Journal of the American Society of CLU and ChFC* (January 1991): 66–79.

Gibby, Douglas A., and Carolanne Dorer. "How Much Retirement Income Do Employees Need?" *Compensational and Benefits Management* (Autumn 1988): 25–34.

Haas, Donald Ray. "Diversifying Retirement Investment Portfolios." *National Underwriter,* July 3, 1990, pp. 5, 26.

Hamilton, Patricia W. "How to Choose a Financial Planner." *D&B Reports* (May-June 1990): 40–41.

International Board of Standards and Practices for Certified Financial Planners, Inc. *General Information Booklet.* Denver, Col.: 1990.

Jackson, Daniel H., and William J. McDonnell. "What's behind the Switch to Defined Contribution Plans?" *Pension World* (August 1990): 40–41.

Malkiel, Burton G. *A Random Walk down Wall Street,* 5th ed. New York: W.W. Norton, 1991.

Smith, Maurice. "The Five-Twentys of Successful Investing." *Agency Sales Magazine* (February 1990): 51–52.

Topolnicki, Denise M. "The Surprising Truth about Getting Out Early." *Money,* Fall 1990, pp. 78–81.

Verespej, Michael A. "Retirement Blues: Not Enough Bucks." *Industry Week,* September 4, 1989, pp. 31–32.

Willis, Clint. "Retiring Soonest with the Mostest." *Money,* November 1988, pp. 78–87.

Appendixes

APPENDIX A-1

The Investment Analysis Software

APPENDIX A-2

Review of Analytical Techniques

APPENDIX A-3

Mathematical Terms, Symbols, and Key Formulas

APPENDIX A-4

Compound and Present Value Tables

APPENDIX A-5

Standard Normal Cumulative Probability Distribution and Student t Distribution

APPENDIX A-1

The Investment Analysis Software

INTRODUCTION

The Investment Analysis Software (IAS) was prepared specifically for *Fundamentals of Investments* by Dr. Carol Billingham of Central Michigan University. It is designed for IBM personal computers and compatibles. IAS, using Lotus 1-2-3, may be run from either a floppy disk drive or a hard disk drive.

The purpose of this appendix is to provide a step-by-step guide for the use of IAS. The software is menu driven, and each application follows the same general procedure. Once the user is familiar with IAS, the "Key to the Investment Analysis Software" (Key to IAS) sections at the end of appropriate chapters can be used without having to refer to this appendix (a page reference to this appendix is provided in each Key to IAS section for every calculation). Access procedures for IAS are presented in the Key to IAS section for all equations in a chapter preceded by a computer disk symbol, . The calculations described in the Key to IAS section can be helpful in answering many of the end-of-chapter problems. In addition, IAS contains a Personal Financial Planning and Analysis category of programs that can be used for preparing personal financial statements, maintaining records and analyzing personal portfolios, and performing a rent-or-buy analysis for a personal residence.

IAS has the following general structure:

1. The main menu, BEGIN, permits the user to select from the six general categories of programs: statistical programs (STATISTICAL), financial statement analysis (FINANCIAL), security valuation models (VALUATION), capital asset pricing model applications (CAPITAL), options (OPTIONS), and personal financial planning and investment analysis (PERSONAL). The user can also select instructions (INSTRUCT) or quit Lotus (QUIT) through the main menu.
2. Each of the six general category menus allows the user to select among subprograms in that category or return to the main menu, BEGIN, by selecting BACK.
3. Menus within each subprogram contain a number of options:
   - The user may enter data from the keyboard (MANUAL), from previously created data files (COMBINE), or make a template (TEMPLATE).
   - After the data have been entered and the ENTER or RETURN key has been pressed an additional time, the user may choose to edit the

data (EDIT), compute the results with the data as currently entered (COMPUTE), or return to the main menu (BACK).

- After computation, the menu allows the user to print the results (PRINT), edit the existing data (EDIT), enter a new set of data to the same program (AGAIN), save the file to a formatted disk or a hard disk (SAVE), or return to the menu from which the program was originally selected (BACK). In addition, where appropriate, several programs offer the option of viewing a graph of the results (GRAPH or a specific command).

GETTING STARTED

Depending on your equipment, you may run Lotus from either a floppy disk or a hard disk drive. IAS runs with Lotus version 2.0 or higher.

• Two Floppy Disk Drives

If you have two floppy disk drives, Lotus will run from the A drive, and your programs and data will be accessed from the B drive. To use Lotus, perform the following steps:

1. Put DOS in drive A and turn on the computer.
2. Respond to the date and time commands.
3. At the A> prompt, remove the DOS disk from drive A and replace it with the Lotus program disk.
4. Type LOTUS, then select 123 from the main Lotus menu.
5. To make certain Lotus expects to read the IAS data from the B drive, type /FD (File Directory). This command changes the directory to B. If it does not read B, now is the time to change it by typing "B:" (RET). This will temporarily set the reading of data to the B drive.

To make the B drive your *permanent* data drive, follow these steps:

1. Type /WGDD (*W*orksheet, *G*lobal, *D*efault, *D*irectory).
2. You will see the words Directory at Startup: (directory name) \ :.
3. Change the directory name to B: (RET) and select UPDATE.
4. Select QUIT from the menu.

• Hard Disk: Temporary Use of IAS

If Lotus is installed on a hard disk and you would like to work with the IAS files on the floppy disk without *permanently* installing them on the hard disk, you need to instruct the computer where to "look" for these files:

1. Turn on the computer. Respond to the date and time commands.
2. At the C> prompt, type in the directory on which your Lotus program is listed. For example, CD \ 123 (RET): tells the computer to *C*hange *D*irectory from where it now is to a directory called "123."
3. Insert the IAS disk into the floppy disk drive (A).
4. Enter into the Lotus spreadsheet program by typing, at the new "C" prompt, LOTUS (RET).
5. Highlight (by pointing with the arrow keys) "123" (RET) from the Lotus main menu.
6. At this point, issue a "Change File Directory" command as follows, /FD. The response to this will be C: \ 123. To change the directory, type A:, which tells the computer to look in drive A for the information, not in drive C.
7. The BEGIN file will have to be retrieved manually as follows: /FR (*F*ile *R*etrieve) (RET). Choose BEGIN by highlighting it with the arrow keys and press the ENTER or RETURN key.

• Hard Disk: Permanent Use of IAS

To create a subdirectory into which you may permanently install the IAS program files onto your hard disk drive, follow these steps:

1. Turn on the computer and enter into the Lotus directory on the C drive, but do not begin the Lotus program.
2. Make a subdirectory by typing at the C> prompt "MD INVEST" (*M*ake a *D*irectory called INVEST>).
3. Enter the newly created subdirectory by typing CD \ INVEST (*C*hange *D*irectory to INVEST).
4. To copy the IAS disk, to the INVEST subdirectory, place the disk in the A drive and type COPY A: *.* C:, then press (RET).
5. Now return to the Lotus directory by typing CD \ LOTUS.
6. You are now ready to begin using Lotus, and you will be able to read data from your new subdirectory, INVEST, by following these steps:
   - Enter the Lotus program by typing LOTUS and then selecting 123 from the Lotus menu.
   - Change the file directory so the Lotus program will read data from the INVEST subdirectory by typing /FD C: \ 123 \ INVEST. This will allow you to read data from the INVEST subdirectory for the current session. Just remember that when you want to use the IAS file, you must switch to the subdirectory of 123 \ INVEST.

• Data Entry

In all cases of data entry, you *may* do the following:

1. Modify previously entered data by moving the cursor, by means of the arrow keys, to the entry to be changed and typing the correct version. Pressing (RET) will replace the old entry with the new one.

2. Perform arithmetic calculations at the time of entering data. For example, if the value you wish to enter is the sum of 254, 79, and 332, you may enter the value as +254+79+332, and the sum, 665, will appear in the cell. If the value to be entered is 438 − 276, you may enter it as +438−276, and the value, 162, will appear in the cell. If the value to be entered is 1,059 divided by 76, you may enter it as +1059/76, and the value, 13.9342, will appear in the cell. If the value to be entered is (67 times 5.6) divided by 4.9, you may enter it as +(67*5.6)/4.9, and the value, 76.5714, will appear in the cell. If the value to be entered is 9 raised to the third power, you may enter it as 9^3, and the value, 729, will appear in the cell.

In all cases of data entry you *must* do these things:

1. Enter numeric data, unless specifically told by the program to do otherwise.

2. If entering alphanumeric (nonnumeric) data that begin with a number, precede the number with the symbol '. For example, if you are entering a date in the form 6/23/90, precede it with the symbol '. Type '6/23/90.

3. Enter numeric data *without* dollar signs, commas, percent signs, or any symbols other than one decimal point per value. For example, enter $125.76 as 125.76. Enter 11,572.34 as 11572.34. Enter 14.86% as 14.86. In some cases, the program will request that percentage data be entered in hundredths. This means enter 14.86% as .1486, and enter 107.32% as 1.0732.

• Combining Files

In three different types of situations, a user might want to combine two different files in Lotus:

- ***Situation 1*** Lotus and IAS are both on a hard disk. IAS is probably in a subdirectory of the Lotus directory, and the file to be combined is in the same subdirectory on the hard disk.
- ***Situation 2*** IAS is on a hard disk, probably in a subdirectory of the Lotus directory, and the file to be combined is on a floppy disk, in either drive A or drive B.
- ***Situation 3*** Lotus is in drive A and IAS is in drive B.

Assume that the data file is called TEST and that the data portion of the file that is to be combined has a range name, DATA. The range name has been created prior to saving the file, TEST, with the commands *R*ange *N*ame *C*reate DATA, and the entire field of data has been indicated.

To combine the range, DATA, from the file, TEST, into another file:

1. Have the receiving file on the screen. The cursor will be at the first data element to be combined.

2. Select COMBINE and follow the directions on the screen for the appropriate situation.

• Saving Files

A user may want to save files as well as have the option of printing them. As indicated earlier, the programs offer a SAVE option. The user may save the file, under a user-created name, to a separate formatted floppy disk or to a subdirectory on a hard disk. After saving a file, the user may retrieve it by the Lotus command

/FR (filename)

The save option is very helpful when the user wishes to modify data entries after completing a particular analysis. For example, assume a user was regressing the holding period returns of stock A against the holding period returns of the market for 10 years of quarterly data (40 entries for both the stock and the market). After completing the regression analysis, the user wants to do the same type of regression analysis for stock B. By saving the results from the first regression, the user can simply replace the holding period returns of stock A (using the EDIT option) with those of stock B and rerun the regression analysis without having to reenter the 40 holding period returns for the market. The user can then save these second results under a different file name.

PROGRAM DESCRIPTIONS

In the sections that follow, the following format will be used:

1. The section head will identify the general category of programs (e.g., STATISTICAL, FINANCIAL, VALUATION, and so on).

2. The names and a description of the subprograms are provided.

3. Any special cautions about data entry, possible error conditions, or results are indicated.

The discussion begins with the assumption that Lotus has been accessed, the IAS disk is in the B drive or has been installed on the hard disk, /FR (file retrieve) has been entered, and the user has selected BEGIN from the menu.

At this point the user has the option of selecting INSTRUCT, QUIT, or one of the six general categories of programs:

STATISTICAL FINANCIAL VALUATION CAPITAL OPTIONS PERSONAL

• STATISTICAL

STATISTICAL contains programs for seven widely used procedures. When STATISTICAL is accessed, the user has the option of accessing the subprograms described in the next paragraphs.

DESCRIP The DESCRIP program computes the arithmetic mean, standard deviation, coefficient of variation, and variance for any series of numbers. The data items to be entered under the column DATA are simply the list of positive and negative numbers.

PORT The PORT program allows the user to compute the weighted average return of a portfolio. The data entries consist of the proportion of each asset's market value to the market value of the total portfolio (WEIGHT column) and the holding period return of each asset (HPR column). The sum of the weights must equal 1.

GEOM The geometric mean program (GEOM) provides the geometric mean for a series of percentage values. Since all numbers must be positive to calculate a geometric mean, the data must be entered in the DATA column as 1 plus the percentage change expressed in hundredths. For example, to enter 23.25 percent, type 1.2325. To enter a 4.3 percent decline (−4.3 percent), type 1−.043. The geometric mean results will be expressed as a percent.

DISCRETE The discrete probability distribution analysis calculated by the DISCRETE program provides an estimate of expected value, variance, and standard deviation given possible outcomes and their probabilities. The probabilities are entered in the PROBABILITY column in decimal form and must sum to 1. The values associated with each probability are entered in the POSSIBLE OUTCOME column. Up to 20 probabilities and their possible outcomes can be entered into the program.

CORR The CORR program calculates the Pearson correlation coefficient, coefficient of determination, covariance, and the alpha and beta for the line of best fit; it also computes a t value for the correlation coefficient. Data for the two variables are entered in the X and Y columns; up to 200 observations can be entered. If the computer will perform graphics, the GRAPH option can be selected to see the scattergram with the line of best fit imposed upon it.

REGRESS The regression program (REGRESS) accepts values for one dependent variable (the Y column) and from one to six independent variables (the X columns), with as many as 200 observations per column. Its output consists of the constant for the regression equation, the standard error of the *y* (dependent variable) estimate, the coefficient of determination (labeled R^2), the number of observations read for each variable, the number of degrees of freedom, the coefficients of the independent variables and their standard errors and computed *t* values, the critical *t* value, an indication as to whether or not each of the independent variables makes a significant contribution to the regression equation at the .05 significance level, and the *F* ratio, from which the significance of the overall regression equation can be determined.

If the computer will perform graphics, the user has the option of viewing a graph (GRAPH) that plots the values of the dependent variable, as computed by the regression equation, against the actual values.

HPR The holding period return program (HPR) computes both single (ONE) and mutiple (MANY) holding period returns. The results for the multiple holding period returns for as many as 40 periods are presented in five forms:

1. A return for each individual period.
2. The total return over all the periods.
3. The geometric average return.
4. The arithmetic average return.
5. A cumulative value of reinvested income or a wealth relative.

It should be noted that when using the multiple holding period program, the first entry represents the acquisition cost of the asset, and you are prevented from entering income beside the first investment value. The term, "NO DATA!", is entered in the INCOME DURING THE PERIOD column.

• FINANCIAL

FINANCIAL requires as a starting point the entry of three years of balance sheet and income statement data. The formats for the balance sheet and income statement have been made as generic as possible, but the user must make certain that entries from the financial statements of the company being analyzed are placed in the appropriate categories in the financial statements contained in the program.

To make creation of company statements relatively easy, this program permits you to enter financial statement data on a special template, apart from the program, and then add that file to any data you have previously entered into the program.

The special template is on the IAS disk under the file name TEMPLATE. To employ the ADDFILES option on the menu, you must use the special template for data entry because this template includes range names required by the program.

To create a template for use with the ADDFILES option, follow these steps:

1. Copy TEMPLATE.WK1 from your IAS disk to a blank formatted disk, or to an appropriate subdirectory on your hard drive, by using the COPY command in DOS.

2. Enter Lotus and retrieve the file named TEMPLATE from your floppy disk or your hard drive subdirectory.

3. Type the desired data on the template and save the newly created file under its own unique name. The name of the company to which the data pertain is a good file name.

To use your newly created template in the FINANCIAL programs, follow these steps:

1. Enter the FINANCIAL programs in Lotus by typing /FR BEGIN (RET).

2. From the main menu, select the program FINANCIAL.

3. When the FINANCIAL menu appears on your screen, you will have two options:

   - If you are reading data from a floppy disk, follow these steps:

     Remove the IAS program disk.

     Insert your own data disk that contains the file(s) to be combined.

     From the main menu on the screen, select ADDFILES.

     Respond to the prompt for a file name by entering the name of the file you created.

     After the file has been added, replace the IAS program disk and continue operating the programs.

   - If you are reading data from a subdirectory on your hard drive, you will have placed your data file in that subdirectory, and you need simply respond to the prompt for a file name and continue with the program.

4. You may add more files in the same way if you have created several templates and given them different names. When you have finished combining files, you may compute and then print your results, and/or you may continue with the financial analysis.

When you enter data into the financial statements, your balance sheet will *always* balance, because the program computations force a balance. However, if you enter erroneous data, you will have an erroneous statement. Under those circumstances, errors will be evident in retained earnings and shareholders' equity, as these values are computed by the program as the balancing numbers.

Once the financial statements have been created, either by inputting the data manually (INPUT) or by using the special template (ADDFILES), select CALCULATE from the menu. The sums for the blank areas (e.g., Total Current Assets) will be completed.

The financial statements are longer than the 20 lines that can be seen on the screen at one time. To see the rest of the statements, select VIEW from the menu. The VIEW option permits you to move up or down one screen at a time to see the entire statement. If you select PRINT, you will obtain a two-page printout of the balance sheet and income statement.

Following the creation of the financial statements, the user can select FINANCIALS from the menu to access the following subprograms:

1. *COMMON* By selecting COMMON, the user obtains a set of common-size financial statements. The common-size balance sheets express each asset and liability as a percentage of total assets. The common-size income statements express each item on the income statement as a percentage of total sales. These statements can be examined using the VIEW option.
2. *GROWTH* The GROWTH menu allows the user to obtain the two-year average growth rates for the key financial variables on the balance sheet and income statement.
3. *RATIOS* If RATIOS is selected from the menu, the user will obtain a set of 16 financial ratios relating to liquidity, financial leverage, activity, and profitability. In addition, the dividend payout and price-earnings ratios are also calculated.
4. *FORECAST* This program provides forecasted income statements for the next three years. The program applies the average annual rate of growth in sales for the past two years to each of the next three years. The user may change the growth rate assumption by selecting CHANGE from the FORECAST menu. The sales level of the most recent past year is used as the base for compounding. All income statement items are computed in dollars on the basis of the most recent past year common-size income statement. This type of income statement forecast is entirely mechanical and would be used by an analyst only as a starting point for making an earnings forecast.

• VALUATION

VALUATION contains programs for the valuation of bonds, stocks, and convertible securities. Each of these subprograms offers the user options for valuing the type of security selected in the subprogram.

BONDS Three sets of computations used for bond analysis are presented in the bond valuation models portion of IAS. These include choices of bond value (VALUE), bond yield to maturity (YIELD), and bond duration (DURATION).

1. VALUE VALUE is used to calculate the price of a bond and requires the user to provide the years to maturity (to the nearest tenth of a year), the annual coupon payment in dollars, the maturity value (usually $1,000), and the required rate of return (usually the yield to maturity).

2. YIELD The yield-to-maturity program (YIELD) is used to compute the discount rate (called the yield to maturity), which equates the present value of the bond (the bond's current price) with the present value of the stream of coupon income to be received over the remaining term of the bond plus the present value of the maturity value of the bond. The user has the choice of selecting the yield to maturity for a zero-coupon bond (ZERO) or an interest-paying bond (ORDINARY), or the bond yield to the nearest call date (CALL). The data required from the user for each of these calculations are requested on the screen.

3. DURATION This program computes a bond's present value weighted average time to maturity and is computed based on both annual and semiannual compounding of interest. The data required from the user for the DURATION calculation are requested on the screen.

STOCKS The programs in this group consist of four models used for deriving the intrinsic value of a share of stock. The three valuation models are based on the dividend discount model and include choices of a zero dividend growth model (NONE), a constant dividend growth model (CONSTANT), and a three-phase dividend growth model (THREE). The fourth program, the corrected earnings per share model (EPSCORRECT), computes a forecast of corrected earnings per share if retained earnings are reinvested by a company at a designated return on equity.

1. NONE This program computes the value of a share of stock using the assumption that the dividend will remain constant over time. The user provides estimates of the constant cash dividend and the investor's required rate of return.

2. CONSTANT In this program, the value of a share of stock is estimated using the assumption that the dividend will grow indefinitely at a constant rate. The user provides an estimate of the anticipated dividend in the next period, the expected constant growth rate, and the investor's required rate of return.

3. THREE This program computes the value of a share of stock using the assumption that the dividend is expected to grow at a relatively high rate for a given number of years and then follow a straight-line decline in growth during another period of years until the growth rate reaches a relatively low rate that will continue indefinitely. The user provides the current dividend, an estimate of the initial (high) growth rate, the number of years the initial growth rate will continue, the final (low) growth rate, the number of years from the present until the final growth rate begins, and the investor's required rate of return.

4. EPSCORRECT The corrected earnings per share model recognizes the fact that corporations can achieve higher earnings per share simply by the retention of earnings. Part of this apparent growth is illusory if the retained earnings are reinvested by the company at a rate of return equal to or below the stockholders' required rate of return. This program estimates the corrected earnings per share by removing from the reported earnings per share the cumulative return earned on retained earnings at the stockholders' required return on equity. The user provides the most recent reported earnings per share, the estimated constant growth rate in earnings, the dividend payout ratio, and the stockholders' required rate of return.

CONVERTIBLES Upon selecting CONVERTIBLES, the user has the choice of analyzing convertible debentures (DEBS) or convertible preferred stock (PFD). The user will be asked to supply the characteristics of the convertible (either the debenture or preferred stock), the current price and dividend of the underlying common stock, and the current price of a comparable nonconvertible (straight) debenture or preferred stock. The results of the analysis include the following:

1. The conversion value of the convertible.
2. The minimum value of the convertible (the higher of the straight value or conversion value).
3. The premium on the convertible above both its straight value and conversion value.
4. The conversion price for the common stock.
5. The conversion parity price for the common stock (current price of the convertible/conversion ratio).
6. The current yield on the convertible and the common stock.
7. The yield spread between the convertible and the common stock.
8. A payback analysis of the premium on the convertible.

• CAPITAL

CAPITAL contains programs for applying capital market theory. These programs allow the user to estimate a stock's beta; view plots of the stock's characteristic line, the capital market line, and the security market line; identify and view dominant investments (single securities or portfolios); and analyze portfolio performance using the Sharpe, Jensen, and Treynor techniques.

CAPM The CAPM program requires as input the historical holding period returns for a market index and an individual stock, as well as estimates of the risk-free rate of return and the return on the market index. The computations provide the user with estimates of the stock's alpha and beta, the correlation coefficient of the stock's returns with the returns of the market index, and an estimate of the stock's expected (required) return.

If the computer will perform graphics, after computing CAPM, the user can select LINECAP to view the capital market line, SML to view the security market line, and CHAR to view the stock's characteristic line.

DOMINANT The DOMINANT program identifies investments (single securities or portfolios) that lie on an efficient frontier as determined by the risk and return measures of the population of possible investments entered as data. This is *not* a Markowitz-based portfolio analysis using quadratic programming to simultaneously estimate the minimum portfolio risk at each level of expected return for many possible investments.

The data to be entered are the standard deviation and expected return for each portfolio. The computations provide the user with a "YES" indication if the portfolio is not dominated by any of the other portfolios. The user can see the results in graph form by selecting GRAPH.

PERFORM The programs contained in this group allow for the evaluation of portfolio performance on a risk-adjusted basis using the techniques developed by Treynor (TREYNOR), Sharpe (SHARPE), and Jensen (JENSEN). TREYNOR and SHARPE require the average risk-free rate of return, the average holding period return of the market (benchmark) index, and the average holding period return of the portfolio over the period being evaluated. In addition, TREYNOR requires a portfolio beta, and SHARPE requires a standard deviation for returns on the market index and for returns on the portfolio over the evaluation period. JENSEN requires as data the risk premiums for the portfolio and market (benchmark) index.

The computations for TREYNOR and SHARPE provide the measure of portfolio performance and a comparison of the portfolio's performance measure with the performance of the benchmark (market index) portfolio. The computation for JENSEN provides the risk premiums for the market and the portfolio and the difference between these risk premiums, which is Jensen's performance measure or alpha.

• OPTIONS

OPTIONS, using the Black-Scholes model, contains a program for the valuation of European-style equity options. After selecting OPTIONS, you are asked to provide the stock price, the striking price of the option, the number of months until the option expires, the risk free rate of return, and the standard deviation of the stock's return. The program will provide the user with the estimated value of the call option, the hedge ratio, and the estimated value of the put option.

• PERSONAL

PERSONAL contains programs for constructing personal financial statements, managing and analyzing a portfolio, and performing a rent-versus-buy analysis for a personal residence.

STATEMENTS After selecting STATEMENTS, the user has a choice of creating a personal balance sheet (NETWORTH) or a personal income statement (INCOME). After selecting NETWORTH and entering the requested data, a personal balance sheet and an analysis section will be computed. After selecting INCOME and entering the requested income and expense items for the last year and the forecasted amount for the coming year, a personal income statement and the amount available for savings will be computed. The user may also select GRAPH from the menu to see a pie chart of forecasted personal expenses and savings. The pie chart will only be accurate if the forecasted savings are positive.

PORTFOLIO The PORTFOLIO programs allow you to create a new stock portfolio (CREATE) or update an existing portfolio (UPDATE). When creating a new stock portfolio, the first item you are asked to enter is the current date. After entering the date as a value, the cursor will move to the requested data entries for each stock (columns A through M). The maximum number of stocks that can be entered is 100. The column headings under which you are required to enter data are highlighted or shown in green on a color monitor. If you wish to incorporate brokerage fees into the portfolio analysis, you may do so by computing the per-share price paid at purchase and the per-share price to be received at sale to include commission charges.

If you are not interested in computing portfolio beta or do not have the betas for each of the stocks, you may use 1 as the beta for each stock so the portfolio analysis program will operate.

When you select COMPUTE, all columns requiring calculations will be completed, and an analysis of the portfolio will also be shown. In addition, the stock names can be entered in any order as they will be sorted into alphabetical order.

After you have saved your file and wish to update it, select UPDATE. You will then have the choice of entering new data (ENTER), changing existing data (MODIFY), or deleting a stock you have sold (DELETE). After you have made the appropriate changes and computed the new values, the file can be saved until it is time for the next update.

REALESTATE Using a five-year horizon, the real estate program computes and presents the rate of return you would earn on your investment in a personal dwelling if you were to purchase rather than rent comparable living quarters. After selecting REALESTATE, the introductory screen describes the data input required. Two precautions must be taken with respect to data entry. First, the mortgage must run for more than five years; otherwise the results will be erroneous. Second, the total annual payments for the mortgage must be equal to or greater than the interest required on the debt; negative debt amortization will yield erroneous results. After computing the results, you can select MODIFY to change one or more data entries and recompute the buy-versus-lease analysis.

Review of Analytical Techniques

EXAMPLES OF ADJUSTING HOLDING PERIOD RETURNS

Annualizing Holding Period Returns

1. To convert an HPR calculated for a holding period less than one year to an annualized HPR:

$$\text{AHPR} = (1 + \text{HPR})^{N/n} - 1$$

where

n = actual length of the holding period in days, weeks, months, or other units of time
N = total number of days, weeks, months, or other units of time in one year

For example, if the weekly HPR = .003, then the AHPR assuming weekly compounding is

$$\text{AHPR} = (1 + .003)^{52/1} - 1 = .1686$$

2. For an example of the conversion of an HPR calculated for a holding period longer than one year to an annualized HPR, assume an HPR of .18 occurred over a 16-month holding period. With annual compounding, the annualized HPR is

$$\text{AHPR} = (1 + .18)^{12/16} - 1 = .1322$$

Calculating an Effective Holding Period Return

1. The effective annual HPR can be calculated as

$$\text{EAHPR} = (1 + \text{HPR}/m)^{m} - 1$$

where

EAHPR = effective annual holding period return
HPR = stated HPR
m = number of compounding periods in one year

For example, the EAHPR for a HPR of 10% per year compounded monthly is

$$\text{EAHPR} = (1 + .1/12)^{12} - 1 = .1047$$

2. The effective HPR for a holding period less than one year can be calculated as

$$EHPR = (1 + HPR)^{1/m} - 1$$

For example, assume the annual HPR is .1. The effective *quarterly* HPR would be

$$EQHPR = (1 + .1)^{1/4} - 1 = .0241$$

PROBABILITY DISTRIBUTIONS

Discrete Distributions

Discrete probability distributions have a finite number of possible outcomes or states of nature. For example, an analyst may assume that there are only three possible economic environments that can exist next year: recession, slow growth, or rapid growth. In making the economic forecast, the analyst would estimate probabilities associated with each possible outcome and the likely rate of growth in real GNP.

Suppose the analyst makes the following estimates:

State of the economy	Probability	Real GNP growth rate
1. Recession	.2	−2.0%
2. Slow growth	.5	1.0
3. Rapid growth	..3	3.0

The discrete probability distribution for these estimates is shown in Figure A2.1.

FIGURE A2.1
Discrete Probability Distribution

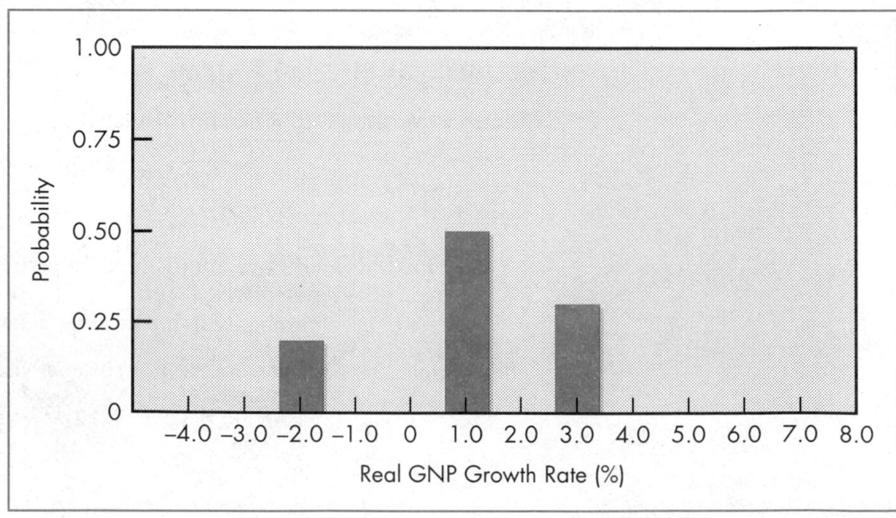

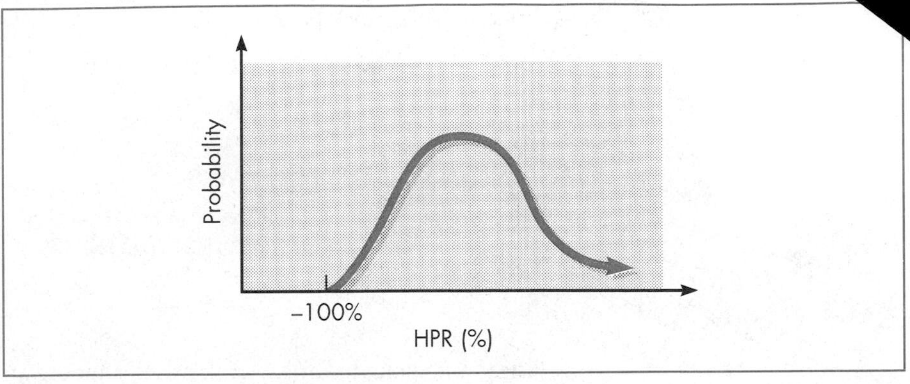

FIGURE A2.2
Continuous HPR Distribution

Continuous Distributions

Continuous probability distributions have an infinite number of possible outcomes or states of nature. For example, assume you purchase a stock today for \$20 per share. In theory, at least, your HPR can be between −100 percent and infinity. If the company fails and the stock becomes worthless, your HPR is −100 percent. If the company does extremely well, the HPR may be very high. Since the future stock price can be almost any value between zero and infinity, essentially an infinite number of HPRs are possible. Thus, the stock's HPR distribution is continuous and may have a distribution like that in Figure A2.2.

DESCRIPTIVE STATISTICS

Investment analysis often involves probability distributions that may be discrete or continuous. The data may be historical (ex-post) or an ex-ante forecast. It is often useful to calculate descriptive statistics for the data.

Measures of Central Tendency

Measures of central tendency such as a mean or expected value are designed to identify a single value from the sample or distribution that best represents all of the observed values.

Consider the following historical stock prices:

	Price of stock (X)
	\$ 2
	3
	5
	2
	8
Sum	\$20

1. Arithmetic mean stock price:

$$\bar{X} = \frac{\Sigma X}{n} = \frac{\$20}{5} = \$4$$

2. Geometric mean stock price:

$$\begin{aligned} \bar{X}_g &= (\pi X)^{1/n} \\ &= [(2)(3)(5)(2)(8)]^{1/5} \\ &= (480)^{.2} \\ &= \$3.44 \end{aligned}$$

Instead of having historical stock prices, suppose an analyst estimates the following discrete distribution:

State of nature (j)	Price of stock (X)	Probability (P_j)
1	\$3	.2
2	4	.7
3	5	.1

3. Expected stock price:

$$\begin{aligned} E(X) &= \sum_{j=1}^{n} P_j X_j \\ &= .2(3) + .7(4) + .1(5) \\ &= .60 + 2.80 + .50 \\ &= \$3.90 \end{aligned}$$

Measures of Variability

Measures of variability such as the range, variance, or standard deviation indicate how much dispersion is present in the data. Variability measures are often used as risk proxies in investment analysis. The previous data on stock prices can be used to illustrate these measures.

1. Range of historical stock prices:

$$\begin{aligned} \text{range} &= \text{highest value} - \text{lowest value} \\ &= \$8 - \$2 \\ &= \$6 \end{aligned}$$

2. Variance and standard deviation of historical stock prices:

$$\begin{aligned}
\sigma_X^2 &= 1/n\, \Sigma\, (X - \bar{X})^2 \\
&= (1/5)[(2-4)^2 + (3-4)^2 + (5-4)^2 + (2-4)^2 + (8-4)^2] \\
&= .2(4 + 1 + 1 + 4 + 16) \\
&= .2(26) \\
&= 5.20 \\
\sigma_X &= \sqrt{\sigma^2} \\
&= \sqrt{5.20} \\
&= \$2.28
\end{aligned}$$

3. Coefficient of variation of historical stock prices:

$$CV_X = \frac{\sigma_X}{\bar{X}} = \frac{\$2.28}{\$4.00} = .57$$

4. Variance and standard deviation of forecasted stock prices:

$$\begin{aligned}
\sigma_X^2 &= \sum_{j=1}^{n} (P_j)(X_j - E(X))^2 \\
&= .2(3 - 3.90)^2 + .7(4 - 3.90)^2 + .1(5 - 3.90)^2 \\
&= .2(.81) + .7(.01) + .1(1.21) \\
&= .162 + .007 + .121 \\
&= .29 \\
\sigma_X &= \sqrt{\sigma^2} \\
&= \sqrt{.29} \\
&= \$.5385
\end{aligned}$$

5. Coefficient of variation of forecasted stock prices:

$$CV_X = \frac{\sigma_X}{E(X)} = \frac{\$.5385}{\$3.90} = .1381$$

TECHNIQUES FOR ESTIMATING THE RELATIONSHIP BETWEEN VARIABLES

Investment analysis often involves the comparison of two or more alternatives. It is essential in the comparison to determine what, if any, relationship exists between the alternatives. For example, do the prices of two stocks move together or in opposite directions, or do their movements appear to be unrelated? Commonly used techniques to measure the relationship between two variables are the correlation coefficient, beta, and regression analysis.

Correlation Coefficient

The correlation coefficient measures the degree of linear relationship between two variables. Values of the correlation coefficient range between −1.0 and 1.0. The sign of the correlation indicates the direction of the relationship. A negative sign indicates that the variables tend to move in the opposite direction while a positive sign indicates they tend to move in the same direction. If the correlation coefficient is close to zero, movements in the two variables are not related.

Consider the following historical HPRs on common stock i and a benchmark portfolio m:

	HPRs	
Year	*Stock i*	*Benchmark m*
1987	.10	.08
1988	−.05	−.01
1989	.12	.10
1990	.18	.12
1991	−.06	−.08

correlation between i and $m = \rho_{i,m}$

$$\rho_{i,m} = \frac{1/n \sum_{t=1}^{n} (\text{HPR}_{it} - \overline{\text{HPR}}_i)(\text{HPR}_{mt} - \overline{\text{HPR}}_m)}{\sigma_i \sigma_m}$$

$$\begin{aligned}
\overline{\text{HPR}}_i &= 1/5(.1 - .05 + .12 + .18 - .06) \\
&= 1/5(.29) \\
&= .058
\end{aligned}$$

$$\begin{aligned}
\overline{\text{HPR}}_m &= 1/5(.08 - .01 + .10 + .12 - .08) \\
&= 1/5(.21) \\
&= .042
\end{aligned}$$

$$\begin{aligned}
\sigma_i^2 &= 1/5[(.1 - .058)^2 + (-.05 - .058)^2 + (.12 - .058)^2 \\
&\quad + (.18 - .058)^2 + (-.06 - .058)^2] \\
&= 1/5(.0018 + .0117 + .0038 + .0149 + .0139) \\
&= 1/5(.0461) \\
\sigma_i^2 &= .0092
\end{aligned}$$

$$\sigma_i = \sqrt{.0092} = .0960$$

$$\begin{aligned}
\sigma_m^2 &= 1/5[(.08 - .042)^2 + (-.01 - .042)^2 + (.10 - .042)^2 \\
&\quad + (.12 - .042)^2 + (-.08 - .042)^2] \\
&= 1/5(.0014 + .0027 + .0034 + .0061 + .0149) \\
&= 1/5(.0285) \\
\sigma_m^2 &= .0057 \\
\sigma_m &= \sqrt{.0057} = .0755
\end{aligned}$$

	Col 1	Col 2	
Year	$HPR_{i,t} - \overline{HPR}_i$	$HPR_{m,t} - \overline{HPR}_m$	Col 1 × Col 2
1987	.0420	.0380	.0016
1988	−.1080	−.0520	.0056
1989	.0620	.0580	.0036
1990	.1220	.0780	.0095
1991	−.1180	−.1220	.0144
			.0347

$$\rho_{i,m} = \frac{1/5(.0347)}{(.0960)(.0755)} = \frac{.0069}{.0072} = .9583$$

Beta

$$\beta_i = \frac{COV_{j,m}}{\sigma_m^2} = \frac{\rho_{i,m}\sigma_i\sigma_m}{\sigma_m^2}$$

$$= \frac{(.9583)(.0960)(.0755)}{.0057}$$

$$= \frac{.0069}{.0057} = 1.21$$

Regression Analysis

The purpose of regression analysis is to find the best fitting linear equation between a dependent variable y and an independent variable x. The procedure for estimating the regression equation minimizes the squared errors between the predicted value of y, $\hat{y}$, and the actual values of y. Therefore, once the regression equation is determined, it can be used to forecast values of $\hat{y}$ given new values for x. The general form of a regression equation is

$$\hat{y} = \hat{a} + \hat{b}x$$

where

$\hat{a}$ = estimate of the constant or intercept of the regression line
$\hat{b}$ = estimate of the slope of the regression line

Consider the following historical data on a company's sales and EPS:

Year	y EPS	x Sales (Millions)
1987	\$.25	\$360
1988	.80	420
1989	.20	380
1990	.75	450
1991	.85	470

The intercept and slope of the regression equation can be found using the following procedure

$$\hat{b} = \frac{\Sigma xy - \dfrac{\Sigma x \Sigma y}{n}}{\Sigma x^2 - \dfrac{(\Sigma x)^2}{n}}$$

$$\hat{a} = \bar{y} - b\bar{x}$$

The following table provides the necessary values to calculate $\hat{b}$ and $\hat{a}$:

Year	y	x	y^2	x^2	xy
1987	$ .25	$ 360	.0625	129,600	90.0
1988	.80	420	.6400	176,400	336.0
1989	.20	380	.0400	144,400	76.0
1990	.75	450	.5625	202,500	337.5
1991	.85	470	.7225	220,900	399.5
Sum	2.85	2,080	2.0275	873,800	1,239.0
Mean	.57	416			

$$\hat{b} = \frac{1239.0 - \dfrac{(2{,}080)(2.85)}{5}}{873{,}800 - \dfrac{(2{,}080)^2}{5}}$$

$$= \frac{1239.0 - 1{,}185.6}{873{,}800 - 865{,}280}$$

$$= \frac{53.40}{8{,}520}$$

$$\hat{b} = .0063$$

$$\hat{a} = .57 - .0063(416)$$

$$= .57 - 2.62$$

$$\hat{a} = -\$2.05$$

The regression equation is

$$\hat{y} = -\$2.05 + .0063x$$

To forecast EPS using the regression equation, assume the sales forecast for 1992 is $500 million. The forecast of EPS for 1992 is

$$EPS_{1992} = -\$2.05 + .0063(500)$$

$$= -2.05 + 3.15$$

$$= \$1.10$$

Appendix A-5 illustrates how the student t distribution can be used to test to see if $\hat{a}$ and $\hat{b}$ are statistically significant.

Coefficient of Determination

It is usually a good idea to check on the goodness of fit of the regression equation. Using the previous example, this analysis can be used to indicate how much of the EPS variability is explained by sales variability. The statistic used for this test is the coefficient of determination, which is simply the square of the correlation coefficient. The coefficient of determination indicates the percentage of the variability of the dependent variable explained by the independent variable.

To calculate the coefficient of determination, R^2, first calculate the correlation coefficient by either using the procedure outlined previously or the following equation:

$$R = \frac{\Sigma\, xy - \dfrac{\Sigma\, x\, \Sigma\, y}{n}}{\left\{\left[\Sigma\, x^2 - \dfrac{(\Sigma\, x)^2}{n}\right]\left[\Sigma\, y^2 - \dfrac{(\Sigma\, y)^2}{n}\right]\right\}^{.5}}$$

$$= \frac{1{,}239 - \dfrac{(2{,}080)(2.85)}{5}}{\left\{\left[873{,}800 - \dfrac{(2{,}080)^2}{5}\right]\left[2.0275 - \dfrac{(2.85)^2}{5}\right]\right\}^{.5}}$$

$$= \frac{1{,}239 - 1{,}185.6}{[(8{,}520)(.4030)]^{.5}}$$

$$= \frac{53.40}{(3{,}433.56)^{.5}}$$

$$= \frac{53.40}{58.60}$$

$$= .91$$

$$R^2 = (.91)^2$$

$$= .828$$

Thus 82.8 percent of the variability in EPS is explained by the variability in sales.

APPENDIX A-3

Mathematical Terms, Symbols, and Key Formulas

Mathematical Terms and Symbols

α_j (alpha)	Vertical intercept from the market model regression. Also represents Jensen's portfolio performance measure.
$\hat{a}$ (a hat)	Estimate of the intercept of a regression line.
b	Earnings retention rate.
$\hat{b}$ (b hat)	Estimate of the slope of a regression line.
β_j (beta)	Indicates the level of systematic risk for security or portfolio j.
β_M	Beta of the market portfolio.
C_t	Anticipated dollar coupon for a bond in period t.
CEPS	Corrected earnings per share.
COV(i, j)	Covariance between variables i and j; also written as $\text{COV}_{i,j}$.
CV_j	Coefficient of variation for security or portfolio j.
D_j	Duration of security or portfolio j.
D_t	Dividends per share for period t; also written as DPS_t and DIV_t.
D/E	Dividends per share divided by earnings per share or the dividend payout ratio.
Δ (delta)	Amount of change in the value of a variable.
δ_i (delta)	Ex-post sample risk factor i.
E_t	Percentage change in the currency exchange rate for period t.
EPS_t	Earnings per share for period t; also written as E_t.
$\tilde{e}_i$ (e tilde)	Security-specific or idiosyncratic (residual) return for security i.
e_t	Random error term from a regression model for period t.
E_i	Ex-ante expected return for asset i.
$E(X)$	Expected value of random variable X.
e^x	Antilog of base e logarithm where $e = 2.71828$.
$E(\text{HPR}_j)$	Expected holding period return for security or portfolio j.
$E(R_j)$	Market-determined required rate of return for asset j.

$E(R_m)$	Expected rate of return on the market portfolio.
g	Annual growth rate in dividends or earnings per share.
HPR_t	Holding period return for period *t*.
HPR_j	Holding period return for security or portfolio *j*.
$\overline{\text{HPR}}_j$	Arithmetic mean holding period return for security or portfolio *j*.
$\overline{\text{HPR}}_g$	Geometric mean holding period return for security or portfolio *j*.
HPR_E	Holding period return adjusted for currency exchange risk.
i_j	Yield to maturity for bond *j*.
I_t	Actual or ex-post dollar interest received on a bond in period *t;* also used to indicate the income on a portfolio in period *t*.
K_j	Investor's required rate of return for security *j*.
λ_j (lambda)	Market price of risk (risk premium) for risk factor *j*.
$\ln(X)$	Natural or base *e* logarithm of *X*.
M_N	Maturity or face value of a bond at time period *N*.
M_t	Estimated price per share to earnings per share for common stock in period *t*.
N	Term to maturity of a bond or the time period when the last cash flow is received.
$N(Z)$	Cumulative normal probability.
$N(d_1)$	Hedge ratio calculated using the Black-Scholes call option valuation model.
NOI_t	Net operating income for period *t*.
NAV_t	Net asset value of a mutual fund in period *t*.
P_i	Probability that event *i* will occur.
P_j	Market price of security *j*.
P_t	Market price of a security in period *t*.
Π (*pi*)	Symbol used to indicate that variables in an equation should be multiplied.
P/E	Price per share divided by earnings per share.
R^2	Coefficient of determination or square of the correlation coefficient.
ROA	Return on assets.
ROE	Return on equity, also written as *r*.
$\rho_{i,j}$ (rho)	Correlation coefficient between variables *i* and *j;* also denoted as *R*.
RP_j	Risk premium on asset *j*.
S	Striking or exercise price on a call or put option or subscription price on a right.
Σ (sigma)	Symbol used to indicate that variables in an equation should be summed.

σ_j (sigma)	Standard deviation of security j.
σ_j^2 (sigma squared)	Variance of security j.
S_p	Sharpe's performance measure for portfolio.
S_M	Sharpe's performance measure for market portfolio.
T_p	Treynor's performance measure for portfolio.
T_M	Treynor's performance measure for the market portfolio.
V_0	Intrinsic value of a security today.
X_j	Weight or relative importance of asset j in a portfolio.

Key Formulas

RETURN MEASURES FOR SECURITIES

1. Historical or ex-post

A. Holding period return

$$\text{HPR} = \frac{P_{t+1} - P_t + D_{t+1} \text{ or } I_{t+1}}{P_t}$$

B. Arithmetic mean holding period return

$$\overline{\text{HPR}}_j = \sum_{t=1}^{n} (\text{HPR}_t)/n$$

C. Geometric mean holding period return

$$\overline{\text{HPR}}_g = \prod_{t=1}^{n} (1 + \text{HPR}_t)^{1/n} - 1$$

2. Expected or ex-ante

A. Expected rate of return

$$E(\text{HPR}) = \sum_{j=1}^{n} P_j \text{HPR}_j$$

B. Required rate of return

$$E(R_j) = R_f + \beta_j[E(R_M) - R_f]$$

RISK MEASURES FOR SECURITIES

1. Range

$$\text{range} = \text{maximum HPR} - \text{minimum HPR}$$

2. Variance

A. Historical or ex-post

$$\sigma_j^2 = 1/n \sum_{t=1}^{n} (\text{HPR}_t - \overline{\text{HPR}}_j)^2$$

B. Expected or ex-ante

$$\sigma_j^2 = \sum_{j=1}^{n} (P_j)(\text{HPR}_j - E(\text{HPR}))^2$$

3. Coefficient of variation

$$\text{CV}_j = \frac{\sigma_j}{\overline{\text{HPR}}_j}$$

4. Covariance

$$\text{COV}_{ij} = 1/n \sum_{t=1}^{n} (\text{HPR}_{it} - \overline{\text{HPR}}_i)(\text{HPR}_{jt} - \overline{\text{HPR}}_j)$$

$$\text{COV}_{ij} = \rho_{ij}\sigma_i\sigma_j$$

5. Correlation

$$\rho_{ij} = \frac{1/n \sum_{t=1}^{n} (\text{HPR}_{it} - \overline{\text{HPR}}_i)(\text{HPR}_{jt} - \overline{\text{HPR}}_j)}{\sigma_i\sigma_j}$$

$$\rho_{ij} = \frac{\text{COV}_{ij}}{\sigma_i\sigma_j}$$

6. Beta

$$B_j = \frac{\text{COV}_{jm}}{\sigma_m^2}$$

RETURN MEASURES FOR PORTFOLIOS

1. Historical or ex-post

$$\text{HPR}_p = \frac{V_{t+1} - V_t + I_t}{V_t}$$

2. Expected or ex-ante

A. Expected rate of return

$$E(\mathrm{HPR}_p) = \sum_{j=1}^{n} X_j E(\mathrm{HPR}_j)$$

$$E(R_p) = R_f + \beta_p[E(R_M) - R_f]$$

RISK MEASURES FOR PORTFOLIOS

1. Variance for a two-security portfolio

$$\sigma_p^2 = X_1^2\sigma_1^2 + X_2^2\sigma_2^2 + 2X_1X_2\mathrm{COV}_{1,2}$$

2. Variance for a three-security portfolio

$$\sigma_p^2 = X_1^2\sigma_1^2 + X_2^2\sigma_2^2 + X_3^2\sigma_3^2 + 2X_1X_2\mathrm{COV}_{1,2} + 2X_1X_3\mathrm{COV}_{1,3} + 2X_2X_3\mathrm{COV}_{2,3}$$

3. Variance for an *n*-security portfolio

$$\sigma_p^2 = \sum_{i=1}^{n}\sum_{j=1}^{n} X_iX_j\mathrm{COV}_{i,j}$$

4. Beta for a portfolio

$$\beta_p = \sum_{j=1}^{n} X_j\beta_j$$

5. Duration for a portfolio

$$D_p = \sum_{j=1}^{n} X_jD_j$$

BOND VALUATION

1. Zero coupon bond

$$V_0 = \frac{M_N}{(1 + i)^N}$$

2. Perpetuity (consol)

$$V_0 = \frac{C}{i}$$

3. Finite maturity

$$V_0 = C\left[\frac{1 - \dfrac{1}{(1+i)^N}}{i}\right] + \frac{M_N}{(1+i)^N}$$

BOND RISK MEASURE

Duration

$$D = \frac{\displaystyle\sum_{t=1}^{N} \frac{tC_t}{(1+i)^t} + \frac{NM_N}{(1+i)^N}}{\displaystyle\sum_{t=1}^{N} \frac{C_t}{(1+i)^t} + \frac{M_N}{(1+i)^N}}$$

PREFERRED STOCK VALUATION

Assuming constant dividends

$$V_0 = \frac{D}{K}$$

COMMON STOCK VALUATION

1. Zero dividend growth

$$V_0 = \frac{D}{K}$$

2. Constant dividend growth

$$V_0 = \frac{E_0(1-b)(1+br)}{K-br} = \frac{D_0(1+g)}{K-g} = \frac{D_1}{K-g}$$

3. H-model

$$V_0 = \frac{D_0}{K-g_2}\left[(1+g_2) + \frac{A+B}{2}(g_1 - g_2)\right]$$

4. CEPS model

$$V_0 = \frac{\text{CEPS}(1+g_{\text{CEPS}})}{K-g_{\text{CEPS}}}$$

OPTION VALUATION

1. Call option

$$V_c = P_s N(d_1) - Se^{-rt} N(d_2)$$

2. Put option

$$V_p = p_t e^{-rt} + V_c - P_s$$

ASSET PRICING MODELS

1. Capital asset pricing model

$$E(R_j) = R_f + \beta_j [E(R_M) - R_f]$$

2. Arbitrage pricing model

$$E_i = \lambda_0 + \lambda_1 b_{i1} + \lambda_2 b_{i2} + \cdots + \lambda_k b_{ik}$$

PORTFOLIO PERFORMANCE EVALUATION TECHNIQUES

1. Treynor's technique:

A. Portfolio

$$T_p = \frac{\overline{\text{HPR}}_p - \bar{R}_f}{\beta_p}$$

B. Benchmark or market

$$T_M = \frac{\overline{\text{HPR}}_M - \bar{R}_f}{\beta_M}$$

2. Sharpe's technique:

A. Portfolio

$$S_p = \frac{\overline{\text{HPR}}_p - \bar{R}_f}{\sigma_p}$$

B. Benchmark or market

$$S_M = \frac{\overline{\text{HPR}}_M - \bar{R}_f}{\sigma_M}$$

3. Jensen's technique:

A. Portfolio

$$R_{jt} - R_{ft} = \hat{\alpha}_j + \hat{\beta}_j (R_{Mt} - R_{ft}) + e_{jt}$$

B. Benchmark or market

$$\hat{\alpha}_M = 0$$

APPENDIX A-4

Compound and Present Value Tables

TIME VALUE OF MONEY FORMULAS

1. Future value

$$P_n = P_0(1 + i)^n$$

2. Present value

$$P_0 = \frac{P_n}{(1 + i)^n}$$

3. Future value of an annuity

$$\text{FVA}_n = A \sum_{t=0}^{n-1} (1 + i)^t = A\left[\frac{(1 + i)^n - 1}{i}\right]$$

4. Present value of an annuity

$$\text{PVA}_n = A \sum_{t=1}^{n} \frac{1}{(1 + i)^t} = A\left[\frac{1 - \frac{1}{(1 + i)^n}}{i}\right]$$

TABLE A4.1 • Future Values of One Dollar, P_n

Period n	1%	2%	3%	4%	5%	6%	7%	8%	9%	10%	11%	12%
1	1.0100	1.0200	1.0300	1.0400	1.0500	1.0600	1.0700	1.0800	1.0900	1.1000	1.1100	1.1200
2	1.0201	1.0404	1.0609	1.0816	1.1025	1.1236	1.1449	1.1664	1.1881	1.2100	1.2321	1.2544
3	1.0303	1.0612	1.0927	1.1249	1.1576	1.1910	1.2250	1.2597	1.2950	1.3310	1.3676	1.4049
4	1.0406	1.0824	1.1255	1.1699	1.2155	1.2625	1.3108	1.3605	1.4116	1.4641	1.5181	1.5735
5	1.0510	1.1041	1.1593	1.2167	1.2763	1.3382	1.4026	1.4693	1.5386	1.6105	1.6851	1.7623
6	1.0615	1.1262	1.1941	1.2653	1.3401	1.4185	1.5007	1.5869	1.6771	1.7716	1.8704	1.9738
7	1.0721	1.1487	1.2299	1.3159	1.4071	1.5036	1.6058	1.7138	1.8280	1.9487	2.0762	2.2107
8	1.0829	1.1717	1.2668	1.3686	1.4775	1.5938	1.7182	1.8509	1.9926	2.1436	2.3045	2.4760
9	1.0937	1.1951	1.3048	1.4233	1.5513	1.6895	1.8385	1.9990	2.1719	2.3579	2.5580	2.7731
10	1.1046	1.2190	1.3439	1.4802	1.6289	1.7908	1.9672	2.1589	2.3674	2.5937	2.8394	3.1058
11	1.1157	1.2434	1.3842	1.5395	1.7103	1.8983	2.1049	2.3316	2.5804	2.8531	3.1518	3.4785
12	1.1268	1.2682	1.4258	1.6010	1.7959	2.0122	2.2522	2.5182	2.8127	3.1384	3.4985	3.8960
13	1.1381	1.2936	1.4685	1.6651	1.8856	2.1329	2.4098	2.7196	3.0658	3.4523	3.8833	4.3635
14	1.1495	1.3195	1.5126	1.7317	1.9799	2.2609	2.5785	2.9372	3.3417	3.7975	4.3104	4.8871
15	1.1610	1.3459	1.5580	1.8009	2.0789	2.3966	2.7590	3.1722	3.6425	4.1772	4.7846	5.4736
16	1.1726	1.3728	1.6047	1.8730	2.1829	2.5404	2.9522	3.4259	3.9703	4.5950	5.3109	6.1304
17	1.1843	1.4002	1.6528	1.9479	2.2920	2.6928	3.1588	3.7000	4.3276	5.0545	5.8951	6.8660
18	1.1961	1.4282	1.7024	2.0258	2.4066	2.8543	3.3799	3.9960	4.7171	5.5599	6.5436	7.6900
19	1.2081	1.4568	1.7535	2.1068	2.5270	3.0256	3.6165	4.3157	5.1417	6.1159	7.2633	8.6128
20	1.2202	1.4859	1.8061	2.1911	2.6533	3.2071	3.8697	4.6610	5.6044	6.7275	8.0623	9.6463
21	1.2324	1.5157	1.8603	2.2788	2.7860	3.3996	4.1406	5.0338	6.1088	7.4002	8.9492	10.804
22	1.2447	1.5460	1.9161	2.3699	2.9253	3.6035	4.4304	5.4365	6.6586	8.1403	9.9336	12.100
23	1.2572	1.5769	1.9736	2.4647	3.0715	3.8197	4.7405	5.8715	7.2579	8.9543	11.026	13.552
24	1.2697	1.6084	2.0328	2.5633	3.2251	4.0489	5.0724	6.3412	7.9111	9.8497	12.239	15.179
25	1.2824	1.6406	2.0938	2.6658	3.3864	4.2919	5.4274	6.8485	8.6231	10.835	13.585	17.000
26	1.2953	1.6734	2.1566	2.7725	3.5557	4.5494	5.8074	7.3964	9.3992	11.918	15.080	19.040
27	1.3082	1.7069	2.2213	2.8834	3.7335	4.8223	6.2139	7.9881	10.245	13.110	16.739	21.325
28	1.3213	1.7410	2.2879	2.9987	3.9201	5.1117	6.6488	8.6271	11.167	14.421	18.580	23.884
29	1.3345	1.7758	2.3566	3.1187	4.1161	5.4184	7.1143	9.3173	12.172	15.863	20.624	26.750
30	1.3478	1.8114	2.4273	3.2434	4.3219	5.7435	7.6123	10.063	13.268	17.449	22.892	29.960
35	1.4166	1.9999	2.8139	3.9461	5.5160	7.6861	10.677	14.785	20.414	28.102	38.575	52.800
40	1.4889	2.2080	3.2620	4.8010	7.0400	10.286	14.974	21.725	31.409	45.259	65.001	93.051
45	1.5648	2.4379	3.7816	5.8412	8.9850	13.765	21.002	31.920	48.327	72.890	109.53	163.99
50	1.6446	2.6916	4.3839	7.1067	11.467	18.420	29.457	46.902	74.358	117.39	184.56	289.00

(continued)

TABLE A4.1 (continued)

Period *n*	13%	14%	15%	16%	17%	18%	19%	20%	25%	30%	35%	40%	50%
1	1.1300	1.1400	1.1500	1.1600	1.1700	1.1800	1.1900	1.2000	1.2500	1.3000	1.3500	1.4000	1.5000
2	1.2769	1.2996	1.3225	1.3456	1.3689	1.3924	1.4161	1.4400	1.5625	1.6900	1.8225	1.9600	2.2500
3	1.4429	1.4815	1.5209	1.5609	1.6016	1.6430	1.6852	1.7280	1.9531	2.1970	2.4604	2.7440	3.3750
4	1.6305	1.6890	1.7490	1.8106	1.8739	1.9388	2.0053	2.0736	2.4414	2.8561	3.3215	3.8416	5.0625
5	1.8424	1.9254	2.0114	2.1003	2.1924	2.2878	2.3864	2.4833	3.0518	3.7129	4.4840	5.3782	7.5938
6	2.0820	2.1950	2.3131	2.4364	2.5652	2.6996	2.8398	2.9860	3.8147	4.8268	6.0534	7.5295	11.391
7	2.3526	2.5023	2.6600	2.8262	3.0012	3.1855	3.3793	3.5832	4.7684	6.2749	8.1722	10.541	17.086
8	2.6584	2.8526	3.0590	3.2784	3.5115	3.7589	4.0214	4.2998	5.9605	8.1573	11.032	14.758	25.629
9	3.0040	3.2519	3.5179	3.8030	4.1084	4.4355	4.7854	5.1598	7.4506	10.604	14.894	20.661	38.443
10	3.3946	3.7072	4.0456	4.4114	4.8068	5.2338	5.6947	6.1917	9.3132	13.786	20.107	28.925	57.665
11	3.8359	4.2262	4.6524	5.1173	5.6240	6.1759	6.7767	7.4301	11.642	17.922	27.144	40.496	86.498
12	4.3345	4.8179	5.3503	5.9360	6.5801	7.2876	8.0642	8.9161	14.552	23.298	36.644	56.694	129.75
13	4.8980	5.4924	6.1528	6.8858	7.6987	8.5994	9.5964	10.699	18.190	30.288	49.470	79.371	194.62
14	5.5348	6.2613	7.0757	7.9875	9.0075	10.147	11.420	12.839	22.737	39.374	66.784	111.12	291.93
15	6.2543	7.1379	8.1371	9.2655	10.539	11.974	13.590	15.407	28.422	51.186	90.158	155.57	437.89
16	7.0673	8.1372	9.3576	10.748	12.330	14.129	16.172	18.488	35.527	66.542	121.71	217.80	656.84
17	7.9861	9.2765	10.761	12.468	14.426	16.672	19.244	22.186	44.409	86.504	164.31	304.91	985.26
18	9.0243	10.575	12.375	14.463	16.879	19.673	22.901	26.623	55.511	112.46	221.82	426.88	1477.9
19	10.197	12.056	14.232	16.777	19.748	23.214	27.252	31.948	69.389	146.19	299.46	597.63	2216.8
20	11.523	13.743	16.367	19.461	23.106	27.393	32.429	38.338	86.736	190.05	404.27	836.68	3325.3
21	13.021	15.668	18.822	22.574	27.034	32.324	38.591	46.005	108.42	247.06	545.77	1171.4	4987.9
22	14.714	17.861	21.645	26.186	31.629	38.142	45.923	55.206	135.53	321.18	736.79	1639.9	7481.8
23	16.627	20.362	24.891	30.376	37.006	45.008	54.649	66.247	169.41	417.54	994.66	2295.9	11223.
24	18.788	23.212	28.625	35.236	43.297	53.109	65.032	79.497	211.76	542.80	1342.8	3214.2	16834.
25	21.231	26.462	32.919	40.874	50.658	62.669	77.388	95.396	264.70	705.64	1812.8	4499.9	25251.
26	23.991	30.167	37.857	47.414	59.270	73.949	92.092	114.48	330.87	917.33	2447.2	6299.8	37877.
27	27.109	34.390	43.535	55.000	69.345	87.260	109.59	137.37	413.59	1192.5	3303.8	8819.8	56815.
28	30.633	39.204	50.066	63.800	81.134	102.97	130.41	164.84	516.99	1550.3	4460.1	12348.	85223.
29	34.616	44.693	57.575	74.009	94.927	121.50	155.19	197.81	646.23	2015.4	6021.1	17287.	*
30	39.116	50.950	66.212	85.850	111.06	143.37	184.68	237.38	807.79	2620.0	8128.5	24201.	*
35	72.069	98.100	133.18	180.31	243.50	328.00	440.70	590.67	2465.2	9727.9	36449.	*	*
40	132.78	188.88	267.86	378.72	533.87	750.38	1051.7	1469.8	7523.2	36119.	*	*	*
45	244.64	363.68	538.77	795.44	1170.5	1716.7	2509.7	3657.3	22959.	*	*	*	*
50	450.74	700.23	1083.7	1670.7	2566.2	3927.4	5988.9	9100.4	70065.	*	*	*	*

*Interest factors exceed 99.999

TABLE A4 2 • Future Values of an Annuity of One Dollar, FVA_n

Period n	1%	2%	3%	4%	5%	6%	7%	8%	9%	10%	11%	12%
1	1.0000	1.0000	1.0000	1.0000	1.0000	1.0000	1.0000	1.0000	1.0000	1.0000	1.0000	1.0000
2	2.0100	2.0200	2.0300	2.0400	2.0500	2.0600	2.0700	2.0800	2.0900	2.1000	2.1100	2.1200
3	3.0301	3.0604	3.0909	3.1216	3.1525	3.1836	3.2149	3.2464	3.2781	3.3100	3.3421	3.3744
4	4.0604	4.1216	4.1836	4.2465	4.3101	4.3746	4.4399	4.5061	4.5731	4.6410	4.7097	4.7793
5	5.1010	5.2040	5.3091	5.4163	5.5256	5.6371	5.7507	5.8666	5.9847	6.1051	6.2278	6.3528
6	6.1520	6.3081	6.4684	6.6330	6.8019	6.9753	7.1533	7.3359	7.5233	7.7156	7.9129	8.1152
7	7.2135	7.4343	7.6625	7.8983	8.1420	8.3938	8.6540	8.9228	9.2004	9.4872	9.7833	10.089
8	8.2857	8.5830	8.8923	9.2142	9.5491	9.8975	10.260	10.637	11.028	11.436	11.859	12.300
9	9.3685	9.7546	10.159	10.583	11.027	11.491	11.978	12.488	13.021	13.579	14.164	14.776
10	10.462	10.950	11.464	12.006	12.578	13.181	13.816	14.487	15.193	15.937	16.722	17.549
11	11.567	12.169	12.808	13.486	14.207	14.972	15.784	16.645	17.560	18.531	19.561	20.655
12	12.683	13.412	14.192	15.026	15.917	16.870	17.888	18.977	20.141	21.384	22.713	24.133
13	13.809	14.680	15.618	16.627	17.713	18.882	20.141	21.495	22.953	24.523	26.212	28.029
14	14.947	15.974	17.086	18.292	19.599	21.015	22.550	24.215	26.019	27.975	30.095	32.393
15	16.097	17.293	18.599	20.024	21.579	23.276	25.129	27.152	29.361	31.772	34.405	37.280
16	17.258	18.639	20.157	21.825	23.657	25.673	27.888	30.324	33.003	35.950	39.190	42.753
17	18.430	20.012	21.762	23.698	25.840	28.213	30.840	33.750	36.974	40.545	44.501	48.884
18	19.615	21.412	23.414	25.645	28.132	30.906	33.999	37.450	41.301	45.599	50.396	55.750
19	20.811	22.841	25.117	27.671	30.539	33.760	37.379	41.446	46.018	51.159	56.939	63.440
20	22.019	24.297	26.870	29.778	33.066	36.786	40.995	45.762	51.160	57.275	64.203	72.052
21	23.239	25.783	28.676	31.969	35.719	39.993	44.865	50.423	56.765	64.002	72.265	81.699
22	24.472	27.299	30.537	34.248	38.505	43.392	49.006	55.457	62.873	71.403	81.214	92.503
23	25.716	28.845	32.453	36.618	41.430	46.996	53.436	60.893	69.532	79.543	91.148	104.60
24	26.973	30.422	34.426	39.083	44.502	50.816	58.177	66.765	76.790	88.497	102.17	118.16
25	28.243	32.030	36.459	41.646	47.727	54.865	63.249	73.106	84.701	98.347	114.41	133.33
26	29.526	33.671	38.553	44.312	51.113	59.156	68.676	79.954	93.324	109.18	128.00	150.33
27	30.821	35.344	40.710	47.084	54.669	63.706	74.484	87.351	102.72	121.10	143.08	169.37
28	32.129	37.051	42.931	49.968	58.403	68.528	80.698	95.339	112.97	134.21	159.82	190.70
29	33.450	38.792	45.219	52.966	62.323	73.640	87.347	103.97	124.14	148.63	178.40	214.58
30	34.785	40.568	47.575	56.085	66.439	79.058	94.461	113.28	136.31	164.49	199.02	241.33
35	41.660	49.994	60.462	73.652	90.320	111.43	138.24	172.32	215.71	271.02	341.59	431.66
40	48.886	60.402	75.401	95.026	120.80	154.76	199.64	259.06	337.88	442.59	581.83	767.09
45	56.481	71.893	92.720	121.03	159.70	212.74	285.75	386.51	525.86	718.90	986.64	1358.2
50	64.463	84.579	112.80	152.67	209.35	290.34	406.53	573.77	815.08	1163.9	1668.8	2400.0

(continued)

TABLE A4.2 (continued)

Period *n*	13%	14%	15%	16%	17%	18%	19%	20%	25%	30%	35%	40%	50%
1	1.0000	1.0000	1.0000	1.0000	1.0000	1.0000	1.0000	1.0000	1.0000	1.0000	1.0000	1.0000	1.0000
2	2.1300	2.1400	2.1500	2.1600	2.1700	2.1800	2.1900	2.2000	2.2500	2.3000	2.3500	2.4000	2.5000
3	3.4069	3.4396	3.4725	3.5056	3.5389	3.5724	3.6061	3.6400	3.8125	3.9900	4.1725	4.3600	4.7500
4	4.8498	4.9211	4.9934	5.0665	5.1405	5.2154	5.2913	5.3680	5.7656	6.1870	6.6329	7.1040	8.1250
5	6.4803	6.6101	6.7424	6.8771	7.0144	7.1542	7.2966	7.4416	8.2070	9.0431	9.9544	10.946	13.188
6	8.3227	8.5355	8.7537	8.9775	9.2068	9.4420	9.6830	9.9299	11.259	12.756	14.438	16.324	20.781
7	10.405	10.730	11.067	11.414	11.772	12.142	12.523	12.916	15.073	17.583	20.492	23.853	32.172
8	12.757	13.233	13.727	14.240	14.773	15.327	15.902	16.499	19.842	23.858	28.664	34.395	49.258
9	15.416	16.085	16.786	17.519	18.285	19.086	19.923	20.799	25.802	32.015	39.696	49.153	74.887
10	18.420	19.337	20.304	21.321	22.393	23.521	24.709	25.959	33.253	42.619	54.590	69.814	113.33
11	21.814	23.045	24.349	25.733	27.200	28.755	30.404	32.150	42.566	56.405	74.697	98.739	171.00
12	25.650	27.271	29.002	30.850	32.824	34.931	37.180	39.581	54.208	74.327	101.84	139.23	257.49
13	29.985	32.089	34.352	36.786	39.404	42.219	45.244	48.497	68.760	97.625	138.48	195.93	387.24
14	34.883	37.581	40.505	43.672	47.103	50.818	54.841	59.196	86.949	127.91	187.95	275.30	581.86
15	40.417	43.842	47.580	51.660	56.110	60.965	66.261	72.035	109.69	167.29	254.74	386.42	873.79
16	46.672	50.980	55.717	60.925	66.649	72.939	79.850	87.442	138.11	218.47	344.90	541.99	1311.7
17	53.739	59.118	65.075	71.673	78.979	87.068	96.022	105.93	173.64	285.01	466.61	759.78	1968.5
18	61.725	68.394	75.836	84.141	93.406	103.74	115.27	128.12	218.04	371.52	630.92	1064.7	2953.8
19	70.749	78.969	88.212	98.603	110.28	123.41	138.17	154.74	273.56	483.97	852.75	1491.6	4431.7
20	80.947	91.025	102.44	115.38	130.03	146.63	165.42	186.69	342.94	630.17	1152.2	2089.2	6648.5
21	92.470	104.77	118.81	134.84	153.14	174.02	197.85	225.03	429.68	820.22	1556.5	2925.9	9973.8
22	105.49	120.44	137.63	157.41	180.17	206.34	236.44	271.03	538.10	1067.3	2102.3	4097.2	14962.
23	120.20	138.30	159.28	183.60	211.80	244.49	282.36	326.24	673.63	1388.5	2839.0	5737.1	22443.
24	136.83	158.66	184.17	213.98	248.81	289.49	337.01	392.48	843.03	1806.0	3833.7	8033.0	33666.
25	155.62	181.87	212.79	249.21	292.10	342.60	402.04	471.98	1054.8	2348.8	5176.5	11247.	50500.
26	176.85	208.33	245.71	290.09	342.76	405.27	479.43	567.38	1319.5	3054.4	6989.3	15747.	75752.
27	200.84	238.50	283.57	337.50	402.03	479.22	571.52	681.85	1650.4	3971.8	9436.5	22047.	*
28	227.95	272.89	327.10	392.50	471.38	566.48	681.11	819.22	2064.0	5164.3	12740.	30867.	*
29	258.58	312.09	377.17	456.30	552.51	669.45	811.52	984.07	2580.9	6714.6	17200.	43214.	*
30	293.20	356.79	434.75	530.31	647.44	790.95	966.71	1181.9	3227.2	8730.0	23222.	60501.	*
35	546.68	693.57	881.17	1120.7	1426.5	1816.7	2314.2	2948.3	9856.8	32423.	*	*	*
40	1013.7	1342.0	1779.1	2360.8	3134.5	4163.2	5529.8	7343.9	30089.	*	*	*	*
45	1874.2	2590.6	3585.1	4965.3	6879.3	9531.6	13203.	18281.	91831.	*	*	*	*
50	3459.5	4994.5	7217.7	10436.	15090.	21813.	31515.	45497.	*	*	*	*	*

*Interest factors exceed 99.999

TABLE A4.3 • Present Values of One Dollar, P_0

Period *n*	1%	2%	3%	4%	5%	6%	7%	8%	9%	10%	11%	12%
1	.9901	.9804	.9709	.9615	.9524	.9434	.9346	.9259	.9174	.9091	.9009	.8929
2	.9803	.9612	.9426	.9246	.9070	.8900	.8734	.8573	.8417	.8264	.8116	.7972
3	.9706	.9423	.9151	.8890	.8638	.8396	.8163	.7938	.7722	.7513	.7312	.7118
4	.9610	.9238	.8885	.8548	.8227	.7921	.7629	.7350	.7084	.6830	.6587	.6355
5	.9515	.9057	.8626	.8219	.7835	.7473	.7130	.6806	.6499	.6209	.5935	.5674
6	.9420	.8880	.8375	.7903	.7462	.7050	.6663	.6302	.5963	.5645	.5346	.5066
7	.9327	.8706	.8131	.7599	.7107	.6651	.6227	.5835	.5470	.5132	.4817	.4523
8	.9235	.8535	.7894	.7307	.6768	.6274	.5820	.5403	.5019	.4665	.4339	.4039
9	.9143	.8368	.7664	.7026	.6446	.5919	.5439	.5002	.4604	.4241	.3909	.3606
10	.9053	.8203	.7441	.6756	.6139	.5584	.5083	.4632	.4224	.3855	.3522	.3220
11	.8963	.8043	.7224	.6496	.5847	.5268	.4751	.4289	.3875	.3505	.3173	.2875
12	.8874	.7885	.7014	.6246	.5568	.4970	.4440	.3971	.3555	.3186	.2858	.2567
13	.8787	.7730	.6810	.6006	.5303	.4688	.4150	.3677	.3262	.2897	.2575	.2292
14	.8700	.7579	.6611	.5775	.5051	.4423	.3878	.3405	.2992	.2633	.2320	.2046
15	.8613	.7430	.6419	.5553	.4810	.4173	.3624	.3152	.2745	.2394	.2090	.1827
16	.8528	.7284	.6232	.5339	.4581	.3936	.3387	.2919	.2519	.2176	.1883	.1631
17	.8444	.7142	.6050	.5134	.4363	.3714	.3166	.2703	.2311	.1978	.1696	.1456
18	.8360	.7002	.5874	.4936	.4155	.3503	.2959	.2502	.2120	.1799	.1528	.1300
19	.8277	.6864	.5703	.4746	.3957	.3305	.2765	.2317	.1945	.1635	.1377	.1161
20	.8195	.6730	.5537	.4564	.3769	.3118	.2584	.2145	.1784	.1486	.1240	.1037
21	.8114	.6598	.5375	.4388	.3589	.2942	.2415	.1987	.1637	.1351	.1117	.0926
22	.8034	.6468	.5219	.4220	.3418	.2775	.2257	.1839	.1502	.1228	.1007	.0826
23	.7954	.6342	.5067	.4057	.3256	.2618	.2109	.1703	.1378	.1117	.0907	.0738
24	.7876	.6217	.4919	.3901	.3101	.2470	.1971	.1577	.1264	.1015	.0817	.0659
25	.7798	.6095	.4776	.3751	.2953	.2330	.1842	.1460	.1160	.0923	.0736	.0588
26	.7720	.5976	.4637	.3607	.2812	.2198	.1722	.1352	.1064	.0839	.0663	.0525
27	.7644	.5859	.4502	.3468	.2678	.2074	.1609	.1252	.0976	.0763	.0597	.0469
28	.7568	.5744	.4371	.3335	.2551	.1956	.1504	.1159	.0895	.0693	.0538	.0419
29	.7493	.5631	.4243	.3207	.2429	.1846	.1406	.1073	.0822	.0630	.0485	.0374
30	.7419	.5521	.4120	.3083	.2314	.1741	.1314	.0994	.0754	.0573	.0437	.0334
35	.7059	.5000	.3554	.2534	.1813	.1301	.0937	.0676	.0490	.0356	.0259	.0189
40	.6717	.4529	.3066	.2083	.1420	.0972	.0668	.0460	.0318	.0221	.0154	.0107
45	.6391	.4102	.2644	.1712	.1113	.0727	.0476	.0313	.0207	.0137	.0091	.0061
50	.6080	.3715	.2281	.1407	.0872	.0543	.0339	.0213	.0134	.0085	.0054	.0035

(*continued*)

TABLE A4.3 (continued)

Period *n*	13%	14%	15%	16%	17%	18%	19%	20%	25%	30%	35%	40%	50%
1	.8850	.8772	.8696	.8621	.8547	.8475	.8403	.8333	.8000	.7692	.7407	.7143	.6667
2	.7831	.7695	.7561	.7432	.7305	.7182	.7062	.6944	.6400	.5917	.5487	.5102	.4444
3	.6931	.6750	.6575	.6407	.6244	.6086	.5934	.5787	.5120	.4552	.4064	.3644	.2963
4	.6133	.5921	.5718	.5523	.5337	.5158	.4987	.4823	.4096	.3501	.3011	.2603	.1975
5	.5428	.5194	.4972	.4761	.4561	.4371	.4190	.4019	.3277	.2693	.2230	.1859	.1317
6	.4803	.4556	.4323	.4104	.3898	.3704	.3521	.3349	.2621	.2072	.1652	.1328	.0878
7	.4251	.3996	.3759	.3538	.3332	.3139	.2959	.2791	.2097	.1594	.1224	.0949	.0585
8	.3762	.3506	.3269	.3050	.2848	.2660	.2487	.2326	.1678	.1226	.0906	.0678	.0390
9	.3329	.3075	.2843	.2630	.2434	.2255	.2090	.1938	.1342	.0943	.0671	.0484	.0260
10	.2946	.2697	.2472	.2267	.2080	.1911	.1756	.1615	.1074	.0725	.0497	.0346	.0173
11	.2607	.2366	.2149	.1954	.1778	.1619	.1476	.1346	.0859	.0558	.0368	.0247	.0116
12	.2307	.2076	.1869	.1685	.1520	.1372	.1240	.1122	.0687	.0429	.0273	.0176	.0077
13	.2042	.1821	.1625	.1452	.1299	.1163	.1042	.0935	.0550	.0330	.0202	.0126	.0051
14	.1807	.1597	.1413	.1252	.1110	.0985	.0876	.0779	.0440	.0254	.0150	.0090	.0034
15	.1599	.1401	.1229	.1079	.0949	.0835	.0736	.0649	.0352	.0195	.0111	.0064	.0023
16	.1415	.1229	.1069	.0930	.0811	.0708	.0618	.0541	.0281	.0150	.0082	.0046	.0015
17	.1252	.1078	.0929	.0802	.0693	.0600	.0520	.0451	.0225	.0116	.0061	.0033	.0010
18	.1108	.0946	.0808	.0691	.0592	.0508	.0437	.0376	.0180	.0089	.0045	.0023	.0007
19	.0981	.0829	.0703	.0596	.0506	.0431	.0367	.0313	.0144	.0068	.0033	.0017	.0005
20	.0868	.0728	.0611	.0514	.0443	.0365	.0308	.0261	.0115	.0053	.0025	.0012	.0003
21	.0768	.0638	.0531	.0443	.0370	.0309	.0259	.0217	.0092	.0040	.0018	.0009	.0002
22	.0680	.0560	.0462	.0382	.0316	.0262	.0218	.0181	.0074	.0031	.0014	.0006	.0001
23	.0601	.0491	.0402	.0329	.0270	.0222	.0183	.0151	.0059	.0024	.0010	.0004	.0001
24	.0532	.0431	.0349	.0284	.0231	.0188	.0154	.0126	.0047	.0018	.0007	.0003	.0001
25	.0471	.0378	.0304	.0245	.0197	.0160	.0129	.0105	.0038	.0014	.0006	.0002	.0000
26	.0417	.0331	.0264	.0211	.0169	.0135	.0109	.0087	.0030	.0011	.0004	.0002	.0000
27	.0369	.0291	.0230	.0182	.0144	.0115	.0091	.0073	.0024	.0008	.0003	.0001	.0000
28	.0326	.0255	.0200	.0157	.0123	.0097	.0077	.0061	.0019	.0006	.0002	.0001	.0000
29	.0289	.0224	.0174	.0135	.0105	.0082	.0064	.0051	.0015	.0005	.0002	.0001	.0000
30	.0256	.0196	.0151	.0116	.0090	.0070	.0054	.0042	.0012	.0004	.0001	.0000	.0000
35	.0139	.0102	.0075	.0055	.0041	.0030	.0023	.0017	.0004	.0001	.0000	.0000	.0000
40	.0075	.0053	.0037	.0026	.0019	.0013	.0010	.0007	.0001	.0000	.0000	.0000	.0000
45	.0041	.0027	.0019	.0013	.0009	.0006	.0004	.0003	.0000	.0000	.0000	.0000	.0000
50	.0022	.0014	.0009	.0006	.0004	.0003	.0002	.0001	.0000	.0000	.0000	.0000	.0000

TABLE A4.4 • Present Values of an Annuity of One Dollar, PVA_n

Period n	1%	2%	3%	4%	5%	6%	7%	8%	9%	10%	11%	12%
1	0.9901	0.9804	0.9709	0.9615	0.9524	0.9434	0.9346	0.9259	0.9174	0.9091	0.9009	0.8929
2	1.9704	1.9416	1.9135	1.8861	1.8594	1.8334	1.8080	1.7833	1.7591	1.7355	1.7125	1.6901
3	2.9410	2.8839	2.8286	2.7751	2.7232	2.6730	2.6243	2.5771	2.5313	2.4869	2.4437	2.4018
4	3.9020	3.8077	3.7171	3.6299	3.5460	3.4651	3.3872	3.3121	3.2397	3.1699	3.1024	3.0373
5	4.8534	4.7135	4.5797	4.4518	4.3295	4.2124	4.1002	3.9927	3.8897	3.7908	3.6959	3.6048
6	5.7955	5.6014	5.4172	5.2421	5.0757	4.9173	4.7665	4.6229	4.4859	4.3553	4.2305	4.1114
7	6.7282	6.4720	6.2303	6.0021	5.7864	5.5824	5.3893	5.2064	5.0330	4.8684	4.7122	4.5638
8	7.6517	7.3255	7.0197	6.7327	6.4632	6.2098	5.9713	5.7466	5.5348	5.3349	5.1461	4.9676
9	8.5660	8.1622	7.7861	7.4353	7.1078	6.8017	6.5152	6.2469	5.9952	5.7590	5.5370	5.3282
10	9.4713	8.9826	8.5302	8.1109	7.7217	7.3601	7.0236	6.7101	6.4177	6.1446	5.8892	5.6502
11	10.368	9.7868	9.2526	8.7605	8.3064	7.8869	7.4987	7.1390	6.8052	6.4951	6.2065	5.9377
12	11.255	10.575	9.9540	9.3851	8.8633	8.3838	7.9427	7.5361	7.1607	6.8137	6.4924	6.1944
13	12.134	11.348	10.635	9.9856	9.3936	8.8527	8.3577	7.9038	7.4869	7.1034	6.7499	6.4235
14	13.004	12.106	11.296	10.563	9.8986	9.2950	8.7455	8.2442	7.7862	7.3667	6.9819	6.6282
15	13.865	12.849	11.938	11.118	10.380	9.7122	9.1079	8.5595	8.0607	7.6061	7.1909	6.8109
16	14.718	13.578	12.561	11.652	10.838	10.106	9.4466	8.8514	8.3126	7.8237	7.3792	6.9740
17	15.562	14.292	13.166	12.166	11.274	10.477	9.7632	9.1216	8.5436	8.0216	7.5488	7.1196
18	16.398	14.992	13.754	12.659	11.690	10.828	10.059	9.3719	8.7556	8.2014	7.7016	7.2497
19	17.226	15.678	14.324	13.134	12.085	11.158	10.336	9.6036	8.9501	8.3649	7.8393	7.3658
20	18.046	16.351	14.877	13.590	12.462	11.470	10.594	9.8181	9.1285	8.5136	7.9633	7.4694
21	18.857	17.011	15.415	14.029	12.821	11.764	10.836	10.017	9.2922	8.6487	8.0751	7.5620
22	19.660	17.658	15.937	14.451	13.163	12.042	11.061	10.201	9.4424	8.7715	8.1757	7.6446
23	20.456	18.292	16.444	14.857	13.489	12.303	11.272	10.371	9.5802	8.8832	8.2664	7.7184
24	21.243	18.914	16.936	15.247	13.799	12.550	11.469	10.529	9.7066	8.9847	8.3481	7.7843
25	22.023	19.523	17.413	15.622	14.094	12.783	11.654	10.675	9.8226	9.0770	8.4217	7.8431
26	22.795	20.121	17.877	15.983	14.375	13.003	11.826	10.810	9.9290	9.1609	8.4881	7.8957
27	23.560	20.707	18.327	16.330	14.643	13.211	11.987	10.935	10.027	9.2372	8.5478	7.9426
28	24.316	21.281	18.764	16.663	14.898	13.406	12.137	11.051	10.116	9.3066	8.6016	7.9844
29	25.066	21.844	19.188	16.984	15.141	13.591	12.278	11.158	10.198	9.3696	8.6501	8.0218
30	25.808	22.396	19.600	17.292	15.372	13.765	12.409	11.258	10.274	9.4269	8.6938	8.0552
35	29.409	24.999	21.487	18.665	16.374	14.498	12.948	11.655	10.567	9.6442	8.8552	8.1755
40	32.835	27.355	23.115	19.793	17.159	15.046	13.332	11.925	10.757	9.7791	8.9511	8.2438
45	36.095	29.490	24.519	20.720	17.774	15.456	13.606	12.108	10.881	9.8628	9.0079	8.2825
50	39.196	31.424	25.730	21.482	18.256	15.762	13.801	12.233	10.962	9.9148	9.0417	8.3045

(continued)

TABLE A4.4 (continued)

Period n	13%	14%	15%	16%	17%	18%	19%	20%	25%	30%	35%	40%	50%
1	0.8850	0.8772	0.8696	0.8621	0.8547	0.8475	0.8403	0.8333	0.8000	0.7692	0.7407	0.7143	0.6667
2	1.6681	1.6467	1.6257	1.6052	1.5852	1.5656	1.5465	1.5278	1.4400	1.3609	1.2894	1.2245	1.1111
3	2.3612	2.3216	2.2832	2.2459	2.2096	2.1743	2.1399	2.1065	1.9520	1.8161	1.6959	1.5889	1.4074
4	2.9745	2.9137	2.8550	2.7982	2.7432	2.6901	2.6386	2.5887	2.3616	2.1662	1.9969	1.8492	1.6049
5	3.5172	3.4331	3.3522	3.2743	3.1993	3.1272	3.0576	2.9906	2.6893	2.4356	2.2200	2.0352	1.7366
6	3.9975	3.8887	3.7845	3.6847	3.5892	3.4976	3.4098	3.3255	2.9514	2.6427	2.3852	2.1680	1.8244
7	4.4226	4.2883	4.1604	4.0386	3.9224	3.8115	3.7057	3.6046	3.1611	2.8021	2.5075	2.2628	1.8829
8	4.7988	4.6389	4.4873	4.3436	4.2072	4.0776	3.9544	3.8372	3.3289	2.9247	2.5982	2.3306	1.9220
9	5.1317	4.9464	4.7716	4.6065	4.4506	4.3030	4.1633	4.0310	3.4631	3.0190	2.6653	2.3790	1.9480
10	5.4262	5.2161	5.0188	4.8332	4.6586	4.4941	4.3389	4.1925	3.5705	3.0915	2.7150	2.4136	1.9653
11	5.6869	5.4527	5.2337	5.0286	4.8364	4.6560	4.4865	4.3271	3.6564	3.1473	2.7519	2.4383	1.9769
12	5.9176	5.6603	5.4206	5.1971	4.9884	4.7932	4.6105	4.4392	3.7251	3.1903	2.7792	2.4559	1.9846
13	6.1218	5.8424	5.5831	5.3423	5.1183	4.9095	4.7147	4.5327	3.7801	3.2233	2.7994	2.4685	1.9897
14	6.3025	6.0021	5.7245	5.4675	5.2293	5.0081	4.8023	4.6106	3.8241	3.2487	2.8144	2.4775	1.9931
15	6.4624	6.1422	5.8474	5.5755	5.3242	5.0916	4.8759	4.6755	3.8593	3.2682	2.8255	2.4839	1.9954
16	6.6039	6.2651	5.9542	5.6685	5.4053	5.1624	4.9377	4.7296	3.8874	3.2832	2.8337	2.4885	1.9970
17	6.7291	6.3729	6.0472	5.7487	5.4746	5.2223	4.9897	4.7746	3.9099	3.2948	2.8398	2.4918	1.9980
18	6.8399	6.4674	6.1280	5.8178	5.5339	5.2732	5.0333	4.8122	3.9279	3.3037	2.8443	2.4941	1.9986
19	6.9380	6.5504	6.1982	5.8775	5.5845	5.3162	5.0700	4.8435	3.9424	3.3105	2.8476	2.4958	1.9991
20	7.0248	6.6231	6.2593	5.9288	5.6278	5.3527	5.1009	4.8696	3.9539	3.3158	2.8501	2.4970	1.9994
21	7.1016	6.6870	6.3125	5.9731	5.6648	5.3837	5.1268	4.8913	3.9631	3.3198	2.8519	2.4979	1.9996
22	7.1695	6.7429	6.3587	6.0113	5.6964	5.4099	5.1486	4.9094	3.9705	3.3230	2.8533	2.4985	1.9997
23	7.2297	6.7921	6.3988	6.0442	5.7234	5.4321	5.1668	4.9245	3.9764	3.3254	2.8543	2.4989	1.9998
24	7.2829	6.8351	6.4338	6.0726	5.7465	5.4509	5.1822	4.9371	3.9811	3.3272	2.8550	2.4992	1.9999
25	7.3300	6.8729	6.4641	6.0971	5.7662	5.4669	5.1951	4.9476	3.9849	3.3286	2.8556	2.4994	1.9999
26	7.3717	6.9061	6.4906	6.1182	5.7831	5.4804	5.2060	4.9563	3.9879	3.3297	2.8560	2.4996	1.9999
27	7.4086	6.9352	6.5135	6.1364	5.7975	5.4919	5.2151	4.9636	3.9903	3.3305	2.8563	2.4997	2.0000
28	7.4412	6.9607	6.5335	6.1520	5.8099	5.5016	5.2228	4.9697	3.9923	3.3312	2.8565	2.4998	2.0000
29	7.4701	6.9830	6.5509	6.1656	5.8204	5.5098	5.2292	4.9747	3.9938	3.3317	2.8567	2.4999	2.0000
30	7.4957	7.0027	6.5660	6.1772	5.8294	5.5168	5.2347	4.9789	3.9950	3.3321	2.8568	2.4999	2.0000
35	7.5856	7.0700	6.6166	6.2153	5.8582	5.5386	5.2512	4.9915	3.9984	3.3330	2.8571	2.5000	2.0000
40	7.6344	7.1050	6.6418	6.2335	5.8713	5.5482	5.2582	4.9966	3.9995	3.3332	2.8571	2.5000	2.0000
45	7.6609	7.1232	6.6543	6.2421	5.8773	5.5523	5.2611	4.9986	3.9998	3.3333	2.8571	2.5000	2.0000
50	7.6752	7.1327	6.6605	6.2463	5.8801	5.5541	5.2623	4.9995	3.9999	3.3333	2.8571	2.5000	2.0000

APPENDIX A-5

Standard Normal Cumulative Probability Distribution and Student t Distribution

USING THE STANDARD NORMAL CUMULATIVE PROBABILITY DISTRIBUTION

Table A5.1 provides cumulative probabilities for the standard normal cumulative probability distribution. As the table indicates, the probabilities start at zero and increase to one. This occurs because the probabilities for an entire distribution must sum to 1. Also notice that the probability of .5000 in the table occurs for a standardized Z value of .00. Thus, 50 percent of the values are below the mean of .00, and 50 percent are above. Finally, notice that the lowest Z is -3.9 and the largest is 3.9. In a standard normal distribution, all values must be between ± 3.9 standard deviations from the mean.

To use the table for any distribution that is normally distributed (bell shaped), the distribution must be standardized. In other words, the distribution must have a mean of zero and a standard deviation of one. The standardization is performed by using the following formula:

$$Z = \frac{X - \mu}{\sigma}$$

where

Z = standard normal random variable
X = value of random variable
μ = mean of random variable
σ = standard deviation of random variable

For example, assume you want to estimate the probability that a stock price of \$20 or less will occur for a particular stock. Assume the stock price is normally distributed with a mean of \$30 and standard deviation of \$8.27.

$$Z = \frac{\$20 - \$30}{\$8.27}$$

$$Z = -1.21$$

Reading from Table A5.1, Prob (Price $\leq$ \$20) = .1131.

FIGURE A5.1 • Standard Normal and Standard Normal Cumulative Distributions

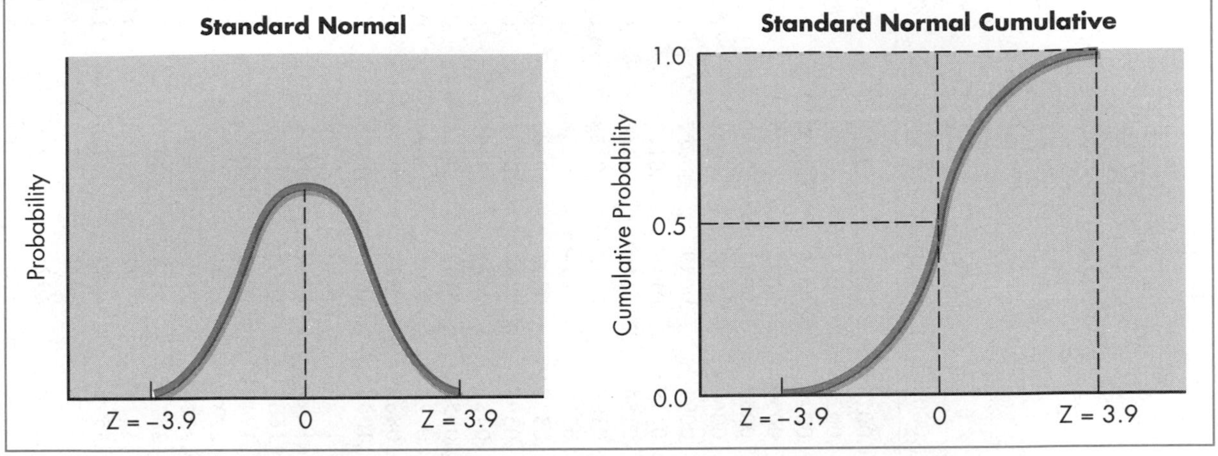

Notice that the table provides values for Z that are calculated to two decimal places for $-2.99 \leq Z \leq 2.99$ but for only one decimal place for $-3.0 \leq Z \leq -3.9$ (the first row of the table) and for $3.0 \leq Z \leq 3.9$ (the last row of the table). Using only one decimal place for very low and very high Z values simply makes the table somewhat shorter.

The probability distribution graphs in Figure A5.1 illustrate the differences between a standard normal distribution and a standard normal cumulative distribution.

USING THE STUDENT *t* DISTRIBUTION

Table A5.2 provides upper-tail student t distribution values for a specified number of degrees of freedom. The columns in the table represent α (alpha) or the significant level selected for the hypothesis test. Notice that the alphas begin at .4 and decline to .0005. For example, if an alpha of .05 is selected, the table indicates the minimum value of t that will be needed to have a .95 probability that the null hypothesis is correct. Since the table provides only the values for the upper-tail area of the distribution, an alpha of .05 is the significance level for a one-sided test of the hypothesis. Usually, however, you will want a two-sided test so you can determine whether an estimate is less than or greater than a certain hypothesized value. For example, suppose you want to test the null hypothesis that the beta for a particular stock is equal to zero. The alternative hypothesis is that the beta is not equal to zero. A two-tail test considers the possibility that the beta can be negative or positive. A one-tail test would test to see if the beta is positive (upper-tail area of distribution) or negative (lower-tail area of distribution).

Since Table A5.2 provides upper-tail values, a two-tail test requires that the selected alpha value or significance level be adjusted to $\alpha/2$. For example, if a .05 level of significance is selected, the correct alpha to use for a two-tailed test is .025.

To continue with the hypothesis test that the true beta of a particular stock (β_j) is zero, assume that the regression estimate of beta, b_j, is .75 with a standard error of the

TABLE A5.1 • Values for the Standard Normal Cumulative Probability Distribution

z	0	1	2	3	4	5	6	7	8	9
−3.	.0013	.0010	.0007	.0005	.0003	.0002	.0002	.0001	.0001	.0000
−2.9	.0019	.0018	.0017	.0017	.0016	.0016	.0015	.0015	.0014	.0014
−2.8	.0026	.0025	.0024	.0023	.0023	.0022	.0021	.0021	.0020	.0019
−2.7	.0035	.0034	.0033	.0032	.0031	.0030	.0029	.0028	.0027	.0026
−2.6	.0047	.0045	.0044	.0043	.0041	.0040	.0039	.0038	.0037	.0036
−2.5	.0062	.0060	.0059	.0057	.0055	.0054	.0052	.0051	.0049	.0048
−2.4	.0082	.0080	.0078	.0075	.0073	.0071	.0069	.0068	.0066	.0064
−2.3	.0107	.0104	.0102	.0099	.0096	.0094	.0091	.0089	.0087	.0084
−2.2	.0139	.0136	.0132	.0129	.0126	.0122	.0119	.0116	.0113	.0110
−2.1	.0179	.0174	.0170	.0166	.0162	.0158	.0154	.0150	.0146	.0143
−2.0	.0228	.0222	.0217	.0212	.0207	.0202	.0197	.0192	.0188	.0183
−1.9	.0287	.0281	.0274	.0268	.0262	.0256	.0250	.0244	.0238	.0233
−1.8	.0359	.0352	.0344	.0336	.0329	.0322	.0314	.0307	.0300	.0294
−1.7	.0446	.0436	.0427	.0418	.0409	.0401	.0392	.0384	.0375	.0367
−1.6	.0548	.0537	.0526	.0516	.0505	.0495	.0485	.0475	.0465	.0455
−1.5	.0668	.0655	.0643	.0630	.0618	.0606	.0594	.0582	.0570	.0559
−1.4	.0808	.0793	.0778	.0764	.0749	.0735	.0722	.0708	.0694	.0681
−1.3	.0968	.0951	.0934	.0918	.0901	.0885	.0869	.0853	.0838	.0823
−1.2	.1151	.1131	.1112	.1093	.1075	.1056	.1038	.1020	.1003	.0985
−1.1	.1357	.1335	.1314	.1292	.1271	.1251	.1230	.1210	.1190	.1170
−1.0	.1587	.1562	.1539	.1515	.1492	.1469	.1446	.1423	.1401	.1379
−.9	.1841	.1814	.1788	.1762	.1736	.1711	.1685	.1660	.1635	.1611
−.8	.2119	.2090	.2061	.2033	.2005	.1977	.1949	.1922	.1894	.1867
−.7	.2420	.2389	.2358	.2327	.2297	.2266	.2236	.2206	.2177	.2148
−.6	.2743	.2709	.2676	.2643	.2611	.2578	.2546	.2514	.2483	.2451
−.5	.3085	.3050	.3015	.2981	.2946	.2912	.2877	.2843	.2810	.2776
−.4	.3446	.3409	.3372	.3336	.3300	.3264	.3228	.3192	.3156	.3121
−.3	.3821	.3783	.3745	.3707	.3669	.3632	.3594	.3557	.3520	.3483
−.2	.4207	.4168	.4129	.4090	.4052	.4013	.3974	.3936	.3897	.3859
−.1	.4602	.4562	.4522	.4483	.4443	.4404	.4364	.4325	.4286	.4247
−.0	.5000	.4960	.4920	.4880	.4840	.4801	.4761	.4721	.4681	.4641

TABLE A5.1 (continued)

z	0	1	2	3	4	5	6	7	8	9
.0	.5000	.5040	.5080	.5120	.5160	.5199	.5239	.5279	.5319	.5359
.1	.5398	.5438	.5478	.5517	.5557	.5596	.5636	.5675	.5714	.5753
.2	.5793	.5832	.5871	.5910	.5948	.5987	.6026	.6064	.6103	.6141
.3	.6179	.6217	.6255	.6293	.6331	.6368	.6406	.6443	.6480	.6517
.4	.6554	.6591	.6628	.6664	.6700	.6736	.6772	.6808	.6844	.6879
.5	.6915	.6950	.6985	.7019	.7054	.7088	.7123	.7157	.7190	.7224
.6	.7257	.7291	.7324	.7357	.7389	.7422	.7454	.7486	.7517	.7549
.7	.7580	.7611	.7642	.7673	.7703	.7734	.7764	.7794	.7823	.7852
.8	.7881	.7910	.7939	.7967	.7995	.8023	.8051	.8078	.8106	.8133
.9	.8159	.8186	.8212	.8238	.8264	.8289	.8315	.8340	.8365	.8389
1.0	.8413	.8438	.8461	.8485	.8508	.8531	.8554	.8577	.8599	.8621
1.1	.8643	.8665	.8686	.8708	.8729	.8749	.8770	.8790	.8810	.8830
1.2	.8849	.8869	.8888	.8907	.8925	.8944	.8962	.8980	.8997	.9015
1.3	.9032	.9049	.9066	.9082	.9099	.9115	.9131	.9147	.9162	.9177
1.4	.9192	.9207	.9222	.9236	.9251	.9265	.9278	.9292	.9306	.9319
1.5	.9332	.9345	.9357	.9370	.9382	.9394	.9406	.9418	.9430	.9441
1.6	.9452	.9463	.9474	.9484	.9495	.9505	.9515	.9525	.9535	.9545
1.7	.9554	.9564	.9573	.9582	.9591	.9599	.9608	.9616	.9625	.9633
1.8	.9641	.9648	.9656	.9664	.9671	.9678	.9686	.9693	.9700	.9706
1.9	.9713	.9719	.9726	.9732	.9738	.9744	.9750	.9756	.9762	.9767
2.0	.9772	.9778	.9783	.9788	.9793	.9798	.9803	.9808	.9812	.9817
2.1	.9821	.9826	.9830	.9834	.9838	.9842	.9846	.9850	.9854	.9857
2.2	.9861	.9864	.9868	.9871	.9874	.9878	.9881	.9884	.9887	.9890
2.3	.9893	.9896	.9898	.9901	.9904	.9906	.9909	.9911	.9913	.9916
2.4	.9918	.9920	.9922	.9925	.9927	.9929	.9931	.9932	.9934	.9936
2.5	.9938	.9940	.9941	.9943	.9945	.9946	.9948	.9949	.9951	.9952
2.6	.9953	.9955	.9956	.9957	.9959	.9960	.9961	.9962	.9963	.9964
2.7	.9965	.9966	.9967	.9968	.9969	.9970	.9971	.9972	.9973	.9974
2.8	.9974	.9975	.9976	.9977	.9977	.9978	.9979	.9979	.9980	.9981
2.9	.9981	.9982	.9982	.9983	.9984	.9984	.9985	.9985	.9986	.9986
3.	.9987	.9990	.9993	.9995	.9997	.9998	.9998	.9999	.9999	1.000

TABLE A5.2 • Student t Distribution

Degrees of Freedom	Upper-Tail Area α									
	.4	.25	.1	.05	.025	.01	.005	.0025	.001	.0005
1	0.325	1.000	3.078	6.314	12.706	31.821	63.657	127.32	318.31	636.62
2	.289	.816	1.886	2.920	4.303	6.965	9.925	14.089	22.327	31.598
3	.277	.765	1.638	2.353	3.182	4.541	5.841	7.453	10.214	12.924
4	.271	.741	1.533	2.132	2.776	3.747	4.604	5.598	7.173	8.610
5	0.267	0.727	1.476	2.015	2.571	3.365	4.032	4.773	5.893	6.869
6	.265	.718	1.440	1.943	2.447	3.143	3.707	4.317	5.208	5.959
7	.263	.711	1.415	1.895	2.365	2.998	3.499	4.029	4.785	5.408
8	.262	.706	1.397	1.860	2.306	2.896	3.355	3.833	4.501	5.041
9	.261	.703	1.383	1.833	2.262	2.821	3.250	3.690	4.297	4.781
10	0.260	0.700	1.372	1.812	2.228	2.764	3.169	3.581	4.144	4.587
11	.260	.697	1.363	1.796	2.201	2.718	3.106	3.497	4.025	4.437
12	.259	.695	1.356	1.782	2.179	2.681	3.055	3.428	3.930	4.318
13	.259	.694	1.350	1.771	2.160	2.650	3.012	3.372	3.852	4.221
14	.258	.692	1.345	1.761	2.145	2.624	2.977	3.326	3.787	4.140
15	0.258	0.691	1.341	1.753	2.131	2.602	2.947	3.286	3.733	4.073
16	.258	.690	1.337	1.746	2.120	2.583	2.921	3.252	3.686	4.015
17	.257	.689	1.333	1.740	2.110	2.567	2.898	3.222	3.646	3.965
18	.257	.688	1.330	1.734	2.101	2.552	2.878	3.197	3.610	3.922
19	.257	.688	1.328	1.729	2.093	2.539	2.861	3.174	3.579	3.883
20	0.257	0.687	1.325	1.725	2.086	2.528	2.845	3.153	3.552	3.850
21	.257	.686	1.323	1.721	2.080	2.518	2.831	3.135	3.527	3.819
22	.256	.686	1.321	1.717	2.074	2.508	2.819	3.119	3.505	3.792
23	.256	.685	1.319	1.714	2.069	2.500	2.807	3.104	3.485	3.767
24	.256	.685	1.318	1.711	2.064	2.492	2.797	3.091	3.467	3.745
25	0.256	0.684	1.316	1.708	2.060	2.485	2.787	3.078	3.450	3.725
26	.256	.684	1.315	1.706	2.056	2.479	2.779	3.067	3.435	3.707
27	.256	.684	1.314	1.703	2.052	2.473	2.771	3.057	3.421	3.690
28	.256	.683	1.313	1.701	2.048	2.467	2.763	3.047	3.408	3.674
29	.256	.683	1.311	1.699	2.045	2.462	2.756	3.038	3.396	3.659
30	0.256	0.683	1.310	1.697	2.042	2.457	2.750	3.030	3.385	3.646
40	.255	.681	1.303	1.684	2.021	2.423	2.704	2.971	3.307	3.551
60	.254	.679	1.296	1.671	2.000	2.390	2.660	2.915	3.232	3.460
120	.254	.677	1.289	1.658	1.980	2.358	2.617	2.860	3.160	3.373
∞	.253	.674	1.282	1.645	1.960	2.326	2.576	2.807	3.090	3.291

beta estimate, σ_b, of .25. Assume that 22 months of data were used to estimate beta resulting in 20 degrees of freedom. The critical t value is

$$t = \frac{\hat{b}_j - \beta_j}{\sigma_b} = \frac{.75 - 0}{.25} = 3.0$$

For $\alpha = .1/2 = .05$ and 20 degrees of freedom, the value in Table A5.2 is 1.725. Since the calculated value of t of 3.0 is not between -1.725 and $+1.725$, we reject the null hypothesis that the stock's beta is zero. Thus, the test indicates that there is a significant relationship between the stock and benchmark portfolio.

As a second example of the use of Table A5.2, assume that Jensen's portfolio performance measure (see Chapter 21) for a particular portfolio, $\hat{a}$, is 3.50 percent. The standard error of the estimate of the regression intercept, σ_a, is 3.0 percent. Ten years of annual HPRs were used to estimate Jensen's measure, resulting in $n - 2$ or 8 degrees of freedom for the t-test. Assume we want to test the hypothesis that the true Jensen's measure, A, is greater than zero (a one-tailed test) at the .05 level of significance:

$$t = \frac{\hat{a} - A}{\sigma_a} = \frac{3.50 - 0}{3.0} = 1.167$$

For 8 degrees of freedom and a significance level of .05, the value in Table A5.2 is 1.860. Since the calculated value of t of 1.167 is within the range of -1.860 and $+1.860$, we accept the null hypothesis that the portfolio manager did not earn a statistically significant risk-adjusted excess return over the evaluation period.

Figure A5.2 illustrates the student t distribution for the values in Table A5.2.

FIGURE A5.2
Student t Distribution

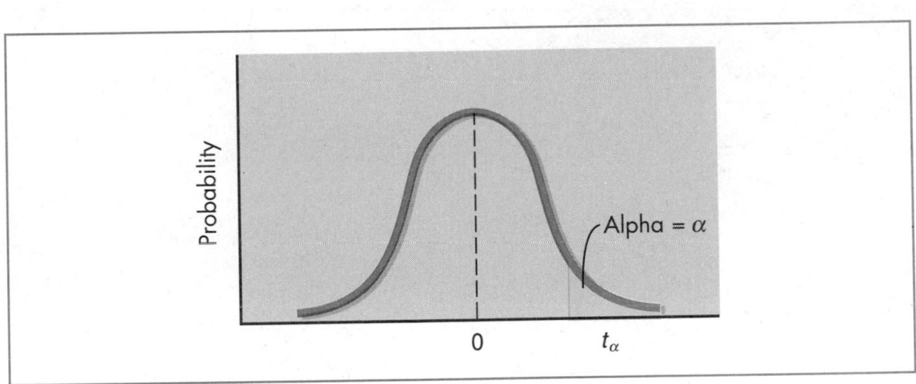

Glossary of Key Terms

This glossary provides a brief definition/explanation of the key terms listed at the end of each chapter. The number(s) in parentheses after the definition or explanation indicates the chapter(s) in the book in which the key term is presented.

Accounting earnings The reported earnings on a firm's income statement (9).

Active strategy An investment strategy designed to exploit market inefficiencies and achieve risk-adjusted excess returns (7).

Adjustable rate mortgage A mortgage that initially has interest rates below those of corresponding fixed rate mortgages, but whose interest rate periodically changes to reflect the movement of some specified measure of the current interest rate (1).

Adjustable rate preferred stock (ARPS) A preferred stock where dividends are adjusted to provide market yields, thereby eliminating interest rate risk (12).

Alpha *See* Jensen's technique.

American depository receipts (ADRs) A certificate issued by a major bank that represents ownership of a foreign security (6).

American Stock Exchange (AMEX) The second largest, national, organized security exchange in the United States (3).

American-style options Stock options that may be exercised by the holder at any time after they are purchased until they expire (15).

Annual report A published report prepared by a publicly traded firm that contains audited financial statements, reviews the operations of the firm over the preceding years, and discusses the future prospects for the company (4).

Arbitrage An investment strategy based on the reasonable and straightforward intuition that in efficient capital markets, assets with similar risk must have similar expected rates of return. The opportunity for investors to add to their wealth without investing dollars or facing risk (7, 20).

Arbitrage pricing theory (APT) An equilibrium theory of expected return. Its central thesis is that more than one systematic factor may affect the long-term average return on financial assets (20).

Asset allocation An investment strategy that refers to the way investment dollars are divided among different types of investment vehicles (7).

Asset allocation fund A mutual fund that invests in different categories of securities such as money market securities, bonds, common stocks, and international stocks and bonds (5).

Asset-backed securities A financial asset in which existing assets, such as automobile loans, credit card receivables, and home mortgages, serve as collateral for the security (3).

Asset utilization ratio The ratio of sales to total assets (9).

Attainable set The set of all possible portfolios (19).

Basis The difference between the futures price and the current spot price (17).

Best-efforts offering A new security offering in which the investment banker acts only as an agent for the issuing company. The investment banker does not underwrite the issue but merely uses its best efforts to sell the issue to the public (3).

Beta An indicator of the systematic or nondiversifiable risk of an asset or portfolio. It measures how an asset's returns react to changes in the returns of the market. Assets with beta values above 1.0 are classified as aggressive, and assets with beta values less than 1.0 are classified as defensive (2, 20).

Bid-ask spread The difference between the bid price a dealer is willing to pay to buy the security and the asked price at which the dealer is willing to sell (12).

Black-Scholes option pricing model A mathematical model for valuing European-type call options on stocks that do not pay cash dividends (15).

Blue-chip stock The common stock of a very large, firmly established corporation (12).

Bond A type of fixed-income security issued by a borrowing entity in which the amount to be paid to the investor is specified in the investment contract or indenture (10).

Bond rating A grade assigned to a bond that reflects the likelihood that the issuer will default on the payments of interest and/or principal (10).

Book value per share A per-share-based ratio calculated by dividing the total common equity on the balance sheet (book) by the number of common shares outstanding (12).

Borrowing portfolio A portfolio formed by borrowing, at the risk-free rate, a portion of the funds needed to take a position in a portfolio on the efficient frontier (19).

Breadth of the market A technical indicator of stock market direction that describes the relationship between the number of stocks that are advancing in price versus those that are declining (8).

Bridge loans Financing made available to borrowers that span the time when cash is needed and the time when permanent financing can be acquired (3).

Budget deficit A deficiency in which a country's expenditures exceed its receipts (8).

Bullion Gold or silver in the form of bars (18).

Bullion coins Coins issued by countries that are valued by the quality and quantity of their precious metal (gold) content (18).

Business cycle A means of indicating the level of economic activity (8).

Business risk The uncertainty about the rate of return from an investment caused by the nature of the business. The most frequently discussed causes of business risk are uncertainty about the firm's future sales and operating expenses (2).

Busted convertible A convertible security that has a conversion price substantially above the market price of the common stock (16).

Call (option) A stock option that grants the holder the right to purchase the shares of the underlying stock, at a specified price, within a specified period of time (15).

Call risk (convertible) The uncertainty associated with the call provision of convertible securities (16).

Capital asset pricing model (CAPM) An expected return model derived from capital market theory. A model that relates an investment's required return to its beta (2, 20).

Capital market line (CML) The linear efficient frontier; defines the relationship between total risk and expected return for efficient portfolios consisting of the risk-free asset and the market portfolio (20).

Capital market theory An equilibrium model of asset price determination; a theory that postulates the ex-ante risk-return relationship of individual assets as well as portfolios under equilibrium conditions (20).

Carrying cost The costs incurred to keep a commodity in inventory until its delivery date (17).

Cash flow per share (CFPS) The profits after taxes and after preferred dividends plus noncash expenses (depreciation and amortization) divided by the weighted average number of shares of common stock outstanding (13).

CEPS model A procedure that can be used to estimate the impact of dividend policy and the firm's profitability on future earnings. CEPS is an acronym for corrected earnings per share (14).

Characteristic line The line of best fit of a linear regression model reflecting the relationship between an asset's returns and those of the market portfolio (20).

Chart services A published, subscription service for technicians (4).

Chartered Financial Analyst (CFA) A professional designation awarded by the Association for Investment Management and Research (22).

Chartered Financial Consultant (ChFC) A professional designation awarded by the American College (22).

Certified Financial Planner (CFP) A professional designation awarded by the International Board of

Standards and Practices for Certified Financial Planners (22).

Clearing corporation An intermediary between the buyer and the seller of a futures contract that guarantees the performance of all participants in the market (17).

Closed-end fund An investment company with a fixed number of shares of common stock outstanding (5).

Coefficient of variation (CV) The standard deviation of returns divided by the mean return. A measure of the risk per unit of return (2).

Coincident composite index A combination of four economic variables that indicates the current phase of the business cycle (8).

Coincident indicators Economic time series produced by the National Bureau of Economic Research that can be used to indicate current trends in the economy (4).

Collateralized mortgage obligations Securities that are similar to mortgage-backed securities issued by the Government National Mortgage Association ("Ginnie Mae"), but they offer a range of maturities, more predictable cash flows, and monthly interest income (18).

Collectibles Tangible or real assets that have value because they are in limited supply and are in demand by collectors (18).

Commission brokers Employees of a brokerage firm that is a member of the New York Stock Exchange who execute buy and sell orders for the firm's clients (3).

Commodity-backed bonds Bonds whose coupons and/or maturity values are indexed to the price of specific commodities such as gold or silver (18).

Commodity funds Professionally managed limited partnerships, offered to investors by prospectus, that buy and sell futures contracts (17).

Commodity futures A contract entered into by a buyer and seller in which the underlying asset is to be delivered in the future (17).

Commodity futures option An option in which the underlying asset is a futures contract that allows the investor to buy or sell the underlying commodity at a fixed price (15).

Common-size statements Financial statements converted to percentages; the income statement items are expressed as a percentage of total sales, and the balance sheet items are expressed as a percentage of total assets (9).

Common stock A representation of an ownership interest in a corporation. Shareholders generally have voting rights and receive cash dividends if they are declared by the board of directors (12).

Common stock equivalents Options and warrants that can be used to purchase common stock from a company; also certain convertible securities (13).

Computerized data bases An organized collection of information that contains both historical and current financial information (4).

Confidence hedge An investment, such as gold, that is viewed as "insurance" against the collapse of the international monetary system (18).

Confidence index A technical indicator of market sentiment that compares the yield on high-grade bonds to the yield on medium-grade bonds (8).

Consensus EPS forecast An average of the forecasts of earnings per share produced by financial analysts (13).

Consensus economic forecast An average of published economic forecasts (8).

Consol A bond with an infinite term to maturity (11).

Constant growth DDM A dividend discount stock valuation model that assumes dividends will grow at a constant rate over time (14).

Constant growth P/E model A P/E stock valuation model that assumes earnings and dividends will grow at a constant rate over time (14).

Contango A hypothesis that suggests that the futures price will be an upward-biased estimate of the expected future spot price (17).

Convergence The decline in the basis as the commodity delivery month approaches (17).

Conversion price The price per share at which a convertible security can be exchanged for common stock (16).

Conversion ratio The number of shares of common stock that will be received at conversion for each convertible security (16).

Conversion value The total market value of the common stock received at conversion (16).

Convertible bond A bond that allows the investor the option of exchanging the bond for common stock using a specified fixed conversion ratio or conversion price (10, 16).

Convertible preferred stock A preferred stock that allows the investor the option of exchanging the preferred stock for common stock using a specified conversion ratio or conversion price (12, 16).

Corporate bond A long-term debt instrument issued by corporations (10).

Coupon The nominal interest rate paid on a bond. It is established at the time a bond is issued and is stated as an annual percentage rate that can be applied to the denomination or face value of the bond to calculate the dollar interest (10).

Correlation coefficient A statistic that measures the relationship between two series of data. The correlation coefficient can take on a range of values between +1.0 and −1.0 (2, 19).

Council of Economic Advisers A select group of economists charged with the responsibility of advising the president on economic issues (8).

Country fund A closed-end investment company that invests only in the securities issued by companies located in a particular country (5).

Covariance A statistic that measures the relationship between two series of data. A positive covariance indicates the two series move together, and a negative covariance indicates the two series move inversely (2, 19).

Covered equity warrants Warrants issued by companies (usually investment or financial institutions) other than the company that issued the underlying stock. The company that issues the warrant has a position in the underlying common stock (16).

Covered option The writer of the option has a position in the underlying common stock (15).

Credit risk The risk associated with the financial condition of a firm (16).

Crossing Security transactions occurring directly between a buyer and a seller without the assistance of a broker (3).

Cross-sectional analysis A comparison of financial ratios of firms within the same industry (9).

Cumulative (preferred stock) A feature of preferred stock in which any omitted dividends accrue to the preferred stockholders and must be paid in full before any dividends can be paid on the common stock (12).

Cumulative voting A method of electing the board of directors in which the common stockholder can cast all his or her votes (usually one vote per share of common stock owned) for a single candidate (12).

Currency exchange warrant A warrant that allows the holder to acquire, at a specified price, a fixed amount of foreign currency from the issuer (16).

Currency futures A contract entered into by a buyer and seller in which the underlying asset to be delivered is a foreign currency. Such contracts are used to decrease currency exchange risk in international trade and investing (17).

Currency options Options in which the underlying asset is a foreign currency (15).

Currency risk The risk that a particular currency may depreciate in value relative to another currency (6).

Current yield A bond return measure that is calculated by dividing the annual dollar coupon by the current market price of the bond (11).

Cyclical stock A common stock that is influenced by economic and industry cycles (12).

Debenture A bond that has no specific collateral and is unsecured except for the general creditworthiness of the issuer (10).

Default risk The risk related to the possibility that some or all of the initial investment will not be returned. The degree of default risk is closely related to the financial condition of the company issuing the security and the security's rank in claims on the company's assets in the event of bankruptcy (2, 11).

Defensive stock A common stock that is not susceptible to economic cycles (12).

Defined benefit plan A pension plan that specifies the benefits that will be received by the employee at retirement (22).

Defined contribution plan A pension plan that specifies the contribution that employers (and/or employees) will make to the plan, but not the level of pension benefits (22).

Derivative security A security whose value depends on the price of an underlying asset or security such as common stock (15).

Dilution The negative impact on earnings per share caused by an increase in the number of common stock shares outstanding (16).

Discount brokers A brokerage firm that does not provide research and advice to its customers and charges brokerage commissions that are between 20 and 70 percent less than those charged by full-service brokerage firms (3).

Disintermediation (insurance) The cancellation of life insurance policies by policyholders and the removal of the cash reserve or savings (22).

Diversifiable risk Risk that has as its source company or industry factors. It is also called unsystematic risk because it is not common to all marketable securities and can be eliminated through appropriate diversification of a portfolio (2, 20).

Diversification Including more than one alternative or category of assets in a portfolio and including more than one asset from each category. Diversification may significantly reduce portfolio risk without a corresponding reduction in the expected rate of return on the portfolio (1, 2).

Dividend discount model (DDM) A stock valuation model that, in its simplest form, defines the intrinsic value of a share of stock as the present value of future dividends (14).

Dividend reinvestment plan An option offered to shareholders that allows them to automatically purchase additional shares of common stock with their cash dividends (12).

Dividend yield A measure of return earned on dividend income. It is calculated by dividing the current annual cash dividend by the current price of the stock (14).

Dollar-cost averaging The investment of the same amount of money at regular intervals over a long period of time. It is used to avoid the investment timing issue (1).

Dominance principle For any given level of risk, investors prefer assets with a higher expected return to assets with a lower expected return; for assets with the same expected return, investors prefer lower to higher risk (19).

Dual fund A closed-end investment company that has two types of shares, income and capital. The income shareholder receives all interest and dividends, while the capital shareholder receives all capital gain distributions (5).

Duration The weighted average number of years that cash flows occur for a bond (11).

Dutch auction rate preferred stock (DARPS) A preferred stock in which the yield is adjusted by auction between both current and potential investors every seven weeks (12).

Earnings per share (EPS) The per-share profits after taxes and after preferred stock dividends that are available to the common stockholders (13).

Economic earnings The real (adjusted for inflation) excess cash flows that a firm generates from a constant level of net assets (9).

Efficient frontier The set of portfolios that dominate all other portfolios in the attainable set (19).

Efficient market hypothesis (EMH) A theory dealing with the market's ability to price securities correctly and instantaneously change security prices to reflect new information. The weak form of the EMH asserts that price changes are random (hence the term random walk) and do not reflect any distinguishable pattern. The semistrong form of the EMH indicates that security prices reflect all publicly available information. The strong form of the EMH suggests that all available information (public or private) is fully reflected in security prices (7, 21).

Efficient portfolio A portfolio that at a given level of risk (expected return) provides the highest (lowest) level of expected return (risk) (19).

Endowment life insurance Life insurance priced to cover the mortality factor for the policy period, plus loading, in the same manner as whole life. Savings are accumulated at a much faster rate than with whole life, since they must equal the face value of the policy in a specified number of years, at which time the policy matures and requires no additional premium payments (22).

Equilibrium A condition in which there are no underpriced or overpriced securities in the capital markets (20).

Equity index option An option in which the underlying "asset" is a broad-based or narrow-based index of stocks (15).

Equity option An option in which the underlying asset is a specific common stock (15).

Eurocurrency market The arena for international short-term investing. It is made up of large banks (called Eurobanks) that are willing to accept short-term deposits in foreign currencies and lend these deposits to corporations and governments in need of short-term funds (6).

European-style options Stock options that may be exercised by the holder only during a specified period, which may end on the expiration date or for a designated period prior to the expiration date (15).

Event study An analysis of the pattern and speed of stock price adjustments to specific types of new information that reaches the market (21).

Ex-ante return An unknown, future expected rate of return from an investment (2).

Exchange rate risk The risk associated with the conversion of the currency of one country into the currency of another country (6).

Exercise (striking) price The price at which the stock may be acquired or sold if the investor exercises a stock option (15).

Expectation hypothesis A theory that suggests that futures prices are unbiased estimates of expected future spot prices (17).

Expected rate of return The rate of return anticipated by the investor based upon the estimate of the cash receipts (e.g., dividends or interest) over the holding period and the expected ending, or selling, price of the asset. The expected rate of return is an ex-ante, or unknown, future return (2, 11).

Expense ratio The operating expenses of a mutual fund, excluding brokerage costs, divided by the net asset value of the fund (5).

Expiration date (stock option) The Saturday following the third Friday of the expiration month (15).

Ex-post return Actual historical rate of return from an investment (2).

Factor model A means of identifying the major forces that influence the returns of a security (20).

Federal Home Loan Mortgage Corporation (FHLMC) A federal agency that issues mortgage-backed securities to increase the funds available for home mortgages (10).

Federal National Mortgage Association (FNMA) A federal agency that issues mortgage-backed securities to increase the funds available for home mortgages (10).

Filter rule A mechanical trading rule based on security price changes that can be used to simulate buying and selling individual securities (21).

Filters Financial criteria used to screen (select) companies for analysis (9).

Financial assets A classification of investment alternatives that includes common stock, preferred stock, bonds, convertibles, warrants, rights, commodity futures, financial futures, and options. Financial assets represent claims on income produced by real assets (1).

Financial futures A contract entered into by a buyer and seller in which the underlying "asset" to be delivered consists of a specified amount of a financial asset such as a debt security, foreign currency, or an index of common stocks (17).

Financial leverage ratio The ratio of total assets to stockholders' equity (9).

Financial planning A process of identifying lifetime goals and determining the level and proper management of financial resources needed to accomplish these goals (22).

Financial risk The uncertainty about the rate of return from an investment caused by the firm's capital structure or sources of financing. The higher the fixed financing charges (interest and preferred dividends), the higher the degree of financial leverage and financial risk (2).

Financial services industry A broad term that includes individuals and companies that are involved in providing investment advice to individual investors (1).

Floating exchange rates The unregulated fluctuation in the price of a unit of one country's currency in terms of another country's currency (6).

Floor brokers Independent owners of a seat on the New York Stock Exchange. Also known as "broker's brokers," they accept and execute orders for the commission brokers when trading activity is high (3).

Floor traders Members of the New York Stock Exchange who buy and sell solely for their own accounts (3).

Forward contract A formal agreement between a buyer and seller in which the buyer agrees to accept delivery of a specified quantity of a commodity, on a specific date, at a fixed price (17).

401(k) plan A tax-sheltered retirement plan that allows before-tax contributions by an employee and tax-deductible contributions by the employer (22).

Fourth market *See* crossing.

Full-service broker A brokerage firm that not only executes orders for customers but also maintains a research staff that provides economic reports and information on industries and firms to its customers (3).

Fully diluted EPS Earnings per share assuming all options and warrants are exercised and all convertible securities are converted (13).

Fundamental analysis The in-depth study of the financial condition of a company, its risk, and other determinants of stock value (7).

Futures option A contract that gives the holder the right to buy or sell a specified futures contract, at a fixed price, within a specified period of time (17).

General obligation municipal bond A debt obligation in which the taxing authority and taxing power of the municipality can be used to satisfy the interest and principal payments (10).

Generally accepted accounting principles (GAAP) The accounting practices and procedures authorized by the Financial Accounting Standards Board (FASB) that are used in preparing financial statements and reports (9).

Geometric mean return The rate of return that would make the initial investment equal to the ending investment value. It is calculated by taking the $1/n$th root of the product of 1 plus the n individual rates of return and subtracting 1 from the results (2).

Gold- and silver-mining stocks The publicly traded common stock of gold- and silver-mining companies (18).

Gold certificates Certificates issued to investors by financial institutions that have bullion in storage as collateral (18).

Gold futures A contract in which the issuer promises to deliver 100 troy ounces of gold, at a specified price, at a specified time in the future (18).

Government National Mortgage Association (GNMA) A federal agency that issues mortgage-backed securities backed by the full credit of the U.S. government to increase the funds available for home mortgages (10).

Growth stock A common stock that is likely to experience above-average price appreciation (12).

Hedge ratio The necessary number of shares of stock, relative to one option contract, that is needed to form a risk-free hedged position (15).

Hedging An attempt by an investor to modify or eliminate risk by undertaking investment positions such that the gain on one investment counterbalances the loss on another (7, 15).

Hedging (currency risk) The use of the futures exchange market to reduce exchange rate risk (6).

H-model A dividend discount stock valuation model that allows for three phases of dividend growth: rapid growth, transition growth, and steady-state growth (14).

Holding period return (HPR) The total return received from an investment over a specified period expressed as a percentage of the initial investment. Total return includes any increase in the asset's price or capital appreciation and any cash receipts such as dividends or interest payments (2, 11).

Income stock A common stock that has a long-term record of stable cash dividends (12).

Indenture The investment contract specifying the agreement between the bondholder and the bond issuer (10).

Index arbitrage The simultaneous trading of a large block of common stock and opposing positions in stock index futures, index options, or index futures options to earn a riskless profit (17).

Index fund A mutual fund that forms a portfolio that duplicates the performance of a market indicator portfolio like the S&P 500 (5).

Index model (single-index model or market model) A model of stock returns, using a market index, that is used to explain the relationship between risk and expected return (20).

Indifference curve A representation of an investor's preference for risk and return. A curve connecting investment alternatives in which each investment alternative has the same utility for the investor (19).

Individual Retirement Account (IRA) A tax-sheltered retirement plan that allows individuals to contribute up to $2,000 per year to the account or $2,250 for a spousal IRA if the spouse does not work (22).

Industry A group of companies with common products and services (8).

Industry beta An indicator of the systematic risk of an industry. A measure of the tendency of an industry's returns to respond to movements in the market (8).

Industry effect The impact of an industry on an individual company's performance (8).

Inflation hedge An asset that provides returns above the observed rate of inflation and consequently provides a positive real return (17, 18).

Initial margin (commodity futures) The minimum deposit required on a commodity futures contract; expressed as a percentage of the contract's value (17).

Initial margin (equity) The minimum percentage of the total security purchase amount that must be provided by an investor (7).

Initial public offering (IPO) The first-time sale of common stock by an issuer to the public (3, 12).

Integrated markets An indication that asset returns are closely related across countries (6).

Interest rate futures A contract that represents a promise to buy or sell a specified amount of a fixed-income security at a specified future time (17).

Interest rate options Options in which the underlying "asset" is an index of short-term or long-term interest rates (15).

Interest rate parity The relationship between spot and forward exchange rates that compensates for interest rate differentials (6).

Interest rate risk The uncertainty of the value of an investment caused by fluctuations in interest rates. Although interest rate risk is most commonly associated with bond price movements, movements in interest rates affect the prices of almost all investment alternatives (2, 19).

International closed-end funds An investment company with a fixed number of shares of common stock outstanding. They are usually nondiversified and concentrate their holdings on the securities issued by companies located in one country (6).

International mutual funds An investment company that manages funds for investors that buy shares in the company. The funds are similar to those of domestic mutual funds except that they include foreign securities in their portfolios (6).

Intrinsic value The value of a security that is justified by financial factors such as asset value, earnings, dividends, and other fundamental and market factors (7, 11, 14).

Intrinsic value (stock option) The difference between the stock price and the exercise or striking price (15).

Investment advisory services Firms that publish reports, with an annual cost, that use objective procedures and provide detailed information on a range of securities (4).

Investment banker A firm that specializes in the placement for original sale of new securities to the public (3).

Investment Company Act of 1940 An act designed to protect investors from abuses that were common in the 1920s and to eliminate conflicts of interest for mutual fund managers; it is administered by the Securities and Exchange Commission (5).

Investment horizon The length of time money will be invested. The investment horizon affects the return and risk characteristics of the investment alternatives (1).

Investment objective The desire of the investor to increase systematically his or her wealth, defined as assets minus liabilities (1).

Investment newsletters A published, subscription service that offers investment advice (4).

Investment strategies Strategies dealing with the selection of investment alternatives, the timing of investment purchases and sales, and the degree of portfolio diversification (1, 7).

Investment timing The decision relating to the ability of an investor to purchase an asset just before it is likely to increase in value and to sell the asset just before it is likely to decrease in value (1).

January effect The study of the effect of the month of the year on risk-adjusted holding period returns (21).

Jensen's technique A portfolio performance measure that estimates the average risk-adjusted excess HPRs, alpha, over the evaluation period (21).

Junk bonds Publicly traded debt obligations rated as noninvestment grade by at least one of the major independent rating agencies (3).

Keogh plan A tax-sheltered retirement plan that is essentially a profit-sharing plan that can be used to shelter self-employment income (22).

Lagging composite index A combination of seven economic variables that indicate where the economy has recently been (8).

Lagging indicators Economic time series produced by the National Bureau of Economic Research that can be used to indicate past trends in the economy (4).

Leading composite index A combination of 11 key economic variables that lead economic activity (8).

Leading indicators Economic time series produced by the National Bureau of Economic Research that can be used to indicate future trends in the economy (4).

Lending portfolio A portfolio composed of the risk-free asset and a portfolio on the efficient frontier (19).

Leverage effect (options) The influence on the returns and risks of an option reflecting the fact that the quoted price for a stock option (premium) is a fraction of the cost of a position in the underlying common stock (15).

Life-cycle planning The changes in financial planning over an individual's lifetime (22).

Limit order An order to buy or sell securities that must be transacted at a price set by the buyer or seller or at a better price (3).

Liquid yield option note (LYON) A type of zero coupon bond that is convertible, callable, and puttable (11).

Liquidity ratios Measures used to indicate a firm's ability to pay its short-term obligations (9).

Liquidity risk The risk associated with uncertainty created by the inability to sell an investment quickly for cash (2).

Load fund A mutual fund that charges sales commissions on the purchases, or on the sale of shares (5).

Loading An all-inclusive expression that includes all expenses associated with marketing and servicing a life insurance policy, plus profits and contingency charges (22).

Long position The purchase of a security in anticipation of an increase in the price of the security (7).

Low-load fund A mutual fund that charges a relatively low sales commission on the purchase, or on the sale of shares (5).

Maintenance call A notification of a requirement for an investor to provide additional equity to a margined account in order to meet the minimum maintenance margin (7).

Maintenance (variation) margin (commodity) The minimum required percentage of a commodity's contract amount that must be maintained in an account. Typically, the maintenance margin is 75 percent of the initial margin on the contract (17).

Maintenance margin (equity) The minimum percentage of equity that must be maintained in a margin account (7).

Management risk The risk associated with decisions made by a firm's management and board of directors (2).

Margin call (futures) A request to deposit additional cash or U.S. Treasury bills to a futures account as a result of the initial margin declining below the required maintenance margin (17).

Market efficiency The market's ability to price securities correctly and instantaneously change security prices to reflect new information (21).

Market order An order to buy or sell securities that is transacted at the last price available when the order reaches the floor of the exchange (3).

Market plane approach An approach for stock selection developed by Wells Fargo Bank in which the expected returns of stocks are plotted against their beta coefficients. Stocks that plot above the regression line offer high expected returns relative to their beta and may therefore be undervalued (14).

Market portfolio A portfolio constructed in such a way that each risky asset is represented in the portfolio in proportion to its value relative to the value of all risky assets (2, 20).

Market price of risk The slope of the capital market line. (20).

Marking to market The daily settlement by the clearing house of each futures' account reflecting the gains or losses due to price changes (17).

Minimum value (convertible) A floor or lower limit for the market value of a convertible security. The higher of a convertible's conversion value or straight value (16).

Money market fund A mutual fund that gives the small investor the opportunity to invest in money market securities (5).

Mortality The cost of dying. It represents the face value of a life insurance policy that will be paid at death by the insurance company (22).

Mortgage-backed security An ownership interest in a pool of home mortgages or a debt obligation secured by a pool of home mortgages (10).

Mortgage bond A bond that has specific real estate pledged as collateral (10).

Multinational companies Companies with subsidiaries based in foreign countries (6).

Municipal bond A debt security issued by a state, county, city, or other governmental units to finance public needs. Interest received from this type of security is generally exempt from federal income taxes (10).

Municipal revenue bond A debt obligation in which the funds used to pay the principal and interest are derived from specific municipality-owned projects such as hospitals, waterworks, or sewage systems (10).

Mutual fund An investment company that manages funds for investors who buy shares in the company (5).

Mutual funds cash position An indicator of the level of liquidity of mutual funds used to forecast the movement of stock prices (8).

Naïve diversification The process of diversifying a portfolio by randomly adding additional securities to the portfolio (11, 20).

NASDAQ A computerized network for obtaining bid and ask quotations on over-the-counter securities that have at least two market makers and meet certain requirements regarding capital and assets (3).

Net asset value (NAV) The total market value of the securities owned by an investment company, less any liabilities, divided by the number of shares outstanding (5).

New York Stock Exchange (NYSE) The largest of the organized securities exchanges in the United States (3).

No-load fund A mutual fund with no sales charges (5).

Nominal GNP The estimate of the total dollar value of the nation's output of goods and services expressed in current dollars (8).

Nondiversifiable risk Risk that has as its source factors that affect all marketable assets and thus cannot be diversified away. It is also called systematic risk, which reflects its source as being market pervasive (2, 20).

Normal backwardation A hypothesis that suggests that the futures price will be a downward-biased estimate of the expected future spot price (17).

Odd lot Less than 100 shares of stock (3).

Open-end fund A mutual fund that stands ready to issue new shares or redeem outstanding shares on a continual basis (5).

Open interest The total number of commodity or financial futures contracts outstanding at a given point in time (17).

Optimal portfolio A portfolio on the efficient frontier that is at the point of tangency with an investor's indifference curve (19).

Option A contract that gives the holder the right to buy or sell a specified amount of the underlying asset at a fixed price within a specified period of time (15).

Options clearing corporation (OCC) A corporation owned by the stock exchanges and the National Association of Security Dealers and regulated by the Securities and Exchange Commission that acts as an intermediary between the buyers and writers of options (15).

Options on gold futures A contract that gives the holder the right to buy or sell a specified gold futures contract at a fixed price within a specified period of time (18).

Original issue discount (OID) bond A bond issued with coupons below prevailing market yields, and sold at a discount (11).

Over-the-counter (OTC) market A network of broker-dealers who deal (negotiate) for their own accounts with each other over the telephone or through computer terminals. All security transactions not taking place on the organized exchanges are considered over-the-counter transactions (3).

Participating preferred stock A nonvoting share in a corporation in which the holder participates with the common stockholders in receiving income above a certain level of earnings (12).

Passive strategy An investment strategy that does not attempt to outperform the market or earn risk-adjusted excess returns (7).

Payback period (convertibles) A strategy for the analysis of convertible securities in which the premium is divided by the difference between the coupon yield on the convertible and the dividend yield on the underlying common stock. The result is an indication of the number of years required to recover the premium (16).

P/E effect The study of the effect of the level of P/E ratios on risk-adjusted holding period returns (21).

Pension fund An investment portfolio that is established to provide retirement benefits to employees of an organization (22).

Per-share-based ratios Financial information, such as earnings and book value, expressed on the basis of a share of common stock outstanding (9).

Political risk The risk associated with a government's policies associated with such factors as regulations, subsidies, and taxes (8).

Portfolio effect The reduction in total risk resulting from combining individual assets into a portfolio (2, 19).

Portfolio insurance A hedging strategy, using financial futures, designed to protect or insure an underlying stock or bond portfolio against price declines (17).

Portfolio return The weighted average of the expected returns of the individual assets in the portfolio. The weights are the proportion of the investor's wealth invested in each asset (19).

Portfolio risk The volatility of a portfolio's returns; estimated by combining the measures of individual asset risk (variance or standard deviation), relative asset weights, and the co-movement of the assets' returns (covariance or correlation coefficient) (19).

Portfolio turnover An indicator of security trading over a certain period of time. For mutual funds, it is usually calculated as the lesser of security purchases or sales divided by average portfolio assets (5).

Precious metals Real or tangible assets such as gold, silver, copper, aluminum, platinum, and palladium (18).

Preemptive right A feature of common stock that gives existing shareholders the first option to purchase a proportionate interest in a new common stock issue of the corporation (12).

Preferred stock A nonvoting share in a corporation that typically receives a fixed dollar dividend (12).

Premium (convertible security) The difference between the market price and the conversion value (or straight value for a busted convertible). The premium is usually expressed as a percentage of conversion value or straight value for a busted convertible (16).

Premium (option) The quoted price for a stock option that represents the price for the right to buy or sell one share of the underlying stock (15).

Price-earnings (P/E) model A stock valuation model that uses the product of estimates of the P/E ratio and earnings per share to estimate intrinsic value (14).

Price limits The maximum daily price range allowed on commodity futures (17).

Price risk The fluctuation in bond prices caused by changes in market interest rates (11).

Price-weighted averages An average, such as the Dow Jones averages, computed by adding the prices of the securities in the sample and dividing by a divisor that is adjusted for stock splits, stock dividends in excess of 10 percent, and the substitution of companies in the sample (4).

Primary EPS The profits after taxes reflecting common stock equivalents and preferred stock dividends divided by the weighted average number of shares of common stock outstanding (13).

Primary markets The market for the original sale of securities by an issuer to the public (3).

Prime A prescribed right to income and maximum equity created by an investment trust holding a blue-chip common stock. The security is analogous to an income share of a dual fund (5).

Principle of risk compensation For a portfolio on the capital market line, the expected return is equal to the risk-free rate plus a return proportional to the total risk of the portfolio (20).

Private placement The direct sales of new security issues to financial institutions or other large investors (3).

Profitability ratio The ratio of net income to sales (9).

Pro forma income statement A projected or forecasted income statement based on the key variables that determine earnings (13).

Program trading *See* index arbitrage.

Prospectus A registration statement approved by the Securities and Exchange Commission. In addition to the information contained in a registration statement, a final prospectus will state the price and date of the offering (3).

Purchasing power risk The risk associated with inflation. Inflation erodes the purchasing power of the dollar and increases investor risk (2, 11).

Put (option) A stock option that grants the holder the right to sell the shares of the underlying stock, at a specified price, within a specified period of time (15).

Put-call parity A principle expressing the appropriate relationship between the prices of put and call options (15).

Put-call ratio The relationship (ratio) of the number of puts and calls; it is used to give an indication of the bullish or bearish sentiment of option market participants (8).

Put feature A provision that allows the investor to "put" or sell the security back to the issuer at a specified price (16).

Random walk *See* efficient market hypothesis.

Range The maximum value in a distribution minus the minimum value (2).

Rate of return The percentage return an investor receives or expects to receive from an investment alternative (1).

Real assets A classification of investments alternatives that includes assets such as real estate, precious metals, and collectibles (1, 18).

Real estate investment trust (REIT) A closed-end investment company that may invest in real estate in several ways, including lending for construction purposes, providing intermediate- and long-term mortgages on properties, buying equity positions in property, and combinations of these activities (18).

Real estate limited partnership A form of real estate syndication that allows the revenues and expenses to be "passed through" to individual investors for tax purposes. The limited partners have limited liability (18).

Real GNP (constant dollar GNP) The estimate of the total dollar value of the nation's output of goods and services adjusted for inflation (8).

Real rate of return The pure time value of money that is equivalent to the growth in purchasing power from an investment that is needed to compensate the investor for deferring consumption (2).

Recession A decline in real gross national product for two consecutive quarters (8).

Red herring A preliminary prospectus that states that the information in the prospectus is being reviewed by the Securities and Exchange Commission and that the prospectus is not a solicitation to sell. The difference between a red herring and a final prospectus is that the preliminary prospectus does not state the security's price or date of the offering (3).

Regional exchanges Stock exchanges that operate in basically the same manner as the national exchanges, but list securities of firms that are too small to meet the listing requirements of the national exchanges; in addition, they dually list some securities of firms on the national exchanges (3).

Registration statement A document on a new security that must be filed with the Securities and Exchange Commission by the originating investment banker. The statement provides information on the firm issuing the new security, the type and amount of the security being offered, and the proposed use of the proceeds from the sale (3).

Reinvestment rate risk The uncertainty associated with the rates of return that will be available when the coupons and principal payments from a bond are to be reinvested (11, 19).

Relative strength A technique used by analysts to select industries and individual companies by comparing a company or industry measure, such as price, to an equivalent measure for the market (8, 21).

Required rate of return The rate of return necessary to compensate the investor for deferred consumption (real rate of return), expected inflation, and risk. Return estimated by the CAPM (2).

Return on assets (ROA) The ratio of operating income to total assets (9).

Return on equity (ROE) The ratio of net income to stockholders' equity. ROE can also be defined as the product of the measures of asset utilization, profitability, and financial leverage (9).

Reversion value The net proceeds from the sale of real estate at the end of the investment holding period (18).

Riding the yield curve An active bond investment strategy that involves buying longer-term bonds during a period of a stable, upward-sloping yield curve in anticipation of capital gains occurring as the remaining maturity of the bond declines (11).

Rights Securities issued by a corporation that give existing common stock shareholders the opportunity to acquire a proportionate share of a new issue of common stock (16).

Risk The variability of possible rates of return around the expected return of an investment. Risk is generally measured by the variance or standard deviation around the expected or historical return (1).

Risk-averse investor An investor who requires additional returns to compensate for additional risk (19).

Risk-free asset An asset whose future rate of return is known with certainty (19).

Risk-free rate The interest rate paid by a risk-free asset; a rate of return earned with certainty (19).

"Risk-neutral" A term used to describe an investor who is willing to accept equal levels of expected return for higher levels of risk (19).

Risk premium (inflation and risk) The return above the real rate of return required by investors as compensation for facing inflation and risk (2).

Risk premium (market) The slope of the security market line. The expected return of the market portfolio less the return of the risk-free asset (20).

Risk premium (portfolio evaluation) The average holding period return on the portfolio over the evaluation period minus the average risk-free return over the same period (21).

"Risk-taker" An investor who is willing to accept lower levels of expected return for higher levels of risk (19).

Round lot One hundred shares of stock or multiples of 100 shares (3).

Rule 12b–1 A Securities and Exchange Commission rule that allows mutual funds to charge distribution and marketing expenses, directly or indirectly, to net asset value (5).

Runs test A statistical test that can be used to test for dependence in successive security price changes (21).

Savings/reserve The accumulated investment by the policyholder of a whole life insurance policy. The policyholder accumulates savings because the annual premium is in excess of the amount needed to pay for mortality and loading expenses in the early years of the policy (22).

Score A special claim on residual equity created by an investment trust holding a blue-chip common stock. The security resembles a capital share of a dual fund (5).

Screening The process by which companies are selected for analysis using financial criteria called filters (9).

Secondary markets The market where already-existing securities are bought and sold. The secondary markets comprise the organized securities exchanges and the over-the-counter market (3).

Security Investor Protection Corporation (SIPC) Established by the Securities Investor Protection Act of 1970, the SIPC provides insurance to protect investors in the event that brokerage firms fail. Customer accounts are insured for up to $500,000 with only $100,000 of the amount applying to cash balances (3).

Security market line (SML) A graphical representation of the relationship between the indicator of systematic risk, beta, and the required return of an asset; also the CAPM (2, 20).

Segmented markets An indication that asset returns are not closely related across countries (6).

Selection A decision involving the identification of appropriate investment alternatives or categories and the selection of individual securities or assets in each category (1).

Semistrong form EMH *See* efficient market hypothesis.

Separation theorem A theorem that separates the problem of selecting the appropriate risk level (amount of lending and borrowing) from the problem of choosing the risky assets to be included in the portfolio (20).

Serial correlation A statistic that measures the relationship of an observed variable to its time-lagged values (21).

Series EE savings bond A U.S. savings bond that has a market-based interest rate that is 85 percent of the market average for five-year Treasury securities (10).

Series HH savings bond A U.S. savings bond that pays semiannual interest (10).

Settle price A specified price that can be used to terminate a position in a commodity or financial future (17).

Sharpes technique A portfolio performance measure that uses the ratio of the average risk premium of the portfolio over the evaluation period divided by the standard deviation of the portfolio's HPRs over the evaluation period (21).

Short interest The number of shares of common stock that have been sold short during a particular time period.

Short position The sale of a security that the investor does not currently own in anticipation of a decline in the price of the security (7).

Simple EPS The profits after taxes and after preferred dividends divided by the number of shares of common stock outstanding (13).

Sinking fund (bond) A provision of a bond that requires the issuer to either periodically allocate funds to repay the principal or use the funds to purchase the bonds in the market and effectively retire the bond before maturity (10).

Sinking fund (preferred stock) A provision in a preferred stock issue in which the issuer allocates funds to buy the stock directly in the market and thus improve the marketability of the issue for investors (12).

Size effect The study of the effect of the size of a firm on risk-adjusted holding period returns (21).

Small stock A relative categorization of common stocks based on the total capitalization of the company (12).

Specialist A stock exchange member responsible for maintaining a "fair and orderly market" in the securities to which he or she is assigned. Specialists perform two functions. First, as brokers, they must handle "limit" and other special orders entered in their book for commission brokers. Second, they act as dealers, buying and selling the stocks they are assigned in order to maintain an orderly market (3).

Speculation Investing in risky assets over a short time horizon with limited information (7).

Speculative stock A classification of common stock that relates to the way the investor feels about stock's risk (12).

Spread (commodity futures) A trader simultaneously taking both a long position and a short position in a futures contract in the same commodity. The two contracts will differ only in their delivery dates (17).

Spread (options) A general type of straddle in which a trader takes simultaneous positions in a put and a call on the same security; the put and call may have different striking prices and/or expiration dates (15).

Spread (underwriting) The difference between the price an underwriter agrees to pay the issuer of new securities and the price of the new issue to the public (3).

Standard deviation The square root of the variance (2).

Standard industrial classification (SIC) A detailed system of industry classification developed by the federal government through the Office of Management and Budget (8).

Standardized options Options with consistent features issued by the Options Clearing Corporation (OCC) so that the buyer may rely on the OCC rather than the individual writer to fulfill the obligations of the option (15).

Stock dividend A dividend paid in the form of additional shares of common stock (12).

Stock index futures A futures contract written on a stock market index with all delivery settlements made in cash (17).

Stock quality ratings A grade assigned to a common stock that is designed to indicate likely long-term risk-return performance (12).

Stock split The issuance by a corporation of additional shares to existing stockholders in proportion to the number of shares currently held (12).

Stop order An order placed in the specialist's book to sell a stock when its price reaches a certain level below its current price. Also known as a stop-loss order, this type of order becomes a market order when the common stock price reaches the designated level (3).

Straddle (options) A trader simultaneously taking a position in a put and a call on the same security, with the same striking price and expiration date (15).

Straight value The value of a nonconvertible security that is identical to the convertible in all other characteristics (16).

Straight voting A method of electing the board of directors in which the common stockholder is allowed one vote per share for each director (12).

Strips Securities issued by the U.S. Treasury in which zero coupon bonds have been created by "stripping" the coupons and principal payments. An acronym for Separate Trading on Registered Interest and Principal Securities (11).

Strong form EMH *See* efficient market hypothesis.

Structuring maturities An active strategy of combining bonds with different maturities into a bond portfolio (11).

Summary plan description The details about vesting and distribution options of a pension plan (22).

Swaps An active bond investment strategy designed to earn short-term gains by exploiting perceived inefficiencies in the bond market. The most frequently used swaps are substitution, yield pickup, and tax swaps (11).

Systematic risk *See* nondiversifiable risk.

Tangible asset mutual funds Investment companies that specialize in investments in gold and other precious metals (18).

Tax consequences Since the government taxes most sources of income received by individuals, the appropriate rate of return to consider when choosing among alternative investments is the net after-tax return (1).

Technical analysis The use of historical price and volume data and determinants of future supply and demand factors in order to resolve the investment timing issue (7, 8).

Term life insurance Life insurance that is usually purchased on a yearly basis and in which the insured does not accumulate cash value (22).

Third market The trading of securities listed on the organized exchanges on the over-the-counter market (3).

Time-series analysis A comparison of financial ratios for the same firm over time (9).

Time value (option) The difference between a stock option price and the option's intrinsic value (15).

Trade deficit A deficiency in a country's exports relative to its imports (8).

Treasury bill A fixed-income security issued by the U.S. government with a term to maturity of one year or less (10).

Treasury bond A fixed-income security issued by the U.S. government with a term to maturity of over ten years (10).

Treasury note A fixed-income security issued by the U.S. government with a term to maturity between one and ten years (10).

Treasury stock Previously outstanding common stock that has been bought back (and held) by the corporation (12).

Treynor's technique A portfolio performance measure that uses the ratio of the average risk premium of the portfolio over the evaluation period divided by the portfolio's beta over the evaluation period (21).

Trustee The representative (usually a large commercial bank) of the collective interests of bond investors (10).

Uncovered ("naked") option An option in which the writer does not have a position in the underlying common stock (15).

Underwriting An agreement by an investment banker to purchase new securities from an issuing company at a specified price (3).

Unexpected earnings Actual earnings per share that differ significantly from the consensus forecast of earnings (13).

Unit trust A special type of investment company in which a "unit" or ownership interest represents a claim to a fixed portfolio of securities (5).

Universal life insurance An interest-sensitive life insurance policy that has numerous options for changing premiums, cash values, and death benefits (22).

Unsystematic risk *See* diversifiable risk.

Utility A measure of the level of investor well-being or satisfaction (19).

Value-weighted index An index, such as the Standard & Poor's stock indexes, computed by summing the market value of all securities in the index and dividing by the aggregate market value of the securities in the base period (4).

Variable life insurance A life insurance policy that consists of two parts: (1) a whole life policy and (2) a separate investment account (22).

Variance The expected value of the squared deviation of returns from the mean return; standard deviation squared (2).

Vested (pension plan) The entitlement of an employee to benefits from a pension plan (22).

Warrants A contract issued by a corporation that grants the holder the option to purchase that corporation's common stock, at a stated price, within a stated period of time (16).

Weak form EMH *See* efficient market hypothesis.

Whitbeck-Kisor model An econometric model used for the estimation of theoretical P/E ratios (14).

Whole life insurance Life insurance that is designed to provide protection until death and in which premiums are paid until death. The policy results in an annual savings/reserve increment, which accumulates over the life of the policy (22).

Yield to first call A bond return measure calculated for callable bonds that represents the annual rate of return for a bond if the bond is redeemed at the call price at the first call date (11).

Yield to maturity A bond return measure that represents the annual rate of return that will occur for a bond if the bond is held to maturity, the issuer does not default on interest and principal payments, the bond is not called or redeemed by the issuer before maturity, and coupon receipts are reinvested at a rate of return equal to the yield to maturity (11).

Zero A bond that does not pay interest and sells at a discount (11).

Zero growth DDM A dividend discount stock valuation model that assumes dividends will be constant over time (14).

Zero growth P/E model A P/E stock valuation model that assumes dividends will be constant over time (14).

Corporation and Organization Name Index

Name Index

Subject Index